FAMILY BIBLE RECORDS

IN THE

WASHINGTON COUNTY
FREE LIBRARY

HAGERSTOWN
MARYLAND

Marsha Lynne Fuller, CGRS

HERITAGE BOOKS
2009

HERITAGE BOOKS
AN IMPRINT OF HERITAGE BOOKS, INC.

Books, CDs, and more—Worldwide

For our listing of thousands of titles see our website
at
www.HeritageBooks.com

Published 2009 by
HERITAGE BOOKS, INC.
Publishing Division
100 Railroad Ave. #104
Westminster, Maryland 21157

Copyright © 2003 Washington County Free Library

Other Heritage Books by Marsha Lynne Fuller, CGRS:
African American Manumissions of Washington County, Maryland
Naturalizations of Washington County, Maryland, Prior to 1880
St. Mary's Catholic Church Records: 1818–1900, Hagerstown, Washington County, Maryland

All rights reserved. No part of this book may be reproduced or transmitted in any form or by any means, electronic or mechanical, including photocopying, recording or by any information storage and retrieval system without written permission from the author, except for the inclusion of brief quotations in a review.

International Standard Book Numbers
Paperbound: 978-1-58549-879-6
Clothbound: 978-0-7884-8238-0

Acknowledgements:

The State of Maryland did not officially register births and deaths until 1898, thus leaving a void for persons doing family research prior to that date. Even though marriages have been recorded throughout the State's history, that record is only recorded in the county in which the marriage was performed, there being no statewide register.

This publication of family Bible records will help to fill that void. Bible records and infant baptism church records are the only substitutes for the lack of official recording by the State.

Over the past three decades, the staff of the Washington County Free Library has been copying Bible records submitted by patrons. This cooperation has furnished the information in this volume that totals over 8,000 entries. There were several Bible records written in old German script that we were unable to translate. These photocopies can be viewed in the Western Maryland Room.

A special word of appreciation to those patrons who furnished Bibles, to staff members who did the copying, to Marsha Fuller for compiling and indexing, and to the RIGGS CONARD TRUST for funding this project.

JOHN C. FRYE, DIRECTOR
WESTERN MARYLAND ROOM

KEY

Each entry is numbered for ease of finding; there are no page numbers. Entry numbers are in numerical order and correspond to the numbers in the index.

Fields are numbered and listed at the top of each page. The corresponding fields are numbered in each entry.

Field #	Field Name	Description
1-	Last Name, First Name	Name of person
2-	Event	Born, christened, confirmed, married, died, obituary
3-	Date	Date when event occurred
4-	Event Location	Location of event
5-	Age	Age of person on date of event
6-	Other	Any other information in the record
7-	Spouse's Last, First	Name of spouse
8-	Groom's Residence	Place that groom lived at time of marriage
9-	Bride's Residence	Place that bride lived at time of marriage
10-	Minister	Name of minister performing the ceremony
11-	Minister's Location	Home church of minister performing the ceremony
12-	Father's Last, First	Name of father of person
13-	Mother's Last, First	Name of mother of person
14-	Transcribed	"Yes" in this field indicates that record had been transcribed; copy of original Bible not available
15-	Family Bible	Name of Family Bible from which this record came

Example:

#1, 1-Funkhouser, Clarence Paul, 2-born, 3-Friday, 24 Aug 1900, 15-Funkhouser

This is entry #1; the person's name was Clarence Paul Funkhouser; he was born on Friday, August 24, 1900; this information came from the Funkhouser Family Bible.

The researcher is encouraged to check the photocopied Bible Records in the Family Files in the Western Maryland Room. There is additional genealogical information in them; we chose to transcribe only the vital records.

A last name that is in parentheses is the woman's maiden name. Example: Jane (Doe) Smith = this woman was given the name of Jane Doe at birth and, later, married a man with the last name of Smith. When information is in quotes, it is an exact quotation from the Bible record.

There were several records written in old German script that we could not translate. We have attempted to list most of the names in these records but were unable to translate the vital statistics associated with them.

Family Bible Records

in the

Washington County Free Library,

Hagerstown, Maryland

FAMILY BIBLE RECORDS IN THE WASHINGTON COUNTY FREE LIBRARY, HAGERSTOWN, MARYLAND

Entry #, 1-Last Name, First Name, 2-Event, 3-Date, 4-Event Location, 5-Age, 6-Other,
7-Spouse's Last, First, 8-Groom's Residence, 9-Bride's Residence, 10-Minister, 11-Minister's Location,
12-Father's Last, First, 13-Mother's Last, First, 14-Transcribed, 15-Family Bible

```
#1,  1-Funkhouser, Clarence Paul, 2-born, 3-Friday, 24 Aug 1900, 15-Funkhouser
#2,  1-Funkhouser, Roy Nelson, 2-born, 3-11 pm, Friday, 18 Nov 1904, 15-Funkhouser
#3,  1-Funkhouser, Hazel Estelle, 2-born, 3-3 pm, Friday, 11 Jan 1907, 15-Funkhouser
#4,  1-Funkhouser, Pauline Catherine, 2-born, 3-3 pm, Friday, 21 Mar 1911, 15-
     Funkhouser
#5,  1-Funkhouser, Godfrey, 2-died, 3-6 Jan 1890, 15-Funkhouser
#6,  1-Funkhouser, Mary Jane, 2-died, 3-2 Sep 1893, 15-Funkhouser
#7,  1-Funkhouser, Mary Catharine, 2-born, 3-1 Feb 1893, 15-Funkhouser
#8,  1-Funkhouser, John Albert, 2-born, 3-5 Dec 1868, 15-Funkhouser
#9,  1-Funkhouser, John Albert, 2-died, 3-5 Oct 1958, 15-Funkhouser
#10, 1-Funkhouser, Franklin Lhist[?], 2-born, 3-27 Dec 1870, 15-Funkhouser
#11, 1-Funkhouser, Mary Catharine, 2-born, 3-9 Apr 1873, 15-Funkhouser
#12, 1-Funkhouser, Victor Godfrey, 2-born, 3-4 Apr 1875, 15-Funkhouser
#13, 1-Funkhouser, Victor Godfrey, 2-died, 3-17 May 1959, 15-Funkhouser
#14, 1-Funkhouser, William Steele, 2-born, 3-11 May 1877, 15-Funkhouser
#15, 1-Funkhouser, Ralph August, 2-born, 3-8 Aug 1879, 15-Funkhouser
#16, 1-Funkhouser, Ralph August, 2-died, 3-29 Apr 1918, 15-Funkhouser
#17, 1-Funkhouser, Thomas Jefferson, 2-born, 3-22 Jan 1882, 15-Funkhouser
#18, 1-Funkhouser, Thomas Jefferson, 2-died, 3-27 Oct 1960, 15-Funkhouser
#19, 1-Funkhouser, Robert Lee, 2-born, 3-5 Feb 1885, 15-Funkhouser
#20, 1-Funkhouser, Robert Lee, 2-died, 3-11 Jun 1955, 15-Funkhouser
#21, 1-Funkhouser, Winona Jackson, 2-born, 3-17 Feb 1888, 15-Funkhouser
#22, 1-Funkhouser, Winona Jackson, 2-died, 3-17[?] Jul 1972, 15-Funkhouser
#23, 1-Funkhouser, Beatrice Ellen, 2-born, 3-26 Mar 1890, 15-Funkhouser
#24, 1-Funkhouser, Beatrice Ellen, 2-died, 3-Dec, 15-Funkhouser
#25, 1-Williams, Sarah Catharine, 2-born, 3-30 Oct 1867, 15-Funkhouser
#26, 1-Funkhouser, Gracie Edith, 2-born, 3-Friday, 19 Dec 1890, 15-Funkhouser
#27, 1-Funkhouser, Mamie Constance, 2-born, 3-3 am, Thursday, 19 Oct 1895, 15-
     Funkhouser
#28, 1-Funkhouser, Keller Herbert, 2-born, 3-6 am, Tuesday, 19 Nov 1895, 15-
     Funkhouser
#29, 1-Funkhouser, Pearl Dexter, 2-born, 3-11 pm, Sunday, 24 Jul 1898, 15-
     Funkhouser
#30, 1-Funkhouser, Pearl Dexter, 2-died, 3-9 Aug 1972, 15-Funkhouser
#31, 1-Somerville, Florence Regenia, 2-born, 3-10:30 pm, 5 Sep 1900, 4-Hillen Road,
     Morton Estate, 15-Somerville
#32, 1-Somerville, Gertrude Elaine, 2-born, 3-9 am, Thursday, 26 Mar 1903, 4-Hillen
     Road, Morton Estate, 15-Somerville
#33, 1-Somerville, Harry Francis, 2-born, 3-3 am, Thursday, 15 Jun 1905, 4-Hillen
     Road, Morton Estate, 15-Somerville
#34, 1-Jamison, Mary E., 2-died, 3-28 Jun 1892, 15-Somerville
#35, 1-Hebb, John H., 2-married, 3-23 Jan 1866, 7-Seiss, Mary C., 15-Hebb
#36, 1-Hebb, Emma R., 2-married, 3-1 Mar 1893, 7-McCauley, Wm. Harvey, 15-Hebb
#37, 1-Hebb, William A., 2-married, 3-3 Jan 1894, 7-Miller, M. Alice, 15-Hebb
#38, 1-Hebb, Clyde E., 2-married, 3-1914, 7-Myers, Edith, 15-Hebb
#39, 1-Snavely, Ada R., 2-married, 3-28 Jun 1885, 7-Kretzer, Hyatt, 15-Hebb
#40, 1-Hebb, Henry C., 2-married, 3-Nov 1929, 7-Malotte, Frances, 15-Hebb
#41, 1-Hebb, Henry C., 2-married, 3-22 Apr 1939, 7-Miller, Estella Rachel, 15-Hebb
#42, 1-Hebb, John Hanson, 2-born, 3-15 Jun 1835, 15-Hebb
#43, 1-Hebb, Mary Catharine, 2-born, 3-4 Apr 1838, 15-Hebb
#44, 1-Snavely, Ada Rebecca, 2-born, 3-22 Feb 1863, 6-"our adopted daughter", 15-
     Hebb
#45, 1-Hebb, William Adams, 2-born, 3-7 am, 26 Jun 1870, 15-Hebb
#46, 1-Hebb, Emma Roberts, 2-born, 3-4 pm, 13 Nov 1873, 15-Hebb
#47, 1-Hebb, Kate Elizabeth, 2-born, 3-2 am, 25 Oct 1875, 15-Hebb
```

FAMILY BIBLE RECORDS IN THE WASHINGTON COUNTY FREE LIBRARY, HAGERSTOWN, MARYLAND

Entry #, 1-Last Name, First Name, 2-Event, 3-Date, 4-Event Location, 5-Age, 6-Other,
7-Spouse's Last, First, 8-Groom's Residence, 9-Bride's Residence, 10-Minister, 11-Minister's Location,
12-Father's Last, First, 13-Mother's Last, First, 14-Transcribed, 15-Family Bible

```
#48, 1-Hebb, Florance Simmons, 2-born, 3-15 Feb 1880, 15-Hebb
#49, 1-Hebb, Clyde Edwin, 2-born, 3-8 Jan 1896, 15-Hebb
#50, 1-Hebb, Henry Clifford, 2-born, 3-23 Mar 1906, 15-Hebb
#51, 1-Hebb, Patricia Ann, 2-born, 3-20 Sep 1931, 15-Hebb
#52, 1-Hebb, Mary C., 2-died, 3-29 Apr 1883, 6-"devoted Christian - most faithful
     Loving Wife and Mother", 15-Hebb
#53, 1-Hebb, Johon H., 2-died, 3-25 Sep 1896, 15-Hebb
#54, 1-Hebb, Mary Alice, 2-died, 3-3 Aug 1918, 6-"Devoted Faithful Wife of Wm. A.
     Hebb", 15-Hebb
#55, 1-Hebb, Anna Myrtle, 2-died, 3-5 Mar 1940, 6-"Second Wife of W.A. Hebb", 15-
     Hebb
#56, 1-Hebb, Wm. A., 2-died, 3-26 Jun 1945, 6-died on his 75th birthday, 15-Hebb
#57, 1-Hebb, William Adam, 2-married, 3-3 Jan 1894, 7-Miller, Mary Alice, 15-Hebb
#58, 1-Hebb, William Adam, 2-born, 3-26 Jun 1870, 15-Hebb
#59, 1-Hebb, William Adam, 2-died, 3-26 Jun 1945, 15-Hebb
#60, 1-Miller, Mary Alice, 2-died, 3-3 Aug 1918, 15-Hebb
#61, 1-Hebb, Clyde Edgar, 2-born, 3-8 Jan 1896, 6-son of William Adam Hebb and Mary
     Alice Miller, 15-Hebb
#62, 1-Hebb, Glenn Edwin, 2-born, 12-Hebb, Clyde Edgar, 13-Myers, Edith, 15-Hebb
#63, 1-Hebb, Henry Clifford, 2-born, 3-23 Mar 1906, 12-Hebb, William Adam, 13-
     Miller, Mary Alice, 15-Hebb
#64, 1-Hebb, Henry Clifford, 2-married, 3-Thanksgiving 192_, 7-Malotte, Frances,
     12-Hebb, William Adam, 13-Miller, Mary Alice, 15-Hebb
#65, 1-Malotte, Frances, 2-[?], 3-26 Oct 1907, 15-Hebb
#66, 1-Malotte, Frances, 2-died, 3-2 Dec 1932, 15-Hebb
#67, 1-Hebb, Patricia Ann, 2-[?], 3-20 Sep 1931, 12-Hebb, Henry Clifford, 13-
     Malotte, Frances, 15-Hebb
#68, 1-Hebb, Henry Clifford, 2-married, 3-20 Apr 1939, 15-Hebb
#69, 1-Miller, Estella Rachel, 2-born, 3-26 Jun 1906, 15-Hebb
#70, 1-Landis, Lillian Mae, 2-married, 3-17 Dec 1912, 4-"at home, near
     Williamsport", 7-Liskey, Sr., Robert Brown, 15-Landis
#71, 1-Buff, Argielle Mozelle, 2-married, 3-18 Jan 1946, 4-Naval Chapel, Oakland,
     California, 7-Liskey, Jr., Robert Brown, 15-Landis
#72, 1-Landis, Joseph, 2-born, 3-1 Jul 1848, 15-Landis
#73, 1-Landis, Rebecca Ripple, 2-born, 3-21 Aug 1845, 15-Landis
#74, 1-Landis, Hattie E., 2-born, 3-8 Nov 1882, 15-Landis
#75, 1-Landis, Lillie May, 2-born, 3-25 Jul 1885, 15-Landis
#76, 1-Liskey, Jr., Robert Brown, 2-born, 3-25 Oct 1916, 15-Landis
#77, 1-Liskey, Lloyd Wayne, 2-born, 3-2 Mar 1955, 15-Landis
#78, 1-Liskey, Argielle Buff, 2-born, 3-11 Apr 1920, 15-Landis
#79, 1-Beckley, Ann Elizabeth Ripple, 2-born, 3-9 May 1844, 15-Landis
#80, 1-Liskey, Sr., Robert Brown, 2-born, 3-21 Jun 1887, 15-Landis
#81, 1-Landis, Joseph, 2-died, 3-23 Oct 1925, 15-Landis
#82, 1-Landis, Rebecca, 2-died, 3-5 Feb 1921, 15-Landis
#83, 1-Liskey, Lillian Mae (Landis), 2-died, 3-3 May 1951, 15-Landis
#84, 1-Landis, Harriet Elizabeth, 2-died, 3-17 Aug 1959, 15-Landis
#85, 1-Liskey, Sr., Robert Brown, 2-died, 3-6 Aug 1964, 15-Landis
#86, 1-Landis, Joseph, 2-died, 3-23 Oct 1925, 5-77 years, 15-Landis
#87, 1-Sutton, Richard Eskridge, 2-born, 3-15 Sep 1831, 15-Sutton
#88, 1-Green, Harrietta Clotilda, 2-born, 3-9 Aug 1833, 15-Sutton
#89, 1-Green, Harrietta Clotilda, 2-married, 3-24 Sep 1854, 7-Sutton, Richard
     Eskridge, 15-Sutton
#90, 1-Flandrau, Ruth Hungerford, 2-born, 3-24 Feb 1863, 15-Sutton
#91, 1-Whyte, Arthur Titherington, 2-born, 3-6 Apr 1864, 4-Southport, Lancashire,
     15-Sutton
```

FAMILY BIBLE RECORDS IN THE WASHINGTON COUNTY FREE LIBRARY, HAGERSTOWN, MARYLAND

Entry #, 1-Last Name, First Name, 2-Event, 3-Date, 4-Event Location, 5-Age, 6-Other,
7-Spouse's Last, First, 8-Groom's Residence, 9-Bride's Residence, 10-Minister, 11-Minister's Location,
12-Father's Last, First, 13-Mother's Last, First, 14-Transcribed, 15-Family Bible

```
#92,  1-Sutton, Henry Carroll, 2-born, 3-6 Aug 1856, 15-Sutton
#93,  1-Sutton, Francis Eskridge, 2-born, 3-23 Dec 1859, 15-Sutton
#94,  1-Sutton, Mary Louise, 2-born, 3-2 Nov 1869, 15-Sutton
#95,  1-Flandrau, Ruth Hungerford, 2-born, 3-24 Feb 1863, 15-Sutton
#96,  1-Whyte, Anne Harriet, 2-born, 3-28 Apr 1903, 15-Sutton
#97,  1-Aldridge, Clayson Wheeler, 2-born, 3-19 Oct 1899, 15-Sutton
#98,  1-Aldridge, Clayson Wheeler, 2-died, 3-30 Mar 1944, 15-Sutton
#99,  1-Sutton, Henry Carroll, 2-married, 3-3 Jun 1891, 7-Flandrau, Ruth Hungerford,
      15-Sutton
#100, 1-Whyte, Arthur Titherington, 2-married, 3-30 Jul 1902, 7-Sutton, Mary
      Louise, 15-Sutton
#101, 1-Whyte, Anne Harriet, 2-married, 3-30 Apr 1932, 7-Aldridge, Clayson Wheeler,
      15-Sutton
#102, 1-Sutton, Francis Eskridge (Lieutenant), 2-died, 3-16 Mar 1889, 4-harbor at
      Apid, Samoa, 6-"washed overboard from the ship Vandalia in the hurricane",
      15-Sutton
#103, 1-Sutton, Harriett, 2-died, 3-24 Jul 1890, 15-Sutton
#104, 1-Sutton, Richard Eskridge (Dr.), 2-died, 3-10 Nov 1897, 15-Sutton
#105, 1-Sutton, Henry Carroll (Dr.), 2-died, 3-5 Mar 1907, 4-DeSoto Sanitarium,
      Jacksonville, Florida, 15-Sutton
#106, 1-Whyte, Arthur Titherington, 2-died, 3-18 Apr 1949, 15-Sutton
#107, 1-Whyte, Mary Sutton, 2-born, 3-2 Nov 1869, 15-Sutton
#108, 1-Whyte, Mary Sutton, 2-died, 3-13 Jan 1959, 15-Sutton
#109, 1-Sparrow, Allen, 2-born, 3-10 Feb 1810, 15-Sparrow
#110, 1-Sparrow, Eliza, 2-born, 3-26 Oct 1818, 15-Sparrow
#111, 1-Sparrow, Elizabeth Aanna, 2-born, 3-1 Aug 1837, 15-Sparrow
#112, 1-Sparrow, William Thomas, 2-born, 3-20 Feb 1839, 15-Sparrow
#113, 1-Sparrow, Howard Edwin, 2-born, 3-18 Apr 1841, 15-Sparrow
#114, 1-Sparrow, Martha Ellen, 2-born, 3-26 Jun 1843, 15-Sparrow
#115, 1-Sparrow, Allen _____[?], 2-born, 3-6 May 1845, 15-Sparrow
#116, 1-Sparrow, Mary Florance, 2-born, 3-22 Sep 1847, 15-Sparrow
#117, 1-Sparrow, Charles Alferd, 2-born, 3-13 Dec 1849, 15-Sparrow
#118, 1-Sparrow, Emory Melvin, 2-born, 3-20 Feb 1853, 15-Sparrow
#119, 1-Sparrow, Henry Clay, 2-born, 3-30 Mar 1854, 15-Sparrow
#120, 1-Sparrow, Anna Eliza Frances[?], 2-born, 3-24 May 1859, 15-Sparrow
#121, 1-Sparrow, Herbert C., 2-died, 3-4 Jul 1960, 15-Sparrow
#122, 1-Sparrow, William H., 2-died, 3-23 Oct 1962, 15-Sparrow
#123, 1-Sparrow, Mary E., 2-born, 3-5:50 am, 10 Jul 1907, 15-Sparrow
#124, 1-Sparrow, William H., 2-born, 3-8 am, 19 Mar 1910, 15-Sparrow
#125, 1-Sparrow, Martin H., 2-born, 3-11:55 pm, 26 May 1912, 15-Sparrow
#126, 1-Sparrow, Effie Mary (Martin), 2-born, 3-29 Aug 1882, 15-Sparrow
#127, 1-Sparrow, Herbert C., 2-born, 3-28 Oct 1878, 15-Sparrow
#128, 1-Sparrow, Lelia (Shank), 2-born, 3-8 Jul 1882, 15-Sparrow
#129, 1-Sparrow, Emma J., 2-died, 3-4 Apr 1895, 15-Sparrow
#130, 1-Crabill, Ella M., 2-died, 3-Oct 1915, 15-Sparrow
#131, 1-Sparrow, Howard E., 2-died, 3-26 Jan 1918, 15-Sparrow
#132, 1-Sparrow, Effie Martin, 2-died, 3-17 Feb 1924, 6-"A dear & Loving Mother & a
      devoted wife.  May her life be a example for us.  Trusting god may we meet
      her in heaven. H.E.S.", 15-Sparrow
#133, 1-Sparrow, Harvey M., 2-died, 3-24 Mar 1935, 15-Sparrow
#134, 1-Sparrow, Ella May, 2-born, 3-18 Dec 1867, 15-Sparrow
#135, 1-Sparrow, Allen Kestor, 2-born, 3-7 Feb 1861, 15-Sparrow
#136, 1-Sparrow, Harry[?] Menard[?], 2-born, 3-16 Apr 1870, 15-Sparrow
#137, 1-Sparrow, Willie[?] Edwin, 2-born, 3-13 Oct 1876[?], 15-Sparrow
#138, 1-Sparrow, Herbert Cory[?], 2-born, 3-28 Oct 1878[?], 15-Sparrow
```

FAMILY BIBLE RECORDS IN THE WASHINGTON COUNTY FREE LIBRARY, HAGERSTOWN, MARYLAND

Entry #, 1-Last Name, First Name, 2-Event, 3-Date, 4-Event Location, 5-Age, 6-Other, 7-Spouse's Last, First, 8-Groom's Residence, 9-Bride's Residence, 10-Minister, 11-Minister's Location, 12-Father's Last, First, 13-Mother's Last, First, 14-Transcribed, 15-Family Bible

```
#139, 1-Sparrow, Charley Leslie[?], 2-born, 3-28 ___[?] 1886, 15-Sparrow
#140, 1-Sparrow, Emma Jane, 2-born, 3-6 Jan 1844, 15-Sparrow
#141, 1-Sparrow, Emma Jane, 2-died, 3-4 Apr 1895, 5-51 years 2 months 24 days, 6-"A
      Loving & kind Mother. May her Death be for our eternal good.", 15-Sparrow
#142, 1-Sparrow, Charles L., 2-died, 3-1 Jan 1939, 15-Sparrow
#143, 1-Sparrow, Willie Edwin, 2-died, 3-4 Jun 1947, 5-70 years, 15-Sparrow
#144, 1-Corby, Emma Jane, 2-obituary, 12-Corby, William, 15-Sparrow
#145, 1-Jamison, Mary E., 2-died, 3-28 Apr 1921, 15-Jamison
#146, 1-Jamison, Maude Ellen (Shoemaker), 2-born, 3-Nov 1887, 15-Jamison
#147, 1-Jamison, Maude Ellen (Shoemaker), 2-died, 3-Feb 1943, 15-Jamison
#148, 1-Jamison, James, 2-died, 3-1 Apr 1915, 15-Jamison
#149, 1-Jamison, Lestser Martin, 2-born, 3-15 Aug 1908, 15-Jamison
#150, 1-Jamison, Alf, 2-died, 3-15 Feb 1923, 15-Jamison
#151, 1-Jamison, Harvey Lester, 2-born, 3-22 Jan 1887, 15-Jamison
#152, 1-Jamison, Harvey Lester, 2-died, 3-3 May 1963, 15-Jamison
#153, 1-Crampton, Mabel Ruth, 2-born, 3-Aug 1920, 15-Jamison
#154, 1-Crampton, Mabel Ruth, 2-died, 3-16 Jul 1938, 15-Jamison
#155, 1-Jamison, Martha May (Brill), 2-born, 3-11 Feb 1917, 15-Jamison
#156, 1-Jamerson, John, 2-born, 3-6 Oct 1861, 15-Jamison
#157, 1-Jamerson, Charles, 2-born, 3-17 Aug 1863, 15-Jamison
#158, 1-Jamerson, Thomas W., 2-born, 3-21 Oct 1865, 15-Jamison
#159, 1-Jamerson, Susan E., 2-born, 3-26 Jan 1864[?], 15-Jamison
#160, 1-Jamerson, Minny V., 2-born, 3-20 Feb 1870, 15-Jamison
#161, 1-Jamison, James, 2-born, 3-29 Jan 1835, 15-Jamison
#162, 1-Jamison, Mary E., 2-born, 3-11 Jun 1839, 15-Jamison
#163, 1-Jamison, James, 2-born, 3-27 Mar 1872, 15-Jamison
#164, 1-Jamison, Birtha M., 2-born, 3-21 Aug 1874, 15-Jamison
#165, 1-Jamison, Worthington J., 2-born, 3-21 Sep 1876, 15-Jamison
#166, 1-Jamison, Clinton H., 2-born, 3-27 Mar 1879, 15-Jamison
#167, 1-Jamison, Blanche D., 2-born, 3-26 Jul 1881, 15-Jamison
#168, 1-Jamison, George W., 2-born, 3-27 Feb 1884, 15-Jamison
#169, 1-Jamison, Harvey L., 2-born, 3-22 Jan 1887, 15-Jamison
#170, 1-Jamison, Dannie Lee, 2-born, 3-20 Mar 1935, 15-Jamison
#171, 1-Herb, Daniel S., 2-born, 3-26 Oct 1834, 4-Little Mahaney Tp.,
      Northumberland Co., PA, 15-Herb
#172, 1-Hilbish, Henrietta, 2-born, 3-9 Jul 1836, 4-Jackson Township,
      Northumberland Co., PA, 15-Herb
#173, 1-Herb, Lillian, 2-born, 3-2 Aug 1858, 10-Rev. Rittenhouse, 12-Herb, D.S.,
      13-Herb, Henrietta, 15-Herb
#174, 1-Herb, James Newton, 2-born, 3-3 Jan 1861, 10-Rev. Fritzinger, 12-Herb,
      Daniel S., 13-Herb, Henrietta, 15-Herb
#175, 1-Herb, Daniel S., 2-married, 3-18 Oct 1857, 8-Treverton, PA, 15-Herb
#176, 1-Hilbish, Henrietta, 2-married, 3-18 Oct 1857, 8-Jackson Township,
      Northumberland Co., PA, 15-Herb
#177, 1-Herb, J. Newton, 2-married, 3-27 Oct 1886, 7-Lerch, Susin O., 8-
      Lewisburg[?], 9-Lewisburg, 15-Herb
#178, 1-Herb, Lillian, 2-died, 3-11 Feb 1860, 5-1 year 6 months 9 days, 6-"Text
      Mat. 18:14", 12-Herb, Daniel S., 13-Herb, Henrietta, 15-Herb
#179, 1-Herb, Daniel S. , 2-died, 3-9 Apr 1865, 4-Jarvis Hospital, 5-30 years 5
      months 13 days, 6-"Sergt. Major of 100th Regt. Ohio Vol.; died of wounds
      received at the battle of Wilminton N.C.", 15-Herb
#180, 1-Herb, James Newton, 3-1937, 15-Herb
#181, 1-Herb, Susan O., 3-23 Feb 1957, 15-Herb
#182, 1-Croft, Catharine, 2-died, 3-3:07 pm, Friday, 20 Nov 1891, 15-Croft/Kroft
```

FAMILY BIBLE RECORDS IN THE WASHINGTON COUNTY FREE LIBRARY, HAGERSTOWN, MARYLAND

Entry #, 1-Last Name, First Name, 2-Event, 3-Date, 4-Event Location, 5-Age, 6-Other, 7-Spouse's Last, First, 8-Groom's Residence, 9-Bride's Residence, 10-Minister, 11-Minister's Location, 12-Father's Last, First, 13-Mother's Last, First, 14-Transcribed, 15-Family Bible

#183, 1-Croft, Catharine (Ross), 2-obituary, 3-Nov 1891, 4-Hamilton Township, Franklin Co., PA, 5-82 years 10 months 3 days, 6-widow of Abraham Croft; born in Chambersburg, PA, 15-Croft/Kroft

#184, 1-Croft, John R., 2-died, 3-27 Jan[?] 1898, 5-10 years 5 months 11 days, 15-Croft/Kroft

#185, 1-Kroft, Abraham, 2-born, 3-25 Jan 1802, 6-husband of Catherine (Ross) Kroft, 15-Croft/Kroft

#186, 1-Kroft, Catherine (Ross), 2-born, 3-17 Jan 1809, 6-wife of Abraham Kroft, 15-Croft/Kroft

#187, 1-Kroft, Abraham, 2-married, 3-2 Nov 1826, 4-German R. Church, Chambersburg, PA, 7-Ross, Catherine, 10-Rev. Frederick Rahauser, 15-Croft/Kroft

#188, 1-Kroft, John, 2-born, 3-21 Aug 1827, 15-Croft/Kroft

#189, 1-Kroft, David, 2-born, 3-25 Nov 1829, 15-Croft/Kroft

#190, 1-Kroft, Elizabeth, 2-born, 3-13 Jul 1831, 15-Croft/Kroft

#191, 1-Kroft, Drusilla Katherine, 2-born, 3-5 Sep 1833, 15-Croft/Kroft

#192, 1-Kroft, Mary Jane, 2-born, 3-14 May 1835, 15-Croft/Kroft

#193, 1-Kroft, Sarah Ann, 2-born, 3-20 Apr 1837, 15-Croft/Kroft

#194, 1-Kroft, Charlotte, 2-born, 3-5 Jul 1839, 15-Croft/Kroft

#195, 1-Kroft, Katharine, 2-died, 3-10 Aug 1834, 15-Croft/Kroft

#196, 1-Ross, Catharine, 2-born, 3-1 Jan 1783, 15-Croft/Kroft

#197, 1-Ross, Catharine, 2-died, 3-26 Nov 1844, 15-Croft/Kroft

#198, 1-Croft, David, 2-born, 3-3 Aug 1765, 15-Croft/Kroft

#199, 1-Croft, David, 2-died, 3-18 Dec 1845, 5-80 years 4 months 12 days , 15-Croft/Kroft

#200, 1-Croft, Abraham, 2-died, 3-16 Apr 1885, 5-83 years 2 months 21 days, 15-Croft/Kroft

#201, 1-Croft, Catharine (Mrs.), 2-died, 3-20 Nov 1891, 4-Franklin Co., PA, 5-82 years 10 months 3 days, 6-wife of Abraham Croft, 15-Croft/Kroft

#202, 1-Croft, John R. (Mrs.)[?], 2-born, 3-2_ Aug 1827, 15-Croft/Kroft

#203, 1-Croft, John R. (Mrs.)[?], 2-died, 3-9 Feb 1895[?], 15-Croft/Kroft

#204, 1-Wolf, David, 2-married, 3-11 Feb 1846, 7-Long, Mary, 15-Wolf

#205, 1-Wolf, David, 2-born, 3-4 Apr 1821, 15-Wolf

#206, 1-Wolf, Mary, 2-born, 3-16 Jan 1824, 15-Wolf

#207, 1-Wolf, Daniel Elmer, 2-born, 3-17 Mar 1847, 12-Wolf, David, 13-Wolf, Mary, 15-Wolf

#208, 1-Wolf, Joseph Albert, 2-born, 3-24 Dec 1851, 12-Wolf, David, 13-Wolf, Mary, 15-Wolf

#209, 1-Wolf, Mary Elen, 2-born, 3-24 Jan 1853, 12-Wolf, David, 13-Wolf, Mary, 15-Wolf

#210, 1-Wolf, Lizzie Angela, 2-born, 3-21 Jul 1857, 12-Wolf, David, 13-Wolf, Mary, 15-Wolf

#211, 1-Wolf, Victor Ellsworth, 2-born, 3-13 Jul 1862, 12-Wolf, David, 13-Wolf, Mary, 15-Wolf

#212, 1-Wolf, Joseph Albert, 2-died, 3-8 Jan 1852, 12-Wolf, David, 13-Wolf, Mary, 15-Wolf

#213, 1-Wolf, Mary Elen, 2-died, 3-11 Dec 1860, 12-Wolf, David, 13-Wolf, Mary, 15-Wolf

#214, 1-Milliken, Andrew, 2-married, 3-5 Mar 1859, 7-Mahon, Louise J., 10-Rev. John Todd, 15-Milliken

#215, 1-Milliken, Thomas Edgar, 2-born, 3-Sunday, 4 Dec 1859, 15-Milliken

#216, 1-Milliken, Elizabeth Bell, 2-born, 3-Wednesday, 16 Oct 1861, 15-Milliken

#217, 1-Milliken, Jane Mary, 2-born, 3-Thursday, 27 Aug 1863, 15-Milliken

#218, 1-Jacques, Mary, 2-born, 3-Wednesday, 15 Feb 1835, 12-Jacques, Lancelot, 13-Jacques, Mary, 15-Milliken

#219, 1-Lowe, Robert, 2-born, 3-23 Jan 1765, 6-husband of Elizabeth Lowe, 15-Lowe

FAMILY BIBLE RECORDS IN THE WASHINGTON COUNTY FREE LIBRARY, HAGERSTOWN, MARYLAND

Entry #, 1-Last Name, First Name, 2-Event, 3-Date, 4-Event Location, 5-Age, 6-Other,
7-Spouse's Last, First, 8-Groom's Residence, 9-Bride's Residence, 10-Minister, 11-Minister's Location,
12-Father's Last, First, 13-Mother's Last, First, 14-Transcribed, 15-Family Bible

```
#220, 1-Lowe, Elizabeth, 2-born, 3-29 May 1765, 6-wife of Robert Lowe, 15-Lowe
#221, 1-Lowe, Maria, 2-born, 3-17 Apr 1791, 12-Lowe, Robert, 13-Lowe, Elizabeth,
      15-Lowe
#222, 1-Lowe, Mary, 2-born, 3-25 Feb 1792, 15-Lowe
#223, 1-Lowe, Susannah, 2-born, 3-17 Aug 1793, 15-Lowe
#224, 1-Lowe, Joseph, 2-born, 3-29 Aug 1795, 15-Lowe
#225, 1-Lowe, Cephias, 2-born, 3-23 Jul 1797, 15-Lowe
#226, 1-Lowe, Charles Swearingin, 2-born, 3-24 Sep 1798, 15-Lowe
#227, 1-Lowe, Elisa, 2-born, 3-7 Jan 1800, 15-Lowe
#228, 1-Lowe, John Booth, 2-born, 3-8 Feb 1802, 15-Lowe
#229, 1-Lowe, Dousilla, 2-born, 3-30 Aug 1803, 15-Lowe
#230, 1-Lehman, John S., 2-married, 3-27 Dec 1860, 4-Chambersburg, 6-witnesses were
      T. Lehman and J. Middlekauff, 7-Middlekauff, Lizzie, 8-Washington Co., MD, 9-
      Washington Co., MD, 10-Rev. Nickolson, 15-Lehman
#231, 1-Lehman, Clegget M., 2-married, 3-5 Feb 1885, 7-Funk, Ida M., 8-Washington
      Co., 9-Wingerton, PA, 15-Lehman
#232, 1-Spessard, Woodward E., 2-married, 3-28 Dec 1898, 7-Lehman, Lizzie M., 8-
      Chewsville, 9-Hagerstown, 15-Lehman
#233, 1-Lehman, J. William, 2-married, 3-2 Aug 1899, 6-bride from Hagerstown, MD,
      7-Lowery, Bettie B., 15-Lehman
#234, 1-Strock, Henry F., 2-married, 3-25 Jan 1900, 6-bride from Hagerstown, MD, 7-
      Lehman, Maud, 15-Lehman
#235, 1-Lehman, John S., 2-born, 3-28 Jan 1833, 15-Lehman
#236, 1-Lehman, Lizzie A., 2-born, 3-10 Aug 1837, 15-Lehman
#237, 1-Lehman, Cleggett Middlekauff, 2-born, 3-27 Oct 1861, 12-Lehman, John S.,
      13-Lehman, Lizzie A., 15-Lehman
#238, 1-Lehman, Emma Florence, 2-born, 3-19 Jun 1863, 12-Lehman, John S., 13-
      Lehman, Lizzie A., 15-Lehman
#239, 1-Lehman, Anna May, 2-born, 3-13 Jan 1866, 12-Lehman, John S., 13-Lehman,
      Lizzie A., 15-Lehman
#240, 1-Lehman, Minnie Kate, 2-born, 3-26 Oct 1867, 12-Lehman, John S., 13-Lehman,
      Lizzie A., 15-Lehman
#241, 1-Lehman, Maud, 2-born, 3-15 May 1870, 12-Lehman, John S., 13-Lehman, Lizzie
      A., 15-Lehman
#242, 1-Lehman, Lizzie, 2-born, 3-9 Nov 1872, 12-Lehman, John S., 13-Lehman, Lizzie
      A., 15-Lehman
#243, 1-Lehman, John William, 2-born, 3-16 Sep 1877, 12-Lehman, John S., 13-Lehman,
      Lizzie A., 15-Lehman
#244, 1-Lehman, Elizabeth A., 2-died, 3-3 am, 19 Oct 1901, 5-64 years 2 months 9
      days, 15-Lehman
#245, 1-Lehman, John F., 2-died, 3-20 Jan 1911, 15-Lehman
#246, 1-Lehman, Cleggett M., 2-died, 3-27 Oct 1894, 12-Lehman, John F., 13-Lehman,
      Elizabeth A., 15-Lehman
#247, 1-Lehman, Annie M., 2-died, 3-16 May 1904, 12-Lehman, John F., 13-Lehman,
      Elizabeth A., 15-Lehman
#248, 1-Lehman, John F., 2-died, 3-20 Jan 1910[?], 12-Lehman, John F., 13-Lehman,
      Elizabeth A., 15-Lehman
#249, 1-Lehman, Minnie K., 2-died, 3-27 Sep 1919, 12-Lehman, John F., 13-Lehman,
      Elizabeth A., 15-Lehman
#250, 1-Witmer, Andrew S., 2-married, 3-7 Apr 1841[or 1847], 7-Witmer, Sarah, 10-
      Rev. John Robaugh, 15-Witmer
#251, 1-Witmer, Andrew S., 2-born, 3-1 Feb 1819, 15-Witmer
#252, 1-Witmer, Sarah, 2-born, 3-18 Oct 1822, 15-Witmer
#253, 1-Witmer, Emily S., 2-born, 3-10 Jul 1848, 15-Witmer
#254, 1-Witmer, Jacob A., 2-born, 3-16 Oct 1847, 15-Witmer
```

FAMILY BIBLE RECORDS IN THE WASHINGTON COUNTY FREE LIBRARY, HAGERSTOWN, MARYLAND

Entry #, 1-Last Name, First Name, 2-Event, 3-Date, 4-Event Location, 5-Age, 6-Other,
7-Spouse's Last, First, 8-Groom's Residence, 9-Bride's Residence, 10-Minister, 11-Minister's Location,
12-Father's Last, First, 13-Mother's Last, First, 14-Transcribed, 15-Family Bible

```
#255, 1-Witmer, Joseph M., 2-born, 3-4 Dec 1851, 15-Witmer
#256, 1-Witmer, Ann Elizabeth, 2-born, 3-7 Sep 1853, 15-Witmer
#257, 1-Witmer, Leander S., 2-born, 3-21 Oct 1855, 15-Witmer
#258, 1-Witmer, Henry J., 2-born, 3-28 Jan 1858, 15-Witmer
#259, 1-Witmer, Sarah Catherine, 2-born, 3-13 Feb 1861, 15-Witmer
#260, 1-Witmer, Elizabeth, 2-born, 3-25 Mar 1822, 15-Witmer
#261, 1-Witmer, Martha, 2-born, 3-11 Apr 1825, 15-Witmer
#262, 1-Witmer, Lydia, 2-born, 3-2 Jun 1833, 15-Witmer
#263, 1-Witmer, Sr., Jacob, 2-born, 3-31 Oct 1789, 15-Witmer
#264, 1-Witmer, Amos, 2-born, 3-27 Apr 1793, 15-Witmer
#265, 1-Witmer, Emily S., 2-died, 3-24 Nov 1848, 5-6 months 14 days, 15-Witmer
#266, 1-Witmer, Sarah Catherine, 2-died, 3-11 Apr 1862, 5-1 year 1 months 28 days,
      15-Witmer
#267, 1-Witmer, Sr., Jacob, 2-died, 3-6 Sep 1856, 5-66 years 10 months 6 days, 15-
      Witmer
#268, 1-Witmer, Nancy, 2-died, 3-19 Jul 1857, 5-64 years 2 months 22 days, 15-
      Witmer
#269, 1-Witmer, A.S., 2-died, 3-15 Sep 1863, 5-44 years 6 months 15 days, 15-Witmer
#270, 1-Beachley, Ralph Gregory, 2-born, 3-12 Aug 1895, 4-Hagerstown, MD, 6-
      baptized 1 Aug 1896 by Rev. S.M. Hartsock, 15-Beachley
#271, 1-Beachley, Katherine Louise, 2-born, 3-20 Sep 1901, 15-Beachley
#272, 1-Beachley, Jack Hanson, 2-born, 3-28 May 1903, 4-Hagerstown, MD, 15-Beachley
#273, 1-Beachley, Eleanor Louise Gregory, 2-born, 3-Jan 1922, 4-Hagerstown, MD, 15-
      Beachley
#274, 1-Beachley, JoAnn, 2-born, 3-3 Mar 1831, 4-Hagerstown, MD, 15-Beachley
#275, 1-Beachley, Yvonne, 2-born, 3-21 Mar 1832, 4-Hagerstown, MD, 15-Beachley
#276, 1-Kilcher, Katherine Starr , 2-born, 3-29 Apr 1954, 4-Hagerstown, MD, 6-
      baptized St. Paul's Methodist Church, Hagerstown, MD by Rev. J. Turnbull
      Spicknall, DD, 15-Beachley
#277, 1-Kilcher, Ann Candace , 2-born, 3-14 Jul 1956, 4-Hagerstown, MD, 15-Beachley
#278, 1-Wells, III, Samuel Robert , 2-born, 3-18 Jan 1960, 4-Hagerstown, MD, 6-
      baptized St. Paul's Methodist Church, Hagerstown, MD by Rev. J. Turnbull
      Spicknall, DD, 15-Beachley
#279, 1-Wells, David Beachley, 2-born, 3-6 Jun 1962, 4-Hagerstown, MD, 6-baptized
      St. Paul's Methodist Church, Hagerstown, MD by Rev. J. Turnbull Spicknall,
      DD, 15-Beachley
#280, 1-Beachley, Harry Knode, 2-married, 3-12 Sep 1888, 4-St. Paul's Methodist
      Church, Hagerstown, MD, 7-Witmer, Clara, 15-Beachley
#281, 1-Beachley, Harry Knode, 2-married, 3-19 Apr 1893, 4-Hagerstown, MD, 7-
      Taylor, Alice, 10-Rev. S.M. Hartsock, 15-Beachley
#282, 1-Beachley, MD, Jack H., 2-married, 3-2 Jul 1929, 4-Baltimore, MD, 7-Morgart,
      RN, Julia Helen, 10-Rev. Frank Bayley, DD, 15-Beachley
#283, 1-Beachley, MD, Jack H., 2-married, 3-16 May 1940, 4-Claredon Methodist
      Church, Arlington Co., VA, 7-Funk, Anna Louise, 10-Rev. J. Martin Gillum, 15-
      Beachley
#284, 1-Beachley, JoAnn, 2-married, 3-14 Jun 1951, 4-St. Paul's Methodist Church,
      Hagerstown, MD, 7-Kilcher, James Conrad, 10-Rev. J. Turnbull Spicknall, DD,
      15-Beachley
#285, 1-Beachley, Yvonne, 2-married, 3-17 Jun 1952, 4-St. Paul's Methodist Church,
      Hagerstown, MD, 7-Wells, Jr., Samuel R., 10-Rev. J. Turnbull Spicknall, DD,
      15-Beachley
#286, 1-Beachley, Clara, 2-died, 3-31 Oct 1891, 6-buried Rose Hill Cemetery,
      Hagerstown, MD, 15-Beachley
#287, 1-Beachley, Harry Knode, 2-died, 3-27 Dec 1918, 6-buried Rose Hill Cemetery,
      Hagerstown, MD, 15-Beachley
```

FAMILY BIBLE RECORDS IN THE WASHINGTON COUNTY FREE LIBRARY, HAGERSTOWN, MARYLAND

Entry #, 1-Last Name, First Name, 2-Event, 3-Date, 4-Event Location, 5-Age, 6-Other,
7-Spouse's Last, First, 8-Groom's Residence, 9-Bride's Residence, 10-Minister, 11-Minister's Location,
12-Father's Last, First, 13-Mother's Last, First, 14-Transcribed, 15-Family Bible

#288, 1-Beachley, Alice (Taylor), 2-died, 3-25 Apr 1928, 6-buried Rose Hill Cemetery, Hagerstown, MD, 15-Beachley

#289, 1-Beachley, Helen Morgart, 2-died, 3-7 Apr 1932, 6-buried Rose Hill Cemetery, Hagerstown, MD, 15-Beachley

#290, 1-Benson, Laura Taylor, 2-born, 3-18 Jul 1868, 6-wife of J. Edward Benson, 15-Beachley

#291, 1-Benson, Laura Taylor, 2-died, 3-14 Aug 1955, 6-wife of J. Edward Benson; buried Jessops Cemetery, Cockeysville, MD, 15-Beachley

#292, 1-Taylor, John Milton, 2-died, 6-buried Hancock, MD cemetery, 15-Beachley

#293, 1-Beachley, Ralph Gregory, 2-died, 3-25 Jan 1969, 4-Arlington, VA, 6-buried Columbia Gardens Cemetery, Arlington, VA, 15-Beachley

#294, 1-Barnes, Levi Y., 2-married, 3-21 Jan 1847, 7-Sellman, Matilda, 15-Barnes

#295, 1-Barnes, Levi Y., 2-born, 3-19 Nov 1827, 15-Barnes

#296, 1-Barnes, Matilda, 2-born, 3-4 Jul 1824, 6-wife of Levi Y. Barnes, 15-Barnes

#297, 1-Barnes, Catharine V., 2-born, 3-19 Jan 1849, 15-Barnes

#298, 1-Barnes, Emily J. C., 2-born, 3-24 Dec 1851, 15-Barnes

#299, 1-Barnes, Joshua B., 2-born, 3-11 Mar 1853, 15-Barnes

#300, 1-Barnes, Sarah N. E.[?], 2-born, 3-11 Jul 1854, 15-Barnes

#301, 1-Barnes, Liza Jane, 2-born, 3-14 Oct 1861, 15-Barnes

#302, 1-Neibert, Scott Alvey, 2-born, 3-24 Oct 1910, 4-Broadfording, MD, 15-Neibert

#303, 1-Neibert, Scott Alvey, 2-married, 3-25 Dec 1931, 4-Hagerstown, MD, 7-Coffinberger, Leda Cornelia, 15-Neibert

#304, 1-Neibert, Scott Alvey, 2-died, 3-13 Oct 1989, 15-Neibert

#305, 1-Coffinberger, Leda Cornelia, 2-born, 3-19 Nov 1912, 4-Shepherdstown, WV, 15-Neibert

#306, 1-Neibert, Betty Jeanene, 2-born, 3-26 May 1933, 4-54 E. Baltimore St., Hagerstown, MD, 12-Neibert, Scott Alvey, 13-Coffinberger, Leda Cornelia, 15-Neibert

#307, 1-Neibert, Richard Duane, 2-born, 3-20 Oct 1934, 4-55 E. Baltimore St., Hagerstown, MD, 12-Neibert, Scott Alvey, 13-Coffinberger, Leda Cornelia, 15-Neibert

#308, 1-Neibert, Faye Rene, 2-born, 3-29 Apr 1937, 4-56 E. Baltimore St., Hagerstown, MD, 12-Neibert, Scott Alvey, 13-Coffinberger, Leda Cornelia, 15-Neibert

#309, 1-Neibert, Betty Jeanene, 2-married, 3-22 May 1954, 4-Hagerstown, MD, 7-Crider, Wayne Stewart, 12-Neibert, Scott Alvey, 13-Coffinberger, Leda Cornelia, 15-Neibert

#310, 1-Neibert, Betty Jeanene, 2-married, 7-Crowe, John, 8-Hagerstown, MD, 12-Neibert, Scott Alvey, 13-Coffinberger, Leda Cornelia, 15-Neibert

#311, 1-Neibert, Richard Duane, 2-married, 4-Clear Spring, 7-Ferris, Hazel Virginia, 12-Neibert, Scott Alvey, 13-Coffinberger, Leda Cornelia, 15-Neibert

#312, 1-Neibert, Faye Rene, 2-married, 4-St. John's Lutheran, 7-Elgin, Robert, 12-Neibert, Scott Alvey, 13-Coffinberger, Leda Cornelia, 15-Neibert

#313, 1-Neibert, Faye Rene, 2-married, 4-Methodist Church, 7-Fowler, David, 12-Neibert, Scott Alvey, 13-Coffinberger, Leda Cornelia, 15-Neibert

#314, 1-Crider, Wayne Stewart, 2-born, 3-30 May 1955, 12-Crider, Wayne Stewart, 13-Neibert, Betty Jeanene, 15-Neibert

#315, 1-Crider, Catherine Carrol, 2-born, 3-19 Jan 1957, 12-Crider, Wayne Stewart, 13-Neibert, Betty Jeanene, 15-Neibert

#316, 1-Elgin, Karan Sue, 2-born, 3-Apr 1962, 12-Elgin, Robert, 13-Neibert, Faye Rene, 15-Neibert

#317, 1-Elgin, Karan Sue, 2-married, 7-Kendall, Larry, 15-Neibert

#318, 1-Neibert, Edgar, 12-Neibert, Christian Phillip, 13-Coffinberger, Bessie Kershner, 15-Neibert

FAMILY BIBLE RECORDS IN THE WASHINGTON COUNTY FREE LIBRARY, HAGERSTOWN, MARYLAND

Entry #, 1-Last Name, First Name, 2-Event, 3-Date, 4-Event Location, 5-Age, 6-Other,
7-Spouse's Last, First, 8-Groom's Residence, 9-Bride's Residence, 10-Minister, 11-Minister's Location,
12-Father's Last, First, 13-Mother's Last, First, 14-Transcribed, 15-Family Bible

#319, 1-Neibert, Scott A., 12-Neibert, Christian Phillip, 13-Coffinberger, Bessie Kershner, 15-Neibert

#320, 1-Neibert, Alice, 12-Neibert, Christian Phillip, 13-Coffinberger, Bessie Kershner, 15-Neibert

#321, 1-Neibert, Lillian, 12-Neibert, Christian Phillip, 13-Coffinberger, Bessie Kershner, 15-Neibert

#322, 1-Neibert, Ella, 12-Neibert, Christian Phillip, 13-Coffinberger, Bessie Kershner, 15-Neibert

#323, 1-Kershner, Bessie, 12-Coffinberger, William Elmer, 13-Link, Margaret May, 15-Neibert

#324, 1-Kershner, Myrtle, 12-Coffinberger, William Elmer, 13-Link, Margaret May, 15-Neibert

#325, 1-Coffinberger, Leda Cornelia, 2-born, 3-19 Nov 1912, 12-Coffinberger, Wm. Elmer, 13-Link, Margaret M., 15-Coffinberger

#326, 1-Coffinberger, Holland R., 2-born, 12-Coffinberger, Wm. Elmer, 13-Link, Margaret M., 15-Coffinberger

#327, 1-Coffinberger, Grace O'Lee, 2-born, 3-24 Mar, 12-Coffinberger, Wm. Elmer, 13-Link, Margaret M., 15-Coffinberger

#328, 1-Coffinberger, Walter W.S., 2-born, 3-30 Mar, 12-Coffinberger, Wm. Elmer, 13-Link, Margaret M., 15-Coffinberger

#329, 1-Coffinberger, Elmer May, 2-born, 3-1 Jun, 12-Coffinberger, Wm. Elmer, 13-Link, Margaret M., 15-Coffinberger

#330, 1-Coffinberger, Bertha L___, 2-born, 3-9 Oct, 12-Coffinberger, Wm. Elmer, 13-Link, Margaret M., 15-Coffinberger

#331, 1-Coffinberger, Wm. Calvin, 2-born, 3-11 Jul 1923, 12-Coffinberger, Wm. Elmer, 13-Link, Margaret M., 15-Coffinberger

#332, 1-Coffinberger, Wm. Calvin, 2-died, 3-24 Jan 1947, 12-Coffinberger, Wm. Elmer, 13-Link, Margaret M., 15-Coffinberger

#333, 1-Link, Margaret M., 2-born, 12-Link, Wm., 13-Daniels, Martha, 15-Coffinberger

#334, 1-Link, John, 2-born, 12-Link, Wm., 13-Daniels, Martha, 15-Coffinberger

#335, 1-Link, Adam, 2-born, 12-Link, Wm., 13-Daniels, Martha, 15-Coffinberger

#336, 1-Link, Wesley, 2-born, 12-Link, Wm., 13-Daniels, Martha, 15-Coffinberger

#337, 1-Link, Bill, 2-born, 12-Link, Wm., 13-Daniels, Martha, 15-Coffinberger

#338, 1-Link, Dennis, 2-born, 12-Link, Wm., 13-Daniels, Martha, 15-Coffinberger

#339, 1-Link, Lester, 2-born, 12-Link, Wm., 13-Daniels, Martha, 15-Coffinberger

#340, 1-Link, Rebecca, 2-born, 12-Link, Wm., 13-Daniels, Martha, 15-Coffinberger

#341, 1-Link, Sally, 2-born, 12-Link, Wm., 13-Daniels, Martha, 15-Coffinberger

#342, 1-Link, Martha, 2-born, 12-Link, Wm., 13-Daniels, Martha, 15-Coffinberger

#343, 1-Coffinberger, Elmer, 2-born, 12-Coffinberger, James, 13-Engle, Cornelia, 15-Coffinberger

#344, 1-Coffinberger, James, 2-born, 12-Coffinberger, James, 13-Engle, Cornelia, 15-Coffinberger

#345, 1-Coffinberger, Nan, 2-born, 12-Coffinberger, James, 13-Engle, Cornelia, 15-Coffinberger

#346, 1-Coffinberger, Bess, 2-born, 12-Coffinberger, James, 13-Engle, Cornelia, 15-Coffinberger

#347, 1-Coffinberger, Amada, 2-born, 12-Coffinberger, James, 13-Engle, Cornelia, 15-Coffinberger

#348, 1-Beckley, David, 2-married, 3-23 Feb 1853, 7-Watkins, Margaret, 15-Beckley

#349, 1-Beckley, David, 2-born, 3-18 May 1825, 15-Beckley

#350, 1-Watkins, Margaret A., 2-born, 3-28 Oct 1836, 15-Beckley

#351, 1-Beckley, John Clinton, 2-born, 3-26 Dec 1853, 15-Beckley

#352, 1-Beckley, Richard P. H__[?], 2-born, 3-16[?] Apr 1855, 6-baptized by Rev. J. Unger[?], 15-Beckley

FAMILY BIBLE RECORDS IN THE WASHINGTON COUNTY FREE LIBRARY, HAGERSTOWN, MARYLAND

Entry #, 1-Last Name, First Name, 2-Event, 3-Date, 4-Event Location, 5-Age, 6-Other, 7-Spouse's Last, First, 8-Groom's Residence, 9-Bride's Residence, 10-Minister, 11-Minister's Location, 12-Father's Last, First, 13-Mother's Last, First, 14-Transcribed, 15-Family Bible

#353, 1-Beckley, Mary Alice, 2-born, 3-22 Oct 1856, 6-baptized by Rev. Crowe[?], 15-Beckley

#354, 1-Beckley, William Henry, 2-born, 3-11 Aug 1858, 15-Beckley

#355, 1-Beckley, Charles Elmer, 2-born, 3-15 Feb 1861, 12-Beckley, David, 13-Beckley, Margaret, 15-Beckley

#356, 1-Beckley, R_____ [?}, 2-born, 3-26 Oct 1862, 15-Beckley

#357, 1-Beckley, Alen Clark, 2-born, 3-18 Nov 1864, 6-baptized by Rev. J. Evans, 12-Beckley, David, 13-Beckley, Margaret, 15-Beckley

#358, 1-Beckley, ____[?] Gertrude, 2-born, 3-10 Jul 1869, 6-baptized by H.J. Watkins, 12-Beckley, David, 13-Beckley, Margaret, 15-Beckley

#359, 1-Beckley, David Luther, 2-born, 3-4 Jan 1872, 6-baptized by Rev. Do. McCron, 12-Beckley, David, 13-Beckley, Margaret, 15-Beckley

#360, 1-Beckley, Walter Scott, 2-born, 3-14 Feb 1874, 6-baptized by Rev.[?] Startzman, 12-Beckley, David, 13-Beckley, Margaret, 15-Beckley

#361, 1-Beckley, Margie Lee, 2-born, 3-6 am, Sunday, 23 Jul 1876, 6-"baptized at home, on the Schindel property, Williamsport Pike by Rev. Keller", 12-Beckley, David, 13-Beckley, Margaret, 15-Beckley

#362, 1-Beckley, Rosa May, 2-died, 3-2 Feb 1902, 5-39 years 4 months, 12-Beckley, David, 13-Beckley, Margaret, 15-Beckley

#363, 1-Kershner, Fannie G., 2-died, 3-20 Feb 1924, 5-54 years, 6-wife of Andrew E. Kershner, 15-Beckley

#364, 1-Beckley, William H., 2-died, 3-11 Oct 1860, 5-2 months, 6-"Blessed art thou dearest Willie", 12-Beckley, D., 13-Beckley, M., 15-Beckley

#365, 1-Beckley, John[?] Clinton, 2-died, 3-16 Jan 1861, 5-7 years 20 days, 12-Beckley, David, 13-Beckley, Margaret, 15-Beckley

#366, 1-Beckley, Allen Clark, 2-died, 3-6 Jan 1866, 5-1 years 1 months 18 days, 12-Beckley, D., 13-Beckley, M., 15-Beckley

#367, 1-Beckley, Margaret A., 2-died, 3-8 Dec 1896, 5-60 years 1 mo 10 days, 6-wife of David Beckley, 15-Beckley

#368, 1-Beckley, David, 2-died, 3-9 Jul[?] 1900, 5-74 years 8 months 21 days, 15-Beckley

#369, 1-Beckley, Margia L., 2-died, 3-2 Jun 1901, 5-24 years 10 months 10 days, 6-wife of Franklin H. Kershner, 12-Beckley, David, 13-Beckley, Margaret, 15-Beckley

#370, 1-Beckley, Margia L., 2-married, 7-Kershner, Franklin H., 15-Beckley

#371, 1-Backus, G.H. Clifford, 2-born, 3-2 Nov 1834, 12-Backhus, Geoerge, 13-Backus, Catharine, 15-Boetler/Boteler

#372, 1-Langdon, Lilian E., 2-born, 3-21 Nov 1856, 12-Langdon, William, 13-Langdon, Almira, 15-Boetler/Boteler

#373, 1-Backus, Kate Kable[?], 2-born, 3-22 Jul 1878, 12-Backus, G. H. Clifford, 13-Backus, Lillie E., 15-Boetler/Boteler

#374, 1-Backus, Wilmira Clifford, 2-born, 3-7 Oct 1879, 15-Boetler/Boteler

#375, 1-Backus, G. H. Clifford, 2-married, 3-8 May 1877, 4-"Mr. T.E.C. Eddy's in Millwood, VA", 7-Langdon, Lilian E., 10-Rev. A.B. Dolly, 15-Boetler/Boteler

#376, 1-Backus, Katie Kable, 2-died, 3-25 Feb 1880, 4-Ripon, WV, 5-1 years 7 months 3 days, 15-Boetler/Boteler

#377, 1-Johnson, Benjamin F., 2-married, 3-22 Feb 1894, 4-Huyetts, 7-Needy, Cora E., 8-Huyetts, 10-A.M. Evers, 15-Johnson

#378, 1-Johnson, Benjamin Franklin, 2-born, 3-12 Dec 1868, 4-Wilson, 15-Johnson

#379, 1-Johnson, Benjamin Franklin, 2-married, 3-22 Feb 1894, 7-Johnson, Cora Elizabeth, 8-Wilson, 9-Huyetts, 15-Johnson

#380, 1-Johnson, Benjamin Franklin, 2-died, 3-4 pm, 26 Mar 1957, 15-Johnson

#381, 1-Johnson, Cora Elizabeth, 2-born, 3-1 Sep 1870, 15-Johnson

#382, 1-Johnson, Cora Elizabeth, 2-died, 3-6:30 am, 12 Oct 1946, 15-Johnson

#383, 1-Johnson, Mary Grace, 2-born, 3-12 Feb 1895, 4-Williamsport, 15-Johnson

FAMILY BIBLE RECORDS IN THE WASHINGTON COUNTY FREE LIBRARY, HAGERSTOWN, MARYLAND

Entry #, 1-Last Name, First Name, 2-Event, 3-Date, 4-Event Location, 5-Age, 6-Other, 7-Spouse's Last, First, 8-Groom's Residence, 9-Bride's Residence, 10-Minister, 11-Minister's Location, 12-Father's Last, First, 13-Mother's Last, First, 14-Transcribed, 15-Family Bible

```
#384, 1-Johnson, Olive Louise, 2-born, 3-19 Apr 1896, 4-Williamsport, 15-Johnson
#385, 1-Johnson, Olive Louise, 2-died, 3-14 Apr 1904, 4-Williamsport, 15-Johnson
#386, 1-Johnson, Paul William, 2-born, 3-2 Nov 1897, 4-Williamsport, 15-Johnson
#387, 1-Johnson, Paul William, 2-married, 3-27 Mar 1924, 15-Johnson
#388, 1-Johnson, Paul William, 2-died, 3-7 Aug 1974, 15-Johnson
#389, 1-Johnson, Benjamin Samuel, 2-born, 3-4 Feb 1899, 4-Williamsport, 15-Johnson
#390, 1-Johnson, Benjamin Samuel, 2-married, 3-20 Jun 1925, 15-Johnson
#391, 1-Johnson, Benjamin Samuel, 2-died, 3-4:30, 12 Apr 1955, 15-Johnson
#392, 1-Johnson, Rhoda Myrtle, 2-born, 3-27 Sep 1900, 4-Williamsport, 15-Johnson
#393, 1-Johnson, Rhoda Myrtle, 2-married, 3-6 Jun 1923, 15-Johnson
#394, 1-Johnson, Agnes Elizabeth, 2-born, 3-6 Jul 1902, 4-Williamsport, 15-Johnson
#395, 1-Johnson, Agnes Elizabeth, 2-married, 3-12 Feb 1925, 15-Johnson
#396, 1-Johnson, Agnes Elizabeth, 2-died, 3-7 pm, 22 Jun 1971, 15-Johnson
#397, 1-Johnson, Frederick Foltz, 2-born, 3-9 May 1904, 4-Williamsport, 15-Johnson
#398, 1-Johnson, Frederick Foltz, 2-died, 3-18 May 1904, 15-Johnson
#399, 1-Johnson, Irvin Wertz, 2-born, 3-28 Mar 1905, 4-Williamsport, 15-Johnson
#400, 1-Johnson, Irvin Wertz, 2-married, 3-7 Aug 1926, 15-Johnson
#401, 1-Johnson, Edwin Franklin, 2-born, 3-5 Mar 1907, 4-Williamsport, 15-Johnson
#402, 1-Johnson, Edwin Franklin, 2-married, 3-6 Nov 1954, 15-Johnson
#403, 1-Johnson, Maurice Needy, 2-born, 3-1 Feb 1909, 4-Williamsport, 15-Johnson
#404, 1-Johnson, Maurice Needy, 2-married, 3-25 Apr 1931, 15-Johnson
#405, 1-Johnson, Maurice Needy, 2-died, 3-16 Aug 1960, 15-Johnson
#406, 1-Johnson, Helen Francis, 2-born, 3-30 Jun 1910, 4-Williamsport, 15-Johnson
#407, 1-Johnson, Helen Francis, 2-married, 3-4 Aug 1933, 15-Johnson
#408, 1-Johnson, Clarence Francis, 2-born, 3-9 Apr 1912, 4-Williamsport, 15-Johnson
#409, 1-Johnson, Clarence Francis, 2-married, 3-15 Sep 1945, 15-Johnson
#410, 1-Johnson, Arthur Bair, 2-born, 3-2 Dec 1914, 4-Williamsport, 15-Johnson
#411, 1-Johnson, Arthur Bair, 2-married, 3-25 Jul 1943, 15-Johnson
#412, 1-Ringer, Robert, 2-died, 3-18 Jan 1835, 5-72 years 5 months 6 days, 15-
      Ringer
#413, 1-Ringer, Julean, 2-died, 3-12 Jan 1837, 5-64 years 3 months 22 days, 15-
      Ringer
#414, 1-Ringer, Mary, 2-died, 3-14 Mar 1848, 5-43 years 9 months, 15-Ringer
#415, 1-Ringer, John (of R), 2-died, 3-22 Dec 1860, 5-65 years 3[?] months 5 days,
      15-Ringer
#416, 1-Line, Thomas Franklin, 2-born, 3-20 May 1841, 15-Line
#417, 1-Line, Malinda Cathrine, 2-born, 3-31 Jul 1849, 15-Line
#418, 1-Line, Florra Bell, 2-born, 3-14 Jul 1872, 15-Line
#419, 1-Line, Ida Elizabeth, 2-born, 3-21 Oct 1874, 15-Line
#420, 1-Line, Clara Virginia, 2-born, 3-27 Aug 1876, 15-Line
#421, 1-Line, F_____[?], 2-born, 3-4 Sep 1879, 15-Line
#422, 1-Line, Thomas Franklin, 2-died, 3-22 Jul 1893, 15-Line
#423, 1-Line, Malinda Catherine, 2-died, 3-29 May 1918, 15-Line
#424, 1-Line, Ida Elizabeth, 2-died, 3-19 Sep 1926, 15-Line
#425, 1-Line, Clara Virginia, 2-died, 3-8 Nov 1927, 15-Line
#426, 1-Line, Flora B., 2-died, 3-31 Mar 1957, 15-Line
#427, 1-Line, Frank Howard, 2-died, 3-23 Aug 1963, 15-Line
#428, 1-Line, Malinda C., 2-obituary, 3-29 May 1918, 6-widow of Thomas Line, 15-
      Line
#429, 1-Bartle, William, 2-married, 3-14 Jan 1879, 4-Hagerstown, MD, 6-witnesses
      were J.Q.[?] Stevens and Daniel Dunry, 7-King, Ella, 8-Washington Co., MD, 9-
      Washington Co., MD, 10-Rev. J. Spangler Kieffer, 11-Hagerstown, MD, 15-Bartle
#430, 1-Bartle, Elmer Vinson, 2-born, 3-29 Jan 1880, 12-Bartle, William, 13-King,
      Ella, 15-Bartle
```

FAMILY BIBLE RECORDS IN THE WASHINGTON COUNTY FREE LIBRARY, HAGERSTOWN, MARYLAND

Entry #, 1-Last Name, First Name, 2-Event, 3-Date, 4-Event Location, 5-Age, 6-Other,
7-Spouse's Last, First, 8-Groom's Residence, 9-Bride's Residence, 10-Minister, 11-Minister's Location,
12-Father's Last, First, 13-Mother's Last, First, 14-Transcribed, 15-Family Bible

```
#431, 1-Bartle, Jeremiah Herman, 2-born, 3-7 Jul 1881, 12-Bartle, William, 13-King,
      Ella, 15-Bartle
#432, 1-Bartle, Effie Naomi, 2-born, 3-17 Dec 1882, 12-Bartle, William, 13-King,
      Ella, 15-Bartle
#433, 1-Bartle, Victor Orville, 2-born, 3-25 Feb 1884, 12-Bartle, William, 13-King,
      Ella, 15-Bartle
#434, 1-Bartle, Luther Cleveland, 2-born, 3-16 Jun 1885, 12-Bartle, William, 13-
      King, Ella, 15-Bartle
#435, 1-Bartle, Lloyd Elgin, 2-born, 3-27 Sep 1886, 12-Bartle, William, 13-King,
      Ella, 15-Bartle
#436, 1-Bartle, Harry Richard, 2-born, 3-10 Apr 1888, 12-Bartle, William, 13-King,
      Ella, 15-Bartle
#437, 1-Bartle, Roy Raymond, 2-born, 3-10 Oct 1889, 12-Bartle, William, 13-King,
      Ella, 15-Bartle
#438, 1-Bartle, Alaxander Rudolph, 2-born, 3-10 Apr 1891, 12-Bartle, William, 13-
      King, Ella, 15-Bartle
#439, 1-Bartle, Percy Glenn, 2-born, 3-24 Dec 1892, 12-Bartle, William, 13-King,
      Ella, 15-Bartle
#440, 1-Bartle, Isaac Newton, 2-born, 3-24 Nov 1894, 12-Bartle, William, 13-King,
      Ella, 15-Bartle
#441, 1-Bartle, Elnora Susan, 2-born, 3-1856, 15-Bartle
#442, 1-Bartle, Elnora Susan, 2-died, 3-3 Jun 1923, 5-67 years 9 months, 15-Bartle
#443, 1-Bartle, Elmer V., 2-died, 3-27 Dec 1945, 15-Bartle
#444, 1-Bartle, Luther C., 2-died, 3-30 Dec 1909, 15-Bartle
#445, 1-Bartle, Harry R., 2-died, 3-4 Jul 1906, 15-Bartle
#446, 1-Bartle, Raymond, 2-died, 3-2 Jan 1969, 15-Bartle
#447, 1-Bartle, Alaxander Rudolph, 2-died, 3-29 Dec 1891, 15-Bartle
#448, 1-Bartle, Percy Glenn, 2-died, 3-15 Aug 1955, 15-Bartle
#449, 1-Bartle, Isaac Neuton, 2-died, 3-24 Feb 1963, 15-Bartle
#450, 1-Bartle, William, 2-born, 3-14 Mar 1846, 15-Bartle
#451, 1-Bartle, William , 2-died, 3-27 Aug 1931, 5-85 years 5 months 12 days, 15-
      Bartle
#452, 1-Perrott, Alexander Rudolph, 2-born, 3-3 Jan 1906, 15-Bartle
#453, 1-Perrott, Hazel Louise, 2-born, 3-14 Aug 1907, 15-Bartle
#454, 1-Perrott, Martin Reichard, 2-born, 3-20 Jan 1909, 15-Bartle
#455, 1-Perrott, Wilbur Vincent, 2-born, 3-21 Feb 1911, 15-Bartle
#456, 1-Perrott, John Rohyer, 2-born, 3-28 Oct 1912, 15-Bartle
#457, 1-Perrott, Laura Susan, 2-born, 3-18 Sep 1914, 15-Bartle
#458, 1-Perrott, Effie Elnora, 2-born, 3-2 Aug 1917, 15-Bartle
#459, 1-Perrott, Robert Lee, 2-born, 3-11 Nov 1919, 15-Bartle
#460, 1-Perrott, Maud Irene, 2-born, 3-9 Jan 1922, 15-Bartle
#461, 1-Perrott, Elva Virginia, 2-born, 3-27 Jun 1925, 15-Bartle
#462, 1-Perrott, Elva Virginia, 2-died, 3-Mar 1926, 15-Bartle
#463, 1-Lowe, John B., 2-born, 3-8 Feb 1802, 12-Lowe, Robert, 13-Lowe, Elizabeth,
      15-Lowe
#464, 1-Smith, Rhody Lowe, 2-born, 3-3 Aug 1808, 12-Smith, Joshua, 13-Smith, Mary,
      15-Lowe
#465, 1-Lowe, David Smith, 2-born, 3-6 Jan 1831, 15-Lowe
#466, 1-Lowe, Robert Bothe[?], 2-born, 3-10 Nov 1832, 15-Lowe
#467, 1-Lowe, Joshua Smith, 2-born, 3-18 Sep 1834, 15-Lowe
#468, 1-Lowe, Joseph, 2-born, 3-23 Mar 1837, 15-Lowe
#469, 1-Lowe, John, 2-born, 3-12 Apr 1839, 15-Lowe
#470, 1-Lowe, Benjamin Franklin, 2-born, 3-6 Aug 1841, 15-Lowe
#471, 1-Lowe, Charles S., 2-born, 3-3 Jan 1844, 15-Lowe
#472, 1-Lowe, Doro. E., 2-born, 3-31 May 1853, 15-Lowe
```

FAMILY BIBLE RECORDS IN THE WASHINGTON COUNTY FREE LIBRARY, HAGERSTOWN, MARYLAND

Entry #, 1-Last Name, First Name, 2-Event, 3-Date, 4-Event Location, 5-Age, 6-Other,
7-Spouse's Last, First, 8-Groom's Residence, 9-Bride's Residence, 10-Minister, 11-Minister's Location,
12-Father's Last, First, 13-Mother's Last, First, 14-Transcribed, 15-Family Bible

#473, 1-Lowe, Martin Luther, 2-born, 3-9[?] Sep 1857, 15-Lowe
#474, 1-Lowe, John B., 2-married, 3-18[?] Sep 1828, 6-bride is daughter of Joshua and Mary Smith, 7-Smith, Rhody, 12-Lowe, Robert, 13-Lowe, Elizabeth, 15-Lowe
#475, 1-Lowe, John B., 2-married, 3-11 Mar 1852, 6-bride is daughter of Daniel and Sarah Robinson, 7-Foreman[?], Susan, 15-Lowe
#476, 1-Lowe, Elizabeth, 2-born, 3-25 Jul 1842, 15-Lowe
#477, 1-Lowe, Eveline, 2-born, 15-Lowe
#478, 1-Lowe, Eliza, 2-born, 3-Jun 1850, 15-Lowe
#479, 1-Lowe, Linthy[?], 2-born, 3-23 Dec 1852, 15-Lowe
#480, 1-Lowe, Mary Almeda, 2-born, 3-31 Jan 1856, 15-Lowe
#481, 1-Lowe, William, 2-born, 3-16 Feb 1857, 1Elisabeth, 15-Lowe
#482, 1-Lowe, James Edmun, 2-born, 3-7 Jul 1858, 15-Lowe
#483, 1-Lowe, Elizabeth[?] Etta[?], 3-1860, 15-Lowe
#484, 1-Lowe, Margret, 2-born, 3-28 Sep 1863, 1Elisabeth, 15-Lowe
#485, 1-Lowe, Frederic, 2-born, 3-1847, 15-Lowe
#486, 1-Lowe, Sinthanna[?], 2-born, 3-23 Dec 1852, 15-Lowe
#487, 1-Lowe, Joseph, 2-died, 3-16 Jan 1849, 15-Lowe
#488, 1-Lowe, Robert Boothe[?], 2-died, 3-23 Jul 1850, 15-Lowe
#489, 1-Lowe, Doro Elphrada, 2-died, 3-4 May 1861, 15-Lowe
#490, 1-Lowe, Charles S., 2-died, 3-7 Oct 1880, 15-Lowe
#491, 1-Lowe, Rhodai, 2-died, 3-30 May 1849, 15-Lowe
#492, 1-Lowe, John B., 2-died, 3-29 Jun 1876, 15-Lowe
#493, 1-Lowe, Susan R., 2-died, 3-30 Mar 1871, 6-notation reads, Second Wife", 15-Lowe
#494, 1-Good, Elizabeth (Miss), 3-1 Jan 1851, 6-contributed money to purchase Bible for Young Men's Temple of Knowledge, 15-Leiter
#495, 1-Zeigler, Kate E., 3-2 Jan 1851, 6-contributed money to purchase Bible for Young Men's Temple of Knowledge, 15-Leiter
#496, 1-Hays, Ann B., 3-3 Jan 1851, 6-contributed money to purchase Bible for Young Men's Temple of Knowledge, 15-Leiter
#497, 1-Leiter, Joseph (Mrs.), 3-4 Jan 1851, 6-contributed money to purchase Bible for Young Men's Temple of Knowledge, 15-Leiter
#498, 1-Leiter, James M. (Mrs.), 3-5 Jan 1851, 6-contributed money to purchase Bible for Young Men's Temple of Knowledge, 15-Leiter
#499, 1-Ritter, Servis (Mrs.), 3-6 Jan 1851, 6-contributed money to purchase Bible for Young Men's Temple of Knowledge, 15-Leiter
#500, 1-Hays, Abner (Mrs.), 3-7 Jan 1851, 6-contributed money to purchase Bible for Young Men's Temple of Knowledge, 15-Leiter
#501, 1-Lyday, Samuel (Mrs.), 3-8 Jan 1851, 6-contributed money to purchase Bible for Young Men's Temple of Knowledge, 15-Leiter
#502, 1-Kissell, Emanuel M. (Mrs.), 3-9 Jan 1851, 6-contributed money to purchase Bible for Young Men's Temple of Knowledge, 15-Leiter
#503, 1-Kissell, Jacob (Mrs.), 3-10 Jan 1851, 6-contributed money to purchase Bible for Young Men's Temple of Knowledge, 15-Leiter
#504, 1-Zeigler, Mary C. (Miss), 3-11 Jan 1851, 6-contributed money to purchase Bible for Young Men's Temple of Knowledge, 15-Leiter
#505, 1-Wolfinger, Mary I.[?] (Miss), 3-12 Jan 1851, 6-contributed money to purchase Bible for Young Men's Temple of Knowledge, 15-Leiter
#506, 1-Bell, Elizabeth (Miss), 3-13 Jan 1851, 6-contributed money to purchase Bible for Young Men's Temple of Knowledge, 15-Leiter
#507, 1-Clarke, Catherine (Miss), 3-14 Jan 1851, 6-contributed money to purchase Bible for Young Men's Temple of Knowledge, 15-Leiter
#508, 1-Knouff, Sarah (Miss), 3-15 Jan 1851, 6-contributed money to purchase Bible for Young Men's Temple of Knowledge, 15-Leiter

FAMILY BIBLE RECORDS IN THE WASHINGTON COUNTY FREE LIBRARY, HAGERSTOWN, MARYLAND

Entry #, 1-Last Name, First Name, 2-Event, 3-Date, 4-Event Location, 5-Age, 6-Other,
7-Spouse's Last, First, 8-Groom's Residence, 9-Bride's Residence, 10-Minister, 11-Minister's Location,
12-Father's Last, First, 13-Mother's Last, First, 14-Transcribed, 15-Family Bible

```
#509, 1-Sndier, Harriet (Miss), 3-16 Jan 1851, 6-contributed money to purchase
      Bible for Young Men's Temple of Knowledge, 15-Leiter
#510, 1-Burkett, Caroline (Miss), 3-17 Jan 1851, 6-contributed money to purchase
      Bible for Young Men's Temple of Knowledge, 15-Leiter
#511, 1-Wampler, Helen (Miss), 3-18 Jan 1851, 6-contributed money to purchase Bible
      for Young Men's Temple of Knowledge, 15-Leiter
#512, 1-Brown, Hester (Miss), 3-19 Jan 1851, 6-contributed money to purchase Bible
      for Young Men's Temple of Knowledge, 15-Leiter
#513, 1-Deshey, Mary Jane (Miss), 3-20 Jan 1851, 6-contributed money to purchase
      Bible for Young Men's Temple of Knowledge, 15-Leiter
#514, 1-Deshey, Ellen (Miss), 3-21 Jan 1851, 6-contributed money to purchase Bible
      for Young Men's Temple of Knowledge, 15-Leiter
#515, 1-Bell, Julia Ann (Miss), 3-22 Jan 1851, 6-contributed money to purchase
      Bible for Young Men's Temple of Knowledge, 15-Leiter
#516, 1-Poe, Sophia (Miss), 3-23 Jan 1851, 6-contributed money to purchase Bible
      for Young Men's Temple of Knowledge, 15-Leiter
#517, 1-Poe, Matilda (Miss), 3-24 Jan 1851, 6-contributed money to purchase Bible
      for Young Men's Temple of Knowledge, 15-Leiter
#518, 1-Hartman, Rebecca (Miss), 3-25 Jan 1851, 6-contributed money to purchase
      Bible for Young Men's Temple of Knowledge, 15-Leiter
#519, 1-Good, Sarah (Miss), 3-26 Jan 1851, 6-contributed money to purchase Bible
      for Young Men's Temple of Knowledge, 15-Leiter
#520, 1-Grey, Ann (Miss), 3-27 Jan 1851, 6-contributed money to purchase Bible for
      Young Men's Temple of Knowledge, 15-Leiter
#521, 1-Shank, Esther (Miss), 3-28 Jan 1851, 6-contributed money to purchase Bible
      for Young Men's Temple of Knowledge, 15-Leiter
#522, 1-Leiter, James Freeland, 2-married, 3-18 Dec 1855, 7-Lantz, Martha Hadessah,
      15-Leiter
#523, 1-Leiter, Joseph, 2-married, 3-1 May 1828, 7-Ziegler, Ann, 10-Rev. Henry
      Hroh[?], 15-Leiter
#524, 1-Leiter, Joseph, 2-born, 3-13 Dec 1805, 15-Leiter
#525, 1-Leiter, Ann, 2-born, 3-16 Oct 1805, 15-Leiter
#526, 1-Leiter, Mary Elizebth [sic], 2-born, 3-20 Oct 1819, 15-Leiter
#527, 1-Ziegler, Barbara, 2-born, 3-12 Oct 1775, 15-Leiter
#528, 1-Ziegler, Barbara, 2-died, 3-13 Apr 1853, 5-77 years 6 months 1 day, 15-
      Leiter
#529, 1-Leiter, James F., 2-born, 3-11 Jul 1829, 15-Leiter
#530, 1-Lantz, Martha H.[?], 2-born, 3-1 Oct 1834, 15-Leiter
#531, 1-Leiter, Anna Mary, 2-baptized, 3-1857, 6-baptized by Rev. Joseph Santee,
      15-Leiter
#532, 1-Leiter, Titus Benton, 2-baptized, 3-1859, 6-baptized by Rev. Joseph Santee,
      15-Leiter
#533, 1-Leiter, Barbara Virginia, 2-baptized, 3-1860, 6-baptized by Rev. Christian
      Lepley, 15-Leiter
#534, 1-Leiter, Leevi Ziegler, 2-baptized, 3-1862, 6-baptized by Rev. Joseph
      Santee, 15-Leiter
#535, 1-Leiter, Joseph G., 2-baptized, 3-1865, 6-baptized by Rev. Joseph Santee,
      15-Leiter
#536, 1-Leiter, Lizzie Carver, 2-baptized, 3-17 Apr 1868, 6-baptized by Rev. Joseph
      Santee, 15-Leiter
#537, 1-Leiter, Anna Mary, 2-born, 3-29 Sep 1856, 15-Leiter
#538, 1-Leiter, Titus Benton, 2-born, 3-2 Sep 1858, 15-Leiter
#539, 1-Leiter, Barbara Virginia, 2-born, 3-10 Oct 1860, 15-Leiter
#540, 1-Leiter, Levi Zeigler, 2-born, 3-25 Nov 1861, 15-Leiter
#541, 1-Leiter, Joseph G., 2-born, 3-13 Apr 1864, 15-Leiter
```

FAMILY BIBLE RECORDS IN THE WASHINGTON COUNTY FREE LIBRARY, HAGERSTOWN, MARYLAND

Entry #, 1-Last Name, First Name, 2-Event, 3-Date, 4-Event Location, 5-Age, 6-Other,
7-Spouse's Last, First, 8-Groom's Residence, 9-Bride's Residence, 10-Minister, 11-Minister's Location,
12-Father's Last, First, 13-Mother's Last, First, 14-Transcribed, 15-Family Bible

```
#542, 1-Leiter, Lizzie Carver, 2-born, 3-8 Sep 1867, 15-Leiter
#543, 1-Leiter, Vannie[?] Kate, 2-born, 3-9 Sep 1870, 15-Leiter
#544, 1-Leiter, Vannie[?] Kate, 2-baptized, 3-25 Sep 1870, 6-baptized by Rev.
     J.N.[?] Santee, 15-Leiter
#545, 1-Leiter, James William, 2-born, 3-13 Jan 1873, 15-Leiter
#546, 1-Leiter, James William, 2-baptized, 3-29 Jun 1873, 6-baptized by Rev. J. W.
     Santee, 15-Leiter
#547, 1-Leiter, Martha Alice, 2-born, 3-19 Jan 1879, 15-Leiter
#548, 1-Leiter, Martha Alice, 2-baptized, 6-baptized by Rev. Richerson, 15-Leiter
#549, 1-Leiter, Barbara Virginia, 2-died, 3-3 Dec 1860, 5-1 months 23 days, 15-
     Leiter
#550, 1-Leiter, Lizzie Carver, 2-died, 3-24 Sep 1868, 5-1 year 17 days, 15-Leiter
#551, 1-Leiter, Joseph, 2-died, 3-25 Jul 1862, 15-Leiter
#552, 1-Leiter, Ann, 2-died, 3-18 Dec 1863, 15-Leiter
#553, 1-Leiter, George Abraham, 2-died, 3-20 Aug 1864, 15-Leiter
#554, 1-Leiter, James W.[?], 2-died, 3-6 Aug 1885[?], 15-Leiter
#555, 1-Leiter, James Freeland, 2-died, 3-19 Mar 1897, 4-Leitersburg, MD, 15-Leiter
#556, 1-Leiter, Barbara Virginia, 2-obituary, 6-died at A. Leiter's Mill in
     Williamsport district, 15-Leiter
#557, 1-Leiter, Lizzie Carrie, 2-obituary, 12-Leiter, James F., 13-Leiter,
     Marsha[?] H., 15-Leiter
#558, 1-Lantz, Mary B., 2-obituary, 4-Leitersburg, MD, 5-68 years 7 months 24 days
     , 15-Leiter
#559, 1-Leiter, Levi Zeigler, 2-died, 3-23 May 1899, 4-Hagerstown, MD, 15-Leiter
#560, 1-Leiter, Titus Benton, 2-died, 3-10 Dec 1899, 15-Leiter
#561, 1-McGraw , Fannie (Leiter), 2-died, 3-7 Sep 1903, 15-Leiter
#562, 1-Wolfinger, Annie Mary (Leiter), 2-died, 3-8 Feb 1908, 15-Leiter
#563, 1-Leiter, George A., 2-born, 3-17 Jun 1832, 15-Leiter
#564, 1-Leiter, Leevi Ziegler, 2-born, 3-22 Nov 1834, 15-Leiter
#565, 1-Leiter, Elizabeth M., 2-born, 3-8 Aug 1841, 15-Leiter
#566, 1-Leiter, J. Harry, 2-born, 3-17 Nov 1860, 15-Leiter
#567, 1-Leiter, J. Carrington, 2-born, 3-1 Nov 1862, 15-Leiter
#568, 1-Leiter, J. Harry, 2-died, 3-29 Sep 1861, 15-Leiter
#569, 1-Leiter, Mary Elizabeth, 2-died, 3-12 Dec 1907, 15-Leiter
#570, 1-Lantz, Martha, 3-6 Dec 1851, 4-Leitersburg, MD, 6-confirmation certificate
     from Ev. Luth. Church of Smithsburg, MD, 10-Rev. D.H. Bittle[?], 15-Leiter
#571, 1-Leiter, James F., 2-married, 3-18 Dec 1855, 7-Lantz, Martha U.[?] (Miss),
     8-Washington Co., MD, 9-Washington Co., MD, 10-Rev. E. Breidenbaugh, 11-
     Evang. Luth. Church I nGreencastle, PA, 15-Leiter
#572, 1-Cost, Catharine (Mrs.), 2-obituary, 4-Keedysville, MD, 5-66 years 5 months
     29 days, 15-Leiter
#573, 1-Hamilton, Lucile, 2-obituary, 5-4 months 18 days, 6-died 11 Jul, 12-
     Hamilton, William, 13-Hamilton, Clara, 15-Leiter
#574, 1-Ebbrecht, William (Mrs.), 2-obituary, 5-advanced age, 15-Leiter
#575, 1-Harman, Alice (Miss), 2-obituary, 4-residence of Mrs. Snyder in the western
     part of the town, 5-18 years, 6-died of cramp colic, 15-Leiter
#576, 1-Spreacher, Bessie Bell, 2-obituary, 4-near Williamsport, 5-8 months 25
     days, 12-Sprecher, William H., 13-Sprecher, Eliza A., 15-Leiter
#577, 1-Ryan, Malvina (Miss), 2-obituary, 3-4 Jul 1876, 4-Hancock, MD, 5-about 45
     years, 15-Leiter
#578, 1-Leiter, Jeremiah, 2-born, 3-31 Mar 1981, 12-Leiter, David, 13-Downing,
     Theresa, 15-Leiter
#579, 1-Leiter, David, 2-born, 3-1953, 12-Leiter, Jr., Samuel, 13-Eckstine,
     Virginia, 15-Leiter
```

FAMILY BIBLE RECORDS IN THE WASHINGTON COUNTY FREE LIBRARY, HAGERSTOWN, MARYLAND

Entry #, 1-Last Name, First Name, 2-Event, 3-Date, 4-Event Location, 5-Age, 6-Other, 7-Spouse's Last, First, 8-Groom's Residence, 9-Bride's Residence, 10-Minister, 11-Minister's Location, 12-Father's Last, First, 13-Mother's Last, First, 14-Transcribed, 15-Family Bible

#580, 1-Leiter, Theresa (Downing), 2-born, 3-1956, 12-Downing, Richard, 13-Malott, Harriett, 15-Leiter

#581, 1-Leiter, Jr., Samuel, 2-born, 3-1925, 12-Leiter, Sr., Samuel, 13-Martin, Edna, 15-Leiter

#582, 1-Leiter, Virginia (Eckstine), 2-born, 3-1930, 12-Eckstine, Earl, 13-Moore, Beatrice C., 15-Leiter

#583, 1-Leiter, Sr., Samuel, 2-born, 3-1890, 12-Leiter, 15-Leiter

#584, 1-Eckstine, Earl, 2-born, 3-1902, 15-Leiter

#585, 1-Leiter, Edna (Martin), 2-born, 3-1892, 15-Leiter

#586, 1-Fox, Beatrice (Moore) (Eckstine), 2-born, 3-1911, 15-Leiter

#587, 1-Downing, Richard, 2-born, 3-1929, 12-Downing, Merrill, 13-Applegate, Iris, 15-Leiter

#588, 1-Malott, Harriett, 2-born, 3-1931, 12-Malott, Francis, 13-Pence, Eva, 15-Leiter

#589, 1-Pence, Eva, 2-born, 3-1914, 15-Leiter

#590, 1-Mullendore, Daniel, 2-born, 3-2 Nov 1807, 15-Mullendore

#591, 1-Mullendore, Sophia, 2-born, 3-3 Feb 1812, 15-Mullendore

#592, 1-Mullendore, Violetta Matilda, 2-born, 3-9 Feb 1834, 15-Mullendore

#593, 1-Mullendore, Cecelia Elizabeth, 2-born, 3-6 May 1836, 15-Mullendore

#594, 1-Potter, William D., 2-born, 3-3 Aug 1865, 15-Mullendore

#595, 1-Prichard, Annie E., 3-Sep 1879, 6-Bible presented by N. Hibbarel from the Library of her grandmother, M.P. J.[?] Prichard, 15-Prichard

#596, 1-Hibbarel, N., 3-Sep 1880, 6-Bible presented by N. Hibbarel from the Library of her grandmother, M.P. J.[?] Prichard, 15-Prichard

#597, 1-Prichard, George, 2-married, 3-5 Jun 1844, 4-Worcester, 7-Brooks, Elizabeth F., 10-Rev. Elan Smalley, D.D., 11-Old South Church, 15-Prichard

#598, 1-Rice, John, 2-married, 3-22 Sep 1841, 4-Worcester, 7-Eldridge, Rhoda B., 10-Rev. Seth Sweetsiy[?], 11-Central Church, 15-Prichard

#599, 1-Rice, Edrie[?], 2-married, 3-18 Sep 1879, 4-Worcester, 7-Prichard, Annie E., 10-Rev. George W. Phillips, 11-Plymouth Church, 15-Prichard

#600, 1-Prichard, George, 2-born, 3-19 Nov 1819, 4-Bradford, Vermont, 15-Prichard

#601, 1-Brooks, Elizabeth F., 2-born, 3-8 Jun 1826, 4-Worcester, Mass., 15-Prichard

#602, 1-Prichard, Annie E., 2-born, 3-1 Jul 1854, 4-Bradford, Vermont, 15-Prichard

#603, 1-Rice, John, 2-born, 3-10 Nov 1815, 4-Marlboro, Mass., 15-Prichard

#604, 1-Eldridge, Rhoda B., 2-born, 3-14 Dec 1819, 4-Quincy, Mass., 15-Prichard

#605, 1-Rice, Edrie J., 2-born, 3-5 Sep 1851, 4-Worcester, Mass., 15-Prichard

#606, 1-Rice, John, 2-died, 3-14 Jun 1886, 4-Worcester, Mass., 15-Prichard

#607, 1-Prichard, Elizabeth F., 2-died, 3-27 Feb 1888, 4-Worcester, Mass., 15-Prichard

#608, 1-Prichard, George, 2-died, 3-13 Jun 1898, 4-Worcester, Mass., 15-Prichard

#609, 1-Rice, Rhoda B., 2-died, 3-10 Nov 1904, 4-Worcester, Mass., 15-Prichard

#610, 1-Clopper, John H., 2-married, 3-25 Dec 1884, 4-Clavick Hall, PA, 7-Barnhardf[?], Martha E., 8-Clear Spring, MD, 9-Clear Spring, MD, 10-Rev. Bricker, 11-Church of Brethren, 15-Clopper

#611, 1-Clopper, John H., 2-born, 3-7 Oct 1863, 15-Clopper

#612, 1-Clopper, Martha E., 2-born, 3-11 Jun 1860, 15-Clopper

#613, 1-Clopper, Geo. D., 2-born, 3-6 Nov 1885, 12-Clopper, John H., 13-Barnhardf[?], Martha E., 15-Clopper

#614, 1-Clopper, Saml. E., 2-born, 3-7 Nov 1887, 12-Clopper, John H., 13-Barnhardf[?], Martha E., 15-Clopper

#615, 1-Clopper, Chas. W., 2-born, 3-11 Dec 1889, 12-Clopper, John H., 13-Barnhardf[?], Martha E., 15-Clopper

#616, 1-Clopper, Mary M., 2-born, 3-1 Jan 1890, 12-Clopper, John H., 13-Barnhardf[?], Martha E., 15-Clopper

FAMILY BIBLE RECORDS IN THE WASHINGTON COUNTY FREE LIBRARY, HAGERSTOWN, MARYLAND

Entry #, 1-Last Name, First Name, 2-Event, 3-Date, 4-Event Location, 5-Age, 6-Other,
7-Spouse's Last, First, 8-Groom's Residence, 9-Bride's Residence, 10-Minister, 11-Minister's Location,
12-Father's Last, First, 13-Mother's Last, First, 14-Transcribed, 15-Family Bible

#617, 1-Clopper, Leroy , 2-born, 3-15 Dec 1893, 12-Clopper, John H., 13-Barnhardf[?], Martha E., 15-Clopper

#618, 1-Clopper, Minnie M., 2-born, 3-15 Jul 1895, 12-Clopper, John H., 13-Barnhardf[?], Martha E., 15-Clopper

#619, 1-Clopper, Harry C., 2-born, 3-1 Nov 1898, 12-Clopper, John H., 13-Barnhardf[?], Martha E., 15-Clopper

#620, 1-Clopper, Sallie K.[?], 2-born, 3-8 Dec 1900, 12-Clopper, John H., 13-Barnhardf[?], Martha E., 15-Clopper

#621, 1-Clopper, Julia M., 2-born, 3-10 Oct 1902, 12-Clopper, John H., 13-Barnhardf[?], Martha E., 15-Clopper

#622, 1-Clopper, Julia M., 2-born, 3-3 Jul 1900, 6-"adopted", 12-Clopper, John H., 13-Barnhardf[?], Martha E., 15-Clopper

#623, 1-Clopper, Chas W., 2-died, 3-Aug 1890, 15-Clopper

#624, 1-Braxton, William, 2-born, 3-12 Mar 1837, 15-Braxton

#625, 1-Braxton, Heniretta V., 2-born, 3-28 Apr 1842, 6-wife of William Braxton, 15-Braxton

#626, 1-Braxton, Henry Victor, 2-born, 3-28 May 1865, 12-Braxton, William, 13-Braxton, Henrietta, 15-Braxton

#627, 1-Braxton, Mattie Virginia, 2-born, 3-24 May 1868, 12-Braxton, William, 13-Braxton, Henrietta, 15-Braxton

#628, 1-Braxton, Perry Edward, 2-born, 3-6 Aug 1869, 12-Braxton, William, 13-Braxton, Henrietta, 15-Braxton

#629, 1-Dorsey, Lucretia, 2-born, 3-7 Jan 1844, 6-"Our Aunt", 15-Braxton

#630, 1-Curtis, Jane Henrietta, 2-born, 3-15 Mar 1903, 12-Curtis, Charles E., 13-Braxton, Mattie V., 15-Braxton

#631, 1-Smith, William Daniel, 2-born, 3-1 Aug 1906, 12-Smith, William , 13-Smith, Mattie V., 15-Braxton

#632, 1-Smith, Mattie Leutishia, 2-born, 3-16 Jan 1908, 12-Smith, William , 13-Smith, Mattie V., 15-Braxton

#633, 1-Braxton, William, 2-died, 3-4 May 1891, 5-54 years 1 months 22 days, 6-"Our father", 15-Braxton

#634, 1-Smith, Mattie Virginia (Braxton), 2-died, 3-1957, 15-Braxton

#635, 1-Somerville, Jane Henrietta (Curtis), 2-died, 3-5 Aug 1977, 15-Braxton

#636, 1-Beckenbaugh, M.D., John M., 2-married, 3-19 Nov 1868, 4-Shepherdstown, VA, 6-bride is daughter of Rev. Robt. Douglas, 7-Douglas, Nannie Cowan[?], 15-Beckenbaugh

#637, 1-Cotton, Henry Evan (Rev.), 2-married, 3-28 Jun 1899, 4-Hagerstown, MD, 6-bride is daughter of John M. & Nannie C. Beckenbaugh, 7-Beckenbaugh, Helen Douglas, 10-Bishop Paret, 15-Beckenbaugh

#638, 1-Beckenbaugh, Jno. Kyd, 2-married, 3-10 Sep 1902, 6-bride is daughtaer of Geo. W. & Lucy H. Howard, 7-Howard, Harriet Louise, 10-Rev. Henry Evan Cotton, 15-Beckenbaugh

#639, 1-Beckenbaugh, Martha Ligget, 2-born, 3-2 Mar 1870, 12-Beckenbaugh, Jno. M. (Dr.), 13-Beckenbaugh, Nannie C., 15-Beckenbaugh

#640, 1-Beckenbaugh, Helen Douglas, 2-born, 3-26 Jan 1872, 12-Beckenbaugh, Jno. M. (Dr.), 13-Beckenbaugh, Nannie C., 15-Beckenbaugh

#641, 1-Beckenbaugh, John, 2-born, 3-14 Jan 1874, 12-Beckenbaugh, Jno. M. (Dr.), 13-Beckenbaugh, Nannie C., 15-Beckenbaugh

#642, 1-Cotton, Henry Douglas, 2-born, 3-18 Apr 1900, 12-Cotton, Henry Evan (Rev.), 13-Beckenbaugh, Helen Douglas, 15-Beckenbaugh

#643, 1-Cotton, Dudley Page, 2-born, 3-9 Sep 1901, 12-Cotton, Henry Evan (Rev.), 13-Beckenbaugh, Helen Douglas, 15-Beckenbaugh

#644, 1-Beckenbaugh, John Howard, 2-born, 3-6 Aug 1903, 12-Beckenbaugh, Jno. Kyd, 13-Beckenbaugh, Harriet Louise, 15-Beckenbaugh

FAMILY BIBLE RECORDS IN THE WASHINGTON COUNTY FREE LIBRARY, HAGERSTOWN, MARYLAND

Entry #, 1-Last Name, First Name, 2-Event, 3-Date, 4-Event Location, 5-Age, 6-Other, 7-Spouse's Last, First, 8-Groom's Residence, 9-Bride's Residence, 10-Minister, 11-Minister's Location, 12-Father's Last, First, 13-Mother's Last, First, 14-Transcribed, 15-Family Bible

#645, 1-Beckenbaugh, Louise Douglas, 2-born, 3-4 Aug 1904, 12-Beckenbaugh, Jno. Kyd, 13-Beckenbaugh, Harriet Louise, 15-Beckenbaugh

#646, 1-Douglas, Robt. (Rev.), 2-died, 3-20 Aug 1867, 5-59 years 10 months, 15-Beckenbaugh

#647, 1-Legget, Jno. E. (Dr.), 2-died, 3-21 Apr 1869, 5-54 years, 15-Beckenbaugh

#648, 1-Beckenbaugh, J.J. (Dr.), 2-died, 3-13 May 1869, 5-32 years 6 months 26 days, 15-Beckenbaugh

#649, 1-Beckenbaugh, Martha Ligget, 2-died, 3-2 Mar 1870, 5-14 hours, 15-Beckenbaugh

#650, 1-Douglas, Robert, 2-died, 3-18 Dec 1872, 5-26 years 4 months 12 days, 12-Douglas, Robert (Rev.), 13-Douglas, Helen B., 15-Beckenbaugh

#651, 1-Beckenbaugh, John In.[?], 2-died, 3-21 Jul 1873, 5-35 years 4 months 2 days, 15-Beckenbaugh

#652, 1-Beckenbaugh, George, 2-died, 3-14 Apr 1878, 15-Beckenbaugh

#653, 1-Beckenbaugh, T.L. (Dr.), 2-died, 3-15 Feb 1881, 15-Beckenbaugh

#654, 1-Douglas, Helen B., 2-died, 3-30 Jan 1882, 6-"wife of Rev. Robt. Douglas", 15-Beckenbaugh

#655, 1-Douglas, Henry Kyd, 2-died, 3-18 Dec 1903, 5-65 years 3 months, 15-Beckenbaugh

#656, 1-Cotton, Helen Douglas, 2-died, 3-1 Jan 1926, 5-53 years 11 months 5 days, 15-Beckenbaugh

#657, 1-Beckenbaugh, John Kyd, 2-died, 3-5 Oct 1940, 5-66 years 8 months 21 days, 15-Beckenbaugh

#658, 1-Highbarger, Catharine, 2-born, 3-15 Jul 1809, 15-Cookerly

#659, 1-Cookerly, Ann Catharine[?], 2-born, 3-7 Feb 1833, 15-Cookerly

#660, 1-Cookerly, William, 2-born, 3-5 Aug 1834, 15-Cookerly

#661, 1-Cookerly, Mary, 2-born, 3-28 Mar 1837, 15-Cookerly

#662, 1-Cookerly, Clenar[?], 2-born, 3-31 May 1839, 15-Cookerly

#663, 1-Cookerly, John Wierton[?], 2-born, 3-28 May 1841, 15-Cookerly

#664, 1-Cookerly, Mary, 2-born, 3-9 Mar 1843, 15-Cookerly

#665, 1-Fiery, Joseph H., 2-married, 3-19 May 1858, 4-Hagerstown, MD, 7-Ridenour, Mary C. (Miss), 8-Washington Co., MD, 9-Washington Co., MD, 10-Reuben Hill, Pastor loci, 11-Hagerstown, MD, 15-Fiery

#666, 1-Polling, Albert W., 2-married, 3-23 Mar 1871, 4-the house of G.W. Cross, 6-witnesses were A.J. Poling and Cordelia Cross, 7-Moore, Catharine, 8-Barbour Co., WV, 9-Barbour Co., WV, 10-Rev. David R. Poling, 15-Polling

#667, 1-Poling, Albert W., 2-born, 3-9 Jul 1854, 12-Poling, Martin B., 13-Poling, Ruth, 15-Polling

#668, 1-Poling, Catharine, 2-born, 3-24 Feb 1851, 12-Moore, Franklin J., 13-Moore, Elisabeth, 15-Polling

#669, 1-Poling, Columbus Hall, 2-born, 3-13 May 1876, 12-Poling, Albert W., 13-Poling, Catharine, 15-Polling

#670, 1-Poling, Wendell Idleman, 2-born, 3-22 Oct 1908, 15-Polling

#671, 1-Poling, Mary Alice, 2-born, 3-5 Feb 1910, 15-Polling

#672, 1-Poling, Newton Lyon, 2-born, 3-25 Mar 1914, 15-Polling

#673, 1-Poling, Baby, 2-born, 3-16 Nov 1917, 15-Polling

#674, 1-Poling, Ruth, 2-born, 3-23 Mar 1817, 15-Polling

#675, 1-Poling, Ruth, 2-died, 3-29 Aug 1890, 15-Polling

#676, 1-Poling, James Newton, 2-born, 3-14 Dec 1942, 12-Poling, Newton, 13-Poling, Virginia S., 15-Polling

#677, 1-Poling, Harry Emerson, 2-born, 3-7 Dec 1945, 12-Poling, Newton, 13-Poling, Virginia S., 15-Polling

#678, 1-Poling, Edward Lee, 2-born, 3-10 Oct 1947, 12-Poling, Newton, 13-Poling, Virginia S., 15-Polling

FAMILY BIBLE RECORDS IN THE WASHINGTON COUNTY FREE LIBRARY, HAGERSTOWN, MARYLAND

Entry #, 1-Last Name, First Name, 2-Event, 3-Date, 4-Event Location, 5-Age, 6-Other,
7-Spouse's Last, First, 8-Groom's Residence, 9-Bride's Residence, 10-Minister, 11-Minister's Location,
12-Father's Last, First, 13-Mother's Last, First, 14-Transcribed, 15-Family Bible

#679, 1-Poling, Rebecca Jeanne, 2-born, 3-9 Aug 1951, 12-Poling, Newton, 13-Poling, Virginia S., 15-Polling

#680, 1-Poling, A.W., 2-married, 3-23 Mar 1871, 6-bride is daughter of F.J. & E. Moore, 7-Moore, C., 12-Poling, M.B., 13-Poling, R., 15-Polling

#681, 1-Poling, C.H., 2-married, 3-14 Aug 1907, 7-Idle, Willyi[?] A., 15-Polling

#682, 1-Poling, Newton L., 2-married, 3-26 May 1941, 7-Smith, Virginia Dare, 15-Polling

#683, 1-Poling, James Newton, 2-married, 3-17 Aug 1953, 7-Werking, Nancy Luetta, 15-Polling

#684, 1-Poling, Harry Emerson, 2-married, 3-2 Jun 1968, 7-Mabe, Marcella Ann, 15-Polling

#685, 1-Poling, Edward Lee, 2-married, 3-21 Jun 1969, 7-Miller, Marjorie Eileen, 15-Polling

#686, 1-Poling, Rebecca Jeanne, 2-married, 3-9 Jun 1973, 7-Karras, Philip, 15-Polling

#687, 1-Poling, Catharine, 2-died, 3-19 Feb 1921, 6-wife of A.W. Poling, 15-Polling

#688, 1-Poling, Wendell J., 2-died, 3-11 May 1921, 12-Poling, C.H., 13-Poling, W.A., 15-Polling

#689, 1-Poling, Mary Alice, 2-died, 3-11 Feb 1925, 15-Polling

#690, 1-Poling, Albert W., 2-died, 3-21 Jun 1932, 15-Polling

#691, 1-Poling, Columbus Hall, 2-died, 3-12 Jun 1934, 12-Poling, Albert, 13-Moore, Catharine, 15-Polling

#692, 1-Poling, Willye Idelman, 2-died, 3-14 Nov 1944, 4-Scherr, WV, 15-Polling

#693, 1-Poling, Newton Lyon, 2-married, 3-26 May 1941[?], 4-Elgin, Illinois, 6-bride is daughter of Leander and Mary Smith, 7-Smith, Virginia D., 15-Polling

#694, 1-Poling, Christina Lynn, 2-born, 3-12 Oct 1966, 4-Chicago, IL, 12-Poling, James, 13-Werking, Nancy, 15-Polling

#695, 1-Poling, James Nathan, 2-born, 3-18 Jul 1968, 4-Takoma Park, MD, 12-Poling, James, 13-Werking, Nancy, 15-Polling

#696, 1-Poling, John Robert, 2-born, 3-10 Dec 1972, 4-Pittsburgh, PA, 12-Poling, Emerson, 13-Mabe, Ann, 15-Polling

#697, 1-Poling, Mark Edward, 2-born, 3-18 Feb 1975, 4-Winchester, VA, 12-Poling, Emerson, 13-Mabe, Ann, 15-Polling

#698, 1-Poling, Chandler Miller, 2-born, 3-29 Jan 1974, 4-Reading, PA, 12-Poling, Edward L., 13-Miller, Marjorie, 15-Polling

#699, 1-Poling, Travis Edward, 2-born, 3-8 Aug 1978, 4-Lebanon, PA, 12-Poling, Edward L., 13-Miller, Marjorie, 15-Polling

#700, 1-Karras, Elicia Poling, 2-born, 3-27 Jun 1980, 4-Washington, DC area, 12-Karras, Philip, 13-Poling, Rebecca, 15-Polling

#701, 1-Karras, Justin Poling, 2-born, 3-22 Apr 1983, 4-Washington, DC area, 12-Karras, Philip, 13-Poling, Rebecca, 15-Polling

#702, 1-Heard, Albert, 2-married, 3-27 Apr 1887, 4-Hagerstown, MD, 7-Fiery, Mollie E. (Miss), 10-Rev. S.W.[?] Owen, 11-St. John's Luth. Church , 15-Heard

#703, 1-Heard, Albert, 2-born, 3-28 Aug 1860, 15-Heard

#704, 1-Heard, Mollie E., 2-born, 3-13 Nov 1861, 15-Heard

#705, 1-Heard, Hellen Firey, 2-born, 3-22 Jul 1888 , 12-Heard, Albert, 13-Heard, Mollie E., 15-Heard

#706, 1-Heard, Mary Catharine, 2-born, 3-16 Aug 1891, 12-Heard, Albert, 13-Heard, Mollie E., 15-Heard

#707, 1-Heard, Alberta, 2-born, 3-30 Oct 1894, 12-Heard, Albert, 13-Heard, Mollie E., 15-Heard

#708, 1-Heard, Mary Catharine, 2-died, 3-12 Sep 1892, 5-1 years 27 days, 15-Heard

#709, 1-Heard, Alberta, 2-died, 3-Tuesday, 7 Nov 1894, 5-8 days, 15-Heard

#710, 1-Heard, Mollie E., 2-died, 3-15 Oct 1921, 6-would have been 60 years old on 13 Nov 1921, 15-Heard

FAMILY BIBLE RECORDS IN THE WASHINGTON COUNTY FREE LIBRARY, HAGERSTOWN, MARYLAND

Entry #, 1-Last Name, First Name, 2-Event, 3-Date, 4-Event Location, 5-Age, 6-Other, 7-Spouse's Last, First, 8-Groom's Residence, 9-Bride's Residence, 10-Minister, 11-Minister's Location, 12-Father's Last, First, 13-Mother's Last, First, 14-Transcribed, 15-Family Bible

#711, 1-Bushong, William, 2-died, 3-31 Mar 1875, 15-Bushong

#712, 1-Bushong, Rachel, 2-died, 3-18 Aug 1894, 15-Bushong

#713, 1-Bushong, Sarah, 2-born, 3-25 Jun 1934, 12-Bushong, John, 13-Bushong, Catharine, 15-Bushong

#714, 1-Bushong, William, 2-born, 3-12 Aug 1804, 12-Bushong, John, 13-Bushong, Magdalena, 15-Bushong

#715, 1-Bushong, Jacob, 2-born, 3-27 Jun 1806, 12-Bushong, John, 13-Bushong, Magdalena, 15-Bushong

#716, 1-Bushong, Mary, 2-born, 3-22 Nov 1808, 12-Bushong, John, 13-Bushong, Magdalena, 15-Bushong

#717, 1-Bushong, Andrew, 2-born, 3-11 Oct 1811, 12-Bushong, John, 13-Bushong, Magdalena, 15-Bushong

#718, 1-Bushong, Susannah, 2-born, 3-25 Aug 1815, 12-Bushong, John, 13-Bushong, Magdalena, 15-Bushong

#719, 1-Bushong, Elizabeth, 2-born, 3-24 Apr 1818, 12-Bushong, John, 13-Bushong, Magdalena, 15-Bushong

#720, 1-Bushong, John, 2-born, 3-19 Jan 1781, 12-Bushong, John, 13-Bushong, Elizabeth, 15-Bushong

#721, 1-McInturff[?], Frederick, 2-born, 3-4 Mar 1814, 15-Bushong

#722, 1-McInturff[?], Maryann, 2-born, 3-29 Mar 1819, 15-Bushong

#723, 1-McInturff[?], Frederick, 2-married, 3-14 Feb 1850, 7-[no maiden name given], Maryann, 15-Bushong

#724, 1-Bushong, William, 2-married, 3-27 Mar 1834, 7-Clem, Rachel, 10-Rev. Jacob F. Dieffenbacher, 11-Woodstock, VA, 15-Bushong

#725, 1-Baxter, William E., 2-married, 3-3 Jul 1888, 4-bride's home, Mechanicstown, MD, 6-witnesses were Mr. & Mrs. D.L. Wilhide and Edward Baxter, 7-Willhide, Emma R., 8-Mechanicstown, MD, 9-Mechanicstown, MD, 10-Rev. G.J. Roudabush, 11-U.B. Church, 15-Baxter

#726, 1-Baxter, William E., 2-married, 3-6 Oct 1896, 7-Jones, Annie L., 15-Baxter

#727, 1-Baxter, William E., 2-born, 3-16 Jun 1867, 15-Baxter

#728, 1-Baxter, Emma R., 2-born, 3-30 Aug 1870, 6-baptized by Rev. J.N.[?] Helane[?], 15-Baxter

#729, 1-Baxter, Ethel Alverda, 2-born, 3-24 Apr 1889, 6-baptized by Rev. G.A. Whitmore[?], 15-Baxter

#730, 1-Baxter, Raymond Erlandis, 2-born, 3-9 Jan 1892, 6-baptized by Rev. G.J. Roudabuch, 15-Baxter

#731, 1-Baxter, Edgar Theodore, 2-born, 3-22 Nov 1892, 6-baptized by Rev. W. L. Martin, 15-Baxter

#732, 1-Baxter, Ruth Elline, 2-born, 3-15 Jul 1897, 6-baptized by Rev. G.A. Whitmore, 15-Baxter

#733, 1-Baxter, Annie L., 2-born, 3-29 Dec 1867, 6-baptized by Rev. Statton, 15-Baxter

#734, 1-Baxter, Hilda Catherine, 2-born, 3-25 Oct 1899, 15-Baxter

#735, 1-Baxter, Nellie Grace, 2-born, 3-24 Feb 1903, 15-Baxter

#736, 1-Baxter, Edith Mildreth, 2-born, 3-24 Feb 1903, 15-Baxter

#737, 1-Wolfe, William Leroy, 2-born, 3-22 Sep 1922, 15-Baxter

#738, 1-Baxter, Raymond E., 2-died, 3-30 Aug 1891, 15-Baxter

#739, 1-Baxter, Emma R., 2-died, 3-5 Oct 1893, 5-23 years 1 months 5 days, 15-Baxter

#740, 1-Baxter, Edgar Theo.[?], 2-died, 3-15 Feb 1913, 15-Baxter

#741, 1-Baxter, Willima E., 2-died, 3-1 May 1942, 15-Baxter

#742, 1-Baxter, Annie L., 2-died, 3-11 May 1951, 15-Baxter

#743, 1-Murdock, John, 2-obituary, 4-Boonsboro, 5-77 years, 7-Barber, Harriett, 15-Murdock

FAMILY BIBLE RECORDS IN THE WASHINGTON COUNTY FREE LIBRARY, HAGERSTOWN, MARYLAND

Entry #, 1-Last Name, First Name, 2-Event, 3-Date, 4-Event Location, 5-Age, 6-Other,
7-Spouse's Last, First, 8-Groom's Residence, 9-Bride's Residence, 10-Minister, 11-Minister's Location,
12-Father's Last, First, 13-Mother's Last, First, 14-Transcribed, 15-Family Bible

#744, 1-Storm, Hattie, 2-obituary, 3-17 Sep, 5-6 months 7 days, 12-Storm, Frank E., 13-Storm, Katie E., 15-Murdock

#745, 1-Metzel, John, 2-obituary, 3-18 Sep, 4-Antietam Iron Works, 5-32 years, 15-Murdock

#746, 1-Murdock, John, 2-married, 3-23 Sep 1844, 4-New Market, MD, 7-Barbour, Harriet C., 8-Frederick Co., MD, 9-Frederick Co., MD, 10-Rev. Margan, 15-Murdock

#747, 1-Storm, Frances E., 2-married, 3-Apr 1881, 7-Falconer, Katie C., 15-Murdock

#748, 1-Storm, Hattie, 2-born, 3-10 Mar 1882, 15-Murdock

#749, 1-Murdock, John, 2-born, 3-Aug, 15-Murdock

#750, 1-Barbour, Harriet C., 2-born, 3-13 Aug 1823, 15-Murdock

#751, 1-Barbour, Clementine E., 2-born, 3-16 Aug 1831, 15-Murdock

#752, 1-Falconer, Oliver L., 2-born, 3-10 Oct 1831, 15-Murdock

#753, 1-Falconer, Lucian E., 2-born, 3-5 Aug 1853, 15-Murdock

#754, 1-Falconer, Clemintine L.K., 2-born, 3-20 Dec 1855, 15-Murdock

#755, 1-Barbour, Caroline M., 2-born, 3-7 Jul 1825, 15-Murdock

#756, 1-Barbour, Achsah[?] A., 2-born, 3-5 Jan 1835, 15-Murdock

#757, 1-Storm, Hattie, 2-died, 3-17 Sep 1882, 5-6 months 7 days, 15-Murdock

#758, 1-Barbour, Catharine, 2-died, 3-20 Sep 1853, 15-Murdock

#759, 1-Barbour, Johnsy, 2-died, 3-1869, 15-Murdock

#760, 1-Cochran, Alexander, 2-born, 3-Mar 1788, 4-Frederick Co., MD, 15-Cochran

#761, 1-Crawmer, Mary, 2-born, 3-20 Jan 1793, 4-Frederick Co., MD, 15-Cochran

#762, 1-Cochran, William H., 2-born, 3-15 Jun 1817, 4-Frederick Co., MD, 15-Cochran

#763, 1-Cochran, John P., 2-born, 3-31 Jul 1818, 4-Washington Co., MD, 15-Cochran

#764, 1-Cochran, Thomas B., 2-born, 3-9 Aug 1821, 4-Washington Co., MD, 15-Cochran

#765, 1-Cochran, Cornwallis, 2-born, 3-19 Oct 1825, 4-Washington Co., MD, 15-Cochran

#766, 1-Cochran, Samuel A., 2-born, 3-10 Aug 1823, 4-Washington Co., MD, 15-Cochran

#767, 1-Cochran, Isaiah Y., 2-born, 3-5 May 1827, 4-Washington Co., MD, 15-Cochran

#768, 1-Cochran, Catharine J., 2-born, 3-22 Mar 1829, 4-Washington Co., MD, 15-Cochran

#769, 1-Cochran, Elizabeth A., 2-born, 3-10 Jan 1833, 4-Washington Co., MD, 15-Cochran

#770, 1-Cochran, Alexander, 2-married, 3-5 Nov 1815, 7-Crawmer, Mary, 15-Cochran

#771, 1-Cochran, Alexander, 2-died, 3-19 Mar 1858, 4-near Newark, Licking Co., Ohio, 5-70 years, 15-Cochran

#772, 1-Cochran, Mary (Mrs.), 2-died, 3-31 Aug 1870, 4-near Newark, Licking Co., Ohio, 5-77 years 9 months 11 days, 15-Cochran

#773, 1-Cochran, Samuel A., 2-died, 3-10 Sep 1825, 5-2 years 1 months, 15-Cochran

#774, 1-Cochran, Cornwallis, 2-died, 3-14 Jan 1883, 5-58 years 2 months 25 days, 15-Cochran

#775, 1-Cochran, William H., 2-died, 3-8 Mar 1891, 4-near Newark, Licking Co., Ohio, 5-73 years 8 months 21 days, 15-Cochran

#776, 1-Cochran, John P., 2-died, 3-27 Dec 1896, 4-Newark, Ohio, 5-78 years 4 months 27 days, 15-Cochran

#777, 1-Cochran, Isaiah Y., 2-died, 3-28 Dec 1904, 4-near Newark, Licking Co., Ohio, 5-77 years 7 months 23 days, 15-Cochran

#778, 1-Cochran, Thomas B., 2-died, 3-22 Nov 1908, 4-near Newark, Licking Co., Ohio, 5-87 years 3 months 13 days, 15-Cochran

#779, 1-Cochran, John P., 2-died, 3-27 Dec 1890, 4-Newark, Ohio, 5-78 years 4 months 27 days, 6-"Our Father", 15-Cochran

#780, 1-Cochran, Mary Wade Davis, 2-died, 3-25 Feb 1916, 4-"on the farm", 5-85 years 6 months 25 days, 15-Cochran

#781, 1-Ball, Lawrence (Mrs.), 2-obituary, 3-12 Mar 1942, 6-Harry is son, 15-Cochran

FAMILY BIBLE RECORDS IN THE WASHINGTON COUNTY FREE LIBRARY, HAGERSTOWN, MARYLAND

Entry #, 1-Last Name, First Name, 2-Event, 3-Date, 4-Event Location, 5-Age, 6-Other,
7-Spouse's Last, First, 8-Groom's Residence, 9-Bride's Residence, 10-Minister, 11-Minister's Location,
12-Father's Last, First, 13-Mother's Last, First, 14-Transcribed, 15-Family Bible

#782, 1-Dalph, Catharine J. (Cochran), 2-died, 3-20 Dec 1910, 4-Newark, Ohio, 5-81 years 8 months 28 days, 15-Cochran

#783, 1-Lees[?], Elizabeth Ann (Cochran), 2-died, 4-Newark, Ohio, 15-Cochran

#784, 1-Ball, Mary Hortense (Cochran), 2-died, 3-12 Mar 1942, 4-in her home in Newark, Ohio, 5-84 years 1 months, 15-Cochran

#785, 1-Cochran, Henry Clay, 2-died, 3-25 Nov 1947, 5-85 years 7 months, 15-Cochran

#786, 1-Cochran, Lydia Brice, 2-died, 3-18 Jan 1945, 5-80 years 5 months 11 days, 15-Cochran

#787, 1-Grice, Peter N., 2-married, 3-12 Jan 1886, 7-Hoffmaster, Sarah V.J., 15-Grice

#788, 1-Grice, John Cleveland, 2-married, 3-1 Jan 1910, 7-Dorsey, Elta Marie, 15-Grice

#789, 1-Grice, Peter N., 2-born, 3-3 Feb 1861, 15-Grice

#790, 1-Hoffmaster, Sarah V.J., 2-born, 3-10 Nov 1853, 15-Grice

#791, 1-Grice, Victor O., 2-born, 3-17 Jan 1887, 12-Grice, Peter N., 13-Hoffmaster, Sarah V.J., 15-Grice

#792, 1-Grice, John Cleveland, 2-born, 3-6 Jul 1888, 12-Grice, Peter N., 13-Hoffmaster, Sarah V.J., 15-Grice

#793, 1-Grice, Nellie May, 2-born, 3-16 Jan 1890, 12-Grice, Peter N., 13-Hoffmaster, Sarah V.J., 15-Grice

#794, 1-Grice, Lucy Neuten, 2-born, 3-4 Jul 1891, 12-Grice, Peter N., 13-Hoffmaster, Sarah V.J., 15-Grice

#795, 1-Grice, Oliver Franklin, 2-born, 3-16 Mar 1893, 12-Grice, Peter N., 13-Hoffmaster, Sarah V.J., 15-Grice

#796, 1-Grice, Martha Virginia, 2-born, 3-12 Jul 1913, 15-Grice

#797, 1-Grice, Charles Cleveland, 2-born, 3-10 Jul 1916, 15-Grice

#798, 1-Grice, Peter Neuton, 2-died, 3-Tuesday, 2:25 pm, 22 Apr 1913, 4-Sharpsburg, MD, 15-Grice

#799, 1-Grice, Sarah Virginia Jefferson, 2-died, 3-Sunday, 2:20 am, 20 Mar 1921, 4-814 Oak Hill Ave., Hagerstown, MD, 15-Grice

#800, 1-Grice, Oliver Franklin, 2-died, 3-Friday, 6:35 pm, 20 May 1921, 4-815 Oak Hill Ave., Hagerstown, MD, 15-Grice

#801, 1-Merckle, Robert E.L., 2-born, 3-14 Jul 1904, 4-McMechen, WV, 15-Merckle

#802, 1-Merckle, Anna Emogene, 2-born, 3-15 Nov 1906, 4-Keyser, WV, 15-Merckle

#803, 1-Merckle, Frances Helene, 2-born, 3-29 Dec 1910, 4-Keyser, WV, 15-Merckle

#804, 1-Merckle, Claude Owen, 2-born, 3-23 Jan 1920, 4-Brunswick, MD, 15-Merckle

#805, 1-Soles, Hattie, 3-29 Feb 1896, 5-13 years, 6-given Bible by brother, Josephus Soles, 15-Merckle

#806, 1-Soles, Josephus, 3-29 Feb 1896, 6-gave Bible to his sister, Hattie Soles, 15-Merckle

#807, 1-Merckle, Frances H., 2-died, 3-Jun 1913, 15-Merckle

#808, 1-Merckle, Robert Lee, 2-obituary, 3-30 Sep 1966, 4-Dunedin, Florida, 15-Merckle

#809, 1-Merckle, Robert Lee, 2-born, 3-12 Mar 1933, 4-Gettysburg, PA, 15-Merckle

#810, 1-Merckle, Robert E., 2-obituary, 3-27 Aug 1972, 4-Keyser, WV, 15-Merckle

#811, 1-Merckle, Claudia Frances, 2-died, 5-18 months, 12-Merckle, Robert C., 13-Herney, Helen M., 15-Merckle

#812, 1-Merckle, Esby Franklin, 2-born, 3-11 Jan 1893, 4-Monroe Co., Ohio, 12-Merckle, Mathis, 13-Holsworth, Elizabeth, 15-Merckle

#813, 1-Merckle, Edward E., 2-obituary, 5-61 years, 15-Merckle

#814, 1-Merckle, Robert L. (Sgt.), 2-obituary, 4-Dunedin, Florida, 12-Merckle, Robert E., 13-Merckle, Robert E. (Mrs.), 15-Merckle

#815, 1-Delauter, Otho Victor, 2-born, 3-24 Sep 1883, 4-Wolfsville, MD, 15-Delauter

#816, 1-Delauter, Otho Victor, 2-married, 3-26 May 1907, 15-Delauter

#817, 1-Delauter, Bertha Ruth, 2-born, 3-6 Jul 1890, 4-Wolfsville, MD, 15-Delauter

FAMILY BIBLE RECORDS IN THE WASHINGTON COUNTY FREE LIBRARY, HAGERSTOWN, MARYLAND

Entry #, 1-Last Name, First Name, 2-Event, 3-Date, 4-Event Location, 5-Age, 6-Other,
7-Spouse's Last, First, 8-Groom's Residence, 9-Bride's Residence, 10-Minister, 11-Minister's Location,
12-Father's Last, First, 13-Mother's Last, First, 14-Transcribed, 15-Family Bible

```
#818, 1-Delauter, Bertha Ruth, 2-married, 3-26 May 1907, 15-Delauter
#819, 1-Delauter, Bertha Ruth, 2-died, 3-17 Oct 1918, 15-Delauter
#820, 1-Delauter, Evylon Grace, 2-born, 3-22 Dec 1907, 4-Waynesboro, PA, 15-
      Delauter
#821, 1-Delauter, Margaret Teressa, 2-born, 3-29 Jul 1910, 4-Foxville, MD, 15-
      Delauter
#822, 1-Delauter, George Woodrow, 2-born, 3-3 Dec 1913, 4-Pleasant Walk, MD, 15-
      Delauter
#823, 1-Delauter, DeWitt Elmer, 2-born, 3-18 May 1916, 4-Pleasant Walk, MD, 15-
      Delauter
#824, 1-Delauter, Catharine Marie, 2-born, 3-26 Jun 1922, 4-Williamsport, MD, 15-
      Delauter
#825, 1-Delauter, Eva C., 2-born, 3-12 Nov 1899, 4-Pleasant Walk, MD, 15-Delauter
#826, 1-Delauter, Hilda Jane, 2-born, 3-13 Jul 1924, 4-Williamsport, MD, 15-
      Delauter
#827, 1-Delauter, Eva C., 2-married, 3-24 Mar 1921, 15-Delauter
#828, 1-Delauter, Hilda Jane, 2-died, 3-6 Jun 1925, 15-Delauter
#829, 1-Delauter, Martha Melchor, 2-born, 3-22 Feb 1926, 4-Williamsport, MD, 15-
      Delauter
#830, 1-Delauter, Jr., Otha Victer, 2-born, 3-4 Mar 1928, 4-Williamsport, MD, 15-
      Delauter
#831, 1-Delauter, Reba Mae, 2-born, 3-29 Aug 1930, 4-Williamsport, MD, 15-Delauter
#832, 1-Delauter, William Byron, 2-born, 3-8 May 1933, 4-Williamsport, MD, 15-
      Delauter
#833, 1-Delauter, Claude Ennis, 2-born, 3-16 Jun 1938, 4-Williamsport, MD, 15-
      Delauter
#834, 1-Pittenger, David L., 2-married, 3-31 Dec 1854, 7-Spickler, Mary Ann, 15-
      Pittenger
#835, 1-Pittenger, D.S., 2-born, 3-30 May 1835, 15-Pittenger
#836, 1-Spickler, Mary A., 2-born, 3-10 Dec, 15-Pittenger
#837, 1-Pittenger, W.D., 2-born, 3-9 Jun 1956, 15-Pittenger
#838, 1-Pittenger, H.F., 2-born, 3-22 Jul 1858, 15-Pittenger
#839, 1-Pittenger, Louisa J., 2-born, 3-26 May 1861, 15-Pittenger
#840, 1-Pittenger, Isabella S., 2-born, 3-8 Dec 1863, 15-Pittenger
#841, 1-Pittenger, Lillie May, 2-born, 3-29 Aug 1866, 15-Pittenger
#842, 1-Pittenger, Harry Tecumseh Sherman, 2-born, 3-22 Feb 1969, 15-Pittenger
#843, 1-Pittenger, Thomas Alvey, 2-born, 3-4 Jul 1872, 15-Pittenger
#844, 1-Pittenger, George B. McClellen, 2-born, 3-29 Jan 1875, 15-Pittenger
#845, 1-Koons, Rayetta, 2-born, 3-19 Mar 1891[or 1897], 15-Pittenger
#846, 1-Koons, G. Clinton, 2-born, 3-27 May 1893, 15-Pittenger
#847, 1-Koons, Harry C., 2-born, 3-10 Jun 1914, 15-Pittenger
#848, 1-Koons, Margaret V., 2-born, 3-11 Oct 1915, 15-Pittenger
#849, 1-Koons, Donald W., 2-born, 3-19 Dec 1917, 15-Pittenger
#850, 1-Koons, Ruth N., 2-born, 3-18 Oct 1920, 15-Pittenger
#851, 1-Koons, Anna Bell, 2-born, 3-27 Sep 1923, 15-Pittenger
#852, 1-Koons, Melvin[?] F., 2-born, 3-20 Jul 1929, 15-Pittenger
#853, 1-Koons, Nancy Lee, 2-born, 3-21 Jun 1935, 15-Pittenger
#854, 1-Hartle, Lea Blanch, 2-born, 3-12 Nov 1890, 15-Hartle
#855, 1-Hartle, William Berkley, 2-born, 3-7 Jan 1892, 15-Hartle
#856, 1-Hartle, Edna Lavene, 2-born, 3-17 Feb 1894, 15-Hartle
#857, 1-Hartle, Ralph Harland, 2-born, 3-26 Dec 1895, 15-Hartle
#858, 1-Hartle, Ellen Grace, 2-born, 3-6 Nov 1897, 15-Hartle
#859, 1-Hartle, Asiaah Mearl, 2-born, 3-23 Oct 1899, 15-Hartle
#860, 1-Hartle, Dorothy Irene, 2-born, 3-1 Feb 1902, 15-Hartle
#861, 1-Hartle, Charles Elles, 2-born, 3-20 Mar 1906, 15-Hartle
```

FAMILY BIBLE RECORDS IN THE WASHINGTON COUNTY FREE LIBRARY, HAGERSTOWN, MARYLAND

Entry #, 1-Last Name, First Name, 2-Event, 3-Date, 4-Event Location, 5-Age, 6-Other,
7-Spouse's Last, First, 8-Groom's Residence, 9-Bride's Residence, 10-Minister, 11-Minister's Location,
12-Father's Last, First, 13-Mother's Last, First, 14-Transcribed, 15-Family Bible

#862, 1-Hartle, Frank Albert, 2-born, 3-30 Sep 1910, 15-Hartle
#863, 1-Smith, Doris Rose, 2-born, 3-8 Mar 1920, 15-Hartle
#864, 1-Poffenberger, Jack Ruddoff, 2-born, 3-30 Mar 1925, 15-Hartle
#865, 1-Hartle, W.B., 2-died, 3-26 Feb 1893, 15-Hartle
#866, 1-Hartle, Leah B., 2-died, 3-22 Oct 1918, 15-Hartle
#867, 1-Hartle, Edna L., 2-died, 3-May, 15-Hartle
#868, 1-Hartle, W.B., 2-died, 3-18 Oct 1933, 15-Hartle
#869, 1-Hartle, Sarah Ann, 2-died, 3-7 Feb 1947, 15-Hartle
#870, 1-Hartle, Ralph H., 2-died, 3-12 Nov 1950, 15-Hartle
#871, 1-Hartle, Isaac M., 2-died, 3-12 Sep, 15-Hartle
#872, 1-Poffenberger, Jack Rudolph, 2-died, 3-24 Apr 1974, 15-Hartle
#873, 1-Pensinger, William J., 2-married, 3-15 Nov 1866, 4-Harrisburg, PA, 6-bride is daughter of Joseph & Catherine Jane Newman; witnesses were Isaac H. Whitmore and Christiann E. Whitmore, 7-Newman, Maria B., 10-Rev. G.F. Stelling, 11-First Lutheran Church, 12-Pensinger, Henry, 13-Pensinger, Rebecca, 15-Pensinger
#874, 1-Pensinger, William J., 2-born, 3-9 Jun 1845, 15-Pensinger
#875, 1-Pensinger, Maria B., 2-born, 3-1 Nov 1848, 6-wife of William J. Pensinger, 15-Pensinger
#876, 1-Pensinger, Linford Roy N., 2-born, 3-13 Dec 1885, 12-Pensinger, William J., 13-Newman, Maria B., 15-Pensinger
#877, 1-Shrader, Susan I., 2-born, 3-20 Nov 1864, 15-Pensinger
#878, 1-Pensinger, Maria Jane, 2-born, 3-11 Apr 1911, 15-Pensinger
#879, 1-Pensinger, Mary Evelyn, 2-born, 3-17 Dec 1916, 15-Pensinger
#880, 1-Pensinger, Lorraine Elizabeth, 2-born, 3-22 Jan 1918, 15-Pensinger
#881, 1-Pensinger, Linford Snyder, 2-born, 3-20 Dec 1919, 15-Pensinger
#882, 1-Pensinger, Harry Richard, 2-born, 3-30 Jun 1921, 15-Pensinger
#883, 1-Pensinger, Virginia Raye, 2-born, 3-26 Nov 1924, 15-Pensinger
#884, 1-Pensinger, Anna Lee, 2-born, 3-11 Jan 1927, 15-Pensinger
#885, 1-Pensinger, Linford Roy N., 2-married, 3-11 Jun 1908, 6-bride is daughter of Emanuel & Emma J. Snyder, 7-Snyder, Mary E., 10-Rev. A.B. Statton, 11-Hagerstown, MD, 12-Pensinger, William J., 13-Pensinger, Maria B., 15-Pensinger
#886, 1-Pensinger, Linford S., 2-married, 3-23 Sep 1950, 7-McNeal, Marguerite, 15-Pensinger
#887, 1-Pensinger, Virginia Raye, 2-married, 3-23 Sep 1950, 7-Mowen, Kenneth F., 15-Pensinger
#888, 1-Pensinger, Anna Lee, 2-married, 3-11 Jan 1952, 7-Diehl, Wm. A., 15-Pensinger
#889, 1-Pensinger, M. Jane, 2-married, 3-22 Feb 1958, 7-Shupp, Isaac Hamilton, 15-Pensinger
#890, 1-Pensinger, Lorraine Elizabeth, 2-married, 3-22 Jan 1961, 7-Phillips, Carl, 15-Pensinger
#891, 1-Pensinger, Maria B., 2-died, 3-1 Aug 1909, 15-Pensinger
#892, 1-Pensinger, William J., 2-died, 3-23 May 1923, 15-Pensinger
#893, 1-Pensinger, M. Evelyn, 2-died, 3-10 Feb 1917, 15-Pensinger
#894, 1-Bryan, Susan Shrader, 2-died, 3-22 Apr 1927, 15-Pensinger
#895, 1-Pensinger, Harry Richard, 2-died, 3-8 Jul 1944, 6-died in World War II, 12-Pensinger, L. Roy, 13-Pensinger, Mary, 15-Pensinger
#896, 1-Trumpower, Thomas, 2-married, 3-25 Mar 1858, 7-Holbird, Mary Jane, 15-Holbird (Holbert)
#897, 1-Holbird, Sarah Ann, 2-died, 3-3 Jun 1871, 5-70 years 7 months 18 days, 15-Holbird (Holbert)
#898, 1-Holbird, Jr.[?], James[?], 2-died, 3-24 Apr 1872, 5-50 years, 15-Holbird (Holbert)

FAMILY BIBLE RECORDS IN THE WASHINGTON COUNTY FREE LIBRARY, HAGERSTOWN, MARYLAND

Entry #, 1-Last Name, First Name, 2-Event, 3-Date, 4-Event Location, 5-Age, 6-Other, 7-Spouse's Last, First, 8-Groom's Residence, 9-Bride's Residence, 10-Minister, 11-Minister's Location, 12-Father's Last, First, 13-Mother's Last, First, 14-Transcribed, 15-Family Bible

#899, 1-Yeager, Elisbeth Ann, 2-died, 3-8 Oct 1891, 5-62 years 3[?] months 20 days, 15-Holbird (Holbert)
#900, 1-Trumpower, Clyde Oscar, 2-born, 3-1 May 1888, 15-Holbird (Holbert)
#901, 1-Trumpower, Vernon Blaine, 2-born, 3-20 Sep 1889, 15-Holbird (Holbert)
#902, 1-Trumpower, Iva Belle, 2-born, 3-2 Jul 1891, 15-Holbird (Holbert)
#903, 1-Trumpower, Beulah Mayble, 2-born, 3-23 Oct 1892, 15-Holbird (Holbert)
#904, 1-Trumpower, Alma Elizabeth, 2-born, 3-18 Feb 1894, 15-Holbird (Holbert)
#905, 1-Trumpower, Walter Lloyd, 2-born, 3-2 Feb 1899, 15-Holbird (Holbert)
#906, 1-Trumpower, Harold Percy, 2-born, 3-2 Feb 1899, 15-Holbird (Holbert)
#907, 1-Trumpower, Findley Frisby, 2-born, 3-8 Jan 1901, 15-Holbird (Holbert)
#908, 1-McAllister, George W., 2-married, 3-30 Sep 1872, 4-Franklin Co., PA, 6-married by Justice of the Peace, Jno. McLaughlin; witnesses were Joseph Winger and Bell McLaughlin, 7-Trumpower, Mary Jane, 15-Holbird (Holbert)
#909, 1-Trumpower, Andrew N., 2-born, 3-29 Apr 1859, 15-Holbird (Holbert)
#910, 1-Trumpower, Calven, 2-born, 3-1 Aug 1861, 15-Holbird (Holbert)
#911, 1-Trumpower, Joseph P., 2-born, 3-3 Sep 1863, 15-Holbird (Holbert)
#912, 1-Trumpower, John William, 2-born, 3-_[?] ___[?] 1869, 15-Holbird (Holbert)
#913, 1-Trumpower, Percy H., 2-died, 3-13 May 1901, 5-2 years 3 months 8 days, 12-Trumpower, Joseph, 15-Holbird (Holbert)
#914, 1-McAllister, Geo. W., 2-born, 3-13 Mar 1822, 15-Holbird (Holbert)
#915, 1-McAllister, Geo. W., 2-died, 3-Saturday, 4 am, 14 Jan 1899, 4-Hicksville, 5-76 years 10 months 1 day, 6-2nd husband of Mary Jane (Holbird) Trumpower), 15-Holbird (Holbert)
#916, 1-Trumpower, Thomas, 2-born, 3-11 May 1836, 15-Holbird (Holbert)
#917, 1-Holbird, Mary Jane, 2-born, 3-11 Jun 1841, 15-Holbird (Holbert)
#918, 1-Holbird, Henry B., 2-died, 3-30 Sep 1866, 5-28 years, 15-Holbird (Holbert)
#919, 1-Holbird, James, 2-died, 3-19 Nov 1866, 5-77 years, 15-Holbird (Holbert)
#920, 1-Leonard, Laura, 2-married, 3-13 Oct 1912, 7-Cook, Monroe E., 10-Rev. Hanner, 11-Wallace[?], VA, 15-Leonard
#921, 1-Leonard, Walter, 2-married, 3-21 Apr 1888, 4-Wallace, VA, 6-witnesses were William and Lilly Jackson, 7-Jackson, Matiedan, 8-Wallace, VA, 9-Wallace, VA, 10-William Done, 15-Leonard
#922, 1-Leonard, Walter, 2-born, 3-12 Oct 1866, 15-Leonard
#923, 1-Leonard, Matilda, 2-born, 3-12 Feb 1872, 15-Leonard
#924, 1-Leonard, Anamay, 2-born, 3-20 Oct 1890, 15-Leonard
#925, 1-Leonard, Maggie C., 2-born, 3-12 Jan 1892, 15-Leonard
#926, 1-Leonard, Lara Lee, 2-born, 3-22 Jun 1894, 15-Leonard
#927, 1-Leonard, Cary, 2-born, 3-28 Jun 1897, 15-Leonard
#928, 1-Leonard, William Henry, 2-born, 3-18 Jun 1903, 15-Leonard
#929, 1-Leonard, Anamay, 2-married, 3-21 Sep 1908, 7-Williams, Marion, 15-Leonard
#930, 1-Leonard, Laura Lee, 2-married, 3-13 Oct 1812, 7-Cock, Monroe, 15-Leonard
#931, 1-Leonard, Maggie, 2-married, 3-19 Jan 1916, 7-Forest, Lee, 15-Leonard
#932, 1-Cock, Virginia Elizabeth, 2-married, 3-12 Jun 1934, 7-Sowers, Howard Winter, 15-Leonard
#933, 1-Cock, Joel Wilson, 2-married, 3-12 Nov 1934, 7-Grams[?], Blanche, 15-Leonard
#934, 1-Cock, Frances Louise, 2-married, 3-28 Sep 1941, 7-Hellane, Jr., Joseph Glen, 15-Leonard
#935, 1-Jackson, Maggie, 2-died, 3-2 Jul 1903, 15-Leonard
#936, 1-Leonard, William Henry, 2-died, 3-3 Mar 1905, 15-Leonard
#937, 1-Leonard, Cary, 2-died, 3-28 Jun 1897, 15-Leonard
#938, 1-Jackson, William, 2-died, 3-21 Jan 1932, 15-Leonard
#939, 1-Leonard, Walter, 2-died, 3-12 Jan 1940, 15-Leonard
#940, 1-Jackson, Jennie, 2-died, 3-28 Dec 1946, 15-Leonard
#941, 1-Jackson, Lillie, 2-died, 3-28 Nov 1848, 15-Leonard

FAMILY BIBLE RECORDS IN THE WASHINGTON COUNTY FREE LIBRARY, HAGERSTOWN, MARYLAND

Entry #, 1-Last Name, First Name, 2-Event, 3-Date, 4-Event Location, 5-Age, 6-Other,
7-Spouse's Last, First, 8-Groom's Residence, 9-Bride's Residence, 10-Minister, 11-Minister's Location,
12-Father's Last, First, 13-Mother's Last, First, 14-Transcribed, 15-Family Bible

```
#942, 1-Williams, Anamay, 2-died, 3-13 Sep 1949, 15-Leonard
#943, 1-Leonard, Matilda, 2-died, 3-28 Jun 1954, 15-Leonard
#944, 1-Cock, Joel Wilson, 2-died, 3-25 Dec 1955, 15-Leonard
#945, 1-Cock, Monroe Edmond, 2-died, 3-13 Feb 1957, 15-Leonard
#946, 1-Sowers, Virginia Elizabeth Cock, 2-died, 3-29 Dec 1975, 15-Leonard
#947, 1-Cock, Blanche Grams[?], 2-died, 3-14 Aug 1980, 15-Leonard
#948, 1-Cock, Charles Monroe, 2-born, 3-2 Nov 1935, 6-grandchild of Monroe and
       Laura Cock, 15-Leonard
#949, 1-Sowers, Bonnie Lee, 2-born, 3-20 Feb 1937, 6-grandchild of Monroe and Laura
       Cock, 15-Leonard
#950, 1-Cock, Connie Marie, 2-born, 3-11 Feb 1940, 6-grandchild of Monroe and Laura
       Cock, 15-Leonard
#951, 1-Cock, Laura Lee, 2-born, 3-22 Jun 1944, 6-grandchild of Monroe and Laura
       Cock, 15-Leonard
#952, 1-Cock, Joel J., 2-born, 3-Jul 1947, 6-grandchild of Monroe and Laura Cock,
       15-Leonard
#953, 1-Hellane, Joseph Glen, 2-born, 3-6 Oct 1946, 6-grandchild of Monroe and
       Laura Cock, 15-Leonard
#954, 1-Hellane, David Lee, 2-born, 3-2 Apr 1948, 6-grandchild of Monroe and Laura
       Cock, 15-Leonard
#955, 1-Cock, Joel Wilson, 2-born, 3-9 Aug 1914, 12-Cock, Monroe, 13-Cock, Laura,
       15-Leonard
#956, 1-Cock, Virginia Elizabeth, 2-born, 3-29 Mar 1919[?], 12-Cock, Monroe, 13-
       Cock, Laura, 15-Leonard
#957, 1-Cock, Frances Louise, 2-born, 3-17 Feb 1921, 12-Cock, Monroe, 13-Cock,
       Laura, 15-Leonard
#958, 1-Leonard, Walter, 2-died, 3-12 Jan 1940, 15-Leonard
#959, 1-Williams, Anamay, 2-died, 3-13 Sep 1949, 15-Leonard
#960, 1-Leonard, Matilda, 2-died, 3-28 Jun 1954, 15-Leonard
#961, 1-Cock, Joel Wilson, 2-died, 3-25 Dec 1956, 15-Leonard
#962, 1-Cock, Monroe Edamond, 2-died, 3-13 Feb 1957, 15-Leonard
#963, 1-Sowers, Virginia E., 2-died, 3-29 Dec 1975, 15-Leonard
#964, 1-Cock, Blanche Grams[?], 2-died, 3-14 Aug 1980, 15-Leonard
#965, 1-Cooper[?], Carrie (Mrs.), 2-died, 3-19 Aug 1980, 15-Leonard
#966, 1-Jennings, Jr.[?], Samuel, 2-born, 3-28 Dec 1849, 15-Jennings
#967, 1-Jennings, Jr.[?], Samuel, 2-died, 3-24 Aug 1925, 5-75 years 7 months 27
       days, 15-Jennings
#968, 1-Jennings, Annie (Spielman), 2-born, 3-1[or15] Jun 1854, 15-Jennings
#969, 1-Spielman, Jr., William H., 2-born, 3-1[or15] Jun 1855, 15-Jennings
#970, 1-Jennings, Laura Elizabeth, 2-born, 3-1 Feb 1882, 15-Jennings
#971, 1-Jennings, Laura Elizabeth, 2-married, 3-1 May 1913, 7-Lorcch[?], D.B., 15-
       Jennings
#972, 1-Lorcch[?], D.B., 2-died, 3-27 Oct 1930, 5-68 years 6 months 27 days, 15-
       Jennings
#973, 1-Jennings, William[?] S., 2-born, 3-23 Sep 1884[?], 15-Jennings
#974, 1-Jennings, William[?] S., 2-married, 3-17[?] Feb 1915, 7-Coffman,
       Catherine[?], 15-Jennings
#975, 1-Jennings, Nellie S., 2-born, 3-15 Oct 1888, 15-Jennings
#976, 1-Jennings, Nellie S., 2-married, 3-20 Mar 1913, 7-Kaetge[?], Ira L., 15-
       Jennings
#977, 1-Fonch, Lora E., 2-born, 3-6 Jun 1915, 15-Jennings
#978, 1-Fonch, David S., 2-born, 3-30 Nov 1916, 15-Jennings
#979, 1-Fonch, Anna M., 2-born, 3-6 Aug 1919, 15-Jennings
#980, 1-Jennings[?], Anna Estelle, 2-born, 3-23 Oct 1917[?], 15-Jennings
#981, 1-Kaetgel, Sterling[?] Dayne[?], 2-born, 3-7 Mar 1918, 15-Jennings
```

FAMILY BIBLE RECORDS IN THE WASHINGTON COUNTY FREE LIBRARY, HAGERSTOWN, MARYLAND

Entry #, 1-Last Name, First Name, 2-Event, 3-Date, 4-Event Location, 5-Age, 6-Other,
7-Spouse's Last, First, 8-Groom's Residence, 9-Bride's Residence, 10-Minister, 11-Minister's Location,
12-Father's Last, First, 13-Mother's Last, First, 14-Transcribed, 15-Family Bible

```
#982,  1-Kaetgel, Miriam Ea_____[?], 2-born, 3-17 Aug 1932, 15-Jennings
#983,  1-Yerty, Daniel, 2-born, 3-6 Jun 1807, 15-Jennings
#984,  1-Yerty, Elizabeth, 2-born, 3-13 Nov 1807, 15-Jennings
#985,  1-Nichols, Jacob, 2-born, 3-25 Dec 1815, 15-Jennings
#986,  1-Rohrback, Barbara, 2-born, 3-18 Aug 1785, 15-Jennings
#987,  1-Rohrback, Jacob, 2-born, 3-29 Nov 1812, 15-Jennings
#988,  1-Rohrback, Henry B., 2-born, 3-29 Nov 1812, 15-Jennings
#989,  1-Rohrback, Elias, 2-born, 3-16 Feb 1820, 15-Jennings
#990,  1-Rohrback, Cornelious, 2-born, 3-1 Sep 1827, 15-Jennings
#991,  1-Yerty, Daniel, 2-died, 3-11 Nov 1841, 15-Jennings
#992,  1-Nichols, Jacob, 2-died, 3-22 Jul 1880, 5-64 years 6 months 27 days, 15-
       Jennings
#993,  1-Nichols, Elizabeth, 2-died, 3-6 Aug 1888, 5-80 years 8 months 24 days, 15-
       Jennings
#994,  1-Rohrback, Henry, 2-born, 3-17 Jan 1783, 15-Jennings
#995,  1-Rohrback, Henry, 2-died, 3-17 Aug 1851, 5-68 years 7 months, 15-Jennings
#996,  1-Rohrback, Barbara (Barks), 2-born, 3-18 Aug 1785, 6-wife of Henry Rohrback,
       15-Jennings
#997,  1-Rohrback, Barbara (Barks), 2-died, 3-30 Sep 1855, 5-70 years 1 months 12
       days, 6-wife of Henry Rohrback, 15-Jennings
#998,  1-Rohrback, Jacob, 2-died, 3-4 Jul 1864, 5-51 years 7 months 5 days, 15-
       Jennings
#999,  1-Rohrback, Elias, 2-died, 3-21 Nov 1862, 5-42 years 9 months 5 days, 15-
       Jennings
#1000, 1-Rohrback, Cornelious, 2-died, 3-2 Nov 1858, 5-31 years 2 months 1 days,
       15-Jennings
#1001, 1-Yerty, Daniel, 2-married, 3-19 Feb 1835, Elizabeth, 15-Jennings
#1002, 1-Nichols, Jacob, 2-married, 3-5 Mar 1844, Elizabeth, 15-Jennings
#1003, 1-Barks, Barbara, 2-born, 3-18 Aug 1785, 15-Jennings
#1004, 1-Rohrback, John H., 2-born, 3-4 Sep 1806, 15-Jennings
#1005, 1-Rohrback, John H., 2-died, 3-11 Oct 1833, 5-27 years 1 months 7 days, 12-
       Rohrback, Henry, 13-Barks, Barbara, 15-Jennings
#1006, 1-Rohrback, Elizabeth, 2-born, 3-13 Nov 1807, 6-possibly married a Yerty
       also, 7-Nichols, 12-Rohrback, Henry, 13-Barks, Barbara, 15-Jennings
#1007, 1-Rohrback, Elizabeth, 2-died, 3-6 Aug 1888, 5-80 years 8 months 24 days,
       12-Rohrback, Henry, 13-Barks, Barbara, 15-Jennings
#1008, 1-Rohrback, Mary, 2-born, 3-23 Feb 1809, 7-Hont[?], 12-Rohrback, Henry, 13-
       Barks, Barbara, 15-Jennings
#1009, 1-Rohrback, Mary, 2-died, 3-4 Jan 1887, 5-77 years 10 months 12 days, 12-
       Rohrback, Henry, 13-Barks, Barbara, 15-Jennings
#1010, 1-Rohrback, Catharine, 2-born, 3-12 Dec 1810, 7-Haskins, 12-Rohrback, Henry,
       13-Barks, Barbara, 15-Jennings
#1011, 1-Rohrback, Catharine, 2-died, 3-4 Apr 1886, 5-75 years 3 months 23 days,
       12-Rohrback, Henry, 13-Barks, Barbara, 15-Jennings
#1012, 1-Rohrback, Jacob H., 2-born, 3-29 Nov 1812, 12-Rohrback, Henry, 13-Barks,
       Barbara, 15-Jennings
#1013, 1-Rohrback, Jacob H., 2-died, 3-4 Jul 1864, 5-51 years 7 months 5 days, 12-
       Rohrback, Henry, 13-Barks, Barbara, 15-Jennings
#1014, 1-Rohrback, Henry Barks, 2-born, 3-29 Nov 1812, 12-Rohrback, Henry, 13-
       Barks, Barbara, 15-Jennings
#1015, 1-Rohrback, Henry Barks, 2-died, 3-29 Dec 1890, 5-78 years 1 months, 12-
       Rohrback, Henry, 13-Barks, Barbara, 15-Jennings
#1016, 1-Rohrback, Daniel, 2-born, 3-10 Apr 1815, 12-Rohrback, Henry, 13-Barks,
       Barbara, 15-Jennings
```

FAMILY BIBLE RECORDS IN THE WASHINGTON COUNTY FREE LIBRARY, HAGERSTOWN, MARYLAND

Entry #, 1-Last Name, First Name, 2-Event, 3-Date, 4-Event Location, 5-Age, 6-Other,
7-Spouse's Last, First, 8-Groom's Residence, 9-Bride's Residence, 10-Minister, 11-Minister's Location,
12-Father's Last, First, 13-Mother's Last, First, 14-Transcribed, 15-Family Bible

```
#1017, 1-Rohrback, Daniel, 2-died, 3-19 Jan 1877, 5-61 years 9 months 9 days, 12-
    Rohrback, Henry, 13-Barks, Barbara, 15-Jennings
#1018, 1-Rohrback, Barbara, 2-born, 3-9 Apr 1817, 7-Hedrick, 12-Rohrback, Henry,
    13-Barks, Barbara, 15-Jennings
#1019, 1-Rohrback, Barbara, 2-died, 3-4 Feb 1857, 5-39 years 9 months 26 days, 12-
    Rohrback, Henry, 13-Barks, Barbara, 15-Jennings
#1020, 1-Rohrback, Elias, 2-born, 3-16 Feb 1820, 12-Rohrback, Henry, 13-Barks,
    Barbara, 15-Jennings
#1021, 1-Rohrback, Elias, 2-died, 3-21 Nov 1862, 5-42 years 9 months 5 days, 12-
    Rohrback, Henry, 13-Barks, Barbara, 15-Jennings
#1022, 1-Rohrback, Noah, 2-born, 3-13 Aug 1822, 12-Rohrback, Henry, 13-Barks,
    Barbara, 15-Jennings
#1023, 1-Rohrback, Noah, 2-died, 3-3 Jan 1881, 5-58 years 4 months 20 days, 12-
    Rohrback, Henry, 13-Barks, Barbara, 15-Jennings
#1024, 1-Rohrback, Anna Mary, 2-born, 3-27 Sep 1824, 7-Spielman, 12-Rohrback,
    Henry, 13-Barks, Barbara, 15-Jennings
#1025, 1-Rohrback, Anna Mary, 2-died, 3-9 May 1878, 5-58 years 1 months 12 days,
    12-Rohrback, Henry, 13-Barks, Barbara, 15-Jennings
#1026, 1-Rohrback, Cornelius, 2-born, 3-1 Sep 1827, 12-Rohrback, Henry, 13-Barks,
    Barbara, 15-Jennings
#1027, 1-Rohrback, Cornelius, 2-died, 3-2 Nov 1858, 5-31 years 2 months 1 days, 12-
    Rohrback, Henry, 13-Barks, Barbara, 15-Jennings
#1028, 1-Howard, William H., 2-born, 3-26 Jul 1812, 15-Howard
#1029, 1-Howard, Lois Ann, 2-born, 3-25 Aug 1811, 15-Howard
#1030, 1-Howard, George W., 2-born, 3-18 Sep 1833, 15-Howard
#1031, 1-Howard, Margaret Ann, 2-born, 3-18 Jan 1836, 15-Howard
#1032, 1-Howard, William Daniel, 2-born, 3-10 Jul 1839, 15-Howard
#1033, 1-Howard, Christopher Leroy, 2-born, 3-2 Sep 1841, 12-Howard, Wm., 13-
    Howard, Lois, 15-Howard
#1034, 1-Howard, James Hatten, 2-born, 3-25 Apr 1843, 12-Howard, Wm., 13-Howard,
    Lois Ann, 15-Howard
#1035, 1-Howard, Leonard Credle, 2-born, 3-12 Aug 1845, 12-Howard, Wm., 13-Howard,
    Lois Ann, 15-Howard
#1036, 1-Howard, Thomas Pasteur, 2-born, 3-11 Feb 1848, 12-Howard, Wm., 13-Howard,
    Lois Ann, 15-Howard
#1037, 1-Howard, Hinman, 2-born, 3-5 Oct 1850, 12-Howard, Wm., 13-Howard, Lois Ann,
    15-Howard
#1038, 1-Cridle[?], Lucretia A., 2-born, 3-11[or16] Feb 1818, 15-Howard
#1039, 1-Myers, Lucy H., 2-born, 3-17 Mar 1838, 15-Howard
#1040, 1-Howard, Lucy H., 2-died, 3-28 Apr 1914, 7-Howard, George N.[?], 15-Howard
#1041, 1-Howard, Mary M., 2-born, 3-30 Apr 1859, 12-Howard, Geo. W., 13-Howard,
    Lucy H., 15-Howard
#1042, 1-Howard, William H., 2-born, 3-3 Jul 1861, 12-Howard, Geo. W., 13-Howard,
    Lucy H., 15-Howard
#1043, 1-Howard, Lois A., 2-born, 3-7 Nov 1863, 12-Howard, Geo. W., 13-Howard, Lucy
    H., 15-Howard
#1044, 1-Howard, John M., 2-born, 3-21 Jan 1866, 12-Howard, Geo. W., 13-Howard,
    Lucy H., 15-Howard
#1045, 1-Howard, Luca A., 2-born, 3-13 Feb 1868, 12-Howard, Geo. W., 13-Howard,
    Lucy H., 15-Howard
#1046, 1-Howard, Geo. W., 2-born, 3-10 Feb 1871, 12-Howard, Geo. W., 13-Howard,
    Lucy H., 15-Howard
#1047, 1-Howard, Waltor H., 2-born, 3-3 May 1873, 12-Howard, Geo. W., 13-Howard,
    Lucy H., 15-Howard
```

FAMILY BIBLE RECORDS IN THE WASHINGTON COUNTY FREE LIBRARY, HAGERSTOWN, MARYLAND

Entry #, 1-Last Name, First Name, 2-Event, 3-Date, 4-Event Location, 5-Age, 6-Other, 7-Spouse's Last, First, 8-Groom's Residence, 9-Bride's Residence, 10-Minister, 11-Minister's Location, 12-Father's Last, First, 13-Mother's Last, First, 14-Transcribed, 15-Family Bible

#1048, 1-Howard, Harriet L., 2-born, 3-7 Jun 1875, 12-Howard, Geo. W., 13-Howard, Lucy H., 15-Howard

#1049, 1-Howard, O.Z.[?], 2-born, 3-6 Dec 1876, 12-Howard, Geo. W., 13-Howard, Lucy H., 15-Howard

#1050, 1-Howard, Emma Wilson, 2-born, 3-10 Apr 1880, 12-Howard, Geo. W., 13-Howard, Lucy H., 15-Howard

#1051, 1-Howard, Lois A., 2-died, 3-28 Sep 1864, 12-Howard, Geo. W., 13-Howard, Lucy H., 15-Howard

#1052, 1-Howard, Harriett L., 2-died, 3-3 Jan 1876, 12-Howard, Geo. W., 13-Howard, Lucy H., 15-Howard

#1053, 1-Howard, O.Z., 2-died, 3-20 Dec 1917, 12-Howard, Geo. W., 13-Howard, Lucy H., 15-Howard

#1054, 1-Howard, Harriet L., 2-born, 3-4 Jul 1882, 15-Howard

#1055, 1-Howard, G.W., 2-died, 3-7 Mar 1895, 12-Howard, W.[?] H., 13-Howard, Lois A., 15-Howard

#1056, 1-Howard, Christopher Leroy, 2-died, 3-6 Nov 1841, 12-Howard, Wm., 13-Howard, Lois, 15-Howard

#1057, 1-Howard, Lois A., 2-died, 3-25 Aug 1851, 7-Howard, Will. H., 15-Howard

#1058, 1-Howard, Leonard C., 2-died, 3-29 Sep 1855, 12-Howard, Will., 13-Howard, Lois, 15-Howard

#1059, 1-Howard, Will. H., 2-died, 3-23 May 1857, 15-Howard

#1060, 1-Howard, William D., 2-died, 3-5 Jun 1863, 6-died of wound received near Fredericksburg, in skermish, ball passed through left lung, survived[?] but a few hours", 12-Howard, Will. H., 13-Howard, Lois A., 15-Howard

#1061, 1-Howard, Walter H., 2-died, 3-30 Dec 1863, 12-Howard, Will. H., 13-Howard, Lois A., 15-Howard

#1062, 1-Howard, Lucretia A., 2-died, 3-Jan 1867, 6-"last wife", 7-Howard, Will H., 15-Howard

#1063, 1-Howard, Daniel Cridle, 2-born, 3-13 Oct 1787, 15-Howard

#1064, 1-Howard, Daniel Cridle, 2-died, 3-30 Mar 1845, 15-Howard

#1065, 1-Howard, Precilla[?] Easter, 2-born, 3-27 Apr 1787, 15-Howard

#1066, 1-Howard, Precilla[?] Easter, 2-died, 3-6 Mar 1830, 15-Howard

#1067, 1-Howard, Geo. W., 2-born, 3-2 Sep 1814, 12-Howard, William, 15-Howard

#1068, 1-Howard, Geo. W., 2-died, 3-23 Jan 1844, 15-Howard

#1069, 1-Howard, William, 2-born, 3-15 Mar 1776, 12-Howard, George, 13-Howard, Anna, 15-Howard

#1070, 1-Mason, Agnes, 2-born, 3-15 Dec 1780, 12-Mason, Joshua, 13-Mason, Nancy, 15-Howard

#1071, 1-Howard, William, 2-married, 3-28 May 1800, 7-Mason, Agnes, 15-Howard

#1072, 1-Howard, Nancy, 2-born, 3-15 Mar 1801, 12-Howard, William, 13-Howard, Agnes, 15-Howard

#1073, 1-Howard, Thurza, 2-born, 3-6 Nov 1803, 12-Howard, William, 13-Howard, Agnes, 15-Howard

#1074, 1-Howard, Eliza Bradley, 2-born, 3-29 Sep 1808, 12-Howard, William, 13-Howard, Agnes, 15-Howard

#1075, 1-Howard, Parliament [female], 2-born, 3-1 May 1810, 12-Howard, William, 13-Howard, Agnes, 15-Howard

#1076, 1-Howard, William H., 2-born, 3-26 Jul 1812, 12-Howard, William, 13-Howard, Agnes, 15-Howard

#1077, 1-Howard, George W., 2-born, 3-2 Sep 1814, 12-Howard, William, 13-Howard, Agnes, 15-Howard

#1078, 1-Shillingburg, Lewis D., 2-born, 3-1832, 15-Shillingburg

#1079, 1-Shillingburg, Lewis D., 2-died, 3-23 Mar 1885, 15-Shillingburg

#1080, 1-Shillingburg, Lewis D., 2-married, 3-27 Sep 1860, 7-Moomau, Lydia, 9-Shenandoah Co., VA, 15-Shillingburg

FAMILY BIBLE RECORDS IN THE WASHINGTON COUNTY FREE LIBRARY, HAGERSTOWN, MARYLAND

Entry #, 1-Last Name, First Name, 2-Event, 3-Date, 4-Event Location, 5-Age, 6-Other,
7-Spouse's Last, First, 8-Groom's Residence, 9-Bride's Residence, 10-Minister, 11-Minister's Location,
12-Father's Last, First, 13-Mother's Last, First, 14-Transcribed, 15-Family Bible

```
#1081, 1-Moomau, Lydia, 2-born, 3-26 Jul 1889, 15-Shillingburg
#1082, 1-Moomau, Lydia, 2-died, 3-1902, 15-Shillingburg
#1083, 1-Shillingburg, Sarah F., 2-married, 3-12 Sep 1883, 7-Balckburn, Ephriam G.,
    15-Shillingburg
#1084, 1-Shillingburg, Hannah, 2-married, 3-17 Oct 1844, 7-Streets , Wm., 15-
    Shillingburg
#1085, 1-Shillingburg, Ann Amelia, 2-married, 3-10 Mar 1852, 7-Kitzmiller,
    Nathaniel, 15-Shillingburg
#1086, 1-Shillingburg, Isabella, 2-married, 3-15 Dec 1853, 7-Cooper, Enos Boston,
    15-Shillingburg
#1087, 1-Shillingburg, William, 2-born, 3-1799, 15-Shillingburg
#1088, 1-Shillingburg, William, 2-died, 3-22 Sep 1880, 15-Shillingburg
#1089, 1-Shillingburg, Elizabeth Kitzmiller, 2-born, 3-1794, 15-Shillingburg
#1090, 1-Shillingburg, Elizabeth Kitzmiller, 2-died, 3-19 Aug 1845, 15-Shillingburg
#1091, 1-Shillingburg, Rebecca, 2-died, 3-Mar 1868, 15-Shillingburg
#1092, 1-Streets, Charles Cunnungham, 2-died, 3-1 Oct 1845, 12-Streets, Wm., 13-
    Streets, Hannah, 15-Shillingburg
#1093, 1-Streets, Charles Cunnungham, 2-born, 3-23 Sep 1845, 15-Shillingburg
#1094, 1-Streets, John Green, 2-born, 3-4 Sep 1846, 15-Shillingburg
#1095, 1-Streets, Streit Lingham, 2-born, 3-6 Dec 1852, 15-Shillingburg
#1096, 1-Cooper, William Howard, 2-born, 3-20 Oct 1854, 12-Cooper, Enos, 13-Cooper,
    Isabella, 15-Shillingburg
#1097, 1-Cooper, Jacob Wellington, 2-born, 3-1 Jul 1856, 15-Shillingburg
#1098, 1-Shillingburg, Lydia, 2-born, 3-26 Jul 1839, 15-Shillingburg
#1099, 1-Shillingburg, Sarah Francis, 2-born, 3-15 Oct 1863, 15-Shillingburg
#1100, 1-Shillingburg, James Gibson, 2-born, 3-16 Sep 1871, 15-Shillingburg
#1101, 1-Shillingburg, Grover C., 2-married, 3-19 Mar 1914, 7-Taylor, Edith M., 15-
    Shillingburg
#1102, 1-Shillingburg, Ledah, 2-married, 3-5 Jun 1916, 7-Hanline, Elmer, 15-
    Shillingburg
#1103, 1-Shillingburg, Edward S., 2-married, 3-11 Aug 1887, 4-J.C. Shavers home, 7-
    Blackburn, Mary A., 10-Rev. Nihiser, 15-Shillingburg
#1104, 1-Shillingburg, Grover Cleveland, 2-born, 3-19 May 1889, 12-Shillingburg,
    Edward S., 13-Balckburn, Mary A., 15-Shillingburg
#1105, 1-Shillingburg, Olin Lee, 2-born, 3-29 Aug 1891, 12-Shillingburg, Edward S.,
    13-Balckburn, Mary A., 15-Shillingburg
#1106, 1-Shillingburg, Infant, 2-born, 3-1894, 12-Shillingburg, Edward S., 13-
    Balckburn, Mary A., 15-Shillingburg
#1107, 1-Shillingburg, Infant, 2-died, 3-1894, 12-Shillingburg, Edward S., 13-
    Balckburn, Mary A., 15-Shillingburg
#1108, 1-Shillingburg, Ledah Ann Frances, 2-born, 3-12 May 1896, 12-Shillingburg,
    Edward S., 13-Balckburn, Mary A., 15-Shillingburg
#1109, 1-Shillingburg, Russel Bryon, 2-born, 3-14 Oct 1898, 12-Shillingburg, Edward
    S., 13-Balckburn, Mary A., 15-Shillingburg
#1110, 1-Shillingburg, Bertha Mildred, 2-born, 3-15 Jun 1905, 12-Shillingburg,
    Edward S., 13-Balckburn, Mary A., 15-Shillingburg
#1111, 1-Shillingburg, Beall Davis, 2-born, 3-8 May 1906, 12-Shillingburg, Edward
    S., 13-Balckburn, Mary A., 15-Shillingburg
#1112, 1-Shillingburg, James G., 2-married, 3-21 Apr 1889, 4-"D.J. and Lydia A.
    (Shillingburg) Bosleys home at Alkire Farm near Stony River Bridge where U.S.
    50 crosses", 7-Sollars, Amelia Frances, 10-Rev. Samuel Fike , 11-Brethren
    Church, 15-Shillingburg
#1113, 1-Shillingburg, Carrie, 2-born, 3-22 Mar 1890, 12-Shillingburg, James G.,
    13-Sollars , Amelia Frances, 15-Shillingburg
```

FAMILY BIBLE RECORDS IN THE WASHINGTON COUNTY FREE LIBRARY, HAGERSTOWN, MARYLAND

Entry #, 1-Last Name, First Name, 2-Event, 3-Date, 4-Event Location, 5-Age, 6-Other,
7-Spouse's Last, First, 8-Groom's Residence, 9-Bride's Residence, 10-Minister, 11-Minister's Location,
12-Father's Last, First, 13-Mother's Last, First, 14-Transcribed, 15-Family Bible

#1114, 1-Shillingburg, John King, 2-born, 3-14 Oct 1891, 12-Shillingburg, James G., 13-Sollars , Amelia Frances, 15-Shillingburg

#1115, 1-Shillingburg, Tony Wilson, 2-born, 3-11 May 1894, 12-Shillingburg, James G., 13-Sollars , Amelia Frances, 15-Shillingburg

#1116, 1-Shillingburg, Samuel Sollars, 2-born, 3-15 Dec 1895, 12-Shillingburg, James G., 13-Sollars , Amelia Frances, 15-Shillingburg

#1117, 1-Shillingburg, James Bryan, 2-born, 3-30 May 1897, 12-Shillingburg, James G., 13-Sollars , Amelia Frances, 15-Shillingburg

#1118, 1-Shillingburg, Ella Rea, 2-born, 3-27 May 1902, 12-Shillingburg, James G., 13-Sollars , Amelia Frances, 15-Shillingburg

#1119, 1-Shillingburg, Leona Mae, 2-born, 3-30 Apr 1904, 12-Shillingburg, James G., 13-Sollars , Amelia Frances, 15-Shillingburg

#1120, 1-Shillingburg, Sarah Isabella, 2-born, 3-6 Sep 1898, 12-Shillingburg, James G., 13-Sollars , Amelia Frances, 15-Shillingburg

#1121, 1-Shillingburg, James G., 2-born, 3-14 Sep 1865, 4-Gibson Farm, 15-Shillingburg

#1122, 1-Sollars, Amelia Frances, 2-born, 3-26 Jul 1862, 15-Shillingburg

#1123, 1-Shillingburg, Carrie, 2-married, 3-1 Jul 1917, 7-Blackburn, Clarence A., 15-Shillingburg

#1124, 1-Shillingburg, Tony Wilson, 2-married, 3-22 Feb 1918, 7-Kitzmiller, Blanche, 15-Shillingburg

#1125, 1-Shillingburg, John King, 2-married, 3-23 Jul 1919, 7-Kitzmiller, Margaret M., 15-Shillingburg

#1126, 1-Blackburn, Carrie (Shillingburg), 2-married, 3-22 Sep 1925, 7-Jones, Frank C., 15-Shillingburg

#1127, 1-Shillingburg, Leona May, 2-married, 3-10 Mar 1938, 7-Parks, Lester A., 15-Shillingburg

#1128, 1-Shillingburg, James B., 2-died, 3-14 Jul 1897, 15-Shillingburg

#1129, 1-Shillingburg, Sarah I., 2-died, 3-3 Oct 1898, 15-Shillingburg

#1130, 1-Shillingburg, Tony W., 2-died, 3-22 Jul 1918, 4-France, 6-"killed in Action in France", 15-Shillingburg

#1131, 1-Shillingburg, Amelia Frances (Sollars), 2-died, 3-13 Nov 1921, 15-Shillingburg

#1132, 1-Shillingburg, James G., 2-died, 3-1937, 6-copied from gravestone, 15-Shillingburg

#1133, 1-Shillingburg, Lewis D., 2-died, 3-23 Mar 1885, 5-52 years 4 months 8 days, 6-copied from gravestone, 15-Shillingburg

#1134, 1-Aronhalt, Rebecca, 2-born, 3-17 Oct 1835, 15-Aronhalt [2nd page of Shillingburg records]

#1135, 1-Aronhalt, Samuel Wheeler, 2-born, 3-20 Sep 1854, 15-Aronhalt [2nd page of Shillingburg records]

#1136, 1-Aronhalt, Mary Margaret, 2-born, 3-27 Jun 1856, 15-Aronhalt [2nd page of Shillingburg records]

#1137, 1-Aronhalt, Thomas Edmund, 2-born, 3-6 Apr 1858, 15-Aronhalt [2nd page of Shillingburg records]

#1138, 1-Aronhalt, Amos Wright, 2-born, 3-2 Dec 1859, 15-Aronhalt [2nd page of Shillingburg records]

#1139, 1-Aronhalt, Eliza Ellen, 2-born, 3-12 Nov 1861, 15-Aronhalt [2nd page of Shillingburg records]

#1140, 1-Aronhalt, David, 2-born, 3-14 Sep 1863, 15-Aronhalt [2nd page of Shillingburg records]

#1141, 1-Aronhalt, Martha A., 2-born, 3-14 Jun 1865, 15-Aronhalt [2nd page of Shillingburg records]

#1142, 1-Aronhalt, Keziah F., 2-born, 3-1 May 1867, 15-Aronhalt [2nd page of Shillingburg records]

FAMILY BIBLE RECORDS IN THE WASHINGTON COUNTY FREE LIBRARY, HAGERSTOWN, MARYLAND

**Entry #, 1-Last Name, First Name, 2-Event, 3-Date, 4-Event Location, 5-Age, 6-Other,
7-Spouse's Last, First, 8-Groom's Residence, 9-Bride's Residence, 10-Minister, 11-Minister's Location,
12-Father's Last, First, 13-Mother's Last, First, 14-Transcribed, 15-Family Bible**

#1143, 1-Aronhalt, Job M., 2-born, 3-21 Jan 1869, 15-Aronhalt [2nd page of Shillingburg records]

#1144, 1-Aronhalt, Jacob L., 2-born, 3-18 Dec 1870, 15-Aronhalt [2nd page of Shillingburg records]

#1145, 1-Aronhalt, Rebecca V., 2-born, 3-27 May 1873, 15-Aronhalt [2nd page of Shillingburg records]

#1146, 1-Aronhalt, Isaac, 2-born, 3-27 Dec 1875, 15-Aronhalt [2nd page of Shillingburg records]

#1147, 1-Aronhalt, Myra J., 2-born, 3-12 Dec 1878, 15-Aronhalt [2nd page of Shillingburg records]

#1148, 1-Aronhalt, Flora L., 2-born, 3-12 Oct 1880, 15-Aronhalt [2nd page of Shillingburg records]

#1149, 1-Aronhalt, John William, 2-born, 3-3 Jan 1832, 15-Aronhalt [2nd page of Shillingburg records]

#1150, 1-Aronhalt, John William, 2-married, 3-Dec 1853, 7-Hays, Rebecca, 15-Aronhalt [2nd page of Shillingburg records]

#1151, 1-Aronhalt, Mary M., 2-married, 3-30 Oct 1878, 7-Moreland, David W., 15-Aronhalt [2nd page of Shillingburg records]

#1152, 1-Aronhalt, Samuel W., 2-married, 3-12 Mar 1879, 7-Hanline, Mary Susan, 15-Aronhalt [2nd page of Shillingburg records]

#1153, 1-Aronhalt, John Wm., 2-died, 3-10 Jun 1884, 15-Aronhalt [2nd page of Shillingburg records]

#1154, 1-Aronhalt, Eliza Ellen, 2-died, 3-22 Nov 1881, 15-Aronhalt [2nd page of Shillingburg records]

#1155, 1-Aronhalt, Myra Jane, 2-died, 3-10 Dec 1881, 15-Aronhalt [2nd page of Shillingburg records]

#1156, 1-Aronhalt, Thomas Wright, 2-died, 3-10 Dec 1885, 15-Aronhalt [2nd page of Shillingburg records]

#1157, 1-Aronhalt, Rebecca, 2-died, 3-4 Jan 1901, 15-Aronhalt [2nd page of Shillingburg records]

#1158, 1-Larew, Noah, 2-died, 3-22 Aug 1827, 15-Larew [3rd page in Shillingburg records]

#1159, 1-Larew, Rachel, 2-died, 3-23 Aug 1827, 15-Larew [3rd page in Shillingburg records]

#1160, 1-Larew, Abraham, 2-died, 3-19 Aug 1825, 15-Larew [3rd page in Shillingburg records]

#1161, 1-Larew, Jacob, 3-14 Mar 1829, 6-appeared before church session, 15-Larew [3rd page in Shillingburg records]

#1162, 1-Neal, Charles Benton, 2-born, 3-30 Jan 1860, 12-Neal, Emry, 13-Neal, Sarah, 15-Neal

#1163, 1-Neal, Eliza Adel, 2-born, 3-2 May 1861, 15-Neal

#1164, 1-Neal, Mary Malindia, 2-born, 3-25 Mar 1862, 12-Neal, S.[?] L., 13-Neal, Eliza[?] G., 15-Neal

#1165, 1-Neal, James E.[?], 2-born, 3-2 Jan 1864, 15-Neal

#1166, 1-Neal, Adam, 2-born, 3-31 Aug 1867, 12-Neal, S.L., 13-Neal, Eliza[?], 15-Neal

#1167, 1-Neal, Elley, 2-born, 3-24 Mar 1869, 12-Neal, S.L., 13-Neal, Eliza J., 15-Neal

#1168, 1-Neal, Captolia, 2-born, 3-21 Feb 1872, 12-Neal, S.L., 13-Neal, Eliza J., 15-Neal

#1169, 1-Neal, Stansbary [?] L., 2-born, 3-5 Oct 1880, 15-Neal

#1170, 1-Neal, J.C.W., 2-died, 3-1 Jun 1822, 15-Neal

#1171, 1-Neal, Charles Wesley, 2-died, 3-3 Apr 1825, 15-Neal

#1172, 1-Neal, Emory Nelson, 2-died, 3-12 Jun 18__[blank], 15-Neal

#1173, 1-Neal, Frances Asbury, 2-died, 3-17 Nov 1844, 15-Neal

FAMILY BIBLE RECORDS IN THE WASHINGTON COUNTY FREE LIBRARY, HAGERSTOWN, MARYLAND

Entry #, 1-Last Name, First Name, 2-Event, 3-Date, 4-Event Location, 5-Age, 6-Other,
7-Spouse's Last, First, 8-Groom's Residence, 9-Bride's Residence, 10-Minister, 11-Minister's Location,
12-Father's Last, First, 13-Mother's Last, First, 14-Transcribed, 15-Family Bible

```
#1174, 1-Neal, James (Mrs.), 2-died, 3-29 Sep 1862, 15-Neal
#1175, 1-Neal, James Emry, 2-died, 3-4 May 1862, 15-Neal
#1176, 1-Neal, Mary Malindia, 2-died, 3-31 Oct 1862, 12-Neal, S.L., 13-Eliza[?] J.,
    15-Neal
#1177, 1-Neal, James E., 2-died, 3-14 Nov 1864, 15-Neal
#1178, 1-Neal, James, 2-married, 3-10 Mar 1818, 7-Jones, Nancy, 15-Neal
#1179, 1-Neal, L.[?] S.[?], 2-married, 3-2 Aug 1860, 7-Charlton, Elize J., 15-Neal
#1180, 1-Neal, William, 2-born, 3-15 May 1819, 12-Neal, James, 13-Neal, Nancy, 15-
    Neal
#1181, 1-Neal, John Curtis, 2-born, 3-7 Sep 1821, 12-Neal, James, 13-Neal, Nancy,
    15-Neal
#1182, 1-Neal, Emory Nelson, 2-born, 3-14 Mar 1823, 12-Neal, James, 13-Neal, Nancy,
    15-Neal
#1183, 1-Neal, Charles Wesley, 2-born, 3-22 Feb 1825, 12-Neal, James, 13-Neal,
    Nancy, 15-Neal
#1184, 1-Neal, Mary Elizabeth, 2-born, 3-12 Jul 1827, 12-Neal, James, 13-Neal,
    Nancy, 15-Neal
#1185, 1-Neal, Enoch Jones, 2-born, 3-13 Aug 1830, 12-Neal, James, 13-Neal, Nancy,
    15-Neal
#1186, 1-Neal, Ann Eliza, 2-born, 3-12 Jun 1833, 12-Neal, James, 13-Neal, Nancy,
    15-Neal
#1187, 1-Neal, James Emory, 2-born, 3-16 Jun 1836, 12-Neal, James, 13-Neal, Nancy,
    15-Neal
#1188, 1-Neal, Stansbury Lawrence, 2-born, 3-3 Mar 1840, 12-Neal, James, 13-Neal,
    Nancy, 15-Neal
#1189, 1-Neal, Francis Asbury, 2-born, 3-28 May 18__ [blank], 12-Neal, James, 13-
    Neal, Nancy, 15-Neal
#1190, 1-Crabtree, Ann Maria, 2-died, 3-22 Aug 1857, 5-21 years 5 months 19 days,
    7-Crabtree, Reason L., 12-Shryock, Lewis P., 13-Shryock, Phebe, 15-Shyrock
#1191, 1-Shryock, Lewis Justin, 2-born, 3-11 Feb 1806, 15-Shyrock
#1192, 1-Shryock, Lewis Justin, 2-died, 3-21 Aug 1874, 5-68 years 6 months 10 days,
    15-Shyrock
#1193, 1-Shryock, George French, 2-born, 3-11 Nov 1831, 15-Shyrock
#1194, 1-Shryock, George French, 2-died, 3-14 Feb 1875, 5-43 years 3 months 13
    days, 15-Shyrock
#1195, 1-Shryock, Phebe, 2-born, 3-10 Mar 1814, 15-Shyrock
#1196, 1-Shryock, Phebe, 2-died, 3-2 Jan 1894, 5-79 years 9 months 23 days, 15-
    Shyrock
#1197, 1-Shryock, Henry R., 2-born, 3-4 Oct 1833, 15-Shyrock
#1198, 1-Shryock, Henry R., 2-died, 3-30 Apr 1910, 5-76 years, 15-Shyrock
#1199, 1-Shryock, Lenol Martin, 2-died, 3-26 Jan 1920, 5-79 years 4 months 26 days,
    15-Shyrock
#1200, 1-Shryock, Lenol Martin, 2-born, 3-31 Aug 1840, 15-Shyrock
#1201, 1-Lupton, Joseph, 2-born, 3-5 Mar 1719 [?-see Other column], 6-father of
    David Lupton; born the 5th of the 1st Mo. Now the 3rd Month 1719", 12-Lupton,
    Joseph, 13-Lupton, Mary, 15-Lupton
#1202, 1-Lupton, Joseph, 2-died, 3-9 Nov 1791, 5-73 years, 15-Lupton
#1203, 1-Lupton, Rachel, 2-died, 4-Nathan Updegraff's in Ohio, 15-Lupton
#1204, 1-Hollingsworth, Isaac, 2-born, 3-22 Feb 1722, 15-Lupton
#1205, 1-Hollingsworth, Rachel, 2-born, 3-3 Jan 1724/1725", 15-Lupton
#1206, 1-Hollingsworth, Isaac, 2-died, 3-10 Sep 1759, 15-Lupton
#1207, 1-Hollingsworth, Rachel, 2-died, 3-8 Oct 1805, 15-Lupton
#1208, 1-Jackson, Spencer, 2-born, 3-4 Feb 1806, 15-Richardson [MD Genealogical
    Bulletin]
```

FAMILY BIBLE RECORDS IN THE WASHINGTON COUNTY FREE LIBRARY, HAGERSTOWN, MARYLAND

Entry #, 1-Last Name, First Name, 2-Event, 3-Date, 4-Event Location, 5-Age, 6-Other, 7-Spouse's Last, First, 8-Groom's Residence, 9-Bride's Residence, 10-Minister, 11-Minister's Location, 12-Father's Last, First, 13-Mother's Last, First, 14-Transcribed, 15-Family Bible

#1209, 1-Jackson, Spencer, 2-died, 3-24 Oct 1868, 15-Richardson [MD Genealogical Bulletin]

#1210, 1-Jackson, Spencer, 2-married, 3-31 Aug 1834, 7-Richardson, Mary Anette, 15-Richardson [MD Genealogical Bulletin]

#1211, 1-Richardson, Mary Anette, 2-born, 3-10 Jul 1816, 15-Richardson [MD Genealogical Bulletin]

#1212, 1-Richardson, Mary Anette, 2-died, 3-26 Feb 1869, 15-Richardson [MD Genealogical Bulletin]

#1213, 1-Jackson, Andrew, 2-born, 3-28 Jun 1838, 12-Jackson, Spencer, 13-Richardson, Mary Anette, 15-Richardson [MD Genealogical Bulletin]

#1214, 1-Jackson, Rachel, 2-born, 3-25 Sep 1839, 15-Richardson [MD Genealogical Bulletin]

#1215, 1-Jackson, Rachel, 2-died, 3-11 Sep 1840, 15-Richardson [MD Genealogical Bulletin]

#1216, 1-Jackson, Amelia P., 2-born, 3-8 Apr 1841, 15-Richardson [MD Genealogical Bulletin]

#1217, 1-Jackson, Amelia P., 2-married, 6-has one child, a girl, 7-Fox, Amos, 15-Richardson [MD Genealogical Bulletin]

#1218, 1-Jackson, John Tyler P., 2-born, 3-31 Nov 1842, 15-Richardson [MD Genealogical Bulletin]

#1219, 1-Jackson, Arabella E., 2-born, 3-8 Jan 1845, 15-Richardson [MD Genealogical Bulletin]

#1220, 1-Jackson, Arabella E., 2-married, 3-5 Dec 1875, 6-no children, 7-Winston, A.O., 15-Richardson [MD Genealogical Bulletin]

#1221, 1-Jackson, Thomas J., 2-born, 3-20 Aug 1846, 15-Richardson [MD Genealogical Bulletin]

#1222, 1-Jackson, Thomas J., 2-married, 3-1 Jun 1881, 4-Fort Worth, Texas, 6-one child, a boy, 7-Loving, Ruth, 15-Richardson [MD Genealogical Bulletin]

#1223, 1-Jackson, Mary L., 2-born, 3-20 Nov 1847, 6-died young, 15-Richardson [MD Genealogical Bulletin]

#1224, 1-Jackson, Lucy A., 2-born, 3-15 May 1850, 15-Richardson [MD Genealogical Bulletin]

#1225, 1-Jackson, Lucy A., 2-married, 6-had three children, 7-Keblinger, W., 15-Richardson [MD Genealogical Bulletin]

#1226, 1-Jackson, Jr., Spencer, 2-born, 3-15 Mar 1853, 6-"died young", 15-Richardson [MD Genealogical Bulletin]

#1227, 1-Jackson, Agnes D., 2-born, 3-9 Apr 1856, 6-"died young", 15-Richardson [MD Genealogical Bulletin]

#1228, 1-Jackson, Maria Louisa, 2-born, 3-16 Jun 1857, 15-Richardson [MD Genealogical Bulletin]

#1229, 1-Jackson, Maria Louisa, 2-married, 7-Kise, M., 15-Richardson [MD Genealogical Bulletin]

#1230, 1-Jackson, Maria Louisa, 2-died, 6-died in childbirth; child died a few weeks later, 15-Richardson [MD Genealogical Bulletin]

#1231, 1-Jackson, Penelope, 2-born, 3-23 Sep 1859, 15-Richardson [MD Genealogical Bulletin]

#1232, 1-Jackson, Penelope, 2-married, 3-17 Apr 1882, 4-Fort Worth, Texas, 7-Fitzhugh, F. (Dr.), 15-Richardson [MD Genealogical Bulletin]

#1233, 1-Richardson, Richard Alexander, 2-married, 3-Sep 1841, 7-Roberdeau, Heriot Triplett, 9-Centerville, Fairfax Co., VA, 15-Richardson [MD Genealogical Bulletin]

#1234, 1-Richardson, Alice Morris, 2-died, 6-died in infancy, 12-Richardson, Richard Alexander, 13-Roberdeau, Heriot Triplett, 15-Richardson [MD Genealogical Bulletin]

FAMILY BIBLE RECORDS IN THE WASHINGTON COUNTY FREE LIBRARY, HAGERSTOWN, MARYLAND

Entry #, 1-Last Name, First Name, 2-Event, 3-Date, 4-Event Location, 5-Age, 6-Other, 7-Spouse's Last, First, 8-Groom's Residence, 9-Bride's Residence, 10-Minister, 11-Minister's Location, 12-Father's Last, First, 13-Mother's Last, First, 14-Transcribed, 15-Family Bible

#1235, 1-Richardson, James William, 2-born, 3-1845, 12-Richardson, Richard Alexander, 13-Roberdeau, Heriot Triplett, 15-Richardson [MD Genealogical Bulletin]

#1236, 1-Richardson, James William, 2-died, 3-Apr 1865, 6-"He enlisted in the Confederate Army at the age of 16, and was killed in the last battle of Appomattox", 12-Richardson, Richard Alexander, 13-Roberdeau, Heriot Triplett, 15-Richardson [MD Genealogical Bulletin]

#1237, 1-Richardson, Hariot Virginia, 2-married, 3-3 Jan 1872, 7-Triplett, Hayward, 12-Richardson, Richard Alexander, 13-Roberdeau, Heriot Triplett, 15-Richardson [MD Genealogical Bulletin]

#1238, 1-Richardson, Mary Anette, 2-died, 6-unmarried, 12-Richardson, Richard Alexander, 13-Roberdeau, Heriot Triplett, 15-Richardson [MD Genealogical Bulletin]

#1239, 1-Richardson, Martha Linton, 2-died, 6-unmarried, 12-Richardson, Richard Alexander, 13-Roberdeau, Heriot Triplett, 15-Richardson [MD Genealogical Bulletin]

#1240, 1-Triplett, Roberdeau, 2-born, 3-17 Oct 1872, 12-Triplett, Hayward, 13-Richardson, Hariot Virginia, 15-Richardson [MD Genealogical Bulletin]

#1241, 1-Triplett, Roderick, 2-born, 3-29 Apr 1874, 12-Triplett, Hayward, 13-Richardson, Hariot Virginia, 15-Richardson [MD Genealogical Bulletin]

#1242, 1-Triplett, Hayward, 2-born, 3-12 Nov 1875, 12-Triplett, Hayward, 13-Richardson, Hariot Virginia, 15-Richardson [MD Genealogical Bulletin]

#1243, 1-Triplett, Edna Linton, 2-born, 3-11 Nov 1876, 12-Triplett, Hayward, 13-Richardson, Hariot Virginia, 15-Richardson [MD Genealogical Bulletin]

#1244, 1-Triplett, Alexander, 2-born, 3-31 Jul 1878, 12-Triplett, Hayward, 13-Richardson, Hariot Virginia, 15-Richardson [MD Genealogical Bulletin]

#1245, 1-Triplett, Pelham, 2-born, 3-22 Mar 1880, 12-Triplett, Hayward, 13-Richardson, Hariot Virginia, 15-Richardson [MD Genealogical Bulletin]

#1246, 1-Richardson, Maria Louisa, 2-married, 3-7 Aug 1850, 7-Mitchell, John E., 12-Richardson, William P., 15-Richardson [MD Genealogical Bulletin]

#1247, 1-Mitchell, Florence V., 2-born, 3-3 Mar 1852, 12-Mitchell, John E., 13-Richardson, Maria Louisa, 15-Richardson [MD Genealogical Bulletin]

#1248, 1-Mitchell, Florence V., 2-married, 6-had three children, 12-Mitchell, John E., 13-Richardson, Maria Louisa, 15-Richardson [MD Genealogical Bulletin]

#1249, 1-Mitchell, John E., 2-born, 3-13 Jun 1854, 12-Mitchell, John E., 13-Richardson, Maria Louisa, 15-Richardson [MD Genealogical Bulletin]

#1250, 1-Glasgow, Nancy, 2-born, 3-about 1771, 12-Glasgow, Adam, 13-Willson, 15-George [MD Genealogical Bulletin]

#1251, 1-Glasgow, Nancy, 2-married, 6-came to America in 1800 from Londonderry, 7-Stewart, John, 15-George [MD Genealogical Bulletin]

#1252, 1-Stewart, Mary Ellen, 2-born, 3-circa 1800, 4-Scotland, 6-a few months old when family came to America in 1800, 12-Stewart, John, 13-Glasgow, Nancy, 15-George [MD Genealogical Bulletin]

#1253, 1-Stewart, John, 2-born, 4-New Castle, 12-Stewart, John, 13-Glasgow, Nancy, 15-George [MD Genealogical Bulletin]

#1254, 1-Stewart, Margaret, 2-born, 4-Baltimore, 12-Stewart, John, 13-Glasgow, Nancy, 15-George [MD Genealogical Bulletin]

#1255, 1-Stewart, Mary Ellen, 2-married, 6-married at 17 yrs, 7-George, James B., 15-George [MD Genealogical Bulletin]

#1256, 1-Stewart, Margaret, 2-married, 7-Russell, George M., 15-George [MD Genealogical Bulletin]

#1257, 1-Stewart, John, 2-married, 6-married three times, 15-George [MD Genealogical Bulletin]

#1258, 1-Stewart, John, 2-died, 4-St. Louis, 15-George [MD Genealogical Bulletin]

#1259, 1-Wood, William, 2-born, 4-Baltimore, 15-Wood [MD Genealogical Bulletin]

FAMILY BIBLE RECORDS IN THE WASHINGTON COUNTY FREE LIBRARY, HAGERSTOWN, MARYLAND

Entry #, 1-Last Name, First Name, 2-Event, 3-Date, 4-Event Location, 5-Age, 6-Other, 7-Spouse's Last, First, 8-Groom's Residence, 9-Bride's Residence, 10-Minister, 11-Minister's Location, 12-Father's Last, First, 13-Mother's Last, First, 14-Transcribed, 15-Family Bible

#1260, 1-Barton, Charlotte, 2-born, 3-28 Oct 1771, 4-Baltimore, 15-Wood [MD Genealogical Bulletin]

#1261, 1-Wood, H.H., 2-born, 3-22 Feb 1791, 15-Wood [MD Genealogical Bulletin]

#1262, 1-Wood, H.H., 2-married, 3-28 Jul 1813, Rebecca, 15-Wood [MD Genealogical Bulletin]

#1263, 1-Wood, Rebecca, 2-born, 3-15 Mar 1796, 15-Wood [MD Genealogical Bulletin]

#1264, 1-Wood, Caroline, 2-born, 3-26 Apr 1814, 12-Wood, H.H., 13-Wood, Rebecca, 15-Wood [MD Genealogical Bulletin]

#1265, 1-Wood, Caroline, 2-married, 7-Atkinson, Samuel, 8-Baltimore, 12-Wood, H.H., 13-Wood, Rebecca, 15-Wood [MD Genealogical Bulletin]

#1266, 1-Wood, Caroline, 2-married, 3-13 Jan 1841, 6-had 4 children, 7-Rawlings, Frederick, 12-Wood, H.H., 13-Wood, Rebecca, 15-Wood [MD Genealogical Bulletin]

#1267, 1-Wood, Caroline, 2-died, 3-14 Apr 1854, 12-Wood, H.H., 13-Wood, Rebecca, 15-Wood [MD Genealogical Bulletin]

#1268, 1-Atkinson, Samuel, 12-Atkinson, Samuel, 13-Wood, Caroline, 15-Wood [MD Genealogical Bulletin]

#1269, 1-Wood, H.W., 2-born, 3-25 Jan 1816, 12-Wood, H.H., 13-Wood, Rebecca, 15-Wood [MD Genealogical Bulletin]

#1270, 1-Wood, Oscar, 2-born, 3-25 Jan 1816, 12-Wood, H.H., 13-Wood, Rebecca, 15-Wood [MD Genealogical Bulletin]

#1271, 1-Wood, William A., 2-born, 3-17 Nov 1818, 12-Wood, H.H., 13-Wood, Rebecca, 15-Wood [MD Genealogical Bulletin]

#1272, 1-Wood, Eliza Jane, 2-born, 3-9 Jan 1820, 12-Wood, H.H., 13-Wood, Rebecca, 15-Wood [MD Genealogical Bulletin]

#1273, 1-Wood, Oliver C., 2-born, 3-14 Feb 1821, 12-Wood, H.H., 13-Wood, Rebecca, 15-Wood [MD Genealogical Bulletin]

#1274, 1-Wood, Charles, 2-born, 3-21 Sep 1823, 12-Wood, H.H., 13-Wood, Rebecca, 15-Wood [MD Genealogical Bulletin]

#1275, 1-Wood, Lafayette, 2-born, 3-20 Jul 1825, 12-Wood, H.H., 13-Wood, Rebecca, 15-Wood [MD Genealogical Bulletin]

#1276, 1-Wood, Tumeson(?), 2-born, 3-16 Feb 1828, 12-Wood, H.H., 13-Wood, Rebecca, 15-Wood [MD Genealogical Bulletin]

#1277, 1-Wood, Elizabeth, 2-born, 3-26 Feb 1831, 12-Wood, H.H., 13-Wood, Rebecca, 15-Wood [MD Genealogical Bulletin]

#1278, 1-Wood, Ann Rebecca, 2-born, 3-26 Feb 1831, 12-Wood, H.H., 13-Wood, Rebecca, 15-Wood [MD Genealogical Bulletin]

#1279, 1-Wood, Wm. A., 2-married, 3-10 [rest blank], 7-Merriken, Alphonza Elizabeth (Miss), 10-Rev. Mr. Rolfe, 15-Wood [MD Genealogical Bulletin]

#1280, 1-Rawlings, Frederick, 2-born, 3-28 Aug 1802, 7-Wood, Caroline, 15-Wood [MD Genealogical Bulletin]

#1281, 1-Rawlings, Frederick, 2-died, 3-25 Nov 1851, 7-Wood, Caroline, 15-Wood [MD Genealogical Bulletin]

#1282, 1-Woltz, Elie, 2-born, 3-27 Apr 1789, 15-VFC - George Woltz file

#1283, 1-Woltz, Eliza, 2-born, 3-23 Sep 1797, 15-VFC - George Woltz file

#1284, 1-Woltz, James Walling, 2-born, 3-9 Sep 1817, 15-VFC - George Woltz file

#1285, 1-Woltz, George Washington, 2-born, 3-13 Jan 1820, 15-VFC - George Woltz file

#1286, 1-Woltz, Charles William, 2-born, 3-23 Jan 1821, 15-VFC - George Woltz file

#1287, 1-Woltz, Samuel Armstrong, 2-born, 3-10 Apr 1823, 15-VFC - George Woltz file

#1288, 1-Woltz, John Reynolds, 2-born, 3-26 Dec 1825, 15-VFC - George Woltz file

#1289, 1-Woltz, Mary Eliza, 2-born, 3-19 Mar 1829, 15-VFC - George Woltz file

#1290, 1-Woltz, Francis Jane, 2-born, 3-22 Sep 1832, 15-VFC - George Woltz file

#1291, 1-Woltz, Herman Dorsey, 2-born, 3-27 Jul 1836, 15-VFC - George Woltz file

#1292, 1-Woltz, Martin Startzman, 2-born, 3-17 Dec 1837, 15-VFC - George Woltz file

FAMILY BIBLE RECORDS IN THE WASHINGTON COUNTY FREE LIBRARY, HAGERSTOWN, MARYLAND

Entry #, 1-Last Name, First Name, 2-Event, 3-Date, 4-Event Location, 5-Age, 6-Other, 7-Spouse's Last, First, 8-Groom's Residence, 9-Bride's Residence, 10-Minister, 11-Minister's Location, 12-Father's Last, First, 13-Mother's Last, First, 14-Transcribed, 15-Family Bible

```
#1293, 1-Walling, Mercy (Miss), 2-married, 3-5 Dec 1809, 15-VFC - George Woltz file
#1294, 1-Woltz, Elie, 2-married, 3-2 Jul 1816, 7-Walling, Eliza (Miss), 15-VFC -
    George Woltz file
#1295, 1-Walling, James, 2-born, 3-31 Aug 1789, 15-VFC - George Woltz file
#1296, 1-Walling, Mercy, 2-born, 3-28 Mar 1791, 15-VFC - George Woltz file
#1297, 1-Walling, Elizabeth, 2-born, 3-23 Sep 1797, 15-VFC - George Woltz file
#1298, 1-Walling, Herman Dorsey, 2-born, 3-27 Jul 1835, 12-Woltz, Elie, 13-Woltz,
    Elizabeth, 15-VFC - George Woltz file
#1299, 1-Walling, Herman Dorsey, 2-baptized, 3-17 Feb 1836, 10-Joab Bernard, 15-VFC
    - George Woltz file
#1300, 1-Woltz, Frances Jane, 2-born, 3-22 Sep 1832, 12-Woltz, Eliee, 13-Woltz,
    Elizabeth, 15-VFC - George Woltz file
#1301, 1-Woltz, Frances Jane, 2-baptized, 3-20 Dec 1832, 10-R.S. Vinton[?], 15-VFC
    - George Woltz file
#1302, 1-Walling, Eliza, 2-born, 3-23 Sep 1797, 15-VFC - George Woltz file
#1303, 1-Woltz, Mary Eliza, 2-born, 3-19 Mar 1829, 15-VFC - George Woltz file
#1304, 1-Walling, James (Col.), 2-died, 3-20 Oct 1811, 5-84 years 1 months, 15-VFC
    - George Woltz file
#1305, 1-Walling, James (Capt.), 2-died, 3-12 Mar 1823, 5-33 years 6 months 12
    days, 15-VFC - George Woltz file
#1306, 1-Walling, Mary, 2-died, 3-16 Aug 1825, 5-61 years 6 months, 15-VFC - George
    Woltz file
#1307, 1-Woltz, George Washington, 2-died, 3-22 Jan 1820, 5-9 days, 15-VFC - George
    Woltz file
#1308, 1-Woltz, Frances Jane, 2-died, 3-7 Jul 1835, 15-VFC - George Woltz file
#1309, 1-Woltz, Martin S., 2-died, 3-2 May 1839, 15-VFC - George Woltz file
#1310, 1-Woltz, Herman Dorsey, 2-died, 3-14[or 4] Apr 1856, 5-19 years 3 months,
    15-VFC - George Woltz file
#1311, 1-Woltz, Eli, 2-died, 3-19 Nov 1858, 5-69 years 6 months 2 weeks, 15-VFC -
    George Woltz file
#1312, 1-Woltz, Eliza, 2-died, 3-2 May 1867, 5-69 years 7 months 9 days, 15-VFC -
    George Woltz file
#1313, 1-Swayne, Isabela, 2-born, 3-17 Sep 1851, 15-Swain
#1314, 1-Swayne, Samuel Lewis, 2-born, 3-4 Mar 1855, 15-Swain
#1315, 1-Swayne, Charles Reuben, 2-born, 3-14 Sep 1853, 15-Swain
#1316, 1-Swain, Emma Traphenia[?], 2-born, 3-2 Dec 1857, 15-Swain
#1317, 1-Swain, Manzela Virginia, 2-born, 3-28 Oct 1861, 15-Swain
#1318, 1-Swain, William B., 2-born, 3-14 Dec 1863, 15-Swain
#1319, 1-Swain, Benny, 2-born, 3-17 Aug 1866, 15-Swain
#1320, 1-Swain, Charles Luther, 2-born, 3-24 Jun 1868, 15-Swain
#1321, 1-Swayne, Susan Elizabeth, 2-born, 3-4 Jan 1835, 15-Swain
#1322, 1-Swain, James Fleven[?], 2-born, 3-20 Aug 1871, 15-Swain
#1323, 1-Swain, Samuel, 2-married, 3-30 Sep , 7-Eicheldugin[?], Carrie F.[?], 15-
    Swain
#1324, 1-Swain, John P., 2-died, 3-9 May 1860, 15-Swain
#1325, 1-Swain, Charls Rubin, 2-died, 3-11 Nov 1850[?], 15-Swain
#1326, 1-Swain, William, 2-died, 3-2 Feb 1864, 15-Swain
#1327, 1-Swain, Benjimine, 2-died, 3-21 Jan 1886, 5-67 years, 15-Swain
#1328, 1-Schidleman, Emma T. (Mrs.), 2-died, 3-24 Apr 1885, 5-27 years 4 months 22
    days, 15-Swain
#1329, 1-Swain, Susan Elizabeth (Mrs.), 2-died, 3-24 Dec 1915, 5-80 years 11 months
    20 days, 15-Swain
#1330, 1-Swayne, Isabella, 2-born, 3-17 Sep 1851, 15-Swain
#1331, 1-Swayne, Charles Reuben, 2-born, 3-14 Sep 1853, 15-Swain
#1332, 1-Swain, John P., 2-born, 3-11 Mar 1859[?], 15-Swain
```

FAMILY BIBLE RECORDS IN THE WASHINGTON COUNTY FREE LIBRARY, HAGERSTOWN, MARYLAND

**Entry #, 1-Last Name, First Name, 2-Event, 3-Date, 4-Event Location, 5-Age, 6-Other,
7-Spouse's Last, First, 8-Groom's Residence, 9-Bride's Residence, 10-Minister, 11-Minister's Location,
12-Father's Last, First, 13-Mother's Last, First, 14-Transcribed, 15-Family Bible**

#1333, 1-Boyers, Susan Elizabeth, 2-married, 3-22 Jun 1851, 7-Swayne, Benjamine, 15-Swain

#1334, 1-Swain, Benjmine, 2-married, 3-16 Oct 1890, 7-Poffenberger, Maggie (Miss), 15-Swain

#1335, 1-Wilson, Isaac, 2-married, 3-16 Nov 1848, 4-Bakersville, 7-Baker, Susan Rebecca, 8-Bakersville, 9-Bakersville, 10-Rev. William Hunt, 14-Yes, 15-Wilson

#1336, 1-Wilson, Isaac, 2-born, 3-17 Feb 1825, 14-Yes, 15-Wilson

#1337, 1-Baker, Susan Rebecca, 2-born, 3-14 Nov 1831, 14-Yes, 15-Wilson

#1338, 1-Wilson, Charles Walter, 2-born, 3-12 May 1850, 12-Wilson, Isaac, 13-Baker, Susan Rebecca, 14-Yes, 15-Wilson

#1339, 1-Wilson, Elias Baker, 2-born, 3-1 Dec 1851, 12-Wilson, Isaac, 13-Baker, Susan Rebecca, 14-Yes, 15-Wilson

#1340, 1-Wilson, Anna Louisa, 2-born, 3-26 Mar 1853, 12-Wilson, Isaac, 13-Baker, Susan Rebecca, 14-Yes, 15-Wilson

#1341, 1-Wilson, Mary Elenora, 2-born, 3-25 Apr 1855, 12-Wilson, Isaac, 13-Baker, Susan Rebecca, 14-Yes, 15-Wilson

#1342, 1-Grove, Richard Duckett, 2-born, 3-Saturday, 4 Nov 1899, 14-Yes, 15-Wilson

#1343, 1-Grove, Frances Louise, 2-born, 3-Saturday, 16 Feb 1901, 14-Yes, 15-Wilson

#1344, 1-Grove, Jeannette Baker, 2-born, 3-Saturday, 20 Dec 1902, 14-Yes, 15-Wilson

#1345, 1-Boteler, Anna Louise Duckett, 2-born, 3-7:30pm, Friday, 19 Jun 1914, 6-Dr. B. Snively's midwife, Saua, 14-Yes, 15-Wilson

#1346, 1-Grove, Harry Clyde (Dr.), 2-born, 3-3:00am, Monday, 27 Nov 1916, 6-became a dentist , 14-Yes, 15-Wilson

#1347, 1-Grove, Jr., Harry Clyde (Dr.), 2-died, 3-12 Dec 1955, 5-39 years, 12-Grove, Harry Clyde, 13-Duckett, Susan, 14-Yes, 15-Wilson

#1348, 1-Wilson, Isaac, 2-died, 3-10 Mar 1892, 4-Bakersville, MD, 5-67 years, 14-Yes, 15-Wilson

#1349, 1-Wilson, Susan Rebecca (Baker), 2-died, 3-8 Feb 1907, 4-Waynesboro, PA, 5-75 years, 7-Wilson, Isaac, 14-Yes, 15-Wilson

#1350, 1-Grove, Harry Clyde, 2-died, 3-16 Sep 1943, 4-Lappans, MD, 5-69 years, 6-farmer, 14-Yes, 15-Wilson

#1351, 1-Boteler, Sophie (Duckett), 2-died, 3-Tuesday, 6 Jun 1944, 4-Elizabeth, NJ, 14-Yes, 15-Wilson

#1352, 1-Grove, Harry C., 2-married, 3-9 Feb 1899, 4-Frederick Co., MD, 7-Duckett, Susan E., 10-Rev. E.R. Eschback, 11-Reformed Church, 14-Yes, 15-Wilson

#1353, 1-Duckett, Joseph Gabby, 2-died, 3-14 Sep 1861, 4-near Potomac River, 6-shot in chest, 12-Duckett, T.B. (Dr.), 14-Yes, 15-Wilson

#1354, 1-Gabby, Eliza C., 2-married, 7-Duckett, T.B. (Dr.), 12-Gabby, Joseph, 14-Yes, 15-Wilson

#1355, 1-Duckett, Joseph Gabby, 2-born, 3-Wednesday, 1 Jun 1842, 14-Yes, 15-Wilson

#1356, 1-Duckett, Richard Jacob, 2-born, 3-Wednesday, 7 Feb 1844, 14-Yes, 15-Wilson

#1357, 1-[blank], Tommy, 2-born, 3-1 Jan 1855, 6-given to Mrs. E.C. Duckett until reaching 21 yrs., 13-[blank], Jane, 14-Yes, 15-Wilson

#1358, 1-[blank], Lally Earle, 2-born, 3-20 Jan 1853, 6-given to Mrs. E.C. Duckett until reaching 21 yrs.; Jane's oldest child, 13-[blank], Jane, 14-Yes, 15-Wilson

#1359, 1-Gabby, John, 2-died, 3-25 Jan 1810, 14-Yes, 15-Wilson

#1360, 1-Gabby, Ann, 2-died, 3-6 Jan 1852, 14-Yes, 15-Wilson

#1361, 1-Gabby, William, 2-died, 3-6 Sep 1820, 14-Yes, 15-Wilson

#1362, 1-McDowell, Emily (Gabby), 3-10 Jan 1853, 14-Yes, 15-Wilson

#1363, 1-Gabby, J., 3-30 Nov 1856, 14-Yes, 15-Wilson

#1364, 1-Gabby, Joseph, 2-died, 3-30 Nov 1856, 14-Yes, 15-Wilson

#1365, 1-Duckett, Elizabeth, 2-died, 3-24 Jun 1861, 14-Yes, 15-Wilson

#1366, 1-Gabby, Joseph, 2-married, 3-28 Mar 1805, 7-Cummins, Ann, 14-Yes, 15-Wilson

FAMILY BIBLE RECORDS IN THE WASHINGTON COUNTY FREE LIBRARY, HAGERSTOWN, MARYLAND

Entry #, 1-Last Name, First Name, 2-Event, 3-Date, 4-Event Location, 5-Age, 6-Other, 7-Spouse's Last, First, 8-Groom's Residence, 9-Bride's Residence, 10-Minister, 11-Minister's Location, 12-Father's Last, First, 13-Mother's Last, First, 14-Transcribed, 15-Family Bible

#1367, 1-Johnson, M.D., James, 2-married, 3-10 Nov 1829, 7-Gabby, Jane, 14-Yes, 15-Wilson

#1368, 1-McDowell, Nathan, 2-married, 3-14 Jan 1834, 7-Gabby, Emily, 14-Yes, 15-Wilson

#1369, 1-Duckett, Buchanan, 2-married, 3-13 Mar 1839, 7-Gabby, Elizabeth, 14-Yes, 15-Wilson

#1370, 1-Gabby, Elizabeth, 2-born, 3-12 Jun 1806, 14-Yes, 15-Wilson

#1371, 1-Gabby, Jane, 2-born, 3-28 Sep 1807, 14-Yes, 15-Wilson

#1372, 1-Gabby, John, 2-born, 3-11 Sep 1809, 14-Yes, 15-Wilson

#1373, 1-Gabby, Emily, 2-born, 3-24 Jan 1811, 14-Yes, 15-Wilson

#1374, 1-Gabby, William, 2-born, 3-17 Jul 1813, 14-Yes, 15-Wilson

#1375, 1-Gabby, Joseph, 2-born, 3-25 Apr 1879, 14-Yes, 15-Wilson

#1376, 1-Cummins, Ann, 2-born, 3-25 Apr 1879, 14-Yes, 15-Wilson

#1377, 1-Baker, Harry Wilson, 2-born, 3-14 Sep 1878, 14-Yes, 15-Wilson

#1378, 1-Baker, William Frances, 2-born, 3-8 Oct 1878, 14-Yes, 15-Wilson

#1379, 1-Baker, Essie May, 2-born, 3-25 Aug 1881, 14-Yes, 15-Wilson

#1380, 1-Baker, Isaac Wilson, 2-born, 3-5 Jul 1883, 14-Yes, 15-Wilson

#1381, 1-Baker, Charles Oliver, 2-born, 3-18 Mar 1885, 14-Yes, 15-Wilson

#1382, 1-Grove, Susan (Duckett), 2-died, 3-12 Dec 1956, 4-Funkstown, MD, 7-Grove, Sr., Harry Clyde, 14-Yes, 15-Wilson

#1383, 1-Snyder, Adam, 2-married, 3-22 May 1845, 7-Hull, Hannah, 15-Froehlich

#1384, 1-Kiracofe, J.W., 2-married, 3-22 Oct 1863, 7-Snyder, C.W.[or V.], 15-Froehlich

#1385, 1-Clemmer, J.H., 2-married, 3-24 Mar 1870, 7-Snyder, S.J., 15-Froehlich

#1386, 1-Clemmer, James F., 2-married, 3-22 Apr 1877, 7-Snyder, Lizzie E., 15-Froehlich

#1387, 1-Kiracofe, Alice J., 2-married, 3-18 Apr 1888, 4-Newvill, PA, 7-Needy, E.L., 15-Froehlich

#1388, 1-Needy, Edna M., 2-married, 3-25 Jun 1914, 4-Hagerstown, 7-Bell, Geo. F., 15-Froehlich

#1389, 1-Needy, Katharine L., 2-married, 3-12 Nov 1923, 4-Baltimore, 7-Froehlich, H. Roy, 15-Froehlich

#1390, 1-Froehlich, Barbara E., 2-married, 3-15 Jun 1946, 7-Horne, Ned V., 15-Froehlich

#1391, 1-Froehlich, Phyllis V., 2-married, 3-17 Jun 1950, 7-Layman, Wm., 15-Froehlich

#1392, 1-Froehlich, Patricia Lee, 2-married, 3-7 Jun 1958, 7-Satterfield, Thomas, 15-Froehlich

#1393, 1-Snyder, Adam, 2-born, 3-28 Aug 1808, 15-Froehlich

#1394, 1-Snyder, Hannah, 2-born, 3-20 Sep 1816, 7-Snyder, Adam, 15-Froehlich

#1395, 1-Snyder, Catharine V.[?], 2-born, 3-10 Apr 1846, 15-Froehlich

#1396, 1-Snyder, Sarah J., 2-born, 3-17 Jul 1847, 15-Froehlich

#1397, 1-Snyder, Mary J., 2-born, 3-21 Jul 1848, 15-Froehlich

#1398, 1-Snyder, Larncia[?] A., 2-born, 3-20 Jun 1852, 15-Froehlich

#1399, 1-Snyder, Elisabeth E., 2-born, 3-20 Sep 1856, 15-Froehlich

#1400, 1-Snyder, John W., 2-born, 3-24 Sep 1863, 15-Froehlich

#1401, 1-Kiracofe, Mary Josephine, 2-born, 3-13 Sep 1867, 15-Froehlich

#1402, 1-Needy, Alice J. (Kiracofe), 2-born, 3-11 Apr 1866, 15-Froehlich

#1403, 1-Needy, E.L., 2-born, 3-21 Jul 1862, 15-Froehlich

#1404, 1-Needy, Edna Myrtle, 2-born, 3-1 Oct 1889, 15-Froehlich

#1405, 1-Needy, Earl Kiracofe, 2-born, 3-21 May 1892, 15-Froehlich

#1406, 1-Needy, Hazel Ruth, 2-born, 3-10 Jan 1896, 15-Froehlich

#1407, 1-Needy, Katharine Louise, 2-born, 3-25 Sep 1899, 15-Froehlich

#1408, 1-Horne, Michael, 2-born, 3-28 Sep 1958, 12-Horne, Ned, 13-Horne, Barbara, 15-Froehlich

FAMILY BIBLE RECORDS IN THE WASHINGTON COUNTY FREE LIBRARY, HAGERSTOWN, MARYLAND

Entry #, 1-Last Name, First Name, 2-Event, 3-Date, 4-Event Location, 5-Age, 6-Other, 7-Spouse's Last, First, 8-Groom's Residence, 9-Bride's Residence, 10-Minister, 11-Minister's Location, 12-Father's Last, First, 13-Mother's Last, First, 14-Transcribed, 15-Family Bible

#1409, 1-Horne, Cindy Louise, 2-born, 3-4 May 1963, 12-Horne, Ned, 13-Horne, Barbara, 15-Froehlich

#1410, 1-Laymon, Diana, 2-born, 3-8 Oct 1951, 12-Laymon, William, 13-Laymon, Phyllis, 15-Froehlich

#1411, 1-Laymon, Jr., William H., 2-born, 3-20 Aug 1954, 12-Laymon, William, 13-Laymon, Phyllis, 15-Froehlich

#1412, 1-Laymon, Clifford Roy, 2-born, 3-23 Mar 1959, 12-Laymon, William, 13-Laymon, Phyllis, 15-Froehlich

#1413, 1-Laymon, Dawn Marie, 2-born, 3-4 Aug 1961, 12-Laymon, William, 13-Laymon, Phyllis, 15-Froehlich

#1414, 1-Laymon, John Carroll, 2-born, 3-7 Jun 1963, 12-Laymon, William, 13-Laymon, Phyllis, 15-Froehlich

#1415, 1-Froehlich, H. Roy, 2-born, 3-11 Oct 1893, 15-Froehlich

#1416, 1-Needy, Katharine L., 2-born, 3-25 Sep 1899, 7-Froehlich, H.R., 15-Froehlich

#1417, 1-Froehlich, Barbara E., 2-born, 3-15 Jun 1925, 15-Froehlich

#1418, 1-Froehlich, Phyllis Virginia, 2-born, 3-21 Apr 1932, 15-Froehlich

#1419, 1-[blank], Kathleen Marie, 2-born, 3-31 Jan 1964, 12-[blank], Tom, 13-[blank], Patricia, 15-Froehlich

#1420, 1-[blank], Tracy Lynn, 2-born, 3-1 Aug 1968, 12-[blank], Tom, 13-[blank], Patricia, 15-Froehlich

#1421, 1-Snyder, Mary J., 2-died, 3-3 Oct 1860, 15-Froehlich

#1422, 1-Snyder, Larncia A., 2-died, 3-6 Oct 1860, 15-Froehlich

#1423, 1-Snyder, John W., 2-died, 3-25 Sep 1863, 15-Froehlich

#1424, 1-Snyder, David[?], 2-died, 3-15 Jul 1871, 15-Froehlich

#1425, 1-Needy, Hazel Ruth, 2-died, 3-18 Aug 1896, 15-Froehlich

#1426, 1-Snyder, Adam, 2-died, 3-15 Mar 1879, 15-Froehlich

#1427, 1-Needy, E.L., 2-died, 3-29 Aug 1904, 15-Froehlich

#1428, 1-Needy, Earle Kiracofe, 2-died, 3-5 Mar 1923, 15-Froehlich

#1429, 1-Needy, Alice J. (Kiracofe), 2-died, 3-14 Dec 1927, 15-Froehlich

#1430, 1-Kiracofe, M. Josephine, 2-died, 3-26 Sep 1942, 15-Froehlich

#1431, 1-Kiracofe, Hannah May, 2-died, 3-21 Aug 1869, 12-Kiracofe, J.W., 13-Kiracofe, C.V., 15-Froehlich

#1432, 1-Kiracofe, Catharine Virginia, 2-died, 3-11 Jan 1870, 4-Georgetown, MD, 7-Kiracofe, J.W., 12-Snyder, Adam, 13-Snyder, Hannah, 15-Froehlich

#1433, 1-Clemmer, Delia Irene, 2-died, 3-22 Feb 1879, 12-Clemmer, J.F., 13-Clemmer, Lizzie E., 15-Froehlich

#1434, 1-Kiracofe, John Wesley (Rev.), 2-born, 3-25 Aug 1841, 15-Froehlich

#1435, 1-Kiracofe, John Wesley (Rev.), 2-died, 3-29 Sep 1914, 15-Froehlich

#1436, 1-Bell, Edna N., 2-died, 3-23 Mar 1956, 15-Froehlich

#1437, 1-Heck, John, 2-born, 3-Jul 1832, 15-Caruthers

#1438, 1-Caruthers, Elizabeth P., 2-born, 3-13[?] Mar 1827, 15-Caruthers

#1439, 1-Heck, Josephine D., 2-born, 3-24 Nov 1858, 12-Heck, John, 13-Caruthers, Elizabeth P., 15-Caruthers

#1440, 1-Heck, John N., 2-born, 3-12 Mar 1860, 12-Heck, John, 13-Caruthers, Elizabeth P., 15-Caruthers

#1441, 1-Heck, Mary E., 2-born, 3-6 Apr 1862, 12-Heck, John, 13-Caruthers, Elizabeth P., 15-Caruthers

#1442, 1-Heck, Harriet J., 2-born, 3-25 Jul 1863, 12-Heck, John, 13-Caruthers, Elizabeth P., 15-Caruthers

#1443, 1-Heck, George W., 2-born, 3-12 Aug 1866, 12-Heck, John, 13-Caruthers, Elizabeth P., 15-Caruthers

#1444, 1-Heck, Willie W., 2-born, 3-3 Apr 1868, 12-Heck, John, 13-Caruthers, Elizabeth P., 15-Caruthers

FAMILY BIBLE RECORDS IN THE WASHINGTON COUNTY FREE LIBRARY, HAGERSTOWN, MARYLAND

Entry #, 1-Last Name, First Name, 2-Event, 3-Date, 4-Event Location, 5-Age, 6-Other,
7-Spouse's Last, First, 8-Groom's Residence, 9-Bride's Residence, 10-Minister, 11-Minister's Location,
12-Father's Last, First, 13-Mother's Last, First, 14-Transcribed, 15-Family Bible

```
#1445, 1-Heck, John, 2-married, 3-9 Mar 1856, 7-Caruthers, Elizabeth P., 15-
    Caruthers
#1446, 1-Heck, Mary E., 2-died, 3-21 Aug 1862, 15-Caruthers
#1447, 1-Heck, Harriet J., 2-died, 3-27 Aug 1863, 15-Caruthers
#1448, 1-Heck, Willie W., 2-died, 3-10 Dec 1868, 15-Caruthers
#1449, 1-Caruther, Sr., Ann, 2-died, 3-20 Aug 1839, 15-Caruthers
#1450, 1-Caruther, Sarah, 2-died, 3-1 Aug 1819, 7-Caruther, Isaac, 12-Davis, Jason,
    13-Davis, Rachel, 15-Caruthers
#1451, 1-Caruther, Sarah, 2-died, 3-18 Dec 1872, 7-Caruthers, Isaac, 12-Hindman[?],
    John[?], 15-Caruthers
#1452, 1-Caruthers, Sr., Isaac, 2-died, 3-5 Oct 1858, 15-Caruthers
#1453, 1-Caruthers, Elizabeth Isabella, 2-died, 3-16 Aug 1899, 7-Heck, John, 15-
    Caruthers
#1454, 1-Heck, John, 2-died, 3-20 Jun 1911, 15-Caruthers
#1455, 1-Caruthers, Sarah Ann, 2-died, 3-15 Oct 1823, 12-Caruthers, Isaac, 13-
    Caruthers, Sarah, 15-Caruthers
#1456, 1-Caruthers, John Hindman, 2-died, 3-10 Sep 1825, 15-Caruthers
#1457, 1-Caruthers, Isaac, 2-died, 3-11 Apr 1826, 15-Caruthers
#1458, 1-Caruthers, Isaac Woodrough, 2-died, 3-15 Aug 1837, 15-Caruthers
#1459, 1-Conard, Rachel Caruthers (Mrs.), 2-died, 3-Sep 1842, 15-Caruthers
#1460, 1-Mathers , Mary Jane, 2-died, 3-5 Mar 1895, 12-Caruthers, Isaac, 13-
    Caruthers, Sarah, 15-Caruthers
#1461, 1-Caruthers, Leiths[?], 2-died, 3-1890, 15-Caruthers
#1462, 1-Caruthers, Isaac, 2-married, 3-1808, 7-Davis, Sarah, 15-Caruthers
#1463, 1-Caruthers, Isaac, 2-married, 3-20 Feb 1821, 7-Hindman, Sarah, 15-Caruthers
#1464, 1-Caruthers, Mary Jane, 2-married, 3-28 Nov 1841, 7-Wagner, Samuel, 12-
    Caruthers, Isaac, 13-Caruthers, Sarah, 15-Caruthers
#1465, 1-Caruthers, Leythe, 2-married, 3-28 Dec 1841, 7-McKilley[?], Margaret Ann,
    15-Caruthers
#1466, 1-Caruthers, William Franklin, 2-married, 3-17 Mar 1844, 7-Spear, Martha,
    15-Caruthers
#1467, 1-Caruthers, Jason, 2-married, 3-Jun 1845, 7-Pennington, Sarah, 15-Caruthers
#1468, 1-Heck, John, 2-married, 3-9 Mar 1856, 7-Caruthers, Elizabeth J., 15-
    Caruthers
#1469, 1-Heck, George Washington, 2-married, 3-11am, Wednesday, 27 Jun 1894, 4-
    bride's home on Second St., possibly in Brunswick, MD, 7-McBee, Mary Gertrude
    (Miss), 10-Rev. I.C. Yeakel, 11-Presbyterian Church, 15-Caruthers
#1470, 1-Hindman, John, 2-born, 3-22 Apr 1782, 12-Hindman, John, 13-Hindman,
    Isabaella, 15-Caruthers
#1471, 1-Hindman, William, 2-born, 3-8 Jan 1785, 12-Hindman, John, 13-Hindman,
    Isabaella, 15-Caruthers
#1472, 1-Hindman, Jane, 2-born, 3-24 Oct 1786, 12-Hindman, John, 13-Hindman,
    Isabaella, 15-Caruthers
#1473, 1-Hindman, Sarah, 2-born, 3-26 Nov 1788, 12-Hindman, John, 13-Hindman,
    Isabaella, 15-Caruthers
#1474, 1-Hindman, Anne, 2-born, 3-10 Oct 1794, 12-Hindman, John, 13-Hindman,
    Isabaella, 15-Caruthers
#1475, 1-Hindman, James, 2-born, 3-24 Oct 1796, 12-Hindman, John, 13-Hindman,
    Isabaella, 15-Caruthers
#1476, 1-Hindman, Mary, 2-born, 3-24 Jul 1799, 12-Hindman, John, 13-Hindman,
    Isabaella, 15-Caruthers
#1477, 1-Hindman, Elizabeth, 2-born, 3-31 Mar 1801, 12-Hindman, John, 13-Hindman,
    Isabaella, 15-Caruthers
#1478, 1-Hindman, Margaret, 2-born, 3-9 Jan 1803, 12-Hindman, John, 13-Hindman,
    Isabaella, 15-Caruthers
```

FAMILY BIBLE RECORDS IN THE WASHINGTON COUNTY FREE LIBRARY, HAGERSTOWN, MARYLAND

Entry #, 1-Last Name, First Name, 2-Event, 3-Date, 4-Event Location, 5-Age, 6-Other, 7-Spouse's Last, First, 8-Groom's Residence, 9-Bride's Residence, 10-Minister, 11-Minister's Location, 12-Father's Last, First, 13-Mother's Last, First, 14-Transcribed, 15-Family Bible

#1479, 1-Collins, Isabella, 2-born, 3-22 Apr 1818, 12-Collins, 13-Hindman, Mary, 15-Caruthers

#1480, 1-Heck, William Gary, 2-born, 3-20 Mar 1897, 15-Caruthers

#1481, 1-Heck, Italene Commella, 2-born, 3-28 Jul 1898, 15-Caruthers

#1482, 1-Heck, Elizabeth (Mrs.), 2-born, 3-13 Mar 1828, 15-Caruthers

#1483, 1-Heck, Elizabeth (Mrs.), 2-obituary, 3-16 Aug 1899, 4-Jamestown, Kansas, 5-72 years 6 months 4 days, 15-Caruthers

#1484, 1-Caruthers, Ann, 2-born, 3-31 Oct 174_, 15-Caruthers

#1485, 1-Caruthers, Isaac, 2-born, 3-10 Sep 1780, 13-Caruthers, Ann, 15-Caruthers

#1486, 1-Caruthers, Rachel, 2-born, 3-16 Jun 1809, 12-Caruthers, Isaac, 13-Davis, Sarah, 15-Caruthers

#1487, 1-Caruthers, Lytle, 2-born, 3-17 Nov 1810, 15-Caruthers

#1488, 1-Caruthers, William Franklin, 2-born, 3-5 Nov 1814, 15-Caruthers

#1489, 1-Caruthers, Isaac, 2-born, 3-15 Nov 1812, 15-Caruthers

#1490, 1-Caruthers, Jason Davis, 2-born, 3-10 Dec 1816, 15-Caruthers

#1491, 1-Caruthers, Mary Jane, 2-born, 3-30 Jan 1822, 12-Caruthers, Isaac, 13-Hindman, Sarah, 15-Caruthers

#1492, 1-Caruthers, Sarah Ann, 2-born, 3-16 Apr 1823, 15-Caruthers

#1493, 1-Caruthers, John Hindman, 2-born, 3-27 Jun 1825, 15-Caruthers

#1494, 1-Caruthers, Elizabeth Isabella, 2-born, 3-13 Mar 1827, 15-Caruthers

#1495, 1-Caruthers, Isaac Woodrough, 2-born, 3-16 Sep 1830, 15-Caruthers

#1496, 1-Crouse, John, 2-born, 3-3 Jul 1782 [or 1772], 15-Crouse

#1497, 1-Crouse, Elizabeth, 2-born, 3-2 Feb 1784, 15-Crouse

#1498, 1-Crouse, Jr., John, 2-born, 3-14 Sep 1811, 15-Crouse

#1499, 1-Crouse, Michel, 2-born, 3-5 Mar 1815, 15-Crouse

#1500, 1-Crouse, Elizabeth, 2-born, 3-7 Aug 1813, 15-Crouse

#1501, 1-Crouse, John, 2-died, 3-17 Feb 1816, 15-Crouse

#1502, 1-Crous, Michel, 2-died, 3-16 Oct 1817, 15-Crouse

#1503, 1-Crous, Jacob, 2-died, 3-3 Nov 1821, 15-Crouse

#1504, 1-Crouse, John, 2-married, 3-9 Sep 1806, 7-Werner, Elizabeth, 15-Crouse

#1505, 1-Crouse, Elizabeth, 2-died, 3-2 May 1872, 15-Crouse

#1506, 1-Crous, peter, 2-born, 3-9 Sep 1816, 15-Crouse

#1507, 1-Crous, Levi, 2-born, 3-25 Oct 1818, 15-Crouse

#1508, 1-Crous, Jacob, 2-born, 3-7 Sep 1820, 15-Crouse

#1509, 1-Crous, Margret, 2-born, 3-28 Jun 1822, 15-Crouse

#1510, 1-Crouse, Elizabeth, 2-born, 3-13 Aug 1845, 12-Crouse, Levi, 13-Crouse, Catherine, 15-Crouse

#1511, 1-Crouse, Elizabeth, 2-married, 3-12 Jan 1813[?], 7-Avery, Thomas, 15-Crouse

#1512, 1-Crouse, Guy L., 2-obituary, 3-9:30pm, Sunday, May 1957, 15-Crouse

#1513, 1-Crouse, Guy L., 2-born, 3-4 Oct 1893, 12-Crouse, John M., 13-Cochran, Minnie Victoria, 15-Crouse

#1514, 1-Crouse, Guy L., 2-married, 7-Lightle, Leora M., 15-Crouse

#1515, 1-Cochran, Thomas B., 2-born, 3-9 Aug 1821, 4-Washington Co., MD, 6-father of Minnie Victoria (Cochran) Crouse, 15-Crouse

#1516, 1-Firey, Jos. H., 2-married, 3-19 May 1858, 7-Ridenour, Mary C., 10-Rev. Reuben Hill, 15-Firey

#1517, 1-Firey, Mary Elizabeth, 2-married, 3-27 Apr 1887, 7-Heard, Albert, 10-Rev. S.W.[?] Owen, 15-Firey

#1518, 1-Firey, John Baxton, 2-married, 3-12 Jul 1894, 7-Happel, Sue rosalie, 10-Rev. Sebastian Rabbais[?], 15-Firey

#1519, 1-Firey, Jos. Frederick, 2-married, 3-16 Aug 1899, 7-McClearey, Eleanor, 10-Rev. J.S. Kieffer, 15-Firey

#1520, 1-Firey, Leilah, 2-married, 3-8 Jan 1908, 7-Oswald, Geo. B., 10-Rev. S.W. Owen, 15-Firey

#1521, 1-Firey, William Henry, 2-born, 3-21 Jun 1859, 15-Firey

FAMILY BIBLE RECORDS IN THE WASHINGTON COUNTY FREE LIBRARY, HAGERSTOWN, MARYLAND

Entry #, 1-Last Name, First Name, 2-Event, 3-Date, 4-Event Location, 5-Age, 6-Other, 7-Spouse's Last, First, 8-Groom's Residence, 9-Bride's Residence, 10-Minister, 11-Minister's Location, 12-Father's Last, First, 13-Mother's Last, First, 14-Transcribed, 15-Family Bible

#1522, 1-Firey, Mary Lizzie, 2-born, 3-13 Nov 1861, 15-Firey
#1523, 1-Firey, Sally, 2-born, 3-12 Nov 1863, 15-Firey
#1524, 1-Firey, Lelah, 2-born, 3-7 Mar 1867, 15-Firey
#1525, 1-Firey, John Baxton, 2-born, 3-26 Jul 1868, 15-Firey
#1526, 1-Firey, Robert Bruce, 2-born, 3-11 Mar 1873, 15-Firey
#1527, 1-Firey, Joseph Frederick, 2-born, 3-2 Apr 1875, 15-Firey
#1528, 1-Firey, Nora, 2-born, 3-15 Jun 1877, 15-Firey
#1529, 1-Oswald, Geo. B., 2-died, 3-26 Apr 1908, 4-Baldwin Hotel, Hagerstown, MD, 5-65 years 4 months 1 day, 15-Firey
#1530, 1-Firey, Sally, 2-died, 3-2 Jun 1864, 5-6 months 20 days, 15-Firey
#1531, 1-Firey, Robert Bruce, 2-died, 3-2 May 1876, 5-3 years 1 mo 22 days, 15-Firey
#1532, 1-Firey, Nora, 2-died, 3-28 Jul 1877, 5-1 months 13 days, 15-Firey
#1533, 1-Firey, William H., 2-died, 3-1 Mar 1895, 5-35 years 8 months 10 days, 15-Firey
#1534, 1-Firey, Jos. Henry, 2-died, 3-2 Jun 1890, 5-57 years 7 months 28 days, 15-Firey
#1535, 1-Firey, John Burton, 2-died, 3-17 Jul 1901, 5-32 years 11 months 21 days, 15-Firey
#1536, 1-Firey, Joseph Henry, 2-born, 3-4 Oct 1832, 15-Firey
#1537, 1-Ridenour, Mary C., 2-born, 3-6 May 1834, 15-Firey
#1538, 1-Hagan, Helen, 6-15 yrs old when her father died, 15-Hagan
#1539, 1-Hagan, Gerald Frank, 2-born, 3-26 Sep 1940, 15-Hagan
#1540, 1-Hagan, Beverly Syvle[?] Jean[?], 2-born, 3-6 Mar 1938, 15-Hagan
#1541, 1-Turner, Nancy Jean, 2-born, 3-24 Oct 1938, 15-Hagan
#1542, 1-Hagan, Clayton Eugene, 2-born, 3-3 Jul 1939, 15-Hagan
#1543, 1-Hagan, John Heflebower, 2-born, 3-25 Feb 1875, 15-Hagan
#1544, 1-Norris, Daisy May, 2-born, 3-28 Jul 1881, 15-Hagan
#1545, 1-Hagan, Leon Viola, 2-born, 3-29 Mar 1901, 15-Hagan
#1546, 1-Hagan, Thos. Hefflebower, 2-born, 3-1 Jun 1902, 15-Hagan
#1547, 1-Hagan, Thos. Hefflebower, 2-died, 3-26 Apr 1971, 15-Hagan
#1548, 1-Hagan, Mary Susan, 2-born, 3-18 Aug 1903, 15-Hagan
#1549, 1-Turner, Joan Eileen, 2-born, 3-16 Jul 1945, 15-Hagan
#1550, 1-Turner, Joan Eileen, 2-died, 3-8 Feb 1951, 5-5 years 6 months 23 days, 15-Hagan
#1551, 1-Hagan, Joseph Norris, 2-born, 3-2 Jan 1906, 15-Hagan
#1552, 1-Hagan, Joseph Norris, 2-died, 3-1 May 1983, 15-Hagan
#1553, 1-Hagan, Harold Lawrence, 2-born, 3-31 Aug 1908, 15-Hagan
#1554, 1-Hagan, Harold Lawrence, 2-died, 3-12 Jun 1960, 15-Hagan
#1555, 1-Hagan, Ralph Samuel, 2-born, 3-29 Apr 1911, 15-Hagan
#1556, 1-Hagan, Howard Luther, 2-born, 3-8 Dec 1913, 15-Hagan
#1557, 1-Hagan, John Vernon, 2-born, 3-8 Apr 1916, 15-Hagan
#1558, 1-Hagan, John Vernon, 2-died, 3-23 Jul 1975, 15-Hagan
#1559, 1-Hagan, Mable Hellen Velettie[?], 2-born, 3-23 Sep 1918, 15-Hagan
#1560, 1-Hagan, Mable Hellen Velettie[?], 2-died, 3-25 Jun 1970, 15-Hagan
#1561, 1-Hagan, Lillian Viola, 2-died, 3-18 Aug 1901, 15-Hagan
#1562, 1-Hagan, Mary Susie, 2-died, 3-10 Nov 1920, 5-17 years, 15-Hagan
#1563, 1-Hagan, Howard L., 2-died, 3-10 Nov 1944, 5-31 years, 15-Hagan
#1564, 1-Hagan, John Heflebower, 2-died, 3-21 May 1933, 5-58 years 2 months 26 days, 15-Hagan
#1565, 1-Hagan, Ralph Samuel, 2-died, 3-12 Apr 1938, 5-26 years 11 months 17 days, 15-Hagan
#1566, 1-Hagan, Daisy May, 2-died, 3-22 Jul 1941, 5-59 years, 15-Hagan
#1567, 1-Hagan, Charlette Joesephine, 2-born, 3-19 Dec 1926, 15-Hagan
#1568, 1-[blank], Sherley Mareget, 2-born, 3-10 Jul 1929, 15-Hagan

FAMILY BIBLE RECORDS IN THE WASHINGTON COUNTY FREE LIBRARY, HAGERSTOWN, MARYLAND

Entry #, 1-Last Name, First Name, 2-Event, 3-Date, 4-Event Location, 5-Age, 6-Other,
7-Spouse's Last, First, 8-Groom's Residence, 9-Bride's Residence, 10-Minister, 11-Minister's Location,
12-Father's Last, First, 13-Mother's Last, First, 14-Transcribed, 15-Family Bible

```
#1569, 1-Hagan, Harlen Huffer, 2-born, 3-3 Apr 1929, 15-Hagan
#1570, 1-Hagan, Ralph Austin, 2-born, 3-7 May 1931, 15-Hagan
#1571, 1-Hagan, Betres, 2-born, 3-18 Jul 1832, 15-Hagan
#1572, 1-Hagan, Betres, 2-died, 3-19 Jul 1932, 5-1 day, 15-Hagan
#1573, 1-Hagan, Jophes Lee, 2-born, 3-8 Feb 1933 *, 6-*9 is written at the top of
    the 8, 15-Hagan
#1574, 1-Hagan, Bernice Jane, 2-born, 3-1 Nov 1833, 15-Hagan
#1575, 1-Hagan, Mary Etta, 2-born, 3-4 Aug 1934, 15-Hagan
#1576, 1-Hagan, Freda Louise, 2-born, 3-12 Feb 1935, 15-Hagan
#1577, 1-Turner, Richard Lee, 2-born, 3-28 Mar 1936, 15-Hagan
#1578, 1-Hagan, Harry Lee, 2-born, 3-21 Oct 1937, 6-"born dead", 15-Hagan
#1579, 1-Hagan, Harry Lee, 2-died, 3-21 Oct 1937, 15-Hagan
#1580, 1-Hagan, Joseph Lee, 2-born, 3-9 Feb 1933, 15-Hagan
#1581, 1-Hagan, Patricia Ann Wheeler, 2-born, 3-13 Apr 1937, 15-Hagan
#1582, 1-Hagan, Timothy Lee, 2-born, 3-13 Aug 1959, 15-Hagan
#1583, 1-Hagan, Thomas Wayne, 2-born, 3-13 Aug 1959, 15-Hagan
#1584, 1-Hagan, JoAnn Eusebia, 2-born, 3-6 Apr 1969, 15-Hagan
#1585, 1-Hagan, Timothy Lee, 2-married, 3-5 Jul ____, 7-Smallwood, Kimberly Jane,
    15-Hagan
#1586, 1-Hagan, Timothy Howard, 2-born, 3-6 Oct 1980, 12-Hagan, Timothy Lee, 13-
    Smallwood, Kimberly Jane, 15-Hagan
#1587, 1-Hagan, Thomas Wayne, 2-married, 3-20 Mar 1981, 7-Fost, Paulette Jean, 15-
    Hagan
#1588, 1-Hagan, John Thomas, 2-born, 3-19 Feb 1982, 12-Hagan, Thomas Wayne, 13-
    Fost, Paulette Jean, 15-Hagan
#1589, 1-Hagan, Joseph Clayton, 2-born, 3-27 Jun 1985, 12-Hagan, Thomas Wayne, 13-
    Fost, Paulette Jean, 15-Hagan
#1590, 1-Hagan, JoAnn Eusebia, 2-married, 3-10 Oct 1987, 7-Myers, Patrick Eugene,
    15-Hagan
#1591, 1-Flory, Daniel, 2-married, 3-3 Jun 1830, 7-McLanahan, Catherine A., 10-Rev.
    T. Harshour, 15-Flory
#1592, 1-Flory, Amanda, 2-married, 3-9 Sep 1857, 4-St. Peter's Church, Clear
    Spring, 7-Wise, John C., 10-Rev. Bowers, 15-Flory
#1593, 1-Flory, Amelia, 2-married, 3-7 pm, 2 Sep 1863, 4-Clear Spring, 7-Lesher,
    John, 10-Rev. Grabill, 15-Flory
#1594, 1-Flory, David H., 2-married, 3-18 Aug 1864, 7-Mathews, Merce, 10-Rev.
    Acres, 15-Flory
#1595, 1-Flory, Alexander M., 2-married, 3-20 Dec 1864, 7-Jacques, Libie, 10-Rev.
    Grabill, 15-Flory
#1596, 1-Flory, Alexander M., 2-born, 3-7 May 1831, 15-Flory
#1597, 1-Flory, Ann E., 2-born, 3-16 May 1832, 15-Flory
#1598, 1-Flory, Ann E., 2-baptized, 3-21 Aug 1833, 10-Rev. I. Kline, 15-Flory
#1599, 1-Flory, Healen, 2-born, 3-17 Nov 1833, 15-Flory
#1600, 1-Flory, Healen, 2-baptized, 3-23 Nov 1834, 10-Rev. I. Kline, 15-Flory
#1601, 1-Flory, Amanda, 2-born, 3-4 Apr 1835, 15-Flory
#1602, 1-Flory, Amanda, 2-baptized, 3-22 Dec 1855, 10-Thos. Monroe, 15-Flory
#1603, 1-Flory, David H., 2-born, 3-3 Jul 1837, 15-Flory
#1604, 1-Flory, David H., 2-baptized, 3-22 Dec 1855, 10-Rev. Thos. Monroe, 15-Flory
#1605, 1-Flory, Amelia, 2-born, 3-13 Apr 1839, 15-Flory
#1606, 1-Flory, Amelia, 2-baptized, 3-22 Dec 1855, 10-Rev. Thos. Monroe, 15-Flory
#1607, 1-Flory, Daniel W., 2-born, 3-15 Jun 1842, 15-Flory
#1608, 1-Wise, Harry, 2-born, 3-6:30 pm, 17 Jun 1858, 4-Clear Spring, MD, 12-Wise,
    John C., 13-Flory, Amanda, 15-Flory
#1609, 1-Wise, Harry, 2-baptized, 3-27 Sep 1858[?], 10-____ Shoaff, 12-Wise, John
    C., 13-Flory, Amanda, 15-Flory
```

FAMILY BIBLE RECORDS IN THE WASHINGTON COUNTY FREE LIBRARY, HAGERSTOWN, MARYLAND

Entry #, 1-Last Name, First Name, 2-Event, 3-Date, 4-Event Location, 5-Age, 6-Other,
7-Spouse's Last, First, 8-Groom's Residence, 9-Bride's Residence, 10-Minister, 11-Minister's Location,
12-Father's Last, First, 13-Mother's Last, First, 14-Transcribed, 15-Family Bible

#1610, 1-Wise, Charly _oise[?], 2-born, 3-23 Oct 1860, 4-Mankato, Minnesota, 12-Wise, John C., 13-Flory, Amanda, 15-Flory

#1611, 1-Wise, Sarah Catherine, 2-born, 3-14 Jul 1864, 4-Mankato, Minnesota, 12-Wise, John C., 13-Flory, Amanda, 15-Flory

#1612, 1-Wise, John Eeloise[?], 2-born, 3-14 Apr 1866, 12-Wise, John C., 13-Flory, Amanda, 15-Flory

#1613, 1-Lesher, Nancy Katherine, 2-born, 3-22 May 1864, 12-Lesher, John, 13-Flory, Amelia, 15-Flory

#1614, 1-Flory, Adam, 2-born, 3-17 Aug 1802, 12-Flory, John, 13-Lyday, Anna, 15-Flory

#1615, 1-Flory, David, 2-born, 3-10 Apr 1804, 12-Flory, John, 13-Lyday, Anna, 15-Flory

#1616, 1-Flory, John, 2-born, 3-27 Jul 1806, 12-Flory, John, 13-Lyday, Anna, 15-Flory

#1617, 1-Flory, Daniel, 2-born, 3-14 Apr 1808, 12-Flory, John, 13-Lyday, Anna, 15-Flory

#1618, 1-Flory, Rebecca, 2-born, 3-7 Apr 1810, 12-Flory, John, 13-Lyday, Anna, 15-Flory

#1619, 1-Flory, Sarah, 2-born, 3-15 Sep 1812, 12-Flory, John, 13-Lyday, Anna, 15-Flory

#1620, 1-Flory, Solomon, 2-born, 3-24 Oct 1814, 12-Flory, John, 13-Lyday, Anna, 15-Flory

#1621, 1-Flory, Ann S., 2-born, 3-23 Dec 1819, 12-Flory, John, 13-Lyday, Anna, 15-Flory

#1622, 1-Flory, Mary A., 2-born, 3-30 Jun 1823, 12-Flory, John, 13-Lyday, Anna, 15-Flory

#1623, 1-Funk, Anna, 2-born, 3-26 Jul 1780, 15-Flory

#1624, 1-McLanahan, Catherine A., 2-born, 3-13 Mary 1812, 15-Flory

#1625, 1-McLanahan, A.C.H., 2-born, 3-9 Oct 1813, 15-Flory

#1626, 1-McLanahan, Amelia, 2-born, 3-27 Oct 1815, 15-Flory

#1627, 1-Flory , Ann E., 2-died, 3-22 Aug 1833, 15-Flory

#1628, 1-Flory , Healin, 2-died, 3-26 Nov 1834, 15-Flory

#1629, 1-Flory , Daniel W., 2-died, 3-10 Feb 1843, 15-Flory

#1630, 1-Wise, Harry, 2-died, 3-18 Jan 1860, 4-Mankato, Minnesota, 12-Wise, John C., 13-Amanda, Flory, 15-Flory.

#1631, 1-Wise, Amanda (Flory), 2-died, 3-7:35 am, Sunday, 11 Jan 1885, 4-Mankato, Blue Earth County, Minnesota, 15-Flory

#1632, 1-McLanahan, Anna, 2-died, 3-14 Nov 1832, 15-Flory

#1633, 1-McLanahan, A.C.H., 2-died, 3-22 Jul 1849, 15-Flory

#1634, 1-Flory, Catherine A., 2-died, 3-8:00 am, 12 Sep 1867, 4-Clear Spring, MD, 6-buried 1:00, 15 Sep, Lutheran graveyard, 7-Flory, Daniel, 15-Flory

#1635, 1-Flory, Daniel, 2-died, 3-11 pm, 24 Mar 1876, 6-buried 11 am, Sunday, 10-Rev. Swope, 11-Lutheran, 15-Flory

#1636, 1-Flory, Mercer[?] (Mathews), 2-born, 3-2 Nov 1843, 15-Flory

#1637, 1-Flory, 2-died, 3-20 Oct 1870, 15-Flory

#1638, 1-Flory, Alex Murphy, 2-born, 3-11 Jan 1865, 12-Flory, D.H., 13-Mathews, Mercer, 15-Flory

#1639, 1-Flory, Alex Murphy, 2-died, 3-14 Feb 1871, 12-Flory, D.H., 13-Mathews, Mercer, 15-Flory

#1640, 1-Flory, Daniel, 2-born, 3-17 Apr 1866, 12-Flory, D.H., 13-Mathews, Mercer, 15-Flory

#1641, 1-Flory, David Hammett, 2-born, 3-3 Aug 1867, 12-Flory, D.H., 13-Mathews, Mercer, 15-Flory

#1642, 1-Flory, Ann Catharine, 2-born, 3-24 Feb 1869, 12-Flory, D.H., 13-Mathews, Mercer, 15-Flory

FAMILY BIBLE RECORDS IN THE WASHINGTON COUNTY FREE LIBRARY, HAGERSTOWN, MARYLAND

Entry #, 1-Last Name, First Name, 2-Event, 3-Date, 4-Event Location, 5-Age, 6-Other, 7-Spouse's Last, First, 8-Groom's Residence, 9-Bride's Residence, 10-Minister, 11-Minister's Location, 12-Father's Last, First, 13-Mother's Last, First, 14-Transcribed, 15-Family Bible

#1643, 1-Flory, David H., 2-married, 3-2 Nov 1871, 7-Flory, Hannah Mary, 15-Flory

#1644, 1-Flory, Maria Amanda, 2-born, 3-21 Aug 1873, 12-Flory, D.H., 13-Flory, Hannah Mary, 15-Flory

#1645, 1-Flory, Grant, 2-born, 3-15 Dec 1874, 12-Flory, D.H., 13-Flory, Hannah Mary, 15-Flory

#1646, 1-Flory, Grant, 2-died, 3-18 Oct 1875, 12-Flory, D.H., 13-Flory, Hannah Mary, 15-Flory

#1647, 1-Flory, Ross Leon, 2-born, 3-10 Jun 1878, 12-Flory, D.H., 13-Flory, Hannah Mary, 15-Flory

#1648, 1-Flory, Ross Leon, 2-died, 3-30 Jun 1878, 12-Flory, D.H., 13-Flory, Hannah Mary, 15-Flory

#1649, 1-Flory, David Hammett, 2-died, 3-22 May 1907, 6-buried Saturday, 28 Mar at St. Paul's, 10-Rev. E.H. Smilli[?], 15-Flory

#1650, 1-Flory, Hannah Mary, 2-died, 3-16 Sep 1918, 6-buried at St. Paul's Cemetery, 15-Flory

#1651, 1-Flory, Maria Amanda, 2-married, 3-20 Jan 1904, 7-Ankeney, Isaac, 10-Rev. J.H. Smith, 11-Methodist Episcopal Church, Clear Spring, 15-Flory

#1652, 1-Ankeney, Isaac, 2-born, 3-22 Dec 1862, 15-Flory

#1653, 1-Ankeney, Maria (Flory), 2-born, 3-21 Aug 1873, 4-Clear Spring, MD, 15-Flory

#1654, 1-Ankeney, Jr., Isaac, 2-died, 3-3 Dec 1938, 6-buried St. Paul's Cemetery, 10-Rev. C.E. Wolf, 15-Flory

#1655, 1-Ankeney, Isaac Donald, 2-born, 3-26 Dec 1905, 4-Garden Spot Farm, 12-Ankeney, Jr., Isaac, 13-Ankeney, Maria F., 15-Flory

#1656, 1-Ankeney, David Hammett, 2-born, 3-18 Jan 1907, 4-Garden Spot Farm, 12-Ankeney, Jr., Isaac, 13-Ankeney, Maria F., 15-Flory

#1657, 1-Ankeney, William Henry, 2-born, 3-30 Sep 1909, 4-Clear Spring, 12-Ankeney, Jr., Isaac, 13-Ankeney, Maria F., 15-Flory

#1658, 1-Ankeney, Jane Flory, 2-born, 3-30 Jul 1912, 4-Clear Spring, 12-Ankeney, Jr., Isaac, 13-Ankeney, Maria F., 15-Flory

#1659, 1-Ankeney, Maria A. (Flory), 2-died, 3-12 Mar 1942, 6-buried Sunday, 15 March, St. Paul's Cemetery, 10-Rev. Clarence E. Wolfe, 15-Flory

#1660, 1-Ankeney, David Hammett, 2-died, 3-16 Jul 1945, 6-buried Rose Hil Cemetery, Hagerstown, 15-Flory

#1661, 1-Ankeney, Jane Flory, 2-married, 3-8 Nov 1940, 4-Clear Spring, 7-Stansbury, Carroll ____, 10-Benj. Machs[?], 15-Flory

#1662, 1-Ankeney, David Hammett, 2-married, 3-Aug 1934, 7-Hassett, Elizabeth Haines, 15-Flory

#1663, 1-Ankeney, David Hassett, 2-born, 3-26 Aug 1937, 12-Ankeney, David Hammett, 13-Hassett, Elizabeth Haines, 15-Flory

#1664, 1-Ardinger, Christian, 2-married, 3-3 Feb 1812, 7-[blank], Hannah, 14-Yes, 15-Ardinger

#1665, 1-Ardinger, John, 2-born, 3-22 Aug 1815, 14-Yes, 15-Ardinger

#1666, 1-Ardinger, Elizabeth, 2-born, 3-25 Feb 1815, 14-Yes, 15-Ardinger

#1667, 1-Ardinger, Elizabeth, 2-died, 3-2 Mar 1816, 14-Yes, 15-Ardinger

#1668, 1-Ardinger, Jacob Christian, 2-born, 3-18 Oct 1816, 14-Yes, 15-Ardinger

#1669, 1-Ardinger, William, 2-born, 3-2 Oct 1818, 14-Yes, 15-Ardinger

#1670, 1-Ardinger, William, 2-died, 3-11 Jun 1821, 14-Yes, 15-Ardinger

#1671, 1-Ardinger, Moses, 2-born, 3-29 Aug 1820, 14-Yes, 15-Ardinger

#1672, 1-Ardinger, Moses, 2-died, 3-22 Jun 1821, 14-Yes, 15-Ardinger

#1673, 1-Ardinger, Maryan, 2-born, 3-3 Apr 1822, 14-Yes, 15-Ardinger

#1674, 1-Ardinger, Benjamin Kurtz, 2-born, 3-3 Feb 1825, 14-Yes, 15-Ardinger

#1675, 1-Ardinger, Joseph, 2-born, 3-3 Mar 1827, 14-Yes, 15-Ardinger

#1676, 1-Ardinger, Mary Elizabeth, 2-born, 3-16 Sep 1830, 14-Yes, 15-Ardinger

#1677, 1-Ardinger, Georgette, 2-born, 3-27 Oct 1856, 14-Yes, 15-Ardinger

FAMILY BIBLE RECORDS IN THE WASHINGTON COUNTY FREE LIBRARY, HAGERSTOWN, MARYLAND

Entry #, 1-Last Name, First Name, 2-Event, 3-Date, 4-Event Location, 5-Age, 6-Other,
7-Spouse's Last, First, 8-Groom's Residence, 9-Bride's Residence, 10-Minister, 11-Minister's Location,
12-Father's Last, First, 13-Mother's Last, First, 14-Transcribed, 15-Family Bible

```
#1678, 1-Ardinger, Benjamin, 2-born, 3-18 Mar 1858, 14-Yes, 15-Ardinger
#1679, 1-Ardinger, William, 2-born, 3-2 Sep 1859, 14-Yes, 15-Ardinger
#1680, 1-Malone, Hannah, 2-born, 3-11 Aug 1818, 14-Yes, 15-Ardinger
#1681, 1-Ardinger, Mary Emma, 2-born, 3-3 Sep 1861, 14-Yes, 15-Ardinger
#1682, 1-Ardinger, Hannah Rebecca, 2-born, 3-10 Dec 1866, 14-Yes, 15-Ardinger
#1683, 1-Ardinger, Mary Lee, 2-born, 3-26 Nov 1864, 14-Yes, 15-Ardinger
#1684, 1-Ardinger, Katherine, 2-born, 3-15 Feb 1868, 14-Yes, 15-Ardinger
#1685, 1-Ardinger, Jessie, 2-born, 3-17 Aug 1871, 14-Yes, 15-Ardinger
#1686, 1-Ardinger, Stonewall J., 2-born, 3-20 Mar 1869, 14-Yes, 15-Ardinger
#1687, 1-[blank], Cecelia Agnes, 2-born, 3-21 Sep 1873, 14-Yes, 15-Ardinger
#1688, 1-Ardinger, Christian, 2-died, 3-4 Nov 1817[or 1827?], 14-Yes, 15-Ardinger
#1689, 1-Ardinger, Elizabeth, 2-died, 3-21 Mar 1815, 14-Yes, 15-Ardinger
#1690, 1-Ardinger, William, 2-died, 3-31 Jan 1831, 14-Yes, 15-Ardinger
#1691, 1-Ardinger, Moses, 2-died, 3-29 Jan 1821, 14-Yes, 15-Ardinger
#1692, 1-Ardinger, Hannah Rebecca, 2-died, 3-10 Dec 1861, 14-Yes, 15-Ardinger
#1693, 1-Ardinger, Hannah Rebecca, 2-died, 3-7 Jan 1864, 14-Yes, 15-Ardinger
#1694, 1-Crisman, Elizabeth, 2-died, 3-8 Jan 1829, 14-Yes, 15-Ardinger
#1695, 1-Bowers, Hanner, 2-died, 3-10 Jan 1829, 14-Yes, 15-Ardinger
#1696, 1-Zeller, Ellen (Ardinger), 2-died, 3-21 Mar 1977, 14-Yes, 15-Ardinger
#1697, 1-Ardinger, Henry Zeller, 2-married, 3-9 Jul 1902, 4-Hagerstown, MD, 7-
    Garrish, Clara Elizabeth, 14-Yes, 15-Ardinger
#1698, 1-Ardinger, Ellen Betty, 2-married, 3-22 Dec 1941, 4-Winchester, VA, 7-
    Zeller, Dennis Tobias, 12-Ardinger, Henry Zeller, 13-Garrish, Clara
    Elizabeth, 14-Yes, 15-Ardinger
#1699, 1-Ardinger, Hannah, 2-married, 4-Virginia, 7-Hummer, Leo, 12-Ardinger, Henry
    Zeller, 13-Garrish, Clara Elizabeth, 14-Yes, 15-Ardinger
#1700, 1-Ardinger, Joseph Henry, 2-married, 4-Stroudsburg, PA, 7-Roth, Althea, 12-
    Ardinger, Henry Zeller, 13-Garrish, Clara Elizabeth, 14-Yes, 15-Ardinger
#1701, 1-Ardinger, Clara Ellen, 2-born, 12-Ardinger, Joseph Henry, 13-Roth, Althea,
    14-Yes, 15-Ardinger
#1702, 1-Hummer, Katherine, 2-born, 12-Hummer, Leo, 13-Ardinger, Hannah, 14-Yes,
    15-Ardinger
#1703, 1-Hummer, Katherine, 2-married, 7-Wood, Robert, 12-Hummer, Leo, 13-Ardinger,
    Hannah, 14-Yes, 15-Ardinger
#1704, 1-Wood, Dallas, 2-born, 12-Wood, Robert, 13-Hummer, Katherine, 14-Yes, 15-
    Ardinger
#1705, 1-Wood, Hannah, 2-born, 12-Wood, Robert, 13-Hummer, Katherine, 14-Yes, 15-
    Ardinger
#1706, 1-Wood, Mattie Ellen, 2-born, 12-Wood, Robert, 13-Hummer, Katherine, 14-Yes,
    15-Ardinger
#1707, 1-Wood, Roberta Ann, 2-born, 12-Wood, Robert, 13-Hummer, Katherine, 14-Yes,
    15-Ardinger
#1708, 1-Ardinger, Henry Zeller, 2-died, 3-1 Feb 1933, 4-Williamsport, MD, 6-buried
    at Riverview Cemetery, Williamsport, 14-Yes, 15-Ardinger
#1709, 1-Ardinger, Clara Elizabeth (Garrish), 2-died, 3-21 Aug 1949, 4-
    Williamsport, MD, 6-buried at Riverview Cemetery, Williamsport, 14-Yes, 15-
    Ardinger
#1710, 1-Ardinger, Peter, 2-married, 3-22 Jan 1839, 7-Steinmetz, Hannah, 14-Yes,
    15-Ardinger
#1711, 1-Steinmetz, Hannah, 2-born, 12-Steinmetz, Henry, 14-Yes, 15-Ardinger
#1712, 1-Ardinger, Peter, 2-married, 3-15 Aug 1866, 6-Maria is widow of John Smith,
    7-Smith, Maria Ardinger, 14-Yes, 15-Ardinger
#1713, 1-Ardinger, Henry Z., 2-married, 3-9 Jul 1902, 4-Hagerstown, MD, 7-Garrish,
    Clara, 12-Ardinger, Peter, 14-Yes, 15-Ardinger
```

FAMILY BIBLE RECORDS IN THE WASHINGTON COUNTY FREE LIBRARY, HAGERSTOWN, MARYLAND

Entry #, 1-Last Name, First Name, 2-Event, 3-Date, 4-Event Location, 5-Age, 6-Other,
7-Spouse's Last, First, 8-Groom's Residence, 9-Bride's Residence, 10-Minister, 11-Minister's Location,
12-Father's Last, First, 13-Mother's Last, First, 14-Transcribed, 15-Family Bible

#1714, 1-Ardinger, Ellen Betty, 2-married, 3-22 Dec 1941, 7-Zeller, Dennis T., 12-Ardinger, Henry Z., 14-Yes, 15-Ardinger

#1715, 1-Ardinger, Frances, 2-born, 3-5 Apr 1840, 12-Ardinger, Peter, 13-Steinmetz, Hannah, 14-Yes, 15-Ardinger

#1716, 1-Ardinger, Caroline, 2-born, 3-15 Sep 1841, 12-Ardinger, Peter, 13-Steinmetz, Hannah, 14-Yes, 15-Ardinger

#1717, 1-Ardinger, Emma E., 2-born, 3-24 Dec 1843, 12-Ardinger, Peter, 13-Steinmetz, Hannah, 14-Yes, 15-Ardinger

#1718, 1-Ardinger, Alen, 2-born, 3-3 Oct 1845, 12-Ardinger, Peter, 13-Steinmetz, Hannah, 14-Yes, 15-Ardinger

#1719, 1-Ardinger, Clara, 2-born, 3-9 Feb 1848, 12-Ardinger, Peter, 13-Steinmetz, Hannah, 14-Yes, 15-Ardinger

#1720, 1-Ardinger, Buena Vista, 2-born, 3-5 Jun 1850, 12-Ardinger, Peter, 13-Steinmetz, Hannah, 14-Yes, 15-Ardinger

#1721, 1-Ardinger, James, 2-born, 3-1852, 12-Ardinger, Peter, 13-Steinmetz, Hannah, 14-Yes, 15-Ardinger

#1722, 1-Ardinger, Hannah, 2-born, 3-16 Mar 1853, 12-Ardinger, Peter, 13-Steinmetz, Hannah, 14-Yes, 15-Ardinger

#1723, 1-Ardinger, Henry Z., 2-born, 3-16 Oct 1856, 12-Ardinger, Peter, 13-Steinmetz, Hannah, 14-Yes, 15-Ardinger

#1724, 1-Ardinger, Bettie, 2-born, 3-1 Jun 1860, 12-Ardinger, Peter, 13-Steinmetz, Hannah, 14-Yes, 15-Ardinger

#1725, 1-Ardinger, James, 2-died, 3-1853, 12-Ardinger, Peter, 13-Steinmetz, Hannah, 14-Yes, 15-Ardinger

#1726, 1-Ardinger, Peter, 2-born, 3-6 Jul 1814, 14-Yes, 15-Ardinger

#1727, 1-Ardinger, Maria, 2-born, 3-9 Oct 1816, 14-Yes, 15-Ardinger

#1728, 1-Ardinger, Henry Z., 2-married, 3-9 Jul 1902, 4-Hagerstown, 7-Garrish, Clara, 14-Yes, 15-Ardinger

#1729, 1-Ardinger, Clara, 2-born, 3-26 Sep 1881, 14-Yes, 15-Ardinger

#1730, 1-Ardinger, Clara, 2-died, 3-21 Aug 1949, 14-Yes, 15-Ardinger

#1731, 1-Ardinger, Ellen Betty, 2-born, 3-13 Mar 1904, 12-Ardinger, Henry Z., 13-Garrish, Clara, 14-Yes, 15-Ardinger

#1732, 1-Ardinger, Hannah Steinmetz, 2-born, 3-26 Dec 1906, 12-Ardinger, Henry Z., 13-Garrish, Clara, 14-Yes, 15-Ardinger

#1733, 1-Ardinger, Joseph Henry, 2-born, 3-13 May 1908, 12-Ardinger, Henry Z., 13-Garrish, Clara, 14-Yes, 15-Ardinger

#1734, 1-Ardinger, Hannah (Mrs.), 2-died, 3-8 Mar 1866, 7-Ardinger, Peter, 14-Yes, 15-Ardinger

#1735, 1-Ardinger, Peter, 2-died, 3-7 May 1900, 14-Yes, 15-Ardinger

#1736, 1-Ardinger, Mariah (Mrs.), 2-died, 3-5 Aug 1904, 14-Yes, 15-Ardinger

#1737, 1-Ardinger, William Hamilton, 2-died, 3-20 Sep 1907, 14-Yes, 15-Ardinger

#1738, 1-Crow, Effie, 2-died, 3-28 Mar 1908, 14-Yes, 15-Ardinger

#1739, 1-Ardinger, Henry Zeller, 2-died, 3-1 Feb 1933, 14-Yes, 15-Ardinger

#1740, 1-Crow, Betty Ardinger, 2-died, 4-Williamsport, MD, 14-Yes, 15-Ardinger

#1741, 1-Bowser, Hannah Ardinger, 2-died, 4-Williamsport, MD, 14-Yes, 15-Ardinger

#1742, 1-McCoy, Clara Ardinger, 2-died, 4-Hagerstown, MD, 14-Yes, 15-Ardinger

#1743, 1-Zeller, Dennis T. (Mrs.), 2-died, 3-21 Mar 1977, 14-Yes, 15-Ardinger

#1744, 1-Bovey, Henry, 2-married, 3-18 Apr 1842, Maria Ellen, 14-Yes, 15-Bovey

#1745, 1-Bovey, Henry, 2-born, 3-16 Jan 1819, 12-Bovey, G., 13-Bovey, C., 14-Yes, 15-Bovey

#1746, 1-Martin, Maria Ellen, 2-born, 3-21 Dec 1821, 12-Martin, H., 13-Martin, M., 14-Yes, 15-Bovey

#1747, 1-Bovey, Lavinia Jane, 2-born, 3-21 Jan 1845, 12-Bovey, Henry, 13-Martin, Maria, 14-Yes, 15-Bovey

FAMILY BIBLE RECORDS IN THE WASHINGTON COUNTY FREE LIBRARY, HAGERSTOWN, MARYLAND

Entry #, 1-Last Name, First Name, 2-Event, 3-Date, 4-Event Location, 5-Age, 6-Other,
7-Spouse's Last, First, 8-Groom's Residence, 9-Bride's Residence, 10-Minister, 11-Minister's Location,
12-Father's Last, First, 13-Mother's Last, First, 14-Transcribed, 15-Family Bible

```
#1748, 1-Bovey, Mary Catharine, 2-born, 3-29 Mar 1846, 12-Bovey, Henry, 13-Martin,
    Maria, 14-Yes, 15-Bovey
#1749, 1-Bovey, Luther Martin, 2-born, 3-4 Aug 1847, 12-Bovey, Henry, 13-Martin,
    Maria, 14-Yes, 15-Bovey
#1750, 1-Bovey, George Henry, 2-born, 3-18 Feb 1850, 12-Bovey, Henry, 13-Martin,
    Maria, 14-Yes, 15-Bovey
#1751, 1-Bovey, Ellen Mussouri, 2-born, 3-11 Oct 1851, 12-Bovey, Henry, 13-Martin,
    Maria, 14-Yes, 15-Bovey
#1752, 1-Bovey, Anna Cecelia, 2-born, 3-31 May 1854, 12-Bovey, Henry, 13-Martin,
    Maria, 14-Yes, 15-Bovey
#1753, 1-Bovey, Millard Claggett, 2-born, 3-26 Feb 1857, 12-Bovey, Henry, 13-
    Martin, Maria, 14-Yes, 15-Bovey
#1754, 1-Bovey, Lillie May, 2-born, 3-26 Mar 1859, 12-Bovey, Henry, 13-Martin,
    Maria, 14-Yes, 15-Bovey
#1755, 1-Bovey, Jacob, 2-born, 3-18 Feb 1861, 12-Bovey, Henry, 13-Martin, Maria,
    14-Yes, 15-Bovey
#1756, 1-Bovey, Flora Belle, 2-born, 3-1865, 12-Bovey, Henry, 13-Martin, Maria, 14-
    Yes, 15-Bovey
#1757, 1-Bovey, Edward O., 2-born, 3-8 Dec 1868, 12-Bovey, Henry, 13-Martin, Maria,
    14-Yes, 15-Bovey
#1758, 1-Bovey, Ellen Missouri, 2-died, 3-Mar 1855, 5-3 years, 14-Yes, 15-Bovey
#1759, 1-Bovey, Jacob Reel, 2-died, 3-21 Feb 1862, 5-1 month 23 days, 14-Yes, 15-
    Bovey
#1760, 1-Bovey, Flora Belle, 2-died, 3-5 Oct 1864, 5-1 years 2 months 5 days, 14-
    Yes, 15-Bovey
#1761, 1-Bovey, Maria Ellen, 2-died, 3-18 Oct 1888, 5-66  years 9 months 27 days,
    14-Yes, 15-Bovey
#1762, 1-Bovey, Henry, 2-died, 3-13 Dec 1902, 5-85 years 10 months 26 days, 14-Yes,
    15-Bovey
#1763, 1-Bovey, Mary Catharine, 2-died, 3-9 Jul 1914, 5-65 years 3 months 10 days,
    14-Yes, 15-Bovey
#1764, 1-Bovey, Edward O., 2-died, 3-15 Apr 1931, 5-62 years 4 months 7 days, 14-
    Yes, 15-Bovey
#1765, 1-Bovey, Anna C., 2-died, 3-12 Sep 1933, 5-79 years 4 months 5 days, 14-Yes,
    15-Bovey
#1766, 1-Cordell, David C., 2-born, 3-21 Jun 1847, 14-Yes, 15-Cordell
#1767, 1-Cordell, David C., 2-died, 3-22 Dec 1915, 14-Yes, 15-Cordell
#1768, 1-Cordell, John Andrew, 2-born, 3-11 Feb 1882, 14-Yes, 15-Cordell
#1769, 1-Cordell, Benjamin Franklin, 2-born, 3-16 Sep 1890, 14-Yes, 15-Cordell
#1770, 1-Cordell, Samuel David, 2-born, 3-16 Jun 1897, 14-Yes, 15-Cordell
#1771, 1-Cordell, Lucye V., 2-born, 3-29 Jun 1904, 14-Yes, 15-Cordell
#1772, 1-Stull, Dorothy, 2-born, 3-26 Jan 1810, 14-Yes, 15-Cordell
#1773, 1-Cordell, John Andrew, 2-died, 3-17 Mar 1883, 14-Yes, 15-Cordell
#1774, 1-Cordell, Benjamin Franklin, 2-born, 3-6 Oct 1911, 14-Yes, 15-Cordell
#1775, 1-Cordell, Ruth Irine, 2-born, 3-23 Mar 1913, 14-Yes, 15-Cordell
#1776, 1-Kuhn, Edward A., 2-died, 3-15 Mar 1931, 14-Yes, 15-Kuhn
#1777, 1-Kuhn, Harry G., 2-died, 3-22 Dec 1941, 12-Kuhn, John, 13-Kuhn, Mahala, 14-
    Yes, 15-Kuhn
#1778, 1-Kuhn, Harry G., 2-born, 3-21 Mar 1866, 12-Kuhn, John, 13-Kuhn, Mahala, 14-
    Yes, 15-Kuhn
#1779, 1-Kuhn, John, 2-died, 3-16 Aug 1910, 14-Yes, 15-Kuhn
#1780, 1-Kuhn, Mahala, 2-died, 3-20 Mar 1920, 7-Kuhn, John, 14-Yes, 15-Kuhn
#1781, 1-Brewer, Antoinette, 2-died, 3-31 Dec 1921, 6-sister of Mahala Brewer Kuhn,
    14-Yes, 15-Kuhn
```

FAMILY BIBLE RECORDS IN THE WASHINGTON COUNTY FREE LIBRARY, HAGERSTOWN, MARYLAND

Entry #, 1-Last Name, First Name, 2-Event, 3-Date, 4-Event Location, 5-Age, 6-Other, 7-Spouse's Last, First, 8-Groom's Residence, 9-Bride's Residence, 10-Minister, 11-Minister's Location, 12-Father's Last, First, 13-Mother's Last, First, 14-Transcribed, 15-Family Bible

#1782, 1-Kuhn, Anna Amelia, 2-died, 3-4 Sep 1868, 12-Kuhn, John, 13-Brewer, Mahala, 14-Yes, 15-Kuhn

#1783, 1-Kuhn, Anna Amelia, 2-born, 3-20 Jun 1867, 12-Kuhn, John, 13-Brewer, Mahala, 14-Yes, 15-Kuhn

#1784, 1-Kuhn, Minnie Amanda, 2-died, 3-7 May 1876, 12-Kuhn, John, 13-Brewer, Mahala, 14-Yes, 15-Kuhn

#1785, 1-Kuhn, John Joseph, 2-died, 3-25 Mar 1893, 12-Kuhn, John, 13-Brewer, Mahala, 14-Yes, 15-Kuhn

#1786, 1-Kuhn, John Joseph, 2-born, 3-22 Feb 1873, 12-Kuhn, John, 13-Brewer, Mahala, 14-Yes, 15-Kuhn

#1787, 1-Kuhn, Frank, 2-died, 3-22 Jul 1930, 12-Kuhn, John, 13-Brewer, Mahala, 14-Yes, 15-Kuhn

#1788, 1-Kuhn, Frank, 2-born, 3-28 Dec 1879, 12-Kuhn, John, 13-Brewer, Mahala, 14-Yes, 15-Kuhn

#1789, 1-Kuhn, John, 2-born, 3-23 Nov 1841, 12-Kuhn, Jacob, 13-Lutz, Nancy, 14-Yes, 15-Kuhn

#1790, 1-Kuhn, John, 2-died, 3-16 Aug 1910, 12-Kuhn, Jacob, 13-Lutz, Nancy, 14-Yes, 15-Kuhn

#1791, 1-Kuhn, Mahala (Brewer), 2-born, 3-19 Nov 1844, 12-Brewer, Joseph, 13-Snyder, Hester, 14-Yes, 15-Kuhn

#1792, 1-Kuhn, Mahala (Brewer), 2-died, 3-20 Mar 1920, 12-Brewer, Joseph, 13-Snyder, Hester, 14-Yes, 15-Kuhn

#1793, 1-Kuhn, Harry G., 2-died, 3-22 Dec 1941, 12-Kuhn, John, 13-Brewer, Mahala, 14-Yes, 15-Kuhn

#1794, 1-Kuhn, Jacob Frederick, 2-died, 3-7 Mar 1954, 12-Kuhn, John, 13-Brewer, Mahala, 14-Yes, 15-Kuhn

#1795, 1-Kuhn, Jacob Frederick, 2-born, 3-13 Dec 1874, 12-Kuhn, John, 13-Brewer, Mahala, 14-Yes, 15-Kuhn

#1796, 1-Kuhn, Mary Amanda, 2-died, 3-7 May 1876, 12-Kuhn, John, 13-Brewer, Mahala, 14-Yes, 15-Kuhn

#1797, 1-Kuhn, Mary Amanda, 2-born, 3-20 Jan 1869, 12-Kuhn, John, 13-Brewer, Mahala, 14-Yes, 15-Kuhn

#1798, 1-Kuhn, Edward Abraham, 2-born, 3-4 May 1871, 12-Kuhn, John, 13-Brewer, Mahala, 14-Yes, 15-Kuhn

#1799, 1-Kuhn, Edward Abraham, 2-died, 3-15 Mar 1931, 12-Kuhn, John, 13-Brewer, Mahala, 14-Yes, 15-Kuhn

#1800, 1-Kuhn, Ada Viola, 2-born, 3-2 Jul 1877, 12-Kuhn, John, 13-Brewer, Mahala, 14-Yes, 15-Kuhn

#1801, 1-Kuhn, Ada Viola, 2-died, 3-13 Sep 1960, 12-Kuhn, John, 13-Brewer, Mahala, 14-Yes, 15-Kuhn

#1802, 1-Kuhn, Libbie G., 2-born, 3-10 Jan 1881, 12-Kuhn, John, 13-Brewer, Mahala, 14-Yes, 15-Kuhn

#1803, 1-Kuhn, John, 2-born, 3-23 Nov 1841, 14-Yes, 15-Kuhn

#1804, 1-Kuhn, Mahalah, 2-born, 3-19 Nov 1844, 14-Yes, 15-Kuhn

#1805, 1-Kuhn, Harry, 2-born, 3-21 Mar 1866, 14-Yes, 15-Kuhn

#1806, 1-Kuhn, Anna Amelia, 2-born, 3-30 Jun 1867, 14-Yes, 15-Kuhn

#1807, 1-Kuhn, Minnie Amanda, 2-born, 3-20 Jan 1869, 14-Yes, 15-Kuhn

#1808, 1-Kuhn, Edward A., 2-born, 3-4 May 1871, 14-Yes, 15-Kuhn

#1809, 1-Kuhn, John Joseph, 2-born, 3-22 Feb 1873, 14-Yes, 15-Kuhn

#1810, 1-Kuhn, Jacob Frederic, 2-born, 3-13 Dec 1874, 14-Yes, 15-Kuhn

#1811, 1-Kuhn, Ada Violet, 2-born, 3-2 Jul 1877, 14-Yes, 15-Kuhn

#1812, 1-Kuhn, Frank Brewer, 2-born, 3-28 Dec 1879, 14-Yes, 15-Kuhn

#1813, 1-Kuhn, Libbie, 2-born, 3-10 Jan 1881, 14-Yes, 15-Kuhn

#1814, 1-Kuhn, Elva Louise, 2-born, 3-1 Dec 1883, 14-Yes, 15-Kuhn

FAMILY BIBLE RECORDS IN THE WASHINGTON COUNTY FREE LIBRARY, HAGERSTOWN, MARYLAND

Entry #, 1-Last Name, First Name, 2-Event, 3-Date, 4-Event Location, 5-Age, 6-Other,
7-Spouse's Last, First, 8-Groom's Residence, 9-Bride's Residence, 10-Minister, 11-Minister's Location,
12-Father's Last, First, 13-Mother's Last, First, 14-Transcribed, 15-Family Bible

```
#1815, 1-Ingram, J. Wilbur, 2-born, 3-11 Aug 1908, 12-Ingram, J. Roy, 13-Kuhn,
    Elva, 14-Yes, 15-Kuhn
#1816, 1-Ingram, R. Leon, 2-born, 3-12 Apr 1923, 12-Ingram, J. Roy, 13-Kuhn, Elva,
    14-Yes, 15-Kuhn
#1817, 1-Ingram, Ada Viola, 2-born, 3-Jul 1877, 14-Yes, 15-Kuhn
#1818, 1-Ingram, Ada Viola, 2-died, 3-13 Sep 1960, 14-Yes, 15-Kuhn
#1819, 1-Smith, George Howard, 2-born, 3-20 Aug 1876, 14-Yes, 15-Kuhn
#1820, 1-Smith, George Howard, 2-died, 3-13 Jan 1957, 14-Yes, 15-Kuhn
#1821, 1-Smith, Howard Cage, 2-born, 3-22 Aug 1906, 12-Smith, Howard, 13-Kuhn, Ada,
    14-Yes, 15-Kuhn
#1822, 1-Smith, Helen Kuhn, 2-born, 3-30 Nov 1911, 6-Thanksgiving Day, 12-Smith,
    Howard, 13-Kuhn, Ada, 14-Yes, 15-Kuhn
#1823, 1-Sands, Samuel A., 3-Dec 1834, 14-Yes, 15-Fasnacht
#1824, 1-Fasnacht, Lidia, 3-14 Feb 1858, 14-Yes, 15-Fasnacht
#1825, 1-Fasnacht, Henry, 2-born, 3-26 Jan 1812, 14-Yes, 15-Fasnacht
#1826, 1-Ross, Lidia, 2-born, 3-26 Nov 1911, 14-Yes, 15-Fasnacht
#1827, 1-Fasnacht, Elizabeth Ann, 2-born, 3-30 May 1848, 14-Yes, 15-Fasnacht
#1828, 1-Fasnacht, Sarah Jane, 2-born, 3-19 May 1851, 14-Yes, 15-Fasnacht
#1829, 1-Fasnacht, Henry, 2-died, 3-19 Nov 1857, 14-Yes, 15-Fasnacht
#1830, 1-Fasnacht, Lidia, 2-died, 3-11 Jul 1891, 14-Yes, 15-Fasnacht
#1831, 1-Zeller, Henry S., 2-married, 3-30 Dec 1834, 7-Zeller, Amelia, 14-Yes, 15-
    Zeller
#1832, 1-Zeller, Henry S., 2-married, 3-30 Dec 1857, 7-Zeller, Annsecelia, 14-Yes,
    15-Zeller
#1833, 1-Zeller, Daniel E., 2-married, 3-22 Dec 1875, 7-Cunningham, Mary L., 14-
    Yes, 15-Zeller
#1834, 1-Cunningham, Mary, 2-born, 3-24 Jun 1852, 14-Yes, 15-Zeller
#1835, 1-Zeller, Charles G., 2-married, 3-30 Jan 1907, 7-Kohr, Ethel B., 14-Yes,
    15-Zeller
#1836, 1-Zeller, Dennis T., 2-married, 3-2 Sep 1925, 7-Wilkes, Olive, 14-Yes, 15-
    Zeller
#1837, 1-Zeller, Dennis T., 2-married, 3-22 Dec 1841, 4-Winchester, VA, 7-Ardinger,
    Ellen, 9-Williamsport, MD, 14-Yes, 15-Zeller
#1838, 1-Zeller, Henry S., 2-born, 3-24 Feb 1829, 4-Washington Co., MD, 14-Yes, 15-
    Zeller
#1839, 1-Zeller, Henry S., 2-died, 3-26 Feb 1906, 14-Yes, 15-Zeller
#1840, 1-Zeller, Anna C., 2-born, 3-15 Aug 1830, 4-Washington Co., MD, 14-Yes, 15-
    Zeller
#1841, 1-Zeller, Rachel E., 2-born, 3-18 Apr 1884, 4-Washington Co., MD, 12-Zeller,
    Daniel E., 14-Yes, 15-Zeller
#1842, 1-Zeller, Rachel E., 2-died, 3-13 Dec 1937, 12-Zeller, Daniel E., 14-Yes,
    15-Zeller
#1843, 1-Zeller, Bruce, 2-born, 3-10 Oct 1876, 4-Washington Co., MD, 12-Zeller,
    Daniel E., 14-Yes, 15-Zeller
#1844, 1-Zeller, Charles G., 2-born, 3-3 Nov 18880, 4-Washington Co., MD, 12-
    Zeller, Daniel E., 14-Yes, 15-Zeller
#1845, 1-Zeller, William Wayne, 12-Zeller, Daniel E., 14-Yes, 15-Zeller
#1846, 1-Zeller, Tobias D., 2-born, 3-18 Oct 1890, 4-Washington Co., MD, 12-Zeller,
    Daniel E., 14-Yes, 15-Zeller
#1847, 1-Zeller, Daniel E., 2-born, 3-2 Jan 1852, 4-Washington Co., MD, 6-baptized
    15 Dec 1861, 14-Yes, 15-Zeller
#1848, 1-Zeller, Mary E., 2-born, 3-15 May 1853, 4-Washington Co., MD, 6-baptized
    15 Dec 1862, 14-Yes, 15-Zeller
#1849, 1-Zeller, Rachel E., 2-born, 3-27 Nov 1855, 4-Washington Co., MD, 6-baptized
    15 Dec 1863, 14-Yes, 15-Zeller
```

FAMILY BIBLE RECORDS IN THE WASHINGTON COUNTY FREE LIBRARY, HAGERSTOWN, MARYLAND

Entry #, 1-Last Name, First Name, 2-Event, 3-Date, 4-Event Location, 5-Age, 6-Other, 7-Spouse's Last, First, 8-Groom's Residence, 9-Bride's Residence, 10-Minister, 11-Minister's Location, 12-Father's Last, First, 13-Mother's Last, First, 14-Transcribed, 15-Family Bible

#1850, 1-Zeller, Ann Amelia, 2-born, 3-12 Nov 1857, 4-Washington Co., MD, 6-baptized 15 Dec 1864, 14-Yes, 15-Zeller

#1851, 1-Zeller, Charles, 2-born, 3-4 Dec 1860, 4-Washington Co., MD, 6-baptized 15 Dec 1865, 14-Yes, 15-Zeller

#1852, 1-Zeller, William Wagner, 2-died, 3-8 Aug 1864, 14-Yes, 15-Zeller

#1853, 1-Zeller, William W., 2-born, 3-12 Feb 1864, 4-Washington Co., MD, 14-Yes, 15-Zeller

#1854, 1-Zeller, William W., 2-died, 3-8 Sep 1864, 14-Yes, 15-Zeller

#1855, 1-Zeller, Margaret Louise, 2-born, 3-21 Sep 1865, 4-Washington Co., MD, 6-baptized 27 May 1866, 14-Yes, 15-Zeller

#1856, 1-Zeller, David H., 2-born, 3-29 Dec 1868, 4-Washington Co., MD, 14-Yes, 15-Zeller

#1857, 1-Cunningham, Elizabeth, 2-died, 3-14 Mar 1901, 14-Yes, 15-Zeller

#1858, 1-Zeller, Daniel, 2-died, 3-20 Oct 1923, 14-Yes, 15-Zeller

#1859, 1-Zeller, Mary Louise (Cunningham), 2-died, 3-17 Mar 1941, 5-88 years 8 months 23 days, 14-Yes, 15-Zeller

#1860, 1-Zeller, Charles Garfield, 2-died, 3-27 Nov 1962, 4-Hagerstown, MD, 6-buried Salem Church Cemetery, Cearfoss, MD, 14-Yes, 15-Zeller

#1861, 1-Zeller, Daniel Edward, 6-owned home in Broadfording in 1895, 7-Zeller, Mary Louise (Cunningham), 14-Yes, 15-Zeller

#1862, 1-Zeller, Rachel Elizabeth, 2-born, 3-18 Apr 1884, 4-near Cearfoos, MD, 14-Yes, 15-Zeller

#1863, 1-Zeller, Rachel Elizabeth, 2-married, 3-26 Sep 1908, 7-Stouffer, James Lee, 14-Yes, 15-Zeller

#1864, 1-Stouffer, James Lee, 2-born, 3-8 Aug 1887, 14-Yes, 15-Zeller

#1865, 1-Stouffer, Frances Louise, 2-born, 3-27 Sep 1912, 4-Hagerstown, MD, 12-Stouffer, James Lee, 13-Zeller, Rachel Elizabeth, 14-Yes, 15-Zeller

#1866, 1-Stouffer, Frances Louise, 2-married, 3-29 May 1935, 7-Stackhouse, Jr., Will, 12-Stouffer, James Lee, 13-Zeller, Rachel Elizabeth, 14-Yes, 15-Zeller

#1867, 1-Stouffer, Almira Virginia, 2-born, 3-29 May 1917, 12-Stouffer, James Lee, 13-Zeller, Rachel Elizabeth, 14-Yes, 15-Zeller

#1868, 1-Stouffer, Almira Virginia, 2-married, 3-27 Aug 1938, 7-Kline, Richard, 12-Stouffer, James Lee, 13-Zeller, Rachel Elizabeth, 14-Yes, 15-Zeller

#1869, 1-Kline, Richard, 2-born, 3-23 Aug 1917, 14-Yes, 15-Zeller

#1870, 1-Lafferty, Van, 2-born, 3-24 Oct 1812, 15-Backhouse

#1871, 1-Backhouse, Mary Ellen, 2-born, 3-2 May 1827, 15-Backhouse

#1872, 1-Backhouse, Anna Potts, 2-born, 3-7 Jan 1832, 15-Backhouse

#1873, 1-Backhouse, Geo. Harvey[?] Clifford, 2-born, 3-2 Nov 1835, 15-Backhouse

#1874, 1-Backhouse, David Harrison, 2-born, 3-14 Apr 1837, 15-Backhouse

#1875, 1-Backhouse, Edward Mortimer Clay, 2-born, 3-3 Jul 1839, 15-Backhouse

#1876, 1-Backhouse, Sarah Amanda, 2-born, 3-5 Oct 1841, 15-Backhouse

#1877, 1-Backhouse, Margaret Francess[?], 2-born, 3-13 Jan 1844, 15-Backhouse

#1878, 1-Ridenour, Catharine M., 2-born, 3-28 Aug 1801, 7-Backhouse, Geo., 12-Ridenour, Christopher, 13-Ridenour, Elizabeth, 15-Backhouse

#1879, 1-Lafferty, Van, 2-died, 3-1:00 pm, 26 Sep 1813, 15-Backhouse

#1880, 1-Backhouse, Thomas, 2-born, 3-23 Jul 1767, 12-Backhouse, John, 13-Backhouse, Mary, 15-Backhouse

#1881, 1-Backhouse, Anna, 2-born, 3-26 Nov 1774, 12-Potts, Ezekiel, 13-Potts, Elisabeth, 15-Backhouse

#1882, 1-Backhouse, George, 2-born, 3-15 Feb 1803, 12-Backhouse, Thos., 13-Backhouse, Anna, 15-Backhouse

#1883, 1-Backhouse, Pleasey[?], 2-born, 3-19 Mar 1806, 12-Backhouse, Thos., 13-Backhouse, Anna, 15-Backhouse

#1884, 1-Backhouse, Thomas[?] Christopher, 2-born, 3-27 Feb 1821, 12-Backhouse, George, 13-Backhouse, Catharine, 15-Backhouse

FAMILY BIBLE RECORDS IN THE WASHINGTON COUNTY FREE LIBRARY, HAGERSTOWN, MARYLAND

Entry #, 1-Last Name, First Name, 2-Event, 3-Date, 4-Event Location, 5-Age, 6-Other, 7-Spouse's Last, First, 8-Groom's Residence, 9-Bride's Residence, 10-Minister, 11-Minister's Location, 12-Father's Last, First, 13-Mother's Last, First, 14-Transcribed, 15-Family Bible

#1885, 1-Backhouse, Elizabeth Ann[?] (Potts), 2-born, 3-1 Feb 1823, 12-Backhouse, George, 13-Backhouse, Catharine, 15-Backhouse
#1886, 1-Backhouse, Jane Catharine, 2-born, 3-22 Jul 1825, 12-Backhouse, George, 13-Backhouse, Catharine, 15-Backhouse
#1887, 1-Backhouse, Pleasey Corbiner[?], 2-born, 3-19 Sep 1829, 12-Backhouse, George, 13-Backhouse, Catharine, 15-Backhouse
#1888, 1-Backhouse, Thomas, 2-died, 3-Monday, 11:00, 20 Jul 1807, 6-buried in Ezekiel Potts family graveyard, Loudoun County, 15-Backhouse
#1889, 1-Lafferty, Anna, 2-died, 3-Sunday, 12:10, 16 Jul 1840, 6-buried in Ezekiel Potts family graveyard, Loudoun County, 7-Backhouse, Thomas, 15-Backhouse
#1890, 1-Backhouse, Thomas C., 2-died, 3-12 Oct 1855, 5-34 years 7 months 15 days, 6-buried in Ezekiel Potts family graveyard, Loudoun County, 15-Backhouse
#1891, 1-Backhouse, Geo. B., 2-died, 3-20 Sep 1867, 5-66 years, 6-buried in Charles Town cemetery, 15-Backhouse
#1892, 1-Milton, Mary Ellen, 2-died, 3-22 Dec 1880, 5-53 years 7 months, 15-Backhouse
#1893, 1-Backhouse, Catharine M., 2-died, 3-15 Mar 1879, 5-73 years, 15-Backhouse
#1894, 1-Backhouse, Catharine M., 2-died, 3-15 Mar 1874, 5-73 years, 15-Backhouse
#1895, 1-Mead, Samiel, 2-died, 3-Friday, 7 Nov 1860, 15-Backhouse
#1896, 1-Backhouse, Jane Catharine, 2-born, 3-22 Jul 1825, 12-Backhouse, Geo., 13-Backhouse, Cath., 15-Backhouse
#1897, 1-Backhouse, Pleasey Corbiner, 2-born, 3-19 Sep 1829, 12-Backhouse, Geo., 13-Backhouse, Cath., 15-Backhouse
#1898, 1-Lafferty, Van, 2-born, 3-24 Oct 1812, 15-Backhouse
#1899, 1-Lafferty, Van, 2-died, 3-1:02 pm, 26 Sep 1813, 15-Backhouse
#1900, 1-Backhouse, Mary Ellen, 2-born, 3-2 May 1827, 15-Backhouse
#1901, 1-Backhouse, Anna Potts, 2-born, 3-7 Jan 1832, 15-Backhouse
#1902, 1-Backhouse, Geo. Henry Clifford, 2-born, 3-2 Nov 1834, 15-Backhouse
#1903, 1-Backhouse, David Harrison, 2-born, 3-14 Apr 1837, 15-Backhouse
#1904, 1-Backhouse, Edward Mortimer Clay, 2-born, 3-3 Jul 1839, 15-Backhouse
#1905, 1-Backhouse, Sarah Amanda, 2-born, 3-5 Oct 1841, 15-Backhouse
#1906, 1-Backhouse, Margaret Francessa, 2-born, 3-13 Jan 1844, 15-Backhouse
#1907, 1-Ridenour, Catharine M., 2-born, 3-28 Aug 1801, 7-Backhouse, George, 12-Ridenour, Christopher, 13-Ridenour, Eliz., 15-Backhouse
#1908, 1-Backhouse, Mary, 2-born, 3-11 Sep 1768, 6-sister of Thomas Backhouse, 12-Backhouse, John, 13-Backhouse, Mary, 15-Backhouse
#1909, 1-Backhouse, Thomas, 2-married, 3-12 May 1801, Anna, 15-Backhouse
#1910, 1-Lafferty, George, 2-married, 3-19 Jan 1811, 7-Backhouse, Anna, 15-Backhouse
#1911, 1-Backhouse, George, 2-married, 3-4 Apr 1820, Catharine, 15-Backhouse
#1912, 1-Hurst, Juliet Frances, 2-died, 5-10 years, 12-Hurst, William, 13-Hurst, Mary, 15-Backhouse
#1913, 1-Hurst, Lucy, 2-obituary, 12-Hurst, William, 13-Hurst, Mary, 15-Backhouse
#1914, 1-Gunnell, John J. H., 2-obituary, 5-40 years, 6-cholera, 15-Backhouse
#1915, 1-Fulton, Lemuel W., 2-obituary, 5-17 years, 6-cholera, 12-Fulton, Robert, 15-Backhouse
#1916, 1-Stephens, Benjamin, 2-obituary, 3-10, 4-Sheperdstown, WV, 5-18 months, 12-Stephens, Thomas, 13-Stephens, Nancy, 15-Backhouse
#1917, 1-Crowl, Mary, 2-obituary, 4-Sheperdstown, WV, 5-69 years, 15-Backhouse
#1918, 1-Griffiths, Mary (Mrs.), 2-obituary, 3-Wednesday, 1:00, 7 Aug, 4-Cincinnati, 5-66 years, 6-cholera, 7-Griffiths, Sr., John, 15-Backhouse
#1919, 1-McDonald, John William, 2-obituary, 5-5 months 1 days, 12-McDonald, Jackson, 13-McDonald, Esther Ann, 15-Backhouse
#1920, 1-Llewelyn, Cordelia Reese, 2-obituary, 4-Camp Hill, 5-15 months, 6-cholera, 12-Llewelyn, Thomas, 13-Llewelyn, Elizabeth, 15-Backhouse

FAMILY BIBLE RECORDS IN THE WASHINGTON COUNTY FREE LIBRARY, HAGERSTOWN, MARYLAND

Entry #, 1-Last Name, First Name, 2-Event, 3-Date, 4-Event Location, 5-Age, 6-Other, 7-Spouse's Last, First, 8-Groom's Residence, 9-Bride's Residence, 10-Minister, 11-Minister's Location, 12-Father's Last, First, 13-Mother's Last, First, 14-Transcribed, 15-Family Bible

#1921, 1-Greer, Maria (Mrs.), 2-obituary, 4-Harpers Ferry, 5-56 years, 6-billious diarrhea, 7-Greer, William, 15-Backhouse

#1922, 1-[blank], Benjamin Augustus, 2-born, 3-5 Jul 1823, 15-Backhouse

#1923, 1-Crowl, Michael, 2-obituary, 3-14, 4-Gerrardstown, Berkeley Co., WV, 5-62 years, 6-cholera, 15-Backhouse

#1924, 1-Crowl, Elizabeth (Mrs.), 2-obituary, 4-Gerrardstown, Berkeley Co., WV, 5-50 years, 6-cholera, 15-Backhouse

#1925, 1-Crowl, Jacob, 2-obituary, 3-17, 4-Gerrardstown, Berkeley Co., WV, 5-27 years, 6-leaves wife and 2 children, 12-Crowl, Michael, 15-Backhouse

#1926, 1-Conrad, Nathan, 2-obituary, 3-12, 4-near Hillsborough, Loudoun Co., 5-21 years, 6-cholera, 15-Backhouse

#1927, 1-Wooddy, John Wm., 2-obituary, 3-Sunday morning, 5-11 months, 12-Wooddy, John W., 13-Wooddy, Mary A., 15-Backhouse

#1928, 1-Hutchinson, Thomas Hunter, 2-obituary, 3-5, 4-Martinsburg, WV, 5-19 months, 12-Hutchinson, Wm. E., 13-Hutchinson, Rachel A., 15-Backhouse

#1929, 1-Irvin, James Wm., 2-obituary, 3-3, 4-Martinsburg, WV, 5-11 years 6 months 12 days, 12-Irvin, Benjamin, 13-Irvin, Mary Jane, 15-Backhouse

#1930, 1-Zerger, Geo. W., 2-obituary, 4-Bolivar, WV, 5-36 years, 6-billious dysentery, 15-Backhouse

#1931, 1-Simpson, Wm., 2-obituary, 4-Island of Virginus, 5-46 years, 6-cholera, 15-Backhouse

#1932, 1-Simpson, [female], 2-obituary, 4-Island of Virginus, 5-3 years, 6-cholera, 12-Simpson, Wm., 15-Backhouse

#1933, 1-Griggs, Thomas, 2-obituary, 4-Boliver, WV, 6-cholera, 15-Backhouse

#1934, 1-Thompson, Chatharine L. (Miss), 2-obituary, 4-Harpers Ferry, WV, 5-19 years, 6-typhoid fever, 15-Backhouse

#1935, 1-Boteler, Elias L., 2-died, 3-23 Jan 1828, 15-Backhouse

#1936, 1-Boteler, Sr., Henry A., 2-died, 3-3 Oct 1843, 5-77 years, 15-Backhouse

#1937, 1-Boteler, Mary, 2-died, 3-24 Jun 1858, 5-82 years, 15-Backhouse

#1938, 1-Necholls, Maryann, 2-died, 3-22 Feb 1860, 5-52 years 11 months 6 days, 15-Backhouse

#1939, 1-Boteler, Jane, 2-married, 3-6 May 1819, 7-Fling, Owen, 15-Backhouse

#1940, 1-Boteler, E.L., 2-married, 3-4 Sep 1832, 7-Cheney, Prudence[?], 15-Backhouse

#1941, 1-Magruder, Henry, 2-married, 3-19 Aug 1826, 15-Backhouse

#1942, 1-Boteler, Henry, 2-born, 3-7 Aug 1766, 15-Backhouse

#1943, 1-Boteler, Edward L., 2-born, 3-5 Dec 1796, 15-Backhouse

#1944, 1-Boteler, Jane, 2-born, 3-17 Mar 1798, 15-Backhouse

#1945, 1-Boteler, Elizabeth, 2-born, 3-11 Aug 1801, 15-Backhouse

#1946, 1-Boteler, Elias[?] L., 2-born, 3-4 Aug 1805, 15-Backhouse

#1947, 1-Boteler, Marryann, 2-born, 3-28 Mar 1807, 15-Backhouse

#1948, 1-Boteler, Jr., Henry, 2-born, 3-20 Mar 1808, 15-Backhouse

#1949, 1-Boteler, Susannah, 2-born, 3-20 Oct 1811, 15-Backhouse

#1950, 1-Boteler, Sarah, 2-born, 3-10 Nov 1813, 15-Backhouse

#1951, 1-Boteler, Catherine C., 2-born, 3-27 Feb 1816, 15-Backhouse

#1952, 1-Fling, Henry, 2-born, 3-19 Feb 1820, 12-Fling, Owen, 15-Backhouse

#1953, 1-Phillips, Amanda, 2-born, 3-17 Oct 1831, 15-Backhouse

#1954, 1-Phillips, Thomas, 2-born, 3-14 Apr 1833, 15-Backhouse

#1955, 1-Darnel[?] or Farrel, William H., 2-born, 3-28 Dec 1834, 15-Backhouse

#1956, 1-Gittings, Robert C., 2-obituary, 3-5, 4-Brownsville, MD, 5-18 months, 6-dysentery, 12-Gittings, Edward L., 13-Gittings, Annetta V., 15-Boteler

#1957, 1-Boteler, Robert Lingan, 2-obituary, 4-Weverton, MD, 6-buried in Magnolia Cemetery, 12-Boteler, R.H.E. (Dr.), 13-Boteler, Rebecca, 15-Boteler

#1958, 1-Boteler, Louise, 2-born, 12-Boteler, Robert Lingan, 15-Boteler

#1959, 1-Boteler, Elizabeth, 2-died, 3-1940, 15-Boteler

FAMILY BIBLE RECORDS IN THE WASHINGTON COUNTY FREE LIBRARY, HAGERSTOWN, MARYLAND

Entry #, 1-Last Name, First Name, 2-Event, 3-Date, 4-Event Location, 5-Age, 6-Other,
7-Spouse's Last, First, 8-Groom's Residence, 9-Bride's Residence, 10-Minister, 11-Minister's Location,
12-Father's Last, First, 13-Mother's Last, First, 14-Transcribed, 15-Family Bible

```
#1960, 1-Ball, Athalia, 2-died, 3-Jun 1947, 15-Boteler
#1961, 1-Boteler, Jane, 2-born, 3-12 Apr 1870, 7-Brown, 15-Boteler
#1962, 1-O'Neal[?], Elia[?], 3-18 Jul 1894, 5-86 years 7 months 7 days, 15-Boteler
#1963, 1-O'Neal, Elias, 3-17 Jan 1801, 15-Boteler
#1964, 1-O'Neal, Rober, 3-17 Jan 1801, 15-Boteler
#1965, 1-O'Neal, E.D.[?], 3-11 Dec 1807, 15-Boteler
#1966, 1-[blank], Maria Susan, 3-20 Jun 1810, 15-Boteler
#1967, 1-Fletcher, Leander M., 3-1 Dec 1818, 15-Boteler
#1968, 1-Fletcher, Leander M., 3-22 Apr 1787, 15-Boteler
#1969, 1-Hammond, John, 2-married, 7-Shupe, Catharine, 15-Boteler
#1970, 1-Wagoner, John, 3-25 Oct 1827, 7-Hammond, Eleanor, 15-Boteler
#1971, 1-Witmer, Ben, 3-18 Dec 1832, 7-Hammond, Cath., 15-Boteler
#1972, 1-Hanm[?], John, 3-31 Dec 1833, 7-O'N., E., 15-Boteler
#1973, 1-Ham, David, 3-12 Mar 1829, 7-Newcomer, Ann, 15-Boteler
#1974, 1-Philip, Joh Hann[?], 3-27 May 1774, 7-Ham[?], Elizabeth, 15-Boteler
#1975, 1-Shupe, Catha., 3-17 Dec 1776, 12-Shupe, Adam, 13-Shupe, Dorothy, 15-
    Boteler
#1976, 1-H., David, 3-11 Oct 1798, 12-H., Joh, 13-H., C., 15-Boteler
#1977, 1-H., Elonore, 3-17 Nov 1802, 7-C., J., 15-Boteler
#1978, 1-H., J., 3-9 Mar 1808, 7-C., J., 15-Boteler
#1979, 1-H., G., 3-27 Aug 1811, 7-C., J., 15-Boteler
#1980, 1-H., A., 3-19 Jan 1835, 15-Boteler
#1981, 1-H., B.[?]C., 3-11 Jan 1837, 15-Boteler
#1982, 1-H., C.G., 3-22 Apr 1838, 15-Boteler
#1983, 1-H., S.M., 3-31 Dec 1839, 15-Boteler
#1984, 1-H., D., 3-4 Mar 1842, 15-Boteler
#1985, 1-H., A.C., 3-6 Nov 1844, 15-Boteler
#1986, 1-H., E., 3-2 Aug 1846, 15-Boteler
#1987, 1-H., W.O.N., 3-30 Dec 1848, 15-Boteler
#1988, 1-H., F.I., 3-20 Jun 1852, 15-Boteler
#1989, 1-H., Joh, 3-22 Feb 1849, 1P.[?], 1E., 15-Boteler
#1990, 1-H., E., 3-10 Dec 1866, P.[?], 15-Boteler
#1991, 1-[blanl], Susan Marie, 3-1 Nov 1846, 15-Boteler
#1992, 1-H., John, 3-15 Jan 1886, 1J., 1C., 15-Boteler
#1993, 1-Boteler, Robert Henry Ezekiel, 2-born, 3-30 Aug 1833, 15-Boteler
#1994, 1-Boteler, Elizabeth Jane, 2-born, 3-19 Nov 1835, 15-Boteler
#1995, 1-Boteler, Jely[?] Bond, 2-born, 3-26 Jun 1837, 15-Boteler
#1996, 1-Boteler, Martha Washington, 2-born, 3-4 Dec 1838, 15-Boteler
#1997, 1-Boteler, Annette Virginia, 2-born, 3-26 Sep 1840, 15-Boteler
#1998, 1-Boteler, Prudence (Cheney), 2-born, 3-23 May 1842, 15-Boteler
#1999, 1-Boteler, Mary Maka, 2-born, 3-22 Jan 1844, 15-Boteler
#2000, 1-Boteler, Rachel Elizabeth, 2-born, 3-13 Jul 1845, 15-Boteler
#2001, 1-Boteler, Matilda Ellen, 2-born, 3-3 Mar 1849, 15-Boteler
#2002, 1-Boteler, William Edward, 2-born, 3-16 Oct 1851, 15-Boteler
#2003, 1-Boteler, E.S., 2-married, 3-4 Sep 1832, 7-Cheney, Prudence, 15-Boteler
#2004, 1-Boteler, Robert H., 2-married, 3-17 Mar 1857, 7-Hammond, Rebecca, 15-
    Boteler
#2005, 1-Boteler, Martha W., 2-married, 3-19 Nov 1863, 7-Garrott, Wm. M., 15-
    Boteler
#2006, 1-Boteler, Annett V., 2-married, 3-8 Jan 1868, 7-Gittings, E.L., 15-Boteler
#2007, 1-Boteler, Prudence C., 2-married, 3-22 Dec 1868, 7-Elgan, Henry Clay, 15-
    Boteler
#2008, 1-Boteler, Rachel E., 2-married, 3-28 Nov 1872, 7-Elgan, P. Luther, 15-
    Boteler
#2009, 1-Boteler, Edward Hammond, 2-born, 3-Tuesday, 15 Dec 1857, 15-Boteler
```

FAMILY BIBLE RECORDS IN THE WASHINGTON COUNTY FREE LIBRARY, HAGERSTOWN, MARYLAND

Entry #, 1-Last Name, First Name, 2-Event, 3-Date, 4-Event Location, 5-Age, 6-Other,
7-Spouse's Last, First, 8-Groom's Residence, 9-Bride's Residence, 10-Minister, 11-Minister's Location,
12-Father's Last, First, 13-Mother's Last, First, 14-Transcribed, 15-Family Bible

#2010, 1-Boteler, Athalia V., 2-born, 3-15 Oct 1859, 15-Boteler
#2011, 1-Boteler, Elizabeth, 2-born, 3-6 Dec 1861, 15-Boteler
#2012, 1-Boteler, Lorena Amelia, 2-born, 3-29 Oct 1863, 15-Boteler
#2013, 1-Boteler, Prudence Chaney, 2-born, 3-21 Jun 1866, 15-Boteler
#2014, 1-Boteler, Jane E., 2-born, 3-12 Apr 1870, 15-Boteler
#2015, 1-Boteler, Robert Henry, 2-born, 3-9 Jul 1873, 15-Boteler
#2016, 1-Boteler, Mary Catharine, 2-born, 3-2 Mar 1876, 15-Boteler
#2017, 1-Boteler, Edward Hammond, 2-born, 3-12 Oct 1863, 15-Boteler
#2018, 1-Boteler, Rosa Nelson, 2-died, 3-27 Oct 1881, 5-4 months 4 days, 15-Boteler
#2019, 1-Emmert, Prudence Boteler, 2-died, 3-28 Feb, 15-Boteler
#2020, 1-Boteler, Robert L., 2-died, 3-9 Apr 1934, 15-Boteler
#2021, 1-Boteler, R.H.E., 2-born, 3-30 Aug 1833, 15-Boteler
#2022, 1-Hammond, Rebecca, 2-born, 3-11 Jan 1837, 7-Boteler, R.H.E., 15-Boteler
#2023, 1-Boteler, Ellen R., 2-born, 3-11 Jan 1879, 15-Boteler
#2024, 1-Boteler, Rosa Nelson, 2-born, 3-22 Jun 1881, 15-Boteler
#2025, 1-Boteler, Robert H.E., 2-died, 3-21 Oct 1892, 12-Boteler, E.L. (Dr.), 15-Boteler
#2026, 1-Boteler, Rebecca C., 2-died, 3-10 Sep 1905, 15-Boteler
#2027, 1-Boteler, R.H.E., 2-married, 3-Tuesday, 17 Mar 1857, 7-Hammond, Rebecca C., 15-Boteler
#2028, 1-Boteler, E.L. (Dr.), 2-died, 3-[blank], 15-Boteler
#2029, 1-Boteler, Prudence, 2-died, 3-27 Feb 1876, 15-Boteler
#2030, 1-Boteler, Henry A., 2-born, 3-1776, 15-Boteler
#2031, 1-Estburn, Mary, 2-born, 3-1776, 15-Boteler
#2032, 1-Boteler, Sr., Henry A., 2-died, 3-3 Oct 1843, 15-Boteler
#2033, 1-Boteler, Mary, 3-24 Jun 1858, 15-Boteler
#2034, 1-Cheney, Sr., Robert, 3-12 Aug 1836[or 1830], 5-63 years 5 months 4 days, 15-Boteler
#2035, 1-Cheney, Jelijs[?], 2-died, 3-13 May 1888, 5-82 years 4 months 15 days, 15-Boteler
#2036, 1-Boteler, July[?] Bond, 2-died, 3-2 Aug 1838, 15-Boteler
#2037, 1-Boteler, Elizabeth Jane, 2-died, 3-26 May 1839, 15-Boteler
#2038, 1-Boteler, Matilda Ellen, 2-died, 3-13 Mar 1850, 15-Boteler
#2039, 1-Boteler, Prudence Cheney, 2-died, 3-28 Feb 1875[?], 15-Boteler
#2040, 1-Boteler, E.L. (Dr.), 2-died, 3-27 May 1881, 15-Boteler
#2041, 1-Elgin, Rachel E., 2-died, 3-6 Jul 1884, 15-Boteler
#2042, 1-Gittings, Winebert[?] L., 2-died, 3-22 Oct 1898, 15-Boteler
#2043, 1-Boteler, Mary Makle, 2-died, 3-21 Mar 1919, 15-Boteler
#2044, 1-Boteler, William Edward, 2-died, 3-24 Jul 1924, 15-Boteler
#2045, 1-Elgin, Prudence Chaney (Boteler), 2-died, 3-26 May 1919, 15-Boteler
#2046, 1-Boteler, E.L., 2-born, 3-5 Dec 1796, 15-Boteler
#2047, 1-Boteler, Prudence Cheney, 2-born, 3-14 Apr 1808, 15-Boteler
#2048, 1-Gittings, Wurbert[?] Livingston, 2-born, 3-13 Nov 1868, 15-Boteler
#2049, 1-Backhouse, Thomas, 2-born, 3-25 Jul 1767, 12-Backhouse, John, 13-Backhouse, Mary, 15-Boteler
#2050, 1-Backhouse, Anna, 2-born, 3-26 Nov 1774, 12-[blank], Ezekiel, 13-[blank], Elizabeth, 15-Boteler
#2051, 1-Backhouse, George, 2-born, 3-15 Feb 1803, 12-Backhouse, Thomas, 13-Backhouse, Anna, 15-Boteler
#2052, 1-Backhouse, Pleasey, 2-born, 3-19 Mar 1806, 12-Backhouse, Tom, 13-Backhouse, Ann, 15-Boteler
#2053, 1-Backhouse, Thomas Christopher, 2-born, 3-27 Feb 1821, 12-Backhouse, Geo., 13-Backhouse, Cathar., 15-Boteler
#2054, 1-Cotts[?], Elizabeth A., 2-born, 3-1 Feb 1823, 12-Backhouse, Geo., 13-Backhouse, C., 15-Boteler

FAMILY BIBLE RECORDS IN THE WASHINGTON COUNTY FREE LIBRARY, HAGERSTOWN, MARYLAND

Entry #, 1-Last Name, First Name, 2-Event, 3-Date, 4-Event Location, 5-Age, 6-Other,
7-Spouse's Last, First, 8-Groom's Residence, 9-Bride's Residence, 10-Minister, 11-Minister's Location,
12-Father's Last, First, 13-Mother's Last, First, 14-Transcribed, 15-Family Bible

```
#2055, 1-Boullt, Wm., 2-married, 3-11 Dec 1802, 7-Hammond, Eliza, 15-Boullt
#2056, 1-Boullt, Thomas, 2-married, 3-22 Sep 1774, 7-Watts, Elizabeth, 15-Boullt
#2057, 1-Watts, Elizabeth, 2-born, 12-Watts, Wm., 13-Watts, Sarah, 15-Boullt
#2058, 1-Boullt, Wm., 2-born, 3-22 Jul 1775, 12-Boullt, Thomas, 13-Boullt,
      Elizabeth, 15-Boullt
#2059, 1-Boullt, Wm. Hammett, 2-born, 3-24[?] Jul 1804, 12-Boullt, Wm., 13-Boullt,
      Elizabeth, 15-Boullt
#2060, 1-Boullt, Hellen Elizabeth, 2-born, 3-10 Jan 1807, 12-Boullt, Wm., 13-
      Boullt, Elizabeth, 15-Boullt
#2061, 1-Boullt, Henery Watts, 2-born, 3-23 Jan 1809, 12-Boullt, Wm., 13-Boullt,
      Elizabeth, 15-Boullt
#2062, 1-Boullt, Cristianna A., 2-born, 3-5 Dec 1811, 12-Boullt, Wm., 13-Boullt,
      Elizabeth, 15-Boullt
#2063, 1-Boullt, [twin sister of Cristianna A.], 2-born, 3-5 Dec 1811, 12-Boullt,
      Wm., 13-Boullt, Elizabeth, 15-Boullt
#2064, 1-Boullt, David Hammett, 2-born, 3-29 Aug 1813, 12-Boullt, Wm., 13-Boullt,
      Elizabeth, 15-Boullt
#2065, 1-Boullt, Thomas Alexander Smith Holings Watts, 2-born, 3-1[?] Nov 1816, 12-
      Boullt, Wm., 13-Boullt, Elizabeth, 15-Boullt
#2066, 1-Boullt, George Washington Colombus, 2-born, 3-4 Dec 1818, 12-Boullt, Wm.,
      13-Boullt, Elizabeth, 15-Boullt
#2067, 1-Boullt, [twin sister of Christianna A.], 2-died, 3-5 Nov 1811, 15-Boullt
#2068, 1-Boullt, G.W.C., 2-died, 3-8 Dec 1818, 15-Boullt
#2069, 1-Boullt, Thos. A., 2-married, 3-14 Dec 1847, 7-Henry[? Or Harry], Tarma
      Bell, 15-Boullt
#2070, 1-Boullt, Thos. A., 2-married, 6-ENTRY UNREADABLE, 7-P_____, H.C., 15-Boullt
#2071, 1-Boullt, Rosa[?], 2-married, 3-21 Feb 1878, 7-[unreadable], Warren, 15-
      Boullt
#2072, 1-Boullt, Susan Bell[?], 2-died, 3-1 Apr 1854, 15-Boullt
#2073, 1-Boullt, William, 2-died, 3-5 Sep 1888, 15-Boullt
#2074, 1-Boullt, Sarah Bell, 2-died, 3-13 Dec 1871, 15-Boullt
#2075, 1-Boullt, Thos. Alex., 2-died, 3-5 Feb[?] 1876, 15-Boullt
#2076, 1-[unreadable], Warren, 2-died, 3-11 Oct 1888, 15-Boullt
#2077, 1-Boullt, Elizabeth, 2-died, 3-30 Sep 1830, 7-Boullt, William, 15-Boullt
#2078, 1-Boullt, William, 2-born, 3-11 Sep 18_8, 15-Boullt
#2079, 1-Boullt, Susan Bell, 2-born, 3-4 Feb 1860, 15-Boullt
#2080, 1-Boullt, Anna Curtis[?], 2-born, 3-30 Nov 185_, 15-Boullt
#2081, 1-Boullt, Clasine[?] Marshall, 2-born, 3-4 Jan 1856, 15-Boullt
#2082, 1-Boullt, Thos. Alex, 2-born, 3-18 Sep 1864, 15-Boullt
#2083, 1-Boullt, Harry, 2-born, 3-26 Oct 1871, 15-Boullt
#2084, 1-Magaruder[?], Florence Stevinson, 2-born, 3-25 Oct 1808[or 1868 or 1878],
      15-Boullt
#2085, 1-Williamson, Bessie, 2-born, 3-29 Jan 1880, 15-Boullt
#2086, 1-Sollers[?], Anna, 2-born, 3-25[?] Oct 1887, 15-Boullt
#2087, 1-[blank], Anna, 3-21 Jan 1886, 15-Boullt
#2088, 1-Boullt, Susanna, 2-born, 3-8 Dec 1776, 12-Boullt, Thos., 13-Boullt,
      Elizabeth, 15-Boullt
#2089, 1-Boullt, Thomas H., 2-born, 3-11 Mar 1779, 15-Boullt
#2090, 1-Boullt, Kenelam, 2-born, 3-4 Mar 1781, 15-Boullt
#2091, 1-Boullt, Sarah, 2-born, 3-18 Jun 1783, 15-Boullt
#2092, 1-Boullt, Ann, 2-born, 3-21 Oct 1785, 15-Boullt
#2093, 1-Boullt, Jane[?], 2-born, 3-16 Jan 1787, 15-Boullt
#2094, 1-Boullt, Elizabeth, 2-born, 3-1 Jan 1788, 15-Boullt
#2095, 1-Boullt, Jean[?], 2-born, 3-Jan 1791, 15-Boullt
```

FAMILY BIBLE RECORDS IN THE WASHINGTON COUNTY FREE LIBRARY, HAGERSTOWN, MARYLAND

Entry #, 1-Last Name, First Name, 2-Event, 3-Date, 4-Event Location, 5-Age, 6-Other, 7-Spouse's Last, First, 8-Groom's Residence, 9-Bride's Residence, 10-Minister, 11-Minister's Location, 12-Father's Last, First, 13-Mother's Last, First, 14-Transcribed, 15-Family Bible

#2096, 1-Boullt, Susanna, 2-died, 3-18 Sep 1780, 12-Boullt, Thos., 13-Boullt, Elizabeth, 15-Boullt

#2097, 1-Boullt, Kenelam, 2-died, 3-8 Aug 1783, 15-Boullt

#2098, 1-Boullt, Ann, 2-died, 3-15 Nov 1786, 15-Boullt

#2099, 1-Boullt, Jean, 2-died, 3-24 Jan 1788, 15-Boullt

#2100, 1-Boullt, Tho. H., 2-died, 3-3 Jun 1796, 15-Boullt

#2101, 1-Boullt, Jean, 2-died, 3-Jan 1791, 15-Boullt

#2102, 1-Boullt, Thomas, 2-died, 3-18 May 1804, 15-Boullt

#2103, 1-Sward[?], Sarah, 2-died, 3-8 Dec 1809, 15-Boullt

#2104, 1-Boullt, William, 2-died, 3-30 Nov 1845, 5-70 years 4 months 29 days, 15-Boullt

#2105, 1-Boullt, Elizabeth, 2-died, 3-30 Sep 1830, 5-52 years 8 months, 15-Boullt

#2106, 1-Boullt, Helen E., 2-died, 3-22 Aug 1840, 15-Boullt

#2107, 1-Hawkins, Thomas Alexander, 2-born, 3-1 Nov 1816, 12-Boullt, William, 13-Boullt, Elizabeth, 15-Boullt

#2108, 1-Hawkins, Thomas Alexander, 2-baptized, 3-9 Nov 1816, 6-private baptism, 10-Jos. Jackson, 15-Boullt

#2109, 1-Hammett, Wm., 2-died, 3-12 midnight, 10 Feb 1797, 5-65 years, 15-Boullt

#2110, 1-Harry, George I.[?], 2-born, 12-Harry, Joseph, 15-Boullt

#2111, 1-Harry, George I.[?], 2-married, 7-Knode, Amelia, 15-Boullt

#2112, 1-Harry, George I.[?], 2-married, 6-wife is sister to William D. Bell, 7-Bell, Susan, 15-Boullt

#2113, 1-Harry, [female], 2-married, 7-Murphy, Dennis (Dr.), 12-Harry, George I., 13-Bell, Susan, 15-Boullt

#2114, 1-Harry, [female], 2-married, 7-Boultt, T.A., 12-Harry, George I., 13-Bell, Susan, 15-Boullt

#2115, 1-Harry, [female], 2-married, 7-Syester, A.K. (Hon.), 12-Harry, George I., 13-Bell, Susan, 15-Boullt

#2116, 1-Harry, [female], 2-married, 7-Lane[?], William (Rev.), 12-Harry, George I., 13-Bell, Susan, 15-Boullt

#2117, 1-Boullt, Thomas A., 2-obituary, 3-Oct 1876, 5-60 years, 6-buried Presbyterian Cemetery, 15-Boullt

#2118, 1-McIlvaine, Robert, 3-1770, 6-will from Lancaster Co., PA, 15-Boullt

#2119, 1-McElvain, George, 3-1775, 6-military paper, 15-Boullt

#2120, 1-Lerch, Reuben, 2-born, 3-1 Dec 1825, 4-Lower Lancon Township, Northampton Co., PA, 12-Lerch, Joseph, 13-Lerch, Susan, 15-Lerch

#2121, 1-Lerch, Reuben, 2-christened, 10-Rev. Thomas Pomss[?], 12-Lerch, Joseph, 13-Lerch, Susan, 15-Lerch

#2122, 1-Knauss, Sarah Lousia, 2-born, 3-26 Oct 1832, 4-Hanover Township, Northampton Co., PA, 12-Knauss, Antonis, 13-Knauss, Anna, 15-Lerch

#2123, 1-Lerch, Miranda Adaline, 2-born, 3-21 Nov 1854, 4-Freemansburg[?], Northampton Co., PA, 12-Lerch, Reuben, 13-Lerch, Sarah, 15-Lerch

#2124, 1-Lerch, Anna Elizabeth, 2-born, 3-27 May 1856, 4-Freemansburg, Northampton Co., PA, 12-Lerch, Reuben, 13-Lerch, Sarah, 15-Lerch

#2125, 1-Lerch, Harvey Joseph, 2-born, 3-6 Jun 1858, 4-Freemansburg, Northampton Co., PA, 12-Lerch, Reuben, 13-Lerch, Sarah, 15-Lerch

#2126, 1-Lerch, Hiram Anthony, 2-born, 3-6 Jun 1858, 4-Freemansburg, Northampton Co., PA, 12-Lerch, Reuben, 13-Lerch, Sarah, 15-Lerch

#2127, 1-Lerch, Susan Ottila, 2-born, 3-4 Oct 1863, 4-Freemansburg, Northampton Co., PA, 12-Lerch, Reuben, 13-Lerch, Sarah, 15-Lerch

#2128, 1-Lerch, Reuben, 2-married, 3-4 Oct 1853, 7-Knauss, Sarah Louisa, 10-Rev. Q.[?] C. Becker, 12-Lerch, Joseph, 13-Lerch, Susan, 15-Lerch

#2129, 1-Knauss, Sarah Louisa, 2-married, 3-4 Oct 1853, 12-Knauss, Anthony, 13-Knauus, Anna, 15-Lerch

FAMILY BIBLE RECORDS IN THE WASHINGTON COUNTY FREE LIBRARY, HAGERSTOWN, MARYLAND

Entry #, 1-Last Name, First Name, 2-Event, 3-Date, 4-Event Location, 5-Age, 6-Other,
7-Spouse's Last, First, 8-Groom's Residence, 9-Bride's Residence, 10-Minister, 11-Minister's Location,
12-Father's Last, First, 13-Mother's Last, First, 14-Transcribed, 15-Family Bible

#2130, 1-Lerch, Harvey Joseph, 2-died, 3-6 Apr 1859, 5-10 months 10 days, 12-Lerch, Reuben, 13-Lerch, Sarah, 15-Lerch

#2131, 1-Lerch, Hiram Anthony, 2-died, 3-26 Mar 1863, 5-4 years 9 months 20 days, 12-Lerch, Reuben, 13-Lerch, Sarah, 15-Lerch

#2132, 1-Herb, Susan O., 2-died, 3-23 Feb 1957, 5-93 years 4 months 19 days, 15-Lerch

#2133, 1-Lerch, Reubon O., 2-died, 3-1896, 15-Lerch

#2134, 1-Lerch, Sarah Louisa (Knauss), 2-died, 3-16 Jan 1907, 15-Lerch

#2135, 1-Miller, Anna Elizabeth (Lerch), 2-died, 3-1943, 15-Lerch

#2136, 1-Lerch, Miranda Adaline, 2-died, 3-1941, 15-Lerch

#2137, 1-Singer, Raymond Frederick, 2-baptized, 3-6 Jan 1907, 12-Singer, Frederick, 13-Getz, Rosa, 15-Lerch

#2138, 1-Singer, Raymond Frederick, 2-born, 3-10 Sep 1906, 4-Westside, 12-Singer, Frederick, 13-Getz, Rosa, 15-Lerch

#2139, 1-Daily, Grace Marguerite, 2-born, 3-4 Oct 1906, 12-Daily, George J., 13-Schantz, Ida, 15-Lerch

#2140, 1-Daily, Grace Marguerite, 2-baptized, 3-27 Jan 1907, 12-Daily, George J., 13-Schantz, Ida, 15-Lerch

#2141, 1-Stein, Evalyn Marguerite, 2-born, 3-14 Jan 1907, 6-sponsors: Clara Ackerman, John W. Smith, 12-Stein, Harvey E., 13-Smith, E., 15-Lerch

#2142, 1-Brany, Emil B., 2-married, 3-26 Jan 1907, 7-Sencenbach, Maude L. (Miss), 15-Lerch

#2143, 1-Lerch, Sarah Louise (Mrs.), 2-obituary, 3-16 Jan 1907, 5-75 years, 15-Lerch

#2144, 1-Dech, Cathrine Barbara (Mrs.), 2-obituary, 3-31 Jan 1907, 4-Allentown, PA, 5-76 years, 12-Clause, Daniel, 15-Lerch

#2145, 1-Dech, Cathrine Barbara (Mrs.), 2-born, 3-9 Sep 1831, 15-Lerch

#2146, 1-Dech, Cathrine Barbara (Mrs.), 2-baptized, 10-Father Thomas Pomp, 15-Lerch

#2147, 1-Dech, Cathrine Barbara (Mrs.), 2-married, 7-Dech, John K., 15-Lerch

#2148, 1-Lerch, Reuben O., 2-born, 3-1 Dec 1825, 4-Lower Saucon Township, 6-from obituary, 12-Lerch, Joseph, 13-Oberly, Susan, 15-Lerch

#2149, 1-Lerch, Reuben O., 2-obituary, 5-71 years, 15-Lerch

#2150, 1-Lerch, Susie O., 2-married, 3-27 Oct 1868, 4-Lewisburg, PA, 7-Herb, J. Newton, 9-J. F. DeLong, 15-Lerch

#2151, 1-Hoffman, Mary, 2-died, 3-28 Jul 1890, 14-Yes, 15-Embich

#2152, 1-Hoffman, Jr., John Adams, 2-died, 3-2 Mar 1891, 14-Yes, 15-Embich

#2153, 1-Hoffman, Donald, 2-born, 3-9 Oct 1891, 14-Yes, 15-Embich

#2154, 1-Embich, Christopher, 2-married, 3-1752, 6-bride's father is Engelhard Kutern, 7-Kutern, Maria Elizabeth, 8-Lancaster Co., PA, 9-Lancaster Co., PA, 14-Yes, 15-Embich

#2155, 1-Embich, Christopher, 2-born, 3-7 Nov 1756, 4-Lancaster Co., PA, 12-Embich, Christopher, 13-Kutern, Maria Elizabeth, 14-Yes, 15-Embich

#2156, 1-Embich, Christopher, 2-died, 3-1 Jul 1837, 4-Lancaster, OH, 5-81 years 8 months, 12-Embich, Christopher, 13-Kutern, Maria Elizabeth, 14-Yes, 15-Embich

#2157, 1-Albright, Anna Maria, 2-born, 3-25 Jun 1758, 7-Embich, Christopher, 14-Yes, 15-Embich

#2158, 1-Albright, Anna Maria, 2-died, 3-1 Sep 1846, 4-Logan, Hocking Co., OH, 7-Embich, Christopher, 14-Yes, 15-Embich

#2159, 1-Embich, Christopher, 2-married, 3-20 Jan 1779, 7-Albright, Anna Maria, 14-Yes, 15-Embich

#2160, 1-Embich, Elizabeth, 2-born, 3-26 Oct 1779, 12-Embich, Christopher, 13-Albright, Anna Maria, 14-Yes, 15-Embich

#2161, 1-Embich, Elizabeth, 2-married, 7-Bigham, Wm., 12-Embich, Christopher, 13-Albright, Anna Maria, 14-Yes, 15-Embich

FAMILY BIBLE RECORDS IN THE WASHINGTON COUNTY FREE LIBRARY, HAGERSTOWN, MARYLAND

Entry #, 1-Last Name, First Name, 2-Event, 3-Date, 4-Event Location, 5-Age, 6-Other, 7-Spouse's Last, First, 8-Groom's Residence, 9-Bride's Residence, 10-Minister, 11-Minister's Location, 12-Father's Last, First, 13-Mother's Last, First, 14-Transcribed, 15-Family Bible

#2162, 1-Embich, Elizabeth, 2-died, 4-Hagerstown, MD, 12-Embich, Christopher, 13-Albright, Anna Maria, 14-Yes, 15-Embich

#2163, 1-Embich, Jacob, 2-died, 4-Lancaster, OH, 12-Embich, Christopher, 13-Albright, Anna Maria, 14-Yes, 15-Embich

#2164, 1-Embich, Philemon, 12-Embich, Jacob, 14-Yes, 15-Embich

#2165, 1-Embich, Phillip, 2-born, 3-8 Sep 1789, 12-Embich, Christopher, 13-Albright, Anna Maria, 14-Yes, 15-Embich

#2166, 1-Embich, Phillip, 2-married, 7-Dugan, Miss, 9-PA, 12-Embich, Christopher, 13-Albright, Anna Maria, 14-Yes, 15-Embich

#2167, 1-Embich, Phillip, 2-died, 4-Cincinnati, OH, 12-Embich, Christopher, 13-Albright, Anna Maria, 14-Yes, 15-Embich

#2168, 1-Embich, Mary, 2-married, 7-Sifferd, 12-Embich, Christopher, 13-Albright, Anna Maria, 14-Yes, 15-Embich

#2169, 1-Embich, Mary, 2-died, 4-Lancaster, OH, 12-Embich, Christopher, 13-Albright, Anna Maria, 14-Yes, 15-Embich

#2170, 1-Embich, Michael, 2-born, 12-Embich, Christopher, 13-Albright, Anna Maria, 14-Yes, 15-Embich

#2171, 1-Embich, Mary, 2-born, 3-12 May 1797, 4-Lebanon, PA, 12-Embich, Christopher, 13-Albright, Anna Maria, 14-Yes, 15-Embich

#2172, 1-Embich, Mary, 2-married, 7-Smith, John Adams, 12-Embich, Christopher, 13-Albright, Anna Maria, 14-Yes, 15-Embich

#2173, 1-Embich, Mary, 2-died, 4-Logan, Hocking Co., OH, 12-Embich, Christopher, 13-Albright, Anna Maria, 14-Yes, 15-Embich

#2174, 1-Embich, Frederick, 2-born, 3-4 Jul 1799, 12-Embich, Christopher, 13-Albright, Anna Maria, 14-Yes, 15-Embich

#2175, 1-Embich, Frederick, 2-died, 4-Xenia, OH, 12-Embich, Christopher, 13-Albright, Anna Maria, 14-Yes, 15-Embich

#2176, 1-Embich, Eleanor, 2-born, 3-1800-1803, 4-Hagerstown, MD, 12-Embich, Christopher, 13-Albright, Anna Maria, 14-Yes, 15-Embich

#2177, 1-Embich, Eleanor, 2-married, 4-Lancaster, OH, 5-26 years, 7-Harrison, T.L., 12-Embich, Christopher, 13-Albright, Anna Maria, 14-Yes, 15-Embich

#2178, 1-Embich, Eleanor, 2-died, 4-Napoleon, OH, 12-Embich, Christopher, 13-Albright, Anna Maria, 14-Yes, 15-Embich

#2179, 1-Harrison, Mary E., 2-married, 3-circa 1847, 7-Taylor, H.D., 8-Providence, OH, 12-Harrison, T.L., 13-Embich, Eleanor, 14-Yes, 15-Embich

#2180, 1-Harrison, Mary E., 2-died, 4-Napoleon, OH, 12-Harrison, T.L., 13-Embich, Eleanor, 14-Yes, 15-Embich

#2181, 1-Smith, Robert, 2-born, 3-1 Nov 1753, 4-Chambersburg, PA, 14-Yes, 15-Embich

#2182, 1-Smith, Susan Line, 2-born, 3-1766, 14-Yes, 15-Embich

#2183, 1-Smith, Susan Line, 2-married, 3-12 May 1791, 4-Chambersburg, PA, 7-Smith, Robert, 14-Yes, 15-Embich

#2184, 1-Smith, John Adams, 2-born, 3-10 May 1799, 4-Chambersburg, PA, 12-Smith, Robert, 13-Line, Susan, 14-Yes, 15-Embich

#2185, 1-Smith, John Adams, 2-married, 3-12 Sep 1824, 4-Lancaster, OH, 7-Embich, Mary, 10-Michael Steck, 14-Yes, 15-Embich

#2186, 1-Smith, Mary Jane, 2-born, 3-3 Jan 1828, 4-Logan, Hocking Co., OH, 12-Smith, John Adams, 13-Embich, Mary, 14-Yes, 15-Embich

#2187, 1-Smith, Mary Jane, 2-married, 3-5 Sep 1850, 4-Logan, Hocking Co., OH, 7-Brown, Edgar T. (Dr.), 10-Rev. J.B. Shelton, 12-Smith, John Adams, 13-Embich, Mary, 14-Yes, 15-Embich

#2188, 1-Brown, Edgar T. (Dr.), 2-died, 3-1 Jun 1855, 14-Yes, 15-Embich

#2189, 1-Brown, Ella Sophia, 2-born, 14-Yes, 15-Embich

#2190, 1-Smith, Mary Jane, 2-married, 3-14 Sep 1856, 7-Officer, Samuel P., 8-Chicago, IL, 10-Rev. T.D. Martindale, 14-Yes, 15-Embich

FAMILY BIBLE RECORDS IN THE WASHINGTON COUNTY FREE LIBRARY, HAGERSTOWN, MARYLAND

Entry #, 1-Last Name, First Name, 2-Event, 3-Date, 4-Event Location, 5-Age, 6-Other,
7-Spouse's Last, First, 8-Groom's Residence, 9-Bride's Residence, 10-Minister, 11-Minister's Location,
12-Father's Last, First, 13-Mother's Last, First, 14-Transcribed, 15-Family Bible

```
#2191, 1-Brown, Ella Sophia, 2-born, 3-2 Jun 1851, 4-Logan, Hocking Co., OH, 12-
     Brown, Edgar T. (Dr.), 13-Smith, Mary Jane, 14-Yes, 15-Embich
#2192, 1-Officer, Edgar T., 2-born, 3-21 Jun 1857, 4-Chicago, IL, 12-Officer,
     Samuel P., 13-Smith, Mary Jane, 14-Yes, 15-Embich
#2193, 1-Officer, Jennie C., 2-born, 3-9 Aug 1862, 4-Meadville, PA, 12-Officer,
     Samuel P., 13-Smith, Mary Jane, 14-Yes, 15-Embich
#2194, 1-Officer, Gertrude H., 2-born, 3-21 Jul 1865, 4-Meadville, PA, 12-Officer,
     Samuel P., 13-Smith, Mary Jane, 14-Yes, 15-Embich
#2195, 1-Officer, Arthur H., 2-born, 3-27 Nov 1863, 4-Meadville, PA, 12-Officer,
     Samuel P., 13-Smith, Mary Jane, 14-Yes, 15-Embich
#2196, 1-Officer, Florence M., 2-born, 3-3 Feb 1867, 4-Meadville, PA, 12-Officer,
     Samuel P., 13-Smith, Mary Jane, 14-Yes, 15-Embich
#2197, 1-Officer, Robert A., 2-born, 3-16 Jan 1870, 4-Meadville, PA, 12-Officer,
     Samuel P., 13-Smith, Mary Jane, 14-Yes, 15-Embich
#2198, 1-Officer, Arthur H., 2-married, 3-30 Nov 1884, 4-Blooming Valley, PA, 14-
     Yes, 15-Embich
#2199, 1-Smith, Emily , 2-born, 3-18 Jan 1830, 4-Logan, Hocking Co., OH, 12-Smith,
     John A., 13-Embrich, Mary, 14-Yes, 15-Embich
#2200, 1-Smith, Emily, 2-married, 3-16 Nov 1848, 4-Logan, OH, 7-Hoffman, David
     Allen (Dr.), 10-Rev. W.R. Litsinger, 14-Yes, 15-Embich
#2201, 1-Hoffman, Edgar Brown, 2-born, 3-21 Aug 1849, 4-Jackson C.H., OH, 12-
     Hoffman, David Allen (Dr.), 13-Smith, Emily, 14-Yes, 15-Embich
#2202, 1-Hoffman, John Adams, 2-born, 3-23 Apr 1851, 4-Jackson C.H., OH, 12-
     Hoffman, David Allen (Dr.), 13-Smith, Emily, 14-Yes, 15-Embich
#2203, 1-Hoffman, Effie Louise, 2-born, 3-13 May 1853, 4-Jackson C.H., OH, 12-
     Hoffman, David Allen (Dr.), 13-Smith, Emily, 14-Yes, 15-Embich
#2204, 1-Hoffman, Ripley Christian (Dr.), 2-born, 3-12 Nov 1860, 4-Logan, Hocking
     Co., OH, 12-Hoffman, David Allen (Dr.), 13-Smith, Emily, 14-Yes, 15-Embich
#2205, 1-Hoffman, Edgar Brown, 2-married, 3-21[or 24] Jun 1879, 4-Oskaloosa, Iowa,
     10-Rev. W.H. H. Pillsbury, 14-Yes, 15-Embich
#2206, 1-Hoffman, Effie R., 2-born, 12-Hoffman, Edgar Brown, 14-Yes, 15-Embich
#2207, 1-Hoffman, David A., 2-born, 12-Hoffman, Edgar Brown, 14-Yes, 15-Embich
#2208, 1-Hoffman, Russell Embich, 2-born, 12-Hoffman, Edgar Brown, 14-Yes, 15-
     Embich
#2209, 1-Hoffman, Victor, 2-born, 12-Hoffman, Edgar Brown, 14-Yes, 15-Embich
#2210, 1-Hoffman, Verona, 2-born, 12-Hoffman, Edgar Brown, 14-Yes, 15-Embich
#2211, 1-Hoffman, John Adams, 2-married, 3-15 Dec 1875, 4-Mt. Pleasant, Iowa, 7-
     Wallace, Anna, 10-Rev. D.S. Tappan, 14-Yes, 15-Embich
#2212, 1-Hoffman, Wallace, 2-born, 12-Hoffman, John Adams, 13-Wallace, Anna, 14-
     Yes, 15-Embich
#2213, 1-Hoffman, Mary, 2-born, 12-Hoffman, John Adams, 13-Wallace, Anna, 14-Yes,
     15-Embich
#2214, 1-Hoffman, Ripley C., 2-born, 12-Hoffman, John Adams, 13-Wallace, Anna, 14-
     Yes, 15-Embich
#2215, 1-Hoffman, David A., 2-born, 12-Hoffman, John Adams, 13-Wallace, Anna, 14-
     Yes, 15-Embich
#2216, 1-Hoffman, John Adams, 2-born, 12-Hoffman, John Adams, 13-Wallace, Anna, 14-
     Yes, 15-Embich
#2217, 1-Hoffman, Mary , 2-died, 5-12 years, 12-Hoffman, John Adams, 13-Wallace,
     Anna, 14-Yes, 15-Embich
#2218, 1-Hoffman, Effie Louise, 2-married, 3-25 Apr 1880, 4-Oskaloosa, Iowa, 7-
     Rogers, John F., 10-Rev. J.C.W. Coxe, 14-Yes, 15-Embich
#2219, 1-Rogers, Emily J., 2-born, 3-13 Mar 1882, 4-Great Bend, Barton Co., Kansas,
     12-Rogers, John F., 13-Hoffman, Effie Louise, 14-Yes, 15-Embich
#2220, 1-Rogers, John F., 2-died, 3-9 Aug 1883, 14-Yes, 15-Embich
```

FAMILY BIBLE RECORDS IN THE WASHINGTON COUNTY FREE LIBRARY, HAGERSTOWN, MARYLAND

Entry #, 1-Last Name, First Name, 2-Event, 3-Date, 4-Event Location, 5-Age, 6-Other, 7-Spouse's Last, First, 8-Groom's Residence, 9-Bride's Residence, 10-Minister, 11-Minister's Location, 12-Father's Last, First, 13-Mother's Last, First, 14-Transcribed, 15-Family Bible

#2221, 1-Smith, Horace Christopher, 2-born, 3-22 Jun 1832, 4-Logan, OH, 14-Yes, 15-Embich

#2222, 1-Smith, Horace Christopher, 2-married, 3-14 Mar 1865, 4-Logan, OH, 7-Steinman, Sophia E., 10-Rev. C.C. Hart, 14-Yes, 15-Embich

#2223, 1-Steinman, Sophia E., 2-born, 3-2 Dec 1842, 4-Lancaster, OH, 14-Yes, 15-Embich

#2224, 1-Smith, John Adams, 12-Smith, Horace Christopher, 13-Steinman, Sophia, 14-Yes, 15-Embich

#2225, 1-Smith, Augustus Kenley, 12-Smith, Horace Christopher, 13-Steinman, Sophia, 14-Yes, 15-Embich

#2226, 1-Smith, Warren, 12-Smith, Horace Christopher, 13-Steinman, Sophia, 14-Yes, 15-Embich

#2227, 1-Smith, Sophia, 12-Smith, Horace Christopher, 13-Steinman, Sophia, 14-Yes, 15-Embich

#2228, 1-Smith, Mary, 12-Smith, Horace Christopher, 13-Steinman, Sophia, 14-Yes, 15-Embich

#2229, 1-Smith, Robert, 2-married, 3-27 Apr 1779, 14-Yes, 15-Smith

#2230, 1-Smith, Jean, 2-born, 3-27 Mar 1780, 14-Yes, 15-Smith

#2231, 1-Smith, William, 2-born, 3-19 Jun 1782, 14-Yes, 15-Smith

#2232, 1-Smith, Emily, 2-born, 3-3 Feb 1784, 14-Yes, 15-Smith

#2233, 1-Smith, Julean, 2-born, 3-31 Jul 1786, 14-Yes, 15-Smith

#2234, 1-Smith, Matilda, 2-born, 3-28 Jun 1788, 14-Yes, 15-Smith

#2235, 1-Smith, Margrete, 2-died, 3-1 Dec 1788, 14-Yes, 15-Smith

#2236, 1-Smith, Robert, 2-married, 3-4 Aug 1789, 7-Fleming, Elizabeth, 14-Yes, 15-Smith

#2237, 1-Smith, Elizabeth, 2-died, 3-13 Jun 1790, 14-Yes, 15-Smith

#2238, 1-Smith, Robert, 2-married, 3-12 May 1791, 7-Line, Suana (Susan?), 14-Yes, 15-Smith

#2239, 1-Smith, Betsey, 2-died, 3-7 Mar 1792, 14-Yes, 15-Smith

#2240, 1-Smith, George W., 2-born, 3-2 Dec 1792, 14-Yes, 15-Smith

#2241, 1-Smith, Benjamin F., 2-born, 3-17 Oct 1794, 14-Yes, 15-Smith

#2242, 1-Smith, John A., 2-born, 3-10 May 1799, 4-Chambersburg, PA, 14-Yes, 15-Smith

#2243, 1-Smith, Robert, 2-died, 3-9 Mar 1813, 5-60 years, 14-Yes, 15-Smith

#2244, 1-Smith, Susan, 2-died, 3-28 Sep 1821, 5-55 years, 14-Yes, 15-Smith

#2245, 1-Smith, John A., 2-married, 3-12 Sep 1824, 4-Lancaster, OH, 7-Embich, Mary, 10-Michael Steck, 14-Yes, 15-Smith

#2246, 1-Smith, Mary Jane, 2-born, 3-3 Jan 1828, 4-Logan, Hocking Co., OH, 14-Yes, 15-Smith

#2247, 1-Smith, Emily, 2-born, 3-30 Jan 1830, 4-Logan, OH, 14-Yes, 15-Smith

#2248, 1-Smith, Horace C., 2-born, 3-22 Jun 1832, 4-Logan, OH, 14-Yes, 15-Smith

#2249, 1-Bass, John, 2-born, 3-27 Nov 1738, 14-Yes, 15-Bass

#2250, 1-Bass, Martha, 2-born, 3-17 Apr 1762, 12-Bass, John, 13-Bass, Tabitha, 14-Yes, 15-Bass

#2251, 1-Bass, Tabitha, 2-born, 3-3 Oct 1763, 12-Bass, John, 13-Bass, Tabitha, 14-Yes, 15-Bass

#2252, 1-Bass, Agnes, 2-born, 3-23 May 1765, 12-Bass, John, 13-Bass, Tabitha, 14-Yes, 15-Bass

#2253, 1-Bass, Ezebath, 2-born, 3-27 Feb 1767, 12-Bass, John, 13-Bass, Tabitha, 14-Yes, 15-Bass

#2254, 1-Bass, Mary, 2-born, 3-24 Aug 1768, 12-Bass, John, 13-Bass, Tabitha, 14-Yes, 15-Bass

#2255, 1-Bass, Frances, 2-born, 3-14 ___ 1770, 12-Bass, John, 13-Bass, Tabitha, 14-Yes, 15-Bass

FAMILY BIBLE RECORDS IN THE WASHINGTON COUNTY FREE LIBRARY, HAGERSTOWN, MARYLAND

Entry #, 1-Last Name, First Name, 2-Event, 3-Date, 4-Event Location, 5-Age, 6-Other,
7-Spouse's Last, First, 8-Groom's Residence, 9-Bride's Residence, 10-Minister, 11-Minister's Location,
12-Father's Last, First, 13-Mother's Last, First, 14-Transcribed, 15-Family Bible

```
#2256, 1-Bass, John, 2-born, 3-14 Mar 1772, 12-Bass, John, 13-Bass, Tabitha, 14-
    Yes, 15-Bass
#2257, 1-Bass, Edward, 2-born, 3-24 Apr 1776, 12-Bass, John, 13-Bass, Tabitha, 14-
    Yes, 15-Bass
#2258, 1-Bass, Nancy, 2-born, 3-20 Nov 1777, 12-Bass, John, 13-Bass, Tabitha, 14-
    Yes, 15-Bass
#2259, 1-Bass, Lucy, 2-born, 3-18 Sep 1781, 12-Bass, John, 13-Bass, Tabitha, 14-
    Yes, 15-Bass
#2260, 1-Dyson, Richard E., 2-born, 3-19 Nov 1837, 14-Yes, 15-Bass
#2261, 1-Dyson, H.H., 2-born, 3-29 Dec 1840, 14-Yes, 15-Bass
#2262, 1-Dyson, Tabitha, 2-died, 3-25 Jun 1845, 14-Yes, 15-Bass
#2263, 1-Dyson, [baby], 2-born, 3-9 May 1843, 12-Dyson, Thomas, 13-Bass, Tabitha,
    14-Yes, 15-Bass
#2264, 1-Dyson, Thomas W., 2-died, 3-12 May 1856, 14-Yes, 15-Bass
#2265, 1-Dyson, Harry H., 2-born, 3-29 Dec 18__, 14-Yes, 15-Bass
#2266, 1-Dyson, E.R., 2-died, 3-18 Mar 1945, 4-Medical College Virginia, 14-Yes,
    15-Bass
#2267, 1-Dyson, Tabitha, 2-died, 3-25 Jun 1843, 14-Yes, 15-Bass
#2268, 1-Dyson, [baby], 2-born, 3-9 May 1843, 12-Dyson, Thomas, 13-Bass, Tabitha,
    14-Yes, 15-Bass
#2269, 1-Bukey, John (Colonel), 2-married, 4-New Jersey, 7-Dunn, Jemima, 9-Sussex
    Co., NJ, 14-Yes, 15-Bukey
#2270, 1-Dunn, Jemima, 2-born, 12-Dunn, Hezekiah, 13-Dunn, Marcia, 14-Yes, 15-Bukey
#2271, 1-Bukey, John (Colonel), 2-died, 3-circa Feb 1778, 14-Yes, 15-Bukey
#2272, 1-Bukey, Jr., John, 2-born, 3-22 Feb 1761, 12-Bukey, John (Colonel), 14-Yes,
    15-Bukey
#2273, 1-Bukey, Jr., John, 2-died, 3-18 Oct 1815, 12-Bukey, John (Colonel), 14-Yes,
    15-Bukey
#2274, 1-Bukey, Jr., John, 2-married, 7-McMahon, Nancy, 12-Bukey, John (Colonel),
    14-Yes, 15-Bukey
#2275, 1-McMahon, Nancy, 2-born, 3-4 Aug 1775, 12-McMahon, John (Major), 14-Yes,
    15-Bukey
#2276, 1-McMahon, Nancy, 2-died, 3-Jul 1860, 12-McMahon, John (Major), 14-Yes, 15-
    Bukey
#2277, 1-Bukey, Marcia, 2-married, 3-1798, 7-Greathouse, Harmon (Colonel), 12-
    Bukey, John (Colonel), 14-Yes, 15-Bukey
#2278, 1-Bukey, Elizabeth, 2-married, 7-Rowland, Abraham, 12-Bukey, John (Colonel),
    14-Yes, 15-Bukey
#2279, 1-Bukey, Elizabeth, 2-died, 3-1850, 4-West Liberty, WV, 14-Yes, 15-Bukey
#2280, 1-Bukey, Mary, 2-married, 7-McColloch, John (Major), 12-Bukey, John
    (Colonel), 14-Yes, 15-Bukey
#2281, 1-Bukey, Hezekiah, 2-born, 3-25 Apr 1770, 4-New Jersey, 12-Bukey, John
    (Colonel), 14-Yes, 15-Bukey
#2282, 1-Bukey, Hezekiah, 2-died, 3-31 Dec 1827, 6-buried Bukey Farm, Williamstown,
    WV, 14-Yes, 15-Bukey
#2283, 1-Bukey, Hezekiah, 2-married, 3-1 Jan 1798, 7-Tomlinson, Drusilla, 14-Yes,
    15-Bukey
#2284, 1-Tomlinson, Drusilla, 2-born, 3-17 Apr 1777, 12-Tomlinson, Joseph
    (Colonel), 14-Yes, 15-Bukey
#2285, 1-Tomlinson, Drusilla, 2-died, 3-22 Apr 1854, 12-Tomlinson, Joseph
    (Colonel), 14-Yes, 15-Bukey
#2286, 1-Tomlinson, Rudolf Adolfus, 2-married, 7-Briscoe, Sarah, 12-Bukey, John
    (Colonel), 14-Yes, 15-Bukey
#2287, 1-Tomlinson, Jemima, 2-born, 3-5 Apr 1777, 12-Bukey, John (Colonel), 14-Yes,
    15-Bukey
```

FAMILY BIBLE RECORDS IN THE WASHINGTON COUNTY FREE LIBRARY, HAGERSTOWN, MARYLAND

Entry #, 1-Last Name, First Name, 2-Event, 3-Date, 4-Event Location, 5-Age, 6-Other,
7-Spouse's Last, First, 8-Groom's Residence, 9-Bride's Residence, 10-Minister, 11-Minister's Location,
12-Father's Last, First, 13-Mother's Last, First, 14-Transcribed, 15-Family Bible

```
#2288, 1-Tomlinson, Jemima, 2-died, 3-25 Sep 1829, 4-Wellsburg, VA, 14-Yes, 15-
     Bukey
#2289, 1-Tomlinson, Jemima, 2-married, 3-4 May 1794, 7-Dodderidge, Joseph (Dr.),
     14-Yes, 15-Bukey
#2290, 1-Bukey, Nancy, 12-Bukey, Jr., John, 13-McMahon, Nancy, 14-Yes, 15-Bukey
#2291, 1-Bukey, William, 12-Bukey, Jr., John, 13-McMahon, Nancy, 14-Yes, 15-Bukey
#2292, 1-Bukey, Jemima, 12-Bukey, Jr., John, 13-McMahon, Nancy, 14-Yes, 15-Bukey
#2293, 1-Bukey, III, John, 12-Bukey, Jr., John, 13-McMahon, Nancy, 14-Yes, 15-Bukey
#2294, 1-Bukey, Mary, 12-Bukey, Jr., John, 13-McMahon, Nancy, 14-Yes, 15-Bukey
#2295, 1-Bukey, James, 12-Bukey, Jr., John, 13-McMahon, Nancy, 14-Yes, 15-Bukey
#2296, 1-Bukey, Fleming, 12-Bukey, Jr., John, 13-McMahon, Nancy, 14-Yes, 15-Bukey
#2297, 1-Bukey, Susannah, 12-Bukey, Jr., John, 13-McMahon, Nancy, 14-Yes, 15-Bukey
#2298, 1-Bukey, Joseph, 12-Bukey, Jr., John, 13-McMahon, Nancy, 14-Yes, 15-Bukey
#2299, 1-Bukey, Elizabeth Ann, 12-Bukey, Jr., John, 13-McMahon, Nancy, 14-Yes, 15-
     Bukey
#2300, 1-Bukey, Massey, 12-Bukey, Jr., John, 13-McMahon, Nancy, 14-Yes, 15-Bukey
#2301, 1-Greathouse, Luther, 12-Greathouse, Harmon (Colonel), 13-Bukey, Marcia, 14-
     Yes, 15-Bukey
#2302, 1-Greathouse, Isaac, 12-Greathouse, Harmon (Colonel), 13-Bukey, Marcia, 14-
     Yes, 15-Bukey
#2303, 1-Greathouse, John, 12-Greathouse, Harmon (Colonel), 13-Bukey, Marcia, 14-
     Yes, 15-Bukey
#2304, 1-Greathouse, Joseph , 12-Greathouse, Harmon (Colonel), 13-Bukey, Marcia,
     14-Yes, 15-Bukey
#2305, 1-Bukey, Lucinda, 12-Bukey, Hezekiah, 13-Tomlinson, Drusilla, 14-Yes, 15-
     Bukey
#2306, 1-Bukey, Elizabeth, 12-Bukey, Hezekiah, 13-Tomlinson, Drusilla, 14-Yes, 15-
     Bukey
#2307, 1-Bukey, Tabitha, 12-Bukey, Hezekiah, 13-Tomlinson, Drusilla, 14-Yes, 15-
     Bukey
#2308, 1-Bukey, Mary Ann, 12-Bukey, Hezekiah, 13-Tomlinson, Drusilla, 14-Yes, 15-
     Bukey
#2309, 1-Bukey, Spencer Tomlinson, 12-Bukey, Hezekiah, 13-Tomlinson, Drusilla, 14-
     Yes, 15-Bukey
#2310, 1-Bukey, Van Hartness, 12-Bukey, Hezekiah, 13-Tomlinson, Drusilla, 14-Yes,
     15-Bukey
#2311, 1-Bukey, William S., 12-Bukey, Hezekiah, 13-Tomlinson, Drusilla, 14-Yes, 15-
     Bukey
#2312, 1-Bukey, John, 12-Bukey, Hezekiah, 13-Tomlinson, Drusilla, 14-Yes, 15-Bukey
#2313, 1-Bukey, Isaac W., 12-Bukey, Hezekiah, 13-Tomlinson, Drusilla, 14-Yes, 15-
     Bukey
#2314, 1-Bukey, Susannah, 12-Bukey, Hezekiah, 13-Tomlinson, Drusilla, 14-Yes, 15-
     Bukey
#2315, 1-Bukey, Julius, 12-Bukey, Rudolf, 13-Brisco, Sarah, 14-Yes, 15-Bukey
#2316, 1-Bukey, Elizabeth, 12-Bukey, Rudolf, 13-Brisco, Sarah, 14-Yes, 15-Bukey
#2317, 1-Bukey, Caroline, 12-Bukey, Rudolf, 13-Brisco, Sarah, 14-Yes, 15-Bukey
#2318, 1-Bukey, Harriet, 12-Bukey, Rudolf, 13-Brisco, Sarah, 14-Yes, 15-Bukey
#2319, 1-Gilchrist, Sr., Malcolm, 2-born, 3-8 Feb 1744, 4-Cantyre, Scotland, 6-from
     gravestone, 14-Yes, 15-Gilchrist
#2320, 1-Gilchrist, Sr., Malcolm, 2-died, 3-12 Apr 1821, 5-77 years 2 months 4
     days, 6-from gravestone, 14-Yes, 15-Gilchrist
#2321, 1-Gilchrist, Catharine, 2-born, 3-30 Jun 1752, 4-Cumberland Co, NC, 6-from
     gravestone, 7-Gilchrist, Sr., Malcolm, 14-Yes, 15-Gilchrist
#2322, 1-Gilchrist, Catharine, 2-died, 3-5 Oct 1839, 5-87 years 3 months 5 days, 6-
     from gravestone, 14-Yes, 15-Gilchrist
```

FAMILY BIBLE RECORDS IN THE WASHINGTON COUNTY FREE LIBRARY, HAGERSTOWN, MARYLAND

Entry #, 1-Last Name, First Name, 2-Event, 3-Date, 4-Event Location, 5-Age, 6-Other, 7-Spouse's Last, First, 8-Groom's Residence, 9-Bride's Residence, 10-Minister, 11-Minister's Location, 12-Father's Last, First, 13-Mother's Last, First, 14-Transcribed, 15-Family Bible

#2323, 1-Brahan, John C., 2-born, 3-1 Dec 1819, 4-Huntsville, AL, 6-from gravestone, 12-Brahan, John (General), 13-Weakley, Mary, 14-Yes, 15-Brahan

#2324, 1-Brahan, John C., 2-died, 3-29 Jun 1888, 4-Panola Co., MS, 6-from gravestone, 14-Yes, 15-Brahan

#2325, 1-Brahan, Mary C., 2-born, 4-Franklin Co., NC, 6-from gravestone, 14-Yes, 15-Brahan

#2326, 1-Brahan, Mary C., 2-died, 3-9 Nov 1848, 4-Panola Co., MS, 5-25 years, 6-from gravestone, 7-Brahan, John C., 12-Haywood, John, 13-Haywood, John, 14-Yes, 15-Brahan

#2327, 1-Gilchrist, Daniel, 2-born, 3-22 Dec 1788, 6-from gravestone, 14-Yes, 15-Gilchrist

#2328, 1-Gilchrist, Daniel, 2-died, 3-24 Jul 1855, 6-from gravestone, 14-Yes, 15-Gilchrist

#2329, 1-Gilchrist, Nancy A., 2-born, 3-21 Jan 1793, 6-from gravestone, 14-Yes, 15-Gilchrist

#2330, 1-Gilchrist, Nancy A., 2-died, 3-May 1863, 6-from gravestone, 14-Yes, 15-Gilchrist

#2331, 1-Brown, Jesse Jacob, 2-married, 3-30 May 1908, 4-Hagerstown, MD, 7-Brown, Marjorie Clyde, 8-Foxville, Frederick Co., MD, 9-Mt. Bethel, Frederick Co., MD, 10-A.M. Evers, 15-Brown

#2332, 1-Brown, Jesse Jacob, 2-born, 12-Brown, George W., 13-Swope, Mary Ann, 15-Brown

#2333, 1-Brown, Marjorie C., 2-born, 12-Brown, David C., 13-Lumn, Sara Alice, 15-Brown

#2334, 1-Swope, Mary Ann, 2-born, 13-Swope, Louisa, 15-Brown

#2335, 1-Brown, David C., 2-born, 12-Brown, Ezra, 13-Smiths, Mary D., 15-Brown

#2336, 1-Lumn, Sara Alice, 2-born, 12-Lumn, Henry, 13-Haynes, Sara Lavina, 15-Brown

#2337, 1-Haynes, Sara Lavina, 2-died, 3-11 Aug 1865, 5-32[?] years 1 months 2 days, 15-Brown

#2338, 1-Brown, Mahlon J., 2-born, 12-Brown, Jesse J., 13-Brown, Marjorie C., 15-Brown

#2339, 1-Brown, Mahlon J., 2-married, 7-Toms, Viola, 15-Brown

#2340, 1-Brown, Robert, 2-born, 3-1931, 12-Brown, Mahlon J., 13-Toms, Viola, 15-Brown

#2341, 1-Brown, Donald, 2-born, 3-1933, 12-Brown, Mahlon J., 13-Toms, Viola, 15-Brown

#2342, 1-Brown, Gladys, 2-born, 3-1934, 12-Brown, Mahlon J., 13-Toms, Viola, 15-Brown

#2343, 1-Brown, Nina P., 2-born, 3-1912, 12-Brown, Jesse J., 13-Brown, Marjorie C., 15-Brown

#2344, 1-Brown, Nina P., 2-married, 7-Glenn, Herman C., 15-Brown

#2345, 1-Brown, Nina P., 2-married, 7-Bohn, Melvin, 15-Brown

#2346, 1-Brown, Nina P., 2-died, 3-1959, 15-Brown

#2347, 1-Glenn/Bohn, Herman, 2-born, 3-1931, 13-Brown, Nina P., 15-Brown

#2348, 1-Glenn/Bohn, Nancy, 2-born, 3-1833, 13-Brown, Nina P., 15-Brown

#2349, 1-Glenn/Bohn, Rethabelle, 2-born, 3-1936, 13-Brown, Nina P., 15-Brown

#2350, 1-Glenn/Bohn, Betty, 2-born, 3-1938, 13-Brown, Nina P., 15-Brown

#2351, 1-Glenn/Bohn, Donna, 2-born, 3-1942, 13-Brown, Nina P., 15-Brown

#2352, 1-Glenn/Bohn, Peggy, 2-born, 3-1948, 13-Brown, Nina P., 15-Brown

#2353, 1-Glenn/Bohn, Butch, 2-born, 3-1951, 13-Brown, Nina P., 15-Brown

#2354, 1-Glenn, Herman C., 2-born, 3-1907, 15-Brown

#2355, 1-Brown, Carmen I., 2-born, 3-12 Jun 1915, 12-Brown, Jesse J., 13-Brown, Marjorie C., 15-Brown

#2356, 1-Brown, Jesse David, 2-born, 3-Jun 1919, 12-Brown, Jesse J., 13-Brown, Marjorie C., 15-Brown

FAMILY BIBLE RECORDS IN THE WASHINGTON COUNTY FREE LIBRARY, HAGERSTOWN, MARYLAND

Entry #, 1-Last Name, First Name, 2-Event, 3-Date, 4-Event Location, 5-Age, 6-Other,
7-Spouse's Last, First, 8-Groom's Residence, 9-Bride's Residence, 10-Minister, 11-Minister's Location,
12-Father's Last, First, 13-Mother's Last, First, 14-Transcribed, 15-Family Bible

```
#2357, 1-Brown, Ruby K., 2-born, 3-1921, 12-Brown, Jesse J., 13-Brown, Marjorie C.,
    15-Brown
#2358, 1-Brown, Carmen I., 2-married, 7-Smith, Gilbert, 15-Brown
#2359, 1-Smith, Jackie, 12-Smith, Gilbert, 13-Brown, Carmen I., 15-Brown
#2360, 1-Smith, Patsy, 12-Smith, Gilbert, 13-Brown, Carmen I., 15-Brown
#2361, 1-Smith, Peggy, 12-Smith, Gilbert, 13-Brown, Carmen I., 15-Brown
#2362, 1-Smith, Roberta, 12-Smith, Gilbert, 13-Brown, Carmen I., 15-Brown
#2363, 1-Smith, Doris, 12-Smith, Gilbert, 13-Brown, Carmen I., 15-Brown
#2364, 1-Brown, Jesse David, 2-married, 7-Piper, Beula, 15-Brown
#2365, 1-Brown, David, 12-Brown, Jesse David, 13-Piper, Beula, 15-Brown
#2366, 1-Brown, John, 12-Brown, Jesse David, 13-Piper, Beula, 15-Brown
#2367, 1-Brown, Richard, 12-Brown, Jesse David, 13-Piper, Beula, 15-Brown
#2368, 1-Brown, Irene, 12-Brown, Jesse David, 13-Piper, Beula, 15-Brown
#2369, 1-Brown, Terry, 12-Brown, Jesse David, 13-Piper, Beula, 15-Brown
#2370, 1-Brown, Mary Ann, 12-Brown, Jesse David, 13-Piper, Beula, 15-Brown
#2371, 1-Brown, Robert, 12-Brown, Jesse David, 13-Piper, Beula, 15-Brown
#2372, 1-Brown, Ruby K., 2-married, 7-Sowers, Charles, 12-Brown, Jesse David, 13-
    Piper, Beula, 15-Brown
#2373, 1-Sowers, Alice, 12-Sowers, Charles, 13-Brown, Ruby K., 15-Brown
#2374, 1-Sowers, Wilma, 12-Sowers, Charles, 13-Brown, Ruby K., 15-Brown
#2375, 1-Sowers, Karen, 12-Sowers, Charles, 13-Brown, Ruby K., 15-Brown
#2376, 1-Sowers, Becky, 12-Sowers, Charles, 13-Brown, Ruby K., 15-Brown
#2377, 1-Sowers, Janice, 12-Sowers, Charles, 13-Brown, Ruby K., 15-Brown
#2378, 1-Delauter, Charles R., 2-died, 4-Korea, 15-Brown
#2379, 1-Brown, Dixie F., 2-born, 3-1929, 15-Brown
#2380, 1-Brown, Wayne, 2-born, 3-10-Oct-52, 15-Brown
#2381, 1-Brown, Judith D., 2-born, 3-Aug 1955, 15-Brown
#2382, 1-Brown, Rosalie G., 2-born, 3-9 Nov 1956, 15-Brown
#2383, 1-Liskey, Robert Clinton, 2-married, 3-15 Jul 1879, 4-home of John M. Brown,
    7-Brown, Ida Catherine, 14-Yes, 15-Liskey
#2384, 1-Liskey, Roberft Clinton, 2-born, 3-13 Jul 1855, 14-Yes, 15-Liskey
#2385, 1-Liskey, Roberft Clinton, 2-died, 3-18 May 1915, 14-Yes, 15-Liskey
#2386, 1-Liskey, Ida Catherine (Brown), 2-born, 3-7 Sep 1860, 14-Yes, 15-Liskey
#2387, 1-Liskey, Ida Catherine (Brown), 2-died, 3-Sep 1938, 14-Yes, 15-Liskey
#2388, 1-Liskey, Luther Harring, 2-born, 3-30 Jun 1880, 12-Liskey, Robert Clinton,
    13-Brown, Ida Catherine, 14-Yes, 15-Liskey
#2389, 1-Liskey, Luther Harring, 2-died, 3-8 Dec 1880, 12-Liskey, Robert Clinton,
    13-Brown, Ida Catherine, 14-Yes, 15-Liskey
#2390, 1-Liskey, John Michael, 2-born, 3-2 Apr 1883, 12-Liskey, Robert Clinton, 13-
    Brown, Ida Catherine, 14-Yes, 15-Liskey
#2391, 1-Liskey, John Michael, 2-died, 3-23-Oct-55, 12-Liskey, Robert Clinton, 13-
    Brown, Ida Catherine, 14-Yes, 15-Liskey
#2392, 1-Liskey, Emma Theresa, 2-born, 3-13 Dec 1881, 12-Liskey, Robert Clinton,
    13-Brown, Ida Catherine, 14-Yes, 15-Liskey
#2393, 1-Liskey, Stella Pearl, 2-born, 3-31 Jan 1885, 12-Liskey, Robert Clinton,
    13-Brown, Ida Catherine, 14-Yes, 15-Liskey
#2394, 1-Liskey, Stella Pearl, 2-died, 3-7 May, 12-Liskey, Robert Clinton, 13-
    Brown, Ida Catherine, 14-Yes, 15-Liskey
#2395, 1-Liskey, Winnie D., 2-born, 3-20 Sep 1886, 12-Liskey, Robert Clinton, 13-
    Brown, Ida Catherine, 14-Yes, 15-Liskey
#2396, 1-Liskey, Winnie D., 2-died, 3-19 Mar 1958, 12-Liskey, Robert Clinton, 13-
    Brown, Ida Catherine, 14-Yes, 15-Liskey
#2397, 1-Liskey, Robert Brown, 2-born, 3-21 Jun 1887[or 1888], 12-Liskey, Robert
    Clinton, 13-Brown, Ida Catherine, 14-Yes, 15-Liskey
```

FAMILY BIBLE RECORDS IN THE WASHINGTON COUNTY FREE LIBRARY, HAGERSTOWN, MARYLAND

Entry #, 1-Last Name, First Name, 2-Event, 3-Date, 4-Event Location, 5-Age, 6-Other,
7-Spouse's Last, First, 8-Groom's Residence, 9-Bride's Residence, 10-Minister, 11-Minister's Location,
12-Father's Last, First, 13-Mother's Last, First, 14-Transcribed, 15-Family Bible

#2398, 1-Liskey, Robert Brown, 2-died, 3-8 Aug 1964, 12-Liskey, Robert Clinton, 13-Brown, Ida Catherine, 14-Yes, 15-Liskey

#2399, 1-Liskey, Leon Wilson, 2-born, 3-16 Apr 1890, 12-Liskey, Robert Clinton, 13-Brown, Ida Catherine, 14-Yes, 15-Liskey

#2400, 1-Liskey, Leon Wilson, 2-died, 3-7 Mar 1950, 12-Liskey, Robert Clinton, 13-Brown, Ida Catherine, 14-Yes, 15-Liskey

#2401, 1-Liskey, Catherine Marie, 2-born, 3-9-Oct-00, 12-Liskey, Robert Clinton, 13-Brown, Ida Catherine, 14-Yes, 15-Liskey

#2402, 1-Liskey, Franklin Clyde, 2-born, 3-11 Jul 1902, 12-Liskey, Robert Clinton, 13-Brown, Ida Catherine, 14-Yes, 15-Liskey

#2403, 1-Nalley, William H., 2-married, 3-24 Dec 1902, 4-Hagerstown, MD, 7-Armstrong, Mary S., 8-Hagerstown, MD, 9-Hagerstown, MD, 10-Rev. A.H. Irvine, 11-Evangelical Church, 15-Nally

#2404, 1-Armstrong, Mary Susan, 2-married, 3-24 Dec 1902, 7-Nalley, William H., 15-Nally

#2405, 1-Nalley, Hilda Irene, 2-married, 3-3 Feb 1922, 7-Nussear, Henry Arthur, 15-Nally

#2406, 1-Nalley, William H., 2-born, 3-19 Nov 1866, 15-Nally

#2407, 1-Armstrong, Mary Susan, 2-born, 3-19 Apr 1872, 15-Nally

#2408, 1-Nalley, Leroy Edward, 2-born, 3-11 Nov 1903, 15-Nally

#2409, 1-Shenk, William Gordon, 2-born, 3-19 Sep 1920, 15-Nally

#2410, 1-Nalley, Hilda Irene, 2-born, 3-26 Sep 1904, 15-Nally

#2411, 1-Nalley, William Richard, 2-born, 3-8 Jun 1917, 15-Nally

#2412, 1-Nussear, Mary Norma, 2-born, 3-9 Dec 1922, 15-Nally

#2413, 1-Nussear, Jr., Henry Arthur, 2-born, 3-21 Jun 1924, 15-Nally

#2414, 1-Perry, Clifton Edward, 2-born, 3-15 Oct 1938, 15-Nally

#2415, 1-Nalley, Leroy Edward, 2-died, 3-14 Nov 1903, 5-3 days, 15-Nally

#2416, 1-Shenk, William Gordon, 2-died, 3-26 Dec 1920, 5-3 months 1 week, 15-Nally

#2417, 1-Nussear, Agnes (Mrs.), 2-died, 3-21 Jan 1940[?], 15-Nally

#2418, 1-[blank], "Mother", 2-born, 3-22 Nov 1843, 15-Nally

#2419, 1-[blank], "Father", 2-born, 3-17 Dec 1841, 15-Nally

#2420, 1-Nally, Joseph J., 2-born, 3-16 Jan 1865, 15-Nally

#2421, 1-Nally, Clara B., 2-born, 3-12 Aug 1869, 15-Nally

#2422, 1-Perry[?], Clifton Edward, 2-born, 3-15 Oct 1938, 15-Nally

#2423, 1-[blank], "Mother", 2-died, 3-23 Jan 1870, 5-26 years 2 months 1 day, 15-Nally

#2424, 1-Nally, Johon H., 2-died, 3-18 Jul 1915, 5-73 years 7 months 1 day, 15-Nally

#2425, 1-Nally, Joseph J., 2-died, 3-20 May 1926, 5-61 years 4 months 4 days, 15-Nally

#2426, 1-Nally, Clara Bell, 2-died, 3-26 Dec 1926, 5-57 years 4 months 14 days, 15-Nally

#2427, 1-Kitzmiller, Augustus, 2-married, 3-18 Mar 1875, 4-Wm. Wilson's home, Metal, PA, 7-Wilson, Clementine A., 8-Keedysville, MD, 9-Metal, PA, 10-Rev. J. Smith Gordon, 15-Kitzmiller

#2428, 1-Kitzmiller, Augustus, 2-married, 3-18 Mar 1875, 7-Wilson, Clementine A., 15-Kitzmiller

#2429, 1-Kitzmiller, Bertie L., 2-married, 3-29 Nov 1899, 7-Knadler, Edward B., 15-Kitzmiller

#2430, 1-Kitzmiller, Augustus, 2-born, 3-11 Mar 1850, 15-Kitzmiller

#2431, 1-Wilson, Clementine A., 2-born, 3-4 Oct 1850, 7-Kitzmiller, Augustus, 15-Kitzmiller

#2432, 1-Kitzmiller, [infant son], 2-born, 3-8 Oct 1876, 15-Kitzmiller

#2433, 1-Kitzmiller, [infant son], 2-died, 3-8 Oct 1876, 15-Kitzmiller

#2434, 1-Kitzmiller, Bertie Lorena, 2-born, 3-27 Dec 1877, 15-Kitzmiller

FAMILY BIBLE RECORDS IN THE WASHINGTON COUNTY FREE LIBRARY, HAGERSTOWN, MARYLAND

Entry #, 1-Last Name, First Name, 2-Event, 3-Date, 4-Event Location, 5-Age, 6-Other,
7-Spouse's Last, First, 8-Groom's Residence, 9-Bride's Residence, 10-Minister, 11-Minister's Location,
12-Father's Last, First, 13-Mother's Last, First, 14-Transcribed, 15-Family Bible

#2435, 1-Kitzmiller, Mary Wilson, 2-born, 3-12 Oct 1881, 15-Kitzmiller
#2436, 1-Knadler, Frances Etelka, 2-born, 3-5 Dec 1902, 12-Knadle, E.B., 13-Kitzmiller Bertie L., 15-Kitzmiller
#2437, 1-Knadler, Ruth Wilson, 2-born, 3-7 Jun 1904, 12-Knadle, E.B., 13-Kitzmiller Bertie L., 15-Kitzmiller
#2438, 1-Knadler, Dorothy Margaret, 2-born, 3-2 Oct 1910, 12-Knadle, E.B., 13-Kitzmiller Bertie L., 15-Kitzmiller
#2439, 1-Kitzmiller, William, 2-born, 3-7 Nov 1853, 12-Kitzmiller, Washington, 13-Kitzmiller, Susan, 15-Kitzmiller
#2440, 1-Kitzmiller, William, 2-died, 3-10 Oct 1921, 5-67 years 11 months 3 days, 12-Kitzmiller, Washington, 13-Kitzmiller, Susan, 15-Kitzmiller
#2441, 1-Kitzmiller, Clementine (Wilson), 2-born, 3-4 Oct 1850, 7-Kitzmiller, Augustus, 15-Kitzmiller
#2442, 1-Kitzmiller, Clementine (Wilson), 2-died, 3-10 Mar 1923, 5-72 years 5 months 6 days, 7-Kitzmiller, Augustus, 15-Kitzmiller
#2443, 1-Kitzmiller, Augustus Ambrose, 2-born, 3-11 Mar 1850, 15-Kitzmiller
#2444, 1-Kitzmiller, Augustus Ambrose, 2-died, 3-22 Sep 1924, 5-74 years 6 months 11 days, 15-Kitzmiller
#2445, 1-Knadler, Bertie Lorena, 2-born, 3-27 Dec 1877, 7-Knadler, E.B., 12-Kitzmiller, Augustus Ambrose, 13-Wilson, Clementine, 15-Kitzmiller
#2446, 1-Knadler, Bertie Lorena, 2-died, 3-1 Sep 1929, 5-51 years 9 months 4 days, 7-Knadler, E.B., 15-Kitzmiller
#2447, 1-Knadler, Edward B., 2-died, 3-10 Apr 1955, 5-87 years, 7-Knadler, Bertie K., 15-Kitzmiller
#2448, 1-Kitzmiller, William, 2-died, 3-10 Oct 1921, 5-67 years 11 months 3 days, 12-Kitzmiller, Washington, 13-Kitzmiller, Susan, 15-Kitzmiller
#2449, 1-Kitzmiller, Mary V., 2-died, 3-1 Apr 1967, 12-Kitzmiller, Augustus, 13-Kitzmiller, Clementine, 15-Kitzmiller
#2450, 1-Baker, Ezra, 2-obituary, 3-8 Dec 1895, 4-Keedysville, MD, 5-82 years 5 months 23 days, 15-Kitzmiller
#2451, 1-Baker, Ezra, 2-married, 3-24 Feb 1835, 7-Line, Catharine, 15-Kitzmiller
#2452, 1-Wilson, William, 2-married, 3-22 Oct 1833, 15-Kitzmiller
#2453, 1-Wyand, Willie C., 2-obituary, 3-8 Jan 1894, 5-29 years 2 months 23 days, 6-buried Fairview Cemetery, 12-Wyand, D.H., 13-Wyand, Kate E., 15-Kitzmiller
#2454, 1-Wyand, Willie C., 2-born, 3-15 Jul 1864, 12-Wyand, D.H., 13-Wyand, Kate E., 15-Kitzmiller
#2455, 1-Wyand, Willie C., 2-married, 3-11 Oct 1893, 4-Washington, DC, 7-Davis, Frances L. (Miss), 12-Wyand, D.H., 13-Wyand, Kate E., 15-Kitzmiller
#2456, 1-Knadler, Ruth Wilson, 2-born, 3-7 Jun 1904, 4-Keedsyville, MD, 15-Kitzmiller
#2457, 1-Perrott, Alexander Rudolph, 2-born, 3-3 Jan 1906, 15-Perrott
#2458, 1-Perrott, Hazel Louise, 2-born, 3-14 Aug 1907, 15-Perrott
#2459, 1-Perrott, Martin Reichard, 2-born, 3-20 Jan 1909, 15-Perrott
#2460, 1-Perrott, Wilbur Vincen, 2-born, 3-21 Feb 1911, 15-Perrott
#2461, 1-Perrott, John Rohyer, 2-born, 3-28 Oct 1912, 15-Perrott
#2462, 1-Perrott, Laura Mildred Susan, 2-born, 3-18 Sep 1914, 15-Perrott
#2463, 1-Perrott, Effie Elnora, 2-born, 3-2 Aug 1917, 15-Perrott
#2464, 1-Perrott, Robert Lee, 2-born, 3-11 Nov 1919, 15-Perrott
#2465, 1-Perrott, Maud Irene, 2-born, 3-9 Jan 1922, 15-Perrott
#2466, 1-Perrott, Elva Virginia, 2-born, 3-27 Jun 1925, 15-Perrott
#2467, 1-Munday, Jr., John Henry, 2-born, 3-26 Apr 1952, 15-Perrott
#2468, 1-Perrott, Elva V., 2-died, 3-Mar 1926, 15-Perrott
#2469, 1-Perrott, Jacob Martin, 2-died, 3-16 Jun 1947, 15-Perrott
#2470, 1-Perrott, Alexander R., 2-died, 3-28 Oct 1967, 12-Perrott, Jacob Martin, 13-Perrott, Effie Naomi, 15-Perrott

FAMILY BIBLE RECORDS IN THE WASHINGTON COUNTY FREE LIBRARY, HAGERSTOWN, MARYLAND

Entry #, 1-Last Name, First Name, 2-Event, 3-Date, 4-Event Location, 5-Age, 6-Other,
7-Spouse's Last, First, 8-Groom's Residence, 9-Bride's Residence, 10-Minister, 11-Minister's Location,
12-Father's Last, First, 13-Mother's Last, First, 14-Transcribed, 15-Family Bible

```
#2471, 1-Perrott, Effie Naomi, 2-died, 3-25 Jul 1973, 15-Perrott
#2472, 1-Perrott, Wilbur V., 2-died, 3-11 Dec 1974, 15-Perrott
#2473, 1-Perrott, Jacob M., 2-married, 3-1 Feb 1905, 4-Hagerstown, MD, 7-Bartle,
    Effie V.[?], 10-S.N.[?] Owen, 11-St. John's Evan. Lutheran, 15-Perrott
#2474, 1-Timmins, David B., 2-married, 3-24 Dec 1868, 4-[unreadable], 7-Gabler,
    Mary Ann, 15-Timmons
#2475, 1-Timmins, David Byers, 2-born, 3-18 Nov 1841, 4-Roxbury, PA, 15-Timmons
#2476, 1-Timmins, Mary Ann, 2-born, 3-18 Apr 1846, 4-Letterkenny Township, Franklin
    Co., PA, 15-Timmons
#2477, 1-Timmins, Ida May, 2-born, 3-20 Dec 1869, 4-Letterkenny Township, Franklin
    Co., PA, 12-Timmins, David Byers, 13-Gabler, Mary Ann, 15-Timmons
#2478, 1-Timmins, William Lane, 2-born, 3-8 Aug 1871, 4-Letterkenny Township,
    Franklin Co., PA, 12-Timmins, David Byers, 13-Gabler, Mary Ann, 15-Timmons
#2479, 1-Timmins, Emma Almeda, 2-born, 3-23 Jul 1875, 4-Letterkenny Township,
    Franklin Co., PA, 12-Timmins, David Byers, 13-Gabler, Mary Ann, 15-Timmons
#2480, 1-Timmins, Joseph Edward, 2-born, 3-13 Dec 1878, 4-Letterkenny Township,
    Franklin Co., PA, 12-Timmins, David Byers, 13-Gabler, Mary Ann, 15-Timmons
#2481, 1-Timmins, Frank Elmer, 2-born, 3-4 Nov 1880, 4-Letterkenny Township,
    Franklin Co., PA, 12-Timmins, David Byers, 13-Gabler, Mary Ann, 15-Timmons
#2482, 1-Timmins, Denton Hartzell, 2-born, 3-26 Jun 1884, 4-Letterkenny Township,
    Franklin Co., PA, 12-Timmins, David Byers, 13-Gabler, Mary Ann, 15-Timmons
#2483, 1-Timmins, Daniel Bird, 2-born, 3-8 Oct 1888, 4-Letterkenny Township,
    Franklin Co., PA, 12-Timmins, David Byers, 13-Gabler, Mary Ann, 15-Timmons
#2484, 1-Timmins, David Byers, 2-died, 3-6 May 1923, 15-Timmons
#2485, 1-Timmins, Mary Ann, 2-died, 3-15 Jun 1924, 15-Timmons
#2486, 1-Timmins, Ida May, 2-died, 3-20 Apr 1947, 15-Timmons
#2487, 1-Timmins, William Lane, 2-died, 3-5 Apr 1962, 15-Timmons
#2488, 1-Burgner, Emma (Timmins), 2-died, 3-22 May 1952, 15-Timmons
#2489, 1-Timmins, Joseph Edward, 2-died, 3-22 Jan 1959, 15-Timmons
#2490, 1-Timmins, Frank Elmer, 2-died, 3-9 Dec 1966, 15-Timmons
#2491, 1-Timmins, Denton Hartzell, 2-died, 3-25 Nov 1962, 15-Timmons
#2492, 1-Timmins, David Bird, 2-died, 3-13 Apr 1932, 15-Timmons
#2493, 1-Timmins, Emma Almeda, 2-married, 3-25 Dec 1902, 7-Burgner, Harry Angle, 8-
    Upper Strasburg PA, 9-Roxbury, PA, 15-Timmons
#2494, 1-Timmins, Rebecca Jane, 2-died, 3-11:00 am, 24 Aug 1838, 5-16 months, 15-
    Timmons
#2495, 1-Timmins, William Walls, 2-died, 3-28 Jun 1853, 4-Bobo house in Port
    Gibson, Clayborn Co., MS, 5-28 years 4 months 28 days, 15-Timmons
#2496, 1-Timmins, Harry O., 2-obituary, 3-6 Apr, 4-near Fulton, IL, 15-Timmons
#2497, 1-Timmins, Harry O., 2-born, 3-24 Sep 1848, 15-Timmons
#2498, 1-Timmins, Harry O., 2-married, 7-Miller, Sarie C. (Miss), 15-Timmons
#2499, 1-Timmins, Anna Maria (Mrs.), 2-obituary, 4-Keefer's Valley, 5-77 years 6
    months 15 days, 7-Timmins, Wm. W., 15-Timmons
#2500, 1-Timmins, David Byers, 2-obituary, 4-Upper Strasburg, PA, 6-buried
    Methodist cemetery, 15-Timmons
#2501, 1-Timmins, David Byers, 2-born, 3-18 Nov 1841, 15-Timmons
#2502, 1-McKee, Mary Elizabeth (Mrs.), 2-obituary, 4-S. Main Street, 5-83 years 3
    months 15 days, 6-buried Keefer's Graveyard, 15-Timmons
#2503, 1-Timmons, Howell, 2-obituary, 12-Timmons, W.E., 15-Timmons
#2504, 1-Timmins, Daniel Reifsnider, 2-born, 3-10 Oct 1827[?], 15-Timmons
#2505, 1-Timmins, William Ward, 2-born, 3-15 Oct 1800, 15-Timmons
#2506, 1-Reifsnider, Anna Mariah, 2-born, 3-24 Apr 1805, 15-Timmons
#2507, 1-Timmins, Daniel Reifsnider, 2-born, 3-10 Oct 1827[?], 15-Timmons
#2508, 1-Timmins, William Walls, 2-born, 3-30 Jan 1830, 15-Timmons
#2509, 1-Timmins, Philip Shoemaker, 2-born, 3-15 Nov 1831, 15-Timmons
```

FAMILY BIBLE RECORDS IN THE WASHINGTON COUNTY FREE LIBRARY, HAGERSTOWN, MARYLAND

Entry #, 1-Last Name, First Name, 2-Event, 3-Date, 4-Event Location, 5-Age, 6-Other,
7-Spouse's Last, First, 8-Groom's Residence, 9-Bride's Residence, 10-Minister, 11-Minister's Location,
12-Father's Last, First, 13-Mother's Last, First, 14-Transcribed, 15-Family Bible

```
#2510, 1-Timmins, Emlyetta, 2-born, 3-1 Aug 1833, 15-Timmons
#2511, 1-Timmins, Susann, 2-born, 3-26 Sep 1835, 15-Timmons
#2512, 1-Timmins, Rebecca Jane, 2-born, 3-24 Apr 1837, 15-Timmons
#2513, 1-Timmins, Matilda, 2-born, 3-22 Mar 1839, 15-Timmons
#2514, 1-Timmins, David Byers, 2-born, 3-18 Nov 1841, 15-Timmons
#2515, 1-Timmins, Joseph, 2-born, 3-18 Nov 1843, 15-Timmons
#2516, 1-Timmins, Mary Elizabeth, 2-born, 3-23 Nov 1845, 15-Timmons
#2517, 1-Timmins, Henry Clay, 2-born, 3-24 Sep 1848, 15-Timmons
#2518, 1-Timmins, Anna Mariah, 2-born, 3-24 Sep 1848, 15-Timmons
#2519, 1-Stake, William Elmer, 2-born, 3-29 May 1861, 15-Timmons
#2520, 1-Timmins, William, 2-married, 3-18 Jan 1827, 7-Reifsnider, Anna Mariah, 15-
    Timmons
#2521, 1-Sole, Willliam D., 2-born, 3-19 Feb 184_, 15-Sole
#2522, 1-Hoskinson, Oliva[?], 3-25 Apr 184_, 15-Sole
#2523, 1-Sole, W. D., 2-married, 3-16 Apr 1861, 7-Haskinson, Oliva , 15-Sole
#2524, 1-Sole, A.B., 2-died, 3-9 Jun 1862, 15-Sole
#2525, 1-Sole, H.E., 2-died, 3-16 Apr 1889, 15-Sole
#2526, 1-Sole, John E., 2-died, 3-11 Nov 1902, 15-Sole
#2527, 1-Hotchinson[?], Elenora C., 2-died, 3-21 Dec 1928[?], 15-Sole
#2528, 1-Sole, Josephus H., 2-died, 3-13 Aug 1934, 15-Sole
#2529, 1-Sole, W.D., 2-died, 3-4 Jul 1922, 15-Sole
#2530, 1-Sole, Olivia, 2-died, 3-14 Jul 1901[?], 15-Sole
#2531, 1-Sole, A.B., 2-born, 3-4 May 1862, 15-Sole
#2532, 1-Sole, Joseph H., 2-born, 3-2 Apr 1863, 15-Sole
#2533, 1-Sole, George M., 2-born, 3-19 Feb 1866, 15-Sole
#2534, 1-Sole, Hugh E., 2-born, 3-22 May 1867, 15-Sole
#2535, 1-Sole, John E., 2-born, 3-29 May 1869, 15-Sole
#2536, 1-Sole, Elenora C., 2-born, 3-17[?] Oct 1871, 15-Sole
#2537, 1-Sole, Josepus H., 2-born, 3-31[?] Jul 1873, 15-Sole
#2538, 1-Sole, Jonas O., 2-born, 3-20 May 1875, 15-Sole
#2539, 1-Sole, William C., 2-born, 3-4 Aug 1877, 15-Sole
#2540, 1-Sole, Charels E., 2-born, 3-31 May 1879, 15-Sole
#2541, 1-Sole, Groves C., 2-born, 3-24 Feb 1881, 15-Sole
#2542, 1-Sole, Hattie V.[?], 2-born, 3-27 Sep 1883, 15-Sole
#2543, 1-Sole, Joseph Henry, 2-obituary, 3-18 Sep 1938, 4-Bremen, OH, 5-75 years 5
    months 16 days, 12-Sole, William, 13-Sole, Oliva, 15-Sole
#2544, 1-Sole, Joseph Henry, 2-born, 3-2 Apr 1863, 4-Sardis, OH, 15-Sole
#2545, 1-Sole, W.C., 2-obituary, 3-21 Feb 1953, Nora, 15-Sole
#2546, 1-Sole, W.C., 2-born, 3-4 Aug 1877, 4-Sardis, OH, 15-Sole
#2547, 1-Sole, W.D., 2-obituary, 4-Sardis, OH, 15-Sole
#2548, 1-Sole, Charles Ephriam Dutch", 2-obituary, 3-11:50 am, 30 Dec 1948, 15-Sole
#2549, 1-Sole, Charles Ephriam Dutch", 2-born, 3-30 May 1883, 4-Sardis, OH, 12-
    Sole, William, 15-Sole
#2550, 1-Sole, Charles Ephriam Dutch", 2-married, 3-1910, 4-New Martinsville, WV,
    7-Thompson, Ella, 15-Sole
#2551, 1-Sole, William C., 2-obituary, 3-21 Feb 1953, 15-Sole
#2552, 1-Sole, William C., 2-born, 3-Aug 1877, 15-Sole
#2553, 1-Sole, Nonnie (Goddard), 2-obituary, 3-10 Jul 1943, 15-Sole
#2554, 1-Sole, Nonnie (Goddard), 2-born, 3-21 Jan 1881, 4-Sardis, OH, 12-Goddard,
    James M., 13-Goddard, Louise, 15-Sole
#2555, 1-Sole, Nonnie (Goddard), 2-married, 3-15 Apr 1906, 7-Sole, Grover C., 15-
    Sole
#2556, 1-Hutchison, Nora (Sole), 2-obituary, 3-21 Dec 1928, 7-Hutchison, Frank R.,
    15-Sole
#2557, 1-Sole, W.C., 2-obituary, 3-21 Feb 1953, 15-Sole
```

FAMILY BIBLE RECORDS IN THE WASHINGTON COUNTY FREE LIBRARY, HAGERSTOWN, MARYLAND

**Entry #, 1-Last Name, First Name, 2-Event, 3-Date, 4-Event Location, 5-Age, 6-Other,
7-Spouse's Last, First, 8-Groom's Residence, 9-Bride's Residence, 10-Minister, 11-Minister's Location,
12-Father's Last, First, 13-Mother's Last, First, 14-Transcribed, 15-Family Bible**

```
#2558, 1-Sole, W.C., 2-born, 3-4 Aug 1877, 15-Sole
#2559, 1-Sole, Grover C., 2-obituary, 3-8 Jan 1953, 4-Lyons, Kansas, 15-Sole
#2560, 1-Sole, Grover C., 2-born, 3-24 Feb 1880, 4-Sardis, OH, 12-Sole, William,
    15-Sole
#2561, 1-Sole, Grover C., 2-married, 3-1906, 7-Goddard, Nonie Inez, 15-Sole
#2562, 1-Sole, Grover C., 2-married, 3-1949, 7-Day, May (Mrs.), 15-Sole
#2563, 1-Gardner, Audrey D., 2-obituary, 3-16 Nov 1941, 4-Wink, TX, 15-Sole
#2564, 1-Reed, Reuben Walter, 2-obituary, 4-Hagerstown, MD, 5-72 years, 15-Sole
#2565, 1-Reed, Reuben Walter, 2-born, 4-Castleman, Somerset Co., PA, 15-Sole
#2566, 1-Wilson, Rufus H., 2-married, 3-22 Nov 1849, 7-Brewer, Elizabeth, 8-
    Washington Co., MD, 9-Franklin Co., PA, 14-Yes, 15-Wilson
#2567, 1-Wilson, John H., 2-married, 3-29 Jun 1876, 7-Huyett, Margaretta Ozella, 8-
    Washington Co., MD, 9-Washington Co., MD, 14-Yes, 15-Wilson
#2568, 1-Wilson, Clyde Huyett, 2-married, 3-25 Dec 1899, 7-Adams, Mary Anders, 8-
    Washington Co., MD, 9-Washington Co., MD, 14-Yes, 15-Wilson
#2569, 1-Wilson, Margaretta Helen, 2-married, 3-12 Apr 1911, 7-Hayman, Edgar
    Thomas, 8-Washington Co., MD, 9-Anne Arundel Co., MD, 14-Yes, 15-Wilson
#2570, 1-Hayman, Edgar Thomas, 2-born, 4-Anne Arundel Co., MD, 14-Yes, 15-Wilson
#2571, 1-Wilson, Mary Adams, 2-married, 7-Jones, Maurice Hepborn, 8-Kent Co., Md,
    9-Washington Co., MD, 14-Yes, 15-Wilson
#2572, 1-Jones, Mary Wilson, 2-married, 7-Cooke, Addison Barnwell, 9-Washington
    Co., MD, 14-Yes, 15-Wilson
#2573, 1-Wilson, Sr., Rufus H., 2-born, 3-18 Feb 1815, 4-Calvert Co., MD, 14-Yes,
    15-Wilson
#2574, 1-Wilson, Elizabeth, 2-born, 3-25 Nov 1825, 4-Franklin Co., PA, 14-Yes, 15-
    Wilson
#2575, 1-Wilson, John Hamilton, 2-born, 3-31 Aug 1850, 4-Washington Co., MD, 14-
    Yes, 15-Wilson
#2576, 1-Wilson, Mary Elizabeth, 2-born, 3-19 Oct 1851, 4-Washington Co., MD, 14-
    Yes, 15-Wilson
#2577, 1-Wilson, Jr., Rufus Hilliary, 2-born, 3-21 Mar 1853, 4-Washington Co., MD,
    14-Yes, 15-Wilson
#2578, 1-Huyett, Margaretta O., 2-born, 3-2 Jan 1858, 4-Washington Co., MD, 12-
    Huyett, Daniel, 13-Huyett, Margaretta Brinham, 14-Yes, 15-Wilson
#2579, 1-Huyett, Margaretta O., 2-died, 3-3 Jul 1936, 12-Huyett, Daniel, 13-Huyett,
    Margaretta Brinham, 14-Yes, 15-Wilson
#2580, 1-Wilson, Clyde Huyett, 2-born, 3-12 Jul 1878, 4-Washington Co., MD, 14-Yes,
    15-Wilson
#2581, 1-Adams, Mary Anders, 2-born, 3-2 Aug 1877, 4-Washington Co., MD, 12-Adams,
    John U., 13-Adams, Elizabeth, 14-Yes, 15-Wilson
#2582, 1-Wilson, Margaretta Helen, 2-born, 3-4 Jul 1889, 4-Washington Co., MD, 12-
    Wilson, John H., 13-Wilson, Margaretta O., 14-Yes, 15-Wilson
#2583, 1-Hayman, Edgar Thomas, 2-born, 3-19 Oct 1885, 4-Worcester Co., MD, 12-
    Hayman, Elijah R., 13-Payne, Margaret, 14-Yes, 15-Wilson
#2584, 1-Wilson, Mary Adams, 2-born, 3-2 Aug 1900, 4-Washington Co., MD, 12-Wilson,
    Clyde H., 13-Wilson, Mary A., 14-Yes, 15-Wilson
#2585, 1-Jones, Maurice Hepborn, 2-born, 3-22 Apr 1896, 4-Kent Co., MD, 12-Jones,
    Harrison Piper, 13-Jones, Minnie A., 14-Yes, 15-Wilson
#2586, 1-Cooke, Addison Barnwell, 2-born, 3-10 Dec 1902, 4-Baltimore, MD, 12-Cooke,
    Addison, 13-Cooke, Mary Sams, 14-Yes, 15-Wilson
#2587, 1-Cooke, Mary Wilson, 2-born, 4-Wilson's, Washington Co., MD, 6-buried St.
    Paul's Cemetery, 14-Yes, 15-Wilson
#2588, 1-Cooke, Mary Wilson, 2-died, 3-26 Jun 1966, 14-Yes, 15-Wilson
#2589, 1-Cooke, Mary Wilson, 2-married, 7-Jones, Maurice Hepborn, 14-Yes, 15-Wilson
```

FAMILY BIBLE RECORDS IN THE WASHINGTON COUNTY FREE LIBRARY, HAGERSTOWN, MARYLAND

Entry #, 1-Last Name, First Name, 2-Event, 3-Date, 4-Event Location, 5-Age, 6-Other,
7-Spouse's Last, First, 8-Groom's Residence, 9-Bride's Residence, 10-Minister, 11-Minister's Location,
12-Father's Last, First, 13-Mother's Last, First, 14-Transcribed, 15-Family Bible

#2590, 1-Cooke, Mary Wilson, 2-married, 7-Cooke, Addison Barnwell, 14-Yes, 15-Wilson

#2591, 1-Wilson, Mary Elizabeth, 2-died, 3-3 Feb 1854, 5-2 years 3 months 14 days, 14-Yes, 15-Wilson

#2592, 1-Wilson, Jr., Rufus Hilery, 2-died, 3-25 Sep 1854, 5-1 year. 6 months 4 days, 14-Yes, 15-Wilson

#2593, 1-Wilson, Elizabeth, 2-died, 3-1 Dec 1854, 5-29 years 6 days, 14-Yes, 15-Wilson

#2594, 1-Wilson, Rufus Hillery, 2-died, 3-25 Nov 1882, 5-67 years 9 months 7 days, 6-mother from Calvert Co., MD, 12-Wilson, Jr., Lancelot, 13-Wilson, Harriet Hillery, 14-Yes, 15-Wilson

#2595, 1-Wilson, John Hamilton, 2-died, 3-6 May 1924, 5-73 years 8 months 6 days, 12-Wilson, Rufus Hillery, 13-Wilson, Elizabeth Brewer , 14-Yes, 15-Wilson

#2596, 1-Wilson, Margaretta O., 2-died, 3-3 Jul 1936, 5-78 years 6 months 1 day, 7-Wilson, John H., 14-Yes, 15-Wilson

#2597, 1-Wilson, Mary (Adams), 2-died, 3-6 Jan 1933, 5-56 years 5 months 4 days, 14-Yes, 15-Wilson

#2598, 1-Wilson, Clyde Huyett, 2-died, 3-6 Jan 1950, 5-71 years 5 months 25 days, 14-Yes, 15-Wilson

#2599, 1-Cooke, Addison Barnwell, 2-died, 3-12 Aug 1958, 5-55 years 8 months 2 day, 7-Wilson, Mary A., 14-Yes, 15-Wilson

#2600, 1-Hayman, Edgar Thomas, 2-died, 3-12 Jan 1963, 12-Hayman, Elijah Robert, 13-Payne, Margaret, 14-Yes, 15-Wilson

#2601, 1-Brewer, John, 2-married, 7-Fiery, Elizabeth, 14-Yes, 15-Wilson

#2602, 1-Brewer, Elizabeth, 2-married, 7-Wilson, Rufus, 12-Brewer, John, 13-Fiery, Elizabeth, 14-Yes, 15-Wilson

#2603, 1-Brewer, James R.E., 2-died, 3-6 Jul 1936, 4-Wilson's, Washington Co., MD, 14-Yes, 15-Wilson

#2604, 1-Wilson, Jr., Lancelot [or Lawrence], 2-married, 3-1815, 7-Hilliary, Harriet, 8-Calvert Co., MD, 9-Prince Georges Co., MD, 14-Yes, 15-Wilson

#2605, 1-Wilson, Rufus Hillary, 2-born, 12-Wilson, Jr., Lancelot [or Lawrence], 13-Hilliary, Harriet, 14-Yes, 15-Wilson

#2606, 1-Wilson, John H., 2-married, 3-1876, 7-Huyett, Margaretta O., 10-Dr. S.W. Owen, 11-St. John's Lutheran, Hagerstown, MD, 14-Yes, 15-Wilson

#2607, 1-Wilson, Margaretta H., 2-married, 3-1911, 7-Hayman, E.T., 10-Dr. S.W. Owen, 11-St. John's Lutheran, Hagerstown, MD, 14-Yes, 15-Wilson

#2608, 1-Sanders, David Benjamin Franklin, 2-died, 3-Jun 1939, 5-74 years, 6-African American; with the wilson family for 56 years, 14-Yes, 15-Wilson

#2609, 1-Hilleary, George, 2-born, 12-Hilleary, Henry, 14-Yes, 15-Wilson

#2610, 1-Hilleary, Thomas, 2-born, 12-Hilleary, Henry, 14-Yes, 15-Wilson

#2611, 1-Hilleary, Harriett, 2-married, 7-Wilson, Law., 12-Hilleary, Henry, 14-Yes, 15-Wilson

#2612, 1-Bowie, Thomas John Davis, 2-born, 3-23 Jan 1834, 12-Bowie, Thomas John, 13-McBride, Catharine, 15-Bowie

#2613, 1-Beatty, Elizabeth Ch___, 2-born, 3-26 Apr 1835, 12-Beatty, Edward W.[?], 13-Beatty, Maria A., 15-Bowie

#2614, 1-Bowie, Edward Beatty, 2-born, 3-18 Jun 1857, 12-Bowie, Thomas John David, 13-Bowie, Elizabeth, 15-Bowie

#2615, 1-Bowie, Catharine Davis, 2-born, 3-31 Jan 1859, 12-Bowie, Thomas John David, 13-Bowie, Elizabeth, 15-Bowie

#2616, 1-Bowie, Allen Thomas, 2-born, 3-7 Nov 1861, 12-Bowie, Thomas John David, 13-Bowie, Elizabeth, 15-Bowie

#2617, 1-Bowie, Maria Williams, 2-born, 3-21 Jul 1863, 12-Bowie, Thomas John David, 13-Bowie, Elizabeth, 15-Bowie

FAMILY BIBLE RECORDS IN THE WASHINGTON COUNTY FREE LIBRARY, HAGERSTOWN, MARYLAND

Entry #, 1-Last Name, First Name, 2-Event, 3-Date, 4-Event Location, 5-Age, 6-Other, 7-Spouse's Last, First, 8-Groom's Residence, 9-Bride's Residence, 10-Minister, 11-Minister's Location, 12-Father's Last, First, 13-Mother's Last, First, 14-Transcribed, 15-Family Bible

#2618, 1-Beatty, Elizabeth Chew, 2-married, 3-21 Nov 1855, 4-St. John's Lutheran, Hagerstown, MD, 7-Bowie, Thomas John Davis, 10-Rev. Walter Ayrault[?], 15-Bowie

#2619, 1-Bowie, Edward Beatty, 2-married, 3-9 Dec 1885, 7-Vass[?], Eleanor, 15-Bowie

#2620, 1-Bowie, Robert Edward, 2-married, 3-10 Dec 1917, 7-Ridd, Edna, 15-Bowie

#2621, 1-Bowie, Allen Thomas, 2-married, 3-1893, 7-Paull, Mary, 15-Bowie

#2622, 1-Bowie, Elizabeth C., 2-died, 3-25 May 1868, 4-near Mechanicsville, Montgomery Co., MD, 15-Bowie

#2623, 1-Bowie, Thomas John, 2-died, 3-Feb 1921, 15-Bowie

#2624, 1-Bowie, Allen Thomas, 2-died, 3-4 Feb 1914, 15-Bowie

#2625, 1-Bowie, Edward Beattty, 2-died, 3-7 May 1929, 15-Bowie

#2626, 1-Bowie, Catharine Davis, 2-died, 3-4 Jan 1942, 15-Bowie

#2627, 1-Bowie, John, 2-born, 3-1688, 4-Scotland, 15-Bowie

#2628, 1-Bowie, John, 2-married, 7-Mullikin, Mary, 15-Bowie

#2629, 1-Bowie, John, 2-died, 3-1759, 4-Prince Georges Co., MD, 15-Bowie

#2630, 1-Bowie, Jr., John, 2-born, 12-Bowie, John, 13-Mullikin, Mary, 15-Bowie

#2631, 1-Bowie, Eleanor, 2-born, 12-Bowie, John, 13-Mullikin, Mary, 15-Bowie

#2632, 1-Bowie, James, 2-born, 12-Bowie, John, 13-Mullikin, Mary, 15-Bowie

#2633, 1-Bowie, Allen, 2-born, 12-Bowie, John, 13-Mullikin, Mary, 15-Bowie

#2634, 1-Bowie, William, 2-born, 12-Bowie, John, 13-Mullikin, Mary, 15-Bowie

#2635, 1-Bowie, Thomas, 2-born, 12-Bowie, John, 13-Mullikin, Mary, 15-Bowie

#2636, 1-Bowie, Mary, 2-born, 12-Bowie, John, 13-Mullikin, Mary, 15-Bowie

#2637, 1-Bowie, Jr., John, 2-born, 3-1708, 15-Bowie

#2638, 1-Bowie, Jr., John, 2-married, 7-Beall, Mary, 15-Bowie

#2639, 1-Bowie, William, 2-born, 12-Bowie, Jr., John, 13-Beall, Mary, 15-Bowie

#2640, 1-Bowie, Molly, 2-born, 12-Bowie, Jr., John, 13-Beall, Mary, 15-Bowie

#2641, 1-Bowie, Jr., John, 2-married, 7-Pottinger, Elizabeth, 15-Bowie

#2642, 1-Bowie, Jr., Allen, 2-born, 15-Bowie

#2643, 1-Bowie, Jr., James, 2-born, 15-Bowie

#2644, 1-Bowie, Jr., John (Rev.), 2-born, 15-Bowie

#2645, 1-Bowie, Jr., John, 2-died, 3-1753, 15-Bowie

#2646, 1-Pottinger, Elizabeth, 2-married, 7-Cramphin[?], Thomas, 15-Bowie

#2647, 1-Pottinger, Elizabeth, 2-died, 3-1775, 15-Bowie

#2648, 1-Bowie, Jr., Allen (Colonel), 2-born, 3-1736, 15-Bowie

#2649, 1-Bowie, Jr., Allen (Colonel), 2-married, 7-Cramphin[?], 15-Bowie

#2650, 1-Bowie, Jr., Allen (Colonel), 2-died, 3-1803, 6-buried Rockville, MD, 15-Bowie

#2651, 1-Bowie, Thomas, 2-born, 12-Bowie, Jr., Allen (Colonel), 13-Cramphin[?], Ruth, 15-Bowie

#2652, 1-Bowie, John (Dr.), 2-born, 12-Bowie, Jr., Allen (Colonel), 13-Cramphin[?], Ruth, 15-Bowie

#2653, 1-Bowie, Elizabeth, 2-born, 12-Bowie, Jr., Allen (Colonel), 13-Cramphin[?], Ruth, 15-Bowie

#2654, 1-Bowie, Mary, 2-born, 12-Bowie, Jr., Allen (Colonel), 13-Cramphin[?], Ruth, 15-Bowie

#2655, 1-Bowie, Washington, 2-born, 12-Bowie, Jr., Allen (Colonel), 13-Cramphin[?], Ruth, 15-Bowie

#2656, 1-Bowie, Allen, 2-born, 12-Bowie, Jr., Allen (Colonel), 13-Cramphin[?], Ruth, 15-Bowie

#2657, 1-Bowie, Hannah, 2-born, 12-Bowie, Jr., Allen (Colonel), 13-Cramphin[?], Ruth, 15-Bowie

#2658, 1-Bowie, Richard, 2-born, 12-Bowie, Jr., Allen (Colonel), 13-Cramphin[?], Ruth, 15-Bowie

#2659, 1-Bowie, Washington (Colonel), 2-born, 3-1776, 15-Bowie

FAMILY BIBLE RECORDS IN THE WASHINGTON COUNTY FREE LIBRARY, HAGERSTOWN, MARYLAND

Entry #, 1-Last Name, First Name, 2-Event, 3-Date, 4-Event Location, 5-Age, 6-Other, 7-Spouse's Last, First, 8-Groom's Residence, 9-Bride's Residence, 10-Minister, 11-Minister's Location, 12-Father's Last, First, 13-Mother's Last, First, 14-Transcribed, 15-Family Bible

```
#2660, 1-Bowie, Washington (Colonel), 2-married, 7-Johns , Margaret Crabb, 15-Bowie
#2661, 1-Bowie, Thomas John, 2-born, 12-Bowie, Washington (Colonel), 13-Johns,
       Margaret Crabb, 15-Bowie
#2662, 1-Bowie, Mary, 2-born, 12-Bowie, Washington (Colonel), 13-Johns, Margaret
       Crabb, 15-Bowie
#2663, 1-Bowie, Margaret, 2-born, 12-Bowie, Washington (Colonel), 13-Johns,
       Margaret Crabb, 15-Bowie
#2664, 1-Bowie, Jr., Washington, 2-born, 12-Bowie, Washington (Colonel), 13-Johns,
       Margaret Crabb, 15-Bowie
#2665, 1-Bowie, Richard Johns (Judge), 2-born, 12-Bowie, Washington (Colonel), 13-
       Johns, Margaret Crabb, 15-Bowie
#2666, 1-Bowie, Robert Gilmer[?], 2-born, 12-Bowie, Washington (Colonel), 13-Johns,
       Margaret Crabb, 15-Bowie
#2667, 1-Bowie, Sarah Hollyday, 2-born, 12-Bowie, Washington (Colonel), 13-Johns,
       Margaret Crabb, 15-Bowie
#2668, 1-Bowie, Thomas Johns (Colonel), 2-born, 3-1800, 15-Bowie
#2669, 1-Bowie, Thomas Johns (Colonel), 2-married, 7-Davis, Catharine W., 15-Bowie
#2670, 1-Bowie, Thomas Johns (Colonel), 2-died, 3-1850, 15-Bowie
#2671, 1-Bowie, Catharine W. (Davis), 2-died, 3-1888, 15-Bowie
#2672, 1-Bowie, Thomas John Davis, 2-born, 12-Bowie, Thomas Johns (Colonel), 13-
       Davis, Catharine W., 15-Bowie
#2673, 1-Bowie, Sarah Hollyday, 2-born, 12-Bowie, Thomas Johns (Colonel), 13-Davis,
       Catharine W., 15-Bowie
#2674, 1-Bowie, Ellen Ruth, 2-born, 12-Bowie, Thomas Johns (Colonel), 13-Davis,
       Catharine W., 15-Bowie
#2675, 1-Bowie, Washington, 2-born, 12-Bowie, Thomas Johns (Colonel), 13-Davis,
       Catharine W., 15-Bowie
#2676, 1-Bowie, Thomas Johns Davis, 2-born, 3-1884, 15-Bowie
#2677, 1-Bowie, Thomas Johns Davis, 2-died, 3-1921, 15-Bowie
#2678, 1-Bowie, Thomas Johns Davis, 2-married, 3-24 Nov 1855, 7-Beatty, Elizabeth
       Chew, 15-Bowie
#2679, 1-Beatty, Elizabeth Chew, 2-died, 3-25 May 1868, 15-Bowie
#2680, 1-Bowie, Edward Beatty, 2-born, 12-Bowie, Thomas John Davis, 13-Beatty,
       Elizabeth Chew, 15-Bowie
#2681, 1-Bowie, Catharine Davis, 2-born, 12-Bowie, Thomas John Davis, 13-Beatty,
       Elizabeth Chew, 15-Bowie
#2682, 1-Bowie, Allen Thomas, 2-born, 12-Bowie, Thomas John Davis, 13-Beatty,
       Elizabeth Chew, 15-Bowie
#2683, 1-Bowie, Maria Williams, 2-born, 12-Bowie, Thomas John Davis, 13-Beatty,
       Elizabeth Chew, 15-Bowie
#2684, 1-Bowie, Edward Beatty, 2-born, 3-1857, 15-Bowie
#2685, 1-Bowie, Edward Beatty, 2-married, 3-1885, 7-Vars[?], Eleanor, 15-Bowie
#2686, 1-Bowie, Robert Edward, 2-born, 3-1886, 12-Bowie, Edwawrd Beatty, 13-
       Vars[?], Eleanor, 15-Bowie
#2687, 1-Bowie, Allen Davis, 2-born, 3-1885, 12-Bowie, Edwawrd Beatty, 13-Vars[?],
       Eleanor, 15-Bowie
#2688, 1-Bowie, Robert Edward, 2-married, 7-Hidd[?], Ednor[?] Mary, 15-Bowie
#2689, 1-Bowie, Allen Davis, 2-married, 7-Jacobs, Virginia, 15-Bowie
#2690, 1-Bowie, Mary Eleanor, 2-born, 12-Bowie, Allen Davis, 13-Jacobs, Virginia,
       15-Bowie
#2691, 1-Bowie, Catharine Davis, 2-born, 3-1859, 15-Bowie
#2692, 1-Bowie, Catharine Davis, 2-married, 7-Windle, James E., 15-Bowie
#2693, 1-Bowie, Allen Thomas, 2-born, 3-1861, 15-Bowie
#2694, 1-Bowie, Allen Thomas, 2-married, 3-1893, 7-Paul, Mary, 15-Bowie
#2695, 1-Bowie, Allen Thomas, 2-died, 3-4 Feb 1814, 15-Bowie
```

FAMILY BIBLE RECORDS IN THE WASHINGTON COUNTY FREE LIBRARY, HAGERSTOWN, MARYLAND

Entry #, 1-Last Name, First Name, 2-Event, 3-Date, 4-Event Location, 5-Age, 6-Other,
7-Spouse's Last, First, 8-Groom's Residence, 9-Bride's Residence, 10-Minister, 11-Minister's Location,
12-Father's Last, First, 13-Mother's Last, First, 14-Transcribed, 15-Family Bible

```
#2696, 1-Bowie, Georgia Pauls, 2-married, 7-Hazlett[?], Henry, 12-Bowie, Allen
    Thomas, 13-Pauls, Mary, 15-Bowie
#2697, 1-Hazlett[?], Mary Pauls, 2-born, 3-1917, 12-Hazlett[?], Henry, 13-Bowie,
    Georgia Pauls, 15-Bowie
#2698, 1-Bowie, Maria Williams, 2-born, 3-21 Jul 1863, 15-Bowie
#2699, 1-Bowie, Thomas, 2-born, 3-1722, 12-Bowie, Sr., John, 15-Bowie
#2700, 1-Bowie, Thomas, 2-married, 3-1758, 7-Lee, Hannah, 15-Bowie
#2701, 1-Bowie, Barbara, 2-born, 3-1759, 12-Bowie, Thomas, 13-Lee, Hannah, 15-Bowie
#2702, 1-Bowie, Barbara, 2-died, 3-1805, 12-Bowie, Thomas, 13-Lee, Hannah, 15-Bowie
#2703, 1-Bowie, Barbara, 2-married, 7-Hall, James, 12-Bowie, Thomas, 13-Lee,
    Hannah, 15-Bowie
#2704, 1-Hall, Elizabeth Bowie, 2-married, 7-Williams, Otho Holland (Gen.), 12-
    Hall, James, 13-Bowie, Barbara, 15-Bowie
#2705, 1-Williams, Catharine L., 12-Williams, Otho Holland (Gen.), 13-Hall,
    Elizabeth Bowie, 15-Bowie
#2706, 1-Williams, Laura, 12-Williams, Otho Holland (Gen.), 13-Hall, Elizabeth
    Bowie, 15-Bowie
#2707, 1-Williams, Covela[?], 12-Williams, Otho Holland (Gen.), 13-Hall, Elizabeth
    Bowie, 15-Bowie
#2708, 1-Williams, Maria, 2-married, 7-Beatty, Edward, 12-Williams, Otho Holland
    (Gen.), 13-Hall, Elizabeth Bowie, 15-Bowie
#2709, 1-Beatty, Edward, 2-born, 12-Beatty, Eli, 15-Bowie
#2710, 1-Beatty, Edward, 2-died, 3-1863, 15-Bowie
#2711, 1-Beatty, Elizabeth Chew, 2-married, 7-Bowie, Thomas Johns Davis, 12-Beatty,
    Edward, 13-Williams, Maria, 15-Bowie
#2712, 1-Beatty, Kate, 12-Beatty, Edward, 13-Williams, Maria, 15-Bowie
#2713, 1-Beatty, Edward, 2-died, 3-1864, 12-Beatty, Edward, 13-Williams, Maria, 15-
    Bowie
#2714, 1-Beatty, Laura, 2-married, 7-Magruder[?], Bradley[?], 12-Beatty, Edward,
    13-Williams, Maria, 15-Bowie
#2715, 1-Gaul, John F., 2-married, 3-23 Dec 1863, 7-Urian, Abbie A., 10-Rev.
    Charles ____, 11-St. John's Church, 15-Gaul
#2716, 1-Gaul, Harriet Rothwell, 2-born, 3-4 Jan 1869, 12-Gaul, John F., 13-Gaul,
    Abbie A., 15-Gaul
#2717, 1-Gaul, Sarah Elizabeth, 2-born, 3-13 Oct 1871, 12-Gaul, John F., 13-Gaul,
    Abbie A., 15-Gaul
#2718, 1-Gaul, Adam Simon, 2-born, 3-27 Jun 1875, 12-Gaul, John F., 13-Gaul, Abbie
    A., 15-Gaul
#2719, 1-Gaul, John Frederick, 2-born, 3-28 Jun 1875, 12-Gaul, John F., 13-Gaul,
    Abbie A., 15-Gaul
#2720, 1-Gaul, John F., 2-born, 3-6 Jun 1838, 12-Gaul, Adam, 13-Gaul, Harriet, 15-
    Gaul
#2721, 1-Urian, Abbie A., 2-born, 3-5 Feb 1836, 12-O'Brian, George A., 13-Urian,
    Phoebe, 15-Gaul
#2722, 1-Gaul, George Henry, 2-born, 3-22 Dec 1864, 12-Gaul, John F., 13-Urian,
    Abbie A., 15-Gaul
#2723, 1-Gaul, Annie Brandt, 2-born, 3-4 Feb 1867, 12-Gaul, John F., 13-Urian,
    Abbie A., 15-Gaul
#2724, 1-Gaul, Sarah Elizabeth, 2-died, 3-11 Nov 1875[?], 5-4 years 1 months, 12-
    Gaul, John F., 13-Urian, Abbie A., 15-Gaul
#2725, 1-Urian, Abbie A., 2-died, 3-16 Jul 1876, 5-40 years 5 months, 7-Gaul, John
    F., 15-Gaul
#2726, 1-Urian, Adam S., 2-died, 3-1 Aug 1876, 5-13 months 4 days, 12-Gaul, John
    F., 13-Urian, Abbie A., 15-Gaul
```

FAMILY BIBLE RECORDS IN THE WASHINGTON COUNTY FREE LIBRARY, HAGERSTOWN, MARYLAND

Entry #, 1-Last Name, First Name, 2-Event, 3-Date, 4-Event Location, 5-Age, 6-Other, 7-Spouse's Last, First, 8-Groom's Residence, 9-Bride's Residence, 10-Minister, 11-Minister's Location, 12-Father's Last, First, 13-Mother's Last, First, 14-Transcribed, 15-Family Bible

#2727, 1-Urian, John Frederick, 2-died, 3-5 Aug 1906, 5-31 years 1 months 8 days, 12-Gaul, John F., 13-Urian, Abbie A., 15-Gaul

#2728, 1-Lum, William S., 2-married, 3-21 Aug 1873, 4-Boonsboro, 7-Beachey[?], Elizabeth C.[?], 8-Smoketown, Washington Co., MD, 9-Balarar[?], 10-J.W. Karicoff, 15-Lum

#2729, 1-Lum, Samuel S., 2-married, 3-7:30 pm, 4 Mar 1897, 7-Loudenslager, Mary E., 15-Lum

#2730, 1-Lum, John Alvy, 2-married, 3-2:30 pm, 23 Nov 1899, 7-Rowe, Minnie May, 15-Lum

#2731, 1-Lum, William E., 2-married, 3-7:30 pm, 18 Oct 1900, 7-Bowers, Edith, 15-Lum

#2732, 1-Lum, Oscar A., 2-married, 3-2:00 pm, 15 Feb 1900, 7-Summers, Mary Lizzie, 15-Lum

#2733, 1-Lum, Mary E.M., 2-married, 7-Linebaugh, Benjamin F., 15-Lum

#2734, 1-Lum, Martha Van Della, 2-married, 3-9 Feb 1903, 7-Hoffman, Albert, 15-Lum

#2735, 1-Lum, Alta V., 2-married, 3-21 Dec 1911, 7-Barnhart, Lester H., 15-Lum

#2736, 1-Lum, William Sihon, 2-born, 3-28 May 1853, 15-Lum

#2737, 1-Lum, Elizebeth Cathrine, 2-born, 3-3 Jul 1853, 15-Lum

#2738, 1-Lum, Samuel Luther, 2-born, 3-21 Mar 1874, 15-Lum

#2739, 1-Lum, John Alvy, 2-born, 3-6 Sep 1875, 15-Lum

#2740, 1-Lum, William Emory, 2-born, 3-29 Sep 1877, 15-Lum

#2741, 1-Lum, Charles Ausker, 2-born, 3-16 Sep 1880, 15-Lum

#2742, 1-Lum, Mary Esty May, 2-born, 3-12 Nov 1882, 15-Lum

#2743, 1-Lum, Martha Van Dela, 2-born, 3-10 Apr 1885, 15-Lum

#2744, 1-Lum, Clara Elizebeth, 2-born, 3-19 Mar 1887, 15-Lum

#2745, 1-Lum, Birtha Viola, 2-born, 3-24 Nov 1889, 15-Lum

#2746, 1-Lum, Alta Virginia, 2-born, 3-12 Jul 1891, 15-Lum

#2747, 1-Lum, Clara Elizebeth, 2-died, 3-18 Apr 1888, 5-1 years 1 months, 15-Lum

#2748, 1-Lum, Birtha Viola, 2-died, 3-23 May 1890, 5-6 months, 15-Lum

#2749, 1-Lum, William E., 2-died, 3-Jun 1931, 5-54 years, 15-Lum

#2750, 1-Lum, Samuel Luther, 2-died, 3-29 Jul 1843, 5-69 years, 15-Lum

#2751, 1-Lum, Elizebeth C., 2-died, 3-25 Mar 1819[?], 5-65 years 8 months 22 days, 15-Lum

#2752, 1-Lum, William S., 2-died, 3-27 Jan 1927, 5-73 years 8 months, 15-Lum

#2753, 1-Lumm, William E., 2-obituary, 5-54 years, 15-Lum

#2754, 1-Lum, Catherine (Mrs.), 2-obituary, 4-Mt. Lena, 5-65 years, 13-Beachley, John H. (Mrs.), 15-Lum

#2755, 1-Cronise, Annie M. (Miss), 2-married, 4-bride's house, 7-Beachley, William W., 10-Rev. L.O. Burtner, 15-Lum

#2756, 1-Linebaugh, Mary E. (Mrs.), 2-obituary, 4-between Leitersburg & Ringgold, 5-53 years 1 months 14 days, 15-Lum

#2757, 1-Lumm, W.E., 2-obituary, 4-Mt. Lena, Washington Co., MD, 5-70 years, 15-Lum

#2758, 1-Lum, Minnie M. (Mrs.), 2-obituary, 3-30 Jul, 4-Mt. Lena, Washington Co., MD, 5-65 years, 15-Lum

#2759, 1-Hoffman, Martha Dandelia (Mrs.), 2-obituary, 4-Mt. Lena, Washington Co., MD, 5-63 years, 12-Beachley, William S., 13-Beachley, Elizabeth, 15-Lum

#2760, 1-Lum, John A., 2-obituary, 3-17 Nov, 5-66 years, 15-Lum

#2761, 1-Long, Joshua, 2-married, 3-1 Jan 1880, 4-Hagerstown, 7-Welty, Ida Cora, 10-Rev. J. Tombaugh, 11-First Brethren Church, Hagerstown, MD, 15-Long

#2762, 1-Long, Ina Pearle, 2-married, 3-17 Nov 1899, 7-Baker, George R., 15-Long

#2763, 1-Rohrer, Wm. A., 2-married, 3-11 Aug 1920, 7-Baker, Verda M., 15-Long

#2764, 1-Baker, Raymond L., 2-married, 3-7 Jan 1921, 7-Davis, Lillian, 15-Long

#2765, 1-Baker, Guy L., 2-married, 3-Apr 1925, 7-Crider, Thelma S., 15-Long

#2766, 1-Jamison, David W., 2-married, 3-12 Oct 1935, 7-Baker, Urla G., 15-Long

#2767, 1-Baker, Joshua J., 2-married, 3-2 Jul 1936, 7-Grove, Hope, 15-Long

FAMILY BIBLE RECORDS IN THE WASHINGTON COUNTY FREE LIBRARY, HAGERSTOWN, MARYLAND

Entry #, 1-Last Name, First Name, 2-Event, 3-Date, 4-Event Location, 5-Age, 6-Other, 7-Spouse's Last, First, 8-Groom's Residence, 9-Bride's Residence, 10-Minister, 11-Minister's Location, 12-Father's Last, First, 13-Mother's Last, First, 14-Transcribed, 15-Family Bible

#2768, 1-Jamison, Harvey L., 2-married, 3-7 Mar 1936, 7-Baker, Wanda A., 15-Long
#2769, 1-Culler, Paul M., 2-married, 3-25 Dec 1938, 7-Baker, Evelyn L., 15-Long
#2770, 1-Mentzer, Walter H., 2-married, 3-29 Apr 1939, 7-Baker, Anita E., 15-Long
#2771, 1-Miller, Harold E., 2-married, 3-14 Sep 1957, 7-Jamison, Barbara A., 15-Long
#2772, 1-Jamison, Marvin L., 2-married, 7-Sigler, Jane[?], 15-Long
#2773, 1-Jamison, Wayne B., 2-married, 7-Diebert, Lorraine, 15-Long
#2774, 1-Long, Joshua, 2-born, 3-10 Mar 1857, 15-Long
#2775, 1-Long, Ida C., 2-born, 3-5 Feb 1855, 15-Long
#2776, 1-Long, I. Peaerle, 2-born, 3-16 Nov 1880, 4-Carlisle, PA, 15-Long
#2777, 1-Long, Guy Mohler, 2-born, 3-18 Dec 1882, 4-Downsville Store, Washington Co., MD, 15-Long
#2778, 1-Long, Earl Downey, 2-born, 3-26 Oct 1884, 4-Downsville, MD, 15-Long
#2779, 1-Long, Simon Wlety, 2-born, 3-6 Jun 1886, 4-old house near Downsville, MD, 15-Long
#2780, 1-Long, Lola Blanche, 2-born, 3-20 Nov 1889, 4-new house near Downsville, MD, 15-Long
#2781, 1-Long, Joshua, 2-died, 3-24 Nov 1935, 4-his home in Downsville, MD, 5-78 years 8 months 14 days, 15-Long
#2782, 1-Long, Ida C., 2-died, 3-18 Feb 1940, 4-below Downsville, MD, 5-85 years __ days, 15-Long
#2783, 1-Baker, I. Pearl (Long), 2-died, 3-22 Mar 1921, 4-Tilghmanton, MD, 5-40 years _ months 7 days, 15-Long
#2784, 1-Long, Simon Welty, 2-died, 3-18 Apr 1947, 4-Greensboro, NC, 15-Long
#2785, 1-Long, Lola Blanche, 2-died, 3-5 May 1935, 4-Baltimore, MD, 15-Long
#2786, 1-Long, Joshua, 2-baptized, 3-16 Jul 1882, 4-"in the pond at home", 6-German Baptist, 10-Elder Daniel Wolf, 15-Long
#2787, 1-Long, Ida C., 2-baptized, 3-Feb 1876, 4-"in the pond at home", 6-Disciple Profession, 10-Elder Mathews, 11-Beaver Creek, 15-Long
#2788, 1-Long, Ida C., 2-baptized, 3-9 Nov 1888, 6-Brethren Faith, 10-Elder Isaac D. Bowman, 15-Long
#2789, 1-Baker, Verda Mary, 2-born, 3-26 Apr 1900, 4-Papa Long's house in Downsville, 12-Baker, Geo. R., 13-Long, I. Pearle, 15-Long
#2790, 1-Baker, Raymond LaMar Teddy", 2-born, 3-19 Aug 1901, 4-Papa Long's house in Downsville, 12-Baker, Geo. R., 13-Long, I. Pearle, 15-Long
#2791, 1-Baker, Thelma Lola, 2-born, 3-4 Oct 1903, 4-Mt. Moriah, MD, 12-Baker, Geo. R., 13-Long, I. Pearle, 15-Long
#2792, 1-Baker, Guy Long, 2-born, 3-2 Apr 1906, 4-Mt. Moriah, MD, 12-Baker, Geo. R., 13-Long, I. Pearle, 15-Long
#2793, 1-Baker, Urla Grace, 2-born, 3-10 Jun 1908, 4-Mt. Moriah, MD, 12-Baker, Geo. R., 13-Long, I. Pearle, 15-Long
#2794, 1-Baker, Joshua Jacob, 2-born, 3-26 Aug 1910, 4-Mt. Moriah, MD, 12-Baker, Geo. R., 13-Long, I. Pearle, 15-Long
#2795, 1-Baker, Wanda Arlene, 2-born, 3-19 Jun 1916, 4-South's Farm below Funkstown, MD, 12-Baker, Geo. R., 13-Long, I. Pearle, 15-Long
#2796, 1-Baker, Evelyn Lorraine, 2-born, 3-20 Feb 1918, 4-Vance Farm south of Hagerstown, MD, 12-Baker, Geo. R., 13-Long, I. Pearle, 15-Long
#2797, 1-Baker, Anita Elizabeth, 2-born, 3-21 Sep 1919, 4-Vance Farm south of Hagerstown, MD, 12-Baker, Geo. R., 13-Long, I. Pearle, 15-Long
#2798, 1-Rohrer, William Arthur, 2-born, 3-27 Feb 1899, 4-Samples Manor on John Brown farm, 7-Baker, Verda, 12-Rohrer, W. Newton, 13-Morrow, Martha Ellen, 15-Long
#2799, 1-Baker, George Raymond, 2-born, 3-4 Nov 1878, 4-E. Berlin, PA, 12-Baker, Jacob, 13-Mummert, Mary, 15-Long

FAMILY BIBLE RECORDS IN THE WASHINGTON COUNTY FREE LIBRARY, HAGERSTOWN, MARYLAND

Entry #, 1-Last Name, First Name, 2-Event, 3-Date, 4-Event Location, 5-Age, 6-Other, 7-Spouse's Last, First, 8-Groom's Residence, 9-Bride's Residence, 10-Minister, 11-Minister's Location, 12-Father's Last, First, 13-Mother's Last, First, 14-Transcribed, 15-Family Bible

#2800, 1-Rohrer, LaVerne Baker, 2-born, 3-25 Mar 1921, 4-Chas. Coffman farm, Tilghmanton, MD, 12-Rohrer, Wm., 13-Baker, Verda, 15-Long

#2801, 1-Rohrer, Nelda Jean, 2-born, 3-5 Sep 1924, 4-Chas. Coffman farm, Tilghmanton, MD, 12-Rohrer, Wm., 13-Baker, Verda, 15-Long

#2802, 1-Rohrer, Miriam Lee, 2-born, 3-4 Jan 1926, 4-Chas. Coffman farm, Tilghmanton, MD, 12-Rohrer, Wm., 13-Baker, Verda, 15-Long

#2803, 1-Rohrer, Nelda Jean, 2-died, 3-25 May 1934, 5-9 years 3 months 10 days, 15-Long

#2804, 1-Long, Joshua Papa", 2-born, 3-10 Mar 1857, 4-Long farm, Downsville, MD, 15-Long

#2805, 1-Long, Ida C., 2-born, 3-5 Feb 1855, 4-right-hand side of Manor Rd. off Sharpsburg Pike at Tilghmanton, MD, 15-Long

#2806, 1-Long, Minnie (Burgan), 2-died, 3-20 Nov 1910, 7-Long, Guy, 15-Long

#2807, 1-Long, Helen, 2-born, 3-29 Jun 1907, 12-Long, Guy, 13-Burgan, Minnie, 15-Long

#2808, 1-Long, Helen, 2-died, 3-13 Aug 1908, 5-1 years 5 months 14 days, 6-cause of death: thrush, 12-Long, Guy, 13-Burgan, Minnie, 15-Long

#2809, 1-Long, Merle Chester, 2-born, 3-24 May 1908, 12-Long, Guy, 13-Burgan, Minnie, 15-Long

#2810, 1-Long, Merle Chester, 2-died, 3-28 Dec 1954, 5-54 years 7 months 4 day, 6-cause of death: heart attack, 12-Long, Guy, 13-Burgan, Minnie, 15-Long

#2811, 1-Long, Lena, 2-born, 3-6 Nov 1910, 12-Long, Guy, 13-Burgan, Minnie, 15-Long

#2812, 1-Long, Lena, 2-died, 3-4 Aug 1911, 5-9 months, 6-cause of death: spasms, 12-Long, Guy, 13-Burgan, Minnie, 15-Long

#2813, 1-Long, Guy, 2-married, 7-Cox, Bessie, 15-Long

#2814, 1-Long, Guy, 2-married, 7-Dellinger, Ida Rhodes, 15-Long

#2815, 1-Cunningham, Sallie L., 2-married, 7-Cunningham, S.S., 15-Long

#2816, 1-Long, Ann Elizabeth, 3-12 Aug 1818, 6-owned Bible, 15-Long

#2817, 1-Long, Abram Devenport, 3-27 Mar 1790, 15-Long

#2818, 1-Long, Ann Elizabeth, 2-born, 3-17 Feb 1795, 15-Long

#2819, 1-Long, Abram D., 2-married, 3-22 May 1817, 7-Long, Ann E., 15-Long

#2820, 1-Long, Elizabeth, 2-born, 3-29 Mar 1818, 15-Long

#2821, 1-Long, James, 2-born, 3-13 Jun 1820, 15-Long

#2822, 1-Long, James, 2-died, 3-23 Nov 1820, 15-Long

#2823, 1-Long, John, 2-died, 3-2 Sep 1821, 15-Long

#2824, 1-Long, John, 2-born, 3-9 Jan 1822, 15-Long

#2825, 1-Ha_____, Jacob, 2-died, 3-19 Nov 1822, 6-father of Ann E. Long, 15-Long

#2826, 1-Long, Elizabeth D., 2-died, 3-5 Sep 1823, 5-5 years 5 months 7 days, 15-Long

#2827, 1-Long, Elizabeth Mary, 2-born, 3-11 Jul 1824, 12-Long, Abram D., 13-Long, Ann E., 15-Long

#2828, 1-Long, Saly, 2-born, 3-22 Sep 1826, 12-Long, Abram D., 13-Long, Ann E., 15-Long

#2829, 1-Long, Abram D., 2-died, 3-18 Feb 1829, 15-Long

#2830, 1-Long, Abram D., 2-born, 3-2 Mar 1829, 15-Long

#2831, 1-Long, Elizabeth M., 2-married, 3-10 Feb 1847, 7-Anderson, Jas. H., 15-Long

#2832, 1-Leatherman, William Brown, 2-married, 3-21 Dec 1898, 4-Bakersville Church, 7-Young, Elva Viola, 10-A.K. Kerlin, 15-Leatherman

#2833, 1-Leatherman, William Brown, 2-born, 3-6 Jun 1876, 15-Leatherman

#2834, 1-Leatherman, Elva (Young), 2-born, 3-1 Mar 1879, 15-Leatherman

#2835, 1-Leatherman, Lloyd Young, 2-born, 3-12 May 1902, 15-Leatherman

#2836, 1-Koontz, Blanche, 2-died, 3-20 Aug 1893, 15-Koontz

#2837, 1-Koontz, Fred E., 2-died, 3-26 Jan 1904, 15-Koontz

#2838, 1-Koontz, Harry C., 2-died, 3-27 Apr 1924, 15-Koontz

#2839, 1-Koontz, Henry C., 2-died, 3-25 Apr 1931, 15-Koontz

FAMILY BIBLE RECORDS IN THE WASHINGTON COUNTY FREE LIBRARY, HAGERSTOWN, MARYLAND

Entry #, 1-Last Name, First Name, 2-Event, 3-Date, 4-Event Location, 5-Age, 6-Other, 7-Spouse's Last, First, 8-Groom's Residence, 9-Bride's Residence, 10-Minister, 11-Minister's Location, 12-Father's Last, First, 13-Mother's Last, First, 14-Transcribed, 15-Family Bible

```
#2840, 1-Koontz, Willie V., 2-died, 3-3 Feb 1942, 15-Koontz
#2841, 1-Fletcher, Edna E., 2-died, 3-29 May 1943, 15-Koontz
#2842, 1-Koontz, Leona V., 2-died, 3-24 Apr 1956, 15-Koontz
#2843, 1-Koontz, Floyd L., 2-died, 3-29 Dec 1957, 15-Koontz
#2844, 1-Koontz, Henry C., 2-born, 3-16 Oct 1869, 15-Koontz
#2845, 1-Koontz, Willie M., 2-born, 3-19 Oct 1872, 15-Koontz
#2846, 1-Koontz, Blanche M., 2-born, 3-3 Dec 1892, 15-Koontz
#2847, 1-Koontz, Agnes C., 2-born, 3-6 May 1894, 15-Koontz
#2848, 1-Koontz, Fred E., 2-born, 3-8 May 1896, 15-Koontz
#2849, 1-Koontz, Edna E., 2-born, 3-26 Oct 1898, 15-Koontz
#2850, 1-Koontz, Harry C., 2-born, 3-4 Sep 1901, 15-Koontz
#2851, 1-Koontz, Gladys F., 2-born, 3-12 Nov 1903, 15-Koontz
#2852, 1-Koontz, Floyd L., 2-born, 3-31 May 1906, 15-Koontz
#2853, 1-Koontz, Elmer W., 2-born, 3-6 Jul 1908, 15-Koontz
#2854, 1-Koontz, Leona V., 2-born, 3-11 Sep 1910, 15-Koontz
#2855, 1-Koontz, Willmina Virginia (Mrs.), 2-obituary, 4-Sharpsburg, MD, 5-69
    years, 7-Koontz, Henry C., 12-Showe, William Henry, 13-McCoy, Amelia
    Catherine, 15-Koontz
#2856, 1-Koontz, Floyd Leslie, 2-obituary, 4-Hagerstown, MD, 5-51 years, 15-Koontz
#2857, 1-Koontz, 2-married, 7-Sagle, Mabel, 15-Koontz
#2858, 1-Fletcher, Edna (Koontz) (Mrs.), 2-obituary, 4-Hagerstown, MD, 5-44 years,
    6-cause of death: heart attack, 7-Fletcher, Morris, 15-Koontz
#2859, 1-Fletcher, Leona Virginia, 2-obituary, 4-Hagerstown, MD, 5-45 years, 15-
    Koontz
#2860, 1-Fletcher, 2-born, 4-Roxbury, Washington Co., MD, 12-Koontz, H.C., 13-
    Showe, Wilimina, 15-Koontz
#2861, 1-Koontz, Henry C., 2-married, 3-7 Jul 1892, 4-Manor Church, 7-Showe, Willia
    M.[?], 10-Elder Daniel Wolf, 15-Koontz
#2862, 1-Stewart, Maryann, 2-born, 3-21 Nov 1788, 12-Stewart, Thomas, 13-Stewart,
    Martha, 15-Stewart
#2863, 1-Leslie, Mary Elisabeth, 2-born, 3-May 1843, 12-Leslie, James, 13-Leslie,
    Jane, 15-Stewart
#2864, 1-Leslie, James H., 2-born, 3-4[?] Aug 1845, 12-Leslie, James, 13-Leslie,
    Jane, 15-Stewart
#2865, 1-Leslie, Susan J.[?], 2-born, 3-12 Mar 1847, 12-Leslie, James, 13-Leslie,
    Jane, 15-Stewart
#2866, 1-Bowling, Elisabeth, 2-born, 3-14 Apr 1822, 12-Bowling, George, 13-Bowling,
    Marcy, 15-Stewart
#2867, 1-Bowling, Jean, 2-born, 3-29 Mar 1824, 12-Bowling, George, 13-Bowling,
    Marcy, 15-Stewart
#2868, 1-Bowling, Thomas William, 2-born, 3-3 Feb 1826, 12-Bowling, George, 13-
    Bowling, Marcy, 15-Stewart
#2869, 1-Bowling, Marthey Ann, 2-born, 3-18 May 1830, 15-Stewart
#2870, 1-Conrad, Mary Francies, 2-born, 3-24[?] Nov 1858[?], 12-Conrad, William,
    13-Conrad, Martha, 15-Stewart
#2871, 1-Stewart, Martha Jane, 2-born, 3-25 May 1835, 12-Stewart, Thomas, 13-
    Stewart, Elizabeth, 15-Stewart
#2872, 1-Stewart, George William, 2-born, 3-14 May 1838, 12-Stewart, Thomas, 13-
    Stewart, Elizabeth, 15-Stewart
#2873, 1-Conrad, William E., 2-born, 3-5 Oct 1867[?], 12-Conrad, William, 13-
    Conrad, Martha, 15-Stewart
#2874, 1-Conrad, William E., 2-died, 3-17 Jul 1897, 15-Stewart
#2875, 1-Conrad, Emma Virginia, 2-born, 3-5 May 1870, 15-Stewart
#2876, 1-Conrad, Emma Virginia, 2-died, 3-5 Oct 1871, 15-Stewart
```

FAMILY BIBLE RECORDS IN THE WASHINGTON COUNTY FREE LIBRARY, HAGERSTOWN, MARYLAND

Entry #, 1-Last Name, First Name, 2-Event, 3-Date, 4-Event Location, 5-Age, 6-Other, 7-Spouse's Last, First, 8-Groom's Residence, 9-Bride's Residence, 10-Minister, 11-Minister's Location, 12-Father's Last, First, 13-Mother's Last, First, 14-Transcribed, 15-Family Bible

#2877, 1-Davis, Marathey An[?], 2-born, 3-29 Jul 1826, 12-Davis, Samuel, 13-Davis, Jane, 15-Stewart

#2878, 1-Davis, John William, 2-born, 3-10 Nov 1829, 15-Stewart

#2879, 1-Leslie, James H.[?], 2-born, 3-9 Aug 1845, 12-Leslie, James, 13-Leslie, Jane, 15-Stewart

#2880, 1-Hoff, Francis C., 2-born, 3-5 Dec 1846, 12-Hoff, Harison, 13-Hoff, Martha, 15-Stewart

#2881, 1-Stewart, Jane, 2-born, 3-5 Jun 1789, 12-Stewart, Thomas, 13-Stewart, Martha, 15-Stewart

#2882, 1-Knode, Blackford Westenhaver, 2-married, 7-Staley, Carolyn Elizabeth, 15-Stewart

#2883, 1-Knode, Ella, 2-born, 12-Knode, Blackford Westenhaver, 13-Staley, Carolyn Elizabeth, 15-Stewart

#2884, 1-Knode, William, 2-born, 12-Knode, Blackford Westenhaver, 13-Staley, Carolyn Elizabeth, 15-Stewart

#2885, 1-Knode, Lula, 2-born, 12-Knode, Blackford Westenhaver, 13-Staley, Carolyn Elizabeth, 15-Stewart

#2886, 1-Knode, Alonzo, 2-born, 12-Knode, Blackford Westenhaver, 13-Staley, Carolyn Elizabeth, 15-Stewart

#2887, 1-Knode, John Calvin, 2-born, 3-Sep 1873, 15-Stewart

#2888, 1-Knode, John Calvin, 2-died, 3-Feb 1952, 15-Stewart

#2889, 1-Knode, Willard Westenhaver, 2-born, 3-11 Apr 1903, 15-Stewart

#2890, 1-Knode, John Ott[?], 2-born, 3-20 Dec 1907, 15-Stewart

#2891, 1-Knode, Louise Blackford, 2-born, 3-26 Dec 1911, 15-Stewart

#2892, 1-Knode, Louise Blackford, 2-died, 3-1983, 15-Stewart

#2893, 1-Benner, Cora May, 2-born, 3-9 Jan 1892, 12-Benner, George W., 15-Stewart

#2894, 1-Benner, Lena Francis, 2-born, 3-23 Oct 1894, 12-Benner, George W., 15-Stewart

#2895, 1-Rhineman, Minnie Edington, 2-born, 3-Jul 1873, 12-Rhineman, John, 13-Rhineman, Mary Jane, 15-Stewart

#2896, 1-Rhineman, Minnie Edington, 2-died, 3-Mar 1951, 15-Stewart

#2897, 1-Knode, John Ott, 2-born, 3-20 Dec, 15-Stewart

#2898, 1-Knode, John Ott, 2-married, 7-Cadwallader, Frances, 15-Stewart

#2899, 1-Knode, John Cadwallader, 2-born, 3-Aug 1938, 12-Knode, John Ott, 13-Cadwallader, Frances, 15-Stewart

#2900, 1-Knode, Louise Blackford, 2-married, 3-15 Jul 1934, 7-Hollis, Philip Boyd, 15-Stewart

#2901, 1-Hollis, Phyllis Bowling, 2-born, 3-12 Oct 1935, 12-Hollis, Philip Boyd, 13-Knode, Louise Blackford, 15-Stewart

#2902, 1-Hollis, Phyllis Bowling, 2-married, 3-3 Oct 1958, 7-Poppen, Daniel Victor, 15-Stewart

#2903, 1-Poppen, Daniel Victor, 2-born, 3-18 Nov 1931, 12-Poppen, Alvin W., 13-Poppen, Grace, 15-Stewart

#2904, 1-Poppen, Kimberly Hollis, 2-born, 3-20 Feb 1975, 12-Poppen, Daniel Victor, 13-Hollis, Phyllis Bowling, 15-Stewart

#2905, 1-Hollis, Philip, 2-born, 3-14 Mar 1913, 12-Hollis, C.W., 13-Barr, Grace, 15-Stewart

#2906, 1-Hollis, Mary Louise, 2-born, 3-14 Feb 1938, 12-Hollis, Philip Boyd, 13-Knode, Louise Blackford, 15-Stewart

#2907, 1-Hollis, Mary Louise, 2-married, 7-Coleman, John H., 15-Stewart

#2908, 1-Coleman, John H., 2-born, 3-8 Nov 1931, 12-Coleman, John, 13-Gaines, Nellie, 15-Stewart

#2909, 1-Coleman, Lou Nell, 2-born, 3-12 Apr 1961, 12-Coleman, John H., 13-Hollis, Mary Louise, 15-Stewart

FAMILY BIBLE RECORDS IN THE WASHINGTON COUNTY FREE LIBRARY, HAGERSTOWN, MARYLAND

Entry #, 1-Last Name, First Name, 2-Event, 3-Date, 4-Event Location, 5-Age, 6-Other, 7-Spouse's Last, First, 8-Groom's Residence, 9-Bride's Residence, 10-Minister, 11-Minister's Location, 12-Father's Last, First, 13-Mother's Last, First, 14-Transcribed, 15-Family Bible

#2910, 1-Coleman, John Boyd, 2-born, 3-21 Feb 1964, 12-Coleman, John H., 13-Hollis, Mary Louise, 15-Stewart

#2911, 1-Coleman, Phyllis Josphine, 2-born, 3-11 Jun 1967, 12-Coleman, John H., 13-Hollis, Mary Louise, 15-Stewart

#2912, 1-Knode, Charles Lane, 2-died, 3-10 Aug 1866, 4-Boonsboro, MD, 5-3 months 16 days, 12-Knode, Saml., 13-Knode, Mary C., 15-Stewart

#2913, 1-Lane, Mary Catharine, 2-died, 3-4 Nov 1919, 4-Boonsboro, MD, 5-78 years 4 months 6 days, 7-Knode, Samuel C., 12-Lane, John C., 13-Horine, Elizabeth, 15-Stewart

#2914, 1-Knode, Samuel C., 2-born, 3-6 Aug 1838, 15-Stewart

#2915, 1-Lane, Mary Catharine, 2-born, 3-29 Jun 1841, 15-Stewart

#2916, 1-Knode, Edgar Lane, 2-born, 3-6 Oct 1863, 12-Knode, Samuel C., 13-Lane, Mary Catharine, 15-Stewart

#2917, 1-Knode, Charles Lane, 2-born, 3-25 Apr 1866, 4-Boonsboro, MD, 15-Stewart

#2918, 1-Knode, John Hubert, 2-born, 3-24 Apr 1868, 4-Boonsboro, MD, 15-Stewart

#2919, 1-Knode, Samuel, 2-married, 3-11 Dec 1862, 4-Frederick, MD, 7-Lane, Mary Catharine, 10-Rev. Dr. Ross, 15-Stewart

#2920, 1-Kendall, Winifred Belle, 2-died, 3-31 Dec 1918, 5-62 years 2 months 3 days, 14-Yes, 15-Kendall

#2921, 1-Myers, Mabel Kendall, 2-died, 3-22 May 1927, 5-46 years 3 months 17 days, 14-Yes, 15-Kendall

#2922, 1-Kendall, Findly J., 2-died, 3-28 Jun 1928, 5-49 years, 14-Yes, 15-Kendall

#2923, 1-Kendall, Roy McNaughton, 2-died, 3-8 Sep 1963, 5-79 years 10 months, 14-Yes, 15-Kendall

#2924, 1-Kendall, Mabel Louise, 2-died, 3-4 Jan 1918, 6-granddaughter of Robert McNaughton Kendall, 14-Yes, 15-Kendall

#2925, 1-Myers, Mabel Virginia , 2-died, 3-24 Feb 1918, 6-granddaughter of Robert McNaughton Kendall, 14-Yes, 15-Kendall

#2926, 1-Wilson, William C., 2-died, 3-1918, 6-Son-in-law of Robert McNaughton Kendall, 14-Yes, 15-Kendall

#2927, 1-Shoap, Hugh W., 2-died, 3-1918, 6-Son-in-law of Robert McNaughton Kendall, 14-Yes, 15-Kendall

#2928, 1-Shimer, Orpha Kendall, 2-died, 3-29 Dec 1918, 12-Kendall, Robert McNaughton, 14-Yes, 15-Kendall

#2929, 1-Kendall, Winifred Belle, 2-died, 3-31 Dec 1918, 7-Kendall, Robert McNaughton, 14-Yes, 15-Kendall

#2930, 1-Pittman, Sarah Ellen, 2-died, 3-5 Dec 1919, 5-91 years 1 months 2 days, 14-Yes, 15-Kendall

#2931, 1-Kendall, Roy McNaughton, 2-married, 3-16 Dec 1908, 7-Nelson, Elizabeth Johnston, 14-Yes, 15-Kendall

#2932, 1-Kendall, Alma Nelson, 2-born, 3-11 Nov 1910, 14-Yes, 15-Kendall

#2933, 1-Kendall, Mabel Louise, 2-born, 3-17 Apr 1914, 14-Yes, 15-Kendall

#2934, 1-Kendall, Katie Elizabeth, 2-born, 3-21 Apr 1916, 14-Yes, 15-Kendall

#2935, 1-Kendall, Dorothy Winifred, 2-born, 3-30 May 1918, 14-Yes, 15-Kendall

#2936, 1-Kendall, John McNaughton, 2-born, 3-24 Apr 1927, 14-Yes, 15-Kendall

#2937, 1-Kendall, Robert McNaughton, 2-died, 3-8 Feb 1910, 5-63 years 1 months 21 days, 14-Yes, 15-Kendall

#2938, 1-Wilson, Frances Kendall, 2-died, 3-5 Nov 1911, 14-Yes, 15-Kendall

#2939, 1-Kendall, Mabel Louise, 2-died, 3-4 Jan 1918, 5-3 years 8 months 18 days, 14-Yes, 15-Kendall

#2940, 1-Myers, Mabel Virginia, 2-died, 3-24 Feb 1918, 5-3 years 4 months, 14-Yes, 15-Kendall

#2941, 1-Shimer, Orpha Kendall, 2-died, 3-29 Dec 1918, 5-29 years 6 months 18 days, 14-Yes, 15-Kendall

FAMILY BIBLE RECORDS IN THE WASHINGTON COUNTY FREE LIBRARY, HAGERSTOWN, MARYLAND

Entry #, 1-Last Name, First Name, 2-Event, 3-Date, 4-Event Location, 5-Age, 6-Other, 7-Spouse's Last, First, 8-Groom's Residence, 9-Bride's Residence, 10-Minister, 11-Minister's Location, 12-Father's Last, First, 13-Mother's Last, First, 14-Transcribed, 15-Family Bible

```
#2942, 1-Kausler, Catarina, 2-married, 3-9 Jun 1795, 6-original in German; typed
    English translation, 7-Weis, Heinrich, 14-Yes, 15-Kausler
#2943, 1-Weis, Johannes, 2-born, 3-16 Oct 1796, 12-Weis, Heinrich, 13-Kausler,
    Catarina, 14-Yes, 15-Kausler
#2944, 1-Weis, Johannes, 2-baptized, 3-20 Nov 1796, 12-Weis, Heinrich, 13-Kausler,
    Catarina, 14-Yes, 15-Kausler
#2945, 1-Weis, Samuel, 2-born, 3-10 Aug 1798, 12-Weis, Heinrich, 13-Kausler,
    Catarina, 14-Yes, 15-Kausler
#2946, 1-Weis, Samuel, 2-baptized, 3-2 Sep 1798, 12-Weis, Heinrich, 13-Kausler,
    Catarina, 14-Yes, 15-Kausler
#2947, 1-Weis, Amalia, 2-born, 3-12 Feb 1801, 12-Weis, Heinrich, 13-Kausler,
    Catarina, 14-Yes, 15-Kausler
#2948, 1-Weis, Amalia, 2-baptized, 3-22 Mar 1801, 12-Weis, Heinrich, 13-Kausler,
    Catarina, 14-Yes, 15-Kausler
#2949, 1-Weis, Heinrich Kausler, 2-born, 3-14 May 1803, 12-Weis, Heinrich, 13-
    Kausler, Catarina, 14-Yes, 15-Kausler
#2950, 1-Weis, Heinrich Kausler, 2-baptized, 3-3 ___ 1803, 12-Weis, Heinrich, 13-
    Kausler, Catarina, 14-Yes, 15-Kausler
#2951, 1-Weis, William Jacob, 2-born, 3-18 Aug 1805, 12-Weis, Heinrich, 13-Kausler,
    Catarina, 14-Yes, 15-Kausler
#2952, 1-Weis, William Jacob, 2-baptized, 3-22 Oct 1805, 12-Weis, Heinrich, 13-
    Kausler, Catarina, 14-Yes, 15-Kausler
#2953, 1-Weis, Anna Maria Elizabeth, 2-born, 3-11 Sep 1808, 12-Weis, Heinrich, 13-
    Kausler, Catarina, 14-Yes, 15-Kausler
#2954, 1-Weis, Anna Maria Elizabeth, 2-baptized, 3-25 Oct 1808, 12-Weis, Heinrich,
    13-Kausler, Catarina, 14-Yes, 15-Kausler
#2955, 1-Weis, James Hendricks, 2-born, 3-20 Mar 1811, 12-Weis, Heinrich, 13-
    Kausler, Catarina, 14-Yes, 15-Kausler
#2956, 1-Weis, James Hendricks, 2-baptized, 3-3 Apr 1811, 12-Weis, Heinrich, 13-
    Kausler, Catarina, 14-Yes, 15-Kausler
#2957, 1-Weis, Alfred, 2-born, 3-5 Jan 1814, 12-Weis, Heinrich, 13-Kausler,
    Catarina, 14-Yes, 15-Kausler
#2958, 1-Weis, Alfred, 2-baptized, 3-10 Feb 1814, 12-Weis, Heinrich, 13-Kausler,
    Catarina, 14-Yes, 15-Kausler
#2959, 1-Weis, Catarina Christina, 2-born, 3-4 Apr 1816, 12-Weis, Heinrich, 13-
    Kausler, Catarina, 14-Yes, 15-Kausler
#2960, 1-Weis, Catarina Christina, 2-baptized, 3-5 May 1816, 12-Weis, Heinrich, 13-
    Kausler, Catarina, 14-Yes, 15-Kausler
#2961, 1-Weis, Georg Weigandt, 2-born, 3-4 Jun 1819, 12-Weis, Heinrich, 13-Kausler,
    Catarina, 14-Yes, 15-Kausler
#2962, 1-Weis, Georg Weigandt, 2-baptized, 3-18 Jul 1819, 12-Weis, Heinrich, 13-
    Kausler, Catarina, 14-Yes, 15-Kausler
#2963, 1-Wise, Augustus Joseph, 2-born, 3-15 Sep 1821, 4-Brownsville, PA, 14-Yes,
    15-Kausler
#2964, 1-Kaetzel, Lewis, 2-married, 3-26 Feb 1880, 4-near Brownsville, MD, 7-Fouch,
    Laura M., 10-Cornelius Castle, 15-Kaetzel
#2965, 1-Spessard, Sr., Charles W., 2-married, 3-24 May 1913, 4-Washington, DC, 5-
    24 years, 6-bride was 22 yrs., 7-Kaetzel, Addie M., 15-Kaetzel
#2966, 1-Spessard, Jr., Charles W., 2-born, 3-11 Aug 1916, 12-Spessard, Sr.,
    Charles W., 13-Kaetzel, Addie M., 15-Kaetzel
#2967, 1-Spessard, Leon Aldine, 2-born, 3-12 May 1921, 12-Spessard, Sr., Charles
    W., 13-Kaetzel, Addie M., 15-Kaetzel
#2968, 1-Spessard, Lewis Cleggett, 2-born, 3-9 Aug 1923, 12-Spessard, Sr., Charles
    W., 13-Kaetzel, Addie M., 15-Kaetzel
#2969, 1-Kaetzel, Lewis P.[?], 2-born, 3-29 Sep 1853, 15-Kaetzel
```

FAMILY BIBLE RECORDS IN THE WASHINGTON COUNTY FREE LIBRARY, HAGERSTOWN, MARYLAND

Entry #, 1-Last Name, First Name, 2-Event, 3-Date, 4-Event Location, 5-Age, 6-Other,
7-Spouse's Last, First, 8-Groom's Residence, 9-Bride's Residence, 10-Minister, 11-Minister's Location,
12-Father's Last, First, 13-Mother's Last, First, 14-Transcribed, 15-Family Bible

```
#2970, 1-Kaetzel, Laura M., 2-born, 3-26 Feb 1858, 15-Kaetzel
#2971, 1-Kaetzel, Bessie Corine, 2-born, 3-26 Dec 1880, 12-Kaetzel, Lewis, 13-
    Fouch, Laura M., 15-Kaetzel
#2972, 1-Kaetzel, Pearl Virginie, 2-born, 3-28 Aug 1882, 12-Kaetzel, Lewis, 13-
    Fouch, Laura M., 15-Kaetzel
#2973, 1-Kaetzel, Annie Laura, 2-born, 3-8 Nov 1884, 12-Kaetzel, Lewis, 13-Fouch,
    Laura M., 15-Kaetzel
#2974, 1-Kaetzel, Maud C., 2-born, 3-8 Aug 1886, 12-Kaetzel, Lewis, 13-Fouch, Laura
    M., 15-Kaetzel
#2975, 1-Kaetzel, John Franklin, 2-born, 3-8 Mar 1888, 12-Kaetzel, Lewis, 13-Fouch,
    Laura M., 15-Kaetzel
#2976, 1-Kaetzel, Mary Alice A., 2-born, 3-18 Jul 1890, 12-Kaetzel, Lewis, 13-
    Fouch, Laura M., 15-Kaetzel
#2977, 1-Kaetzel, Laura M. (Mrs.), 2-died, 3-Friday, 4:00 pm, 16 Jul 1915, 5-57
    years 4 months 20 days, 15-Kaetzel
#2978, 1-Kaetzel, Lewis P., 2-died, 3-Thursday, 5:30 pm, 23 Dec 1943, 5-90 years 2
    months 24 days, 6-buried 27 Dec, 4 pm, Rose Hill Cemetery, 15-Kaetzel
#2979, 1-Kaetzel, John Franklin, 2-died, 3-15 Sep 1907, 5-19 years 6 months 7 days,
    15-Kaetzel
#2980, 1-Kaetzel, Harry David, 2-died, 3-Tuesday, 9:30 pm, 24 Mar 1953, 5-55 years
    9 months 23 days, 6-funeral Friday, 2 pm, 15-Kaetzel
#2981, 1-Middlekauff-McBride, Annie L. (Mrs.), 2-died, 3-Friday, 2:00 pm, 13 Feb
    1959, 5-74 years, 6-funeral 2:00 pm, 16 Feb 1959, buried Rose Hill Cemetery,
    15-Kaetzel
#2982, 1-Lowman, Pearl Virginia (Kaetzel), 2-died, 3-8:00 pm, 4 Jul 1959, 5-76
    years 10 months 6 days, 15-Kaetzel
#2983, 1-McBride, William F., 2-died, 3-2 Jun 1961, 5-84 years, 15-Kaetzel
#2984, 1-Curfman, Bessie Cornie (Kaetzel), 2-died, 3-30 Jan 1964, 5-83 years 1
    months 4 days, 6-buried in Rose Hill, 15-Kaetzel
#2985, 1-Spessard, Charles Earl, 2-born, 3-18 Oct 1892, 15-Kaetzel
#2986, 1-Spessard, Russell Leon, 2-born, 3-3 Apr 1895, 15-Kaetzel
#2987, 1-Spessard, Harry David, 2-born, 3-1 Jun 1897, 15-Kaetzel
#2988, 1-Spessard, Jr., Charles William, 2-born, 3-11 Aug 1919, 15-Kaetzel
#2989, 1-Spessard, Aldine Leon, 2-born, 3-12 May 1921, 15-Kaetzel
#2990, 1-Spessard, Lewis Cleggett, 2-born, 3-9 Aug 1923, 15-Kaetzel
#2991, 1-Souders, Ronald Lewis, 2-married, 3-21 Jun 1969, 4-Hagerstown, MD, 7-
    Spessard, Darla Jean, 15-Kaetzel
#2992, 1-Spessard, Charles W., 2-married, 3-24 May 1913, 4-Washington, DC, 7-
    Kaetzel, Adelaide M., 15-Kaetzel
#2993, 1-Hammond, Nora F. (Miss), 2-married, 3-May 1913, 4-Washington, DC, 7-
    Stockslager, David S., 12-Hammond, Charles E., 15-Kaetzel
#2994, 1-Kaetzel, Addie, 2-born, 12-Kaetzel, Lewis P., 15-Kaetzel
#2995, 1-Curfman, Bessie C., 2-obituary, 3-Jan 1964, 4-Stoufferstown, PA, 12-
    Kaetzel, Lewis, 13-Fouch, Laura, 15-Kaetzel
#2996, 1-Middlekauff, Hilda Jean (Miss), 2-married, 3-2 Sep , 4-New Carlisle, 7-
    Eddy, John Alfred, 10-Rev. John C. Middlekauff, 11-Church of the Brethren,
    12-Middlekauff, John C. (Rev.), 15-Kaetzel
#2997, 1-Baumgardner, Barbara Kay, 2-married, 3-16 Mar, 4-St. Paul's United
    Methodist Church, 7-Spessard, Robert Dean, 8-Hagerstown, Md, 9-Waynesboro,
    PA, 10-Lester Kauffman (Rev.), 11-St. Paul's United Methodist Church, 12-
    Baumgardner, Robert B., 15-Kaetzel
#2998, 1-Cushen, Cinda Lou, 2-married, 3-17 Sep, 4-Hagerstown, MD Church of the
    Brethren, 7-Knecht, Robert William, 8-Harpers Ferry, WV, 9-Hagerstown, MD,
    10-DeWitt L. Miller (Rev.), 11-Church of the Brethren, 12-Cushen, Ralph
    Forest, 15-Kaetzel
```

FAMILY BIBLE RECORDS IN THE WASHINGTON COUNTY FREE LIBRARY, HAGERSTOWN, MARYLAND

Entry #, 1-Last Name, First Name, 2-Event, 3-Date, 4-Event Location, 5-Age, 6-Other,
7-Spouse's Last, First, 8-Groom's Residence, 9-Bride's Residence, 10-Minister, 11-Minister's Location,
12-Father's Last, First, 13-Mother's Last, First, 14-Transcribed, 15-Family Bible

```
#2999, 1-Kaetzel, Christian Theobald, 2-born, 3-29 Sep 1857, 15-Kaetzel
#3000, 1-Kaetzel, Mary Elizabeth, 2-born, 3-14 Dec 1859, 15-Kaetzel
#3001, 1-Kaetzel, Cora Elizabeth, 2-born, 3-27 Oct 1800, 15-Kaetzel
#3002, 1-Kaetzel, James Henry, 2-born, 3-17 Aug 1884, 15-Kaetzel
#3003, 1-Kaetzel, Nettie Naomi, 2-born, 3-7 Feb 1887, 15-Kaetzel
#3004, 1-Kaetzel, Edith Virginia, 2-born, 3-8 Aug 1889, 15-Kaetzel
#3005, 1-Kaetzel, Bertie Rebbecca, 2-born, 3-23 Aug 1892, 15-Kaetzel
#3006, 1-Kaetzel, Ethel Viola, 2-born, 3-26 Aug 1895, 15-Kaetzel
#3007, 1-Kaetzel, Garland Bovie[?], 2-born, 3-20 Sep 1898, 15-Kaetzel
#3008, 1-Kaetzel, Katie Mozell[?], 2-born, 3-13 Aug 1901, 15-Kaetzel
#3009, 1-Kaetzel, Robert Lee, 2-born, 3-13 May 1903, 15-Kaetzel
#3010, 1-Weddle, Elizabeth (Mrs.), 2-died, 3-13 May 1882, 5-62 years, 15-Kaetzel
#3011, 1-Kaetzel, Christian, 2-died, 3-31 Dec 1926, 5-69 years, 15-Kaetzel
#3012, 1-Gordon, Joseph, 2-died, 3-19 Sep 1925, 5-77 years, 15-Kaetzel
#3013, 1-Kaetzel, Elizabeth, 2-died, 3-4 Feb 1910, 15-Kaetzel
#3014, 1-Beachley, Mattie[?] V., 2-died, 3-15 Feb 1910, 5-28 years, 15-Kaetzel
#3015, 1-Kaetzel, Blanche L., 2-born, 3-8 May 1914, 15-Kaetzel
#3016, 1-Kaetzel, William L., 2-born, 3-2 Jul 1916, 15-Kaetzel
#3017, 1-Kaetzel, June M., 2-born, 3-23 Nov 1918, 15-Kaetzel
#3018, 1-Kaetzel, Catherain V., 2-born, 3-27 Dec 1921, 15-Kaetzel
#3019, 1-Kaetzel, Charles C., 2-born, 3-30 May 1922, 15-Kaetzel
#3020, 1-Kaetzel, Dorothy G., 2-born, 3-22 Nov 1924, 15-Kaetzel
#3021, 1-Kaetzel, Wanda LaRue, 2-born, 3-27 Jul 1937, 15-Kaetzel
#3022, 1-Wishard, Donna Jean, 2-born, 3-10 Jan 1939, 15-Kaetzel
#3023, 1-Wishard, Lucinda Kay, 2-born, 3-21 Oct 1953, 15-Kaetzel
#3024, 1-Kaetzel, Louise, 2-married, 7-Myers, Leroy, 15-Kaetzel
#3025, 1-Kaetzel, William, 2-married, 7-Young, Pauline, 15-Kaetzel
#3026, 1-Kaetzel, June Marie, 2-married, 7-Wishard, Woodrow, 15-Kaetzel
#3027, 1-Kaetzel, Virginia, 2-married, 7-Font, Robert, 15-Kaetzel
#3028, 1-Kaetzel, Charles Claude, 2-married, 7-Kearns, Mary Jane, 15-Kaetzel
#3029, 1-Kaetzel, Dorothy Grace, 2-married, 7-Gardner, Thomas, 15-Kaetzel
#3030, 1-Shilling, Beatrice Pearl (Mrs.), 2-died, 3-3:15, 8 Sep 1927, 6-funeral
       Trinity Lutheran Church, 10-R. Simon, 15-Kaetzel
#3031, 1-Kaetzel, Edna L., 2-died, 3-24 May 1926, 15-Kaetzel
#3032, 1-Kaetzel, Loretta Jean, 2-died, 3-21 Apr 1950, 15-Kaetzel
#3033, 1-Wishard, Woodrow W., 2-obituary, 3-24 Feb 1976, 6-buried Rose Hill
       Cemetery, 10-Thomas L. Perry (Rev.), 15-Kaetzel
#3034, 1-Wishard, Woodrow W., 2-born, 3-18 Aug 1912, 15-Kaetzel
#3035, 1-Eirley, William H., 2-obituary, 3-5:30 pm, May 1900, 4-S. Walnut St.,
       Hagerstown, MD, 5-75 years, 15-Kaetzel
#3036, 1-Bowers, Eleanora (Mrs.), 2-obituary, 3-Tuesday, 6 pm,, 5-69 years 26 days,
       6-buried Rose Hill Cemetery, 7-Bowers, J.C., 15-Kaetzel
#3037, 1-Kaetzel, William Lewis, 2-obituary, 3-25 Jan 1967, 15-Kaetzel
#3038, 1-Kaetzel, William Lewis, 2-born, 3-3 Jul 1917, 15-Kaetzel
#3039, 1-Brown, Thompson A., 2-married, 3-23 Mar 1916, 4-Baltimore, MD, 7-Huyett,
       Anna Virginia, 14-Yes, 15-Brown
#3040, 1-Brown, Sara V., 2-married, 3-18 Sep 1937, 4-Frederick, MD, 7-Hopkins,
       William F., 14-Yes, 15-Brown
#3041, 1-Brown, Evanna C., 2-married, 3-12 Apr 1941, 4-Baltimore, MD, 7-Ridgely,
       Ruxton M., 14-Yes, 15-Brown
#3042, 1-Brown, T.A., 2-born, 3-5 May 1861, 4-Shady Grove, PA, 14-Yes, 15-Brown
#3043, 1-Brown, T.A., 2-died, 3-26 Jun 1943, 4-Boonsboro, MD, 14-Yes, 15-Brown
#3044, 1-Huyett, Anna Virginia, 2-born, 3-28 Jan 1879, 4-Washington Co., MD, 14-
       Yes, 15-Brown
```

FAMILY BIBLE RECORDS IN THE WASHINGTON COUNTY FREE LIBRARY, HAGERSTOWN, MARYLAND

Entry #, 1-Last Name, First Name, 2-Event, 3-Date, 4-Event Location, 5-Age, 6-Other, 7-Spouse's Last, First, 8-Groom's Residence, 9-Bride's Residence, 10-Minister, 11-Minister's Location, 12-Father's Last, First, 13-Mother's Last, First, 14-Transcribed, 15-Family Bible

#3045, 1-Huyett, Anna Virginia, 2-died, 3-14 Mar 1957, 4-Hagerstown, MD, 14-Yes, 15-Brown

#3046, 1-Hopkins, Wm. F., 2-born, 4-Pennsylvania, 14-Yes, 15-Brown

#3047, 1-Brown, Evanna Connor, 2-born, 3-2 Aug 1917, 4-Hagerstown, MD, 14-Yes, 15-Brown

#3048, 1-Brown, Sara Virginia, 2-born, 3-13 Sep 1918, 4-Hagerstown, MD, 14-Yes, 15-Brown

#3049, 1-Hopkins, Jr., Wm. F., 2-born, 3-13 Jul 1941, 4-Hagerstown, MD, 12-Hopkins, Wm. F., 13-Hopkins, Sara B., 14-Yes, 15-Brown

#3050, 1-Hopkins, John Thompson, 2-born, 3-23 Nov 1945, 4-Hagerstown, MD, 12-Hopkins, Wm. F., 13-Hopkins, Sara B., 14-Yes, 15-Brown

#3051, 1-Hopkins, Angela Marie, 2-born, 3-1 Nov 1951, 4-Hagerstown, MD, 12-Hopkins, Wm. F., 13-Hopkins, Sara B., 14-Yes, 15-Brown

#3052, 1-Hopkins, Samuel Earl, 2-born, 3-2-Sep-58, 4-Hagerstown, MD, 12-Hopkins, Wm. F., 13-Hopkins, Sara B., 14-Yes, 15-Brown

#3053, 1-Huffer, John, 2-born, 3-16 Mar 1806, 15-Huffer

#3054, 1-Huffer, John, 2-died, 3-31 Dec 1868, 15-Huffer

#3055, 1-Huffer, John, 2-married, 3-24 May 1829, 7-Blecher, Leah, 15-Huffer

#3056, 1-Blecher, Leah, 2-born, 3-7 Jan 1805, 15-Huffer

#3057, 1-Blecher, Leah, 2-died, 3-19 Jan 1863, 15-Huffer

#3058, 1-Huffer, Jonas Z.[?], 2-born, 3-12 Jun 1840, 12-Huffer, John, 13-Blecher, Leah, 15-Huffer

#3059, 1-Huffer, Jonas Z.[?], 2-died, 3-1 Mar 1896, 4-Washington Co., MD, 12-Huffer, John, 13-Blecher, Leah, 15-Huffer

#3060, 1-Nikirk, Mollie E., 2-born, 3-12 Mar 1853, 15-Huffer

#3061, 1-Nikirk, Mollie E., 2-died, 3-1 Apr 1884, 4-Washington Co., MD, 15-Huffer

#3062, 1-Nikirk, Mollie E., 2-married, 3-23 Dec 1869, 7-Huffer, Jonas Z.[?], 15-Huffer

#3063, 1-Huffer, Ivy Z.[?], 2-born, 3-28 Aug 1871, 4-Washington Co., MD, 12-Huffer, Jonas Z.[?], 13-Nikirk, Mollie E., 15-Huffer

#3064, 1-Huffer, Ivy Z.[?], 2-died, 3-21 Nov 1956, 12-Huffer, Jonas Z.[?], 13-Nikirk, Mollie E., 15-Huffer

#3065, 1-Huffer, Ivy Z.[?], 2-married, 3-28 Oct 1896, 7-Snyder, J. Edmond, 12-Huffer, Jonas Z.[?], 13-Nikirk, Mollie E., 15-Huffer

#3066, 1-Huffer, Mary G., 2-born, 3-9 Feb 1873, 4-Washington Co., MD, 12-Huffer, Jonas Z.[?], 13-Nikirk, Mollie E., 15-Huffer

#3067, 1-Huffer, Mary G., 2-died, 3-13[?] Sep 1939, 12-Huffer, Jonas Z.[?], 13-Nikirk, Mollie E., 15-Huffer

#3068, 1-Huffer, Mary G., 2-married, 3-20 Dec 1894, 7-Harbaugh, J. Earl, 12-Huffer, Jonas Z.[?], 13-Nikirk, Mollie E., 15-Huffer

#3069, 1-Huffer, Dorah M., 2-born, 3-31 Mar 1874, 4-Washington Co., MD, 12-Huffer, Jonas Z.[?], 13-Nikirk, Mollie E., 15-Huffer

#3070, 1-Huffer, Dorah M., 2-died, 3-5 Jul 1874, 12-Huffer, Jonas Z.[?], 13-Nikirk, Mollie E., 15-Huffer

#3071, 1-Huffer, Sarah A. Huffer, 2-born, 3-3 May 1875, 4-Washington Co., MD, 12-Huffer, Jonas Z.[?], 13-Nikirk, Mollie E., 15-Huffer

#3072, 1-Huffer, Sarah A. Huffer, 2-died, 3-13[?] Jul 1952, 12-Huffer, Jonas Z.[?], 13-Nikirk, Mollie E., 15-Huffer

#3073, 1-Huffer, Sarah A. Huffer, 2-married, 3-Apr 1896, 7-Hammaker, Geo. Wm., 12-Huffer, Jonas Z.[?], 13-Nikirk, Mollie E., 15-Huffer

#3074, 1-Huffer, Clarence E., 2-born, 3-14 Sep 1878, 12-Huffer, Jonas Z.[?], 13-Nikirk, Mollie E., 15-Huffer

#3075, 1-Huffer, Clarence E., 2-married, 7-Spessard, Elizabeth, 12-Huffer, Jonas Z.[?], 13-Nikirk, Mollie E., 15-Huffer

#3076, 1-Snyder, J. Edmond, 2-born, 3-22 Sep 1868, 4-Washington Co., MD, 15-Huffer

FAMILY BIBLE RECORDS IN THE WASHINGTON COUNTY FREE LIBRARY, HAGERSTOWN, MARYLAND

Entry #, 1-Last Name, First Name, 2-Event, 3-Date, 4-Event Location, 5-Age, 6-Other, 7-Spouse's Last, First, 8-Groom's Residence, 9-Bride's Residence, 10-Minister, 11-Minister's Location, 12-Father's Last, First, 13-Mother's Last, First, 14-Transcribed, 15-Family Bible

```
#3077, 1-Snyder, J. Edmond, 2-died, 3-20 Jan 1901, 4-Hagerstown, MD, 15-Huffer
#3078, 1-Snyder, Ivy Z.[?], 2-born, 3-28 Aug 1871, 4-Washington Co., MD, 12-Huffer,
    Jonas Z.[?], 13-Nikirk, Mollie E., 15-Huffer
#3079, 1-Snyder, Ivy Z.[?], 2-died, 3-21 Nov 1956, 4-Washington Co., MD, 12-Huffer,
    Jonas Z.[?], 13-Nikirk, Mollie E., 15-Huffer
#3080, 1-Snyder, Ivy Z.[?], 2-married, 3-28 Oct 1896, 4-White Hall, Washington Co.,
    MD, 7-Snyder, J. Edmond, 10-Chas. Brubaker (Rev.), 12-Huffer, Jonas Z.[?],
    13-Nikirk, Mollie E., 15-Huffer
#3081, 1-Snyder, Irene, 2-born, 3-7 Sep 1898, 4-Hagerstown, MD, 12-Snyder, J.
    Edmond, 13-Huffer, Ivy Z.[?], 15-Huffer
#3082, 1-Huffer, Rhuannah, 2-born, 3-21 Feb 1830, 15-Huffer
#3083, 1-Huffer, Elizabeth, 2-born, 3-1 Feb 1833, 15-Huffer
#3084, 1-Huffer, Elizabeth, 2-died, 5-87 years, 15-Huffer
#3085, 1-Huffer, John, 2-born, 3-24 Oct 1834, 15-Huffer
#3086, 1-Huffer, John, 2-died, 3-22 Mar 1839, 15-Huffer
#3087, 1-Huffer, Alfred, 2-born, 3-8 Oct 1836, 15-Huffer
#3088, 1-Huffer, Alfred, 2-died, 3-1908, 15-Huffer
#3089, 1-Huffer, Jacob, 2-born, 3-21 Jul 1838, 15-Huffer
#3090, 1-Huffer, Jonas Z.[?], 2-born, 3-12 Jun 1846, 15-Huffer
#3091, 1-Huffer, Jonas Z.[?], 2-died, 3-1 Mar 1896, 15-Huffer
#3092, 1-Huffer, Mary, 2-born, 3-7 Oct 1842, 15-Huffer
#3093, 1-Huffer, John, 2-born, 3-1746, 4-Canton of Basle[?], Switzerland, 6-
    migrated to America in 1753, 7-Rohrer, Magdaline, 15-Huffer
#3094, 1-Huffer, Jr., John, 2-born, 3-1771, 4-Washington Co., MD, 12-Huffer, John,
    13-Rohrer, Magdaline, 15-Huffer
#3095, 1-Huffer, Jr., John, 2-died, 3-1842, 15-Huffer
#3096, 1-Huffer, Jr., John, 2-married, 7-Line, Elizabeth, 9-Washington Co., MD, 15-
    Huffer
#3097, 1-Line, Elizabeth, 2-born, 3-1781, 15-Huffer
#3098, 1-Line, Elizabeth, 2-died, 3-1862, 15-Huffer
#3099, 1-Huffer, III, John, 2-born, 3-16 Mar 1806, 4-Washington Co., MD, 12-Huffer,
    Jr., John, 13-Line, Elizabeth, 15-Huffer
#3100, 1-Huffer, III, John, 2-died, 3-31 Dec 1868, 12-Huffer, Jr., John, 13-Line,
    Elizabeth, 15-Huffer
#3101, 1-Huffer, III, John, 2-married, 7-Blecher, Leah, 12-Huffer, Jr., John, 13-
    Line, Elizabeth, 15-Huffer
#3102, 1-Blecher, Leah, 2-born, 3-7 Jan 1805, 15-Huffer
#3103, 1-Blecher, Leah, 2-died, 3-19 Jan 1863, 15-Huffer
#3104, 1-Huffer, Jonas O.[or Q.], 2-born, 3-12 Jun 1840, 4-Washington Co., MD, 12-
    Huffer, III, John, 13-Blecher, Leah, 15-Huffer
#3105, 1-Huffer, Jonas O.[or Q.], 2-died, 3-1 Mar 1896, 12-Huffer, III, John, 13-
    Blecher, Leah, 15-Huffer
#3106, 1-Huffer, Jonas O.[or Q.], 2-married, 7-Nikirk, Mollie E., 12-Huffer, III,
    John, 13-Blecher, Leah, 15-Huffer
#3107, 1-Nikirk, Mollie E., 2-born, 3-12 Mar 1853, 4-Washington Co., MD, 15-Huffer
#3108, 1-Nikirk, Mollie E., 2-died, 3-1 Apr 1884, 15-Huffer
#3109, 1-Hoffman, Isabell, 2-died, 3-17 Oct 1865, 15-Hoffman
#3110, 1-Hoffman, Sarah Elizabeth, 2-died, 3-24 Mar 1872, 15-Hoffman
#3111, 1-Hoffman, Ida, 2-died, 3-28 Mar 1872, 15-Hoffman
#3112, 1-Hoffman, Edith M., 2-died, 3-10 Feb 1876, 15-Hoffman
#3113, 1-Hoffman, Sarah D., 2-died, 3-20 Sep 1895, 15-Hoffman
#3114, 1-Hoffman, Elias, 2-died, 3-1 Mar 1922, 15-Hoffman
#3115, 1-Hill, Willard, 2-died, 3-14 Jun 1922, 15-Hoffman
#3116, 1-Hoffman, Elias, 2-born, 3-9 Apr 1838, 4-Lebanon Township, Stunterdon Co.,
    NJ, 15-Hoffman
```

FAMILY BIBLE RECORDS IN THE WASHINGTON COUNTY FREE LIBRARY, HAGERSTOWN, MARYLAND

Entry #, 1-Last Name, First Name, 2-Event, 3-Date, 4-Event Location, 5-Age, 6-Other, 7-Spouse's Last, First, 8-Groom's Residence, 9-Bride's Residence, 10-Minister, 11-Minister's Location, 12-Father's Last, First, 13-Mother's Last, First, 14-Transcribed, 15-Family Bible

#3117, 1-Hoffman, Sarah D., 2-born, 3-20 Jul 1839, 15-Hoffman

#3118, 1-Hoffman, Mary J., 2-born, 3-3 Aug 1859, 15-Hoffman

#3119, 1-Hoffman, Isabell, 2-born, 3-25 Jan 1865, 15-Hoffman

#3120, 1-Hoffman, Sarah Elizabeth, 2-born, 3-30 Sep 1867, 15-Hoffman

#3121, 1-Hoffman, Ida, 2-born, 3-7 Nov 1872, 15-Hoffman

#3122, 1-Hoffman, Edith M., 2-born, 3-13 Aug 1875, 15-Hoffman

#3123, 1-Mitchell, Carrie B., 2-born, 3-27 Nov 1880, 15-Hoffman

#3124, 1-Hill, Willard, 2-born, 3-29 Apr 1922, 15-Hoffman

#3125, 1-Hoffman, Elias, 2-married, 3-28 Oct 1862, 4-Spruce Run, 7-Garey, Sarah T.[?], 8-Lebanon Township, Stunterdon Co., NJ, 9-Lebanon Township, Stunterdon Co., NJ, 10-Peter A. Struble, 11-Lutheran Parsonage, 15-Hoffman

#3126, 1-Herr, John, 2-married, 3-28 Aug 1810, 4-Hagerstown, MD, 6-married 11 yrs 11 days, 7-Boroff, Catharine, 10-Jonathan Rahauser (Rev.), 14-Yes, 15-Herr

#3127, 1-Herr, John, 2-married, 3-23 Oct 1823, 7-Boroff, Sarah, 14-Yes, 15-Herr

#3128, 1-Herr, Mary Ann, 2-married, 3-Tuesday, 25 Nov 1828, 7-Albert, George, 10-John Winder (Rev.), 14-Yes, 15-Herr

#3129, 1-Herr, Susanna, 2-married, 3-Thursday, 16 Oct 1834, 7-Reynolds, James W., 10-Rev. Harkey, 14-Yes, 15-Herr

#3130, 1-Herr, Eliza, 2-married, 3-Thursday, 5 Sep 1839, 7-Martin, Augustus C., 10-C. Startzman (Rev.), 14-Yes, 15-Herr

#3131, 1-Herr, John P., 2-married, 3-Tuesday, 13 Oct 1840, 7-Fitzpatrick, Sarah H., 9-Lexington, Lafayette Co., Missouri, 14-Yes, 15-Herr

#3132, 1-Herr, Henry C., 2-married, 3-22 Apr 1849, 7-Jennings, Catharine A., 9-Jennings Co, Indianna, 14-Yes, 15-Herr

#3133, 1-Herr, Henry C., 2-married, 3-10 Jul 1851, 4-Indiana, 7-Roberts, Rebecca H., 14-Yes, 15-Herr

#3134, 1-Herr, William L., 2-married, 3-Tuesday, 10 Jan 1854, 4-Culpepper, VA, 7-Chambers, Columbia A., 10-A. H. Spilman (Rev.), 14-Yes, 15-Herr

#3135, 1-Herr, Isabella, 2-married, 3-Wednesday, 21 Nov 1877, 4-Lutheran Church, Shepherdstown, WV, 7-Norris, Thomas W., 10-R.C. Holland (Rev.), 14-Yes, 15-Herr

#3136, 1-Herr, John, 2-born, 3-29 Nov 1789, 14-Yes, 15-Herr

#3137, 1-Herr, Catharine, 2-born, 3-6 Jul 1790, 7-Herr, John, 14-Yes, 15-Herr

#3138, 1-Herr, Sarah, 2-born, 3-3 Aug 1797, 7-Herr, John, 14-Yes, 15-Herr

#3139, 1-Herr, Margaret R., 2-born, 3-6 Sep 1850, 6-twins, 12-Herr, Henry, 13-Herr, Catharine, 14-Yes, 15-Herr

#3140, 1-Herr, Sarah E., 2-born, 3-6 Sep 1850, 6-twins, 12-Herr, Henry, 13-Herr, Catharine, 14-Yes, 15-Herr

#3141, 1-Herr, Mary Ann, 2-born, 3-Thursday, 11 Jul 1811, 12-Herr, John, 13-Herr, Catharine, 14-Yes, 15-Herr

#3142, 1-Herr, Mary Ann, 2-baptized, 3-11 Aug 1811, 4-Hagerstown, MD, 10-Jonathan Rauhauser (Rev.), 12-Herr, John, 13-Herr, Catharine, 14-Yes, 15-Herr

#3143, 1-Herr, Elizabeth, 2-born, 3-Friday, 9 Apr 1813, 12-Herr, John, 13-Herr, Catharine, 14-Yes, 15-Herr

#3144, 1-Herr, Elizabeth, 2-baptized, 3-23 May 1813, 4-Chambersburg, PA, 10-Rev. Houffman, 12-Herr, John, 13-Herr, Catharine, 14-Yes, 15-Herr

#3145, 1-Herr, Susanna, 2-born, 3-Monday, 12 Sep 1814, 12-Herr, John, 13-Herr, Catharine, 14-Yes, 15-Herr

#3146, 1-Herr, Susanna, 2-baptized, 3-27 Nov 1814, 4-Hagerstown, MD, 10-Jonathan Rahauser (Rev.), 12-Herr, John, 13-Herr, Catharine, 14-Yes, 15-Herr

#3147, 1-Herr, Eleanor, 2-born, 3-Tuesday, 19 Mar 1816, 12-Herr, John, 13-Herr, Catharine, 14-Yes, 15-Herr

#3148, 1-Herr, Eleanor, 2-baptized, 3-4 Aug 1816, 4-Hagerstown, MD, 10-Benjamin Kurtz (Rev.), 12-Herr, John, 13-Herr, Catharine, 14-Yes, 15-Herr

FAMILY BIBLE RECORDS IN THE WASHINGTON COUNTY FREE LIBRARY, HAGERSTOWN, MARYLAND

Entry #, 1-Last Name, First Name, 2-Event, 3-Date, 4-Event Location, 5-Age, 6-Other,
7-Spouse's Last, First, 8-Groom's Residence, 9-Bride's Residence, 10-Minister, 11-Minister's Location,
12-Father's Last, First, 13-Mother's Last, First, 14-Transcribed, 15-Family Bible

#3149, 1-Herr, Eliza, 2-born, 3-Tuesday, 19 Mar 1816, 12-Herr, John, 13-Herr, Catharine, 14-Yes, 15-Herr

#3150, 1-Herr, Eliza, 2-baptized, 3-4 Aug 1816, 4-Hagerstown, MD, 10-Benjamin Kurtz (Rev.), 12-Herr, John, 13-Herr, Catharine, 14-Yes, 15-Herr

#3151, 1-Herr, John Peter, 2-born, 3-Monday, 6 Apr 1818, 12-Herr, John, 13-Herr, Catharine, 14-Yes, 15-Herr

#3152, 1-Herr, John Peter, 2-baptized, 3-11 May 1818, 10-Benjamin Kurtz (Rev.), 11-Hagerstown, 12-Herr, John, 13-Herr, Catharine, 14-Yes, 15-Herr

#3153, 1-Herr, George Washington, 2-born, 3-Tuesday, 21 Dec 1819, 12-Herr, John, 13-Herr, Catharine, 14-Yes, 15-Herr

#3154, 1-Herr, George Washington, 2-baptized, 3-9 Jan 1820, 10-James R. Reily (Rev.), 11-Hagerstown, 12-Herr, John, 13-Herr, Catharine, 14-Yes, 15-Herr

#3155, 1-Herr, [daughter], 2-born, 3-Friday, 7 Sep 1821, 6-"stillborn", 12-Herr, John, 13-Herr, Catharine, 14-Yes, 15-Herr

#3156, 1-Herr, [daughter], 2-died, 3-Friday, 7 Sep 1821, 12-Herr, John, 13-Herr, Catharine, 14-Yes, 15-Herr

#3157, 1-Herr, William LaFayette, 2-born, 3-Friday, 24 Dec 1824, 12-Herr, John, 13-Herr, Sarah, 14-Yes, 15-Herr

#3158, 1-Herr, William LaFayette, 2-baptized, 3-23 Jan 1825, 10-Rev. Reily, 12-Herr, John, 13-Herr, Sarah, 14-Yes, 15-Herr

#3159, 1-Herr, Henry Clay, 2-born, 3-Sunday, 21 May 1826, 12-Herr, John, 13-Herr, Sarah, 14-Yes, 15-Herr

#3160, 1-Herr, Henry Clay, 2-baptized, 3-25 Oct 1826, 10-Isaac Keller (Rev.), 12-Herr, John, 13-Herr, Sarah, 14-Yes, 15-Herr

#3161, 1-Herr, Henrietta Catharine, 2-born, 3-Thursday, 20 Sep 1827, 12-Herr, John, 13-Herr, Sarah, 14-Yes, 15-Herr

#3162, 1-Herr, Henrietta Catharine, 2-baptized, 3-2 Apr 1828, 10-John Winter (Rev.), 11-Williamsport, 12-Herr, John, 13-Herr, Sarah, 14-Yes, 15-Herr

#3163, 1-Herr, Edward Green Williams, 2-born, 3-Monday, 30 Mar 1829, 14-Yes, 15-Herr

#3164, 1-Herr, Edward Green Williams, 2-baptized, 3-12 Jan 1830, 10-John Winter (Rev.), 11-Williamsport, 14-Yes, 15-Herr

#3165, 1-Herr, Ann Williams, 2-born, 3-Friday, 3 Sep 1830, 14-Yes, 15-Herr

#3166, 1-Herr, Ann Williams, 2-baptized, 3-23 May 1831, 10-John Winter (Rev.), 11-Williamsport, 14-Yes, 15-Herr

#3167, 1-Herr, Samuel Horatio, 2-born, 3-Thursday, 28 Jun 1832, 14-Yes, 15-Herr

#3168, 1-Herr, Samuel Horatio, 2-baptized, 3-7 Nov 1832, 10-John Winters (Rev.), 14-Yes, 15-Herr

#3169, 1-Herr, Sarah Jane, 2-born, 3-Sunday, 19 Jan 1834, 14-Yes, 15-Herr

#3170, 1-Herr, Sarah Jane, 2-baptized, 3-23 Mar 1835, 10-Isaac Keller (Rev.), 11-Williamsport, 14-Yes, 15-Herr

#3171, 1-Herr, Isabella, 2-born, 3-Sunday, 17 Jan 1836, 14-Yes, 15-Herr

#3172, 1-Herr, Isabella, 2-baptized, 3-29 ___ 1838, 10-John Winter (Rev.), 14-Yes, 15-Herr

#3173, 1-Herr, Elizabeth Beecher, 2-born, 3-Friday, 16 Sep 1838, 14-Yes, 15-Herr

#3174, 1-Herr, Elizabeth Beecher, 2-baptized, 3-9 Jun 1841, 10-Christian Startzman (Rev.), 11-Williamsport, 14-Yes, 15-Herr

#3175, 1-Entler, Elizabeth Beecher (Herr), 2-died, 3-25 Nov 1920, 4-Los Angeles, CA, 14-Yes, 15-Herr

#3176, 1-Herr, Elizabeth, 2-died, 3-Tuesday, 1 Feb 1814, 4-Chambersburg, PA, 5-9 months 23 days, 14-Yes, 15-Herr

#3177, 1-Herr, [daughter], 2-born, 3-Friday, 7 Sep 1821, 4-Williamsport, MD, 6-"stillborn", 14-Yes, 15-Herr

#3178, 1-Herr, [daughter], 2-died, 3-Friday, 7 Sep 1821, 4-Williamsport, MD, 14-Yes, 15-Herr

FAMILY BIBLE RECORDS IN THE WASHINGTON COUNTY FREE LIBRARY, HAGERSTOWN, MARYLAND

Entry #, 1-Last Name, First Name, 2-Event, 3-Date, 4-Event Location, 5-Age, 6-Other,
7-Spouse's Last, First, 8-Groom's Residence, 9-Bride's Residence, 10-Minister, 11-Minister's Location,
12-Father's Last, First, 13-Mother's Last, First, 14-Transcribed, 15-Family Bible

```
#3179, 1-Herr, Catharine, 2-died, 3-Saturday, 4:50 pm, 8 Sep 1821, 4-Williamsport,
    MD, 5-31 years 2 months 2 days, 7-Herr, John, 14-Yes, 15-Herr
#3180, 1-Herr, Eleanor, 2-died, 3-Monday, 9:30 pm, 6 Feb 1837, 4-Williamsport, MD,
    5-20 years, 10 months, 18 days, 14-Yes, 15-Herr
#3181, 1-Reynolds, Susanna, 2-died, 3-Sunday, 4 Aug 1839, 4-Frederick, MD, 5-24
    years 10 months 23 days, 7-Reynolds, James W., 14-Yes, 15-Herr
#3182, 1-Reynolds, James W., 2-died, 3-5 Jul 1849, 14-Yes, 15-Herr
#3183, 1-Herr, Susannah, 2-died, 3-Sunday, 6:00 am, 14 Mar 1841, 4-Greencastle, PA,
    5-79 years 2 months 2 days, 6-mother of John Herr, 14-Yes, 15-Herr
#3184, 1-Albert, Mary Ann, 2-died, 3-Wednesday, 24 Apr 1844, 4-Williamsport, MD, 5-
    32 years, 9 months, 13 days, 7-Albert, George, 14-Yes, 15-Herr
#3185, 1-Herr, John P., 2-died, 3-Monday, 2:00 pm, 26 May 1845, 4-Greencastle, PA,
    5-87 years 9 months 8 days, 6-father of John Herr, 14-Yes, 15-Herr
#3186, 1-Martin, Eliza, 2-died, 3-Friday, 10 Feb 1854, 4-Williamsport, MD, 5-37
    years 10 months 23 days, 7-Martin, A.C., 14-Yes, 15-Herr
#3187, 1-Herr, John, 2-died, 3-Monday, 29 Jan 1855, 4-Williamsport, MD, 5-65 years
    2 months, 14-Yes, 15-Herr
#3188, 1-Herr, Samuel Horatio, 2-died, 3-12 Apr 1870, 4-St. Louis, 5-37 years 9
    months 14 days, 14-Yes, 15-Herr
#3189, 1-Herr, Sarah, 2-died, 3-Friday, 29 Apr 1870, 4-Williamsport, MD, 5-72 years
    8 months 26 days, 14-Yes, 15-Herr
#3190, 1-Cyester, Daniel W., 2-died, 3-4 May 1874, 5-46 years, 7-Cyester,
    Henrietta, 14-Yes, 15-Herr
#3191, 1-Herr, Henrietta Catharine Cyester, 2-died, 3-31 Oct 1904, 4-Williamsport,
    MD, 5-77 years 1 months 13 days, 14-Yes, 15-Herr
#3192, 1-Herr, William L., 2-died, 3-19 Nov 1894, 4-Staunton, VA, 5-69 years 10
    months 25 days, 14-Yes, 15-Herr
#3193, 1-Herr, Edward G.W., 2-died, 3-8 Mar 1901, 4-Jefferson Co., WV, 5-71 years
    11 months 8 days, 14-Yes, 15-Herr
#3194, 1-Norris, Isabella, 2-died, 3-6 Nov 1901, 4-Washington, DC, 5-65 years 9
    months 19 days, 7-Norris, T.T., 14-Yes, 15-Herr
#3195, 1-Osbourn, William, 2-died, 3-8 Jun 1901, 4-Shenandoah, VA, 5-66 years, 7-
    Osbourn, Sarah Jane, 14-Yes, 15-Herr
#3196, 1-Lefevere, Samuel, 2-died, 3-7 Feb 1904, 5-89 years, 7-Lefevere, Ann W.,
    14-Yes, 15-Herr
#3197, 1-Lefevere, Ann W., 2-died, 3-13 Nov 1905, 5-75 years, 14-Yes, 15-Herr
#3198, 1-Osbourne, Sarah Jane, 2-died, 3-4 Feb 1919, 4-Leetown, WV, 5-85 years, 14-
    Yes, 15-Herr
#3199, 1-Herr, [son], 2-born, 3-20 Sep 1857, 6-"stillborn", 14-Yes, 15-Herr
#3200, 1-Herr, [son], 2-died, 3-20 Sep 1857, 14-Yes, 15-Herr
#3201, 1-Herr, Sarah Elizabeth, 2-born, 3-9:00 am, 11 Mar 1838, 4-Williamsport, MD,
    14-Yes, 15-Herr
#3202, 1-Herr, Irene Virginia, 2-born, 3-9:45 am, 28 Sep 1862, 4-Williamsport, MD,
    14-Yes, 15-Herr
#3203, 1-Herr, John, 2-married, 3-23 Oct 1823, 7-Boroff, Sarah, 14-Yes, 15-Herr
#3204, 1-Herr, Henrietta, 2-married, 3-28 Jun 1855, 7-Cyester, Daniel W., 14-Yes,
    15-Herr
#3205, 1-Cyester, Sarah E. (Miss), 2-married, 3-25 Feb 1880, 7-Osbourn, Thomas F.,
    14-Yes, 15-Herr
#3206, 1-Cyester, Irene V., 2-married, 3-14 Oct 1884, 7-Norris, Milton V.A., 14-
    Yes, 15-Herr
#3207, 1-Cyester, Mary B., 2-married, 3-17 Jan 1885, 7-Norris, Upton O., 14-Yes,
    15-Herr
#3208, 1-Norris, H. Pearl, 2-married, 3-16 Jun 1921, 7-Miller, G. Arthur, 14-Yes,
    15-Herr
```

FAMILY BIBLE RECORDS IN THE WASHINGTON COUNTY FREE LIBRARY, HAGERSTOWN, MARYLAND

Entry #, 1-Last Name, First Name, 2-Event, 3-Date, 4-Event Location, 5-Age, 6-Other,
7-Spouse's Last, First, 8-Groom's Residence, 9-Bride's Residence, 10-Minister, 11-Minister's Location,
12-Father's Last, First, 13-Mother's Last, First, 14-Transcribed, 15-Family Bible

#3209, 1-Norris, H. Pearl, 2-died, 3-28 Jul 1969, 5-83 years 3 months less 6 days", 14-Yes, 15-Herr

#3210, 1-Cyester, Daniel W., 2-died, 3-4 May 1874, 5-46 years 2 months 5 days, 14-Yes, 15-Herr

#3211, 1-Herr, John, 2-died, 3-29 Jan 1855, 4-Williamsport, MD, 5-65 years 2 months, 14-Yes, 15-Herr

#3212, 1-Herr, Sarah, 2-died, 3-29 Apr 1870, 4-Williamsport, MD, 5-72 years 8 months 26 days, 14-Yes, 15-Herr

#3213, 1-Cyester, Henrietta Catherine, 2-died, 3-31 Oct 1904, 5-77 years 1 months, 14-Yes, 15-Herr

#3214, 1-Norris, Upton O., 2-died, 3-15 Oct 1931, 14-Yes, 15-Herr

#3215, 1-Norris, Mary B., 2-died, 3-23 Feb 1939, 14-Yes, 15-Herr

#3216, 1-Norris, Upton, 2-born, 3-16 Feb 1862, 4-near Williamsport, MD, 14-Yes, 15-Herr

#3217, 1-Norris, Henrietta Pearl, 2-born, 3-3 May 1886, 4-Williamsport, MD, 14-Yes, 15-Herr

#3218, 1-Norris, Henrietta Pearl, 2-baptized, 3-12 Jul 1887, 10-W.C. Griffith, 14-Yes, 15-Herr

#3219, 1-Hager, Jonathan, 2-born, 3-20 Dec 1792, 15-Hager

#3220, 1-Hogmire, Catharine, 2-born, 3-2 May 1795, 15-Hager

#3221, 1-Hogmire, Catharine, 2-married, 3-21 Apr 1816, 7-Hager, Jonathan, 15-Hager

#3222, 1-Straub, S.D., 2-born, 3-3 Mar 1828, 15-Hager

#3223, 1-Hager, S.E., 2-born, 3-22 Mar 1833, 15-Hager

#3224, 1-Hager, S.E., 2-married, 3-19 Jul 1864, 7-Straub, S.D., 15-Hager

#3225, 1-Hager, William H., 2-born, 3-25 Jan 1817, 15-Hager

#3226, 1-Hager, Daniel, 2-born, 3-25 Dec 1819, 15-Hager

#3227, 1-Hager, Jonas H., 2-born, 3-4 Jul 1821, 15-Hager

#3228, 1-Hager, Andrew H., 2-born, 3-12 Aug 1822, 15-Hager

#3229, 1-Hager, John, 2-born, 3-4 Jul 1824, 15-Hager

#3230, 1-Hager, Jonathan, 2-born, 3-28 Dec 1826, 15-Hager

#3231, 1-Hager, David, 2-born, 3-28 Dec 1828, 15-Hager

#3232, 1-Hager, Susan E., 2-born, 3-22 Mar 1833, 15-Hager

#3233, 1-Hager, Edward, 2-born, 3-15 Jul 1837, 15-Hager

#3234, 1-Hager, Kate K., 2-born, 3-24 Apr 1840, 15-Hager

#3235, 1-Syrus, Frank, 2-born, 3-5 Jan 1861, 6-"colored", 15-Hager

#3236, 1-Syrus, Harry, 2-born, 3-8 Sep 1862, 6-"colored", 15-Hager

#3237, 1-Bird, Harry, 2-born, 3-1 Nov 1863, 6-"colored", 15-Hager

#3238, 1-Hager, Carrie, 2-died, 3-15 Apr, 5-13 years, 15-Hager

#3239, 1-Hager, Johnathan, 2-died, 3-16 Apr 1864, 5-70 years 3 months 25 days, 15-Hager

#3240, 1-Syrus, Harry, 2-died, 3-6 Jul 1863, 5-10 months, 15-Hager

#3241, 1-Straub, Catharine (Hager), 2-born, 3-16 Apr 1865, 15-Hager

#3242, 1-Straub, Harry H., 2-born, 3-15 Jan 1867, 15-Hager

#3243, 1-Straub, Norman B., 2-born, 3-24 Sep 1868, 15-Hager

#3244, 1-Straub, Norman B., 2-died, 3-20 Jul 1869, 5-10 months, 15-Hager

#3245, 1-Miller, Hager, 2-born, 3-25 Aug 1865, 15-Hager

#3246, 1-Miller, Hager, 2-died, 3-11 Nov 1865, 5-2 months 17 days, 15-Hager

#3247, 1-Miller, J. Garvin, 2-obituary, 3-3:00 am , 5-63 years, 15-Hager

#3248, 1-Hager, Sallie A. (Mrs.), 2-obituary, 5-70 years, 7-Hager, Andrew, 15-Hager

#3249, 1-Grove, Daniel S.[or L.], 2-born, 3-21 Apr 1817, 12-Grove, Philip, 15-Grove

#3250, 1-Grove, Philip, 2-married, 3-9 Mar 1800, 7-Hess, Catharina, 15-Grove

#3251, 1-Shafer, Margaret C., 2-born, 3-21 Oct 1824, 15-Grove

#3252, 1-Shafer, Margaret C., 2-married, 3-19 Jan 1843, 7-Grove, Daniel S.[or L.], 15-Grove

FAMILY BIBLE RECORDS IN THE WASHINGTON COUNTY FREE LIBRARY, HAGERSTOWN, MARYLAND

Entry #, 1-Last Name, First Name, 2-Event, 3-Date, 4-Event Location, 5-Age, 6-Other,
7-Spouse's Last, First, 8-Groom's Residence, 9-Bride's Residence, 10-Minister, 11-Minister's Location,
12-Father's Last, First, 13-Mother's Last, First, 14-Transcribed, 15-Family Bible

```
#3253, 1-Grove, Philip, 2-born, 3-10:00 am, 7 Apr 1775, 4-"in the Line[?] Crab",
    15-Grove
#3254, 1-Hess, Catharina, 2-born, 3-28 Mar 1782, 4-"in the Line[?] watterman", 15-
    Grove
#3255, 1-Grove, Mary, 2-born, 3-3:30 pm, 20 Feb 1801, 4-"in the Line tweens", 15-
    Grove
#3256, 1-Grove, Jacob, 2-born, 3-2:15 am, 18 Sep 1802, 4-"in the Line tweens", 15-
    Grove
#3257, 1-Grove, Elias, 2-born, 3-11:45 am, 6 Jun 1804, 4-"in the Line of Steer",
    15-Grove
#3258, 1-Grove, Samuel, 2-born, 3-8:30 pm, 10 Mar 1806, 4-"Line Schetts", 15-Grove
#3259, 1-Grove, Lovina, 2-born, 3-5:45 am, 29 Apr 1808, 4-"in the Line tweens", 15-
    Grove
#3260, 1-Grove, Joseph, 2-born, 3-10:45 am, 15 May 1810, 4-"Line Seales", 15-Grove
#3261, 1-Grove, Harriet, 2-born, 3-10:00 am, 4 Jun 1812, 4-"Lines widder", 15-Grove
#3262, 1-Grove, Daniel, 2-born, 3-10:00 pm, 21 Apr 1817, 4-"in the Line tweens",
    15-Grove
#3263, 1-Grove, Stephen Philip, 2-born, 3-10:45 pm, 24 May 1819, 4-"in Line tween",
    15-Grove
#3264, 1-Grove, Jeremiah, 2-born, 3-6:00 am, 21 Aug 1821, 4-"Line tweens", 15-Grove
#3265, 1-Grove, Catharina, 2-born, 3-1:00 pm, 16 Apr 1824, 15-Grove
#3266, 1-Grove, Catharina, 2-died, 3-6 Apr 1815, 5-33 years 9 days, 6-"lived with
    her husband 15 year & 28 Days. Born to Gitter[?] 4 sons & 3 Daughters, total
    7 Children; first wife of Philip Grove", 15-Grove
#3267, 1-Grove, Harriet B., 2-died, 3-28 Oct 1826, 15-Grove
#3268, 1-Grove, Susan, 2-died, 3-10 Sep 1827, 6-"second wife of Philip Grove", 15-
    Grove
#3269, 1-Hays, Loveney, 2-died, 3-20 Feb 1834, 5-25 years 9 months 20 days, 15-
    Grove
#3270, 1-Grove, Philip, 2-died, 3-Sunday, 13 Jun 1841, 5-66[?] years 2 months 6
    days, 15-Grove
#3271, 1-Reinharat[?], Ann Catharine, 2-died, 3-29 Nov 1865, 7-Reinhart[?],
    Christian, 15-Grove
#3272, 1-Grove, Daniel L., 2-died, 3-4 Feb 1868, 5-50 years 9 months 14 days, 15-
    Grove
#3273, 1-Grove, Elias S., 2-died, 3-26 Feb 1870[?], 5-67 years 8 months 19 days,
    15-Grove
#3274, 1-Locher[?], Mary, 2-died, 3-1 Apr 1873, 5-72 years 1 months 10 days, 15-
    Grove
#3275, 1-Grove, Jacob H., 2-died, 3-15 Jan 1879, 5-76 years 2[?] months 28 days,
    15-Grove
#3276, 1-Grove, Stephen P., 2-died, 3-9 Dec 1886, 5-67 years 6 months ___ days, 15-
    Grove
#3277, 1-Grosh, Frederick, 2-married, 3-23 Jul 1797, Ann Maria, 15-Grosh
#3278, 1-Grosh, Frederick, 2-married, 3-28 Jun 1829, Elizabeth, 15-Grosh
#3279, 1-Grosch, Frederick, 2-born, 3-28 Oct 1774, 15-Grosh
#3280, 1-Grosch, Anna Maria, 2-born, 3-Feb 1781, 15-Grosh
#3281, 1-Grosch, Henry, 2-born, 3-3 Dec 1798, 15-Grosh
#3282, 1-Grosch, Anna Maria, 2-born, 3-23 May 1801, 15-Grosh
#3283, 1-Grosch, Sara, 2-born, 3-18 Dec 1802, 15-Grosh
#3284, 1-Grosch, Amalia, 2-born, 3-26 Nov 1804, 15-Grosh
#3285, 1-Grosch, Cathrine, 2-born, 3-1 Aug 1806, 15-Grosh
#3286, 1-Grosch, Lewis Andrew, 2-born, 3-27 Nov 1808, 15-Grosh
#3287, 1-Grosch, Conradt Clement, 2-born, 3-28 [or 23] Nov 1810, 15-Grosh
#3288, 1-Grosch, Frederick David, 2-born, 3-14 Apr 1813, 15-Grosh
```

FAMILY BIBLE RECORDS IN THE WASHINGTON COUNTY FREE LIBRARY, HAGERSTOWN, MARYLAND

Entry #, 1-Last Name, First Name, 2-Event, 3-Date, 4-Event Location, 5-Age, 6-Other,
7-Spouse's Last, First, 8-Groom's Residence, 9-Bride's Residence, 10-Minister, 11-Minister's Location,
12-Father's Last, First, 13-Mother's Last, First, 14-Transcribed, 15-Family Bible

```
#3289, 1-Grosch, Benjamin Franklin, 2-born, 3-9 Jun 1815, 15-Grosh
#3290, 1-Grosch, Sophia, 2-born, 3-27 Jul 1817, 15-Grosh
#3291, 1-Grosch, Julianna, 2-born, 3-21 Mar 1819, 15-Grosh
#3292, 1-Grosch, George Washington , 2-born, 3-30 Mar 1820, 15-Grosh
#3293, 1-Grosch, John Frederick, 2-born, 3-26 Oct 1822, 15-Grosh
#3294, 1-Grosch, Elisabeth, 2-born, 3-30 Mar 1789[?], 15-Grosh
#3295, 1-Grosh, Sr., Frederick, 2-died, 3-17 Jun 1862, 15-Grosh
#3296, 1-Grosch, Anna Maria, 2-died, 3-3 Oct 1823, 15-Grosh
#3297, 1-Grosch, Anna Maria, 2-died, 3-19 Sep 1823, 15-Grosh
#3298, 1-Hogmire, Amalia, 2-died, 3-10 Apr 1855, 15-Grosh
#3299, 1-[unreadable], Sarah, 2-died, 3-10 Sep 1860, 15-Grosh
#3300, 1-Grosch, Conradt Clement, 2-died, 3-24 Jul 1828, 15-Grosh
#3301, 1-Grosch, Frederick David, 2-died, 3-4 Jun 1821, 15-Grosh
#3302, 1-Grosch, Sophia, 2-died, 3-8 Aug 1817, 15-Grosh
#3303, 1-Grosch, Juliana, 2-died, 3-1 Apr 1819, 15-Grosh
#3304, 1-Grosch, George Washington , 2-died, 3-2 Oct 1842, 15-Grosh
#3305, 1-Grosch, Elisabeth, 2-died, 3-16 Nov 1839, 15-Grosh
#3306, 1-Grosch, Catharine, 2-died, 3-17 Nov 1865, 15-Grosh
#3307, 1-Grosch, Frederick, 2-died, 3-17 Jun 1862, 15-Grosh
#3308, 1-Grosch, Lewis A., 2-died, 3-23 Feb 1874, 5-65 years 3 months 2 days, 15-
    Grosh
#3309, 1-Betts, David, 2-born, 3-12 Jan 1791[?], 15-Grosh
#3310, 1-Betts, Elisabeth, 2-born, 3-3 Mar 1795, 15-Grosh
#3311, 1-Betts, Elisabeth, 2-born, 3-23 Nov[?] 1815, 15-Grosh
#3312, 1-Betts, Cathrine, 2-born, 3-12 Feb 1816, 15-Grosh
#3313, 1-Betts, Cathrine, 2-died, 3-1845, 15-Grosh
#3314, 1-Betts, Susanna, 2-born, 3-3 Oct 1818, 15-Grosh
#3315, 1-Betts, Susanna, 2-died, 3-11 Dec, 15-Grosh
#3316, 1-Betts, Daniel L.[?], 2-born, 3-10 Jan 1820, 15-Grosh
#3317, 1-Betts, Rosenia, 2-born, 3-11 May 1821, 15-Grosh
#3318, 1-Betts, John V., 2-died, 3-2 Oct 1823, 15-Grosh
#3319, 1-Betts, "The Twins", 2-born, 3-13 Oct 1826, 15-Grosh
#3320, 1-Betts, Cardine[?], 2-born, 3-3 Nov 1825, 15-Grosh
#3321, 1-Betts, Lutter[?] David, 2-born, 3-5 May 1828, 15-Grosh
#3322, 1-Betts, Jacob, 2-born, 3-12 Nov 1830, 15-Grosh
#3323, 1-Betts, Aalferd[?], 2-born, 3-14 Feb 1833, 15-Grosh
#3324, 1-Grosh, Ann E.L., 2-born, 3-10 Apr 1833, 15-Grosh
#3325, 1-Grosh, Henry I.F., 2-born, 3-31 Aug 1836, 15-Grosh
#3326, 1-Grosh, Otis S., 2-born, 3-15 May 1840, 15-Grosh
#3327, 1-Grosh, Sr., Henry, 2-died, 3-4 Jan 1841, 15-Grosh
#3328, 1-Grosh, Catharine E., 2-died, 3-19 Apr 1861, 5-52 years, 15-Grosh
#3329, 1-Grosh, George W., 2-died, 3-22 Mar 1862, 5-56 years, 15-Grosh
#3330, 1-Grosh, Otis S.[?], 2-died, 3-24 May 1962, 5-22 years 9 days, 15-Grosh
#3331, 1-Grosh, Ann E.L. Snyder, 2-died, 3-4 Sep 1907, 12-Grosh, George, 13-Grosh,
    Catherine, 15-Grosh
#3332, 1-Grosh, Henry Levin Fisher, 2-died, 3-2 Oct 1914, 4-Haysville, Sedgewick
    Co., Kansas, 5-78 years 1 months 2 days, 15-Grosh
#3333, 1-Snyder, Mary Otis, 2-died, 3-13 Oct 1866, 5-16 months 4 days, 15-Grosh
#3334, 1-Grosh, George W., 2-married, 3-27 Sep 1827, 7-Fisher, Cath. E., 15-Grosh
#3335, 1-Grosh, Ann E., 2-married, 3-28 Jan 1864, 7-Snyder, Wm. B., 8-Clear Spring,
    MD, 9-Clear Spring, MD, 10-J. B. Akers, 12-Grosh, Geo., 13-Grosh, Catharine,
    15-Grosh
#3336, 1-Snyder, Wm. B., 2-born, 12-Snyder, Leonard, 13-Snyder, Rebecca, 15-Grosh
#3337, 1-Grosh, Henry I.F., 2-married, 3-Jun 1867, 4-Franklin, ___gan Co.,
    Illinois, 7-Hays, Marian, 15-Grosh
```

FAMILY BIBLE RECORDS IN THE WASHINGTON COUNTY FREE LIBRARY, HAGERSTOWN, MARYLAND

Entry #, 1-Last Name, First Name, 2-Event, 3-Date, 4-Event Location, 5-Age, 6-Other, 7-Spouse's Last, First, 8-Groom's Residence, 9-Bride's Residence, 10-Minister, 11-Minister's Location, 12-Father's Last, First, 13-Mother's Last, First, 14-Transcribed, 15-Family Bible

#3338, 1-Snyder, Mary Otis, 2-born, 3-9 Jun 1865, 12-Snyder, Wm. B., 13-Snyder, A.E., 15-Grosh

#3339, 1-Snyder, Mary Otis, 2-baptized, 3-12 Oct 1866, 12-Snyder, Wm. B., 13-Snyder, A.E., 15-Grosh

#3340, 1-Snyder, Viola Willetta, 2-born, 3-12 May 1867, 12-Snyder, Wm. B., 13-Snyder, A.E., 15-Grosh

#3341, 1-Snyder, Viola Willetta, 2-baptized, 3-Aug 1870, 12-Snyder, Wm. B., 13-Snyder, A.E., 15-Grosh

#3342, 1-Snyder, Ella Dellinger, 2-born, 3-26 Dec 1868, 12-Snyder, Wm. B., 13-Snyder, A.E., 15-Grosh

#3343, 1-Snyder, Ella Dellinger, 2-baptized, 3-Aug 1870, 12-Snyder, Wm. B., 13-Snyder, A.E., 15-Grosh

#3344, 1-Snyder, Leonard P., 2-born, 3-15 Jul 1871, 12-Snyder, Wm. B., 13-Snyder, A.E., 15-Grosh

#3345, 1-Snyder, Leonard P., 2-baptized, 3-1872, 12-Snyder, Wm. B., 13-Snyder, A.E., 15-Grosh

#3346, 1-Grimm, John, 6-buried in U.B. Cemetery, Rohrersville, MD, 15-Grim

#3347, 1-Grimm, Mary Franck, 6-buried in U.B. Cemetery, Rohrersville, MD, 15-Grim

#3348, 1-Grimm, Frederick A., 2-born, 3-18 May 1802, 12-Grimm, John, 13-Grimm, Mary Franck, 15-Grim

#3349, 1-Grimm, Elizabeth, 2-born, 3-12 Aug 1805, 12-Grimm, John, 13-Grimm, Mary Franck, 15-Grim

#3350, 1-Grimm, John I., 2-born, 3-12 Feb 1808, 12-Grimm, John, 13-Grimm, Mary Franck, 15-Grim

#3351, 1-Grimm, Thomas G., 2-born, 3-24 Jul 1810, 12-Grimm, John, 13-Grimm, Mary Franck, 15-Grim

#3352, 1-Grimm, Joseph S., 2-born, 3-8 May 1812, 12-Grimm, John, 13-Grimm, Mary Franck, 15-Grim

#3353, 1-Grimm, Margaret, 2-born, 3-18 Nov 1814, 12-Grimm, John, 13-Grimm, Mary Franck, 15-Grim

#3354, 1-Grimm, Daniel B., 2-born, 3-4 May 1817, 12-Grimm, John, 13-Grimm, Mary Franck, 15-Grim

#3355, 1-Grimm, Susanna, 2-born, 3-3 Jan 1820, 12-Grimm, John, 13-Grimm, Mary Franck, 15-Grim

#3356, 1-Grimm, Joseph Y., 2-born, 3-8 May 1812, 15-Grim

#3357, 1-Grimm, Joseph Y., 2-died, 3-10 Mar 1892, 6-buried in Rohrersville Cemetery, 15-Grim

#3358, 1-Grimm, Sarah, 2-born, 3-4 May 1817, 15-Grim

#3359, 1-Grimm, Sarah, 2-died, 3-12 Feb 1904, 6-buried in Rohrersville Cemetery, 15-Grim

#3360, 1-Grim, William Otterbein, 2-born, 3-Friday, 14 Jul 1837, 6-"Sign of the Bowman", 15-Grim

#3361, 1-Grim, William Otterbein, 2-died, 3-24 Aug 1896, 6-buried in Rohrersville Cemetery, 15-Grim

#3362, 1-Grimm, John Wesley, 2-born, 3-Monday, 24 Jun 1839, 6-"Sign of Bowman", 15-Grim

#3363, 1-Grimm, John Wesley, 2-died, 3-15 Feb 1921, 6-buried at Prospect Hill Cemetery, York, PA, 15-Grim

#3364, 1-Grimm, Martha Ann, 2-died, 3-Oct 1926, 6-"Sign Balance; buried near Salina, Kansas, 15-Grim

#3365, 1-Grimm, Martha Ann, 2-born, 3-Thursday, 14 Jan 1841, 15-Grim

#3366, 1-Grimm, Jacob Luther, 2-born, 3-Sunday, 27 Nov 1842, 6-"In Sign of Balance", 15-Grim

#3367, 1-Grimm, Jacob Luther, 2-died, 3-22 Aug 1905, 4-Baltimore, MD, 6-buried Druid Ridge Cemetery, Pikesville, MD, 15-Grim

FAMILY BIBLE RECORDS IN THE WASHINGTON COUNTY FREE LIBRARY, HAGERSTOWN, MARYLAND

Entry #, 1-Last Name, First Name, 2-Event, 3-Date, 4-Event Location, 5-Age, 6-Other, 7-Spouse's Last, First, 8-Groom's Residence, 9-Bride's Residence, 10-Minister, 11-Minister's Location, 12-Father's Last, First, 13-Mother's Last, First, 14-Transcribed, 15-Family Bible

#3368, 1-Grimm, Sophia Cecilia, 2-born, 3-Sunday, 16 Feb 1845, 6-"Sign of the Turns", 15-Grim

#3369, 1-Grimm, Sophia Cecilia, 2-baptized, 3-26 Oct 1845, 15-Grim

#3370, 1-Grimm, Sophia Cecilia, 2-died, 3-25 Apr 1904, 6-buried Church Cemetery at Rohrersville, MD, 15-Grim

#3371, 1-Grimm, Amanda Mariah, 2-born, 3-Friday, 15 Jan 1847, 6-"Sign of Goat or Capriconus", 15-Grim

#3372, 1-Grimm, Amanda Mariah, 2-died, 3-2_ Jan 1923, 4-Hagerstown, 6-buried Rose Hil Cemetery, Hagerstown, 15-Grim

#3373, 1-Grimm, Joseph Samuel, 2-born, 3-14 Feb 1849, 6-"Sign Scorpis[?], 15-Grim

#3374, 1-Grimm, Joseph Samuel, 2-baptized, 3-5 Nov 1849, 15-Grim

#3375, 1-Grimm, Joseph Samuel, 2-died, 3-Sep 1921, 6-buried Rohrersville Cemetery, 15-Grim

#3376, 1-Grimm, Sarah Susan, 2-born, 3-Monday, 18 Aug 1851, 15-Grim

#3377, 1-Grimm, Sarah Susan, 2-baptized, 3-6 Feb 1855, 10-E. Witte, 15-Grim

#3378, 1-Grimm, Sarah Susan, 2-died, 3-1 Jun 1935, 6-buried in cemetery at Locust Grove, 15-Grim

#3379, 1-Grimm, Mary Elizabeth, 2-born, 3-15 Jun 1853, 4-near Rohrersville, MD, 15-Grim

#3380, 1-Grimm, Mary Elizabeth, 2-married, 7-Ruff, John K., 15-Grim

#3381, 1-Grimm, Mary Elizabeth, 2-died, 3-18 Apr 1941, 6-buried Church Cemetery, rohrersville, MD, 15-Grim

#3382, 1-Grimm, Irwin Randolph, 2-born, 3-25 Apr 1855, 15-Grim

#3383, 1-Grimm, Irwin Randolph, 2-died, 3-25 Apr 1933, 6-buried Rose Hill Cemetery, Hagerstown, 15-Grim

#3384, 1-Grimm, Harmon Milton, 2-born, 3-6 Oct 1857, 15-Grim

#3385, 1-Grimm, Harmon Milton, 2-died, 3-27 Nov 1928, 6-buried in Rohrersville Cemetery, 15-Grim

#3386, 1-Grimm, Barbara Ella, 2-born, 3-20 Feb 1860, 15-Grim

#3387, 1-Grimm, Barbara Ella, 2-died, 3-6 Apr 1860, 5-6 weeks 4 days, 6-buried at Rohrersville, 15-Grim

#3388, 1-Grimm, Betty [possibly Barbara Ellen], 2-baptized, 5-"infancy", 10-H.[?[Markwood, 15-Grim

#3389, 1-Grimm, Irwin, 2-baptized, 5-"infancy", 10-H.[?[Markwood, 15-Grim

#3390, 1-Grimm, Harmon, 2-baptized, 5-"infancy", 10-H.[?[Markwood, 15-Grim

#3391, 1-Grimm, Emma Althea, 2-born, 3-27 Dec 1861, 15-Grim

#3392, 1-Grimm, Emma Althea, 2-baptized, 3-29 Aug 1870, 10-H.[?] Weaver, 15-Grim

#3393, 1-Grimm, Joseph L., 2-married, 3-22 Nov 1836, 7-Huffer, Sarah, 15-Grim

#3394, 1-Grimm, William O., 2-married, 3-16 Mar 1865, 7-Mullendore, Martha A., 10-Geo. W. Stattan, 15-Grim

#3395, 1-Grimm, John Wesley, 2-married, 3-17 Jun 1867, 7-Hoffman, Lizzie Catharine, 10-Bishop J.J. Gloss Crenner[?], 15-Grim

#3396, 1-Grimm, Martha A., 2-married, 3-2 Dec 1866, 7-Gloss, Siman, 10-A.M. Evers, 15-Grim

#3397, 1-Grimm, Jacob Luther, 2-married, 3-10 Feb 1870, 7-Harp, Mary Ellen, 10-Wm.[?] T. Lower, 15-Grim

#3398, 1-Grimm, Amanda M., 2-married, 3-14 Oct 1869, 7-Smith, Hiram J., 10-C.T. Steam, 15-Grim

#3399, 1-Grimm, Sarah Susan, 2-married, 3-10 Oct 1872, 7-Smith, Albert H., 10-James W. Hott, 15-Grim

#3400, 1-Grimm, Joseph S., 2-married, 3-10 Feb 1874, 7-Thomas, Beatie E., 10-H.A. Bovey, 15-Grim

#3401, 1-Grimm, Sophia C., 2-married, 3-25 Oct 1879, 7-Smith, Mahlon H.[?], 10-Wm. W. Grimm, 15-Grim

FAMILY BIBLE RECORDS IN THE WASHINGTON COUNTY FREE LIBRARY, HAGERSTOWN, MARYLAND

Entry #, 1-Last Name, First Name, 2-Event, 3-Date, 4-Event Location, 5-Age, 6-Other, 7-Spouse's Last, First, 8-Groom's Residence, 9-Bride's Residence, 10-Minister, 11-Minister's Location, 12-Father's Last, First, 13-Mother's Last, First, 14-Transcribed, 15-Family Bible

#3402, 1-Grimm, Irvin, 2-married, 3-2 Dec 1885, 7-Beard, Lila V., 10-J.L. Grimm, 15-Grim

#3403, 1-Grimm, Harmon M., 2-married, 3-24 Dec 1886, 7-Huntzberry, Etta May, 10-Rev. J.S. Grimm, father of the groom, 15-Grim

#3404, 1-Rohrer, Samuel J., 2-obituary, 12-Rohrer, Daniel A., 13-Beeler, Violetta, 15-Grim

#3405, 1-Rohrer, Samuel J., 2-married, 3-25 May 1899, 7-Brown, Lulu (Miss), 15-Grim

#3406, 1-Brown, Lulu (Miss), 2-died, 3-Jan 1902, 7-Rohrer, Samuel J., 12-Brown, Eli, 15-Grim

#3407, 1-Rohrer, Elizabeth, 2-born, 12-Rohrer, Samuel J., 13-Brown, Lulu, 15-Grim

#3408, 1-Rohrer, Samuel J., 2-married, 3-1903, 7-Slifer, Virgie (Miss), 15-Grim

#3409, 1-Rohrer, Margaret, 2-born, 3-circa 1906, 12-Rohrer, Samuel J., 13-Slifer, Virgie, 15-Grim

#3410, 1-Rohrer, Daniel, 2-born, 3-circa 1909, 12-Rohrer, Samuel J., 13-Slifer, Virgie, 15-Grim

#3411, 1-Grimm, Joseph S. (Rev.), 2-born, 3-8 May 1812, 15-Grim

#3412, 1-Grimm, Joseph S. (Rev.), 2-died, 3-10 Mar 1892, 4-near Rohrersville, MD, 5-79 years 10 months 2 days, 15-Grim

#3413, 1-Grimm, Harry T., 2-obituary, 3-Jan 1914, 4-Montana, 6-buried Rohrersville Cemetery, 12-Grimm, Joseph S., 15-Grim

#3414, 1-Slifer, Rodney LaTaine, 2-married, 3-31 Jan, 7-Linger, Margaret Ruth (Miss), 8-Rohrersville, MD, 9-Buckhannon, WV, 10-Rev. Norman L. Trott, 12-Slifer, L.B., 15-Grim

#3415, 1-Grimm, Hubert, 2-died, 5-"died young", 15-Grim

#3416, 1-Grimm, Nellie, 2-married, 7-McCune, Walter A., 15-Grim

#3417, 1-Grimm, Annie E., 2-married, 7-Hammond, Charles W., 15-Grim

#3418, 1-Grimm, Iva M., 2-married, 7-Smith, Earl H., 15-Grim

#3419, 1-Grimm, Karl M., 2-married, 7-[blank], Marion, 15-Grim

#3420, 1-Grimm, Ethel, 2-married, 7-Gabriel, Grover C. (Rev.), 15-Grim

#3421, 1-Grimm, Mabel, 2-married, 7-Gabriel, Grover C. (Rev.), 15-Grim

#3422, 1-Grimm, Nettie, 2-married, 7-Davenport, Harris, 15-Grim

#3423, 1-Grimm, Anna, 2-married, 7-Winkleblack, Orvis, 15-Grim

#3424, 1-Grimm, Charles I., 2-married, 7-Cunningham, Pearl, 15-Grim

#3425, 1-Grimm, Martha, 2-married, 7-Glass/Gloss, Simon, 15-Grim

#3426, 1-Grimm, William N.G., 2-married, 7-Rohrer, Winifred, 15-Grim

#3427, 1-Grimm, William N.G., 2-married, 7-Talley, Pearl, 15-Grim

#3428, 1-Grimm, Mamie, 2-died, 5-"died young", 15-Grim

#3429, 1-Grimm, Edward L., 2-married, 7-Spielman, Cora, 15-Grim

#3430, 1-Grimm, Robert W., 2-married, 7-Rogerson, Maud, 15-Grim

#3431, 1-Grimm, Ira R., 2-married, 7-Wright, Lucille, 15-Grim

#3432, 1-Grimm, Lela B., 2-married, 7-Miller, Joseph, 15-Grim

#3433, 1-Grimm, Lester, 2-died, 5-"died young", 15-Grim

#3434, 1-Grimm, Arthur G., 2-married, 7-Ashmull, Florence, 15-Grim

#3435, 1-Grimm, William A., 2-married, 7-Miller, Mae L., 15-Grim

#3436, 1-Grimm, M. Luther, 2-married, 7-Dick, Ella, 15-Grim

#3437, 1-Grimm, Myra E., 2-married, 7-Steele, Axel W., 15-Grim

#3438, 1-Grimm, Luther O., 2-married, 7-Gloss, Fannie, 15-Grim

#3439, 1-Grimm, Paul H., 2-married, 7-Snyder, Mae Esther, 15-Grim

#3440, 1-Grimm, Orpha M., 2-married, 7-Slifer, Luther, 15-Grim

#3441, 1-Grimm, William C., 2-married, 7-Metz, Myrtle, 15-Grim

#3442, 1-Grimm, Walter L., 2-married, 7-Wiles, Nellie, 15-Grim

#3443, 1-Grimm, Wilbur M., 2-married, 7-Danner, Edna, 15-Grim

#3444, 1-Grimm, Annie M., 2-married, 7-Green, George, 15-Grim

#3445, 1-Grimm, Lester, 2-married, 7-Swope, May, 15-Grim

#3446, 1-Grimm, William E., 2-died, 5-"died young", 15-Grim

FAMILY BIBLE RECORDS IN THE WASHINGTON COUNTY FREE LIBRARY, HAGERSTOWN, MARYLAND

Entry #, 1-Last Name, First Name, 2-Event, 3-Date, 4-Event Location, 5-Age, 6-Other,
7-Spouse's Last, First, 8-Groom's Residence, 9-Bride's Residence, 10-Minister, 11-Minister's Location,
12-Father's Last, First, 13-Mother's Last, First, 14-Transcribed, 15-Family Bible

```
#3447, 1-Grimm, Claude, 2-died, 5-"died young", 15-Grim
#3448, 1-Grimm, J. Wesley, 2-married, 7-Huffman, Elizabeth, 15-Grim
#3449, 1-Grimm, J. Lower, 2-married, 7-Appenzellar, Lillie, 15-Grim
#3450, 1-Grimm, Charlie, 2-married, 7-Mickey, Sallie, 15-Grim
#3451, 1-Grimm, Nellie, 2-married, 7-Shue, Alan (Rev.), 15-Grim
#3452, 1-Grimm, Virgie, 2-married, 7-Kottcamp, A.Francis, 15-Grim
#3453, 1-Grimm, Odo R., 2-married, 7-Algird[?], Harry C. (Dr.), 15-Grim
#3454, 1-Grimm, Elsie M., 2-married, 7-Baldwin, Warren, 15-Grim
#3455, 1-Garlinger, Benj. A., 2-married, 3-4 Jan 1847, 7-Rosenstal, Joanna M., 10-
    Rev. John Rebaugh, 15-Garlinger
#3456, 1-Garlinger, Benj. Aaron, 2-born, 3-8 Jun 1825, 15-Garlinger
#3457, 1-Garlinger, Benj. Aaron, 2-died, 3-4:45 am, 20 Jan[?] 1897, 5-71 years 7
    months 12 days, 15-Garlinger
#3458, 1-Rosensteel[?], Joanna Margaret, 2-born, 3-18 Jan 1829, 15-Garlinger
#3459, 1-Garlinger, Mahlon Fredrick McClure, 2-born, 3-6 May 1848, 15-Garlinger
#3460, 1-Garlinger, Benj. Ryland, 2-born, 3-20 Jan 1850, 15-Garlinger
#3461, 1-Garlinger, Howard Rosensteel, 2-born, 3-23 Nov 1865, 15-Garlinger
#3462, 1-Garlinger, Rachel, 2-born, 3-23 Mar 1852, 15-Garlinger
#3463, 1-Garlinger, Anna Margaret, 2-born, 3-9 Dec 1853, 15-Garlinger
#3464, 1-Garlinger, Jacob Harry, 2-born, 3-3 Mar 1864, 15-Garlinger
#3465, 1-Garlinger, Aaron, 2-born, 3-7 Apr 1856, 15-Garlinger
#3466, 1-Garlinger, Dixon Nesbitt, 2-born, 3-23 Feb 1858, 15-Garlinger
#3467, 1-Garlinger, McVitty Burnside, 2-born, 3-5 Oct 1861, 15-Garlinger
#3468, 1-Garlinger, Benj. Ryland, 2-died, 3-13 Aug 1851, 5-1 year 6 months 23 days,
    15-Garlinger
#3469, 1-Garlinger, McVitty Burnside, 2-died, 3-10 Dec 1862, 5-1 year 1 months 16
    days, 15-Garlinger
#3470, 1-Garlinger, Jacob Harry, 2-died, 3-28 Aug 1864, 5-5 months 25 days, 15-
    Garlinger
#3471, 1-Garlinger, Mahlon F. McClure, 2-died, 3-28 Aug 1871, 5-23 years 3 months
    22 days, 15-Garlinger
#3472, 1-Garlinger, Anna M., 2-died, 3-11:30, 23 Nov 1881, 15-Garlinger
#3473, 1-Garlinger, Joanna M., 2-died, 3-11 Apr 1892, 5-63 years 2 months 13 days,
    15-Garlinger
#3474, 1-Fry, David, 2-married, 3-1 Aug 1841, 7-Ridenour, Susan, 10-Rev. John P.
    Cline, 15-Fry
#3475, 1-Fry, John Henry, 2-born, 3-20 Jun 1845, 15-Fry
#3476, 1-Fry, Elizabeth Mary, 2-born, 3-5 Mar 1845, 15-Fry
#3477, 1-Fry, Sarah Louisa, 2-born, 3-27 Jan 1847, 15-Fry
#3478, 1-Fry, Lidia Ann, 2-born, 3-21 Jan 1849, 15-Fry
#3479, 1-Fry, Margaret Virginia, 2-born, 3-28 Aug 1850, 15-Fry
#3480, 1-Fry, Clarah Kate, 2-born, 3-9 Apr 1853, 15-Fry
#3481, 1-Fry, Emma Susan, 2-born, 3-26 Aug 1855, 6-twin, 15-Fry
#3482, 1-Fry, Hannah Barbara, 2-born, 3-26 Aug 1855, 6-twin, 15-Fry
#3483, 1-Fry, David Lewis, 2-born, 3-21 Oct 1857, 15-Fry
#3484, 1-Fry, Helen Rebecka, 2-born, 3-6 Nov 1859, 15-Fry
#3485, 1-Fry, David, 2-born, 3-12 Feb 1814, 15-Fry
#3486, 1-Fry, Susan, 2-born, 3-18 Mar 1822, 15-Fry
#3487, 1-Fry, Lilly Irene, 2-born, 3-11 Apr 1862, 15-Fry
#3488, 1-Fry, Martha Allice, 2-born, 3-23 May 1864, 15-Fry
#3489, 1-Frey, Joseph Samuel, 2-born, 3-29 Jan 1870, 15-Fry
#3490, 1-Shank, Noah , 2-born, 3-28 Mar 1821, 15-Fry
#3491, 1-Frey, Joseph S., 2-died, 3-17 Nov 1943, 15-Fry
#3492, 1-Frey, Lillie S. (Funkhouser), 2-died, 3-9 Dec 1948, 7-Frey, Joseph S., 15-
    Fry
```

FAMILY BIBLE RECORDS IN THE WASHINGTON COUNTY FREE LIBRARY, HAGERSTOWN, MARYLAND

Entry #, 1-Last Name, First Name, 2-Event, 3-Date, 4-Event Location, 5-Age, 6-Other,
7-Spouse's Last, First, 8-Groom's Residence, 9-Bride's Residence, 10-Minister, 11-Minister's Location,
12-Father's Last, First, 13-Mother's Last, First, 14-Transcribed, 15-Family Bible

```
#3493, 1-Fry, John Henry, 2-died, 3-10 Oct 1844, 15-Fry
#3494, 1-Fry, David Lewis, 2-died, 3-18 Sep 1861, 15-Fry
#3495, 1-Fry, Helen Rebecka, 2-died, 3-27 Sep 1862, 15-Fry
#3496, 1-Fry, Ludia Ann, 2-died, 3-8 Oct 1862, 15-Fry
#3497, 1-Frey, Emma Susan, 2-died, 3-8 Apr 1866, 15-Fry
#3498, 1-Frey, David, 2-died, 3-2 Oct 1878, 15-Fry
#3499, 1-Shank, Susan (Frey), 2-died, 3-21 Feb 1895, 15-Fry
#3500, 1-Ridenour, David A., 2-died, 3-2 Aug 1888, 5-64 years 7 months 13 days, 15-
    Fry
#3501, 1-Yeakle[?], Sara Lousisa, 2-died, 3-2 Oct 1902[?], 5-58[?] years 8 months
    28 days, 15-Fry
#3502, 1-Winters, David B., 2-obituary, 4-Cavetown, MD, 5-40 years, 12-Winters,
    John, 15-Fry
#3503, 1-Edwards, Catharine (Hughes) (Mrs.), 2-obituary, 3-Sunday, 12 Jan, 4-
    Hagerstown, MD, 6-buried Rose Hill Cemetery, Hagerstown, 7-Edwards, Tryon
    (Rev. Dr.), 12-Hughes, Samuel, 15-Fry
#3504, 1-Shank, Susan (Mrs.), 2-obituary, 3-6:00 am, Thursday, __ Feb 1895, 4-
    Leitersburg, MD, 5-75 years, 6-Leitersburg Lutheran Church Cemetery, 7-Shank,
    Noah, 15-Fry
#3505, 1-Fry, Susan, 2-married, 3-10 Dec 1846, 15-Fry
#3506, 1-Fry, John P.[?], 2-married, 3-29 Oct 1857, 15-Fry
#3507, 1-Fry, Margaret Ann, 2-married, 3-25 Aug 1859, 7-Grubb, Joseph Lewis, 10-
    Rev. J.B. Anthony, 15-Fry
#3508, 1-Tery[?], Butbr[?], 2-married, 3-13 Apr 1882, 15-Fry
#3509, 1-Fry, Ann G., 2-married, 3-11 Jan 1885, 15-Fry
#3510, 1-Fry, Peter, 2-born, 3-20 Oct 1800, 15-Fry
#3511, 1-Tritefoe, Sarah, 2-born, 3-5 Oct 1805, 15-Fry
#3512, 1-Tritefoe, Sarah, 2-baptized, 3-9 Mar 1806, 15-Fry
#3513, 1-Fry, Anjaline, 2-born, 3-27 July 1824, 15-Fry
#3514, 1-Fry, Susan Catharine, 2-born, 3-27 Jun 1827, 15-Fry
#3515, 1-Fry, Elizabeth, 2-born, 3-1 Mar 1830, 15-Fry
#3516, 1-Fry, John P., 2-born, 3-12 Feb 1833, 15-Fry
#3517, 1-Fry, Margaretan[?], 2-born, 3-29 Dec 1835, 15-Fry
#3518, 1-Fry, George W., 2-born, 3-13 Apr 1838, 15-Fry
#3519, 1-Vincel, Sarah Elizabeth, 2-born, 3-1 Nov 1847, 15-Fry
#3520, 1-Vincel, Luisa Virginia, 2-born, 3-16 Jul 1849, 15-Fry
#3521, 1-Vincel, Laura Jane, 2-born, 3-6 Feb 1851[?], 15-Fry
#3522, 1-Vincel, Earling Amanda, 2-born, 3-23 Sep 1855, 15-Fry
#3523, 1-Fry, Catharine Alvinda, 2-born, 3-8 Mar 1856, 15-Fry
#3524, 1-Fry, Orrow[?] May, 2-born, 3-31 Jul 1882, 15-Fry
#3525, 1-Fry, Ann Jane Bertha[?], 2-born, 3-3 Jul 1858, 15-Fry
#3526, 1-Fry, George L. Bottler, 2-born, 3-8 Oct 1859, 15-Fry
#3527, 1-Fry, John W., 2-born, 3-29 Sep 1861, 14-Yes, 15-Fry
#3528, 1-Fry, Edker P., 2-born, 3-15 Oct 1863, 14-Yes, 15-Fry
#3529, 1-Fry, Elen U., 2-born, 3-8 Mar 1865, 14-Yes, 15-Fry
#3530, 1-Fry, Arthur I., 2-born, 3-25 Jun 1867, 14-Yes, 15-Fry
#3531, 1-Fry, Orrow[?] May, 2-born, 3-31 Jul 1882, 14-Yes, 15-Fry
#3532, 1-Young[?], John M.[?], 2-born, 3-29 Sep 1861, 15-Fry
#3533, 1-Fry, Edker[?] P., 2-born, 3-15[?] Oct 1863, 15-Fry
#3534, 1-Frey[?], Elon A., 2-born, 3-8 Mar 1865, 15-Fry
#3535, 1-Fry[?], Luthor[?], 2-born, 3-25 Jun 1864, 15-Fry
#3536, 1-Fry, Susan, 2-died, 3-3 Dec 1866, 15-Fry
#3537, 1-Fry, George W., 2-died, 3-19 Feb 1872, 15-Fry
#3538, 1-Fry, Anjalene, 2-died, 3-6 Mar 1875, 15-Fry
#3539, 1-Fry, Catharine Alverda, 2-died, 3-7 Mar 1876, 15-Fry
```

FAMILY BIBLE RECORDS IN THE WASHINGTON COUNTY FREE LIBRARY, HAGERSTOWN, MARYLAND

Entry #, 1-Last Name, First Name, 2-Event, 3-Date, 4-Event Location, 5-Age, 6-Other,
7-Spouse's Last, First, 8-Groom's Residence, 9-Bride's Residence, 10-Minister, 11-Minister's Location,
12-Father's Last, First, 13-Mother's Last, First, 14-Transcribed, 15-Family Bible

```
#3540, 1-Fry, Peter, 2-died, 3-26 Feb 1879, 15-Fry
#3541, 1-Fry, Ann J., 2-died, 3-7 Jan 1884[?], 15-Fry
#3542, 1-Fry, Harry Clinton, 2-born, 3-11 Jul 1886, 15-Fry
#3543, 1-Fry, Pearl Va., 2-born, 3-5 Nov 1884, 15-Fry
#3544, 1-Fry, John P., 2-died, 3-4 Oct 1888, 15-Fry
#3545, 1-Fry, Paul, 2-born, 3-5 Feb 1768, 14-Yes, 15-Fry
#3546, 1-Fry, Elizabeth, 2-born, 3-24 Jul 1770, 7-Fry, Paul, 14-Yes, 15-Fry
#3547, 1-Fry, [male], 2-born, 3-13 Oct 1792, 12-Fry, Paul, 13-Fry, Elizabeth, 14-
    Yes, 15-Fry
#3548, 1-Fry, Mary, 2-born, 3-11 Jul 1798, 12-Fry, Paul, 13-Fry, Elizabeth, 14-Yes,
    15-Fry
#3549, 1-Fry, [female], 2-born, 3-1 Sep 1800, 12-Fry, Paul, 13-Fry, Elizabeth, 14-
    Yes, 15-Fry
#3550, 1-Fry, [male], 2-born, 3-13 Jun 1804, 12-Fry, Paul, 13-Fry, Elizabeth, 14-
    Yes, 15-Fry
#3551, 1-Fry, Joshua, 2-born, 3-29 Nov 1794, 14-Yes, 15-Fry
#3552, 1-Fry, Ann, 2-born, 3-5 Oct 1795, 14-Yes, 15-Fry
#3553, 1-Fry, Isaac, 2-born, 3-12 Sep 1823, 14-Yes, 15-Fry
#3554, 1-Fry, Mary Ann, 2-born, 3-8 Jul 1829, 14-Yes, 15-Fry
#3555, 1-Fry, Joshua, 2-died, 3-14 Jan 1874, 5-79 years 1 months 16 days, 14-Yes,
    15-Fry
#3556, 1-Fry, Ann, 2-died, 3-29 Jan 1885, 5-89 years 3 months 24 days, 14-Yes, 15-
    Fry
#3557, 1-Fry, Isaac, 2-died, 3-11 Apr 1900, 5-74 years 9 months 8 days, 14-Yes, 15-
    Fry
#3558, 1-Fry, B. Franklin, 2-died, 3-10 Feb 1908, 5-46 years 23 days, 14-Yes, 15-
    Fry
#3559, 1-Fox, Ann, 2-baptized, 3-19 May 1819, 14-Yes, 15-Fry
#3560, 1-Frey, Josua, 2-married, 3-3 Dec 1822, 4-New Hanover, Montgomery Co., PA,
    7-Fox, Anna (Miss), 8-Upper Providence Township, Montgomery Co., PA, 9-Upper
    Providence, Montgomery Co., PA, 10-H. Miller, 11-Lutheran minister, 14-Yes,
    15-Fry
#3561, 1-Fouch, David, 2-born, 3-18 Dec 1820, 15-Fouch
#3562, 1-Fouch, Louisa (Grim), 2-born, 3-10 Dec 1828, 15-Fouch
#3563, 1-Fouch, John Jacob, 2-born, 3-31 Jul 1846, 15-Fouch
#3564, 1-Fouch, Mary Elizabeth, 2-born, 3-19 Nov 1849, 15-Fouch
#3565, 1-Fouch, Geoerge Washington, 2-born, 3-1 May 1855, 15-Fouch
#3566, 1-Fouch, Lara Manzilla, 2-born, 3-26 Feb 1858, 15-Fouch
#3567, 1-Fouch, Margreat Elen, 2-born, 3-26 Jan 1860, 15-Fouch
#3568, 1-Fouch, David Birnside, 2-born, 3-31 Mar 1862, 15-Fouch
#3569, 1-Fouch, Emma Fransis, 2-born, 3-21 May 1864, 15-Fouch
#3570, 1-Fouch, Martha Ann Catharine, 2-born, 3-31 Mar 1866, 15-Fouch
#3571, 1-Fouch, Edwin Oscar, 2-born, 3-7 Jun 1869, 15-Fouch
#3572, 1-Fouch, Bertha May, 2-born, 3-26 Jan 1872, 15-Fouch
#3573, 1-Fouch, Ada Leah, 2-born, 3-5 May 1874, 15-Fouch
#3574, 1-Fouch, Louisa, 2-died, 3-17 May 1847, 15-Fouch
#3575, 1-Fouch, David, 2-died, 3-31 Jul 1888, 15-Fouch
#3576, 1-Fouch, Matilda, 2-died, 3-1 Aug 1915, 15-Fouch
#3577, 1-Fouch, David, 2-married, 3-12 Jun 1845, 7-Grim, Louisa, 15-Fouch
#3578, 1-Foltz, Henry, 2-married, 3-27 Feb 1855, 7-Forney, Annamaia, 14-Yes, 15-
    Foltz
#3579, 1-Witmer, Milton, 2-born, 3-18__, 14-Yes, 15-Foltz
#3580, 1-Witmer, Milton, 2-married, 3-14 Feb 1860, 7-Foltz, Sarah A., 14-Yes, 15-
    Foltz
#3581, 1-Foltz, Henry, 2-born, 3-7 Jan 1798, 14-Yes, 15-Foltz
```

FAMILY BIBLE RECORDS IN THE WASHINGTON COUNTY FREE LIBRARY, HAGERSTOWN, MARYLAND

**Entry #, 1-Last Name, First Name, 2-Event, 3-Date, 4-Event Location, 5-Age, 6-Other,
7-Spouse's Last, First, 8-Groom's Residence, 9-Bride's Residence, 10-Minister, 11-Minister's Location,
12-Father's Last, First, 13-Mother's Last, First, 14-Transcribed, 15-Family Bible**

```
#3582, 1-Stouffer, Nancy, 2-born, 3-2 Jul 1796, 14-Yes, 15-Foltz
#3583, 1-Foltz, Henry, 2-born, 3-22 Apr 1835, 14-Yes, 15-Foltz
#3584, 1-Foltz, Sarah A., 2-born, 3-30 Oct 1836, 14-Yes, 15-Foltz
#3585, 1-Foltz, Marann Catherine, 2-born, 3-23 Nov 1855, 14-Yes, 15-Foltz
#3586, 1-Foltz, Lewis Henry, 2-born, 3-30 Jan 1857, 14-Yes, 15-Foltz
#3587, 1-Foltz, Amey Elly, 2-born, 3-7 Jul 1858, 14-Yes, 15-Foltz
#3588, 1-Foltz, Laura Jane, 2-born, 3-7 Mar 1860, 14-Yes, 15-Foltz
#3589, 1-Foltz, Clara Bell, 2-born, 3-22 Aug 1862, 14-Yes, 15-Foltz
#3590, 1-Foltz, Celia Rose[?], 2-born, 3-27 May 1864, 14-Yes, 15-Foltz
#3591, 1-Foltz, Willie Edwin, 2-born, 3-30 Jan 1869, 14-Yes, 15-Foltz
#3592, 1-Foltz, Jacob Forny, 2-born, 3-18 Jul 1871, 14-Yes, 15-Foltz
#3593, 1-Foltz, Samuel Oswalt, 2-born, 3-4 Jan 1874, 14-Yes, 15-Foltz
#3594, 1-Foltz, Ulysses Grant, 2-born, 3-12 Apr 1875, 14-Yes, 15-Foltz
#3595, 1-Foltz, Ulysses Grant, 2-died, 3-12 Apr 1875, 5-hours, 14-Yes, 15-Foltz
#3596, 1-Forney, Annamaria, 2-born, 3-12 Oct 1833, 14-Yes, 15-Foltz
#3597, 1-Foltz, Henry, 2-died, 3-2 Dec 1860, 5-62 years 10 months 25 days, 14-Yes,
    15-Foltz
#3598, 1-Foltz, Nancy, 2-died, 3-26 Jan 1868, 5-61 years 6 months 24 days, 14-Yes,
    15-Foltz
#3599, 1-Witmer, Sarah A., 2-died, 3-19 Jul 1876, 5-39 years 8 months 18 days, 14-
    Yes, 15-Foltz
#3600, 1-Foltz, Clara, 2-died, 3-30 Dec 1886, 5-24 years 5 months 8 days, 14-Yes,
    15-Foltz
#3601, 1-Shafer, Ellen Newcomer, 2-died, 3-1 May 1885, 5-4 months 9 days, 6-
    "granddaughter of Henry & Annamaria Foltz", 14-Yes, 15-Foltz
#3602, 1-Foltz, Anna M., 2-died, 3-26 Dec 1892, 6-buried 30 Dec 1892, 14-Yes, 15-
    Foltz
#3603, 1-Foltz, Henry J., 2-died, 3-18 May 1899, 6-buried 21 May 1899, 14-Yes, 15-
    Foltz
#3604, 1-Foltz, Willie E., 2-died, 3-15 Apr 1896, 14-Yes, 15-Foltz
#3605, 1-Fisher, Alta L___[?], 2-born, 3-Friday, 4 Mar 1927, 14-Yes, 15-Fisher
#3606, 1-Fisher, Bruce Mills, 2-born, 3-Tuesday, 2 Apr 1929, 14-Yes, 15-Fisher
#3607, 1-Fisher, Sara Eileen, 2-born, 3-Monday, 31 May 1937, 14-Yes, 15-Fisher
#3608, 1-Fisher, Barbara Ann, 2-born, 3-Thursday, 21 Sep 1939, 14-Yes, 15-Fisher
#3609, 1-Cash, Laura, 2-born, 3-20 Feb 1960, 14-Yes, 15-Fisher
#3610, 1-Cluts[?], Bruce Fisher, 2-born, 3-5 Mar 1963, 14-Yes, 15-Fisher
#3611, 1-Fisher, Timothy Craig, 2-born, 3-7 May 1970, 14-Yes, 15-Fisher
#3612, 1-Hood, Pamela, 2-born, 3-12 May 1962, 14-Yes, 15-Fisher
#3613, 1-Cash, Robert Rocky O., 2-born, 3-13 May 1964, 14-Yes, 15-Fisher
#3614, 1-Hood, Michael, 2-born, 3-15 May 1964, 14-Yes, 15-Fisher
#3615, 1-Cash, Amy Lynn, 2-born, 3-29 May 1962, 14-Yes, 15-Fisher
#3616, 1-Fisher, Virginia, 2-born, 3-22 Jul 1930, 14-Yes, 15-Fisher
#3617, 1-Fisher, Terri, 2-born, 3-21 Sep 1958, 14-Yes, 15-Fisher
#3618, 1-Cash, Sheila[?], 2-born, 3-25 Oct 1958, 14-Yes, 15-Fisher
#3619, 1-Thompson, Tommy, 2-born, 3-20 Nov 1958, 14-Yes, 15-Fisher
#3620, 1-Thompson, Wm. K., 2-born, 3-27 Jan 1956, 14-Yes, 15-Fisher
#3621, 1-Fisher, Timothy Craig, 2-born, 3-7 May 1970, 14-Yes, 15-Fisher
#3622, 1-Hood, Pete, 2-born, 3-5 Dec 1932, 14-Yes, 15-Fisher
#3623, 1-Stratton, Edward, 2-born, 3-2 Aug 1924, 14-Yes, 15-Fisher
#3624, 1-Cash, Jr., Robert Owen, 2-born, 3-16 Dec 1927, 14-Yes, 15-Fisher
#3625, 1-Fisher, Janet E., 2-died, 3-28 Dec 1948, 14-Yes, 15-Fisher
#3626, 1-Fisher, Barbara Jean Weeks, 2-died, 3-10 Aug 1967, 14-Yes, 15-Fisher
#3627, 1-Fisher, Bruce M., 3-15 Aug 1901, 14-Yes, 15-Fisher
#3628, 1-Fisher, Janet Mills, 3-28 Sep 1901, 14-Yes, 15-Fisher
#3629, 1-Fisher, Margaret M., 3-15 Sep 1901, 14-Yes, 15-Fisher
```

FAMILY BIBLE RECORDS IN THE WASHINGTON COUNTY FREE LIBRARY, HAGERSTOWN, MARYLAND

Entry #, 1-Last Name, First Name, 2-Event, 3-Date, 4-Event Location, 5-Age, 6-Other, 7-Spouse's Last, First, 8-Groom's Residence, 9-Bride's Residence, 10-Minister, 11-Minister's Location, 12-Father's Last, First, 13-Mother's Last, First, 14-Transcribed, 15-Family Bible

#3630, 1-Fisher, Ray Monroe, 2-died, 3-7 Mar 1903, 4-Robinsville, 14-Yes, 15-Fisher

#3631, 1-Fisher, Maxwell Wynwood, 2-died, 3-18 Jul 1906, 4-Robinsville, 14-Yes, 15-Fisher

#3632, 1-Fisher, Marsahll Albert, 2-died, 3-5 Sep 1908, 4-Robinsville, 14-Yes, 15-Fisher

#3633, 1-Fisher, Paul Waynfield[?], 2-died, 3-27 Sep 1910, 4-Robinsville, 14-Yes, 15-Fisher

#3634, 1-Fisher, Bruce M., 2-[blank], 3-15 Aug 1901, 14-Yes, 15-Fisher

#3635, 1-Fisher, Bruce M., 2-[blank], 3-27 Dec 19_6, 14-Yes, 15-Fisher

#3636, 1-Fisher, Bruce M., 2-married, 3-17 Jun 1926, 7-Mills[?], Janet E., 14-Yes, 15-Fisher

#3637, 1-Fisher, Bruce M., 2-married, 3-27 Dec 1949, 7-McVicker, Margaret Rae, 14-Yes, 15-Fisher

#3638, 1-Stratton, Edward, 2-married, 3-29 Aug 1948, 7-Fisher, Alta L., 14-Yes, 15-Fisher

#3639, 1-Fisher, Bruce Mills, 2-married, 3-7 Jul 1950[?], 7-Weeks[?], Barbara Jean, 14-Yes, 15-Fisher

#3640, 1-Cash, Jr., Robert O., 2-married, 3-17 Aug 1957, 7-Fisher, Sara Eileen, 14-Yes, 15-Fisher

#3641, 1-Hood, Peter, 2-married, 3-1 Apr 1961, 7-Fisher, Barbara Ann, 14-Yes, 15-Fisher

#3642, 1-Fisher, Bruce Mills, 2-married, 3-17 Aug 1968, 7-Thompson, Virginia, 14-Yes, 15-Fisher

#3643, 1-Emmert, Leonard D., 2-married, 3-12 Aug 1913, 7-Remsburg, Annie[?] E., 15-Emmert

#3644, 1-Emmert, Leonard Remsburg , 2-born, 3-10[?] Aug 1914, 15-Emmert

#3645, 1-Emmert, Ann Cathrine, 2-born, 3-3 Sep 1921, 15-Emmert

#3646, 1-Emmert, Leonard R., 2-married, 3-5 Oct 1940, 7-Kelley, Margaret L., 15-Emmert

#3647, 1-Emmert, Anne Catherine, 2-married, 3-21 Jun 1946, 7-Lambert, Donald ____, 15-Emmert

#3648, 1-Lambert, Dale Kirkham[?], 2-born, 3-17 Jun 1950, 15-Emmert

#3649, 1-Lambert, David Orien, 2-born, 3-10 Aug 1952, 15-Emmert

#3650, 1-Emmert, Bessie R., 2-married, 3-7 Jan 1914, 7-Wingert[?] Lewis P., 15-Emmert

#3651, 1-Wingert, Lewis Emmert, 2-born, 3-28 Mar 1916, 15-Emmert

#3652, 1-Wingert, Lewis Emmert, 2-married, 3-23 Feb 1952, 7-Pennington, Sarah Rochester, 15-Emmert

#3653, 1-Wingert, Philip Carter, 2-born, 3-20 Nov 1953, 15-Emmert

#3654, 1-Wingert, Theresa, 2-born, 3-11 Aug 1960, 15-Emmert

#3655, 1-Lambert, Catherine, 2-born, 3-8-Oct-58, 15-Emmert

#3656, 1-Lambert, Kristie Anne, 2-born, 3-24 Nov 1955, 15-Emmert

#3657, 1-Emmert, Anne[?] Craft, 2-born, 3-9 May 1947, 15-Emmert

#3658, 1-Emmert, Lewis[?] Cookerly, 2-born, 3-2 Apr 1950, 15-Emmert

#3659, 1-Emmert, Mamie Barbara, 2-died, 3-10 Sep 1903, 15-Emmert

#3660, 1-Emmert, Mary Naomi[?], 2-died, 3-27 Apr 1905, 15-Emmert

#3661, 1-Emmert, Joseph Martin, 2-died, 3-29 Apr 1906, 15-Emmert

#3662, 1-Emmert, Leonard David, 2-died, 3-28 May 1935, 15-Emmert

#3663, 1-Emmert, Annie[?] R., 2-died, 3-30 Jan 1958, 7-Emmert, Leonard David, 15-Emmert

#3664, 1-Emmert, Mary C. (Young), 2-died, 3-10 Apr 1909, 15-Emmert

#3665, 1-Emmert, Isaac, 2-died, 3-31 Mar 1920, 15-Emmert

#3666, 1-Wingert, Lewis Peters, 2-born, 3-4 Sep 1872, 15-Emmert

#3667, 1-Wingert, Lewis Peters, 2-died, 3-7 Feb 1955[?], 15-Emmert

FAMILY BIBLE RECORDS IN THE WASHINGTON COUNTY FREE LIBRARY, HAGERSTOWN, MARYLAND

Entry #, 1-Last Name, First Name, 2-Event, 3-Date, 4-Event Location, 5-Age, 6-Other, 7-Spouse's Last, First, 8-Groom's Residence, 9-Bride's Residence, 10-Minister, 11-Minister's Location, 12-Father's Last, First, 13-Mother's Last, First, 14-Transcribed, 15-Family Bible

#3668, 1-Wingert, Bessie (Emmert), 2-died, 3-24 Apr 1979[?], 7-Wingert, Lewis Peters, 15-Emmert

#3669, 1-Ecton, Charles R., 2-married, 3-23 Dec 1886, 7-Show, Maggie E., 15-Ecton

#3670, 1-Ecton, Sarah Jane, 2-married, 3-May 1886, 7-Show, John A., 15-Ecton

#3671, 1-Show, Annie F., 2-married, 3-1 Jan 1889, 7-Jacobs, William H., 15-Ecton

#3672, 1-Show, Charles W., 2-married, 3-24 May 1889, 7-Benner, Viola, 15-Ecton

#3673, 1-Show, William Henry, 2-born, 3-10 Dec 1834, 15-Ecton

#3674, 1-McCoy, Amelia Catherine, 2-born, 3-[blank], 15-Ecton

#3675, 1-Show, John Andrew, 2-born, 3-24 Nov 1859, 15-Ecton

#3676, 1-Show, Ann Mary, 2-born, 3-2 May 1861, 15-Ecton

#3677, 1-Show, Margaret Elizabeth, 2-born, 3-18 Mar 1864, 15-Ecton

#3678, 1-Show, Charles Wesley, 2-born, 3-7 Mar 1867, 15-Ecton

#3679, 1-Show, Ann Francis[?], 2-born, 3-10 Dec[?] 1869, 15-Ecton

#3680, 1-Show, Ann Mary, 2-died, 3-18 Nov 1862, 15-Ecton

#3681, 1-Show, George Elmer, 2-died, 3-29 Aug 1880, 15-Ecton

#3682, 1-Show, Amelia C., 2-died, 3-12 Nov 1899, 15-Ecton

#3683, 1-Ecton, Charles William, 2-born, 3-26 Dec 188_, 15-Ecton

#3684, 1-Ecton, Flossie Virginia, 2-born, 3-11 Nov 1891, 15-Ecton

#3685, 1-Ecton, Mary Cathern, 2-born, 3-18[?] Dec 1894, 15-Ecton

#3686, 1-Ecton, Dora Francis, 2-born, 3-13 Dec 1898, 15-Ecton

#3687, 1-Show, Willmenia Massa Virginia, 2-born, 3-19 Oct 1872, 15-Ecton

#3688, 1-Show, William Henry, 2-born, 3-26 May 1875, 15-Ecton

#3689, 1-Show, Sarah Cathren, 2-born, 3-21 Oct 1877, 15-Ecton

#3690, 1-Show, George Elmer, 2-born, 3-24 Mar 1880, 15-Ecton

#3691, 1-Ecton, Nina May, 2-born, 3-22 Sep 1887, 15-Ecton

#3692, 1-Show, Winnie Frances, 2-born, 3-28 Jan 1888, 15-Ecton

#3693, 1-Downey, Lewis, 2-born, 3-19 Sep 1812, 14-Yes, 15-Downey

#3694, 1-Downey, Hadassah, 2-born, 3-14 Dec 1815, 14-Yes, 15-Downey

#3695, 1-Downey, Maria, 2-born, 3-3 Aug 1836, 12-Downey, Lewis, 13-Downey, Hadassah, 14-Yes, 15-Downey

#3696, 1-Downey, Elizabeth, 2-born, 3-2 Mar 1838, 12-Downey, Lewis, 13-Downey, Hadassah, 14-Yes, 15-Downey

#3697, 1-Downey, Catharine, 2-born, 3-23 May 1840, 12-Downey, Lewis, 13-Downey, Hadassah, 14-Yes, 15-Downey

#3698, 1-Downey, Anna, 2-born, 3-1 Jan 1842, 12-Downey, Lewis, 13-Downey, Hadassah, 14-Yes, 15-Downey

#3699, 1-Downey, George, 2-born, 3-1 Dec 1843, 12-Downey, Lewis, 13-Downey, Hadassah, 14-Yes, 15-Downey

#3700, 1-Downey, Ella, 2-born, 3-27 Dec 1845, 12-Downey, Lewis, 13-Downey, Hadassah, 14-Yes, 15-Downey

#3701, 1-Downey, Lewis, 2-born, 3-29 Jul 1848, 12-Downey, Lewis, 13-Downey, Hadassah, 14-Yes, 15-Downey

#3702, 1-Downey, Lewis, 2-married, 3-28 Aug 1834, 7-Brown, Hadassah, 14-Yes, 15-Downey

#3703, 1-Downey, Maria, 2-married, 3-18 Dec 1856, 7-Downs, Lewis O., 14-Yes, 15-Downey

#3704, 1-Downey, Elizabeth, 2-married, 3-25 Jun 1863, 7-Coffman, John D., 14-Yes, 15-Downey

#3705, 1-Downey, George, 2-married, 3-16 Dec 1869, 7-Hibarger, Alice, 14-Yes, 15-Downey

#3706, 1-Downey, Lewis, 2-married, 3-26 Nov 1872, 7-Hagerman, Anna, 14-Yes, 15-Downey

#3707, 1-Downey, Lewis, 2-died, 3-15 Mar 1848, 5-35 years 5 months 25 days, 14-Yes, 15-Downey

FAMILY BIBLE RECORDS IN THE WASHINGTON COUNTY FREE LIBRARY, HAGERSTOWN, MARYLAND

Entry #, 1-Last Name, First Name, 2-Event, 3-Date, 4-Event Location, 5-Age, 6-Other, 7-Spouse's Last, First, 8-Groom's Residence, 9-Bride's Residence, 10-Minister, 11-Minister's Location, 12-Father's Last, First, 13-Mother's Last, First, 14-Transcribed, 15-Family Bible

#3708, 1-Long, Hadassah (Downey), 2-died, 3-28 Mar 1901, 5-85 years 3 months 14 days, 14-Yes, 15-Downey

#3709, 1-Downey, Ella, 2-died, 3-7 Jul 1882, 5-36 years 6 months 10 days, 14-Yes, 15-Downey

#3710, 1-Downs, Lewis O., 2-died, 3-15 Apr 1894, 5-68 years 4 months 28 days, 14-Yes, 15-Downey

#3711, 1-Downey, George, 2-died, 3-4 Jan 1911, 5-67 years 1 months 4 days, 14-Yes, 15-Downey

#3712, 1-Coffman, John D., 2-died, 3-8 May 1913, 5-75 years 10 months 4 days, 14-Yes, 15-Downey

#3713, 1-Downey, Anna, 2-died, 3-1 Oct 1914, 5-72 years 9 months, 14-Yes, 15-Downey

#3714, 1-Downey, Catharine, 2-died, 3-28 Aug 1917, 5-77 years 3 months 5 days, 14-Yes, 15-Downey

#3715, 1-Downey, Maria, 2-died, 3-24 Jul 1885, 5-67 years 2months 24 days, 6-"sister of Lewis Downey, Sr.", 14-Yes, 15-Downey

#3716, 1-Clingan, A. Maria, 2-died, 3-5 Jul 1848, 5-1 months 24 days, 15-Clingan

#3717, 1-Clingan, Juliet A., 2-died, 3-18 Sep 1853, 15-Clingan

#3718, 1-Clingan, Elenor[?] Jane, 2-died, 3-29 Oct[?] 1863, 15-Clingan

#3719, 1-Clingan, William Henry, 2-died, 3-20 Feb 1864, 15-Clingan

#3720, 1-Clingan, McClean, 2-died, 3-18 May 1876, 5-59 years 19 days, 15-Clingan

#3721, 1-Folk, Virginia, 2-died, 3-15 Dec 1900, 5-77 years, 15-Clingan

#3722, 1-Clingan, Thomas F., 2-died, 3-7 Apr 1924, 15-Clingan

#3723, 1-Clingan, Robert S., 2-died, 3-18 Jan 1938, 5-76 years 9 months, 15-Clingan

#3724, 1-Clingan, John Bell, 2-died, 3-3 Aug 1939, 15-Clingan

#3725, 1-Clingan, McClean, 2-born, 3-29 Mar 1817[?], 15-Clingan

#3726, 1-Clingan, Juliet A. (Miss), 2-born, 3-8 Mar 1812, 15-Clingan

#3727, 1-Clingan, Mary Elizabeth, 2-born, 3-10 Oct 1845, 15-Clingan

#3728, 1-Clingan, An Maria, 2-born, 3-11 May 1848, 15-Clingan

#3729, 1-Clingan, Samuel Walker, 2-born, 3-28 Mar 1850, 15-Clingan

#3730, 1-Clingan, William Henry, 2-born, 3-3 Mar 1856, 15-Clingan

#3731, 1-Clingan, Thomas Franklin, 2-born, 3-11 Jul 1857, 15-Clingan

#3732, 1-Clingan, elenor Jane, 2-born, 3-10 May 1859, 15-Clingan

#3733, 1-Clingan, John Bell, 2-born, 3-1 Oct 1860, 15-Clingan

#3734, 1-Clingan, Qunnen[?] Jackson, 2-born, 3-9 Jul 1862, 15-Clingan

#3735, 1-Clingan, James Semmerville, 2-born, 3-1 Jan 1866, 15-Clingan

#3736, 1-Clingan, Robert Snoden, 2-born, 3-20 Apr 1867, 15-Clingan

#3737, 1-Clingan, McClean, 2-married, 3-15 Jan 1845, 7-Wilson, Juliet A., 15-Clingan

#3738, 1-Clingan, McClean, 2-married, 3-13 Mar 1855, 7-Bound[?], Virginia, 15-Clingan

#3739, 1-Clingan, Virginia (Mrs.), 2-married, 3-24 Jan 1878, 7-Folk, John, 15-Clingan

#3740, 1-Cheney, William, 2-born, 3-9 Aug 1776, 15-Cheney

#3741, 1-Hatch, Tryphena, 2-born, 3-29 Feb 1784, 15-Cheney

#3742, 1-Cheney, Chloe, 2-born, 3-30 Aug 1801, 12-Cheney, William, 13-Hatch, Tryphena, 15-Cheney

#3743, 1-Cheney, Chloe, 2-died, 3-1875, 12-Cheney, William, 13-Hatch, Tryphena, 15-Cheney

#3744, 1-Cheney, Philena, 2-born, 3-3 Jan 1803, 12-Cheney, William, 13-Hatch, Tryphena, 15-Cheney

#3745, 1-Cheney, Peosis[?] Hatch, 2-born, 3-29 Apr 1805, 12-Cheney, William, 13-Hatch, Tryphena, 15-Cheney

#3746, 1-Cheney, Peosis[?] Hatch, 2-died, 3-1861, 12-Cheney, William, 13-Hatch, Tryphena, 15-Cheney

FAMILY BIBLE RECORDS IN THE WASHINGTON COUNTY FREE LIBRARY, HAGERSTOWN, MARYLAND

Entry #, 1-Last Name, First Name, 2-Event, 3-Date, 4-Event Location, 5-Age, 6-Other, 7-Spouse's Last, First, 8-Groom's Residence, 9-Bride's Residence, 10-Minister, 11-Minister's Location, 12-Father's Last, First, 13-Mother's Last, First, 14-Transcribed, 15-Family Bible

#3747, 1-Cheney, William Hutchinson, 2-born, 3-5 Mar 1807, 12-Cheney, William, 13-Hatch, Tryphena, 15-Cheney

#3748, 1-Cheney, Tryphena, 2-born, 3-31 Dec 1808, 12-Cheney, William, 13-Hatch, Tryphena, 15-Cheney

#3749, 1-Cheney, Sophia, 2-born, 3-21 Jul 1810, 12-Cheney, William, 13-Hatch, Tryphena, 15-Cheney

#3750, 1-Cheney, George Hallet, 2-born, 3-29 Mar 1812, 12-Cheney, William, 13-Hatch, Tryphena, 15-Cheney

#3751, 1-Cheney, George Hallet, 2-died, 3-1871, 12-Cheney, William, 13-Hatch, Tryphena, 15-Cheney

#3752, 1-Cheney, Alice, 2-born, 3-13 Jun 1814, 12-Cheney, William, 13-Hatch, Tryphena, 15-Cheney

#3753, 1-Cheney, Prentice, 2-born, 3-2 Mar 1816, 12-Cheney, William, 13-Hatch, Tryphena, 15-Cheney

#3754, 1-Cheney, James Monroe, 2-born, 3-9 Dec 1817, 12-Cheney, William, 13-Hatch, Tryphena, 15-Cheney

#3755, 1-Cheney, Charles Franklin, 2-born, 3-11 Apr 1819, 12-Cheney, William, 13-Hatch, Tryphena, 15-Cheney

#3756, 1-Cheney, James Edwin, 2-born, 3-10 Apr 1821, 12-Cheney, William, 13-Hatch, Tryphena, 15-Cheney

#3757, 1-Cheney, Rosette[?] Maria, 2-born, 3-15 Feb 1824, 12-Cheney, William, 13-Hatch, Tryphena, 15-Cheney

#3758, 1-Cheney, Henry Martin, 2-born, 3-21 Mar 1830, 12-Cheney, William, 13-Hatch, Tryphena, 15-Cheney

#3759, 1-Foster, Marine[?] Frederic A., 2-married, 3-13 Nov 1817, 7-Arnold, Sarah, 15-Cheney

#3760, 1-Arnold, Sarah, 2-born, 3-2 Oct 1800, 15-Cheney

#3761, 1-Foster, Peregrine Dwight, 2-born, 3-18 Feb 1819, 15-Cheney

#3762, 1-Foster, Henry Bowman, 2-born, 3-28 Dec 1820, 15-Cheney

#3763, 1-Foster, Maria Louisa, 2-born, 3-25 Mar 1825, 15-Cheney

#3764, 1-Foster, Frederea[?] Augustus, 2-born, 3-4 Jan 1833, 15-Cheney

#3765, 1-Foster, Sarah Jane, 2-born, 3-19 Dec 1834, 15-Cheney

#3766, 1-Holmes , John F., 2-born, 3-31 Dec 1833, 15-Cheney

#3767, 1-Foster, Martha Ellen, 2-born, 3-21 Feb 1837, 15-Cheney

#3768, 1-Foster, William Beck, 2-born, 3-11 Nov 1838, 15-Cheney

#3769, 1-Foster, Wilson Parkman, 2-born, 3-15 Sep 1845, 15-Cheney

#3770, 1-Foster, Theodore[?] Newton, 2-born, 3-28 Aug 1847, 15-Cheney

#3771, 1-Foster, Clara Belle, 2-born, 3-1 Aug 1871, 12-Foster, Wilson Parkman, 13-Larque, Jenie[?] A.[?], 15-Cheney

#3772, 1-Foster, Peregrine Dwight, 2-married, 7-Duble, Margaret M., 15-Cheney

#3773, 1-Foster, Peregrine Dwight, 2-married, 7-B____an[?], Martha, 15-Cheney

#3774, 1-Foster, Charles Frederick, 2-born, 3-9 Jun 1847, 12-Foster, Peregrine Dwight, 13-Duble, Margaret M., 15-Cheney

#3775, 1-Foster, Henry Arnold, 2-born, 3-1849, 12-Foster, Peregrine Dwight, 13-Duble, Margaret M., 15-Cheney

#3776, 1-Foster, Henry Arnold, 2-died, 3-1850, 15-Cheney

#3777, 1-Foster, Maria Louisa, 2-married, 7-Cheney, James Edwin, 15-Cheney

#3778, 1-Cheney, James Edwin, 2-born, 3-12 Jul 1847, 15-Cheney

#3779, 1-Cheney, Foster Hallet, 2-born, 3-6 Feb 1850, 15-Cheney

#3780, 1-Foster, Sarah Jane, 2-married, 3-12 Jun 1856, 7-Holmes, John F.[?], 15-Cheney

#3781, 1-Foster, Wilson Parkman, 2-married, 3-1870, 7-Larque, Jenie[?] A.[?], 15-Cheney

#3782, 1-Cheney, Foster Hallet, 2-married, 3-2 Oct 1873, 7-Blackburn, Martha Rosanna, 15-Cheney

FAMILY BIBLE RECORDS IN THE WASHINGTON COUNTY FREE LIBRARY, HAGERSTOWN, MARYLAND

Entry #, 1-Last Name, First Name, 2-Event, 3-Date, 4-Event Location, 5-Age, 6-Other,
7-Spouse's Last, First, 8-Groom's Residence, 9-Bride's Residence, 10-Minister, 11-Minister's Location,
12-Father's Last, First, 13-Mother's Last, First, 14-Transcribed, 15-Family Bible

#3783, 1-Blackburn, Martha Rosanna, 2-born, 3-31 Dec 1851, 12-Blackburn, Thos., 15-Cheney

#3784, 1-Cheney, Reginald Foster, 2-born, 3-2 Jul 1874, 12-Cheney, Foster Hallet, 13-Blackburn, Martha Rosanna, 15-Cheney

#3785, 1-Cheney, William, 2-married, 7-Hatch, Tryphina, 15-Cheney

#3786, 1-Cheney, Philence[?], 2-married, 3-24 Sep 1822, 7-Prentice, Eliza P., 15-Cheney

#3787, 1-Cheney, Persis H., 2-married, 3-30 May 1824, 7-Forbes, Charles, 15-Cheney

#3788, 1-Cheney, Chloe, 2-married, 3-13 Sep 1824, 7-Metcalf, Horace, 15-Cheney

#3789, 1-Cheney, Tryphena, 2-married, 3-9 Jul 1827, 7-King, Alonzo (Rev.), 15-Cheney

#3790, 1-Cheney, W.H., 2-married, 3-22 Sep 1830, 7-Whittney, Caroline H., 15-Cheney

#3791, 1-Cheney, Sophia, 2-married, 3-25 Apr 1833, 7-Manning, Franklin, 15-Cheney

#3792, 1-Cheney, George H., 2-married, 3-30 Jul 1833, 7-Davis, Sarah D., 15-Cheney

#3793, 1-Cheney, Alice, 2-married, 3-28 Jan 1835, 7-Dodge, O.A. (Rev.), 15-Cheney

#3794, 1-Cheney, James Edwin, 2-married, 3-15 Jul 1846, 7-Foster, Maria L., 15-Cheney

#3795, 1-Cheney, Tryhena[?] (Mrs.), 2-married, 7-Farnsworth, [blank], 15-Cheney

#3796, 1-King, Tryphena C. (Mrs.), 2-married, 7-Penson[?], Ira (Rev.), 15-Cheney

#3797, 1-Foster, Henry Bowman, 2-died, 3-18 Sep 1831, 5-10 years 8 months 21 days, 15-Cheney

#3798, 1-Foster, Martha Ellen, 2-died, 3-24 Apr 1837, 5-2 months, 15-Cheney

#3799, 1-Foster, Sarah (Mrs.), 2-died, 3-21 Aug 1842, 5-41 years 10 months 19 days, 15-Cheney

#3800, 1-Foster, Sr., Frederic Augustus, 2-born, 3-7 May 1791, 4-Providence, Rhoide Island, 15-Cheney

#3801, 1-Foster, Jr.[?], Frederick A., 2-died, 3-2 Jul 1856, 15-Cheney

#3802, 1-Holmes, Sarah Jane (Miss), 2-died, 3-22 May 1858, 15-Cheney

#3803, 1-Foster, William Black[?], 2-died, 3-28 Jan 1862, 15-Cheney

#3804, 1-Cheney, William, 2-died, 3-15 Jun 1830, 5-54 years, 15-Cheney

#3805, 1-Cheney, Tryphena H. (Mrs.), 2-died, 3-10 Aug 1861, 15-Cheney

#3806, 1-Cheney, James Monroe, 2-died, 3-13 Mar 1818, 5-3 months, 15-Cheney

#3807, 1-Cheney, Rosette Maria, 2-died, 3-15 Oct 1825, 5-20 months, 15-Cheney

#3808, 1-Cheney, Henry Martin, 2-died, 3-30 Apr 1830, 15-Cheney

#3809, 1-Cheney, Charles Franklin, 2-died, 3-31 Jul 1834, 5-15 years, 15-Cheney

#3810, 1-Cheney, Prentice, 2-died, 3-18 Mar 1835, 5-19 years, 15-Cheney

#3811, 1-King, Alonzo (Rev.), 2-died, 3-29 Nov 1835, 4-Westborough, MA, 5-38 years, 15-Cheney

#3812, 1-Dodge, Oliver Augustus (Rev.), 2-died, 3-27 May 1840, 4-Lixington, MA, 5-27 years, 15-Cheney

#3813, 1-Forbes, Charles, 2-died, 3-16 Sep 1849, 4-Cincinnati, OH, 5-50 years, 15-Cheney

#3814, 1-Brown, George, 2-born, 3-19 Aug 1775, 14-Yes, 15-Brown

#3815, 1-Brown, Esther, 2-born, 3-27 Jun 1773, 14-Yes, 15-Brown

#3816, 1-Brown, Elizabeth, 2-born, 3-9 Jul 1801, 12-Brown, George, 13-Brown, Esther, 15-Brown

#3817, 1-Brown, Benjamin, 2-born, 3-17 Apr 1803, 12-Brown, George, 13-Brown, Esther, 15-Brown

#3818, 1-Brown, Susanna, 2-born, 3-26 Nov 1804, 12-Brown, George, 13-Brown, Esther, 15-Brown

#3819, 1-Brown, Eleanor, 2-born, 3-13 Sep 1806, 12-Brown, George, 13-Brown, Esther, 15-Brown

#3820, 1-Brown, Anna, 2-born, 3-5 Jun 1808, 12-Brown, George, 13-Brown, Esther, 15-Brown

FAMILY BIBLE RECORDS IN THE WASHINGTON COUNTY FREE LIBRARY, HAGERSTOWN, MARYLAND

Entry #, 1-Last Name, First Name, 2-Event, 3-Date, 4-Event Location, 5-Age, 6-Other, 7-Spouse's Last, First, 8-Groom's Residence, 9-Bride's Residence, 10-Minister, 11-Minister's Location, 12-Father's Last, First, 13-Mother's Last, First, 14-Transcribed, 15-Family Bible

```
#3821, 1-Brown, George, 2-born, 3-15 Sep 1809, 12-Brown, George, 13-Brown, Esther,
     15-Brown
#3822, 1-Brown, Maria, 2-born, 3-21 Oct 1811, 12-Brown, George, 13-Brown, Esther,
     15-Brown
#3823, 1-Brown, William, 2-born, 3-16 Jun 1813, 12-Brown, George, 13-Brown, Esther,
     15-Brown
#3824, 1-Brown, Hadassah, 2-born, 3-14 Dec 1815, 12-Brown, George, 13-Brown,
     Esther, 15-Brown
#3825, 1-Leary, Hadassah , 2-born, 3-1 Jan 1825, 12-Leary, Edward, 13-Leary,
     Elizabeth, 15-Brown
#3826, 1-Leary, George B., 2-born, 3-10 Apr 1827, 12-Leary, Edward, 13-Leary,
     Elizabeth, 15-Brown
#3827, 1-Brown, Susanna, 2-died, 3-3 Aug 1806, 12-Brown, George, 13-Brown, Esther,
     15-Brown
#3828, 1-Brown, George, 2-died, 3-28 Sep 1809, 12-Brown, George, 13-Brown, Esther,
     15-Brown
#3829, 1-Leary, Hadassah, 2-died, 3-28 Jan 1826, 12-Leary, Edward, 13-Leary,
     Elizabeth, 15-Brown
#3830, 1-Brown, George, 2-married, 3-3 Jun 1799, 7-Morison, Esther, 15-Brown
#3831, 1-Brown, Benjamin, 2-married, 3-22 Feb 1827, 7-Maudy, Matilda, 15-Brown
#3832, 1-Brown, George M., 2-born, 3-27 Dec 1827, 12-Brown, Benjamin, 13-Brown,
     Matilda, 15-Brown
#3833, 1-Brown, Ann Maria, 2-born, 3-27 Sep 1829, 12-Brown, Benjamin, 13-Brown,
     Matilda, 15-Brown
#3834, 1-Brown, Amanda, 2-born, 3-3 Jan 1832, 12-Brown, Benjamin, 13-Brown,
     Matilda, 15-Brown
#3835, 1-Brown, George, 2-died, 3-4 Dec 1828, 7-Brown, Esther, 15-Brown
#3836, 1-Brown, Esther, 2-died, 3-21 Sep 1829, 7-Brown, George, 15-Brown
#3837, 1-Brown, Benjamin, 2-died, 3-23 Mar 1833, 12-Brown, George, 13-Brown,
     Esther, 15-Brown
#3838, 1-Miller, Anna (Brown), 2-died, 3-24 Feb 1856, 15-Brown
#3839, 1-Leary, Elizabeth (Brown), 2-died, 3-17 Sep 1873, 15-Brown
#3840, 1-Leary, Edward, 2-died, 3-22 Apr 1876, 15-Brown
#3841, 1-Brown, Eleanor, 2-died, 3-16 Mar 1879, 15-Brown
#3842, 1-Cooley, Maria (Brown), 2-died, 3-10 Aug 1887, 15-Brown
#3843, 1-Long, Hadassah (Brown), 2-died, 3-28 Mar 1901, 15-Brown
#3844, 1-Bowman, Andrew, 2-died, 3-15 Jun 1854, 15-Bowman
#3845, 1-Boman, Melia, 2-born, 3-2 Feb 1808, 15-Bowman
#3846, 1-Bowman, Emmanual, 2-born, 3-8 Aug 1809, 15-Bowman
#3847, 1-Bowman, _____[?] L., 2-born, 3-20 Oct 1811, 15-Bowman
#3848, 1-Bowman, Couseau[?], 2-born, 3-30 Oct 1813, 15-Bowman
#3849, 1-Bowman, Audry[?], 2-born, 3-15 Nov 1815, 15-Bowman
#3850, 1-Bowman, Johnathan, 2-born, 3-22 Dec 1817, 15-Bowman
#3851, 1-Bowman, William, 2-born, 3-20 Sep 1819, 15-Bowman
#3852, 1-Bowman, Samuel, 2-born, 3-10 May 182_[?], 15-Bowman
#3853, 1-Bowman, David R., 2-born, 3-14 Sep 1824, 15-Bowman
#3854, 1-Stoner[?], Aron, 2-born, 3-5 Jun 1824, 15-Bowman
#3855, 1-Bowman, Jacob, 2-died, 3-23 Sep 1824[?], 15-Bowman
#3856, 1-Weeks[?], Simon, 2-born, 3-3 ___[?] 1830, 15-Bowman
#3857, 1-Bowman, Elizabeth, 2-born, 3-15 Jan 1789[?], 15-Bowman
#3858, 1-Bowie, Thomas John Davis, 2-born, 3-23 Jan 1834, 12-Bowie, Thomas John,
     13-Bowie, Catharine _.[?], 15-Bowie
#3859, 1-Beatty, Elizabeth Chew, 2-born, 3-26 Apr 1835, 12-Beatty, Edward W., 13-
     Beatty, Maria A., 15-Bowie
```

FAMILY BIBLE RECORDS IN THE WASHINGTON COUNTY FREE LIBRARY, HAGERSTOWN, MARYLAND

Entry #, 1-Last Name, First Name, 2-Event, 3-Date, 4-Event Location, 5-Age, 6-Other, 7-Spouse's Last, First, 8-Groom's Residence, 9-Bride's Residence, 10-Minister, 11-Minister's Location, 12-Father's Last, First, 13-Mother's Last, First, 14-Transcribed, 15-Family Bible

#3860, 1-Bowie, Edward Beatty, 2-born, 3-18 Jun 1857, 12-Bowie, Thomas John Davis, 13-Bowie, Elizabeth, 15-Bowie

#3861, 1-Bowie, Catharine Davis, 2-born, 3-31 Jan 1859, 12-Bowie, Thomas John Davis, 13-Bowie, Elizabeth, 15-Bowie

#3862, 1-Bowie, Allen Thomas, 2-born, 3-7 Nov 1861, 12-Bowie, Thomas John Davis, 13-Bowie, Elizabeth, 15-Bowie

#3863, 1-Bowie, Maria Williams, 2-born, 3-21 Jul 1863, 12-Bowie, Thomas John Davis, 13-Bowie, Elizabeth, 15-Bowie

#3864, 1-Beatty, Elizabeth Chew, 2-married, 3-21 Nov 1855, 4-St. John's Church, Hagerstown, 7-Bowie, Thomas John Davis, 10-Rev. Walter Ayrault[?], 15-Bowie

#3865, 1-Bowie, Edward Beatty, 2-born, 3-9 Dec 1885, 15-Bowie

#3866, 1-Bowie, Robert Edward, 2-born, 3-10 Dec 1917, 15-Bowie

#3867, 1-Bowie, Allen Thomas, 2-married, 3-1893, 7-Paull, Mary, 15-Bowie

#3868, 1-Bowie, John, 2-born, 3-1688, 4-Scotland, 15-Bowie

#3869, 1-Bowie, John, 2-married, 4-America, 7-Mullikin, Mary, 15-Bowie

#3870, 1-Bowie, John, 2-died, 3-1759, 6-buried Brookefield, Prince Georges Co., MD, 15-Bowie

#3871, 1-Bowie, Jr., John, 2-born, 3-1708, 12-Bowie, John, 13-Mullikin, Mary, 15-Bowie

#3872, 1-Bowie, Eleanor, 2-born, 12-Bowie, John, 13-Mullikin, Mary, 15-Bowie

#3873, 1-Bowie, James, 2-born, 12-Bowie, John, 13-Mullikin, Mary, 15-Bowie

#3874, 1-Bowie, Allen, 2-born, 12-Bowie, John, 13-Mullikin, Mary, 15-Bowie

#3875, 1-Bowie, William, 2-born, 12-Bowie, John, 13-Mullikin, Mary, 15-Bowie

#3876, 1-Bowie, Thomas, 2-born, 12-Bowie, John, 13-Mullikin, Mary, 15-Bowie

#3877, 1-Bowie, Mary, 2-born, 12-Bowie, John, 13-Mullikin, Mary, 15-Bowie

#3878, 1-Bowie, Jr., John, 2-married, 7-Beall, Mary, 15-Bowie

#3879, 1-Bowie, William, 2-born, 12-Bowie, Jr., John, 13-Beall, Mary, 15-Bowie

#3880, 1-Bowie, Mary, 2-born, 12-Bowie, Jr., John, 13-Beall, Mary, 15-Bowie

#3881, 1-Bowie, Jr., John, 2-married, 7-Pollinger, Elizabeth, 15-Bowie

#3882, 1-Bowie, Jr., Allen, 2-born, 12-Bowie, Jr., John, 13-Pollinger, Elizabeth, 15-Bowie

#3883, 1-Bowie, James, 2-born, 15-Bowie

#3884, 1-Bowie, John (Rev.), 2-born, 15-Bowie

#3885, 1-Bowie, Jr., John, 2-died, 3-1753, 6-buried Thorpland[?], Prince George's Co., MD, 15-Bowie

#3886, 1-Bowie, Mary (Beall), 2-died, 3-1778, 6-buried Rock Creek Cemetery, 15-Bowie

#3887, 1-Bowie, Jr., Allen (Col.), 2-born, 3-1736, 15-Bowie

#3888, 1-Bowie, Jr., Allen (Col.), 2-married, 7-Cramptin, Ruth, 15-Bowie

#3889, 1-Bowie, Jr., Allen (Col.), 2-died, 3-1803, 6-buried Union Cemetery, Rockville, MD, 15-Bowie

#3890, 1-Bowie, Ruth (Cramptin), 2-born, 6-buried Union Cemetery, Rockville, MD, 15-Bowie

#3891, 1-Bowie, Thomas, 2-born, 12-Bowie, Jr., Allen (Col.), 13-Cramptin, Ruth, 15-Bowie

#3892, 1-Bowie, John, 2-born, 12-Bowie, Jr., Allen (Col.), 13-Cramptin, Ruth, 15-Bowie

#3893, 1-Bowie, Elizabeth, 2-born, 12-Bowie, Jr., Allen (Col.), 13-Cramptin, Ruth, 15-Bowie

#3894, 1-Bowie, Mary, 2-born, 12-Bowie, Jr., Allen (Col.), 13-Cramptin, Ruth, 15-Bowie

#3895, 1-Bowie, Washington, 2-born, 12-Bowie, Jr., Allen (Col.), 13-Cramptin, Ruth, 15-Bowie

#3896, 1-Bowie, Allen, 2-born, 12-Bowie, Jr., Allen (Col.), 13-Cramptin, Ruth, 15-Bowie

FAMILY BIBLE RECORDS IN THE WASHINGTON COUNTY FREE LIBRARY, HAGERSTOWN, MARYLAND

Entry #, 1-Last Name, First Name, 2-Event, 3-Date, 4-Event Location, 5-Age, 6-Other,
7-Spouse's Last, First, 8-Groom's Residence, 9-Bride's Residence, 10-Minister, 11-Minister's Location,
12-Father's Last, First, 13-Mother's Last, First, 14-Transcribed, 15-Family Bible

#3897, 1-Bowie, Hannah, 2-born, 12-Bowie, Jr., Allen (Col.), 13-Cramptin, Ruth, 15-Bowie

#3898, 1-Bowie, Richard, 2-born, 12-Bowie, Jr., Allen (Col.), 13-Cramptin, Ruth, 15-Bowie

#3899, 1-Bowie, Washington (Col.), 2-born, 3-1776, 12-Bowie, Jr., Allen (Col.), 13-Cramptin, Ruth, 15-Bowie

#3900, 1-Bowie, Washington (Col.), 2-married, 7-Johns, Margaret Crabb, 15-Bowie

#3901, 1-Bowie, Washington (Col.), 2-died, 3-1825, 6-buried Oatland, Olney, Montgomery Co., MD, 15-Bowie

#3902, 1-Bowie, Margaret Crabb (Johns), 2-died, 6-buried Oatland, Olney, Montgomery Co., MD, 15-Bowie

#3903, 1-Bowie, Thomas John, 2-born, 12-Bowie, Washington (Col.), 13-Johns, Margaret Crabb, 15-Bowie

#3904, 1-Bowie, Mary, 2-born, 12-Bowie, Washington (Col.), 13-Johns, Margaret Crabb, 15-Bowie

#3905, 1-Bowie, Margaret, 2-born, 12-Bowie, Washington (Col.), 13-Johns, Margaret Crabb, 15-Bowie

#3906, 1-Bowie, Jr., Washington, 2-born, 12-Bowie, Washington (Col.), 13-Johns, Margaret Crabb, 15-Bowie

#3907, 1-Bowie, Richard Johns, 2-born, 12-Bowie, Washington (Col.), 13-Johns, Margaret Crabb, 15-Bowie

#3908, 1-Bowie, Robert Gilmor[?], 2-born, 12-Bowie, Washington (Col.), 13-Johns, Margaret Crabb, 15-Bowie

#3909, 1-Bowie, Sarah Hollyday, 2-born, 12-Bowie, Washington (Col.), 13-Johns, Margaret Crabb, 15-Bowie

#3910, 1-Bowie, Thomas Johns (Col.), 2-born, 3-1800, 12-Bowie, Washington (Col.), 13-Johns, Margaret Crabb, 15-Bowie

#3911, 1-Bowie, Thomas Johns (Col.), 2-died, 3-1850, 6-buried Oatland in private Bowie cemetery, 15-Bowie

#3912, 1-Bowie, Thomas Johns (Col.), 2-married, 7-Davis, Catharine W., 15-Bowie

#3913, 1-Davis, Catharine W., 2-died, 3-1888, 6-buried Oatland in private Bowie cemetery, 15-Bowie

#3914, 1-Bowie, Thomas John Davis, 2-born, 3-1834, 12-Bowie, Thomas Johns (Col.), 13-Davis, Catharine W., 15-Bowie

#3915, 1-Bowie, Sarah Hollyday, 2-born, 12-Bowie, Thomas Johns (Col.), 13-Davis, Catharine W., 15-Bowie

#3916, 1-Bowie, Ellen Ruth, 2-born, 12-Bowie, Thomas Johns (Col.), 13-Davis, Catharine W., 15-Bowie

#3917, 1-Bowie, Washington, 2-born, 12-Bowie, Thomas Johns (Col.), 13-Davis, Catharine W., 15-Bowie

#3918, 1-Bowie, Thomas John Davis, 2-died, 3-1921, 6-buried Union Cemetery, Rockville, MD, 12-Bowie, Thomas Johns (Col.), 13-Davis, Catharine W., 15-Bowie

#3919, 1-Bowie, Thomas John Davis, 2-married, 3-24 Nov 1854, 15-Bowie

#3920, 1-Bowie, Elizabeth Chew (Beatty), 2-died, 3-25 May 1868, 15-Bowie

#3921, 1-Bowie, Edward Beatty, 2-born, 3-1857, 12-Bowie, Thomas John Davis, 13-Beatty, Elizabeth Chew, 15-Bowie

#3922, 1-Bowie, Catharine Davis, 2-born, 12-Bowie, Thomas John Davis, 13-Beatty, Elizabeth Chew, 15-Bowie

#3923, 1-Bowie, Allen Thomas, 2-born, 12-Bowie, Thomas John Davis, 13-Beatty, Elizabeth Chew, 15-Bowie

#3924, 1-Bowie, Maria Williams, 2-born, 12-Bowie, Thomas John Davis, 13-Beatty, Elizabeth Chew, 15-Bowie

#3925, 1-Bowie, Edward Beatty, 2-married, 3-1885, 7-Vars[?], Eleanor, 12-Bowie, Thomas John Davis, 13-Beatty, Elizabeth Chew, 15-Bowie

FAMILY BIBLE RECORDS IN THE WASHINGTON COUNTY FREE LIBRARY, HAGERSTOWN, MARYLAND

Entry #, 1-Last Name, First Name, 2-Event, 3-Date, 4-Event Location, 5-Age, 6-Other,
7-Spouse's Last, First, 8-Groom's Residence, 9-Bride's Residence, 10-Minister, 11-Minister's Location,
12-Father's Last, First, 13-Mother's Last, First, 14-Transcribed, 15-Family Bible

```
#3926, 1-Bowie, Robert Edward, 2-born, 12-Bowie, Edward Beatty, 13-Vars[?],
    Eleanor, 15-Bowie
#3927, 1-Bowie, Allen Davis, 2-born, 3-1885, 12-Bowie, Edward Beatty, 13-Vars[?],
    Eleanor, 15-Bowie
#3928, 1-Bowie, Robert Edward, 2-born, 3-1886, 12-Bowie, Edward Beatty, 13-Vars[?],
    Eleanor, 15-Bowie
#3929, 1-Bowie, Robert Edward, 2-married, 7-Kidd, Ednor Mary, 12-Bowie, Edward
    Beatty, 13-Vars[?], Eleanor, 15-Bowie
#3930, 1-Bowie, Allen Davis, 2-married, 7-Jacobs, Virginia, 12-Bowie, Edward
    Beatty, 13-Vars[?], Eleanor, 15-Bowie
#3931, 1-Bowie, Mary Eleanor, 2-born, 12-Bowie, Allen Davis, 13-Jacobs, Virginia,
    15-Bowie
#3932, 1-Bowie, Catharine Davis, 2-born, 3-1859, 15-Bowie
#3933, 1-Bowie, Catharine Davis, 2-married, 7-Windle, James B.[?], 15-Bowie
#3934, 1-Bowie, Allen Thomas, 2-born, 3-1861, 15-Bowie
#3935, 1-Bowie, Allen Thomas, 2-married, 3-1893, 7-Paul[?], Mary, 15-Bowie
#3936, 1-Bowie, Allen Thomas, 2-died, 3-4 Feb 1914, 6-buried Union Cemetery,
    Rockville, MD, 15-Bowie
#3937, 1-Bowie, Georgia Paul, 2-born, 15-Bowie
#3938, 1-Bowie, Georgia Paul, 2-married, 7-Hazlett, Henry, 12-Bowie, Allen Thomas,
    13-Paul, Mary, 15-Bowie
#3939, 1-Hazlett, Mary Paul, 2-born, 3-1917, 12-Hazlett, Henry, 13-Bowie, Georgia
    Paul, 15-Bowie
#3940, 1-Bowie, Maria Williams, 2-born, 3-21 Jul 1863, 15-Bowie
#3941, 1-Bowie, Thomas, 2-born, 3-1712, 15-Bowie
#3942, 1-Bowie, Thomas, 2-married, 7-Lee, Hannah, 12-Bowie, Sr., John, 15-Bowie
#3943, 1-Bowie, Barbara, 2-born, 3-1756, 12-Bowie, Thomas, 13-Lee, Hannah, 15-Bowie
#3944, 1-Bowie, Barbara, 2-died, 3-1805, 12-Bowie, Thomas, 13-Lee, Hannah, 15-Bowie
#3945, 1-Bowie, Barbara, 2-married, 7-Hall, James, 12-Bowie, Thomas, 13-Lee,
    Hannah, 15-Bowie
#3946, 1-Hall, Elizabeth Bowie, 2-married, 7-Williams, Otho Holland (Gen.), 12-
    Hall, James, 13-Bowie, Barbara, 15-Bowie
#3947, 1-Williams, Catharine L., 2-born, 12-Williams, Otho Holland (Gen.), 13-Hall,
    Elizabeth Bowie, 15-Bowie
#3948, 1-Williams, Laura, 2-born, 12-Williams, Otho Holland (Gen.), 13-Hall,
    Elizabeth Bowie, 15-Bowie
#3949, 1-Williams, Covah[?], 2-born, 12-Williams, Otho Holland (Gen.), 13-Hall,
    Elizabeth Bowie, 15-Bowie
#3950, 1-Williams, Maria, 2-born, 12-Williams, Otho Holland (Gen.), 13-Hall,
    Elizabeth Bowie, 15-Bowie
#3951, 1-Williams, Maria, 2-married, 7-Beatty, Edward, 15-Bowie
#3952, 1-Beatty, Edward, 2-born, 12-Beatty, Eli, 15-Bowie
#3953, 1-Beatty, Edward, 2-died, 3-1863, 4-Harrisonville, VA [?], 15-Bowie
#3954, 1-Beatty, Elizabeth Chew, 2-born, 15-Bowie
#3955, 1-Beatty, Elizabeth Chew, 2-married, 7-Bowie, Thomas Johns Davis, 15-Bowie
#3956, 1-Beatty, Kate, 2-born, 3-1859, 15-Bowie
#3957, 1-Beatty, Edward, 2-died, 3-1864, 15-Bowie
#3958, 1-Beatty, Laura[?], 2-married, 7-Magruder, Bradley, 15-Bowie
#3959, 1-Bair, Isaac, 2-married, 3-11 Feb 1868, 4-Parsonage, 7-Barnes, Catherine
    Virginia, 10-Rev. Philip Boyle, 15-Bair
#3960, 1-Bair, Isaac, 2-born, 3-29 Jul 1848, 15-Bair
#3961, 1-Bair, Isaac, 2-died, 3-11 Oct 1937, 15-Bair
#3962, 1-Barnes, Catherine Virginia, 2-born, 3-19 Jan 1849, 15-Bair
#3963, 1-Barnes, Catherine Virginia, 2-died, 3-5 Feb 1935, 15-Bair
```

FAMILY BIBLE RECORDS IN THE WASHINGTON COUNTY FREE LIBRARY, HAGERSTOWN, MARYLAND

Entry #, 1-Last Name, First Name, 2-Event, 3-Date, 4-Event Location, 5-Age, 6-Other,
7-Spouse's Last, First, 8-Groom's Residence, 9-Bride's Residence, 10-Minister, 11-Minister's Location,
12-Father's Last, First, 13-Mother's Last, First, 14-Transcribed, 15-Family Bible

#3964, 1-Bair, Florence B., 2-born, 3-Nov, 4-Warfieldsburg, 12-Bair, Isaac, 13-Barnes, Catherine Virginia, 15-Bair

#3965, 1-Bair, Florence B., 2-died, 3-Jan, 12-Bair, Isaac, 13-Barnes, Catherine Virginia, 15-Bair

#3966, 1-Bair, William H., 2-born, 3-15 May 1872, 4-near New Windsor, 12-Bair, Isaac, 13-Barnes, Catherine Virginia, 15-Bair

#3967, 1-Bair, William H., 2-married, 3-23 Apr 1905, 12-Bair, Isaac, 13-Barnes, Catherine Virginia, 15-Bair

#3968, 1-Bair, William H., 2-died, 3-5 Jan 1920, 12-Bair, Isaac, 13-Barnes, Catherine Virginia, 15-Bair

#3969, 1-Bair, Arthur E., 2-born, 3-29 Apr 1875, 4-Westminster, 12-Bair, Isaac, 13-Barnes, Catherine Virginia, 15-Bair

#3970, 1-Bair, Arthur E., 2-married, 3-13 Jan 1895, 12-Bair, Isaac, 13-Barnes, Catherine Virginia, 15-Bair

#3971, 1-Bair, Arthur E., 2-died, 3-1974, 12-Bair, Isaac, 13-Barnes, Catherine Virginia, 15-Bair

#3972, 1-Bair, Luther H., 2-born, 3-28 Jan 1879[?], 4-Westminster, 12-Bair, Isaac, 13-Barnes, Catherine Virginia, 15-Bair

#3973, 1-Bair, Luther H., 2-married, 3-9 Jun 1907, 12-Bair, Isaac, 13-Barnes, Catherine Virginia, 15-Bair

#3974, 1-Bair, Charley N., 2-born, 3-21 Jul 1882, 4-Westminster, 12-Bair, Isaac, 13-Barnes, Catherine Virginia, 15-Bair

#3975, 1-Bair, Charley N., 2-died, 3-20 Jul 1968, 12-Bair, Isaac, 13-Barnes, Catherine Virginia, 15-Bair

#3976, 1-Bair, Grace E., 2-born, 3-Nov 1883, 4-Westminster, 12-Bair, Isaac, 13-Barnes, Catherine Virginia, 15-Bair

#3977, 1-Bair, Grace E., 2-died, 3-Sep, 12-Bair, Isaac, 13-Barnes, Catherine Virginia, 15-Bair

#3978, 1-Bair, Lena V., 2-born, 3-10 Mar 1885, 4-Westminster, 12-Bair, Isaac, 13-Barnes, Catherine Virginia, 15-Bair

#3979, 1-Bair, Lena V., 2-married, 3-29[?] 1902, 12-Bair, Isaac, 13-Barnes, Catherine Virginia, 15-Bair

#3980, 1-Bair, Maude E., 2-born, 3-10 Nov 1888, 4-Westminster, 12-Bair, Isaac, 13-Barnes, Catherine Virginia, 15-Bair

#3981, 1-Bair, Maude E., 2-married, 3-31 Mar 1907, 12-Bair, Isaac, 13-Barnes, Catherine Virginia, 15-Bair

#3982, 1-Bair, Mabel, 2-born, 3-Mar, 4-Westminster, 12-Bair, Isaac, 13-Barnes, Catherine Virginia, 15-Bair

#3983, 1-Bair, Mabel, 2-died, 3-Sep, 12-Bair, Isaac, 13-Barnes, Catherine Virginia, 15-Bair

#3984, 1-Bair, Howard S., 2-born, 3-21 Feb 1895, 12-Bair, Arthur E., 15-Bair

#3985, 1-Bair, Russell T., 2-born, 3-5 Mar 1896, 12-Bair, Arthur E., 15-Bair

#3986, 1-Bair, Carl E., 2-born, 3-19 Apr 1901, 12-Bair, Arthur E., 15-Bair

#3987, 1-Bair, Alma V., 2-born, 3-2 Nov 1903, 12-Bair, Arthur E., 15-Bair

#3988, 1-Bair, Robert F., 2-born, 3-11 Feb 1906, 12-Bair, Arthur E., 15-Bair

#3989, 1-Bair, Helen L., 2-born, 3-1 Mar 1908, 12-Bair, Arthur E., 15-Bair

#3990, 1-Bair, Helen L., 2-died, 3-26 Feb 1911, 12-Bair, Arthur E., 15-Bair

#3991, 1-Bair, Herald C., 2-born, 3-24 Nov 1907, 12-Bair, Luther H., 15-Bair

#3992, 1-Bair, Herald C., 2-died, 3-7 Jan 1911, 12-Bair, Luther H., 15-Bair

#3993, 1-Bair, Leon I., 2-born, 3-1 May 1910, 12-Bair, Charley N., 15-Bair

#3994, 1-Bair, Leonard W., 2-born, 3-30 Mar 1904, 12-Bair, Charley N., 15-Bair

#3995, 1-Bair, Ralph, 2-born, 3-16 Jul 1906, 12-Bair, Charley N., 15-Bair

#3996, 1-Bair, Herald E., 2-born, 3-23 Feb 1917, 12-Bair, Charley N., 15-Bair

#3997, 1-Bair, Herald E., 2-died, 3-13 Aug 1917, 12-Bair, Charley N., 15-Bair

#3998, 1-[blank], Floyd W., 2-born, 3-17 Jun 1903, 12-Bair, Lena V., 15-Bair

FAMILY BIBLE RECORDS IN THE WASHINGTON COUNTY FREE LIBRARY, HAGERSTOWN, MARYLAND

Entry #, 1-Last Name, First Name, 2-Event, 3-Date, 4-Event Location, 5-Age, 6-Other,
7-Spouse's Last, First, 8-Groom's Residence, 9-Bride's Residence, 10-Minister, 11-Minister's Location,
12-Father's Last, First, 13-Mother's Last, First, 14-Transcribed, 15-Family Bible

```
#3999, 1-[blank], Kathleen J., 2-born, 3-10 Jan 1906, 12-Bair, Lena V., 15-Bair
#4000, 1-[blank], Clyde H., 2-born, 3-9 May 1911, 12-Bair, Lena V., 15-Bair
#4001, 1-[blank], Frances V., 2-born, 3-27 Oct 1907, 12-Bair, Maude E., 15-Bair
#4002, 1-[blank], Frances V., 2-died, 3-2 Dec 1932, 12-Bair, Maude E., 15-Bair
#4003, 1-Bair, Howard S., 2-died, 3-30 Jun 1937, 15-Bair
#4004, 1-Bair, Carl E., 2-died, 3-Apr 1939, 15-Bair
#4005, 1-Barnes, Levi Y., 2-married, 3-21 Jan 1847, 7-Sellman, Matilda, 15-Bair
#4006, 1-Barnes, Levi Y., 2-born, 3-19 Nov 1827, 15-Bair
#4007, 1-Barnes, Matilda, 2-born, 3-4 Jul 1824, 15-Bair
#4008, 1-Barnes, Catharine V., 2-born, 3-19 Jan 1849, 15-Bair
#4009, 1-Barnes, Emily J.C.[?], 2-born, 3-__ ___ 1851, 15-Bair
#4010, 1-Barnes, Joshua B., 2-born, 3-11 Mar 1853, 15-Bair
#4011, 1-Barnes, Sarah _._.[?], 2-born, 3-11 Jul 1854, 15-Bair
#4012, 1-Barnes, Eliza Jane, 2-born, 3-14 Oct 1861, 15-Bair
#4013, 1-Baker, George R., 2-married, 3-5 Nov 1899, 4-Hagerstown, 6-witnesses were
    Mr. & Mrs. J.B. Bausman  , 7-Long, Pearle, 8-Downsville, MD, 9-Downsville,
    MD, 10-J.M. Tombaugh, 15-Baker
#4014, 1-Baker, David Ellsworth, 2-born, 3-16 Jul 1927, 4-Tilghmanton, MD, 15-Baker
#4015, 1-Baker, George William, 2-born, 3-29 Oct 1928, 4-Tilghmanton, MD, 15-Baker
#4016, 1-Baker, George Raymond, 2-born, 3-4 Nov 1878, 4-East Berlin, PA, 15-Baker
#4017, 1-Baker, George Raymond, 2-died, 3-30 Dec 1956, 5-78 years 1 month 26 days,
    6-funeral 2 Jan 1957, 15-Baker
#4018, 1-Long, Ina Pearle, 2-born, 3-16 Nov 1880, 4-Carlisle, PA, 15-Baker
#4019, 1-Long, Ina Pearle, 2-died, 3-22 Mar 1928, 15-Baker
#4020, 1-Baker, Verda Mary, 2-born, 3-26 Apr 1900, 4-Downsville, MD, 15-Baker
#4021, 1-Baker, Raymond Lamar, 2-born, 3-19 Aug 1901, 4-Downsville, MD, 15-Baker
#4022, 1-Baker, Raymond Lamar, 2-died, 3-1 Feb 1974, 15-Baker
#4023, 1-Long, Hadassah, 2-born, 3-14 Dec 1815, 15-Baker
#4024, 1-Long, Hadassah, 2-died, 3-28 Mar 1901, 5-85 years 3 months 14 days, 15-
    Baker
#4025, 1-Welty, Susan, 2-born, 3-12 Feb 1836, 15-Baker
#4026, 1-Welty, Susan, 2-died, 3-15 Jan 1906, 4-Colo, Icwa, 15-Baker
#4027, 1-Long, Helen Saxton, 2-born, 3-29 Jan 1907, 15-Baker
#4028, 1-Long, Helen Saxton, 2-died, 3-13 Aug 1908, 5-1 year 6 months 13 days, 15-
    Baker
#4029, 1-Long, Minnie S., 2-died, 3-20 Nov 1910, 4-Downsville, MD, 5-23 years, 15-
    Baker
#4030, 1-Long, Lena M., 2-died, 3-Aug 1910, 5-9 months, 15-Baker
#4031, 1-Long, Simon, 2-died, 3-4 Jan 1913, 5-86 years 5 months 17 days, 15-Baker
#4032, 1-Long, Isaac S., 2-died, 3-21 Mar 1918, 15-Baker
#4033, 1-Baker, Lulu Thelma, 2-born, 3-Sunday, 4 Oct 1903, 4-Mt. Moriah, MD, 15-
    Baker
#4034, 1-Baker, Lulu Thelma, 2-died, 3-11 Feb 1982, 15-Baker
#4035, 1-Baker, Guy Long, 2-born, 3-2 Apr 1906, 4-Mt. Moriah, MD, 15-Baker
#4036, 1-Baker, Urla Grace, 2-born, 3-Wednesday, 10 Jun 1908, 4-Mt. Moriah, MD, 15-
    Baker
#4037, 1-Baker, Joshua Jacob, 2-born, 3-Friday evening, 26 Aug 1910, 4-Mt. Moriah,
    MD, 15-Baker
#4038, 1-Baker, Joshua Jacob, 2-died, 3-5 Jul 1983, 15-Baker
#4039, 1-Baker, Wanda Arlene, 2-born, 3-Monday, 6 am, 19 Jun 1916, 4-South Farm,
    near Funkstown, MD, 15-Baker
#4040, 1-Baker, Wanda Arlene, 2-died, 3-29 Dec 1968, 5-52 years 6 months 10 days,
    15-Baker
#4041, 1-Baker, Evelyn Lorraine, 2-born, 3-Wednesday, 1 am, 20 Feb 1918, 4-Vance
    farm, 15-Baker
```

FAMILY BIBLE RECORDS IN THE WASHINGTON COUNTY FREE LIBRARY, HAGERSTOWN, MARYLAND

Entry #, 1-Last Name, First Name, 2-Event, 3-Date, 4-Event Location, 5-Age, 6-Other, 7-Spouse's Last, First, 8-Groom's Residence, 9-Bride's Residence, 10-Minister, 11-Minister's Location, 12-Father's Last, First, 13-Mother's Last, First, 14-Transcribed, 15-Family Bible

#4042, 1-Baker, Evelyn Lorraine, 2-died, 3-3 Feb 1978, 15-Baker

#4043, 1-Baker, Anita Elizabeth, 2-born, 3-Sunday, 10 am, 21 Sep 1919, 4-Vance farm, 15-Baker

#4044, 1-Baker, George R., 2-baptized, 3-27 Nov 1909, 6-triune immersion baptism, 10-J. I. Hall, 11-Brethren Church, 15-Baker

#4045, 1-Baker, Wanda (Miss), 2-married, 7-Jamison, Harvey, 8-Downsville, MD, 9-Downsville, MD, 10-Rev. W.S. Baker, 11-First Brethren Church, St. James, MD, 15-Baker

#4046, 1-Baker, Charles Russell, 2-married, 3-7 Jul 1938, 4-Frederick, MD, 7-Miller, Myrtle Virginia, 10-Rev. Schmidt, 11-Centennial Memorial Church, United Brethren in Christ, 15-Baker

#4047, 1-Miller, Grace Yvonne, 2-married, 3-5 Dec 1945, 7-Custer, James W., 10-Rev. Wallington, 11-First Baptist Church, Hagerstown, 15-Baker

#4048, 1-Baker, Mary Florence, 2-born, 3-21 Jul 1939, 4-626 Maryland Ave., Hagersotwn, MD, 6-Doctor was S. Earl Young, MD, 12-Baker, Charles, 13-Baker, Virginia, 15-Baker

#4049, 1-Baker, Mildred Joanne, 2-born, 3-8 Nov 1941, 4-Security, MD, 6-Doctor was Arthur Baptisti, MD, 15-Baker

#4050, 1-Baker, Virginia Marie, 2-born, 3-11 pm (during blackout) 19 Jul 1943, 4-1105 Ballast Court, Baltimore, MD, 6-Doctor was Dr. Imre Neunbauer, 15-Baker

#4051, 1-Baker, Charlene Ruth, 2-born, 3-9 Mar 1947, 4-Washington Co. Hospital, Hagerstown, MD, 15-Baker

#4052, 1-Baker, Paula Elizabeth, 2-born, 3-30 Aug 1951, 4-Washington Co. Hospital, Hagerstown, MD, 15-Baker

#4053, 1-Baker, Myrtle Virginia (Miller), 2-born, 3-7 Jan 1923, 15-Baker

#4054, 1-Baker, Myrtle Virginia (Miller), 2-died, 3-3:45 am, 11 Jun 1973, 4-Washington Co. Hospital, Hagerstown, MD, 6-malignant tumor in right kidney, 15-Baker

#4055, 1-Baker, Florence Elizabeth (Mrs.), 2-died, 3-19 Sep 1939, 4-Washington Co. Hospital, Hagerstown, MD, 15-Baker

#4056, 1-Miller, Mary Cecil (Mrs.), 2-died, 3-9:15, 26 Apr 1946, 4-845 Chestnut St., Hagerstown, MD, 6-buried Rest Haven Cemetery, 15-Baker

#4057, 1-Fisher, Charles H., 2-died, 3-11 Oct 1957, 4-Washington Co. Hospital, Hagerstown, MD, 5-88 years, 6-buried 13 Oct 1957, 15-Baker

#4058, 1-Frey, Margaret Ann (Miss), 2-married, 3-14 Mar, 4-Smithsburg, MD, 6-Ridenour, 7-Sidney Mark, 12-Frey, Harry R., 15-Baker

#4059, 1-Bachtell, Martin Luther, 2-born, 3-29 Jul 1854, 4-Washington Co., MD, 14-Yes, 15-Bachtell

#4060, 1-Bachtell, Martin Luther, 2-married, 3-18 May 1879, 4-Sylvan, Franklin Co., PA, 7-Keefer, Catharine Margaretta, 10-Rev. Jacob Miller, 11-Dunkard Church, 14-Yes, 15-Bachtell

#4061, 1-Keefer, Catharine Margaretta, 2-born, 3-15 Apr 1852, 4-Franklin Co., PA, 14-Yes, 15-Bachtell

#4062, 1-Bachtell, Lucetia Blanch, 2-born, 3-3 Apr 1880, 12-Bachtell, Martin Luther, 13-Keefer, Catharine Margaretta, 14-Yes, 15-Bachtell

#4063, 1-Bachtell, Emerson Guy, 2-born, 3-3 Sep 1883, 12-Bachtell, Martin Luther, 13-Keefer, Catharine Margaretta, 14-Yes, 15-Bachtell

#4064, 1-Bachtell, Clifton Macedon, 2-born, 3-29 Mar 1895, 12-Bachtell, Martin Luther, 13-Keefer, Catharine Margaretta, 14-Yes, 15-Bachtell

#4065, 1-Bachtell, Raymond Paul, 2-born, 3-May 1894, 12-Bachtell, Martin Luther, 13-Keefer, Catharine Margaretta, 14-Yes, 15-Bachtell

#4066, 1-Bachtell, Mabel Achsah, 2-born, 3-1 Nov 1898, 12-Bachtell, Martin Luther, 13-Keefer, Catharine Margaretta, 14-Yes, 15-Bachtell

#4067, 1-Bachtell, Jr., Clifton Macedon, 2-born, 3-17 Aug 1916, 14-Yes, 15-Bachtell

#4068, 1-Bachtell, Lucetia Blanche, 2-died, 3-13 Apr 1908, 14-Yes, 15-Bachtell

FAMILY BIBLE RECORDS IN THE WASHINGTON COUNTY FREE LIBRARY, HAGERSTOWN, MARYLAND

Entry #, 1-Last Name, First Name, 2-Event, 3-Date, 4-Event Location, 5-Age, 6-Other, 7-Spouse's Last, First, 8-Groom's Residence, 9-Bride's Residence, 10-Minister, 11-Minister's Location, 12-Father's Last, First, 13-Mother's Last, First, 14-Transcribed, 15-Family Bible

```
#4069, 1-Bachtell, Ruby Heil, 2-died, 3-28 Mar 1955, 14-Yes, 15-Bachtell
#4070, 1-Bachtell, Sr., Clifton M., 2-died, 3-28 Sep 1955, 14-Yes, 15-Bachtell
#4071, 1-Bachtell, Ruth V. Peck, 2-died, 3-19 Jun 1956, 14-Yes, 15-Bachtell
#4072, 1-Ardinger, Christian, 2-married, 3-9 Feb 1812, 7-[blank], Hannah, 15-
    Ardinger
#4073, 1-Ardinger, John, 2-born, 3-22 Aug 1813, 15-Ardinger
#4074, 1-Ardinger, Elizabeth, 2-born, 3-25 Feb 1815, 15-Ardinger
#4075, 1-Ardinger, Elizabeth, 2-died, 3-21 Mar 1816, 15-Ardinger
#4076, 1-Ardinger, Jacob Christian, 2-born, 3-18 Oct 1816, 15-Ardinger
#4077, 1-Ardinger, William, 2-born, 3-4 am, 21 Oct 1818, 15-Ardinger
#4078, 1-Ardinger, William, 2-died, 3-31 Jun 1821, 15-Ardinger
#4079, 1-Ardinger, Moses, 2-born, 3-Thursday, 8:48 am, 29 Aug 1820, 15-Ardinger
#4080, 1-Ardinger, Moses, 2-died, 3-22 Jun 1821, 15-Ardinger
#4081, 1-Ardinger, Maryan, 2-born, 3-3 Apr 1822, 15-Ardinger
#4082, 1-Ardinger, Benjamin Kurts, 2-born, 3-Monday 11 pm, 7 Feb 1825, 15-Ardinger
#4083, 1-Ardinger, Joseph Finley, 2-born, 3-18 Mar 1827, 15-Ardinger
#4084, 1-Ardinger, Mary Elizabeth, 2-born, 3-16 Sep 1830, 15-Ardinger
#4085, 1-Ardinger, Georgetta, 2-born, 3-27 Oct 1856, 15-Ardinger
#4086, 1-Ardinger, Benjamin, 2-born, 3-18 Mar 1858, 15-Ardinger
#4087, 1-Ardinger, William, 2-born, 3-12[?] Sep 1859, 15-Ardinger
#4088, 1-Ardinger, Joseph Finley, 2-died, 3-2 Aug 1828, 15-Ardinger
#4089, 1-Malone, Hannah, 2-born, 3-11 Aug 1818, 15-Ardinger
#4090, 1-Ardinger, Mary Emmie, 2-born, 3-3 Sep 1861, 15-Ardinger
#4091, 1-Ardinger, Hannah Rebecca, 2-born, 3-10 Dec 1865, 15-Ardinger
#4092, 1-Ardinger, Harry Lee, 2-born, 3-26 Nov 1864, 15-Ardinger
#4093, 1-Ardinger, Katherine[?], 2-born, 3-15 Feb 1868, 6-"Aunt Kate", 15-Ardinger
#4094, 1-Ardinger, Jessie F., 2-born, 3-17 Aug 1871, 15-Ardinger
#4095, 1-Ardinger, Stonewall J., 2-born, 3-20 Mar 1869, 15-Ardinger
#4096, 1-Ardinger, Cecilia Agnes, 2-born, 3-21 Sep 1873, 15-Ardinger
#4097, 1-Ardinger, Christian, 2-died, 3-4 Nov 1827, 15-Ardinger
#4098, 1-Ardinger, Elizabeth, 2-died, 3-21 Mar 1815[?], 15-Ardinger
#4099, 1-Ardinger, William, 2-died, 3-31 Jan 1821, 15-Ardinger
#4100, 1-Ardinger, Moses, 2-died, 3-29 Jan 1821, 15-Ardinger
#4101, 1-Ardinger, Hanah Rebecca, 2-born, 3-10 Dec 1869, 15-Ardinger
#4102, 1-Ardinger, Hanah Rebecca, 2-died, 3-7 Jan 1864, 15-Ardinger
#4103, 1-Crisman, Elizabeth, 2-died, 3-8 Jan 1829, 15-Ardinger
#4104, 1-Bowers, Hanner, 2-died, 3-10 Jan 1829, 15-Ardinger
#4105, 1-Ardinger, Jr., Benjamin, 2-born, 3-Mar 1858, 15-Ardinger
#4106, 1-Ardinger, Peter, 2-married, 3-22 Jan 1839, 7-Stinemetz, Hannah, 15-
    Ardinger
#4107, 1-Stinemetz, Hannah, 2-born, 12-Stinemetz, Henry, 15-Ardinger
#4108, 1-Ardinger, Peter, 2-married, 3-15 Aug 1866, 7-Smith, Maria, 15-Ardinger
#4109, 1-Smith, Maria, 2-married, 6-widowed, 7-Smith, John, 15-Ardinger
#4110, 1-Ardinger, Henry Z., 2-married, 3-9 Jul 1902, 4-Hagerstown, MD, 7-Garrish,
    Clara, 12-Ardinger, Peter, 15-Ardinger
#4111, 1-Ardinger, Clara Elizabeth (Garriah), 2-born, 3-26 Sep 1881, 4-
    Williamsport, MD, 15-Ardinger
#4112, 1-Ardinger, Clara Elizabeth (Garriah), 2-died, 3-Sunday, 6:35 pm, 21 Aug
    1949, 15-Ardinger
#4113, 1-Ardinger, Ellen Betty, 2-married, 3-22 Dec 1941, 4-Winchester, VA, 7-
    Zeller, Dennis Tobias, 12-Ardinger, Henry Z., 13-Garrish, Clara Elizabeth,
    15-Ardinger
#4114, 1-Ardinger, Francis, 2-born, 3-5 Apr 1840, 12-Ardinger, Peter, 13-Ardinger,
    Hanah, 15-Ardinger
```

FAMILY BIBLE RECORDS IN THE WASHINGTON COUNTY FREE LIBRARY, HAGERSTOWN, MARYLAND

Entry #, 1-Last Name, First Name, 2-Event, 3-Date, 4-Event Location, 5-Age, 6-Other,
7-Spouse's Last, First, 8-Groom's Residence, 9-Bride's Residence, 10-Minister, 11-Minister's Location,
12-Father's Last, First, 13-Mother's Last, First, 14-Transcribed, 15-Family Bible

#4115, 1-Ardinger, Caroline, 2-born, 3-15 Sep 1841, 12-Ardinger, Peter, 13-Ardinger, Hanah, 15-Ardinger

#4116, 1-Ardinger, Emma E., 2-born, 3-24 Dec 1843, 12-Ardinger, Peter, 13-Ardinger, Hanah, 15-Ardinger

#4117, 1-Ardinger, Alex. H., 2-born, 3-3 Oct 1845, 12-Ardinger, Peter, 13-Ardinger, Hanah, 15-Ardinger

#4118, 1-Ardinger, Clara, 2-born, 3-9 Feb 1846, 12-Ardinger, Peter, 13-Ardinger, Hanah, 15-Ardinger

#4119, 1-Ardinger, Clara, 2-died, 3-22 Feb 1931, 12-Ardinger, Peter, 13-Ardinger, Hanah, 15-Ardinger

#4120, 1-Ardinger, Bun Vista, 2-born, 3-5 Jun 1850, 12-Ardinger, Peter, 13-Ardinger, Hanah, 15-Ardinger

#4121, 1-Ardinger, James, 2-born, 3-1852, 12-Ardinger, Peter, 13-Ardinger, Hanah, 15-Ardinger

#4122, 1-Ardinger, James, 2-died, 3-1853, 12-Ardinger, Peter, 13-Ardinger, Hanah, 15-Ardinger

#4123, 1-Ardinger, Hannah, 2-born, 3-16 Mar 1853, 12-Ardinger, Peter, 13-Ardinger, Hanah, 15-Ardinger

#4124, 1-Ardinger, Henry Z., 2-born, 3-16 Oct 1856, 4-Williamsport, MD, 12-Ardinger, Peter, 13-Ardinger, Hanah, 15-Ardinger

#4125, 1-Ardinger, Bettie, 2-born, 3-1 Jun 1864, 12-Ardinger, Peter, 13-Ardinger, Hanah, 15-Ardinger

#4126, 1-Ardinger, Peter, 2-born, 3-16 Jul 1814, 15-Ardinger

#4127, 1-Ardinger, Maria, 2-born, 3-9 Oct 1816, 15-Ardinger

#4128, 1-Ardinger, Ellen Betty, 2-born, 3-Sunday, 7 am, 13 Mar 1904, 4-103 W. Potomac St., Williamsport, MD, 12-Ardinger, Henry, 13-Garriah, Clara, 15-Ardinger

#4129, 1-Ardinger, Hannah Steinmetz, 2-born, 3-Tuesday, 11:20 am, 26 Dec 1906, 4-104 W. Potomac St., Williamsport, MD, 12-Ardinger, Henry, 13-Garriah, Clara, 15-Ardinger

#4130, 1-Ardinger, Joseph Henry, 2-born, 3-13 May 1908, 4-105 W. Potomac St., Williamsport, MD, 12-Ardinger, Henry, 13-Garriah, Clara, 15-Ardinger

#4131, 1-Ardinger, Hanah (Mrs.), 2-died, 3-8 Mar 1866, 15-Ardinger

#4132, 1-Ardinger, Peter, 2-died, 3-7 May 1900, 15-Ardinger

#4133, 1-Ardinger, Mariah (Mrs.), 2-died, 3-5 Aug 1904, 15-Ardinger

#4134, 1-Ardinger, William Hamilton, 2-died, 3-20 Sep 1907, 15-Ardinger

#4135, 1-Crow, Effie, 2-died, 3-Tuesday, 28 Mar 1908, 15-Ardinger

#4136, 1-Ardinger, Henry Zellers, 2-died, 3-1 Feb 1933, 4-Williamsport, MD, 15-Ardinger

#4137, 1-Crow, Betty Ardinger, 2-died, 4-Williamsport, MD, 15-Ardinger

#4138, 1-Bower, Hannah Ardinger, 2-died, 4-Williamsport, MD, 15-Ardinger

#4139, 1-McCoy, Clara Ardinger, 2-died, 4-Hagerstown, MD, 15-Ardinger

#4140, 1-Garrish, Joseph H., 2-married, 3-20 Oct 1873, 4-Cumberland, MD, 6-witnesses were Mrs. Alice McCardell and J.J. Valliant, 7-Ardinger, Georgietta, 8-Williamsport, MD, 9-Williamsport, MD, 10-Austin H. Courtney, 11-Beford Street M.E. Church, 15-Ardinger

#4141, 1-Garrish, Osman Latrobe, 2-born, 3-16 Mar 1899, 15-Ardinger

#4142, 1-Garrish, Thomas Rhodes, 2-born, 3-17 Oct 1901, 15-Ardinger

#4143, 1-Garrish, Sprigg Dixon, 2-born, 3-19 Oct 1874, 12-Garrish, Joseph, 13-Ardinger, Georgietta, 15-Ardinger

#4144, 1-Garrish, Joseph Benjamin, 2-born, 3-24 Dec 1875, 12-Garrish, Joseph, 13-Ardinger, Georgietta, 15-Ardinger

#4145, 1-Garrish, George Jacob, 2-born, 3-9 Oct 1877, 12-Garrish, Joseph, 13-Ardinger, Georgietta, 15-Ardinger

FAMILY BIBLE RECORDS IN THE WASHINGTON COUNTY FREE LIBRARY, HAGERSTOWN, MARYLAND

Entry #, 1-Last Name, First Name, 2-Event, 3-Date, 4-Event Location, 5-Age, 6-Other, 7-Spouse's Last, First, 8-Groom's Residence, 9-Bride's Residence, 10-Minister, 11-Minister's Location, 12-Father's Last, First, 13-Mother's Last, First, 14-Transcribed, 15-Family Bible

#4146, 1-Garrish, Lutie Albert, 2-born, 3-14 Sep 1879, 12-Garrish, Joseph, 13-Ardinger, Georgietta, 15-Ardinger

#4147, 1-Garrish, Clara Elizabeth, 2-born, 3-26 Sep 1881, 12-Garrish, Joseph, 13-Ardinger, Georgietta, 15-Ardinger

#4148, 1-Garrish, Maggie Thompson[?], 2-born, 3-28 Sep 1885, 12-Garrish, Joseph, 13-Ardinger, Georgietta, 15-Ardinger

#4149, 1-Garrish, Isaac Thompson, 2-born, 3-24 Sep 1887, 12-Garrish, Joseph, 13-Ardinger, Georgietta, 15-Ardinger

#4150, 1-Garrish, Lutie Albert, 2-died, 3-24 Aug 1881, 5-1 year 11 months 10 days, 12-Garrish, Joseph, 13-Ardinger, Georgietta, 15-Ardinger

#4151, 1-Garrish, Allen Stewart, 2-died, 3-18 Jul 1885, 5-1 year 7 months 18 days, 12-Garrish, Joseph, 13-Ardinger, Georgietta, 15-Ardinger

#4152, 1-Garrish, Florance K., 2-born, 3-10 Apr 1897, 15-Ardinger

#4153, 1-Garrish, Florance K., 2-died, 3-22 Feb 1902, 5-5 years 5 days, 15-Ardinger

#4154, 1-Garrish, Joseph Henry, 2-born, 3-14 Feb 1844, 15-Ardinger

#4155, 1-Garrish, Georgietta, 2-born, 3-27 Oct 1856, 7-Garrish, Joseph Henry, 15-Ardinger

#4156, 1-Garrish, Bruce William, 2-born, 3-1 Oct 1889, 12-Garrish, Joseph H., 13-Garrish, Georgietta, 15-Ardinger

#4157, 1-Garrish, Lewis E. McComas, 2-born, 3-18 Jul 1890, 12-Garrish, Joseph H., 13-Garrish, Georgietta, 15-Ardinger

#4158, 1-Garrish, Frank Thomas Goddard, 2-born, 3-10 Jun 1893, 12-Garrish, Joseph H., 13-Garrish, Georgietta, 15-Ardinger

#4159, 1-Garrish, Isabell Ridell, 2-born, 3-16 May 1895, 12-Garrish, Joseph H., 13-Garrish, Georgietta, 15-Ardinger

#4160, 1-Hummer, Hannah Ardinger, 2-obituary, 3-1 May 1969, 4-Springfield, VA, 7-Hummer, Andrew Leo, 15-Ardinger

#4161, 1-Hummer, Hannah Ardinger, 2-born, 3-26 Dec 1905, 4-Williamsport, MD, 15-Ardinger

#4162, 1-Hummer, Hannah Ardinger, 2-married, 7-Hummer, Leo, 15-Ardinger

#4163, 1-Hummer, Katherine Elizabeth, 2-born, 3-26 Jan 1924, 4-Bradbury Heights, Prince Georges Co., MD, 12-Hummer, Andrew Leo, 13-Ardinger, Hannah Steinmetz, 15-Ardinger

#4164, 1-Hummer, Katherine Elizabeth, 2-married, 7-Wood, Robert, 15-Ardinger

#4165, 1-Ardinger, Joseph Henry, 2-married, 4-Stroudsburg, PA, 7-Roth, Althea, 15-Ardinger

#4166, 1-Ardinger, Clara Ellen, 2-born, 12-Ardinger, Joseph Henry, 13-Roth, Althea, 15-Ardinger

#4167, 1-Wood, Dallas, 2-born, 12-Wood, Robert, 13-Hummer, Katherine Elizabeth, 15-Ardinger

#4168, 1-Wood, Hannah, 2-born, 12-Wood, Robert, 13-Hummer, Katherine Elizabeth, 15-Ardinger

#4169, 1-Wood, Mattie Ellen, 2-born, 12-Wood, Robert, 13-Hummer, Katherine Elizabeth, 15-Ardinger

#4170, 1-Wood, Roberta Ann, 2-born, 12-Wood, Robert, 13-Hummer, Katherine Elizabeth, 15-Ardinger

#4171, 1-Ardinger, Henry Zeller, 2-died, 3-1 Feb 1933, 4-103 W. Potomac St., Williamsport, MD, 6-buried in Riverview Cemetery, Williamsport, MD, 15-Ardinger

#4172, 1-Ardinger, Clara Elizabeth (Garrish), 2-died, 3-21 Aug 1949, 4-104 W. Potomac St., Williamsport, MD, 6-buried in Riverview Cemetery, Williamsport, MD, 15-Ardinger

#4173, 1-Ardinger, Charles G., 2-married, 3-1 Jan 1837, 4-Williamsport, MD, 7-Shook, Jane, 10-Rev. Miller, 15-Ardinger

FAMILY BIBLE RECORDS IN THE WASHINGTON COUNTY FREE LIBRARY, HAGERSTOWN, MARYLAND

Entry #, 1-Last Name, First Name, 2-Event, 3-Date, 4-Event Location, 5-Age, 6-Other,
7-Spouse's Last, First, 8-Groom's Residence, 9-Bride's Residence, 10-Minister, 11-Minister's Location,
12-Father's Last, First, 13-Mother's Last, First, 14-Transcribed, 15-Family Bible

#4174, 1-Ardinger, Emma Rachael, 2-married, 3-20 Nov 1866, 4-Hagerstown, MD, 7-Newcomer, Henry M., 10-Rev. Titus, 15-Ardinger

#4175, 1-Newcomer, John B., 2-married, 3-19 Dec 1895, 4-Williamsport, MD, 7-Corby, Lillie[?], 10-Rev. Chas. S. Biggs, 15-Ardinger

#4176, 1-Newcomer, Mary J., 2-married, 3-29 Oct 1889, 4-Williamsport, MD, 7-Harsh, John W., 10-Rev. Arrond, 15-Ardinger

#4177, 1-Newcomer, Grason E., 2-married, 3-24 Apr 1907, 4-Williamsport, MD, 7-Spickler, Besse V., 10-Rev. Guy A. Tuttrell, 15-Ardinger

#4178, 1-Ardinger, Charles G., 2-born, 3-28 Mar 1812, 15-Ardinger

#4179, 1-Ardinger, Jane (Shook), 2-born, 3-31 Aug 1819, 15-Ardinger

#4180, 1-Ardinger, John W., 2-born, 3-31 Dec 1837, 12-Ardinger, Charles G., 13-Shook, Jane, 15-Ardinger

#4181, 1-Ardinger, James C., 2-born, 3-16 Nov 1839, 12-Ardinger, Charles G., 13-Shook, Jane, 15-Ardinger

#4182, 1-Ardinger, Mary Ellen, 2-born, 3-2 Mar 1842, 12-Ardinger, Charles G., 13-Shook, Jane, 15-Ardinger

#4183, 1-Ardinger, Joseph T. Van Lear, 2-born, 3-3 Jan 1844, 12-Ardinger, Charles G., 13-Shook, Jane, 15-Ardinger

#4184, 1-Ardinger, Emma R., 2-born, 3-17 Mar 1846, 12-Ardinger, Charles G., 13-Shook, Jane, 15-Ardinger

#4185, 1-Ardinger, Margret I.[?], 2-born, 3-13 Feb 1849, 12-Ardinger, Charles G., 13-Shook, Jane, 15-Ardinger

#4186, 1-Ardinger, Charles A., 2-born, 3-26 Nov 1851, 12-Ardinger, Charles G., 13-Shook, Jane, 15-Ardinger

#4187, 1-Ardinger, Henry Zellers, 2-born, 3-2 Jun 1854, 12-Ardinger, Charles G., 13-Shook, Jane, 15-Ardinger

#4188, 1-Ardinger, Amanda Virginia, 2-born, 3-8 Apr 1857, 12-Ardinger, Charles G., 13-Shook, Jane, 15-Ardinger

#4189, 1-Ardinger, George W., 2-born, 3-15 May 1861, 12-Ardinger, Charles G., 13-Shook, Jane, 15-Ardinger

#4190, 1-Newcomer, Nellie Inez, 2-born, 3-25 Aug 1867, 15-Ardinger

#4191, 1-Newcomer, Charles Jacob, 2-born, 3-10 Oct 1868, 15-Ardinger

#4192, 1-Newcomer, John Brewer, 2-born, 3-8 Jun 1870, 15-Ardinger

#4193, 1-Newcomer, Mary Jane Jen", 2-born, 3-19 Aug 1871, 15-Ardinger

#4194, 1-Newcomer, Susan Emma, 2-born, 3-4 Dec 1873, 15-Ardinger

#4195, 1-Newcomer, Henry Martin, 2-born, 3-16 Mar 1876, 15-Ardinger

#4196, 1-Newcomer, Samuel Cadwell, 2-born, 3-2 Nov 1877, 15-Ardinger

#4197, 1-Newcomer, Edmond Motter, 2-born, 3-23 Aug 1879, 15-Ardinger

#4198, 1-Newcomer, William Rudolph, 2-born, 3-5 Oct 1880, 15-Ardinger

#4199, 1-Newcomer, Grason Earle, 2-born, 3-6 Sep 1882, 15-Ardinger

#4200, 1-Newcomer, George Lester, 2-born, 3-10 Oct 1884, 15-Ardinger

#4201, 1-Newcomer, John Brewer[?], 2-born, 3-8 Jun[?] 1870, 15-Ardinger

#4202, 1-Corby, Lillie[?], 2-born, 3-8 Aug 1873, 15-Ardinger

#4203, 1-Newcomer, Keefer Brewer, 2-born, 3-29 Sep 1897, 15-Ardinger

#4204, 1-Newcomer, Altha Massinne[?], 2-born, 3-24 Jan 1901, 15-Ardinger

#4205, 1-Newcomer, Emma Margarette, 2-born, 3-4 Aug 1902, 15-Ardinger

#4206, 1-Newcomer, Guy Luttrell, 2-born, 3-26 Feb 1906, 15-Ardinger

#4207, 1-Newcomer, Julia E., 2-born, 3-26 Oct 1907, 15-Ardinger

#4208, 1-Newcomer, Joseph G. Joe", 2-born, 3-25 Nov 1910, 15-Ardinger

#4209, 1-Ardinger, Charles G., 2-died, 3-19 Mar 1891, 5-79 years 9 days, 15-Ardinger

#4210, 1-Ardinger, Mary Ellen, 2-died, 3-16 Oct 1854, 5-12 years 7 months 14 days, 15-Ardinger

#4211, 1-Ardinger, James C., 2-died, 3-5 Dec 1876, 5-37 years 19 days, 15-Ardinger

FAMILY BIBLE RECORDS IN THE WASHINGTON COUNTY FREE LIBRARY, HAGERSTOWN, MARYLAND

Entry #, 1-Last Name, First Name, 2-Event, 3-Date, 4-Event Location, 5-Age, 6-Other,
7-Spouse's Last, First, 8-Groom's Residence, 9-Bride's Residence, 10-Minister, 11-Minister's Location,
12-Father's Last, First, 13-Mother's Last, First, 14-Transcribed, 15-Family Bible

```
#4212, 1-Newcomer, John Brewer, 2-died, 3-21 Nov 1916, 5-46 years 5 months 13 days,
    15-Ardinger
#4213, 1-Newcomer, Harry M., 2-died, 3-2 May 1919, 5-43 years, 15-Ardinger
#4214, 1-Newcomer, Emma R., 2-died, 3-27 Mar 1926, 5-80 years 10 days, 15-Ardinger
#4215, 1-Steffey, Nellie J.[?], 2-died, 3-5 Aug 1930, 5-62 years 11 months 20 days,
    15-Ardinger
#4216, 1-Ardinger, Jane, 2-died, 3-14 Dec 1886, 5-67 years, 15-Ardinger
#4217, 1-Newcomer, Henry M., 2-died, 3-19 Apr 1884, 5-35 years 2 months 11 days,
    15-Ardinger
#4218, 1-Newcomer, Charles Jacob, 2-died, 3-22 Dec 1890, 5-22 years 2 months 12
    days, 15-Ardinger
#4219, 1-Newcomer, Susan Emma, 2-died, 3-23 Jan 1891, 5-18 years 1 mo 19 days, 15-
    Ardinger
#4220, 1-Newcomer, Edmund M., 2-died, 3-10 Jul 1898, 5-18 years, 15-Ardinger
#4221, 1-Newcomer, Samuel C., 2-died, 3-19 Mar 1906, 5-28 years 4 months 17 days,
    15-Ardinger
#4222, 1-Newcomer, William D., 2-died, 3-3 Jul 1938, 5-58 years, 15-Ardinger
#4223, 1-Harsle, Jennie Newcomer, 2-died, 3-15 Apr 1947, 5-75 years, 15-Ardinger
#4224, 1-Newcomer, George L., 2-died, 3-4 Jul 1947, 5-62 years, 15-Ardinger
#4225, 1-Gaylor, Rachael M. (Harsh), 2-died, 3-8 Apr 1959, 15-Ardinger
#4226, 1-Newcomer, Grason Earle, 2-died, 4-13 W. Salisbury St., Williamsport, MD,
    6-buried Riverview Cemetery, Williamsport, MD, 15-Ardinger
#4227, 1-Newcomer, Besse (Spickler), 2-died, 4-14 W. Salisbury St., Williamsport,
    MD, 6-buried Riverview Cemetery, Williamsport, MD, 15-Ardinger
#4228, 1-Armor, Samuel, 2-married, 3-3 Oct 1788, 7-Swan, Jane Savanah[?], 14-Yes,
    15-Armor
#4229, 1-Armor, Mary, 2-married, 3-5 Dec 1810, 7-Bennett, George, 14-Yes, 15-Armor
#4230, 1-Armor, John, 2-married, 3-15 Oct 1815, 4-Hagerstown, MD, 7-Seidenstricker,
    14-Yes, 15-Armor
#4231, 1-Armor, Joseph Guyton, 2-married, 3-15 Oct 1839, 7-Scobey[?], Rachel, 14-
    Yes, 15-Armor
#4232, 1-Armor, George F., 2-married, 3-21 May 1845, 7-Adrean[?], Emily Ann Delico,
    14-Yes, 15-Armor
#4233, 1-Armor, George F., 2-married, 3-4 Dec 1873, 7-Dickson, Jennie Reid, 14-Yes,
    15-Armor
#4234, 1-Bennett, William, 2-died, 3-10 Jan 1811, 14-Yes, 15-Armor
#4235, 1-Bennett, Elizabeth Ann, 2-died, 3-1 Aug 1812[or 1814], 14-Yes, 15-Armor
#4236, 1-Armor, Thomas, 2-died, 3-23 Mar 1814, 12-Armor, Samuel, 13-Armor, Susan,
    14-Yes, 15-Armor
#4237, 1-Armor, Susan, 2-died, 3-28 Feb 1815, 7-Armor, Samuel, 14-Yes, 15-Armor
#4238, 1-Armor, George Bennett, 2-died, 3-9 Sep 1819, 12-Armor, John, 13-Armor,
    Mary, 14-Yes, 15-Armor
#4239, 1-Armor, Samuel, 2-died, 3-9 Oct 1827, 14-Yes, 15-Armor
#4240, 1-Armor, Jane O., 2-died, 3-30 Jun 1831, 5-34 years 11 months, 14-Yes, 15-
    Armor
#4241, 1-Spicer[?], Soppia, 2-died, 3-28 Apr 1838, 5-28 years 6 months, 14-Yes, 15-
    Armor
#4242, 1-Armor, Samuel, 2-died, 3-2 Dec 1840, 5-23 years, 12-Armor, William, 13-
    Armor, Margaret, 14-Yes, 15-Armor
#4243, 1-Armor, John, 2-died, 3-11 Oct 1859, 5-64 years, 14-Yes, 15-Armor
#4244, 1-Armor, George Maxwell, 2-died, 3-15 Sep 1955, 14-Yes, 15-Armor
#4245, 1-Armor, Louise Haas, 2-died, 3-17 Nov 1957, 7-Armor, George M., 14-Yes, 15-
    Armor
#4246, 1-Armor, Samuel, 2-born, 3-24 Dec 1766, 14-Yes, 15-Armor
#4247, 1-Armor, William, 2-born, 3-10 Aug 1789, 12-Armor, Samuel, 14-Yes, 15-Armor
```

FAMILY BIBLE RECORDS IN THE WASHINGTON COUNTY FREE LIBRARY, HAGERSTOWN, MARYLAND

Entry #, 1-Last Name, First Name, 2-Event, 3-Date, 4-Event Location, 5-Age, 6-Other, 7-Spouse's Last, First, 8-Groom's Residence, 9-Bride's Residence, 10-Minister, 11-Minister's Location, 12-Father's Last, First, 13-Mother's Last, First, 14-Transcribed, 15-Family Bible

```
#4248, 1-Armor, Thomas, 2-born, 3-3 Apr 1791, 14-Yes, 15-Armor
#4249, 1-Armor, Mary, 2-born, 3-25 Nov 1792, 14-Yes, 15-Armor
#4250, 1-Armor, John, 2-born, 3-25 Mar 1795, 14-Yes, 15-Armor
#4251, 1-Armor, Jr., Samuel, 2-born, 3-25 Dec 1797, 14-Yes, 15-Armor
#4252, 1-Armor, Jane Thompson, 2-born, 3-13 Jul 1805, 14-Yes, 15-Armor
#4253, 1-Armor, George Maxwell, 2-born, 3-4 Feb 1875, 12-Armor, George F., 13-
    Armor, Jennie R., 14-Yes, 15-Armor
#4254, 1-Armor, Jennie Wooldridge, 2-born, 3-11 Dec 1876, 12-Armor, George F., 13-
    Armor, Jennie R., 14-Yes, 15-Armor
#4255, 1-Armor, Ida, 2-born, 3-24 Apr 1878, 12-Armor, George F., 13-Armor, Jennie
    R., 14-Yes, 15-Armor
#4256, 1-Armor, William Hunter, 2-born, 3-8 Jan 1880, 12-Armor, George F., 13-
    Armor, Jennie R., 14-Yes, 15-Armor
#4257, 1-Armor, Anne, 2-born, 3- 10 Nov, 14-Yes, 15-Armor
#4258, 1-Bennett, William T., 2-born, 3-27 Aug 1811, 14-Yes, 15-Armor
#4259, 1-Bennett, Elizabeth Ann, 2-born, 3-27 Feb 1814, 14-Yes, 15-Armor
#4260, 1-Armor, Joseph G., 2-born, 3-3 Jan 1817, 14-Yes, 15-Armor
#4261, 1-Armor, George F., 2-born, 3-9 Jul 1820, 14-Yes, 15-Armor
#4262, 1-Armor, William Thomas, 2-born, 3-13 Aug 1823, 12-Armor, John, 13-Armor,
    Mary, 14-Yes, 15-Armor
#4263, 1-Armor, John, 2-born, 3-26 Feb 1826, 12-Armor, John, 13-Armor, Mary, 14-
    Yes, 15-Armor
#4264, 1-Armor, Charles Huffman, 2-born, 3-7 Aug 1827, 14-Yes, 15-Armor
#4265, 1-Armor, Josephine, 2-born, 3-13 Aug 1840, 12-Armor, Joseph, 13-Armor,
    Rachel, 14-Yes, 15-Armor
#4266, 1-Armor, Sedonia Coleman, 2-born, 3-29 Sep 1842, 12-Armor, Joseph, 13-Armor,
    Rachel, 14-Yes, 15-Armor
#4267, 1-Armor, Mary Anna Fonerdin, 2-born, 3-15 May 1845, 12-Armor, Joseph, 13-
    Armor, Rachel, 14-Yes, 15-Armor
#4268, 1-Armor, Mary Anna, 2-born, 3-15 May 1846, 12-Armor, Joseph, 13-Armor,
    Rachel, 14-Yes, 15-Armor
#4269, 1-Armor, Leonidas, 2-born, 3-9 Oct 1849, 12-Armor, Joseph, 13-Armor, Rachel,
    14-Yes, 15-Armor
#4270, 1-Armor, Emma Elizabeth, 2-born, 3-13 Nov 1851, 12-Armor, Joseph, 13-Armor,
    Rachel, 14-Yes, 15-Armor
#4271, 1-Armor, Iola, 2-born, 3-19 Mar 1853, 12-Armor, Joseph, 13-Armor, Rachel,
    14-Yes, 15-Armor
#4272, 1-Price, Alfred Armor, 2-born, 3-11 Sep 1882, 12-Price, Augustus, 13-Price,
    Emma, 14-Yes, 15-Armor
#4273, 1-Price, Augustus Richard, 2-born , 3-27 Feb 1894, 12-Price, Augustus, 13-
    Price, Emma, 14-Yes, 15-Armor
#4274, 1-Armor, Joseph Guyton, 2-married, 3-15 Oct 1839, 7-Scobey, Rachel, 10-Rev.
    John C. Backus, 14-Yes, 15-Armor
#4275, 1-Armor, Mary Annie, 2-married, 3-Dec 1866, 7-Holmes, Thomas, 10-Rev.
    Dickson, 14-Yes, 15-Armor
#4276, 1-Armor, Sedonia, 2-married, 3-1868, 7-Dungan, Harry G., 10-Rev. Richard
    Fuller, 14-Yes, 15-Armor
#4277, 1-Armor, Emma E., 2-married, 3-30 Nov 1881, 7-Price, Augustus W., 10-Rev.
    Gill, 14-Yes, 15-Armor
#4278, 1-Armor, John, 2-died, 3-9 Oct 1859, 14-Yes, 15-Armor
#4279, 1-Armor, Mary, 2-died, 3-15 Mar 1864, 14-Yes, 15-Armor
#4280, 1-Scobey, Mary Ann, 2-died, 3-23 Jul 1865, 14-Yes, 15-Armor
#4281, 1-Armor, Rachel, 2-died, 3-18 Jan 1898, 14-Yes, 15-Armor
#4282, 1-Price, Augustus W., 2-died, 3-24 Mar 1905, 14-Yes, 15-Armor
#4283, 1-Armor, Josephine, 2-died, 3-14 Mar 1929, 5-88 years, 14-Yes, 15-Armor
```

FAMILY BIBLE RECORDS IN THE WASHINGTON COUNTY FREE LIBRARY, HAGERSTOWN, MARYLAND

Entry #, 1-Last Name, First Name, 2-Event, 3-Date, 4-Event Location, 5-Age, 6-Other, 7-Spouse's Last, First, 8-Groom's Residence, 9-Bride's Residence, 10-Minister, 11-Minister's Location, 12-Father's Last, First, 13-Mother's Last, First, 14-Transcribed, 15-Family Bible

```
#4284, 1-Armor, Ida, 2-died, 3-13 Oct 1872, 14-Yes, 15-Armor
#4285, 1-Holmes, Nellie Armor, 2-obituary, 4-Brooklyn, NY , 6-congestion of the
    lungs, 12-Holmes, Thomas, 13-Holmes, Minnie, 14-Yes, 15-Armor
#4286, 1-Armor, Joseph G., 2-obituary, 3-17 Dec, 4-San Francisco, 5-52 years, 6-
    congestion of the brain, 14-Yes, 15-Armor
#4287, 1-Price, Alfred A., 2-obituary, 3-6 Mar 1943, 7-Price, Amelia Wild, 14-Yes,
    15-Armor
#4288, 1-Price, Emma Elizabeth (Armor), 2-obituary, 3-23 Dec 1945, 4-705 Beaumont
    Ave., 14-Yes, 15-Armor
#4289, 1-Hott, J.W. (Bishop), 2-obituary, 3-9 Jan 1902, 15-Wyand
#4290, 1-Hott, J.W. (Bishop), 2-born, 3-15 Nov 1844, 15-Wyand
#4291, 1-Wyand, Caleb, 2-married, 3-5 Jan 1865, 7-Blessing, Sarah Ann Penelope, 10-
    Rev. C. Startzman, 15-Wyand
#4292, 1-Wyand, Caleb, 2-born, 3-13 May 1840, 15-Wyand
#4293, 1-Wyand, Sarah A.P. (Blessing), 2-born, 3-14 Jun 1844, 15-Wyand
#4294, 1-Wyand, [male], 2-born, 3-6 Nov 1865, 15-Wyand
#4295, 1-Wyand, Emory Elmer, 2-born, 3-4 Nov 1866, 15-Wyand
#4296, 1-Wyand, Ora Blessing, 2-born, 3-9 May 1869, 15-Wyand
#4297, 1-Wyand, Merta Catharine, 2-born, 3-9 Sep 1871, 15-Wyand
#4298, 1-Wyand, Lurilla[?] Penelope, 2-born, 3-20 Jun 1874, 15-Wyand
#4299, 1-Wyand, Perlie Naomi, 2-born, 3-14 Feb 1880, 15-Wyand
#4300, 1-Wyand, Eva Luaretta, 2-born, 3-11 May 1883, 15-Wyand
#4301, 1-Wyand, Emory C., 2-married, 3-24 Dec 1885, 7-Hoffman, Sue M., 10-Rev. J.K.
    Nelson, 15-Wyand
#4302, 1-Wyand, Mertie C., 2-married, 3-21 Dec 1893, 7-Poffenberger, Woodward M.,
    10-Rev. E.C. B. Castle, 15-Wyand
#4303, 1-Wyand, Pearl N., 2-married, 3-19 Apr 1900, 7-Wilson, edwin C., 10-Rev.
    S.L. Rice, 15-Wyand
#4304, 1-Wyand, Ora B., 2-married, 3-5 Feb 1902, 7-Vinson, Eva M., 10-Dr. W.H.
    Stone, 15-Wyand
#4305, 1-Wyand, Eva L., 2-married, 3-20 May 1910, 7-Noble, Fred B., 10-Rev. J.P.
    Anthony, 15-Wyand
#4306, 1-Wyand, Lurilla Penelope, 2-died, 3-19 Nov 1879, 5-5 years 4 months 29
    days, 15-Wyand
#4307, 1-Wyand, Emery E., 2-died, 3-30 Aug 1905[?], 5-38 years 9 months 26 days,
    15-Wyand
#4308, 1-Wilson, Edwin C., 2-died, 3-10 Jan 1912, 5-4_[?] years, 15-Wyand
#4309, 1-Wyand, Caleb, 2-died, 3-21 Aug 1913, 5-73 years 3 months 8 days, 15-Wyand
#4310, 1-Wyand, Sarah (Blessing), 2-died, 3-2 Aug 1921, 5-77 years 2 months 28
    days, 15-Wyand
#4311, 1-Wyand, Ora B., 2-died, 3-18 Apr 1923, 5-53 years 11 months 9 days, 15-
    Wyand
#4312, 1-Wyand, Eva M., 2-died, 3-2 Jan 1938, 5-63 years 11 months 22 days, 15-
    Wyand
#4313, 1-Wilson, Pearl N., 2-died, 3-13 Nov 1927, 5-47 years 8 months 29 days, 15-
    Wyand
#4314, 1-Lockwood, Henrietta M., 2-born, 3-12 Mar 1851, 15-Wood
#4315, 1-England, James H., 2-born, 3-17 Jul 1857, 15-Wood
#4316, 1-England, James Albert, 2-born, 3-4 Oct 1873, 15-Wood
#4317, 1-England, Theodore Austin, 2-born, 3-6 May 1876, 15-Wood
#4318, 1-England, Stuart Alanson, 2-born, 3-15 Jan 1878, 15-Wood
#4319, 1-England, Edith Jackson, 2-born, 3-7 Oct 1881, 15-Wood
#4320, 1-Wood, Henry Millard, 2-born, 3-21 Dec 1882, 15-Wood
#4321, 1-Wood, Carlton Emerson, 2-born, 3-2 Feb 1884, 15-Wood
#4322, 1-England, James, 2-born, 12-England, Carlton Emerson, 15-Wood
```

FAMILY BIBLE RECORDS IN THE WASHINGTON COUNTY FREE LIBRARY, HAGERSTOWN, MARYLAND

Entry #, 1-Last Name, First Name, 2-Event, 3-Date, 4-Event Location, 5-Age, 6-Other, 7-Spouse's Last, First, 8-Groom's Residence, 9-Bride's Residence, 10-Minister, 11-Minister's Location, 12-Father's Last, First, 13-Mother's Last, First, 14-Transcribed, 15-Family Bible

#4323, 1-England, Ralph, 2-born, 12-England, Carlton Emerson, 15-Wood

#4324, 1-England, Ruth, 2-born, 12-England, Carlton Emerson, 15-Wood

#4325, 1-England, Louise, 2-born, 12-England, James A., 15-Wood

#4326, 1-England, Elizabeth, 2-born, 12-England, James A., 15-Wood

#4327, 1-England, James, 2-born, 12-England, James A., 15-Wood

#4328, 1-England, Mary Elizabeth, 2-born, 3-8 Feb 1911, 4-Cincinatti, OH, 12-Wood, 13-England, Edith, 15-Wood

#4329, 1-England, Jean Millard, 2-born, 3-13 Mar 1915, 4-Cincinatti, OH, 12-Wood, 13-England, Edith, 15-Wood

#4330, 1-Heymering, Jr., Marinus, 2-born, 3-6 Feb 1948, 4-Hagerstown, MD, 12-Heymering, Henry, 13-Wood, Mary Elizabeth, 15-Wood

#4331, 1-Heymering, Henry Wood, 2-born, 3-8 Mar 1950, 4-Hagerstown, MD, 12-Heymering, Henry, 13-Wood, Mary Elizabeth, 15-Wood

#4332, 1-England, James H., 2-married, 3-5 Jun 1872, 7-Lockwood, Marietta Maria, 10-Rev. A.[?] B. Goodrich, 15-Wood

#4333, 1-England, Carlton E., 2-married, Bertha, 15-Wood

#4334, 1-England, James A., 2-married, 3-15 Mar 1905, 4-Wilmington, DE, 7-Loflin, Lola, 15-Wood

#4335, 1-England, Edith Jackson, 2-married, 3-13 Jun 1907, 7-Wood, Henry Millard, 15-Wood

#4336, 1-Wood, Jean Millard, 2-married, 3-1 Jun 1940, 7-Myers, George Summer, 10-Rev. Maxwell B. Long, 11-Church fo the Redeemer, Cincinnati, OH, 13-Wood, Edith (England), 15-Wood

#4337, 1-Wood, Mary Elizabeth, 2-born, 3-8 Feb 1911, 15-Wood

#4338, 1-Wood, Mary Elizabeth, 2-married, 3-15 Apr 1944, 7-Heymering, Marinus, 10-Rev. Maxwell B. Long, 11-Church fo the Redeemer, Cincinnati, OH, 15-Wood

#4339, 1-Heymering, Marinus, 2-born, 3-11-Sep-00, 15-Wood

#4340, 1-Heymering, Jr., Marinus, 2-married, 3-14 Feb 1969, 4-Meadville, PA, 7-Piersel, Barbara, 10-Allegheny College chaplain, 15-Wood

#4341, 1-Heymering, Henry Wood, 2-married, 3-3 Nov 1973, 4-St. Mary's of the Hills, Boylston, MA, 7-Coderre, Dolores Jean, 15-Wood

#4342, 1-England, Theodore Austin, 2-died, 3-16 Jun 1883, 15-Wood

#4343, 1-England, James H., 2-died, 3-4 Jun 1890, 15-Wood

#4344, 1-England, Stuart Alanson, 2-died, 3-25 Oct 1895, 15-Wood

#4345, 1-England, Marietta M., 2-died, 3-24 Jan 1922, 15-Wood

#4346, 1-England, Carlton Emerson, 2-died, 3-2 Aug 1924, 15-Wood

#4347, 1-England, James Albert, 2-died, 3-6 Mar 1940, 15-Wood

#4348, 1-Wood, Henry Millard, 2-died, 3-19 Mar 1967, 4-Cincinnati, OH, 6-buried Utica, NY, 15-Wood

#4349, 1-Wood, Edith E., 2-died, 3-5 Oct 1972, 4-Indianapolis, IN, 6-buried Utica, NY, 15-Wood

#4350, 1-Wood, Mary Elizabeth, 2-born, 3-8 Feb 1911, 4-Cincinnati, Ohio, 14-Yes, 15-Wood

#4351, 1-Wood, Mary Elizabeth, 2-married, 3-15 Apr 1944, 7-Heymering, Marinus, 14-Yes, 15-Wood

#4352, 1-Heymering, Jr., Marinus, 2-born, 3-6 Feb 1948, 4-Hagerstown, MD, 15-Wood

#4353, 1-Heymering, Henry Wood, 2-born, 3-8 Mar 1850, 4-Hagerstown, MD, 15-Wood

#4354, 1-Winter, Thomas, 2-married, 3-16 May 1827, 7-Fortney, Elizabeth, 10-D.F. Scheafer, 15-Winter

#4355, 1-Winter, Francis B., 2-married, 3-3 May 1858, 4-Washington, DC, 7-Stone, Lucy Alvera, 9-Georgetown, DC, 10-Rev. Dr. F. Swentzel, 15-Winter

#4356, 1-Winter, Yempre[?], 2-married, 3-14 Nov 1861, 7-Keating, John A., 8-Washington City, 10-Rev. Joseph Trapnel[?], 15-Winter

#4357, 1-Winter, Anne Matilda, 2-married, 3-21 Feb 1866, 7-Shaffer, Christian[?] M., 8-Martinsburg, WV, 10-Rev. Joseph Trapmill[?], 15-Winter

FAMILY BIBLE RECORDS IN THE WASHINGTON COUNTY FREE LIBRARY, HAGERSTOWN, MARYLAND

Entry #, 1-Last Name, First Name, 2-Event, 3-Date, 4-Event Location, 5-Age, 6-Other, 7-Spouse's Last, First, 8-Groom's Residence, 9-Bride's Residence, 10-Minister, 11-Minister's Location, 12-Father's Last, First, 13-Mother's Last, First, 14-Transcribed, 15-Family Bible

#4358, 1-Winter, John T.[?] (Dr.), 2-married, 3-20 Oct 1869, 4-Foundry Chappell, Washington City, DC, 7-First[?], Alphonso Roberts (Miss), 10-Rev. J.M.[?] Gibson, 15-Winter

#4359, 1-Winter, E.C.C., 2-married, 3-25 Dec 1869, 4-Washington, DC, 7-Garrott, E.V., 10-Rev. A.A.[?] Wilson, 15-Winter

#4360, 1-Winter, Alvina E., 2-married, 3-20 Jun 1871, 7-Phleegen[?], L.H., 10-Rev. McMann[?], 15-Winter

#4361, 1-Winter, Mary E., 2-married, 3-26 Dec 1872, 7-Smith, Edward (Rev.), 10-Rev. Mr. Masser [or McMann?], 15-Winter

#4362, 1-Winter, E.C.C., 2-married, 3-29 Jan 1896, 4-129 D Street, NW, Washington, DC, 7-Yingling, Blanche H., 10-Rev. Chas. Bauldiven, 15-Winter

#4363, 1-Winter, Francis E., 2-born, 3-9 Oct 1870, 12-Winter, E.C.C., 13-Winter, E.V., 15-Winter

#4364, 1-Winter, Francis E., 2-baptized, 10-Rev. Jno. Trapnell, 15-Winter

#4365, 1-Winter, Maud A., 2-born, 3-28 Nov 1871, 12-Winter, E.C.C., 13-Winter, E.V., 15-Winter

#4366, 1-Winter, Maud A., 2-baptized, 10-Rev. Bro. Shipley, 15-Winter

#4367, 1-Winter, Thomas, 2-born, 3-4 Jan 1805, 4-Washington Co., MD, 15-Winter

#4368, 1-Fortney, Elizabeth Ann, 2-born, 3-31 Mar 1806, 4-Frederick Co., MD, 12-Fortney, David, 13-Fortney, Elizabeth, 15-Winter

#4369, 1-Winter, Ann Matilda, 2-born, 3-6 Feb 1828, 12-Winter, Thomas, 13-Winter, Elizabeth, 15-Winter

#4370, 1-Winter, Ann Matilda, 2-baptized, 3-26 May 1828, 4-Frederick, MD, 10-Rev. David F. Schaefer, 11-Lutheran Church, Frederick, MD, 15-Winter

#4371, 1-Winter, Mary Ellen, 2-born, 3-Friday, 27 Aug 1830, 12-Winter, T., 13-Winter, E., 15-Winter

#4372, 1-Winter, Mary Ellen, 2-baptized, 3-16 Nov 1830, 4-Frederick, MD, 10-Francis Ruth, 15-Winter

#4373, 1-Winter, Francis Benjamin, 2-born, 3-Wednesday evening[?], 26 Dec 1832, 12-Winter, T., 13-Winter, E., 15-Winter

#4374, 1-Winter, Francis Benjamin, 2-baptized, 3-30 Jun 1833, 4-Manor Church, 10-Rev. D.F. Scheafer, 11-Frederick, MD, 15-Winter

#4375, 1-Winter, Charles Thomas, 2-born, 3-4 Jul 1836, 12-Winter, T., 13-Winter, E., 15-Winter

#4376, 1-Winter, Charles Thomas, 2-baptized, 3-2 Apr 1837, 10-Rev. Boteler, 11-Methodist Episcopal Church, 15-Winter

#4377, 1-Winter, Alvina Elizabeth, 2-born, 3-10 Feb 1838, 12-Winter, T., 13-Winter, E., 15-Winter

#4378, 1-Winter, Alvina Elizabeth, 2-baptized, 3-16 Sep 1838, 10-Rev. Hankey[?], 11-Lutheran Church, Frederick, MD, 15-Winter

#4379, 1-Winter, Templeanna Mason, 2-born, 3-Thursday morning, 27 Feb 1840, 12-Winter, T., 13-Winter, E., 15-Winter

#4380, 1-Winter, Templeanna Mason, 2-baptized, 10-Rev. M. Wachter, 11-Pastor, Lutheran Church, Middletown, MD, 15-Winter

#4381, 1-Winter, John Thomas, 2-born, 3-26 Apr 1842, 12-Winter, T., 13-Winter, E., 15-Winter

#4382, 1-Winter, John Thomas, 2-baptized, 10-W.F. Eyster, 15-Winter

#4383, 1-Winter, Eugene Charles Curtis, 2-born, 3-Sunday night, 13 Aug 1848, 15-Winter

#4384, 1-Winter, Eugene Charles Curtis, 2-baptized, 4-Paner[?] Hill School House, 10-Rev. J.[?]P. Smeltzer, 15-Winter

#4385, 1-Winter, Estelle Vannet, 2-born, 3-22 Sep 1859, 4-Washington City, 12-Winter, Francis, 13-Winter, L.A., 15-Winter

#4386, 1-Winter, Frank Benjamin, 2-born, 3-25 Dec 1861, 4-Washington, DC, 12-Winter, Francis, 13-Winter, L.A., 15-Winter

FAMILY BIBLE RECORDS IN THE WASHINGTON COUNTY FREE LIBRARY, HAGERSTOWN, MARYLAND

Entry #, 1-Last Name, First Name, 2-Event, 3-Date, 4-Event Location, 5-Age, 6-Other,
7-Spouse's Last, First, 8-Groom's Residence, 9-Bride's Residence, 10-Minister, 11-Minister's Location,
12-Father's Last, First, 13-Mother's Last, First, 14-Transcribed, 15-Family Bible

```
#4387, 1-Winter, Louisa Ellen, 2-born, 3-20 Oct 1865, 12-Winter, Francis, 13-
     Winter, L.A., 15-Winter
#4388, 1-Winter, Emma Temple, 2-born, 3-22 Nov 1868, 12-Winter, Francis, 13-Winter,
     L.A., 15-Winter
#4389, 1-Winter, Odilon Fortney, 6-[rest of entry blank], 12-Winter, Francis, 13-
     Winter, L.A., 15-Winter
#4390, 1-Keating, Lillie Marshall, 2-born, 3-31 May 1864, 4-Washington, 12-Keating,
     John, 13-Winter, Templeanna, 15-Winter
#4391, 1-Keating, Lillie Marshall, 2-died, 3-29 Jul 1864, 4-Petersville, 15-Winter
#4392, 1-Keating, Fannie Winter, 2-born, 3-20 Mar 1866, 15-Winter
#4393, 1-Keating, Fannie Winter, 2-christened, 10-Rev. Joseph Trapnell, 15-Winter
#4394, 1-Keating, Fannie Winter, 2-died, 3-4 Mar 1867, 6-buried by Rev. Joseph
     Trapnell, 15-Winter
#4395, 1-Keating, Lottie Russell, 2-born, 3-2 Sep 1868, 15-Winter
#4396, 1-Keating, Lottie Russell, 2-christened, 10-Rev. Joseph Trapnell, 11-St.
     Marks Parish, 15-Winter
#4397, 1-Keating, George Winter, 2-born, 3-17 Feb 1871, 4-Norfolk, 15-Winter
#4398, 1-Keating, George Winter, 2-died, 3-7 Jun 1873, 4-Washington, 5-2 years 3
     months 20 days, 15-Winter
#4399, 1-Keating, John Marshall, 2-born, 3-25 Nov 1872, 4-Washington, 15-Winter
#4400, 1-Keating, John Marshall, 2-died, 3-10 Jun 1873, 5-6 months 16 days, 15-
     Winter
#4401, 1-Burrows, Elizabeth, 2-died, 3-11 Jul 1827, 6-buried in Lutheran Church
     yard, Frederick, MD, 7-Burrows, Thomas, 12-Winter, Benjamin, 13-Winter,
     Catharine, 15-Winter
#4402, 1-Winter, Sr., Benjamin, 2-died, 3-27 Jun 1827, 6-buried in Lutheran Church
     yard, Frederick, MD, 15-Winter
#4403, 1-Bast, Catharine, 2-died, 3-27 Apr 1837, 6-buried Mount Zion Church, 15-
     Winter
#4404, 1-Winter, John (Rev.), 2-died, 3-26 Mar 1854, 5-54 years , 6-buried Clear
     Spring, MD, 15-Winter
#4405, 1-Winter, Luther G.[?], 2-died, 3-29[?] Apr 1849, 5-24 years, 15-Winter
#4406, 1-Winter, Catharine, 2-died, 3-9 Mar 1847[?], 5-76 years, 15-Winter
#4407, 1-Winter, Charles Thomas, 2-died, 3-13 Apr 1837, 5-9 months 9 days, 6-buried
     Episcopal Church yard, St. Marks Parrish, Maryland Tract, 15-Winter
#4408, 1-Winter, Francis C., 2-died, 3-10 Jul 1871, 5-9 months 1 days, 6-buried
     Episcopal Church yard, St. Marks Parrish, Maryland Tract, 12-Winter, E.C.,
     13-Winter, E.V., 15-Winter
#4409, 1-Winter, Maud Alvira, 2-died, 3-3pm, 15 Mar 1876, 4-Washington, DC, 5-4
     years 3 months 17 days, 6-buried St. Marks yard Petersville, MD, 17 Mar 1876,
     12-Winter, E.C.C., 13-winter, Lillie V., 15-Winter
#4410, 1-Winter, E.C.C. (Dr.), 2-died, 3-9 am, 20 Mar 1916, 4-Cherry Dale, VA, 6-
     buried Oak Hill, Washington, DC, 15-Winter
#4411, 1-Winter, Sarah E., 2-died, 3-27 Jan 1866, 7-Winter, Johon (Rev.), 15-Winter
#4412, 1-Keating, Maggie Mason, 2-born, 3-27 Mar 1874, 12-Keating, John, 13-Winter,
     Tempie[?], 15-Winter
#4413, 1-Keating, Percy Varnell[?], 2-born, 3-9 Nov 1875, 12-Keating, John, 13-
     Winter, Tempie[?], 15-Winter
#4414, 1-Keating, Edward Smith , 2-born, 3-6 Feb 1877, 12-Keating, John, 13-Winter,
     Tempie[?], 15-Winter
#4415, 1-Keating, Howard Thomas, 2-born, 3-25 Mar 1878, 12-Keating, John, 13-
     Winter, Tempie[?], 15-Winter
#4416, 1-Keating, Marion, 2-born, 3-5 Mar 1880, 12-Keating, John, 13-Winter,
     Tempie[?], 15-Winter
```

FAMILY BIBLE RECORDS IN THE WASHINGTON COUNTY FREE LIBRARY, HAGERSTOWN, MARYLAND

Entry #, 1-Last Name, First Name, 2-Event, 3-Date, 4-Event Location, 5-Age, 6-Other, 7-Spouse's Last, First, 8-Groom's Residence, 9-Bride's Residence, 10-Minister, 11-Minister's Location, 12-Father's Last, First, 13-Mother's Last, First, 14-Transcribed, 15-Family Bible

#4417, 1-Keating, Templie Eugenia, 2-born, 3-2 Mar 1884[?], 12-Keating, John, 13-Winter, Tempie[?], 15-Winter

#4418, 1-Keating, Templie Eugenia, 2-died, 3-19 Apr 1886, 12-Keating, John, 13-Winter, Tempie[?], 15-Winter

#4419, 1-Winter, Francis Benjamin, 2-died, 3-19 Dec 1896, 4-Washington, DC, 5-64 years, 6-entire entry crossed out; buried at Oak Hill, 15-Winter

#4420, 1-Winter, Lucy Alvira, 2-died, 3-7 Jul 1879, 6-buried at Oak Hill, 7-Winter, Francis Benjamin, 15-Winter

#4421, 1-Shaffer, Ann Matilda (Winter), 2-died, 3-26 Apr 1902, 4-Washington, DC, 6-buried Martinsburg, WV, 15-Winter

#4422, 1-Winter, John Thomas, 2-died, 3-22 Jun 1902, 4-Washington, DC, 6-buried Oak Hill Cemetery, 15-Winter

#4423, 1-Keating, John M., 2-died, 3-18 Feb 1902, 4-Washington, DC, 6-buried Petersville, MD, 15-Winter

#4424, 1-Winter, Thomas, 2-died, 3-6 Dec 1881, 4-Washington, DC, 5-77 years, 6-buried St. Marks Church yard, Petersville, MD, 15-Winter

#4425, 1-Winter, Elizabeth Ann, 2-died, 3-19 Jan 1875, 5-69 years, 6-buried St. Marks Church yard, Petersville, MD, 7-Winter, Thomas, 15-Winter

#4426, 1-Winter, Francis Benjamin, 2-died, 3-19 Dec 1896, 4-Anacostia, DC, 5-64 years, 15-Winter

#4427, 1-Winter, Homer Gibson, 2-died, 3-10 Apr 1874, 15-Winter

#4428, 1-Winter, Elizabeth A., 2-died, 3-19 Jan [no year], 4-Petersville, MD, 5-68 years, 7-Winter, Thos., 15-Winter

#4429, 1-Winter, Thomas, 2-died, 3-6 Dec 1881, 4-Washington, DC, 5-77 years, 6-buried Petersville, MD, 15-Winter

#4430, 1-Winter, Eugene C.C. (Dr.), 2-obituary, 3-3/20/1916 9:15, 4-Dominion Heights, Cherrydale, VA, 6-buried Oak Hill Cemetery, 7-Winter, Blanche, 15-Winter

#4431, 1-Winter, Louisa Ellen, 2-born, 3-20 Oct 1865, 12-Winter, Francis B., 13-Winter, Lucy Alvira, 15-Winter

#4432, 1-Winter, Emma Temple, 2-born, 3-1868, 15-Winter

#4433, 1-Winter, Maud Alvira, 2-born, 3-28 Nov 1871, 12-Winter, E.C.C., 13-Winter, L., 15-Winter

#4434, 1-Winter, Jno. Thomas Hirst[?], 2-born, 3-16 May 1870, 12-Winter, J.[?]T.[?], 15-Winter

#4435, 1-Winter, Minsia[?] Sherman, 2-born, 3-26 Nov 1871, 12-Winter, J.[?]T.[?], 15-Winter

#4436, 1-Winter, Homer Gibson, 2-born, 3-3 Dec 1873, 12-Winter, J.[?]T.[?], 15-Winter

#4437, 1-Shaffer, Francis Winter, 6-[no other info], 15-Winter

#4438, 1-Shaffer, _____ M., 2-born, 3-8 Jun 1868, 12-Shaffer, C.M., 13-Shaffer, Ann, 15-Winter

#4439, 1-Shaffer, Charles Hamil[?], 2-born, 3-9 Apr 1870, 12-Shaffer, C.M., 13-Shaffer, Ann, 15-Winter

#4440, 1-Phleeges[?], John Winter, 3-1872, 6-page torn off so no other info, 12-Shaffer, C.M., 13-Shaffer, Ann, 15-Winter

#4441, 1-Fortney, Elizabeth, 2-died, 3-1 Jun 1847, 5-68 years, 15-Winter

#4442, 1-Fortney, David, 2-died, 3-29 Mar 1851, 5-70 years 6 months 16 days, 15-Winter

#4443, 1-Myers, Rebecca, 2-died, 3-6 Jan 1865, 5-60 years 6 months, 7-Myers, Peter, 15-Winter

#4444, 1-Myers, Peter, 2-died, 3-26 Jul 1870, 5-75 years 2 days, 15-Winter

#4445, 1-Winter, Luly A., 2-died, 3-17 Jul 1879, 4-Washington, DC, 5-39 years, 6-buried Oak Hill, Georgetown, DC, 7-Winter, F.B., 15-Winter

FAMILY BIBLE RECORDS IN THE WASHINGTON COUNTY FREE LIBRARY, HAGERSTOWN, MARYLAND

Entry #, 1-Last Name, First Name, 2-Event, 3-Date, 4-Event Location, 5-Age, 6-Other, 7-Spouse's Last, First, 8-Groom's Residence, 9-Bride's Residence, 10-Minister, 11-Minister's Location, 12-Father's Last, First, 13-Mother's Last, First, 14-Transcribed, 15-Family Bible

#4446, 1-Shrigley, Enoch Murry, 2-married, 3-26 May 1836, 7-Norton[?], Martha Elizabeth, 15-Winter

#4447, 1-Shrigley, Enoch Murry, 2-born, 3-__ Apr 1801, 15-Winter

#4448, 1-Slingley, Martha Elizabeth, 2-born, 3-22 Dec 1813[?], 15-Winter

#4449, 1-Shrigley, Mary Luesa Penelope, 2-born, 3-19 Feb 1837, 12-Shrigley, Enoch M., 13-Shrigley, Martha, 15-Winter

#4450, 1-Shrigley, Caroline Susan Rebeca, 2-born, 3-24 Sep 1838, 15-Winter

#4451, 1-Shrigley, Joseph Thomas Hanson, 2-born, 3-23 Oct 1840, 15-Winter

#4452, 1-Shrigley, John Henry Dill, 2-born, 3-29 Aug 1842, 15-Winter

#4453, 1-Shrigley, Enoch Raylord[?], 2-born, 3-19 Nov 1844, 15-Winter

#4454, 1-Shrigley, James Andrew Winfield Scott, 2-born, 3-7 Dec 1846, 15-Winter

#4455, 1-Shrigley, Ellon Agusta Mas[?], 2-born, 3-15 Jun 1849, 15-Winter

#4456, 1-Shrigley, Ida Ann Florence, 2-born, 3-25 Mar [year torn off], 15-Winter

#4457, 1-Shrigley, Thadeus Langley, 2-born, 3-16 May 1853, 4-Springfield, Clark Co., 6-notations about family fight, 15-Winter

#4458, 1-Shrigley, James Vincent, 6-no other info, 15-Winter

#4459, 1-Shrigley, Lewelin Marshall, 6-no other info, 15-Winter

#4460, 1-Warenfeltz, George Marelous, 2-born, 3-25 Jan 1866, 15-Warrenfeltz

#4461, 1-Warenfeltz, Josiah Jefferson, 2-born, 3-28 Sep 1849, 15-Warrenfeltz

#4462, 1-Warenfeltz, Philip Terrances, 2-born, 3-7 Nov 1851, 15-Warrenfeltz

#4463, 1-Warenfeltz, Maryan Elizabeth, 2-born, 3-23 Oct 1853, 6-appears to have married a Bussard, 15-Warrenfeltz

#4464, 1-Warenfeltz, Jacob Wiliam, 2-born, 3-22 Mar 1855[?], 15-Warrenfeltz

#4465, 1-Warenfeltz, Adam Nicholos, 2-born, 3-16 Sep 1857, 15-Warrenfeltz

#4466, 1-Warenfeltz, Sarah Jane Rebecca, 2-born, 3-30 Apr 1858, 6-appears to have married a Dutrow, 15-Warrenfeltz

#4467, 1-Warenfeltz, Charls Frederick Santee, 2-born, 3-28 Jul 1860, 15-Warrenfeltz

#4468, 1-Warenfeltz, Martha E., 2-born, 3-3 Dec 1863, 15-Warrenfeltz

#4469, 1-Warenfeltz, Martha E., 2-died, 5-2 years, 15-Warrenfeltz

#4470, 1-Warenfeltz, Henry Mlow[?], 2-born, 3-15 Jan 1864, 15-Warrenfeltz

#4471, 1-Warenfels, John, 2-born, 3-17 Aug 1822, 15-Warrenfeltz

#4472, 1-Warenfels, Jacob, 2-born, 3-16 Apr 1824, 15-Warrenfeltz

#4473, 1-Warenfels, Josiah, 2-born, 3-Jun 1826, 15-Warrenfeltz

#4474, 1-Warenfels, Adam, 2-born, 3-4 Apr 1828, 15-Warrenfeltz

#4475, 1-Warrenfeltz, Susan, 2-born, 3-24 Aug 1823, 6-either was a Luty before marriage, or married a Luty, 15-Warrenfeltz

#4476, 1-Warenfelz, John Godfrey, 2-born, 3-7 Aug 1844, 15-Warrenfeltz

#4477, 1-Warenfels, Evean Catharine, 2-born, 3-18 Dec 1845, 15-Warrenfeltz

#4478, 1-Warenfels, Daniel Theodore, 2-born, 3-16 Oct 1847, 15-Warrenfeltz

#4479, 1-Warenfels, John, 2-born, 3-21 Sep 1785, 15-Warrenfeltz

#4480, 1-Warenfels, Frederick, 2-born, 3-14 Sep 1810, 15-Warrenfeltz

#4481, 1-Warenfels, Catharine, 2-born, 3-24 Dec 1812, 15-Warrenfeltz

#4482, 1-Warenfels, Daniel, 2-born, 3-19 Nov 1814, 15-Warrenfeltz

#4483, 1-Warenfels, Margret, 2-born, 3-3 Feb 1816, 15-Warrenfeltz

#4484, 1-Warenfels, Sarah, 2-born, 3-19 Dec 1817, 15-Warrenfeltz

#4485, 1-Warenfels, Magdalena, 2-born, 3-5 Mar 1820, 15-Warrenfeltz

#4486, 1-Warrenfels, Catharina, 2-born, 3-24 Dec 1812, 15-Warrenfeltz

#4487, 1-Warrenfels, Daniel, 2-born, 3-19 Nov 1814, 15-Warrenfeltz

#4488, 1-Warrenfels, Rebecca, 2-born, 3-3 Feb 1816, 15-Warrenfeltz

#4489, 1-Warrenfels, Sarah, 2-born, 3-19 Dec 1817, 15-Warrenfeltz

#4490, 1-Warrenfels, Magdalene, 2-born, 3-5 Mar 1820, 15-Warrenfeltz

#4491, 1-Warrenfels, John, 2-born, 3-17 Aug 1822, 15-Warrenfeltz

#4492, 1-Warrenfels, Jacob, 2-born, 3-16 Apr 1824, 15-Warrenfeltz

#4493, 1-[blank], Daniel, 2-born, 3-23 Dec 1799, 15-Warrenfeltz

#4494, 1-Leatherman, Godfrey, 2-born, 3-10 Feb 1748, 15-Warrenfeltz

FAMILY BIBLE RECORDS IN THE WASHINGTON COUNTY FREE LIBRARY, HAGERSTOWN, MARYLAND

Entry #, 1-Last Name, First Name, 2-Event, 3-Date, 4-Event Location, 5-Age, 6-Other, 7-Spouse's Last, First, 8-Groom's Residence, 9-Bride's Residence, 10-Minister, 11-Minister's Location, 12-Father's Last, First, 13-Mother's Last, First, 14-Transcribed, 15-Family Bible

#4495, 1-Twigg, Wm., 2-married, 3-7 Apr 1836, 7-Midlar[?], Mary Jane, 15-Twigg

#4496, 1-Midlar[?], Mary Jane, 2-born, 12-Midlar[?], Sebastian, 13-Midlar[?], Jane, 15-Twigg

#4497, 1-Twigg, Wm., 2-married, 3-16 Apr 1844, 7-Cunningham, Martha, 15-Twigg

#4498, 1-Cunningham, Martha, 2-born, 12-Cunningham, Walter, 13-Cunningham, Nancy, 15-Twigg

#4499, 1-Twigg, John W., 2-married, 3-14 Jan 1869, 7-Kline, Rose E., 15-Twigg

#4500, 1-Kline, Rose E., 2-born, 12-Kline, David, 13-Kline, Charlott, 15-Twigg

#4501, 1-Twigg, Essie Anna, 2-married, 3-28 ___ 1907, 7-Kitzmiller[?], LeRoy Iller, 15-Twigg

#4502, 1-Twigg, Wm., 2-born, 3-5 Oct 1814, 15-Twigg

#4503, 1-Twigg, Mary Jane, 2-born, 3-24 Mar 1818, 7-Twigg, Wm., 15-Twigg

#4504, 1-Twigg, Martha, 2-born, 3-14 Sep 1826, 7-Twigg, Wm., 15-Twigg

#4505, 1-Twigg, Sarah Catharine, 2-born, 3-24 Feb 1838, 12-Twigg, Wm., 13-Twigg, Mary Jane, 15-Twigg

#4506, 1-Twigg, Elizabeth, 2-born, 3-1 Feb 1840, 12-Twigg, Wm., 13-Twigg, Mary Jane, 15-Twigg

#4507, 1-Twigg, John Wesley, 2-born, 3-2 Apr 1845, 12-Twigg, Wm., 13-Twigg, Martha, 15-Twigg

#4508, 1-Twigg, Wm. Albert, 2-born, 3-23 May 1847, 12-Twigg, Wm., 13-Twigg, Martha, 15-Twigg

#4509, 1-Twigg, Daniel Fenton, 2-born, 3-26 Jan 1849, 12-Twigg, Wm., 13-Twigg, Martha, 15-Twigg

#4510, 1-Twigg, Henry Martin, 2-born, 3-19 Aug 1850, 12-Twigg, Wm., 13-Twigg, Martha, 15-Twigg

#4511, 1-Twigg, Samuel Mirchant, 2-born, 3-6 Oct 1852, 15-Twigg

#4512, 1-Twigg, Leucizer Marthar Matilda, 2-born, 3-15 Mar 1855, 15-Twigg

#4513, 1-Twigg, David Finley[?], 2-born, 3-6 May 185_, 15-Twigg

#4514, 1-Kitzmiller, Eve ___rene, 2-born, 3-19 Sep 1908, 15-Twigg

#4515, 1-Kitzmiller, Melvin LeRoy, 2-born, 3-23 Oct 1910, 15-Twigg

#4516, 1-Kitzmiller, Nevin David, 2-born, 3-16 Jun 1916, 15-Twigg

#4517, 1-Kitzmiller, Raymond Eugene, 2-born, 3-1 Feb 1919, 15-Twigg

#4518, 1-Twigg, Rose E., 2-born, 3-6 May 1845, 15-Twigg

#4519, 1-Twigg, Martha Ellen, 2-born, 3-29 Nov 1869, 12-Twigg, John, 13-Twigg, Rose E., 15-Twigg

#4520, 1-Twigg, William Edward, 2-born, 3-20 Apr 1872[?], 12-Twigg, John, 13-Twigg, Rose E., 15-Twigg

#4521, 1-Twigg, Essie Anna, 2-born, 3-8 May 1889, 15-Twigg

#4522, 1-Kitzmiller, LeRoy Iller, 2-born, 3-1 Oct 1882, 15-Twigg

#4523, 1-Twigg, Wm., 2-baptized, 5-infancy, 15-Twigg

#4524, 1-Twigg, Martha, 2-baptized, 3-14 Apr 1845, 7-Twigg, Wm., 15-Twigg

#4525, 1-Twigg, John Wesley, 2-baptized, 3-14 Apr 1845, 12-Twigg, Wm., 13-Twigg, Martha, 15-Twigg

#4526, 1-Twigg, Wm. Albert, 2-baptized, 3-25 Jul 1848, 12-Twigg, Wm., 13-Twigg, Martha, 15-Twigg

#4527, 1-Twigg, Henry Martin, 2-baptized, 3-15 Sep 1850, 12-Twigg, Wm., 13-Twigg, Martha, 15-Twigg

#4528, 1-Twigg, Samuel Mirchant, 2-baptized, 3-10 Oct 1853, 12-Twigg, Wm., 13-Twigg, Martha, 15-Twigg

#4529, 1-Twigg, Leuezesa[?] Marthar Matilda, 2-baptized, 3-28 Jan 1856, 12-Twigg, Wm., 13-Twigg, Martha, 15-Twigg

#4530, 1-Twigg, David Finley, 2-baptized, 3-12 Sep 1858, 15-Twigg

#4531, 1-Twigg, Martha Ellen, 2-baptized, 3-30 Dec 1872, 10-Rev. Howe, 15-Twigg

#4532, 1-Kitzmiller, Evelyn Irene, 2-baptized, 3-17 Jun 1921, 10-Rev. Kabele, 15-Twigg

FAMILY BIBLE RECORDS IN THE WASHINGTON COUNTY FREE LIBRARY, HAGERSTOWN, MARYLAND

Entry #, 1-Last Name, First Name, 2-Event, 3-Date, 4-Event Location, 5-Age, 6-Other,
7-Spouse's Last, First, 8-Groom's Residence, 9-Bride's Residence, 10-Minister, 11-Minister's Location,
12-Father's Last, First, 13-Mother's Last, First, 14-Transcribed, 15-Family Bible

```
#4533, 1-Kitzmiller, Melvin[?], 2-baptized, 3-23 Apr 1927, 15-Twigg
#4534, 1-Kitzmiller, Laverne Earl, 2-baptized, 3-28 Jun 1942, 10-Rev. Hightower,
    15-Twigg
#4535, 1-Twigg, Mary Jane, 2-died, 3-15 Feb 1840, 7-Twigg, Wm., 15-Twigg
#4536, 1-Twigg, Elizabeth, 2-died, 3-14 Feb 1840, 5-infant, 12-Twigg, Wm., 13-
    Twigg, Mary Jane, 15-Twigg
#4537, 1-Twigg, Sarah Catharine, 2-died, 3-1 Oct 1847, 15-Twigg
#4538, 1-Twigg, Daniel Fenton, 2-died, 3-1 Nov 1849, 12-Twigg, Wm., 13-Twigg,
    Martha, 15-Twigg
#4539, 1-Twigg, Wm. Albert, 2-died, 3-16 Jun 1853, 12-Twigg, Wm., 13-Twigg, Martha,
    15-Twigg
#4540, 1-Twigg, Martha, 2-died, 3-7 Jun 1867, 7-Twigg, Wm., 15-Twigg
#4541, 1-Kitzmiller, Raymond Eugene, 2-died, 3-24 Jun 1919, 15-Twigg
#4542, 1-Trovinger, Joseph, 2-born, 3-11 Dec 1790, 15-Trovinger
#4543, 1-Trovinger, Elizabeth, 2-born, 3-11 Sep 1804, 7-Trovinger, Joseph, 15-
    Trovinger
#4544, 1-Trovinger, John, 2-born, 3-3 Jun 1823, 15-Trovinger
#4545, 1-Trovinger, Joseph, 2-born, 3-30 Aug 1824, 15-Trovinger
#4546, 1-Trovinger, Samuel, 2-born, 3-13 Jan 1826, 15-Trovinger
#4547, 1-Trovinger, Barbary, 2-born, 3-20 Aug 1827, 15-Trovinger
#4548, 1-Trovinger, Elizabeth, 2-born, 3-5 Feb 1829, 15-Trovinger
#4549, 1-Trovinger, Daniel, 2-born, 3-9 Feb 1831, 15-Trovinger
#4550, 1-Trovinger, Joseph, 2-born, 3-16 Dec 1832, 15-Trovinger
#4551, 1-Trovinger, Benton, 2-born, 3-26 Nov 1834, 15-Trovinger
#4552, 1-Trovinger, Ann Malinda, 2-born, 3-26 Aug 1836, 15-Trovinger
#4553, 1-Trovinger, Fanny, 2-born, 3-30 Sep 1837, 15-Trovinger
#4554, 1-Trovinger, Emily, 2-born, 3-30 May 1839, 15-Trovinger
#4555, 1-Trovinger, Franklin, 2-born, 3-31 May 1841, 15-Trovinger
#4556, 1-Trovinger, Catharine, 2-born, 3-26 Nov 1842, 15-Trovinger
#4557, 1-Trovinger, Nancy Amelia, 2-born, 3-11 Jan 1845, 15-Trovinger
#4558, 1-Trovinger, Martin Luther, 2-born, 3-22 Jan 1847, 15-Trovinger
#4559, 1-Trovinger, Joseph, 2-died, 3-11 May 1851, 5-60 years 5 months, 15-
    Trovinger
#4560, 1-Trovinger, Joseph, 2-died, 3-7 Apr 1825, 5-7 months 7 days, 15-Trovinger
#4561, 1-Trovinger, Barbary, 2-died, 3-4 May 1830, 5-2 years 8 months 15 days, 15-
    Trovinger
#4562, 1-Trovinger, Fanny, 2-died, 3-30 Sep 1837, 15-Trovinger
#4563, 1-Trovinger, Sarah E., 2-died, 3-11 Oct 1853, 5-22 years 7 months 6 days, 7-
    Trovinger, John, 15-Trovinger
#4564, 1-Clopper, Grandmother, 2-died, 3-8 Dec 1858, 5-82 years 8 months 23 days,
    15-Trovinger
#4565, 1-Trovinger, John, 2-died, 3-21 Jul 1882, 5-59 years 1 months 18 days, 15-
    Trovinger
#4566, 1-Trovinger, Samuel, 2-died, 3-1 Jun 1886, 5-60 years 5 months 27 days, 15-
    Trovinger
#4567, 1-Trovinger, Daniel, 2-died, 3-24 May 1890, 5-59 years 3 months 8 days, 15-
    Trovinger
#4568, 1-Kershner, Elizabeth, 2-died, 3-21 Jan 1892, 5-62 years 11 months 16 days,
    15-Trovinger
#4569, 1-Middlekauff, Susan (Mrs.), 2-obituary, 3-Apr 1925, 4-Hagerstown, MD, 5-99
    years 4 months 26 days, 6-buried Rose Hill Cemetery, 7-Middlekauff,
    Cornelius, 12-Trovinger, Joseph, 13-Clopper, Elizabeth, 15-Trovinger
#4570, 1-Kershner, Benjamin F., 2-married, 3-8 ___ ____, 7-Freaner, Rebecca (Miss),
    15-Trovinger
```

FAMILY BIBLE RECORDS IN THE WASHINGTON COUNTY FREE LIBRARY, HAGERSTOWN, MARYLAND

Entry #, 1-Last Name, First Name, 2-Event, 3-Date, 4-Event Location, 5-Age, 6-Other, 7-Spouse's Last, First, 8-Groom's Residence, 9-Bride's Residence, 10-Minister, 11-Minister's Location, 12-Father's Last, First, 13-Mother's Last, First, 14-Transcribed, 15-Family Bible

#4571, 1-Turner, John D., 2-married, 3-13 ___ ____, 7-McIlhenny, Mary (Miss), 8-Berkeley Co., WV, 15-Trovinger

#4572, 1-Albert, Alfred, 2-obituary, 3-11 ___ ____, 5-2 years 10 months, 12-Albert, Jacob, 13-Albert, Mary, 15-Trovinger

#4573, 1-Trovinger, Joseph (Major), 2-obituary, 15-Summer

#4574, 1-Summer, John, 2-married, 3-8 Sep 1857, 7-Bachtel, Ann M.E., 15-Summer

#4575, 1-Rinehart, Mary Magdalene (Summer), 2-died, 3-25 May 1920, 5-42 years 4 months 21 days, 15-Summer

#4576, 1-Stoner, Emma J. (Summer), 2-died, 3-16 Apr 1936[?], 5-74 years 5 months 5 days, 15-Summer

#4577, 1-Summer, Benjamin R., 2-died, 3-19 Sep 1940, 5-82 years 19 days, 15-Summer

#4578, 1-Summer, Thomas H., 2-died, 3-24 Jun 1942, 5-69 years, 15-Summer

#4579, 1-Shank, Barbara E., 2-died, 3-28 Dec 1943, 5-76 years, 15-Summer

#4580, 1-Summer, Benjamin R., 2-born, 3-31 Aug 1858, 15-Summer

#4581, 1-Summer, Alvey B., 2-born, 3-11 Oct 1859[?], 15-Summer

#4582, 1-Summer, Emma J., 2-born, 3-11 Nov 1861, 15-Summer

#4583, 1-Summer, Barbara E., 2-born, 3-20 May 1866, 15-Summer

#4584, 1-Summer, Charles C., 2-born, 3-13 Nov 1863, 15-Summer

#4585, 1-Summer, Sarah E., 2-born, 3-10 Feb 1868, 15-Summer

#4586, 1-Summer, John G., 2-born, 3-31 Jan 1870, 15-Summer

#4587, 1-Summer, Edward Clinton, 2-born, 3-5 May 1872, 6-twin, 15-Summer

#4588, 1-Summer, William J., 2-born, 3-5 May 1872, 6-twin, 15-Summer

#4589, 1-Summer, Thomas H., 2-born, 3-18 Nov 1873, 15-Summer

#4590, 1-Summer, Anna Maria, 2-born, 3-14 Feb 1876, 15-Summer

#4591, 1-Summer, Mary Magdalene, 2-born, 3-4 Jan 1878, 15-Summer

#4592, 1-Summer, Sarah E., 2-died, 3-1 Oct 1868, 5-7 months 21 days, 15-Summer

#4593, 1-Summer, Edward C., 2-died, 3-28 Jul 1872, 5-2 months 25 days, 15-Summer

#4594, 1-Summer, William J., 2-died, 3-11 Aug 1872, 5-3 months 6 days, 15-Summer

#4595, 1-Summer, John G., 2-died, 3-1 May 1890, 5-20 years 3 months 1 days, 15-Summer

#4596, 1-Summer, Charles C., 2-died, 3-28 Dec 1890, 5-27 years 1 months 15 days, 15-Summer

#4597, 1-Summer, Alvey B., 2-died, 3-22 Mar 1896, 5-36 years 5 months 6 days, 15-Summer

#4598, 1-Summer, John, 2-born, 3-2 Jul 1854, 15-Summer

#4599, 1-Bachtel, Ann M.E., 2-born, 3-2 Sep 1855, 15-Summer

#4600, 1-Summer, John, 2-died, 3-15 Aug 1901, 5-67 years 1 months 6 days, 15-Summer

#4601, 1-Summer, Ann M.E., 2-died, 3-8 Mar 1905, 5-69 years 7 months 6 days, 15-Summer

#4602, 1-McCollister, Amby[?], 2-born, 3-20 Oct 1870[?], 15-Summer

#4603, 1-McCollister, Lavina (Miss), 2-born, 3-19[?] Aug 1830, 15-Summer

#4604, 1-McCollister, Margaret (Miss), 2-born, 3-29 Aug 1856, 15-Summer

#4605, 1-McCollister, Mathas[?] James, 2-born, 3-17 Oct 1860, 15-Summer

#4606, 1-McCollister, Mary Ellen, 2-born, 3-13 Dec 1863, 15-Summer

#4607, 1-McCollister, Murten[?] William, 2-born, 3-16 Jul 1866, 15-Summer

#4608, 1-Zittle, Michael, 2-born, 3-5 Oct 1798, 15-Summer

#4609, 1-Zittle, Michael, 2-died, 3-12 Jul 1877, 15-Summer

#4610, 1-Summers, Simon P., 2-born, 3-8 Nov 1841, 15-Summer

#4611, 1-Summers, Emma, 2-born, 3-28 Apr 1838, 15-Summer

#4612, 1-Summers, Michael F., 2-born, 3-27 Jan 1864, 15-Summer

#4613, 1-Summers, James V., 2-born, 3-25[?] Jun 1865, 15-Summer

#4614, 1-Summers, Mary E., 2-born, 3-19 Mar 1867, 15-Summer

#4615, 1-Summers, Emma A., 2-born, 3-22 Sep 1869, 15-Summer

#4616, 1-Summers, Caroline M., 2-born, 3-2_[?] Aug 1871, 15-Summer

#4617, 1-Summers, Ezra D., 2-born, 3-5 May 1873, 15-Summer

FAMILY BIBLE RECORDS IN THE WASHINGTON COUNTY FREE LIBRARY, HAGERSTOWN, MARYLAND

Entry #, 1-Last Name, First Name, 2-Event, 3-Date, 4-Event Location, 5-Age, 6-Other, 7-Spouse's Last, First, 8-Groom's Residence, 9-Bride's Residence, 10-Minister, 11-Minister's Location, 12-Father's Last, First, 13-Mother's Last, First, 14-Transcribed, 15-Family Bible

```
#4618, 1-Summers, Dolly M., 2-born, 3-8 Oct 1876, 15-Summer
#4619, 1-Summers, Simon P., 2-died, 3-27 Apr 1878, 5-37 years 5 months 19 days, 15-
    Summer
#4620, 1-Summers, Emma (Mrs.), 2-died, 3-5 Jul 1919, 5-81 years 3 months 5 days,
    15-Summer
#4621, 1-Summers, James Eugene, 2-died, 15-Summer
#4622, 1-Summers, Ezra Daniel, 2-died, 3-3 Feb 1940, 15-Summer
#4623, 1-Moser, Mary E. (Summers) (Mrs.), 2-died, 3-27 Apr 1947, 5-80 years 1
    months 10 days, 15-Summer
#4624, 1-Wolfe, Dollie (Summers), 2-died, 15-Summer
#4625, 1-Flook, Minnie (Summers), 2-died, 15-Summer
#4626, 1-Summers, Michael Francis, 6-"no one knowd what become of him", 15-Summer
#4627, 1-Summers, Simon P., 2-obituary, 3-1964, 5-81 years, 7-Summers, Sarah Ann,
    12-Summers, James, 13-Summers, Rebecca, 15-Summer
#4628, 1-Wolfe, Melvin E., 2-obituary, 12-Wolfe, Sherman, 15-Summer
#4629, 1-Flook, Minnie Ellen (Mrs.), 2-obituary, 5-86 years, 7-Flook, John P., 12-
    Summers, Simon, 13-Zittle, Emmaline, 15-Summer
#4630, 1-Lowery, Frank E., 2-obituary, 5-64 years, 12-Lowery, William L. (Rev.),
    13-Nicholson, Matilda, 15-Summer
#4631, 1-Summers, Emma (Mrs.), 2-obituary, 5-81 years, 7-Summers, Simon G., 15-
    Summer
#4632, 1-Hutzel, Elizabeth, 2-born, 6-list of grandchildren follows, 15-Summer
#4633, 1-Hutzel, Septimus, 2-born, 12-Hutzel, John, 15-Summer
#4634, 1-Hutzel, George, 2-born, 12-Hutzel, John, 15-Summer
#4635, 1-Hutzel, Calren[?], 2-born, 12-Hutzel, John, 15-Summer
#4636, 1-Hutzel, Charley, 2-born, 12-Hutzel, John, 15-Summer
#4637, 1-Hutzel, Clemmie, 2-born, 12-Hutzel, John, 15-Summer
#4638, 1-Hagerman, Nanie, 2-born, 13-Hagerman, Mary, 15-Summer
#4639, 1-Hagerman, Alice, 2-born, 13-Hagerman, Mary, 15-Summer
#4640, 1-Hagerman, Adie, 2-born, 13-Hagerman, Mary, 15-Summer
#4641, 1-Hagerman, Luther, 2-born, 13-Hagerman, Mary, 15-Summer
#4642, 1-Hagerman, Willy, 2-born, 13-Hagerman, Mary, 15-Summer
#4643, 1-Rohrer, Carrie, 2-born, 13-Rohrer, Becca[?], 15-Summer
#4644, 1-Stine[?], Samy[?], 2-born, 6-twice married, 13-Rohrer, Becca[?], 15-Summer
#4645, 1-Hutzel, Vernon, 2-born, 12-Hutzel, Jonas , 15-Summer
#4646, 1-Hutzel, Russell, 2-born, 12-Hutzel, Jonas , 15-Summer
#4647, 1-Hutzel, Webster, 2-born, 12-Hutzel, Samuel, 15-Summer
#4648, 1-Hutzel, Ellsworth, 2-born, 12-Hutzel, Samuel, 15-Summer
#4649, 1-Hutzel, Alice, 2-born, 12-Hutzel, Luther, 15-Summer
#4650, 1-Hutzel, Corma[?], 2-born, 12-Hutzel, Luther, 15-Summer
#4651, 1-Hutzel, Maude, 2-born, 12-Hutzel, Luther, 15-Summer
#4652, 1-Hutzel, Elesis[?], 2-born, 12-Hutzel, Luther, 15-Summer
#4653, 1-Hutzel, Elmer, 2-born, 12-Hutzel, Luther, 15-Summer
#4654, 1-Zittle, Michael, 2-born, 3-5 Oct 1798, 15-Summer
#4655, 1-Zittle, Michael, 2-died, 3-12 Jul 1877, 15-Summer
#4656, 1-Summer, J.W., 2-married, 3-13 Feb 1851, 7-Hart, Kate, 10-Rev. E. Butler,
    11-Methodist Episcopal Church, 15-Summer
#4657, 1-Summer, J. Wesley, 2-born, 3-12 Dec 1823, 15-Summer
#4658, 1-Hart, Kate, 2-born, 3-6 Jun 1828, 15-Summer
#4659, 1-Summer, Ellie May, 2-born, 3-29 Jan 1852, 12-Summer, J.W., 13-Summer,
    H.[or K.?], 15-Summer
#4660, 1-Summer, Bettie Barten[?], 2-born, 3-19 Mar 1853, 15-Summer
#4661, 1-Summer, Lillian Ka____[?], 2-born, 3-__ Aug ____, 15-Summer
#4662, 1-Summer, Mary[?] , 2-born, 3-16 Aug 1859[?], 15-Summer
#4663, 1-Summers, John W., 2-obituary, 3-1860, 15-Summer
```

FAMILY BIBLE RECORDS IN THE WASHINGTON COUNTY FREE LIBRARY, HAGERSTOWN, MARYLAND

Entry #, 1-Last Name, First Name, 2-Event, 3-Date, 4-Event Location, 5-Age, 6-Other, 7-Spouse's Last, First, 8-Groom's Residence, 9-Bride's Residence, 10-Minister, 11-Minister's Location, 12-Father's Last, First, 13-Mother's Last, First, 14-Transcribed, 15-Family Bible

#4664, 1-Hart, John Dewit[?], 2-died, 3-2 Jun 1854, 15-Summer
#4665, 1-Hart, Elizabeth, 2-died, 3-Feb 1837, 15-Summer
#4666, 1-Summers, Ellie Mary, 2-died, 3-4 Feb 1854, 15-Summer
#4667, 1-Summers, Bettie Baxter[?], 2-died, 3-30 Jun 1854, 15-Summer
#4668, 1-Summers, Sarah Waring[?], 2-died, 3-9 May 1824, 15-Summer
#4669, 1-Summers, Nathaniel, 2-died, 3-17 Aug 1855, 5-65 years, 15-Summer
#4670, 1-Summers, J. Wesley, 2-died, 3-7 Dec 1859, 15-Summer
#4671, 1-Summers, Wallie Waring, 2-died, 3-19 Jan 1862, 15-Summer
#4672, 1-Summers, Kate (Hart), 2-died, 3-9 Dec 1894, 15-Summer
#4673, 1-Summers, Kate (Hart), 2-obituary, 3-9 Dec 1894, 7-Summers, J.W., 12-Hart, John DeWit (Capt.), 15-Summer
#4674, 1-Bowles, Mary Ann (Mrs.), 2-obituary, 5-79 years, 7-Bowles, William A., 15-Summer
#4675, 1-Stouffer, William H., 2-married, 3-13 Sep 1880, 7-Sigler, Lillie V. (Miss), 15-Stouffer
#4676, 1-Stouffer, M.V., 2-born, 3-17 Apr 1881, 4-Cavetown, MD, 15-Stouffer
#4677, 1-Stouffer, D.[?] C., 2-born, 3-12 Jun 1882, 4-Cavetown, MD, 15-Stouffer
#4678, 1-Stouffer, Ranskin[?] A., 2-born, 3-17 Feb 1881[?], 4-Cavetown, MD, 15-Stouffer
#4679, 1-Stouffer, William V., 2-born, 3-8 Sep 1885, 4-Cavetown, MD, 15-Stouffer
#4680, 1-Stouffer, James L., 2-born, 3-6 Aug 1887, 4-Cavetown, MD, 15-Stouffer
#4681, 1-Stouffer, Lois Ann, 2-born, 3-9 Feb 1889, 4-Cavetown, MD, 15-Stouffer
#4682, 1-Stouffer, Frank McKaig, 2-born, 3-16 Jun[?] 1891, 4-Hagerstown, MD, 15-Stouffer
#4683, 1-Stouffer, Fred Hallle[?], 2-born, 3-20 Nov 1893[?], 4-Hagerstown, MD, 15-Stouffer
#4684, 1-Stouffer, Richard Z.[?], 2-born, 3-22 Sep 1894, 4-Hagerstown, MD, 15-Stouffer
#4685, 1-Stouffer, Joseph P., 2-born, 3-15 Feb 1896, 4-Hagerstown, MD, 15-Stouffer
#4686, 1-Stouffer, Edith G., 2-born, 3-29[?] Jul 1898, 4-Hagerstown, MD, 15-Stouffer
#4687, 1-Storm, Frank E., 2-married, 3-13 Apr 1881, 4-John Murdock's, 7-Falconer, Katie C., 8-Boonsboro, MD, 9-Boonsboro, MD, 10-Geo. H. Beckley, 11-Boonsboro, 15-Storm
#4688, 1-Storm, Hattie, 2-born, 3-10 Mar 1882, 15-Storm
#4689, 1-Storm, Allice C., 2-born, 3-5 Aug 1883, 15-Storm
#4690, 1-Storm, Pauline S., 2-born, 3-31 Mar 1888, 15-Storm
#4691, 1-Storm, John F., 2-born, 3-20 Jan 1890, 15-Storm
#4692, 1-Storm, Harriet C., 2-born, 3-30 Jun 1892, 15-Storm
#4693, 1-Storm, Frances M., 2-born, 3-16 Apr 1894, 15-Storm
#4694, 1-Storm, Hattie, 2-died, 3-17 Sep 1882, 15-Storm
#4695, 1-Startzman, Daniel R., 2-married, 3-24 May 1877, 7-Startzman, Lily, 15-Startzman
#4696, 1-Startzman, R. Newton, 2-married, 3-26 Sep 1901, 7-Middlekauff, Nellie F., 15-Startzman
#4697, 1-Startzman, Laura V., 2-married, 3-2 Aug 1911, 7-Martin, W. Edgar, 15-Startzman
#4698, 1-Startzman, Clara E., 2-married, 3-1 Jan 1917, 7-Hendry, James, 15-Startzman
#4699, 1-Startzman, Max W., 2-married, 3-27 Feb 1919, 7-Ensminger, Malissa J., 15-Startzman
#4700, 1-Startzman, Paul Raymond, 2-married, 3-1930, 7-Summer, Madeline, 15-Startzman
#4701, 1-Startzman, Daniel R., 2-died, 3-26 Apr 1903, 5-50 years 17 days, 15-Startzman

FAMILY BIBLE RECORDS IN THE WASHINGTON COUNTY FREE LIBRARY, HAGERSTOWN, MARYLAND

Entry #, 1-Last Name, First Name, 2-Event, 3-Date, 4-Event Location, 5-Age, 6-Other,
7-Spouse's Last, First, 8-Groom's Residence, 9-Bride's Residence, 10-Minister, 11-Minister's Location,
12-Father's Last, First, 13-Mother's Last, First, 14-Transcribed, 15-Family Bible

```
#4702, 1-Startzman, Lillie, 2-died, 3-14 Jul 1911, 5-52 years 3 months 14 days, 15-
    Startzman
#4703, 1-Startzman, Richard Newton, 2-died, 3-27 Oct 1935, 5-10 months 11 days, 15-
    Startzman
#4704, 1-Startzman, Susan, 2-died, 3-14 Apr 1910, 5-23 years 4 months 6 days, 15-
    Startzman
#4705, 1-Startzman, Charles Christian, 2-died, 3-10 Feb 1960, 5-79 years 6 months
    10 days, 15-Startzman
#4706, 1-Startzman, Max W., 2-died, 3-22 Feb 1971, 5-81 years 4 months 17 days, 15-
    Startzman
#4707, 1-Martin, Laura V., 2-died, 3-19 Sep 1974, 5-90 years 6 months, 15-Startzman
#4708, 1-Startzman, Mary E. [or C.], 2-died, 3-7 Apr 1975, 5-82 years 7 months 26
    days, 15-Startzman
#4709, 1-Martin, Helene Jane, 2-born, 3-11 Jun 1912, 12-Martin, W.E., 13-Martin,
    Laura V., 15-Startzman
#4710, 1-Startzman, Esther Cornelia, 2-born, 3-7 Nov 1912, 12-Startzman, Richard
    Newton, 13-Startzman, Nellie F., 15-Startzman
#4711, 1-Martin, Edgar Thuston, 2-born, 3-13 Apr 1915, 12-Martin, W.E., 13-Martin,
    Laura V., 15-Startzman
#4712, 1-Startzman, Vernon Newton, 2-born, 3-14 May 1915, 12-Startzman, R. Newton,
    13-Startzman, Nellie F., 15-Startzman
#4713, 1-Startzman, Rosalie, 2-born, 3-23 Jul 1918, 12-Startzman, R. Newton, 13-
    Startzman, Nellie F., 15-Startzman
#4714, 1-Martin, Robert Startzman, 2-born, 3-4 May 1917, 15-Startzman
#4715, 1-Startzman, Daniel R., 2-born, 3-9 Apr 1853, 15-Startzman
#4716, 1-Startzman, Lily, 2-born, 3-21 May 1858, 15-Startzman
#4717, 1-Startzman, Richard Newton, 2-born, 3-16 Jan 1878, 15-Startzman
#4718, 1-Startzman, Charles Christian, 2-born, 3-31 Jul 1880, 15-Startzman
#4719, 1-Startzman, Laura Virginia, 2-born, 3-19 Mar 1884, 15-Startzman
#4720, 1-Startzman, Susan, 2-born, 3-6 Dec 1886, 15-Startzman
#4721, 1-Startzman, Max William, 2-born, 3-5 Oct 1889, 15-Startzman
#4722, 1-Startzman, Mary Elizabeth, 2-born, 3-11 Aug 1892, 15-Startzman
#4723, 1-Startzman, Clara Ellen, 2-born, 3-3 Aug 1895, 15-Startzman
#4724, 1-Startzman, Paul R., 2-born, 3-25 Aug 1898, 15-Startzman
#4725, 1-Grayston, James, 2-married, 3-25 Dec 1875, 7-Grayston, Margaret, 15-
    Grayston
#4726, 1-Grayston, James, 2-born, 3-28 Nov 1856, 15-Grayston
#4727, 1-Grayston, Margaret, 2-born, 3-22 Mar 1856, 15-Grayston
#4728, 1-Grayston, John Thomas, 2-born, 3-14 Oct 1876, 15-Grayston
#4729, 1-Grayston, Mary Ann, 2-born, 3-15 Dec 1878, 15-Grayston
#4730, 1-Grayston, James Edward, 2-born, 3-14 Apr 1881, 15-Grayston
#4731, 1-Grayston, William Albert, 2-born, 3-23 Oct 1883, 15-Grayston
#4732, 1-Grayston, Margaret Alice, 2-born, 3-2 Dec 1885, 15-Grayston
#4733, 1-Grayston, Francis, 2-born, 3-28 May 1888, 15-Grayston
#4734, 1-Grayston, Amelia Ellen, 2-born, 3-10 Jul 1891, 15-Grayston
#4735, 1-Grayston, Gladys Matilda, 2-born, 3-26 Nov 1895, 15-Grayston
#4736, 1-Grayston, Agnes Ada, 2-born, 3-14 Dec 1897, 15-Grayston
#4737, 1-Grayston, Mary Ann, 2-married, 3-26 Dec 1899, 7-Stoakes, Frank, 15-
    Grayston
#4738, 1-Grayston, William Albert, 2-married, 3-18 Mar 1905, 7-Mount, Ann Jane, 15-
    Grayston
#4739, 1-Grayston, Margaret Alice, 2-born, 3-10 May 1913, 7-Brown, Wm. Henry, 15-
    Grayston
#4740, 1-Grayston, Amelia Ellen, 2-born, 3-22 Mar 1913, 7-Hargreaves, Harold, 15-
    Grayston
```

FAMILY BIBLE RECORDS IN THE WASHINGTON COUNTY FREE LIBRARY, HAGERSTOWN, MARYLAND

Entry #, 1-Last Name, First Name, 2-Event, 3-Date, 4-Event Location, 5-Age, 6-Other, 7-Spouse's Last, First, 8-Groom's Residence, 9-Bride's Residence, 10-Minister, 11-Minister's Location, 12-Father's Last, First, 13-Mother's Last, First, 14-Transcribed, 15-Family Bible

#4741, 1-Grayston, Francis, 2-married, 3-23-Oct-15, 7-Schofield, Gertrude Annie, 15-Grayston

#4742, 1-Grayston, Gladys Matilda, 2-married, 3-4 Sep 1920, 7-Kneale, Harry, 15-Grayston

#4743, 1-Grayston, Agnes Ada, 2-married, 3-22 Sep 1923, 7-Ambler, Cecil Parker, 15-Grayston

#4744, 1-Grayston, James Edward, 2-died, 3-28[?] Dec 1904, 15-Grayston

#4745, 1-Grayston, Francis, 2-died, 3-6 Jun 1931, 15-Grayston

#4746, 1-Grayston, James , 2-died, 3-16 Dec 1934, 6-"father", 15-Grayston

#4747, 1-Grayston, Margaret , 2-died, 3-30 Mar 1936, 6-"mother", 15-Grayston

#4748, 1-Grayston, Mary Ann, 2-died, 3-3 Oct 1943, 15-Grayston

#4749, 1-Grayston, Agnes Ada, 2-died, 3-29-Sep-45, 15-Grayston

#4750, 1-Grayston, John Thomas, 2-died, 3-27 May 1949, 15-Grayston

#4751, 1-Grayston, William Albert, 2-died, 3-7 Dec 1952, 15-Grayston

#4752, 1-Kneale, Gladys Matilda (Grayston), 2-died, 3-12 Feb 1971, 15-Grayston

#4753, 1-Brown, Margaret Alice (Grayston), 2-died, 3-7 Mar 1975, 15-Grayston

#4754, 1-Hargreaves, Amelia Ellen (Grayston), 2-died, 3-23 Aug 1975, 15-Grayston

#4755, 1-Tweedy, John, 2-born, 3-5 Feb 1825, 15-Tweedy

#4756, 1-Tweedy, Maria, 2-born, 3-13 May 1831, 15-Tweedy

#4757, 1-Tweedy, Eliza Jane, 2-born, 3-3 Mar 1850, 15-Tweedy

#4758, 1-Tweedy, Samuel, 2-born, 3-19 Sep 1851, 15-Tweedy

#4759, 1-Tweedy, Elenor, 2-born, 3-28 Dec 1853, 15-Tweedy

#4760, 1-Tweedy, Mary Ann, 2-born, 3-5 Mar 1855, 15-Tweedy

#4761, 1-Tweedy, William, 2-born, 3-21 Jan 1857, 15-Tweedy

#4762, 1-Tweedy, John, 2-born, 3-5 Apr 1859, 15-Tweedy

#4763, 1-Tweedy, Martha Maria, 2-born, 3-21 May 1861, 15-Tweedy

#4764, 1-Tweedy, Robert L., 2-born, 3-3 Jun 1863, 15-Tweedy

#4765, 1-Tweedy, James, 2-born, 3-22 Jan 1865, 15-Tweedy

#4766, 1-Tweedy, James B., 2-born, 3-11 Feb 1867, 15-Tweedy

#4767, 1-Tweedy, Johnston W., 2-born, 3-1 Aug 1869, 15-Tweedy

#4768, 1-Tweedy, Sarah E., 2-born, 3-1 May 1871, 15-Tweedy

#4769, 1-Tweedy, James, 2-died, 3-9 Jan 1865, 15-Tweedy

#4770, 1-Tweedy, William, 2-died, 3-15 Jan 1879, 15-Tweedy

#4771, 1-Tweedy, Sarah Edith[?], 2-died, 3-1 Oct 1888, 15-Tweedy

#4772, 1-Tweedy, James[?] Bell[?], 2-died, 3-25 Jan 1888[?], 15-Tweedy

#4773, 1-Tweedy, Eliza Jane, 2-married, 3-1867, 15-Tweedy

#4774, 1-Tweedy, Mary Ann, 2-married, 3-May 1871, 15-Tweedy

#4775, 1-Tweedy, Samuel, 2-married, 3-1878, 15-Tweedy

#4776, 1-Tweedy, Martha, 2-married, 3-11 Jun 1884, 15-Tweedy

#4777, 1-Stapleford, Edmund, 2-married, 3-8 Jun 1898, 4-Merritton, 7-Dale, Lillie, 8-St. Catharines, 9-Thorold, 15-Stapleford

#4778, 1-Stapleford, Edmund, 2-born, 3-26 Jul 1872, 4-St. Catharines, 15-Stapleford

#4779, 1-Stapleford, Lillie, 2-born, 3-17 Jun 1874, 4-Thorold, 15-Stapleford

#4780, 1-Stapleford, Edmund Russell Blake, 2-born, 3-11 Jul 1901, 4-St. Catharines, 15-Stapleford

#4781, 1-Stapleford, Lillie Dale, 2-born, 3-31 Sep 1903, 4-St. Catharines, 15-Stapleford

#4782, 1-Dunn, Jane Elizabeth, 2-obituary, 3-Thursday, 8 Mar 1917, 4-Thorold, 5-75 years, 6-buried Lakeview Cemetery, 7-Dunn, W.H., 15-Stapleford

#4783, 1-Dunn, William Henwood, 2-obituary, 3-16 Sun 1917, 4-Thorold, 5-77 years 7 months 10 days, 6-buried Lakeview Cemetery, Thorold, 15-Stapleford

#4784, 1-Dale, James, 2-obituary, 15-Stapleford

#4785, 1-Spealman, Mary Ann, 2-born, 3-27 Aug 1818, 12-Spealman, John, 15-Spielman

#4786, 1-Spealman, Susan, 2-born, 3-14 Jul 1820, 12-Spealman, John, 15-Spielman

FAMILY BIBLE RECORDS IN THE WASHINGTON COUNTY FREE LIBRARY, HAGERSTOWN, MARYLAND

Entry #, 1-Last Name, First Name, 2-Event, 3-Date, 4-Event Location, 5-Age, 6-Other,
7-Spouse's Last, First, 8-Groom's Residence, 9-Bride's Residence, 10-Minister, 11-Minister's Location,
12-Father's Last, First, 13-Mother's Last, First, 14-Transcribed, 15-Family Bible

#4787, 1-Spealman, William H., 2-born, 3-30 Jan 1822, 12-Spealman, John, 15-Spielman
#4788, 1-Spealman, Jacob, 2-born, 3-17 Jan 1824, 12-Spealman, John, 15-Spielman
#4789, 1-Spealman, John, 2-born, 3-3 Mar 1826, 12-Spealman, John, 15-Spielman
#4790, 1-Spealman, Joseph, 2-born, 3-5 Nov 1827, 12-Spealman, John, 15-Spielman
#4791, 1-Spealman, David, 2-born, 3-8 Oct 1829, 12-Spealman, John, 15-Spielman
#4792, 1-Spealman, Daniel, 2-born, 3-11 Jul 1831, 12-Spealman, John, 15-Spielman
#4793, 1-Spealman, Emanuel, 2-born, 3-11 Sep 1833, 12-Spealman, John, 15-Spielman
#4794, 1-Spealman, Ezra, 2-born, 3-3 Dec 1835, 12-Spealman, John, 15-Spielman
#4795, 1-Spealman, Ezra, 2-died, 3-16 Nov 1915, 5-79 years 11 months, 12-Spealman, John, 15-Spielman
#4796, 1-Spealman, Losson, 2-born, 3-3 Mar 1838, 6-buried Chadwick Cemetery, 12-Spealman, John, 15-Spielman
#4797, 1-Sigler, Mary, 2-born, 3-20 Feb 1794, 12-Spealman, John, 15-Spielman
#4798, 1-Sigler, Mary, 2-died, 3-1874, 5-80 years 9 months, 12-Spealman, John, 15-Spielman
#4799, 1-Spealman, John [father], 2-born, 3-17 Jul 1800, 15-Spielman
#4800, 1-Spealman, John [father], 2-died, 3-30 Jul 185_[?], 15-Spielman
#4801, 1-Spealman, John, 2-died, 3-6 Mar 1839, 15-Spielman
#4802, 1-Spealman, Sr., John, 2-died, 3-30 Jul 1850, 15-Spielman
#4803, 1-Spealman, Emanuel, 2-died, 3-1 Jul 1893, 4-Carroll Co., IL, 15-Spielman
#4804, 1-Spealman, Lawson, 2-died, 3-6 Jun 1894, 4-Chadwick, Carroll Co., IL, 15-Spielman
#4805, 1-Spealman, Sr., Mary, 2-died, 3-1874, 15-Spielman
#4806, 1-Spielman, Ezra, 2-died, 3-16 Nov 1915, 5-79 years 11 months, 15-Spielman
#4807, 1-Spielman, Mary Elizabeth, 2-died, 3-1902, 5-69 years, 7-Spielman, Ezra, 15-Spielman
#4808, 1-Spielman, Wm., 2-died, 3-19 Jul 1889, 5-67 years 6 months, 15-Spielman
#4809, 1-Spielman, Ann, 2-died, 3-9 May 1878, 5-53 years 7 months, 7-Spielman, Wm., 15-Spielman
#4810, 1-Spielman, Jacob, 2-born, 3-13 ___ 1805, 15-Spielman
#4811, 1-Spielman, Jacob, 2-died, 3-1 Sep 1847, 5-11 years 9 months 18 days, 6-[note discrepancy in dates of birth, death, and age], 15-Spielman
#4812, 1-Spielman, Joseph, 2-died, 3-1907, 6-buried Chadwick[?] Cemetery, Carroll Co., IL, 15-Spielman
#4813, 1-Spielman, Emanuel, 2-died, 3-1 Jul 1893, 6-buried Chadwick[?] Cemetery, Carroll Co., IL, 15-Spielman
#4814, 1-Spielman, Mary Ann, 2-married, 3-26 Sep 1840, 15-Spielman
#4815, 1-Spielaman, Jason, 2-married, 3-14 Jan 1842, 15-Spielman
#4816, 1-Spielman, Jacob, 2-married, 3-23 Apr 1846, 15-Spielman
#4817, 1-Spielman, Emanuel, 2-married, 3-1 Oct 1871, 7-Tigh, Margery, 15-Spielman
#4818, 1-Spielman, Effie May, 2-married, 3-15 Jan 1896, 4-Chadwick, Carroll Co., IL, 7-Wbee[?], Henry, 15-Spielman
#4819, 1-Spielman, Harvey Loomer[?], 2-married, 3-20 Jun 1901, 7-Showalter, Olive Stover[?], 15-Spielman
#4820, 1-Spielman, Martin Lewis[?], 2-married, 3-5 Feb 1903, 7-Stover, Mae Elverta[?], 15-Spielman
#4821, 1-Spielman, Herbert, 2-married, 3-8 Jun 1937, 7-Strawn[?], Juanita, 12-Spealman, Harvey, 15-Spielman
#4822, 1-Spielman, Violet, 2-married, 3-18 Jan 1920[?], 4-Mt. Carroll, IL, 7-Frank, John[?], 15-Spielman
#4823, 1-Spielman, Evelyn, 6-entry is unreadable, 15-Spielman
#4824, 1-Spealman, William H., 2-married, 3-12 Jun 1849, 7-Spealman, Ann M., 15-Spielman
#4825, 1-Spealman, William H., 2-born, 3-30 Jan 1822, 15-Spielman

FAMILY BIBLE RECORDS IN THE WASHINGTON COUNTY FREE LIBRARY, HAGERSTOWN, MARYLAND

**Entry #, 1-Last Name, First Name, 2-Event, 3-Date, 4-Event Location, 5-Age, 6-Other,
7-Spouse's Last, First, 8-Groom's Residence, 9-Bride's Residence, 10-Minister, 11-Minister's Location,
12-Father's Last, First, 13-Mother's Last, First, 14-Transcribed, 15-Family Bible**

```
#4826, 1-Spealman, Ann M., 2-born, 3-27 Sep 1824, 15-Spielman
#4827, 1-Spealman, Barbara E., 2-born, 3-3 Mar 1850, 15-Spielman
#4828, 1-Spealman, Mary Alice, 2-born, 3-8 Nov 1851, 15-Spielman
#4829, 1-Spealman, Anne Mary, 2-born, 3-15 Jun 1854, 6-twin, 15-Spielman
#4830, 1-Spealman, William Henry, 2-born, 3-15 Jun 1854, 6-twin, 15-Spielman
#4831, 1-Spealman, Martha Jane, 2-born, 3-8 Jul 1856, 15-Spielman
#4832, 1-Spielman, George Noah, 2-born, 3-3 Oct 1858, 15-Spielman
#4833, 1-Spielman, Jacob Everett, 2-born, 3-19 Jul 1860, 15-Spielman
#4834, 1-Spielman, Elizabeth, 2-born, 3-9 Dec 1863, 15-Spielman
#4835, 1-Spielman, Harvey A., 2-born, 3-9 Sep 1865, 15-Spielman
#4836, 1-Spielman, Otha Aten.[?], 2-born, 3-15 Mar 1868, 15-Spielman
#4837, 1-Spielman, Jacob Everett, 2-died, 3-5 Mar 1863, 5-2 years 1 months 14 days,
    15-Spielman
#4838, 1-Spielman, Ann M., 2-died, 3-9 May 1878, 5-53 years 7 months 12 days, 15-
    Spielman
#4839, 1-Spielman, William H., 2-died, 3-19 Jul 1889, 5-67 years 5 months 19 days,
    15-Spielman
#4840, 1-Spielman, Mary M. , 2-died, 3-11 Oct 1874, 5-80 years 9 months 21 days, 6-
    "grandmother", 15-Spielman
#4841, 1-Spielman, Mary M. , 2-born, 3-20 Dec 1793, 6-"grandmother", 15-Spielman
#4842, 1-Hellane, Louisa, 2-obituary, 3-25 Oct 1858, 5-12 years 4 months 25 days,
    15-Spielman
#4843, 1-Rhorback, Cornelius, 2-obituary, 3-2 Nov 1858, 4-Sharpsburg, MD, 5-31
    years 2 months 1 days, 15-Spielman
#4844, 1-Rohrback, William Wagner, 2-obituary, 3-16 Jun 1859, 4-Sharpsburg, MD, 5-1
    years 7 months, 12-Rohrback, Franklin, 13-Rohrback, Ann S., 15-Spielman
#4845, 1-Rohrback, William, 2-obituary, 3-2 Jul 1859, 4-Sharpsburg, MD, 5-74 years
    5 months 25 days, 15-Spielman
#4846, 1-Rohrback, Joseph L., 2-obituary, 3-20 Oct, 4-Sharpsburg, MD, 5-28 years 5
    months, 15-Spielman
#4847, 1-Rohrback, Mary (Mrs.), 2-obituary, 3-24 Aug 1866, 4-Sharpsburg, MD, 5-66
    years, 7-Rohrback, Jacob (Col.), 15-Spielman
#4848, 1-Schaeffer, Sophia C. (Mrs.), 2-obituary, 4-Berlin, Frederick Co., 5-25
    years 2 months 21 days, 7-Schaeffer, Frederick, 15-Spielman
#4849, 1-Spielman, Mary M. (Mrs.), 2-obituary, 3-1874, 4-Monroe, 5-__[?] years 9
    months 21 days, 15-Spielman
#4850, 1-Spielman, Anna M. (Mrs.), 2-obituary, 3-9 ___ 1878, 4-Keedysville, MD, 5-
    53 years 7 months 12 days, 7-Spielman, William, 15-Spielman
#4851, 1-Cost, Barbara E., 2-died, 3-8 Sep 1912, 5-62 years 6 months 5 days, 15-
    Spielman
#4852, 1-Cost, Conatencims[?] S., 2-died, 3-6 Apr 1911, 15-Spielman
#4853, 1-Divelbiss, Mary A.[?], 2-died, 3-3 Aug 1910, 5-58 years 8 months 26 days,
    15-Spielman
#4854, 1-Divelbiss, John, 2-died, 3-3 Aug 1910, 15-Spielman
#4855, 1-Spielman[?], Mary Magdalene, 2-born, 3-20 Dec 1793[?], 15-Spielman
#4856, 1-Spielman[?], Mary Magdalene, 2-died, 3-11 Oct 1874, 5-80 years 9 months 21
    days, 15-Spielman
#4857, 1-Spielman, Sr., William H., 2-born, 3-30 Jan 1822, 15-Spielman
#4858, 1-Spielman, Sr., William H., 2-died, 3-19 Jul 1889, 5-67 years 5 months 19
    days, 15-Spielman
#4859, 1-Spielman, Anna Mary, 2-born, 3-27 Sep 1824, 7-Spielman, Sr., William H.,
    15-Spielman
#4860, 1-Spielman, Anna Mary, 2-died, 3-9 May 1878, 5-53 years 7 months 12 days,
    15-Spielman
```

FAMILY BIBLE RECORDS IN THE WASHINGTON COUNTY FREE LIBRARY, HAGERSTOWN, MARYLAND

Entry #, 1-Last Name, First Name, 2-Event, 3-Date, 4-Event Location, 5-Age, 6-Other,
7-Spouse's Last, First, 8-Groom's Residence, 9-Bride's Residence, 10-Minister, 11-Minister's Location,
12-Father's Last, First, 13-Mother's Last, First, 14-Transcribed, 15-Family Bible

```
#4861, 1-Spielman, Barbara Ellen, 2-born, 3-3 Mar 1850, 7-Cost, 12-Spielman, Sr.,
    William H., 13-Spielman, Anna Mary, 15-Spielman
#4862, 1-Spielman, Barbara Ellen, 2-died, 3-8 Sep 1912, 5-62 years 6 months 5 days,
    12-Spielman, Sr., William H., 13-Spielman, Anna Mary, 15-Spielman
#4863, 1-Spielman, Mary Alice, 2-born, 3-8 Nov 1851, 7-Divelbiss, 12-Spielman, Sr.,
    William H., 13-Spielman, Anna Mary, 15-Spielman
#4864, 1-Spielman, Mary Alice, 2-died, 3-4 Aug 1910, 5-58 years 8 months 27 days,
    12-Spielman, Sr., William H., 13-Spielman, Anna Mary, 15-Spielman
#4865, 1-Spielman, Anna Mary, 2-born, 3-15 Jun 1854, 6-twin, 7-Jennings, 12-
    Spielman, Sr., William H., 13-Spielman, Anna Mary, 15-Spielman
#4866, 1-Spielman, Anna Mary, 2-died, 3-27 Mar 1934, 12-Spielman, Sr., William H.,
    13-Spielman, Anna Mary, 15-Spielman
#4867, 1-Spielman, William Henry, 2-born, 3-15 Jun 1854, 6-twin, 12-Spielman, Sr.,
    William H., 13-Spielman, Anna Mary, 15-Spielman
#4868, 1-Spielman, William Henry, 2-died, 3-24 Mar 1937, 12-Spielman, Sr., William
    H., 13-Spielman, Anna Mary, 15-Spielman
#4869, 1-Spielman, Martha Jane, 2-born, 3-8 Jul 1856, 7-Line, 12-Spielman, Sr.,
    William H., 13-Spielman, Anna Mary, 15-Spielman
#4870, 1-Spielman, Martha Jane, 2-died, 3-23 Oct 1919, 5-63 years 3 months 15 days,
    12-Spielman, Sr., William H., 13-Spielman, Anna Mary, 15-Spielman
#4871, 1-Spielman, George Noah, 2-born, 3-3 Oct 1858, 12-Spielman, Sr., William H.,
    13-Spielman, Anna Mary, 15-Spielman
#4872, 1-Spielman, George Noah, 2-died, 3-Sep 1931, 12-Spielman, Sr., William H.,
    13-Spielman, Anna Mary, 15-Spielman
#4873, 1-Spielman, Jacob Everett, 2-born, 3-19 Jul 1860, 12-Spielman, Sr., William
    H., 13-Spielman, Anna Mary, 15-Spielman
#4874, 1-Spielman, Jacob Everett, 2-died, 3-Mar, 5-2 years 7 months, 12-Spielman,
    Sr., William H., 13-Spielman, Anna Mary, 15-Spielman
#4875, 1-Spielman, Elizabeth Catherine, 2-born, 3-9 Dec 1862, 7-Huffer, 12-
    Spielman, Sr., William H., 13-Spielman, Anna Mary, 15-Spielman
#4876, 1-Spielman, Harvey Albert, 2-born, 3-9 Sep 1865, 12-Spielman, Sr., William
    H., 13-Spielman, Anna Mary, 15-Spielman
#4877, 1-Spielman, Otha Allen, 2-born, 3-15 Mar 1868, 12-Spielman, Sr., William H.,
    13-Spielman, Anna Mary, 15-Spielman
#4878, 1-Rohrback, Henry, 2-born, 3-17 Jan 1783, 15-Spielman
#4879, 1-Rohrback, Henry, 2-died, 3-7 Aug 1851, 5-68 years 7 months, 15-Spielman
#4880, 1-Barks, Barbara, 2-born, 3-18 Aug 1785, 7-Rohrback, Henry, 15-Spielman
#4881, 1-Barks, Barbara, 2-died, 3-30 Sep 1855, 5-70 years 1 months 12 days, 7-
    Rohrback, Henry, 15-Spielman
#4882, 1-Rohrback, John H., 2-born, 3-4 Sep 1806, 12-Rohrback, Henry, 13-Barks,
    Barbara, 15-Spielman
#4883, 1-Rohrback, John H., 2-died, 3-11 Oct 1833, 5-27 years 1 months 7 days, 12-
    Rohrback, Henry, 13-Barks, Barbara, 15-Spielman
#4884, 1-Rohrback, Elizabeth, 2-born, 3-13 Nov 1807, 7-Yerty (1st husband); Nichols
    (2nd husband), 12-Rohrback, Henry, 13-Barks, Barbara, 15-Spielman
#4885, 1-Rohrback, Elizabeth, 2-died, 3-6 Aug 1888, 5-80 years 8 months 24 days,
    12-Rohrback, Henry, 13-Barks, Barbara, 15-Spielman
#4886, 1-Rohrback, Mary, 2-born, 3-23 Feb 1809, 7-Hout, 12-Rohrback, Henry, 13-
    Barks, Barbara, 15-Spielman
#4887, 1-Rohrback, Mary, 2-died, 3-4 Jan 1887, 5-77 years 10 months 12 days, 12-
    Rohrback, Henry, 13-Barks, Barbara, 15-Spielman
#4888, 1-Rohrback, Catherine, 2-born, 3-12 Dec 1810, 7-Hoskins, 12-Rohrback, Henry,
    13-Barks, Barbara, 15-Spielman
#4889, 1-Rohrback, Catherine, 2-died, 3-4 Apr 1886, 5-75 years 3 months 23 days,
    12-Rohrback, Henry, 13-Barks, Barbara, 15-Spielman
```

FAMILY BIBLE RECORDS IN THE WASHINGTON COUNTY FREE LIBRARY, HAGERSTOWN, MARYLAND

Entry #, 1-Last Name, First Name, 2-Event, 3-Date, 4-Event Location, 5-Age, 6-Other, 7-Spouse's Last, First, 8-Groom's Residence, 9-Bride's Residence, 10-Minister, 11-Minister's Location, 12-Father's Last, First, 13-Mother's Last, First, 14-Transcribed, 15-Family Bible

#4890, 1-Rohrback, Jacob H., 2-born, 3-29 Nov 1812, 12-Rohrback, Henry, 13-Barks, Barbara, 15-Spielman

#4891, 1-Rohrback, Jacob H., 2-died, 3-14 Jul 1864, 5-51 years 7 months 5 days, 12-Rohrback, Henry, 13-Barks, Barbara, 15-Spielman

#4892, 1-Rohrback, Henry B., 2-born, 3-29 Nov 1812, 12-Rohrback, Henry, 13-Barks, Barbara, 15-Spielman

#4893, 1-Rohrback, Henry B., 2-died, 3-29 Dec 1890, 5-78 years 1 months, 12-Rohrback, Henry, 13-Barks, Barbara, 15-Spielman

#4894, 1-Rohrback, Daniel, 2-born, 3-10 Apr 1815, 12-Rohrback, Henry, 13-Barks, Barbara, 15-Spielman

#4895, 1-Rohrback, Daniel, 2-died, 3-19 Jan 1877, 5-61 years 9 months 9 days, 12-Rohrback, Henry, 13-Barks, Barbara, 15-Spielman

#4896, 1-Rohrback, Barbara, 2-born, 3-9 Apr 1817, 7-Hedrick, 12-Rohrback, Henry, 13-Barks, Barbara, 15-Spielman

#4897, 1-Rohrback, Barbara, 2-died, 3-4 Feb 1857, 5-39 years 9 months 26 days, 12-Rohrback, Henry, 13-Barks, Barbara, 15-Spielman

#4898, 1-Rohrback, Elias, 2-born, 3-16 Feb 1820, 12-Rohrback, Henry, 13-Barks, Barbara, 15-Spielman

#4899, 1-Rohrback, Elias, 2-died, 3-21 Nov 1862, 5-42 years 9 months 5 days, 12-Rohrback, Henry, 13-Barks, Barbara, 15-Spielman

#4900, 1-Rohrback, Noah, 2-born, 3-13 Aug 1822, 12-Rohrback, Henry, 13-Barks, Barbara, 15-Spielman

#4901, 1-Rohrback, Noah, 2-died, 3-31 Jan 1881, 5-58 years 4 months 20 days, 12-Rohrback, Henry, 13-Barks, Barbara, 15-Spielman

#4902, 1-Rohrback, Anna Mary, 2-born, 3-27 Sep 1824, 7-Spielman, 12-Rohrback, Henry, 13-Barks, Barbara, 15-Spielman

#4903, 1-Rohrback, Anna Mary, 2-died, 3-9 May 1878, 5-58 years 7 months 12 days, 12-Rohrback, Henry, 13-Barks, Barbara, 15-Spielman

#4904, 1-Rohrback, Cornelius, 2-born, 3-1 Sep 1827, 12-Rohrback, Henry, 13-Barks, Barbara, 15-Spielman

#4905, 1-Rohrback, Cornelius, 2-died, 3-2 Nov 1858, 5-31 years 2 months 1 days, 12-Rohrback, Henry, 13-Barks, Barbara, 15-Spielman

#4906, 1-Show, John Andrew, 2-born, 3-20 Nov 1859, 14-Yes, 15-Show

#4907, 1-Show, Ann Mary, 2-born, 3-2 May 1861, 14-Yes, 15-Show

#4908, 1-Show, Margaret Elizabeth, 2-born, 3-18 Mar 1864, 14-Yes, 15-Show

#4909, 1-Show, Charles W., 2-born, 14-Yes, 15-Show

#4910, 1-Show, Annie F., 2-born, 14-Yes, 15-Show

#4911, 1-Show, Willmina M.V., 2-born, 3-19 Oct 1872, 14-Yes, 15-Show

#4912, 1-Show, Jr., William Henry, 2-born, 3-26 May 1875, 14-Yes, 15-Show

#4913, 1-Show, Sarah Cathien, 2-born, 3-21 Oct 1879, 14-Yes, 15-Show

#4914, 1-Show, George Elmer, 2-born, 3-24 Mar 1880, 14-Yes, 15-Show

#4915, 1-Show, John Andrew, 2-died, 3-6 May 1892, 14-Yes, 15-Show

#4916, 1-Show, Ann Mary, 2-died, 3-18 Nov 1862, 14-Yes, 15-Show

#4917, 1-Show, Willmina M.V., 2-died, 3-3 Feb 1942, 14-Yes, 15-Show

#4918, 1-Show, Jr., William Henry, 2-died, 3-14 Jul 1926, 14-Yes, 15-Show

#4919, 1-Show, George Elmer, 2-died, 3-29 Aug 1880, 14-Yes, 15-Show

#4920, 1-Show, Amelia Catherine McCoy, 2-died, 3-14 Nov 1899, 14-Yes, 15-Show

#4921, 1-Ecton, Charles William, 2-born, 3-26 Dec 1889, 14-Yes, 15-Show

#4922, 1-Ecton, Flossie Virginia, 2-born, 3-11 Nov 1891, 14-Yes, 15-Show

#4923, 1-Ecton, Mary Cathern, 2-born, 3-18 Dec 1894, 14-Yes, 15-Show

#4924, 1-Ecton, Mary Frances, 2-born, 3-13 Dec 1898, 14-Yes, 15-Show

#4925, 1-Show, John Andrew, 2-married, 3-May 1886, 7-Ecton, Sarah Jane, 14-Yes, 15-Show

#4926, 1-Show, Margaret Elizabeth, 2-married, 3-23 Dec 1886, 7-Ecton, Charles R., 14-Yes, 15-Show

FAMILY BIBLE RECORDS IN THE WASHINGTON COUNTY FREE LIBRARY, HAGERSTOWN, MARYLAND

Entry #, 1-Last Name, First Name, 2-Event, 3-Date, 4-Event Location, 5-Age, 6-Other,
7-Spouse's Last, First, 8-Groom's Residence, 9-Bride's Residence, 10-Minister, 11-Minister's Location,
12-Father's Last, First, 13-Mother's Last, First, 14-Transcribed, 15-Family Bible

```
#4927, 1-Show, Charles W., 2-married, 3-24 May 1889, 7-Benner, Viola, 14-Yes, 15-
    Show
#4928, 1-Show, Annie F., 2-married, 3-1 Jan 1889, 6-[note the Viola Benner is
    listed twice], 7-Benner [sic], Viola [sic], 14-Yes, 15-Show
#4929, 1-Show, Annie F., 2-married, 3-24 Jan 1889, 7-Jacobs, William, 14-Yes, 15-
    Show
#4930, 1-Show, Willmina M.V., 2-married, 3-17 Jul 1892, 7-Koontz, Henry C., 14-Yes,
    15-Show
#4931, 1-Show, Jr., William Henry, 2-married, Sarah J., 14-Yes, 15-Show
#4932, 1-Roulette, William, 2-born, 3-11 Jul 1825, 15-Roulette
#4933, 1-Roulette, Margaret Ann, 2-born, 3-12 Oct 1829, 7-Roulette, William, 15-
    Roulette
#4934, 1-Roulette, Annie Elizabeth, 2-born, 3-16 Jul 1849, 15-Roulette
#4935, 1-Roulette, John Daniel, 2-born, 3-23 Apr 1851, 15-Roulette
#4936, 1-Roulette, Joseph Clinton, 2-born, 3-22 Jun 1852, 15-Roulette
#4937, 1-Roulette, Otho William, 2-born, 3-6 Oct 1853, 15-Roulette
#4938, 1-Roulette, Susan Rebecca, 2-born, 3-27 Jan 1857, 15-Roulette
#4939, 1-Roulette, Benjamin Franklin, 2-born, 3-29 Aug 1858, 15-Roulette
#4940, 1-Roulette, Carrie May, 2-born, 3-23 Feb 1860, 15-Roulette
#4941, 1-Roulette, Ulyssis Sheridan, 2-born, 3-15 Oct 1864, 15-Roulette
#4942, 1-Miller, Absam, 2-born, 3-31 Jul 1831, 15-Roulette
#4943, 1-Roulette, William, 2-married, 3-4 Mar 1847, 7-Miller, Margaret Ann, 15-
    Roulette
#4944, 1-Roulette, William, 2-married, 3-19 Jun 1889, 4-Lancaster, PA, 7-Smith,
    Elizabeth B.G., 10-Rev. _____ Gerhert, 15-Roulette
#4945, 1-Roulette, Otho William, 2-died, 3-12 Jul 1856, 15-Roulette
#4946, 1-Roulette, Carrie May, 2-died, 3-21 Oct 1862, 15-Roulette
#4947, 1-Roulette, Margaret Ann, 2-died, 3-19 Feb 1883, 15-Roulette
#4948, 1-Roulette, William, 2-died, 3-27 Feb 1901, 15-Roulette
#4949, 1-Rowland, John S., 2-married, 3-6 Oct 1825, 7-Gossart[?], Nancy, 15-Rowland
#4950, 1-Rowland, Ann _____, 2-married, 3-15 Oct 1850, 7-Wodf[?], Daniel, 15-
    Rowland
#4951, 1-Rowland, Benjamin, 2-married, 3-9 Jan 1855, 7-Funk[?], Elisa, 15-Rowland
#4952, 1-Rowland, Lena, 2-married, 3-7 Jan 1858[?], 7-McCauley, James, 15-Rowland
#4953, 1-Rowland, Catharine, 2-married, 3-9 Jan 1859, 7-Funk, Solmin[?], 15-Rowland
#4954, 1-Rowland, Joseph M., 2-married, 3-Oct 1866, 7-Emmert[?], [?], 15-Rowland
#4955, 1-Rowland, Nancy H., 2-married, 3-10 May 1867, 7-Hitt, John W., 15-Rowland
#4956, 1-Rowland, Mary E., 2-married, 3-1 Jan 1868, 7-Marshall[?], George H., 15-
    Rowland
#4957, 1-Rowland, John E., 2-married, 3-4 Mar 1868, 7-McCauley, Lizzie, 15-Rowland
#4958, 1-Rowland, Henry, 2-born, 3-24 May 1750[?], 4-Lancaster Co., PA, 15-Rowland
#4959, 1-Rowland, Mary (Shively), 2-born, 3-20 Aug 1755, 4-Franklin Co., PA, 15-
    Rowland
#4960, 1-Rowland, John Shively, 2-born, 3-22 Mar 1795, 4-Washington Co., MD, 15-
    Rowland
#4961, 1-Rowland, Nancy Emmert, 2-born, 3-12 Sep 1803, 4-Washington Co., MD, 15-
    Rowland
#4962, 1-Rowland, Benjamin Henry, 2-born, 3-19 Oct 1826, 15-Rowland
#4963, 1-Rowland, Ann Maria, 2-born, 3-19 Dec 1820[?], 15-Rowland
#4964, 1-Rowland, Catharine, 2-born, 3-8 Jan 1831, 15-Rowland
#4965, 1-Rowland, Lena, 2-born, 3-Sunday, 10 Mar 1833, 4-Washington Co., MD, 15-
    Rowland
#4966, 1-Rowland, Nancy H., 2-born, 3-22 Oct 1835, 15-Rowland
#4967, 1-Rowland, John Emmert, 2-born, 3-13 Oct 1837, 15-Rowland
#4968, 1-Rowland, Mary Ellen, 2-born, 3-4 Aug 1840, 15-Rowland
```

FAMILY BIBLE RECORDS IN THE WASHINGTON COUNTY FREE LIBRARY, HAGERSTOWN, MARYLAND

Entry #, 1-Last Name, First Name, 2-Event, 3-Date, 4-Event Location, 5-Age, 6-Other, 7-Spouse's Last, First, 8-Groom's Residence, 9-Bride's Residence, 10-Minister, 11-Minister's Location, 12-Father's Last, First, 13-Mother's Last, First, 14-Transcribed, 15-Family Bible

```
#4969, 1-Rowland, Joseph Martin, 2-born, 3-19 Dec 1842, 15-Rowland
#4970, 1-Rowland, Samuel David, 2-born, 3-15 Apr 1846, 15-Rowland
#4971, 1-Rowland, Henry, 2-died, 3-30 Jan 1833, 5-82 years 8 months 8 days, 15-
    Rowland
#4972, 1-Rowland, Mary (Shively), 2-died, 3-10 Oct 1831, 5-76 years 1 months 20
    days, 15-Rowland
#4973, 1-Rowland, Benjamin H., 2-died, 3-4 Aug 1863, 5-36 years 9 months 5 days,
    15-Rowland
#4974, 1-Rowland, Samuel David, 2-died, 3-24 May 1848, 5-2 years 1 months 9 days,
    15-Rowland
#4975, 1-Rowland, John Shively, 2-died, 3-1 May 1898, 5-83 years 1 months 8 days,
    15-Rowland
#4976, 1-Rowland, Nancy Emmert, 2-died, 3-4 Mar 1903, 5-99 years 5 months 23 days,
    15-Rowland
#4977, 1-Rowland, John Emmert[?], 2-died, 3-23 Feb 1904, 5-66 years 4 months 10
    days, 15-Rowland
#4978, 1-Rowland, Ann Maria, 2-died, 3-21 Oct 1912, 5-83 years 10 months __ days,
    12-[?], John, 13-Rowland, Nancy, 15-Rowland
#4979, 1-Funk, Solomon, 2-died, 3-23 Dec 1874, 5-72 years, 15-Rowland
#4980, 1-Wolf, Daniel, 2-died, 3-18 Aug 1899, 5-74 years, 15-Rowland
#4981, 1-McCauley, James, 2-died, 3-Mar 1902, 5-72 years, 15-Rowland
#4982, 1-Hitt, John Wesley, 2-died, 3-3 Sep 1903[?], 5-72 years, 15-Rowland
#4983, 1-Rowland, Eliza, 2-died, 3-Mar 1901, 7-Rowland, Benjamin, 15-Rowland
#4984, 1-Hitt, Nancy, 2-died, 3-28[?] Aug 1913, 5-77 years 10 months 2 days, 7-
    Hitt, John W., 15-Rowland
#4985, 1-McCauley, Lena R., 2-died, 3-14 Jan 1918, 5-84 years 11 months, 7-
    McCauley, James, 15-Rowland
#4986, 1-Rohrer, Henry, 2-born, 3-28 Aug 1826, 12-Rohrer, Jr., John M., 13-Rohrer,
    Mary, 15-Rohrer
#4987, 1-Rohrer, Joseph, 2-born, 3-15 Sep 1828, 12-Rohrer, Jr., John M., 13-Rohrer,
    Mary, 15-Rohrer
#4988, 1-Rohrer, David, 2-born, 3-28 Sep 1830, 12-Rohrer, Jr., John M., 13-Rohrer,
    Mary, 15-Rohrer
#4989, 1-Rohrer, John, 2-born, 3-11 Oct 1832, 12-Rohrer, Jr., John M., 13-Rohrer,
    Mary, 15-Rohrer
#4990, 1-Rohrer, William, 2-born, 3-17 Apr 1835, 12-Rohrer, Jr., John M., 13-
    Rohrer, Mary, 15-Rohrer
#4991, 1-Rohrer, Winfield S.[?], 2-born, 3-13 Oct 1852, 12-Rohrer, Jr., John M.,
    13-Rohrer, Mary, 15-Rohrer
#4992, 1-Rohrer, Margaret Ellen, 2-born, 3-26 Apr 1837, 12-Rohrer, Jr., John M.,
    13-Rohrer, Mary, 15-Rohrer
#4993, 1-Rohrer, Sophia Jane, 2-born, 3-26 Oct 1839, 12-Rohrer, Jr., John M., 13-
    Rohrer, Mary, 15-Rohrer
#4994, 1-Rohrer, Maryan ____[?], 2-born, 3-18 Jan 1842, 12-Rohrer, Jr., John M.,
    13-Rohrer, Mary, 15-Rohrer
#4995, 1-Rohrer, Martha E., 2-born, 3-15[?] Feb 1844, 12-Rohrer, Jr., John M., 13-
    Rohrer, Mary, 15-Rohrer
#4996, 1-Rohrer, Jacob A., 2-born, 3-29 Dec 1846, 12-Rohrer, Jr., John M., 13-
    Rohrer, Mary, 15-Rohrer
#4997, 1-Rohrer, Jr., John M., 2-born, 3-16 Jan 1804, 12-Rohrer, John M., 13-
    Rohrer, Elizabeth, 15-Rohrer
#4998, 1-Heldabrand, Mary, 2-born, 3-13 Nov 1806, 12-Heldabrand, Jacob, 13-
    Heldabrand, Maryan M., 15-Rohrer
#4999, 1-Rohrer, Harriet Matilda, 2-born, 3-29 Jun 1849, 12-Rohrer, Jr., John M.,
    13-Rohrer, Mary, 15-Rohrer
```

FAMILY BIBLE RECORDS IN THE WASHINGTON COUNTY FREE LIBRARY, HAGERSTOWN, MARYLAND

Entry #, 1-Last Name, First Name, 2-Event, 3-Date, 4-Event Location, 5-Age, 6-Other,
7-Spouse's Last, First, 8-Groom's Residence, 9-Bride's Residence, 10-Minister, 11-Minister's Location,
12-Father's Last, First, 13-Mother's Last, First, 14-Transcribed, 15-Family Bible

```
#5000, 1-Rohrer, David, 2-died, 3-66 Nov 1833, 12-Rohrer, Jr., John M., 13-Rohrer,
    Mary, 15-Rohrer
#5001, 1-Rohrer, William, 2-died, 3-26 Feb 1837, 12-Rohrer, Jr., John M., 13-
    Rohrer, Mary, 15-Rohrer
#5002, 1-Rohrer, Harriet Matilda, 2-died, 3-11 Sep 1850, 12-Rohrer, Jr., John M.,
    13-Rohrer, Mary, 15-Rohrer
#5003, 1-Rohrer, Flora M., 2-died, 3-5 Oct 1918, 12-Rohrer, Jacob M., 13-Rohrer,
    Lillie M., 15-Rohrer
#5004, 1-Rohrer, Edgar F.[?], 2-died, 3-10-Oct-18, 12-Rohrer, Jacob M., 13-Rohrer,
    Lillie M., 15-Rohrer
#5005, 1-Beachley, Cora R., 2-died, 3-19 Oct 1911[or 17?], 12-Rohrer, Jacob M., 13-
    Rohrer, Lillie M., 15-Rohrer
#5006, 1-Rohrer, Clarence Henry, 2-died, 3-21 Oct 1966, 15-Rohrer
#5007, 1-Rohrer, Albert Martin, 2-died, 3-7 Aug 1880, 5-9 months 2 days, 12-Rohrer,
    Jacob M., 13-Rohrer, Lillie M., 15-Rohrer
#5008, 1-Rohrer, Jacob M., 2-died, 3-26 Aug 1___[?], 6-"father", 15-Rohrer
#5009, 1-Rohrer, Lillie M. , 2-died, 3-11 Jun 1929[?], 6-"mother", 15-Rohrer
#5010, 1-Rohrer, Corah[?] Ellen, 2-born, 3-20 Jan 1881, 12-Rohrer, Jacob M., 13-
    Rohrer, Lillie M., 15-Rohrer
#5011, 1-Rohrer, Clarence Henry, 2-born, 3-18 Jul 1882, 12-Rohrer, Jacob M., 13-
    Rohrer, Lillie M., 15-Rohrer
#5012, 1-Rohrer, Florie May, 2-born, 3-21 Jun 1884, 12-Rohrer, Jacob M., 13-Rohrer,
    Lillie M., 15-Rohrer
#5013, 1-Rohrer, Albert Martin, 2-born, 3-5 Nov 1885, 12-Rohrer, Jacob M., 13-
    Rohrer, Lillie M., 15-Rohrer
#5014, 1-Rohrer, Edger Frank, 2-born, 3-1 Dec 1887, 12-Rohrer, Jacob M., 13-Rohrer,
    Lillie M., 15-Rohrer
#5015, 1-Rohrer, Jacob M., 2-married, 3-16 Dec 1879, 7-Rohrer, Lillie M., 15-Rohrer
#5016, 1-Rohrer, Clarence H., 2-married, 3-20 Dec 1910, 7-Rohrer, Anna[?] R., 15-
    Rohrer
#5017, 1-Rohrer, Clarence H., 2-married, 3-24 Jan 1933, 7-Rohrer, Marie C., 15-
    Rohrer
#5018, 1-Rohrer, Ivon Delmar, 2-married, 3-3 Dec 1938, 7-Rohrer, Louise S., 15-
    Rohrer
#5019, 1-Rohrer, Jr., Ivon Delmar, 2-married, 3-11 Nov 1955, 7-Rohrer, Helen H.,
    15-Rohrer
#5020, 1-Ruck, Daniel, 2-married, 3-5 Feb 1885, 4-Hagerstown, MD, 7-Bishop, Kate
    (Miss), 8-Beaver Creek, 9-Smoketown, 10-Rev. J. Spangler Keiffer, 11-1st
    Reformed Church, Hagerstown, 15-Ridenour
#5021, 1-Ridenour, John L., 2-married, 3-28 Jan 1904, 7-Welty, Jennie , 8-Beaver
    Creek, 9-Beaver Creek, 10-Rev. Charles Fisher, 15-Ridenour
#5022, 1-Ruch, Daniel, 2-died, 3-25 Sep 1900, 5-58 years 3 months 4 days, 15-
    Ridenour
#5023, 1-Ruch, Kate (Bishop), 2-died, 3-30 Mar 1933, 5-79 years 6 months 6 days, 7-
    Ruch, Dan'l, 15-Ridenour
#5024, 1-Ridenour, John L., 2-died, 3-25 Apr 1925, 5-54 years 7 months 2 days, 15-
    Ridenour
#5025, 1-Ridenour, Jennie G., 2-died, 3-23 Sep 1932, 5-58 years, 15-Ridenour
#5026, 1-Ruch, Daniel, 2-born, 3-21 Jun 1842, 15-Ridenour
#5027, 1-Ruch, Kate, 2-born, 3-24 Sep 1853, 15-Ridenour
#5028, 1-Ridenour, John L., 2-born, 3-23 Sep 1870, 15-Ridenour
#5029, 1-Ridenour, Jennie Gertrude, 2-born, 3-23 Sep 1874, 15-Ridenour
#5030, 1-Ridenour, Edna Jane, 2-born, 3-21 Dec 1904, 15-Ridenour
#5031, 1-Ridenour, Welty Andrew, 2-born, 3-3 Apr 1906, 15-Ridenour
#5032, 1-Ridenour, Catharine Elizabeth, 2-born, 3-26 Jan 1908, 15-Ridenour
```

FAMILY BIBLE RECORDS IN THE WASHINGTON COUNTY FREE LIBRARY, HAGERSTOWN, MARYLAND

Entry #, 1-Last Name, First Name, 2-Event, 3-Date, 4-Event Location, 5-Age, 6-Other, 7-Spouse's Last, First, 8-Groom's Residence, 9-Bride's Residence, 10-Minister, 11-Minister's Location, 12-Father's Last, First, 13-Mother's Last, First, 14-Transcribed, 15-Family Bible

```
#5033, 1-Ridenour, Doris Gertrude, 2-born, 3-3 Dec 1915, 6-Bright's Disease, 12-
    Kaylor, John W., 13-Kaylor, Isouria, 15-Ridenour
#5034, 1-Kaylor, Mary (Miss), 2-obituary, 4-Beaver Creek, 15-Ridenour
#5035, 1-Foltz, John H., 2-died, 4-Mapleville, MD, 5-76 years 3 months 26 days, 6-
    Paralysis, 15-Ridenour
#5036, 1-Eikelberger, Mary E., 2-born, 3-29 Dec 1896, 15-Ridenour
#5037, 1-Eikelberger, Mary E., 2-died, 3-30 Aug 1969, 6-buried Rest Haven Cemetery,
    15-Ridenour
#5038, 1-Byers, Catherine Oleig (Mrs.), 2-obituary, 5-72 years, 7-Byers, George,
    15-Ridenour
#5039, 1-Muck, Elizabeth Ann (Mrs.), 2-obituary, 4-Hagerstown, MD, 5-77 years, 7-
    Muck, Abraham F., 15-Ridenour
#5040, 1-Eccard, Burnice Susie (Mrs.), 2-obituary, 4-Baltimore, MD, 5-78 years, 7-
    Eccard, Claude G., 12-Ridenour, David, 13-Reese, Lydia, 15-Ridenour
#5041, 1-Krouse, Mazie K. (Mrs.), 2-obituary, 4-Beaver Creek, 5-32 years, 7-Krouse,
    Geo. E., 12-Long, John W., 15-Ridenour
#5042, 1-Waltz, John E.K., 2-married, 3-30 Dec, 4-Beaver Creek, 7-Detrow, Ida S.
    (Miss), 10-Rev. W.S. Hoye, 15-Ridenour
#5043, 1-Wise, William E., 2-married, 3-30 Dec, 4-Boonsboro, MD, 7-Long, Georgia A.
    (Miss), 8-Middletown, MD, 9-Boonsboro, MD, 10-Rev. J.A. Hopkins, 11-Boonsboro
    Christian Church, 15-Ridenour
#5044, 1-Beachley, Laura A. (Mrs.), 2-obituary, 4-Hagerstown, MD, 5-62 years, 6-
    heart trouble, 7-Beachley, Charles E., 15-Ridenour
#5045, 1-Chaney, Laura (Mrs.), 2-obituary, 4-Benevola, 5-72 years, 7-Chaney,
    Ezekiel, 12-Harp, Joshua, 15-Ridenour
#5046, 1-Moore, Mary (Mrs.), 2-obituary, 4-Sharpsburg, MD, 5-82 years, 7-Moore,
    L.T. (Col.), 15-Ridenour
#5047, 1-Faulder, Susan (Mrs.), 2-obituary, 4-South Mountain, 5-32 years 7 months 2
    days, 7-Faulder, Joshua, 12-Beachley, John Henry, 15-Ridenour
#5048, 1-Ridenour, David M., 2-obituary, 5-63 years, 15-Ridenour
#5049, 1-Ridenour, John L., 2-obituary, 4-Mt. Lena, 5-54 years, 6-buried in
    Funkstown cemetery, 15-Ridenour
#5050, 1-Ridenour, Courtney A., 2-obituary, 3-17 Jun, 4-Woodward, 5-88 years, 6-
    buried in Mooreland Cemetery, 15-Ridenour
#5051, 1-Ridenour, Courtney A., 2-born, 3-12 Sep 1886, 4-Boonsboro, MD, 12-
    Ridenour, John, 13-Ridenour, Jane, 15-Ridenour
#5052, 1-Ridenour, Samuel, 2-married, 3-9 May 1833, 7-Burkhart, Elizabeth, 10-Rev.
    Hofhour, 15-Ridenour
#5053, 1-Ridenour, Mary Cornelia, 2-born, 3-6 May 1834, 12-Ridenour, Samuel, 13-
    Burkhart, Elizabeth, 15-Ridenour
#5054, 1-Ridenour, Sophia Ann, 2-born, 3-6 Nov 1836, 12-Ridenour, Samuel, 13-
    Burkhart, Elizabeth, 15-Ridenour
#5055, 1-Ridenour, Laura Virginia, 2-born, 3-22 Sep 1837, 12-Ridenour, Samuel, 13-
    Burkhart, Elizabeth, 15-Ridenour
#5056, 1-Ridenour, Oliver Burkhart, 2-born, 3-16 Jun 1840, 12-Ridenour, Samuel, 13-
    Burkhart, Elizabeth, 15-Ridenour
#5057, 1-Ridenour, Charles Augustus, 2-born, 3-23 Dec 1842, 12-Ridenour, Samuel,
    13-Burkhart, Elizabeth, 15-Ridenour
#5058, 1-Ridenour, Emma Jane, 2-born, 3-6 Mar 1845, 12-Ridenour, Samuel, 13-
    Burkhart, Elizabeth, 15-Ridenour
#5059, 1-Ridenour, James William, 2-born, 3-23 Jun 1847, 12-Ridenour, Samuel, 13-
    Burkhart, Elizabeth, 15-Ridenour
#5060, 1-Ridenour, John Edward, 2-born, 3-29 Nov 1849, 12-Ridenour, Samuel, 13-
    Burkhart, Elizabeth, 15-Ridenour
```

FAMILY BIBLE RECORDS IN THE WASHINGTON COUNTY FREE LIBRARY, HAGERSTOWN, MARYLAND

**Entry #, 1-Last Name, First Name, 2-Event, 3-Date, 4-Event Location, 5-Age, 6-Other,
7-Spouse's Last, First, 8-Groom's Residence, 9-Bride's Residence, 10-Minister, 11-Minister's Location,
12-Father's Last, First, 13-Mother's Last, First, 14-Transcribed, 15-Family Bible**

```
#5061, 1-Ridenour, Alice, 2-born, 3-16 Mar 1851, 12-Ridenour, Samuel, 13-Burkhart,
    Elizabeth, 15-Ridenour
#5062, 1-Ridenour, Frank Leslie, 2-born, 3-21 Nov 1854, 12-Ridenour, Samuel, 13-
    Burkhart, Elizabeth, 15-Ridenour
#5063, 1-Ridenour, Mary Kate, 2-born, 3-13 Oct 1857, 12-Ridenour, Samuel, 13-
    Burkhart, Elizabeth, 15-Ridenour
#5064, 1-Ridenour, Samuel, 2-born, 3-25 Oct 1802, 15-Ridenour
#5065, 1-Burkhart, Elizabeth, 2-born, 3-7 May 1812, 15-Ridenour
#5066, 1-Ridenour, Sophia Ann, 2-died, 3-27 Nov 1836, 15-Ridenour
#5067, 1-Ridenour, Emma Jane, 2-died, 3-14 Aug 1846, 15-Ridenour
#5068, 1-Ridenour, Alice, 2-died, 3-1 Feb 1852, 15-Ridenour
#5069, 1-Ridenour, Frank Leslie, 2-died, 3-13 Jun 1883, 15-Ridenour
#5070, 1-Ridenour, John Edward, 2-died, 3-31 Aug 1888, 5-38 years 9 months 2 days,
    15-Ridenour
#5071, 1-Wantz, Laura Virginia, 2-died, 3-9 Dec 1888, 5-51 years 3 months 17 days,
    15-Ridenour
#5072, 1-Ridenour, Elizabeth, 2-died, 3-7 Jul 1873, 5-61 years 2 months, 15-
    Ridenour
#5073, 1-Ridenour, Samuel, 2-died, 3-20 Feb 1886, 5-83 years 3 months 25 days, 15-
    Ridenour
#5074, 1-Souders, William A., 2-born, 3-30 Sep 1872, 15-Souders
#5075, 1-Souders, Lillie M., 2-born, 3-22 Jul 1874, 15-Souders
#5076, 1-Souders, Birdie M.B., 2-born, 3-18 Feb 1898, 15-Souders
#5077, 1-Souders, Nathan J., 2-born, 3-21 Dec 1899, 15-Souders
#5078, 1-Souders, Daniel L., 2-born, 3-10 Sep 1901, 15-Souders
#5079, 1-Souders, Leon Summers, 2-born, 3-3 Feb 1904, 15-Souders
#5080, 1-Souders, Elcie Elizabeth, 2-born, 3-15 Mar 1905, 15-Souders
#5081, 1-Souders, Lovease Barbria, 2-born, 3-23 Apr 1913, 15-Souders
#5082, 1-Ruck, Ralph R., 2-born, 3-12 Feb 1904, 15-Souders
#5083, 1-Perrott, Oliver, 2-born, 3-5 Jan 1890, 15-Souders
#5084, 1-Souders, Lilly May (Mrs.), 2-died, 3-11 Mar 1918, 15-Souders
#5085, 1-Perrott, Oliver, 2-died, 3-15 Dec 1931, 15-Souders
#5086, 1-Ramsey, W.H., 2-married, 3-21 Nov 1897, 4-Hagerstown, MD, 7-Miller, Flora
    B., 8-Funkstown, MD, 9-Funkstown, MD, 10-Rev. Van Arsdale, 11-Methodist, 15-
    Ramsey
#5087, 1-Ramsey, W.H., 2-born, 3-5 Nov 1871, 4-Beaver Creek, MD, 15-Ramsey
#5088, 1-Ramsey, Flora B., 2-born, 3-9 Sep 1878, 4-Funkstown, MD, 15-Ramsey
#5089, 1-Ramsey, Jessie Beatrice, 2-born, 3-9 Jul 1898, 4-Funkstown, MD, 15-Ramsey
#5090, 1-Ramsey, Chester Sylvester, 2-born, 3-18 Oct 1899, 4-Funkstown, MD, 15-
    Ramsey
#5091, 1-Ramsey, Margaret M., 2-born, 3-25 Sep 1901, 4-Hagestown, MD, 15-Ramsey
#5092, 1-Ramsey, Laura Jane, 2-born, 3-1 Nov 1904, 4-Hagestown, MD, 15-Ramsey
#5093, 1-Ramsey, Lena Gray, 2-born, 3-29 Aug 1906, 4-Hagestown, MD, 15-Ramsey
#5094, 1-Ramsey, Wiliam L., 2-born, 3-20 Jan 1912, 4-Hagestown, MD, 15-Ramsey
#5095, 1-Ramsey, Vivian Belle, 2-born, 3-7 Jul 1914, 4-Funkstown, MD, 15-Ramsey
#5096, 1-Miller, Laura, 2-died, 3-6 Oct 1905, 5-55 years 5 months 6 days, 15-Ramsey
#5097, 1-Miller, Martin L., 2-died, 3-3[?] Sep 1914, 5-63 years, 15-Ramsey
#5098, 1-Ramsey, Sylvester, 2-died, 15-Ramsey
#5099, 1-Ramsey, Flora B., 2-died, 3-24 Jan 1937, 4-Hagerstown, MD, 15-Ramsey
#5100, 1-Ramsey, Sarah J., 2-died, 3-6 Nov 1939, 15-Ramsey
#5101, 1-Poffenberger, Harvey L., 2-married, 3-5 Feb 1890, 4-Hagerstown, MD, 7-
    Myers, N. Effie, 15-Poffenberger
#5102, 1-Poffenberger, Harvey Line, 2-born, 3-22 Aug 1864, 15-Poffenberger
#5103, 1-Myers, Noah Etta, 2-born, 3-25 Apr 1863, 15-Poffenberger
#5104, 1-Poffenberger, Elizabeth Ray, 2-born, 3-1 Jun 1891, 15-Poffenberger
```

FAMILY BIBLE RECORDS IN THE WASHINGTON COUNTY FREE LIBRARY, HAGERSTOWN, MARYLAND

Entry #, 1-Last Name, First Name, 2-Event, 3-Date, 4-Event Location, 5-Age, 6-Other, 7-Spouse's Last, First, 8-Groom's Residence, 9-Bride's Residence, 10-Minister, 11-Minister's Location, 12-Father's Last, First, 13-Mother's Last, First, 14-Transcribed, 15-Family Bible

```
#5105, 1-Poffenberger, Jacob Evans, 2-born, 3-17 Feb 1894, 15-Poffenberger
#5106, 1-Poffenberger, Mary Ann Francis, 2-born, 3-17 Nov 1895, 15-Poffenberger
#5107, 1-Poffenberger, Norman Myers, 2-born, 3-13 Feb 1899, 15-Poffenberger
#5108, 1-Poffenberger, Harvey Cecil, 2-born, 3-16 Feb 1902, 15-Poffenberger
#5109, 1-Poffenberger, Ettie Pauline, 2-born, 3-28 Aug 1907, 15-Poffenberger
#5110, 1-Myers, Charles M., 2-married, 3-3 Jun 1888, 7-Myers, Annie M., 15-
      Poffenberger
#5111, 1-Myers, Evans M., 2-married, 3-12 Jun 1912, 7-Torbitt[?], Bessie, 15-
      Poffenberger
#5112, 1-Myers, Elizabeth, 2-died, 3-13 Jul 1897, 5-59 years 4 months 25 days, 15-
      Poffenberger
#5113, 1-Myers, Elizabeth, 2-born, 3-12 Mar 1838, 15-Poffenberger
#5114, 1-Myers, Jacob A., 2-died, 3-22 Nov 1901, 5-68 years 3 months 14 days, 15-
      Poffenberger
#5115, 1-Myers, Rosa Almy, 2-died, 3-5 May 1861, 5-1 years 4 months 6 days, 15-
      Poffenberger
#5116, 1-Myers, Evans Miller, 2-died, 3-29 Apr 1913, 5-37 years 4 months 24 days,
      15-Poffenberger
#5117, 1-Poffenberger, Christian M., 2-died, 3-10 Oct 1910, 5-71 years 11 months 22
      days, 15-Poffenberger
#5118, 1-Poffenberger, Mary Ann R., 2-died, 3-20 Oct 1895, 5-50 years 10 months 3
      days, 15-Poffenberger
#5119, 1-Poffenberger, Noah Ettie, 2-died, 3-12 May 1935, 5-72 years 17 days, 15-
      Poffenberger
#5120, 1-Myers, Annie Mary, 2-died, 3-29 Mar 1936, 5-70 years 8 months 15 days, 15-
      Poffenberger
#5121, 1-Poffenberger, Harvey Line, 2-died, 3-7 Mar 1953, 5-88 years 6 months 15
      days, 15-Poffenberger
#5122, 1-Poffenberger, Norman Myers, 2-died, 3-11 Dec 1971, 5-72 years 9 months 11
      days, 15-Poffenberger
#5123, 1-Poffenberger, Jacob Evans, 2-died, 3-3 Mar 1972, 5-78 years 17 days, 15-
      Poffenberger
#5124, 1-Poffenberger, Elizabeth Raye, 2-died, 3-22 May 1975, 5-84 years 5 months
      22 days, 15-Poffenberger
#5125, 1-Poffenberger, Harvey Cecil, 2-died, 3-9 Mar 1982, 5-80 years 21 days, 15-
      Poffenberger
#5126, 1-Poffenberger, Mary Ann Frances, 2-died, 3-5 Sep 1983, 5-87 years 10 months
      12 days, 15-Poffenberger
#5127, 1-Plummer, Henry E., 2-married, 3-1 Dec 1887, 4-Hagerstown, MD, 7-Worenfels,
      Alice E., 8-Washington Co., MD, 9-Frederick Co., MD, 10-C.J.B. Brane, 15-
      Plummer
#5128, 1-Plummer, Henry E., 2-born, 3-15 Jan 1852, 15-Plummer
#5129, 1-Plummer, Alice E., 2-born, 3-6 Aug 1864, 15-Plummer
#5130, 1-Plummer, Fannie Virginia, 2-born, 3-26 Jul 1888, 15-Plummer
#5131, 1-Plummer, Mary Ellen, 2-born, 3-28 Oct 1889, 15-Plummer
#5132, 1-Plummer, Gertrude May, 2-born, 3-8 Feb 1891, 15-Plummer
#5133, 1-Plummer, Alice Estella, 2-born, 3-3 Nov 1892, 15-Plummer
#5134, 1-Plummer, Henry Edward, 2-born, 3-26 Jan 1905, 15-Plummer
#5135, 1-Plummer, Fannie Virginia, 2-died, 3-14 Jun 1897, 5-8 years 10 months 19
      days, 15-Plummer
#5136, 1-Plummer, Henry E., 2-died, 3-29 Aug 1937, 15-Plummer
#5137, 1-Plummer, Alice E., 2-died, 3-15 Jun 1953, 15-Plummer
#5138, 1-Flory, Mary Ellen, 2-died, 3-1 Mar 1965, 15-Plummer
#5139, 1-Plummer, Henry E., 2-died, 3-18 Jun 1968, 15-Plummer
#5140, 1-Burkholder, Alice Estella, 2-died, 3-24 Dec 1969, 15-Plummer
```

FAMILY BIBLE RECORDS IN THE WASHINGTON COUNTY FREE LIBRARY, HAGERSTOWN, MARYLAND

Entry #, 1-Last Name, First Name, 2-Event, 3-Date, 4-Event Location, 5-Age, 6-Other, 7-Spouse's Last, First, 8-Groom's Residence, 9-Bride's Residence, 10-Minister, 11-Minister's Location, 12-Father's Last, First, 13-Mother's Last, First, 14-Transcribed, 15-Family Bible

#5141, 1-Norris, John F., 2-married, 3-18 Nov 1875, 4-Keedysville, MD, 7-Rucker, Genie M., 10-H.A. Bovey, 11-Keedysville, 15-Norris

#5142, 1-Norris, Ma__le Ellin, 2-born, 3-4 Jul 1872, 12-Norris, John F., 15-Norris

#5143, 1-Norris, Mary Etta, 2-born, 3-2 Aug 1880, 15-Norris

#5144, 1-Norris, William Henry Fenton, 2-born, 3-14 Jan 1883, 15-Norris

#5145, 1-Norris, Thomas Envey, 2-born, 3-24 Oct 1885, 15-Norris

#5146, 1-Norris, Mary Elizabeth, 2-born, 3-5 Aug 1887, 12-Norris, John F., 13-Norris, Virginia M., 15-Norris

#5147, 1-Norris, John Scott, 2-born, 3-16 Apr 1892, 15-Norris

#5148, 1-Norris, John Scott, 2-died, 3-14 Dec 1966, 15-Norris

#5149, 1-Norris, Evente[?] Earl, 2-born, 3-4 Aug 1894, 15-Norris

#5150, 1-Norris, Evente[?] Earl, 2-died, 3-19 Jan 1966, 4-Sharpsburg, MD, 15-Norris

#5151, 1-Norris, William Earl, 2-born, 3-20 Apr 1903, 12-Norris, Wm. A., 15-Norris

#5152, 1-Norris, William Henry Fenton, 3-Tuesday, 24 Mar 1885, 6-"taking Sick with pneumonia", 15-Norris

#5153, 1-Norris, Pearl Frances Regina, 2-born, 3-12 Feb 1914, 12-Norris, Scott, 13-Norris, Marguerite, 15-Norris

#5154, 1-Norris, Willard Hodges, 2-born, 3-21 Nov 1916, 15-Norris

#5155, 1-Norris, Willard Hodges, 2-died, 3-10 Jan 1918, 5-2 years 1 months, 15-Norris

#5156, 1-Norris, Marvin Scott, 2-born, 3-24 Mar 1919, 15-Norris

#5157, 1-Norris, John Marion, 2-born, 3-4 Oct 1922, 15-Norris

#5158, 1-Norris, Minnie Ellen, 2-died, 3-15 Aug 1879, 12-Norris, John F., 13-Norris, Genie M., 15-Norris

#5159, 1-Norris, Mary Etta, 2-died, 3-3 Feb 1883, 5-2 years 6 months, 12-Norris, John F., 13-Norris, Genie M., 15-Norris

#5160, 1-Rickird, Kattie M., 2-died, 3-12 Mar 1899, 5-23 years 7 months 12 days, 12-Norris, John F., 13-Norris, Genie M., 15-Norris

#5161, 1-Norris, Elizbeth (Mrs.), 2-died, 3-20 Sep 1900, 5-78 years, 15-Norris

#5162, 1-Scott, Ellen, 2-died, 3-26 Feb 1908, 15-Norris

#5163, 1-Norris, Virginia M., 2-died, 3-6 Nov 1925, 5-70 years, 7-Norris, John F., 15-Norris

#5164, 1-Norris, John Scott, 2-died, 3-14 Dec 1966, 4-Sandy Hook, MD, 5-74 years, 15-Norris

#5165, 1-Norris, William H., 2-born, 4-Calham House, Sandy Hook, MD, 15-Norris

#5166, 1-Norris, Thomas E., 2-born, 4-"in the old hous at the mouten", 15-Norris

#5167, 1-Norris, Mary Elizabeth, 2-born, 4-"in the old hous at the mouten", 15-Norris

#5168, 1-Norris, John F., 2-born, 3-1852, 15-Norris

#5169, 1-Norris, Elen, 2-born, 3-1849, 15-Norris

#5170, 1-Norris, John F., 2-born, 3-24 Feb 1852, 12-Norris, John A., 15-Norris

#5171, 1-Norris, Virginia M., 2-born, 3-12 Aug 1855, 15-Norris

#5172, 1-Norris, Minnie Ellin, 2-born, 3-4 Jul 1878, 15-Norris

#5173, 1-Scott, William Henry, 2-born, 3-1870, 15-Norris

#5174, 1-Scott, William Henry, 2-died, 3-1871, 15-Norris

#5175, 1-Norris, John F., 2-married, 3-18 Nov 1875, 7-Rucker, Virginia, 12-Norris, John A., 15-Norris

#5176, 1-Norris, Henry, 2-born, 3-8 Feb 1867, 15-Norris

#5177, 1-Norris, Annie[?] E., 2-born, 3-26 Mar 1869, 15-Norris

#5178, 1-Norris, Daniel W., 2-born, 3-[?], 15-Norris

#5179, 1-Norris, Mary C., 3-2 Jun 1871, 15-Norris

#5180, 1-Norris, Charles W., 2-born, 3-7 Jun 1872, 15-Norris

#5181, 1-Norris, Daniel E., 2-born, 3-20 Jun 1873, 15-Norris

#5182, 1-Norris, Daissy V., 2-born, 3-26 ___ 1875, 15-Norris

#5183, 1-Norris, Daissy V., 3-6 Feb 1879, 15-Norris

FAMILY BIBLE RECORDS IN THE WASHINGTON COUNTY FREE LIBRARY, HAGERSTOWN, MARYLAND

Entry #, 1-Last Name, First Name, 2-Event, 3-Date, 4-Event Location, 5-Age, 6-Other, 7-Spouse's Last, First, 8-Groom's Residence, 9-Bride's Residence, 10-Minister, 11-Minister's Location, 12-Father's Last, First, 13-Mother's Last, First, 14-Transcribed, 15-Family Bible

```
#5184, 1-Norris, Mary Jane, 2-born, 3-4 Mar 1877, 15-Norris
#5185, 1-Norris, Maclen[?], 2-born, 3-12 Sep 1881, 15-Norris
#5186, 1-Norris, Minnie Ellen, 2-died, 3-15 Aug 1878, 15-Norris
#5187, 1-Bayly, Mary Jane, 2-died, 3-7 Jul 1880[?], 15-Norris
#5188, 1-Norris, Wm. A., 2-died, 3-23 Jan 1910, 15-Norris
#5189, 1-Scott, Ellen, 2-died, 3-26 ___ 1909, 15-Norris
#5190, 1-Norris, Henry, 2-born, 3-8 Feb 1867, 15-Norris
#5191, 1-Norris, Annie E., 2-born, 3-24 Mar 1869, 15-Norris
#5192, 1-Norris, Daniel W., 2-born, 3-5 Jun 1871, 15-Norris
#5193, 1-Norris, Mary C., 2-born, 3-8 Jun 1873, 15-Norris
#5194, 1-Norris, Charts[?] W., 2-born, 3-20 Jun 1875, 15-Norris
#5195, 1-Norris, Daniel E., 2-born, 3-26 Jun 1876, 15-Norris
#5196, 1-Norris, Daisy V., 2-born, 3-2 Nov 1878, 15-Norris
#5197, 1-Norris, Mary J., 2-born, 3-6 Mar 1880, 15-Norris
#5198, 1-Norris, Emma E., 2-born, 3-12 Sep 1882, 15-Norris
#5199, 1-Norris, Jennie M., 2-born, 3-18 Feb 1887, 15-Norris
#5200, 1-Norris, Patrick, 2-born, 3-31 Mar 1782, 15-Norris
#5201, 1-Norris, Patrick, 2-died, 3-7 Jan 1857, 15-Norris
#5202, 1-Norris, Sarah, 2-born, 3-9 Jun 1791, 7-Norris, Patrick, 15-Norris
#5203, 1-Norris, Sarah, 2-died, 3-16 Jul 1865, 7-Norris, Patrick, 15-Norris
#5204, 1-Heskett, William, 2-born, 3-12 Apr 1780, 15-Norris
#5205, 1-Heskett, William, 2-died, 3-11 Jan 1865, 15-Norris
#5206, 1-Heskett, Clarissa Amanda, 2-born, 3-1 May 1798, 7-Heskett, Wm., 15-Norris
#5207, 1-Heskett, Clarissa Amanda, 2-died, 3-15 Jan 1832, 7-Heskett, Wm., 15-Norris
#5208, 1-Norris, John, 2-born, 3-4 Mar 1816, 15-Norris
#5209, 1-Posey, Sarah A., 2-born, 3-5 Aug 1803, 7-Norris, John, 15-Norris
#5210, 1-Heskett, Alcinda L., 2-born, 3-22 Sep 1828, 7-Norris, John, 15-Norris
#5211, 1-Hawkins, Reuben Waeton[?], 2-born, 3-4 Aug 1864, 15-Norris
#5212, 1-Norris, John, 2-married, 3-5 Jan 1836, 6-1st wife, 7-Posey, Sarah, 15-
    Norris
#5213, 1-Norris, John, 2-married, 3-19 Oct 1854, 6-2nd wife, 7-Smith, Catharine,
    15-Norris
#5214, 1-Norris, John, 2-married, 3-11 Jun 1857, 6-3rd wife, 7-Heskett, Alcinda L.,
    15-Norris
#5215, 1-Norris, Emma V., 2-married, 3-21 Oct 1888, 7-Hawkins, Rueben W., 15-Norris
#5216, 1-Hawkins, Rua A., 2-married, 3-12 Jan 1911, 7-McQuiller, Joseph M., 15-
    Norris
#5217, 1-Forrest, Douglas, 2-married, 3-Oct 1910, 7-Hawkins, Agnes L., 15-Norris
#5218, 1-Deavers, Harry N., 2-married, 3-23 Dec 1919, 7-Hawkins, Maggie M., 15-
    Norris
#5219, 1-Mitchell, Clarence F., 2-married, 3-30 Dec 1919, 7-Hawkins, Ethel L., 15-
    Norris
#5220, 1-Hawkins, Kathleen Gertrude, 2-married, 3-6 Dec 1931, 7-Merriman[?],
    Robert, 15-Norris
#5221, 1-Donovan, Janie A., 2-married, 3-3 Sep 1932, 7-Hawkins, Virginia, 15-Norris
#5222, 1-Norris, Amanda, 2-born, 3-8 Oct 1836, 12-Norris, John, 13-Norris, Sarah
    A., 15-Norris
#5223, 1-Norris, Sarah Elizabeth, 2-born, 3-24 Mar 1839, 12-Norris, John, 13-
    Norris, Sarah A., 15-Norris
#5224, 1-Norris, Mary Jane, 2-born, 3-22 Jun 1841, 12-Norris, John, 13-Norris,
    Sarah A., 15-Norris
#5225, 1-Norris, Patrick, 2-born, 3-27 Aug 1842, 12-Norris, John, 13-Norris, Sarah
    A., 15-Norris
#5226, 1-Norris, John William, 2-born, 3-27 Nov 1843, 12-Norris, John, 13-Norris,
    Sarah A., 15-Norris
```

FAMILY BIBLE RECORDS IN THE WASHINGTON COUNTY FREE LIBRARY, HAGERSTOWN, MARYLAND

Entry #, 1-Last Name, First Name, 2-Event, 3-Date, 4-Event Location, 5-Age, 6-Other, 7-Spouse's Last, First, 8-Groom's Residence, 9-Bride's Residence, 10-Minister, 11-Minister's Location, 12-Father's Last, First, 13-Mother's Last, First, 14-Transcribed, 15-Family Bible

```
#5227, 1-Norris, Annie Eliza, 2-born, 3-29 Apr 1860, 12-Norris, John, 13-Norris,
    Alcinda L., 15-Norris
#5228, 1-Norris, Charlotte Louisa, 2-born, 3-9 Oct 1863, 12-Norris, John, 13-
    Norris, Alcinda L., 15-Norris
#5229, 1-Norris, Emma Virginia, 2-born, 3-25 Oct 1868, 12-Norris, John, 13-Norris,
    Alcinda L., 15-Norris
#5230, 1-Norris, Sarah A., 2-died, 3-18 Mar 1853, 6-1st wife, 7-Norris, John, 15-
    Norris
#5231, 1-Norris, Catharine, 2-died, 3-27 May 1856, 6-2nd wife, 7-Norris, John, 15-
    Norris
#5232, 1-Norris, Amanda, 2-died, 3-16 Oct 1852, 15-Norris
#5233, 1-Norris, Annie Eliza, 2-died, 3-27 Aug 1865, 15-Norris
#5234, 1-Norris, Patrick H., 2-died, 3-19 Dec 1865, 15-Norris
#5235, 1-Norris, John W., 2-died, 3-16 Nov 1866, 15-Norris
#5236, 1-Norris, John, 2-died, 3-21 Nov 1893, 15-Norris
#5237, 1-Forrest, Agnes L., 2-died, 3-26 Nov 1911, 15-Norris
#5238, 1-Norris, Alcinda L., 2-died, 3-1 May 1905, 15-Norris
#5239, 1-Hawkins, Geneieve W., 2-died, 3-Sep 1909[?], 15-Norris
#5240, 1-Hawkins, Benjaman F.N., 2-died, 3-9 Aug 1895, 15-Norris
#5241, 1-Hawkins, Jr., Reuben W., 2-died, 3-31 Aug 1903, 15-Norris
#5242, 1-Hawkins, Vera F., 2-died, 3- Jul 1910, 15-Norris
#5243, 1-Hawkins, William A., 2-died, 3- 7 Aug 1902, 15-Norris
#5244, 1-Hawkins, Charles Leo, 2-died, 3-28 May 1906, 15-Norris
#5245, 1-Hawkins, Reuben W., 2-died, 3- 3 Oct 1944, 15-Norris
#5246, 1-Hawkins, Emma V., 2-died, 3-13 May 1949, 15-Norris
#5247, 1-[blank], Rua, 2-born, 3-9 Aug 1889, 15-Norris
#5248, 1-[blank], Agnes, 2-born, 3-21 Dec 1891, 15-Norris
#5249, 1-[blank], Franklin, 2-born, 3-1 Aug 1894, 15-Norris
#5250, 1-[blank], Maggie, 2-born, 3-26 Jun 1896, 15-Norris
#5251, 1-[blank], Charles, 2-born, 3-13 Jan 1898, 15-Norris
#5252, 1-[blank], Ethel, 2-born, 3-21 Aug 1900, 15-Norris
#5253, 1-[blank], Albert, 2-born, 3-6 Jul 1902, 15-Norris
#5254, 1-[blank], Walter, 2-born, 3-21 Aug 1903, 15-Norris
#5255, 1-[blank], Kathleen, 2-born, 3-4 Nov[?] 1906, 15-Norris
#5256, 1-[blank], Geneieve[?], 2-born, 3-19 Jun 1908, 15-Norris
#5257, 1-[blank], Virginia, 2-born, 3-14 Oct 1909, 15-Norris
#5258, 1-[blank], Vera, 2-born, 3-15 May 1911, 15-Norris
#5259, 1-Norris, Charles E., 2-born, 3-8 Sep 1870, 15-Norris
#5260, 1-Norris, Ida R., 2-born, 3-27 Mar 1877, 15-Norris
#5261, 1-Norris, Claud M., 2-born, 3-30 Sep 1896, 15-Norris
#5262, 1-Norris, Mary, 2-born, 3-5 Oct 18__[?], 15-Norris
#5263, 1-Norris, Carlton E., 2-born, 3-22 Jan 1901, 15-Norris
#5264, 1-Norris, Franklin W., 2-born, 3-17 Sep 1903, 15-Norris
#5265, 1-Norris, William F.[?], 2-born, 3-23 Dec 1905, 15-Norris
#5266, 1-Norris, Arthur J., 2-born, 3-17 Dec 1908, 15-Norris
#5267, 1-Norris, Earl W., 2-born, 3-26 Oct 1910, 15-Norris
#5268, 1-Norris, Joseph A., 2-born, 3-11 Jan 1913, 15-Norris
#5269, 1-Norris, Paul L., 2-born, 3-19[?] May 1914, 15-Norris
#5270, 1-Norris, Preston B., 2-born, 3-13 ___ 1920, 15-Norris
#5271, 1-Norris, Mary, 2-died, 3-17 Dec 1899, 15-Norris
#5272, 1-Norris, Earl, 2-died, 3-6 ___ 1911, 15-Norris
#5273, 1-Norris, Paul, 2-died, 3-1 Dec 1914, 15-Norris
#5274, 1-Norris, Ida, 2-died, 3-6 Aug 1921, 15-Norris
#5275, 1-Norris, Charles E., 2-died, 3-5 Jan 1932, 15-Norris
#5276, 1-Norris, Carlton E., 2-died, 3-[illegible], 15-Norris
```

FAMILY BIBLE RECORDS IN THE WASHINGTON COUNTY FREE LIBRARY, HAGERSTOWN, MARYLAND

Entry #, 1-Last Name, First Name, 2-Event, 3-Date, 4-Event Location, 5-Age, 6-Other, 7-Spouse's Last, First, 8-Groom's Residence, 9-Bride's Residence, 10-Minister, 11-Minister's Location, 12-Father's Last, First, 13-Mother's Last, First, 14-Transcribed, 15-Family Bible

```
#5277, 1-Norris, John, 2-married, 3-11 Jun 1857, 4-Sandy Hook, MD, 7-Hiskett,
    Alcinda L., 15-Norris
#5278, 1-Needy, E.L., 2-born, 3-21 Jul 1862, 15-Needy
#5279, 1-Needy, Alice J.E., 2-born, 3-11 Apr 1866, 15-Needy
#5280, 1-Needy, Edna Myrtle, 2-born, 3-1 Oct 1889, 15-Needy
#5281, 1-Needy, Earl Kiracofe, 2-born, 3-21 May 1892, 15-Needy
#5282, 1-Needy, Ruth Hazel, 2-born, 3-10 Jan 1896, 15-Needy
#5283, 1-Needy, Katharine Louise, 2-born, 3-25 Sep 1899, 15-Needy
#5284, 1-Froehlich, Barbara Elizabeth, 2-born, 3-15 Jun 1925, 12-Froehlich, Roy,
    13-Froehlich, Katharine, 15-Needy
#5285, 1-Froehlich, Patricia Lee, 2-born, 3-23 Jan 1929, 15-Needy
#5286, 1-Froehlich, Phyllis Virginia, 2-born, 3-21 Apr 1932, 15-Needy
#5287, 1-Layman, Diana Lynn, 2-born, 3-8 Oct 1951, 15-Needy
#5288, 1-Laymon, Wm. H., 2-born, 3-20 Aug 1954, 15-Needy
#5289, 1-Laymon, Deana Lynn, 2-born, 3-8-Oct-51, 12-Laymon, Dilliom[?], 13-
    Froehlich, Phyllis, 15-Needy
#5290, 1-Laymon, Jr., Wm. H., 2-born, 3-20 Aug 1954, 12-Laymon, Dilliom[?], 13-
    Froehlich, Phyllis, 15-Needy
#5291, 1-Laymon, Clifford R., 2-born, 3-23 Mar 1959, 12-Laymon, Dilliom[?], 13-
    Froehlich, Phyllis, 15-Needy
#5292, 1-Laymon, Dawn Marie, 2-born, 3-4 Aug 1961, 12-Laymon, Dilliom[?], 13-
    Froehlich, Phyllis, 15-Needy
#5293, 1-Laymon, John C., 2-born, 3-7 Jun 1963, 12-Laymon, Dilliom[?], 13-
    Froehlich, Phyllis, 15-Needy
#5294, 1-Horne, Michael, 2-born, 3-28 Sep 1958, 12-Horne, Ned, 13-Froehlich,
    Barbara, 15-Needy
#5295, 1-Horne, Cindy Louise, 2-born, 3-May 1963, 12-Horne, Ned, 13-Froehlich,
    Barbara, 15-Needy
#5296, 1-Satterfield, Kathleen Marie, 2-born, 3-31 Jan 1964, 12-Satterfield,
    Thomas, 13-Froehlich, Patricia Lee, 15-Needy
#5297, 1-Satterfield, Tracy Lynn, 2-born, 3-1 Aug 1968, 12-Satterfield, Thomas, 13-
    Froehlich, Patricia Lee, 15-Needy
#5298, 1-Kiracofe, Alic J., 2-married, 3-18 Apr 1888, 4-Lewville,[?] PA, 7-Needy,
    E.L., 15-Needy
#5299, 1-Needy, Edna M., 2-married, 3-25 Jun 1914, 4-Hagerstown, Md, 7-Bell, George
    Y., 15-Needy
#5300, 1-Needy, Katharine L., 2-married, 3-12 Nov 1923, 4-Baltimore, MD, 7-
    Froehlich, H. Roy, 15-Needy
#5301, 1-Froehlich, Barbara E., 2-married, 3-15 Jun 1946[?], 7-Horne, Ned V., 15-
    Needy
#5302, 1-Froehlich, Phyllis V., 2-married, 3-17 Jun 1950, 7-Laymon, William, 15-
    Needy
#5303, 1-Froehlich, Patricia Lee, 2-married, 3-7 Jun 1958, 7-Satterfield, Thomas,
    15-Needy
#5304, 1-Needy, Hazel Ruth, 2-died, 3-18[?] Aug 1896, 15-Needy
#5305, 1-Needy, Edward L., 2-died, 3-29 Aug 1904, 15-Needy
#5306, 1-Needy, Earle Kiracofe, 2-died, 3-5 Mar 1923, 5-30 years 9 months 12 days,
    15-Needy
#5307, 1-Needy, Alice J., 2-died, 3-14 Dec 1927, 5-61 years 8 months 3 days, 15-
    Needy
#5308, 1-Kiracofe, M. Josephine, 2-died, 3-26 Sep 1942, 5-15 years, 15-Needy
#5309, 1-Bell, Edna N., 2-died, 3-23 Mar 1956, 5-66 years, 15-Needy
#5310, 1-Myers, Jacob, 2-born, 3-26 Dec 1832, 15-Myers
#5311, 1-Myers, Ann C., 2-born, 3-7 Feb 1833, 15-Myers
#5312, 1-Myers, Mary cathern, 2-born, 3-4 Sep 1855, 15-Myers
```

FAMILY BIBLE RECORDS IN THE WASHINGTON COUNTY FREE LIBRARY, HAGERSTOWN, MARYLAND

Entry #, 1-Last Name, First Name, 2-Event, 3-Date, 4-Event Location, 5-Age, 6-Other,
7-Spouse's Last, First, 8-Groom's Residence, 9-Bride's Residence, 10-Minister, 11-Minister's Location,
12-Father's Last, First, 13-Mother's Last, First, 14-Transcribed, 15-Family Bible

```
#5313, 1-Myers, Margaret Ellen, 2-born, 3-4 Aug 1857, 15-Myers
#5314, 1-Myers, John William, 2-born, 3-4 Mar 1859, 15-Myers
#5315, 1-Myers, Benjamin F., 2-born, 3-6 Dec 1860, 15-Myers
#5316, 1-Myers, Charles M., 2-born, 3-3 Jul 1862, 15-Myers
#5317, 1-Myers, Carrie M., 2-born, 3-11 Mar 1864, 15-Myers
#5318, 1-Myers, Ulysses S., 2-born, 3-24 Feb 1866, 15-Myers
#5319, 1-Myers, Noah W., 2-born, 3-1 Sep 1867, 15-Myers
#5320, 1-Myers, Minnie F., 2-born, 3-3 Aug 1869, 15-Myers
#5321, 1-Myers, Cora E., 2-born, 3-6 Aug 1871, 15-Myers
#5322, 1-Myers, Bertha V., 2-born, 3-16 Mar 1874, 15-Myers
#5323, 1-Myers, Harry G., 2-born, 3-8 May 1876, 15-Myers
#5324, 1-Myers, Jacob, 2-married, 3-26 Feb 1853, 7-Cookerly, Ann Cathern, 15-Myers
#5325, 1-Myers, Benjamin F., 2-died, 3-27 Mar 1872, 15-Myers
#5326, 1-Myers, Ann C. [mother], 2-died, 3-4 May 1895, 15-Myers
#5327, 1-Myers, Jacob C. [father], 2-died, 3-14 Aug 1904, 15-Myers
#5328, 1-Myers, Carrie May, 2-died, 3-17 Feb 1919, 15-Myers
#5329, 1-Remsburg, Mary Catherine, 2-died, 3-4 Nov 1919, 15-Myers
#5330, 1-Myers, John William, 2-died, 3-7 Feb 1920, 15-Myers
#5331, 1-Remsburg, Peter, 2-died, 3-25 Apr 1924, 15-Myers
#5332, 1-Myers, Noah Washington, 2-died, 3-5 Nov 1926, 15-Myers
#5333, 1-Myers, Ulysses S., 2-died, 3-26 Jun 1934, 15-Myers
#5334, 1-Myers, Chas. McC., 2-died, 3-18 Mar 1938, 15-Myers
#5335, 1-Miller, Minnie F., 2-died, 3-16 Jun 1944, 15-Myers
#5336, 1-Myers, Harry Grafton, 2-died, 3-7 Sep 1945, 15-Myers
#5337, 1-Myers, Bertha V., 2-died, 3-17 Nov 1948, 15-Myers
#5338, 1-Myers, Margaret E., 2-died, 3-12 Jan 1950, 15-Myers
#5339, 1-Myers, Ida Virginia, 2-died, 3-18 Jan 1863, 5-7 years 3 months 27 days,
       15-Myers
#5340, 1-Myers, Charles Learitt, 2-died, 3-22 Jan 1863, 5-2 years 8 months, 15-
       Myers
#5341, 1-Myers, Jno. [father], 2-died, 3-15 Feb 1888, 5-75 years 7 months 13 days,
       15-Myers
#5342, 1-Myers, John D., 2-died, 3-20 Jun 1931, 5-68 years 10 months 20 days, 15-
       Myers
#5343, 1-Myers, Mary Elizabeth, 2-died, 3-18 Jul 1915, 5-88 years 4 months, 15-
       Myers
#5344, 1-Myers, Henry Samuel, 2-died, 3-23 Jan 1923, 4-Vienna, VA, 6-buried Mt.
       Olivett Cemetery, Frederick MD, 15-Myers
#5345, 1-Myers, Lemuel Edgar, 2-died, 3-23 Jan 1933, 5-64 years, 15-Myers
#5346, 1-Laurence, William, 2-died, 3-9 Nov 1866, 5-25 years 11 months, 15-Myers
#5347, 1-Myers, Mary Lantz, 2-died, 3-11 Sep 1896, 4-Smithsburg, MD, 6-diptheria
       croup, 15-Myers
#5348, 1-Laurence, William, 2-married, 3-12 Nov 1862, 7-Lantz, Annie C., 15-Myers
#5349, 1-Myers, Jno. D., 2-married, 3-10 Sep 1889, 4-Hagerstown, MD, 7-Lawrence,
       Mary E., 10-Dr. J.W. Santee, 15-Myers
#5350, 1-Laurence, Mary E., 2-born, 3-8 May 1864, 12-Laurence, William, 13-
       Laurence, Annie C., 15-Myers
#5351, 1-Laurence, Emma V.[?], 2-born, 3-14 Sep 1865, 12-Laurence, William, 13-
       Laurence, Annie C., 15-Myers
#5352, 1-Laurence, Willie K., 2-born, 3-14 Apr 1867, 12-Laurence, William, 13-
       Laurence, Annie C., 15-Myers
#5353, 1-Myers, Jno. D., 2-born, 3-12 Aug 1862, 4-Wolfesville, MD, 15-Myers
#5354, 1-Myers, Mary E., 2-born, 3-8 May 1864, 4-Leitersburg, MD, 15-Myers
#5355, 1-Myers, Mary Lantz, 2-born, 3-28 Apr 1891, 4-Smithsburg, MD, 15-Myers
#5356, 1-Myers, Kathrian, 2-born, 3-26 Nov 1896, 4-Hagerstown, MD, 15-Myers
```

FAMILY BIBLE RECORDS IN THE WASHINGTON COUNTY FREE LIBRARY, HAGERSTOWN, MARYLAND

Entry #, 1-Last Name, First Name, 2-Event, 3-Date, 4-Event Location, 5-Age, 6-Other, 7-Spouse's Last, First, 8-Groom's Residence, 9-Bride's Residence, 10-Minister, 11-Minister's Location, 12-Father's Last, First, 13-Mother's Last, First, 14-Transcribed, 15-Family Bible

```
#5357, 1-Myers, John, 2-born, 3-2 Jul 1812, 15-Myers
#5358, 1-Myers, Mary Elizabeth, 2-born, 3-18 Mar 1827, 15-Myers
#5359, 1-Myers, Henry Samuel, 2-born, 3-3 Sep 1850, 15-Myers
#5360, 1-Myers, Ida Virginia, 2-born, 3-22 Sep 1855, 15-Myers
#5361, 1-Myers, Charles Leavitt, 2-born, 3-22 May 1860, 15-Myers
#5362, 1-Myers, John Daniel, 2-born, 3-12 Aug 1862, 15-Myers
#5363, 1-Myers, Marshall Howard, 2-born, 3-2 Mar 1865, 15-Myers
#5364, 1-Myers, Lemuel Edgar, 2-born, 3-11 Feb 1869, 15-Myers
#5365, 1-Mills, Alta May E., 2-born, 3-28 Sep 1890, 15-Mills
#5366, 1-Mills, Izora Alverta, 2-born, 3-24 Feb 1893, 15-Mills
#5367, 1-Mills, Daisy Viola, 2-born, 3-16 Oct 1895, 15-Mills
#5368, 1-Mills, Ida Camilla, 2-born, 3-9 Dec 1897, 15-Mills
#5369, 1-Mills, David Elmer, 2-born, 3-1 Jan 1867[?], 15-Mills
#5370, 1-Mills, Alice Virginia, 2-born, 3-29 Jun 1872, 15-Mills
#5371, 1-Mills, Mary Catherine, 2-born, 3-30 May 1899, 15-Mills
#5372, 1-Mills, Elmer Franklin, 2-born, 3-18-Sep-01, 15-Mills
#5373, 1-Mills, Eda Louise Ellen, 2-born, 3-24 May 1904, 15-Mills
#5374, 1-Mills, Robt. L., 2-born, 3-16 May 1849, 15-Mills
#5375, 1-Mills, Lizzie J., 2-born, 3-29 Aug 1859, 15-Mills
#5376, 1-Mills, Amos Calvin, 2-born, 3-15 Nov 1875, 15-Mills
#5377, 1-Mills, Mary E.W., 2-born, 3-26 Oct 1877, 15-Mills
#5378, 1-Mills, Charles H., 2-born, 3-26 Jul 1880, 15-Mills
#5379, 1-Mills, William Ellsworth, 2-born, 3-221 Jul 1882, 15-Mills
#5380, 1-Mills, Pleasant Gertrude, 2-born, 3-8 Sep 1884, 15-Mills
#5381, 1-Mills, Joseph, 2-died, 3-28 Feb 1890, 15-Mills
#5382, 1-Mills, Robert S., 2-born, 3-12 Feb 1841, 15-Mills
#5383, 1-Mills, Daisy R., 2-born, 3-30 Mar 1903[?], 15-Mills
#5384, 1-Mills, Lulu May, 2-born, 3-4 Jul 1904, 15-Mills
#5385, 1-Mills, George Anne, 2-born, 3-13 Sep 1906, 15-Mills
#5386, 1-Mills, Eva/Iva Irene, 2-born, 3-Apr 1909, 15-Mills
#5387, 1-Mills, Robert Sheridan, 3-30 Jun 1910, 15-Mills
#5388, 1-Mills, Albert Franklin, 2-born, 3-Sunday, 29 Sep 1921, 15-Mills
#5389, 1-Mills, Joseph F., 2-died, 3-28 Feb 1891, 15-Mills
#5390, 1-Mills, Lizie, 2-died, 3-28 Dec 1891, 15-Mills
#5391, 1-Mills, James J., 2-married, 3-6 Dec 1864, 7-Bookman, Mary E., 15-Mills
#5392, 1-Mills, Mary E., 2-born, 3-17 Mar 1848, 15-Mills
#5393, 1-Mills, Dewitt Clinton, 2-born, 3-19 Jan 1867, 12-Mills, James J., 13-
     Mills, Mary E., 15-Mills
#5394, 1-Mills, Asa Marion, 2-born, 3-6 Nov 1868, 12-Mills, James J., 13-Mills,
     Mary E., 15-Mills
#5395, 1-Mills, Minnie May, 2-born, 3-24 Dec 1871, 12-Mills, James J., 13-Mills,
     Mary E., 15-Mills
#5396, 1-Mills, Charles Johnson, 2-born, 3-16 Sep 1874, 12-Mills, James J., 13-
     Mills, Mary E., 15-Mills
#5397, 1-Mills, Orlando B., 2-born, 3-28 Apr 1866, 12-Mills, James J., 13-Mills,
     Mary E., 15-Mills
#5398, 1-Mills, Rober[?], 2-married, 3-20 Oct 1853, 7-Clair, Mahlia (Miss), 15-
     Mills
#5399, 1-Mills, Aslander, 2-married, 3-15 Jul 1884, 7-Maasty[?], Ellin B., 15-Mills
#5400, 1-Mills, Sarah Annie, 2-born, 3-2 Jun 1871, 15-Mills
#5401, 1-Mills, George F., 2-married, 3-14 Dec 1886, 7-Shrader, Marget E., 15-Mills
#5402, 1-Mills, Aslander, 2-married, 3-28 Aug 1884, 7-McCaitey, Barbery, 15-Mills
#5403, 1-Mills, George F., 2-married, 3-14 Dec 1886, 7-Shrader, Marget E., 15-Mills
#5404, 1-Mills, William E.B., 2-born, 3-8 Sep 1854, 15-Mills
#5405, 1-Mills, Sarah Catharine, 2-born, 3-7 Jun 1857, 15-Mills
```

FAMILY BIBLE RECORDS IN THE WASHINGTON COUNTY FREE LIBRARY, HAGERSTOWN, MARYLAND

Entry #, 1-Last Name, First Name, 2-Event, 3-Date, 4-Event Location, 5-Age, 6-Other, 7-Spouse's Last, First, 8-Groom's Residence, 9-Bride's Residence, 10-Minister, 11-Minister's Location, 12-Father's Last, First, 13-Mother's Last, First, 14-Transcribed, 15-Family Bible

```
#5406, 1-Mills, John Allenwood, 2-born, 3-1 Sep 1860, 15-Mills
#5407, 1-Mills, Groege Franklin Webster, 2-born, 3-29 Oct 1862, 15-Mills
#5408, 1-Mills, Nelson anladey[?], 2-born, 3-4 Feb 1865, 15-Mills
#5409, 1-Mills, George Franklin Webster, 2-born, 3-29 Oct 1862, 15-Mills
#5410, 1-Mills, Alte[?] Lizze May, 2-born, 3-16 Jul 1885, 15-Mills
#5411, 1-Mills, Elmer, 2-born, 3-1 Jan 1867, 15-Mills
#5412, 1-Mills, Oscar, 2-born, 3-7 Jun 1869, 6-entire entry crossed out, 15-Mills
#5413, 1-Mills, Oscar T.B., 2-born, 3-7 Jun 1869, 15-Mills
#5414, 1-Mills, Denton W., 2-born, 3-11 Oct 1872, 15-Mills
#5415, 1-Mills, Charles Edgar, 2-born, 3-27 Sep 1876, 15-Mills
#5416, 1-Mills, Charles William Edgare, 2-born, 3-11 Jul 1880, 15-Mills
#5417, 1-Mills, Mahala, 2-died, 3-2[?] Sep [year unreadable], 5-65 years 5 months
    23 days, 15-Mills
#5418, 1-Mills, Daisy Viola, 2-died, 3-1[?] Nov, 5-1 months 1 days, 15-Mills
#5419, 1-Mills, Ida Camilla, 2-died, 3-3 Jun, 5-1 years 5 months 25 days, 15-Mills
#5420, 1-Mills, Robert S., 2-died, 3-13 Feb, 5-84 years 7 days, 15-Mills
#5421, 1-Mills, Alice V., 2-died, 3-8 Nov, 5-34 years 4 months 8 days, 15-Mills
#5422, 1-Mills, Maria, 2-died, 3-25 Jun 1915, 5-35 years 3 months 24 days, 15-Mills
#5423, 1-Mills, Sarah Annie, 2-born, 3-2 Jun 1817, 15-Mills
#5424, 1-Mills, David E., 2-married, 3-28[?] Oct 1889, 7-[unreadable], Alice V.,
    15-Mills
#5425, 1-Mills, Sarah[?] Annie, 2-born, 3-2 Jun 1871, 15-Mills
#5426, 1-Blair, Jane Louise, 2-born, 3-6[?] Apr 1850, 15-Mills
#5427, 1-Mills, William E. Bruffey, 2-born, 3-8 Sep 1854, 15-Mills
#5428, 1-Mills, Robert, 2-born, 3-6 Feb 1819, 15-Mills
#5429, 1-Mills, Samuel J.[?], 2-born, 3-15 Jun 1840, 15-Mills
#5430, 1-Mills, James J., 2-born, 3-15 Mar 1842, 15-Mills
#5431, 1-Mills, Amos A., 2-born, 3-4 Feb 1844, 15-Mills
#5432, 1-Mills, John D., 2-born, 3-16 Apr 1846, 15-Mills
#5433, 1-Mills, Sarah Ann, 2-born, 3-30 Jun 1822, 15-Mills
#5434, 1-Mills, Robert J.[?], 2-born, 3-13 May 1849, 15-Mills
#5435, 1-Mills, Mary G.[?], 2-born, 3-8 May 1841[?], 15-Mills
#5436, 1-Mills, Nancy Ann, 2-born, 3-1 May 1843, 15-Mills
#5437, 1-Mills, Sary[?] Cathrine, 2-born, 3-7 Jun 1857[?], 15-Mills
#5438, 1-Mills, John Allen Wood, 2-born, 3-12 Sep 1860, 15-Mills
#5439, 1-Mills, George Walter, 2-born, 3-15 Sep 1887, 15-Mills
#5440, 1-Mills, Franklin Webster, 2-born, 3-7 Nov 1888, 15-Mills
#5441, 1-Mills, Carry Mahala, 2-born, 3-4 Mar 1891[?], 15-Mills
#5442, 1-Mills, John A., 2-died, 3-10 Dec 1861, 15-Mills
#5443, 1-Mills, Charles E., 2-died, 3-22 Jul 1876, 15-Mills
#5444, 1-Mills, James J., 2-died, 3-17 Dec 1874, 15-Mills
#5445, 1-Mills, Orlando B., 2-died, 3-28 Apr 1866, 12-Mills, James J., 13-Mills,
    Mary E., 15-Mills
#5446, 1-Mills, William E.B., 2-died, 3-4 Aug 1880, 15-Mills
#5447, 1-Turlang, Annie L., 2-died, 3-8 Feb 1889, 15-Mills
#5448, 1-Mills, Nelsan Arlander, 2-died, 3-30 Jul 1889, 15-Mills
#5449, 1-Mills, Nickler Raman, 2-born, 3-10 May 1890, 15-Mills
#5450, 1-Mills, Sarah Ann, 2-died, 3-3 Jul 1853, 15-Mills
#5451, 1-Mills, Nancy Ann, 2-died, 3-5 Aug 1853, 15-Mills
#5452, 1-Mills, Charles P.[?], 2-died, 3-22 Feb 1877, 15-Mills
#5453, 1-Mills, Allie Lizzey May, 2-born, 3-16 Jul 1885, 15-Mills
#5454, 1-Mills, Charles Amos Calvin, 2-born, 3-1 May 1887, 15-Mills
#5455, 1-Mills, Bruffe , 2-born, 3-19 Jun 1889, 12-Mills, Arlander, 15-Mills
#5456, 1-Mills, Hare[?] Milton Arlander, 2-born, 3-11 May 1892, 15-Mills
#5457, 1-Mills, Mahala, 2-died, 3-23 Sep 1897, 15-Mills
```

FAMILY BIBLE RECORDS IN THE WASHINGTON COUNTY FREE LIBRARY, HAGERSTOWN, MARYLAND

Entry #, 1-Last Name, First Name, 2-Event, 3-Date, 4-Event Location, 5-Age, 6-Other,
7-Spouse's Last, First, 8-Groom's Residence, 9-Bride's Residence, 10-Minister, 11-Minister's Location,
12-Father's Last, First, 13-Mother's Last, First, 14-Transcribed, 15-Family Bible

```
#5458, 1-Mills, Ida Comila, 2-died, 3-3 Jun 1898, 15-Mills
#5459, 1-Miller, Jacob Henry, 2-born, 3-2 Mar 1797, 4-Tahlhiem, Oberampt Heilbron,
       Wurtemburg, 15-Miller
#5460, 1-Miller, Jacob Henry, 2-baptized, 3-Saturday afternoon, 1819, 4-Baltimore,
       6-immigrated from Bremen - 70 days at sea, 15-Miller
#5461, 1-Miller, Henry, 2-married, 3-11 Jan 1821, 7-Hoffman, Elisabeth, 15-Miller
#5462, 1-Miller, Henry, 2-born, 3-2 Mar 1797, 15-Miller
#5463, 1-Hoffman, Elis.th. [Elisabeth], 2-born, 3-26 Jun 1797, 15-Miller
#5464, 1-Hoffman, Nicholas, 2-born, 3-6 Oct 1776, 15-Miller
#5465, 1-Shank, Rachel, 2-born, 3-1 Apr 1771, 15-Miller
#5466, 1-Hoffman, Jos.h. [Joseph], 2-born, 3-25 Aug 1801, 12-Hoffman, Nichol, 13-
       Hoffman, Rachel, 15-Miller
#5467, 1-Hoffman, Susan, 2-born, 3-9 Jun 1799, 12-Hoffman, Nichol, 13-Hoffman,
       Rachel, 15-Miller
#5468, 1-Hoffman, Christena, 2-born, 3-29 Oct 1802, 12-Hoffman, Nichol, 13-Hoffman,
       Rachel, 15-Miller
#5469, 1-Miller, Catharina, 2-born, 3-4 Nov 1821, 12-Miller, Henry, 13-Miller,
       Elisabeth, 15-Miller
#5470, 1-Miller, Susanna, 2-born, 3-18 Jun 1825, 12-Miller, Henry, 13-Miller,
       Elisabeth, 15-Miller
#5471, 1-Miller, Johannes, 2-born, 3-8 Sep 1827, 12-Miller, Henry, 13-Miller,
       Elisabeth, 15-Miller
#5472, 1-Miller, Hannah, 2-born, 3-3 Jun 1833, 12-Miller, Henry, 13-Miller,
       Elisabeth, 15-Miller
#5473, 1-Miller, Rachel, 2-born, 3-8 Jul 1837, 12-Miller, Henry, 13-Miller,
       Elisabeth, 15-Miller
#5474, 1-Miller, Jac.b. [Jacob] Henry, 2-born, 3-17 Oct 1839, 12-Miller, Henry, 13-
       Miller, Elisabeth, 15-Miller
#5475, 1-Miller, Catharina, 2-died, 3-10 Aug 1834, 15-Miller
#5476, 1-Hoffman, Nicolas, 2-died, 3-4 Jan 1849, 15-Miller
#5477, 1-Miller, Elizabeth, 2-died, 3-31 Mar 1865, 5-67 years 9 months 5 days, 15-
       Miller
#5478, 1-Miller, Henry, 2-died, 3-16 Jul 1875, 5-78 years 4 months 14 days, 15-
       Miller
#5479, 1-Hoffman, Rachel, 2-died, 3-11 Jan 1806, 5-31 years 9 months 10 days, 7-
       Hoffman, Nicholas, 15-Miller
#5480, 1-Hoffman, Jos.h. [Joseph], 2-died, 3-27 Sep 180_ [page torn off], 5-1 months
       2 days, 12-Hoffman, Nicholas, 13-Hoffman, Rachel, 15-Miller
#5481, 1-Thomas, Rachel (Heiller[?]), 2-died, 3-14 Apr 1873[?], 5-35 years 9
       months, 15-Miller
#5482, 1-Miller, Martin, 2-married, 3-17 Jan 1869, 7-Earick, Laura C., 10-Rev. T.T.
       Tittus, 15-Miller
#5483, 1-Warrenfeltz, Jacob M., 2-married, 3-11 Oct 1916, 4-Funkstown, MD, 7-McCoy,
       Ethel L.[?], 10-Rev. Ramsburg, 15-Miller
#5484, 1-Moser[?], Josiah, 2-born, 3-23 Feb 1841, 15-Miller
#5485, 1-Miller, Ezra[?] M., 2-born, 3-4 Dec 1869, 15-Miller
#5486, 1-Nickels, Joseph, 2-died, 3-10 Dec 1864, 5-76 years, 15-Miller
#5487, 1-Earick, Catherine, 12-Nickels, Joseph, 15-Miller
#5488, 1-Miller, Laurra C., 13-Earick, Catherine, 15-Miller
#5489, 1-McCoy, Violetta, 13-Miller, Laura C., 15-Miller
#5490, 1-Warrenfeltz, Ethel Irene, 13-McCoy, Violetta, 15-Miller
#5491, 1-Warrenfeltz, Stuart Martin, 2-died, 3-4 Sep 1938, 5-21 years, 13-
       Warrenfeltz, Ethel Irene, 15-Miller
#5492, 1-Miller, David, 2-died, 5-72 years, 15-Miller
```

FAMILY BIBLE RECORDS IN THE WASHINGTON COUNTY FREE LIBRARY, HAGERSTOWN, MARYLAND

Entry #, 1-Last Name, First Name, 2-Event, 3-Date, 4-Event Location, 5-Age, 6-Other,
7-Spouse's Last, First, 8-Groom's Residence, 9-Bride's Residence, 10-Minister, 11-Minister's Location,
12-Father's Last, First, 13-Mother's Last, First, 14-Transcribed, 15-Family Bible

#5493, 1-Miller, Magdalana Sager, 2-died, 3-11 Jan 1909, 5-85 years, 7-Miller, David, 15-Miller
#5494, 1-Miller, Martin Luther, 13-Miller, Magdalana Sager, 15-Miller
#5495, 1-McCoy, Theodore Elsworth, 2-died, 3-10 Feb 1942, 5-71 years, 15-Miller
#5496, 1-Miller, Nannie, 2-died, 3-24 Jan 1947, 5-85 years, 15-Miller
#5497, 1-Miller, Nannie, 2-born, 3-23 Nov 1861, 15-Miller
#5498, 1-Daywalt, Jennie (Aunt), 2-died, 3-1 Aug 1944, 15-Miller
#5499, 1-O'Donnell, Lester, 2-born, 3-18 Nov 1899, 12-O'Donnell, Frank, 13-Miller, Sue, 15-Miller
#5500, 1-Hout, Henry R.T.S., 2-born, 3-8 Feb 1831, 15-Miller
#5501, 1-Miller, Urilah V.[?], 2-born, 3-8 Nov 1834, 15-Miller
#5502, 1-Hout, Susie May S., 2-born, 3-4 Jun 1881, 15-Miller
#5503, 1-Rohrer, Estella May, 2-born, 3-1 Apr 1883, 15-Miller
#5504, 1-Miller, Goldie V., 2-born, 3-Aug 1884, 15-Miller
#5505, 1-Otto, Ruth E.V., 2-born, 3-5 Jul 1892, 15-Miller
#5506, 1-Hout, Henry R.T.S., 2-married, 3-21 Jan 1869, 7-Miller, Urillah V., 15-Miller
#5507, 1-Miller, Mother, 2-died, 3-5 Jul 1872, 15-Miller
#5508, 1-Miller, Father, 2-died, 3-10 Nov 1891, 15-Miller
#5509, 1-Hout, H.R.W., 2-died, 3-7 May 1899, 15-Miller
#5510, 1-Hout, Urillah V., 2-died, 3-27 Aug 1915, 5-80 years 9 months 19 days, 15-Miller
#5511, 1-Middlekauff, Jonathan, 2-married, 3-30 Dec 1845, 7-Shindle, Ann M., 15-Middlekauff
#5512, 1-Middlekauff, Emma K., 2-married, 3-12 Dec 1872, 15-Middlekauff
#5513, 1-Middlekauff, Wm. C., 2-married, 3-20 Nov 1883, 15-Middlekauff
#5514, 1-Middlekauff, Jonathan, 2-born, 3-3 Mar 1820, 15-Middlekauff
#5515, 1-Middlekauff, Ann M., 2-born, 3-2 Feb 1822, 15-Middlekauff
#5516, 1-Middlekauff, Joseph Melvin, 2-born, 3-9 Nov 1846, 15-Middlekauff
#5517, 1-Middlekauff, Samuel Osker, 2-born, 3-1 Apr 1850, 15-Middlekauff
#5518, 1-Middlekauff, Emma C., 2-born, 3-26 Sep 1852, 15-Middlekauff
#5519, 1-Middlekauff, Julia A.P., 2-born, 3-20 Feb 1856, 15-Middlekauff
#5520, 1-Middlekauff, William C., 2-born, 3-28 Jan 1858, 15-Middlekauff
#5521, 1-Middlekauff, Jonathan B., 2-born, 3-8 Jun 1859, 15-Middlekauff
#5522, 1-Middlekauff, Joseph M., 2-born, 3-9 Nov 1846, 15-Middlekauff
#5523, 1-Middlekauff, Joseph M., 2-died, 3-14 Apr 1849, 5-2 years 5 months 5 days, 15-Middlekauff
#5524, 1-Middlekauff, Saml. O., 2-born, 3-1 Apr 1850, 15-Middlekauff
#5525, 1-Middlekauff, Saml. O., 2-died, 3-30 Jun 1858, 5-8 years 2 months, 15-Middlekauff
#5526, 1-Middlekauff, Julia A.P., 2-born, 3-20 Feb 1856, 15-Middlekauff
#5527, 1-Middlekauff, Julia A.P., 2-died, 3-5 Jun 1858, 5-2 years 3 months 16 days, 15-Middlekauff
#5528, 1-Middlekauff, Jonathan B., 2-born, 3-8 Jun 1859, 15-Middlekauff
#5529, 1-Middlekauff, Jonathan B., 2-died, 3-2 Aug 1859, 5-1 months 25 days, 15-Middlekauff
#5530, 1-Middlekauff, Ann Maria, 2-born, 3-3 Feb 1822, 15-Middlekauff
#5531, 1-Middlekauff, Ann Maria, 2-died, 3-12:30 pm, 9 Apr 1903, 5-81 years 2 months 6 days, 15-Middlekauff
#5532, 1-Middlekauff, Emma C., 2-born, 3-26 Sep 1852, 15-Middlekauff
#5533, 1-Middlekauff, Emma C., 2-died, 3-31 Mar 1907, 5-54 years 6 months, 15-Middlekauff
#5534, 1-Middlekauff, Jonathan, 2-born, 3-3 Mar 1820, 15-Middlekauff
#5535, 1-Middlekauff, Jonathan, 2-died, 3-Sunday, 8:30 pm, 19 Dec 1909, 5-89 years 9 months 16 days, 15-Middlekauff

FAMILY BIBLE RECORDS IN THE WASHINGTON COUNTY FREE LIBRARY, HAGERSTOWN, MARYLAND

Entry #, 1-Last Name, First Name, 2-Event, 3-Date, 4-Event Location, 5-Age, 6-Other,
7-Spouse's Last, First, 8-Groom's Residence, 9-Bride's Residence, 10-Minister, 11-Minister's Location,
12-Father's Last, First, 13-Mother's Last, First, 14-Transcribed, 15-Family Bible

```
#5536, 1-Middlekauff, Daniel , 2-born, 3-6 Aug 1779, 15-Middlekauff
#5537, 1-Middlekauff, Marea, 2-born, 3-23 Jul 1781, 15-Middlekauff
#5538, 1-Middlekauff, Marea, 2-married, 3-3 Oct 1822, 7-Middlekauff, Daniel, 15-
    Middlekauff
#5539, 1-Middlekauff, Susan, 2-born, 3-27 Aug 1803, 15-Middlekauff
#5540, 1-Middlekauff, Marea, 2-born, 3-4 Nov 1805, 15-Middlekauff
#5541, 1-Middlekauff, Barbara, 2-born, 3-23 Oct 1807, 15-Middlekauff
#5542, 1-Middlekauff, Samual, 2-born, 3-17 Nov 1809, 15-Middlekauff
#5543, 1-Middlekauff, Daniel, 2-born, 3-3 Oct 1811, 15-Middlekauff
#5544, 1-Middlekauff, Peter, 2-born, 3-23 Dec 1817, 15-Middlekauff
#5545, 1-Middlekauff, Jonnaton, 2-born, 3-3 Mar 1820, 15-Middlekauff
#5546, 1-Middlekauff, Jacob, 2-born, 3-5 Nov 1822, 6-twin, 15-Middlekauff
#5547, 1-Middlekauff, Josebh [sic], 2-born, 3-5 Nov 1822, 6-twin, 15-Middlekauff
#5548, 1-Middlekauff, Emma, 2-died, 3-6 Feb 1927, 15-Middlekauff
#5549, 1-Saler, Catrin, 2-born, 3-28 Mar 1785, 15-Middlekauff
#5550, 1-Saler, Nancy Ann, 2-born, 3-3 Sep 1799, 15-Middlekauff
#5551, 1-Toms, Oscar Ray, 2-died, 3-12 Sep 1930, 15-Middlekauff
#5552, 1-Middlekauff, William L., 2-died, 3-10-Oct-45, 15-Middlekauff
#5553, 1-Stine, Mildred Phyllis, 2-died, 3-15 Jan 1945, 15-Middlekauff
#5554, 1-Robertson, Lois (Middlekauff), 15-Middlekauff
#5555, 1-Howard, John Preston, 2-died, 3-18 Jan 1951, 15-Middlekauff
#5556, 1-Lynch, Martin Edward, 2-died, 3-2 Dec 1950, 15-Middlekauff
#5557, 1-Middlekauff, Jane, 2-died, 3-24 Feb 1919, 15-Middlekauff
#5558, 1-Middlekauff, William Clyde, 2-died, 3-26 Nov 1964, 15-Middlekauff
#5559, 1-Lynch, Mildred Catherine (Middlekauff) Toms, 2-died, 3-15 Nov 1976, 15-
    Middlekauff
#5560, 1-Howard, Mary Leah (Middlekauff), 2-died, 3-18 Jun 1971, 15-Middlekauff
#5561, 1-Middlekauff, Naomi Supinger, 2-died, 3-11 Apr 1968, 15-Middlekauff
#5562, 1-Stine, Victor F., 2-died, 3-29 Oct 1958, 15-Middlekauff
#5563, 1-Middlekauff, William L., 2-married, 3-20 Oct 1886, 7-Mullen, Emma, 15-
    Middlekauff
#5564, 1-Middlekauff, Leah Mary, 2-married, 3-25 Jul 1907, 7-Howard, John Preston,
    15-Middlekauff
#5565, 1-Middlekauff, Franklin Earl, 2-married, 3-3 Mar 1909, 7-Reynolds, Ruth
    Estella, 15-Middlekauff
#5566, 1-Middlekauff, William Clyde, 2-married, 3-25 Dec 1916, 7-Supinger, Naomi,
    15-Middlekauff
#5567, 1-Middlekauff, Ruth, 2-married, 3-29 Dec 1915, 7-Stine, Victor Francis, 15-
    Middlekauff
#5568, 1-Middlekauff, Mildred, 2-married, 3-7 Nov 1923, 7-Toms, Oscar Ray, 15-
    Middlekauff
#5569, 1-Middlekauff, Emma Irene, 2-married, 3-6 Dec 1929, 7-Ellsworth, Donald
    Monroe, 15-Middlekauff
#5570, 1-Middlekauff, Mildred C., 2-married, 3-20 Nov 1933, 7-Lynch, Martin Edward,
    15-Middlekauff
#5571, 1-Middlekauff, Mildred Catherine, 2-born, 3-26 Jan 1900, 15-Middlekauff
#5572, 1-Middlekauff, William Lycurgus[?], 2-born, 3-2 Oct 1858, 15-Middlekauff
#5573, 1-Middlekauff, Emma Mariah, 2-born, 3-4 Jul 1862, 15-Middlekauff
#5574, 1-Middlekauff, Franklin Earl, 2-born, 3-30 Jul 1887, 15-Middlekauff
#5575, 1-Middlekauff, Mary Leah, 2-born, 3-26 Jul 1888, 15-Middlekauff
#5576, 1-Middlekauff, William Clyde, 2-born, 3-20 Apr 1891, 15-Middlekauff
#5577, 1-Middlekauff, Ruth, 2-born, 3-19 Aug 1894, 15-Middlekauff
#5578, 1-Middlekauff, Emma Irene, 2-born, 3-3 Sep 1904, 15-Middlekauff
#5579, 1-Michael, Jonathan, 2-married, 7-Schmiding, Anna Maria, 14-Yes, 15-Michael
#5580, 1-Schmiding, Anna Maria, 2-died, 3-Nov 1852, 14-Yes, 15-Michael
```

FAMILY BIBLE RECORDS IN THE WASHINGTON COUNTY FREE LIBRARY, HAGERSTOWN, MARYLAND

Entry #, 1-Last Name, First Name, 2-Event, 3-Date, 4-Event Location, 5-Age, 6-Other,
7-Spouse's Last, First, 8-Groom's Residence, 9-Bride's Residence, 10-Minister, 11-Minister's Location,
12-Father's Last, First, 13-Mother's Last, First, 14-Transcribed, 15-Family Bible

```
#5581, 1-Michael, Johann Christoph, 2-born, 3-1825, 14-Yes, 15-Michael
#5582, 1-Michael, Jacob Jonathan, 2-born, 3-1826, 14-Yes, 15-Michael
#5583, 1-Michael, Jacob Jonathan, 2-died, 3-1829, 14-Yes, 15-Michael
#5584, 1-Michael, Johann Gottlieb, 2-born, 3-1827, 14-Yes, 15-Michael
#5585, 1-Michael, Johann Gottlieb, 2-died, 3-1854, 5-26 years 5 months 24 days, 14-
    Yes, 15-Michael
#5586, 1-Michael, Anna Maria, 2-born, 3-1835, 14-Yes, 15-Michael
#5587, 1-Michael, Heinrich Christan, 2-born, 3-1838, 14-Yes, 15-Michael
#5588, 1-Michael, Georg Willhelm, 2-born, 3-1840, 14-Yes, 15-Michael
#5589, 1-Michael, Georg Willhelm, 2-died, 3-1842, 14-Yes, 15-Michael
#5590, 1-Michael, Johann Willhelm, 2-born, 3-1843, 14-Yes, 15-Michael
#5591, 1-Michael, Johann Willhelm, 2-died, 3-1844, 14-Yes, 15-Michael
#5592, 1-Michael, Matilda, 2-born, 3-1846, 14-Yes, 15-Michael
#5593, 1-Michael, Matilda, 2-died, 3-1847, 14-Yes, 15-Michael
#5594, 1-Martin, Solomon W., 2-born, 3-23 Nov 1830, 15-Martin
#5595, 1-Martin, Annah H., 2-born, 3-20 Aug 1838, 15-Martin
#5596, 1-Martin, Jacob M., 2-born, 3-24 Feb 1864, 15-Martin
#5597, 1-Martin, Daniel M., 2-born, 3-24[?] Jul 1865, 15-Martin
#5598, 1-Martin, Elizann M., 2-born, 3-26 Oct 1866, 15-Martin
#5599, 1-Martin, Solomon M., 2-born, 3-6 Nov 1868, 15-Martin
#5600, 1-Martin, Martha M., 2-born, 3-31 Jul 1870, 15-Martin
#5601, 1-Martin, John M., 2-born, 3-19 Nov 1871, 15-Martin
#5602, 1-Martin, Fanney M., 2-born, 3-29 Aug 1873, 15-Martin
#5603, 1-Martin, Ely M., 2-born, 3-13 Oct 1875, 15-Martin
#5604, 1-Martin, Leda M., 2-born, 3-5 Mar 1878, 15-Martin
#5605, 1-Martin, Jonas M., 2-born, 3-9 Sep 1880, 15-Martin
#5606, 1-Martin, Jacob M., 2-married, 3-9 Dec 1888, 7-Rhodes, Elizabeth, 9-
    Virginia, 10-Bisup Abraham Shank, 15-Martin
#5607, 1-Martin, M.D., Solomon M., 2-married, 3-1 Nov 1891, 4-Grabil at Bairvill,
    Lancaster Co., PA, 7-Good, Helteie C., 9-Vaarerland, 15-Martin
#5608, 1-Martin, Daniel, 2-married, 3-18 Dec 1895, 7-McNamee, Sallie V., 9-
    Marigans[?] Mill, MD, 15-Martin
#5609, 1-Martin, Mattie, 2-married, 3-26 Jul 1896, 7-Hamlin, Marceltells[?], 8-
    Lancaster Co., PA, 9-Washington Co., MD, 15-Martin
#5610, 1-Martin, Lydia, 2-married, 3-30 Aug 1896, 7-Witmor, Pharas B., 8-Lancaster
    Co., PA, 9-Washington Co., MD, 15-Martin
#5611, 1-Martin, Fannie E., 2-married, 3-13 Dec 1896, 7-Frankhouser, Diller[?] G.,
    8-Lancaster[?] Co., PA, 9-Washington Co., MD, 15-Martin
#5612, 1-Martin, Solomon W., 2-born, 3-14 Feb 1863, 4-Jacob Martin's , 7-Martin,
    Annah H., 8-Lancaster Co., PA, 9-Washington Co., MD, 10-Peter Estlyman[?],
    Bishup, 11-Washington Co., MD, 15-Martin
#5613, 1-McKee, John, 2-born, 3-28 Feb 1787, 15-McKee
#5614, 1-McKee, Isabella, 2-born, 3-30 Apr 1789, 15-McKee
#5615, 1-McKee, James, 2-born, 3-15 Sep 1808, 15-McKee
#5616, 1-McKee, Elisajane, 2-born, 3-27 Mar 1810, 15-McKee
#5617, 1-McKee, Robert, 2-born, 3-12 Dec 1811, 15-McKee
#5618, 1-McKee, William, 2-born, 3-24 Oct 1813, 15-McKee
#5619, 1-McKee, Ferdinand, 2-born, 3-25 Sep 1815, 15-McKee
#5620, 1-McKee, Evaline, 2-born, 3-2 Sep 1817, 15-McKee
#5621, 1-McKee, John, 2-born, 3-16 Dec 1819, 15-McKee
#5622, 1-McKee, Leander, 2-born, 3-29 Nov 1821, 15-McKee
#5623, 1-McKee, Laura, 2-born, 3-23 Feb 1806, 15-McKee
#5624, 1-McKee, Ann Louisa Henrietta, 2-born, 3-23 Feb 1806, 15-McKee
#5625, 1-McKee, Elisajane, 2-died, 3-24 Jan 18__[?], 5-10 months **, 6-** 10 months
    lacking 3 days", 15-McKee
```

FAMILY BIBLE RECORDS IN THE WASHINGTON COUNTY FREE LIBRARY, HAGERSTOWN, MARYLAND

Entry #, 1-Last Name, First Name, 2-Event, 3-Date, 4-Event Location, 5-Age, 6-Other, 7-Spouse's Last, First, 8-Groom's Residence, 9-Bride's Residence, 10-Minister, 11-Minister's Location, 12-Father's Last, First, 13-Mother's Last, First, 14-Transcribed, 15-Family Bible

#5626, 1-McKee, Evaline, 2-died, 3-19 Sep 1846, 5-29 years 17 days, 15-McKee
#5627, 1-McKee, Isabella, 2-died, 3-17 Dec 1851, 5-62 years 7 months 17 days, 15-McKee
#5628, 1-McKee, William B., 2-died, 3-1854, 15-McKee
#5629, 1-McKee, John, 2-died, 3-13 Mar 1860, 4-Francivile[?], MO, 5-40 years 2 months 8 days, 15-McKee
#5630, 1-McKee, Ferdonand, 2-died, 3-Mar 1861, 5-45 years 6 months, 15-McKee
#5631, 1-McKee, John, 2-died, 3-8 Jan 1871, 5-84 years, 15-McKee
#5632, 1-McKee, Leander, 15-McKee
#5633, 1-McKee, James B., 2-died, 3-Monday, 4:30 pm, 18 Aug 1890, 15-McKee
#5634, 1-McKee, John, 2-married, 3-10 Dec 1807, 7-Dinwiddie, Isabella, 15-McKee
#5635, 1-McKee, John, 2-married, 3-10 May 1853, 7-Spangle, Louise, 15-McKee
#5636, 1-Main, Marthe, 2-born, 3-28 Oct 1825, 15-Main
#5637, 1-Main, Henry Luther, 2-born, 3-19 Apr 1849, 12-Main, John, 13-Main, Martha, 15-Main
#5638, 1-Mehn, Georg Adam, 2-married, 3-14 Aug 1791, 7-Jautze, Margaretha, 14-Yes, 15-Main
#5639, 1-Menn, May Adam, 2-born, 3-15 May 1746, 14-Yes, 15-Main
#5640, 1-Main, George, 2-married, 3-14 Apr 1816, 7-Derr, Anamaria, 14-Yes, 15-Main
#5641, 1-Main, Anna Mary, 2-died, 3-21 Jan 1872, 5-79 years 4 months 5 days, 7-Main, George, 14-Yes, 15-Main
#5642, 1-Main, John, 2-born, 3-14 Jan 1817, 14-Yes, 15-Main
#5643, 1-Main, Elisabeth, 2-born, 3-15 Apr 1819, 14-Yes, 15-Main
#5644, 1-Main, George Adam, 2-born, 3-8 Jun 1821, 14-Yes, 15-Main
#5645, 1-Bruchey, Mary Catherine, 2-born, 3-18 Dec 1844, 14-Yes, 15-Main
#5646, 1-Bruchey, Frederick, 2-born, 3-19 Feb 1807, 14-Yes, 15-Main
#5647, 1-Bruchey, Margaret Ellen, 2-born, 3-21 Dec 1846, 14-Yes, 15-Main
#5648, 1-Mehn, Adam, 2-married, 3-1770, 7-Weil, Abelohen [Apollonia]", 14-Yes, 15-Main
#5649, 1-Mehn, Elisabeth, 2-born, 3-27 Mar 1772, 12-Mehn, Adam, 13-Weil, Apollonia, 14-Yes, 15-Main
#5650, 1-Mehn, John Frederick, 2-born, 3-Apr 1774, 12-Mehn, Adam, 13-Weil, Apollonia, 14-Yes, 15-Main
#5651, 1-Mehn, Maria Magdalena, 2-born, 3-22 ___ [page torn] 1785, 12-Mehn, Adam, 13-Weil, Apollonia, 14-Yes, 15-Main
#5652, 1-Mehn, John George, 2-born, 3-29 Jul 1792, 12-Mehn, Adam, 13-Weil, Apollonia, 14-Yes, 15-Main
#5653, 1-Main, Mary Elizabeth, 2-born, 3-4 Apr 1845, 14-Yes, 15-Main
#5654, 1-Main, John George, 2-born, 3-29 Jul 1792, 12-Main, George A., 14-Yes, 15-Main
#5655, 1-Main, John George, 2-died, 3-30 Aug 1787, 5-86 years 1 months 1 days, 12-Main, George A., 14-Yes, 15-Main
#5656, 1-Heron, Robert, 2-born, 3-29 Oct 1709, 14-Yes, 15-Heron
#5657, 1-Heron, Robert, 2-married, 3-13 Jun 1730, 14-Yes, 15-Heron
#5658, 1-Heron, John, 2-born, 3-17 Dec 1739, 14-Yes, 15-Heron
#5659, 1-Heron, Robert, 2-born, 3-8[?] Apr 1742, 14-Yes, 15-Heron
#5660, 1-Heron, Margaret, 2-born, 3-7 May 1747, 14-Yes, 15-Heron
#5661, 1-Heron, Helen, 2-born, 3-12 Apr 1752, 14-Yes, 15-Heron
#5662, 1-Heron, Jean, 2-born, 3-5 May, 14-Yes, 15-Heron
#5663, 1-Heron, John, 2-married, 3-10 Oct 1763, 7-Climie, Jo Joan, 14-Yes, 15-Heron
#5664, 1-Heron, Robert, 2-born, 3-6 Nov 1764, 12-Heron, John, 13-Climie, Jo Joan, 14-Yes, 15-Heron
#5665, 1-Heron, Jean, 2-born, 3-29 Nov 1766, 12-Heron, John, 13-Climie, Jo Joan, 14-Yes, 15-Heron

FAMILY BIBLE RECORDS IN THE WASHINGTON COUNTY FREE LIBRARY, HAGERSTOWN, MARYLAND

Entry #, 1-Last Name, First Name, 2-Event, 3-Date, 4-Event Location, 5-Age, 6-Other, 7-Spouse's Last, First, 8-Groom's Residence, 9-Bride's Residence, 10-Minister, 11-Minister's Location, 12-Father's Last, First, 13-Mother's Last, First, 14-Transcribed, 15-Family Bible

```
#5666, 1-Heron, Grefel, 2-born, 3-7 Jan 1769, 12-Heron, John, 13-Climie, Jo Joan,
    14-Yes, 15-Heron
#5667, 1-Heron, Elazabath, 2-born, 3-17 May 1771, 12-Heron, John, 13-Climie, Jo
    Joan, 14-Yes, 15-Heron
#5668, 1-Heron, Agnes[?], 2-born, 3-17 Jul 1773, 12-Heron, John, 13-Climie, Jo
    Joan, 14-Yes, 15-Heron
#5669, 1-Heron, John, 2-born, 3-18 Oct 1776, 12-Heron, John, 13-Climie, Jo Joan,
    14-Yes, 15-Heron
#5670, 1-Heron, Mary, 2-born, 3-11 Oct 1779, 12-Heron, John, 13-Climie, Jo Joan,
    14-Yes, 15-Heron
#5671, 1-Heron, Elazabeth, 2-born, 3-27 May 1782, 12-Heron, John, 13-Climie, Jo
    Joan, 14-Yes, 15-Heron
#5672, 1-Heron, John, 2-married, 3-8 Jun 1795, 7-[blank], Helen, 14-Yes, 15-Heron
#5673, 1-Heron, William, 2-born, 3-10 Jun 1798, 12-Heron, John, 13-Heron, Helen,
    14-Yes, 15-Heron
#5674, 1-Heron, John, 2-born, 3-9 May 1800[?], 12-Heron, John, 13-Heron, Helen, 14-
    Yes, 15-Heron
#5675, 1-Kirby, Charles H., 2-born, 3-31 Aug 1847, 14-Yes, 15-Kirby
#5676, 1-Kirby, Edward S., 2-born, 3-25 Nov 1848, 14-Yes, 15-Kirby
#5677, 1-Kirby, Susan E., 2-born, 3-26 Jun 1851, 14-Yes, 15-Kirby
#5678, 1-Kirby, Sarah J., 2-born, 3-30 Jul 1853, 14-Yes, 15-Kirby
#5679, 1-Kirby, MaryE., 2-born, 3-8 Oct 1858, 14-Yes, 15-Kirby
#5680, 1-Kirby, John A., 2-born, 3-25 Sep 1860, 14-Yes, 15-Kirby
#5681, 1-Kirby, Eliza, 2-born, 3-1822, 14-Yes, 15-Kirby
#5682, 1-Kirby, Eliza, 2-died, 5-73 years 5 months 2 days, 14-Yes, 15-Kirby
#5683, 1-Kirby, James, 2-born, 3-4 Jul 1806, 14-Yes, 15-Kirby
#5684, 1-Kirby, John, 2-born, 3-9 Oct 1808, 14-Yes, 15-Kirby
#5685, 1-Kirby, Edward, 2-born, 3-25 Nov 1810, 14-Yes, 15-Kirby
#5686, 1-Kirby, Hannah, 2-born, 3-3 Jan 1813, 14-Yes, 15-Kirby
#5687, 1-Kirby, Sarah, 2-born, 3-9 Dec 1815, 14-Yes, 15-Kirby
#5688, 1-Kirby, Lucy, 2-born, 3-27 Dec 1818, 14-Yes, 15-Kirby
#5689, 1-Kirby, Stephen, 2-born, 3-12 Sep 1821, 14-Yes, 15-Kirby
#5690, 1-Kirby, Catharine, 2-born, 3-20Apr 1824, 14-Yes, 15-Kirby
#5691, 1-Kirby, Elizabeth, 2-born, 3-18 Apr 1827, 14-Yes, 15-Kirby
#5692, 1-Kirby, Joseph, 2-born, 3-26 Oct 1829, 14-Yes, 15-Kirby
#5693, 1-Jones, Joseph C., 2-married, 3-8 Aug 183_[?], 7-Curby, Catharine, 14-Yes,
    15-Kirby
#5694, 1-Jones, Catharine, 2-married, 3-28 Oct 1847, 7-Hood, John Westly, 14-Yes,
    15-Kirby
#5695, 1-Jones, Mary Elizabeth, 2-married, 3-13 Jan 185_[?], 7-Hood, Luke, 14-Yes,
    15-Kirby
#5696, 1-Jones, MaryElizabeth, 2-born, 3-10 Jul 1840, 14-Yes, 15-Kirby
#5697, 1-Jones, Charles Edward, 2-born, 3-10 Oct 1842, 14-Yes, 15-Kirby
#5698, 1-Jones, Joseph Chiswell, 2-born, 3-10 May 1847, 14-Yes, 15-Kirby
#5699, 1-Hood, William Aron, 2-born, 3-1 Feb 1851[or 1850], 14-Yes, 15-Kirby
#5700, 1-Hood, John Pope, 2-born, 3-11 Sep 1854, 14-Yes, 15-Kirby
#5701, 1-Hood, Luke Pearce, 2-born, 3-13 Jun 1858, 14-Yes, 15-Kirby
#5702, 1-Miller, James E., 2-born, 3-18 Oct 1844, 14-Yes, 15-Kirby
#5703, 1-Wright, Flosie Bell, 2-born, 3-6 Apr 1874, 14-Yes, 15-Kirby
#5704, 1-Smice, Peter, 2-born, 3-21 Dec 1801, 15-Smice
#5705, 1-Parks, Elisabeth, 2-born, 3-1806[?], 15-Smice
#5706, 1-Smice, Peter, 2-married, 3-27 Jun 1924, 7-Parks, Elisabeth, 15-Smice
#5707, 1-Smice, Margaret, 2-born, 3-7 Sep 1826, 15-Smice
#5708, 1-Smice, Susannah, 2-born, 3-15 Mar 1828, 15-Smice
#5709, 1-Smice, Elisabeth, 2-born, 3-27 Dec 1832, 15-Smice
```

FAMILY BIBLE RECORDS IN THE WASHINGTON COUNTY FREE LIBRARY, HAGERSTOWN, MARYLAND

Entry #, 1-Last Name, First Name, 2-Event, 3-Date, 4-Event Location, 5-Age, 6-Other, 7-Spouse's Last, First, 8-Groom's Residence, 9-Bride's Residence, 10-Minister, 11-Minister's Location, 12-Father's Last, First, 13-Mother's Last, First, 14-Transcribed, 15-Family Bible

```
#5710, 1-Smice, Maria, 2-born, 3-Feb 1830, 15-Smice
#5711, 1-Smice, Maria, 2-died, 3-Dec 1832, 15-Smice
#5712, 1-Smice, John, 2-born, 3-23 Oct 1834, 15-Smice
#5713, 1-Smice, George, 2-born, 3-12 Apr 1837, 15-Smice
#5714, 1-Smice, Amelia, 2-born, 3-13 Mar 1841, 15-Smice
#5715, 1-Smice, Thomas, 2-born, 3-18 Nov 1843, 15-Smice
#5716, 1-Smice, Thomas, 2-died, 3-2 Sep 1843[?], 15-Smice
#5717, 1-Smice, Mary, 2-born, 3-25 Dec 1845[?], 15-Smice
#5718, 1-Smice, Nage[?], 2-born, 3-25 Dec 1845[?], 15-Smice
#5719, 1-Smice, Elizabeth, 2-died, 3-3 Oct 1849, 5-33 years, 15-Smice
#5720, 1-Smice, Mary L., 2-born, 3-25 Dec 18__, 15-
#5721, 1-Smice, Mary L., 2-married, 3-7 Feb 1868[?], 15-
#5722, 1-[blank], Mary Ellen, 15-
#5723, 1-[blank], Lewis[?], 2-born, 3-6 Dec, 15-
#5724, 1-Smice, George Washington, 2-born, 3-18 Apr 1838, 4-Washington Co., MD, 15-
    Smice
#5725, 1-Netty, Clara Maria, 2-born, 3-30 Mar 1850, 4-Washington Co., MD, 15-Smice
#5726, 1-Smice, Lydia Ellen, 2-born, 3-27 Nov 1869, 4-Grand Detour Township, Ogle
    Co., IL, 15-Smice
#5727, 1-Smice, William Henry, 2-born, 3-19 Apr 1877, 4-Grand Detour Township, Ogle
    Co., IL, 15-Smice
#5728, 1-Smice, Bertie Eugene, 2-born, 3-30 Aug 1879, 4-Pine Creek Township, Ogle
    Co., IL, 6-twin, 15-Smice
#5729, 1-Smice, Bertha Irine, 2-born, 3-30 Aug 1879, 4-Pine Creek Township, Ogle
    Co., IL, 6-twin, 15-Smice
#5730, 1-Smice, Ada Belle, 2-born, 3-9 May 1887, 4-Dixon Township, Lee Co., IL, 15-
    Smice
#5731, 1-Bohlken, Esther May, 2-born, 3-17 May 1909, 4-Dixon Township, Lee Co., IL,
    15-Smice
#5732, 1-Smice, Bobert Eugene, 2-born, 3-29 May 1909, 4-Dixon Township, Lee Co.,
    IL, 15-Smice
#5733, 1-Smice, Frances Ruthanna, 2-born, 3-3 Dec 1910, 4-Dixon Township, Lee Co.,
    IL, 15-Smice
#5734, 1-Smice, Geo. W., 2-married, 3-1 Feb 1866, 4-Oregon, Ogle Co., IL, 7-Netty,
    Clara M., 15-Smice
#5735, 1-Smice, Lydia C., 2-married, 3-21 Jan 1886, 4-Dixon, Lee Co., IL, 7-Heaton,
    Andrew J., 15-Smice
#5736, 1-Smice, Ada B., 2-married, 3-24 Dec 1907, 4-Rockford, IL, 7-Bohlken,
    Charles, 15-Smice
#5737, 1-Smice, Beit E., 2-married, 3-3 Jun 1908, 4-Dixon, Lee Co., IL, 7-Sanford,
    Ruthann, 15-Smice
#5738, 1-Smice, William, 2-married, 3-25 Jan 1926, 4-Freeport, IL, 7-Brooke, Hazel,
    15-Smice
#5739, 1-Smice, Bertha Irine, 2-died, 3-18 Mar 1884, 4-Dixon Township, Lee Co., IL,
    15-Smice
#5740, 1-Smice, George Washington, 2-died, 3-24 Aug 1920, 5-83[?] years 4 months 12
    days, 15-Smice
#5741, 1-Smice, Clara Maria, 2-died, 3-6 Mar 1941, 15-Smice
#5742, 1-Smice, Geo. W., 2-born, 3-18 Apr 1838, 4-Washington Co., MD, 15-Smice
#5743, 1-Netty, Clara Maria, 2-born, 3-30 Mar 1850, 4-Washington Co., MD, 15-Smice
#5744, 1-Netty, Lydia Ellen, 2-born, 3-27 Nov 1869, 4-Grand Detour Township, Ogle
    Co., IL, 12-Smice, Geo. W., 13-Netty, Clara Maria, 15-Smice
#5745, 1-Netty, William Henry, 2-born, 3-9 Apr 1877, 4-Grand Detour Township, Ogle
    Co., IL, 12-Smice, Geo. W., 13-Netty, Clara Maria, 15-Smice
```

FAMILY BIBLE RECORDS IN THE WASHINGTON COUNTY FREE LIBRARY, HAGERSTOWN, MARYLAND

Entry #, 1-Last Name, First Name, 2-Event, 3-Date, 4-Event Location, 5-Age, 6-Other, 7-Spouse's Last, First, 8-Groom's Residence, 9-Bride's Residence, 10-Minister, 11-Minister's Location, 12-Father's Last, First, 13-Mother's Last, First, 14-Transcribed, 15-Family Bible

#5746, 1-Netty, Bertie Eugene, 2-born, 3-30 Aug 1880, 4-Pine Creek Township, Ogle Co., IL, 6-twin, 12-Smice, Geo. W., 13-Netty, Clara Maria, 15-Smice

#5747, 1-Netty, Bertha Irene, 2-born, 3-30 Aug 1880, 4-Pine Creek Township, Ogle Co., IL, 6-twin, 12-Smice, Geo. W., 13-Netty, Clara Maria, 15-Smice

#5748, 1-Netty, Ada Belle, 2-born, 3-9 May 1887, 4-Dixon Township, Lee Co., IL, 12-Smice, Geo. W., 13-Netty, Clara Maria, 15-Smice

#5749, 1-Sanford, Joseph Francis, 2-born, 3-10 Jul 1810, 4-Prospect, CT, 7-Parker, Ruthanna, 15-Smice

#5750, 1-Parker, Ruthanna, 2-born, 3-1804, 4-New York, 7-Sanford, Joseph Francis, 15-Smice

#5751, 1-Sanford, Francis Parker, 2-born, 3-11 Nov 1838, 4-Byron, Ogle Co., IL, 15-Smice

#5752, 1-Sanford, George Pinkney, 2-born, 3-24 Dec 1843, 4-Byron, Ogle Co., IL, 15-Smice

#5753, 1-Sanford, Frances Ruthanna, 2-born, 3-9 Feb 1888, 4-Byron, Igle Co., IL, 15-Smice

#5754, 1-Sanford, Robert Parker, 2-born, 3-15 Jan 1890, 4-Byron, Ogle Co., IL, 15-Smice

#5755, 1-Rabuck, Sarah Jane, 2-born, 3-14 Jul 1860, 4-Lavalle, Sank Co., WI, 15-Smice

#5756, 1-Smice, Geo. W., 2-married, 3-1 Feb 1866, 4-Origon, Ogle Co., IL, 7-Nety, Clara M., 15-Smice

#5757, 1-Smice, Lydia E., 2-married, 3-2 Jan 1886, 4-Dixon, Lee Co., IL, 7-Heatin, Andrew J., 15-Smice

#5758, 1-Smice, Ada Belle, 2-married, 3-Dec 1907, 4-Rockford, IL, 7-Bohlken, Charles, 15-Smice

#5759, 1-Smice, Bert E., 2-married, 3-3 Jun 1908, 4-Dixon, IL, 7-Sanford, F.[?] Ruthanna, 15-Smice

#5760, 1-Sanford, Joseph Francis, 2-married, 3-Feb 1886, 4-Dixon, IL, 7-Parker, Ruthanna, 15-Smice

#5761, 1-Sanford, Francis Parker, 2-married, 3-1882, 4-Lacross, WI, 7-Rabuck, Sarah Jane, 15-Smice

#5762, 1-Smice, Bert E., 2-born, 3-30 Aug 1879 [1880 crossed out], 15-Smice

#5763, 1-Sanford, Frances Ruthanna, 2-born, 3-9 Feb 1888, 15-Smice

#5764, 1-Smice, Bobert Eugene, 2-born, 3-29 May 1909, 4-Dixon, IL, 12-Smice, Bert E., 13-Sanford, Frances Ruthanna, 15-Smice

#5765, 1-Smice, Frances Ruthanna, 2-born, 3-3 Dec 1910, 4-Dixon, IL, 12-Smice, Bert E., 13-Sanford, Frances Ruthanna, 15-Smice

#5766, 1-Smice, Bert Raymond, 2-born, 3-30 Jul 1922, 4-Dixon, IL, 12-Smice, Bert E., 13-Sanford, Frances Ruthanna, 15-Smice

#5767, 1-Smice, Bertha Irene, 2-died, 3-18 Mar 1884, 4-Dixon Township, Lee Co., IL, 15-Smice

#5768, 1-Sanford, Ruthanna Parker, 2-died, 15-Smice

#5769, 1-Sanford, Joseph Francis, 2-died, 15-Smice

#5770, 1-Sanford, George Pinkney, 2-died, 15-Smice

#5771, 1-Sanford, Sarah Jane, 2-died, 3-10 Feb 1920, 15-Smice

#5772, 1-Smice, Geo. W., 2-died, 3-Aug 1920, 15-Smice

#5773, 1-Sanford, F.[?] P.[?], 2-died, 3-22 Jun 1922, 15-Smice

#5774, 1-Crowe, Sarah Jane, 2-born, 3-4 Oct 1840, 12-Crowe, William, 13-Crowe, Margret, 15-Crowe

#5775, 1-Crowe, Davis W., 2-born, 3-15 Apr 1842, 12-Crowe, William, 13-Crowe, Margret, 15-Crowe

#5776, 1-Crowe, Mariah, 2-born, 3-6 Oct 1804, 15-Crowe

#5777, 1-Crowe, John, 2-born, 3-1 Sep 1806, 15-Crowe

#5778, 1-Crowe, James, 2-born, 3-10 May 1808, 15-Crowe

FAMILY BIBLE RECORDS IN THE WASHINGTON COUNTY FREE LIBRARY, HAGERSTOWN, MARYLAND

Entry #, 1-Last Name, First Name, 2-Event, 3-Date, 4-Event Location, 5-Age, 6-Other,
7-Spouse's Last, First, 8-Groom's Residence, 9-Bride's Residence, 10-Minister, 11-Minister's Location,
12-Father's Last, First, 13-Mother's Last, First, 14-Transcribed, 15-Family Bible

```
#5779, 1-Crowe, Elisabeth, 2-born, 3-27 May 1810, 15-Crowe
#5780, 1-Crowe, Catharine Griffith, 2-born, 3-1 Feb 1812, 6-twin, 15-Crowe
#5781, 1-Crowe, Christian__[?] Paullstin[?], 2-born, 3-1 Feb 1812, 6-twin, 15-Crowe
#5782, 1-Crowe, William, 2-born, 3-27 Sep 1815, 15-Crowe
#5783, 1-Crow, Maria, 2-died, 3-30 Jul 1879, 7-McGlaughlin, 12-Crow, Parmenas, 13-
    Crow, Jane, 15-Crowe
#5784, 1-Crow, Christiana R., 2-died, 3-17 Oct 1880, 12-Crow, Parmenas, 13-Crow,
    Jane, 15-Crowe
#5785, 1-Crow, Catharine G., 2-died, 3-14 Sep 1881, 12-Crow, Parmenas, 13-Crow,
    Jane, 15-Crowe
#5786, 1-Crow, Eliza Houston, 2-died, 3-9 Apr 1882, 12-Crow, Parmenas, 13-Crow,
    Jane, 15-Crowe
#5787, 1-Crowe, William, 2-died, 3-21 Sep 1883, 12-Crowe, Parmenas, 13-Crowe, Jane,
    15-Crowe
#5788, 1-Crowe, James L., 2-died, 3-28 Mar 1885, 12-Crow, Parmenas, 13-Crow, Jane,
    15-Crowe
#5789, 1-Crowe, Margaret, 2-died, 7-Crowe, James L., 15-Crowe
#5790, 1-Crowe, John, 2-died, 3-30 Aug 1815, 5-8 years 11 months 30 days, 12-Crow,
    Paremnas, 13-Crow, Jane, 15-Crowe
#5791, 1-Crowe, Jane, 2-died, 3-19 Mar 1845, 5-65 years 1 months 19 days, 7-Crow,
    Parmenas, 15-Crowe
#5792, 1-Crowe, Permnes, 2-died, 3-4 Dec 1851, 5-70 years, 6-buried Forks of the
    Brandywine Pres. Church, 15-Crowe
#5793, 1-Hoffman, Conrod, 2-died, 3-11 Aug 1874, 5-58 years 2 months 2[?] days, 15-
    Hoffman
#5794, 1-Hoffman, Randolph, 2-died, 3-10[?] Aug 1874, 5-65 years 3 months 20 days,
    15-Hoffman
#5795, 1-Hoffman, Goege, 2-married, 3-30[?] Oct 1808, 7-Yong, Mary, 15-Hoffman
#5796, 1-Hoffman, Mary, 2-died, 3-23 Oct 1865, 5-82[?] years 7 months 2 days, 7-
    Hoffman, George, 15-Hoffman
#5797, 1-Hoffman, George, 2-died, 3-25 Sep 1873, 5-88 years 11 months 4 days, 15-
    Hoffman
#5798, 1-Wolfkiel, losson[?], 2-born, 3-24 Jul 1848, 15-Hoffman
#5799, 1-Wolfkiel, John, 2-born, 3-30 Sep 1851[or 7], 15-Hoffman
#5800, 1-Wolfkiel, Allice, 2-born, 3-12 Oct 1853, 15-Hoffman
#5801, 1-Wolfkiel, Curtis, 2-born, 3-6 Feb 1857, 15-Hoffman
#5802, 1-Wolfkiel, Lorrenzo, 2-died, 3-18 Apr 1886, 5-63 years, 15-Hoffman
#5803, 1-Hoffman, George, 2-born, 3-21 Oct 1784, 15-Hoffman
#5804, 1-Hoffman, Mary, 2-born, 3-21 Mar 1783, 7-Hoffman, George, 15-Hoffman
#5805, 1-Hoffman, Randolph, 2-born, 3-20 Apr 1809, 15-Hoffman
#5806, 1-Hoffman, Sarah, 2-born, 3-3 Mar 1811, 15-Hoffman
#5807, 1-Hoffman, Conrod, 2-born, 3-16 May 1816, 15-Hoffman
#5808, 1-Hoffman, Elizabeth, 2-born, 3-28 Apr 1818, 15-Hoffman
#5809, 1-Hoffman, Mary, 2-born, 3-4 Apr 1820, 15-Hoffman
#5810, 1-Hoffman, John, 2-born, 3-3 Feb 1823, 15-Hoffman
#5811, 1-Hoffman, Annrebecca, 2-born, 3-18 Jul 1825, 15-Hoffman
#5812, 1-Miller, Henry, 2-born, 3-17 Sep 1838, 15-Miller
#5813, 1-Miller, Susan, 2-born, 3-29 Aug 1842, 15-Miller
#5814, 1-Miller, Bessie Lind, 2-born, 3-15 Jul 1884, 15-Miller
#5815, 1-Miller, Mary Alice, 2-born, 3-13 Sep 1866, 15-Miller
#5816, 1-Miller, Ida Frances, 2-born, 3-31 Mar 1869, 15-Miller
#5817, 1-Miller, Henry Carlton, 2-born, 3-31 Mar 1871, 15-Miller
#5818, 1-Miller, Emma Kate, 2-born, 3-22 Aug 1874, 15-Miller
#5819, 1-Miller, Frank Edson, 2-born, 3-27 Jul 1876, 15-Miller
#5820, 1-Miller, Annie Florence, 2-born, 3-12 Dec 1878, 15-Miller
```

FAMILY BIBLE RECORDS IN THE WASHINGTON COUNTY FREE LIBRARY, HAGERSTOWN, MARYLAND

**Entry #, 1-Last Name, First Name, 2-Event, 3-Date, 4-Event Location, 5-Age, 6-Other,
7-Spouse's Last, First, 8-Groom's Residence, 9-Bride's Residence, 10-Minister, 11-Minister's Location,
12-Father's Last, First, 13-Mother's Last, First, 14-Transcribed, 15-Family Bible**

```
#5821, 1-Miller, Henry, 2-married, 3-18 May 1865, 7-Schriver, Susann, 15-Miller
#5822, 1-Miller, Susan, 2-died, 3-20 Oct 1911, 15-Miller
#5823, 1-Miller, Henry, 2-died, 3-14 Jul 1914, 15-Miller
#5824, 1-Hill, Ida Frances, 2-died, 3-3 May 1939, 15-Miller
#5825, 1-Hebb, Emma Kate, 2-died, 3-17 May 1952, 15-Miller
#5826, 1-Miller, Bessie Lind, 2-died, 3-15 Sep 1957, 15-Miller
#5827, 1-Miller, Henry, 2-died, 3-14 Jul 1914, 15-Miller
#5828, 1-Hebb, Mary Alice, 2-died, 3-3 Aug 1918, 15-Miller
#5829, 1-Miller, Henry Carlton, 2-died, 3-26 Aug 1926, 15-Miller
#5830, 1-Miller, Frank Edson, 2-died, 3-24 Mar 1929, 15-Miller
#5831, 1-Miller, John, 2-born, 3-15 Jun 1766, 4-Frederick Co., MD, 15-Miller
#5832, 1-Miller, Susanna, 2-born, 3-17 Feb 1771, 7-Miller, John, 15-Miller
#5833, 1-Miller, Elizabeth, 2-born, 3-23 Mar 1793, 12-Miller, John, 13-Miller,
    Susanna, 15-Miller
#5834, 1-Miller, Barbra, 2-born, 3-14 Feb 1795, 12-Miller, John, 13-Miller,
    Susanna, 15-Miller
#5835, 1-Miller, Susanna, 2-born, 3-27 Sep 1797, 12-Miller, John, 13-Miller,
    Susanna, 15-Miller
#5836, 1-Miller, Esther, 2-born, 3-7 Mar 1800, 12-Miller, John, 13-Miller, Susanna,
    15-Miller
#5837, 1-Miller, Daniel, 2-born, 3-2 Jun 1802, 12-Miller, John, 13-Miller, Susanna,
    15-Miller
#5838, 1-Miller, Mary, 2-born, 3-11 Aug 1804, 12-Miller, John, 13-Miller, Susanna,
    15-Miller
#5839, 1-Miller, Sophia, 2-born, 3-27 Feb 1807, 12-Miller, John, 13-Miller,
    Susanna, 15-Miller
#5840, 1-Miller, Samuel, 2-born, 3-13 Sep 1812, 15-Miller
#5841, 1-Shotts, Henry, 2-born, 3-29 Oct 1796, 12-Shotts, Philip, 13-Shotts,
    Katharine, 15-Miller
#5842, 1-Shotts, Henry, 12-Shotts, Henry, 13-Shotts, Elizabeth, 15-Miller
#5843, 1-Shotts, Peter Philip, 2-born, 3-26 Sep 1821, 12-Shotts, Henry, 13-Shotts,
    Elizabeth, 15-Miller
#5844, 1-Shotts, Michael Christian, 2-born, 3-8 Feb 1823, 12-Shotts, Henry, 13-
    Shotts, Elizabeth, 15-Miller
#5845, 1-Shotts, Samuel Henry, 2-born, 3-25 Jul 1824, 15-Miller
#5846, 1-Shotts, Mary Elizabeth, 2-born, 3-15 Jan 1852, 12-Shotts, Michael[?], 15-
    Miller
#5847, 1-Shotts, Daniel, 2-born, 3-4 Sep 1853, 15-Miller
#5848, 1-Shotts, Daniel, 2-died, 3-23 Oct 1853, 5-7 w, 15-Miller
#5849, 1-Shotts, Samuel Henry, 2-born, 3-11 Mar 1854[?], 15-Miller
#5850, 1-Shotts, Samuel Henry, 2-died, 3-26 Aug 1854[?], 5-5 months 16 days, 15-
    Miller
#5851, 1-Miller, John, 2-married, 3-25 Mar 1792, 7-Kemp, Susanna, 15-Miller
#5852, 1-Miller, Elizabeth, 2-married, 3-17 Dec 1820, 7-Shotts, Henry, 12-Miller,
    John, 13-Kemp, Susanna, 15-Miller
#5853, 1-Shotts, Michael C., 2-married, 3-10 Nov 1850, 7-Kentner, Cristena, 12-
    Shotts, Henry, 13-Shotts, Elizabeth, 15-Miller
#5854, 1-Kentner, Cristena, 2-born, 12-Kentner, Jacob, 13-Kentner, Elizabeth, 15-
    Miller
#5855, 1-Shotts, Samuel H., 2-married, 3-4 Jan 1857, 7-Long, Maria, 12-Shotts,
    Henry, 13-Shotts, Elizabeth, 15-Miller
#5856, 1-Long, Maria, 2-born, 12-Long, Anthony, 13-Long, Catherine, 15-Miller
#5857, 1-Miller, John, 2-died, 3-11 Aug 1824, 15-Miller
#5858, 1-Miler, Sophia, 2-died, 3-3 Feb 1833, 15-Miller
#5859, 1-Gaver, Harrit, 2-died, 3-18 Apr 1833, 15-Miller
```

FAMILY BIBLE RECORDS IN THE WASHINGTON COUNTY FREE LIBRARY, HAGERSTOWN, MARYLAND

Entry #, 1-Last Name, First Name, 2-Event, 3-Date, 4-Event Location, 5-Age, 6-Other,
7-Spouse's Last, First, 8-Groom's Residence, 9-Bride's Residence, 10-Minister, 11-Minister's Location,
12-Father's Last, First, 13-Mother's Last, First, 14-Transcribed, 15-Family Bible

```
#5860, 1-Shotts, Peter P., 2-died, 3-8 Feb 1834, 15-Miller
#5861, 1-Kemp, Granmother, 2-died, 3-1 Jan 1840, 5-99 years 8 days, 15-Miller
#5862, 1-Miller, Susannah, 2-died, 3-3 May 1843, 5-74 years, 15-Miller
#5863, 1-Gaver, Barbara, 2-died, 3-27[?] Apr 1845, 15-Miller
#5864, 1-Shotts, Martha R., 2-died, 3-20 Oct 1860, 12-Shotts, Samuel H., 13-Shotts,
    Maria, 15-Miller
#5865, 1-Shotts, Mary E., 2-died, 3-23 Mar 1866, 12-Shotts, Michael, 13-Shotts,
    Cristena, 15-Miller
#5866, 1-Shotts, Elizabeth, 2-died, 3-1 Dec 1877, 15-Miller
#5867, 1-Shotts, Christena, 2-died, 3-[unreadable], 15-Miller
#5868, 1-Johns, Julia M., 2-born, 3-10 Oct 1833, 4-Geneseo, Livingston Co., NY, 15-
    Johns
#5869, 1-Johns, John, 2-born, 3-6 Apr 1834, 4-Barriser[?], Cornwell, England, 15-
    Johns
#5870, 1-Johns, Margret Louisia, 2-born, 3-11 May 1859, 4-Hanover, Luzerne Co., PA,
    15-Johns
#5871, 1-Johns, James  Saml., 2-born, 3-30 Aug 1861, 4-Wilkes Barre, Luzerne Co.,
    PA, 15-Johns
#5872, 1-Johns, John Nelson, 2-born, 3-2 Aug 1864, 4-Wilkes Barre, Luzerne Co., PA,
    15-Johns
#5873, 1-Johns, Emma Julia, 2-born, 3-13 Apr 1866, 4-Wilkes Barre, Luzerne Co., PA,
    15-Johns
#5874, 1-Johns, Stella Malissa, 2-born, 3-5 Aug 1868, 4-Wilkes Barre, Luzerne Co.,
    PA, 12-Johns, John, 13-Johns, Julia, 15-Johns
#5875, 1-Johns, Julia Marinda, 2-born, 3-7 Sep 1872, 4-Plymouth, Puzene Co., PA,
    12-Johns, John, 13-Johns, Julia, 15-Johns
#5876, 1-Johns, Luther Rinehard[?], 2-born, 3-7 May 1878, 4-Plymouth, Puzene Co.,
    PA, 12-Johns, John, 13-Johns, Julia, 15-Johns
#5877, 1-Atwell, Hannah May, 2-born, 3-4 Sep 1910, 4-Parksville, Luzerne Co., PA,
    12-Atwell, George, 13-Atwell, Julia, 15-Johns
#5878, 1-Atwell, Mame Alice, 2-born, 3-27 Sep 1914, 4-Wilkes Barre, Luzerne Co.,
    PA, 12-Atwell, George, 13-Atwell, Julia, 15-Johns
#5879, 1-Anderson, Ernest Nelson, 2-born, 3-9 Nov 1895, 4-Plymouth, Luzern Co., PA,
    12-Anderson, Joe, 13-Anderson, Julia, 15-Johns
#5880, 1-Anderson, Leona Mable, 2-born, 3-13 Feb 1902, 4-Plymouth, Luzerne Co., PA,
    12-Anderson, Joe, 13-Anderson, Julia, 15-Johns
#5881, 1-Atwell, Fredrick John, 2-born, 3-23 Jun 1906[?], 4-Plymouth, Luzerne Co.,
    PA, 12-Atwell, George, 13-Atwell, Julia, 15-Johns
#5882, 1-Atwell, Martha Elizabeth, 2-born, 3-1 Nov 1908, 4-Royelville, Moyming[?]
    Co., PA, 12-Atwell, George, 13-Atwell, Julia, 15-Johns
#5883, 1-Johns, Emma Julia, 2-baptized, 3-18 Apr 1869, 15-Johns
#5884, 1-Johns, John, 2-married, 3-10 Sep 1857, 7-Johns, Julia M., 15-Johns
#5885, 1-Atwell, George, 2-married, 3-22 Jun 1905, 7-Atwell, Julia M., 15-Johns
#5886, 1-Johns, John Nelson, 2-died, 3-28 Aug 1864, 15-Johns
#5887, 1-Johns, James Samuel, 2-died, 3-29 Mar 1866, 15-Johns
#5888, 1-Johns, Emma Julia, 2-died, 3-12 May 1867, 15-Johns
#5889, 1-Johns, Luther Richard, 2-died, 3-3 Sep 1878, 15-Johns
#5890, 1-Atwell, Julia M., 2-died, 3-25 Dec 1925, 5-53 years, 15-Johns
#5891, 1-Atwell, George W., 2-died, 3-2 May 1934, 6-buried 5 May 1934, 15-Johns
#5892, 1-Ostrander, Martha Atwell, 2-died, 3-5 Jul 1934, 15-Johns
#5893, 1-Ostrander, Robert, 2-died, 3-Feb 1935, 13-Ostrander, Martha, 15-Johns
#5894, 1-Johns, John, 2-died, 3-25 Jun 1903, 15-Johns
#5895, 1-Johns, Julia M., 2-died, 3-13 Nov 1916, 15-Johns
#5896, 1-Anderson, Clara May, 2-born, 3-25 Nov 1893, 15-Johns
#5897, 1-Anderson, Clara May, 2-died, 3-29 Aug 1894, 15-Johns
```

FAMILY BIBLE RECORDS IN THE WASHINGTON COUNTY FREE LIBRARY, HAGERSTOWN, MARYLAND

Entry #, 1-Last Name, First Name, 2-Event, 3-Date, 4-Event Location, 5-Age, 6-Other,
7-Spouse's Last, First, 8-Groom's Residence, 9-Bride's Residence, 10-Minister, 11-Minister's Location,
12-Father's Last, First, 13-Mother's Last, First, 14-Transcribed, 15-Family Bible

```
#5898, 1-Atwell, Laurisa[?], 2-died, 3-Jan 1919, 15-Johns
#5899, 1-Atwell, Frederick John, 2-died, 3-11 May 1974, 15-Johns
#5900, 1-Eastwood, Martha Lela , 2-born, 3-30 Dec 1891, 4-Port Allegheny, PA, 7-
    Noble, Thomas William, 12-Eastwood, Samuel B., 13-Lewis, Almira, 15-Johns
#5901, 1-Eastwood, Samuel B., 2-born, 3-13 Sep 1857, 4-Port Allegheny, 15-Johns
#5902, 1-Lewis, Almira, 2-born, 3-1 Dec 1851, 4-Coudersport, PA, 15-Johns
#5903, 1-Noble, Thomas, 2-born, 3-16 Mar 1883, 4-Whitby, Yorkshire, England, 15-
    Johns
#5904, 1-Noble, Norman Geo., 2-born, 3-11 Aug 1911, 4-Oswego, NY, 15-Johns
#5905, 1-Atwell, Alice Susanna, 2-born, 3-29 Sep 1914, 4-Wilkes Barre, PA, 15-Johns
#5906, 1-Nobel, Norman, 2-married, 3-25 May 1938, 7-Atwell, Alice, 15-Johns
#5907, 1-Nobel, Beverly Alice, 2-born, 3-29 Dec 1940, 4-Berwick, PA, 12-Nobel,
    Norman, 13-Atwell, Alice, 15-Johns
#5908, 1-Nobel, Norma May, 2-born, 3-30 Apr 1945, 4-West Pittston, PA, 12-Nobel,
    Norman, 13-Atwell, Alice, 15-Johns
#5909, 1-Spindle, Benjm. T., 2-married, 3-15 May 1856, 7-Rose, H. Adelaide, 8-VA,
    9-VA, 10-Rev. Holmead, 11-Washington, DC, 15-Spindle
#5910, 1-Spindle, Benj. T., 2-married, 3-15 Jan 1866, 4-residence of groom's
    mother, 7-Lyons[?], Martha E., 8-Fairfax, VA, 9-Fairfax, VA, 10-Elder
    Marders, 15-Spindle
#5911, 1-Lee, Matthew R., 2-married, 3-9 Jan 1891, 4-Davidson's home, 7-Spindle,
    Martha A., 10-Davidson, 15-Spindle
#5912, 1-Lee, Mary M., 2-married, 3-11 Nov 1938, 4-Clarksville, MD, 7-Hobbs,
    Kenneth L., 10-Rev. Geo. Stocksdale, 15-Spindle
#5913, 1-Spindle, Benj. T., 2-born, 3-13 Nov 1835, 4-Prince William Co., VA, 15-
    Spindle
#5914, 1-Spindle, H. Addelaide, 2-born, 3-14 Jun 1840, 4-Alexandria, VA, 7-Spindle,
    Benjm. T., 15-Spindle
#5915, 1-Spindle, Martha E., 2-born, 3-3 Aug 1840, 4-Fairfax Co., VA, 6-2nd wife ,
    7-Spindle, Benjm. T., 15-Spindle
#5916, 1-Spindle, Martha Adelaide, 2-born, 3-7:30 am, 24 Sep 1867, 4-Centreville,
    Fairfax Co., VA, 15-Spindle
#5917, 1-Spindle, Pansly[?] Purington, 2-born, 3-7:30 am, 31 Oct 1870, 4-
    Centreville, Fairfax Co., VA, 15-Spindle
#5918, 1-Spindle, Addison Beebe, 2-born, 3-7:30 am, 14 Jul 1872, 4-Centreville,
    Fairfax Co., VA, 15-Spindle
#5919, 1-Spindle, Forris[?] Thomas, 2-born, 3-5:00 am, 2 Aug 1875, 4-Centreville,
    VA, 15-Spindle
#5920, 1-Hobbs, Kenneth L., 2-born, 3-17 Feb 1895, 4-Clarksville, Howard Co., MD,
    15-Spindle
#5921, 1-Hobbs, Mary Lee, 2-born, 3-6 Nov 1903, 4-Centreville, Fairfax Co., VA, 7-
    Hobbs, Kenneth L., 15-Spindle
#5922, 1-Spindle, H. Adelaide, 2-died, 3-30 Dec 1859[?], 4-Fayette Co., TX, 15-
    Spindle
#5923, 1-Spindle, Forris[?] Thomas, 2-died, 3-midnight-1am, 21 Mar 1876, 4-
    Centreville, VA, 15-Spindle
#5924, 1-Spindle, Benjm., 2-died, 3-11 pm, 7 Aug 1898, 4-Centreville, VA, 15-
    Spindle
#5925, 1-Spindle, Martha E., 2-died, 3-7 am, 14 Jan 1919, 4-Herndon, VA, 15-Spindle
#5926, 1-Hobbs, Kenneth L., 2-died, 3-early morning, 27 Mar 1978, 4-Sharon Nursing
    Home, Olney, MD, 15-Spindle
#5927, 1-Lee, Richard Auburn, 2-died, 3-7 pm, 9 Oct 1918, 4-Herndon, VA, 15-Spindle
#5928, 1-Lee, Matthew Richard, 2-died, 3-4 pm, 16 Apr 1920, 4-Herndon, VA, 15-
    Spindle
```

FAMILY BIBLE RECORDS IN THE WASHINGTON COUNTY FREE LIBRARY, HAGERSTOWN, MARYLAND

Entry #, 1-Last Name, First Name, 2-Event, 3-Date, 4-Event Location, 5-Age, 6-Other, 7-Spouse's Last, First, 8-Groom's Residence, 9-Bride's Residence, 10-Minister, 11-Minister's Location, 12-Father's Last, First, 13-Mother's Last, First, 14-Transcribed, 15-Family Bible

#5929, 1-Lee, Martha Adelaide, 2-died, 3-8:40 am, 19 Mar 1935, 4-Herndon, VA, 15-Spindle

#5930, 1-Lee, Chas. Bery, 2-died, 3-2 am, 2 Jul 1935, 4-Hanover, PA, 15-Spindle

#5931, 1-Spindle, Benjm. T., 2-baptized, 3-5 May 1867, 4-Broad Run, 10-Elder R.C. Leashman, 15-Spindle

#5932, 1-Lee, Matthew R., 2-baptized, 3-14 May 1914, 10-Rev. Simms, 11-Baptist Church, 15-Spindle

#5933, 1-Lee, Martha A., 2-baptized, 3-14 May 1914, 10-Rev. Simms, 11-Baptist Church, 15-Spindle

#5934, 1-Lee, Auburn R., 2-baptized, 3-14 May 1914, 10-Rev. Simms, 11-Baptist Church, 12-Lee, Matthew R., 13-Lee, Martha A., 15-Spindle

#5935, 1-Lee, Estelle, 2-baptized, 3-14 May 1914, 10-Rev. Simms, 11-Baptist Church, 12-Lee, Matthew R., 13-Lee, Martha A., 15-Spindle

#5936, 1-Lee, Mary, 2-baptized, 3-14 May 1914, 10-Rev. Simms, 11-Baptist Church, 12-Lee, Matthew R., 13-Lee, Martha A., 15-Spindle

#5937, 1-Lee, Grace, 2-baptized, 3-14 May 1914, 10-Rev. Simms, 11-Baptist Church, 12-Lee, Matthew R., 13-Lee, Martha A., 15-Spindle

#5938, 1-Lee, Martha A., 2-baptized, 3-16 Sep 1922, 6-"making a change", 10-U.D. Pickard, 11-Seventhday Adventist, 15-Spindle

#5939, 1-Lee, Grace A., 2-baptized, 3-16 Sep 1922, 6-"making a change", 10-U.D. Pickard, 11-Seventhday Adventist, 15-Spindle

#5940, 1-Lee, Harold Mathew, 2-died, 3-10 Jan 1984, 4-Salem, VA, 15-Spindle

#5941, 1-Lee, Matthew R., 2-born, 3-21 Jul 1864, 15-Spindle

#5942, 1-Lee, Martha A., 2-born, 3-24 Sep 1867, 7-Lee, Matthew R., 15-Spindle

#5943, 1-Lee, Charles B., 2-born, 3-Friday, 12 Feb 1892, 15-Spindle

#5944, 1-Lee, Ruth E., 2-born, 3-Thursday, 20 Feb 1894, 15-Spindle

#5945, 1-Lee, Richard A., 2-born, 3-Thursday, 18 Feb 1897, 15-Spindle

#5946, 1-Lee, Farris C., 2-born, 3-Saturday, 4 Nov 1898, 15-Spindle

#5947, 1-Lee, Martha E., 2-born, 3-Thursday, 13 Sep 1900, 15-Spindle

#5948, 1-Lee, Mary M., 2-born, 3-Friday, 6 Nov 1903, 15-Spindle

#5949, 1-Lee, Mace Alta, 2-born, 3-Tuesday, 4 Apr 1906, 6-twin, 15-Spindle

#5950, 1-Lee, Grace Adelaide, 2-born, 3-Tuesday, 4 Apr 1906, 6-twin, 15-Spindle

#5951, 1-Lee, Harold Matthew, 2-born, 3-Monday, 7 Mar 1908, 15-Spindle

#5952, 1-Lee, Clarence C., 2-born, 3-21 Mar 1910, 15-Spindle

#5953, 1-Walmsley, Robt. M., 3-m, 4-10 pm, 15 Feb 1827, 7-Beard, Margaret, 15-Walmsley

#5954, 1-Walmsley, Robt. M., 2-married, 3-11 Oct 1847, 7-McCauley, Harriet, 15-Walmsley

#5955, 1-Walmsley, Robert M., 2-married, 3-1785, 4-Sassafras, Cecil Co., MD, 7-Gorden[?], Margaret, 15-Walmsley

#5956, 1-Walmsley, Louisa J., 2-married, 3-Dec 1852, 4-M.E. Church, Elkton, MD, 7-Ricktis[?], George, 15-Walmsley

#5957, 1-Walmsley, Robert M., 2-married, 3-May 1853, 4-New Castle, DE, 7-Barr, Eavie[?], 15-Walmsley

#5958, 1-Walmsley, Robert M., 2-married, 3-Feb 1856, 4-Dubuque, Iowa, Williams, 8-Carrie Gracie[?], 15-Walmsley

#5959, 1-Walmsley, John M., 2-married, 3-Jun 1880, 4-Philadelphia, PA, 7-Vickers[?], Jennie, 15-Walmsley

#5960, 1-Walmsley, James G., 2-married, 3-15 Jan 1885, 4-Baltimore, MD, 7-Barrick, Emma, 15-Walmsley

#5961, 1-Walmsley, Robert M., 2-born, 3-26 Feb 1804, 4-Sassafras, 15-Walmsley

#5962, 1-Walmsley, Louisa Jane, 2-born, 3-1 Jan 1828, 4-Cecil Co., MD, 15-Walmsley

#5963, 1-Walmsley, Philip McCauley, 2-born, 3-16 Jul 1829, 4-Cecil Co., MD, 15-Walmsley

FAMILY BIBLE RECORDS IN THE WASHINGTON COUNTY FREE LIBRARY, HAGERSTOWN, MARYLAND

Entry #, 1-Last Name, First Name, 2-Event, 3-Date, 4-Event Location, 5-Age, 6-Other, 7-Spouse's Last, First, 8-Groom's Residence, 9-Bride's Residence, 10-Minister, 11-Minister's Location, 12-Father's Last, First, 13-Mother's Last, First, 14-Transcribed, 15-Family Bible

#5964, 1-Walmsley, Charles Edward, 2-born, 3-13 May 1831, 4-Cecil Co., MD, 15-Walmsley

#5965, 1-Walmsley, Robt. M., 2-born, 3-5 Mar 1833, 4-Cecil Co., MD, 15-Walmsley

#5966, 1-Walmsley, Hugh Beard, 2-born, 3-18 Jan 1835, 4-Cecil Co., MD, 15-Walmsley

#5967, 1-Walmsley, William Gibbs, 2-born, 3-5 Nov 1837, 4-Cecil Co., MD, 15-Walmsley

#5968, 1-Walmsley, Margaret Beard, 2-born, 3-27 Dec 1804, 4-Cecil Co., MD, 15-Walmsley

#5969, 1-Walmsley, Harriet McClauley, 2-born, 3-22 Feb 1814, 4-Cecil Co., MD, 15-Walmsley

#5970, 1-Walmsley, Daniel McCullough, 2-born, 3-2 Jan 1839, 4-Cecil Co., MD, 15-Walmsley

#5971, 1-Walmsley, Peggy Eliza, 2-born, 3-6 Aug 1840, 15-Walmsley

#5972, 1-Walmsley, Robert M., 2-born, 3-1764, 4-Sassafras Neck, Cecil Co., 15-Walmsley

#5973, 1-Walmsley, Robert M., 2-died, 3-1814, 4-Bel Hill, Cecil Co., MD, 6-"buried on the farm afterward moved to Old M.E. Cemetery, Elkton, MD", 15-Walmsley

#5974, 1-Gooding, Margaret, 2-born, 3-1762[or 1765], 4-Sassafras Neck, 6-"buried on Bell Hill Farm. Afterward moved to M.E. Cemetery Elkton", 7-Walmsley, R.M., 15-Walmsley

#5975, 1-Walmsley, Harriet Vickers, 2-born, 3-21 Apr 1887, 4-Buffalo, NY, 12-Walsmely, John, 13-Vickers, Jennie, 15-Walmsley

#5976, 1-Walmsley, Harriet Vickers, 2-died, 3-5:45 pm, 7 May 1947, 4-Union Hospital, Elkton, MD, 5-60 years 15 days, 6-buried 2pm, May 10, 1947, Elkton Methodist Church, interment in family lot in Elkton Cemetery, 15-Walmsley

#5977, 1-Walmsley, James Gooding, 2-born, 3-14 Mar 1843, 4-near Elkton, Md, 15-Walmsley

#5978, 1-Walmsley, MaryCarroll, 2-born, 3-25 Sep 1844, 4-Elkton, MD, 15-Walmsley

#5979, 1-Walmsley, Anne Elizabeth, 2-born, 3-26 Sep 1846, 4-Elkton, MD, 15-Walmsley

#5980, 1-Walmsley, John McCauley, 2-born, 3-31 Aug 1849, 4-Elkton, MD, 15-Walmsley

#5981, 1-Walmsley, James Gooding, 2-baptized, 3-Mar 1857, 10-E.J. Way, 11-Methodist Episcopal Church, 15-Walmsley

#5982, 1-Walmsley, Mary Carroll, 2-baptized, 3-Mar 1857, 4-Elkton, MD, 10-E.J. Way, 11-Methodist Episcopal Church, 15-Walmsley

#5983, 1-Walmsley, Anne Elizabeth, 2-baptized, 3-Mar 1857, 4-Methodist Episcopal Church, Elkton, MD, 10-E.J. Way, 11-Methodist Episcopal Church, 15-Walmsley

#5984, 1-Walmsley, John McCauley, 2-baptized, 3-Mar 1857, 4-Methodist Episcopal Church, 10-E.J. Way, 11-Methodist Episcopal Church, 15-Walmsley

#5985, 1-Walmsley, Margaret Beard, 2-died, 3-19 Nov 1840, 5-36 years, 6-buried at New[?] Leeds, 15-Walmsley

#5986, 1-Walmsley, Philip M., 2-died, 3-29 Oct 1853, 5-24 years, 6-buried in old Methodist Cemetery, 12-Walmsley, Robert, 13-Walmsley, Margaret B., 15-Walmsley

#5987, 1-Walmsley, Harriet McCauley, 2-died, 3-5 Nov 1885, 5-71 years, 6-heart disease; buried in Elkton Cemetery, 15-Walmsley

#5988, 1-Walmsley, John McCauley, 2-died, 3-18 Feb 1887, 6-consumption; buried Elkton Cemetery, 12-Walmsley, Robert M., 13-Walmsley, Harriet M., 15-Walmsley

#5989, 1-Walmsley, Jennie Vickers, 2-died, 3-27 Sep 1891, 4-Philadelphia, 6-pneumonia; buried Elkton Cemetery, 7-Walmsley, John M., 15-Walmsley

#5990, 1-Walmsley, Robt. M., 2-died, 3-22 Jul 1879, 5-75 years 5 months, 6-buried in Elkton Cemetery, 15-Walmsley

#5991, 1-Walmsley, Mary Gooding, 2-died, 3-20 Nov 1879, 5-70 years, 6-buried Elkton Cemetery, 15-Walmsley

#5992, 1-Walmsley, Hugh Beard, 2-died, 3-4 Dec 1888, 4-Natchitoches, LA, 6-buried Natchitoches, LA, 12-Walmsley, Robert H.[?], 13-Beard, Margaret, 15-Walmsley

FAMILY BIBLE RECORDS IN THE WASHINGTON COUNTY FREE LIBRARY, HAGERSTOWN, MARYLAND

Entry #, 1-Last Name, First Name, 2-Event, 3-Date, 4-Event Location, 5-Age, 6-Other, 7-Spouse's Last, First, 8-Groom's Residence, 9-Bride's Residence, 10-Minister, 11-Minister's Location, 12-Father's Last, First, 13-Mother's Last, First, 14-Transcribed, 15-Family Bible

#5993, 1-Hart, Rebecca P., 2-died, 3-Nov[?] 1866, 6-buried M.E. Cemetery, Elkton, MD, 12-Walmsley, Robert M., 13-Gooding, Margaret, 15-Walmsley

#5994, 1-Walmsley, James Gooding, 2-died, 3-21 Sep 1924, 4-Baltimore, 12-Walmsley, Robt., 13-Walmsley, Harriet, 15-Walmsley

#5995, 1-Walmsley, Anne Elizabeth, 2-died, 3-25 Feb 1914, 4-Elkton, MD, 6-buried Elkton Cemetery; neuralgia of the heart", 12-Walmsley, Robert M., 13-McCauley, Harriet, 15-Walmsley

#5996, 1-Ricketts, Louisa Jane, 2-died, 3-Dec 1905, 6-buried Elkton Cemetery; paralysis aftaer ten days illness", 7-Ricketts, George, 12-Walmsley, Robert Miller, 13-Beard, Margaret, 15-Walmsley

#5997, 1-Walmsley, Mary C., 2-died, 3-6 am, 22 Jan 1931, 6-buried Elkton Cemetery, a stroke of parlysis", 12-Walmsley, Robert M., 13-McCauley, Harriet, 15-Walmsley

#5998, 1-Williams, Caroline Gratia[?], 2-died, 3-21 Aug 1905, 4-"at their summer home, Essex, NY", 5-68 years, 6-"wife of Robert M. Walmsley of New Orleans", 7-Walmsley, Robert M., 15-Walmsley

#5999, 1-Ricketts, George, 2-died, 3-8 Dec 1902, 4-"at their home 'Brookside' near Elkton", 6-buried Elkton Cemetery, 7-Walmsley, Louisa Jane, 12-Ricketts, Thomas, 13-Ricketts, Jane, 15-Walmsley

#6000, 1-Walmsley, Robert Miller, 2-died, 3-26 Dec 1919, 4-New Orleans, at his house, 6-buried New Orleans, 15-Walmsley

#6001, 1-Oyeman, Robert T.[?], 2-married, 3-26 Dec 1876, 7-Gontrum, Anna M., 15-Oyeman

#6002, 1-Oyeman, John F.[?], 2-born, 3-3 am, Sunday, 13 Jan 1878, 15-Oyeman

#6003, 1-Oyeman, John F.[?], 2-died, 3-14 Feb 1878, 5-1months 1 days, 15-Oyeman

#6004, 1-Oyeman, Robert T.[?], 2-born, 3-7 pm, Thursday, 21 Nov 1878, 15-Oyeman

#6005, 1-Oyeman, Robert T.[?], 2-died, 3-21 Dec 1878, 5-1 months, 15-Oyeman

#6006, 1-Oyeman, Johann Herman, 2-married, 3-9 Feb 1847, 7-Yellman, Anna Chatarina Margaretha, 14-Yes, 15-Oyeman

#6007, 1-Dietrich, Johann Heinrich, 2-born, 3-2:30 am, 13 Oct 1847, 14-Yes, 15-Oyeman

#6008, 1-Luciman, Adelheid, 2-born, 3-11:45 pm, 22 Feb 1850, 14-Yes, 15-Oyeman

#6009, 1-[blank], Emma Catharina, 2-born, 3-5:30 am, 16 Dec 1851, 14-Yes, 15-Oyeman

#6010, 1-[blank], Robert Theodore, 2-born, 3-3:45 am, 14 Aug 1853, 14-Yes, 15-Oyeman

#6011, 1-Oyeman, Johann Herman, 2-born, 3-10 Oct 1815, 14-Yes, 15-Oyeman

#6012, 1-Yellman, Anna Catharina Margaretha, 2-born, 3-18 Sep 1827, 14-Yes, 15-Oyeman

#6013, 1-Dietrich, Juergen, 2-died, 3-6 Nov 1846, 14-Yes, 15-Oyeman

#6014, 1-Dietrich, Johann Heinrich, 2-died, 3-2 Mar 1849, 5-1 years 4 months 3 days, 14-Yes, 15-Oyeman

#6015, 1-[blank], Emma Chatarina, 2-died, 3-19 Apr 1852, 5-4 months 3 days, 14-Yes, 15-Oyeman

#6016, 1-Oyeman, Johann Herman, 2-died, 3-22 Feb 1856, 5-40 years 4 months 12 days, 14-Yes, 15-Oyeman

#6017, 1-Lucinna, Adelheid, 2-died, 3-9 Feb 1858, 5-8 years monthsinus 13 days, 14-Yes, 15-Oyeman

#6018, 1-Oyeman, Anna Catharina Margeretha, 2-died, 3-15 Jan 1865, 14-Yes, 15-Oyeman

#6019, 1-Oyeman, Geo. F.C., 2-married, 3-9 Dec 1903, 4-Grace Lutheran Church, Baltimore, 7-Fucie, Katharine M., 8-Baltimore, 9-Baltimore, 10-Rev. Wm. S. Freus, 15-Oyeman

#6020, 1-Oyeman, Henrietta Marie, 2-born, 3-5 Oct 1904, 15-Oyeman

#6021, 1-Oyeman, Robert Theodore, 2-born, 3-13 Nov 1907, 15-Oyeman

#6022, 1-Oyeman, Evalena Dorothy, 2-born, 3-8 Dec 1909, 15-Oyeman

FAMILY BIBLE RECORDS IN THE WASHINGTON COUNTY FREE LIBRARY, HAGERSTOWN, MARYLAND

Entry #, 1-Last Name, First Name, 2-Event, 3-Date, 4-Event Location, 5-Age, 6-Other,
7-Spouse's Last, First, 8-Groom's Residence, 9-Bride's Residence, 10-Minister, 11-Minister's Location,
12-Father's Last, First, 13-Mother's Last, First, 14-Transcribed, 15-Family Bible

```
#6023, 1-Oyeman, William Fricke, 2-born, 3-24 Nov 1912, 15-Oyeman
#6024, 1-Oyeman, William Fricke, 2-died, 3-26 Feb 1913, 15-Oyeman
#6025, 1-Musser, George, 2-born, 3-11 Jul 1777, 12-Musser, George, 13-Musser,
    Christiana, 15-Musser
#6026, 1-Musser, Mary, 2-born, 3-25 Mar 1783, 7-Musser, George, 12-Graff,
    Sebastian, 15-Musser
#6027, 1-Musser, George, 2-married, 3-18 May 1807, 7-Graff, Mary, 15-Musser
#6028, 1-Musser, William, 2-born, 3-5 Mar 1808, 12-Musser, Geo., 13-Musser, Mary,
    15-Musser
#6029, 1-Musser, Sebastian Graff, 2-born, 3-24 Aug 1810, 12-Musser, G., 13-Musser,
    M., 15-Musser
#6030, 1-Musser, Christiana Catharine, 2-born, 3-8 Sep 1812, 12-Musser, G., 13-
    Musser, M., 15-Musser
#6031, 1-Musser, Mary Elleanor, 2-born, 3-2 Aug 1814, 12-Musser, G., 13-Musser, M.,
    15-Musser
#6032, 1-Musser, George, 2-married, 3-17 Oct 1817, 7-Graeff, Sarah, 15-Musser
#6033, 1-Musser, George, 2-born, 3-31 Aug 1818, 12-Musser, Geo., 13-Musser, Sarah,
    15-Musser
#6034, 1-Musser, Jacob Graeff, 2-born, 3-3 Sep 1819, 12-Musser, G., 13-Musser, S.,
    15-Musser
#6035, 1-Musser, Sarah Elizabeth, 2-born, 3-2 Nov 1820, 12-Musser, G., 13-Musser,
    S., 15-Musser
#6036, 1-Musser, George, 2-died, 3-26 May 1868, 15-Musser
#6037, 1-Musser, Mary, 2-died, 3-31 Aug 1816, 15-Musser
#6038, 1-Musser, William, 2-died, 3-16 Jun 1891, 15-Musser
#6039, 1-Musser, Sebatian Graff, 2-died, 3-Apr 1861, 15-Musser
#6040, 1-Musser, Christianna Catharine, 2-died, 3-1 Nov 1894, 15-Musser
#6041, 1-Musser, Sarah, 2-died, 3-17 Aug 1874, 12-Graeff, 15-Musser
#6042, 1-Musser, George, 2-died, 3-25 Jan 1884, 12-Musser, George, 13-Musser,
    Sarah, 15-Musser
#6043, 1-Musser, Susanna, 2-born, 3-7 Jan 1822, 12-Musser, G., 13-Musser, S., 15-
    Musser
#6044, 1-Musser, Emma, 2-born, 3-27 Jan 1823, 12-Musser, G., 13-Musser, S., 15-
    Musser
#6045, 1-Musser, Anna Maria, 2-born, 3-27 Mar 1824, 12-Musser, G., 13-Musser, S.,
    15-Musser
#6046, 1-Musser, Henry Young, 2-born, 3-14 Feb 1826, 12-Musser, G., 13-Musser, S.,
    15-Musser
#6047, 1-Musser, Margaretta Schaum, 2-born, 3-26 Feb 1833, 12-Musser, G., 13-
    Musser, S., 15-Musser
#6048, 1-Musser, Anna Maria, 2-died, 3-Feb 1894, 15-Musser
#6049, 1-Musser, H.Y. [Henry Young], 2-died, 3-Dec 1831, 15-Musser
#6050, 1-Musser, Margaretta Schaum, 2-died, 3-5 Jan 1877, 12-Musser, George, 13-
    Musser, Sarah, 15-Musser
#6051, 1-Musser, William, 2-born, 3-5 Mar 1808, 12-Musser, George, 13-Musser, Mary,
    15-Musser
#6052, 1-Henderson, Sarah Anne, 2-born, 3-5 Nov 1813, 7-Musser, William, 12-
    Henderson, James, 13-Henderson, Sarah, 15-Musser
#6053, 1-Musser, George James, 2-born, 3-28 Sep 1835, 4-Montgomery Co., MD, 15-
    Musser
#6054, 1-Musser, George James, 2-baptized, 10-Jno. Mines[?], 15-Musser
#6055, 1-Musser, Sarah, 2-born, 3-30 Jul 1837, 4-Montgomery Co., MD, 12-Musser,
    William, 13-Musser, Sarah Anne, 15-Musser
#6056, 1-Musser, Flavel Augustus, 2-born, 3-21 Jul 1839, 4-Montgomery Co., MD, 12-
    Musser, William, 13-Musser, Sarah Anne, 15-Musser
```

FAMILY BIBLE RECORDS IN THE WASHINGTON COUNTY FREE LIBRARY, HAGERSTOWN, MARYLAND

Entry #, 1-Last Name, First Name, 2-Event, 3-Date, 4-Event Location, 5-Age, 6-Other, 7-Spouse's Last, First, 8-Groom's Residence, 9-Bride's Residence, 10-Minister, 11-Minister's Location, 12-Father's Last, First, 13-Mother's Last, First, 14-Transcribed, 15-Family Bible

```
#6057, 1-Musser, William, 2-died, 3-1[?] Jun 1891, 5-83 years, 15-Musser
#6058, 1-Musser, Sarah Anne, 2-died, 3-2:30 pm, Sunday, 23 Sep 1855, 15-Musser
#6059, 1-Musser, George James, 2-died, 3-17 Mar 1895, 15-Musser
#6060, 1-Musser, George, 2-born, 3-27 Mar 1741, 4-Falkner Levam[?], Berks Co., PA,
    12-Musser, Paul, 13-Musser, [unreadable], 15-Musser
#6061, 1-Musser, George, 2-died, 3-17 Jul 1806, 4-Lancaster, PA, 5-65 years 3
    months 20 days, 12-Musser, Paul, 13-Musser, [unreadable], 15-Musser
#6062, 1-Musser, Christiana, 2-born, 3-11 Sep 1748, 15-Musser
#6063, 1-Musser, George, 2-married, 3-1765, 4-Lancaster, 7-Young, Christiana, 15-
    Musser
#6064, 1-Musser, Rebecca, 2-born, 3-5 Aug 1766, 12-Musser, George, 13-Young,
    Christiana, 15-Musser
#6065, 1-Musser, Rebecca, 2-died, 3-26 Jan 1840, 15-Musser
#6066, 1-Musser, John, 2-born, 3-25 Sep 1768, 12-Musser, George, 13-Young,
    Christiana, 15-Musser
#6067, 1-Musser, Ann Maria, 2-born, 3-8 Apr 1771, 12-Musser, George, 13-Young,
    Christiana, 15-Musser
#6068, 1-Musser, Ann Maria, 2-died, 3-27 Jan 1827, 12-Musser, George, 13-Young,
    Christiana, 15-Musser
#6069, 1-Musser, Elizabeth, 2-born, 3-29 Mar 1773, 12-Musser, George, 13-Young,
    Christiana, 15-Musser
#6070, 1-Musser, Sarah (Salome)", 2-born, 3-9 Jul 1774, 12-Musser, George, 13-
    Young, Christiana, 15-Musser
#6071, 1-Musser, Sarah (Salome)", 2-died, 3-20 Oct 1854, 12-Musser, George, 13-
    Young, Christiana, 15-Musser
#6072, 1-Musser, John, 2-born, 3-10 May 1776, 12-Musser, George, 13-Young,
    Christiana, 15-Musser
#6073, 1-Musser, George, 2-born, 3-11 Jul 1777, 12-Musser, George, 13-Young,
    Christiana, 15-Musser
#6074, 1-Musser, George, 2-died, 3-26 May 1868, 12-Musser, George, 13-Young,
    Christiana, 15-Musser
#6075, 1-Musser, Jacob, 2-born, 3-16 Oct 1779, 12-Musser, George, 13-Young,
    Christiana, 15-Musser
#6076, 1-Musser, Catharine, 2-born, 3-30 Jan 1781, 12-Musser, George, 13-Young,
    Christiana, 15-Musser
#6077, 1-Musser, Catharine, 2-died, 3-26 Jul 1868, 12-Musser, George, 13-Young,
    Christiana, 15-Musser
#6078, 1-Musser, Jaub[?], 2-born, 3-30 May 1783, 12-Musser, George, 13-Young,
    Christiana, 15-Musser
#6079, 1-Musser, Matthias, 2-born, 3-2 Apr 1785, 12-Musser, George, 13-Young,
    Christiana, 15-Musser
#6080, 1-Musser, Matthias, 2-died, 3-22 Feb 1833, 12-Musser, George, 13-Young,
    Christiana, 15-Musser
#6081, 1-Musser, John Adam, 2-born, 3-3 Apr 1787, 12-Musser, George, 13-Young,
    Christiana, 15-Musser
#6082, 1-Musser, John Adam, 2-died, 3-18 Sep 1837, 12-Musser, George, 13-Young,
    Christiana, 15-Musser
#6083, 1-Musser, William, 2-born, 3-17 Aug 1789, 12-Musser, George, 13-Young,
    Christiana, 15-Musser
#6084, 1-Musser, William, 2-died, 3-17 May 1881, 12-Musser, George, 13-Young,
    Christiana, 15-Musser
#6085, 1-Musser, Henry, 2-born, 3-11 Mar 1791, 4-Augusta, Georgia, 12-Musser,
    George, 13-Young, Christiana, 15-Musser
#6086, 1-Musser, Henry, 2-died, 3-26 Jul 1822, 12-Musser, George, 13-Young,
    Christiana, 15-Musser
```

FAMILY BIBLE RECORDS IN THE WASHINGTON COUNTY FREE LIBRARY, HAGERSTOWN, MARYLAND

Entry #, 1-Last Name, First Name, 2-Event, 3-Date, 4-Event Location, 5-Age, 6-Other,
7-Spouse's Last, First, 8-Groom's Residence, 9-Bride's Residence, 10-Minister, 11-Minister's Location,
12-Father's Last, First, 13-Mother's Last, First, 14-Transcribed, 15-Family Bible

#6087, 1-Musser, Abraham, 2-born, 3-15 May 1793, 12-Musser, George, 13-Young, Christiana, 15-Musser

#6088, 1-Musser, Abraham, 2-died, 3-12 Nov 1828, 12-Musser, George, 13-Young, Christiana, 15-Musser

#6089, 1-Musser, Henrietta (Harriet)", 2-born, 3-26 Nov 1794, 12-Musser, George, 13-Young, Christiana, 15-Musser

#6090, 1-Musser, Henrietta (Harriet)", 2-died, 3-25 Dec 1886, 12-Musser, George, 13-Young, Christiana, 15-Musser

#6091, 1-Musser, Adam, 2-died, 3-26 Jan 1823, 4-Reamstown[?], 6-"Uncle Adam, grandfather's brother", 15-Musser

#6092, 1-Musser, William, 2-married, 3-30 Mar 1815, 4-Philadelphia, 7-Greis____[?], Susan Elizabeth, 12-Musser, George, 13-Musser, Christiana, 15-Musser

#6093, 1-Greis____[?], Susan Elizabeth, 2-born, 3-27 Mar 1795, 4-Philadelphia, 15-Musser

#6094, 1-Greis____[?], Susan Elizabeth, 2-died, 3-14 Sep 1867, 15-Musser

#6095, 1-Krug, Rebecca, 2-died, 3-11 Dec 1831, 5-80 years 19 days, 6-sister of Christiann Musser, 15-Musser

#6096, 1-Musser, Christiana, 2-died, 3-31 Mar 1828, 5-79 years 6 months, 7-Musser, George, 15-Musser

#6097, 1-Linger, Sr., John, 2-died, 3-13 May[?] 1829, 15-Musser

#6098, 1-Linger, Sr., John, 2-born, 3-11 Mar 1763, 15-Musser

#6099, 1-Dering, George Small, 2-born, 12-Dering, 13-Musser, Rebecca, 15-Musser

#6100, 1-Dering, Maria Christiana, 2-born, 7-Evans, 12-Dering, 13-Musser, Rebecca, 15-Musser

#6101, 1-Dering, Harriet, 2-born, 7-Lowry, 12-Dering, 13-Musser, Rebecca, 15-Musser

#6102, 1-Dering, Henry Young, 2-born, 12-Dering, 13-Musser, Rebecca, 15-Musser

#6103, 1-Dering, William Musser, 2-born, 12-Dering, 13-Musser, Rebecca, 15-Musser

#6104, 1-Dering, Sophia, 2-born, 12-Dering, 13-Musser, Rebecca, 15-Musser

#6105, 1-Dering, John Franklin, 2-born, 12-Dering, 13-Musser, Rebecca, 15-Musser

#6106, 1-Dering, Frederick Augustus, 2-born, 12-Dering, 13-Musser, Rebecca, 15-Musser

#6107, 1-Dering, Mary R., 2-born, 7-Lorentz, 12-Dering, F.A., 15-Musser

#6108, 1-Dering, William W., 12-Dering, F.A., 15-Musser

#6109, 1-Dering, Ellie E., 12-Dering, F.A., 15-Musser

#6110, 1-Dering, M. Augustus, 12-Dering, F.A., 15-Musser

#6111, 1-Dering, H. Ray, 12-Dering, F.A., 15-Musser

#6112, 1-Dering, D. Lida, 12-Dering, F.A., 15-Musser

#6113, 1-Lowrie[?], Delia, 7-Allen, 13-Lowrie, Harriet, 15-Musser

#6114, 1-Lowrie[?], Jane, 7-Kagans[?], 13-Lowrie, Harriet, 15-Musser

#6115, 1-Lowrie[?], Eliza, 6-twin, 7-Chadwick, 13-Lowrie, Harriet, 15-Musser

#6116, 1-Lowrie[?], Martha, 6-twin, 13-Lowrie, Harriet, 15-Musser

#6117, 1-Dering, Ann, 7-Chadwick, 12-Dering, Wm. Musser, 15-Musser

#6118, 1-Dering, Ellen, 7-Mills, 12-Dering, Wm. Musser, 15-Musser

#6119, 1-Dering, Laura G., 7-Pickenpaugh, 12-Dering, Wm. Musser, 15-Musser

#6120, 1-Dering, Harriet L., 12-Dering, Wm. Musser, 15-Musser

#6121, 1-Dering, Henry, 12-Dering, George Small, 15-Musser

#6122, 1-Dering, Mary Ann, 12-Dering, George Small, 15-Musser

#6123, 1-Dering, Rebecca, 12-Dering, George Small, 15-Musser

#6124, 1-Dering, Harriet, 12-Dering, George Small, 15-Musser

#6125, 1-Dering, Sarah, 12-Dering, George Small, 15-Musser

#6126, 1-Evans, George Dering, 13-Evans, Maria, 15-Musser

#6127, 1-Evans, Henry, 13-Evans, Maria, 15-Musser

#6128, 1-Evans, William Musser, 13-Evans, Maria, 15-Musser

#6129, 1-Evans, Harriet Lowry, 13-Evans, Maria, 15-Musser

#6130, 1-Evans, Sophia Eliza, 13-Evans, Maria, 15-Musser

FAMILY BIBLE RECORDS IN THE WASHINGTON COUNTY FREE LIBRARY, HAGERSTOWN, MARYLAND

Entry #, 1-Last Name, First Name, 2-Event, 3-Date, 4-Event Location, 5-Age, 6-Other,
7-Spouse's Last, First, 8-Groom's Residence, 9-Bride's Residence, 10-Minister, 11-Minister's Location,
12-Father's Last, First, 13-Mother's Last, First, 14-Transcribed, 15-Family Bible

```
#6131, 1-Evans, Elizabeth, 13-Evans, Maria, 15-Musser
#6132, 1-Evans, Mary, 13-Evans, Maria, 15-Musser
#6133, 1-Evans, Rebecca, 13-Evans, Maria, 15-Musser
#6134, 1-Evans, Sarah, 13-Evans, Maria, 15-Musser
#6135, 1-Lowry, Juliet Rebecca, 13-Lowry, Harriet, 15-Musser
#6136, 1-Lowry, Delia Maria, 13-Lowry, Harriet, 15-Musser
#6137, 1-Lowry, Jane Sophia, 13-Lowry, Harriet, 15-Musser
#6138, 1-Lowry, Harriet Eliza, 6-twin, 13-Lowry, Harriet, 15-Musser
#6139, 1-Lowry, Martha Ann, 6-twin, 13-Lowry, Harriet, 15-Musser
#6140, 1-Musser, William, 2-married, 3-19 Aug 1834, 7-Henderson, Sarah Anne, 8-
    Lancaster, PA, 9-Montgomery Co., MD, 10-Lio[?] Mines[?], 12-Musser, George,
    15-Musser
#6141, 1-Henderson, Sarah Anne, 2-born, 12-Henderson, James, 13-Henderson, Sarah,
    15-Musser
#6142, 1-Musser, William, 2-married, 3-10 Mar 1857, 7-Cromwell, Maria Catherine, 8-
    Lancaster, PA, 10-Rev. D. Metzer, 12-Musser, George, 15-Musser
#6143, 1-Cromwell, Maria Catherine, 2-born, 12-Cromwell, William, 13-Cromwell,
    Sarah, 15-Musser
#6144, 1-Musser, George James, 2-married, 3-12 Apr 1859, 4-Washington, DC, 7-
    Hutchinson, Sarah, 10-Rev. P.D. Curleny[?], 12-Musser, William, 13-Musser,
    Sarah Anne, 15-Musser
#6145, 1-Musser, William Henderson, 2-married, 3-30 May 1883, 7-Fairfax, Mary
    Jett.[?], 12-Musser, William, 13-Musser, Sarah Anne, 15-Musser
#6146, 1-Musser, Henry M., 2-married, 3-Oct 1882, 7-Burdette, MaryE., 12-Musser,
    William, 13-Musser, Sarah Anne, 15-Musser
#6147, 1-Musser, Caroline Beall, 2-married, 3-19 Dec 1893, 7-Graff, James William,
    10-Rev. L.R. Milburne, 15-Musser
#6148, 1-Musser, William, 2-born, 3-5 Mar 1808, 12-Musser, George, 13-Musser, Mary,
    15-Musser
#6149, 1-Musser, Sarah Anne, 2-born, 3-5 Nov 1813, 7-Musser, William, 12-Henderson,
    James, 13-Henderson, Sarah, 15-Musser
#6150, 1-Musser, George James, 2-born, 3-28 Sep 1835, 4-Montgomery Co., MD, 12-
    Musser, William, 13-Musser, Sarah Anne, 15-Musser
#6151, 1-Musser, George James, 2-baptized, 10-Rev. Jno.[?] Mines, 12-Musser,
    William, 13-Musser, Sarah Anne, 15-Musser
#6152, 1-Musser, Sarah Marie, 2-born, 3-30 Jul 1837, 4-Montgomery Co., MD, 12-
    Musser, William, 13-Musser, Sarah Anne, 15-Musser
#6153, 1-Musser, Sarah Marie, 2-baptized, 10-Rev. Jno[?] Mines, 12-Musser, William,
    13-Musser, Sarah Anne, 15-Musser
#6154, 1-Musser, Flavel Augustus, 2-born, 3-21 Jul 1839, 4-Montgomery Co., MD, 12-
    Musser, William, 13-Musser, Sarah Anne, 15-Musser
#6155, 1-Musser, Flavel Augustus, 2-baptized, 10-Rev. Jno[?] Mines, 12-Musser,
    William, 13-Musser, Sarah Anne, 15-Musser
#6156, 1-Musser, Christina Catherine, 2-born, 3-10 Oct 1841, 4-Montgomery Co., MD,
    12-Musser, William, 13-Musser, Sarah Anne, 15-Musser
#6157, 1-Musser, Christina Catherine, 2-baptized, 10-Rev. Jno[?] Mines, 12-Musser,
    William, 13-Musser, Sarah Anne, 15-Musser
#6158, 1-Musser, Susan Jane, 2-born, 3-4 Aug 1843, 4-Montgomery Co., MD, 12-Musser,
    William, 13-Musser, Sarah Anne, 15-Musser
#6159, 1-Musser, Susan Jane, 2-baptized, 10-Rev. R.T. Berry[?], 12-Musser, William,
    13-Musser, Sarah Anne, 15-Musser
#6160, 1-Musser, William Henderson, 2-born, 3-8 Aug 1845, 4-Montgomery Co., MD, 12-
    Musser, William, 13-Musser, Sarah Anne, 15-Musser
#6161, 1-Musser, William Henderson, 2-baptized, 10-Rev. S.J. Baird, 12-Musser,
    William, 13-Musser, Sarah Anne, 15-Musser
```

FAMILY BIBLE RECORDS IN THE WASHINGTON COUNTY FREE LIBRARY, HAGERSTOWN, MARYLAND

Entry #, 1-Last Name, First Name, 2-Event, 3-Date, 4-Event Location, 5-Age, 6-Other, 7-Spouse's Last, First, 8-Groom's Residence, 9-Bride's Residence, 10-Minister, 11-Minister's Location, 12-Father's Last, First, 13-Mother's Last, First, 14-Transcribed, 15-Family Bible

#6162, 1-Musser, Caroline Beall, 2-born, 3-8 Aug 1847, 4-Montgomery Co., MD, 12-Musser, William, 13-Musser, Sarah Anne, 15-Musser

#6163, 1-Musser, Caroline Beall, 2-baptized, 10-Rev. S.J. Baird, 12-Musser, William, 13-Musser, Sarah Anne, 15-Musser

#6164, 1-Musser, Mary Ellen, 2-born, 3-18 Sep 1849, 4-Montgomery Co., MD, 12-Musser, William, 13-Musser, Sarah Anne, 15-Musser

#6165, 1-Musser, Mary Ellen, 2-baptized, 10-Rev. A.M. Hershey, 12-Musser, William, 13-Musser, Sarah Anne, 15-Musser

#6166, 1-Musser, Henry Martyn, 2-born, 3-17 Oct 1850, 4-Montgomery Co., MD, 12-Musser, William, 13-Musser, Sarah Anne, 15-Musser

#6167, 1-Musser, Henry Martyn, 2-baptized, 10-Rev. A.M. Hershey, 12-Musser, William, 13-Musser, Sarah Anne, 15-Musser

#6168, 1-Musser, Sarah Anne, 2-died, 3-23 Sep 1855, 7-Musser, William, 15-Musser

#6169, 1-Musser, Maria C., 2-died, 3-12 Jun 1860, 7-Musser, William, 15-Musser

#6170, 1-Musser, William, 2-died, 3-16 Jun 1891, 15-Musser

#6171, 1-Musser, Henry M., 2-died, 3-30 Sep 1894, 15-Musser

#6172, 1-Musser, George J., 2-died, 3-17 Mar 1895, 15-Musser

#6173, 1-Musser, William H., 2-died, 3-26 May 1899, 15-Musser

#6174, 1-Musser, Christianie C., 2-died, 3-5 Nov 1908, 15-Musser

#6175, 1-Musser, Sarah M., 2-died, 3-6 Aug 1916, 15-Musser

#6176, 1-Musser, Susan J., 2-died, 3-9 May 1918, 15-Musser

#6177, 1-Musser, Flavel A., 2-died, 3-1923, 15-Musser

#6178, 1-Graff, Caroline Beall, 2-died, 3-26 Jun 1924, 15-Musser

#6179, 1-Musser, George James, 2-born, 3-28 Sep 1835, 15-Musser

#6180, 1-Musser, George James, 2-married, 3-12 Apr 1859, 4-Washington, DC, 7-Hutchinson, Sarah E., 10-Rev. P.D. Curley, 15-Musser

#6181, 1-Musser, Anne Catherine, 2-born, 3-19 Jan 1861, 12-Musser, George James, 13-Hutchinson, Sarah E., 15-Musser

#6182, 1-Musser, Elizabeth Mary, 2-born, 3-16 Mar 1863, 12-Musser, George James, 13-Hutchinson, Sarah E., 15-Musser

#6183, 1-Musser, William, 2-born, 3-Dec 1866, 12-Musser, George James, 13-Hutchinson, Sarah E., 15-Musser

#6184, 1-Musser, Sarah Elizabeth, 2-born, 3-30 Oct 1869, 12-Musser, George James, 13-Hutchinson, Sarah E., 15-Musser

#6185, 1-Musser, Sarah Elizabeth, 2-married, 3-12 Nov 1894, 7-Randal, Walter B., 15-Musser

#6186, 1-Musser, William Henderson, 2-born, 3-8 Aug 1845, 15-Musser

#6187, 1-Fairfax, Mary Jett, 2-born, 3-1 Apr 1858, 15-Musser

#6188, 1-Musser, William Henderson, 2-married, 3-30 May 1883, 4-Montross, VA, 7-Fairfax, Mary Jett, 15-Musser

#6189, 1-Musser, Minnie Palmer, 2-born, 3-30 Mar 1884, 12-Musser, William H., 13-Musser, Mary J., 15-Musser

#6190, 1-Musser, Annie Laurie, 2-born, 3-21 Aug 1885, 12-Musser, William H., 13-Musser, Mary J., 15-Musser

#6191, 1-Musser, Sarah Fairfax, 2-born, 3-5 Jan 1889, 12-Musser, William H., 13-Musser, Mary J., 15-Musser

#6192, 1-Musser, Ada Cary, 2-born, 3-20 Apr 1891, 12-Musser, William H., 13-Musser, Mary J., 15-Musser

#6193, 1-Musser, Mary Jett, 2-born, 3-27 Jan 1899, 12-Musser, William H., 13-Musser, Mary J., 15-Musser

#6194, 1-Musser, Frances E., 2-born, 3-6 Feb 1888, 15-Musser

#6195, 1-Musser, Henry Marcellus, 2-born, 3-26 Jan 1881, 15-Musser

#6196, 1-Musser, Susie, 2-born, 3-21 May 1895, 15-Musser

#6197, 1-Musser, Minnie Palmer, 2-married, 3-21 Jun 1909, 4-Rockville, 7-Hawkins, Edward Mack Curtis, 10-Rev. Samuel White, 12-Musser, William H., 15-Musser

FAMILY BIBLE RECORDS IN THE WASHINGTON COUNTY FREE LIBRARY, HAGERSTOWN, MARYLAND

Entry #, 1-Last Name, First Name, 2-Event, 3-Date, 4-Event Location, 5-Age, 6-Other, 7-Spouse's Last, First, 8-Groom's Residence, 9-Bride's Residence, 10-Minister, 11-Minister's Location, 12-Father's Last, First, 13-Mother's Last, First, 14-Transcribed, 15-Family Bible

#6198, 1-Musser, Sarah Fairfax, 2-married, 3-3 Jul 1907, 4-Fort Smith, Arkansas, 7-Burall, Harrison, 12-Musser, William H., 15-Musser

#6199, 1-Musser, Annie Laurie, 2-married, 3-26 Sep 1912, 4-London, 7-Stevens, Neill Graham, 12-Musser, William H., 15-Musser

#6200, 1-Musser, Mary Jett, 2-died, 3-16 ___ 1909, 15-Musser

#6201, 1-Musser, Frances E., 2-born, 3-6 Feb 1888, 12-Musser, Henry M., 13-Musser, Elisabeth, 15-Musser

#6202, 1-Musser, Henry Marcellus, 2-born, 3-26 Jan 1891, 12-Musser, Henry M., 13-Musser, Elisabeth, 15-Musser

#6203, 1-Musser, Susie, 2-born, 3-12 May 1895, 12-Musser, Henry M., 13-Musser, Elisabeth, 15-Musser

#6204, 1-Musser, George, 2-born, 3-27 Mar 1741, 14-Yes, 15-Musser

#6205, 1-Musser, George, 2-married, 3-16 Jul 1765, 7-Young, Christina, 14-Yes, 15-Musser

#6206, 1-Musser, George, 2-died, 3-12 Jul 1806, 14-Yes, 15-Musser

#6207, 1-Young, Christina, 2-born, 3-11 Sep 1748, 7-Musser, George, 14-Yes, 15-Musser

#6208, 1-Young, Christina, 2-died, 3-31 Mar 1828[?], 7-Musser, George, 14-Yes, 15-Musser

#6209, 1-Musser, Rebecca, 2-born, 3-5 Aug 1766, 12-Musser, George, 13-Young, Christina, 14-Yes, 15-Musser

#6210, 1-Musser, Johannes, 2-born, 3-25 Sep 1768, 12-Musser, George, 13-Young, Christina, 14-Yes, 15-Musser

#6211, 1-Musser, Johannes, 2-died, 3-7 May 1773, 12-Musser, George, 13-Young, Christina, 14-Yes, 15-Musser

#6212, 1-Musser, Anna Maria, 2-born, 3-8 Aug 1771, 12-Musser, George, 13-Young, Christina, 14-Yes, 15-Musser

#6213, 1-Musser, Elizabeth, 2-born, 3-29 Mar 1773, 12-Musser, George, 13-Young, Christina, 14-Yes, 15-Musser

#6214, 1-Musser, Salmi (Salome), 2-born, 3-9 Jul 1774, 12-Musser, George, 13-Young, Christina, 14-Yes, 15-Musser

#6215, 1-Musser, Johannes, 2-born, 3-10 May 1776, 12-Musser, George, 13-Young, Christina, 14-Yes, 15-Musser

#6216, 1-Musser, George, 2-born, 3-11 Jul 1777, 12-Musser, George, 13-Young, Christina, 14-Yes, 15-Musser

#6217, 1-Musser, Jacob, 2-born, 3-16 Oct 1779, 12-Musser, George, 13-Young, Christina, 14-Yes, 15-Musser

#6218, 1-Musser, Catharine, 2-born, 3-30 Jan 1781, 12-Musser, George, 13-Young, Christina, 14-Yes, 15-Musser

#6219, 1-Musser, Jacob, 2-born, 3-30 May 1783, 12-Musser, George, 13-Young, Christina, 14-Yes, 15-Musser

#6220, 1-Musser, Mattheus, 2-born, 3-2 Apr 1785, 12-Musser, George, 13-Young, Christina, 14-Yes, 15-Musser

#6221, 1-Musser, Mattheus, 2-died, 3-1833, 12-Musser, George, 13-Young, Christina, 14-Yes, 15-Musser

#6222, 1-Musser, Johan Adam, 2-born, 3-3 Apr 1787, 12-Musser, George, 13-Young, Christina, 14-Yes, 15-Musser

#6223, 1-Musser, Johan Adam, 2-died, 3-18 Sep 1837, 12-Musser, George, 13-Young, Christina, 14-Yes, 15-Musser

#6224, 1-Musser, Wilhelm, 2-born, 3-17 Aug 1789, 12-Musser, George, 13-Young, Christina, 14-Yes, 15-Musser

#6225, 1-Musser, Henrich, 2-born, 3-11 Mar 1791, 12-Musser, George, 13-Young, Christina, 14-Yes, 15-Musser

#6226, 1-Musser, Abraham, 2-born, 3-15 May 1793, 12-Musser, George, 13-Young, Christina, 14-Yes, 15-Musser

FAMILY BIBLE RECORDS IN THE WASHINGTON COUNTY FREE LIBRARY, HAGERSTOWN, MARYLAND

Entry #, 1-Last Name, First Name, 2-Event, 3-Date, 4-Event Location, 5-Age, 6-Other, 7-Spouse's Last, First, 8-Groom's Residence, 9-Bride's Residence, 10-Minister, 11-Minister's Location, 12-Father's Last, First, 13-Mother's Last, First, 14-Transcribed, 15-Family Bible

#6227, 1-Musser, Abraham, 2-died, 3-11 Nov 1828, 12-Musser, George, 13-Young, Christina, 14-Yes, 15-Musser

#6228, 1-Musser, Henrieta, 2-born, 3-2 Nov 1794, 12-Musser, George, 13-Young, Christina, 14-Yes, 15-Musser

#6229, 1-Musser, George, 2-born, 3-11 Jul 1777, 14-Yes, 15-Musser

#6230, 1-Musser, George, 2-married, 3-18 May 1807, 14-Yes, 15-Musser

#6231, 1-Musser, Mary, 2-born, 3-25 Mar 1783, 14-Yes, 15-Musser

#6232, 1-Musser, William, 2-born, 3-5 Mar 1808, 14-Yes, 15-Musser

#6233, 1-Musser, Sebastian Graff, 2-born, 3-24 Aug 1810, 14-Yes, 15-Musser

#6234, 1-Musser, Sebastian Graff, 2-died, 3-23 Apr 1861, 14-Yes, 15-Musser

#6235, 1-Musser, Christiana Catharine, 2-born, 3-8 Sep 1812, 14-Yes, 15-Musser

#6236, 1-Musser, Christiana Catharine, 2-died, 3-1 Nov 1895, 14-Yes, 15-Musser

#6237, 1-Musser, Mary Ellen, 2-born, 3-2 Aug 1814, 14-Yes, 15-Musser

#6238, 1-Musser, Mary Ellen, 2-died, 3-22 Dec 1898, 14-Yes, 15-Musser

#6239, 1-Musser, George, 2-married, 3-23 Oct 1817, 7-Graff, Sarah, 14-Yes, 15-Musser

#6240, 1-Musser, George, 2-born, 3-31 Aug 1818, 14-Yes, 15-Musser

#6241, 1-Musser, Jacob Graff, 2-born, 3-3 Sep 1819, 14-Yes, 15-Musser

#6242, 1-Musser, Sarah Elizabeth, 2-born, 3-2 Nov 1820, 14-Yes, 15-Musser

#6243, 1-Musser, Susanna, 2-born, 3-7 Jan 1822, 14-Yes, 15-Musser

#6244, 1-Musser, Emma, 2-born, 3-27 Jan 1823, 14-Yes, 15-Musser

#6245, 1-Musser, Ann Maria, 2-born, 3-27 Mar 1824, 14-Yes, 15-Musser

#6246, 1-Musser, Ann Maria, 2-died, 3-11 Feb 1894, 14-Yes, 15-Musser

#6247, 1-Musser, Henry Young, 2-born, 3-12 Feb 1826, 14-Yes, 15-Musser

#6248, 1-Musser, Margaretta Schaum, 2-born, 3-27 Feb 1833, 14-Yes, 15-Musser

#6249, 1-Musser, Margaretta Schaum, 2-died, 3-5 Jan 1877, 14-Yes, 15-Musser

#6250, 1-Hardwick, Sadie Alma, 2-born, 3-Saturday, 12 noon, 26 Apr 1879, 4-58[?] Greenmount Avenue, 12-Hardwick, William Charles, 13-Hardwick, Mollie, 15-Hardwick

#6251, 1-Hardwick, Sadie Alma, 2-baptized, 10-J.J.G. Webster, 12-Hardwick, William Charles, 13-Hardwick, Mollie, 15-Hardwick

#6252, 1-Hardwick, William Murdock Webster, 2-born, 3-Saturday afternoon, 2 Jul 1881, 4-50 Greenmount Avenue, 12-Hardwick, William Charles, 13-Hardwick, Mollie, 15-Hardwick

#6253, 1-Hardwick, William Murdock Webster, 2-baptized, 3-May 1882, 4-45 East Eager, 10-Rev. L.T. Weiderman, 12-Hardwick, William Charles, 13-Hardwick, Mollie, 15-Hardwick

#6254, 1-Hardwick, Mollie A., 2-born, 3-19 Jan 1853, 12-Shomaker, George, 15-Hardwick

#6255, 1-Hardwick, William Charles, 2-born, 3-22 Sep 1854, 4-58 Greenmount Avenue, 15-Hardwick

#6256, 1-Hardwick, Sadie Alma, 2-died, 3-11 am, Wednesday, 25 Mar 1964, 4-6200 Brook Avenue, Baltimore, 5-85 years, 15-Hardwick

#6257, 1-Shomaker, George, 2-died, 3-8 Mar 1880, 4-at his home 5 miles from York, PA, 5-64 years 11 days, 6-father of Mollie Hardwick, 15-Hardwick

#6258, 1-Shomaker, George, 2-born, 3-26 Feb 1816, 15-Hardwick

#6259, 1-Hardwick, Henry Th., 2-married, 3-15 May 1849, 4-St. Paul's Church, Knightsbridge, London, England, 6-"Left London for America June 1 1849, Arrived in Baltimore August 4, 1849", 7-Powell, Sarah, 15-Hardwick

#6260, 1-Hardwick, Sarah Elisabeth, 2-baptized, 3-15 Jun 1851, 15-Hardwick

#6261, 1-Hardwick, Henry William, 2-baptized, 3-25 Jul 1852, 15-Hardwick

#6262, 1-Hardwick, William Charles, 2-baptized, 3-31 Dec 1854, 15-Hardwick

#6263, 1-Hardwick, Arthur James, 2-baptized, 3-24 Jul 1858, 15-Hardwick

#6264, 1-Hardwick, Harry William Rynn, 2-baptized, 3-1876, 10-Rev. A.S. Hank, 15-Hardwick

FAMILY BIBLE RECORDS IN THE WASHINGTON COUNTY FREE LIBRARY, HAGERSTOWN, MARYLAND

Entry #, 1-Last Name, First Name, 2-Event, 3-Date, 4-Event Location, 5-Age, 6-Other, 7-Spouse's Last, First, 8-Groom's Residence, 9-Bride's Residence, 10-Minister, 11-Minister's Location, 12-Father's Last, First, 13-Mother's Last, First, 14-Transcribed, 15-Family Bible

```
#6265, 1-Hardwick, Charles Jones, 2-baptized, 3-1877, 10-Rev. Bishop, 15-Hardwick
#6266, 1-Hardwick, Robert Henry, 2-baptized, 3-Sunday, 21 Aug 1898, 4-816 Green Mt.
      Avenue, 10-Rev. George Maydwell, 15-Hardwick
#6267, 1-Hardwick, Sarah, 2-obituary, 3-7 Sep 1909, 5-83 years, 15-Hardwick
#6268, 1-Hardwicke, Elizabeth, 2-married, 7-Pymont, 14-Yes, 15-Hardwick
#6269, 1-Hardwicke, Elizabeth, 2-died, 3-13 Dec 1876, 4-England, 14-Yes, 15-
      Hardwick
#6270, 1-Hardwicke, Mary, 2-married, 4-England, 6-came to America in 1849, 7-Conn,
      William Robert, 14-Yes, 15-Hardwick
#6271, 1-Powell, William, 2-died, 3-18 Apr 1860, 4-England, 6-father of Sarah
      Powell, 14-Yes, 15-Hardwick
#6272, 1-Hardwicke, Henry Thomas, 2-born, 3-23 Sep 1825, 14-Yes, 15-Hardwick
#6273, 1-Hardwicke, Henry Thomas, 2-died, 3-22 Oct 1888, 14-Yes, 15-Hardwick
#6274, 1-Hardwicke, Henry Thomas, 2-married, 3-15 May 1849, 4-St. Paul's Church,
      Knightsbridge, London, 6-"They left London for America june 1,1849; arrived
      in Baltimore, Md. Aug. 10, 1849", 7-Powell, Sarah, 9-London, England, 14-Yes,
      15-Hardwick
#6275, 1-Powell, Sarah, 2-born, 3-25 Apr 1827, 14-Yes, 15-Hardwick
#6276, 1-Hardwick, Arthur James, 2-born, 3-17 Jan 1876, 12-Hardwick, Henry Thomas,
      13-Powell, Sarah, 14-Yes, 15-Hardwick
#6277, 1-Hardwick, Arthur James, 2-died, 3-8 Nov 1876, 12-Hardwick, Henry Thomas,
      13-Powell, Sarah, 14-Yes, 15-Hardwick
#6278, 1-Hardwick, William Charles, 2-born, 3-22 Sep 1854, 12-Hardwick, Henry
      Thomas, 13-Powell, Sarah, 14-Yes, 15-Hardwick
#6279, 1-Hardwick, William Charles, 2-died, 3-17 May 1920, 12-Hardwick, Henry
      Thomas, 13-Powell, Sarah, 14-Yes, 15-Hardwick
#6280, 1-Hardwick, Sarah Elizabeth, 2-born, 3-21 Feb 1850, 12-Hardwick, Henry
      Thomas, 13-Powell, Sarah, 14-Yes, 15-Hardwick
#6281, 1-Hardwick, Sarah Elizabeth, 2-died, 3-15 Jun 1851, 12-Hardwick, Henry
      Thomas, 13-Powell, Sarah, 14-Yes, 15-Hardwick
#6282, 1-Hardwick, Harry (Henry) William, 2-born, 3-25 Apr 1852, 12-Hardwick, Henry
      Thomas, 13-Powell, Sarah, 14-Yes, 15-Hardwick
#6283, 1-Hardwick, Harry (Henry) William, 2-died, 3-24 Feb 1911, 12-Hardwick, Henry
      Thomas, 13-Powell, Sarah, 14-Yes, 15-Hardwick
#6284, 1-Hardwick, Harry (Henry) William, 2-married, 3-Apr 1874, 4-Parsonage of
      Strawbridge M.E.[?] Church, 7-Otty, Phebe, 12-Hardwick, Henry Thomas, 13-
      Powell, Sarah, 14-Yes, 15-Hardwick
#6285, 1-Hardwick, Harry William Byrne, 2-born, 3-12 Sep 1875, 12-Hardwick, Harry,
      13-Hardwick, Phebe, 14-Yes, 15-Hardwick
#6286, 1-Hardwick, Charles Jones, 2-born, 3-29 Jan 1877, 12-Hardwick, Harry, 13-
      Hardwick, Phebe, 14-Yes, 15-Hardwick
#6287, 1-Hardwick, Charles Jones, 2-died, 5-infancy, 12-Hardwick, Harry, 13-
      Hardwick, Phebe, 14-Yes, 15-Hardwick
#6288, 1-Hardwick, Albert Birtwell, 2-born, 3-19 Sep 1879, 12-Hardwick, Harry, 13-
      Hardwick, Phebe, 14-Yes, 15-Hardwick
#6289, 1-Hardwick, Albert Birtwell, 2-died, 3-1955, 12-Hardwick, Harry, 13-
      Hardwick, Phebe, 14-Yes, 15-Hardwick
#6290, 1-Hardwick, Elsie, 2-born, 3-23 Apr 1885, 12-Hardwick, Harry, 13-Hardwick,
      Phebe, 14-Yes, 15-Hardwick
#6291, 1-Hardwick, Ambrose Smedley, 2-born, 3-16 Dec 1887, 12-Hardwick, Harry, 13-
      Hardwick, Phebe, 14-Yes, 15-Hardwick
#6292, 1-Hardwick, Jessie, 2-born, 12-Hardwick, Harry, 13-Hardwick, Phebe, 14-Yes,
      15-Hardwick
#6293, 1-Hardwick, Jessie, 2-died, 5-infancy, 12-Hardwick, Harry, 13-Hardwick,
      Phebe, 14-Yes, 15-Hardwick
```

FAMILY BIBLE RECORDS IN THE WASHINGTON COUNTY FREE LIBRARY, HAGERSTOWN, MARYLAND

Entry #, 1-Last Name, First Name, 2-Event, 3-Date, 4-Event Location, 5-Age, 6-Other, 7-Spouse's Last, First, 8-Groom's Residence, 9-Bride's Residence, 10-Minister, 11-Minister's Location, 12-Father's Last, First, 13-Mother's Last, First, 14-Transcribed, 15-Family Bible

#6294, 1-Hardwick, Jr., Harry William, 2-born, 12-Hardwick, Harry, 13-Hardwick, Phebe, 14-Yes, 15-Hardwick

#6295, 1-Hardwick, Jr., Harry William, 2-married, 7-Fitchett, Nora, 12-Hardwick, Harry, 13-Hardwick, Phebe, 14-Yes, 15-Hardwick

#6296, 1-Hardwick, Mildred, 2-married, 7-Walker, John E., 12-Hardwick, Jr., Harry William, 13-Fitchett, Nora, 14-Yes, 15-Hardwick

#6297, 1-Hardwick, Albert, 2-married, 7-Becker, Carrie, 12-Hardwick, Jr., Harry William, 13-Fitchett, Nora, 14-Yes, 15-Hardwick

#6298, 1-Hardwick, Elizabeth , 2-born, 12-Hardwick, Albert, 13-Becker, Carrie, 14-Yes, 15-Hardwick

#6299, 1-Hardwick, Alberta, 2-born, 12-Hardwick, Albert, 13-Becker, Carrie, 14-Yes, 15-Hardwick

#6300, 1-Hardwick, Elsie, 2-married, 7-Tapman, John, 12-Hardwick, Albert, 13-Becker, Carrie, 14-Yes, 15-Hardwick

#6301, 1-Tapman, John Allen, 2-married, 7-Yingling, Elizabeth, 12-Tapman, John, 13-Hardwick, Elsie, 14-Yes, 15-Hardwick

#6302, 1-Tapman, Edward Brent, 2-married, 7-Fogel, Verna, 12-Tapman, John, 13-Hardwick, Elsie, 14-Yes, 15-Hardwick

#6303, 1-Tapman, Ambrose Smedley, 2-married, 7-Sandlass, Viola, 12-Tapman, John, 13-Hardwick, Elsie, 14-Yes, 15-Hardwick

#6304, 1-Tapman, Harold, 2-born, 12-Tapman, Ambrose Smedley, 13-Sandlass, Viola, 14-Yes, 15-Hardwick

#6305, 1-Tapman, Marjorie, 2-married, 7-Jones, 12-Tapman, Ambrose Smedley, 13-Sandlass, Viola, 14-Yes, 15-Hardwick

#6306, 1-Shomaker, Mollie Amanda, 2-born, 3-17 Jan 1860, 14-Yes, 15-Hardwick

#6307, 1-Shomaker, Mollie Amanda, 2-married, 3-16 Aug 1877, 4-groom's residence, 7-Hardwick, William Charles, 8-58 Greenount Ave., 10-Rev. J.J.G. Webster, 11-Monument Street M.E. Church, 14-Yes, 15-Hardwick

#6308, 1-Shomaker, Mollie Amanda, 2-died, 3-29 May 1882, 14-Yes, 15-Hardwick

#6309, 1-Hardwick, William Charles, 2-married, 3-19 Oct 1897, 7-Ringleb, Mary Ida, 14-Yes, 15-Hardwick

#6310, 1-Hardwick, Robert Henry, 2-born, 3-3 May 1898, 12-Hardwick, William Charles, 13-Ringleb, Mary Ida, 14-Yes, 15-Hardwick

#6311, 1-Hardwick, Robert Henry, 2-died, 3-25 Aug 1898, 12-Hardwick, William Charles, 13-Ringleb, Mary Ida, 14-Yes, 15-Hardwick

#6312, 1-Hardwick, Sadie Alma, 2-born, 3-26 Apr 1879, 12-Hardwick, William Charles, 13-Shomaker, Mollie Amanda, 14-Yes, 15-Hardwick

#6313, 1-Hardwick, Sadie Alma, 2-married, 3-1903, 7-Jackson, Howard Thomas, 12-Hardwick, William Charles, 13-Shomaker, Mollie Amanda, 14-Yes, 15-Hardwick

#6314, 1-Hardwick, William Murdock Webster, 2-born, 3-2 Jul 1881, 12-Hardwick, William Charles, 13-Shomaker, Mollie Amanda, 14-Yes, 15-Hardwick

#6315, 1-Hardwick, William Murdock Webster, 2-died, 3-26 Nov 1941, 12-Hardwick, William Charles, 13-Shomaker, Mollie Amanda, 14-Yes, 15-Hardwick

#6316, 1-Hardwick, William Murdock Webster, 2-married, 7-Baldwin, Bertha Gertrude, 9-York, PA, 12-Hardwick, William Charles, 13-Shomaker, Mollie Amanda, 14-Yes, 15-Hardwick

#6317, 1-Jackson, Jr., Thomas Howard, 2-born, 3-16 Feb 1904, 12-Jackson, Howard, 13-Hardwick, Sadie Alma, 14-Yes, 15-Hardwick

#6318, 1-Jackson, Robert Earle, 2-born, 3-29 Jan 1906, 12-Jackson, Howard, 13-Hardwick, Sadie Alma, 14-Yes, 15-Hardwick

#6319, 1-Jackson, George Willard, 2-born, 3-25 Feb 1908, 12-Jackson, Howard, 13-Hardwick, Sadie Alma, 14-Yes, 15-Hardwick

#6320, 1-Jackson, Gilbert William, 2-born, 3-31 Jul 1909, 12-Jackson, Howard, 13-Hardwick, Sadie Alma, 14-Yes, 15-Hardwick

FAMILY BIBLE RECORDS IN THE WASHINGTON COUNTY FREE LIBRARY, HAGERSTOWN, MARYLAND

Entry #, 1-Last Name, First Name, 2-Event, 3-Date, 4-Event Location, 5-Age, 6-Other, 7-Spouse's Last, First, 8-Groom's Residence, 9-Bride's Residence, 10-Minister, 11-Minister's Location, 12-Father's Last, First, 13-Mother's Last, First, 14-Transcribed, 15-Family Bible

```
#6321, 1-Jackson, William Charles, 2-born, 3-12 Nov 1917, 12-Jackson, Howard, 13-
     Hardwick, Sadie Alma, 14-Yes, 15-Hardwick
#6322, 1-Hardwick, Ida Hazel, 2-born, 3-13 May 1905, 12-Hardwick, William, 14-Yes,
     15-Hardwick
#6323, 1-Hardwick, Ida Hazel, 2-married, 3-25 Dec 1928, 7-DeWeise, Charles W., 12-
     Hardwick, William, 14-Yes, 15-Hardwick
#6324, 1-Hardwick, Webster Melbourne, 2-born, 3-11 Aug 1906, 12-Hardwick, William,
     14-Yes, 15-Hardwick
#6325, 1-Hardwick, Webster Melbourne, 2-married, 3-15 Oct 1928, 7-Smith, Cecelia
     A., 12-Hardwick, William, 14-Yes, 15-Hardwick
#6326, 1-Jackson, William Charles, 2-born, 3-4 Jan 1909, 12-Hardwick, William, 14-
     Yes, 15-Hardwick
#6327, 1-Jackson, Mary May, 2-born, 3-13 Dec 1911, 12-Hardwick, William, 14-Yes,
     15-Hardwick
#6328, 1-Jackson, Harry Thomas, 2-born, 3-9 Nov 1914, 12-Hardwick, William, 14-Yes,
     15-Hardwick
#6329, 1-Jackson, Thomas Howard, 2-married, 7-Oyeman, Henrietta Marie, 14-Yes, 15-
     Hardwick
#6330, 1-Jackson, Dorothy Marie, 2-born, 3-1 Nov 1929, 12-Jackson, Thomas Howard,
     13-Oyeman, Marie, 14-Yes, 15-Hardwick
#6331, 1-Jackson, Dorothy Marie, 2-married, 3-7 Feb 1948, 7-Thomas, William Kirley,
     12-Jackson, Thomas Howard, 13-Oyeman, Marie, 14-Yes, 15-Hardwick
#6332, 1-Jackson, III, Thomas Howard, 2-born, 3-5 Mar 1932, 12-Jackson, Thomas
     Howard, 13-Oyeman, Marie, 14-Yes, 15-Hardwick
#6333, 1-Jackson, Miriam Elizabeth, 2-born, 3-18 May 1945, 12-Jackson, Thomas
     Howard, 13-Oyeman, Marie, 14-Yes, 15-Hardwick
#6334, 1-Jackson, __bert Earle, 2-married, 7-Copenhaver, Anna Clara, 12-Jackson,
     Thomas Howard, 13-Oyeman, Marie, 14-Yes, 15-Hardwick
#6335, 1-Jackson, Jr., Robert Earle, 2-born, 3-19 Apr 1928, 12-Jackson, __bert
     Earle, 13-Copenhavaer, Anna Clara, 14-Yes, 15-Hardwick
#6336, 1-Jackson, Richard Raymond, 2-born, 3-30 Apr 1932, 12-Jackson, __bert Earle,
     13-Copenhavaer, Anna Clara, 14-Yes, 15-Hardwick
#6337, 1-Jackson, Donald Louis, 2-born, 3-27 ___ 1934, 12-Jackson, __bert Earle,
     13-Copenhavaer, Anna Clara, 14-Yes, 15-Hardwick
#6338, 1-Jackson, Dennis Roger, 2-born, 3-11 Apr 1939, 12-Jackson, __bert Earle,
     13-Copenhavaer, Anna Clara, 14-Yes, 15-Hardwick
#6339, 1-Jackson, Alan Edward, 2-born, 3-26 Sep 1945, 12-Jackson, __bert Earle, 13-
     Copenhavaer, Anna Clara, 14-Yes, 15-Hardwick
#6340, 1-Jackson, George Willard, 2-married, 7-Hochrein, Margaret Ellen, 14-Yes,
     15-Hardwick
#6341, 1-Jackson, Arlene Frances, 2-born, 3-8 Feb 1947, 12-Jackson, Geroge Willard,
     13-Hochrein, Margaret Ellen, 14-Yes, 15-Hardwick
#6342, 1-Jackson, _lbert William, 2-married, 7-Jones, Bertha, 14-Yes, 15-Hardwick
#6343, 1-Jackson, William Charles, 2-married, 7-Hefastay, Vivien, 14-Yes, 15-
     Hardwick
#6344, 1-Jackson, Carol Vivien, 2-born, 3-24 Dec 1940, 12-Jackson, William Charles,
     13-Hefastay, Vivien, 14-Yes, 15-Hardwick
#6345, 1-Jackson, Jr., William Charles, 2-born, 3-4 Oct 1947, 12-Jackson, William
     Charles, 13-Hefastay, Vivien, 14-Yes, 15-Hardwick
#6346, 1-Hardwick, Jr., William Charles, 2-born, 3-3 May 1930, 12-Hardwick, William
     Charles, 13-Hoke, Sarah Velma, 14-Yes, 15-Hardwick
#6347, 1-Hardwick, Richard Eugene, 2-born, 3-14 Jul 1931, 12-Hardwick, William
     Charles, 13-Hoke, Sarah Velma, 14-Yes, 15-Hardwick
#6348, 1-Hardwick, Mary (Mollie) May, 2-married, 3-7 Sep 1931, 14-Yes, 15-Hardwick
```

FAMILY BIBLE RECORDS IN THE WASHINGTON COUNTY FREE LIBRARY, HAGERSTOWN, MARYLAND

Entry #, 1-Last Name, First Name, 2-Event, 3-Date, 4-Event Location, 5-Age, 6-Other, 7-Spouse's Last, First, 8-Groom's Residence, 9-Bride's Residence, 10-Minister, 11-Minister's Location, 12-Father's Last, First, 13-Mother's Last, First, 14-Transcribed, 15-Family Bible

```
#6349, 1-Decker, _une Louise, 2-born, 3-7 Jun 1932, 12-Decker, James, 13-Hardwick,
   Mary May, 14-Yes, 15-Hardwick
#6350, 1-Decker, James William, 2-born, 3-4 Jul 1934, 12-Decker, James, 13-
   Hardwick, Mary May, 14-Yes, 15-Hardwick
#6351, 1-Decker, Lois May, 2-born, 3-4 May 1941, 12-Decker, James, 13-Hardwick,
   Mary May, 14-Yes, 15-Hardwick
#6352, 1-Decker, Doris Marie, 2-born, 3-22 Oct 1946, 12-Decker, James, 13-Hardwick,
   Mary May, 14-Yes, 15-Hardwick
#6353, 1-Hardwick, Harry T.H., 2-married, 3-24 Dec 1934, 7-Horn, Edith Maxine, 14-
   Yes, 15-Hardwick
#6354, 1-Hardwick, Stanley Eugene, 2-born, 3-4 Dec 1935, 12-Hardwick, Harry, 13-
   Horn, Edith Maxine, 14-Yes, 15-Hardwick
#6355, 1-Hardwick, Robert Sterling, 2-born, 3-27 Jul 1937, 12-Hardwick, Harry, 13-
   Horn, Edith Maxine, 14-Yes, 15-Hardwick
#6356, 1-Hardwick, Thomas Dean, 2-born, 3-28 May 1940, 12-Hardwick, Harry, 13-Horn,
   Edith Maxine, 14-Yes, 15-Hardwick
#6357, 1-Hardwick, Leonard Paul, 2-born, 3-7 Aug 1946, 12-Hardwick, Harry, 13-Horn,
   Edith Maxine, 14-Yes, 15-Hardwick
#6358, 1-Decker, June Louise, 2-married, 3-15 Sep 1951, 7-Patterson, Carl E., 14-
   Yes, 15-Hardwick
#6359, 1-Patterson, Leon Allen, 2-born, 3-27 Feb 1953, 12-Patterson, Carl E., 13-
   Decker, June Louise, 14-Yes, 15-Hardwick
#6360, 1-Patterson, Leon Allen, 2-died, 3-30 Jun 1953, 12-Patterson, Carl E., 13-
   Decker, June Louise, 14-Yes, 15-Hardwick
#6361, 1-Patterson, Sharon Ann, 2-born, 3-24 Sep 1955, 12-Patterson, Carl E., 13-
   Decker, June Louise, 14-Yes, 15-Hardwick
#6362, 1-Hardwick, William, 2-died, 3-21 Jun 1889, 4-Baltimore County, MD, 5-69
   years, 6-brother of Henry Thomas Hardwicke, 14-Yes, 15-Hardwick
#6363, 1-Hardwick, Ida Hazel, 3-13 May 1905, 15-Hardwick
#6364, 1-Hardwick, Webster Melbourne, 3-11 Aug 1906, 15-Hardwick
#6365, 1-Hardwick, William Charles, 3-4 Jan 1910, 15-Hardwick
#6366, 1-Hardwick, Mary May, 3-13 Dec 1913[?], 15-Hardwick
#6367, 1-Hardwick, Harry Thomas , 3-9 Nov 1914, 15-Hardwick
#6368, 1-Hardwick, Jr., Wm. Charles, 3-3 May 1930, 12-Hardwick, Wm. Charles, 15-
   Hardwick
#6369, 1-Hardwick, Richard Eugene, 3-14 Jul 1931, 12-Hardwick, Wm. Charles, 15-
   Hardwick
#6370, 1-Decker, June Louise, 3-7 Jun 1932, 12-Decker, 13-Hardwick, Mary, 15-
   Hardwick
#6371, 1-Decker, James William, 3-4 Jul 1934, 12-Decker, 13-Hardwick, Mary, 15-
   Hardwick
#6372, 1-Decker, Lois May, 3-4 May 1941, 12-Decker, 13-Hardwick, Mary, 15-Hardwick
#6373, 1-Decker, Doris Marie, 3-22 Oct 1946, 12-Decker, 13-Hardwick, Mary, 15-
   Hardwick
#6374, 1-Hardwick, Stanley Eugene, 3-4 Dec 1935, 12-Hardwick, Harry, 13-Horn,
   Edith, 15-Hardwick
#6375, 1-Hardwick, Robert Sterling, 3-27 Jul 1937, 12-Hardwick, Harry, 13-Horn,
   Edith, 15-Hardwick
#6376, 1-Hardwick, Thomas Dean, 3-28 May 1940, 12-Hardwick, Harry, 13-Horn, Edith,
   15-Hardwick
#6377, 1-Hardwick, Leonard Paul, 3-7 Aug 1946, 12-Hardwick, Harry, 13-Horn, Edith,
   15-Hardwick
#6378, 1-H., W.W., 2-died, 3-26 Nov 1941, 15-Hardwick
#6379, 1-Hardwick, Ida Hazel, 3-13 May 1905, 15-Hardwick
#6380, 1-Hardwick, Webster Melbourne, 3-11 Aug 1906, 15-Hardwick
```

FAMILY BIBLE RECORDS IN THE WASHINGTON COUNTY FREE LIBRARY, HAGERSTOWN, MARYLAND

Entry #, 1-Last Name, First Name, 2-Event, 3-Date, 4-Event Location, 5-Age, 6-Other, 7-Spouse's Last, First, 8-Groom's Residence, 9-Bride's Residence, 10-Minister, 11-Minister's Location, 12-Father's Last, First, 13-Mother's Last, First, 14-Transcribed, 15-Family Bible

```
#6381, 1-Hardwick, Wm. Charles, 3-4 Jan 1910[?], 15-Hardwick
#6382, 1-Hardwick, Mary May, 3-13 Dec 1911, 15-Hardwick
#6383, 1-Hardwick, Harry Thomas, 2-born, 3-9 Nov 1914, 15-Hardwick
#6384, 1-Hardwick, Jr., Wm. C., 3-3 May 1930, 12-Hardwick, Wm. C., 13-Hardwick,
    Sarah, 15-Hardwick
#6385, 1-Hardwick, Richard Eugene, 3-14 Jul 1931, 12-Hardwick, Wm. C., 13-Hardwick,
    Sarah, 15-Hardwick
#6386, 1-Decker, June Louise, 3-7 Jun 1932, 12-Decker, 1Mary May, 15-Hardwick
#6387, 1-Decker, James Wm., 3-4 Jul 1934, 12-Decker, 1Mary May, 15-Hardwick
#6388, 1-Decker, Lois May, 3-4 May 1941, 12-Decker, 1Mary May, 15-Hardwick
#6389, 1-Decker, Doris Marie, 3-22 Oct 1946, 12-Decker, 1Mary May, 15-Hardwick
#6390, 1-Hardwick, William Webster, 2-married, 3-7 Oct 1903, 4-Parsonage of 2nd
    Moravian Church, 679 Rouse Avenue, York, PA, 7-Baldwin, Bertha G., 12-
    Hardwick, Wm. C., 13-Hardwick, Mollie A., 15-Hardwick
#6391, 1-Hardwick, Ida Hazel, 2-born, 3-13 May 1906, 12-Hardwick, William Webster,
    13-Baldwin, Bertha G., 15-Hardwick
#6392, 1-Hardwick, Webster, 2-born, 3-11 Aug 1907, 12-Hardwick, William Webster,
    13-Baldwin, Bertha G., 15-Hardwick
#6393, 1-Hardwick, William Charles, 2-born, 3-4 Jan 1910, 12-Hardwick, William
    Webster, 13-Baldwin, Bertha G., 15-Hardwick
#6394, 1-Hardwick, Molly May, 2-born, 3-13 Dec 1913, 15-Hardwick
#6395, 1-Hardwick, _____ Thomas, 2-born, 3-7 Nov 1917[?], 15-Hardwick
#6396, 1-Hardwick, Stanley Eugene, 3-4 Dec 1935, 12-Hardwick, Harry, 13-Hardwick,
    Edith, 15-Hardwick
#6397, 1-Hardwick, Robert Sterling, 3-27 Jul 1937, 12-Hardwick, Harry, 13-Hardwick,
    Edith, 15-Hardwick
#6398, 1-Hardwick, Thomas Dean, 3-28 May 1940, 12-Hardwick, Harry, 13-Hardwick,
    Edith, 15-Hardwick
#6399, 1-Hardwick, Leonard Paul, 3-7 Aug 1946, 12-Hardwick, Harry, 13-Hardwick,
    Edith, 15-Hardwick
#6400, 1-Jackson, Jr., Thomas Howard, 2-born, 3-16 Feb 1904, 12-Jackson, Thomas
    Howard, 13-Jackson, Sadie A., 15-Hardwick
#6401, 1-Jackson, Robert Earle, 2-born, 3-29 Jan 1906, 12-Jackson, Thomas Howard,
    13-Jackson, Sadie A., 15-Hardwick
#6402, 1-Jackson, George Willard, 2-born, 3-25 Feb 1908, 12-Jackson, Thomas Howard,
    13-Jackson, Sadie A., 15-Hardwick
#6403, 1-Jackson, Gilbert William, 2-born, 3-31 Jul 1909, 12-Jackson, Thomas
    Howard, 13-Jackson, Sadie A., 15-Hardwick
#6404, 1-Jackson, William Charles, 2-born, 3-12 Nov 1917, 12-Jackson, Thomas
    Howard, 13-Jackson, Sadie A., 15-Hardwick
#6405, 1-Jackson, Jr., Thomas Howard, 2-married, 7-Oyeman, Henrietta Marie, 15-
    Hardwick
#6406, 1-Jackson, Dorothy Marie, 2-born, 3-1 Nov 1929, 12-Jackson, Jr., Thomas
    Howard, 13-Oyeman, Henrietta Marie, 15-Hardwick
#6407, 1-Jackson, III, Thomas Howard, 2-born, 3-5 Mar 1932, 15-Hardwick
#6408, 1-Jackson, Mirriam Elizabeth, 2-born, 3-18 May 1945, 15-Hardwick
#6409, 1-Jackson, Dorothy M., 2-married, 3-8 Feb 1948, 7-Thomas, Wm. K., 15-
    Hardwick
#6410, 1-Jackson, Robert Earle, 2-married, 7-Copenhaver, Anna Clara, 15-Hardwick
#6411, 1-Jackson, Jr., Robert Earle, 2-born, 3-19 Apr 1928, 12-Jackson, Robert
    Earle, 13-Copenhaver, Anna Clara, 15-Hardwick
#6412, 1-Jackson, Richard Raymond, 2-born, 3-30 Apr 1930, 12-Jackson, Robert Earle,
    13-Copenhaver, Anna Clara, 15-Hardwick
#6413, 1-Jackson, Donald Louis, 2-born, 3-2 May 1934, 12-Jackson, Robert Earle, 13-
    Copenhaver, Anna Clara, 15-Hardwick
```

FAMILY BIBLE RECORDS IN THE WASHINGTON COUNTY FREE LIBRARY, HAGERSTOWN, MARYLAND

Entry #, 1-Last Name, First Name, 2-Event, 3-Date, 4-Event Location, 5-Age, 6-Other,
7-Spouse's Last, First, 8-Groom's Residence, 9-Bride's Residence, 10-Minister, 11-Minister's Location,
12-Father's Last, First, 13-Mother's Last, First, 14-Transcribed, 15-Family Bible

#6414, 1-Jackson, Dennis Roger, 2-born, 3-11 Apr 1939, 12-Jackson, Robert Earle, 13-Copenhaver, Anna Clara, 15-Hardwick

#6415, 1-Jackson, Alan Edward, 2-born, 3-26 Sep 1945, 12-Jackson, Robert Earle, 13-Copenhaver, Anna Clara, 15-Hardwick

#6416, 1-Jackson, George Willard, 2-married, 7-Hochrein, Margaret Ellen, 15-Hardwick

#6417, 1-Jackson, Arlene Frances, 2-born, 3-8 Feb 1947, 12-Jackson, George Willard, 13-Hochrein, Margaret Ellen, 15-Hardwick

#6418, 1-Hardwick, Harry Wm. Byrne, 2-born, 3-12 Sep 1875, 12-Hardwick, Harry, 13-Ottry, Phebe, 15-Hardwick

#6419, 1-Hardwick, Charles Jones, 2-born, 3-29 Jan 1877, 12-Hardwick, Harry, 13-Ottry, Phebe, 15-Hardwick

#6420, 1-Hardwick, Albert Birtwell, 2-born, 3-19 Sep 1879, 12-Hardwick, Harry, 13-Ottry, Phebe, 15-Hardwick

#6421, 1-Hardwick, Elsie, 2-born, 3-23 Apr 1885, 12-Hardwick, Harry, 13-Ottry, Phebe, 15-Hardwick

#6422, 1-Hardwick, Ambrose Smedley, 2-born, 3-16 Dec 1887, 12-Hardwick, Harry, 13-Ottry, Phebe, 15-Hardwick

#6423, 1-Hardwick, Jessie, 2-born, 12-Hardwick, Harry, 13-Ottry, Phebe, 15-Hardwick

#6424, 1-Hardwick, Jessie, 2-died, 5-infancy, 12-Hardwick, Harry, 13-Ottry, Phebe, 15-Hardwick

#6425, 1-Hardwick, Harry, 2-married, 7-Fitchett, Nora, 15-Hardwick

#6426, 1-Hardwick, Mildred, 2-married, 7-Walker, J.E., 12-Hardwick, Harry, 13-Fitchett, Nora, 15-Hardwick

#6427, 1-Hardwick, Albert, 2-married, 7-Becker, Carrie, 15-Hardwick

#6428, 1-Hardwick, Elizabeth, 2-born, 12-Hardwick, Albert, 13-Becker, Carrie, 15-Hardwick

#6429, 1-Hardwick, Alberta, 2-born, 12-Hardwick, Albert, 13-Becker, Carrie, 15-Hardwick

#6430, 1-Hardwick, Elsie, 2-married, 7-Taxman[?], John, 15-Hardwick

#6431, 1-Taxman[?], John Allen, 2-married, 7-Yingling, Elizabeth, 12-Taxman, John, 13-Hardwick, Elsie, 15-Hardwick

#6432, 1-Taxman[?], E. Brent, 2-married, 7-Fogel, Verna, 12-Taxman, John, 13-Hardwick, Elsie, 15-Hardwick

#6433, 1-Hardwick, Ambrose Smedley, 2-married, 7-Sandlass, Viola, 15-Hardwick

#6434, 1-Hardwick, Harold, 2-born, 12-Hardwick, Ambrose Smedley, 13-Sandlass, Viola, 15-Hardwick

#6435, 1-Hardwick, Margorie, 2-born, 12-Hardwick, Ambrose Smedley, 13-Sandlass, Viola, 15-Hardwick

#6436, 1-Hardwick, Wm. C., 2-married, 3-24 Mar 1940, 7-Hefastay, Dorothy Vivien, 15-Hardwick

#6437, 1-Hardwick, Carol Vivien, 2-born, 3-24 Dec 1940, 12-Hardwick, Wm. C., 13-Hefastay, Dorothy Vivien, 15-Hardwick

#6438, 1-Hardwick, Jr., Wm. C., 2-born, 3-4 Oct 1947, 12-Hardwick, Wm. C., 13-Hefastay, Dorothy Vivien, 15-Hardwick

#6439, 1-Hardwick, George W., 2-married, 3-14 Nov 1942, 7-Hochrein, Margaret Ellen, 15-Hardwick

#6440, 1-Hardwick, Arlene Frances, 2-born, 3-8 Feb 194-[?], 12-Hardwick, George W., 13-Hochrein, Margaret Ellen, 15-Hardwick

#6441, 1-Hardwick, Thomas Howard, 2-married, 3-2 Jun 1928, 7-Oyeman, Henrietta Marie, 15-Hardwick

#6442, 1-Hardwick, Dorothy Marie, 2-born, 3-1 Nov 1929, 12-Hardwick, Thomas Howard, 13-Oyeman, Henrietta Marie, 15-Hardwick

#6443, 1-Hardwick, III, Thomas Howard, 2-born, 3-5 Mar 1932, 12-Hardwick, Thomas Howard, 13-Oyeman, Henrietta Marie, 15-Hardwick

FAMILY BIBLE RECORDS IN THE WASHINGTON COUNTY FREE LIBRARY, HAGERSTOWN, MARYLAND

Entry #, 1-Last Name, First Name, 2-Event, 3-Date, 4-Event Location, 5-Age, 6-Other,
7-Spouse's Last, First, 8-Groom's Residence, 9-Bride's Residence, 10-Minister, 11-Minister's Location,
12-Father's Last, First, 13-Mother's Last, First, 14-Transcribed, 15-Family Bible

```
#6444, 1-Hardwick, Miriam Elizabeth, 2-born, 3-18 May 1945, 12-Hardwick, Thomas
    Howard, 13-Oyeman, Henrietta Marie, 15-Hardwick
#6445, 1-Hardwick, Dorothy Marie, 2-married, 3-7 Feb 1948, 7-Thomas, Wm. K., 15-
    Hardwick
#6446, 1-Hardwick, Gilbert Wm., 2-married, 3-1 Jun 1935, 7-Jones, Bertha Catherine,
    15-Hardwick
#6447, 1-Hardwick, Robert Earle, 2-married, 3-3 Sep 1927, 7-Copenhaver, Anna Clara,
    15-Hardwick
#6448, 1-Hardwick, Jr., Robert Earle, 2-born, 3-19 Apr 1928, 12-Hardwick, Robert
    Earle, 13-Copenhaver, Anna Clara, 15-Hardwick
#6449, 1-Hardwick, Richard Raymond, 2-born, 12-Hardwick, Robert Earle, 13-
    Copenhaver, Anna Clara, 15-Hardwick
#6450, 1-Hardwick, Donald Louis, 2-born, 12-Hardwick, Robert Earle, 13-Copenhaver,
    Anna Clara, 15-Hardwick
#6451, 1-Hardwick, Dennis Roger, 2-born, 12-Hardwick, Robert Earle, 13-Copenhaver,
    Anna Clara, 15-Hardwick
#6452, 1-Hardwick, Alan Edward, 2-born, 12-Hardwick, Robert Earle, 13-Copenhaver,
    Anna Clara, 15-Hardwick
#6453, 1-Hardwick, Harry William Byrne, 2-born, 3-12 Sep 1875, 15-Hardwick
#6454, 1-Hardwick, Charles Jones, 2-born, 3-29 Jan 1877, 15-Hardwick
#6455, 1-Hardwick, Albert Birtwell, 2-born, 3-19 Sep 1879, 15-Hardwick
#6456, 1-Hardwick, Elsie, 2-born, 3-23 Apr 1885, 15-Hardwick
#6457, 1-Hardwick, Ambrose Ottey, 2-born, 3-16 Dec 1887, 15-Hardwick
#6458, 1-Hardwick, Jessie, 2-died, 5-infancy, 15-Hardwick
#6459, 1-Hardwick, Albert, 2-married, 7-Becker, Carrie, 15-Hardwick
#6460, 1-Hardwick, Alberta, 2-born, 12-Hardwick, Harry, 13-Becker, Carrie, 15-
    Hardwick
#6461, 1-Hardwick, Elizabeth, 2-born, 12-Hardwick, Harry, 13-Becker, Carrie, 15-
    Hardwick
#6462, 1-Hardwick, Elsie, 2-married, 7-Tapman, John, 15-Hardwick
#6463, 1-Hardwick, Alan, 2-born, 12-Tapman, John, 13-Hardwick, Elsie, 15-Hardwick
#6464, 1-Hardwick, John Brent, 2-born, 12-Tapman, John, 13-Hardwick, Elsie, 15-
    Hardwick
#6465, 1-Hardwick, Ambrose, 2-married, 7-Sandlass, [blank], 15-Hardwick
#6466, 1-Hardwick, Dennis, 3-11 Apr 1939, 15-Hardwick
#6467, 1-Hardwick, Alan, 3-26 Sep 1945, 15-Hardwick
#6468, 1-Hardwick, Harry Wm. Byrne, 3-12 Sep 1875, 15-Hardwick
#6469, 1-Hardwick, Charles Jones, 3-29 Jan 1877, 15-Hardwick
#6470, 1-Hardwick, Elsie, 3-23 Apr 1885, 15-Hardwick
#6471, 1-Hardwick, Ambrose, 3-16 Dec 1887, 15-Hardwick
#6472, 1-Hardwick, Jessie, 15-Hardwick
#6473, 1-Hardwick, Albert Birtwell, 3-19 Sep 1879, 15-Hardwick
#6474, 1-Hardwick, Ambrose Smedley, 2-died, 15-Hardwick
#6475, 1-Graff, Elizabeth A.C., 2-born, 3-Saturday, 20 Jun 1812, 15-Graff
#6476, 1-Graff, Mary Charttas[?], 2-born, 3-Saturday, 27 May 1818[?], 15-Graff
#6477, 1-Graff, Marcus Sebastian, 2-born, 3-25 Oct[?] 1817, 15-Graff
#6478, 1-Graff, Sophia Jane, 2-born, 3-27 Oct 1819, 15-Graff
#6479, 1-Graff, Elie Beatty[?], 2-born, 3-15 ___[?] 1821, 15-Graff
#6480, 1-Graff, Geo.[?] Usher, 2-born, 3-26 Feb 1824, 15-Graff
#6481, 1-Dyer, Ann Elizabeth, 2-born, 3-28 Jun 1825, 15-Graff
#6482, 1-[?], Margaret E. Cross[?] , 2-born, 3-23 Jul 1830, 15-Graff
#6483, 1-Charlton, Daniel E., 2-born, 3-[unreadable], 15-Graff
#6484, 1-Delaplaine[?], Elizabeth Mary, 2-born, 3-Friday, 15 Sep 1835[?], 15-Graff
#6485, 1-Delaplaine[?], Catharine Jane, 2-born, 3-11 Feb 1822, 15-Graff
#6486, 1-Delaplaine[?], John Usher[?], 2-born, 3-14 Jan 1826, 15-Graff
```

FAMILY BIBLE RECORDS IN THE WASHINGTON COUNTY FREE LIBRARY, HAGERSTOWN, MARYLAND

Entry #, 1-Last Name, First Name, 2-Event, 3-Date, 4-Event Location, 5-Age, 6-Other,
7-Spouse's Last, First, 8-Groom's Residence, 9-Bride's Residence, 10-Minister, 11-Minister's Location,
12-Father's Last, First, 13-Mother's Last, First, 14-Transcribed, 15-Family Bible

```
#6487, 1-Delaplaine[?], Sophia[?] Louisa, 2-born, 3-10 Jan 1826, 15-Graff
#6488, 1-Nouier[?], Catharine Elizabeth, 2-born, 3-Sunday, 27[?] Jun 1829, 15-Graff
#6489, 1-Norris[?], Eleanor Jane, 2-born, 15-Graff
#6490, 1-Talbot[?], Ann Elizabeth, 2-born, 3-4 Jan 1853, 15-Graff
#6491, 1-Talbott, John, 2-born, 3-10 Feb 1834, 15-Graff
#6492, 1-Talbott, Joseph, 2-born, 3-1 Sep 1837, 15-Graff
#6493, 1-Graff, Mary Charlton, 2-born, 3-1815, 12-Graff, George, 15-Graff
#6494, 1-Graff, Marcus, 2-born, 3-1817, 12-Graff, George, 15-Graff
#6495, 1-Graff, Eli Beatty, 2-born, 3-1821, 12-Graff, George, 15-Graff
#6496, 1-Graff, George Usher, 2-born, 3-Feb 1824, 12-Graff, George, 15-Graff
#6497, 1-Graff, James Johnson, 2-born, 3-22 Nov 1803, 12-Graff, Andrew, 15-Graff
#6498, 1-Graff, Mary Catharine, 2-born, 3-22 Aug 1809, 12-Graff, Andrew, 15-Graff
#6499, 1-Graff, George Musser, 2-born, 3-21 Dec 1811, 12-Graff, Andrew, 15-Graff
#6500, 1-Graff, Rosanna Jane, 2-born, 3-10 Apr 1815, 12-Graff, Andrew, 15-Graff
#6501, 1-Graff, William Sebastian, 2-born, 3-2 Aug 1818, 12-Graff, Andrew, 15-Graff
#6502, 1-Graff, Robert John, 2-born, 3-1 Sep 1821, 12-Graff, Andrew, 15-Graff
#6503, 1-Fricke, William, 2-born, 3-12[or 10] Jan 1808, 15-Fricke
#6504, 1-Fricke, Henrietta, 2-born, 3-6 Nov 1831, 7-Fricke, William, 15-Fricke
#6505, 1-Fricke, Jr., Henry John, 2-born, 3-15 Mar 1854, 15-Fricke
#6506, 1-Fricke, Jr., William Theodore, 2-born, 3-5 Nov 1863, 15-Fricke
#6507, 1-Oyeman, Julienne[?], 2-born, 3-4[?] Dec[?] 1878, 15-Fricke
#6508, 1-Fricke, William, 2-born, 3-17 Aug 1881, 15-Fricke
#6509, 1-[unreadable], Henrietta, 2-born, 3-27[?] Sep 1882, 15-Fricke
#6510, 1-Fricke, John Henry, 2-born, 3-11 Jun 1833[?], 15-Fricke
#6511, 1-[?], Ernest, 2-born, 15-Fricke
#6512, 1-Fricke, Laura[?], 2-born, 15-Fricke
#6513, 1-Ways[?], Gertrude May Fricke, 2-born, 3-15 Oct 18__, 15-Fricke
#6514, 1-Fricke, Gustar[?] A., 2-born, 3-10 Jun 1894, 15-Fricke
#6515, 1-Schone, Eva[?] A. Fricke, 2-born, 3-21 Jun 1895, 15-Fricke
#6516, 1-Fricke[?], Theodore, 2-born, 3-28 Nov 1901, 15-Fricke
#6517, 1-Fricke, James, 2-born, 3-8 Nov 1901, 15-Fricke
#6518, 1-Fricke, Henriette (Mrs.), 2-died, 3-20 Oct 1866, 15-Fricke
#6519, 1-Fricke, Wm., 2-died, 3-25 Oct 1866, 15-Fricke
#6520, 1-Ways[?], Gertrude May Fricke, 2-died, 3-9 Oct 1919, 15-Fricke
#6521, 1-Ways[?], Ernest, 2-died, 3-17 Jul 1914, 15-Fricke
#6522, 1-Ways[?], John Henry, 2-died, 3-29 Jan 1926, 15-Fricke
#6523, 1-Citie[?], Mace[?] R.M., 2-died, 3-13 May 1900, 15-Fricke
#6524, 1-Fricke, William, 2-married, 3-9 Apr 1853, 7-Carriere, Henrietta, 15-Fricke
#6525, 1-Fricke, John Henry, 2-married, 3-21 Mar 1877, 7-Uter[?], Catherine M., 15-
    Fricke
#6526, 1-Cromwell, William, 2-born, 3-26 Jun 1773, 12-Cromwell, R.C., 13-Cromwell,
    R., 15-Cromwell
#6527, 1-Cromwell, Sarah, 2-born, 3-18 Jun 1778, 7-Cromwell, William, 15-Cromwell
#6528, 1-Cromwell, Maria Catharine, 2-born, 3-18 Feb 1800, 12-Cromwell, W.C., 13-
    Cromwell, S., 15-Cromwell
#6529, 1-Cromwell, Constant Comfort, 2-born, 3-18 Sep 1801, 12-Cromwell, W.C., 13-
    Cromwell, S., 15-Cromwell
#6530, 1-Cromwell, Richard, 2-born, 3-10 Sep 1802, 12-Cromwell, W.C., 13-Cromwell,
    S., 15-Cromwell
#6531, 1-Cromwell, Sebastian Graff, 2-born, 3-4 Apr 1805, 12-Cromwell, W.C., 13-
    Cromwell, S., 15-Cromwell
#6532, 1-Cromwell, Constant Comfort, 2-born, 3-20 Nov 1806, 12-Cromwell, W.C., 13-
    Cromwell, S., 15-Cromwell
#6533, 1-Cromwell, William, 2-born, 3-7 Jan 1809, 12-Cromwell, W.C., 13-Cromwell,
    S., 15-Cromwell
```

FAMILY BIBLE RECORDS IN THE WASHINGTON COUNTY FREE LIBRARY, HAGERSTOWN, MARYLAND

Entry #, 1-Last Name, First Name, 2-Event, 3-Date, 4-Event Location, 5-Age, 6-Other,
7-Spouse's Last, First, 8-Groom's Residence, 9-Bride's Residence, 10-Minister, 11-Minister's Location,
12-Father's Last, First, 13-Mother's Last, First, 14-Transcribed, 15-Family Bible

#6534, 1-Cromwell, W.C., 2-died, 3-27 Mar 1809, 15-Cromwell
#6535, 1-Cromwell, S.C., 2-died, 3-23 Aug 1836, 15-Cromwell
#6536, 1-Cromwell, Maria C., 2-died, 3-12 Jun 1860, 7-Musser, William, 15-Cromwell
#6537, 1-Cromwell, C.C., 2-died, 3-7 Oct 1801, 15-Cromwell
#6538, 1-Cromwell, Richard, 2-died, 3-16 Jun 1868, 15-Cromwell
#6539, 1-Cromwell, S.G., 2-died, 3-8 Sep 1805, 15-Cromwell
#6540, 1-Cromwell, C.C., 2-died, 3-5 May 1828, 15-Cromwell
#6541, 1-Cromwell, Wm., 2-died, 3-22 Nov 1877, 15-Cromwell
#6542, 1-Cromwell, William, 2-born, 3-26 Jun 1773, 6-grandson of Joseph Cromwell and great-grandson of William Cromwell, 12-Cromwell, Richard, 13-Cromwell, Rachael, 15-Cromwell
#6543, 1-Cromwell, Oliver, 2-born, 3-20 Jul 1775, 12-Cromwell, R.C., 13-Cromwell, R., 15-Cromwell
#6544, 1-Cromwell, Richard, 2-born, 3-31 May 1777, 12-Cromwell, R.C., 13-Cromwell, R., 15-Cromwell
#6545, 1-Cromwell, Philemon, 2-born, 3-18 Jan 1780, 12-Cromwell, R.C., 13-Cromwell, R., 15-Cromwell
#6546, 1-Cromwell, Constant Comfort, 2-born, 3-7 Dec 1782, 12-Cromwell, R.C., 13-Cromwell, R., 15-Cromwell
#6547, 1-Cromwell, Nathan, 2-born, 3-14 Apr 1785, 12-Cromwell, R.C., 13-Cromwell, R., 15-Cromwell
#6548, 1-Cromwell, John Cockey, 2-born, 3-9 Dec 1787, 12-Cromwell, R.C., 13-Cromwell, R., 15-Cromwell
#6549, 1-Cromwell, Stephen, 2-born, 3-21 Jan 1790, 12-Cromwell, R.C., 13-Cromwell, R., 15-Cromwell
#6550, 1-Cromwell, Joseph, 2-born, 3-13 Jun 1792, 12-Cromwell, R.C., 13-Cromwell, R., 15-Cromwell
#6551, 1-Cromwell, W., 2-died, 3-27 Mar 1809, 15-Cromwell
#6552, 1-Cromwell, P., 2-died, 3-18 Jul 1814, 15-Cromwell
#6553, 1-Cromwell, C.C., 2-died, 3-3 Sep 1801, 15-Cromwell
#6554, 1-Cromwell, Joseph, 2-born, 3-21 Aug 1707, 12-Cromwell, William, 13-Cromwell, Mary, 15-Cromwell
#6555, 1-Cromwell, Comfort, 2-born, 3-3 Jul 1710, 15-Cromwell
#6556, 1-Cromwell, Nathan, 2-born, 3-17 Mar 1731, 12-Cromwell, J., 13-Cromwell, C., 15-Cromwell
#6557, 1-Cromwell, Ruth, 2-born, 3-20 May 1738, 12-Cromwell, J., 13-Cromwell, C., 15-Cromwell
#6558, 1-Cromwell, Joseph, 2-born, 3-2 Apr 1741, 12-Cromwell, J., 13-Cromwell, C., 15-Cromwell
#6559, 1-Cromwell, Philemon, 2-born, 3-16 Sep 1743, 12-Cromwell, J., 13-Cromwell, C., 15-Cromwell
#6560, 1-Cromwell, Cloe[?], 2-born, 3-1 May 1746, 12-Cromwell, J., 13-Cromwell, C., 15-Cromwell
#6561, 1-Cromwell, Stephen, 2-born, 3-17 Nov 1747, 12-Cromwell, J., 13-Cromwell, C., 15-Cromwell
#6562, 1-Cromwell, Richard, 2-born, 3-30 Nov 1749, 12-Cromwell, J., 13-Cromwell, C., 15-Cromwell
#6563, 1-Cromwell, Comfort, 2-died, 3-12 Jan 1787, 15-Cromwell
#6564, 1-Cromwell, Philemon, 2-died, 3-11 Nov 1767, 15-Cromwell
#6565, 1-Cromwell, Stephen, 2-died, 3-10 Apr 1783, 15-Cromwell
#6566, 1-Cromwell, Richard, 2-died, 3-25 Dec 1802, 15-Cromwell
#6567, 1-Cromwell, Rachael, 2-died, 3-24 Jan 1806, 7-Cromwell, Richard, 15-Cromwell
#6568, 1-Henderson, James, 2-born, 3-15 Jul 1776, 12-Henderson, James, 13-Henderson, Sarah, 15-Cromwell

FAMILY BIBLE RECORDS IN THE WASHINGTON COUNTY FREE LIBRARY, HAGERSTOWN, MARYLAND

Entry #, 1-Last Name, First Name, 2-Event, 3-Date, 4-Event Location, 5-Age, 6-Other,
7-Spouse's Last, First, 8-Groom's Residence, 9-Bride's Residence, 10-Minister, 11-Minister's Location,
12-Father's Last, First, 13-Mother's Last, First, 14-Transcribed, 15-Family Bible

```
#6569, 1-Henderson, Sarah, 2-born, 3-18 Jun 1778, 6-widow of Wm. Cromwell, 7-
     Henderson, Jr., James, 15-Cromwell
#6570, 1-Henderson, Sarah, 2-died, 3-23 Aug 1836, 15-Cromwell
#6571, 1-Henderson, Sarah, 2-died, 3-31 Jan 1817, 7-Henderson, Sr., James, 15-
     Cromwell
#6572, 1-Henderson, Sarah Anne, 2-born, 3-5 Nov 1813, 12-Henderson, James, 13-
     Henderson, Sarah, 15-Cromwell
#6573, 1-Henderson, Sarah Anne, 2-died, 3-23 Sep 1855, 7-Musser, Wm., 15-Cromwell
#6574, 1-Henderson, James Sebastian Hamilton, 2-born, 3-26 Sep 1815, 12-Henderson,
     James, 13-Henderson, Sarah, 15-Cromwell
#6575, 1-Henderson, James, 2-married, 3-15 Nov 1812, 7-Cromwell, Sarah (widow of
     William Cromwell), 8-Frederick Co., MD, 15-Cromwell
#6576, 1-Musser, William, 2-married, 3-19 Aug 1834, 7-Henderson, Sarah Anne, 8-
     Lancaster Co., PA, 9-Montgomery Co., MD, 10-Rev. Jno. Miner[?], 12-Musser,
     Geo., 15-Cromwell
#6577, 1-Henderson, Sarah Anne, 2-born, 12-Henderson, James, 13-Henderson, Sarah,
     15-Cromwell
#6578, 1-Henderson, S.H., 2-married, 3-19 Dec 1843, 7-Neel, Rosanna __ne, 8-
     Montgomery Co., MD, 9-Montgomery Co., MD, 10-Rev. Jno. Miller, 12-Henderson,
     Jas., 13-Henderson, Sarah, 15-Cromwell
#6579, 1-Neel, Rosanna __ne, 2-born, 12-Neel, Joseph, 13-Neel, Isabella, 15-
     Cromwell
#6580, 1-Musser, William, 2-married, 3-10 Mar 1857, 7-Cromwell, Maria Catharine,
     12-Musser, Geo., 15-Cromwell
#6581, 1-Cromwell, Maria Catharine, 2-born, 12-Cromwell, William, 13-Cromwell,
     Sarah, 15-Cromwell
#6582, 1-Cromwell, William, 2-married, 3-22 Jan 1799, 7-Graff, Sarah, 8-Washington
     Co., MD, 9-Lancaster Co., PA, 12-Cromwell, Richard, 15-Cromwell
#6583, 1-Graff, Sarah, 2-born, 12-Graff, Sebastian, 15-Cromwell
#6584, 1-Cromwell, Richard, 2-married, 3-10 Sep 1833, 7-Williams, Elizabeth Ann, 9-
     Montgomery Co., MD, 12-Cromwell, William, 13-Cromwell, Sarah, 15-Cromwell
#6585, 1-Williams, Elizabeth Ann, 2-born, 10-Rev. Mines, 12-Williams, Zachariah,
     13-Williams, Elleonor, 15-Cromwell
#6586, 1-Kretzer, Benj. F., 2-born, 3-24 Decd 1832, 15-Smith
#6587, 1-Kretzer, Henrietta, 2-born, 3-25 Mar 1836, 15-Smith
#6588, 1-Smith, David, 2-born, 15-Smith
#6589, 1-Smith, Mary Ann, 2-born, 15-Smith
#6590, 1-Snavely, Ida C., 2-born, 3-29 Nov 1856, 15-Smith
#6591, 1-Smith, Willard F., 2-born, 3-26 Nov 1852, 15-Smith
#6592, 1-Smith, Fannie C., 2-born, 3-7 Mar 1854, 15-Smith
#6593, 1-Smith, Murta C., 2-born, 3-16 Nov 1874, 15-Smith
#6594, 1-Smith, Claude McPhearson, 2-born, 3-1 Aug 1877, 15-Smith
#6595, 1-Snaveley, Roy Webster, 2-born, 3-2 Oct 1875, 15-Smith
#6596, 1-Smith, Idelia Cordelia, 2-born, 3-17 Jan 1883, 15-Smith
#6597, 1-Smith, Franklin Lester, 2-born, 3-17 Jun 1885, 15-Smith
#6598, 1-Smith, Norman Scott, 2-born, 3-16 Mar 1888, 15-Smith
#6599, 1-Smith, Carlyle Fillmore, 2-born, 3-26 Jun 1891, 15-Smith
#6600, 1-Smith, Fannie Cecelia, 2-born, 3-2 May 1896, 15-Smith
#6601, 1-Eavey, John Wesley, 2-born, 3-2 Aug 1873, 15-Smith
#6602, 1-Smith, Myrta C., 2-married, 3-20 Dec 1899, 7-Wilson, Noah McKendree, 15-
     Smith
#6603, 1-Smith, Idella C., 2-married, 3-16 Jul 1902, 7-Eavey, John Wesley, 15-Smith
#6604, 1-Snavely, Ida C., 2-died, 3-7 Nov 1881, 15-Smith
#6605, 1-Smith, Fannie C., 2-died, 3-8 Jun 1896, 15-Smith
#6606, 1-Smith, Jr., Fannie C., 2-died, 3-7 Aug 1896, 15-Smith
```

FAMILY BIBLE RECORDS IN THE WASHINGTON COUNTY FREE LIBRARY, HAGERSTOWN, MARYLAND

**Entry #, 1-Last Name, First Name, 2-Event, 3-Date, 4-Event Location, 5-Age, 6-Other,
7-Spouse's Last, First, 8-Groom's Residence, 9-Bride's Residence, 10-Minister, 11-Minister's Location,
12-Father's Last, First, 13-Mother's Last, First, 14-Transcribed, 15-Family Bible**

```
#6607, 1-Kretzer, Benjamin F., 2-died, 3-12 Feb 1898, 15-Smith
#6608, 1-Kretzer, Henrietta, 2-died, 3-17 May 1903, 15-Smith
#6609, 1-Smith, Millard Fillmore, 2-died, 3-12 Nov 1925, 15-Smith
#6610, 1-Smith, Claude McPhearson, 2-died, 3-16 Dec 1938, 15-Smith
#6611, 1-Wilson, Myrta Smith, 2-died, 3-19 Jul 1942, 15-Smith
#6612, 1-Smith, Franklin Lester, 2-died, 3-22 Apr 1950, 15-Smith
#6613, 1-Eavey, Idella Cordelia (Smith), 2-died, 3-14Sep 1952, 15-Smith
#6614, 1-Eavey, Rudolph Richard, 2-died, 3-12 Aug 1956, 15-Smith
#6615, 1-Smith, F. Lester, 2-died, 3-22 Apr 1950, 15-Smith
#6616, 1-Eavey, John Wesley, 2-died, 3-20 Jun 1962, 15-Smith
#6617, 1-Smith, Carlyle Fillmore, 2-died, 3-3 Oct 1963, 15-Smith
#6618, 1-Smith, Norman Scott, 2-died, 3-13 Sep 1970, 15-Smith
#6619, 1-Wilson, Edith Louise, 2-born, 3-4 May 1910, 15-Smith
#6620, 1-Wilson, Edith Louise, 2-died, 3-4 Mar 1954, 15-Smith
#6621, 1-Wilson, Millard Calvin, 2-born, 3-13 Oct 1900, 15-Smith
#6622, 1-Wilson, Millard Calvin, 2-died, 3-19 Mar 1968, 15-Smith
#6623, 1-Smith, Frisby, 2-obituary, 3-1 Oct 1926, 4-Sharpsburg, MD, 5-76 years 2
     months 8 days, 6-buried Mountain View Cemetery, Sharpsburg, MD, 12-Smith,
     David, 15-Smith
#6624, 1-Penner, Mary Louise, 2-died, 3-6 Jun 1906, 5-61 years 5 months 10 days,
     15-Penner
#6625, 1-Penner, Samuel, 2-married, 3-30 Mar 1865, 7-Penner, Mary Louise, 15-Penner
#6626, 1-Hastings, Walter Henry, 2-born, 3-18 Jul 1876, 15-Penner
#6627, 1-Hastings, Walter Henry, 2-died, 3-23 Apr 1942, 15-Penner
#6628, 1-Penner, Samuel, 2-born, 3-11 Jul 1840, 15-Penner
#6629, 1-Penner, Mary Louise, 2-born, 3-29 Dec 1842[?], 15-Penner
#6630, 1-Penner, William Henry, 2-born, 3-28 Aug 1865, 15-Penner
#6631, 1-Penner, Daniel Albert, 2-born, 3-2[?] Oct 1867, 15-Penner
#6632, 1-Penner, John J., 2-born, 3-17 Oct 1869, 15-Penner
#6633, 1-Penner, George W., 2-born, 3-11 Sep 1872, 15-Penner
#6634, 1-Penner, George W., 2-died, 3-"either Sep or Oct 1938", 15-Penner
#6635, 1-Hastings, Clarence Henry, 2-born, 3-7 May 1909, 15-Penner
#6636, 1-Hastings, Clarence Henry, 2-died, 3-7 Sep 1970, 15-Penner
#6637, 1-Penner, Edward L., 2-born, 3-21 Sep 1876, 15-Penner
#6638, 1-Penner, Edward L., 2-died, 3-1 Apr 1955, 15-Penner
#6639, 1-Penner, Calvin R., 2-born, 3-23 Apr 1878, 15-Penner
#6640, 1-Penner, Calvin R., 2-died, 3-Feb 1960, 15-Penner
#6641, 1-Penner, Margaret E., 2-born, 3-23 Nov 1880[?], 15-Penner
#6642, 1-Penner, Charles R., 2-born, 3-17 Jul 1883, 15-Penner
#6643, 1-Penner, Charles R., 2-died, 3-14 May 1966, 15-Penner
#6644, 1-Hastings, Margaret Louise, 2-born, 3-Wednesday, 17 Jul 1907, 15-Penner
#6645, 1-Hastings, Margaret Louise, 2-died, 3-4 Nov 1987, 15-Penner
#6646, 1-Penner, William H., 2-died, 3-31 Aug 1869, 15-Penner
#6647, 1-Penner, Daniel Albert, 2-died, 3-28 Aug 1869, 15-Penner
#6648, 1-Penner, William, 2-died, 3-Saturday, 20 Feb 1897, 5-80 years, 15-Penner
#6649, 1-Penner, J.J., 2-died, 3-Wednesday, 11 Jan 1905, 5-35 years 2 months 24
     days, 15-Penner
#6650, 1-Penner, Samuel, 2-died, 3-Friday, 9 Feb 1906, 5-65 years 6 months 28 days,
     15-Penner
#6651, 1-Beck, Howard, 2-married, 3-25 Dec 1881, 4-Waynesboro, PA, 7-Wilson, Alice,
     8-Hagerstown, MD, 9-Hagerstown, MD, 10-Thomas S. Wilcox, 11-M.E. Church, 15-
     Beck
#6652, 1-Beck, Howard Ellsworth, 2-married, 3-25 Dec 1881, 7-Wilson, Susan Alice,
     15-Beck
#6653, 1-Beck, Ada May, 2-married, 3-7 Apr 1904, 7-Snyder, John Leiter, 15-Beck
```

FAMILY BIBLE RECORDS IN THE WASHINGTON COUNTY FREE LIBRARY, HAGERSTOWN, MARYLAND

Entry #, 1-Last Name, First Name, 2-Event, 3-Date, 4-Event Location, 5-Age, 6-Other, 7-Spouse's Last, First, 8-Groom's Residence, 9-Bride's Residence, 10-Minister, 11-Minister's Location, 12-Father's Last, First, 13-Mother's Last, First, 14-Transcribed, 15-Family Bible

```
#6654, 1-Beck, William Granville, 2-married, 3-25 Jun 1914, 7-Baker, Edna Adele,
    15-Beck
#6655, 1-Beck, Billy Baker, 2-born, 12-Beck, William Granville, 13-Baker, Edna
    Adele, 15-Beck
#6656, 1-Beck, Robert Edwin, 2-born, 12-Beck, William Granville, 13-Baker, Edna
    Adele, 15-Beck
#6657, 1-Wilson, Grace Irene, 2-married, 3-7:30 am, 24 Aug 1917, 7-Baker, Otho
    Fout, 15-Beck
#6658, 1-Wilson, Arthur G., 2-married, 3-Saturday, 2 Jun 1934, 4-Washington, DC, 7-
    Nicholson, Nellie Faire, 10-Rev. Perrpout[?], 15-Beck
#6659, 1-Beck, Robert Edwin, 2-married, 3-6 Dec 1969, 4-Hagerstown, MD, 7-Keyes,
    Jean Woodhead, 15-Beck
#6660, 1-Beck, Howard Ellsworth, 2-born, 3-25 Mar 1862, 15-Beck
#6661, 1-Wilson, Susan Alice, 2-born, 3-12 Jul 1864, 15-Beck
#6662, 1-Beck, Ada May, 2-born, 3-25 Mar 1883, 12-Beck, Howard Ellsworth, 13-
    Wilson, Susan Alice, 15-Beck
#6663, 1-Beck, William Granville, 2-born, 3-31 Dec 1884, 12-Beck, Howard Ellsworth,
    13-Wilson, Susan Alice, 15-Beck
#6664, 1-Beck, Billie Baker, 2-born, 3-21 Mar 1915, 15-Beck
#6665, 1-Beck, Robert Edwin, 2-born, 3-8 Oct 1919, 15-Beck
#6666, 1-Beck, Edna Adelle (Baker), 2-born, 3-29 Jan 1889, 15-Beck
#6667, 1-Wilson, Granville, 2-born, 3-27 Jan 1836, 15-Beck
#6668, 1-Wilson, Anna, 2-born, 3-3 Jun 1842, 15-Beck
#6669, 1-Wilson, MaryElen Virginia, 2-born, 3-3 Apr 1861, 15-Beck
#6670, 1-Wilson, Susan Alice, 2-born, 3-12 Jul 1864, 15-Beck
#6671, 1-Wilson, Harry Edward, 2-born, 3-8 Nov 1867, 15-Beck
#6672, 1-Wilson, Florence Isabell, 2-born, 3-6 Mar 1870, 15-Beck
#6673, 1-Wilson, Charles Norton, 2-born, 3-22 Dec 1883, 15-Beck
#6674, 1-Wilson, Grace Irene, 2-born, 3-5 Nov 1886, 15-Beck
#6675, 1-Wilson, Granville, 2-died, 3-29 Dec 1886, 15-Beck
#6676, 1-Hawthorn, Florence (Wilson), 2-died, 3-8 Jul 1903, 15-Beck
#6677, 1-Wilson, Chas. Granville, 2-born, 3-25 May 1907, 12-Wilson, Chas. M, 15-
    Beck
#6678, 1-Wilson, Chas. Granville, 2-died, 3-12 Jul 1908, 12-Wilson, Chas. M, 15-
    Beck
#6679, 1-Wilson, Anna, 2-died, 3-31 Jul 1916, 15-Beck
#6680, 1-Wilson, Edward, 2-died, 3-1 Jan 1914, 15-Beck
#6681, 1-Wilson, Jennie M., 2-died, 3-9 Oct 1930, 15-Beck
#6682, 1-Wilson, Chas. N., 2-died, 3-15 Jul 1934, 6-buried 18 Jul 1934, 15-Beck
#6683, 1-Beck, Susan Alice (Wilson), 2-died, 3-8 Dec 1955, 6-buried 11 Dec 1955,
    15-Beck
#6684, 1-Beck, Howard Ellsworth, 2-died, 3-27 Jul 1933, 5-71 years, 15-Beck
#6685, 1-Beck, John Williams, 2-born, 3-9 Apr 1950, 12-Beck, Robert, 13-Beck, Ruth,
    15-Beck
#6686, 1-Beck, James Ellsworth, 2-born, 3-15 Aug 1947, 12-Beck, Robert Edwin, 15-
    Beck
#6687, 1-Beck, II, William Granville Chip", 2-born, 3-23 Nov 1945, 12-Beck, William
    Baker, 15-Beck
#6688, 1-Wilson, Edward, 2-born, 3-4 Jul 1877, 15-Beck
#6689, 1-Wilson, Arthur Granville, 2-born, 3-13 Dec 1911, 12-Wilson, Chas., 15-Beck
#6690, 1-Hawthorn, Harry Edward, 2-born, 3-19 Sep 1892, 15-Beck
#6691, 1-Baker, Grace Irene (Wilson), 2-died, 3-18 Jan 1952, 5-65 years, 15-Beck
#6692, 1-Snyder, Ada May (Beck), 2-died, 3-21 Dec 1953, 5-71 years, 13-Beck, Susan
    Alice, 15-Beck
#6693, 1-Beck, Susan Alice, 2-died, 3-8 Dec 1955, 5-91 years 5 months, 15-Beck
```

FAMILY BIBLE RECORDS IN THE WASHINGTON COUNTY FREE LIBRARY, HAGERSTOWN, MARYLAND

Entry #, 1-Last Name, First Name, 2-Event, 3-Date, 4-Event Location, 5-Age, 6-Other,
7-Spouse's Last, First, 8-Groom's Residence, 9-Bride's Residence, 10-Minister, 11-Minister's Location,
12-Father's Last, First, 13-Mother's Last, First, 14-Transcribed, 15-Family Bible

```
#6694, 1-Beck, Edna Adelle (Baker), 2-died, 3-2 Feb 1957, 5-68 years, 15-Beck
#6695, 1-Beck, Ruth P., 2-died, 3-28 Feb 1969, 5-48 years, 15-Beck
#6696, 1-Beck, Ruth P., 2-born, 3-15 Mar 1920, 15-Beck
#6697, 1-Beck, William Baker, 2-married, 3-13 Oct 1937, 4-Winchester, VA, 7-Kugler,
    Phyllis, 9-Waynesboro, PA, 12-Beck, William G., 15-Beck
#6698, 1-Beck, Robert Edwin, 2-married, 3-21 Feb 1941, 4-bride's home on N. Potomac
    St., Hagerstown, MD, 7-Powles, Ruth, 9-Hagerstown, MD, 12-Beck, William G.,
    15-Beck
#6699, 1-Beck, Jr., Robert Edwin, 2-born, 3-2 Sep 1944, 12-Beck, Sr., Robert Edwin,
    15-Beck
#6700, 1-Beck, Jr., Howard, 2-married, 3-25 Dec 1861, 4-Waynesboro, PA, 7-Wilson,
    Alice, 8-Hagerstown, MD, 9-Hagerstown, MD, 15-Beck
#6701, 1-Knodle, William, 2-married, 3-11 Jan 1844, 7-Beck, Mary Ann, 15-Beck
#6702, 1-Unger, Harry Benton, 2-married, 3-2 Sep 1886, 4-Hagerstown, MD, 7-Martin,
    Ella David, 15-Beck
#6703, 1-Unger, J. Elvin, 2-married, 3-16 Jun 1917, 4-Frederick, MD, 7-Wolf, Mary
    Margaret, 10-Rev. Dr. Ulysses S.G. Rupp, 11-Lutheran Church, Frederick, MD,
    15-Beck
#6704, 1-Unger, Harry B., 2-married, 3-16 Mar 1899, 7-Beck, Lillie M., 15-Beck
#6705, 1-Beck, Howard E., 2-obituary, 3-27 Jul 1933, 4-117 E. Washington St.,
    Hagerstown, MD, 5-71 years, 6-heart attack, 7-Beck, Alice S., 15-Beck
#6706, 1-Knodle, William, 2-born, 3-1 May 1819, 15-Beck
#6707, 1-Knodle, Mary Ann, 2-born, 3-28 Dec 1818, 15-Beck
#6708, 1-Knodle, Mary A., 2-died, 3-"nearing 5 o'clock Friday evening, 21 Oct 1898,
    15-Beck
#6709, 1-Miller, Susann, 2-born, 3-30 May 1793, 15-Beck
#6710, 1-Miller, Susann, 2-born, 3-18 Feb 1813, 15-Beck
#6711, 1-Miller, John, 2-born, 3-18 Jan 1817, 15-Beck
#6712, 1-Miller, William, 2-born, 3-26 Jun 1823, 15-Beck
#6713, 1-Miller, David, 2-born, 3-28 Aug 1829, 15-Beck
#6714, 1-Grove, Susann, 2-died, 3-6 Jul 1854, 15-Beck
#6715, 1-Beck, Andrew, 2-died, 3-6 May 1831, 5-47 years, 15-Beck
#6716, 1-Beck, Susan, 2-died, 3-11 Aug 1855, 5-62 years 3 months 14 days, 15-Beck
#6717, 1-Grove, William T.[?], 2-died, 3-7 Apr 1865, 5-31 years 2 months 10 days,
    15-Beck
#6718, 1-Unger, Henry Benton, 2-born, 3-2 Dec 1863, 15-Beck
#6719, 1-Unger, Ella David, 2-born, 3-27 Jul 1864, 15-Beck
#6720, 1-Unger, Lillie May, 2-born, 3-3 Mar 1866, 15-Beck
#6721, 1-Unger, John Elvin, 2-born, 3-31 Oct 1892, 15-Beck
#6722, 1-Unger, William Frederick, 2-born, 3-9 Jan 1890, 15-Beck
#6723, 1-Wagner, Harry Martin, 2-born, 3-16 Nov 1883, 15-Beck
#6724, 1-Unger, William Frederick, 2-died, 3-16 Dec 1890, 15-Beck
#6725, 1-Unger, Ella David, 2-died, 3-9 Nov 1892, 15-Beck
#6726, 1-Unger, Henry Benton, 2-died, 3-10 Feb 1925, 15-Beck
#6727, 1-Helferstay, Wm., 2-married, 3-27 Jan 1863, 4-Shepherdstown, WV, 7-
    Gattrell, Harriet E., 8-Martinsburg, WV, 9-Shepherdstown, WV, 10-Rev. Miller,
    15-Helferstay
#6728, 1-Helferstay, William R., 2-born, 3-1[?] Jan 1840, 15-Helferstay
#6729, 1-Gattrell, Harriett Elizabeth, 2-born, 3-1 Sep 1843, 15-Helferstay
#6730, 1-Helferstay, James Oscar, 2-born, 3-10[?] May 1864, 15-Helferstay
#6731, 1-Helferstay, Minnie Lee, 2-born, 3-16 Nov 1866, 15-Helferstay
#6732, 1-Helferstay, Carrie May, 2-born, 3-15 May 1869, 15-Helferstay
#6733, 1-Helferstay, Nellie Mildred, 2-born, 3-14 Oct 1871, 15-Helferstay
#6734, 1-Helferstay, Rena West, 2-born, 3-7 Dec 1873, 15-Helferstay
#6735, 1-Helferstay, Harry Kimble, 2-born, 3-19 Aug 1875, 15-Helferstay
```

FAMILY BIBLE RECORDS IN THE WASHINGTON COUNTY FREE LIBRARY, HAGERSTOWN, MARYLAND

Entry #, 1-Last Name, First Name, 2-Event, 3-Date, 4-Event Location, 5-Age, 6-Other,
7-Spouse's Last, First, 8-Groom's Residence, 9-Bride's Residence, 10-Minister, 11-Minister's Location,
12-Father's Last, First, 13-Mother's Last, First, 14-Transcribed, 15-Family Bible

```
#6736, 1-Helferstay, Nettie Louise, 2-born, 3-22 Sep 1877, 15-Helferstay
#6737, 1-Helferstay, William Gattrell, 2-born, 3-15 Mar 1880, 15-Helferstay
#6738, 1-Helferstay, Leroy Cofron, 2-born, 3-27 Mar 1884, 15-Helferstay
#6739, 1-Helferstay, Mildred V., 2-born, 3-6 Oct 1904, 12-Helferstay, Leroy, 15-
      Helferstay
#6740, 1-Harris, Annie K., 2-born, 3-25 Sep 1887, 13-Helferstay, Minnie, 15-
      Helferstay
#6741, 1-Harris, Charles P., 2-born, 3-31 Jan 1889, 13-Helferstay, Minnie, 15-
      Helferstay
#6742, 1-Harris, Helen J., 2-born, 3-27 Feb 1891, 13-Helferstay, Minnie, 15-
      Helferstay
#6743, 1-Helferstay, Minnie L., 2-married, 3-31 Mar 1887, 7-Harris, C.W., 15-
      Helferstay
#6744, 1-Helferstay, Nellie M., 2-married, 3-22 Feb 1893, 7-Logan, W., 15-
      Helferstay
#6745, 1-Helferstay, Nettie L., 2-married, 3-21 Jun 1907, 7-Foltz, Harry R., 15-
      Helferstay
#6746, 1-Foltz, Julia F., 2-married, 3-15 Jul 1931, 7-Thomas, Milo E., 15-
      Helferstay
#6747, 1-Foltz, E. Louise, 2-married, 3-27 Aug 1937, 7-Brown, Glenn E., 15-
      Helferstay
#6748, 1-Foltz, H. Jane, 2-married, 3-16 Jun 1940, 7-Cash, George B., 15-Helferstay
#6749, 1-Lord, Elizabeth Heather, 2-married, 3-6 Feb 1999, 7-Hudson, Edward
      Carlyle, 15-Helferstay
#6750, 1-Helferstay, James Oscar, 2-died, 3-13 Jun 1865, 15-Helferstay
#6751, 1-Helferstay, Rena West, 2-died, 3-18 Mar 1874, 15-Helferstay
#6752, 1-Helferstay, William G., 2-died, 3-9 Dec 1900, 15-Helferstay
#6753, 1-Helferstay, Harry Kimble, 2-died, 3-22 Feb 1903, 15-Helferstay
#6754, 1-Helferstay, William R., 2-died, 3-10 Apr 1917, 15-Helferstay
#6755, 1-Foltz, Harry, 2-died, 3-26 Jun 1921, 15-Helferstay
#6756, 1-Helferstay, Harriet Elizabeth, 2-died, 3-18 Jan 1922, 15-Helferstay
#6757, 1-Strobel, Carrie May, 2-died, 3-8 Oct 1949, 15-Helferstay
#6758, 1-Sigafoose, Minnie Lee, 2-died, 3-24 Dec 1943, 15-Helferstay
#6759, 1-Foltz, Nettie Louise, 2-died, 3-11 Sep 1950, 15-Helferstay
#6760, 1-Logan, Nellie Mildred, 2-died, 3-14 Jul 1953, 15-Helferstay
#6761, 1-Thomas, Milo Edwin, 2-died, 3-14 Aug 1980, 15-Helferstay
#6762, 1-Thomas, Julia Frances Foltz, 2-died, 3-19 Jun 1982, 15-Helferstay
#6763, 1-Cash, Henrietta Jane Foltz, 2-died, 3-10 Jan 1995, 15-Helferstay
#6764, 1-Brown, Glenn E., 2-died, 3-17 Oct 1996, 15-Helferstay
#6765, 1-Brown, Elizabeth Louise Foltz, 2-died, 3-21 Dec 1996, 15-Helferstay
#6766, 1-Cash, George Byrd, 2-died, 3-23 Feb 1997, 15-Helferstay
#6767, 1-Foltz, Elizabeth Louise, 2-born, 3-14 Jul 1908, 15-Helferstay
#6768, 1-Foltz, Julia Francis, 2-born, 3-18 May 1912, 15-Helferstay
#6769, 1-Foltz, Henrietta Jane, 2-born, 3-10 Sep 1915, 15-Helferstay
#6770, 1-Brown, Laurel Lee, 2-born, 3-20 Dec 1938, 15-Helferstay
#6771, 1-Brown, Mary Louise, 2-born, 3-28 Jul 1942, 15-Helferstay
#6772, 1-Lord, Michelle Louise, 2-born, 3-7 Jul 1971, 15-Helferstay
#6773, 1-Lord, Eizabeth Heather E'Lea[?], 2-born, 3-22 Jun 1974, 15-Helferstay
#6774, 1-Zeigler, George Fredk., 2-married, 3-4 Feb 1928, 4-Hagerstown, MD, 7-
      Eshleman, Thelma, 8-Greencastle, PA, 9-Greencastle, PA, 10-F. Berry Plummer,
      11-St. Paul's United Brethren Church, 15-Zeigler
#6775, 1-Zeigler, Robert Lee, 2-married, 3-9 Feb 1909, 4-Geo. W. Gossard's, 7-
      Gossard, Ruth B., 8-Greencastle, PA, 9-Greencastle, PA, 10-J.E.B. Rice, 15-
      Zeigler
#6776, 1-Speaker, Harman, 2-married, 3-10 Jan 1846, 7-Harsh, Fanny, 15-Speaker
```

FAMILY BIBLE RECORDS IN THE WASHINGTON COUNTY FREE LIBRARY, HAGERSTOWN, MARYLAND

Entry #, 1-Last Name, First Name, 2-Event, 3-Date, 4-Event Location, 5-Age, 6-Other,
7-Spouse's Last, First, 8-Groom's Residence, 9-Bride's Residence, 10-Minister, 11-Minister's Location,
12-Father's Last, First, 13-Mother's Last, First, 14-Transcribed, 15-Family Bible

#6777, 1-Speaker, Hiram, 2-died, 3-17 Feb 1876, 5-60 years 10 months 2 days, 15-Speaker

#6778, 1-Speaker, Anna M., 2-married, 3-24 Dec 1901, 7-Carnelius, Absolmon, 15-Speaker

#6779, 1-Speaker, Sarah E., 2-married, 3-23 Jan 1879, 7-Shank, Abraham, 15-Speaker

#6780, 1-Speaker, Mary V., 2-married, 3-3 Mar 1897, 7-Beckley, John Ashby, 15-Speaker

#6781, 1-Speaker, Harman, 2-born, 3-15 Apr 1815, 15-Speaker

#6782, 1-Speaker, Fanny, 2-born, 3-3 Apr 1823, 15-Speaker

#6783, 1-Speaker, Henry, 2-born, 3-31 Mar 1847, 15-Speaker

#6784, 1-Speaker, Sarah Elizabeth, 2-born, 3-26 Mar 1851, 15-Speaker

#6785, 1-Speaker, Nacey Hellen, 2-born, 3-14 Jan 1856, 15-Speaker

#6786, 1-Speaker, Fanny Neomi, 2-born, 3-29 Apr 1857, 15-Speaker

#6787, 1-Speaker, Ama May, 2-born, 3-13 May 1863, 15-Speaker

#6788, 1-Speaker, Mary Virginia, 2-born, 3-21 Sep 1865, 15-Speaker

#6789, 1-Beckley, [twins], 2-born, 3-1 Jan 1898, 12-Beckley, J.A., 13-Beckley, Mary V., 15-Speaker

#6790, 1-Beckley, John Michael, 2-born, 3-12[?] Jun 1900, 15-Speaker

#6791, 1-Beckley, Frederick Hershey, 2-born, 3-14 Aug 1907, 15-Speaker

#6792, 1-Speaker, Henry, 2-died, 3-16 Oct 1864[?], 5-17 years 6 months 16 days, 6-"prisoner of war at Andersonville, Georgia", 15-Speaker

#6793, 1-Speaker, Hiram, 2-died, 3-17 Feb 1876, 5-60 years 10 months 2 days, 15-Speaker

#6794, 1-Speaker, Fanny, 2-died, 3-9 Jan 1896, 5-72[or 73] years 9[?] months 6 days, 15-Speaker

#6795, 1-Charlton, Wilmer A., 2-died, 3-27 Apr 1893, 5-5 years 6 months, 15-Speaker

#6796, 1-Speaker, Fannie neomi, 2-died, 3-1925, 5-68 years, 15-Speaker

#6797, 1-Startzman, Nancy Helen (Speaker), 2-died, 3-1925, 5-69 years, 15-Speaker

#6798, 1-Beckley, Mary Virginia (Speaker), 2-died, 3-26 Nov 1933, 5-68 years 2 months 5 days, 15-Speaker

#6799, 1-Cornelius, Anna M. (Speaker), 2-died, 3-1936, 5-73 years, 15-Speaker

#6800, 1-Shank, Maria, 2-born, 3-8 Jan 1827, 12-Shank, Henry, 15-Shank

#6801, 1-Shank, Abraham, 2-married, 3-23 Jan 1879, 4-Hagerstown, MD, 7-Speaker, Sarah E., 8-Clear Spring, MD, 9-Clear Spring, MD, 10-J. Spangler Kieffer, 15-Shank

#6802, 1-Speaker, Sarah E., 2-confirmed, 3-3 Feb 1878, 4-Clear Spring Reformed Church, 10-W. Goodrich, 15-Shank

#6803, 1-Shank, M. Bertha, 2-married, 3-5 Jun 1906, 4-bride's home, Clear Spring, MD, 7-Stone, Oscar J., 9-Clear Spring, MD, 10-Rev. Bald, 15-Shank

#6804, 1-Shank, Mary N., 2-married, 3-18 Sep 1910, 4-Hagerstown, MD, 7-Weller, Charles, 10-Rev. Kieffer, 15-Shank

#6805, 1-Shank, Loulia E., 2-married, 3-29 Mar 1926, 4-Reformed parsonage, 7-Seibert, Daniel S., 10-Rev. Peck, 15-Shank

#6806, 1-Shank, John C., 2-married, 3-10 Apr 1926, 4-parsonage of First Brethren Church, Hagerstown, MD, 7-Davis, Lillia E., 10-Rev. G.C. Carpenter, 15-Shank

#6807, 1-Weller, Margaret, 2-married, 3-1 Sep 1934, 7-Tritsch, Roy, 10-Rev. Rider, 11-Hagerstown, 15-Shank

#6808, 1-Weller, William C., 2-married, 3-18 Nov 1937, 4-Reformed parsonage, 7-Sisler, Martha J., 10-Rev. Huffman, 15-Shank

#6809, 1-Tritch, Eric E., 2-married, 3-25 Jan 1958, 4-Reformed parsonage at Clear Spring, 7-Care6y, Irene, 9-Scotland, 10-Rev. Huffman, 15-Shank

#6810, 1-Shank, Abraham, 2-born, 3-30 Jun 1848, 15-Shank

#6811, 1-Speaker, Sarah Elizabeth, 2-born, 3-26 Mar 1851, 15-Shank

#6812, 1-Shank, Fanny Leah, 2-born, 3-18 Oct 1879, 12-Shank, Abraham, 13-Speaker, Sarah Elizabeth, 15-Shank

FAMILY BIBLE RECORDS IN THE WASHINGTON COUNTY FREE LIBRARY, HAGERSTOWN, MARYLAND

Entry #, 1-Last Name, First Name, 2-Event, 3-Date, 4-Event Location, 5-Age, 6-Other,
7-Spouse's Last, First, 8-Groom's Residence, 9-Bride's Residence, 10-Minister, 11-Minister's Location,
12-Father's Last, First, 13-Mother's Last, First, 14-Transcribed, 15-Family Bible

```
#6813, 1-Shank, Fanny Leah, 2-baptized, 10-Rev. Goodrich, 12-Shank, Abraham, 13-
    Speaker, Sarah Elizabeth, 15-Shank
#6814, 1-Shank, Jacob Harman, 2-born, 3-18 Oct 1879, 12-Shank, Abraham, 13-Speaker,
    Sarah Elizabeth, 15-Shank
#6815, 1-Shank, Jacob Harman, 2-baptized, 10-Rev. Goodrich, 12-Shank, Abraham, 13-
    Speaker, Sarah Elizabeth, 15-Shank
#6816, 1-Shank, Charley Abraham, 2-born, 3-16 Nov 1880, 12-Shank, Abraham, 13-
    Speaker, Sarah Elizabeth, 15-Shank
#6817, 1-Shank, Charley Abraham, 2-baptized, 10-Rev. Goodrich, 12-Shank, Abraham,
    13-Speaker, Sarah Elizabeth, 15-Shank
#6818, 1-Shank, Christley Speaker, 2-born, 3-23 Jul 1882, 12-Shank, Abraham, 13-
    Speaker, Sarah Elizabeth, 15-Shank
#6819, 1-Shank, Christley Speaker, 2-baptized, 10-Rev. Goodrich, 12-Shank, Abraham,
    13-Speaker, Sarah Elizabeth, 15-Shank
#6820, 1-Shank, Margaret Bertha, 2-born, 3-18 Mar 1884, 12-Shank, Abraham, 13-
    Speaker, Sarah Elizabeth, 15-Shank
#6821, 1-Shank, Margaret Bertha, 2-baptized, 10-Rev. Goodrich, 12-Shank, Abraham,
    13-Speaker, Sarah Elizabeth, 15-Shank
#6822, 1-Shank, Mary Naomi, 2-born, 3-5 Jun 1886, 12-Shank, Abraham, 13-Speaker,
    Sarah Elizabeth, 15-Shank
#6823, 1-Shank, Mary Naomi, 2-baptized, 10-Rev. Goodrich, 12-Shank, Abraham, 13-
    Speaker, Sarah Elizabeth, 15-Shank
#6824, 1-Shank, Loulia Elizabeth, 2-born, 3-8 Feb 1888, 12-Shank, Abraham, 13-
    Speaker, Sarah Elizabeth, 15-Shank
#6825, 1-Shank, Loulia Elizabeth, 2-baptized, 10-Rev. Goodrich, 12-Shank, Abraham,
    13-Speaker, Sarah Elizabeth, 15-Shank
#6826, 1-Shank, Fredrick Arthur, 2-born, 3-14 Mar 1891, 12-Shank, Abraham, 13-
    Speaker, Sarah Elizabeth, 15-Shank
#6827, 1-Shank, Fredrick Arthur, 2-baptized, 10-Rev. Goodrich, 12-Shank, Abraham,
    13-Speaker, Sarah Elizabeth, 15-Shank
#6828, 1-Shank, John Chester, 2-born, 3-13 Oct 1894, 12-Shank, Abraham, 13-Speaker,
    Sarah Elizabeth, 15-Shank
#6829, 1-Shank, John Chester, 2-baptized, 10-Rev. Goodrich, 12-Shank, Abraham, 13-
    Speaker, Sarah Elizabeth, 15-Shank
#6830, 1-Tritch, Eric Edgar, 2-born, 3-21 Oct 1935, 4-at Hospital, 12-Tritch, Roy,
    13-Tritch, Margaret, 15-Shank
#6831, 1-Tritch, Eric Edgar, 2-baptized, 10-Rev. Huffman, 12-Tritch, Roy, 13-
    Tritch, Margaret, 15-Shank
#6832, 1-Shank, Fanny Leah, 2-died, 3-2 Jan 1880, 5-2 months 14 days, 15-Shank
#6833, 1-Shank, Jacob Harman, 2-died, 3-5 Jan 1880, 5-2 months 17 days, 15-Shank
#6834, 1-Shank, Charley Abraham, 2-died, 3-7 Jul 1882, 5-1 years 7 months 21 days,
    15-Shank
#6835, 1-Shank, Shristley Speaker, 2-died, 3-1 Feb 1901, 5-18 years 6 months 8
    days, 15-Shank
#6836, 1-Shank, Abraham, 2-died, 3-6 Feb 1901, 5-52 years 7 months 7 days, 15-Shank
#6837, 1-Shank, Sarah, 2-died, 3-15 Jun 1910, 5-60 years 3 months, 7-Shank,
    Abraham, 15-Shank
#6838, 1-Weller, Mary N., 2-died, 3-10-Jun-41, 5-55 years, 15-Shank
#6839, 1-Seibert, Louila E., 2-died, 3-12 Jan 1955, 5-66 years, 15-Shank
#6840, 1-Stone, Oscar James, 2-died, 3-29 Mar 1942, 5-57 years, 15-Shank
#6841, 1-Stone, M. Bertha, 2-died, 3-1 Jan 1965, 5-80 years, 15-Shank
#6842, 1-Weller, Loulia Margaret, 2-born, 3-Aug, 15-Shank
#6843, 1-Weller, John Arthur , 2-born, 3-22 Jul 1914, 15-Shank
#6844, 1-Weller, William Charles, 2-born, 3-29 Mar 1916, 15-Shank
#6845, 1-Weller, Roger Francis, 2-born, 3-18 Nov 1918, 15-Shank
```

FAMILY BIBLE RECORDS IN THE WASHINGTON COUNTY FREE LIBRARY, HAGERSTOWN, MARYLAND

Entry #, 1-Last Name, First Name, 2-Event, 3-Date, 4-Event Location, 5-Age, 6-Other,
7-Spouse's Last, First, 8-Groom's Residence, 9-Bride's Residence, 10-Minister, 11-Minister's Location,
12-Father's Last, First, 13-Mother's Last, First, 14-Transcribed, 15-Family Bible

```
#6846, 1-Weller, Anna Mary, 2-born, 3-20 Aug 1923, 15-Shank
#6847, 1-Tritch, Avril May, 2-born, 3-27 Dec 1959, 6-twin, 12-Tritch, Eric, 13-
    Tritch, Irene Carey, 15-Shank
#6848, 1-Tritch, Avril May, 2-baptized, 3-Jul 1960, 4-St. John's Reformed Church,
    10-Rev. Huffman, 12-Tritch, Eric, 13-Tritch, Irene Carey, 15-Shank
#6849, 1-Tritch, Roy Eric, 2-born, 3-27 Dec 1959, 6-twin, 12-Tritch, Eric, 13-
    Tritch, Irene Carey, 15-Shank
#6850, 1-Tritch, Roy Eric, 2-baptized, 3-Jul 1960, 4-St. John's Reformed Church,
    10-Rev. Huffman, 12-Tritch, Eric, 13-Tritch, Irene Carey, 15-Shank
#6851, 1-Weller, Willa Jane, 2-born, 3-17 Oct 1938, 12-Weller, William C., 13-
    Sisler, Martha, 15-Shank
#6852, 1-Weller, Cormorea Lee, 2-born, 3-29 Jun 1940, 12-Weller, William C., 13-
    Sisler, Martha, 15-Shank
#6853, 1-Weller, John Charles, 2-born, 3-3 Nov 1946, 12-Weller, William C., 13-
    Sisler, Martha, 15-Shank
#6854, 1-Weller, William Sisler, 2-born, 3-26 May 1948, 12-Weller, William C., 13-
    Sisler, Martha, 15-Shank
#6855, 1-Weller, Dixie Dee, 2-born, 3-23 Oct 1950, 12-Weller, William C., 13-
    Sisler, Martha, 15-Shank
#6856, 1-Weller, Richard Dudley, 2-born, 3-28 Jun 1952, 12-Weller, William C., 13-
    Sisler, Martha, 15-Shank
#6857, 1-Hager, Jonathan, 2-born, 3-20 Dec 1792, 15-Hager
#6858, 1-Hogmire, Catharine, 2-born, 3-2 May 1795, 15-Hager
#6859, 1-Hogmire, Catharine, 2-married, 3-21 Apr 1816, 7-Hager, Jonathan, 15-Hager
#6860, 1-Straub, L.D., 2-born, 3-3 Mar 1828, 15-Hager
#6861, 1-Hager, L.E., 2-born, 3-22 Mar 1833, 15-Hager
#6862, 1-Hager, L.E., 2-married, 3-19 Jul 1864, 7-Straub, L.D., 15-Hager
#6863, 1-Hager, William H., 2-born, 3-25 Jan 1817, 15-Hager
#6864, 1-Hager, David, 2-born, 3-25 Dec 1819, 15-Hager
#6865, 1-Hager, Jonas H., 2-born, 3-4 Jul 1821, 15-Hager
#6866, 1-Hager, Andrew H., 2-born, 3-12 Aug 1822, 15-Hager
#6867, 1-Hager, John, 2-born, 3-4 Jul 1824, 15-Hager
#6868, 1-Hager, Jonathan, 2-born, 3-28 Dec 1826, 15-Hager
#6869, 1-Hager, David, 2-born, 3-28 Dec 1828, 15-Hager
#6870, 1-Hager, Susan E., 2-born, 3-22 Mar 1833, 15-Hager
#6871, 1-Hager, Edward, 2-born, 3-15 Jul 1837, 15-Hager
#6872, 1-Hager, Kate K.[?], 2-born, 3-24 Apr 1840, 15-Hager
#6873, 1-Syrus, Frank, 2-born, 3-5 Jan 1861, 6-"colored", 15-Hager
#6874, 1-Syrus, Harry, 2-born, 3-8 Sep 1862, 6-"colored", 15-Hager
#6875, 1-Bird, Harry, 2-born, 3-1 Nov 1865, 6-"colored", 15-Hager
#6876, 1-Straub, Catherine Hager, 2-born, 3-16 Apr 1865, 15-Hager
#6877, 1-Straub, Harry H., 2-born, 3-15 Jan 1867, 15-Hager
#6878, 1-Straub, Norman B., 2-born, 3-24 Sep 1868, 15-Hager
#6879, 1-Straub, Norman B., 2-died, 3-20 Jul 1869, 5-10 months, 15-Hager
#6880, 1-Miller, Hager, 2-born, 3-25 Aug 1866, 15-Hager
#6881, 1-Miller, Hager, 2-died, 3-11 Nov 1866, 5-2 months 17 days, 15-Hager
#6882, 1-Hager, Carrie L.[?], 2-died, 3-15 Apr, 5-13 years, 15-Hager
#6883, 1-Hager, Johnathan, 2-died, 3-16 Apr 1864, 5-70 years 3 months 25 days, 15-
    Hager
#6884, 1-Syrus, Harry, 2-died, 3-6 Jul 1863, 5-10 months, 15-Hager
#6885, 1-Loose, Jos. B., 2-married, 3-12 Apr 1844, 7-Baechtel, Henrietta B., 15-
    Loose-Miller
#6886, 1-Loose, Henry C., 2-married, 3-16 Oct 1867, 7-Pearson, Jennie[?], 15-Loose-
    Miller
```

FAMILY BIBLE RECORDS IN THE WASHINGTON COUNTY FREE LIBRARY, HAGERSTOWN, MARYLAND

Entry #, 1-Last Name, First Name, 2-Event, 3-Date, 4-Event Location, 5-Age, 6-Other,
7-Spouse's Last, First, 8-Groom's Residence, 9-Bride's Residence, 10-Minister, 11-Minister's Location,
12-Father's Last, First, 13-Mother's Last, First, 14-Transcribed, 15-Family Bible

```
#6887, 1-Loose, Samuel Baechtel, 2-married, 3-12 Jun 1877, 7-Negley, Rose, 15-
    Loose-Miller
#6888, 1-Loose, M. Frances, 2-married, 3-3 pm, 14 Nov 1895, 7-Smith, Robert
    McLanahan[?], 15-Loose-Miller
#6889, 1-Loose, Laura Virginia, 2-married, 3-noon, 26 Apr 1899, 7-Keedy, Jr., Henry
    H., 15-Loose-Miller
#6890, 1-Loose, Carey, 2-married, 3-10 Oct 1901, 7-Reityet, William R., 15-Loose-
    Miller
#6891, 1-Loose, Nelly, 2-married, 3-noon, 1 Jun 1905, 7-Miller, Jr., Victor D., 15-
    Loose-Miller
#6892, 1-Loose, J. Pearson, 2-married, 3-14 Nov 1905, 7-Heieton, Jean, 15-Loose-
    Miller
#6893, 1-Smith, Frances Loose, 2-married, 3-18 Dec 1919, 7-Howard, William H., 15-
    Loose-Miller
#6894, 1-Miller, Helen Loose, 2-married, 3-2 Jan 1930, 7-Mathias, Philip Heagy, 15-
    Loose-Miller
#6895, 1-Miller, Henry Loose, 2-married, 3-16 Apr 1938, 7-Winroth[?], Esther
    Madelyn, 15-Loose-Miller
#6896, 1-Miller, Victor Davis, 2-married, 3-12 Jan 1946, 7-Gfreen, Catherine, 15-
    Loose-Miller
#6897, 1-Mathias, Anne Louise, 2-married, 3-21 Jul, 7-Schinkel, Robert Downs, 15-
    Loose-Miller
#6898, 1-Mathias, Jane Loose, 2-married, 3-20 Sep 1958, 7-[unreadable], Nelson
    Charlton, 15-Loose-Miller
#6899, 1-Miller, David Scott, 2-married, 3-22 Aug 1964, 7-Kenney, Susan Jean, 15-
    Loose-Miller
#6900, 1-Miller, Susan Winroth, 2-married, 3-23 Nov 1968, 15-Loose-Miller
#6901, 1-Loose, Jos. B., 2-born, 3-14 Aug 1810, 15-Loose-Miller
#6902, 1-Loose, Henrietta B., 2-born, 3-15 Aug 1823, 15-Loose-Miller
#6903, 1-Loose, Henry C., 2-born, 3-4 Apr 1845, 15-Loose-Miller
#6904, 1-Loose, Margaret Francie, 2-born, 3-22 Aug 1850, 15-Loose-Miller
#6905, 1-Loose, Samuel Baechtel, 2-born, 3-10 Aug 1852, 15-Loose-Miller
#6906, 1-Loose, Mary Lizzie, 2-born, 3-12 Jan 1860, 15-Loose-Miller
#6907, 1-Loose, Joseph Edward, 2-born, 3-1 Nov 1861, 15-Loose-Miller
#6908, 1-Loose, Jennie (Laura V. Pearson)", 2-born, 3-13 Aug 1848, 15-Loose-Miller
#6909, 1-Loose, Joseph Pearson, 2-born, 3-17 Oct 1868, 15-Loose-Miller
#6910, 1-Loose, Mary Francie, 2-born, 3-8 Dec 1870, 15-Loose-Miller
#6911, 1-Loose, Laura Virginia, 2-born, 3-29 Jul 1872, 15-Loose-Miller
#6912, 1-Loose, Henrietta A., 2-born, 3-23 Apr 1874, 15-Loose-Miller
#6913, 1-Loose, Carry, 2-born, 3-10 Jan 1876, 15-Loose-Miller
#6914, 1-Loose, Nelly, 2-born, 3-2 Jan 1878, 15-Loose-Miller
#6915, 1-Loose, Grace Cannon[?], 2-born, 3-27 Oct 1879, 15-Loose-Miller
#6916, 1-Loose, Anna, 2-born, 3-3 Jun 1881, 15-Loose-Miller
#6917, 1-Miller, Victor Davis, 2-born, 3-15 Mar 1876, 15-Loose-Miller
#6918, 1-Miller, Helen Loose, 2-born, 3-6 Jan 1907, 15-Loose-Miller
#6919, 1-Miller, Jr., Victor Davis, 2-born, 3-14 Mar 1909, 15-Loose-Miller
#6920, 1-Miller, Henry Loose, 2-born, 3-12 Jun 1912, 15-Loose-Miller
#6921, 1-Mathias, Jane Loose, 2-born, 3-14 Dec 1930, 15-Loose-Miller
#6922, 1-Mathias, Anne Louise, 2-born, 3-16 Apr 1935, 15-Loose-Miller
#6923, 1-Miller, David Scott, 2-born, 3-19 Jan 1944, 15-Loose-Miller
#6924, 1-Miller, Susan Winroth, 2-born, 3-14 Apr 1947, 15-Loose-Miller
#6925, 1-Schenkel, Robert Downs, 2-born, 3-11 Jul 1958, 15-Loose-Miller
#6926, 1-Schenkel, Philip Mathias, 2-born, 3-31 Jul 1963, 4-Baltimore, MD, 15-
    Loose-Miller
```

FAMILY BIBLE RECORDS IN THE WASHINGTON COUNTY FREE LIBRARY, HAGERSTOWN, MARYLAND

Entry #, 1-Last Name, First Name, 2-Event, 3-Date, 4-Event Location, 5-Age, 6-Other,
7-Spouse's Last, First, 8-Groom's Residence, 9-Bride's Residence, 10-Minister, 11-Minister's Location,
12-Father's Last, First, 13-Mother's Last, First, 14-Transcribed, 15-Family Bible

```
#6927, 1-Schenkel, Hunt Hardinge, 2-born, 3-6 Jun 1965, 4-Annapolis, MD, 15-Loose-
    Miller
#6928, 1-Noland, Peter Chilton, 2-born, 3-7 Jul 1959, 4-Hagerstown, MD, 15-Loose-
    Miller
#6929, 1-Noland, Susan Mathias, 2-born, 3-6 May 1961, 4-Hagerstown, MD, 15-Loose-
    Miller
#6930, 1-Miller, Christine Amber, 2-born, 3-13 Jan 1968, 4-Arlington, VA, 15-Loose-
    Miller
#6931, 1-Miller, Scott Richard, 2-born, 3-4 Mar 1969, 4-Winchester, VA, 15-Loose-
    Miller
#6932, 1-Hunt, Heather Susan, 2-born, 3-6 Sep 1974, 4-Hartford, CT, 15-Loose-Miller
#6933, 1-Hunt, Jonathan Ross, 2-born, 3-8 Oct 1977, 4-Hartford, CT, 15-Loose-Miller
#6934, 1-Schenkel, Stuart Pearson, 2-born, 3-14 Oct 1969, 4-Kansas City, KS, 15-
    Loose-Miller
#6935, 1-Miller, Kyle Gregory, 2-born, 3-Dec 1993, 15-Loose-Miller
#6936, 1-Miller, Brian Patrick, 2-born, 3-17 Dec 1995, 15-Loose-Miller
#6937, 1-Libby, Noah W., 2-born, 3-9 Apr 1997, 15-Loose-Miller
#6938, 1-Miller, Carly Nicole, 2-born, 3-3 Aug 1997, 15-Loose-Miller
#6939, 1-Loose, Mary Lizzie, 2-died, 3-14 Jun 1840, 15-Loose-Miller
#6940, 1-Loose, Joseph Edward, 2-died, 3-11 Jan 1865, 15-Loose-Miller
#6941, 1-Loose, Margaret Francis, 2-died, 3-7 Oct 1868, 15-Loose-Miller
#6942, 1-Loose, Joseph B., 2-died, 3-6 Apr 1884, 15-Loose-Miller
#6943, 1-Loose, Henry C., 2-died, 3-20 Mar 1888, 15-Loose-Miller
#6944, 1-Loose, Jennie (Laura Va.)", 2-died, 3-29 May 1896, 15-Loose-Miller
#6945, 1-Loose, Henrietta B., 2-died, 3-26 Nov 1894, 15-Loose-Miller
#6946, 1-Loose, Anna, 2-died, 3-11 Mar 1906, 15-Loose-Miller
#6947, 1-Smith, Robert McL., 2-died, 3-16 Apr 1898, 15-Loose-Miller
#6948, 1-Loose, Joseph Pearson, 2-died, 3-11 Aug 1918, 15-Loose-Miller
#6949, 1-Loose, Henry Clay, 2-died, 3-5 Sep 1918, 12-Loose, J. Pearson, 15-Loose-
    Miller
#6950, 1-Reetzell[?], Carry Pearson Loose, 2-died, 3-19 Dec 1946, 4-Worcester, MA,
    15-Loose-Miller
#6951, 1-Loose, Henrietta Baectell, 2-died, 3-12 Jun 1954, 15-Loose-Miller
#6952, 1-Howard, Frances Loose, 2-died, 3-24 Dec 1955, 15-Loose-Miller
#6953, 1-Keedy, Laura Loose, 2-died, 3-7[?] Mar 1956, 15-Loose-Miller
#6954, 1-Loose, Trace[?] Cannon, 2-died, 3-8 Jun 1961, 15-Loose-Miller
#6955, 1-Miller, Nellie Loose, 2-died, 3-29 Apr 1965, 15-Loose-Miller
#6956, 1-Miller, Jr., Victor D., 2-died, 3-17 Jul 1968, 15-Loose-Miller
#6957, 1-Mathias, Helen Loose Miller, 2-died, 3-19 Sep 1997, 15-Loose-Miller
#6958, 1-Miller, Catherine, 2-died, 3-Apr 1993, 15-Loose-Miller
#6959, 1-Carle, Joseph, 2-born, 3-8 Apr 1789, 4-Hempfield Township, Lancaster Co.,
    PA, 15-Charles
#6960, 1-Herr, Anna, 2-born, 3-10 Dec 1792, 4-Manor Township, Lancasater Co., PA,
    7-Carle, Joseph, 15-Charles
#6961, 1-Herr, Anna, 2-married, 3-19 Jan 1814, 4-Lancaster Co., PA, 7-Carle,
    Joseph, 10-H. Muhlenberg, 15-Charles
#6962, 1-Carle, [son], 2-born, 3-7 Sep 1814, 12-Carle, Joseph, 13-Herr, Anna, 15-
    Charles
#6963, 1-Carle, [son], 2-died, 3-ca. 12 Sep 1814, 5-5 days, 12-Carle, Joseph, 13-
    Herr, Anna, 15-Charles
#6964, 1-Carle, John Joseph, 2-born, 3-7 Oct 1815, 6-"born into the world in the
    sign of the dagger", 12-Carle, Joseph, 13-Herr, Anna, 15-Charles
#6965, 1-Carle, Joel, 2-born, 3-30 Jan 1818, 6-"born into the world in the sign of
    the Scorpion", 12-Carle, Joseph, 13-Herr, Anna, 15-Charles
```

FAMILY BIBLE RECORDS IN THE WASHINGTON COUNTY FREE LIBRARY, HAGERSTOWN, MARYLAND

Entry #, 1-Last Name, First Name, 2-Event, 3-Date, 4-Event Location, 5-Age, 6-Other, 7-Spouse's Last, First, 8-Groom's Residence, 9-Bride's Residence, 10-Minister, 11-Minister's Location, 12-Father's Last, First, 13-Mother's Last, First, 14-Transcribed, 15-Family Bible

#6966, 1-Carle, [son], 2-born, 3-6 Apr 1820, 12-Carle, Joseph, 13-Herr, Anna, 15-Charles

#6967, 1-Carle, [son], 2-died, 3-ca. 18 Apr 1820, 5-12 days, 12-Carle, Joseph, 13-Herr, Anna, 15-Charles

#6968, 1-Carle, Benjamin, 2-born, 3-27 Mar 1821, 12-Carle, Joseph, 13-Herr, Anna, 15-Charles

#6969, 1-Carle, Benjamin, 2-died, 3-26 Nov 1821, 12-Carle, Joseph, 13-Herr, Anna, 15-Charles

#6970, 1-Carle, Henry, 2-born, 3-24 Aug 1822, 12-Carle, Joseph, 13-Herr, Anna, 15-Charles

#6971, 1-Carle, Henry, 2-died, 3-ca. Oct 1822, 5-6 weeks, 12-Carle, Joseph, 13-Herr, Anna, 15-Charles

#6972, 1-Carle, Maria Anna, 2-born, 3-11 Oct 1823, 6-"born into the world in the sign of the Capricorn", 12-Carle, Joseph, 13-Herr, Anna, 15-Charles

#6973, 1-Carle, "Ludwig or Lewis", 2-born, 3-6 Dec 1826, 6-"born into the world in the sign of the Fish", 12-Carle, Joseph, 13-Herr, Anna, 15-Charles

#6974, 1-Carle, Elizabeth, 2-born, 3-5 am, 17 Dec 1829, 12-Carle, Joseph, 13-Herr, Anna, 15-Charles

#6975, 1-Carle, John Joseph, 2-married, 7-Kauffman, Frances, 15-Charles

#6976, 1-Carle, John Joseph, 2-born, 3-8 Apr 1764, 15-Charles

#6977, 1-Carle, John Joseph, 2-died, 3-12 Mar 1849[?], 15-Charles

#6978, 1-Carle, Frances (Kauffman), 2-born, 3-23 Sep 1767, 15-Charles

#6979, 1-Carle, Frances (Kauffman), 2-died, 3-27 J__ 1822, 15-Charles

#6980, 1-Carle, Joseph, 2-born, 3-8 Apr 1789, 15-Charles

#6981, 1-Carle, Joseph, 2-died, 3-1 Sep 1854, 15-Charles

#6982, 1-Carle, Anna (Herr), 2-born, 3-19 Dec 1792, 15-Charles

#6983, 1-Carle, Anna (Herr), 2-died, 3-27 Mar 1857, 15-Charles

#6984, 1-Leiter, Abraham, 2-married, 3-10 Jun 1828, 7-Miller, Louisa, 15-Leiter

#6985, 1-Leiter, Louisa (Miller), 2-born, 3-25 May 1846, 15-Leiter

#6986, 1-Leiter, Emma Susan, 2-born, 3-4 Jun 1848, 15-Leiter

#6987, 1-Leiter, Lydia Ann, 2-born, 3-21 Mar 1851, 15-Leiter

#6988, 1-Ash, Harry G., 2-born, 3-23 Nov 1873, 15-Leiter

#6989, 1-Siter[?], Annie L., 2-born, 3-21 Mar 1871, 15-Leiter

#6990, 1-Sites, William E., 2-born, 3-1 Aug 1874, 15-Leiter

#6991, 1-Leiter, Abraham, 2-born, 3-3 Jun 1806, 15-Leiter

#6992, 1-Miller, Louisa, 2-born, 3-27 Sep 1809, 15-Leiter

#6993, 1-Leiter, Joseph, 2-born, 3-11 Mar 1829, 15-Leiter

#6994, 1-Leiter, Mary Beatty, 2-born, 3-6 May 1831, 15-Leiter

#6995, 1-Leiter, John William, 2-born, 3-20 May 1834, 15-Leiter

#6996, 1-Leiter, George Thompson, 2-born, 3-18 Sep 1836, 15-Leiter

#6997, 1-Leiter, Eliza Jane, 2-born, 3-29 Feb 1839, 15-Leiter

#6998, 1-Leiter, Sarah Drusilla, 2-born, 3-30 Dec 1840, 15-Leiter

#6999, 1-Leiter, Edward Benton, 2-born, 3-25 Jun 1842, 15-Leiter

#7000, 1-Leiter, Mary Catherine, 2-born, 3-11 Apr 1844, 15-Leiter

#7001, 1-Miller, Mary (Mrs.), 2-died, 3-26 Jan 1844, 15-Leiter

#7002, 1-Leiter, Sr., Abraham, 2-died, 3-26 May 1833, 15-Leiter

#7003, 1-Leiter, Jr., Abraham, 2-died, 3-31 Mar 1864, 5-57 years 9 months 28 days, 15-Leiter

#7004, 1-Leiter, Mary Beatty, 2-died, 3-14 May 1832, 5-1 years 8 days, 15-Leiter

#7005, 1-Leiter, Sarah Drusilla, 2-died, 3-3 Feb 1841, 5-1 months 4 days, 15-Leiter

#7006, 1-Leiter, Louisa Miller, 2-died, 3-11 Jun 1847, 5-1 years 15 days, 15-Leiter

#7007, 1-Snyder, Leonard P., 2-born, 3-15 Jul 1871, 15-Snyder

#7008, 1-Snyder, Leonard P., 2-married, 3-26 Oct 1898, 7-Kratz, Elsie, 10-Rev. E.H. Jones, 15-Snyder

#7009, 1-Kratz, Elsie, 2-born, 3-21 Jun 1874, 15-Snyder

FAMILY BIBLE RECORDS IN THE WASHINGTON COUNTY FREE LIBRARY, HAGERSTOWN, MARYLAND

Entry #, 1-Last Name, First Name, 2-Event, 3-Date, 4-Event Location, 5-Age, 6-Other,
7-Spouse's Last, First, 8-Groom's Residence, 9-Bride's Residence, 10-Minister, 11-Minister's Location,
12-Father's Last, First, 13-Mother's Last, First, 14-Transcribed, 15-Family Bible

```
#7010, 1-Snyder, Cornelius Kratz, 2-born, 3-28 Aug 1899, 12-Snyder, Leonard P., 13-
    Kratz, Elsie, 15-Snyder
#7011, 1-Snyder, Syble Lucile, 2-born, 3-7 Apr 1905, 12-Snyder, Leonard P., 13-
    Kratz, Elsie, 15-Snyder
#7012, 1-Snyder, Ralph Leonard, 2-born, 3-14 Feb 1907, 12-Snyder, Leonard P., 13-
    Kratz, Elsie, 15-Snyder
#7013, 1-Snyder, George Grosh, 2-born, 3-25 Apr 1909, 12-Snyder, Leonard P., 13-
    Kratz, Elsie, 15-Snyder
#7014, 1-Snyder, Helen Louise, 2-born, 3-13 Jul 1913, 12-Snyder, Leonard P., 13-
    Kratz, Elsie, 15-Snyder
#7015, 1-Snyder, Luther Peterman, 2-born, 3-20 May 1915, 12-Snyder, Leonard P., 13-
    Kratz, Elsie, 15-Snyder
#7016, 1-Snyder, George G., 2-married, 3-11 Dec 1942, 7-Kamps[?], Margaret A., 10-
    Rev. Allen B.L. Fisher, 11-Methodist Church, Ellicott City, MD, 15-Snyder
#7017, 1-Snyder, Sibyl Lucile, 2-died, 3-27 Sep 1905, 5-5 months 20 days, 15-Snyder
#7018, 1-Snyder, Luther Peterman, 2-died, 3-14 Aug 1917, 5-2 years 2 months 24
    days, 15-Snyder
#7019, 1-Snyder, Ralph Leonard, 2-died, 3-25 Aug 1918, 5-11 years 6 months 11 days,
    15-Snyder
#7020, 1-Snyder, Leonard P., 2-died, 3-2 Jul 1929, 15-Snyder
#7021, 1-Snyder, Cornelius K., 2-died, 3-22 Jan 1947, 15-Snyder
#7022, 1-Dellinger, Jacob H., 2-born, 3-18 Jun 1835, 12-Dellinger, Henry William,
    13-Snyder, Mary Margaret, 15-Snyder
#7023, 1-Dellinger, Jacob H., 2-died, 3-2 Jul 1838, 12-Dellinger, Henry William,
    13-Snyder, Mary Margaret, 15-Snyder
#7024, 1-Dellinger, Anne W., 2-born, 3-18 Jan 1837, 4-Kelso, Washington, 12-
    Dellinger, Henry William, 13-Snyder, Mary Margaret, 15-Snyder
#7025, 1-Dellinger, Anne W., 2-married, 7-Castleman, 12-Dellinger, Henry William,
    13-Snyder, Mary Margaret, 15-Snyder
#7026, 1-Dellinger, Anne W., 2-died, 3-2 Jul 1924, 4-Kelso, Washington, 12-
    Dellinger, Henry William, 13-Snyder, Mary Margaret, 15-Snyder
#7027, 1-Dellinger, Anne W., 2-married, 3-29 Dec 1958, 4-Clear Spring, MD, 6-groom
    of Central Pa M.E. Church Conference Pa.", 7-Castleman, Rev. David, 12-
    Dellinger, Henry William, 13-Snyder, Mary Margaret, 15-Snyder
#7028, 1-Dellinger, Henrietta M., 2-born, 3-16 Feb 1839, 12-Dellinger, Henry
    William, 13-Snyder, Mary Margaret, 15-Snyder
#7029, 1-Dellinger, Henrietta M., 2-died, 3-8 Aug 1909, 12-Dellinger, Henry
    William, 13-Snyder, Mary Margaret, 15-Snyder
#7030, 1-Dellinger, Allmira V.[?], 2-born, 3-10 Mar 1841, 12-Dellinger, Henry
    William, 13-Snyder, Mary Margaret, 15-Snyder
#7031, 1-Dellinger, Emily L., 2-born, 3-10 Mar 1841, 12-Dellinger, Henry William,
    13-Snyder, Mary Margaret, 15-Snyder
#7032, 1-Dellinger, Emily L., 2-died, 3-6 Sep 1870, 12-Dellinger, Henry William,
    13-Snyder, Mary Margaret, 15-Snyder
#7033, 1-Dellinger, Emily L., 2-married, 7-Knepper, Lewis F., 12-Dellinger, Henry
    William, 13-Snyder, Mary Margaret, 15-Snyder
#7034, 1-Knepper, Lewis F., 2-died, 3-31 Oct 1893, 12-Dellinger, Henry William, 13-
    Snyder, Mary Margaret, 15-Snyder
#7035, 1-Dellinger, Catherine C., 2-born, 3-25 Jun 1843, 12-Dellinger, Henry
    William, 13-Snyder, Mary Margaret, 15-Snyder
#7036, 1-Dellinger, Catherine C., 2-married, 7-Lancy, 12-Dellinger, Henry William,
    13-Snyder, Mary Margaret, 15-Snyder
#7037, 1-Dellinger, Ellen Burrows, 2-born, 3-16 Dec 1847, 12-Dellinger, Henry
    William, 13-Snyder, Mary Margaret, 15-Snyder
```

FAMILY BIBLE RECORDS IN THE WASHINGTON COUNTY FREE LIBRARY, HAGERSTOWN, MARYLAND

Entry #, 1-Last Name, First Name, 2-Event, 3-Date, 4-Event Location, 5-Age, 6-Other, 7-Spouse's Last, First, 8-Groom's Residence, 9-Bride's Residence, 10-Minister, 11-Minister's Location, 12-Father's Last, First, 13-Mother's Last, First, 14-Transcribed, 15-Family Bible

#7038, 1-Dellinger, Ellen Burrows, 2-died, 3-22 Jul 1875, 5-27 years, 12-Dellinger, Henry William, 13-Snyder, Mary Margaret, 15-Snyder

#7039, 1-Dellinger, Mary Williams, 2-born, 3-18 Sep 1850, 12-Dellinger, Henry William, 13-Snyder, Mary Margaret, 15-Snyder

#7040, 1-Dellinger, Mary Williams, 2-died, 3-2 Feb 1885, 12-Dellinger, Henry William, 13-Snyder, Mary Margaret, 15-Snyder

#7041, 1-Dellinger, Lucy S., 2-born, 3-28 May 1853, 12-Dellinger, Henry William, 13-Snyder, Mary Margaret, 15-Snyder

#7042, 1-Dellinger, Lucy S., 2-died, 3-19 Jul 1853, 12-Dellinger, Henry William, 13-Snyder, Mary Margaret, 15-Snyder

#7043, 1-Dellinger, Henry Williams, 2-born, 3-30 May 1855, 12-Dellinger, Henry William, 13-Snyder, Mary Margaret, 15-Snyder

#7044, 1-Snyder, Ann Eliza, 2-died, 3-18 Jul 1813, 15-Snyder

#7045, 1-Snyder, John S.B., 2-died, 3-29 Aug 1819, 15-Snyder

#7046, 1-Snyder, Susan Ann, 2-died, 3-21 Oct 1825, 15-Snyder

#7047, 1-Snyder, Tarleton[?], 2-died, 3-1 Jul 1827, 15-Snyder

#7048, 1-Snyder, Harriet Bryan, 2-died, 3-24 Sep 1828, 6-"buried at Park Head, old Snyder burying ground", 7-Snyder, Jacob Casper, 15-Snyder

#7049, 1-Snyder, Jacob C., 2-died, 3-4 Jan 1840, 5-52 years 6 months 15 days, 6-"buried in Lutheran grave yard, Clear Spring", 15-Snyder

#7050, 1-Snyder, Maria, 2-died, 3-3 Oct 1841, 6-"buried in Lutheran graveyard Clear Spring, Md.", 12-Snyder, Jacob Casper, 15-Snyder

#7051, 1-Bryan, John, 2-died, 3-15 Jun 1825, 6-"fatherinlaw of Jacob Casper Snyder", 12-Bryan, James, 15-Snyder

#7052, 1-Bryan, Sary, 2-died, 3-20 Jan 1829, 6-"motherinlaw of Jacob Casper Snyder", 15-Snyder

#7053, 1-Bryan, Mary Margaret, 2-married, 3-1 May 1834, 7-Dellinger, Henry Williams, 12-Snyder, Jacob Casper, 15-Snyder

#7054, 1-Dellinger, Henry Williams, 2-born, 3-11 Jul 1813, 15-Snyder

#7055, 1-Dellinger, Henry Williams, 2-died, 3-1 Nov 1884, 6-"Had 10 children, 2 died in infancy, 4 married and 4 remained single", 15-Snyder

#7056, 1-Snyder, Jacob Casper, 2-married, 3-23 Aug 1812, 7-Bryan, Hariet, 15-Snyder

#7057, 1-Snyder, Hariet (Bryan), 2-born, 12-Bryan, John, 15-Snyder

#7058, 1-Bryan, John, 2-born, 3-Nov 1757, 12-Bryan, James, 15-Snyder

#7059, 1-Bryan, John, 2-married, 3-17 Sep 1762, 7-Bryan, Sary, 15-Snyder

#7060, 1-Bryan, John, 2-died, 3-15 Jun 1825[?], 15-Snyder

#7061, 1-Bryan, Sary, 2-born, 3-17 Sep 1762, 12-Blunt, James R., 13-Blunt, Ann, 15-Snyder

#7062, 1-Bryan, Sarah, 2-died, 3-20 Jan 1829, 15-Snyder

#7063, 1-Bryan, Ann, 2-born, 3-7 Nov 1792, 15-Snyder

#7064, 1-Bryan, Ann, 2-died, 3-14[?] Mar 1828, 15-Snyder

#7065, 1-Bryan, Frederick, 2-born, 3-14 Jul 1795, 15-Snyder

#7066, 1-Bryan, Frederick, 2-died, 3-25 Jul, 5-76 years 17 days, 15-Snyder

#7067, 1-Bryan, Mariah, 2-born, 3-6[?] Jan 1802, 15-Snyder

#7068, 1-Bryan, Mariah, 2-died, 3-20 Oct 1821, 15-Snyder

#7069, 1-Snyder, Jacob C., 2-married, 3-15 Feb 1830, 7-Beard, Sarah, 15-Snyder

#7070, 1-Snyder, Jacob C., 2-born, 3-19 Jun 1787, 15-Snyder

#7071, 1-Snyder, Jacob C., 2-died, 3-4 Jan 1840, 5-52 years 5 months 15 days, 15-Snyder

#7072, 1-Bryan, Harriet, 2-born, 3-18 Mar 1791, 7-Snyder, Jacob C., 15-Snyder

#7073, 1-Snyder, Anne Eliza, 2-born, 3-4 Jul 1813, 12-Snyder, Jacob C., 13-Bryan, Harriet, 15-Snyder

#7074, 1-Snyder, Anne Eliza, 2-died, 3-18 Jul 1813, 12-Snyder, Jacob C., 13-Bryan, Harriet, 15-Snyder

FAMILY BIBLE RECORDS IN THE WASHINGTON COUNTY FREE LIBRARY, HAGERSTOWN, MARYLAND

Entry #, 1-Last Name, First Name, 2-Event, 3-Date, 4-Event Location, 5-Age, 6-Other, 7-Spouse's Last, First, 8-Groom's Residence, 9-Bride's Residence, 10-Minister, 11-Minister's Location, 12-Father's Last, First, 13-Mother's Last, First, 14-Transcribed, 15-Family Bible

#7075, 1-Snyder, Mary Margaret, 2-born, 3-9 Apr 1815, 12-Snyder, Jacob C., 13-Bryan, Harriet, 15-Snyder

#7076, 1-Snyder, Mary Margaret, 2-died, 3-1883, 5-83 years, 15-Snyder

#7077, 1-Snyder, John S.B., 2-born, 3-2 Sep 1817, 12-Snyder, Jacob C., 13-Bryan, Harriet, 15-Snyder

#7078, 1-Snyder, John S.B., 2-died, 3-29 Aug 1819, 12-Snyder, Jacob C., 13-Bryan, Harriet, 15-Snyder

#7079, 1-Snyder, Frederick, 2-born, 3-10 Feb 1820, 12-Snyder, Jacob C., 13-Bryan, Harriet, 15-Snyder

#7080, 1-Snyder, Mariah, 2-born, 3-18 Nov 1821, 12-Snyder, Jacob C., 13-Bryan, Harriet, 15-Snyder

#7081, 1-Snyder, Mariah, 2-died, 3-3 Oct 1841, 12-Snyder, Jacob C., 13-Bryan, Harriet, 15-Snyder

#7082, 1-Snyder, Susan Ann, 2-born, 3-14 Sep 1824, 12-Snyder, Jacob C., 13-Bryan, Harriet, 15-Snyder

#7083, 1-Snyder, Susan Ann, 2-died, 3-21[?] Oct 1825, 12-Snyder, Jacob C., 13-Bryan, Harriet, 15-Snyder

#7084, 1-Snyder, Tarleton[?], 2-born, 3-27 Mar 1827, 12-Snyder, Jacob C., 13-Bryan, Harriet, 15-Snyder

#7085, 1-Snyder, Tarleton[?], 2-died, 3-1 Jul 1827, 12-Snyder, Jacob C., 13-Bryan, Harriet, 15-Snyder

#7086, 1-Snyder, Harriet Henrietta, 2-born, 3-6 Sep 1828, 12-Snyder, Jacob C., 13-Bryan, Harriet, 15-Snyder

#7087, 1-Bryan, Harriet, 2-died, 3-24 Sep 1828, 15-Snyder

#7088, 1-Castleman, Mary W., 2-born, 3-30 May 1860, 6-grandchild of Henry William & Mary Margaret (Snyder) Dellinger, 15-Snyder

#7089, 1-Castleman, Sallie C., 2-born, 3-26 Jun 1862, 6-grandchild of Henry William & Mary Margaret (Snyder) Dellinger, 15-Snyder

#7090, 1-Castleman, Harry W., 2-born, 3-2 Jul 1865, 6-grandchild of Henry William & Mary Margaret (Snyder) Dellinger, 15-Snyder

#7091, 1-Knepper, George, 2-born, 3-19 Dec 1860, 6-grandchild of Henry William & Mary Margaret (Snyder) Dellinger, 15-Snyder

#7092, 1-Knepper, Nellie D., 2-born, 3-14 Nov 1862, 6-grandchild of Henry William & Mary Margaret (Snyder) Dellinger, 15-Snyder

#7093, 1-Knepper, Freddie[?], 2-born, 3-12 Sep 1865, 6-grandchild of Henry William & Mary Margaret (Snyder) Dellinger, 15-Snyder

#7094, 1-Knepper, Myrtle V., 2-born, 3-14 Apr 1868, 6-grandchild of Henry William & Mary Margaret (Snyder) Dellinger, 15-Snyder

#7095, 1-Lancy, Geneva, 2-born, 3-Aug, 6-grandchild of Henry William & Mary Margaret (Snyder) Dellinger, 15-Snyder

#7096, 1-Lancy, Maggie M., 2-born, 3-Nov 1865, 6-grandchild of Henry William & Mary Margaret (Snyder) Dellinger, 15-Snyder

#7097, 1-Greathead, Hattie K., 2-born, 3-Jul, 6-grandchild of Henry William & Mary Margaret (Snyder) Dellinger, 15-Snyder

#7098, 1-Greathead, Fanny M., 2-born, 6-grandchild of Henry William & Mary Margaret (Snyder) Dellinger, 15-Snyder

#7099, 1-Greathead, Willie T., 2-born, 3-Nov, 6-grandchild of Henry William & Mary Margaret (Snyder) Dellinger, 15-Snyder

#7100, 1-Greathead, Robert N., 2-born, 6-grandchild of Henry William & Mary Margaret (Snyder) Dellinger, 15-Snyder

#7101, 1-Greathead, Thornton[?] F.[?], 2-born, 6-grandchild of Henry William & Mary Margaret (Snyder) Dellinger, 15-Snyder

#7102, 1-Greathead, Ormond[?] Leroy[?], 2-born, 6-grandchild of Henry William & Mary Margaret (Snyder) Dellinger, 15-Snyder

FAMILY BIBLE RECORDS IN THE WASHINGTON COUNTY FREE LIBRARY, HAGERSTOWN, MARYLAND

Entry #, 1-Last Name, First Name, 2-Event, 3-Date, 4-Event Location, 5-Age, 6-Other, 7-Spouse's Last, First, 8-Groom's Residence, 9-Bride's Residence, 10-Minister, 11-Minister's Location, 12-Father's Last, First, 13-Mother's Last, First, 14-Transcribed, 15-Family Bible

#7103, 1-Greathead, Arthur D., 2-born, 6-grandchild of Henry William & Mary Margaret (Snyder) Dellinger, 15-Snyder

#7104, 1-Greathead, Emily V., 2-born, 6-grandchild of Henry William & Mary Margaret (Snyder) Dellinger, 15-Snyder

#7105, 1-Dellinger, Henry Williams, 2-died, 3-8 Apr 1930, 15-Snyder

#7106, 1-Snyder, Mary, 2-born, 3-1813[?], 15-Snyder

#7107, 1-Dellinger, Henry Williams, 2-born, 3-10 Jul 1813, 15-Snyder

#7108, 1-Castleman, Anne White (Dellinger) (Mrs.), 2-obituary, 5-87 years 5 months 13 days, 15-Snyder

#7109, 1-Perkins, Wm. H. (Dr.), 2-obituary, 4-Hancock, MD, 5-55 years, 15-Snyder

#7110, 1-Snyder, Leonard, 2-died, 3-30 Sep 1832, 15-Snyder

#7111, 1-Snyder, Sarahan, 2-died, 3-11 Oct 1835, 15-Snyder

#7112, 1-Snyder, Louisa, 2-died, 3-26 Sep 1857, 4-Clear Spring, MD, 7-Ridgeley[?], Richard, 15-Snyder

#7113, 1-Snyder, Rebecca, 2-died, 3-7 Aug 1858, 4-Clear Spring, MD, 7-Snyder, Leonard, 15-Snyder

#7114, 1-Snyder, Otho, 2-died, 3-11 Nov 1870, 4-near Owensboro, Davis Co., KY, 12-Snyder, Leonard, 13-Snyder, Rebecca, 15-Snyder

#7115, 1-Snyder, Jacob C., 2-died, 3-4 Jan 1840, 15-Snyder

#7116, 1-Snyder, William B., 2-died, 3-12 Nov 1888, 4-Clear Spring, MD, 12-Snyder, Leonard, 13-Snyder, Rebecca, 15-Snyder

#7117, 1-Snyder, Mary, 2-died, 3-7 Apr 1896, 4-Dayton, OH, 6-buried Centreville, OH, 7-Nutt, Nelson, 12-Snyder, Leonard, 13-Snyder, Rebecca, 15-Snyder

#7118, 1-Snyder, John Y.[?], 2-died, 3-23 Aug 1895, 4-Clear Spring, MD, 12-Snyder, Leonard, 13-Snyder, Rebecca, 15-Snyder

#7119, 1-Snyder, Peter L., 2-died, 3-10 Sep 1912, 4-Dayton, OH, 6-buried Dayton, OH, 15-Snyder

#7120, 1-Snyder, Maggie M. (Houck), 2-died, 3-25 Dec 1895, 4-Dayton, OH, 6-buried Dayton, OH, 15-Snyder

#7121, 1-Snider, Leonard, 2-born, 3-1 Jan 1795, 15-Snyder

#7122, 1-Snider, Rebecca (Charlton), 2-born, 3-28 Sep 1797, 7-Snider, Leonard, 15-Snyder

#7123, 1-Snider, Otho, 2-born, 3-15 Nov 1819, 15-Snyder

#7124, 1-Snider, Mary, 2-born, 3-24 Aug 1821, 4-Clear Spring, MD, 15-Snyder

#7125, 1-Snider, Louisa, 2-born, 3-17 Sep 1823, 15-Snyder

#7126, 1-Snider, Peter, 2-born, 3-22 Jun 1825, 15-Snyder

#7127, 1-Snider, William B., 2-born, 3-14 Jul 1827, 15-Snyder

#7128, 1-Snider, John T., 2-born, 3-6 Aug 1830, 15-Snyder

#7129, 1-Snider, Sarah Ann, 2-born, 3-31 Jan 1833, 15-Snyder

#7130, 1-Snyder, Peter Leonard, 2-married, 3-4 Mar 1862, 4-Clear Spring, MD, 7-Houck, Margaret M., 12-Snyder, Leonard, 13-Charlton, Rebecca, 15-Snyder

#7131, 1-Houck, Margaret M., 2-born, 12-Houck, Jacob, 13-Houck, Maria, 15-Snyder

#7132, 1-Snyder, Margaret M., 2-died, 3-25 Dec 1895, 6-buried Dayton, OH, 15-Snyder

#7133, 1-Snyder, Peter Leonard, 2-died, 3-10 Sep 1912, 6-buried Dayton, OH, 15-Snyder

#7134, 1-Snyder, Mary, 2-married, 3-10 Apr 1845, 4-Xenia[?], OH, 7-Nutt, Nelson, 10-Rev. Valentine Winters, 12-Snyder, Leonard, 13-Charlton, Rebecca, 15-Snyder

#7135, 1-Nutt, Nelson, 2-born, 3-1 Sep 1818, 4-Centreville, OH, 12-Nutt, Aaron, 13-Nutt, Nancy Jane, 15-Snyder

#7136, 1-Nutt, Nelson, 2-died, 3-3 Oct 1861, 6-buried Centreville, OH, 15-Snyder

#7137, 1-Nutt, Mary (Snyder), 2-died, 3-7 Apr 1895, 6-buried Centreville, OH, 15-Snyder

#7138, 1-Barkman[?], Jacob, 2-born, 3-21 Aug 1767, 15-Snyder

FAMILY BIBLE RECORDS IN THE WASHINGTON COUNTY FREE LIBRARY, HAGERSTOWN, MARYLAND

Entry #, 1-Last Name, First Name, 2-Event, 3-Date, 4-Event Location, 5-Age, 6-Other,
7-Spouse's Last, First, 8-Groom's Residence, 9-Bride's Residence, 10-Minister, 11-Minister's Location,
12-Father's Last, First, 13-Mother's Last, First, 14-Transcribed, 15-Family Bible

#7139, 1-Barkman[?], Jacob, 2-died, 3-18 Jan 1842, 5-71 years 7 months 27 days, 6-buried Lutheran graveyard, 15-Snyder

#7140, 1-Barkman[?], Catherine, 2-died, 3-9 Nov 1855, 5-77 years 4 months 15 days, 6-buried Lutheran graveyard, 15-Snyder

#7141, 1-Schneider, Peter, 2-born, 3-8 Sep 1791, 4-Washington Co., MD, 12-Schneider, Caspar, 13-Schneider, Anna Maria, 15-Snyder

#7142, 1-Schneider, Peter, 2-baptized, 3-16 Apr 1792, 6-sponsor: George Mandy (unmarried), 10-Rev. Goering, 15-Snyder

#7143, 1-Snyder, Leonard, 2-born, 3-1 Jan 1795, 4-near Clear Spring, MD, 6-youngest son of parents, 12-Snyder, Casper, 15-Snyder

#7144, 1-Snyder, Leonard, 2-died, 3-30 Sep 1832, 15-Snyder

#7145, 1-Snyder, Rebecca (Charlton), 2-born, 3-28 Sep 1797, 4-near Clear Spring, 7-Snyder, Leonard, 12-Charlton, Wm., 15-Snyder

#7146, 1-Snyder, Rebecca (Charlton), 2-died, 3-7 Aug 1858, 15-Snyder

#7147, 1-Snyder, Otho A., 2-born, 3-15 Nov 1819, 6-oldest son of parents; moved to Kentucky in 1841, 12-Snyder, Leonard, 13-Snyder, Rebecca, 15-Snyder

#7148, 1-Snyder, Otho A., 2-died, 3-11 Nov 1870, 15-Snyder

#7149, 1-Snyder, Mary, 2-born, 3-24 Aug 1821, 4-near Clear Spring, 6-moved to Ohio in 1842, 15-Snyder

#7150, 1-Snyder, Mary, 2-married, 4-Ohio, 7-Nutt, Nelson, 15-Snyder

#7151, 1-Snyder, Mary, 2-died, 3-7 Apr 1895, 6-died leaving 3 daughters, 15-Snyder

#7152, 1-Barkman, Aunty Katie, 2-died, 3-Oct 1855, 4-Clear Spring, MD, 15-Snyder

#7153, 1-Snyder, Maggie M. (Deahl), 2-born, 3-11 Dec 1897, 12-Deale, Dus, 13-Deale, Jennie, 15-Snyder

#7154, 1-Deale, Jennie, 2-born, 12-Eyerly, Sam'l., 13-Cook, Kate, 15-Snyder

#7155, 1-Snyder, Louisa, 2-born, 3-17 Sep 1823, 4-near Clear Spring, MD, 7-Ridgeley, Richard, 15-Snyder

#7156, 1-Snyder, Louisa, 2-died, 3-26 Sep 1857, 6-consumption, 15-Snyder

#7157, 1-Ridgeley, Mary, 2-born, 12-Ridgeley, Richard, 13-Snyder, Louisa, 15-Snyder

#7158, 1-Ridgeley, Kate, 2-born, 12-Ridgeley, Richard, 13-Snyder, Louisa, 15-Snyder

#7159, 1-Ridgeley, Mary, 2-married, 7-Lorrence, F.D., 15-Snyder

#7160, 1-Snyder, Peter, 2-born, 3-22 Jun 1825, 4-near Clear Spring, MD, 6-moved to Dayton, OH on 1 Apr 1850, 15-Snyder

#7161, 1-Snyder, Peter, 2-married, 3-4 Mar 1862, 7-Houch, Margre M., 15-Snyder

#7162, 1-Houch, Margre M., 2-born, 12-Houch, Jacob, 15-Snyder

#7163, 1-Snyder, Margre M. (Houch), 2-died, 3-25 Dec 1895, 15-Snyder

#7164, 1-Snyder, Wm. B., 2-born, 3-14 Jul 1827, 15-Snyder

#7165, 1-Snyder, Wm. B., 2-died, 3-12 Nov 1888, 15-Snyder

#7166, 1-Snyder, John L., 2-born, 3-30 Aug 1831, 15-Snyder

#7167, 1-Snyder, John L., 2-died, 3-23 Aug 1895, 15-Snyder

#7168, 1-Snyder, Sarah Ann, 2-born, 3-31 Jan 1833, 4-Clear Spring, MD, 15-Snyder

#7169, 1-Snyder, Sarah Ann, 2-died, 3-11 Oct 1835, 15-Snyder

#7170, 1-Ridgeley, Richard, 2-died, 3-Aug 1856, 4-Williamsport, MD, 15-Snyder

#7171, 1-Ridgeley, Richard, 2-married, 3-22 Oct 1841, 10-Rev. Lanahan, 15-Snyder

#7172, 1-Snyder, Peter, 2-died, 3-6 Nov 1859, 4-Clear Spring, MD, 12-Snyder, Casper, 15-Snyder

#7173, 1-Gordon, Susan D., 2-died, 3-13 Apr 1877, 4-Clear Spring, MD, 5-75 years, 6-buried by her husband's side in the Lutheran Grave yard, 7-Snyder, Peter, 15-Snyder

#7174, 1-Snyder, Jacob Casper, 2-born, 3-19 Jun 1878, 15-Snyder

#7175, 1-Snyder, Jacob Casper, 2-died, 3-4 Jan 1840, 15-Snyder

#7176, 1-Snyder, Peter, 2-born, 3-8 Sep 1791, 15-Snyder

#7177, 1-Snyder, Leonard, 2-born, 3-1 Jan 1795, 15-Snyder

#7178, 1-Snyder, Leonard, 2-died, 3-30 Sep 1832, 15-Snyder

#7179, 1-Snyder, Anthony, 2-born, 3-23 Apr 1771, 15-Snyder

FAMILY BIBLE RECORDS IN THE WASHINGTON COUNTY FREE LIBRARY, HAGERSTOWN, MARYLAND

Entry #, 1-Last Name, First Name, 2-Event, 3-Date, 4-Event Location, 5-Age, 6-Other,
7-Spouse's Last, First, 8-Groom's Residence, 9-Bride's Residence, 10-Minister, 11-Minister's Location,
12-Father's Last, First, 13-Mother's Last, First, 14-Transcribed, 15-Family Bible

```
#7180, 1-Snyder, Anthony, 2-died, 3-26 Apr 1817, 15-Snyder
#7181, 1-Snyder, Susan (Mrs.), 2-obituary, 4-Rome, 5-83 years, 15-Snyder
#7182, 1-Bryan, Sarah, 2-died, 3-20 Jun 1820, 5-67 years, 7-Bryan, John, 15-Snyder
#7183, 1-Snyder, Harriet, 2-died, 3-28Sep 1828, 5-37 years, 15-Snyder
#7184, 1-Snyder, Anthony, 2-born, 3-23 Apr 1771, 15-Snyder
#7185, 1-Snyder, Anthony, 2-died, 3-26 Apr 1817, 15-Snyder
#7186, 1-Snyder, Otho A., 2-married, 3-29 Sep 1842, 7-Raney, Susan Ann, 15-Snyder
#7187, 1-Raney, Susan Ann, 2-born, 3-1 Jul 1826, 12-Raney, John T.[?], 15-Snyder
#7188, 1-Snyder, Francis Frederick, 2-born, 3-5 Dec 1843, 12-Snyder, Otho A., 13-
    Raney, Susan Ann, 15-Snyder
#7189, 1-Snyder, Mary Catherine, 2-born, 3-4 Mar 1845, 12-Snyder, Otho A., 13-
    Raney, Susan Ann, 15-Snyder
#7190, 1-Snyder, James Thomas, 2-born, 3-24 Aug 1846, 12-Snyder, Otho A., 13-Raney,
    Susan Ann, 15-Snyder
#7191, 1-Snyder, John Francis, 2-born, 3-26 Apr 1849, 12-Snyder, Otho A., 13-Raney,
    Susan Ann, 15-Snyder
#7192, 1-Snyder, Rebecca Jane, 2-born, 3-28 Dec 1851, 12-Snyder, Otho A., 13-Raney,
    Susan Ann, 15-Snyder
#7193, 1-Snyder, Leonard Williams, 2-born, 3-24 Nov 1854, 15-Snyder
#7194, 1-Snyder, Maria Luisa, 2-born, 3-28 Jan 1858, 15-Snyder
#7195, 1-Snyder, Joseph, 2-born, 3-3 Feb 1863, 15-Snyder
#7196, 1-Snyder, Otho A., 2-died, 3-11 Nov 1870, 12-Snyder, Leonard, 13-Snyder,
    Rebecca, 15-Snyder
#7197, 1-Snyder, John Francis, 2-died, 3-24 Apr 1859, 12-Snyder, Otho, 13-Snyder,
    Susan, 15-Snyder
#7198, 1-Snyder, Leonard Williams, 2-died, 3-27 Dec 1871, 12-Snyder, Otho, 13-
    Snyder, Susan, 15-Snyder
#7199, 1-Nutt, Addie (Miss), 2-obituary, 5-74 years, 15-Snyder
#7200, 1-Nutt, General, 2-born, 3-22 Feb 1846, 4-Lancaster, PA, 15-Snyder
#7201, 1-Nutt, Emma (Miss), 2-obituary, 6-buried Centreville, OH, 15-Snyder
#7202, 1-Nutt, Nellie (Miss), 2-obituary, 3-30 Mar 1892, 6-3rd daughter of parents,
    12-Nutt, Nelson, 13-Snyder, Mary, 15-Snyder
#7203, 1-Nutt, Emma, 2-born, 3-Saturday, 13 Feb 1847, 4-Lancaster, PA, 15-Snyder
#7204, 1-Nutt, Jennie R., 2-born, 3-Saturday, 26 Aug 1848, 4-Lancaster, PA, 15-
    Snyder
#7205, 1-Nutt, Nellie, 2-born, 3-Friday, 3 May 1850, 4-Centerville, OH, 15-Snyder
#7206, 1-Nutt, Viola, 2-born, 3-Monday, 15 Aug 1853, 4-Dayton, OH, 15-Snyder
#7207, 1-Nutt, Mary, 2-born, 3-Thursday, 15 Mar 1855, 4-Dayton, OH, 15-Snyder
#7208, 1-Nutt, Addie, 2-born, 3-Sunday, 20 Feb 1859, 4-Dayton, OH, 15-Snyder
#7209, 1-Nutt, Addie, 2-died, 3-2:45am, Saturday, 3 Dec 1932, 4-St. Joseph Mission,
    Dayton, OH, 6-buried Centerville, OH, 15-Snyder
#7210, 1-Nutt, Emma, 2-died, 3-7pm, Wednesday, 2 Oct 1917, 4-Dayton, OH, 6-buried
    Centerville, OH, 15-Snyder
#7211, 1-Nutt, Nelson, 2-died, 3-Thursday, 3 Oct 1861, 5-43 years 1 months 2 days,
    15-Snyder
#7212, 1-Nutt, General, 2-died, 3-Wednesday, 20 May 1846, 5-2 months 28 days, 15-
    Snyder
#7213, 1-Nutt, Mary, 2-died, 3-Friday, 17 Jul 1855, 5-4 months 2 days, 15-Snyder
#7214, 1-Nutt, Jennie, 2-died, 3-Thursday, 26 Apr 1883, 5-34 years 8 months 5 days,
    15-Snyder
#7215, 1-Nutt, Nellie, 2-died, 3-Wednesday, 30 Mar 1892, 5-41 years 10 months 27
    days, 15-Snyder
#7216, 1-Nutt, Mary (Mrs.), 2-died, 3-Sunday, 7 Apr 1895, 5-73 years 7 months 15
    days, 15-Snyder
#7217, 1-Nutt, Viola, 2-died, 3-Tuesday, 27 Mar 1905, 5-51 years 15 days, 15-Snyder
```

FAMILY BIBLE RECORDS IN THE WASHINGTON COUNTY FREE LIBRARY, HAGERSTOWN, MARYLAND

Entry #, 1-Last Name, First Name, 2-Event, 3-Date, 4-Event Location, 5-Age, 6-Other, 7-Spouse's Last, First, 8-Groom's Residence, 9-Bride's Residence, 10-Minister, 11-Minister's Location, 12-Father's Last, First, 13-Mother's Last, First, 14-Transcribed, 15-Family Bible

#7218, 1-Nutt, Leonard, 2-married, 3-26 Oct 1898, 4-Clear Spring, MD, 7-Kratz, Elsie, 8-Clear Spring, MD, 9-Clear Spring, MD, 10-Rev. E.H. Jones, 11-Clear Spring Lutheran Church, 15-Snyder

#7219, 1-Nutt, Sibyl Lucile, 2-died, 3-27 Sep 1905, 4-Clear Spring, MD, 5-5 months 20 days, 15-Snyder

#7220, 1-Nutt, Luther Peterman, 2-died, 3-14 Aug 1917, 4-Clear Spring, MD, 5-2 years 2 months 24 days, 15-Snyder

#7221, 1-Nutt, Ralph Leonard, 2-died, 3-25 Aug 1918, 4-Clear Spring, MD, 5-11 years 6 months 11 days, 15-Snyder

#7222, 1-Nutt, Leonard P., 2-born, 3-15 Jul 1871, 4-Clear Spring, MD, 15-Snyder

#7223, 1-Kratz, Elsie, 2-born, 3-21 Jun 1874, 4-Cumberland, MD, 15-Snyder

#7224, 1-Snyder, Cornelius Kratz, 2-born, 3-28 Aug 1899, 4-Clear Spring, MD, 15-Snyder

#7225, 1-Snyder, Cornelius Kratz, 2-baptized, 3-28 Aug 1901, 10-Rev. Royer, 15-Snyder

#7226, 1-Snyder, Sibyl Lucile, 2-born, 3-7 Apr 1905, 4-Clear Spring, MD, 15-Snyder

#7227, 1-Snyder, Sibyl Lucile, 2-baptized, 3-27 Sep 1905, 4-Clear Spring, MD, 10-Rev. Royer, 15-Snyder

#7228, 1-Snyder, Ralph Leonard, 2-born, 3-14 Feb 1907, 4-Clear Spring, MD, 15-Snyder

#7229, 1-Snyder, Ralph Leonard, 2-baptized, 3-3 May 1907, 4-Clear Spring, MD, 10-Rev. G.A. Royer, 15-Snyder

#7230, 1-Snyder, George Grosh, 2-born, 3-25 Apr 1909, 4-Clear Spring, MD, 15-Snyder

#7231, 1-Snyder, George Grosh, 2-baptized, 3-3 Jun 1909, 10-Rev. Dehl, 15-Snyder

#7232, 1-Snyder, Helen Louise, 2-born, 3-13 Jul 1913, 4-Clear Spring, MD, 15-Snyder

#7233, 1-Snyder, Helen Louise, 2-baptized, 3-13 Jul 1915, 10-Rev. Deihl, 15-Snyder

#7234, 1-Snyder, Luther Peterman, 2-born, 3-20 May 1915, 4-Clear Spring, MD, 15-Snyder

#7235, 1-Snyder, Luther Peterman, 2-baptized, 3-13 Jul 1915, 10-Rev. Deihl, 15-Snyder

#7236, 1-Kratz, Anna E., 2-died, 3-12 Dec 1922, 4-Clear Spring, MD, 5-72 years 5 months 27 days, 15-Snyder

#7237, 1-Snyder, Leonard P., 2-died, 3-2 Jul 1929, 4-Clear Spring, MD, 5-57 years 11 months 19 days, 15-Snyder

#7238, 1-Snyder, Cornelius K., 2-died, 3-22 Jan 1947, 4-Clear Spring, MD, 5-47 years 4 months 24 days, 15-Snyder

#7239, 1-Snyder, Elsie (Kratz), 2-died, 3-30 Jul 1954, 4-Clear Spring, MD, 5-80 years 1 months 9 days, 15-Snyder

#7240, 1-Snyder, Ralph Leonard, 2-obituary, 4-Clear Spring, MD, 5-11 years 6 months 11 days, 6-buried Lutheran cemetery, Clear Spring, MD, 12-Snyder, Leonard, 13-Kratz, Elsie, 15-Snyder

#7241, 1-Snyder, Cornelius Kratz, 2-born, 3-28 Aug 1899, 15-Snyder

#7242, 1-Snyder, Ralph Leonard, 2-born, 3-14 Feb 1907, 15-Snyder

#7243, 1-Snyder, Ralph Leonard, 2-baptized, 3-3 May 1907, 10-Rev. Royer, 15-Snyder

#7244, 1-Snyder, George Grosh, 2-born, 3-25 Apr 1909, 15-Snyder

#7245, 1-Snyder, George Grosh, 2-baptized, 3-3 Jun 1909, 10-Rev. Diehl, 15-Snyder

#7246, 1-Snyder, Sibyl Lucile, 2-born, 3-7 Apr 1905, 15-Snyder

#7247, 1-Snyder, Sibyl Lucile, 2-died, 3-27 Sep 1905, 5-5 months 20 days, 15-Snyder

#7248, 1-Snyder, Sibyl Lucile, 2-baptized, 3-27 Sep 1905, 10-Rev. A. Royer, 15-Snyder

#7249, 1-Snyder, Luth[?], 5-2 years 3 months 3 days, 15-Snyder

#7250, 1-Snyder, Leonard P., 2-died, 3-2 Jul 1929, 15-Snyder

#7251, 1-Snyder, Cornelius K., 2-died, 3-22 Jan 1947, 15-Snyder

FAMILY BIBLE RECORDS IN THE WASHINGTON COUNTY FREE LIBRARY, HAGERSTOWN, MARYLAND

Entry #, 1-Last Name, First Name, 2-Event, 3-Date, 4-Event Location, 5-Age, 6-Other,
7-Spouse's Last, First, 8-Groom's Residence, 9-Bride's Residence, 10-Minister, 11-Minister's Location,
12-Father's Last, First, 13-Mother's Last, First, 14-Transcribed, 15-Family Bible

#7252, 1-Snyder, Daniel J., 2-married, 3-Thursday, 25 May 1858, 7-McNamee, Elizabeth K. (Miss), 8-Hagerstown, MD, 9-Hagerstown, MD, 10-Rev. Dr. Geisey, 11-Zion Reformed Church, 15-Snyder

#7253, 1-Snyder, Charles Dixon, 2-married, 3-24 Dec 1884, 7-Horn[?], Clara (Miss), 15-Snyder

#7254, 1-Snyder, Daniel Clyde, 2-married, 3-Wednesday, 11 May 1904, 7-Bush, Mary E. (Miss), 15-Snyder

#7255, 1-Snyder, Daniel J., 2-born, 3-6 Feb 1837, 15-Snyder

#7256, 1-Snyder, Elizabeth H.[?], 2-born, 3-15 Jun 1837, 15-Snyder

#7257, 1-Snyder, Charles Dixon, 2-born, 3-3 Feb 1860, 15-Snyder

#7258, 1-Snyder, Mary Emma, 2-born, 3-6 Aug 1863, 15-Snyder

#7259, 1-Snyder, Daniel Clyde, 2-born, 3-15 Aug 1877, 15-Snyder

#7260, 1-Snyder, Bessie Cora, 2-born, 3-2 Apr 1882, 15-Snyder

#7261, 1-Snyder, Daniel J., 2-died, 3-Monday, 17 Oct 1904, 15-Snyder

#7262, 1-Snyder, Elizabeth H. (Mrs.), 2-died, 3-Wednesday, 24 Oct 1917, 15-Snyder

#7263, 1-Snyder, Mary Emma, 2-died, 3-Thursday, 17 Dec 1931, 15-Snyder

#7264, 1-Snyder, Charles Dickson, 2-died, 3-Sunday, 18 Mar 1934, 15-Snyder

#7265, 1-Snyder, Clara, 2-died, 3-Saturday, 24 Oct 1926, 7-Snyder, Dick, 15-Snyder

#7266, 1-Snyder, Charles Bruce, 2-born, 3-14 Jan 1886, 12-Snyder, Dixon, 15-Snyder

#7267, 1-Snyder, William Clyde, 2-born, 3-10 Mar 1905, 12-Snyder, Clyde, 15-Snyder

#7268, 1-Snyder, Elizabeth Louise, 2-born, 3-4 May 1907, 12-Snyder, Clyde, 15-Snyder

#7269, 1-Snyder, Richard Franklin, 2-born, 3-18 Sep 1909, 15-Snyder

#7270, 1-Snyder, Cathrine, 2-born, 3-18 Feb 1916, 12-Snyder, Bruce, 15-Snyder

#7271, 1-Hoffman, Patricia Ann, 2-born, 3-8 Feb 1934, 12-Hoffman, [blank], 13-Snyder, Cathrine, 15-Snyder

#7272, 1-Wagner, Beverly Diane, 2-born, 3-15 Apr 1935, 12-Snyder, Robert, 13-Snyder, Louise, 15-Snyder

#7273, 1-Welty, Michael, 2-married, 3-22 Aug 1839, 7-South, Amelia, 14-Yes, 15-Welty

#7274, 1-Welty, Daniel, 2-born, 3-25 May 1840, 14-Yes, 15-Welty

#7275, 1-Welty, William Geary, 2-born, 3-26 Jun 1841, 14-Yes, 15-Welty

#7276, 1-Welty, Rackel Ann, 2-born, 3-1 Jul 1843, 14-Yes, 15-Welty

#7277, 1-Welty, Sarow Elen, 2-born, 3-21 Jun 1846, 14-Yes, 15-Welty

#7278, 1-Welty, Martin L., 2-born, 3-22 Aug 1850, 14-Yes, 15-Welty

#7279, 1-Welty, William Alforde, 2-born, 3-8 Oct 1853, 14-Yes, 15-Welty

#7280, 1-Welty, Michael, 2-born, 3-27 Sep 1814, 14-Yes, 15-Welty

#7281, 1-Welty, Amelia, 2-born, 3-10 Apr 1816, 14-Yes, 15-Welty

#7282, 1-Welty, Michael, 2-died, 3-27 Oct 1889, 5-75 years 27 days, 14-Yes, 15-Welty

#7283, 1-Welty, Martin Luther, 2-died, 3-29 Mar 1896, 5-45 years 7 months 7 days, 14-Yes, 15-Welty

#7284, 1-Welty, Amelia, 2-died, 3-27 Oct 1867, 5-51 years 6 months 17 days, 14-Yes, 15-Welty

#7285, 1-Welty, William Alfred, 2-died, 3-25 Jan 1920, 5-66 years 3 months 17 days, 14-Yes, 15-Welty

#7286, 1-Walling, Mercy (Miss), 2-married, 3-5 Dec 1809, 14-Yes, 15-Walling

#7287, 1-Walling, Eliza (Miss), 2-married, 3-Tuesday, 2 Jul 1816, 7-Woltz, Elie, 14-Yes, 15-Walling

#7288, 1-Walling, James, 2-born, 3-31 Aug 1789, 14-Yes, 15-Walling

#7289, 1-Walling, Mercy, 2-born, 3-28 Mar 1791, 14-Yes, 15-Walling

#7290, 1-Walling, Elizabeth, 2-born, 3-23 Sep 1797, 14-Yes, 15-Walling

#7291, 1-Woltz, Herman G., 2-born, 3-27 Jul 1835, 12-Woltz, Elie, 13-Walling, Elizabeth, 14-Yes, 15-Walling

FAMILY BIBLE RECORDS IN THE WASHINGTON COUNTY FREE LIBRARY, HAGERSTOWN, MARYLAND

Entry #, 1-Last Name, First Name, 2-Event, 3-Date, 4-Event Location, 5-Age, 6-Other, 7-Spouse's Last, First, 8-Groom's Residence, 9-Bride's Residence, 10-Minister, 11-Minister's Location, 12-Father's Last, First, 13-Mother's Last, First, 14-Transcribed, 15-Family Bible

#7292, 1-Woltz, Herman G., 2-baptized, 3-17 Jul 1836, 10-Joab Bernard, 12-Woltz, Elie, 13-Walling, Elizabeth, 14-Yes, 15-Walling

#7293, 1-Walling, Nancy, 2-born, 3-28 Mar 1791, 14-Yes, 15-Walling

#7294, 1-Woltz, Frances Jane, 2-born, 3-22 Sep 1832, 12-Woltz, Elie, 13-Walling, Elizabeth, 14-Yes, 15-Walling

#7295, 1-Woltz, Frances Jane, 2-baptized, 3-20 Dec 1832, 10-R.L. Vinton, 12-Woltz, Elie, 13-Walling, Elizabeth, 14-Yes, 15-Walling

#7296, 1-Walling, Eliza, 2-born, 3-23 Sep 1797, 14-Yes, 15-Walling

#7297, 1-Woltz, Mary Eliza, 2-born, 3-19 Mar 1829, 14-Yes, 15-Walling

#7298, 1-Woltz, James Walling, 2-born, 3-9 Sep 1817, 14-Yes, 15-Walling

#7299, 1-Woltz, George Washington, 2-born, 3-13 Jan 1820, 14-Yes, 15-Walling

#7300, 1-Woltz, Charles William, 2-born, 3-23 Jan 1821, 14-Yes, 15-Walling

#7301, 1-Woltz, Samuel Armstrong, 2-born, 3-10 Apr 1823, 14-Yes, 15-Walling

#7302, 1-Woltz, John Reynolds, 2-born, 3-26 Dec 1825, 14-Yes, 15-Walling

#7303, 1-Walling, James (Col.), 2-died, 3-20 Oct 1811, 5-84 years 1 months, 14-Yes, 15-Walling

#7304, 1-Walling, James (Capt.), 2-died, 3-12 Mar 1823, 5-33 years 6 months 12 days, 14-Yes, 15-Walling

#7305, 1-Walling, Mary, 2-died, 3-16 Aug 1825, 5-61 years 6 months, 14-Yes, 15-Walling

#7306, 1-Woltz, George Washington , 2-died, 3-22 Jan 1820, 5-9 days, 14-Yes, 15-Walling

#7307, 1-Woltz, Frances Jane, 2-died, 3-7 Jul 1835, 14-Yes, 15-Walling

#7308, 1-Woltz, Martin S., 2-died, 3-2 May 1839, 14-Yes, 15-Walling

#7309, 1-Woltz, Herman Dorsey, 2-died, 3-14 Apr 1856, 5-19 years 3 months, 14-Yes, 15-Walling

#7310, 1-Woltz, Eli, 2-died, 3-19 Nov 1859, 5-69 years 6 months 14 days, 14-Yes, 15-Walling

#7311, 1-Woltz, Eliza, 2-died, 3-2 May 1867, 5-69 years 7 months 9 days, 14-Yes, 15-Walling

#7312, 1-Sherrick, Joseph, 3-2 Oct 1897, 7-Sherick, Anna, 8-Sharpsburg, MD, 9-Funkstown, MD, 14-Yes, 15-Sherrick

#7313, 1-Sherrick, Joseph, 2-married, 3-17 Apr 1828, 7-Ham, Sarah, 14-Yes, 15-Sherrick

#7314, 1-Sherrick, Mary H., 2-married, 3-20 May 1858, 7-Newcomer, Victor H., 14-Yes, 15-Sherrick

#7315, 1-Newcomer, Virginia Sherrick, 2-married, 3-9 Nov 1892, 7-Nicodemus, John L., 14-Yes, 15-Sherrick

#7316, 1-Nicodemus, John Luther, 2-born, 3-8 Dec 1828, 14-Yes, 15-Sherrick

#7317, 1-Nicodemus, John Luther, 2-died, 3-30 Jul 1915, 5-86 years 7 months 21 days, 14-Yes, 15-Sherrick

#7318, 1-Nicodemus, Virginia S., 2-died, 3-30 Jun 1924, 14-Yes, 15-Sherrick

#7319, 1-Sherrick, Joseph, 2-born, 3-12 Nov 1801, 14-Yes, 15-Sherrick

#7320, 1-Ham, Sarah, 2-born, 3-18 Jan 1807, 14-Yes, 15-Sherrick

#7321, 1-Sherrick, Anna, 2-born, 3-22 Jun 1836, 14-Yes, 15-Sherrick

#7322, 1-Newcomer, Victor H., 2-born, 3-16 Sep 1833, 14-Yes, 15-Sherrick

#7323, 1-Newcomer, Virginia Sherrick, 2-born, 3-21 Mar 1859, 14-Yes, 15-Sherrick

#7324, 1-Newcomer, Frank Sherrick, 2-born, 3-8 Jun 1863, 14-Yes, 15-Sherrick

#7325, 1-Sherrick, Barbara, 2-died, 3-11 Nov 1840, 14-Yes, 15-Sherrick

#7326, 1-Sherrick, Joseph, 2-died, 3-17 Mar 1846, 14-Yes, 15-Sherrick

#7327, 1-Sherrick, Jacob, 2-born, 3-2 Mar 1798, 14-Yes, 15-Sherrick

#7328, 1-Sherrick, Jacob, 2-died, 3-25 Aug 1857, 14-Yes, 15-Sherrick

#7329, 1-Sherrick, Joseph, 2-died, 3-11 Aug 1871, 5-69 years 8 months 28 days, 14-Yes, 15-Sherrick

FAMILY BIBLE RECORDS IN THE WASHINGTON COUNTY FREE LIBRARY, HAGERSTOWN, MARYLAND

Entry #, 1-Last Name, First Name, 2-Event, 3-Date, 4-Event Location, 5-Age, 6-Other, 7-Spouse's Last, First, 8-Groom's Residence, 9-Bride's Residence, 10-Minister, 11-Minister's Location, 12-Father's Last, First, 13-Mother's Last, First, 14-Transcribed, 15-Family Bible

#7330, 1-Sherrick, Sarah, 2-died, 3-25 Aug 1874, 5-67 years 7 months 7 days, 14-Yes, 15-Sherrick

#7331, 1-Newcomer, Victor H., 2-died, 3-25 Feb 1894[?], 5-59 years 5 months 9 days, 14-Yes, 15-Sherrick

#7332, 1-Newcomer, Anna Sherrick, 2-died, 3-24 Dec 1904, 5-68 years 6 months 2 days, 14-Yes, 15-Sherrick

#7333, 1-Sherrick, Sarah, 2-obituary, 3-25 Aug 1874, 5-67 years 7 months 7 days, 6-buried Brethren graveyard near Sharpsburg, MD; birthdate given as 18 Jan 1807, 14-Yes, 15-Sherrick

#7334, 1-Alice, Victor H., 2-obituary, 5-59 years, 7-Sherrick, Anna, 12-Newcomer, Henry, 14-Yes, 15-Sherrick

#7335, 1-Kane, John N., 2-married, 3-10 Sep 1848, 4-Hagerstown, MD, 7-Boyce, Margret A., 10-Rev. Philips, 15-Kane

#7336, 1-Kane, John N., 2-born, 3-5 Mar 1831, 15-Kane

#7337, 1-Kane, Margret A., 2-born, 3-21 Sep 1831, 15-Kane

#7338, 1-Kane, John W., 2-born, 3-4 Feb 1850, 15-Kane

#7339, 1-Kane, Ann Rebecca, 2-born, 3-21 Feb 1853, 15-Kane

#7340, 1-Kane, Laura V., 2-born, 3-5 Oct 1854, 15-Kane

#7341, 1-Kane, Comillis P., 2-born, 3-30 May 1856, 15-Kane

#7342, 1-Kane, Albert G., 2-born, 3-9 Nov 1858, 15-Kane

#7343, 1-Kane, Capitolia, 2-born, 3-29 Dec 1862, 15-Kane

#7344, 1-Kane, Walter W., 2-born, 3-16 Jul 1865, 15-Kane

#7345, 1-Kane, Rosa L., 2-born, 3-18 Feb 1870, 15-Kane

#7346, 1-Kane, Frank W., 2-born, 3-16 May 1873, 15-Kane

#7347, 1-Kane, Hattie B., 2-born, 3-22 Feb 1876, 15-Kane

#7348, 1-Kane, John N., 2-died, 3-21 Jul 1917, 5-86 years, 15-Kane

#7349, 1-Kane, Margaret Ann, 2-died, 3-1904, 15-Kane

#7350, 1-Kane, John W., 2-died, 3-12 May 1896, 4-Georgetown, DC, 6-drowned, 7-Newlin, Ida, 15-Kane

#7351, 1-Kane, Maggie, 2-born, 7-Kyle, Marsha, 12-Kane, John W., 13-Newlin, Ida, 15-Kane

#7352, 1-Kane, Ann Rebecca, 2-died, 3-18 Feb 1931, 4-Pittsburgh, PA, 6-gall bladder and heart; died suddenly, 7-McNabb, James H., 15-Kane

#7353, 1-McNabb, Hallie, 2-born, 12-McNabb, James H., 13-Kane, Ann Rebecca, 15-Kane

#7354, 1-McNabb, Francis, 2-born, 12-McNabb, James H., 13-Kane, Ann Rebecca, 15-Kane

#7355, 1-McNabb, Ruth, 2-born, 12-McNabb, James H., 13-Kane, Ann Rebecca, 15-Kane

#7356, 1-McNabb, George, 2-born, 12-McNabb, James H., 13-Kane, Ann Rebecca, 15-Kane

#7357, 1-McNabb, John, 2-born, 6-twin, 12-McNabb, James H., 13-Kane, Ann Rebecca, 15-Kane

#7358, 1-McNabb, Jim, 2-born, 6-twin, 12-McNabb, James H., 13-Kane, Ann Rebecca, 15-Kane

#7359, 1-Kane, Laura Virginia, 2-married, 7-Evans, William, 15-Kane

#7360, 1-Evans, Nettie, 2-born, 7-Cummings, [blank], 12-Evans, William, 13-Kane, Laura Virginia, 15-Kane

#7361, 1-Kane, Laura Virginia, 2-married, 7-Jenkins, Henry, 15-Kane

#7362, 1-Jenkins, Harry, 2-born, 12-Jenkins, Henry, 13-Kane, Laura Virginia, 15-Kane

#7363, 1-Jenkins, Robert, 2-born, 12-Jenkins, Henry, 13-Kane, Laura Virginia, 15-Kane

#7364, 1-Kane, Camillis Powell Mick", 2-married, 7-Kraus, Mollie, 15-Kane

#7365, 1-Kane, Camillis Powell Mick", 2-died, 4-Wheeling, WV, 6-kicked by horse in Cumberland, MD and died in Wheeling, WV, 15-Kane

#7366, 1-Kane, Albert Graichen, 2-married, 7-Shimp, Rossie[?], 9-Winchester, VA, 15-Kane

FAMILY BIBLE RECORDS IN THE WASHINGTON COUNTY FREE LIBRARY, HAGERSTOWN, MARYLAND

Entry #, 1-Last Name, First Name, 2-Event, 3-Date, 4-Event Location, 5-Age, 6-Other, 7-Spouse's Last, First, 8-Groom's Residence, 9-Bride's Residence, 10-Minister, 11-Minister's Location, 12-Father's Last, First, 13-Mother's Last, First, 14-Transcribed, 15-Family Bible

#7367, 1-Kane, Albert Graichen, 2-died, 3-29 Jan 1916, 4-Cumberland, MD, 6-heart and alcoholism, 15-Kane

#7368, 1-Kane, Mora Ethel, 2-born, 12-Kane, Albert Graichen, 13-Shimp, Rossie[?], 15-Kane

#7369, 1-Kane, Theodore Paul, 2-born, 12-Kane, Albert Graichen, 13-Shimp, Rossie[?], 15-Kane

#7370, 1-Kane, Eva Bell, 2-born, 12-Kane, Albert Graichen, 13-Shimp, Rossie[?], 15-Kane

#7371, 1-Kane, Blanche Va., 2-born, 12-Kane, Albert Graichen, 13-Shimp, Rossie[?], 15-Kane

#7372, 1-Kane, James Oscar[?], 2-born, 12-Kane, Albert Graichen, 13-Shimp, Rossie[?], 15-Kane

#7373, 1-Kane, Lillian May, 2-born, 12-Kane, Albert Graichen, 13-Shimp, Rossie[?], 15-Kane

#7374, 1-Kane, Charley Rouse, 2-born, 12-Kane, Albert Graichen, 13-Shimp, Rossie[?], 15-Kane

#7375, 1-Kane, Capitolia Sis", 2-married, 7-Fuller, Charles, 15-Kane

#7376, 1-Fuller, Walter, 2-died, 5-baby, 12-Fuller, Charles, 13-Kane, Capitolia Sis", 15-Kane

#7377, 1-Kane, Capitolia Sis", 2-died, 3-1890, 6-died soon after child died, 15-Kane

#7378, 1-Kane, Walter Joshua, 2-married, 7-Weidman, Mary, 15-Kane

#7379, 1-Kane, Walter Joshua, 2-died, 3-4 Apr 1903, 4-Manheim, PA, 6-died suddenly - heart, 15-Kane

#7380, 1-Kane, Rosa Lillian, 2-married, 7-Fuller, Howard Mason, 15-Kane

#7381, 1-Kane, Rosa Lillian, 2-died, 3-7 May 1946, 6-gall bladder, 15-Kane

#7382, 1-Kane, Frank Ward, 2-married, 7-Barnes, Grace, 15-Kane

#7383, 1-Kane, Frank Ward, 2-married, 7-Campbell, Druzella, 15-Kane

#7384, 1-Kane, Margaret, 2-born, 12-Kane, Frank Ward, 13-Barnes, Grace, 15-Kane

#7385, 1-Kane, Hattie Belle, 2-died, 5-about 6 years, 6-brain absess, 15-Kane

#7386, 1-Fuller, Elijah, 2-married, 3-15 Oct 1843, 7-Kemp, Catharine Ann, 15-Fuller

#7387, 1-Fuller, Alice C., 2-married, 3-8 Oct 1866, 7-Sanner, R.R., 15-Fuller

#7388, 1-Sanner, Alice, 2-died, 3-Aug 1926, 15-Fuller

#7389, 1-Fuller, Cornelia Ann, 2-married, 3-19 Oct 1869, 7-Bare, James V., 15-Fuller

#7390, 1-Fuller, Howard Mason, 2-married, 3-1 Sep 1872, 7-Rizer, Mary Martha, 15-Fuller

#7391, 1-Fuller, Howard Mason, 2-married, 3-27 Sep 1887, 7-Kane, Rosa Lillian, 15-Fuller

#7392, 1-Fuller, Elijah, 2-born, 3-15 Sep 1821, 15-Fuller

#7393, 1-Fuller, Catharine Ann, 2-born, 3-16 Nov 1823, 15-Fuller

#7394, 1-Fuller, James Kemp, 2-born, 3-18 Oct 1844, 12-Fuller, Elijah , 13-Kemp, Catharine Ann, 15-Fuller

#7395, 1-Fuller, Alice Charlotte, 2-born, 3-8 Nov 1846, 12-Fuller, Elijah , 13-Kemp, Catharine Ann, 15-Fuller

#7396, 1-Fuller, Cornelia Ann, 2-born, 3-2 Jul 1849, 12-Fuller, Elijah , 13-Kemp, Catharine Ann, 15-Fuller

#7397, 1-Fuller, Howard Mason, 2-born, 3-6 Sep 1851, 12-Fuller, Elijah , 13-Kemp, Catharine Ann, 15-Fuller

#7398, 1-Fuller, Clifton E., 2-born, 3-1 May 1873, 4-Prospect Square, Cumberland, MD, 12-Fuller, Howard Mason, 13-Rizer, Mary Martha, 15-Fuller

#7399, 1-Fuller, James Ray, 2-born, 3-23 Jul 1874, 4-Polk St., Cumberland, MD, 12-Fuller, Howard Mason, 13-Rizer, Mary Martha, 15-Fuller

#7400, 1-Fuller, Walter Mason, 2-born, 3-1 Mar 1889, 12-Fuller, Howard Mason, 13-Kane, Rosa Lillian, 15-Fuller

FAMILY BIBLE RECORDS IN THE WASHINGTON COUNTY FREE LIBRARY, HAGERSTOWN, MARYLAND

Entry #, 1-Last Name, First Name, 2-Event, 3-Date, 4-Event Location, 5-Age, 6-Other,
7-Spouse's Last, First, 8-Groom's Residence, 9-Bride's Residence, 10-Minister, 11-Minister's Location,
12-Father's Last, First, 13-Mother's Last, First, 14-Transcribed, 15-Family Bible

```
#7401, 1-Fuller, Earl Newton, 2-born, 3-4 Nov 1891, 12-Fuller, Howard Mason, 13-
    Kane, Rosa Lillian, 15-Fuller
#7402, 1-Fuller, Mira Spear, 2-born, 3-11 Aug 1892, 12-Fuller, Howard Mason, 13-
    Kane, Rosa Lillian, 15-Fuller
#7403, 1-Fuller, Arthur Gorman, 2-born, 3-15 Oct 1897, 12-Fuller, Howard Mason, 13-
    Kane, Rosa Lillian, 15-Fuller
#7404, 1-Fuller, Howard Mason, 2-died, 3-16 Jun 1924, 5-72 years 9 months, 15-
    Fuller
#7405, 1-Westrata, Katherine, 2-died, 3-1919, 4-Martinsburg, WV, 7-Westrata, Wm.,
    15-Fuller
#7406, 1-Ridenor, Jacob, 2-born, 3-8 Mar 1828, 14-Yes, 15-Ridenour
#7407, 1-Ridenour, Susanna, 2-born, 3-15 Oct 1824, 14-Yes, 15-Ridenour
#7408, 1-Ridenour, Mary Ellen Rebecca, 2-born, 3-11 Nov 1850, 14-Yes, 15-Ridenour
#7409, 1-Ridenour, John Henry, 2-born, 3-28 Jan 1852, 14-Yes, 15-Ridenour
#7410, 1-Ridenour, Manday Catharine, 2-born, 3-27 Sep 1853, 14-Yes, 15-Ridenour
#7411, 1-Ridenour, George Melanchthon, 2-born, 3-25 Feb 1855, 14-Yes, 15-Ridenour
#7412, 1-Ridenour, Daniel Nuton, 2-born, 3-18 Dec 1856, 14-Yes, 15-Ridenour
#7413, 1-Ridenour, Charles Edward, 2-born, 3-28 Aug 1858, 14-Yes, 15-Ridenour
#7414, 1-Ridenour, Sarah Elizabeth, 2-born, 3-3 Apr 1860, 14-Yes, 15-Ridenour
#7415, 1-Ridenour, Lewis Machelon, 2-born, 3-5 Oct 1861, 14-Yes, 15-Ridenour
#7416, 1-Ridenour, Emma Arbelan, 2-born, 3-27 Feb 1863, 14-Yes, 15-Ridenour
#7417, 1-Ridennour, Daniel Newton, 2-died, 3-19 Sep 1857, 5-9 months 1 days, 14-
    Yes, 15-Ridenour
#7418, 1-Ridenour, Lewis Machelon, 2-died, 3-27 Apr 1862, 14-Yes, 15-Ridenour
#7419, 1-Ridenour, Effa Jane, 2-died, 3-7 Aug 1869, 14-Yes, 15-Ridenour
#7420, 1-Ridenour, Etta, 2-born, 3-13 Sep 1866, 6-twin, 14-Yes, 15-Ridenour
#7421, 1-Ridenour, Effa Jane, 2-born, 3-13 Sep 1866, 6-twin, 14-Yes, 15-Ridenour
#7422, 1-Ridenour, Susannah, 2-born, 3-15 Oct 1824, 14-Yes, 15-Ridenour
#7423, 1-Ridenour, John He, 2-born, 3-24 Sep 1826, 14-Yes, 15-Ridenour
#7424, 1-Ridenour, William, 2-born, 3-6 Oct 1828, 14-Yes, 15-Ridenour
#7425, 1-Ridenour, Daniel, 2-born, 3-12 Feb 1831, 14-Yes, 15-Ridenour
#7426, 1-Poffenberger, Joseph, 2-married, 3-8 Feb 1838, 7-Kauffman, Mary Ann, 14-
    Yes, 15-Frye
#7427, 1-Frye, Clayton, 2-married, 3-9 Oct 1888, 4-Monroeville, OH, 7-Whaley, Susie
    B., 14-Yes, 15-Frye
#7428, 1-Frye, Susie, 2-married, 3-26 Nov 1902, 4-Columbus, OH, 7-Cooper, Geary A.,
    14-Yes, 15-Frye
#7429, 1-Frye, Vira, 2-married, 3-3 Jul 1918, 4-Frostburg, MD, 7-Kight, Casper
    Ellsworth, 14-Yes, 15-Frye
#7430, 1-Poffenberger, Jos., 2-born, 3-26 Jul 1812, 14-Yes, 15-Frye
#7431, 1-Kauffman, MaryAnn, 2-born, 3-23 Oct 1817, 14-Yes, 15-Frye
#7432, 1-Kight, Theodore J., 2-born, 3-2 Nov 1919, 4-Keyser, WV, 12-Kight, Casper
    E., 13-Frye, Vira, 14-Yes, 15-Frye
#7433, 1-Kight, Casper E., 2-born, 3-8 Apr 1926, 4-Piedmont, WV, 12-Kight, Casper
    E., 13-Frye, Vira, 14-Yes, 15-Frye
#7434, 1-Frye, George W., 2-born, 3-19 Apr 1898, 14-Yes, 15-Frye
#7435, 1-Frye, Martha E., 2-born, 3-7 Apr 1842, 14-Yes, 15-Frye
#7436, 1-Frye, William Clayton, 2-born, 3-19 Nov 1863, 14-Yes, 15-Frye
#7437, 1-Nichles, John Ashton, 2-born, 3-6 Oct 1865, 14-Yes, 15-Frye
#7438, 1-Frye, Angeline, 2-born, 3-11 Feb 1868, 14-Yes, 15-Frye
#7439, 1-Frye, Catherine Girmettee, 2-born, 3-3 Dec 1870, 12-Frye, Geo. W., 13-
    Frye, Martha E., 14-Yes, 15-Frye
#7440, 1-Frye, Catherine Girmettee, 2-baptized, 3-21 Jul 1871, 10-Rev. H.J.
    Richardson, 12-Frye, Geo. W., 13-Frye, Martha E., 14-Yes, 15-Frye
#7441, 1-Frye, John Ashton Michelous, 2-born, 3-6 Oct 1865, 14-Yes, 15-Frye
```

FAMILY BIBLE RECORDS IN THE WASHINGTON COUNTY FREE LIBRARY, HAGERSTOWN, MARYLAND

Entry #, 1-Last Name, First Name, 2-Event, 3-Date, 4-Event Location, 5-Age, 6-Other, 7-Spouse's Last, First, 8-Groom's Residence, 9-Bride's Residence, 10-Minister, 11-Minister's Location, 12-Father's Last, First, 13-Mother's Last, First, 14-Transcribed, 15-Family Bible

```
#7442, 1-Frye, John Ashton Michelous, 2-died, 3-22 Mar 1867, 5-1 years 5 months 16
    days, 14-Yes, 15-Frye
#7443, 1-Frye, Martha E., 2-born, 3-7 Apr 1842, 14-Yes, 15-Frye
#7444, 1-Frye, Martha E., 2-died, 3-24 Sep 1874, 5-32 years 5 months 17 days, 14-
    Yes, 15-Frye
#7445, 1-Fry, George W., 2-born, 3-12 Apr 1838, 14-Yes, 15-Frye
#7446, 1-Fry, George W., 2-died, 3-19 Feb 1872, 5-33 years 8 months 7 days, 14-Yes,
    15-Frye
#7447, 1-Frye, William Clayton, 2-born, 3-19 Nov 1863, 14-Yes, 15-Frye
#7448, 1-Frye, William Clayton, 2-christened, 3-11 Sep 1893, 4-Newark, OH, 10-Rev.
    C.W. Gifford, 11-Lutheran Church, 14-Yes, 15-Frye
#7449, 1-Whaley, Susie Belle, 2-born, 3-10 Feb 1868, 14-Yes, 15-Frye
#7450, 1-Whaley, Susie Belle, 2-christened, 3-11 Sep 1893, 4-Newark, OH, 10-Rev.
    C.W. Gifford, 11-Lutheran Church, 14-Yes, 15-Frye
#7451, 1-Frye, Walter Clayton, 2-born, 3-21 Jul 1889, 12-Frye, Clayton, 13-Frey,
    Susie, 14-Yes, 15-Frye
#7452, 1-Frye, Walter Clayton, 2-christened, 3-11 Sep 1893, 4-Newark, OH, 10-Rev.
    C.W. Gifford, 11-Lutheran Church, 14-Yes, 15-Frye
#7453, 1-Frye, Isabella Martha, 2-born, 3-7 Jun 1891, 14-Yes, 15-Frye
#7454, 1-Frye, Isabella Martha, 2-christened, 3-11 Sep 1893, 4-Newark, OH, 10-Rev.
    C.W. Gifford, 11-Lutheran Church, 14-Yes, 15-Frye
#7455, 1-Frye, Vira, 2-born, 3-13 Aug 1893, 14-Yes, 15-Frye
#7456, 1-Frye, Vira, 2-christened, 3-11 Sep 1893, 4-Newark, OH, 10-Rev. C.W.
    Gifford, 11-Lutheran Church, 14-Yes, 15-Frye
#7457, 1-Frye, William Clayton, 2-died, 3-5 Nov 1898, 4-Newark, OH, 5-34 years 11
    months 16 days, 6-buried at Monroeville, OH, 14-Yes, 15-Frye
#7458, 1-Cooper, Susie (Frye), 2-died, 3-19 Feb 1925, 4-Newark, OH, 5-57 years 9
    days, 6-buried at Monroeville, OH, 14-Yes, 15-Frye
#7459, 1-Frye, Isabella M., 2-died, 3-20 Feb 1949, 4-Keyser, WV, 5-57 years 8
    months 13 days, 6-buried at Monroeville, OH, 14-Yes, 15-Frye
#7460, 1-Cooper, Geary A., 2-died, 3-22 Dec 1951, 4-Morgantown, WV, 5-80 years 11
    months 9 days, 6-buried at Monroeville, OH, 14-Yes, 15-Frye
#7461, 1-Frye, Walter Clayton, 2-died, 3-26 Nov 1952, 4-Keyser, WV, 6-buried at
    Monroeville, OH, 14-Yes, 15-Frye
#7462, 1-Fague, John, 2-married, 3-24 Jan 1839, 7-Boone, Kate (Miss), 14-Yes, 15-
    Nikirk
#7463, 1-Fagne, Mary Ellie, 2-born, 3-29 Apr 1840, 4-Boonsboro, MD, 14-Yes, 15-
    Nikirk
#7464, 1-Fagne, Susan Maria, 2-born, 3-2 Jul 1842, 4-Boonsboro, MD, 14-Yes, 15-
    Nikirk
#7465, 1-Fagne, Theodore, 2-born, 3-4 Nov 1844, 4-Boonsboro, MD, 14-Yes, 15-Nikirk
#7466, 1-Fagne, Samuel Edward, 2-born, 3-19 Mar 1847, 4-Boonsboro, MD, 14-Yes, 15-
    Nikirk
#7467, 1-Fagne, William Boone, 2-born, 3-24 Aug 1849, 4-Boonsboro, MD, 14-Yes, 15-
    Nikirk
#7468, 1-Fagne, Theodore F., 2-born, 3-25 Dec 1852, 4-Boonsboro, MD, 14-Yes, 15-
    Nikirk
#7469, 1-Fagne, Millard Gillman, 2-born, 3-21 Apr 1856, 4-Boonsboro, MD, 14-Yes,
    15-Nikirk
#7470, 1-Boone, Catherine, 2-born, 3-8 Jun 1814, 14-Yes, 15-Nikirk
#7471, 1-Fagne, Mary Catherine, 2-born, 3-3 Dec 1874, 14-Yes, 15-Nikirk
#7472, 1-Fagne, John, 2-born, 3-24 Dec 1811, 14-Yes, 15-Nikirk
#7473, 1-Fagne, John, 2-died, 3-1 Oct 1886, 14-Yes, 15-Nikirk
#7474, 1-Fagne, Catherine, 2-died, 3-30 Sep 1902, 14-Yes, 15-Nikirk
#7475, 1-Myers, Will, 2-born, 3-30 Oct 1868, 14-Yes, 15-Nikirk
```

FAMILY BIBLE RECORDS IN THE WASHINGTON COUNTY FREE LIBRARY, HAGERSTOWN, MARYLAND

Entry #, 1-Last Name, First Name, 2-Event, 3-Date, 4-Event Location, 5-Age, 6-Other, 7-Spouse's Last, First, 8-Groom's Residence, 9-Bride's Residence, 10-Minister, 11-Minister's Location, 12-Father's Last, First, 13-Mother's Last, First, 14-Transcribed, 15-Family Bible

```
#7476, 1-Myers, Mary Aileen, 2-born, 3-25 Feb 1875, 14-Yes, 15-Nikirk
#7477, 1-Myers, Melbrey Kate, 2-born, 3-11 Sep 1865, 14-Yes, 15-Nikirk
#7478, 1-Boon, Kate Donekins[?], 2-born, 3-6 Jan 1865, 14-Yes, 15-Nikirk
#7479, 1-Fagne, Theodore, 2-died, 3-5 Apr 1851, 5-6 years 7 months 1 days, 14-Yes,
    15-Nikirk
#7480, 1-Fagne, Millard F., 2-died, 3-5 Aug 1864, 5-8 years 6 months 14 days, 14-
    Yes, 15-Nikirk
#7481, 1-Fagne, Edward E., 2-died, 3-14 Aug 1871, 5-24 years 4 months 26 days, 14-
    Yes, 15-Nikirk
#7482, 1-Fagne, William Boone, 2-died, 3-7 Jul 1876, 5-26 years 10 months 13 days,
    14-Yes, 15-Nikirk
#7483, 1-Fagne, John, 2-died, 3-1 Oct 1886, 14-Yes, 15-Nikirk
#7484, 1-Myers, Sue M., 2-died, 3-27 Feb 1888, 14-Yes, 15-Nikirk
#7485, 1-Nikirk, Joseph, 2-married, 3-19 Apr 1864, 4-Boonsboro, MD, 7-Fagne, Mary
    Ellen, 10-George W. Statton, 11-U.B. Church, 14-Yes, 15-Nikirk
#7486, 1-Nikirk, Joseph, 2-born, 3-18 Jan 1836, 14-Yes, 15-Nikirk
#7487, 1-Fagne, Mary Ellen, 2-born, 3-27 Apr 1840, 14-Yes, 15-Nikirk
#7488, 1-Nikirk, Walter Edward, 2-born, 3-31 Aug 1866, 12-Nikirk, Joseph, 13-Fagne,
    Mary Ellen, 14-Yes, 15-Nikirk
#7489, 1-Nikirk, Ernest Boone, 2-born, 3-24 Oct 1868, 12-Nikirk, Joseph, 13-Fagne,
    Mary Ellen, 14-Yes, 15-Nikirk
#7490, 1-Nikirk, Harry Wilson, 2-born, 3-15 Jun 1870, 12-Nikirk, Joseph, 13-Fagne,
    Mary Ellen, 14-Yes, 15-Nikirk
#7491, 1-Nikirk, Grace May, 2-born, 3-28 Apr 1872, 12-Nikirk, Joseph, 13-Fagne,
    Mary Ellen, 14-Yes, 15-Nikirk
#7492, 1-Nikirk, Albert Russell, 2-born, 3-24 Sep 1874, 12-Nikirk, Joseph, 13-
    Fagne, Mary Ellen, 14-Yes, 15-Nikirk
#7493, 1-Nikirk, William Fagne, 2-born, 3-29 May 1878, 12-Nikirk, Joseph, 13-Fagne,
    Mary Ellen, 14-Yes, 15-Nikirk
#7494, 1-Nikirk, Ellen Catherine, 2-born, 3-11 Mar 1881, 12-Nikirk, Joseph, 13-
    Fagne, Mary Ellen, 14-Yes, 15-Nikirk
#7495, 1-Nikirk, George Roy, 2-born, 3-5 Oct 1883, 12-Nikirk, Joseph, 13-Fagne,
    Mary Ellen, 14-Yes, 15-Nikirk
#7496, 1-Nikirk, William Fagne, 2-died, 3-15 Aug 1878, 14-Yes, 15-Nikirk
#7497, 1-Nikirk, Joseph, 2-died, 3-17 Aug 1897, 14-Yes, 15-Nikirk
#7498, 1-Nikirk, A. Russell, 2-died, 3-Feb 1914, 4-Colorado, 6-died in fall in a
    mine.  His home was in Denver", 14-Yes, 15-Nikirk
#7499, 1-Windsor, Newman, 2-married, 3-12 Aug 1813, 7-Windsor, Fanny, 14-Yes, 15-
    Mealey
#7500, 1-Mealey, Edw. M., 2-married, 3-11 Nov 1841, 7-Windsor, Elizabeth, 14-Yes,
    15-Mealey
#7501, 1-Mealey, Edward Windsor, 2-married, 3-1 Jun 1876, 7-Parks, Laura Gertrude,
    14-Yes, 15-Mealey
#7502, 1-Mealey, Edward Windsor, 2-married, 3-15 Oct 1895, 7-Alderdice[?], Adelaide
    Berry, 14-Yes, 15-Mealey
#7503, 1-Windsor, Newman, 2-born, 3-20 Dec 1789, 14-Yes, 15-Mealey
#7504, 1-Windsor, Fanny, 2-born, 3-29 Aug 1790, 14-Yes, 15-Mealey
#7505, 1-Windsor, Richard T., 2-born, 3-8 Jan 1816, 14-Yes, 15-Mealey
#7506, 1-Windsor, Robert N., 2-born, 3-4 May 1818, 14-Yes, 15-Mealey
#7507, 1-Windsor, Elizabeth H., 2-born, 3-15 Mar 1820, 14-Yes, 15-Mealey
#7508, 1-Windsor, Joseph R., 2-born, 3-17 Dec 1821, 14-Yes, 15-Mealey
#7509, 1-Windsor, John H., 2-born, 3-5 Aug 1824, 14-Yes, 15-Mealey
#7510, 1-Windsor, Emily C., 2-born, 3-1 Jun 1827, 14-Yes, 15-Mealey
#7511, 1-Mealey, Edward Windsor, 2-born, 3-23 Aug 1846, 14-Yes, 15-Mealey
#7512, 1-Mealey, Joseph Albert, 2-born, 3-24 Sep 1848, 14-Yes, 15-Mealey
```

FAMILY BIBLE RECORDS IN THE WASHINGTON COUNTY FREE LIBRARY, HAGERSTOWN, MARYLAND

Entry #, 1-Last Name, First Name, 2-Event, 3-Date, 4-Event Location, 5-Age, 6-Other,
7-Spouse's Last, First, 8-Groom's Residence, 9-Bride's Residence, 10-Minister, 11-Minister's Location,
12-Father's Last, First, 13-Mother's Last, First, 14-Transcribed, 15-Family Bible

```
#7513, 1-Mealey, Richard Clinton, 2-born, 3-17 Jun 1850, 14-Yes, 15-Mealey
#7514, 1-Mealey, Frederick Samson, 2-born, 3-12 Mar 1852, 14-Yes, 15-Mealey
#7515, 1-[blank], Hannah, 2-born, 3-10 Mar 1794, 14-Yes, 15-Mealey
#7516, 1-[blank], Jesse, 2-born, 3-27 mar 1796, 14-Yes, 15-Mealey
#7517, 1-[blank], Jordan, 2-born, 3-29 Aug 1804, 14-Yes, 15-Mealey
#7518, 1-[blank], Agnes, 2-born, 3-8 Jan 1806, 14-Yes, 15-Mealey
#7519, 1-[blank], Ralph, 2-born, 3-20 Dec 1809, 14-Yes, 15-Mealey
#7520, 1-[blank], Frielin, 2-born, 3-12 Nov 1810, 14-Yes, 15-Mealey
#7521, 1-[blank], Mary, 2-born, 3-10 Feb 1814, 14-Yes, 15-Mealey
#7522, 1-[blank], Lindy, 2-born, 3-20 May 1814, 14-Yes, 15-Mealey
#7523, 1-[blank], Jiles, 2-born, 3-17 Jul 1817, 14-Yes, 15-Mealey
#7524, 1-[blank], Jerry, 2-born, 3-12 Mar 1819, 14-Yes, 15-Mealey
#7525, 1-[blank], Ritter, 2-born, 3-29 Apr 1820, 14-Yes, 15-Mealey
#7526, 1-[blank], George, 2-born, 3-20 Jun 1822, 14-Yes, 15-Mealey
#7527, 1-[blank], Ephraim, 2-born, 3-7 Oct 1824, 14-Yes, 15-Mealey
#7528, 1-[blank], Lewis, 2-born, 3-18 Feb 1827, 14-Yes, 15-Mealey
#7529, 1-[blank], Ely, 2-born, 3-25 Nov 1828, 14-Yes, 15-Mealey
#7530, 1-[blank], Lisa, 2-born, 3-31 Mar 1830, 14-Yes, 15-Mealey
#7531, 1-Windsor, Fanny, 2-died, 3-21 Dec 1828, 14-Yes, 15-Mealey
#7532, 1-Windsor, John H., 2-died, 3-Sep 1824, 14-Yes, 15-Mealey
#7533, 1-Windsor, Newman, 2-died, 3-29 Mar 1830, 14-Yes, 15-Mealey
#7534, 1-Windsor, Joseph R., 2-died, 3-25 Dec 1835, 14-Yes, 15-Mealey
#7535, 1-Mealey, Elizabeth Frances (Windsor), 2-died, 3-2 Jul 1891, 14-Yes, 15-
    Mealey
#7536, 1-Windsor, Edward Mealey, 2-died, 3-28 Apr 1911, 14-Yes, 15-Mealey
#7537, 1-Mealey, Joseph Albert, 2-died, 3-13 Apr 1854, 14-Yes, 15-Mealey
#7538, 1-Mealey, Richard Clinton, 2-died, 3-26 Apr 1854, 14-Yes, 15-Mealey
#7539, 1-Mealey, Frederick Samson, 2-died, 3-25 Mar 1856, 14-Yes, 15-Mealey
#7540, 1-Mealey, Edward Merryman, 2-died, 3-26 May 1871, 7-Windsor, Elizabeth
    Frances, 14-Yes, 15-Mealey
#7541, 1-Mealey, Laura Gertrude (Parks), 2-died, 3-20 Sep 1897, 14-Yes, 15-Mealey
#7542, 1-Long, Abram Devenport, 2-born, 3-27 Mar 1790, 14-Yes, 15-Long
#7543, 1-Long, Ann Elizabeth, 2-born, 3-17 Feb 1795, 14-Yes, 15-Long
#7544, 1-Long, Abram D., 2-married, 3-22 May 1817, 7-Long, Ann Elizabeth, 14-Yes,
    15-Long
#7545, 1-Long, Elizabeth, 2-born, 3-29 Mar 1818, 14-Yes, 15-Long
#7546, 1-Long, James, 2-born, 3-13 Jun 1820, 14-Yes, 15-Long
#7547, 1-Long, James, 2-died, 3-23 Nov 1820, 14-Yes, 15-Long
#7548, 1-Long, John, 2-died, 3-2 Sep 1821, 14-Yes, 15-Long
#7549, 1-Long, John, 2-born, 3-9 Jan 1822, 14-Yes, 15-Long
#7550, 1-Hammie, Jacob, 2-died, 3-19 Nov 1822, 14-Yes, 15-Long
#7551, 1-Long, Ann Elizabeth, 2-born, 12-Hammie, Jacob, 14-Yes, 15-Long
#7552, 1-Long, Elizabeth D., 2-died, 3-5 Sep 1823, 5-5 years 5 months 7 days, 14-
    Yes, 15-Long
#7553, 1-Long, Elizabeth Mary, 2-born, 3-11 Jul 1824, 12-Long, Abram D., 13-Long,
    Ann E., 14-Yes, 15-Long
#7554, 1-Long, Sally, 2-born, 3-22 Sep 1826, 12-Long, Abram D., 13-Long, Ann E.,
    14-Yes, 15-Long
#7555, 1-Long, Abram D., 2-died, 3-18 Feb 1829, 14-Yes, 15-Long
#7556, 1-Long, Abram D., 2-born, 3-2 Mar 1829, 14-Yes, 15-Long
#7557, 1-Long, Elizabeth M., 2-married, 3-10 Feb 1847, 7-Anderson, S.H., 14-Yes,
    15-Long
#7558, 1-Latrobe, Benjamin H., 2-married, 3-12 Mar 1833, 4-Salem, NJ, 7-Hazelhurst,
    Juliana Eleanor, 10-Rev. Henry M. Mason, 14-Yes, 15-Latrobe
```

FAMILY BIBLE RECORDS IN THE WASHINGTON COUNTY FREE LIBRARY, HAGERSTOWN, MARYLAND

Entry #, 1-Last Name, First Name, 2-Event, 3-Date, 4-Event Location, 5-Age, 6-Other, 7-Spouse's Last, First, 8-Groom's Residence, 9-Bride's Residence, 10-Minister, 11-Minister's Location, 12-Father's Last, First, 13-Mother's Last, First, 14-Transcribed, 15-Family Bible

#7559, 1-Gamble[?], Letita B., 2-born, 12-Gambla[?], Robert (Col.), 14-Yes, 15-Latrobe

#7560, 1-Gamble[?], Letita B., 2-married, 3-2 Apr 1861, 7-Latrobe, Charles H., 14-Yes, 15-Latrobe

#7561, 1-Latrobe, Agnes Catherine, 2-married, 3-9 Jul 1867, 4-Emmanuel Church, Baltimore, MD, 7-Weston, Cornelius, 14-Yes, 15-Latrobe

#7562, 1-Latrobe, Mary Elizabeth, 2-married, 3-17 Dec 1868, 4-Emmanuel Church, Baltimore, MD, 7-Onderdonk, Henry, 10-Rev. B.H. Latrobe, Jr., 14-Yes, 15-Latrobe

#7563, 1-Latrobe, Charles H., 2-married, 3-14 Dec 1869, 4-Grace Church, Baltimore, MD, 7-Robinson, Rosa W., 10-Rev. B.H. Latrobe, Jr., 14-Yes, 15-Latrobe

#7564, 1-Robinson, Rosa W., 2-born, 12-Robinson, A.C. (Dr.), 14-Yes, 15-Latrobe

#7565, 1-Latrobe, Jr., Benjamin H., 2-married, 3-2 Dec 1873, 4-Church of Our Savior, 7-Yeates, Jenny Estelle, 14-Yes, 15-Latrobe

#7566, 1-Latrobe, Charles Hazelhurst, 2-born, 3-25 Dec 1833, 4-Mrs. Greetham's house on Calvert Street, Baltimore, MD, 14-Yes, 15-Latrobe

#7567, 1-Latrobe, Charles Hazelhurst, 2-baptized, 4-St. Paul's Church, Baltimore, MD, 14-Yes, 15-Latrobe

#7568, 1-Latrobe, Edward, 2-born, 3-31 May 1835, 4-home of Mrs. Hazelhurst in Salem, NJ, 14-Yes, 15-Latrobe

#7569, 1-Latrobe, Edward, 2-baptized, 4-St. John's Church, Salem, NJ, 14-Yes, 15-Latrobe

#7570, 1-Latrobe, Mary Elizabeth, 2-born, 3-27 Aug 1830, 4-St. John's Church, Salem, NJ, 14-Yes, 15-Latrobe

#7571, 1-Latrobe, Mary Elizabeth, 2-baptized, 4-Christ's Church, Baltimore, MD, 14-Yes, 15-Latrobe

#7572, 1-Latrobe, Agnes Catherine, 2-born, 3-25 Dec 1838, 4-"in the house at the corner of Charles and Hamilton Sts., Baltimore", 14-Yes, 15-Latrobe

#7573, 1-Latrobe, Agnes Catherine, 2-baptized, 4-Baltimore, MD, 6-"recorded in St. John's Church, Salem, NJ", 14-Yes, 15-Latrobe

#7574, 1-Latrobe, Benjamin Henry, 2-born, 3-4 Dec 1840, 14-Yes, 15-Latrobe

#7575, 1-Latrobe, Benjamin Henry, 2-baptized, 6-"recorded in Christ's Church, Baltimore", 10-Dr. Johns, 14-Yes, 15-Latrobe

#7576, 1-Latrobe, Maria Eleanor, 2-born, 3-8 Oct 1843, 4-"in the house in Courtland near Franklin Street, Baltimore", 14-Yes, 15-Latrobe

#7577, 1-Latrobe, Maria Eleanor, 2-baptized, 6-"recorded in Christ's Church, Baltimore", 10-Henry Johns, 14-Yes, 15-Latrobe

#7578, 1-Latrobe, Elsie Gamble, 2-born, 3-6 May, 4-Tallahassee, 12-Latrobe, Charles H., 13-Latrobe, Letitia B., 14-Yes, 15-Latrobe

#7579, 1-Latrobe, Eleanor Breckenridge, 2-born, 3-6 Oct 1864, 4-Tallahassee, 14-Yes, 15-Latrobe

#7580, 1-Latrobe, Gamble , 2-born, 3-21 Jan 1866, 4-Baltimore, MD, 12-Latrobe, C.H., 13-Latrobe, L.B., 14-Yes, 15-Latrobe

#7581, 1-Weston, Bnj. Latrobe, 2-born, 3-8 Sep 1868, 4-Lanvale Street, Baltimore, MD, 12-Weston, Corn., 13-Weston, Kate, 14-Yes, 15-Latrobe

#7582, 1-Weston, Henry Bancroft, 2-born, 3-1 Jan 1871, 4-Lanvale Street, Baltimore, MD, 12-Weston, Corn., 13-Weston, Kate, 14-Yes, 15-Latrobe

#7583, 1-Onderdonk, Buy Latrobe, 2-born, 3-12 May 1872, 4-St. James College, 12-Onderdonk, Henry, 13-Latrobe, Mary E., 14-Yes, 15-Latrobe

#7584, 1-Weston, Arthur Hazelhurst, 2-born, 3-18 Aug 1872, 4-St. James College, 12-Weston, Corn., 13-Weston, Kate, 14-Yes, 15-Latrobe

#7585, 1-Latrobe, Laura Riggs, 2-born, 3-25 Mar 1875, 4-340 N. Broadway, Baltimore, MD, 12-Latrobe, Jr., B.H. (Rev.), 14-Yes, 15-Latrobe

#7586, 1-Latrobe, Edward, 2-died, 3-1 Aug 1835, 4-Salem, NJ, 6-"second son of parents, 12-Latrobe, B.H., 13-Latrobe, J.E., 14-Yes, 15-Latrobe

FAMILY BIBLE RECORDS IN THE WASHINGTON COUNTY FREE LIBRARY, HAGERSTOWN, MARYLAND

Entry #, 1-Last Name, First Name, 2-Event, 3-Date, 4-Event Location, 5-Age, 6-Other,
7-Spouse's Last, First, 8-Groom's Residence, 9-Bride's Residence, 10-Minister, 11-Minister's Location,
12-Father's Last, First, 13-Mother's Last, First, 14-Transcribed, 15-Family Bible

```
#7587, 1-Bagden, Ann Catherine, 2-died, 3-11 Nov 1857, 4-Baltimore, MD, 6-buried
    Greenmount Cemetery in B.H. Latrobe lot; aunt of Eleanor Latrobe, 14-Yes, 15-
    Latrobe
#7588, 1-Hazelhurst, Maria Eleanor, 2-died, 3-20 Oct 1861, 4-Baltimore, MD, 6-
    "mother of I.E. Latrobe; buried beside her sister at Greenmont, 14-Yes, 15-
    Latrobe
#7589, 1-Latrobe, Lettie G., 2-died, 3-21 May 1867, 4-NY, 6-buried in Greenmont in
    Baltimore, 7-Latrobe, Charles H., 14-Yes, 15-Latrobe
#7590, 1-Latrobe, Rosa Wirt (Robinson), 2-died, 3-Jul 1870, 4-Baltimore, MD, 6-
    buried in her father's vault in the church yard of the Westminster, 7-
    Latrobe, Charles H., 14-Yes, 15-Latrobe
#7591, 1-Latrobe, Ellen Hazelhurst, 2-died, 3-3 Oct 1872, 6-buried at Greenmont, 7-
    Latrobe, B.H., 14-Yes, 15-Latrobe
#7592, 1-Witherow, William, 2-married, 7-McGinley, Sarah, 14-Yes, 15-Knox
#7593, 1-Witherow, Samuel, 2-married, 7-McLean, Rachel, 12-Witherow, William, 13-
    McGinley, Sarah, 14-Yes, 15-Knox
#7594, 1-Witherow, Margaret, 2-married, 3-15 Mar 1821, 7-Knox, Samuel, 10-Rev. John
    King, 12-Witherow, Samuel, 13-McLean, Rachel, 14-Yes, 15-Knox
#7595, 1-Witherow, Margaret, 2-born, 3-9 Oct 1803, 14-Yes, 15-Knox
#7596, 1-Witherow, Margaret, 2-died, 3-19 Oct 1847, 14-Yes, 15-Knox
#7597, 1-Knox, Samuel, 2-born, 3-21 Dec 1794, 14-Yes, 15-Knox
#7598, 1-Knox, Samuel, 2-died, 3-26 May 1845, 14-Yes, 15-Knox
#7599, 1-Knox, Rachel Rebecca, 2-born, 3-19 Apr 1822, 12-Knox, Samuel, 13-Witherow,
    Margaret, 14-Yes, 15-Knox
#7600, 1-Knox, Rachel Rebecca, 2-died, 3-19 Apr 1908, 12-Knox, Samuel, 13-Witherow,
    Margaret, 14-Yes, 15-Knox
#7601, 1-Knox, Rachel Rebecca, 2-married, 3-5 Dec 1842, 7-Marshall, John H. (Hon.),
    10-Rev. John Knox, 12-Knox, Samuel, 13-Witherow, Margaret, 14-Yes, 15-Knox
#7602, 1-Knox, Samuel, 2-born, 3-10 Oct 1824, 12-Knox, Samuel, 13-Witherow,
    Margaret, 14-Yes, 15-Knox
#7603, 1-Knox, Samuel, 2-died, 3-18 Jul 1887, 12-Knox, Samuel, 13-Witherow,
    Margaret, 14-Yes, 15-Knox
#7604, 1-Knox, Samuel, 2-married, 3-23 Dec 1851, 7-Culbertson, Mary D., 10-Rev.
    James Mason, 12-Knox, Samuel, 13-Witherow, Margaret, 14-Yes, 15-Knox
#7605, 1-Knox, John, 2-born, 3-14 Jan 1827, 12-Knox, Samuel, 13-Witherow, Margaret,
    14-Yes, 15-Knox
#7606, 1-Knox, John, 2-died, 3-20 Jun 1898, 12-Knox, Samuel, 13-Witherow, Margaret,
    14-Yes, 15-Knox
#7607, 1-Knox, John, 2-married, 3-1 Mar 1845, 7-McWhenny [McIlhenny], Margaret A.,
    10-Rev. David Clark, 12-Knox, Samuel, 13-Witherow, Margaret, 14-Yes, 15-Knox
#7608, 1-Knox, Helen Margaret, 2-born, 3-11 Mar 1829, 12-Knox, Samuel, 13-Witherow,
    Margaret, 14-Yes, 15-Knox
#7609, 1-Knox, Helen Margaret, 2-died, 3-1 Apr 1893, 12-Knox, Samuel, 13-Witherow,
    Margaret, 14-Yes, 15-Knox
#7610, 1-Knox, Helen Margaret, 2-married, 3-22 Sep 1859, 7-Marshall, Andrew, 10-
    J.R. Warner, 12-Knox, Samuel, 13-Witherow, Margaret, 14-Yes, 15-Knox
#7611, 1-Knox, Sarah Mary, 2-born, 3-26 Sep 1831, 12-Knox, Samuel, 13-Witherow,
    Margaret, 14-Yes, 15-Knox
#7612, 1-Knox, Sarah Mary, 2-married, 3-20 Nov 1860, 7-Marshall, Benjamin A., 10-
    Dr. J.R. Warner, 12-Knox, Samuel, 13-Witherow, Margaret, 14-Yes, 15-Knox
#7613, 1-Knox, Sarah Mary, 2-married, 3-1898, 7-Blythe, D. Bruce, 10-Rev. Van
    Cleve, 12-Knox, Samuel, 13-Witherow, Margaret, 14-Yes, 15-Knox
#7614, 1-Knox, Euphemia Mason, 2-born, 3-28 Feb 1834, 12-Knox, Samuel, 13-Witherow,
    Margaret, 14-Yes, 15-Knox
```

FAMILY BIBLE RECORDS IN THE WASHINGTON COUNTY FREE LIBRARY, HAGERSTOWN, MARYLAND

Entry #, 1-Last Name, First Name, 2-Event, 3-Date, 4-Event Location, 5-Age, 6-Other, 7-Spouse's Last, First, 8-Groom's Residence, 9-Bride's Residence, 10-Minister, 11-Minister's Location, 12-Father's Last, First, 13-Mother's Last, First, 14-Transcribed, 15-Family Bible

```
#7615, 1-Knox, Euphemia Mason, 2-died, 3-10 Mar 1862, 12-Knox, Samuel, 13-Witherow,
    Margaret, 14-Yes, 15-Knox
#7616, 1-Knox, Euphemia Mason, 2-married, 3-26 Dec 1860, 7-Rinehart, E.T., 10-Rev.
    J.R. Warner, 12-Knox, Samuel, 13-Witherow, Margaret, 14-Yes, 15-Knox
#7617, 1-Knox, Charles McLean, 2-born, 3-7 May 1837, 12-Knox, Samuel, 13-Witherow,
    Margaret, 14-Yes, 15-Knox
#7618, 1-Knox, Charles McLean, 2-died, 3-14 Feb 1894, 12-Knox, Samuel, 13-Witherow,
    Margaret, 14-Yes, 15-Knox
#7619, 1-Knox, Charles McLean, 2-married, 3-12 May 1864, 7-Mason, Meta. R., 10-Jos.
    H. Mason Knox, 12-Knox, Samuel, 13-Witherow, Margaret, 14-Yes, 15-Knox
#7620, 1-Knox, Elizabeth Harriet, 2-born, 3-7 Jun 1841, 12-Knox, Samuel, 13-
    Witherow, Margaret, 14-Yes, 15-Knox
#7621, 1-Knox, Elizabeth Harriet, 2-married, 3-17 Mar 1868, 7-Rankin, S. Johnston,
    10-R.J. Fergueson, 12-Knox, Samuel, 13-Witherow, Margaret, 14-Yes, 15-Knox
#7622, 1-Knox, Martha Virginia, 2-born, 3-26 Jan 1844, 12-Knox, Samuel, 13-
    Witherow, Margaret, 14-Yes, 15-Knox
#7623, 1-Knox, Martha Virginia, 2-married, 3-26 Apr 1861[or 1867?], 7-Boyd, R.
    Hance, 10-J.R. Warner, 12-Knox, Samuel, 13-Witherow, Margaret, 14-Yes, 15-
    Knox
#7624, 1-McLean, Moses, 2-married, 7-Charlesworth, Sarah, 14-Yes, 15-Knox
#7625, 1-McLean, Rachel, 2-born, 12-McLean, Moses, 13-Charlesworth, Sarah, 14-Yes,
    15-Knox
#7626, 1-Knox, Rebecca Hodge (Mrs.), 2-died, 3-1843, 14-Yes, 15-Knox
#7627, 1-McCurdy, James, 2-born, 3-1770, 14-Yes, 15-Knox
#7628, 1-McCurdy, James, 2-married, 6-Brown, 7-Mary, 14-Yes, 15-Knox
#7629, 1-McCurdy, Margaret, 2-married, 6-"settled in Clarion Co., PA", 7-Rankin,
    James, 12-McCurdy, James, 13-Brown, Mary, 14-Yes, 15-Knox
#7630, 1-Rankin, Elizabeth Watson, 2-born, 3-29 Nov 1868, 12-Rankin, Samuel
    Johnston, 13-Knox, Elizabeth, 14-Yes, 15-Knox
#7631, 1-Rankin, Margaret Johston, 2-born, 3-13 Feb 1871, 12-Rankin, Samuel
    Johnston, 13-Knox, Elizabeth, 14-Yes, 15-Knox
#7632, 1-Rankin, Harry Huber, 2-born, 12-Rankin, Jere C., 13-Huber, Annie L., 14-
    Yes, 15-Knox
#7633, 1-Rankin, Mary Jane, 2-born, 3-23 Sep 1875, 12-Rankin, Jere C., 13-Huber,
    Annie L., 14-Yes, 15-Knox
#7634, 1-Rankin, Maria Louise, 2-born, 3-20 Jun 1878, 12-Rankin, Jere C., 13-Huber,
    Annie L., 14-Yes, 15-Knox
#7635, 1-Knox, John, 2-died, 3-20 Jun 1898, 12-Knox, Samuel, 13-Witherow, Margaret,
    14-Yes, 15-Knox
#7636, 1-Marshall, Rachel Rebecca Knox, 2-died, 3-Easter Sunday, 19 Apr 1908, 14-
    Yes, 15-Knox
#7637, 1-Scott, George Marshall, 2-died, 3-Dec 1893, 12-Scott, William, 13-
    Rinehart, Marmie, 14-Yes, 15-Knox
#7638, 1-Knox, Samuel, 2-married, 3-15 Mar 1821, 7-Witherow, Margaret, 10-Rev. John
    King, 14-Yes, 15-Knox
#7639, 1-Knox, Rachel Rebecca, 2-married, 3-5 Dec 1842, 7-Marshall, James H., 10-
    Rev. John Knox, 11-New York City, 12-Knox, Samuel, 13-Witherow, Margaret, 14-
    Yes, 15-Knox
#7640, 1-Knox, Samuel, 2-married, 3-23 Dec 1851, 7-Culbertson, Mary E., 10-Rev.
    James Mason, 12-Knox, Samuel, 13-Witherow, Margaret, 14-Yes, 15-Knox
#7641, 1-Knox, John, 2-married, 3-1 Mar 1854, 7-McSherry, Margaret A., 10-Rev.
    David Clark, 12-Knox, Samuel, 13-Witherow, Margaret, 14-Yes, 15-Knox
#7642, 1-Knox, Helen M., 2-married, 3-22 Sep 1859, 7-Marshall, Andrew, 10-Rev. J.R.
    Warner, 12-Knox, Samuel, 13-Witherow, Margaret, 14-Yes, 15-Knox
```

FAMILY BIBLE RECORDS IN THE WASHINGTON COUNTY FREE LIBRARY, HAGERSTOWN, MARYLAND

Entry #, 1-Last Name, First Name, 2-Event, 3-Date, 4-Event Location, 5-Age, 6-Other, 7-Spouse's Last, First, 8-Groom's Residence, 9-Bride's Residence, 10-Minister, 11-Minister's Location, 12-Father's Last, First, 13-Mother's Last, First, 14-Transcribed, 15-Family Bible

#7643, 1-Knox, Sarah M., 2-married, 3-20 Nov 1860, 7-Marshall, Benjamin A., 10-Rev. J.R. Warner, 12-Knox, Samuel, 13-Witherow, Margaret, 14-Yes, 15-Knox

#7644, 1-Knox, Euphemia M., 2-married, 3-26 Dec 1860, 7-Rinehart, E.T., 10-Rev. J.R. Warner, 12-Knox, Samuel, 13-Witherow, Margaret, 14-Yes, 15-Knox

#7645, 1-Knox, Charles McLean, 2-married, 3-12 May 1864, 7-Mason, Meta R. (Miss), 10-Jos. H. Mason Knox, 12-Knox, Samuel, 13-Witherow, Margaret, 14-Yes, 15-Knox

#7646, 1-Knox, Elizabeth Harriet, 2-married, 3-17 Mar 1868, 7-Rankin, S. Johnston, 10-R.G. Fergueson, 12-Knox, Samuel, 13-Witherow, Margaret, 14-Yes, 15-Knox

#7647, 1-Knox, Martha Virginia, 2-married, 3-26 Apr 1861, 7-Boyd, R. Hance, 10-J.R. Warner, 12-Knox, Samuel, 13-Witherow, Margaret, 14-Yes, 15-Knox

#7648, 1-Rankin, Mary Jane, 2-born, 3-23 Sep 1875, 12-Rankin, Jerry, 14-Yes, 15-Knox

#7649, 1-Rankin, Maria Louise, 2-born, 3-20 Jun 1878, 12-Rankin, Jerry, 14-Yes, 15-Knox

#7650, 1-Knox, Samuel, 2-born, 3-21 Dec 1794, 14-Yes, 15-Knox

#7651, 1-Knox, Margaret, 2-born, 3-9 Oct 1803, 14-Yes, 15-Knox

#7652, 1-Knox, Rachel Rebecca, 2-born, 3-19 Apr 1822, 12-Knox, Samuel, 13-Knox, Margaret, 14-Yes, 15-Knox

#7653, 1-Knox, Samuel, 2-born, 3-16 Oct 1824, 12-Knox, Samuel, 13-Knox, Margaret, 14-Yes, 15-Knox

#7654, 1-Knox, John, 2-born, 3-14 Jan 1827, 12-Knox, Samuel, 13-Knox, Margaret, 14-Yes, 15-Knox

#7655, 1-Knox, Helen Margaret, 2-born, 3-11 Mar 1829, 12-Knox, Samuel, 13-Knox, Margaret, 14-Yes, 15-Knox

#7656, 1-Knox, Sarah Mary, 2-born, 3-26 Sep 1831, 12-Knox, Samuel, 13-Knox, Margaret, 14-Yes, 15-Knox

#7657, 1-Knox, Euphemia Mason, 2-born, 3-28 Feb 1834, 12-Knox, Samuel, 13-Knox, Margaret, 14-Yes, 15-Knox

#7658, 1-Knox, Charles McLean, 2-born, 3-7 May 1837, 12-Knox, Samuel, 13-Knox, Margaret, 14-Yes, 15-Knox

#7659, 1-Knox, [female], 2-born, 3-17 Feb 1840, 12-Knox, Samuel, 13-Knox, Margaret, 14-Yes, 15-Knox

#7660, 1-Knox, Elizabeth Harriet, 2-born, 3-7 Jun 1841, 12-Knox, Samuel, 13-Knox, Margaret, 14-Yes, 15-Knox

#7661, 1-Knox, Martha Virginia, 2-born, 3-26 Jan 1844, 12-Knox, Samuel, 13-Knox, Margaret, 14-Yes, 15-Knox

#7662, 1-Rinehart, Mary Helen, 2-born, 3-3 Mar 1862, 7-Scott, Wm., 14-Yes, 15-Knox

#7663, 1-Rinehart, Mary Helen, 2-died, 3-13 Sep 1894, 14-Yes, 15-Knox

#7664, 1-Scott, Helen, 2-born, 12-Scott, Wm., 13-Rinehart, Mary Helen, 14-Yes, 15-Knox

#7665, 1-Rankin, Elizabeth Watson, 2-born, 3-29 Nov 1868, 12-Rankin, Johnston, 13-Rankin, Elizabeth K., 14-Yes, 15-Knox

#7666, 1-Rankin, Margaret Johnston, 2-born, 3-13 Apr 1871, 12-Rankin, Johnston, 13-Rankin, Elizabeth K., 14-Yes, 15-Knox

#7667, 1-Knox, Rebecca (Mrs.), 2-died, 3-28 May 1843, 14-Yes, 15-Knox

#7668, 1-Knox, Samuel, 2-died, 3-26 May 1845, 14-Yes, 15-Knox

#7669, 1-Knox, Margaret, 2-died, 3-19 Oct 1847, 14-Yes, 15-Knox

#7670, 1-Knox, [female], 2-died, 3-7 Mar 1840, 14-Yes, 15-Knox

#7671, 1-Rinehart, Euphemia Mason, 2-died, 3-10 Mar 1862, 14-Yes, 15-Knox

#7672, 1-Rinehart, Samuel (M.D.), 2-died, 3-18 Jul 1887, 12-Knox, Samuel, 14-Yes, 15-Knox

#7673, 1-Rinehart, Even. Thomas, 2-died, 3-Jun 1891, 14-Yes, 15-Knox

#7674, 1-Rankin, Samuel Johnston, 2-died, 3-21 Dec 1891, 14-Yes, 15-Knox

#7675, 1-Boyd, Robert Hance, 2-died, 3-30 Apr 1892, 14-Yes, 15-Knox

FAMILY BIBLE RECORDS IN THE WASHINGTON COUNTY FREE LIBRARY, HAGERSTOWN, MARYLAND

Entry #, 1-Last Name, First Name, 2-Event, 3-Date, 4-Event Location, 5-Age, 6-Other,
7-Spouse's Last, First, 8-Groom's Residence, 9-Bride's Residence, 10-Minister, 11-Minister's Location,
12-Father's Last, First, 13-Mother's Last, First, 14-Transcribed, 15-Family Bible

```
#7676, 1-Marshall, Helen Margaret, 2-died, 3-1 Apr 1893, 14-Yes, 15-Knox
#7677, 1-Knox, Charles McLean, 2-died, 3-14 Feb 1894, 14-Yes, 15-Knox
#7678, 1-Poffenberger, Ira Grayson, 2-born, 3-15 Jun 1907, 12-Poffenberger, Owen
    Edward, 13-Jones, Bertha E., 14-Yes, 15-Poffenberger
#7679, 1-Poffenberger, Ira Grayson, 2-married, 3-29 Oct 1932, 7-Reeder, Irene
    Elizabeth, 10-Frank L. Stine , 14-Yes, 15-Poffenberger
#7680, 1-Reeder, Irene Elizabeth, 2-born, 3-6 Oct 1915, 12-Reeder, John Luther, 13-
    Alexander, Sarah Ruth, 14-Yes, 15-Poffenberger
#7681, 1-Poffenberger, Janice Marie, 2-born, 3-4 Mar 1935, 14-Yes, 15-Poffenberger
#7682, 1-Poffenberger, Deloris Mae, 2-born, 3-31 Aug 1940, 14-Yes, 15-Poffenberger
#7683, 1-Poffenberger, Irene E. Reeder, 2-born, 3-6 Oct 1915, 14-Yes, 15-
    Poffenberger
#7684, 1-Poffenberger, Ira Grayson, 2-born, 3-15 Jun 1907, 14-Yes, 15-Poffenberger
#7685, 1-Poffenberger, Janice Marie, 2-married, 3-4 Jul 1954, 7-Frye, John Clinton,
    14-Yes, 15-Poffenberger
#7686, 1-Poffenberger, Dolores Mae, 2-married, 3-17 Jan 1960, 7-Grim, Everard
    Therin, 14-Yes, 15-Poffenberger
#7687, 1-Poffenberger, Ira David, 2-born, 3-16 Nov 1932, 14-Yes, 15-Poffenberger
#7688, 1-Poffenberger, Ira David, 2-died, 3-16 Nov 1932, 6-buried Fairview
    Cemetery, Keedysville, MD, 14-Yes, 15-Poffenberger
#7689, 1-Poffenberger, Ira Grayson, 2-died, 3-4 Aug 1980, 5-74 years, 14-Yes, 15-
    Poffenberger
#7690, 1-Reeder, Hiram, 2-born, 3-21 Aug 1818, 15-Poffenberger
#7691, 1-Reeder, Hiram, 2-died, 3-17 Sep 1875, 6-buried Mt. Carmel Church, Rt. 67,
    15-Poffenberger
#7692, 1-Reeder, Rose Ann (Longman), 2-born, 3-6 Jun 1804, 15-Poffenberger
#7693, 1-Reeder, Rose Ann (Longman), 2-died, 3-16 Sep 1888, 15-Poffenberger
#7694, 1-Reeder, Daniel, 2-born, 3-28 Dec 1837, 15-Poffenberger
#7695, 1-Reeder, Daniel, 2-died, 3-17 Feb 1918, 15-Poffenberger
#7696, 1-Reeder, Susan (Beachley), 2-born, 3-1 May 1840, 15-
#7697, 1-Reeder, Susan (Beachley), 2-died, 3-24 Dec 1898, 15-
#7698, 1-Reeder, Otho James, 2-born, 3-17 Oct 1867, 15-
#7699, 1-Reeder, Otho James, 2-died, 3-18 Apr 1948, 15-
#7700, 1-Reeder, Otho James, 2-married, 3-1889, 15-
#7701, 1-Reeder, Betty Cronise, 2-born, 3-2 Sep 1866, 15-
#7702, 1-Reeder, Betty Cronise, 2-died, 3-30 Jul, 15-
#7703, 1-Reeder, John Luther, 2-married, 3-31 Mar 1915, 4-Rohrersville, MD, 7-
    Alexander, Sarah Ruth, 10-Rev. L.A. Stangle, 14-Yes, 15-Poffenberger
#7704, 1-Alexander, Sarah Ruth, 2-born, 3-4 May 1898, 14-Yes, 15-Poffenberger
#7705, 1-Reeder, John Luther, 2-born, 3-18 May 1896, 14-Yes, 15-Poffenberger
#7706, 1-Reeder, Irene Elizabeth, 2-born, 3-6 Oct 1915, 12-Reeder, John Luther, 13-
    Alexander , Sarah Ruth, 14-Yes, 15-Poffenberger
#7707, 1-Reeder, Mae Gertrude, 2-born, 3-7 Jun 1920, 12-Reeder, John Luther, 13-
    Alexander , Sarah Ruth, 14-Yes, 15-Poffenberger
#7708, 1-Reeder, Ernest Winfred, 2-born, 3-10 Feb 1922[or 1923], 12-Reeder, John
    Luther, 13-Alexander , Sarah Ruth, 14-Yes, 15-Poffenberger
#7709, 1-Reeder, Dennis Elwood, 2-born, 3-12 Mar 1925, 12-Reeder, John Luther, 13-
    Alexander , Sarah Ruth, 14-Yes, 15-Poffenberger
#7710, 1-Reeder, Bettie Marie, 2-born, 3-15 Mar 1928, 12-Reeder, John Luther, 13-
    Alexander , Sarah Ruth, 14-Yes, 15-Poffenberger
#7711, 1-Reeder, Marcia Copeland, 2-born, 3-5 May 1930, 12-Reeder, John Luther, 13-
    Alexander , Sarah Ruth, 14-Yes, 15-Poffenberger
#7712, 1-Poffenburger, Janice Marie, 2-born, 3-4 Mar 1935, 14-Yes, 15-Poffenberger
#7713, 1-Pierce, ____h Lewis, 2-born, 3-26 Jun 1917, 15-
#7714, 1-Reeder, Imogene Bernice Hardez, 2-born, 3-3 Feb 1932, 15-
```

FAMILY BIBLE RECORDS IN THE WASHINGTON COUNTY FREE LIBRARY, HAGERSTOWN, MARYLAND

Entry #, 1-Last Name, First Name, 2-Event, 3-Date, 4-Event Location, 5-Age, 6-Other, 7-Spouse's Last, First, 8-Groom's Residence, 9-Bride's Residence, 10-Minister, 11-Minister's Location, 12-Father's Last, First, 13-Mother's Last, First, 14-Transcribed, 15-Family Bible

```
#7715, 1-Poffenburger, Deloris M., 2-born, 3-31 Aug 1940, 15-
#7716, 1-Poffenburger, Ira Grayson, 2-born, 3-15 Jun 1906, 4-Keedysville, MD, 14-
    Yes, 15-Poffenberger
#7717, 1-Reeder, Irene Elizabeth, 2-born, 3-6 Oct 1915, 4-Boonsboro, MD, 14-Yes,
    15-Poffenberger
#7718, 1-Poffenberger, Owen Edward, 2-born, 3-16 Jun 1880, 4-Washington Co., MD,
    14-Yes, 15-Poffenberger
#7719, 1-Poffenberger, Owen Edward, 2-died, 3-25 Aug 1962, 6-buried in Keedysville,
    MD, 14-Yes, 15-Poffenberger
#7720, 1-Jones, Bertha Elizabeth, 2-born, 3-9 Jan 1888, 4-Frederick Co., MD, 14-
    Yes, 15-Poffenberger
#7721, 1-Jones, Bertha Elizabeth, 2-died, 3-14 Dec 1943, 6-buried in Keedysville,
    MD, 14-Yes, 15-Poffenberger
#7722, 1-Reeder, John Luther, 2-born, 3-18 May 1896, 4-Washington Co., MD, 14-Yes,
    15-Poffenberger
#7723, 1-Reeder, John Luther, 2-died, 3-23 Feb 1973, 5-76 years, 6-buried in
    Boonsboro Cemetery, 14-Yes, 15-Poffenberger
#7724, 1-Alexander, Sarah Ruth, 2-born, 3-4 May 1898, 4-Frederick Co., MD, 14-Yes,
    15-Poffenberger
#7725, 1-Alexander, Sarah Ruth, 2-married, 3-31 Mar 1915, 7-Reeder, John Luther,
    14-Yes, 15-Poffenberger
#7726, 1-Alexander, Sarah Ruth, 2-died, 3-14 Oct 1991, 5-93 years 5 months 10 days,
    6-buried Boonsboro Cemetery, Boonsboro, MD, 14-Yes, 15-Poffenberger
#7727, 1-Poffenberger, Ira Grayson, 2-born, 3-15 Jun 1906, 12-Poffenberger, Owen
    Edward, 13-Jones, Bertha Elizabeth, 14-Yes, 15-Poffenberger
#7728, 1-Poffenberger, Ira Grayson, 2-died, 3-4 Aug 1980, 12-Poffenberger, Owen
    Edward, 13-Jones, Bertha Elizabeth, 14-Yes, 15-Poffenberger
#7729, 1-Poffenberger, Agnes Stella, 2-born, 3-17 Sep 1907[?], 12-Poffenberger,
    Owen Edward, 13-Jones, Bertha Elizabeth, 14-Yes, 15-Poffenberger
#7730, 1-Poffenberger, Agnes Stella, 2-died, 3-6 Dec 1961, 12-Poffenberger, Owen
    Edward, 13-Jones, Bertha Elizabeth, 14-Yes, 15-Poffenberger
#7731, 1-Poffenberger, Jr., Owen Edward, 12-Poffenberger, Owen Edward, 13-Jones,
    Bertha Elizabeth, 14-Yes, 15-Poffenberger
#7732, 1-Poffenberger, Clarence Glenwood, 2-born, 3-11 Nov 1910, 12-Poffenberger,
    Owen Edward, 13-Jones, Bertha Elizabeth, 14-Yes, 15-Poffenberger
#7733, 1-Poffenberger, Clarence Glenwood, 2-died, 3-9 Jul 1980, 12-Poffenberger,
    Owen Edward, 13-Jones, Bertha Elizabeth, 14-Yes, 15-Poffenberger
#7734, 1-Poffenberger, Irma Elizabeth, 2-born, 3-14 Oct 1912, 12-Poffenberger, Owen
    Edward, 13-Jones, Bertha Elizabeth, 14-Yes, 15-Poffenberger
#7735, 1-Poffenberger, Irma Elizabeth, 2-married, 3-26 Apr 1936, 12-Poffenberger,
    Owen Edward, 13-Jones, Bertha Elizabeth, 14-Yes, 15-Poffenberger
#7736, 1-Poffenberger, Margie Leona, 2-born, 3-7 Oct 1918, 12-Poffenberger, Owen
    Edward, 13-Jones, Bertha Elizabeth, 14-Yes, 15-Poffenberger
#7737, 1-Poffenberger, Theodore Rosevelt, 2-born, 6-twin, 12-Poffenberger, Owen
    Edward, 13-Jones, Bertha Elizabeth, 14-Yes, 15-Poffenberger
#7738, 1-Poffenberger, Woodrow Wilson, 2-born, 6-twin, 12-Poffenberger, Owen
    Edward, 13-Jones, Bertha Elizabeth, 14-Yes, 15-Poffenberger
#7739, 1-Poffenberger, Alice Louise, 2-born, 3-7 May 1927, 12-Poffenberger, Owen
    Edward, 13-Jones, Bertha Elizabeth, 14-Yes, 15-Poffenberger
#7740, 1-Poffenberger, Leonard Ellsworth, 2-born, 3-21 Feb 1924, 12-Poffenberger,
    Owen Edward, 13-Jones, Bertha Elizabeth, 14-Yes, 15-Poffenberger
#7741, 1-Poffenberger, Irene Isabell, 2-born, 3-15 Sep 1921, 12-Poffenberger, Owen
    Edward, 13-Jones, Bertha Elizabeth, 14-Yes, 15-Poffenberger
#7742, 1-Hager, James Thornton , 2-born, 3-24 Nov 1851, 4-Hagerstown, MD, 14-Yes,
    15-Hager
```

FAMILY BIBLE RECORDS IN THE WASHINGTON COUNTY FREE LIBRARY, HAGERSTOWN, MARYLAND

Entry #, 1-Last Name, First Name, 2-Event, 3-Date, 4-Event Location, 5-Age, 6-Other,
7-Spouse's Last, First, 8-Groom's Residence, 9-Bride's Residence, 10-Minister, 11-Minister's Location,
12-Father's Last, First, 13-Mother's Last, First, 14-Transcribed, 15-Family Bible

#7743, 1-Hall, Mary DuBois, 2-born, 3-7 Nov 1850, 4-Warren, Trumbull Co., OH, 14-Yes, 15-Hager

#7744, 1-Spielman, Mary F., 2-died, 3-7 Jan 1881, 14-Yes, 15-Hager

#7745, 1-Spielman, Amthe[?], 2-died, 3-26 Jun 1883, 14-Yes, 15-Hager

#7746, 1-Turner, John D., 2-married, 3-24 Apr 1879, 4-"bride's parents", 7-Pittenger, Marthe J., 10-Rev. Nicholas, 14-Yes, 15-Turner

#7747, 1-Turner, John D., 2-died, 3-1930, 5-77 years, 13-Turner, Margaret, 14-Yes, 15-Turner

#7748, 1-Hager, Jacob, 2-married, 3-20 Dec 1845, 7-Pritchard, M. Susan (Miss), 12-Hager, Jonathan The Miller", 14-Yes, 15-Hager

#7749, 1-Pritchard, Susan, 2-born, 3-27 Dec 1826, 12-Pritchard, Samuel, 13-Prtichard, Mary, 14-Yes, 15-Hager

#7750, 1-Hager, Eleanor, 2-born, 3-22 Nov 1846, 12-Hager, Jacob, 13-Hager, Susan, 14-Yes, 15-Hager

#7751, 1-Hager, Emma Virginia, 2-born, 3-27 Oct 1849, 12-Hager, Jacob, 13-Hager, Susan, 14-Yes, 15-Hager

#7752, 1-Hager, Anna Bell, 2-born, 3-2 Jun 1852, 12-Hager, Jacob, 13-Hager, Susan, 14-Yes, 15-Hager

#7753, 1-Hager, Jacob C., 2-born, 3-2 Sep 1825, 14-Yes, 15-Hager

#7754, 1-Hager, Willey Gra., 2-born, 3-27 Aug 1859, 14-Yes, 15-Hager

#7755, 1-Hager, Annie, 2-married, 7-Douglas, George, 8-Baltimore, MD, 12-Hager, Jacob, 13-Hager, Susan, 14-Yes, 15-Hager

#7756, 1-Eichelberger, Barbara (Mrs.), 2-died, 3-Sunday night, 14 Apr 1833, 5-67 years, 6-"found dead in bed on Monday morning", 14-Yes, 15-Eichelberger

#7757, 1-Eichelberger, Theobold, 2-died, 3-Thursday, 6 Nov 1845, 5-83 years, 6-buried in old Lutheran Cemetery, 14-Yes, 15-Eichelberger

#7758, 1-Tonhbaugh, Elizabeth (Aunt), 2-died, 3-12 Aug 1846, 5-86 years, 14-Yes, 15-Eichelberger

#7759, 1-Aughinbaugh, J. Philip, 2-married, 3-3 Jun 1828, 7-Hubley, Anna Catharine Rauna, 10-Rev. John F. Moeller, 11-Lutheran clergy, 12-Aughinbaugh, Henry, 14-Yes, 15-Aughinbaugh

#7760, 1-Hubley, Anna Catharine Rauna, 2-born, 12-Hubley, Michael, 14-Yes, 15-Aughinbaugh

#7761, 1-Aughinbaugh, Wm. M., 2-married, 3-24 Oct 1854, 7-Taylor, Mary Jane, 12-Aughinbaugh, Philip, 14-Yes, 15-Aughinbaugh

#7762, 1-Aughinbaugh, Margaret Ann, 2-married, 3-2 Jun 1864, 7-Lachman, G.W., 12-Aughinbaugh, Philip, 14-Yes, 15-Aughinbaugh

#7763, 1-Aughinbaugh, Susanna, 2-married, 7-Bricker, Jerry, 12-Aughinbaugh, Philip, 14-Yes, 15-Aughinbaugh

#7764, 1-Aughinbaugh, Henry, 2-married, 7-Stock, Lizzie, 12-Aughinbaugh, Philip, 14-Yes, 15-Aughinbaugh

#7765, 1-Aughinbaugh, Geo. Besore, 2-married, 3-6 Jun 1865, 7-Lawrence, Laura F.[?], 12-Aughinbaugh, Philip, 14-Yes, 15-Aughinbaugh

#7766, 1-Aughinbaugh, Chas., 2-married, 7-[blank], Lou, 12-Aughinbaugh, Philip, 14-Yes, 15-Aughinbaugh

#7767, 1-Aughinbaugh, Philip, 2-born, 3-17 Nov 1799, 4-Mifflin Township, Cumberland Co., PA, 12-Aughinbaugh, Henry, 13-Aughinbaugh, Eve, 14-Yes, 15-Aughinbaugh

#7768, 1-Aughinbaugh, Anna Catherine Raum, 2-born, 3-3 Jul 1806, 4-Shippensburg, PA, 12-Hubley, Michael, 13-Hubley, Mary, 14-Yes, 15-Aughinbaugh

#7769, 1-Aughinbaugh, Anna Catherine Raum, 2-baptized, 3-13 Jul 1806, 14-Yes, 15-Aughinbaugh

#7770, 1-Aughinbaugh, Anna Catherine Raum, 2-confirmed, 3-1 Apr 1825, 14-Yes, 15-Aughinbaugh

#7771, 1-Aughinbaugh, Mary Elizabeth, 2-born, 3-21 Mar 1829, 4-Waynesboro, PA, 12-Aughinbaugh, Philip, 13-Hubley, Anna Catherine Raum, 14-Yes, 15-Aughinbaugh

FAMILY BIBLE RECORDS IN THE WASHINGTON COUNTY FREE LIBRARY, HAGERSTOWN, MARYLAND

Entry #, 1-Last Name, First Name, 2-Event, 3-Date, 4-Event Location, 5-Age, 6-Other, 7-Spouse's Last, First, 8-Groom's Residence, 9-Bride's Residence, 10-Minister, 11-Minister's Location, 12-Father's Last, First, 13-Mother's Last, First, 14-Transcribed, 15-Family Bible

```
#7772, 1-Aughinbaugh, Mary Elizabeth, 2-baptized, 3-8 Nov 1829, 12-Aughinbaugh,
    Philip, 13-Hubley, Anna Catherine Raum, 14-Yes, 15-Aughinbaugh
#7773, 1-Aughinbaugh, William Michael, 2-born, 3-23 Jun 1831, 4-Waynesboro, PA, 12-
    Aughinbaugh, Philip, 13-Hubley, Anna Catherine Raum, 14-Yes, 15-Aughinbaugh
#7774, 1-Aughinbaugh, William Michael, 2-baptized, 3-28 Aug 1831, 10-Rev. J. Beck,
    12-Aughinbaugh, Philip, 13-Hubley, Anna Catherine Raum, 14-Yes, 15-
    Aughinbaugh
#7775, 1-Aughinbaugh, Susanna, 2-born, 3-25 Mar 1833, 4-Waynesboro, PA, 12-
    Aughinbaugh, Philip, 13-Hubley, Anna Catherine Raum, 14-Yes, 15-Aughinbaugh
#7776, 1-Aughinbaugh, Susanna, 2-baptized, 3-11 Jul 1833, 10-Rev. George W.
    Glesner, 12-Aughinbaugh, Philip, 13-Hubley, Anna Catherine Raum, 14-Yes, 15-
    Aughinbaugh
#7777, 1-Aughinbaugh, Henry Eliphabet, 2-born, 3-29 Jan 1836, 4-Waynesboro, PA, 12-
    Aughinbaugh, Philip, 13-Hubley, Anna Catherine Raum, 14-Yes, 15-Aughinbaugh
#7778, 1-Aughinbaugh, Henry Eliphabet, 2-baptized, 3-5 Jul 1836, 10-Rev. George W.
    Glesner, 12-Aughinbaugh, Philip, 13-Hubley, Anna Catherine Raum, 14-Yes, 15-
    Aughinbaugh
#7779, 1-Aughinbaugh, George Besore, 2-born, 3-10 Jun 1838, 4-Shippensburg, PA, 12-
    Aughinbaugh, Philip, 13-Hubley, Anna Catherine Raum, 14-Yes, 15-Aughinbaugh
#7780, 1-Aughinbaugh, George Besore, 2-baptized, 3-Jul 1838, 10-Rev. Wm. C. Bennet,
    12-Aughinbaugh, Philip, 13-Hubley, Anna Catherine Raum, 14-Yes, 15-
    Aughinbaugh
#7781, 1-Aughinbaugh, Charles Augustus, 2-born, 3-26 Mar 1841, 4-Newburg, PA, 12-
    Aughinbaugh, Philip, 13-Hubley, Anna Catherine Raum, 14-Yes, 15-Aughinbaugh
#7782, 1-Aughinbaugh, Charles Augustus, 2-baptized, 10-Rev. J.C. Gulden, 12-
    Aughinbaugh, Philip, 13-Hubley, Anna Catherine Raum, 14-Yes, 15-Aughinbaugh
#7783, 1-Aughinbaugh, Margaret Ann, 2-born, 3-4 Aug 1843, 4-Newburg, PA, 12-
    Aughinbaugh, Philip, 13-Hubley, Anna Catherine Raum, 14-Yes, 15-Aughinbaugh
#7784, 1-Aughinbaugh, Margaret Ann, 2-baptized, 10-Rev. Hurfmyer, 12-Aughinbaugh,
    Philip, 13-Hubley, Anna Catherine Raum, 14-Yes, 15-Aughinbaugh
#7785, 1-Aughinbaugh, Emma Jane, 2-born, 3-18 Dec 1845, 4-Newburg, PA, 12-
    Aughinbaugh, Philip, 13-Hubley, Anna Catherine Raum, 14-Yes, 15-Aughinbaugh
#7786, 1-Aughinbaugh, Philip , 2-died, 3-10 Nov 1865, 4-memphis, Indianna, 5-66
    years, 14-Yes, 15-Aughinbaugh
#7787, 1-Aughinbaugh, Ann Catherine, 2-died, 3-15 Aug 1883, 4-Shippensburg, PA, 5-
    77 years 1 months 11 days, 14-Yes, 15-Aughinbaugh
#7788, 1-Aughinbaugh, Sarah, 2-died, 3-13 Apr 1866, 4-Carlisle, PA, 5-64 years, 6-
    "sister of Philip Aughinbaugh", 14-Yes, 15-Aughinbaugh
#7789, 1-Aughinbaugh, Laura F., 2-died, 3-12 Jul 1886, 4-Chicago, IL, 5-44 years 3
    months 27 days, 7-Aughinbaugh, George B., 14-Yes, 15-Aughinbaugh
#7790, 1-Aughinbaugh, Lille, 2-died, 3-May 1866, 4-Harrisburg, PA, 5-7 weeks 1
    days, 14-Yes, 15-Aughinbaugh
#7791, 1-Aughinbaugh, Mary Jane, 2-died, 3-2 Jul 1883, 5-52 years, 7-Aughinbaugh,
    Wm., 14-Yes, 15-Aughinbaugh
#7792, 1-Aughinbaugh, Mary Eliz., 2-died, 3-16 Dec 1902, 4-Shippensburg, PA, 12-
    Aughinbaugh, Philip, 14-Yes, 15-Aughinbaugh
#7793, 1-Aughinbaugh, Wm. M., 2-died, 3-10 Jan 1914, 4-Shippensburg, PA, 14-Yes,
    15-Aughinbaugh
#7794, 1-Brecker, Susanna (Aughinbaugh), 2-died, 3-19 Apr 1913, 4-Missouri, 12-
    Aughinbaugh, Philip, 14-Yes, 15-Aughinbaugh
#7795, 1-Bricker, Jerry, 2-died, 3-22 Jul 1904, 4-Missouri, 7-Aughinbaugh, Susanna,
    14-Yes, 15-Aughinbaugh
#7796, 1-Aughinbaugh, Charles, 2-died, 3-11 Dec 1900, 4-Harrisburg, PA, 12-
    Aughinbaugh, Philip, 14-Yes, 15-Aughinbaugh
```

FAMILY BIBLE RECORDS IN THE WASHINGTON COUNTY FREE LIBRARY, HAGERSTOWN, MARYLAND

Entry #, 1-Last Name, First Name, 2-Event, 3-Date, 4-Event Location, 5-Age, 6-Other,
7-Spouse's Last, First, 8-Groom's Residence, 9-Bride's Residence, 10-Minister, 11-Minister's Location,
12-Father's Last, First, 13-Mother's Last, First, 14-Transcribed, 15-Family Bible

```
#7797, 1-Lackman, Margaret (Aughinbaugh), 2-died, 3-10 Jan 1955, 4-Shippensburg,
    PA, 12-Aughinbaugh, Philip, 14-Yes, 15-Aughinbaugh
#7798, 1-Lackman, G.W., 2-died, 3-14 Apr 1896, 4-Shippensburg, PA, 7-Aughinbaugh,
    Margaret, 14-Yes, 15-Aughinbaugh
#7799, 1-Aughinbaugh, Emma Jane, 2-died, 3-26 Oct 1932, 4-Shippensburg, PA, 12-
    Aughinbaugh, Philip, 14-Yes, 15-Aughinbaugh
#7800, 1-Aughinbaugh, John, 2-died, 3-7 Mar 1852, 6-"brother of Philip
    Aughinbaugh", 14-Yes, 15-Aughinbaugh
#7801, 1-McCullough, Elizabeth, 2-died, 3-1875, 7-Aughinbaugh, John, 14-Yes, 15-
    Aughinbaugh
#7802, 1-Aughinbaugh, Adam, 2-died, 3-6 Nov 1875, 4-Chambersburg, PA, 6-"brother of
    Philip Aughinbaugh", 14-Yes, 15-Aughinbaugh
#7803, 1-Aughinbaugh, Harriet McCausland, 2-died, 3-May 1880, 4-Chambersburg, PA,
    7-Aughinbaugh, Adam, 14-Yes, 15-Aughinbaugh
#7804, 1-Aughinbaugh, Alfred, 2-died, 3-26 Nov 1916, 4-Shippensburg, PA, 12-
    Aughinbaugh, M.M., 13-Taylor, Mary J., 14-Yes, 15-Aughinbaugh
#7805, 1-Aughinbaugh, Lillie, 2-died, 4-Gettysburg, PA, 7-Aughinbaugh, Alfred, 14-
    Yes, 15-Aughinbaugh
#7806, 1-Aughinbaugh, J.C., 2-married, 3-8 Mar 1870, 4-Chambersburg, PA, 7-Werner,
    Anna, 10-Rev. David Townsend, 14-Yes, 15-Aughinbaugh
#7807, 1-Aughinbaugh, Charles Edward, 2-married, 3-15 Feb 1898, 7-Gillan, Nell La
    Turner, 14-Yes, 15-Aughinbaugh
#7808, 1-Gillan, Nell La Turner, 2-died, 3-18 Jan 1939, 14-Yes, 15-Aughinbaugh
#7809, 1-Aughinbaugh, Laura Marie, 2-married, 3-1 Apr 1902, 7-McCausland, John
    Glen, 14-Yes, 15-Aughinbaugh
#7810, 1-McCausland, John Glen, 2-died, 3-3 Aug 1937, 14-Yes, 15-Aughinbaugh
#7811, 1-Aughinbaugh, Grayce Estelle, 2-married, 3-11 Apr 1905, 7-Thompson, Richard
    R., 14-Yes, 15-Aughinbaugh
#7812, 1-Thompson, Richard R., 2-died, 3-4 Oct 1923, 14-Yes, 15-Aughinbaugh
#7813, 1-Aughinbaugh, Sidney McLananhan, 2-married, 3-19 Jun 1906, 7-Swigert,
    Dessie, 14-Yes, 15-Aughinbaugh
#7814, 1-Swigert, Dessie, 2-died, 3-19 Mar 1918, 14-Yes, 15-Aughinbaugh
#7815, 1-Aughinbaugh, Bertha Frances, 2-married, 3-15 Mar 1911, 7-Greenawalt, S.
    Miller, 14-Yes, 15-Aughinbaugh
#7816, 1-Greenawalt, S. Miller, 2-died, 3-7 Feb 1952, 14-Yes, 15-Aughinbaugh
#7817, 1-Aughinbaugh, John Carson, 2-born, 3-11 Oct 1840, 14-Yes, 15-Aughinbaugh
#7818, 1-Aughinbaugh, Anna Dorothy, 2-born, 3-14 Oct 1848, 14-Yes, 15-Aughinbaugh
#7819, 1-Aughinbaugh, Charles Edward, 2-born, 3-18 Feb 1871, 14-Yes, 15-Aughinbaugh
#7820, 1-Aughinbaugh, Laura Marie, 2-born, 3-28 Jun 1874, 14-Yes, 15-Aughinbaugh
#7821, 1-Aughinbaugh, Sidney McLanahan, 2-born, 3-12 May 1877, 14-Yes, 15-
    Aughinbaugh
#7822, 1-Aughinbaugh, George , 2-born, 3-18 Sep 1880, 14-Yes, 15-Aughinbaugh
#7823, 1-Aughinbaugh, Grace Estelle, 2-born, 3-30 Jun 1883, 14-Yes, 15-Aughinbaugh
#7824, 1-Aughinbaugh, Bertha Frances, 2-born, 3-8 Jun 1886, 14-Yes, 15-Aughinbaugh
#7825, 1-Aughinbaugh, George, 2-died, 3-14 Nov 1880, 14-Yes, 15-Aughinbaugh
#7826, 1-Aughinbaugh, John Carson, 2-died, 3-17 Jun 1904, 14-Yes, 15-Aughinbaugh
#7827, 1-Aughinbaugh, Anna Dorothy, 2-died, 3-1 Apr 1917, 14-Yes, 15-Aughinbaugh
#7828, 1-Aughinbaugh, Sidney McL., 2-died, 3-4 Jul 1923, 14-Yes, 15-Aughinbaugh
#7829, 1-Aughinbaugh, Laura A., 2-died, 3-6 Feb 1947, 14-Yes, 15-Aughinbaugh
#7830, 1-Aughinbaugh, Charles E., 2-died, 3-28 Aug 1948, 14-Yes, 15-Aughinbaugh
#7831, 1-Aughinbaugh, Roland, 2-born, 3-16 Jun 1900, 12-Aughinbaugh, Charles, 14-
    Yes, 15-Aughinbaugh
#7832, 1-Aughinbaugh, Charles, 2-born, 3-9 Mar 1902, 6-twin, 12-Aughinbaugh,
    Charles, 14-Yes, 15-Aughinbaugh
```

FAMILY BIBLE RECORDS IN THE WASHINGTON COUNTY FREE LIBRARY, HAGERSTOWN, MARYLAND

Entry #, 1-Last Name, First Name, 2-Event, 3-Date, 4-Event Location, 5-Age, 6-Other,
7-Spouse's Last, First, 8-Groom's Residence, 9-Bride's Residence, 10-Minister, 11-Minister's Location,
12-Father's Last, First, 13-Mother's Last, First, 14-Transcribed, 15-Family Bible

```
#7833, 1-Aughinbaugh, Henry, 2-born, 3-9 Mar 1902, 6-twin, 12-Aughinbaugh, Charles,
    14-Yes, 15-Aughinbaugh
#7834, 1-McCausland, Glenn, 2-born, 3-12 Sep 1907, 12-McCausland, 13-Aughinbaugh,
    Laura, 14-Yes, 15-Aughinbaugh
#7835, 1-Greenawalt, Helen, 2-born, 3-14 Feb 1912, 12-Greenawalt, 13-Aughinbaugh,
    Bertha, 14-Yes, 15-Aughinbaugh
#7836, 1-Greenawalt, Kathryn, 2-born, 3-30 Oct 1913, 12-Greenawalt, 13-Aughinbaugh,
    Bertha, 14-Yes, 15-Aughinbaugh
#7837, 1-Greenawalt, Lois, 2-born, 3-20 Sep 1919, 12-Greenawalt, 13-Aughinbaugh,
    Bertha, 14-Yes, 15-Aughinbaugh
#7838, 1-Greenawalt, Mary Ellen, 2-born, 3-30 Nov 1921, 12-Greenawalt, 13-
    Aughinbaugh, Bertha, 14-Yes, 15-Aughinbaugh
#7839, 1-Aughinbaugh, Robert, 2-born, 3-10 Jul 1921, 12-Aughinbaugh, Sidney , 14-
    Yes, 15-Aughinbaugh
#7840, 1-Aughinbaugh, Charles William, 2-born, 3-24 Feb 1923, 12-Aughinbaugh,
    Sidney , 14-Yes, 15-Aughinbaugh
#7841, 1-Thompson, Richard, 2-born, 3-Feb 1921, 12-Thompson, 13-Aughinbaugh, Grace,
    14-Yes, 15-Aughinbaugh
#7842, 1-Thompson, Richard, 2-died, 3-1906, 14-Yes, 15-Aughinbaugh
#7843, 1-Greenawalt, Helen, 2-married, 7-Adams, Daniel Stover, 14-Yes, 15-
    Aughinbaugh
#7844, 1-Adams, Daniel Stover, 2-born, 3-1 Dec 1911, 14-Yes, 15-Aughinbaugh
#7845, 1-Adams, Daniel Stover, 2-died, 3-26 Jan 1957, 14-Yes, 15-Aughinbaugh
#7846, 1-Adams, Frances Brough, 2-born, 3-21 Dec 1935, 12-Adams, Daniel Stover, 13-
    Greenawalt, Helen, 14-Yes, 15-Aughinbaugh
#7847, 1-Adams, Frances Brough, 2-married, 3-15 Jun 1957, 7-Parnell, Ural Clay, 14-
    Yes, 15-Aughinbaugh
#7848, 1-Parnell, Frances Elizabeth, 2-born, 3-3 Apr 1958, 12-Parnell, Ural Clay,
    13-Adams, Frances Brough, 14-Yes, 15-Aughinbaugh
#7849, 1-Parnell, Kathryn Ann, 2-born, 3-2 Dec 1959, 12-Parnell, Ural Clay, 13-
    Adams, Frances Brough, 14-Yes, 15-Aughinbaugh
#7850, 1-Parnell, Daniel, 2-born, 3-4 Mar 1961, 12-Parnell, Ural Clay, 13-Adams,
    Frances Brough, 14-Yes, 15-Aughinbaugh
#7851, 1-Greenawalt, Kathryn, 2-married, 3-23 Feb 1933, 7-Cump, Charles, 14-Yes,
    15-Aughinbaugh
#7852, 1-Cump, Nancy Lou, 2-born, 3-11 May 1937, 12-Cump, Charles, 13-Greenawalt,
    Kathryn, 14-Yes, 15-Aughinbaugh
#7853, 1-Cump, Nancy Lou, 2-married, 7-Severson, Harlan, 12-Cump, Charles, 13-
    Greenawalt, Kathryn, 14-Yes, 15-Aughinbaugh
#7854, 1-Severson, Doyles, 2-born, 3-10 Jan 1957, 12-Severson, Harlan, 13-Cump,
    Nancy Lou, 14-Yes, 15-Aughinbaugh
#7855, 1-Timmins, William, 2-married, 3-18 Jan 1827, 7-Reifsnider, Anna Mariah, 14-
    Yes, 15-Timmins
#7856, 1-Timmins, William Walls, 2-born, 3-15 Oct 1800, 14-Yes, 15-Timmins
#7857, 1-Reifsnider, Anna Mariah, 2-born, 3-24 Apr 1805, 14-Yes, 15-Timmins
#7858, 1-Timmons, Daniel Reifsnider, 2-born, 3-10 Oct 1827, 14-Yes, 15-Timmins
#7859, 1-Timmons, William Walls, 2-born, 3-30 Jan 1830, 14-Yes, 15-Timmins
#7860, 1-Timmons, William Walls, 2-died, 3-28 Jun 1853, 4-Port Gibson, Clayborn
    Co., Mississippi, 14-Yes, 15-Timmins
#7861, 1-Timmons, Philip Shoemaker, 2-born, 3-15 Nov 1831, 14-Yes, 15-Timmins
#7862, 1-Timmons, Philip Shoemaker, 2-died, 4-Andersonville Prison, 6-"Civil War",
    14-Yes, 15-Timmins
#7863, 1-Timmons, Emiyetta[?], 2-born, 3-1 Aug 1833, 14-Yes, 15-Timmins
#7864, 1-Timmons, Susann, 2-born, 3-26 Sep 1835, 14-Yes, 15-Timmins
#7865, 1-Timmons, Rebecca Jane, 2-born, 3-24 Apr 1837, 14-Yes, 15-Timmins
```

FAMILY BIBLE RECORDS IN THE WASHINGTON COUNTY FREE LIBRARY, HAGERSTOWN, MARYLAND

Entry #, 1-Last Name, First Name, 2-Event, 3-Date, 4-Event Location, 5-Age, 6-Other, 7-Spouse's Last, First, 8-Groom's Residence, 9-Bride's Residence, 10-Minister, 11-Minister's Location, 12-Father's Last, First, 13-Mother's Last, First, 14-Transcribed, 15-Family Bible

#7866, 1-Timmons, Rebecca Jane, 2-died, 3-24 Aug 1838, 14-Yes, 15-Timmins
#7867, 1-Timmons, Matilda, 2-born, 3-22 Mar 1839, 14-Yes, 15-Timmins
#7868, 1-Timmons, David Byers, 2-born, 3-18 Nov 1841, 14-Yes, 15-Timmins
#7869, 1-Timmons, Joseph, 2-born, 3-18 Nov 1843, 14-Yes, 15-Timmins
#7870, 1-Timmons, Mary Elizabeth, 2-born, 3-23 Nov 1845, 14-Yes, 15-Timmins
#7871, 1-Timmons, Henry Clay, 2-born, 3-24 Sep 1848, 6-twin, 14-Yes, 15-Timmins
#7872, 1-Timmons, Anna Mariah, 2-born, 3-24 Sep 1848, 6-twin, 14-Yes, 15-Timmins
#7873, 1-Timmons, William Elmer Stake, 2-born, 3-29 May 1861, 14-Yes, 15-Timmins
#7874, 1-Timmons, Anna Mariah (Mrs.), 3-o, 5-77 years 6 months 15 days, 6-lived in Kiefer's Valley; buried in Zion Church Graveyard near Kiefer's Store, 7-Timmins, William W., 14-Yes, 15-Timmins
#7875, 1-Timmons, David B., 2-married, 3-24 Dec 1868, 4-Solomon Gabler's home, 7-Gabler, Mary Ann, 10-Ephraim Dutt, 14-Yes, 15-Timmins
#7876, 1-Timmons, David Byers, 2-born, 3-18 Nov 1841, 4-Roxbury, PA, 14-Yes, 15-Timmins
#7877, 1-Timmons, David Byers, 2-died, 3-6 May 1923, 14-Yes, 15-Timmins
#7878, 1-Timmons, Mary Ann, 2-born, 3-18 Apr 1846, 4-Letterkenny Township, 14-Yes, 15-Timmins
#7879, 1-Timmons, Mary Ann, 2-died, 3-15 Jun 1924, 14-Yes, 15-Timmins
#7880, 1-Timmons, Ida May, 2-born, 3-20 Dec 1869, 4-Letterkenny Township, 14-Yes, 15-Timmins
#7881, 1-Timmons, Ida May, 2-died, 3-20 Apr 1947, 14-Yes, 15-Timmins
#7882, 1-Timmons, William Lane, 2-born, 3-8 Aug 1871, 4-Letterkenny Township, 14-Yes, 15-Timmins
#7883, 1-Timmons, William Lane, 2-died, 3-5Apr 1962, 14-Yes, 15-Timmins
#7884, 1-Timmons, Emma Almeda, 2-born, 3-23 Jul 1875, 4-Letterkenny Township, 14-Yes, 15-Timmins
#7885, 1-Timmons, Emma Almeda, 2-died, 3-22 May 1952, 14-Yes, 15-Timmins
#7886, 1-Timmons, Joseph Edward, 2-born, 3-13 Dec 1878, 4-Letterkenny Township, 14-Yes, 15-Timmins
#7887, 1-Timmons, Joseph Edward, 2-died, 3-22 Jan 1959, 14-Yes, 15-Timmins
#7888, 1-Timmons, Frank Elmer, 2-born, 3-4 Nov 1880, 4-Letterkenny Township, 14-Yes, 15-Timmins
#7889, 1-Timmons, Denton Hartzell, 2-born, 3-26 Jun 1884, 4-Letterkenny Township, 14-Yes, 15-Timmins
#7890, 1-Timmons, Denton Hartzell, 2-died, 3-25 Nov 1962, 14-Yes, 15-Timmins
#7891, 1-Timmons, Daniel Bird, 2-born, 3-8 Oct 1888, 4-Letterkenny Township, 14-Yes, 15-Timmins
#7892, 1-Timmons, Daniel Bird, 2-died, 3-13 Apr 1932, 14-Yes, 15-Timmins
#7893, 1-Greenawalt, Samuel Godfrey, 2-married, 3-11 Dec 1884, 4-Chambersburg, PA, 7-Miller, Mary Ellen, 10-Rev. Ganoe, 14-Yes, 15-Greenawalt
#7894, 1-Greenawalt, S.G., 2-born, 3-3 Jan 1860, 4-Chambersburg, PA, 14-Yes, 15-Greenawalt
#7895, 1-Greenawalt, S.G., 2-married, 3-1884, 14-Yes, 15-Greenawalt
#7896, 1-Greenawalt, S.G., 2-died, 3-7 Mar 1921, 14-Yes, 15-Greenawalt
#7897, 1-Greenawalt, M.E., 2-born, 3-15 Jul 1861, 14-Yes, 15-Greenawalt
#7898, 1-Greenawalt, M.E., 2-married, 3-1884, 14-Yes, 15-Greenawalt
#7899, 1-Greenawalt, M.E., 2-died, 3-28 Jan 1940, 14-Yes, 15-Greenawalt
#7900, 1-Greenawalt, S. Miller, 2-born, 3-15 Mar 1887, 4-Chambersburg, PA, 14-Yes, 15-Greenawalt
#7901, 1-Greenawalt, S. Miller, 2-married, 3-1911, 14-Yes, 15-Greenawalt
#7902, 1-Greenawalt, S. Miller, 2-died, 3-27 Feb 1952, 14-Yes, 15-Greenawalt
#7903, 1-Greenawalt, Margaret B., 2-born, 3-25 Jul 1893, 4-Chambersburg, PA, 14-Yes, 15-Greenawalt
#7904, 1-Greenawalt, Margaret B., 2-married, 3-1917, 14-Yes, 15-Greenawalt

FAMILY BIBLE RECORDS IN THE WASHINGTON COUNTY FREE LIBRARY, HAGERSTOWN, MARYLAND

Entry #, 1-Last Name, First Name, 2-Event, 3-Date, 4-Event Location, 5-Age, 6-Other,
7-Spouse's Last, First, 8-Groom's Residence, 9-Bride's Residence, 10-Minister, 11-Minister's Location,
12-Father's Last, First, 13-Mother's Last, First, 14-Transcribed, 15-Family Bible

```
#7905, 1-Greenawalt, Margaret B., 2-died, 3-16 Jul 1964, 14-Yes, 15-Greenawalt
#7906, 1-Greenawalt, Samuel L., 2-born, 3-26 Jan 1899, 4-Chambersburg, PA, 14-Yes,
    15-Greenawalt
#7907, 1-Greenawalt, Samuel L., 2-married, 3-1927, 14-Yes, 15-Greenawalt
#7908, 1-Greenawalt, Samuel L., 2-died, 3-28 Aug 1964, 14-Yes, 15-Greenawalt
#7909, 1-Greenawalt, William F., 2-born, 3-10 Jul 1903, 4-Chambersburg, PA, 14-Yes,
    15-Greenawalt
#7910, 1-Greenawalt, William F., 2-married, 3-1925, 14-Yes, 15-Greenawalt
#7911, 1-Greenawalt, S. Miller, 2-married, 3-15 Mar 1911, 7-Aughinbaugh, Bertha
    Frances, 14-Yes, 15-Greenawalt
#7912, 1-Aughinbaugh, Bertha Frances, 2-born, 3-8 Jun 1886, 4-Chambersburg, PA, 14-
    Yes, 15-Greenawalt
#7913, 1-Greenawalt, Helen Frances, 2-born, 3-24 Feb 1912, 4-Philadelphia, PA, 12-
    Greenawalt, S. Miller, 13-Aughinbaugh, Bertha Frances, 14-Yes, 15-Greenawalt
#7914, 1-Greenawalt, Helen Frances, 2-married, 3-22 Jul 1934, 7-Adams, Daniel, 12-
    Greenawalt, S. Miller, 13-Aughinbaugh, Bertha Frances, 14-Yes, 15-Greenawalt
#7915, 1-Greenawalt, Kathryn Olivia, 2-born, 3-30 Oct 1913, 4-Chambersburg, PA, 12-
    Greenawalt, S. Miller, 13-Aughinbaugh, Bertha Frances, 14-Yes, 15-Greenawalt
#7916, 1-Greenawalt, Kathryn Olivia, 2-married, 3-22 Feb 1932, 7-Cump, Charles, 12-
    Greenawalt, S. Miller, 13-Aughinbaugh, Bertha Frances, 14-Yes, 15-Greenawalt
#7917, 1-Greenawalt, Lois Jane, 2-born, 3-20 Sep 1919, 4-Chambersburg, PA, 12-
    Greenawalt, S. Miller, 13-Aughinbaugh, Bertha Frances, 14-Yes, 15-Greenawalt
#7918, 1-Greenawalt, Mary Ellen, 2-born, 3-30 Nov 1921, 4-Chambersburg, PA, 12-
    Greenawalt, S. Miller, 13-Aughinbaugh, Bertha Frances, 14-Yes, 15-Greenawalt
#7919, 1-Greenawalt, Margaret B., 2-married, 3-2 Jun 1917, 7-Derbyshire, George
    Henry, 14-Yes, 15-Greenawalt
#7920, 1-Derbyshire, George Henry, 2-born, 3-1 May 1893, 4-Chambersburg, PA, 14-
    Yes, 15-Greenawalt
#7921, 1-Derbyshire, Jr., George Henry, 2-born, 3-31 Mar 1918, 4-Chambersburg, PA,
    12-Derbyshire, George Henry, 13-Greenawalt, Margaret B., 14-Yes, 15-
    Greenawalt
#7922, 1-Derbyshire, Jr., George Henry, 2-married, 3-11 Jan 1941, 7-Cade, Edna, 12-
    Derbyshire, George Henry, 13-Greenawalt, Margaret B., 14-Yes, 15-Greenawalt
#7923, 1-Derbyshire, Henry Godfrey, 2-born, 3-14 Oct 1919, 4-Chambersburg, PA, 12-
    Derbyshire, George Henry, 13-Greenawalt, Margaret B., 14-Yes, 15-Greenawalt
#7924, 1-Derbyshire, Henry Godfrey, 2-married, 3-30 May 1942, 7-Cryder, Barbara,
    12-Derbyshire, George Henry, 13-Greenawalt, Margaret B., 14-Yes, 15-
    Greenawalt
#7925, 1-Derbyshire, Lucille Marie, 2-born, 3-5 May 1925, 4-Ridley Park, PA, 12-
    Derbyshire, George Henry, 13-Greenawalt, Margaret B., 14-Yes, 15-Greenawalt
#7926, 1-Derbyshire, Lucille Marie, 2-married, 3-21 Dec 1946, 7-Granger, Jr.,
    Gordon, 12-Derbyshire, George Henry, 13-Greenawalt, Margaret B., 14-Yes, 15-
    Greenawalt
#7927, 1-Greenawalt, Samuel L., 2-married, 3-8 Oct 1927, 7-Burgner, Mary Josephine,
    14-Yes, 15-Greenawalt
#7928, 1-Burgner, Mary Josephine, 2-born, 3-21 Sep 1905, 4-Lemoyne, PA, 14-Yes, 15-
    Greenawalt
#7929, 1-Greenawalt, Mary Josephine, 2-born, 3-3 Jun 1929, 4-Hagerstown, MD, 12-
    Greenawalt, Samuel L., 13-Burgner, Mary Josephine, 14-Yes, 15-Greenawalt
#7930, 1-Greenawalt, Mary Josephine, 2-married, 3-10 Sep 1949, 7-Murphy, Matthew
    Hilt, 12-Greenawalt, Samuel L., 13-Burgner, Mary Josephine, 14-Yes, 15-
    Greenawalt
#7931, 1-Greenawalt, William F., 2-married, 3-19 Dec 1925, 7-Hollis, Edna, 14-Yes,
    15-Greenawalt
#7932, 1-Hollis, Edna, 2-born, 3-30 Oct 1902, 14-Yes, 15-Greenawalt
```

FAMILY BIBLE RECORDS IN THE WASHINGTON COUNTY FREE LIBRARY, HAGERSTOWN, MARYLAND

Entry #, 1-Last Name, First Name, 2-Event, 3-Date, 4-Event Location, 5-Age, 6-Other, 7-Spouse's Last, First, 8-Groom's Residence, 9-Bride's Residence, 10-Minister, 11-Minister's Location, 12-Father's Last, First, 13-Mother's Last, First, 14-Transcribed, 15-Family Bible

#7933, 1-Greenawalt, Ann Louise, 2-born, 3-25 Feb 1927, 4-Doylestown, PA, 12-Greenawalt, William F., 13-Hollis, Edna, 14-Yes, 15-Greenawalt

#7934, 1-Greenawalt, Ann Louise, 2-married, 3-10 Oct 1948, 7-Haldeman, Harry Harvey, 12-Greenawalt, William F., 13-Hollis, Edna, 14-Yes, 15-Greenawalt

#7935, 1-Greenawalt, Jr., William F., 2-born, 3-23 Dec 1930, 4-Doylestown, PA, 12-Greenawalt, William F., 13-Hollis, Edna, 14-Yes, 15-Greenawalt

#7936, 1-Greenawalt, Carolyn Hollis, 2-born, 3-8 Oct 1934, 4-Doylestown, PA, 12-Greenawalt, William F., 13-Hollis, Edna, 14-Yes, 15-Greenawalt

#7937, 1-Greenawalt, Carolyn Hollis, 2-married, 3-25 Jan 1958, 7-Harris, John Presley, 12-Greenawalt, William F., 13-Hollis, Edna, 14-Yes, 15-Greenawalt

#7938, 1-Greenawalt, Mary Josephine, 2-married, 3-10 Sep 1949, 7-Murphy, Matthew Hilt, 14-Yes, 15-Greenawalt

#7939, 1-Murphy, Matthew Hilt, 2-born, 3-14 Jul 1923, 14-Yes, 15-Greenawalt

#7940, 1-Murphy, Mary Lois, 2-born, 3-11 Feb 1951, 4-Bronxville, NY, 12-Murphy, Matthew Hilt, 13-Greenawalt, Mary Josphine, 14-Yes, 15-Greenawalt

#7941, 1-Murphy, Matthew Samuel, 2-born, 3-10 Jun 1955, 4-Bronxville, NY, 12-Murphy, Matthew Hilt, 13-Greenawalt, Mary Josphine, 14-Yes, 15-Greenawalt

#7942, 1-Bachtel, John Jacob, 2-born, 3-6 Mar 1750, 14-Yes, 15-Bachtell

#7943, 1-Letch, Catharine, 2-born, 3-15 Apr 1755, 7-Bachtel, John Jacob, 14-Yes, 15-Bachtell

#7944, 1-Letch, Catharine, 2-married, 3-16 Mar 1773, 6-"lived also in Conamaughville, near Johnstown, PA", 7-Bachtel, John Jacob, 14-Yes, 15-Bachtell

#7945, 1-Bachtel, John Jacob, 2-born, 3-10 Feb 1774, 6-"eldest John", 14-Yes, 15-Bachtell

#7946, 1-Bachtel, George, 2-born, 3-14 Oct 1775, 14-Yes, 15-Bachtell

#7947, 1-Bachtel, Magdalene, 2-born, 3-3 Dec 1777, 14-Yes, 15-Bachtell

#7948, 1-Bachtel, John Jacob, 2-born, 3-9 Oct 1779, 4-Washington Co., MD, 14-Yes, 15-Bachtell

#7949, 1-Bachtel, Jno. Martin, 2-born, 3-26 Oct 1783, 4-Washington Co., MD, 14-Yes, 15-Bachtell

#7950, 1-Bachtel, Anna Barbara, 2-born, 3-5 Nov 1786, 14-Yes, 15-Bachtell

#7951, 1-Bachtel, Frederick, 2-born, 3-21 Mar 1789, 14-Yes, 15-Bachtell

#7952, 1-Bachtel, Anna Mary, 2-born, 3-5 Nov 1791, 14-Yes, 15-Bachtell

#7953, 1-Bachtel, Daniel, 2-born, 3-28 Aug 1793, 14-Yes, 15-Bachtell

#7954, 1-Bachtel, Thomas, 2-born, 3-17 Feb 1796, 14-Yes, 15-Bachtell

#7955, 1-Bachtel, David, 2-born, 3-13 Jun 1798, 14-Yes, 15-Bachtell

#7956, 1-Hamaker, Sr., Adam, 2-born, 3-1717, 14-Yes, 15-Bachtell

#7957, 1-Hamaker, Sr., Adam, 2-died, 3-1784, 14-Yes, 15-Bachtell

#7958, 1-Hamaker, John Hubrect, 6-brother of Adam Hamaker, Sr., 14-Yes, 15-Bachtell

#7959, 1-Hamaker, Samuel, 2-married, 7-Overdear, Anna, 12-Hamaker, Jr., Adam, 14-Yes, 15-Bachtell

#7960, 1-Overdear, Polly, 2-married, 4-near Williamsport, MD, 7-Miller, 14-Yes, 15-Bachtell

#7961, 1-Hamaker, Peter, 2-born, 3-11 Jan 1792, 14-Yes, 15-Bachtell

#7962, 1-Hamaker, Peter, 2-married, 3-21 Oct 1817, 7-Krouse, Elizabeth, 14-Yes, 15-Bachtell

#7963, 1-Krouse, Elizabeth, 2-born, 3-31 Jul 1795, 12-Krouse, Peter, 13-Krouse, Mary, 14-Yes, 15-Bachtell

#7964, 1-Hamaker, Maria, 2-born, 3-15 Jul 1818, 6-twin, 12-Hamaker, Peter, 13-Krouse, Elizabeth, 14-Yes, 15-Bachtell

#7965, 1-Hamaker, Anna, 2-born, 3-15 Jul 1818, 6-twin, 12-Hamaker, Peter, 13-Krouse, Elizabeth, 14-Yes, 15-Bachtell

#7966, 1-Hamaker, Ephraim, 2-born, 3-Aug 1821, 12-Hamaker, Peter, 13-Krouse, Elizabeth, 14-Yes, 15-Bachtell

FAMILY BIBLE RECORDS IN THE WASHINGTON COUNTY FREE LIBRARY, HAGERSTOWN, MARYLAND

Entry #, 1-Last Name, First Name, 2-Event, 3-Date, 4-Event Location, 5-Age, 6-Other,
7-Spouse's Last, First, 8-Groom's Residence, 9-Bride's Residence, 10-Minister, 11-Minister's Location,
12-Father's Last, First, 13-Mother's Last, First, 14-Transcribed, 15-Family Bible

```
#7967, 1-Hamaker, Ephraim, 2-died, 3-15 Nov 1880, 12-Hamaker, Peter, 13-Krouse,
    Elizabeth, 14-Yes, 15-Bachtell
#7968, 1-Hamaker, Solomon, 2-born, 3-6 Mar 1825, 12-Hamaker, Peter, 13-Krouse,
    Elizabeth, 14-Yes, 15-Bachtell
#7969, 1-Hamaker, Solomon, 2-died, 3-1855, 12-Hamaker, Peter, 13-Krouse, Elizabeth,
    14-Yes, 15-Bachtell
#7970, 1-Hamaker, Sophia, 2-born, 3-13 Mar 1827, 12-Hamaker, Peter, 13-Krouse,
    Elizabeth, 14-Yes, 15-Bachtell
#7971, 1-Hamaker, Sophia, 2-died, 3-27 Aug 1891, 4-Cavetown, MD, 12-Hamaker, Peter,
    13-Krouse, Elizabeth, 14-Yes, 15-Bachtell
#7972, 1-Hamaker, Danl., 2-born, 3-2 Nov 1829, 12-Hamaker, Peter, 13-Krouse,
    Elizabeth, 14-Yes, 15-Bachtell
#7973, 1-Hamaker, Danl., 2-died, 3-1898, 4-Pondsville, 12-Hamaker, Peter, 13-
    Krouse, Elizabeth, 14-Yes, 15-Bachtell
#7974, 1-Hamill, Wm., 2-married, 3-1 Oct 1812, 7-Galbraith, Dorcas, 14-Yes, 15-
    Bachtell
#7975, 1-Hamill, S.B., 2-born, 14-Yes, 15-Bachtell
#7976, 1-Hamill, Mary, 2-born, 3-9 Sep 1816, 14-Yes, 15-Bachtell
#7977, 1-Hamill, Robert, 2-born, 3-19 Apr 1816, 14-Yes, 15-Bachtell
#7978, 1-Hamill, Robert, 2-married, 7-Royer, Jane, 14-Yes, 15-Bachtell
#7979, 1-Hamill, Wm., 2-married, 3-2 Apr 1818, 7-Ashman, Rebecca, 14-Yes, 15-
    Bachtell
#7980, 1-Ashman, Rebecca, 2-born, 3-14 Feb 1790, 14-Yes, 15-Bachtell
#7981, 1-Hamill, Ashman, 2-born, 3-9 Oct 1819, 4-Martinsburg, WV, 12-Hamill, Wm.,
    13-Ashman, Rebecca, 14-Yes, 15-Bachtell
#7982, 1-Hamill, Wm. Cromwell, 2-born, 3-Aug 1821, 12-Hamill, Wm., 13-Ashman,
    Rebecca, 14-Yes, 15-Bachtell
#7983, 1-Hamill, Eliz., 2-born, 3-Jul 1823, 12-Hamill, Wm., 13-Ashman, Rebecca, 14-
    Yes, 15-Bachtell
#7984, 1-Hamill, Eleanor, 2-born, 3-29 Apr 1827, 12-Hamill, Wm., 13-Ashman,
    Rebecca, 14-Yes, 15-Bachtell
#7985, 1-Hamill, Eleanor, 2-married, 7-Wigton, R. Benton, 12-Hamill, Wm., 13-
    Ashman, Rebecca, 14-Yes, 15-Bachtell
#7986, 1-Hamill, Rebecca, 2-born, 3-10 Apr 1830, 12-Hamill, Wm., 13-Ashman,
    Rebecca, 14-Yes, 15-Bachtell
#7987, 1-Hamill, George, 2-born, 3-7 Oct 1823, 4-Jef. Co., VA, 12-Hamill, James,
    13-Hamill, Mary, 14-Yes, 15-Bachtell
#7988, 1-Hamill, E.B. (Dr.), 2-married, 3-22 Nov 1853, 7-Hughes, Irene, 12-Hamill,
    Wm., 13-Ashman, Rebecca, 14-Yes, 15-Bachtell
#7989, 1-Hamill, Mary Eliz., 2-born, 3-15 Dec 1854, 14-Yes, 15-Bachtell
#7990, 1-Hamill, Irene Hughes, 2-born, 3-2 Mar 1856, 14-Yes, 15-Bachtell
#7991, 1-Hamill, Mary Eliz., 2-married, 3-9 Mar 1875, 7-Bullen , W. (Capt.), 14-
    Yes, 15-Bachtell
#7992, 1-Hamill, Irene Hughes, 2-married, 3-25 Jun 1879, 7-Bachtel, H.A. (Prof.),
    14-Yes, 15-Bachtell
#7993, 1-Bullen, Sallie, 2-born, 12-Bullen, W. (Capt.), 13-Hamill, Mary Eliz., 14-
    Yes, 15-Bachtell
#7994, 1-Bullen, Bessie, 2-born, 12-Bullen, W. (Capt.), 13-Hamill, Mary Eliz., 14-
    Yes, 15-Bachtell
#7995, 1-Bullen, Fannie, 2-born, 12-Bullen, W. (Capt.), 13-Hamill, Mary Eliz., 14-
    Yes, 15-Bachtell
#7996, 1-Hooper, Mary Cath., 2-born, 3-24 May 1859, 14-Yes, 15-Bachtell
#7997, 1-Hooper, Mary Cath., 2-died, 3-16 Jan 1897, 4-Martinsusrg, WV, 6-buried
    Greencastle, PA, 14-Yes, 15-Bachtell
#7998, 1-Hamill, Geo. A., 2-born, 3-5 Apr 1860, 14-Yes, 15-Bachtell
```

FAMILY BIBLE RECORDS IN THE WASHINGTON COUNTY FREE LIBRARY, HAGERSTOWN, MARYLAND

Entry #, 1-Last Name, First Name, 2-Event, 3-Date, 4-Event Location, 5-Age, 6-Other,
7-Spouse's Last, First, 8-Groom's Residence, 9-Bride's Residence, 10-Minister, 11-Minister's Location,
12-Father's Last, First, 13-Mother's Last, First, 14-Transcribed, 15-Family Bible

```
#7999, 1-Hamill, DDS, Geo. Ashman (Dr.), 2-died, 3-Apr 1901, 5-45 years, 14-Yes,
    15-Bachtell
#8000, 1-Richardson, Francis Samuel, 2-born, 3-22 Nov 1870, 12-Richardson, Daniel
    Stewart, 13-Richardson, Sallie J., 14-Yes, 15-Bachtell
#8001, 1-Richardson, Clarenc Rich., 2-born, 3-24 Oct 1872, 12-Richardson, Daniel
    Stewart, 13-Richardson, Sallie J., 14-Yes, 15-Bachtell
#8002, 1-Richardson, Wm. Alfred, 2-born, 3-11 Feb 1874, 12-Richardson, Daniel
    Stewart, 13-Richardson, Sallie J., 14-Yes, 15-Bachtell
#8003, 1-Richardson, Robert Howard, 2-born, 3-19 Jul 1876, 12-Richardson, Daniel
    Stewart, 13-Richardson, Sallie J., 14-Yes, 15-Bachtell
#8004, 1-Richardson, Harry Earnest, 2-born, 3-22 Sep 1878, 12-Richardson, Daniel
    Stewart, 13-Richardson, Sallie J., 14-Yes, 15-Bachtell
#8005, 1-Bachtel, Henry A., 2-born, 3-30 Apr 1854, 12-Bachtel, Samuel, 13-Bachtel,
    Anna B., 14-Yes, 15-Bachtell
#8006, 1-Bachtel, Irene H., 2-born, 3-2 Mar 1856, 12-Hamill, E.B. (Dr.), 14-Yes,
    15-Bachtell
#8007, 1-Bachtel, Samuel A., 2-born, 3-21 Mar 1814, 4-"Huyett's, now owned by
    Joshua Houck (1895)", 14-Yes, 15-Bachtell
#8008, 1-Hammaker, Anna, 2-born, 3-15 Jul 1818, 4-Stoner's Mill, near Waynesboro,
    PA, 12-Hammaker, Peter, 13-Krouse, Elizabeth, 14-Yes, 15-Bachtell
#8009, 1-Bachtel, Jacob L., 2-born, 3-26 Oct 1841, 4-Grandfather Hammaker's farm,
    near Shank's Church, 12-Bachtel, Samuel A., 13-Hammaker, Anna, 14-Yes, 15-
    Bachtell
#8010, 1-Bachtel, Peter Cornelius, 2-born, 3-14 Jul 1843, 4-Beard's farm,
    Chewsville, 12-Bachtel, Samuel A., 13-Hammaker, Anna, 14-Yes, 15-Bachtell
#8011, 1-Bachtel, Wm. L., 2-born, 3-22 Mar 1845, 4-Peter Krouse farm, near
    Cavetown, MD, 12-Bachtel, Samuel A., 13-Hammaker, Anna, 14-Yes, 15-Bachtell
#8012, 1-Bachtel, Daniel Stewart, 2-born, 3-10 Mar 1847, 12-Bachtel, Samuel A., 13-
    Hammaker, Anna, 14-Yes, 15-Bachtell
#8013, 1-Bachtel, Mary E., 2-born, 3-22 Feb 1849, 12-Bachtel, Samuel A., 13-
    Hammaker, Anna, 14-Yes, 15-Bachtell
#8014, 1-Bachtel, Benj. H., 2-born, 3-12 Mar 1851, 6-"lived 5 days", 12-Bachtel,
    Samuel A., 13-Hammaker, Anna, 14-Yes, 15-Bachtell
#8015, 1-Bachtel, Margaret Ann, 2-born, 3-12 Feb 1852, 4-"Desert Farm, Beard's
    Church", 12-Bachtel, Samuel A., 13-Hammaker, Anna, 14-Yes, 15-Bachtell
#8016, 1-Bachtel, Henry Alfred, 2-born, 3-30 Apr 1854, 4-above Cavetown, MD, 12-
    Bachtel, Samuel A., 13-Hammaker, Anna, 14-Yes, 15-Bachtell
#8017, 1-Bachtel, Emma S., 2-born, 3-17 Dec 1858, 4-Pondsville, 12-Bachtel, Samuel
    A., 13-Hammaker, Anna, 14-Yes, 15-Bachtell
#8018, 1-Bachtel, Ellen Sophia, 2-born, 3-12 Feb 1862, 4-"near present house, now
    Geo. Noel's, Cavehill, lived there during Civil War", 12-Bachtel, Samuel A.,
    13-Hammaker, Anna, 14-Yes, 15-Bachtell
#8019, 1-Bachtel, Henry Alfred, 2-married, 3-25 Jun 1879, 4-Clear Spring, MD, 7-
    Hamill, Irene Hughes, 10-Rev. C.R. Page, 14-Yes, 15-Bachtell
#8020, 1-Bachtel, Samuel A., 2-married, 3-21 Jan 1840, 4-near Cavetown, MD, 6-
    "lived 28 years", 7-Hammaker, Anna, 14-Yes, 15-Bachtell
#8021, 1-Bachtel, Jacob L., 2-married, 3-10 Jan 1865, 4-Smithsburg, MD, 6-bride is
    described as sister to Frisby Stouffer, 7-Snyder, Kate, 14-Yes, 15-Bachtell
#8022, 1-Bachtel, Daniel S., 2-married, 4-Holden, MO, 7-Richardson, Sallie, 14-Yes,
    15-Bachtell
#8023, 1-Bachtel, Henry A., 2-married, 3-25 Jun 1879, 4-Clear Spring, MD, 7-Hamill,
    Irene Hughes, 14-Yes, 15-Bachtell
#8024, 1-Bachtel, Emma S., 2-married, 3-18 Dec 1885, 7-Oswald, Allen Heck, 14-Yes,
    15-Bachtell
#8025, 1-Bachtel, Mary E., 2-married, 7-Witmer, Milton, 14-Yes, 15-Bachtell
```

FAMILY BIBLE RECORDS IN THE WASHINGTON COUNTY FREE LIBRARY, HAGERSTOWN, MARYLAND

Entry #, 1-Last Name, First Name, 2-Event, 3-Date, 4-Event Location, 5-Age, 6-Other, 7-Spouse's Last, First, 8-Groom's Residence, 9-Bride's Residence, 10-Minister, 11-Minister's Location, 12-Father's Last, First, 13-Mother's Last, First, 14-Transcribed, 15-Family Bible

#8026, 1-Bachtel, Margaret A., 2-married, 7-Stephey, Daniel, 14-Yes, 15-Bachtell

#8027, 1-Bachtel, Samuel Augustua, 2-died, 3-22 Mar 1895, 4-near Cavetown, MD, 5-81 years 1 days, 14-Yes, 15-Bachtell

#8028, 1-Bachtel, Benjamin F., 2-died, 3-17 Mar 1851, 5-5 days, 14-Yes, 15-Bachtell

#8029, 1-Bachtel, Ellen Sophia, 2-died, 3-16 Mar 1863/1864, 14-Yes, 15-Bachtell

#8030, 1-Bachtel, Peter C., 2-died, 3-16 Jul 1865, 14-Yes, 15-Bachtell

#8031, 1-Richardson, Sallie J., 2-died, 3-25 Aug 1880, 7-Bachtel, Danl. S., 14-Yes, 15-Bachtell

#8032, 1-Bachtell, Anna Hammaker Krouse, 2-died, 3-6 Apr 1900, 4-near Cavetown, MD, 14-Yes, 15-Bachtell

#8033, 1-Hammaker, Anna, 2-born, 4-Ingram's Mill near Smithsburg, MD, 14-Yes, 15-Bachtell

#8034, 1-Hammaker, Mary, 2-married, 6-twin of Anna Hammaker Bachtel, 7-Royer, Saul, 14-Yes, 15-Bachtell

#8035, 1-Krouse, [father of Elizabeth], 2-born, 3-1773, 4-Germany, 6-came to Baltimore in 1788, aged 15 years, 14-Yes, 15-Bachtell

#8036, 1-Krouse, [father of Elizabeth], 2-married, 4-1805, 7-Wolf, (Miss), 14-Yes, 15-Bachtell

#8037, 1-Krouse, [father of Elizabeth], 2-died, 3-1843, 6-buried Beard's Church, 14-Yes, 15-Bachtell

#8038, 1-Hammaker, Ephraim, 2-married, 7-Shank, Susan, 14-Yes, 15-Bachtell

#8039, 1-Hammaker, Adam, 12-Hammaker, Ephraim, 13-Shank, Susan, 14-Yes, 15-Bachtell

#8040, 1-Hammaker, Peter, 12-Hammaker, Ephraim, 13-Shank, Susan, 14-Yes, 15-Bachtell

#8041, 1-Hammaker, Amanda, 12-Hammaker, Ephraim, 13-Shank, Susan, 14-Yes, 15-Bachtell

#8042, 1-Hammaker, Amanda, 2-married, 7-Snavely, 12-Hammaker, Ephraim, 13-Shank, Susan, 14-Yes, 15-Bachtell

#8043, 1-Hammaker, Saml., 12-Hammaker, Ephraim, 13-Shank, Susan, 14-Yes, 15-Bachtell

#8044, 1-Hammaker, Stewart, 12-Hammaker, Ephraim, 13-Shank, Susan, 14-Yes, 15-Bachtell

#8045, 1-Hammaker, Lizzie, 12-Hammaker, Ephraim, 13-Shank, Susan, 14-Yes, 15-Bachtell

#8046, 1-Royer, Saml., 2-married, 7-Hammaker, Mary, 14-Yes, 15-Bachtell

#8047, 1-Royer, Dan., 12-Royer, Saml., 13-Hammaker, Mary, 14-Yes, 15-Bachtell

#8048, 1-Royer, Jno., 12-Royer, Saml., 13-Hammaker, Mary, 14-Yes, 15-Bachtell

#8049, 1-Royer, Thos., 12-Royer, Saml., 13-Hammaker, Mary, 14-Yes, 15-Bachtell

#8050, 1-Royer, Mary, 12-Royer, Saml., 13-Hammaker, Mary, 14-Yes, 15-Bachtell

#8051, 1-Royer, Mary, 2-married, 7-Nichols, 12-Royer, Saml., 13-Hammaker, Mary, 14-Yes, 15-Bachtell

#8052, 1-Royer, Lizzie, 12-Royer, Saml., 13-Hammaker, Mary, 14-Yes, 15-Bachtell

#8053, 1-Royer, [female], 12-Royer, Saml., 13-Hammaker, Mary, 14-Yes, 15-Bachtell

#8054, 1-Royer, [female], 2-married, 7-Nichol, 12-Royer, Saml., 13-Hammaker, Mary, 14-Yes, 15-Bachtell

#8055, 1-Royer, Ella, 12-Royer, Saml., 13-Hammaker, Mary, 14-Yes, 15-Bachtell

#8056, 1-Royer, Ella, 2-married, 7-Wassler, 12-Royer, Saml., 13-Hammaker, Mary, 14-Yes, 15-Bachtell

#8057, 1-Fasnacht, Henry, 2-born, 3-26 Jan 1812, 14-Yes, 15-Fasnacht

#8058, 1-Ross, Lidia, 2-born, 3-26 Nov 1811, 14-Yes, 15-Fasnacht

#8059, 1-Fasnacht, Elizabeth Ann, 2-born, 3-30 May 1848, 14-Yes, 15-Fasnacht

#8060, 1-Fasnacht, Sarah Jane, 2-born, 3-19 May 1851, 14-Yes, 15-Fasnacht

#8061, 1-Fasnacht, Henry, 2-died, 3-19 Nov 1857, 14-Yes, 15-Fasnacht

#8062, 1-Fasnacht, Lidia, 2-died, 3-11 Jul 1891, 14-Yes, 15-Fasnacht

#8063, 1-Kuhn, John Joseph, 2-born, 3-22 Feb 1873, 15-Kuhn

FAMILY BIBLE RECORDS IN THE WASHINGTON COUNTY FREE LIBRARY, HAGERSTOWN, MARYLAND

Entry #, 1-Last Name, First Name, 2-Event, 3-Date, 4-Event Location, 5-Age, 6-Other,
7-Spouse's Last, First, 8-Groom's Residence, 9-Bride's Residence, 10-Minister, 11-Minister's Location,
12-Father's Last, First, 13-Mother's Last, First, 14-Transcribed, 15-Family Bible

```
#8064, 1-Kuhn, Jacob Frederic, 2-born, 3-13 Dec 1874, 15-Kuhn
#8065, 1-Kuhn, Ada Viola, 2-born, 3-2 Jul 1877, 15-Kuhn
#8066, 1-Kuhn, Frank Brewer, 2-born, 3-28 Dec 1879, 15-Kuhn
#8067, 1-Kuhn, Libbie, 2-born, 3-10 Jan 1881, 15-Kuhn
#8068, 1-Kuhn, Elva Louise, 2-born, 3-1 Dec 1883, 15-Kuhn
#8069, 1-Ingram, J. Wilbur, 2-born, 3-11 Aug 1908, 15-Kuhn
#8070, 1-Ingram, R. Leon, 2-born, 3-12 Apr 1923, 15-Kuhn
#8071, 1-Kuhn, Anna Amelia, 2-died, 3-4 Sep 1868, 12-Kuhn, John, 13-Kuhn, Mahalah,
    15-Kuhn
#8072, 1-Kuhn, Minnie Amanda, 2-died, 3-7 May6 1876, 12-Kuhn, John, 13-Kuhn,
    Mahalah, 15-Kuhn
#8073, 1-Kuhn, John Joseph, 2-died, 3-25 Mar 1893, 15-Kuhn
#8074, 1-Kuhn, Frank, 2-died, 3-22 Jul 1930, 15-Kuhn
#8075, 1-Kuhn, John, 2-born, 3-23 Nov 1841, 15-Kuhn
#8076, 1-Kuhn, John, 2-died, 3-16 Aug 1910, 12-Kuhn, Jacob, 13-Lutz, Nancy, 15-Kuhn
#8077, 1-Kuhn, Mahala, 2-born, 3-19 Nov 1844, 15-Kuhn
#8078, 1-Kuhn, Mahala, 2-died, 3-20 Mar 1920, 12-Brewer, Joseph, 13-Snyder, Hester,
    15-Kuhn
#8079, 1-Kuhn, Harry G., 2-died, 3-22 Dec 1941, 12-Kuhn, John, 13-Kuhn, Mahala, 15-
    Kuhn
#8080, 1-Brewer, Antoinette , 2-died, 3-31 Dec 1921, 6-sister of Mahala Brewer
    Kuhn, 15-Kuhn
#8081, 1-Kuhn, Jacob Frederick, 2-died, 3-7 Mar 1954, 12-Kuhn, John, 13-Kuhn,
    Mahala, 15-Kuhn
#8082, 1-Kuhn, Anna Amelia, 2-died, 3-4 Sep 1868, 15-Kuhn
#8083, 1-Kuhn, Mary Amanda, 2-died, 3-7 May 1876, 15-Kuhn
#8084, 1-Kuhn, Jacob Frederick, 2-died, 3-7 Mar 1954, 15-Kuhn
#8085, 1-Kuhn, John Joseph, 2-born, 3-22 Feb 1873, 15-Kuhn
#8086, 1-Kuhn, John Joseph, 2-died, 3-25 Mar 1893, 5-20 years 1 months 3 days, 15-
    Kuhn
#8087, 1-Kuhn, Harry Gustavus, 2-born, 3-21 Mar 1866, 12-Kuhn, John, 13-Kuhn,
    Mahala, 15-Kuhn
#8088, 1-Kuhn, Harry Gustavus, 2-died, 3-22 Dec 1941, 12-Kuhn, John, 13-Kuhn,
    Mahala, 15-Kuhn
#8089, 1-Kuhn, Anna Amelia, 2-born, 3-30 Jun 1867, 12-Kuhn, John, 13-Kuhn, Mahala,
    15-Kuhn
#8090, 1-Kuhn, Anna Amelia, 2-died, 3-4 Sep 1868, 12-Kuhn, John, 13-Kuhn, Mahala,
    15-Kuhn
#8091, 1-Kuhn, Mary Amanda, 2-born, 3-20 Jan 1869, 12-Kuhn, John, 13-Kuhn, Mahala,
    15-Kuhn
#8092, 1-Kuhn, Mary Amanda, 2-died, 3-7 May 1876, 12-Kuhn, John, 13-Kuhn, Mahala,
    15-Kuhn
#8093, 1-Kuhn, Edward Abraham, 2-born, 3-4 May 1871, 12-Kuhn, John, 13-Kuhn,
    Mahala, 15-Kuhn
#8094, 1-Kuhn, Edward Abraham, 2-died, 3-15 Mar 1931, 12-Kuhn, John, 13-Kuhn,
    Mahala, 15-Kuhn
#8095, 1-Kuhn, John Joseph, 2-born, 3-22 Feb 1873, 12-Kuhn, John, 13-Kuhn, Mahala,
    15-Kuhn
#8096, 1-Kuhn, John Joseph, 2-died, 3-25 Mar 1893, 12-Kuhn, John, 13-Kuhn, Mahala,
    15-Kuhn
#8097, 1-Kuhn, Jacob Frederic, 2-born, 3-13 Dec 1874, 12-Kuhn, John, 13-Kuhn,
    Mahala, 15-Kuhn
#8098, 1-Kuhn, Jacob Frederic, 2-died, 3-7 Mar 1954, 12-Kuhn, John, 13-Kuhn,
    Mahala, 15-Kuhn
```

FAMILY BIBLE RECORDS IN THE WASHINGTON COUNTY FREE LIBRARY, HAGERSTOWN, MARYLAND

Entry #, 1-Last Name, First Name, 2-Event, 3-Date, 4-Event Location, 5-Age, 6-Other, 7-Spouse's Last, First, 8-Groom's Residence, 9-Bride's Residence, 10-Minister, 11-Minister's Location, 12-Father's Last, First, 13-Mother's Last, First, 14-Transcribed, 15-Family Bible

#8099, 1-Kuhn, Ada Viola, 2-born, 3-2 Jul 1877, 12-Kuhn, John, 13-Kuhn, Mahala, 15-Kuhn

#8100, 1-Kuhn, Ada Viola, 2-died, 3-13 Sep 1960, 12-Kuhn, John, 13-Kuhn, Mahala, 15-Kuhn

#8101, 1-Kuhn, Frank Brewer, 2-born, 3-28 Dec 1879, 12-Kuhn, John, 13-Kuhn, Mahala, 15-Kuhn

#8102, 1-Kuhn, Frank Brewer, 2-died, 3-22 Jul 1930, 12-Kuhn, John, 13-Kuhn, Mahala, 15-Kuhn

#8103, 1-Kuhn, Libbie G., 2-born, 3-10 Jan 1881, 12-Kuhn, John, 13-Kuhn, Mahala, 15-Kuhn

#8104, 1-Kuhn, Elva Louise, 2-born, 3-1 Dec 1883, 12-Kuhn, John, 13-Kuhn, Mahala, 15-Kuhn

#8105, 1-Ingram, J. Wilbur, 2-born, 3-11 Aug 1908, 12-Ingram, J. Roy, 13-Ingram, Elva L., 15-Kuhn

#8106, 1-Ingram, R. Leon, 2-born, 3-12 Apr 1923[?], 12-Ingram, J. Roy, 13-Ingram, Elva L., 15-Kuhn

#8107, 1-Cordell, David C., 2-born, 3-21 Jun 1847, 14-Yes, 15-Cordell

#8108, 1-Cordell, David C., 2-died, 3-22 Dec 1915, 14-Yes, 15-Cordell

#8109, 1-Cordell, John Andrew, 2-born, 3-11 Feb 1882, 14-Yes, 15-Cordell

#8110, 1-Cordell, Benjamin Franklin, 2-born, 3-16 Sep 1890, 14-Yes, 15-Cordell

#8111, 1-Cordell, Samuel David, 2-born, 3-16 Jun 1897, 14-Yes, 15-Cordell

#8112, 1-Cordell, Lucye V., 2-born, 3-29 Jun 1904, 14-Yes, 15-Cordell

#8113, 1-Stull, Dortha, 2-born, 3-26 Jan 1810, 14-Yes, 15-Cordell

#8114, 1-Cordell, John Andrew, 2-died, 3-17 Mar 1883, 14-Yes, 15-Cordell

#8115, 1-Cordell, Benjamin Franklin, 2-born, 3-6 Oct 1911, 14-Yes, 15-Cordell

#8116, 1-Cordell, Ruth Irine, 2-born, 3-23 Mar 1913, 14-Yes, 15-Cordell

#8117, 1-Bovey, Henry, 2-married, 3-18 Apr 1842, 7-[blank], Maria Ellen, 14-Yes, 15-Bovey

#8118, 1-Bovey, Henry, 2-born, 3-16 Jan 1819, 12-Bovey, G., 13-Bovey, C., 14-Yes, 15-Bovey

#8119, 1-Martin, Maria Ellen, 2-born, 3-21 Dec 1821, 12-Martin, H., 13-Martin, M., 14-Yes, 15-Bovey

#8120, 1-Bovey, Lavinia Jane, 2-born, 3-21 Jan 1845, 12-Bovey, Henry, 13-Bovey, Maria, 14-Yes, 15-Bovey

#8121, 1-Bovey, Mary Catharine, 2-born, 3-29 Mar 1846, 12-Bovey, Henry, 13-Bovey, Maria, 14-Yes, 15-Bovey

#8122, 1-Bovey, Luther Martin, 2-born, 3-4 Aug 1847, 12-Bovey, Henry, 13-Bovey, Maria, 14-Yes, 15-Bovey

#8123, 1-Bovey, George Henry, 2-born, 3-18 Feb 1850, 12-Bovey, Henry, 13-Bovey, Maria, 14-Yes, 15-Bovey

#8124, 1-Bovey, Ellen Mussouri[?], 2-born, 3-11 Oct 1851, 12-Bovey, Henry, 13-Bovey, Maria, 14-Yes, 15-Bovey

#8125, 1-Bovey, Anna Cecelia, 2-born, 3-31 May 1854, 12-Bovey, Henry, 13-Bovey, Maria, 14-Yes, 15-Bovey

#8126, 1-Bovey, Millard Claggett, 2-born, 3-26 Feb 1857, 12-Bovey, Henry, 13-Bovey, Maria, 14-Yes, 15-Bovey

#8127, 1-Bovey, Lillie May, 2-born, 3-26 Mar 1859, 12-Bovey, Henry, 13-Bovey, Maria, 14-Yes, 15-Bovey

#8128, 1-Bovey, Jacob, 2-born, 3-18 Feb 1861, 12-Bovey, Henry, 13-Bovey, Maria, 14-Yes, 15-Bovey

#8129, 1-Bovey, Flora Belle, 2-born, 3-1865, 12-Bovey, Henry, 13-Bovey, Maria, 14-Yes, 15-Bovey

#8130, 1-Bovey, Edward O., 2-born, 3-8 Dec 1868, 12-Bovey, Henry, 13-Bovey, Maria, 14-Yes, 15-Bovey

#8131, 1-Bovey, Ellen Missouri, 2-died, 3-Mar 1855, 5-3 years, 14-Yes, 15-Bovey

FAMILY BIBLE RECORDS IN THE WASHINGTON COUNTY FREE LIBRARY, HAGERSTOWN, MARYLAND

Entry #, 1-Last Name, First Name, 2-Event, 3-Date, 4-Event Location, 5-Age, 6-Other,
7-Spouse's Last, First, 8-Groom's Residence, 9-Bride's Residence, 10-Minister, 11-Minister's Location,
12-Father's Last, First, 13-Mother's Last, First, 14-Transcribed, 15-Family Bible

#8132, 1-Bovey, Jacob Reel, 2-died, 3-21 Feb 1862, 5-1 months 23 days, 14-Yes, 15-Bovey

#8133, 1-Bovey, Flora Belle, 2-died, 3-5 Oct 1864, 5-1 years 2 months 5 days, 14-Yes, 15-Bovey

#8134, 1-Bovey, Maria Ellen, 2-died, 3-18 Oct 1888, 5-66 years 9 months 27 days, 14-Yes, 15-Bovey

#8135, 1-Bovey, Henry, 2-died, 3-13 Dec 1902, 5-85 years 10 months 26 days, 14-Yes, 15-Bovey

#8136, 1-Bovey, Mary Catharine, 2-died, 3-9 Jul 1914, 5-65 years 3 months 10 days, 14-Yes, 15-Bovey

#8137, 1-Bovey, Edward O., 2-died, 3-15 Apr 1931, 5-62 years 4 months 7 days, 14-Yes, 15-Bovey

#8138, 1-Bovey, Anna C., 2-died, 3-12 Sep 1933, 5-79 years 4 months 5 days, 14-Yes, 15-Bovey

#8139, 1-Middlekauff, Leonard, 2-born, 3-24 Sep 1807, 14-Yes, 15-Middlekauff

#8140, 1-Middlekauff, Polly, 2-born, 3-22 May 1815, 14-Yes, 15-Middlekauff

#8141, 1-Middlekauff, Corneae Cunningham, 2-born, 3-29 Mar 1834, 14-Yes, 15-Middlekauff

#8142, 1-Middlekauff, An Susen, 2-born, 3-23 May 1836, 14-Yes, 15-Middlekauff

#8143, 1-Schlosser, Elizabeth, 2-born, 3-16 Dec 1809, 4-Bendersvill, Adams Co., PA, 12-Schlosser, John, 14-Yes, 15-Middlekauff

#8144, 1-Middlekauff, Samuel Clenton, 2-born, 3-14 Mar 1864, 14-Yes, 15-Middlekauff

#8145, 1-Middlekauff, Mary A. Eliz.[?], 2-born, 3-18 Dec 1867, 14-Yes, 15-Middlekauff

#8146, 1-Middlekauff, Walter Cornelius, 2-born, 3-15 Feb 1871, 14-Yes, 15-Middlekauff

#8147, 1-Middlekauff, Leonard, 2-married, 3-24 Feb 1831, 7-Bragunier, Mary (Miss), 14-Yes, 15-Middlekauff

#8148, 1-Middlekauff, Jr., Leonard, 2-married, 3-10 Aug 1840, 4-Chambersburg, PA, 7-Schlosser, Eliz., 8-Washington Co., MD, 9-Washington Co., MD, 10-Rev. John Bowen, 14-Yes, 15-Middlekauff

#8149, 1-Middlekauff, Cornelius C., 2-married, 3-31 Dec 1863, 4-Waynesboro, PA, 7-Trovinger, Susan Kate (Miss), 14-Yes, 15-Middlekauff

#8150, 1-Schlosser, John, 2-died, 3-18 May 1841, 4-Chambersburg, PA, 6-"of Adams Co., PA", 12-Schlosser, Peter, 14-Yes, 15-Middlekauff

#8151, 1-Schlosser, Susannah, 2-died, 3-5 Nov 1838, 6-from Adams Co., PA, 7-Schlosser, John, 12-Bender, Conrad, 14-Yes, 15-Middlekauff

#8152, 1-Middlekauff, Leonard, 2-died, 3-26 Jan 1851, 5-87 years 3 months 6 days, 14-Yes, 15-Middlekauff

#8153, 1-Middlekauff, Cornelius C., 2-died, 3-6 May 1873, 4-Harrisburg[?], PA, 14-Yes, 15-Middlekauff

#8154, 1-Trovinger, Joseph, 2-born, 3-11 Dec 1790, 6-note added by original transcriber: Grandmother Middlekauff was Mrs. Susan Kate Middlekauff, widow of Cornelius Middlekauff, dau. Of Joseph & Eliz. Trovenger", 14-Yes, 15-Middlekauff

#8155, 1-Trovinger, Eliz., 2-born, 3-11 Sep 1804, 7-Trovenger, Joseph, 14-Yes, 15-Middlekauff

#8156, 1-Trovinger, John, 2-born, 3-3 Jun 1823, 14-Yes, 15-Middlekauff

#8157, 1-Trovinger, Joseph, 2-born, 3-30 Aug 1824, 14-Yes, 15-Middlekauff

#8158, 1-Trovinger, Samuel, 2-born, 3-13 Jan 1826, 14-Yes, 15-Middlekauff

#8159, 1-Trovinger, Barbary, 2-born, 3-20 Aug 1827, 14-Yes, 15-Middlekauff

#8160, 1-Trovinger, Eliz., 2-born, 3-5 Feb 1829, 14-Yes, 15-Middlekauff

#8161, 1-Trovinger, Daniel, 2-born, 3-9 Feb 1831, 14-Yes, 15-Middlekauff

#8162, 1-Trovinger, Joseph, 2-born, 3-16 Dec 1832, 14-Yes, 15-Middlekauff

#8163, 1-Trovinger, Benton, 2-born, 3-26 Nov 1834, 14-Yes, 15-Middlekauff

FAMILY BIBLE RECORDS IN THE WASHINGTON COUNTY FREE LIBRARY, HAGERSTOWN, MARYLAND

Entry #, 1-Last Name, First Name, 2-Event, 3-Date, 4-Event Location, 5-Age, 6-Other, 7-Spouse's Last, First, 8-Groom's Residence, 9-Bride's Residence, 10-Minister, 11-Minister's Location, 12-Father's Last, First, 13-Mother's Last, First, 14-Transcribed, 15-Family Bible

#8164, 1-Trovinger, Ann Malenda, 2-born, 3-26 Aug 1836, 14-Yes, 15-Middlekauff
#8165, 1-Trovinger, Fanny, 2-born, 3-30 Sep 1837, 14-Yes, 15-Middlekauff
#8166, 1-Trovinger, Emily, 2-born, 3-30 May 1839, 14-Yes, 15-Middlekauff
#8167, 1-Trovinger, Franklen, 2-born, 3-31 May 1841, 14-Yes, 15-Middlekauff
#8168, 1-Trovinger, Catharine, 2-born, 3-26 Nov 1842, 14-Yes, 15-Middlekauff
#8169, 1-Trovinger, Nancy Amelia, 2-born, 3-11 Jan 1845, 14-Yes, 15-Middlekauff
#8170, 1-Trovinger, Marten Luther, 2-born, 3-22 Jan 1847, 14-Yes, 15-Middlekauff
#8171, 1-Fry, Susan, 2-married, 3-10 Dec 1847[?], 15-Fry
#8172, 1-Fry, John N., 2-married, 3-29 Oct 1857, 15-Fry
#8173, 1-Fry, Margaret An, 2-married, 3-25 Aug 1859, 15-Fry
#8174, 1-Fry, Margaret Ann, 2-married, 3-25 Aug 1857, 7-Grubb, Joseph Lewis, 10-Rev. J.B. Anthony, 15-Fry
#8175, 1-Fry, Butler[?], 2-married, 3-15 Apr 1882[?], 15-Fry
#8176, 1-Fry, Anne[?] J.[?], 2-married, 3-1 Jan 1883, 15-Fry
#8177, 1-Fry, Peter, 2-born, 3-20 Oct 1800, 15-Fry
#8178, 1-Tritefoe, Sarah, 2-born, 3-5 Oct 1805, 15-Fry
#8179, 1-Tritefoe, Sarah, 2-baptized, 3-9[?] Mar 1806, 15-Fry
#8180, 1-Fry, Anjaline, 2-born, 3-27 Jul 1824, 15-Fry
#8181, 1-Fry, Susan Catharine, 2-born, 3-27 Jun 1827, 15-Fry
#8182, 1-Fry, Elizabeth, 2-born, 3-1 Mar 1830, 15-Fry
#8183, 1-Fry, John P., 2-born, 3-12 Feb 1833, 15-Fry
#8184, 1-Fry, Margaretan, 2-born, 3-29 Dec 1835, 15-Fry
#8185, 1-Fry, George W., 2-born, 3-13 Apr 1858, 15-Fry
#8186, 1-Vincel, Larah Eizbeth, 2-born, 3-1 Nov 1847, 15-Fry
#8187, 1-Vincel, Luisa Virginia, 2-born, 3-16 Jul 1849, 15-Fry
#8188, 1-Vincel, Laura Jane, 2-born, 3-6 Feb 1852[?], 15-Fry
#8189, 1-Vincel, Earline Amanda, 2-born, 3-28 Sep 1855, 15-Fry
#8190, 1-Fry, Catharine Alvinda, 2-born, 3-6 Mar 1856, 15-Fry
#8191, 1-Fry, Ann Jane a Bertha, 2-born, 3-3 Jul 1858, 15-Fry
#8192, 1-Fry, George L. Botler, 2-born, 3-8 Oct 1859, 15-Fry
#8193, 1-Fry[?], John M., 2-born, 3-29 Sep, 15-Fry
#8194, 1-Fry, Arnold[?] May, 2-born, 3-31[?] Jul 18_9[?], 15-Fry
#8195, 1-Fry, Sarah, 2-died, 3-3 Dec 1866, 15-Fry
#8196, 1-Fry, George W., 2-died, 3-19 Feb 1872, 15-Fry
#8197, 1-Fry, Anjaline, 2-died, 3-5 Mar 1875, 15-Fry
#8198, 1-Fry, Catharene Alvenda[?], 2-died, 3-7 Mar 1876, 15-Fry
#8199, 1-Fry, Peter, 2-died, 3-26 Feb 1879, 15-Fry
#8200, 1-Fry, Ann Y.[?], 2-died, 3-7 Jan 1884, 15-Fry
#8201, 1-Fry, Harry Clinton, 2-born, 3-11[?] Jul 1886, 15-Fry
#8202, 1-Fry, Purle[?] Va[?], 2-born, 3-5 Nov 1884, 15-Fry
#8203, 1-Fry, John P., 2-died, 3-4[?] Oct 1888, 15-Fry
#8204, 1-Henneberger, Alfred, 2-married, 3-23 Dec 1858, 4-Chambersburg, PA, 7-Wampler, Mary E., 8-Waynesboro, PA, 9-Chambersburg, PA, 10-Rev. Samuel Philips, 14-Yes, 15-Henneberger
#8205, 1-Henneberger, Alfred Garfield, 2-born, 3-4:20 am, 8 May 1880, 14-Yes, 15-Henneberger
#8206, 1-Henneberger, Alfred Garfield, 2-baptized, 10-Rev. Roundthaler, 14-Yes, 15-Henneberger
#8207, 1-Henneberger, Lula May, 2-born, 3-11:45 am/pm, Sunday, 25 Jun 1882, 14-Yes, 15-Henneberger
#8208, 1-Henneberger, Lula May, 2-baptized, 10-Rev. Roundthaler, 14-Yes, 15-Henneberger
#8209, 1-Henneberger, Alfred Augustus, 2-born, 3-10 May 1900, 4-Hagerstown, MD, 12-Henneberger, Albertus, 13-Beard, Cora, 14-Yes, 15-Henneberger

FAMILY BIBLE RECORDS IN THE WASHINGTON COUNTY FREE LIBRARY, HAGERSTOWN, MARYLAND

Entry #, 1-Last Name, First Name, 2-Event, 3-Date, 4-Event Location, 5-Age, 6-Other,
7-Spouse's Last, First, 8-Groom's Residence, 9-Bride's Residence, 10-Minister, 11-Minister's Location,
12-Father's Last, First, 13-Mother's Last, First, 14-Transcribed, 15-Family Bible

#8210, 1-Henneberger, Jr., Alfred Augustus, 2-born, 3-12 Sep 1832, 4-Hagerstown, MD, 12-Henneberger, Alfred Augustus, 13-Bitzberger, Evelyn, 14-Yes, 15-Henneberger

#8211, 1-Henneberger, Jr., Alfred Augustus, 2-baptized, 3-25 Dec 1932, 4-Trinity Lutheran Church, 6-weight was 8 lbs., 10-Dr. J.S. Simon, 14-Yes, 15-Henneberger

#8212, 1-Henneberger, Alfred, 2-born, 3-7 Apr 1832, 14-Yes, 15-Henneberger

#8213, 1-Henneberger, Mary Elizabeth, 2-born, 3-1 Oct 1837, 14-Yes, 15-Henneberger

#8214, 1-Henneberger, Mary Catherine, 2-born, 3-27 Oct 1859, 14-Yes, 15-Henneberger

#8215, 1-Henneberger, Mary Catherine, 2-baptized, 4-Chambersburg, PA, 10-Rev. Samuel Philips, 14-Yes, 15-Henneberger

#8216, 1-Henneberger, George Wampler, 2-born, 3-28 Dec 1860, 14-Yes, 15-Henneberger

#8217, 1-Henneberger, George Wampler, 2-baptized, 4-Hagerstown, MD, 10-Rev. Evans, 14-Yes, 15-Henneberger

#8218, 1-Henneberger, Harry Lincoln, 2-born, 3-7 Mar 1865, 14-Yes, 15-Henneberger

#8219, 1-Henneberger, Harry Lincoln, 2-baptized, 4-Hagerstown, MD, 10-Rev. Keefer, 14-Yes, 15-Henneberger

#8220, 1-Henneberger, Albertus, 2-born, 3-9:55 am/pm, 15 Aug 1867, 14-Yes, 15-Henneberger

#8221, 1-Henneberger, Albertus, 2-baptized, 4-Hagerstown, MD, 10-Rev. Keefer, 14-Yes, 15-Henneberger

#8222, 1-Henneberger, Clara, 2-born, 3-"between 9 & 10 o'clock, 30 Mar 1870, 14-Yes, 15-Henneberger

#8223, 1-Henneberger, Clara, 2-baptized, 10-Rev. Thompson, 14-Yes, 15-Henneberger

#8224, 1-Henneberger, Nellie, 2-born, 3-3:25 pm, Sunday, 11 Aug 1872, 14-Yes, 15-Henneberger

#8225, 1-Henneberger, Nellie, 2-baptized, 10-Rev. Thompson, 14-Yes, 15-Henneberger

#8226, 1-Henneberger, Nina, 2-born, 3-12:30 pm, Sunday, 11 Jun 1876, 14-Yes, 15-Henneberger

#8227, 1-Henneberger, Nina, 2-baptized, 10-Rev. Thompson, 14-Yes, 15-Henneberger

#8228, 1-Henneberger, Eva, 2-born, 3-2:10 am, Saturday, 20 Oct 1877, 14-Yes, 15-Henneberger

#8229, 1-Henneberger, Eva, 2-baptized, 10-Rev. Roundthaler, 14-Yes, 15-Henneberger

#8230, 1-Henneberger, Alfred Augustus, 2-obituary, 3-7 Oct 1864, 5-1 years 5 months, 14-Yes, 15-Henneberger

#8231, 1-Henneberger, Mary E., 2-obituary, 3-8 Sep 1904, 5-66 years 11 months 8 days, 14-Yes, 15-Henneberger

#8232, 1-Henneberger, Alfred, 2-obituary, 3-22 Mar 1908, 5-75 years 11 months 22 days, 14-Yes, 15-Henneberger

#8233, 1-Henneberger, III, Alfred Augustus, 2-born, 3-19 Jan 1960, 4-Hagaerstown, MD, 6-weight was 9 lbs., 12-Henneberger, Jr., Alfred Augustus, 13-Schmid, Karel, 14-Yes, 15-Henneberger

#8234, 1-Henneberger, III, Alfred Augustus, 2-baptized, 3-17 Apr 1960, 4-St. Mark's Lutheran Church, Wolfsville, MD, 10-Rev. R. Markley, 12-Henneberger, Jr., Alfred Augustus, 13-Schmid, Karel, 14-Yes, 15-Henneberger

#8235, 1-Henneberger, Mark Wendel, 2-born, 3-25 Feb 1961, 4-Hagerstown, MD, 6-weight was 7 lbs. 9 1/2 oz., 12-Henneberger, Jr., Alfred Augustus, 13-Schmid, Karel, 14-Yes, 15-Henneberger

#8236, 1-Henneberger, Mark Wendel, 2-baptized, 3-16 Apr 1961, 4-St. Mark's Lutheran Church, Wolfsville, MD, 12-Henneberger, Jr., Alfred Augustus, 13-Schmid, Karel, 14-Yes, 15-Henneberger

#8237, 1-Henneberger, John, 2-born, 3-14 Jun 1785, 14-Yes, 15-Henneberger

#8238, 1-Henneberger, Catherine, 2-born, 3-1 Sep 1788, 14-Yes, 15-Henneberger

#8239, 1-Henneberger, William, 2-born, 3-3 Dec 1810, 12-Henneberger, John, 13-Henneberger, Catherine, 14-Yes, 15-Henneberger

FAMILY BIBLE RECORDS IN THE WASHINGTON COUNTY FREE LIBRARY, HAGERSTOWN, MARYLAND

Entry #, 1-Last Name, First Name, 2-Event, 3-Date, 4-Event Location, 5-Age, 6-Other, 7-Spouse's Last, First, 8-Groom's Residence, 9-Bride's Residence, 10-Minister, 11-Minister's Location, 12-Father's Last, First, 13-Mother's Last, First, 14-Transcribed, 15-Family Bible

#8240, 1-Henneberger, Augustus J., 2-born, 3-22 Jul 1812, 12-Henneberger, John, 13-Henneberger, Catherine, 14-Yes, 15-Henneberger

#8241, 1-Henneberger, Sarah Ann, 2-born, 3-27 Apr 1814, 12-Henneberger, John, 13-Henneberger, Catherine, 14-Yes, 15-Henneberger

#8242, 1-Henneberger, John J., 2-born, 3-1 Feb 1816, 12-Henneberger, John, 13-Henneberger, Catherine, 14-Yes, 15-Henneberger

#8243, 1-Henneberger, Catherine, 2-born, 3-17 Nov 1817, 12-Henneberger, John, 13-Henneberger, Catherine, 14-Yes, 15-Henneberger

#8244, 1-Henneberger, Susan, 2-born, 3-22 May 1819, 12-Henneberger, John, 13-Henneberger, Catherine, 14-Yes, 15-Henneberger

#8245, 1-Henneberger, George W., 2-born, 3-22 Jul 1821, 12-Henneberger, John, 13-Henneberger, Catherine, 14-Yes, 15-Henneberger

#8246, 1-Henneberger, Ann Catherine, 2-born, 3-16 Jul 1823, 12-Henneberger, John, 13-Henneberger, Catherine, 14-Yes, 15-Henneberger

#8247, 1-Henneberger, Margaret, 2-born, 3-4 May 1825, 12-Henneberger, John, 13-Henneberger, Catherine, 14-Yes, 15-Henneberger

#8248, 1-Henneberger, Hiram, 2-born, 3-4 Apr 1827, 12-Henneberger, John, 13-Henneberger, Catherine, 14-Yes, 15-Henneberger

#8249, 1-Henneberger, Clinton, 2-born, 3-21 Jun 1829, 12-Henneberger, John, 13-Henneberger, Catherine, 14-Yes, 15-Henneberger

#8250, 1-Henneberger, Alfred, 2-born, 3-7 Apr 1832, 12-Henneberger, John, 13-Henneberger, Catherine, 14-Yes, 15-Henneberger

#8251, 1-Henneberger, William, 2-died, 3-10 Dec 1851, 4-Baltimore, MD, 14-Yes, 15-Henneberger

#8252, 1-Henneberger, George W., 2-died, 3-23 Nov 1858, 4-Hagerstown, MD, 14-Yes, 15-Henneberger

#8253, 1-Henneberger, John, 2-died, 3-11 Sep 1859, 4-Hagerstown, MD, 14-Yes, 15-Henneberger

#8254, 1-Mittag, Ann Catherine, 2-died, 3-5 Sep 1860, 4-Hagerstown, MD, 14-Yes, 15-Henneberger

#8255, 1-Henneberger, Catherine (Mrs.), 2-died, 3-11 Aug 1869, 4-Hagerstown, MD, 14-Yes, 15-Henneberger

#8256, 1-Henneberger, Susan, 2-died, 3-6 Dec 1872, 4-Hagerstown, MD, 14-Yes, 15-Henneberger

#8257, 1-Henneberger, Augustus J., 2-died, 3-2 Jul 1877, 4-Louisville, KY, 14-Yes, 15-Henneberger

#8258, 1-Henneberger, John J., 2-died, 3-7 Jun 1880, 4-Hagerstown, MD, 14-Yes, 15-Henneberger

#8259, 1-Henneberger, Hiram, 2-died, 3-18 May 1892, 4-Waynesboro, PA, 14-Yes, 15-Henneberger

#8260, 1-Henneberger, Sarah Ann, 2-died, 3-3 Nov 1893, 4-Baltimore, MD, 14-Yes, 15-Henneberger

#8261, 1-Henneberger, Clinton, 2-died, 3-25 Oct 1902, 4-Baltimore, MD, 14-Yes, 15-Henneberger

#8262, 1-Henneberger, Margaret, 2-died, 3-11 Apr 1907, 4-Hagerstown, MD, 14-Yes, 15-Henneberger

#8263, 1-Henneberger, Alfred, 2-died, 3-22 Mar 1908, 4-Hagerstown, MD, 14-Yes, 15-Henneberger

#8264, 1-Henneberger, Mark Wendel, 2-married, 3-7 Jun 1985, 4-Brunswick, 7-Robbins, Donna Jeanne, 9-Lewiston, ME, 10-Rev. Ronald Klose, 14-Yes, 15-Henneberger

#8265, 1-Henneberger, Douglas Wade, 2-born, 3-8 Aug 1964, 4-Hagerstown, MD, 6-weight was 8 lbs. 12 oz., 12-Henneberger, Jr., Alfred Augustus, 13-Schmid, Karel Marie, 14-Yes, 15-Henneberger

#8266, 1-Henneberger, Sr., Alfred Augustus, 2-died, 3-9 Jul 1970, 5-70 years, 14-Yes, 15-Henneberger

FAMILY BIBLE RECORDS IN THE WASHINGTON COUNTY FREE LIBRARY, HAGERSTOWN, MARYLAND

Entry #, 1-Last Name, First Name, 2-Event, 3-Date, 4-Event Location, 5-Age, 6-Other, 7-Spouse's Last, First, 8-Groom's Residence, 9-Bride's Residence, 10-Minister, 11-Minister's Location, 12-Father's Last, First, 13-Mother's Last, First, 14-Transcribed, 15-Family Bible

#8267, 1-Henneberger, Sr., Evelyn Bitzberger, 2-died, 3-4 Jul 1977, 5-72 years, 14-Yes, 15-Henneberger

#8268, 1-Henneberger, Jr., Alfred Augustus, 2-married, 3-23 Aug 1958, 4-Haven Lutheran Church, Hagerstown, MD, 7-Schmid, Elgina Marie, 10-Rev. Ray Blanset; Dr. Frank Cauble, 14-Yes, 15-Henneberger

#8269, 1-Henneberger, Sr., Alfred Augustus, 2-married, 3-29 Jan 1929, 4-Calvary Lutheran Church, Baltimore, MD, 7-Bitzberger, Evelyn Gertrude, 10-Rev. J.S. Simon; Dr. Foster Gift; Rev. Jenkins, 14-Yes, 15-Henneberger

#8270, 1-Henneberger, Alfred Augustus, 2-obituary, 3-7 Oct 1864, 5-1 years 5 months, 12-Henneberger, Alfred, 13-Henneberger, Mary E., 14-Yes, 15-Henneberger

#8271, 1-Henneberger, Cather. (Mrs.), 2-obituary, 3-11 Aug, 5-86 years, 7-Henneberger, John, 14-Yes, 15-Henneberger

#8272, 1-Heneberger, Andrew E., 2-married, 3-21 Oct 1846, 7-Effinger, Mary E., 10-Rev. Wm. McK. Ward, 14-Yes, 15-Henneberger

#8273, 1-Heneberger, Mary Ella, 2-married, 3-18 Oct 1870, 7-Grattan, George G., 10-Rev. F. Rice Bowman, 14-Yes, 15-Henneberger

#8274, 1-Heneberger, Lucien G., 2-married, 3-22 Apr 1882, 4-Baltimore, MD, 7-Grymes, Mabel, 10-Rev. Dr. Minkland, 14-Yes, 15-Henneberger

#8275, 1-Heneberger, Edwin Randolph Grymes, 2-married, 3-8 pm, 11 Jan 1941, 4-Presbyterian Church, Upper Tract, WV, 7-Kimble, Mary Maxine, 10-Rev. D.L. Beard, 14-Yes, 15-Henneberger

#8276, 1-Heneberger, Barbara Maxine, 2-married, 3-4:00 pm, 8 Jul 1967, 4-1st Presbyterian Church, Harrisonburg, VA, 7-Bingham, Sammy K., 10-Don Rathen, 14-Yes, 15-Henneberger

#8277, 1-Heneberger, A.E., 2-married, 3-30 Sep 1968, 4-Lexington, VA, 7-Bailey, Lucy L., 10-Rev. Dr. White, 14-Yes, 15-Henneberger

#8278, 1-Heneberger, Mary Breese, 2-married, 3-30 Sep 1896, 4-Harrisonburg, VA, 7-Hening, George Griffin, 10-Rev. Dr. E.P. Palmer, 14-Yes, 15-Henneberger

#8279, 1-Heneberger, Edgar, 2-born, 3-11 Oct 1847, 14-Yes, 15-Henneberger

#8280, 1-Heneberger, Mary Ella, 2-born, 3-20 May 1849, 14-Yes, 15-Henneberger

#8281, 1-Heneberger, Lucien, 2-born, 3-20 Oct 1851, 14-Yes, 15-Henneberger

#8282, 1-Heneberger, Edwin H., 2-born, 3-24 Oct 1853, 14-Yes, 15-Henneberger

#8283, 1-Heneberger, John, 2-born, 3-25 Mar 1856, 14-Yes, 15-Henneberger

#8284, 1-Heneberger, Maggie, 2-born, 3-21 Jul 1861, 14-Yes, 15-Henneberger

#8285, 1-Heneberger, Harry Bailey, 2-born, 3-25 Jul 1869, 14-Yes, 15-Henneberger

#8286, 1-Heneberger, Mary Breese, 2-born, 3-20 Nov 1871, 14-Yes, 15-Henneberger

#8287, 1-Heneberger, Andrew E., 2-born, 3-15 Aug 1822, 14-Yes, 15-Henneberger

#8288, 1-Effinger, Mary E., 2-born, 3-13 Jun 1825, 14-Yes, 15-Henneberger

#8289, 1-Bailey, Lucy L. [or S.], 2-born, 3-9 Feb 1844, 14-Yes, 15-Henneberger

#8290, 1-Heneberger, Andrew Ellis, 2-born, 3-17 Mar 1875, 14-Yes, 15-Henneberger

#8291, 1-Heneberger, Lucien Randolph, 2-born, 3-27 Feb 1883, 4-Washington, DC, 14-Yes, 15-Henneberger

#8292, 1-Hening, Lillian Bailey, 2-born, 3-8 Aug 1897, 14-Yes, 15-Henneberger

#8293, 1-Hening, Jr., George Griffin, 2-born, 3-13 Dec 1898, 14-Yes, 15-Henneberger

#8294, 1-Grattan, Robert, 2-born, 3-20 Dec 1871, 14-Yes, 15-Henneberger

#8295, 1-Heneberger, Edwin Randolph Grymes, 2-born, 3-30 Jun 1906, 4-Harrisonburg, VA, 14-Yes, 15-Henneberger

#8296, 1-Grattan, Jr., George Gilmer, 2-born, 3-5 Jul 1875, 14-Yes, 15-Henneberger

#8297, 1-Heneberger, Edgar, 2-died, 3-27 Jul 1848, 5-9 months 16 days, 14-Yes, 15-Henneberger

#8298, 1-Heneberger, Edwin, 2-died, 3-18 Jul 1855, 5-1 years 8 months 25 days, 14-Yes, 15-Henneberger

#8299, 1-Heneberger, Maggie, 2-died, 3-11 Aug 1861, 5-21 days, 14-Yes, 15-Henneberger

FAMILY BIBLE RECORDS IN THE WASHINGTON COUNTY FREE LIBRARY, HAGERSTOWN, MARYLAND

Entry #, 1-Last Name, First Name, 2-Event, 3-Date, 4-Event Location, 5-Age, 6-Other, 7-Spouse's Last, First, 8-Groom's Residence, 9-Bride's Residence, 10-Minister, 11-Minister's Location, 12-Father's Last, First, 13-Mother's Last, First, 14-Transcribed, 15-Family Bible

#8300, 1-Heneberger, Harry Bailey, 2-died, 3-28 Feb 1876, 5-6 years 7 months 23 days, 14-Yes, 15-Henneberger

#8301, 1-Heneberger, Mabel, 2-died, 3-15 Mar 1883, 4-Washington, DC, 5-21 years 8 months 12 days, 7-Heneberger, Lucien G., 14-Yes, 15-Henneberger

#8302, 1-Heneberger, John, 2-died, 3-25 Jul 1885, 4-Cleveland, OH, 14-Yes, 15-Henneberger

#8303, 1-Heneberger, Mary E., 2-died, 3-21 Jul 1861, 5-36 years 1 months 8 days, 14-Yes, 15-Henneberger

#8304, 1-Heneberger, Andrew E., 2-died, 3-7 Aug 1900, 5-77 years 11 months 23 days, 14-Yes, 15-Henneberger

#8305, 1-Heneberger, Lucien Randolph, 2-died, 3-22 Dec 1910, 4-Ashland, 6-buried Harrisonburg, VA, 14-Yes, 15-Henneberger

#8306, 1-Heneberger, Peter, 2-died, 3-30 Jun 1869, 5-85 years, 14-Yes, 15-Henneberger

#8307, 1-Heneberger, Mary, 2-died, 3-20 Jun 1869, 14-Yes, 15-Henneberger

#8308, 1-Heneberger, Peter, 2-married, 3-26 Aug 1813, 7-Bear , Elizabeth, 14-Yes, 15-Henneberger

#8309, 1-Heneberger, Peter, 2-married, 3-30 Aug 1827, 7-Gibbons, Mary, 14-Yes, 15-Henneberger

#8310, 1-Heneberger, Peter, 2-born, 3-9 Oct 1784, 14-Yes, 15-Henneberger

#8311, 1-Heneberger, Mary Ann, 2-born, 3-7 Aug 1815, 14-Yes, 15-Henneberger

#8312, 1-Heneberger, Frances, 2-born, 3-24 Nov 1819, 14-Yes, 15-Henneberger

#8313, 1-Heneberger, Andrew Eli, 2-born, 3-15 Aug 1822, 14-Yes, 15-Henneberger

#8314, 1-Heneberger, Ellis Clark, 2-born, 3-21 Nov 1824, 14-Yes, 15-Henneberger

#8315, 1-Heneberger, Elizabeth (Bear), 2-born, 3-31 May 1790, 14-Yes, 15-Henneberger

#8316, 1-Heneberger, Elizabeth Catherine, 2-born, 3-9 Oct 1828, 14-Yes, 15-Henneberger

#8317, 1-Heneberger, Susan Jane, 2-born, 3-23 Sep 1831, 14-Yes, 15-Henneberger

#8318, 1-Heneberger, Ellis Clark, 2-died, 3-21 Jun 1825, 5-7 months, 14-Yes, 15-Henneberger

#8319, 1-Heneberger, Elizabeth, 2-died, 3-3 Sep 1826, 5-36 years 3 months 13 days, 14-Yes, 15-Henneberger

#8320, 1-Heneberger, Mary, 2-died, 3-20 Jun 1869, 14-Yes, 15-Henneberger

#8321, 1-Heneberger, Peter, 2-died, 3-30 Jun 1869, 14-Yes, 15-Henneberger

#8322, 1-Danner, Mary H., 2-died, 3-19 Mar 1899, 14-Yes, 15-Henneberger

#8323, 1-Heneberger, Andrew E., 2-died, 3-7 Aug 1900, 5-"nearly 78 years", 14-Yes, 15-Henneberger

#8324, 1-Slonacher, Charles E., 2-married, 3-1 Dec 1877, 4-"house of Samuel Krise", 7-Hess, Addie M., 14-Yes, 15-Henneberger

#8325, 1-Slonaker, C., 2-born, 3-2 Jul 1857, 4-Uniontown, MD, 14-Yes, 15-Henneberger

#8326, 1-Slonaker, C., 2-married, 3-1 Dec 1877, 14-Yes, 15-Henneberger

#8327, 1-Slonaker, C., 2-died, 3-29 Sep 1943, 14-Yes, 15-Henneberger

#8328, 1-Hess, Addie M., 2-born, 3-5 Aug 1851, 4-Taneytown, MD, 14-Yes, 15-Henneberger

#8329, 1-Hess, Addie M., 2-married, 3-1 Dec 1877, 14-Yes, 15-Henneberger

#8330, 1-Hess, Addie M., 2-died, 3-24 Feb 1943, 14-Yes, 15-Henneberger

#8331, 1-[blank], [infant], 2-born, 3-25 Sep 1878, 4-Uniontown, MD, 14-Yes, 15-Henneberger

#8332, 1-[blank], [infant], 2-died, 3-25 Sep 1878, 14-Yes, 15-Henneberger

#8333, 1-Slonaker, C.O., 2-born, 3-25 Sep 1879, 4-Uniontown, MD, 14-Yes, 15-Henneberger

#8334, 1-Slonaker, C.O., 2-died, 3-26 Feb 1958, 14-Yes, 15-Henneberger

#8335, 1-Slonaker, Andrew, 2-died, 3-22 Feb 1901, 14-Yes, 15-Henneberger

FAMILY BIBLE RECORDS IN THE WASHINGTON COUNTY FREE LIBRARY, HAGERSTOWN, MARYLAND

Entry #, 1-Last Name, First Name, 2-Event, 3-Date, 4-Event Location, 5-Age, 6-Other, 7-Spouse's Last, First, 8-Groom's Residence, 9-Bride's Residence, 10-Minister, 11-Minister's Location, 12-Father's Last, First, 13-Mother's Last, First, 14-Transcribed, 15-Family Bible

#8336, 1-Henneberger, Mark Wendel, 2-born, 3-25 Feb 1961, 4-Hagerstown, MD, 12-Henneberger, Jr., Alfred, 13-Henneberger, Karel, 14-Yes, 15-Henneberger

#8337, 1-Henneberger, Mark Wendel, 2-married, 3-7 Jun 1985, 4-Brunswick, ME, 7-Robbins, Donna Jeanne, 14-Yes, 15-Henneberger

#8338, 1-Bitzberger, Fred, 2-born, 3-17 Feb 1884, 4-Huntington, WV, 7-Slonaker, Nettie, 14-Yes, 15-Henneberger

#8339, 1-Bitzberger, Fred, 2-married, 3-26 Nov 1903, 14-Yes, 15-Henneberger

#8340, 1-Bitzberger, Fred, 2-died, 3-26 Oct 1967, 14-Yes, 15-Henneberger

#8341, 1-Henenberger, Sr., Alfred A., 2-born, 3-10 May 1900, 4-Hagerstown, MD, 7-Bitzberger, Evelyn, 14-Yes, 15-Henneberger

#8342, 1-Henenberger, Sr., Alfred A., 2-married, 3-29 Jan 1929, 14-Yes, 15-Henneberger

#8343, 1-Henenberger, Sr., Alfred A., 2-died, 3-9 Jul 1970, 14-Yes, 15-Henneberger

#8344, 1-Slonaker, Nettie G., 2-born, 3-15 Feb 1882, 4-Uniontown, 14-Yes, 15-Henneberger

#8345, 1-Slonaker, Nettie G., 2-married, 3-26 Nov 1903, 14-Yes, 15-Henneberger

#8346, 1-Slonaker, Nettie G., 2-died, 3-5 Oct 1974, 4-Hagerstown, MD, 6-buried Baltimore, MD, 14-Yes, 15-Henneberger

#8347, 1-Slonak, Nora B., 2-born, 3-18 Apr 1884, 4-Uniontown, 14-Yes, 15-Henneberger

#8348, 1-Slonak, Nora B., 2-married, 3-1 Jan 1930, 14-Yes, 15-Henneberger

#8349, 1-Slonak, Nora B., 2-died, 3-3 May 1961, 14-Yes, 15-Henneberger

#8350, 1-Grace[?], Edieth, 2-born, 3-26 Jun 1890, 4-Westminster, 14-Yes, 15-Henneberger

#8351, 1-Grace[?], Edieth, 2-died, 3-13 May 1963, 14-Yes, 15-Henneberger

#8352, 1-Slonaker, Chas. O., 2-born, 3-25 Sep 1879, 4-Uniontown, 14-Yes, 15-Henneberger

#8353, 1-Slonaker, Chas. O., 2-married, 3-15 May 1900, 14-Yes, 15-Henneberger

#8354, 1-Slonaker, Chas. O., 2-died, 3-26 Feb 1955, 14-Yes, 15-Henneberger

#8355, 1-Bitzberger, Evelyn Gertrude, 2-born, 3-25 May 1905, 4-Baltimore, MD, 14-Yes, 15-Henneberger

#8356, 1-Bitzberger, Evelyn Gertrude, 2-married, 3-29 Jan 1929, 14-Yes, 15-Henneberger

#8357, 1-Bitzberger, Evelyn Gertrude, 2-died, 3-4 Jul 1977, 14-Yes, 15-Henneberger

#8358, 1-Henneberger, Jr., Alfred A., 2-born, 3-12 Sep 1932, 4-Hagerstown, MD, 12-Henneberger, Alfred, 13-Henneberger, Evelyn, 14-Yes, 15-Henneberger

#8359, 1-Henneberger, Jr., Alfred A., 2-married, 3-23 Aug 1958, 14-Yes, 15-Henneberger

#8360, 1-Henneberger, III, Alfred A., 2-born, 3-19 Jan 1960, 4-Hagerstown, MD, 12-Henneberger, Alfred, 13-Henneberger, Karel, 14-Yes, 15-Henneberger

#8361, 1-Henneberger, Mark Wendel, 2-born, 3-25 Feb 1961, 4-Hagerstown, MD, 14-Yes, 15-Henneberger

#8362, 1-Henneberger, Mark Wendel, 2-married, 3-7 Jun 1985, 14-Yes, 15-Henneberger

#8363, 1-Henneberger, Douglas Wade, 2-born, 3-8 Aug 1964, 4-Hagerstown, MD, 14-Yes, 15-Henneberger

#8364, 1-Henneberger, Sr., Alfred Augustus, 2-born, 3-10 May 1900, 14-Yes, 15-Henneberger

#8365, 1-Henneberger, Sr., Alfred Augustus, 2-died, 3-9 Jul 1970, 4-Hagerstown, MD, 5-70 years 1 months, 6-died of stroke, 14-Yes, 15-Henneberger

#8366, 1-Henneberger, Evelyn Gertrude, 2-born, 3-25 May 1905, 14-Yes, 15-Henneberger

#8367, 1-Henneberger, Evelyn Gertrude, 2-died, 3-4 Jul 1977, 4-Hagerstown, MD, 5-72 years 1 months 10 days, 6-died of heart disease, 14-Yes, 15-Henneberger

FAMILY BIBLE RECORDS IN THE WASHINGTON COUNTY FREE LIBRARY, HAGERSTOWN, MARYLAND

Entry #, 1-Last Name, First Name, 2-Event, 3-Date, 4-Event Location, 5-Age, 6-Other, 7-Spouse's Last, First, 8-Groom's Residence, 9-Bride's Residence, 10-Minister, 11-Minister's Location, 12-Father's Last, First, 13-Mother's Last, First, 14-Transcribed, 15-Family Bible

#8368, 1-Henneberger, Mark Wendel, 2-married, 3-7 Jun 1985, 4-Brunswick, ME, 7-Robbins, Donna Jeanne, 9-Lewiston, ME, 10-Rev. Ronald Klose, 14-Yes, 15-Henneberger

#8369, 1-Ott, J.D., 2-married, 3-Thursday, 10 May 1832, 7-Quantrill, Mary, 10-Rev. Drane, 15-Quantrill

#8370, 1-Lane, John C., 15-Quantrill

#8371, 1-Leisure, Elijah, 2-married, 3-6 Oct 1811, 7-Miller, Susannah, 15-Quantrill

#8372, 1-Leasure, Christian, 2-married, 3-30 May 1840, 7-Guy___nner[?], Catharine, 10-Rev. Charles F. Shafer, 11-Hagerstown, MD, 15-Quantrill

#8373, 1-Quantrill, J.D.E., 2-married, 3-11 Feb 1831, 7-Lane, Mary, 10-Rev. N. Rothrauff[?], 15-Quantrill

#8374, 1-Lechron[?], Danl. H., 2-married, 3-24 Feb 1831, 7-Quantrill, Eliza, 10-Rev. Bruner[?], 15-Quantrill

#8375, 1-Sensaman, Mariah, 2-born, 3-11 May 1808, 15-Quantrill

#8376, 1-Leisure, Christian, 2-born, 3-9 Nov 1812, 15-Quantrill

#8377, 1-Leisure, Susannah, 2-born, 3-28 Oct 1815, 15-Quantrill

#8378, 1-Leisure, Elizabeth, 2-born, 3-27 Nov 1819, 15-Quantrill

#8379, 1-Leasure, Margaret Allis[?], 2-died, 3-15 Jul 1855, 5-5 months 5 days, 15-Quantrill

#8380, 1-Quantrill, J.D.E., 2-born, 3-19 Aug 1809, 4-Hagerstown, MD, 15-Quantrill

#8381, 1-Lane, Mary, 2-born, 3-7 May 1814, 4-Hagerstown, MD, 15-Quantrill

#8382, 1-Leasure, Anna Atelia[?], 2-born, 3-23 Jan 1852, 15-Quantrill

#8383, 1-Leasure, Anna Atelia[?], 2-died, 3-24 Feb 1923, 5-71 years 10 months 1 days, 15-Quantrill

#8384, 1-Leasure, Sarah Jane, 2-born, 3-3 Mar 1853, 15-Quantrill

#8385, 1-Leasure, Margaret Allis, 2-born, 3-10 Feb 1855, 15-Quantrill

#8386, 1-Leasure, Elijah C.[?], 2-died, 3-18 Jan 1931, 5-81 years 2 months 12 days, 15-Quantrill

#8387, 1-Quantrill, Judith Ann, 2-died, 3-11 Nov 1830, 5-45 years, 7-Quantrill, Thomas, 15-Quantrill

#8388, 1-Quantrill, Mary, 2-died, 3-17 Nov 1804, 7-Quantrill, Pretzman[?], 15-Quantrill

#8389, 1-Quantrill, Pretzman, 2-died, 3-9 Jan 1811, 15-Quantrill

#8390, 1-Quantrill, J.D.E., 2-died, 3-8 Jun 1820, 5-6 years, 12-Quantrill, Thomas, 13-Quantrill, Judith Ann, 15-Quantrill

#8391, 1-Leisure, Elijah, 2-died, 3-22 Oct 1821, 15-Quantrill

#8392, 1-Leasure, Catharine, 2-died, 3-1 Aug 1855, 5-32[?] years, 15-Quantrill

#8393, 1-Lane, Seth, 2-died, 3-Dec 1824, 5-51 years, 15-Quantrill

#8394, 1-Lane, Catherine, 2-died, 3-Apr 1825, 5-48 years, 7-Lane, Seth, 15-Quantrill

#8395, 1-Leasure, William Henry, 2-died, 3-26 Apr 1841, 5-6 months, 15-Quantrill

#8396, 1-Leasure, Martin Luther, 2-died, 3-24 Aug 1845, 5-"9 months all but two days", 15-Quantrill

#8397, 1-Leasure, John Henry, 2-died, 3-5 Jan 1849, 5-5 months 20 days, 15-Quantrill

#8398, 1-Leasure, Sarah Jane, 2-died, 3-23 Sep 1867, 5-14 years 6 months 20 days, 15-Quantrill

#8399, 1-Leasure, William Henry, 2-born, 3-26 Oct 1840, 15-Quantrill

#8400, 1-Leasure, Mary Elizabeth, 2-born, 3-3 May 1843, 15-Quantrill

#8401, 1-Leasure, Martin Luther, 2-born, 3-26 Nov 1844, 15-Quantrill

#8402, 1-Leasure, Susan Catharine, 2-born, 3-26 Aug 1846, 15-Quantrill

#8403, 1-Leasure, John Henry, 2-born, 3-15 Jul 1848, 15-Quantrill

#8404, 1-Leasure, Elijah C., 2-born, 3-6 Nov 1849, 15-Quantrill

#8405, 1-Leasure, Christian, 2-died, 3-7 Nov 1890[?], 5-78 years, 15-Quantrill

#8406, 1-Quantrill, Mary Ann, 2-born, 3-20 Jun 1808, 15-Quantrill

FAMILY BIBLE RECORDS IN THE WASHINGTON COUNTY FREE LIBRARY, HAGERSTOWN, MARYLAND

Entry #, 1-Last Name, First Name, 2-Event, 3-Date, 4-Event Location, 5-Age, 6-Other,
7-Spouse's Last, First, 8-Groom's Residence, 9-Bride's Residence, 10-Minister, 11-Minister's Location,
12-Father's Last, First, 13-Mother's Last, First, 14-Transcribed, 15-Family Bible

```
#8407, 1-Heyser, William, 2-born, 3-19 Aug 1809, 15-Quantrill
#8408, 1-Quantrill, Eliza, 2-born, 3-12 Jun 1811, 15-Quantrill
#8409, 1-Quantrill, Thos. H., 2-born, 3-19 Feb 1813, 15-Quantrill
#8410, 1-Quantrill, Jesse D.E., 2-born, 3-24 Aug 1814, 15-Quantrill
#8411, 1-Quantrill, A.R., 2-born, 3-8 Jan 1816, 15-Quantrill
#8412, 1-Quantrill, Catharine C., 2-born, 3-21 Jan 1822, 15-Quantrill
#8413, 1-Glossbrenner, Elizabeth, 2-died, 3-22 Mar 1880, 5-90 years 1 months, 15-
    Quantrill
#8414, 1-Glossbrenner, Mary Ann, 2-died, 3-11 May 1884, 5-66 years, 15-Quantrill
#8415, 1-Glossbrenner, Susan, 2-died, 3-14 Feb 189_[?], 5-[unreadable], 15-
    Quantrill
#8416, 1-Snyder, Samuel J., 2-born, 3-15 Sep 1858, 4-Keedysville, MD, 15-Snyder
#8417, 1-Snyder, Samuel J., 2-died, 3-1 Jan 1929, 15-Snyder
#8418, 1-Snyder, Samuel J., 2-married, 3-1880, Catharine M., 15-Snyder
#8419, 1-Snyder, Catharine M., 2-born, 3-2 Jun 1860, 15-Snyder
#8420, 1-Snyder, Catharine M., 2-died, 3-13 Dec 1928, 15-Snyder
#8421, 1-Snyder, Nina[?] O., 2-born, 3-27 Nov 1880, 15-Snyder
#8422, 1-Snyder, Nina[?] O., 2-died, 3-7 May 1955, 15-Snyder
#8423, 1-Snyder, Harry G., 2-born, 3-2 Aug 1883, 15-Snyder
#8424, 1-Snyder, Harry G., 2-died, 3-1 Nov 1960, 15-Snyder
#8425, 1-Snyder, Maudy M., 2-born, 3-24 Mar 1887, 15-Snyder
#8426, 1-Snyder, Maudy M., 2-died, 3-22 Jan 1955, 15-Snyder
#8427, 1-Snyder, Howard F.H., 2-born, 3-16 Jun 1889, 15-Snyder
#8428, 1-Snyder, Lela Lucinda, 2-born, 3-29 Oct 1892[?], 15-Snyder
#8429, 1-Snyder, Lela Lucinda, 2-died, 3-16 Nov 1916, 15-Snyder
#8430, 1-Snyder, Roy Samuel, 2-born, 3-4 Jun 1899, 4-Monroe, 15-Snyder
#8431, 1-Snyder, Roy Samuel, 2-died , 3-21 Apr 1954, 15-Snyder
#8432, 1-Snyder, Paul Elbert, 2-born, 3-13 May 1900, 4-Monroe, 15-Snyder
#8433, 1-Snyder, Paul Elbert, 2-died, 3-21[?] Jun 1962, 15-Snyder
#8434, 1-Snyder, Mary Eva[?], 2-born, 3-19 Jun 1904, 4-Monroe, 15-Snyder
#8435, 1-Garrott, Erasmus, 2-married, 3-5 Mar 1805, 7-Garrott, Sarah, 12-Garrott,
    John, 13-Garrott, Mary, 15-Garrott
#8436, 1-Garrott, Sarah, 12-Garrott, Barton, 13-Garrott, Ann, 15-Garrott
#8437, 1-Garrott, Warren, 2-married, 3-2 Oct 1851, 7-Hardey, Priscilla, 12-Garrott,
    Edw., 13-Garrott, Mary Ann, 15-Garrott
#8438, 1-Garrott, Edward, 2-married, 3-26 Sep 1882, 7-Hilleary, Laura Claggett, 12-
    Garrott, Warren, 13-Hardey, Ann P., 15-Garrott
#8439, 1-Garrott, Barton, 2-married, 3-28 Jan 1778, 7-Gray, Ann Buttle, 15-Garrott
#8440, 1-Garrott, Edward, 2-married, 3-14 May 1807, 7-Clagett, Mary Ann, 15-Garrott
#8441, 1-Garrott, Edward, 2-married, 3-28 Dec 1905, 7-Boteler, Lorina A., 12-
    Garrott, Warren, 13-Garrott, Ann P., 15-Garrott
#8442, 1-Boteler, Lorina, 12-Boteler, R.H.E. (Dr.), 13-Hammond, Rebecca, 15-Garrott
#8443, 1-Garrott, Erasmus, 2-born, 3-24 Apr 1777, 12-Garrott, John, 13-Garrott,
    Mary, 15-Garrott
#8444, 1-Garrott, Sarah, 2-born, 3-9 Dec 1782, 12-Garrott, Barton, 13-Garrott, Ann,
    15-Garrott
#8445, 1-Garrott, Elizabeth Ann, 2-born, 3-24 Jul 1808, 15-Garrott
#8446, 1-Garrott, Matilda, 2-born, 3-25 Feb 1810, 15-Garrott
#8447, 1-Garrott, Joseph, 2-born, 3-15 Oct 1778, 15-Garrott
#8448, 1-Garrott, Hanah, 2-born, 3-2 May 1780, 15-Garrott
#8449, 1-Garrott, Elizabeth, 2-born, 3-12 Jul 1781, 15-Garrott
#8450, 1-Garrott, Edward, 2-born, 3-17 Jun 1784, 15-Garrott
#8451, 1-Garrott, Ann, 2-born, 3-1 Apr 1797, 15-Garrott
#8452, 1-Garrott, Sarah, 2-born, 3-3 Sep 1811, 15-Garrott
#8453, 1-Garrott, Warren, 2-born, 3-12 Jan 1813, 15-Garrott
```

FAMILY BIBLE RECORDS IN THE WASHINGTON COUNTY FREE LIBRARY, HAGERSTOWN, MARYLAND

Entry #, 1-Last Name, First Name, 2-Event, 3-Date, 4-Event Location, 5-Age, 6-Other,
7-Spouse's Last, First, 8-Groom's Residence, 9-Bride's Residence, 10-Minister, 11-Minister's Location,
12-Father's Last, First, 13-Mother's Last, First, 14-Transcribed, 15-Family Bible

```
#8454, 1-Garrott, Mary Ann, 2-born, 3-14 Feb 1814, 15-Garrott
#8455, 1-Garrott, Edwd., 2-born, 3-16 Nov[?] 1856, 12-Garrott, Warren, 13-Garrott,
    Priscill, 15-Garrott
#8456, 1-Garrott, Amanda, 2-born, 3-20 Dec 1816, 15-Garrott
#8457, 1-Garrott, Hannah Frances, 2-born, 3-12 Apr 1827, 15-Garrott
#8458, 1-Garrott, Ann Buller, 2-died, 3-25 Apr 1802, 15-Garrott
#8459, 1-Garrott, Barton, 2-died, 3-8 Aug 1804, 15-Garrott
#8460, 1-Garrott, Joseph, 2-died, 3-16 Jul 1816, 15-Garrott
#8461, 1-Garrott, Ann, 2-died, 3-23 Mar 1820, 15-Garrott
#8462, 1-Garrott, Erasmus, 2-died, 3-23[?] Jun 1833, 15-Garrott
#8463, 1-Garrott, Sarah, 2-died, 3-1 Nov 1848, 15-Garrott
#8464, 1-Gray, Hanah , 2-died, 3-1 Nov 1802, 15-Garrott
#8465, 1-Garrott, Mary A., 2-died, 3-25 Sep 1856, 15-Garrott
#8466, 1-Garrott, Edward, 2-died, 3-31 Jan 1861, 5-76 y 7 m 13 d, 15-Garrott
#8467, 1-Garrott, Warren, 2-died, 3-9 Jan 1890, 12-Garrott, Edward, 13-Garrott,
    Mary Ann, 15-Garrott
#8468, 1-Garrott, Laura (Clagett), 2-died, 3-8 Jan 1902, 7-Garrott, Edward, 15-
    Garrott
#8469, 1-Garrott, Ann Priscilla, 2-died, 3-26 Feb 1923, 7-Garrott, Warren, 15-
    Garrott
#8470, 1-French[?], Mary Jane, 2-born, 3-26 Jan 1915, 12-French[?], Edwin S., 13-
    French[?], Ann P., 15-Garrott
#8471, 1-Garrott, Edward, 2-born, 3-20 Oct 1915, 12-Garrott, Warren, 13-Garrott,
    Margaret, 15-Garrott
#8472, 1-Garrott, William Andrew, 2-born, 3-25 Jan 1917, 12-Garrott, Warren, 13-
    Garrott, Margaret, 15-Garrott
#8473, 1-French, Dorothy Warren, 2-born, 3-5 Oct 1918, 12-French, Edwin S., 13-
    French, Ann Priscilla, 15-Garrott
#8474, 1-Garrott, John Warren, 2-born, 3-30 May 1971, 12-Garrott, Warren, 13-
    Garrott, Margaret, 15-Garrott
#8475, 1-Garrott, John Hilleary, 2-born, 3-27 Jan 1926, 12-Garrott, Wm. H., 13-
    Garrott, Mary, 15-Garrott
#8476, 1-Garrott, William Robert, 2-born, 3-3 Nov 1927, 12-Garrott, Warren, 13-
    Garrott, Margaret, 15-Garrott
#8477, 1-Garrott, Warren, 2-born, 3-12 Jan 1813, 12-Garrott, Edward, 13-Garrott,
    Mary Ann, 15-Garrott
#8478, 1-Hardey, Ann Priscilla, 2-born, 3-18 Oct 1836, 12-Hardey, George, 13-
    Hardey, Editha, 15-Garrott
#8479, 1-Garrott, Edward, 2-born, 3-16 Nov 1856, 12-Garrott, Warren, 13-Garrott,
    Ann Priscilla, 15-Garrott
#8480, 1-Hilleary, Laura Claggett, 2-born, 3-28 Aug 1859, 12-Hilleary, Wm. H., 13-
    McGill, Ellen, 15-Garrott
#8481, 1-Garrott, Warren, 2-born, 3-24 Jul 1883, 12-Garrott, Edward, 13-Garrott,
    Laura Claggett, 15-Garrott
#8482, 1-Garrott, Ellen (McGill), 2-born, 3-4 Aug 1885, 12-Garrott, Edward, 13-
    Garrott, Laura Claggett, 15-Garrott
#8483, 1-Garrott, Ann Priscilla, 2-born, 3-9 Feb 1891, 12-Garrott, Edward, 13-
    Garrott, Laura Claggett, 15-Garrott
#8484, 1-Garrott, William Hilleary, 2-born, 3-30 May 1896[?], 12-Garrott, Edward,
    13-Garrott, Laura Claggett, 15-Garrott
#8485, 1-Coleman, Ellen Carey, 2-born, 3-22 Sep 1913, 12-Coleman, Chas. Warren, 13-
    Garrott, Ellen, 15-Garrott
#8486, 1-French, Laura Spruce, 2-born, 3-6 Oct 1913, 12-French, Edwin S., 13-
    French, Ann P., 15-Garrott
#8487, 1-Garrott, Warren, 2-died, 3-9 Jan 1890, 5-76 y 11 m 28 d, 15-Garrott
```

FAMILY BIBLE RECORDS IN THE WASHINGTON COUNTY FREE LIBRARY, HAGERSTOWN, MARYLAND

Entry #, 1-Last Name, First Name, 2-Event, 3-Date, 4-Event Location, 5-Age, 6-Other,
7-Spouse's Last, First, 8-Groom's Residence, 9-Bride's Residence, 10-Minister, 11-Minister's Location,
12-Father's Last, First, 13-Mother's Last, First, 14-Transcribed, 15-Family Bible

```
#8488, 1-Garrott, Laura Claggett (Hilleary), 2-died, 3-8 Jan 1903, 5-43 y 5 m 10 d,
    7-Garrott, Edward, 15-Garrott
#8489, 1-Garrott, Ann Priscilla (Hardy), 2-died, 3-Feb 1924, 7-Garrott, Warren, 15-
    Garrott
#8490, 1-Garrott, William Andrew, 2-died, 3-5 Nov 1927, 12-Garrott, Warren, 13-
    Garrott, Margaret, 15-Garrott
#8491, 1-Garrott, Edward, 2-died, 3-16 Dec 1935, 12-Garrott, Warren, 13-Garrott,
    Margaret, 15-Garrott
#8492, 1-Garrott, Margaret Goode, 2-died, 3-9 Jul 1936, 7-Garrott, Warren, 15-
    Garrott
#8493, 1-Garrott, Edward, 2-died, 3-23 Mar 1938, 15-Garrott
#8494, 1-Garrott, Edward, 2-born, 3-1856, 15-Garrott
#8495, 1-Garrott, William Hilleary, 2-died, 3-6 Apr 1939, 15-Garrott
#8496, 1-Coleman, Ellen McGill Garrott, 2-died, 3-14 Aug 1945, 15-Garrott
#8497, 1-French, Ann Priscilla (Garrott), 2-died, 3-11 Sep 1965, 15-Garrott
#8498, 1-French, Dorothy W., 2-died, 3-29 Oct 1965, 15-Garrott
#8499, 1-Murphy, Ellen Carey (Coleman), 2-died, 3-16 Jul 1980, 12-Coleman, Charles
    Warren, 13-Garrott, Ellen, 15-Garrott
#8500, 1-Garrott, Edward, 2-married, 3-26 Sep 1882, 7-Hilleary, Laura Claggett, 15-
    Garrott
#8501, 1-Garrott, Edward, 2-married, 3-28 Dec 1905, 7-Boteler, Lorena, 15-Garrott
#8502, 1-Coleman, Charles Warren, 2-married, 3-8 Jan 1910, 7-Garrott, Ellen McGill,
    15-Garrott
#8503, 1-French, Edwin S., 2-married, 3-24 Nov 1911, 7-Garrott, Ann Priscilla, 15-
    Garrott
#8504, 1-Garrott, Warren, 2-married, 3-1914, 7-Goode, Margaret, 15-Garrott
#8505, 1-Garrott, William Hilleary, 2-married, 3-16 Apr 1925, 7-Ramacciotti, Mary
    B., 15-Garrott
#8506, 1-French, Laura Spence, 2-married, 7-Ellis, Harley, 15-Garrott
#8507, 1-French, Mary Jane, 2-married, 7-Seigleitz, Frank C., 15-Garrott
#8508, 1-Coleman, Ellen Carey, 2-married, 7-Murphey, John Edmond, 15-Garrott
#8509, 1-Garrott, John Warren, 2-married, 3-23 Jan 1943, 7-Hellane, Julia, 15-
    Garrott
#8510, 1-Garrott, Margaret Priscilla, 2-married, 7-Litten, George M., 15-Garrott
#8511, 1-Garrott, John P., 2-married, 3-16 Apr 1801, 7-Garrott, Elizabeth, 15-
    Garrott
#8512, 1-Garrott, Bartholomew, 2-married, 3-27 May 1830, 7-Burgee, Elen Jane, 15-
    Garrott
#8513, 1-Burgee, Elen Jane, 12-Burgee, Jr., Thomas, 15-Garrott
#8514, 1-Garrott, Bartholomew, 2-married, 3-22 May 1832, 7-Anderson, Priscilla, 15-
    Garrott
#8515, 1-Garrott, Ann Virginia, 2-born, 3-27 Aug 1848, 15-Garrott
#8516, 1-Garrott, Jessie Tolbert, 2-born, 3-10[?] Mar 1849, 15-Garrott
#8517, 1-Farper, Franey B.F., 2-married, 3-23 Apr 1835, 7-Garrott, Mary Elizabeth,
    15-Garrott
#8518, 1-Garrott, Emma Rosalia, 2-born, 3-6 Jan 1853[?], 15-Garrott
#8519, 1-Garrott, Laura Jane, 2-born, 3-18 Apr 1856, 15-Garrott
#8520, 1-Garrott, Aden Anderson, 2-born, 3-15 Feb 1851, 15-Garrott
#8521, 1-Garrott, Barton Van Buren, 2-born, 3-3 Jan 1840, 12-Garrott, Barton, 13-
    Garrott, Mary Priscilla, 15-Garrott
#8522, 1-Garrott, Elen Catharine, 2-born, 3-24 Feb 1842, 15-Garrott
#8523, 1-Garrott, Allen Franklin, 2-born, 3-9 Feb 1844, 15-Garrott
#8524, 1-Garrott, Susan Matilda, 2-born, 3-27 Dec 1845, 15-Garrott
#8525, 1-Garrott, Maryann, 2-born, 3-8 Feb 1802, 15-Garrott
#8526, 1-Garrott, Bartholomew, 2-born, 3-21 Mar 1803, 15-Garrott
```

FAMILY BIBLE RECORDS IN THE WASHINGTON COUNTY FREE LIBRARY, HAGERSTOWN, MARYLAND

Entry #, 1-Last Name, First Name, 2-Event, 3-Date, 4-Event Location, 5-Age, 6-Other, 7-Spouse's Last, First, 8-Groom's Residence, 9-Bride's Residence, 10-Minister, 11-Minister's Location, 12-Father's Last, First, 13-Mother's Last, First, 14-Transcribed, 15-Family Bible

#8527, 1-Garrott, [infant], 2-born, 3-9 Apr 1805, 6-"stillborn", 15-Garrott
#8528, 1-Garrott, Mary Elizabeth, 2-born, 3-1 Mar 1806, 15-Garrott
#8529, 1-Garrott, John P., 2-born, 3-17 Apr 1811, 15-Garrott
#8530, 1-Garrott, Joseph Edward, 2-born, 3-27 May 1819, 15-Garrott
#8531, 1-Garrott, Elizabeth, 2-born, 3-12 Jul 1781, 15-Garrott
#8532, 1-Garrott, Sarah, 2-born, 3-9 Nov 1782, 15-Garrott
#8533, 1-Garrott, Elizabeth Ann, 2-born, 3-25 Jan 1831, 12-Garrott, Barton, 13-Garrott, Elen Jane, 15-Garrott
#8534, 1-Garrott, John Robert, 2-born, 3-14 Jun 1833, 12-Garrott, Barton, 13-Garrott, Mary Priscilla, 15-Garrott
#8535, 1-Garrott, Jared Rice, 2-born, 3-2 Oct 1834, 12-Garrott, Barton, 13-Garrott, Mary Priscilla, 15-Garrott
#8536, 1-Garrott, Sarah Erasmus, 2-born, 3-8 Oct 1836, 12-Garrott, Barton, 13-Garrott, Mary Priscilla, 15-Garrott
#8537, 1-Garrott, Mary Elizabeth Gray, 2-born, 3-19 Jun 1838, 15-Garrott
#8538, 1-Johnson, Catherine, 2-born, 3-21 Mar 1823, 15-Garrott
#8539, 1-Johnson, Ritch, 2-born, 15-Garrott
#8540, 1-Rideout, Eliza, 2-born, 3-Jan 1811, 15-Garrott
#8541, 1-[blank], Caroline, 2-born, 3-Jun 1836, 15-Garrott
#8542, 1-[blank], Coliar, 2-born, 3-31 Jan 1831, 15-Garrott
#8543, 1-[blank], Ann Maria, 2-born, 3-30 Dec 1833, 15-Garrott
#8544, 1-[blank], Harvey[?], 2-born, 3-1 Mar 1835, 15-Garrott
#8545, 1-Green, Mariah, 2-born, 3-6 Aug 1846, 12-Green, Rozelen, 13-Green, Elen, 15-Garrott
#8546, 1-Green, Fanny Franklin, 2-born, 3-17 Jun 1847[?], 15-Garrott
#8547, 1-Washington, Ida , 2-born, 3-10 Jul 1850[?], 15-Garrott
#8548, 1-[blank], Negro Bill, 2-born, 3-5 Jul 1816, 15-Garrott
#8549, 1-[blank], Negro Sam, 2-born , 3-2 Sep 1818, 15-Garrott
#8550, 1-Johson, William, 2-died, 3-13 Jul 1835, 5-17 y 8 d, 15-Garrott
#8551, 1-Johson, William, 2-born, 3-5 Jul 1816, 15-Garrott
#8552, 1-Smallwood, Elizabeth, 2-born, 3-16 Jul 185_[?], 13-Green, Elen S.A., 15-Garrott
#8553, 1-Green, Louisa Flourence, 2-born, 3-2 Jun 1854[?], 15-Garrott
#8554, 1-Green, Caroline Carohelus, 2-born, 3-12 Sep 1856, 15-Garrott
#8555, 1-Garrott, Mary P., 2-died, 3-16 Sep 1891, 15-Garrott
#8556, 1-Garrott, Joseph, 2-died, 3-21 Mar 1891, 15-Garrott
#8557, 1-Garrott, John P., 2-died, 3-26 Apr 1815, 15-Garrott
#8558, 1-Garrott, Elen Jane, 2-died, 3-7 Feb 1831, 15-Garrott
#8559, 1-Garrott, Allen Warren, 2-died, 3-23 Feb 1835, 15-Garrott
#8560, 1-Garrott, Elizabeth, 2-died, 3-16 Dec 1837, 15-Garrott
#8561, 1-Murphey, Catharine, 2-died, 3-6 Mar 1829[?], 15-Garrott
#8562, 1-Fairfax, Mary C., 2-died, 3-29 Nov 1841, 15-Garrott
#8563, 1-Garrott, Joseph E., 2-died, 3-29 Dec 1843?", 15-Garrott
#8564, 1-Garrott, John Robert, 2-died, 3-17 May 1844, 15-Garrott
#8565, 1-Garrott, Sarah, 2-died, 3-1 Nov 1848, 15-Garrott
#8566, 1-Garrott, John P., 2-died, 3-15 Mar 1852, 15-Garrott
#8567, 1-Garrott, Hannah Frances, 2-born, 3-18 Oct 1858, 15-Garrott
#8568, 1-Garrott, Barton, 2-died, 3-31 Jul 1880, 15-Garrott
#8569, 1-Garrott, Sarah Erasmus, 2-married, 3-23 Nov 1858, 7-Carlisle, Robert Barton, 15-Garrott
#8570, 1-Garrott, Mary E.G., 2-married, 3-29 May 1861, 7-Anderson, James, 15-Garrott
#8571, 1-Garrott, Mary, 2-died, 3-1891, 15-Garrott
#8572, 1-Coblentz, Peter, 2-born, 3-22 Sep 1769, 15-Coblentz
#8573, 1-Bowles, Nicklas, 6-could not translate German script, 15-Coblentz

FAMILY BIBLE RECORDS IN THE WASHINGTON COUNTY FREE LIBRARY, HAGERSTOWN, MARYLAND

Entry #, 1-Last Name, First Name, 2-Event, 3-Date, 4-Event Location, 5-Age, 6-Other,
7-Spouse's Last, First, 8-Groom's Residence, 9-Bride's Residence, 10-Minister, 11-Minister's Location,
12-Father's Last, First, 13-Mother's Last, First, 14-Transcribed, 15-Family Bible

```
#8574, 1-Coblentz, Elizabeth, 6-could not translate German script, 15-Coblentz
#8575, 1-Coblentz, Lydia, 6-could not translate German script, 15-Coblentz
#8576, 1-Coblentz, Rebecca, 6-could not translate German script, 15-Coblentz
#8577, 1-Coblentz, John, 6-could not translate German script, 15-Coblentz
#8578, 1-Coblentz, Jacob, 6-could not translate German script, 15-Coblentz
#8579, 1-Coblentz, Catharina, 6-could not translate German script, 15-Coblentz
#8580, 1-Coblentz, 15-Coblentz
#8581, 1-Coblentz, Barbara, 2-died, 3-25 Sep 1823, 5-48 years 8 months 20 days, 15-
    Coblentz
#8582, 1-Beckenbaugh, Magdalena, 6-could not translate German script, 15-Coblentz
#8583, 1-Bowles, Magdalena Bechenbaugh, 6-could not translate German script, 15-
    Coblentz
#8584, 1-Ringer, Eberhard, 2-born, 3-Aug 1702, 6-could not translate German script,
    15-Ringer
#8585, 1-Ringer, Rhegattin Juliana, 2-born, 3-Sep 1794, 6-could not translate
    German script, 15-Ringer
#8586, 1-Ringer, Jacob (Mrs.), 6-could not translate German script, 15-Ringer
#8587, 1-Hager, Jonathan, 6-could not translate German script, 15-Hager
#8588, 1-Hager, Elizabeth, 6-could not translate German script, 15-Hager
#8589, 1-Schneider, Peter, 6-could not translate German script, 15-Schneider
#8590, 1-Schneider, Jacob, 6-could not translate German script, 15-Schneider
#8591, 1-Baker, Johan Nickolas, 6-could not translate German script, 15-Baker
#8592, 1-Baker, Catherine, 6-could not translate German script, 15-Baker
#8593, 1-Sprecher, Mary M., 2-born, 3-17 Feb 1799, 6-could not translate German
    script, 15-Baker
#8594, 1-Sprecher, Mary M., 2-married, 3-30 Dec 1819, 6-could not translate German
    script, 15-Baker
#8595, 1-Baker, Caroline S. [?], 2-born, 3-27 Dec 1820, 6-could not translate
    German script, 15-Baker
#8596, 1-Stickel, Mary Veda (Miss), 2-born, 3-25 Feb 1894, 6-could not translate
    German script, 15-Baker
#8597, 1-Stickel, Mary Veda (Miss), 2-obit, 3-20 Dec 1973, 6-could not translate
    German script, 15-Baker
#8598, 1-Middlekauff, Maria Elizabeth, 6-could not translate German script, 15-
    Middlekauff
#8599, 1-Middlekauff, Johannes, 6-could not translate German script, 15-Middlekauff
```

INDEX
Pages are not numbered; numbers refer to the entry number at the beginning of each record.

Acres, Rev., #1594
Adams, Daniel, #7914
Adams, Daniel Stover, #7843
Adams, Daniel Stover, #7844
Adams, Daniel Stover, #7845
Adams, Daniel Stover, #7846
Adams, Elizabeth, #2581
Adams, Frances Brough, #7846
Adams, Frances Brough, #7847
Adams, Frances Brough, #7848
Adams, Frances Brough, #7849
Adams, Frances Brough, #7850
Adams, John U., #2581
Adams, Mary Anders, #2568
Adams, Mary Anders, #2581
Adrean[?], Emily Ann Delico, #4232
Akers, J.B., #3335
Albert, Alfred, #4572
Albert, George, #3128
Albert, George, #3184
Albert, Jacob, #4572
Albert, Mary, #4572
Albert, Mary Ann, #3184
Albright, Anna Maria, #2157
Albright, Anna Maria, #2158
Albright, Anna Maria, #2159
Albright, Anna Maria, #2160
Albright, Anna Maria, #2161
Albright, Anna Maria, #2162
Albright, Anna Maria, #2163
Albright, Anna Maria, #2165
Albright, Anna Maria, #2166
Albright, Anna Maria, #2167
Albright, Anna Maria, #2168
Albright, Anna Maria, #2169
Albright, Anna Maria, #2170
Albright, Anna Maria, #2171
Albright, Anna Maria, #2172
Albright, Anna Maria, #2173
Albright, Anna Maria, #2174
Albright, Anna Maria, #2175
Albright, Anna Maria, #2176
Albright, Anna Maria, #2177
Albright, Anna Maria, #2178
Alderdice[?], Adelaide Berry, #7502
Aldridge, Clayson Wheeler, #101
Aldridge, Clayson Wheeler, #97
Aldridge, Clayson Wheeler, #98
Alexander, Sarah Ruth, #7680
Alexander, Sarah Ruth, #7703
Alexander, Sarah Ruth, #7704
Alexander, Sarah Ruth, #7724
Alexander, Sarah Ruth, #7725
Alexander, Sarah Ruth, #7726
Alexander , Sarah Ruth, #7706
Alexander , Sarah Ruth, #7707
Alexander , Sarah Ruth, #7708
Alexander , Sarah Ruth, #7709
Alexander , Sarah Ruth, #7710
Alexander , Sarah Ruth, #7711
Algird[?] , Harry C. (Dr.), #3453
Alice, Victor H., #7334
Allegheny College, chaplain, #4340
Allen, , #6113
Amanda, Flory, #1630
Ambler, Cecil Parker, #4743
Anderson, Clara May, #5896
Anderson, Clara May, #5897
Anderson, Ernest Nelson, #5879
Anderson, James, #8570
Anderson, Jas. H., #2831
Anderson, Joe, #5879
Anderson, Joe, #5880
Anderson, Julia, #5879
Anderson, Julia, #5880
Anderson, Leona Mable, #5880
Anderson, Priscilla, #8514
Anderson, S.H., #7557
Ankeney, David Hammett, #1656
Ankeney, David Hammett, #1660
Ankeney, David Hammett, #1662
Ankeney, David Hammett, #1663
Ankeney, David Hassett, #1663
Ankeney, Isaac, #1651
Ankeney, Isaac, #1652
Ankeney, Isaac Donald, #1655
Ankeney, Jane Flory, #1658
Ankeney, Jane Flory, #1661
Ankeney, Maria (Flory), #1653
Ankeney, Maria A. (Flory), #1659
Ankeney, Maria F., #1655
Ankeney, Maria F., #1656
Ankeney, Maria F., #1657
Ankeney, Maria F., #1658
Ankeney, William Henry, #1657
"Ankeney, Jr.", Isaac, #1654
"Ankeney, Jr.", Isaac, #1655
"Ankeney, Jr.", Isaac, #1656
"Ankeney, Jr.", Isaac, #1657
"Ankeney, Jr.", Isaac, #1658
Anthony, J.B., #3507
Anthony, J.B., #8174
Anthony, J.P., #4305
Appenzellar, Lillie, #3449
Applegate, Iris, #587
Ardinger, Alen, #1718
Ardinger, Alex. H., #4117
Ardinger, Amanda Virginia, #4188
Ardinger, Benjamin, #1678
Ardinger, Benjamin, #4086
Ardinger, Benjamin Kurts, #4082
Ardinger, Benjamin Kurtz, #1674
Ardinger, Bettie, #1724
Ardinger, Bettie, #4125
Ardinger, Buena Vista, #1720
Ardinger, Bun Vista, #4120
Ardinger, Caroline, #1716
Ardinger, Caroline, #4115
Ardinger, Cecilia Agnes, #4096
Ardinger, Charles A., #4186
Ardinger, Charles G., #4173
Ardinger, Charles G., #4178
Ardinger, Charles G., #4180
Ardinger, Charles G., #4181
Ardinger, Charles G., #4182
Ardinger, Charles G., #4183
Ardinger, Charles G., #4184
Ardinger, Charles G., #4185
Ardinger, Charles G., #4186
Ardinger, Charles G., #4187
Ardinger, Charles G., #4188
Ardinger, Charles G., #4189
Ardinger, Charles G., #4209
Ardinger, Christian, #1664
Ardinger, Christian, #1688
Ardinger, Christian, #4072
Ardinger, Christian, #4097
Ardinger, Clara, #1719
Ardinger, Clara, #1729
Ardinger, Clara, #1730
Ardinger, Clara, #4118
Ardinger, Clara, #4119
Ardinger, Clara Elizabeth (Garriah), #4111
Ardinger, Clara Elizabeth (Garriah), #4112
Ardinger, Clara Elizabeth (Garrish), #1709
Ardinger, Clara Elizabeth (Garrish), #4172
Ardinger, Clara Ellen, #1701
Ardinger, Clara Ellen, #4166
Ardinger, Elizabeth, #1666
Ardinger, Elizabeth, #1667
Ardinger, Elizabeth, #1689
Ardinger, Elizabeth, #4074
Ardinger, Elizabeth, #4075
Ardinger, Elizabeth, #4098
Ardinger, Ellen, #1837
Ardinger, Ellen Betty, #1698
Ardinger, Ellen Betty, #1714
Ardinger, Ellen Betty, #1731
Ardinger, Ellen Betty, #4113
Ardinger, Ellen Betty, #4128
Ardinger, Emma E., #1717
Ardinger, Emma E., #4116
Ardinger, Emma R., #4184
Ardinger, Emma Rachael, #4174
Ardinger, Frances, #1715
Ardinger, Francis, #4114
Ardinger, George W., #4189
Ardinger, Georgetta, #4085
Ardinger, Georgette, #1677
Ardinger, Georgietta, #4140
Ardinger, Georgietta, #4143
Ardinger, Georgietta, #4144
Ardinger, Georgietta, #4145
Ardinger, Georgietta, #4146
Ardinger, Georgietta, #4147
Ardinger, Georgietta, #4148
Ardinger, Georgietta, #4149
Ardinger, Georgietta, #4150
Ardinger, Georgietta, #4151
Ardinger, Hanah, #4114
Ardinger, Hanah, #4115
Ardinger, Hanah, #4116
Ardinger, Hanah, #4117
Ardinger, Hanah, #4118
Ardinger, Hanah, #4119
Ardinger, Hanah, #4120
Ardinger, Hanah, #4121
Ardinger, Hanah, #4122
Ardinger, Hanah, #4123
Ardinger, Hanah, #4124
Ardinger, Hanah, #4125
Ardinger, Hanah (Mrs.), #4131
Ardinger, Hanah Rebecca, #4101
Ardinger, Hanah Rebecca, #4102
Ardinger, Hannah, #1699
Ardinger, Hannah, #1702
Ardinger, Hannah, #1703
Ardinger, Hannah, #1722
Ardinger, Hannah, #4123
Ardinger, Hannah (Mrs.), #1734
Ardinger, Hannah Rebecca, #1682
Ardinger, Hannah Rebecca, #1692
Ardinger, Hannah Rebecca, #1693
Ardinger, Hannah Rebecca, #4091
Ardinger, Hannah Steinmetz, #1732
Ardinger, Hannah Steinmetz, #4129
Ardinger, Hannah Steinmetz , #4163
Ardinger, Harry Lee, #4092
Ardinger, Henry, #4128
Ardinger, Henry, #4129
Ardinger, Henry, #4130
Ardinger, Henry Z., #1713
Ardinger, Henry Z., #1714
Ardinger, Henry Z., #1723
Ardinger, Henry Z., #1728
Ardinger, Henry Z., #1731
Ardinger, Henry Z., #1732
Ardinger, Henry Z., #1733
Ardinger, Henry Z., #4110
Ardinger, Henry Z., #4113
Ardinger, Henry Z., #4124
Ardinger, Henry Zeller, #1697
Ardinger, Henry Zeller, #1698
Ardinger, Henry Zeller, #1699
Ardinger, Henry Zeller, #1700
Ardinger, Henry Zeller, #1708
Ardinger, Henry Zeller, #1739
Ardinger, Henry Zeller, #4171
Ardinger, Henry Zellers, #4136
Ardinger, Henry Zellers, #4187
Ardinger, Jacob Christian, #1668
Ardinger, Jacob Christian, #4076
Ardinger, James, #1721
Ardinger, James, #1725
Ardinger, James, #4121
Ardinger, James, #4122
Ardinger, James C., #4181
Ardinger, James C., #4211
Ardinger, Jane, #4216
Ardinger, Jane (Shook), #4179
Ardinger, Jessie, #1685
Ardinger, Jessie F., #4094
Ardinger, John, #1665
Ardinger, John, #4073
Ardinger, John W., #4180
Ardinger, Joseph, #1675
Ardinger, Joseph Finley, #4083
Ardinger, Joseph Finley, #4088
Ardinger, Joseph Henry, #1700
Ardinger, Joseph Henry, #1701
Ardinger, Joseph Henry, #1733
Ardinger, Joseph Henry, #4130
Ardinger, Joseph Henry, #4165
Ardinger, Joseph Henry, #4166
Ardinger, Joseph T. Van Lear, #4183

INDEX
Pages are not numbered; numbers refer to the entry number at the beginning of each record.

Ardinger, Katherine, #1684
Ardinger, Katherine[?], #4093
Ardinger, Margret I.[?], #4185
Ardinger, Maria, #1727
Ardinger, Maria, #4127
Ardinger, Mariah (Mrs.), #1736
Ardinger, Mariah (Mrs.), #4133
Ardinger, Mary Elizabeth, #1676
Ardinger, Mary Elizabeth, #4084
Ardinger, Mary Ellen, #4182
Ardinger, Mary Ellen, #4210
Ardinger, Mary Emma, #1681
Ardinger, Mary Emmie, #4090
Ardinger, Mary Lee, #1683
Ardinger, Maryan, #1673
Ardinger, Maryan, #4081
Ardinger, Moses, #1671
Ardinger, Moses, #1672
Ardinger, Moses, #1691
Ardinger, Moses, #4079
Ardinger, Moses, #4080
Ardinger, Moses, #4100
Ardinger, Peter, #1710
Ardinger, Peter, #1712
Ardinger, Peter, #1713
Ardinger, Peter, #1715
Ardinger, Peter, #1716
Ardinger, Peter, #1717
Ardinger, Peter, #1718
Ardinger, Peter, #1719
Ardinger, Peter, #1720
Ardinger, Peter, #1721
Ardinger, Peter, #1722
Ardinger, Peter, #1723
Ardinger, Peter, #1724
Ardinger, Peter, #1725
Ardinger, Peter, #1726
Ardinger, Peter, #1734
Ardinger, Peter, #1735
Ardinger, Peter, #4106
Ardinger, Peter, #4108
Ardinger, Peter, #4110
Ardinger, Peter, #4114
Ardinger, Peter, #4115
Ardinger, Peter, #4116
Ardinger, Peter, #4117
Ardinger, Peter, #4118
Ardinger, Peter, #4119
Ardinger, Peter, #4120
Ardinger, Peter, #4121
Ardinger, Peter, #4122
Ardinger, Peter, #4123
Ardinger, Peter, #4124
Ardinger, Peter, #4125
Ardinger, Peter, #4126
Ardinger, Peter, #4132
Ardinger, Stonewall J., #1686
Ardinger, Stonewall J., #4095
Ardinger, William, #1669
Ardinger, William, #1670
Ardinger, William, #1679
Ardinger, William, #1690
Ardinger, William, #4077
Ardinger, William, #4078
Ardinger, William, #4087
Ardinger, William, #4099

Ardinger, William Hamilton, #1737
Ardinger, William Hamilton, #4134
"Ardinger, Jr.", Benjamin, #4105
Armor, Anne, #4257
Armor, Charles Huffman, #4264
Armor, Emma E., #4277
Armor, Emma Elizabeth, #4270
Armor, George Bennett, #4238
Armor, George F., #4232
Armor, George F., #4233
Armor, George F., #4253
Armor, George F., #4254
Armor, George F., #4255
Armor, George F., #4256
Armor, George F., #4261
Armor, George M., #4245
Armor, George Maxwell, #4244
Armor, George Maxwell, #4253
Armor, Ida, #4255
Armor, Ida, #4284
Armor, Iola, #4271
Armor, Jane O., #4240
Armor, Jane Thompson, #4252
Armor, Jennie R., #4253
Armor, Jennie R., #4254
Armor, Jennie R., #4255
Armor, Jennie R., #4256
Armor, Jennie Wooldridge, #4254
Armor, John, #4230
Armor, John, #4238
Armor, John, #4243
Armor, John, #4250
Armor, John, #4262
Armor, John, #4263
Armor, John, #4263
Armor, John, #4278
Armor, Joseph, #4265
Armor, Joseph, #4266
Armor, Joseph, #4267
Armor, Joseph, #4268
Armor, Joseph, #4269
Armor, Joseph, #4270
Armor, Joseph, #4271
Armor, Joseph G., #4260
Armor, Joseph G., #4286
Armor, Joseph Guyton, #4231
Armor, Joseph Guyton, #4274
Armor, Josephine, #4265
Armor, Josephine, #4283
Armor, Leonidas, #4269
Armor, Louise Haas, #4245
Armor, Margaret, #4242
Armor, Mary, #4229
Armor, Mary, #4238
Armor, Mary, #4249
Armor, Mary, #4262
Armor, Mary, #4263
Armor, Mary, #4279
Armor, Mary Anna, #4268
Armor, Mary Anna Fonerdin, #4267
Armor, Mary Annie, #4275
Armor, Rachel, #4265
Armor, Rachel, #4266
Armor, Rachel, #4267
Armor, Rachel, #4268
Armor, Rachel, #4269

Armor, Rachel, #4270
Armor, Rachel, #4271
Armor, Rachel, #4281
Armor, Samuel, #4228
Armor, Samuel, #4236
Armor, Samuel, #4237
Armor, Samuel, #4239
Armor, Samuel, #4242
Armor, Samuel, #4246
Armor, Samuel, #4247
Armor, Sedonia, #4276
Armor, Sedonia Coleman, #4266
Armor, Susan, #4236
Armor, Susan, #4237
Armor, Thomas, #4236
Armor, Thomas, #4248
Armor, William, #4242
Armor, William, #4247
Armor, William Hunter, #4256
Armor, William Thomas, #4262
"Armor, Jr.", Samuel, #4251
Armstrong, Mary S., #2403
Armstrong, Mary Susan, #2404
Armstrong, Mary Susan, #2407
Arnold, Sarah, #3759
Arnold, Sarah, #3760
Aronhalt, Amos Wright, #1138
Aronhalt, David, #1140
Aronhalt, Eliza Ellen, #1139
Aronhalt, Eliza Ellen, #1154
Aronhalt, Flora L., #1148
Aronhalt, Isaac, #1146
Aronhalt, Jacob L., #1144
Aronhalt, Job M., #1143
Aronhalt, John William, #1149
Aronhalt, John William, #1150
Aronhalt, John Wm., #1153
Aronhalt, Keziah F., #1142
Aronhalt, Martha A., #1141
Aronhalt, Mary M., #1151
Aronhalt, Mary Margaret, #1136
Aronhalt, Myra J., #1147
Aronhalt, Myra Jane, #1155
Aronhalt, Rebecca, #1134
Aronhalt, Rebecca, #1157
Aronhalt, Rebecca V., #1145
Aronhalt, Samuel W., #1152
Aronhalt, Samuel Wheeler, #1135
Aronhalt, Thomas Edmund, #1137
Aronhalt, Thomas Wright, #1156
Arrond, Rev., #4176
Arsdale, Van, #5086
Ash, Harry G., #6988
Ashman, Rebecca, #7979
Ashman, Rebecca, #7980
Ashman, Rebecca, #7981
Ashman, Rebecca, #7982
Ashman, Rebecca, #7983
Ashman, Rebecca, #7984
Ashman, Rebecca, #7985
Ashman, Rebecca, #7986
Ashman, Rebecca, #7988
Ashmull, Florence, #3434
Atkinson, Samuel, #1268
Atkinson, Samuel, #1268
Atkinson, Samuel, #1265
Atwell, Alice, #5906
Atwell, Alice, #5907
Atwell, Alice, #5908
Atwell, Alice Susanna, #5905
Atwell, Frederick John, #5899

Atwell, Fredrick John, #5881
Atwell, George, #5877
Atwell, George, #5878
Atwell, George, #5881
Atwell, George, #5882
Atwell, George, #5885
Atwell, George W., #5891
Atwell, Hannah May, #5877
Atwell, Julia, #5877
Atwell, Julia, #5878
Atwell, Julia, #5881
Atwell, Julia, #5882
Atwell, Julia M., #5885
Atwell, Julia M., #5890
Atwell, Laurisa[?], #5898
Atwell, Mame Alice, #5878
Atwell, Martha Elizabeth, #5882
Aughinbaugh, Adam, #7802
Aughinbaugh, Adam, #7803
Aughinbaugh, Alfred, #7804
Aughinbaugh, Alfred, #7805
Aughinbaugh, Ann Catherine, #7787
Aughinbaugh, Anna Catherine Raum, #7768
Aughinbaugh, Anna Catherine Raum, #7769
Aughinbaugh, Anna Catherine Raum, #7770
Aughinbaugh, Anna Dorothy, #7818
Aughinbaugh, Anna Dorothy, #7827
Aughinbaugh, Bertha, #7835
Aughinbaugh, Bertha, #7836
Aughinbaugh, Bertha, #7837
Aughinbaugh, Bertha, #7838
Aughinbaugh, Bertha Frances, #7815
Aughinbaugh, Bertha Frances, #7824
Aughinbaugh, Bertha Frances, #7911
Aughinbaugh, Bertha Frances, #7912
Aughinbaugh, Bertha Frances, #7913
Aughinbaugh, Bertha Frances, #7914
Aughinbaugh, Bertha Frances, #7915
Aughinbaugh, Bertha Frances, #7916
Aughinbaugh, Bertha Frances, #7917
Aughinbaugh, Bertha Frances, #7918
Aughinbaugh, Charles, #7796
Aughinbaugh, Charles, #7831
Aughinbaugh, Charles, #7832
Aughinbaugh, Charles, #7832
Aughinbaugh, Charles, #7833
Aughinbaugh, Charles Augustus, #7781
Aughinbaugh, Charles Augustus, #7782
Aughinbaugh, Charles E., #7830
Aughinbaugh, Charles Edward, #7807
Aughinbaugh, Charles Edward, #7819
Aughinbaugh, Charles William, #7840
Aughinbaugh, Chas., #7766
Aughinbaugh, Emma Jane, #7785
Aughinbaugh, Emma Jane, #7799
Aughinbaugh, Eve, #7767
Aughinbaugh, Geo. Besore, #7765
Aughinbaugh, George, #7825
Aughinbaugh, George , #7822
Aughinbaugh, George B., #7789
Aughinbaugh, George Besore, #7779
Aughinbaugh, George Besore, #7780
Aughinbaugh, Grace, #7841
Aughinbaugh, Grace Estelle, #7823
Aughinbaugh, Grayce Estelle, #7811
Aughinbaugh, Harriet McCausland, #7803
Aughinbaugh, Henry, #7759

INDEX
Pages are not numbered; numbers refer to the entry number at the beginning of each record.

Aughinbaugh, Henry, #7764
Aughinbaugh, Henry, #7767
Aughinbaugh, Henry, #7833
Aughinbaugh, Henry Eliphabet, #7777
Aughinbaugh, Henry Eliphabet, #7778
Aughinbaugh, J. Philip, #7759
Aughinbaugh, J.C., #7806
Aughinbaugh, John, #7800
Aughinbaugh, John, #7801
Aughinbaugh, John Carson, #7817
Aughinbaugh, John Carson, #7826
Aughinbaugh, Laura, #7834
Aughinbaugh, Laura A., #7829
Aughinbaugh, Laura F., #7789
Aughinbaugh, Laura Marie, #7809
Aughinbaugh, Laura Marie, #7820
Aughinbaugh, Lille, #7790
Aughinbaugh, Lillie, #7805
Aughinbaugh, M.M., #7804
Aughinbaugh, Margaret, #7798
Aughinbaugh, Margaret Ann, #7762
Aughinbaugh, Margaret Ann, #7783
Aughinbaugh, Margaret Ann, #7784
Aughinbaugh, Mary Eliz., #7792
Aughinbaugh, Mary Elizabeth, #7771
Aughinbaugh, Mary Elizabeth, #7772
Aughinbaugh, Mary Jane, #7791
Aughinbaugh, Philip, #7761
Aughinbaugh, Philip, #7762
Aughinbaugh, Philip, #7763
Aughinbaugh, Philip, #7764
Aughinbaugh, Philip, #7765
Aughinbaugh, Philip, #7766
Aughinbaugh, Philip, #7767
Aughinbaugh, Philip, #7771
Aughinbaugh, Philip, #7772
Aughinbaugh, Philip, #7773
Aughinbaugh, Philip, #7774
Aughinbaugh, Philip, #7775
Aughinbaugh, Philip, #7776
Aughinbaugh, Philip, #7777
Aughinbaugh, Philip, #7778
Aughinbaugh, Philip, #7779
Aughinbaugh, Philip, #7780
Aughinbaugh, Philip, #7781
Aughinbaugh, Philip, #7782
Aughinbaugh, Philip, #7783
Aughinbaugh, Philip, #7784
Aughinbaugh, Philip, #7785
Aughinbaugh, Philip, #7792
Aughinbaugh, Philip, #7794
Aughinbaugh, Philip, #7796
Aughinbaugh, Philip, #7797
Aughinbaugh, Philip, #7799
Aughinbaugh, Philip , #7786
Aughinbaugh, Robert, #7839

Aughinbaugh, Roland, #7831
Aughinbaugh, Sarah, #7788
Aughinbaugh, Sidney , #7839
Aughinbaugh, Sidney , #7840
Aughinbaugh, Sidney McL., #7828
Aughinbaugh, Sidney McLanahan, #7821
Aughinbaugh, Sidney McLananhan, #7813
Aughinbaugh, Susanna, #7763
Aughinbaugh, Susanna, #7775
Aughinbaugh, Susanna, #7776
Aughinbaugh, Susanna, #7795
Aughinbaugh, William Michael, #7773
Aughinbaugh, William Michael, #7774
Aughinbaugh, Wm., #7791
Aughinbaugh, Wm. M., #7761
Aughinbaugh, Wm. M., #7793
Avery, Thomas, #1511
Ayrault, Walter, #2618
Ayrault, Walter, #3864
B____an[?], Martha, #3773
Bachtel, Ann M.E., #4574
Bachtel, Ann M.E., #4599
Bachtel, Anna B., #8005
Bachtel, Anna Barbara, #7950
Bachtel, Anna Mary, #7952
Bachtel, Benj. H., #8014
Bachtel, Benjamin F., #8028
Bachtel, Daniel, #7953
Bachtel, Daniel S., #8022
Bachtel, Daniel Stewart, #8012
Bachtel, Danl. S., #8031
Bachtel, David, #7955
Bachtel, Ellen Sophia, #8018
Bachtel, Ellen Sophia, #8029
Bachtel, Emma S., #8017
Bachtel, Emma S., #8024
Bachtel, Frederick, #7951
Bachtel, George, #7946
Bachtel, H.A. (Prof.), #7992
Bachtel, Henry A., #8005
Bachtel, Henry A., #8023
Bachtel, Henry Alfred, #8016
Bachtel, Henry Alfred, #8019
Bachtel, Irene H., #8006
Bachtel, Jacob L., #8009
Bachtel, Jacob L., #8021
Bachtel, Jno. Martin, #7949
Bachtel, John Jacob, #7942
Bachtel, John Jacob, #7943
Bachtel, John Jacob, #7944
Bachtel, John Jacob, #7945
Bachtel, John Jacob, #7948
Bachtel, Magdalene, #7947
Bachtel, Margaret A., #8026
Bachtel, Margaret Ann, #8015
Bachtel, Mary E., #8013
Bachtel, Mary E., #8025
Bachtel, Peter C., #8030
Bachtel, Peter Cornelius, #8010
Bachtel, Samuel, #8005
Bachtel, Samuel A., #8007
Bachtel, Samuel A., #8009
Bachtel, Samuel A., #8010
Bachtel, Samuel A., #8011
Bachtel, Samuel A., #8012
Bachtel, Samuel A., #8013

Bachtel, Samuel A., #8014
Bachtel, Samuel A., #8015
Bachtel, Samuel A., #8016
Bachtel, Samuel A., #8017
Bachtel, Samuel A., #8018
Bachtel, Samuel A., #8020
Bachtel, Samuel Augustua, #8027
Bachtel, Thomas, #7954
Bachtel, Wm. L., #8011
Bachtell, Anna Hammaker Krouse, #8032
Bachtell, Clifton Macedon, #4064
Bachtell, Emerson Guy, #4063
Bachtell, Lucetia Blanch, #4062
Bachtell, Lucetia Blanche, #4068
Bachtell, Mabel Achsah, #4066
Bachtell, Martin Luther, #4059
Bachtell, Martin Luther, #4060
Bachtell, Martin Luther, #4062
Bachtell, Martin Luther, #4063
Bachtell, Martin Luther, #4064
Bachtell, Martin Luther, #4065
Bachtell, Martin Luther, #4066
Bachtell, Raymond Paul, #4065
Bachtell, Ruby Heil, #4069
Bachtell, Ruth V. Peck, #4071
"Bachtell, Jr.", Clifton Macedon, #4067
"Bachtell, Sr.", Clifton M., #4070
Backhouse, Ann, #2052
Backhouse, Anna, #1881
Backhouse, Anna, #1882
Backhouse, Anna, #1883
Backhouse, Anna, #1910
Backhouse, Anna, #2050
Backhouse, Anna, #2051
Backhouse, Anna Potts, #1872
Backhouse, Anna Potts, #1901
Backhouse, C., #2054
Backhouse, Cath., #1896
Backhouse, Cath., #1897
Backhouse, Cathar., #2053
Backhouse, Catharine, #1884
Backhouse, Catharine, #1885
Backhouse, Catharine, #1886
Backhouse, Catharine, #1887
Backhouse, Catharine M., #1893
Backhouse, Catharine M., #1894
Backhouse, David Harrison, #1874
Backhouse, David Harrison, #1903
Backhouse, Edward Mortimer Clay, #1875
Backhouse, Edward Mortimer Clay, #1904
Backhouse, Elizabeth Ann[?] (Potts), #1885
Backhouse, Geo., #1878
Backhouse, Geo., #1896
Backhouse, Geo., #1897
Backhouse, Geo., #2053
Backhouse, Geo., #2054
Backhouse, Geo. B., #1891
Backhouse, Geo. Harvey[?] Clifford, #1873
Backhouse, Geo. Henry Clifford, #1902
Backhouse, George, #1882
Backhouse, George, #1884
Backhouse, George, #1885
Backhouse, George, #1886
Backhouse, George, #1887

Backhouse, George, #1907
Backhouse, George, #1911
Backhouse, George, #2051
Backhouse, Jane Catharine, #1886
Backhouse, Jane Catharine, #1896
Backhouse, John, #1880
Backhouse, John, #1908
Backhouse, John, #2049
Backhouse, Margaret Francess[?], #1877
Backhouse, Margaret Francessa, #1906
Backhouse, Mary, #1880
Backhouse, Mary, #1908
Backhouse, Mary, #1908
Backhouse, Mary, #2049
Backhouse, Mary Ellen, #1871
Backhouse, Mary Ellen, #1900
Backhouse, Pleasey, #2052
Backhouse, Pleasey Corbiner, #1897
Backhouse, Pleasey Corbiner[?], #1887
Backhouse, Pleasey[?], #1883
Backhouse, Sarah Amanda, #1876
Backhouse, Sarah Amanda, #1905
Backhouse, Thomas, #1880
Backhouse, Thomas, #1888
Backhouse, Thomas, #1889
Backhouse, Thomas, #1909
Backhouse, Thomas, #2049
Backhouse, Thomas, #2051
Backhouse, Thomas C., #1890
Backhouse, Thomas Christopher, #2053
Backhouse, Thomas[?] Christopher, #1884
Backhouse, Thos., #1882
Backhouse, Thos., #1883
Backhouse, Tom, #2052
Backhus, Geoerge, #371
Backus, Catharine, #371
Backus, G. H. Clifford, #373
Backus, G. H. Clifford , #375
Backus, G.H. Clifford, #371
Backus, John C., #4274
Backus, Kate Kable[?], #373
Backus, Katie Kable, #376
Backus, Lillie E., #373
Backus, Wilmira Clifford, #374
Baechtel, Henrietta B., #6885
Bagden, Ann Catherine, #7587
Bailey, Lucy L., #8277
Bailey, Lucy L.[or S.], #8289
Bair, Alma V., #3987
Bair, Arthur E., #3969
Bair, Arthur E., #3970
Bair, Arthur E., #3971
Bair, Arthur E., #3984
Bair, Arthur E., #3985
Bair, Arthur E., #3986
Bair, Arthur E., #3987
Bair, Arthur E., #3988
Bair, Arthur E., #3989
Bair, Arthur E., #3990
Bair, Carl E., #3986
Bair, Carl E., #4004
Bair, Charley N., #3974
Bair, Charley N., #3975
Bair, Charley N., #3993
Bair, Charley N., #3994
Bair, Charley N., #3995
Bair, Charley N., #3996
Bair, Charley N., #3997
Bair, Florence B., #3964
Bair, Florence B., #3965

INDEX
Pages are not numbered; numbers refer to the entry number at the beginning of each record.

Bair, Grace E., #3976
Bair, Grace E., #3977
Bair, Helen L., #3989
Bair, Helen L., #3990
Bair, Herald C., #3991
Bair, Herald C., #3992
Bair, Herald E., #3996
Bair, Herald E., #3997
Bair, Howard S., #3984
Bair, Howard S., #4003
Bair, Isaac, #3959
Bair, Isaac, #3960
Bair, Isaac, #3961
Bair, Isaac, #3964
Bair, Isaac, #3965
Bair, Isaac, #3966
Bair, Isaac, #3967
Bair, Isaac, #3968
Bair, Isaac, #3969
Bair, Isaac, #3970
Bair, Isaac, #3971
Bair, Isaac, #3972
Bair, Isaac, #3973
Bair, Isaac, #3974
Bair, Isaac, #3975
Bair, Isaac, #3976
Bair, Isaac, #3977
Bair, Isaac, #3978
Bair, Isaac, #3979
Bair, Isaac, #3980
Bair, Isaac, #3981
Bair, Isaac, #3982
Bair, Isaac, #3983
Bair, Lena V., #3978
Bair, Lena V., #3979
Bair, Lena V., #3998
Bair, Lena V., #3999
Bair, Lena V., #4000
Bair, Leon I., #3993
Bair, Leonard W., #3994
Bair, Luther H., #3972
Bair, Luther H., #3973
Bair, Luther H., #3991
Bair, Luther H., #3992
Bair, Mabel, #3982
Bair, Mabel, #3983
Bair, Maude E., #3980
Bair, Maude E., #3981
Bair, Maude E., #4001
Bair, Maude E., #4002
Bair, Ralph, #3995
Bair, Robert F., #3988
Bair, Russell T., #3985
Bair, William H., #3966
Bair, William H., #3967
Bair, William H., #3968
Baird, S.J., #6161
Baird, S.J., #6163
Baker, Anita E., #2770
Baker, Anita Elizabeth, #2797
Baker, Anita Elizabeth, #4043
Baker, Caroline S. [?], #8595
Baker, Catherine, #8592
Baker, Charlene Ruth, #4051
Baker, Charles, #4048
Baker, Charles Oliver, #1381
Baker, Charles Russell, #4046
Baker, David Ellsworth, #4014
Baker, Edna Adele, #6654
Baker, Edna Adele, #6655

Baker, Edna Adele, #6656
Baker, Essie May, #1379
Baker, Evelyn L., #2769
Baker, Evelyn Lorraine, #2796
Baker, Evelyn Lorraine, #4041
Baker, Evelyn Lorraine, #4042
Baker, Ezra, #2450
Baker, Ezra, #2451
Baker, Florence Elizabeth (Mrs.), #4055
Baker, Geo. R., #2789
Baker, Geo. R., #2790
Baker, Geo. R., #2791
Baker, Geo. R., #2792
Baker, Geo. R., #2793
Baker, Geo. R., #2794
Baker, Geo. R., #2795
Baker, Geo. R., #2796
Baker, Geo. R., #2797
Baker, George R., #2762
Baker, George R., #4013
Baker, George R., #4044
Baker, George Raymond, #2799
Baker, George Raymond, #4016
Baker, George Raymond, #4017
Baker, George William, #4015
Baker, Grace Irene (Wilson), #6691
Baker, Guy L., #2765
Baker, Guy Long, #2792
Baker, Guy Long, #4035
Baker, Harry Wilson, #1377
Baker, I. Pearl (Long), #2783
Baker, Isaac Wilson, #1380
Baker, Jacob, #2799
Baker, Johan Nickolas, #8591
Baker, Joshua J., #2767
Baker, Joshua Jacob, #2794
Baker, Joshua Jacob, #4037
Baker, Joshua Jacob, #4038
Baker, Lulu Thelma, #4033
Baker, Lulu Thelma, #4034
Baker, Mary Florence, #4048
Baker, Mildred Joanne, #4049
Baker, Myrtle Virginia (Miller), #4053
Baker, Myrtle Virginia (Miller), #4054
Baker, Otho Fout, #6657
Baker, Paula Elizabeth, #4052
Baker, Raymond L., #2764
Baker, Raymond Lamar, #4021
Baker, Raymond Lamar, #4022
Baker, "Raymond LaMar ""Teddy", #2790
Baker, Susan Rebecca, #1335
Baker, Susan Rebecca, #1337
Baker, Susan Rebecca, #1338
Baker, Susan Rebecca, #1339
Baker, Susan Rebecca, #1340
Baker, Susan Rebecca, #1341
Baker, Thelma Lola, #2791
Baker, Urla G., #2766
Baker, Urla Grace, #2793
Baker, Urla Grace, #4036
Baker, Verda, #2798
Baker, Verda, #2800
Baker, Verda, #2801
Baker, Verda, #2802
Baker, Verda M., #2763
Baker, Verda Mary, #2789

Baker, Verda Mary, #4020
Baker, Virginia, #4048
Baker, Virginia Marie, #4050
Baker, W.S., #4045
Baker, Wanda (Miss), #4045
Baker, Wanda A., #2768
Baker, Wanda Arlene, #2795
Baker, Wanda Arlene, #4039
Baker, Wanda Arlene, #4040
Baker, William Frances, #1378
Balckburn, Ephriam G., #1083
Balckburn, Mary A., #1104
Balckburn, Mary A., #1105
Balckburn, Mary A., #1106
Balckburn, Mary A., #1107
Balckburn, Mary A., #1108
Balckburn, Mary A., #1109
Balckburn, Mary A., #1110
Balckburn, Mary A., #1111
Bald, Rev., #6803
Baldwin, Bertha G., #6390
Baldwin, Bertha G., #6391
Baldwin, Bertha G., #6392
Baldwin, Bertha G., #6393
Baldwin, Bertha Gertrude, #6316
Baldwin, Warren, #3454
Ball, Athalia, #1960
Ball, Lawrence (Mrs.), #781
Ball, Mary Hortense (Cochran), #784
Barber, Harriett, #743
Barbour, Achsah[?] A., #756
Barbour, Caroline M., #755
Barbour, Catharine, #758
Barbour, Clementine E., #751
Barbour, Harriet C., #746
Barbour, Harriet C., #750
Barbour, Johnsy, #759
Bare, James V., #7389
Barkman, Aunty Katie, #7152
Barkman[?], Catherine, #7140
Barkman[?], Jacob, #7138
Barkman[?], Jacob, #7139
Barks, Barbara, #1003
Barks, Barbara, #1005
Barks, Barbara, #1006
Barks, Barbara, #1007
Barks, Barbara, #1008
Barks, Barbara, #1009
Barks, Barbara, #1010
Barks, Barbara, #1011
Barks, Barbara, #1012
Barks, Barbara, #1013
Barks, Barbara, #1014
Barks, Barbara, #1015
Barks, Barbara, #1016
Barks, Barbara, #1017
Barks, Barbara, #1018
Barks, Barbara, #1019
Barks, Barbara, #1020
Barks, Barbara, #1021
Barks, Barbara, #1022
Barks, Barbara, #1023
Barks, Barbara, #1024
Barks, Barbara, #1025
Barks, Barbara, #1026
Barks, Barbara, #1027
Barks, Barbara, #4880
Barks, Barbara, #4881
Barks, Barbara, #4882
Barks, Barbara, #4883

Barks, Barbara, #4884
Barks, Barbara, #4885
Barks, Barbara, #4886
Barks, Barbara, #4887
Barks, Barbara, #4888
Barks, Barbara, #4889
Barks, Barbara, #4890
Barks, Barbara, #4891
Barks, Barbara, #4892
Barks, Barbara, #4893
Barks, Barbara, #4894
Barks, Barbara, #4895
Barks, Barbara, #4896
Barks, Barbara, #4897
Barks, Barbara, #4898
Barks, Barbara, #4899
Barks, Barbara, #4900
Barks, Barbara, #4901
Barks, Barbara, #4902
Barks, Barbara, #4903
Barks, Barbara, #4904
Barks, Barbara, #4905
Barnes, Catharine V., #297
Barnes, Catharine V., #4008
Barnes, Catherine Virginia, #3959
Barnes, Catherine Virginia, #3962
Barnes, Catherine Virginia, #3963
Barnes, Catherine Virginia, #3964
Barnes, Catherine Virginia, #3965
Barnes, Catherine Virginia, #3966
Barnes, Catherine Virginia, #3967
Barnes, Catherine Virginia, #3968
Barnes, Catherine Virginia, #3969
Barnes, Catherine Virginia, #3970
Barnes, Catherine Virginia, #3971
Barnes, Catherine Virginia, #3972
Barnes, Catherine Virginia, #3973
Barnes, Catherine Virginia, #3974
Barnes, Catherine Virginia, #3975
Barnes, Catherine Virginia, #3976
Barnes, Catherine Virginia, #3977
Barnes, Catherine Virginia, #3978
Barnes, Catherine Virginia, #3979
Barnes, Catherine Virginia, #3980
Barnes, Catherine Virginia, #3981
Barnes, Catherine Virginia, #3982
Barnes, Catherine Virginia, #3983
Barnes, Eliza Jane, #4012
Barnes, Emily J. C., #298
Barnes, Emily J.C.[?], #4009
Barnes, Grace, #7382
Barnes, Grace, #7384
Barnes, Joshua B., #299
Barnes, Joshua B., #4010
Barnes, Levi Y., #294
Barnes, Levi Y., #295
Barnes, Levi Y., #4005
Barnes, Levi Y., #4006
Barnes, Liza Jane, #301
Barnes, Matilda, #296
Barnes, Matilda, #4007
Barnes, Sarah _._.[?], #4011
Barnes, Sarah N. E.[?], #300
Barnhardf[?], Martha E., #610
Barnhardf[?], Martha E., #613
Barnhardf[?], Martha E., #614
Barnhardf[?], Martha E., #615
Barnhardf[?], Martha E., #617
Barnhardf[?], Martha E., #618
Barnhardf[?], Martha E., #619

INDEX
Pages are not numbered; numbers refer to the entry number at the beginning of each record.

Barnhardf[?], Martha E., #620
Barnhardf[?], Martha E., #621
Barnhardf[?], Martha E., #622
Barnhart, Lester H., #2735
Barr, Eavie[?], #5957
Barr, Grace, #2905
Barrick, Emma, #5960
Bartle, Alaxander Rudolph, #438
Bartle, Alaxander Rudolph, #447
Bartle, Effie Naomi, #432
Bartle, Effie V.[?], #2473
Bartle, Elmer V., #443
Bartle, Elmer Vinson, #430
Bartle, Elnora Susan, #441
Bartle, Elnora Susan, #442
Bartle, Harry R., #445
Bartle, Harry Richard, #436
Bartle, Isaac Neuton, #449
Bartle, Isaac Newton, #440
Bartle, Jeremiah Herman, #431
Bartle, Lloyd Elgin, #435
Bartle, Luther C., #444
Bartle, Luther Cleveland, #434
Bartle, Percy Glenn, #439
Bartle, Percy Glenn, #448
Bartle, Raymond, #446
Bartle, Roy Raymond, #437
Bartle, Victor Orville, #433
Bartle, William, #429
Bartle, William, #430
Bartle, William, #431
Bartle, William, #432
Bartle, William, #433
Bartle, William, #434
Bartle, William, #435
Bartle, William, #436
Bartle, William, #437
Bartle, William, #438
Bartle, William, #439
Bartle, William, #440
Bartle, William, #450
Bartle, William, #451
Barton, Charlotte, #1260
Bass, Agnes, #2252
Bass, Edward, #2257
Bass, Ezebath, #2253
Bass, Frances, #2255
Bass, John, #2249
Bass, John, #2250
Bass, John, #2251
Bass, John, #2252
Bass, John, #2253
Bass, John, #2254
Bass, John, #2255
Bass, John, #2256
Bass, John, #2256
Bass, John, #2257
Bass, John, #2258
Bass, John, #2259
Bass, Lucy, #2259
Bass, Martha, #2250
Bass, Mary, #2254
Bass, Nancy, #2258
Bass, Tabitha, #2250
Bass, Tabitha, #2251
Bass, Tabitha, #2251
Bass, Tabitha, #2252

Bass, Tabitha, #2253
Bass, Tabitha, #2254
Bass, Tabitha, #2255
Bass, Tabitha, #2256
Bass, Tabitha, #2257
Bass, Tabitha, #2258
Bass, Tabitha, #2259
Bass, Tabitha, #2263
Bass, Tabitha, #2268
Bast, Catharine, #4403
Bauldiven, Chas., #4362
Baumgardner, Barbara Kay, #2997
Baumgardner, Robert B., #2997
Baxter, Annie L., #733
Baxter, Annie L., #742
Baxter, Edgar Theo.[?], #740
Baxter, Edgar Theodore, #731
Baxter, Edith Mildreth, #736
Baxter, Emma R., #728
Baxter, Emma R., #739
Baxter, Ethel Alverda, #729
Baxter, Hilda Catherine, #734
Baxter, Nellie Grace, #735
Baxter, Raymond E., #738
Baxter, Raymond Erlandis, #730
Baxter, Ruth Elline, #732
Baxter, William E., #725
Baxter, William E., #726
Baxter, William E., #727
Baxter, Willima E., #741
Bayley, Frank, #282
Bayly, Mary Jane, #5187
Beachey[?], Elizabeth C.[?], #2728
Beachley, Alice (Taylor), #288
Beachley, Charles E., #5044
Beachley, Clara, #286
Beachley, Cora R., #5005
Beachley, Eleanor Louise Gregory, #273
Beachley, Elizabeth, #2759
Beachley, Harry Knode, #280
Beachley, Harry Knode, #281
Beachley, Harry Knode, #287
Beachley, Helen Morgart, #289
Beachley, Jack Hanson, #272
Beachley, JoAnn, #274
Beachley, JoAnn, #284
Beachley, John H. (Mrs.), #2754
Beachley, John Henry, #5047
Beachley, Katherine Louise, #271
Beachley, Laura A. (Mrs.), #5044
Beachley, Mattie[?] V., #3014
Beachley, Ralph Gregory, #270
Beachley, Ralph Gregory, #293
Beachley, William S., #2759
Beachley, William W., #2755
Beachley, Yvonne, #275
Beachley, Yvonne, #285
"Beachley, MD", Jack H., #282
"Beachley, MD", Jack H., #283
Beall, Mary, #2638
Beall, Mary, #2639
Beall, Mary, #2640
Beall, Mary, #3878
Beall, Mary, #3879
Beall, Mary, #3880

Bear, Elizabeth, #8308
Beard, Cora, #8209
Beard, D.L., #8275
Beard, Lila V., #3402
Beard, Margaret, #5953
Beard, Margaret, #5992
Beard, Margaret, #5996
Beard, Sarah, #7069
Beatty, Edward, #2708
Beatty, Edward, #2709
Beatty, Edward, #2710
Beatty, Edward, #2711
Beatty, Edward, #2712
Beatty, Edward, #2713
Beatty, Edward, #2713
Beatty, Edward, #2714
Beatty, Edward, #3951
Beatty, Edward, #3952
Beatty, Edward, #3953
Beatty, Edward, #3957
Beatty, Edward W., #3859
Beatty, Edward W.[?], #2613
Beatty, Eli, #2709
Beatty, Eli, #3952
Beatty, Elizabeth Ch___, #2613
Beatty, Elizabeth Chew, #2618
Beatty, Elizabeth Chew, #2678
Beatty, Elizabeth Chew, #2679
Beatty, Elizabeth Chew, #2680
Beatty, Elizabeth Chew, #2681
Beatty, Elizabeth Chew, #2682
Beatty, Elizabeth Chew, #2683
Beatty, Elizabeth Chew, #2711
Beatty, Elizabeth Chew, #3859
Beatty, Elizabeth Chew, #3864
Beatty, Elizabeth Chew, #3921
Beatty, Elizabeth Chew, #3922
Beatty, Elizabeth Chew, #3923
Beatty, Elizabeth Chew, #3924
Beatty, Elizabeth Chew, #3925
Beatty, Elizabeth Chew, #3954
Beatty, Elizabeth Chew, #3955
Beatty, Kate, #2712
Beatty, Kate, #3956
Beatty, Laura, #2714
Beatty, Laura[?], #3958
Beatty, Maria A., #2613
Beatty, Maria A., #3859
Beck, Ada May, #6653
Beck, Ada May, #6662
Beck, Alice S., #6705
Beck, Andrew, #6715
Beck, Billie Baker, #6664
Beck, Billy Baker, #6655
Beck, Edna Adelle (Baker), #6666
Beck, Edna Adelle (Baker), #6694
Beck, Howard, #6651
Beck, Howard E., #6705
Beck, Howard Ellsworth, #6652
Beck, Howard Ellsworth, #6660
Beck, Howard Ellsworth, #6662
Beck, Howard Ellsworth, #6663
Beck, Howard Ellsworth, #6684
Beck, J., #7774
Beck, James Ellsworth, #6686
Beck, John Williams, #6685
Beck, Lillie M., #6704
Beck, Mary Ann, #6701
Beck, Robert, #6685
Beck, Robert Edwin, #6656
Beck, Robert Edwin, #6659

Beck, Robert Edwin, #6665
Beck, Robert Edwin, #6686
Beck, Robert Edwin, #6698
Beck, Ruth, #6685
Beck, Ruth P., #6695
Beck, Ruth P., #6696
Beck, Susan, #6716
Beck, Susan Alice, #6692
Beck, Susan Alice, #6693
Beck, Susan Alice (Wilson), #6683
Beck, William Baker, #6687
Beck, William Baker, #6697
Beck, William G., #6697
Beck, William G., #6698
Beck, William Granville, #6654
Beck, William Granville, #6655
Beck, William Granville, #6656
Beck, William Granville, #6663
"Beck, II", "William Granville ""Chip", #6687
"Beck, Jr.", Howard, #6700
"Beck, Jr.", Robert Edwin, #6699
"Beck, Sr.", Robert Edwin, #6699
Beckenbaugh, George, #652
Beckenbaugh, Harriet Louise, #644
Beckenbaugh, Harriet Louise, #645
Beckenbaugh, Helen Douglas, #637
Beckenbaugh, Helen Douglas, #640
Beckenbaugh, Helen Douglas, #642
Beckenbaugh, Helen Douglas, #643
Beckenbaugh, J.J. (Dr.), #648
Beckenbaugh, Jno. Kyd, #638
Beckenbaugh, Jno. Kyd, #644
Beckenbaugh, Jno. Kyd, #645
Beckenbaugh, Jno. M. (Dr.), #639
Beckenbaugh, Jno. M. (Dr.), #640
Beckenbaugh, Jno. M. (Dr.), #641
Beckenbaugh, John, #641
Beckenbaugh, John Howard, #644
Beckenbaugh, John In.[?], #651
Beckenbaugh, John Kyd, #657
Beckenbaugh, Louise Douglas, #645
Beckenbaugh, Magdalena, #8582
Beckenbaugh, Martha Ligget, #639
Beckenbaugh, Martha Ligget, #649
Beckenbaugh, Nannie C., #639
Beckenbaugh, Nannie C., #640
Beckenbaugh, Nannie C., #641
Beckenbaugh, T.L. (Dr.), #653
"Beckenbaugh, M.D.", John M., #636
Becker, Carrie, #6297
Becker, Carrie, #6298
Becker, Carrie, #6299
Becker, Carrie, #6300
Becker, Carrie, #6427
Becker, Carrie, #6428
Becker, Carrie, #6429
Becker, Carrie, #6459
Becker, Carrie, #6460
Becker, Carrie, #6461
Becker, Q.C., #2128
Beckley, [twins], #6789
Beckley, ___[?] Gertrude, #358
Beckley, Alen Clark, #357
Beckley, Allen Clark, #366
Beckley, Ann Elizabeth Ripple, #79
Beckley, Charles Elmer, #355
Beckley, D., #364
Beckley, D., #366
Beckley, David, #348
Beckley, David, #349

INDEX
Pages are not numbered; numbers refer to the entry number at the beginning of each record.

Beckley, David, #355
Beckley, David, #357
Beckley, David, #358
Beckley, David, #359
Beckley, David, #360
Beckley, David, #361
Beckley, David, #362
Beckley, David, #365
Beckley, David, #368
Beckley, David, #369
Beckley, David Luther, #359
Beckley, Frederick Hershey, #6791
Beckley, Geo. H., #4687
Beckley, J.A., #6789
Beckley, John Ashby, #6780
Beckley, John Clinton, #351
Beckley, John Michael, #6790
Beckley, John[?] Clinton, #365
Beckley, M., #364
Beckley, M., #366
Beckley, Margaret, #355
Beckley, Margaret, #357
Beckley, Margaret, #358
Beckley, Margaret, #359
Beckley, Margaret, #360
Beckley, Margaret, #361
Beckley, Margaret, #362
Beckley, Margaret, #365
Beckley, Margaret, #369
Beckley, Margaret A., #367
Beckley, Margia L., #369
Beckley, Margia L., #370
Beckley, Margie Lee, #361
Beckley, Mary Alice, #353
Beckley, Mary V., #6789
Beckley, Mary Virginia (Speaker), #6798
Beckley, R_____ [?], #356
Beckley, Richard P. H__[?], #352
Beckley, Rosa May, #362
Beckley, Walter Scott, #360
Beckley, William H., #364
Beckley, William Henry, #354
Beeler, Violetta, #3404
Bell, Edna N., #1436
Bell, Edna N., #5309
Bell, Elizabeth (Miss), #506
Bell, Geo. F., #1388
Bell, George Y., #5299
Bell, Julia Ann (Miss), #515
Bell, Susan, #2112
Bell, Susan, #2113
Bell, Susan, #2114
Bell, Susan, #2115
Bell, Susan, #2116
Bender, Conrad, #8151
Benner, Cora May, #2893
Benner, George W., #2893
Benner, George W., #2894
Benner, Lena Francis, #2894
Benner, Viola, #3672
Benner, Viola, #4927
Benner [sic], Viola [sic], #4928
Bennet, Wm. C., #7780
Bennett, Elizabeth Ann, #4235
Bennett, Elizabeth Ann, #4259
Bennett, George, #4229

Bennett, William, #4234
Bennett, William T., #4258
Benson, Laura Taylor, #290
Benson, Laura Taylor, #291
Bernard, Joab, #1299
Bernard, Joab, #7292
Berry, R.T., #6159
Betts, "The Twins", #3319
Betts, Aalferd[?], #3323
Betts, Cardine[?], #3320
Betts, Cathrine, #3312
Betts, Cathrine, #3313
Betts, Daniel L.[?], #3316
Betts, David, #3309
Betts, Elisabeth, #3310
Betts, Elisabeth, #3311
Betts, Jacob, #3322
Betts, John V., #3318
Betts, Lutter[?] David, #3321
Betts, Rosenia, #3317
Betts, Susanna, #3314
Betts, Susanna, #3315
Biggs, Chas. S., #4175
Bigham, Wm., #2161
Bingham, Sammy K., #8276
Bird, Harry, #3237
Bird, Harry, #6875
Bishop, Kate (Miss), #5020
Bishop, Rev., #6265
Bittle, D.H., #570
Bitzberger, Evelyn, #8210
Bitzberger, Evelyn, #8341
Bitzberger, Evelyn Gertrude, #8269
Bitzberger, Evelyn Gertrude, #8355
Bitzberger, Evelyn Gertrude, #8356
Bitzberger, Evelyn Gertrude, #8357
Bitzberger, Fred, #8338
Bitzberger, Fred, #8339
Bitzberger, Fred, #8340
Blackburn, Carrie (Shillingburg), #1126
Blackburn, Clarence A., #1123
Blackburn, Martha Rosanna, #3782
Blackburn, Martha Rosanna, #3783
Blackburn, Martha Rosanna, #3784
Blackburn, Mary A., #1103
Blackburn, Thos., #3783
Blair, Jane Louise, #5426
Blanset, Ray, #8268
Blecher, Leah, #3055
Blecher, Leah, #3056
Blecher, Leah, #3057
Blecher, Leah, #3058
Blecher, Leah, #3059
Blecher, Leah, #3101
Blecher, Leah, #3102
Blecher, Leah, #3103
Blecher, Leah, #3104
Blecher, Leah, #3105
Blecher, Leah, #3106
Blessing, Sarah Ann Penelope, #4291
Blunt, Ann, #7061
Blunt, James R., #7061

Blythe, D. Bruce, #7613
Bohlken, Charles, #5736
Bohlken, Charles, #5758
Bohlken, Esther May, #5731
Bohn, Melvin, #2345
Boman, Melia, #3845
Bookman, Mary E., #5391
Boon, Kate Donekins[?], #7478
Boone, Catherine, #7470
Boone, Kate (Miss), #7462
Boroff, Catharine, #3126
Boroff, Sarah, #3127
Boroff, Sarah, #3203
Boteler, Anna Louise Duckett, #1345
Boteler, Annett V., #2006
Boteler, Annette Virginia, #1997
Boteler, Athalia V., #2010
Boteler, Catherine C., #1951
Boteler, E.L., #1940
Boteler, E.L., #2046
Boteler, E.L. (Dr.), #2025
Boteler, E.L. (Dr.), #2028
Boteler, E.L. (Dr.), #2040
Boteler, E.S., #2003
Boteler, Edward Hammond, #2009
Boteler, Edward Hammond, #2017
Boteler, Edward L., #1943
Boteler, Elias L., #1935
Boteler, Elias[?] L., #1946
Boteler, Elizabeth, #1945
Boteler, Elizabeth, #1959
Boteler, Elizabeth, #2011
Boteler, Elizabeth Jane, #1994
Boteler, Elizabeth Jane, #2037
Boteler, Ellen R., #2023
Boteler, Henry, #1942
Boteler, Henry A., #2030
Boteler, Jane, #1939
Boteler, Jane, #1944
Boteler, Jane, #1961
Boteler, Jane E., #2014
Boteler, Jely[?] Bond, #1995
Boteler, July[?] Bond, #2036
Boteler, Lorena, #8501
Boteler, Lorena Amelia, #2012
Boteler, Lorina, #8442
Boteler, Lorina A., #8441
Boteler, Louise, #1958
Boteler, Marryann, #1947
Boteler, Martha W., #2005
Boteler, Martha Washington, #1996
Boteler, Mary, #1937
Boteler, Mary, #2033
Boteler, Mary Catharine, #2016
Boteler, Mary Maka, #1999
Boteler, Mary Makle, #2043
Boteler, Matilda Ellen, #2001
Boteler, Matilda Ellen, #2038
Boteler, Prudence, #2029
Boteler, Prudence (Cheney), #1998
Boteler, Prudence C., #2007
Boteler, Prudence Chaney, #2013
Boteler, Prudence Cheney, #2039
Boteler, Prudence Cheney, #2047
Boteler, R.H.E., #2021
Boteler, R.H.E., #2022
Boteler, R.H.E., #2027
Boteler, R.H.E. (Dr.), #1957
Boteler, R.H.E. (Dr.), #8442

Boteler, Rachel E., #2008
Boteler, Rachel Elizabeth, #2000
Boteler, Rebecca, #1957
Boteler, Rebecca C., #2026
Boteler, Rev., #4376
Boteler, Robert H., #2004
Boteler, Robert H.E., #2025
Boteler, Robert Henry, #2015
Boteler, Robert Henry Ezekiel, #1993
Boteler, Robert L., #2020
Boteler, Robert Lingan, #1957
Boteler, Robert Lingan, #1958
Boteler, Rosa Nelson, #2018
Boteler, Rosa Nelson, #2024
Boteler, Sarah, #1950
Boteler, Sophie (Duckett), #1351
Boteler, Susannah, #1949
Boteler, William Edward, #2002
Boteler, William Edward, #2044
"Boteler, Jr.", Henry, #1948
"Boteler, Sr.", Henry A., #1936
"Boteler, Sr.", Henry A., #2032
Boullt, [twin sister of Christianna A.], #2067
Boullt, [twin sister of Cristianna A.], #2063
Boullt, Ann, #2092
Boullt, Ann, #2098
Boullt, Anna Curtis[?], #2080
Boullt, Clasine[?] Marshall, #2081
Boullt, Cristianna A., #2062
Boullt, David Hammett, #2064
Boullt, Elizabeth, #2058
Boullt, Elizabeth, #2059
Boullt, Elizabeth, #2060
Boullt, Elizabeth, #2061
Boullt, Elizabeth, #2062
Boullt, Elizabeth, #2063
Boullt, Elizabeth, #2064
Boullt, Elizabeth, #2065
Boullt, Elizabeth, #2066
Boullt, Elizabeth, #2077
Boullt, Elizabeth, #2088
Boullt, Elizabeth, #2094
Boullt, Elizabeth, #2096
Boullt, Elizabeth, #2105
Boullt, Elizabeth, #2107
Boullt, G.W.C., #2068
Boullt, George Washington Colombus, #2066
Boullt, Harry, #2083
Boullt, Helen E., #2106
Boullt, Hellen Elizabeth, #2060
Boullt, Henery Watts, #2061
Boullt, Jane[?], #2093
Boullt, Jean, #2099
Boullt, Jean, #2101
Boullt, Jean[?], #2095
Boullt, Kenelam, #2090
Boullt, Kenelam, #2097
Boullt, Rosa[?], #2071
Boullt, Sarah, #2091
Boullt, Sarah Bell, #2074
Boullt, Susan Bell, #2079
Boullt, Susan Bell[?], #2072
Boullt, Susanna, #2088
Boullt, Susanna, #2096
Boullt, Tho. H., #2100
Boullt, Thomas, #2056
Boullt, Thomas, #2058
Boullt, Thomas, #2102

INDEX
Pages are not numbered; numbers refer to the entry number at the beginning of each record.

Boullt, Thomas A., #2117
Boullt, Thomas Alexander Smith Holings Watts, #2065
Boullt, Thomas H., #2089
Boullt, Thos., #2088
Boullt, Thos., #2096
Boullt, Thos. A., #2069
Boullt, Thos. A., #2070
Boullt, Thos. Alex, #2082
Boullt, Thos. Alex., #2075
Boullt, William, #2077
Boullt, William, #2078
Boullt, William, #2104
Boullt, William, #2107
Boullt, William , #2073
Boullt, Wm., #2055
Boullt, Wm., #2058
Boullt, Wm., #2059
Boullt, Wm., #2060
Boullt, Wm., #2061
Boullt, Wm., #2062
Boullt, Wm., #2063
Boullt, Wm., #2064
Boullt, Wm., #2065
Boullt, Wm., #2066
Boullt, Wm. Hammett, #2059
Boultt, T.A., #2114
Bound[?], Virginia, #3738
Bovey, Anna C., #1765
Bovey, Anna C., #8138
Bovey, Anna Cecelia, #1752
Bovey, Anna Cecelia, #8125
Bovey, C., #1745
Bovey, C., #8118
Bovey, Edward O., #1757
Bovey, Edward O., #1764
Bovey, Edward O., #8130
Bovey, Edward O., #8137
Bovey, Ellen Missouri, #1758
Bovey, Ellen Missouri, #8131
Bovey, Ellen Mussouri, #1751
Bovey, Ellen Mussouri[?], #8124
Bovey, Flora Belle, #1756
Bovey, Flora Belle, #1760
Bovey, Flora Belle, #8129
Bovey, Flora Belle, #8133
Bovey, G., #1745
Bovey, G., #8118
Bovey, George Henry, #1750
Bovey, George Henry, #8123
Bovey, H.A., #3400
Bovey, H.A., #5141
Bovey, Henry, #1744
Bovey, Henry, #1745
Bovey, Henry, #1747
Bovey, Henry, #1748
Bovey, Henry, #1749
Bovey, Henry, #1750
Bovey, Henry, #1751
Bovey, Henry, #1752
Bovey, Henry, #1753
Bovey, Henry, #1754
Bovey, Henry, #1755
Bovey, Henry, #1756
Bovey, Henry, #1757
Bovey, Henry, #1762
Bovey, Henry, #8117
Bovey, Henry, #8118
Bovey, Henry, #8120
Bovey, Henry, #8121

Bovey, Henry, #8122
Bovey, Henry, #8123
Bovey, Henry, #8124
Bovey, Henry, #8125
Bovey, Henry, #8126
Bovey, Henry, #8127
Bovey, Henry, #8128
Bovey, Henry, #8129
Bovey, Henry, #8130
Bovey, Henry, #8135
Bovey, Jacob, #1755
Bovey, Jacob, #8128
Bovey, Jacob Reel, #1759
Bovey, Jacob Reel, #8132
Bovey, Lavinia Jane, #1747
Bovey, Lavinia Jane, #8120
Bovey, Lillie May, #1754
Bovey, Lillie May, #8127
Bovey, Luther Martin, #1749
Bovey, Luther Martin, #8122
Bovey, Maria, #8120
Bovey, Maria, #8121
Bovey, Maria, #8122
Bovey, Maria, #8123
Bovey, Maria, #8124
Bovey, Maria, #8125
Bovey, Maria, #8126
Bovey, Maria, #8127
Bovey, Maria, #8128
Bovey, Maria, #8129
Bovey, Maria, #8130
Bovey, Maria Ellen, #1761
Bovey, Maria Ellen, #8134
Bovey, Mary Catharine, #1748
Bovey, Mary Catharine, #1763
Bovey, Mary Catharine, #8121
Bovey, Mary Catharine, #8136
Bovey, Millard Claggett, #1753
Bovey, Millard Claggett, #8126
Bowen, John, #8148
Bower, Hannah Ardinger, #4138
Bowers, Edith, #2731
Bowers, Eleanora (Mrs.), #3036
Bowers, Hanner, #1695
Bowers, Hanner, #4104
Bowers, J.C., #3036
Bowers, Rev., #1592
Bowie, Allen, #2656
Bowie, Allen, #3874
Bowie, Allen, #3896
Bowie, Allen , #2633
Bowie, Allen Davis, #2687
Bowie, Allen Davis, #2689
Bowie, Allen Davis, #2690
Bowie, Allen Davis, #3927
Bowie, Allen Davis, #3930
Bowie, Allen Davis, #3931
Bowie, Allen Thomas, #2616
Bowie, Allen Thomas, #2624
Bowie, Allen Thomas, #2682
Bowie, Allen Thomas, #2693
Bowie, Allen Thomas, #2694
Bowie, Allen Thomas, #2695
Bowie, Allen Thomas, #2696
Bowie, Allen Thomas, #3862
Bowie, Allen Thomas, #3867
Bowie, Allen Thomas, #3923
Bowie, Allen Thomas, #3934
Bowie, Allen Thomas, #3935
Bowie, Allen Thomas, #3936

Bowie, Allen Thomas, #3938
Bowie, Allen Thomas , #2621
Bowie, Barbara, #2701
Bowie, Barbara, #2702
Bowie, Barbara, #2703
Bowie, Barbara, #2704
Bowie, Barbara, #3943
Bowie, Barbara, #3944
Bowie, Barbara, #3945
Bowie, Barbara, #3946
Bowie, Catharine _.[?], #3858
Bowie, Catharine Davis, #2615
Bowie, Catharine Davis, #2626
Bowie, Catharine Davis, #2681
Bowie, Catharine Davis, #2691
Bowie, Catharine Davis, #2692
Bowie, Catharine Davis, #3861
Bowie, Catharine Davis, #3922
Bowie, Catharine Davis, #3932
Bowie, Catharine Davis, #3933
Bowie, Catharine W. (Davis), #2671
Bowie, Edward Beattty , #2625
Bowie, Edward Beatty, #2614
Bowie, Edward Beatty, #2619
Bowie, Edward Beatty, #2680
Bowie, Edward Beatty, #2684
Bowie, Edward Beatty, #2685
Bowie, Edward Beatty, #3860
Bowie, Edward Beatty, #3865
Bowie, Edward Beatty, #3921
Bowie, Edward Beatty, #3925
Bowie, Edward Beatty, #3926
Bowie, Edward Beatty, #3927
Bowie, Edward Beatty, #3928
Bowie, Edward Beatty, #3929
Bowie, Edward Beatty, #3930
Bowie, Edwawrd Beatty, #2686
Bowie, Edwawrd Beatty, #2687
Bowie, Eleanor, #2631
Bowie, Eleanor, #3872
Bowie, Elizabeth, #2614
Bowie, Elizabeth, #2615
Bowie, Elizabeth, #2616
Bowie, Elizabeth, #2617
Bowie, Elizabeth, #2653
Bowie, Elizabeth, #3860
Bowie, Elizabeth, #3861
Bowie, Elizabeth, #3862
Bowie, Elizabeth, #3863
Bowie, Elizabeth, #3893
Bowie, Elizabeth C., #2622
Bowie, Elizabeth Chew (Beatty), #3920
Bowie, Ellen Ruth, #2674
Bowie, Ellen Ruth, #3916
Bowie, Georgia Paul, #3937
Bowie, Georgia Paul, #3938
Bowie, Georgia Paul, #3939
Bowie, Georgia Pauls, #2696
Bowie, Georgia Pauls, #2697
Bowie, Hannah, #2657
Bowie, Hannah, #3897
Bowie, James, #2632
Bowie, James, #3873
Bowie, James, #3883
Bowie, John, #2627
Bowie, John, #2628
Bowie, John, #2629
Bowie, John, #2630
Bowie, John, #2631

Bowie, John, #2632
Bowie, John, #2633
Bowie, John, #2634
Bowie, John, #2635
Bowie, John, #2636
Bowie, John, #3868
Bowie, John, #3869
Bowie, John, #3870
Bowie, John, #3871
Bowie, John, #3872
Bowie, John, #3873
Bowie, John, #3874
Bowie, John, #3875
Bowie, John, #3876
Bowie, John, #3877
Bowie, John, #3892
Bowie, John (Dr.), #2652
Bowie, John (Rev.), #3884
Bowie, Margaret, #2663
Bowie, Margaret, #3905
Bowie, Margaret Crabb (Johns), #3902
Bowie, Maria Williams, #2617
Bowie, Maria Williams, #2683
Bowie, Maria Williams, #2698
Bowie, Maria Williams, #3863
Bowie, Maria Williams, #3924
Bowie, Maria Williams, #3940
Bowie, Mary, #2636
Bowie, Mary, #2654
Bowie, Mary, #2662
Bowie, Mary, #3877
Bowie, Mary, #3880
Bowie, Mary, #3894
Bowie, Mary, #3904
Bowie, Mary (Beall), #3886
Bowie, Mary Eleanor, #2690
Bowie, Mary Eleanor, #3931
Bowie, Molly, #2640
Bowie, Richard, #2658
Bowie, Richard, #3898
Bowie, Richard Johns, #3907
Bowie, Richard Johns (Judge), #2665
Bowie, Robert Edward, #2620
Bowie, Robert Edward, #2686
Bowie, Robert Edward, #2688
Bowie, Robert Edward, #3866
Bowie, Robert Edward, #3926
Bowie, Robert Edward, #3928
Bowie, Robert Edward, #3929
Bowie, Robert Gilmer[?], #2666
Bowie, Robert Gilmor[?], #3908
Bowie, Ruth (Cramptin), #3890
Bowie, Sarah Hollyday, #2667
Bowie, Sarah Hollyday, #2673
Bowie, Sarah Hollyday, #3909
Bowie, Sarah Hollyday, #3915
Bowie, Thomas, #2635
Bowie, Thomas, #2651
Bowie, Thomas, #2699
Bowie, Thomas, #2700
Bowie, Thomas, #2701
Bowie, Thomas, #2702
Bowie, Thomas, #2703
Bowie, Thomas, #3876
Bowie, Thomas, #3891
Bowie, Thomas, #3941
Bowie, Thomas, #3942
Bowie, Thomas, #3943
Bowie, Thomas, #3944
Bowie, Thomas, #3945
Bowie, Thomas John, #2612

INDEX
Pages are not numbered; numbers refer to the entry number at the beginning of each record.

Bowie, Thomas John, #2623
Bowie, Thomas John, #2661
Bowie, Thomas John, #3858
Bowie, Thomas John, #3903
Bowie, Thomas John David, #2614
Bowie, Thomas John David, #2615
Bowie, Thomas John David, #2616
Bowie, Thomas John David, #2617
Bowie, Thomas John Davis, #2612
Bowie, Thomas John Davis, #2618
Bowie, Thomas John Davis, #2672
Bowie, Thomas John Davis, #2680
Bowie, Thomas John Davis, #2681
Bowie, Thomas John Davis, #2682
Bowie, Thomas John Davis, #2683
Bowie, Thomas John Davis, #3858
Bowie, Thomas John Davis, #3860
Bowie, Thomas John Davis, #3861
Bowie, Thomas John Davis, #3862
Bowie, Thomas John Davis, #3863
Bowie, Thomas John Davis, #3864
Bowie, Thomas John Davis, #3914
Bowie, Thomas John Davis, #3918
Bowie, Thomas John Davis, #3919
Bowie, Thomas John Davis, #3921
Bowie, Thomas John Davis, #3922
Bowie, Thomas John Davis, #3923
Bowie, Thomas John Davis, #3924
Bowie, Thomas John Davis, #3925
Bowie, Thomas Johns (Col.), #3910
Bowie, Thomas Johns (Col.), #3911
Bowie, Thomas Johns (Col.), #3912
Bowie, Thomas Johns (Col.), #3914
Bowie, Thomas Johns (Col.), #3915
Bowie, Thomas Johns (Col.), #3916
Bowie, Thomas Johns (Col.), #3917
Bowie, Thomas Johns (Col.), #3918
Bowie, Thomas Johns (Colonel), #2668
Bowie, Thomas Johns (Colonel), #2669
Bowie, Thomas Johns (Colonel), #2670
Bowie, Thomas Johns (Colonel), #2672
Bowie, Thomas Johns (Colonel), #2673
Bowie, Thomas Johns (Colonel), #2674
Bowie, Thomas Johns (Colonel), #2675
Bowie, Thomas Johns Davis, #2676
Bowie, Thomas Johns Davis, #2677
Bowie, Thomas Johns Davis, #2678
Bowie, Thomas Johns Davis, #2711
Bowie, Thomas Johns Davis, #3955
Bowie, Washington, #2655
Bowie, Washington, #2675
Bowie, Washington, #3895
Bowie, Washington, #3917
Bowie, Washington (Col.), #3899
Bowie, Washington (Col.), #3900
Bowie, Washington (Col.), #3901
Bowie, Washington (Col.), #3903
Bowie, Washington (Col.), #3904
Bowie, Washington (Col.), #3905
Bowie, Washington (Col.), #3906
Bowie, Washington (Col.), #3907
Bowie, Washington (Col.), #3908
Bowie, Washington (Col.), #3909
Bowie, Washington (Col.), #3910
Bowie, Washington (Colonel), #2659
Bowie, Washington (Colonel), #2660
Bowie, Washington (Colonel), #2661
Bowie, Washington (Colonel), #2662
Bowie, Washington (Colonel), #2663
Bowie, Washington (Colonel), #2664
Bowie, Washington (Colonel), #2665
Bowie, Washington (Colonel), #2666
Bowie, Washington (Colonel), #2667
Bowie, William, #2634
Bowie, William, #2639
Bowie, William, #3875
Bowie, William, #3879
"Bowie, Jr.", Allen, #2642
"Bowie, Jr.", Allen, #3882
"Bowie, Jr.", Allen (Col.), #3887
"Bowie, Jr.", Allen (Col.), #3888
"Bowie, Jr.", Allen (Col.), #3889
"Bowie, Jr.", Allen (Col.), #3891
"Bowie, Jr.", Allen (Col.), #3892
"Bowie, Jr.", Allen (Col.), #3893
"Bowie, Jr.", Allen (Col.), #3894
"Bowie, Jr.", Allen (Col.), #3895
"Bowie, Jr.", Allen (Col.), #3896
"Bowie, Jr.", Allen (Col.), #3897
"Bowie, Jr.", Allen (Col.), #3898
"Bowie, Jr.", Allen (Col.), #3899
"Bowie, Jr.", Allen (Colonel), #2648
"Bowie, Jr.", Allen (Colonel), #2649
"Bowie, Jr.", Allen (Colonel), #2650
"Bowie, Jr.", Allen (Colonel), #2651
"Bowie, Jr.", Allen (Colonel), #2652
"Bowie, Jr.", Allen (Colonel), #2653
"Bowie, Jr.", Allen (Colonel), #2654
"Bowie, Jr.", Allen (Colonel), #2655
"Bowie, Jr.", Allen (Colonel), #2656
"Bowie, Jr.", Allen (Colonel), #2657
"Bowie, Jr.", Allen (Colonel), #2658
"Bowie, Jr.", James, #2643
"Bowie, Jr.", John, #2630
"Bowie, Jr.", John, #2637
"Bowie, Jr.", John, #2638
"Bowie, Jr.", John, #2639
"Bowie, Jr.", John, #2640
"Bowie, Jr.", John, #2641
"Bowie, Jr.", John, #2645
"Bowie, Jr.", John, #3871
"Bowie, Jr.", John, #3878
"Bowie, Jr.", John, #3879
"Bowie, Jr.", John, #3880
"Bowie, Jr.", John, #3881
"Bowie, Jr.", John, #3882
"Bowie, Jr.", John, #3885
"Bowie, Jr.", John (Rev.), #2644
"Bowie, Jr.", Washington, #2664
"Bowie, Jr.", Washington, #3906
"Bowie, Sr.", John, #2699
"Bowie, Sr.", John, #3942
Bowles, Magdalena Bechenbaugh, #8583
Bowles, Mary Ann (Mrs.), #4674
Bowles, Nicklas, #8573
Bowles, William A., #4674
Bowling, Elisabeth, #2866
Bowling, George, #2866
Bowling, George, #2867
Bowling, George, #2868
Bowling, Jean, #2867
Bowling, Marcy, #2866
Bowling, Marcy, #2867
Bowling, Marcy, #2868
Bowling, Marthey Ann, #2869
Bowling, Thomas William, #2868
Bowman, _____[?] L., #3847
Bowman, Andrew, #3844
Bowman, Audry[?], #3849
Bowman, Couseau[?], #3848
Bowman, David R., #3853
Bowman, Elizabeth, #3857
Bowman, Emmanual, #3846
Bowman, F.Rice, #8273
Bowman, Isaac D., #2788
Bowman, Jacob, #3855
Bowman, Johnathan, #3850
Bowman, Samuel, #3852
Bowman, William, #3851
Bowser, Hannah Ardinger, #1741
Boyce, Margret A., #7335
Boyd, R. Hance, #7623
Boyd, R. Hance, #7647
Boyd, Robert Hance, #7675
Boyers, Susan Elizabeth, #1333
Boyle, Philip, #3959
Bragunier, Mary (Miss), #8147
Brahan, John (General), #2323
Brahan, John C., #2323
Brahan, John C., #2324
Brahan, John C., #2326
Brahan, Mary C., #2325
Brahan, Mary C., #2326
Brane, C.J.B., #5127
Brany, Emil B., #2142
Braxton, Heniretta V., #625
Braxton, Henrietta, #626
Braxton, Henrietta, #627
Braxton, Henrietta, #628
Braxton, Henry Victor, #626
Braxton, Mattie V., #630
Braxton, Mattie Virginia, #627
Braxton, Perry Edward, #628
Braxton, William, #624
Braxton, William, #626
Braxton, William, #627
Braxton, William, #628
Braxton, William, #633
Brecker, Susanna (Aughinbaugh), #7794
Breidenbaugh, E., #571
Brewer, Antoinette, #1781
Brewer, Antoinette , #8080
Brewer, Elizabeth, #2566
Brewer, Elizabeth, #2602
Brewer, James R.E., #2603
Brewer, John, #2601
Brewer, John, #2602
Brewer, Joseph, #1791
Brewer, Joseph, #1792
Brewer, Joseph, #8078
Brewer, Mahala, #1782
Brewer, Mahala, #1783
Brewer, Mahala, #1784
Brewer, Mahala, #1785
Brewer, Mahala, #1786
Brewer, Mahala, #1787
Brewer, Mahala, #1788
Brewer, Mahala, #1793
Brewer, Mahala, #1794
Brewer, Mahala, #1795
Brewer, Mahala, #1796
Brewer, Mahala, #1797
Brewer, Mahala, #1798
Brewer, Mahala, #1799
Brewer, Mahala, #1800
Brewer, Mahala, #1801

INDEX

Pages are not numbered; numbers refer to the entry number at the beginning of each record.

Brewer, Mahala, #1802	Brown, George, #3822	Brown, Marjorie C., #2357	Bryan, John, #7058
Bricker, Jerry, #7763	Brown, George, #3823	Brown, Marjorie Clyde, #2331	Bryan, John, #7059
Bricker, Jerry, #7795	Brown, George, #3824	Brown, Mary, #7629	Bryan, John, #7060
Bricker, Rev., #610	Brown, George, #3827	Brown, Mary Ann, #2370	Bryan, John, #7182
Brisco, Sarah, #2315	Brown, George, #3828	Brown, Mary Louise, #6771	Bryan, Mariah, #7067
Brisco, Sarah, #2316	Brown, George, #3828	Brown, Matilda, #3832	Bryan, Mariah, #7068
Brisco, Sarah, #2317	Brown, George, #3830	Brown, Matilda, #3833	Bryan, Mary Margaret, #7053
Brisco, Sarah, #2318	Brown, George, #3835	Brown, Matilda, #3834	Bryan, Sarah, #7062
Briscoe, Sarah, #2286	Brown, George, #3836	Brown, Nina P., #2343	Bryan, Sarah, #7182
Brooke, Hazel, #5738	Brown, George, #3837	Brown, Nina P., #2344	Bryan, Sary, #7052
Brooks, Elizabeth F., #597	Brown, George M., #3832	Brown, Nina P., #2345	Bryan, Sary, #7059
Brooks, Elizabeth F., #601	Brown, George W., #2332	Brown, Nina P., #2346	Bryan, Sary, #7061
Brown, Amanda, #3834	Brown, Gladys, #2342	Brown, Nina P., #2347	Bryan, Susan Shrader, #894
Brown, Ann Maria, #3833	Brown, Glenn E., #6747	Brown, Nina P., #2348	Buff, Argielle Mozelle, #71
Brown, Anna, #3820	Brown, Glenn E., #6764	Brown, Nina P., #2349	Bukey, Caroline, #2317
Brown, Benjamin, #3817	Brown, Hadassah, #3702	Brown, Nina P., #2350	Bukey, Elizabeth, #2278
Brown, Benjamin, #3831	Brown, Hadassah, #3824	Brown, Nina P., #2351	Bukey, Elizabeth, #2279
Brown, Benjamin, #3832	Brown, Hester (Miss), #512	Brown, Nina P., #2352	Bukey, Elizabeth, #2306
Brown, Benjamin, #3833	Brown, Ida Catherine, #2383	Brown, Nina P., #2353	Bukey, Elizabeth, #2316
Brown, Benjamin, #3834	Brown, Ida Catherine, #2388	Brown, Richard, #2367	Bukey, Elizabeth Ann, #2299
Brown, Benjamin, #3837	Brown, Ida Catherine, #2389	Brown, Robert, #2340	Bukey, Fleming, #2296
Brown, Carmen I., #2355	Brown, Ida Catherine, #2390	Brown, Robert, #2371	Bukey, Harriet, #2318
Brown, Carmen I., #2358	Brown, Ida Catherine, #2391	Brown, Rosalie G., #2382	Bukey, Hezekiah, #2281
Brown, Carmen I., #2359	Brown, Ida Catherine, #2392	Brown, Ruby K., #2357	Bukey, Hezekiah, #2282
Brown, Carmen I., #2360	Brown, Ida Catherine, #2393	Brown, Ruby K., #2372	Bukey, Hezekiah, #2283
Brown, Carmen I., #2361	Brown, Ida Catherine, #2394	Brown, Ruby K., #2373	Bukey, Hezekiah, #2305
Brown, Carmen I., #2362	Brown, Ida Catherine, #2395	Brown, Ruby K., #2374	Bukey, Hezekiah, #2306
Brown, Carmen I., #2363	Brown, Ida Catherine, #2396	Brown, Ruby K., #2375	Bukey, Hezekiah, #2307
Brown, David, #2365	Brown, Ida Catherine, #2397	Brown, Ruby K., #2376	Bukey, Hezekiah, #2308
Brown, David C., #2333	Brown, Ida Catherine, #2398	Brown, Ruby K., #2377	Bukey, Hezekiah, #2309
Brown, David C., #2335	Brown, Ida Catherine, #2399	Brown, Sara V., #3040	Bukey, Hezekiah, #2310
Brown, Dixie F., #2379	Brown, Ida Catherine, #2400	Brown, Sara Virginia, #3048	Bukey, Hezekiah, #2311
Brown, Donald, #2341	Brown, Ida Catherine, #2401	Brown, Susanna, #3818	Bukey, Hezekiah, #2312
Brown, Edgar T. (Dr.), #2187	Brown, Ida Catherine, #2402	Brown, Susanna, #3827	Bukey, Hezekiah, #2313
Brown, Edgar T. (Dr.), #2188	Brown, Irene, #2368	Brown, T.A., #3042	Bukey, Hezekiah, #2314
Brown, Edgar T. (Dr.), #2191	Brown, Jesse David, #2356	Brown, T.A., #3043	Bukey, Isaac W., #2313
Brown, Eleanor, #3819	Brown, Jesse David, #2364	Brown, Terry, #2369	Bukey, James, #2295
Brown, Eleanor, #3841	Brown, Jesse David, #2365	Brown, Thompson A., #3039	Bukey, Jemima, #2292
Brown, Eli, #3406	Brown, Jesse David, #2366	Brown, Wayne, #2380	Bukey, John, #2312
Brown, Elizabeth, #3816	Brown, Jesse David, #2367	Brown, William, #3823	Bukey, John (Colonel), #2269
Brown, Elizabeth Louise Foltz, #6765	Brown, Jesse David, #2368	Brown, Wm. Henry, #4739	Bukey, John (Colonel), #2271
Brown, Ella Sophia, #2189	Brown, Jesse David, #2369	Brown, , #1961	Bukey, John (Colonel), #2272
Brown, Ella Sophia, #2191	Brown, Jesse David, #2370	Brubaker, Chas., #3080	Bukey, John (Colonel), #2273
Brown, Esther, #3815	Brown, Jesse David, #2371	Bruchey, Frederick, #5646	Bukey, John (Colonel), #2274
Brown, Esther, #3816	Brown, Jesse David, #2372	Bruchey, Margaret Ellen, #5647	Bukey, John (Colonel), #2277
Brown, Esther, #3817	Brown, Jesse J., #2338	Bruchey, Mary Catherine, #5645	Bukey, John (Colonel), #2278
Brown, Esther, #3818	Brown, Jesse J., #2343	Bruner, Rev., #8374	Bukey, John (Colonel), #2280
Brown, Esther, #3819	Brown, Jesse J., #2355	Bryan, Ann, #7063	Bukey, John (Colonel), #2281
Brown, Esther, #3820	Brown, Jesse J., #2356	Bryan, Ann, #7064	Bukey, John (Colonel), #2286
Brown, Esther, #3821	Brown, Jesse J., #2357	Bryan, Frederick, #7065	Bukey, John (Colonel), #2287
Brown, Esther, #3822	Brown, Jesse Jacob, #2331	Bryan, Frederick, #7066	Bukey, Joseph, #2298
Brown, Esther, #3823	Brown, Jesse Jacob, #2332	Bryan, Hariet, #7056	Bukey, Julius, #2315
Brown, Esther, #3824	Brown, John, #2366	Bryan, Harriet, #7072	Bukey, Lucinda, #2305
Brown, Esther, #3827	Brown, Judith D., #2381	Bryan, Harriet, #7073	Bukey, Marcia, #2277
Brown, Esther, #3828	Brown, Laurel Lee, #6770	Bryan, Harriet, #7074	Bukey, Marcia, #2301
Brown, Esther, #3835	Brown, Lulu, #3407	Bryan, Harriet, #7075	Bukey, Marcia, #2302
Brown, Esther, #3836	Brown, Lulu (Miss), #3405	Bryan, Harriet, #7077	Bukey, Marcia, #2303
Brown, Esther, #3837	Brown, Lulu (Miss), #3406	Bryan, Harriet, #7078	Bukey, Marcia, #2304
Brown, Evanna C., #3041	Brown, Mahlon J., #2338	Bryan, Harriet, #7079	Bukey, Mary, #2280
Brown, Evanna Connor, #3047	Brown, Mahlon J., #2339	Bryan, Harriet, #7080	Bukey, Mary, #2294
Brown, Ezra, #2335	Brown, Mahlon J., #2340	Bryan, Harriet, #7081	Bukey, Mary Ann, #2308
Brown, George, #3814	Brown, Mahlon J., #2341	Bryan, Harriet, #7082	Bukey, Massey, #2300
Brown, George, #3816	Brown, Mahlon J., #2342	Bryan, Harriet, #7083	Bukey, Nancy, #2290
Brown, George, #3817	Brown, Margaret Alice (Grayston), #4753	Bryan, Harriet, #7084	Bukey, Rudolf, #2315
Brown, George, #3818		Bryan, Harriet, #7085	Bukey, Rudolf, #2316
Brown, George, #3819	Brown, Maria, #3822	Bryan, Harriet, #7086	Bukey, Rudolf, #2317
Brown, George, #3820	Brown, Marjorie C., #2333	Bryan, Harriet, #7087	Bukey, Rudolf, #2318
Brown, George, #3821	Brown, Marjorie C., #2338	Bryan, James, #7051	Bukey, Spencer Tomlinson, #2309
Brown, George, #3821	Brown, Marjorie C., #2343	Bryan, James, #7058	Bukey, Susannah, #2297
	Brown, Marjorie C., #2355	Bryan, John, #7051	Bukey, Susannah, #2314
	Brown, Marjorie C., #2356	Bryan, John, #7057	Bukey, Tabitha, #2307

INDEX

Pages are not numbered; numbers refer to the entry number at the beginning of each record.

Bukey, Van Hartness, #2310
Bukey, William, #2291
Bukey, William S., #2311
"Bukey, III", John, #2293
"Bukey, Jr.", John, #2272
"Bukey, Jr.", John, #2273
"Bukey, Jr.", John, #2274
"Bukey, Jr.", John, #2290
"Bukey, Jr.", John, #2291
"Bukey, Jr.", John, #2292
"Bukey, Jr.", John, #2293
"Bukey, Jr.", John, #2294
"Bukey, Jr.", John, #2295
"Bukey, Jr.", John, #2296
"Bukey, Jr.", John, #2297
"Bukey, Jr.", John, #2298
"Bukey, Jr.", John, #2299
"Bukey, Jr.", John, #2300
Bullen, Bessie, #7994
Bullen, Fannie, #7995
Bullen, Sallie, #7993
Bullen, W. (Capt.), #7993
Bullen, W. (Capt.), #7994
Bullen, W. (Capt.), #7995
Bullen, W. (Capt.), #7991
Burall, Harrison, #6198
Burdette, MaryE., #6146
Burgan, Minnie, #2807
Burgan, Minnie, #2808
Burgan, Minnie, #2809
Burgan, Minnie, #2810
Burgan, Minnie, #2811
Burgan, Minnie, #2812
Burgee, Elen Jane, #8512
Burgee, Elen Jane, #8513
"Burgee, Jr.", Thomas, #8513
Burgner, Emma (Timmins), #2488
Burgner, Harry Angle, #2493
Burgner, Mary Josephine, #7927
Burgner, Mary Josephine, #7928
Burgner, Mary Josephine, #7929
Burgner, Mary Josephine, #7930
Burkett, Caroline (Miss), #510
Burkhart, Elizabeth, #5052
Burkhart, Elizabeth, #5053
Burkhart, Elizabeth, #5054
Burkhart, Elizabeth, #5055
Burkhart, Elizabeth, #5056
Burkhart, Elizabeth, #5057
Burkhart, Elizabeth, #5058
Burkhart, Elizabeth, #5059
Burkhart, Elizabeth, #5060
Burkhart, Elizabeth, #5061
Burkhart, Elizabeth, #5062
Burkhart, Elizabeth, #5063
Burkhart, Elizabeth, #5065
Burkholder, Alice Estella, #5140
Burrows, Elizabeth, #4401
Burrows, Thomas, #4401
Burtner, L.O., #2755
Bush, Mary E. (Miss), #7254
Bushong, Andrew, #717
Bushong, Catharine, #713
Bushong, Elizabeth, #719
Bushong, Elizabeth, #720

Bushong, Jacob, #715
Bushong, John, #713
Bushong, John, #714
Bushong, John, #715
Bushong, John, #716
Bushong, John, #717
Bushong, John, #718
Bushong, John, #719
Bushong, John, #720
Bushong, John, #720
Bushong, Magdalena, #714
Bushong, Magdalena, #715
Bushong, Magdalena, #716
Bushong, Magdalena, #717
Bushong, Magdalena, #718
Bushong, Magdalena, #719
Bushong, Mary, #716
Bushong, Rachel, #712
Bushong, Sarah, #713
Bushong, Susannah, #718
Bushong, William, #711
Bushong, William, #714
Bushong, William, #724
Butler, E., #4656
Byers, Catherine Oleig (Mrs.), #5038
Byers, George, #5038
C., J., #1977
C., J., #1978
C., J., #1979
Cade, Edna, #7922
Cadwallader, Frances, #2898
Cadwallader, Frances, #2899
Campbell, Druzella, #7383
Care6y, Irene, #6809
Carle, "Ludwig or Lewis", #6973
Carle, [son], #6962
Carle, [son], #6963
Carle, [son], #6966
Carle, [son], #6967
Carle, Anna (Herr), #6982
Carle, Anna (Herr), #6983
Carle, Benjamin, #6968
Carle, Benjamin, #6969
Carle, Elizabeth, #6974
Carle, Frances (Kauffman), #6978
Carle, Frances (Kauffman), #6979
Carle, Henry, #6970
Carle, Henry, #6971
Carle, Joel, #6965
Carle, John Joseph, #6964
Carle, John Joseph, #6975
Carle, John Joseph, #6976
Carle, John Joseph, #6977
Carle, Joseph, #6959
Carle, Joseph, #6960
Carle, Joseph, #6961
Carle, Joseph, #6962
Carle, Joseph, #6963
Carle, Joseph, #6964
Carle, Joseph, #6965
Carle, Joseph, #6966
Carle, Joseph, #6967
Carle, Joseph, #6968
Carle, Joseph, #6969
Carle, Joseph, #6970
Carle, Joseph, #6971
Carle, Joseph, #6972

Carle, Joseph, #6973
Carle, Joseph, #6974
Carle, Joseph, #6980
Carle, Joseph, #6981
Carle, Maria Anna, #6972
Carlisle, Robert Barton, #8569
Carnelius, Absolmon, #6778
Carpenter, G.C., #6806
Carriere, Henrietta, #6524
Caruther, Isaac, #1450
Caruther, Sarah, #1450
Caruther, Sarah, #1451
"Caruther, Sr.", Ann, #1449
Caruthers, Ann, #1484
Caruthers, Ann, #1485
Caruthers, Elizabeth Isabella, #1453
Caruthers, Elizabeth Isabella, #1494
Caruthers, Elizabeth J., #1468
Caruthers, Elizabeth P., #1438
Caruthers, Elizabeth P., #1439
Caruthers, Elizabeth P., #1440
Caruthers, Elizabeth P., #1441
Caruthers, Elizabeth P., #1442
Caruthers, Elizabeth P., #1443
Caruthers, Elizabeth P., #1444
Caruthers, Elizabeth P., #1445
Caruthers, Isaac, #1451
Caruthers, Isaac, #1455
Caruthers, Isaac, #1457
Caruthers, Isaac, #1460
Caruthers, Isaac, #1462
Caruthers, Isaac, #1463
Caruthers, Isaac, #1464
Caruthers, Isaac, #1485
Caruthers, Isaac, #1486
Caruthers, Isaac, #1489
Caruthers, Isaac, #1491
Caruthers, Isaac Woodrough, #1458
Caruthers, Isaac Woodrough, #1495
Caruthers, Jason, #1467
Caruthers, Jason Davis, #1490
Caruthers, John Hindman, #1456
Caruthers, John Hindman, #1493
Caruthers, Leiths[?], #1461
Caruthers, Leythe, #1465
Caruthers, Lytle, #1487
Caruthers, Mary Jane, #1464
Caruthers, Mary Jane, #1491
Caruthers, Rachel, #1486
Caruthers, Sarah, #1455
Caruthers, Sarah, #1460
Caruthers, Sarah, #1464
Caruthers, Sarah Ann, #1455
Caruthers, Sarah Ann, #1492
Caruthers, William Franklin, #1466
Caruthers, William Franklin, #1488
"Caruthers, Sr.", Isaac, #1452
Cash, Amy Lynn, #3615
Cash, George B., #6748
Cash, George Byrd, #6766
Cash, Henrietta Jane Foltz, #6763
Cash, Laura, #3609
Cash, Robert Rocky O., #3613
Cash, Sheila[?], #3618
"Cash, Jr.", Robert O., #3640

"Cash, Jr.", Robert Owen, #3624
Castle, Cornelius, #2964
Castle, E.C.B., #4302
Castleman, Anne White (Dellinger) (Mrs.), #7108
Castleman, Harry W., #7090
Castleman, Mary W., #7088
Castleman, Rev. David, #7027
Castleman, Sallie C., #7089
Castleman, , #7025
Cauble, Frank, #8268
Chadwick, , #6115
Chadwick, , #6117
Chambers, Columbia A., #3134
Chaney, Ezekiel, #5045
Chaney, Laura (Mrs.), #5045
Charlesworth, Sarah, #7624
Charlesworth, Sarah, #7625
Charlton, Daniel E., #6483
Charlton, Elize J., #1179
Charlton, Rebecca, #7130
Charlton, Rebecca, #7134
Charlton, Wilmer A., #6795
Charlton, Wm., #7145
Cheney, Alice, #3752
Cheney, Alice, #3793
Cheney, Charles Franklin, #3755
Cheney, Charles Franklin, #3809
Cheney, Chloe, #3742
Cheney, Chloe, #3743
Cheney, Chloe, #3788
Cheney, Foster Hallet, #3779
Cheney, Foster Hallet, #3782
Cheney, Foster Hallet, #3784
Cheney, George H., #3792
Cheney, George Hallet, #3750
Cheney, George Hallet, #3751
Cheney, Henry Martin, #3758
Cheney, Henry Martin, #3808
Cheney, James Edwin, #3756
Cheney, James Edwin, #3777
Cheney, James Edwin, #3778
Cheney, James Edwin, #3794
Cheney, James Monroe, #3754
Cheney, James Monroe, #3806
Cheney, Jelijs[?], #2035
Cheney, Peosis[?] Hatch, #3745
Cheney, Peosis[?] Hatch, #3746
Cheney, Persis H., #3787
Cheney, Philena, #3744
Cheney, Philence[?], #3786
Cheney, Prentice, #3753
Cheney, Prentice, #3810
Cheney, Prudence, #2003
Cheney, Prudence[?], #1940
Cheney, Reginald Foster, #3784
Cheney, Rosette Maria, #3807
Cheney, Rosette[?] Maria, #3757
Cheney, Sophia, #3749
Cheney, Sophia, #3791
Cheney, Tryhena[?] (Mrs.), #3795
Cheney, Tryphena, #3748
Cheney, Tryphena, #3789
Cheney, Tryphena H. (Mrs.), #3805
Cheney, W.H., #3790
Cheney, William, #3740
Cheney, William, #3742
Cheney, William, #3743
Cheney, William, #3744
Cheney, William, #3745
Cheney, William, #3746

INDEX
Pages are not numbered; numbers refer to the entry number at the beginning of each record.

Cheney, William, #3747
Cheney, William, #3748
Cheney, William, #3749
Cheney, William, #3750
Cheney, William, #3751
Cheney, William, #3752
Cheney, William, #3753
Cheney, William, #3754
Cheney, William, #3755
Cheney, William, #3756
Cheney, William, #3757
Cheney, William, #3758
Cheney, William, #3785
Cheney, William, #3804
Cheney, William Hutchinson, #3747
"Cheney, Sr.", Robert, #2034
Citie[?], Mace[?] R.M., #6523
Clagett, Mary Ann, #8440
Clair, Mahlia (Miss), #5398
Clark, David, #7607
Clark, David, #7641
Clarke, Catherine (Miss), #507
Clause, Daniel, #2144
Clem, Rachel, #724
Clemmer, Delia Irene, #1433
Clemmer, J.F., #1433
Clemmer, J.H., #1385
Clemmer, James F., #1386
Clemmer, Lizzie E., #1433
Cleve, Van, #7613
Climie, Jo Joan, #5663
Climie, Jo Joan, #5664
Climie, Jo Joan, #5665
Climie, Jo Joan, #5666
Climie, Jo Joan, #5667
Climie, Jo Joan, #5668
Climie, Jo Joan, #5669
Climie, Jo Joan, #5670
Climie, Jo Joan, #5671
Cline, John P., #3474
Clingan, A. Maria, #3716
Clingan, An Maria, #3728
Clingan, elenor Jane, #3732
Clingan, Elenor[?] Jane, #3718
Clingan, James Semmerville, #3735
Clingan, John Bell, #3724
Clingan, John Bell, #3733
Clingan, Juliet A., #3717
Clingan, Juliet A. (Miss), #3726
Clingan, Mary Elizabeth, #3727
Clingan, McClean, #3725
Clingan, McClean, #3737
Clingan, McClean, #3738
Clingan, McClean, #3720
Clingan, Qunnen[?] Jackson, #3734
Clingan, Robert S., #3723
Clingan, Robert Snoden, #3736
Clingan, Samuel Walker, #3729
Clingan, Thomas F., #3722
Clingan, Thomas Franklin, #3731

Clingan, Virginia (Mrs.), #3739
Clingan, William Henry, #3719
Clingan, William Henry, #3730
Clopper, Chas W., #623
Clopper, Chas. W., #615
Clopper, Elizabeth, #4569
Clopper, Geo. D., #613
Clopper, Grandmother, #4564
Clopper, Harry C., #619
Clopper, John H., #610
Clopper, John H., #611
Clopper, John H., #613
Clopper, John H., #614
Clopper, John H., #615
Clopper, John H., #616
Clopper, John H., #617
Clopper, John H., #618
Clopper, John H., #619
Clopper, John H., #620
Clopper, John H., #621
Clopper, John H., #622
Clopper, Julia M., #621
Clopper, Julia M., #622
Clopper, Leroy, #617
Clopper, Martha E., #612
Clopper, Mary M., #616
Clopper, Minnie M., #618
Clopper, Sallie K.[?], #620
Clopper, Saml. E., #614
Cluts[?], Bruce Fisher, #3610
Coblentz, Barbara, #8581
Coblentz, Catharina, #8579
Coblentz, Elizabeth, #8574
Coblentz, Jacob, #8578
Coblentz, John, #8577
Coblentz, Lydia, #8575
Coblentz, Peter, #8572
Coblentz, Rebecca, #8576
Coblentz, , #8580
Cochran, Alexander, #760
Cochran, Alexander, #770
Cochran, Alexander, #771
Cochran, Catharine J., #768
Cochran, Cornwallis, #765
Cochran, Cornwallis, #774
Cochran, Elizabeth A., #769
Cochran, Henry Clay, #785
Cochran, Isaiah Y., #767
Cochran, Isaiah Y., #777
Cochran, John P., #763
Cochran, John P., #776
Cochran, John P., #779
Cochran, Lydia Brice, #786
Cochran, Mary (Mrs.), #772
Cochran, Mary Wade Davis, #780
Cochran, Minnie Victoria, #1513
Cochran, Samuel A., #766
Cochran, Samuel A., #773
Cochran, Thomas B., #1515
Cochran, Thomas B., #764
Cochran, Thomas B., #778
Cochran, William H., #762
Cochran, William H., #775
Cock, Blanche Grams[?], #947
Cock, Blanche Grams[?], #964
Cock, Charles Monroe, #948
Cock, Connie Marie, #950
Cock, Frances Louise, #934
Cock, Frances Louise, #957

Cock, Joel J., #952
Cock, Joel Wilson, #933
Cock, Joel Wilson, #944
Cock, Joel Wilson, #955
Cock, Joel Wilson, #961
Cock, Laura, #955
Cock, Laura, #956
Cock, Laura, #957
Cock, Laura Lee, #951
Cock, Monroe, #930
Cock, Monroe, #955
Cock, Monroe, #956
Cock, Monroe, #957
Cock, Monroe Edamond, #962
Cock, Monroe Edmond, #945
Cock, Virginia Elizabeth, #932
Cock, Virginia Elizabeth, #956
Coderre, Dolores Jean, #4341
Coffinberger, Amada, #347
Coffinberger, Bertha L___, #330
Coffinberger, Bess, #346
Coffinberger, Bessie Kershner, #318
Coffinberger, Bessie Kershner, #319
Coffinberger, Bessie Kershner, #320
Coffinberger, Bessie Kershner, #321
Coffinberger, Bessie Kershner, #322
Coffinberger, Elmer, #343
Coffinberger, Elmer May, #329
Coffinberger, Grace O'Lee, #327
Coffinberger, Holland R., #326
Coffinberger, James, #343
Coffinberger, James, #344
Coffinberger, James, #344
Coffinberger, James, #345
Coffinberger, James, #346
Coffinberger, James, #347
Coffinberger, Leda Cornelia, #303
Coffinberger, Leda Cornelia, #305
Coffinberger, Leda Cornelia, #306
Coffinberger, Leda Cornelia, #307
Coffinberger, Leda Cornelia, #308
Coffinberger, Leda Cornelia, #309
Coffinberger, Leda Cornelia, #310
Coffinberger, Leda Cornelia, #311
Coffinberger, Leda Cornelia, #312
Coffinberger, Leda Cornelia, #313
Coffinberger, Leda Cornelia, #325
Coffinberger, Nan, #345
Coffinberger, Walter W.S., #328
Coffinberger, William Elmer, #323
Coffinberger, William Elmer, #324
Coffinberger, Wm. Calvin, #331
Coffinberger, Wm. Calvin, #332
Coffinberger, Wm. Elmer, #325
Coffinberger, Wm. Elmer, #326
Coffinberger, Wm. Elmer, #327
Coffinberger, Wm. Elmer, #328
Coffinberger, Wm. Elmer, #329
Coffinberger, Wm. Elmer, #330
Coffinberger, Wm. Elmer, #331
Coffinberger, Wm. Elmer, #332
Coffman, Catherine[?], #974
Coffman, John D., #3704
Coffman, John D., #3712
Coleman, Charles Warren, #8499
Coleman, Charles Warren, #8502

Coleman, Chas. Warren, #8485
Coleman, Ellen Carey, #8485
Coleman, Ellen Carey, #8508
Coleman, Ellen McGill Garrott, #8496
Coleman, John, #2908
Coleman, John Boyd, #2910
Coleman, John H., #2907
Coleman, John H., #2908
Coleman, John H., #2909
Coleman, John H., #2910
Coleman, John H., #2911
Coleman, Lou Nell, #2909
Coleman, Phyllis Josphine, #2911
Collins, Isabella, #1479
Collins, , #1479
Conard, Rachel Caruthers (Mrs.), #1459
Conn, William Robert, #6270
Conrad, Emma Virginia, #2875
Conrad, Emma Virginia, #2876
Conrad, Martha, #2870
Conrad, Martha, #2873
Conrad, Mary Francies , #2870
Conrad, Nathan, #1926
Conrad, William, #2870
Conrad, William, #2873
Conrad, William E., #2873
Conrad, William E., #2874
Cook, Kate, #7154
Cook, Monroe E., #920
Cooke, Addison, #2586
Cooke, Addison Barnwell, #2572
Cooke, Addison Barnwell, #2586
Cooke, Addison Barnwell, #2590
Cooke, Addison Barnwell, #2599
Cooke, Mary Sams, #2586
Cooke, Mary Wilson, #2587
Cooke, Mary Wilson, #2588
Cooke, Mary Wilson, #2589
Cooke, Mary Wilson, #2590
Cookerly, Ann Catharine[?], #659
Cookerly, Ann Cathern, #5324
Cookerly, Clenar[?], #662
Cookerly, John Wierton[?], #663
Cookerly, Mary, #661
Cookerly, Mary, #664
Cookerly, William, #660
Cooley, Maria (Brown), #3842
Cooper, Enos, #1096
Cooper, Enos Boston, #1086
Cooper, Geary A., #7428
Cooper, Geary A., #7460
Cooper, Isabella, #1096
Cooper, Jacob Wellington, #1097
Cooper, Susie (Frye), #7458
Cooper, William Howard, #1096
Cooper[?], Carrie (Mrs.), #965
Copenhavaer, Anna Clara, #6335
Copenhavaer, Anna Clara, #6336
Copenhavaer, Anna Clara, #6337
Copenhavaer, Anna Clara, #6338
Copenhavaer, Anna Clara, #6339
Copenhaver, Anna Clara, #6334
Copenhaver, Anna Clara, #6410
Copenhaver, Anna Clara, #6411
Copenhaver, Anna Clara, #6412
Copenhaver, Anna Clara, #6413
Copenhaver, Anna Clara, #6414
Copenhaver, Anna Clara, #6415
Copenhaver, Anna Clara, #6447
Copenhaver, Anna Clara, #6448
Copenhaver, Anna Clara, #6449

INDEX
Pages are not numbered; numbers refer to the entry number at the beginning of each record.

Copenhaver, Anna Clara, #6450
Copenhaver, Anna Clara, #6451
Copenhaver, Anna Clara, #6452
Corby, Emma Jane, #144
Corby, Lillie[?], #4175
Corby, Lillie[?], #4202
Corby, William, #144
Cordell, Benjamin Franklin, #1769
Cordell, Benjamin Franklin, #1774
Cordell, Benjamin Franklin, #8110
Cordell, Benjamin Franklin, #8115
Cordell, David C., #1766
Cordell, David C., #1767
Cordell, David C., #8107
Cordell, David C., #8108
Cordell, John Andrew, #1768
Cordell, John Andrew, #1773
Cordell, John Andrew, #8109
Cordell, John Andrew, #8114
Cordell, Lucye V., #1771
Cordell, Lucye V., #8112
Cordell, Ruth Irine, #1775
Cordell, Ruth Irine, #8116
Cordell, Samuel David, #1770
Cordell, Samuel David, #8111
Cornelius, Anna M. (Speaker), #6799
Cost, Barbara E., #4851
Cost, Catharine (Mrs.), #572
Cost, Conatencims[?] S., #4852
Cost, , #4861
Cotton, Dudley Page, #643
Cotton, Helen Douglas, #656
Cotton, Henry Douglas, #642
Cotton, Henry Evan, #638
Cotton, Henry Evan (Rev.), #637
Cotton, Henry Evan (Rev.), #642
Cotton, Henry Evan (Rev.), #643
Cotts[?], Elizabeth A., #2054
Courtney, Austin H., #4140
Cox, Bessie, #2813
Coxe, J.C.W., #2218
Crabill, Ella M., #130
Crabtree, Ann Maria, #1190
Crabtree, Reason L., #1190
Cramphin[?], Ruth, #2651
Cramphin[?], Ruth, #2652
Cramphin[?], Ruth, #2653
Cramphin[?], Ruth, #2654
Cramphin[?], Ruth, #2655
Cramphin[?], Ruth, #2656
Cramphin[?], Ruth, #2657
Cramphin[?], Ruth, #2658
Cramphin[?], Thomas, #2646
Cramphin[?], , #2649
Cramptin, Ruth, #3888
Cramptin, Ruth, #3891
Cramptin, Ruth, #3892
Cramptin, Ruth, #3893
Cramptin, Ruth, #3894

Cramptin, Ruth, #3895
Cramptin, Ruth, #3896
Cramptin, Ruth, #3897
Cramptin, Ruth, #3898
Cramptin, Ruth, #3899
Crampton, Mabel Ruth, #153
Crampton, Mabel Ruth, #154
Crawmer, Mary, #761
Crawmer, Mary, #770
Crenner, J.J. Gloss, #3395
Crider, Catherine Carrol, #315
Crider, Thelma S., #2765
Crider, Wayne Stewart, #309
Crider, Wayne Stewart, #314
Crider, Wayne Stewart, #314
Crider, Wayne Stewart, #315
Cridle[?], Lucretia A., #1038
Crisman, Elizabeth, #1694
Crisman, Elizabeth, #4103
Croft, Abraham, #200
Croft, Catharine, #182
Croft, Catharine (Mrs.), #201
Croft, Catharine (Ross), #183
Croft, David, #198
Croft, David, #199
Croft, John R., #184
Croft, John R. (Mrs.)[?], #202
Croft, John R. (Mrs.)[?], #203
Cromwell, C., #6556
Cromwell, C., #6557
Cromwell, C., #6558
Cromwell, C., #6559
Cromwell, C., #6560
Cromwell, C., #6561
Cromwell, C., #6562
Cromwell, C.C., #6537
Cromwell, C.C., #6540
Cromwell, C.C., #6553
Cromwell, Cloe[?], #6560
Cromwell, Comfort, #6555
Cromwell, Comfort, #6563
Cromwell, Constant Comfort, #6529
Cromwell, Constant Comfort, #6532
Cromwell, Constant Comfort, #6546
Cromwell, J., #6556
Cromwell, J., #6557
Cromwell, J., #6558
Cromwell, J., #6559
Cromwell, J., #6560
Cromwell, J., #6561
Cromwell, J., #6562
Cromwell, John Cockey, #6548
Cromwell, Joseph, #6550
Cromwell, Joseph, #6554
Cromwell, Joseph, #6558
Cromwell, Maria C., #6536
Cromwell, Maria Catharine, #6528
Cromwell, Maria Catharine, #6580
Cromwell, Maria Catharine, #6581
Cromwell, Maria Catharine, #6142
Cromwell, Maria Catharine, #6143
Cromwell, Mary, #6554
Cromwell, Nathan, #6547

Cromwell, Nathan, #6556
Cromwell, Oliver, #6543
Cromwell, P., #6552
Cromwell, Philemon, #6545
Cromwell, Philemon, #6559
Cromwell, Philemon, #6564
Cromwell, R., #6526
Cromwell, R., #6543
Cromwell, R., #6544
Cromwell, R., #6545
Cromwell, R., #6546
Cromwell, R., #6547
Cromwell, R., #6548
Cromwell, R., #6549
Cromwell, R., #6550
Cromwell, R.C., #6526
Cromwell, R.C., #6543
Cromwell, R.C., #6544
Cromwell, R.C., #6545
Cromwell, R.C., #6546
Cromwell, R.C., #6547
Cromwell, R.C., #6548
Cromwell, R.C., #6549
Cromwell, R.C., #6550
Cromwell, Rachael, #6542
Cromwell, Rachael, #6567
Cromwell, Richard, #6530
Cromwell, Richard, #6538
Cromwell, Richard, #6542
Cromwell, Richard, #6562
Cromwell, Richard, #6566
Cromwell, Richard, #6567
Cromwell, Richard, #6582
Cromwell, Richard, #6584
Cromwell, Ruth, #6557
Cromwell, S., #6528
Cromwell, S., #6529
Cromwell, S., #6530
Cromwell, S., #6531
Cromwell, S., #6532
Cromwell, S., #6533
Cromwell, S.C., #6535
Cromwell, S.G., #6539
Cromwell, Sarah, #6143
Cromwell, Sarah, #6527
Cromwell, Sarah, #6581
Cromwell, Sarah, #6584
Cromwell, Sarah (widow of William Cromwell), #6575
Cromwell, Sebatian Graff, #6531
Cromwell, Stephen, #6549
Cromwell, Stephen, #6561
Cromwell, Stephen, #6565
Cromwell, W., #6551
Cromwell, W.C., #6528
Cromwell, W.C., #6529
Cromwell, W.C., #6530
Cromwell, W.C., #6531
Cromwell, W.C., #6532
Cromwell, W.C., #6533
Cromwell, W.C., #6534
Cromwell, William, #6143
Cromwell, William, #6526
Cromwell, William, #6527
Cromwell, William, #6533
Cromwell, William, #6542
Cromwell, William, #6554
Cromwell, William, #6581
Cromwell, William, #6582
Cromwell, William, #6584

Cromwell, Wm., #6541
Cronise, Annie M. (Miss), #2755
Crous, Jacob, #1503
Crous, Jacob, #1508
Crous, Levi, #1507
Crous, Margret, #1509
Crous, Michel, #1502
Crous, peter, #1506
Crouse, Catherine, #1510
Crouse, Elizabeth, #1497
Crouse, Elizabeth, #1500
Crouse, Elizabeth, #1505
Crouse, Elizabeth, #1510
Crouse, Elizabeth, #1511
Crouse, Guy L., #1512
Crouse, Guy L., #1513
Crouse, Guy L., #1514
Crouse, John, #1496
Crouse, John, #1501
Crouse, John, #1504
Crouse, John M., #1513
Crouse, Levi, #1510
Crouse, Michel, #1499
"Crouse, Jr.", John, #1498
Crow, Betty Ardinger, #1740
Crow, Betty Ardinger, #4137
Crow, Catharine G., #5785
Crow, Christiana R., #5784
Crow, Effie, #1738
Crow, Effie, #4135
Crow, Eliza Houston, #5786
Crow, Jane, #5783
Crow, Jane, #5784
Crow, Jane, #5785
Crow, Jane, #5786
Crow, Jane, #5788
Crow, Jane, #5790
Crow, Maria, #5783
Crow, Paremnas, #5790
Crow, Parmenas, #5783
Crow, Parmenas, #5784
Crow, Parmenas, #5785
Crow, Parmenas, #5786
Crow, Parmenas, #5788
Crow, Parmenas, #5791
Crowe, Catharine Griffith, #5780
Crowe, Christian__[?] Paullstin[?], #5781
Crowe, Davis W., #5775
Crowe, Elisabeth, #5779
Crowe, James, #5778
Crowe, James L., #5788
Crowe, James L., #5789
Crowe, Jane, #5787
Crowe, Jane, #5791
Crowe, John, #310
Crowe, John, #5777
Crowe, John, #5790
Crowe, Margaret, #5789
Crowe, Margret, #5774
Crowe, Margret, #5775
Crowe, Mariah, #5776
Crowe, Parmenas, #5787
Crowe, Permnes, #5792
Crowe, Sarah Jane, #5774
Crowe, William, #5774
Crowe, William, #5775
Crowe, William, #5782
Crowe, William, #5787
Crowl, Elizabeth (Mrs.), #1924
Crowl, Jacob, #1925

INDEX
Pages are not numbered; numbers refer to the entry number at the beginning of each record.

Crowl, Mary, #1917
Crowl, Michael, #1923
Crowl, Michael, #1925
Cryder, Barbara, #7924
Culbertson, Mary D., #7604
Culbertson, Mary E., #7640
Culler, Paul M., #2769
Cummings, [blank], #7360
Cummins, Ann, #1366
Cummins, Ann, #1376
Cump, Charles, #7851
Cump, Charles, #7852
Cump, Charles, #7853
Cump, Charles, #7916
Cump, Nancy Lou, #7852
Cump, Nancy Lou, #7853
Cump, Nancy Lou, #7854
Cunningham, Elizabeth, #1857
Cunningham, Martha, #4497
Cunningham, Martha, #4498
Cunningham, Mary, #1834
Cunningham, Mary L., #1833
Cunningham, Nancy, #4498
Cunningham, Pearl, #3424
Cunningham, S.S., #2815
Cunningham, Sallie L., #2815
Cunningham, Walter, #4498
Curby, Catharine, #5693
Curfman, Bessie C., #2995
Curfman, Bessie Cornie (Kaetzel), #2984
Curleny, P.D., #6144
Curley, P.D., #6180
Curtis, Charles E., #630
Curtis, Jane Henrietta, #630
Cushen, Cinda Lou, #2998
Cushen, Ralph Forest, #2998
Custer, James W., #4047
Cyester, Daniel W., #3190
Cyester, Daniel W., #3204
Cyester, Daniel W., #3210
Cyester, Henrietta, #3190
Cyester, Henrietta Catherine, #3213
Cyester, Irene V., #3206
Cyester, Mary B., #3207
Cyester, Sarah E. (Miss), #3205
Daily, George J., #2139
Daily, George J., #2140
Daily, Grace Marguerite, #2139
Daily, Grace Marguerite, #2140
Dale, James, #4784
Dale, Lillie, #4777
Dalph, Catharine J. (Cochran), #782
Daniels, Martha, #333
Daniels, Martha, #334
Daniels, Martha, #335
Daniels, Martha, #336
Daniels, Martha, #337
Daniels, Martha, #338
Daniels, Martha, #339
Daniels, Martha, #340
Daniels, Martha, #341
Daniels, Martha, #342
Danner, Edna, #3443
Danner, Mary H., #8322

Darnel[?] or Farrel, William H., #1955
Davenport, Harris, #3422
Davidson, , #5911
Davis, Catharine W., #2669
Davis, Catharine W., #2672
Davis, Catharine W., #2673
Davis, Catharine W., #2674
Davis, Catharine W., #2675
Davis, Catharine W., #3912
Davis, Catharine W., #3913
Davis, Catharine W., #3914
Davis, Catharine W., #3915
Davis, Catharine W., #3916
Davis, Catharine W., #3917
Davis, Catharine W., #3918
Davis, Frances L. (Miss), #2455
Davis, Jane, #2877
Davis, Jason, #1450
Davis, John William, #2878
Davis, Lillia E., #6806
Davis, Lillian, #2764
Davis, Marathey An[?], #2877
Davis, Rachel, #1450
Davis, Samuel, #2877
Davis, Sarah, #1462
Davis, Sarah, #1486
Davis, Sarah D., #3792
Day, May (Mrs.), #2562
Daywalt, Jennie (Aunt), #5498
Deale, Dus, #7153
Deale, Jennie, #7153
Deale, Jennie, #7154
Deavers, Harry N., #5218
Dech, Cathrine Barbara (Mrs.), #2144
Dech, Cathrine Barbara (Mrs.), #2145
Dech, Cathrine Barbara (Mrs.), #2146
Dech, Cathrine Barbara (Mrs.), #2147
Dech, John K., #2147
Decker, _une Louise, #6349
Decker, Doris Marie, #6352
Decker, Doris Marie, #6373
Decker, Doris Marie, #6389
Decker, James, #6349
Decker, James, #6350
Decker, James, #6351
Decker, James, #6352
Decker, James William, #6350
Decker, James William, #6371
Decker, James Wm., #6387
Decker, June Louise, #6358
Decker, June Louise, #6359
Decker, June Louise, #6360
Decker, June Louise, #6361
Decker, June Louise, #6370
Decker, June Louise, #6386
Decker, Lois May, #6351
Decker, Lois May, #6372
Decker, Lois May, #6388
Decker, , #6370
Decker, , #6371
Decker, , #6372
Decker, , #6373
Decker, , #6386
Decker, , #6387
Decker, , #6388
Decker, , #6389

Dehl, Rev., #7231
Deihl, Rev., #7233
Deihl, Rev., #7235
Delaplaine[?], Catharine Jane, #6485
Delaplaine[?], Elizabeth Mary, #6484
Delaplaine[?], John Usher[?], #6486
Delaplaine[?], Sophia[?] Louisa, #6487
Delauter, Bertha Ruth, #817
Delauter, Bertha Ruth, #818
Delauter, Bertha Ruth, #819
Delauter, Catharine Marie, #824
Delauter, Charles R., #2378
Delauter, Claude Ennis, #833
Delauter, DeWitt Elmer, #823
Delauter, Eva C., #825
Delauter, Eva C., #827
Delauter, Evylon Grace, #820
Delauter, George Woodrow, #822
Delauter, Hilda Jane, #826
Delauter, Hilda Jane, #828
Delauter, Margaret Teressa, #821
Delauter, Martha Melchor, #829
Delauter, Otho Victor, #815
Delauter, Otho Victor, #816
Delauter, Reba Mae, #831
Delauter, William Byron, #832
"Delauter, Jr.", Otha Victer, #830
Dellinger, Allmira V.[?], #7030
Dellinger, Anne W., #7024
Dellinger, Anne W., #7025
Dellinger, Anne W., #7026
Dellinger, Anne W., #7027
Dellinger, Catherine C., #7035
Dellinger, Catherine C., #7036
Dellinger, Ellen Burrows, #7037
Dellinger, Ellen Burrows, #7038
Dellinger, Emily L., #7031
Dellinger, Emily L., #7032
Dellinger, Emily L., #7033
Dellinger, Henrietta M., #7028
Dellinger, Henrietta M., #7029
Dellinger, Henry William, #7022
Dellinger, Henry William, #7023
Dellinger, Henry William, #7024
Dellinger, Henry William, #7025
Dellinger, Henry William, #7026
Dellinger, Henry William, #7027
Dellinger, Henry William, #7028
Dellinger, Henry William, #7029
Dellinger, Henry William, #7030
Dellinger, Henry William, #7031
Dellinger, Henry William, #7032
Dellinger, Henry William, #7033
Dellinger, Henry William, #7034
Dellinger, Henry William, #7035
Dellinger, Henry William, #7036
Dellinger, Henry William, #7037
Dellinger, Henry William, #7038
Dellinger, Henry William, #7039
Dellinger, Henry William, #7040
Dellinger, Henry William, #7041
Dellinger, Henry William, #7042
Dellinger, Henry William, #7043
Dellinger, Henry Williams, #7043
Dellinger, Henry Williams, #7053
Dellinger, Henry Williams, #7054
Dellinger, Henry Williams, #7055

Dellinger, Henry Williams, #7105
Dellinger, Henry Williams, #7107
Dellinger, Ida Rhodes, #2814
Dellinger, Jacob H., #7022
Dellinger, Jacob H., #7023
Dellinger, Lucy S., #7041
Dellinger, Lucy S., #7042
Dellinger, Mary Williams, #7039
Dellinger, Mary Williams, #7040
Derbyshire, George Henry, #7919
Derbyshire, George Henry, #7920
Derbyshire, George Henry, #7921
Derbyshire, George Henry, #7922
Derbyshire, George Henry, #7923
Derbyshire, George Henry, #7924
Derbyshire, George Henry, #7925
Derbyshire, George Henry, #7926
Derbyshire, Henry Godfrey, #7923
Derbyshire, Henry Godfrey, #7924
Derbyshire, Lucille Marie, #7925
Derbyshire, Lucille Marie, #7926
"Derbyshire, Jr.", George Henry, #7921
"Derbyshire, Jr.", George Henry, #7922
Dering, Ann, #6117
Dering, D. Lida, #6112
Dering, Ellen, #6118
Dering, Ellie E., #6109
Dering, F.A., #6107
Dering, F.A., #6108
Dering, F.A., #6109
Dering, F.A., #6110
Dering, F.A., #6111
Dering, F.A., #6112
Dering, Frederick Augustus, #6106
Dering, George Small, #6099
Dering, George Small, #6121
Dering, George Small, #6122
Dering, George Small, #6123
Dering, George Small, #6124
Dering, George Small, #6125
Dering, H. Ray, #6111
Dering, Harriet, #6101
Dering, Harriet, #6124
Dering, Harriet L., #6120
Dering, Henry, #6121
Dering, Henry Young, #6102
Dering, John Franklin, #6105
Dering, Laura G., #6119
Dering, M. Augustus, #6110
Dering, Maria Christiana, #6100
Dering, Mary Ann, #6122
Dering, Mary R., #6107
Dering, Rebecca, #6123
Dering, Sarah, #6125
Dering, Sophia, #6104
Dering, William Musser, #6103
Dering, William W., #6108
Dering, Wm. Musser, #6117
Dering, Wm. Musser, #6118
Dering, Wm. Musser, #6119
Dering, Wm. Musser, #6120
Dering, , #6099
Dering, , #6100
Dering, , #6101
Dering, , #6102
Dering, , #6103
Dering, , #6104
Dering, , #6105
Dering, , #6106
Derr, Anamaria, #5640
Deshey, Ellen (Miss), #514

INDEX
Pages are not numbered; numbers refer to the entry number at the beginning of each record.

Deshey, Mary Jane (Miss), #513
Detrow, Ida S. (Miss), #5042
DeWeise, Charles W., #6323
Dick, Ella, #3436
Dickson, Jennie Reid, #4233
Dickson, Rev., #4275
Diebert, Lorraine, #2773
Dieffenbacher, Jacob F., #724
Diehl, Rev., #7245
Diehl, Wm. A., #888
Dietrich, Johann Heinrich, #6007
Dietrich, Johann Heinrich, #6014
Dietrich, Juergen, #6013
Dinwiddie, Isabella, #5634
Divelbiss, John, #4854
Divelbiss, Mary A.[?], #4853
Divelbiss, , #4863
Dodderidge, Joseph (Dr.), #2289
Dodge, O.A. (Rev.), #3793
Dodge, Oliver Augustus (Rev.), #3812
Dolly, A.B., #375
Done, William , #921
Donovan, Janie A., #5221
Dorsey, Elta Marie, #788
Dorsey, Lucretia, #629
Douglas, George, #7755
Douglas, Helen B., #650
Douglas, Helen B., #654
Douglas, Henry Kyd, #655
Douglas, Nannie Cowan[?], #636
Douglas, Robert, #650
Douglas, Robert (Rev.), #650
Douglas, Robt. (Rev.), #646
Downey, Anna, #3698
Downey, Anna, #3713
Downey, Catharine, #3697
Downey, Catharine, #3714
Downey, Elizabeth, #3696
Downey, Elizabeth, #3704
Downey, Ella, #3700
Downey, Ella, #3709
Downey, George, #3699
Downey, George, #3705
Downey, George, #3711
Downey, Hadassah, #3694
Downey, Hadassah, #3695
Downey, Hadassah, #3696
Downey, Hadassah, #3697
Downey, Hadassah, #3698
Downey, Hadassah, #3699
Downey, Hadassah, #3700
Downey, Hadassah, #3701
Downey, Lewis, #3693
Downey, Lewis, #3695
Downey, Lewis, #3696
Downey, Lewis, #3697
Downey, Lewis, #3698
Downey, Lewis, #3699
Downey, Lewis, #3700
Downey, Lewis, #3701
Downey, Lewis, #3701
Downey, Lewis, #3702
Downey, Lewis, #3706
Downey, Lewis, #3707
Downey, Maria, #3695

Downey, Maria, #3703
Downey, Maria, #3715
Downing, Merrill, #587
Downing, Richard, #580
Downing, Richard, #587
Downing, Theresa, #578
Downs, Lewis O., #3703
Downs, Lewis O., #3710
Drane, Rev., #8369
Duble, Margaret M., #3772
Duble, Margaret M., #3774
Duble, Margaret M., #3775
Duckett, Buchanan, #1369
Duckett, Elizabeth, #1365
Duckett, Joseph Gabby, #1353
Duckett, Joseph Gabby, #1355
Duckett, Richard Jacob, #1356
Duckett, Susan, #1347
Duckett, Susan E., #1352
Duckett, T.B. (Dr.), #1353
Duckett, T.B. (Dr.), #1354
Dugan, Miss, #2166
Dungan, Harry G., #4276
Dunn, Hezekiah, #2270
Dunn, Jane Elizabeth, #4782
Dunn, Jemima, #2269
Dunn, Jemima, #2270
Dunn, Marcia, #2270
Dunn, W.H., #4782
Dunn, William Henwood, #4783
Dutt, Ephraim, #7875
Dyer, Ann Elizabeth, #6481
Dyson, [baby], #2263
Dyson, [baby], #2268
Dyson, E.R., #2266
Dyson, H.H., #2261
Dyson, Harry H., #2265
Dyson, Richard E., #2260
Dyson, Tabitha, #2262
Dyson, Tabitha, #2267
Dyson, Thomas, #2263
Dyson, Thomas, #2268
Dyson, Thomas W., #2264
Earick, Catherine, #5487
Earick, Catherine, #5488
Earick, Laura C., #5482
Eastwood, Martha Lela , #5900
Eastwood, Samuel B., #5900
Eastwood, Samuel B., #5901
Eavey, Idella Cordelia (Smith), #6613
Eavey, John Wesley, #6601
Eavey, John Wesley, #6603
Eavey, John Wesley, #6616
Eavey, Rudolph Richard, #6614
Ebbrecht, William (Mrs.), #574
Eccard, Burnice Susie (Mrs.), #5040
Eccard, Claude G., #5040
Eckstine, Earl, #582
Eckstine, Earl, #584
Eckstine, Virginia, #579
Ecton, Charles R., #3669
Ecton, Charles R., #4926
Ecton, Charles William, #3683
Ecton, Charles William, #4921
Ecton, Dora Francis, #3686
Ecton, Flossie Virginia, #3684
Ecton, Flossie Virginia, #4922
Ecton, Mary Cathern, #3685

Ecton, Mary Cathern, #4923
Ecton, Mary Frances, #4924
Ecton, Nina May, #3691
Ecton, Sarah Jane, #3670
Ecton, Sarah Jane, #4925
Eddy, John Alfred, #2996
Edwards, Catharine (Hughes) (Mrs.), #3503
Edwards, Tryon (Rev. Dr.), #3503
Effinger, Mary E., #8272
Effinger, Mary E., #8288
Eichelberger, Barbara (Mrs.), #7756
Eichelberger, Theobold, #7757
Eicheldugin[?], Carrie F.[?], #1323
Eikelberger, Mary E., #5036
Eikelberger, Mary E., #5037
Eirley, William H., #3035
Eldridge, Rhoda B., #598
Eldridge, Rhoda B., #604
Elgan, Henry Clay, #2007
Elgan, P. Luther, #2008
Elgin, Prudence Chaney (Boteler), #2045
Elgin, Rachel E., #2041
Elgin, Robert, #312
Elgin, Robert, #316
Elgin , Karan Sue, #316
Elgin , Karan Sue, #317
Eliza[?] J., , #1176
Ellis, Harley, #8506
Ellsworth, Donald Monroe, #5569
Embich, Christopher, #2154
Embich, Christopher, #2155
Embich, Christopher, #2155
Embich, Christopher, #2156
Embich, Christopher, #2156
Embich, Christopher, #2157
Embich, Christopher, #2158
Embich, Christopher, #2159
Embich, Christopher, #2160
Embich, Christopher, #2161
Embich, Christopher, #2162
Embich, Christopher, #2163
Embich, Christopher, #2165
Embich, Christopher, #2166
Embich, Christopher, #2167
Embich, Christopher, #2168
Embich, Christopher, #2169
Embich, Christopher, #2170
Embich, Christopher, #2171
Embich, Christopher, #2172
Embich, Christopher, #2173
Embich, Christopher, #2174
Embich, Christopher, #2175
Embich, Christopher, #2176
Embich, Christopher, #2177
Embich, Christopher, #2178
Embich, Eleanor, #2176
Embich, Eleanor, #2177
Embich, Eleanor, #2178
Embich, Eleanor, #2179
Embich, Eleanor, #2180
Embich, Elizabeth, #2160
Embich, Elizabeth, #2161
Embich, Elizabeth, #2162
Embich, Frederick, #2174
Embich, Frederick, #2175
Embich, Jacob, #2163
Embich, Jacob, #2164
Embich, Mary, #2168

Embich, Mary, #2169
Embich, Mary, #2171
Embich, Mary, #2172
Embich, Mary, #2173
Embich, Mary, #2185
Embich, Mary, #2186
Embich, Mary, #2187
Embich, Mary, #2245
Embich, Michael, #2170
Embich, Philemon, #2164
Embich, Phillip, #2165
Embich, Phillip, #2166
Embich, Phillip, #2167
Embrich, Mary, #2199
Emmert, Ann Cathrine, #3645
Emmert, Anne Catherine, #3647
Emmert, Anne[?] Craft, #3657
Emmert, Annie[?] R., #3663
Emmert, Bessie R., #3650
Emmert, Isaac, #3665
Emmert, Joseph Martin, #3661
Emmert, Leonard D., #3643
Emmert, Leonard David, #3662
Emmert, Leonard David, #3663
Emmert, Leonard R., #3646
Emmert, Leonard Remsburg , #3644
Emmert, Lewis[?] Cookerly, #3658
Emmert, Mamie Barbara, #3659
Emmert, Mary C. (Young), #3664
Emmert, Mary Naomi[?], #3660
Emmert, Prudence Boteler, #2019
Emmert[?], [?], #4954
England, Carlton E., #4333
England, Carlton Emerson, #4322
England, Carlton Emerson, #4323
England, Carlton Emerson, #4324
England, Carlton Emerson, #4346
England, Edith, #4328
England, Edith, #4329
England, Edith Jackson, #4319
England, Edith Jackson, #4335
England, Elizabeth, #4326
England, James, #4322
England, James, #4327
England, James A., #4325
England, James A., #4326
England, James A., #4327
England, James A., #4334
England, James Albert, #4316
England, James Albert, #4347
England, James H., #4315
England, James H., #4332
England, James H., #4343
England, Jean Millard, #4329
England, Louise, #4325
England, Marietta M., #4345
England, Mary Elizabeth, #4328
England, Ralph, #4323
England, Ruth, #4324
England, Stuart Alanson, #4318
England, Stuart Alanson, #4344
England, Theodore Austin, #4317
England, Theodore Austin, #4342
Engle, Cornelia, #343
Engle, Cornelia, #344
Engle, Cornelia, #345
Engle, Cornelia, #346
Engle, Cornelia, #347
Ensminger, Malissa J., #4699
Entler, Elizabeth Beecher (Herr), #3175
Eschback, E.R., #1352

INDEX
Pages are not numbered; numbers refer to the entry number at the beginning of each record.

Eshleman, Thelma, #6774
Estburn, Mary, #2031
Estlyman, Peter, #5612
Evans, Elizabeth, #6131
Evans, George Dering, #6126
Evans, Harriet Lowry, #6129
Evans, Henry, #6127
Evans, Maria, #6126
Evans, Maria, #6127
Evans, Maria, #6128
Evans, Maria, #6129
Evans, Maria, #6130
Evans, Maria, #6131
Evans, Maria, #6132
Evans, Maria, #6133
Evans, Maria, #6134
Evans, Mary, #6132
Evans, Nettie, #7360
Evans, Rebecca, #6133
Evans, Rev., #8217
Evans, Sarah, #6134
Evans, Sophia Eliza, #6130
Evans, William, #7359
Evans, William, #7360
Evans, William Musser, #6128
Evans, , #6100
Evers, A.M., #2331
Evers, A.M., #3396
Evers, A.M., #377
Eyerly, Sam'l., #7154
Eyster, W.F., #4382
Fagne, Catherine, #7474
Fagne, Edward E., #7481
Fagne, John, #7472
Fagne, John, #7473
Fagne, John, #7483
Fagne, Mary Catherine, #7471
Fagne, Mary Ellen, #7485
Fagne, Mary Ellen, #7487
Fagne, Mary Ellen, #7488
Fagne, Mary Ellen, #7489
Fagne, Mary Ellen, #7490
Fagne, Mary Ellen, #7491
Fagne, Mary Ellen, #7492
Fagne, Mary Ellen, #7493
Fagne, Mary Ellen, #7494
Fagne, Mary Ellen, #7495
Fagne, Mary Ellie, #7463
Fagne, Millard F., #7480
Fagne, Millard Gillman, #7469
Fagne, Samuel Edward, #7466
Fagne, Susan Maria, #7464
Fagne, Theodore, #7465
Fagne, Theodore, #7479
Fagne, Theodore F., #7468
Fagne, William Boone, #7467
Fagne, William Boone, #7482
Fague, John, #7462
Fairfax, Mary C., #8562
Fairfax, Mary Jett, #6187
Fairfax, Mary Jett, #6188
Fairfax, Mary Jett.[?], #6145
Falconer, Clementine L.K., #754
Falconer, Katie C., #4687
Falconer, Katie C., #747
Falconer, Lucian E., #753
Falconer, Oliver L., #752
Farnsworth, [blank], #3795

Farper, Franey B.F., #8517
Fasnacht, Elizabeth Ann, #1827
Fasnacht, Elizabeth Ann, #8059
Fasnacht, Henry, #1825
Fasnacht, Henry, #1829
Fasnacht, Henry, #8057
Fasnacht, Henry, #8061
Fasnacht, Lidia, #1824
Fasnacht, Lidia, #1830
Fasnacht, Lidia, #8062
Fasnacht, Sarah Jane, #1828
Fasnacht, Sarah Jane, #8060
Father, ,
Faulder, Joshua, #5047
Faulder, Susan (Mrs.), #5047
Fergueson, R.J., #7621
Ferris, Hazel Virginia, #311
Fiery, Elizabeth, #2601
Fiery, Elizabeth, #2602
Fiery, Joseph H., #665
Fiery, Mollie E. (Miss), #702
Fike, Samuel, #1112
Firey, John Baxton, #1518
Firey, John Baxton, #1525
Firey, John Burton, #1535
Firey, Jos. Frederick, #1519
Firey, Jos. H., #1516
Firey, Jos. Henry, #1534
Firey, Joseph Frederick, #1527
Firey, Joseph Henry, #1536
Firey, Leilah, #1520
Firey, Lelah, #1524
Firey, Mary Elizabeth, #1517
Firey, Mary Lizzie, #1522
Firey, Nora, #1528
Firey, Nora, #1532
Firey, Robert Bruce, #1526
Firey, Robert Bruce, #1531
Firey, Sally, #1523
Firey, Sally, #1530
Firey, William H., #1533
Firey, William Henry, #1521
First[?], Alphonso Roberts (Miss), #4358
Fisher, Allen B.L., #7016
Fisher, Alta L., #3638
Fisher, Alta L___[?], #3605
Fisher, Barbara Ann, #3608
Fisher, Barbara Ann, #3641
Fisher, Barbara Jean Weeks, #3626
Fisher, Bruce M., #3627
Fisher, Bruce M., #3634
Fisher, Bruce M., #3635
Fisher, Bruce M., #3636
Fisher, Bruce M., #3637
Fisher, Bruce Mills, #3606
Fisher, Bruce Mills, #3639
Fisher, Bruce Mills, #3642
Fisher, Cath. E., #3334
fisher, Charles, #5021
Fisher, Charles H., #4057
Fisher, Janet E., #3625
Fisher, Janet Mills, #3628
Fisher, Margaret M., #3629
Fisher, Marsahll Albert, #3632
Fisher, Maxwell Wynwood, #3631
Fisher, Paul Waynfield[?], #3633
Fisher, Ray Monroe, #3630

Fisher, Sara Eileen, #3607
Fisher, Sara Eileen, #3640
Fisher, Terri, #3617
Fisher, Timothy Craig, #3611
Fisher, Timothy Craig, #3621
Fisher, Virginia, #3616
Fitchett, Nora, #6295
Fitchett, Nora, #6296
Fitchett, Nora, #6297
Fitchett, Nora, #6425
Fitchett, Nora, #6426
Fitzhugh, F. (Dr.), #1232
Fitzpatrick, Sarah H., #3131
Flandrau, Ruth Hungerford, #90
Flandrau, Ruth Hungerford, #95
Flandrau, Ruth Hungerford, #99
Fleming, Elizabeth, #2236
Fletcher, Edna (Koontz) (Mrs.), #2858
Fletcher, Edna E., #2841
Fletcher, Leander M., #1967
Fletcher, Leander M., #1968
Fletcher, Leona Virginia, #2859
Fletcher, Morris, #2858
Fletcher, , #2860
Fling, Henry, #1952
Fling, Owen, #1939
Fling, Owen, #1952
Flook, John P., #4629
Flook, Minnie (Summers), #4625
Flook, Minnie Ellen (Mrs.), #4629
Flory, Adam, #1614
Flory, Alex Murphy, #1638
Flory, Alex Murphy, #1639
Flory, Alexander M., #1595
Flory, Alexander M., #1596
Flory, Amanda, #1592
Flory, Amanda, #1601
Flory, Amanda, #1602
Flory, Amanda, #1608
Flory, Amanda, #1609
Flory, Amanda, #1610
Flory, Amanda, #1611
Flory, Amanda, #1612
Flory, Amelia, #1593
Flory, Amelia, #1605
Flory, Amelia, #1606
Flory, Amelia, #1613
Flory, Ann Catharine, #1642
Flory, Ann E., #1597
Flory, Ann E., #1598
Flory, Ann S., #1621
Flory, Catherine A., #1634
Flory, D.H., #1638
Flory, D.H., #1639
Flory, D.H., #1640
Flory, D.H., #1641
Flory, D.H., #1642
Flory, D.H., #1644
Flory, D.H., #1645
Flory, D.H., #1646
Flory, D.H., #1647
Flory, D.H., #1648
Flory, Daniel, #1591
Flory, Daniel, #1617
Flory, Daniel, #1634
Flory, Daniel, #1635
Flory, Daniel, #1640
Flory, Daniel W., #1607
Flory, David, #1615
Flory, David H., #1594

Flory, David H., #1603
Flory, David H., #1604
Flory, David H., #1643
Flory, David Hammett, #1641
Flory, David Hammett, #1649
Flory, Grant, #1645
Flory, Grant, #1646
Flory, Hannah Mary, #1643
Flory, Hannah Mary, #1644
Flory, Hannah Mary, #1645
Flory, Hannah Mary, #1646
Flory, Hannah Mary, #1647
Flory, Hannah Mary, #1648
Flory, Hannah Mary, #1650
Flory, Healen, #1599
Flory, Healen, #1600
Flory, John, #1614
Flory, John, #1615
Flory, John, #1616
Flory, John, #1616
Flory, John, #1617
Flory, John, #1618
Flory, John, #1619
Flory, John, #1620
Flory, John, #1621
Flory, John, #1622
Flory, Maria Amanda, #1644
Flory, Maria Amanda, #1651
Flory, Mary A., #1622
Flory, Mary Ellen, #5138
Flory, Mercer[?] (Mathews), #1636
Flory, Rebecca, #1618
Flory, Ross Leon, #1647
Flory, Ross Leon, #1648
Flory, Sarah, #1619
Flory, Solomon, #1620
Flory, , #1637
Flory , Ann E., #1627
Flory , Daniel W., #1629
Flory , Healin, #1628
Fogel, Verna, #6302
Fogel, Verna, #6432
Folk, John, #3739
Folk, Virginia, #3721
Foltz, Amey Elly, #3587
Foltz, Anna M., #3602
Foltz, Celia Rose[?], #3590
Foltz, Clara, #3600
Foltz, Clara Bell, #3589
Foltz, E. Louise, #6747
Foltz, Elizabeth Louise, #6767
Foltz, H. Jane, #6748
Foltz, Harry, #6755
Foltz, Harry R., #6745
Foltz, Henrietta Jane, #6769
Foltz, Henry, #3578
Foltz, Henry, #3581
Foltz, Henry, #3583
Foltz, Henry, #3597
Foltz, Henry J., #3603
Foltz, Jacob Forny, #3592
Foltz, John H., #5035
Foltz, Julia F., #6746
Foltz, Julia Francis, #6768
Foltz, Laura Jane, #3588
Foltz, Lewis Henry, #3586
Foltz, Marann Catherine, #3585
Foltz, Nancy, #3598
Foltz, Nettie Louise, #6759
Foltz, Samuel Oswalt, #3593
Foltz, Sarah A., #3580

INDEX
Pages are not numbered; numbers refer to the entry number at the beginning of each record.

Foltz, Sarah A., #3584
Foltz, Ulysses Grant, #3594
Foltz, Ulysses Grant, #3595
Foltz, Willie E., #3604
Foltz, Willie Edwin, #3591
Fonch, Anna M., #979
Fonch, David S., #978
Fonch, Lora E., #977
Font, Robert, #3027
Forbes, Charles, #3787
Forbes, Charles, #3813
Foreman[?], Susan, #475
Forest, Lee, #931
Forney, Annamaia, #3578
Forney, Annamaria, #3596
Forrest, Agnes L., #5237
Forrest, Douglas, #5217
Fortney, David, #4368
Fortney, David, #4442
Fortney, Elizabeth, #4354
Fortney, Elizabeth, #4368
Fortney, Elizabeth, #4441
Fortney, Elizabeth Ann, #4368
Fost, Paulette Jean, #1587
Fost, Paulette Jean, #1588
Fost, Paulette Jean, #1589
Foster, Charles Frederick, #3774
Foster, Clara Belle, #3771
Foster, Frederea[?] Augustus, #3764
Foster, Henry Arnold, #3775
Foster, Henry Arnold, #3776
Foster, Henry Bowman, #3762
Foster, Henry Bowman, #3797
Foster, Maria L., #3794
Foster, Maria Louisa, #3763
Foster, Maria Louisa, #3777
Foster, Marine[?] Frederic A., #3759
Foster, Martha Ellen, #3767
Foster, Martha Ellen, #3798
Foster, Peregrine Dwight, #3761
Foster, Peregrine Dwight, #3772
Foster, Peregrine Dwight, #3773
Foster, Peregrine Dwight, #3774
Foster, Peregrine Dwight, #3775
Foster, Sarah (Mrs.), #3799
Foster, Sarah Jane, #3765
Foster, Sarah Jane, #3780
Foster, Theodore[?] Newton, #3770
Foster, William Beck, #3768
Foster, William Black[?], #3803
Foster, Wilson Parkman, #3769
Foster, Wilson Parkman, #3771
Foster, Wilson Parkman, #3781
"Foster, Jr.[?]", Frederick A., #3801
"Foster, Sr.", Frederic Augustus, #3800
Fouch, Ada Leah, #3573

Fouch, Bertha May, #3572
Fouch, David, #3561
Fouch, David, #3575
Fouch, David, #3577
Fouch, David Birnside, #3568
Fouch, Edwin Oscar, #3571
Fouch, Emma Fransis, #3569
Fouch, Geoerge Washington, #3565
Fouch, John Jacob, #3563
Fouch, Lara Manzilla, #3566
Fouch, Laura, #2995
Fouch, Laura M., #2964
Fouch, Laura M., #2971
Fouch, Laura M., #2972
Fouch, Laura M., #2973
Fouch, Laura M., #2974
Fouch, Laura M., #2975
Fouch, Laura M., #2976
Fouch, Louisa, #3574
Fouch, Louisa (Grim), #3562
Fouch, Margreat Elen, #3567
Fouch, Martha Ann Catharine, #3570
Fouch, Mary Elizabeth, #3564
Fouch, Matilda, #3576
Fowler, David, #313
Fox, Amos, #1217
Fox, Ann, #3559
Fox, Anna (Miss), #3560
Fox, Beatrice (Moore) (Eckstine), #586
Frank, John[?], #4822
Frankhouser, Diller[?] G., #5611
Freaner, Rebecca (Miss), #4570
French, Ann P., #8486
French, Ann Priscilla, #8473
French, Ann Priscilla (Garrott), #8497
French, Dorothy W., #8498
French, Dorothy Warren, #8473
French, Edwin S., #8473
French, Edwin S., #8486
French, Edwin S., #8503
French, Laura Spence, #8506
French, Laura Spruce, #8486
French, Mary Jane, #8507
French[?], Ann P., #8470
French[?], Edwin S., #8470
French[?], Mary Jane, #8470
Freus, Wm. S., #6019
Frey, David, #3498
Frey, Emma Susan, #3497
Frey, Harry R., #4058
Frey, Joseph S., #3491
Frey, Joseph S., #3492
Frey, Joseph Samuel, #3489
Frey, Josua, #3560
Frey, Lillie S. (Funkhouser), #3492
Frey, Margaret Ann (Miss), #4058
Frey, Susie, #7451
Frey[?], Elon A., #3534
Fricke, Gustar[?] A., #6514
Fricke, Henrietta, #6504
Fricke, Henriette (Mrs.), #6518
Fricke, James, #6517
Fricke, John Henry, #6510
Fricke, John Henry, #6525

Fricke, Laura[?], #6512
Fricke, William, #6503
Fricke, William, #6504
Fricke, William, #6508
Fricke, William, #6524
Fricke, Wm., #6519
"Fricke, Jr.", Henry John, #6505
"Fricke, Jr.", William Theadore, #6506
Fricke[?], Theodore, #6516
Fritzinger, Rev., #174
Froehlich, Barbara, #5294
Froehlich, Barbara, #5295
Froehlich, Barbara E., #1390
Froehlich, Barbara E., #1417
Froehlich, Barbara E., #5301
Froehlich, Barbara Elizabeth, #5284
Froehlich, H. Roy, #1389
Froehlich, H. Roy, #1415
Froehlich, H. Roy, #5300
Froehlich, H.R., #1416
Froehlich, Katharine, #5284
Froehlich, Patricia Lee, #1392
Froehlich, Patricia Lee, #5285
Froehlich, Patricia Lee, #5296
Froehlich, Patricia Lee, #5297
Froehlich, Patricia Lee, #5303
Froehlich, Phyllis, #5289
Froehlich, Phyllis, #5290
Froehlich, Phyllis, #5291
Froehlich, Phyllis, #5292
Froehlich, Phyllis, #5293
Froehlich, Phyllis V., #1391
Froehlich, Phyllis V., #5302
Froehlich, Phyllis Virginia, #1418
Froehlich, Phyllis Virginia, #5286
Froehlich, Roy, #5284
Fry, [female], #3549
Fry, [male], #3547
Fry, [male], #3550
Fry, Anjalene, #3538
Fry, Anjaline, #3513
Fry, Anjaline, #8180
Fry, Anjaline, #8197
Fry, Ann, #3552
Fry, Ann, #3556
Fry, Ann G., #3509
Fry, Ann J., #3541
Fry, Ann Jane a Bertha, #8191
Fry, Ann Jane Bertha[?], #3525
Fry, Ann Y.[?], #8200
Fry, Anne[?] J.[?], #8176
Fry, Arnold[?] May, #8194
Fry, Arthur I., #3530
Fry, B. Franklin, #3558
Fry, Butler[?], #8175
Fry, Catharene Alvenda[?], #8198
Fry, Catharine Alverda, #3539
Fry, Catharine Alvinda, #3523
Fry, Catharine Alvinda, #8190
Fry, Clarah Kate, #3480
Fry, David, #3474
Fry, David, #3485
Fry, David Lewis, #3483
Fry, David Lewis, #3494
Fry, Edker P., #3528
Fry, Edker[?] P., #3533
Fry, Elen U., #3529
Fry, Elizabeth, #3515
Fry, Elizabeth, #3546

Fry, Elizabeth, #3547
Fry, Elizabeth, #3548
Fry, Elizabeth, #3549
Fry, Elizabeth, #3550
Fry, Elizabeth, #8182
Fry, Elizabeth Mary, #3476
Fry, Emma Susan, #3481
Fry, George L. Botler, #8192
Fry, George L. Bottler, #3526
Fry, George W., #3518
Fry, George W., #3537
Fry, George W., #7445
Fry, George W., #7446
Fry, George W., #8185
Fry, George W., #8196
Fry, Hannah Barbara, #3482
Fry, Harry Clinton, #3542
Fry, Harry Clinton, #8201
Fry, Helen Rebecka, #3484
Fry, Helen Rebecka, #3495
Fry, Isaac, #3553
Fry, Isaac, #3557
Fry, John Henry, #3475
Fry, John Henry, #3493
Fry, John N., #8172
Fry, John P., #3516
Fry, John P., #3544
Fry, John P., #8183
Fry, John P., #8203
Fry, John P.[?], #3506
Fry, John W., #3527
Fry, Joshua, #3551
Fry, Joshua, #3555
Fry, Lidia Ann, #3478
Fry, Lilly Irene, #3487
Fry, Ludia Ann, #3496
Fry, Margaret An, #8173
Fry, Margaret Ann, #3507
Fry, Margaret Ann, #8174
Fry, Margaret Virginia, #3479
Fry, Margaretan, #8184
Fry, Margaretan[?], #3517
Fry, Martha Allice, #3488
Fry, Mary, #3548
Fry, Mary Ann, #3554
Fry, Orrow[?] May, #3524
Fry, Orrow[?] May, #3531
Fry, Paul, #3545
Fry, Paul, #3546
Fry, Paul, #3547
Fry, Paul, #3548
Fry, Paul, #3549
Fry, Paul, #3550
Fry, Pearl Va., #3543
Fry, Peter, #3510
Fry, Peter, #3540
Fry, Peter, #8177
Fry, Peter, #8199
Fry, Purle[?] Va[?], #8202
Fry, Sarah, #8195
Fry, Sarah Louisa, #3477
Fry, Susan, #3486
Fry, Susan, #3505
Fry, Susan, #3536
Fry, Susan, #8171
Fry, Susan Catharine, #3514
Fry, Susan Catharine, #8181
Fry[?], John M., #8193
Fry[?], Luthor[?], #3535
Frye, Angeline, #7438
Frye, Catherine Girmettee, #7439

INDEX
Pages are not numbered; numbers refer to the entry number at the beginning of each record.

Frye, Catherine Girmettee, #7440
Frye, Clayton, #7427
Frye, Clayton, #7451
Frye, Geo. W., #7439
Frye, Geo. W., #7440
Frye, George W., #7434
Frye, Isabella M., #7459
Frye, Isabella Martha, #7453
Frye, Isabella Martha, #7454
Frye, John Ashton Michelous, #7441
Frye, John Ashton Michelous, #7442
Frye, John Clinton, #7685
Frye, Martha E., #7435
Frye, Martha E., #7439
Frye, Martha E., #7440
Frye, Martha E., #7443
Frye, Martha E., #7444
Frye, Susie, #7428
Frye, Vira, #7429
Frye, Vira, #7432
Frye, Vira, #7433
Frye, Vira, #7455
Frye, Vira, #7456
Frye, Walter Clayton, #7451
Frye, Walter Clayton, #7452
Frye, Walter Clayton, #7461
Frye, William Clayton, #7436
Frye, William Clayton, #7447
Frye, William Clayton, #7448
Frye, William Clayton, #7457
Fucie, Katharine M., #6019
Fuller, Alice C., #7387
Fuller, Alice Charlotte, #7395
Fuller, Arthur Gorman, #7403
Fuller, Catharine Ann, #7393
Fuller, Charles, #7375
Fuller, Charles, #7376
Fuller, Clifton E., #7398
Fuller, Cornelia Ann, #7389
Fuller, Cornelia Ann, #7396
Fuller, Earl Newton, #7401
Fuller, Elijah, #7386
Fuller, Elijah, #7392
Fuller, Elijah , #7394
Fuller, Elijah , #7395
Fuller, Elijah , #7396
Fuller, Elijah , #7397
Fuller, Howard Mason, #7380
Fuller, Howard Mason, #7390
Fuller, Howard Mason, #7391
Fuller, Howard Mason, #7397
Fuller, Howard Mason, #7398
Fuller, Howard Mason, #7399
Fuller, Howard Mason, #7400
Fuller, Howard Mason, #7401
Fuller, Howard Mason, #7402
Fuller, Howard Mason, #7403
Fuller, Howard Mason, #7404
Fuller, James Kemp, #7394
Fuller, James Ray, #7399
Fuller, Mira Spear, #7402
Fuller, Richard, #4276
Fuller, Walter, #7376
Fuller, Walter Mason, #7400
Fulton, Lemuel W., #1915
Fulton, Robert, #1915
Funk, Anna, #1623
Funk, Anna Louise, #283

Funk, Ida M., #231
Funk, Solmin[?], #4953
Funk, Solomon, #4979
Funk[?], Elisa, #4951
Funkhouser, Beatrice Ellen, #23
Funkhouser, Beatrice Ellen, #24
Funkhouser, Clarence Paul, #1
Funkhouser, Franklin Lhist[?], #10
Funkhouser, Godfrey, #5
Funkhouser, Gracie Edith, #26
Funkhouser, Hazel Estelle, #3
Funkhouser, John Albert, #8
Funkhouser, John Albert, #9
Funkhouser, Keller Herbert, #28
Funkhouser, Mamie Constance, #27
Funkhouser, Mary Catharine, #11
Funkhouser, Mary Catharine, #7
Funkhouser, Mary Jane, #6
Funkhouser, Pauline Catherine, #4
Funkhouser, Pearl Dexter, #29
Funkhouser, Pearl Dexter, #30
Funkhouser, Ralph August, #15
Funkhouser, Ralph August, #16
Funkhouser, Robert Lee, #19
Funkhouser, Robert Lee, #20
Funkhouser, Roy Nelson, #2
Funkhouser, Thomas Jefferson, #17
Funkhouser, Thomas Jefferson, #18
Funkhouser, Victor Godfrey, #12
Funkhouser, Victor Godfrey, #13
Funkhouser, William Steele, #14
Funkhouser, Winona Jackson, #21
Funkhouser, Winona Jackson, #22
Gabby, Ann, #1360
Gabby, Eliza C., #1354
Gabby, Elizabeth, #1369
Gabby, Elizabeth, #1370
Gabby, Emily, #1368
Gabby, Emily, #1373
Gabby, J., #1363
Gabby, Jane, #1367
Gabby, Jane, #1371
Gabby, John, #1359
Gabby, John, #1372
Gabby, Joseph, #1354
Gabby, Joseph, #1364
Gabby, Joseph, #1366
Gabby, Joseph, #1375
Gabby, William, #1361
Gabby, William, #1374
Gabler, Mary Ann, #2474
Gabler, Mary Ann, #2477
Gabler, Mary Ann, #2478
Gabler, Mary Ann, #2479
Gabler, Mary Ann, #2480
Gabler, Mary Ann, #2481
Gabler, Mary Ann, #2482
Gabler, Mary Ann, #2483
Gabler, Mary Ann, #7875

Gabriel, Grover C. (Rev.), #3420
Gabriel, Grover C. (Rev.), #3421
Gaines, Nellie, #2908
Galbraith, Dorcas, #7974
Gambla[?], Robert (Col.), #7559
Gamble[?], Letita B., #7559
Gamble[?], Letita B., #7560
Ganoe, Rev., #7893
Gardner, Audrey D., #2563
Gardner, Thomas, #3029
Garey, Sarah T.[?], #3125
Garlinger, Aaron, #3465
Garlinger, Anna M., #3472
Garlinger, Anna Margaret, #3463
Garlinger, Benj. A., #3455
Garlinger, Benj. Aaron, #3456
Garlinger, Benj. Aaron, #3457
Garlinger, Benj. Ryland, #3460
Garlinger, Benj. Ryland, #3468
Garlinger, Dixon Nesbitt, #3466
Garlinger, Howard Rosensteel, #3461
Garlinger, Jacob Harry, #3464
Garlinger, Jacob Harry, #3470
Garlinger, Joanna M., #3473
Garlinger, Mahlon F. McClure, #3471
Garlinger, Mahlon Fredrick McClure, #3459
Garlinger, McVitty Burnside, #3467
Garlinger, McVitty Burnside, #3469
Garlinger, Rachel, #3462
Garriah, Clara, #4128
Garriah, Clara, #4129
Garriah, Clara, #4130
Garrish, Allen Stewart, #4151
Garrish, Bruce William, #4156
Garrish, Clara, #1713
Garrish, Clara, #1728
Garrish, Clara, #1731
Garrish, Clara, #1732
Garrish, Clara, #1733
Garrish, Clara, #4110
Garrish, Clara Elizabeth, #1697
Garrish, Clara Elizabeth, #1698
Garrish, Clara Elizabeth, #1699
Garrish, Clara Elizabeth, #1700
Garrish, Clara Elizabeth, #4113
Garrish, Clara Elizabeth, #4147
Garrish, Florance K., #4152
Garrish, Florance K., #4153
Garrish, Frank Thomas Goddard, #4158
Garrish, George Jacob, #4145
Garrish, Georgietta, #4155
Garrish, Georgietta, #4156
Garrish, Georgietta, #4157
Garrish, Georgietta, #4158
Garrish, Georgietta, #4159
Garrish, Isaac Thompson, #4149
Garrish, Isabell Ridell, #4159
Garrish, Joseph, #4143
Garrish, Joseph, #4144
Garrish, Joseph, #4145
Garrish, Joseph, #4146
Garrish, Joseph, #4147
Garrish, Joseph, #4148
Garrish, Joseph, #4149
Garrish, Joseph, #4150

Garrish, Joseph, #4151
Garrish, Joseph Benjamin, #4144
Garrish, Joseph H., #4140
Garrish, Joseph H., #4156
Garrish, Joseph H., #4157
Garrish, Joseph H., #4158
Garrish, Joseph H., #4159
Garrish, Joseph Henry, #4154
Garrish, Joseph Henry, #4155
Garrish, Lewis E. McComas, #4157
Garrish, Lutie Albert, #4146
Garrish, Lutie Albert, #4150
Garrish, Maggie Thompson[?], #4148
Garrish, Osman Latrobe, #4141
Garrish, Sprigg Dixon, #4143
Garrish, Thomas Rhodes, #4142
Garrott, [infant], #8527
Garrott, Aden Anderson, #8520
Garrott, Allen Franklin, #8523
Garrott, Allen Warren, #8559
Garrott, Amanda, #8456
Garrott, Ann, #8436
Garrott, Ann, #8444
Garrott, Ann, #8451
Garrott, Ann, #8461
Garrott, Ann Buller, #8458
Garrott, Ann P., #8441
Garrott, Ann Priscilla, #8469
Garrott, Ann Priscilla, #8479
Garrott, Ann Priscilla, #8483
Garrott, Ann Priscilla, #8503
Garrott, Ann Priscilla (Hardy), #8489
Garrott, Ann Virginia, #8515
Garrott, Bartholomew, #8512
Garrott, Bartholomew, #8514
Garrott, Bartholomew, #8526
Garrott, Barton, #8436
Garrott, Barton, #8439
Garrott, Barton, #8444
Garrott, Barton, #8459
Garrott, Barton, #8521
Garrott, Barton, #8533
Garrott, Barton, #8534
Garrott, Barton, #8535
Garrott, Barton, #8536
Garrott, Barton, #8568
Garrott, Barton Van Buren, #8521
Garrott, E.V., #4359
Garrott, Edw., #8437
Garrott, Edward, #8438
Garrott, Edward, #8440
Garrott, Edward, #8441
Garrott, Edward, #8450
Garrott, Edward, #8466
Garrott, Edward, #8467
Garrott, Edward, #8468
Garrott, Edward, #8471
Garrott, Edward, #8477
Garrott, Edward, #8479
Garrott, Edward, #8481
Garrott, Edward, #8482
Garrott, Edward, #8483
Garrott, Edward, #8484
Garrott, Edward, #8488
Garrott, Edward, #8491
Garrott, Edward, #8493
Garrott, Edward, #8494
Garrott, Edward, #8500
Garrott, Edward, #8501
Garrott, Edwd., #8455
Garrott, Elen Catharine, #8522

INDEX

Pages are not numbered; numbers refer to the entry number at the beginning of each record.

Garrott, Elen Jane, #8533
Garrott, Elen Jane, #8558
Garrott, Elizabeth, #8449
Garrott, Elizabeth, #8511
Garrott, Elizabeth, #8531
Garrott, Elizabeth, #8560
Garrott, Elizabeth Ann, #8445
Garrott, Elizabeth Ann, #8533
Garrott, Ellen, #8485
Garrott, Ellen, #8499
Garrott, Ellen (McGill), #8482
Garrott, Ellen McGill, #8502
Garrott, Emma Rosalia, #8518
Garrott, Erasmus, #8435
Garrott, Erasmus, #8443
Garrott, Erasmus, #8462
Garrott, Hanah, #8448
Garrott, Hannah Frances, #8457
Garrott, Hannah Frances, #8567
Garrott, Jared Rice, #8535
Garrott, Jessie Tolbert, #8516
Garrott, John, #8435
Garrott, John, #8443
Garrott, John Hilleary, #8475
Garrott, John P., #8511
Garrott, John P., #8529
Garrott, John P., #8557
Garrott, John P., #8566
Garrott, John Robert, #8534
Garrott, John Robert, #8564
Garrott, John Warren, #8474
Garrott, John Warren, #8509
Garrott, Joseph, #8447
Garrott, Joseph, #8460
Garrott, Joseph, #8556
Garrott, Joseph E., #8563
Garrott, Joseph Edward, #8530
Garrott, Laura (Clagett), #8468
Garrott, Laura Claggett, #8481
Garrott, Laura Claggett, #8482
Garrott, Laura Claggett, #8483
Garrott, Laura Claggett, #8484
Garrott, Laura Claggett (Hilleary), #8488
Garrott, Laura Jane, #8519
Garrott, Margaret, #8471
Garrott, Margaret, #8472
Garrott, Margaret, #8474
Garrott, Margaret, #8476
Garrott, Margaret, #8490
Garrott, Margaret, #8491
Garrott, Margaret Goode, #8492
Garrott, Margaret Priscilla, #8510
Garrott, Mary, #8435
Garrott, Mary, #8443
Garrott, Mary, #8475
Garrott, Mary, #8571
Garrott, Mary A., #8465
Garrott, Mary Ann, #8437
Garrott, Mary Ann, #8454
Garrott, Mary Ann, #8467
Garrott, Mary Ann, #8477
Garrott, Mary E.G., #8570
Garrott, Mary Elizabeth, #8517

Garrott, Mary Elizabeth, #8528
Garrott, Mary Elizabeth Gray, #8537
Garrott, Mary P., #8555
Garrott, Mary Priscilla, #8521
Garrott, Mary Priscilla, #8534
Garrott, Mary Priscilla, #8535
Garrott, Mary Priscilla, #8536
Garrott, Maryann, #8525
Garrott, Matilda, #8446
Garrott, Priscill, #8455
Garrott, Sarah, #8435
Garrott, Sarah, #8436
Garrott, Sarah, #8444
Garrott, Sarah, #8452
Garrott, Sarah, #8463
Garrott, Sarah, #8532
Garrott, Sarah, #8565
Garrott, Sarah Erasmus, #8536
Garrott, Sarah Erasmus, #8569
Garrott, Susan Matilda, #8524
Garrott, Warren, #8437
Garrott, Warren, #8438
Garrott, Warren, #8441
Garrott, Warren, #8453
Garrott, Warren, #8455
Garrott, Warren, #8467
Garrott, Warren, #8469
Garrott, Warren, #8471
Garrott, Warren, #8472
Garrott, Warren, #8474
Garrott, Warren, #8476
Garrott, Warren, #8477
Garrott, Warren, #8479
Garrott, Warren, #8481
Garrott, Warren, #8487
Garrott, Warren, #8489
Garrott, Warren, #8490
Garrott, Warren, #8491
Garrott, Warren, #8492
Garrott, Warren, #8504
Garrott, William Andrew, #8472
Garrott, William Andrew, #8490
Garrott, William Hilleary, #8484
Garrott, William Hilleary, #8495
Garrott, William Hilleary, #8505
Garrott, William Robert, #8476
Garrott, Wm. H., #8475
Garrott, Wm. M., #2005
Gattrell, Harriet E., #6727
Gattrell, Harriett Elizabeth, #6729
Gaul, Abbie A., #2716
Gaul, Abbie A., #2717
Gaul, Abbie A., #2718
Gaul, Abbie A., #2719
Gaul, Adam, #2720
Gaul, Adam Simon, #2718
Gaul, Annie Brandt, #2723
Gaul, George Henry, #2722
Gaul, Harriet, #2720
Gaul, Harriet Rothwell, #2716
Gaul, John F., #2715
Gaul, John F., #2716
Gaul, John F., #2717
Gaul, John F., #2718

Gaul, John F., #2719
Gaul, John F., #2720
Gaul, John F., #2722
Gaul, John F., #2723
Gaul, John F., #2724
Gaul, John F., #2725
Gaul, John F., #2726
Gaul, John F., #2727
Gaul, John Frederick, #2719
Gaul, Sarah Elizabeth, #2717
Gaul, Sarah Elizabeth, #2724
Gaver, Barbara, #5863
Gaver, Harrit, #5859
Gaylor, Rachael M. (Harsh), #4225
Geisey, Rev. Dr., #7252
George, James B., #1255
Gergueson, R.G., #7646
Gerhert, Rev., #4944
Getz, Rosa, #2137
Getz, Rosa, #2138
Gfreen, Catherine, #6896
Gibbons, Mary, #8309
Gibson, J.M., #4358
Gifford, C.W., #7448
Gifford, C.W., #7450
Gifford, C.W., #7452
Gifford, C.W., #7454
Gifford, C.W., #7456
Gift, Foster, #8269
Gilchrist, Catharine, #2321
Gilchrist, Catharine, #2322
Gilchrist, Daniel, #2327
Gilchrist, Daniel, #2328
Gilchrist, Nancy A., #2329
Gilchrist, Nancy A., #2330
"Gilchrist, Sr.", Malcolm, #2319
"Gilchrist, Sr.", Malcolm, #2320
"Gilchrist, Sr.", Malcolm, #2321
Gill, Rev., #4277
Gillan, Nell La Turner, #7807
Gillan, Nell La Turner, #7808
Gillum, J. Martin, #283
Gittings, Annetta V., #1956
Gittings, E.L., #2006
Gittings, Edward L., #1956
Gittings, Robert C., #1956
Gittings, Winebert[?] L., #2042
Gittings, Wurbert[?] Livingston, #2048
Glasgow, Adam, #1250
Glasgow, Nancy, #1250
Glasgow, Nancy, #1251
Glasgow, Nancy, #1252
Glasgow, Nancy, #1253
Glasgow, Nancy, #1254
Glass/Gloss, Simon, #3425
Glenn, Herman C., #2344
Glenn, Herman C., #2354
Glenn/Bohn, Betty, #2350
Glenn/Bohn, Butch, #2353
Glenn/Bohn, Donna, #2351
Glenn/Bohn, Herman, #2347
Glenn/Bohn, Nancy, #2348
Glenn/Bohn, Peggy, #2352
Glenn/Bohn, Rethabelle, #2349
Glesner, George W., #7776
Glesner, George W., #7778
Gloss, Fannie, #3438
Gloss, Siman, #3396
Glossbrenner, Elizabeth, #8413
Glossbrenner, Mary Ann, #8414

Glossbrenner, Susan, #8415
Goddard, James M., #2554
Goddard, Louise, #2554
Goddard, Nonie Inez, #2561
Goering, Rev., #7142
Gontrum, Anna M., #6001
Good, Elizabeth (Miss), #494
Good, Helteie C., #5607
Good, Sarah (Miss), #519
Goode, Margaret, #8504
Gooding, Margaret, #5974
Gooding, Margaret, #5993
Goodrich, A.B., #4332
Goodrich, Rev., #6813
Goodrich, Rev., #6815
Goodrich, Rev., #6817
Goodrich, Rev., #6819
Goodrich, Rev., #6821
Goodrich, Rev., #6823
Goodrich, Rev., #6825
Goodrich, Rev., #6827
Goodrich, Rev., #6829
Goodrich, W., #6802
Gorden[?], Margaret, #5955
Gordon, J. Smith, #2427
Gordon, Joseph, #3012
Gordon, Susan D., #7173
Gossard, Ruth B., #6775
Gossart[?], Nancy, #4949
Grabill, Rev., #1593
Grabill, Rev., #1595
Grace[?], Edieth, #8350
Grace[?], Edieth, #8351
Graeff, Sarah, #6032
Graeff, , #6041
Graff, Andrew, #6497
Graff, Andrew, #6498
Graff, Andrew, #6499
Graff, Andrew, #6500
Graff, Andrew, #6501
Graff, Andrew, #6502
Graff, Caroline Beall, #6178
Graff, Eli Beatty, #6495
Graff, Elie Beatty[?], #6479
Graff, Elizabeth A.C., #6475
Graff, Geo.[?] Usher, #6480
Graff, George, #6493
Graff, George, #6494
Graff, George, #6495
Graff, George, #6496
Graff, George Musser, #6499
Graff, George Usher, #6496
Graff, James Johnson, #6497
Graff, James William, #6147
Graff, Marcus, #6494
Graff, Marcus Sebastian, #6477
Graff, Mary, #6027
Graff, Mary Catharine, #6498
Graff, Mary Charlton, #6493
Graff, Mary Charttas[?], #6476
Graff, Robert John, #6502
Graff, Rosanna Jane, #6500
Graff, Sarah, #6239
Graff, Sarah, #6582
Graff, Sarah, #6583
Graff, Sebastian, #6026
Graff, Sebastian, #6583
Graff, Sophia Jane, #6478
Graff, William Sebastian, #6501
Grams[?], Blanche, #933
"Granger, Jr.", Gordon, #7926

INDEX
Pages are not numbered; numbers refer to the entry number at the beginning of each record.

Grattan, George G., #8273
Grattan, Robert, #8294
"Grattan, Jr.", George Gilmer, #8296
Gray, Ann Buttle, #8439
Gray, Hanah , #8464
Grayston, Agnes Ada, #4736
Grayston, Agnes Ada, #4743
Grayston, Agnes Ada, #4749
Grayston, Amelia Ellen, #4734
Grayston, Amelia Ellen, #4740
Grayston, Francis, #4733
Grayston, Francis, #4741
Grayston, Francis, #4745
Grayston, Gladys Matilda, #4735
Grayston, Gladys Matilda, #4742
Grayston, James, #4725
Grayston, James, #4726
Grayston, James , #4746
Grayston, James Edward, #4730
Grayston, James Edward, #4744
Grayston, John Thomas, #4728
Grayston, John Thomas, #4750
Grayston, Margaret, #4725
Grayston, Margaret, #4727
Grayston, Margaret , #4747
Grayston, Margaret Alice, #4732
Grayston, Margaret Alice, #4739
Grayston, Mary Ann, #4729
Grayston, Mary Ann, #4737
Grayston, Mary Ann, #4748
Grayston, William Albert, #4731
Grayston, William Albert, #4738
Grayston, William Albert, #4751
Greathead, Arthur D., #7103
Greathead, Emily V., #7104
Greathead, Fanny M., #7098
Greathead, Hattie K., #7097
Greathead, Ormond[?] Leroy[?], #7102
Greathead, Robert N., #7100
Greathead, Thornton[?] F.[?], #7101
Greathead, Willie T., #7099
Greathouse, Harmon (Colonel), #2277
Greathouse, Harmon (Colonel), #2301
Greathouse, Harmon (Colonel), #2302
Greathouse, Harmon (Colonel), #2303
Greathouse, Harmon (Colonel), #2304
Greathouse, Isaac, #2302
Greathouse, John, #2303
Greathouse, Joseph , #2304
Greathouse, Luther, #2301

Green, Caroline Carohelus, #8554
Green, Elen, #8545
Green, Elen S.A., #8552
Green, Fanny Franklin, #8546
Green, George, #3444
Green, Harrietta Clotilda, #88
Green, Harrietta Clotilda, #89
Green, Louisa Flourence, #8553
Green, Mariah, #8545
Green, Rozelen, #8545
Greenawalt, Ann Louise, #7933
Greenawalt, Ann Louise, #7934
Greenawalt, Carolyn Hollis, #7936
Greenawalt, Carolyn Hollis, #7937
Greenawalt, Helen, #7835
Greenawalt, Helen, #7843
Greenawalt, Helen, #7846
Greenawalt, Helen Frances, #7913
Greenawalt, Helen Frances, #7914
Greenawalt, Kathryn, #7836
Greenawalt, Kathryn, #7851
Greenawalt, Kathryn, #7852
Greenawalt, Kathryn, #7853
Greenawalt, Kathryn Olivia, #7915
Greenawalt, Kathryn Olivia, #7916
Greenawalt, Lois, #7837
Greenawalt, Lois Jane, #7917
Greenawalt, M.E., #7897
Greenawalt, M.E., #7898
Greenawalt, M.E., #7899
Greenawalt, Margaret B., #7903
Greenawalt, Margaret B., #7904
Greenawalt, Margaret B., #7905
Greenawalt, Margaret B., #7919
Greenawalt, Margaret B., #7921
Greenawalt, Margaret B., #7922
Greenawalt, Margaret B., #7923
Greenawalt, Margaret B., #7924
Greenawalt, Margaret B., #7925
Greenawalt, Margaret B., #7926
Greenawalt, Mary Ellen, #7838
Greenawalt, Mary Ellen, #7918
Greenawalt, Mary Josephine, #7929
Greenawalt, Mary Josephine, #7930
Greenawalt, Mary Josephine, #7938
Greenawalt, Mary Josphine, #7940
Greenawalt, Mary Josphine, #7941
Greenawalt, S. Miller, #7815
Greenawalt, S. Miller, #7816
Greenawalt, S. Miller, #7901
Greenawalt, S. Miller, #7902
Greenawalt, S. Miller, #7911
Greenawalt, S. Miller, #7913
Greenawalt, S. Miller, #7914
Greenawalt, S. Miller, #7915
Greenawalt, S. Miller, #7916
Greenawalt, S. Miller, #7917
Greenawalt, S. Miller, #7918

Greenawalt, S.G., #7894
Greenawalt, S.G., #7895
Greenawalt, S.G., #7896
Greenawalt, Samuel Godfrey, #7893
Greenawalt, Samuel L., #7906
Greenawalt, Samuel L., #7907
Greenawalt, Samuel L., #7908
Greenawalt, Samuel L., #7927
Greenawalt, Samuel L., #7929
Greenawalt, Samuel L., #7930
Greenawalt, William F., #7909
Greenawalt, William F., #7910
Greenawalt, William F., #7931
Greenawalt, William F., #7934
Greenawalt, William F., #7935
Greenawalt, William F., #7936
Greenawalt, William F., #7937
Greenawalt, , #7835
Greenawalt, , #7836
Greenawalt, , #7837
Greenawalt, , #7838
"Greenawalt, Jr.", William F., #7935
Greer, Maria (Mrs.), #1921
Greer, William, #1921
Greis____[?], Susan Elizabeth, #6092
Greis____[?], Susan Elizabeth, #6093
Greis____[?], Susan Elizabeth, #6094
Grey, Ann (Miss), #520
Grice, Charles Cleveland, #797
Grice, John Cleveland, #788
Grice, John Cleveland, #792
Grice, Lucy Neuten, #794
Grice, Martha Virginia, #796
Grice, Nellie May, #793
Grice, Oliver Franklin, #795
Grice, Oliver Franklin, #800
Grice, Peter N., #787
Grice, Peter N., #789
Grice, Peter N., #791
Grice, Peter N., #792
Grice, Peter N., #793
Grice, Peter N., #794
Grice, Peter N., #795
Grice, Peter Neuton, #798
Grice, Sarah Virginia Jefferson, #799
Grice, Victor O., #791
Griffith, W.C., #3218
Griffiths, Mary (Mrs.), #1918
"Griffiths, Sr.", John, #1918
Griggs, Thomas, #1933
Grim, Everard Therin, #7686
Grim, Louisa, #3577
Grim, William Otterbein, #3360
Grim, William Otterbein, #3361
Grimm, Amanda M., #3398
Grimm, Amanda Mariah, #3371
Grimm, Amanda Mariah, #3372
Grimm, Anna, #3423
Grimm, Annie E., #3417
Grimm, Annie M., #3444
Grimm, Arthur G., #3434
Grimm, Barbara Ella, #3386
Grimm, Barbara Ella, #3387

Grimm, Betty [possibly Barbara Ellen], #3388
Grimm, Charles I., #3424
Grimm, Charlie, #3450
Grimm, Claude, #3447
Grimm, Daniel B., #3354
Grimm, Edward L., #3429
Grimm, Elizabeth, #3349
Grimm, Elsie M., #3454
Grimm, Emma Althea, #3391
Grimm, Emma Althea, #3392
Grimm, Ethel, #3420
Grimm, Frederick A., #3348
Grimm, Harmon, #3390
Grimm, Harmon M., #3403
Grimm, Harmon Milton, #3384
Grimm, Harmon Milton, #3385
Grimm, Harry T., #3413
Grimm, Hubert, #3415
Grimm, Ira R., #3431
Grimm, Irvin, #3402
Grimm, Irwin, #3389
Grimm, Irwin Randolph, #3382
Grimm, Irwin Randolph, #3383
Grimm, Iva M., #3418
Grimm, J. Lower, #3449
Grimm, J. Wesley, #3448
Grimm, J.L., #3402
Grimm, J.S., #3403
Grimm, Jacob Luther, #3366
Grimm, Jacob Luther, #3367
Grimm, Jacob Luther, #3397
Grimm, John, #3346
Grimm, John, #3348
Grimm, John, #3349
Grimm, John, #3350
Grimm, John, #3351
Grimm, John, #3352
Grimm, John, #3353
Grimm, John, #3354
Grimm, John, #3355
Grimm, John I., #3350
Grimm, John Wesley, #3362
Grimm, John Wesley, #3363
Grimm, John Wesley, #3395
Grimm, Joseph L., #3393
Grimm, Joseph S., #3352
Grimm, Joseph S., #3400
Grimm, Joseph S., #3413
Grimm, Joseph S. (Rev.), #3411
Grimm, Joseph S. (Rev.), #3412
Grimm, Joseph Samuel, #3373
Grimm, Joseph Samuel, #3374
Grimm, Joseph Samuel, #3375
Grimm, Joseph Y., #3356
Grimm, Joseph Y., #3357
Grimm, Karl M., #3419
Grimm, Lela B., #3432
Grimm, Lester, #3433
Grimm, Lester, #3445
Grimm, Luther O., #3438
Grimm, M. Luther, #3436
Grimm, Mabel, #3421
Grimm, Mamie, #3428
Grimm, Margaret, #3353
Grimm, Martha, #3425
Grimm, Martha A., #3396
Grimm, Martha Ann, #3364
Grimm, Martha Ann, #3365
Grimm, Mary Elizabeth, #3379
Grimm, Mary Elizabeth, #3380

INDEX
Pages are not numbered; numbers refer to the entry number at the beginning of each record.

Grimm, Mary Elizabeth, #3381
Grimm, Mary Franck, #3347
Grimm, Mary Franck, #3348
Grimm, Mary Franck, #3349
Grimm, Mary Franck, #3350
Grimm, Mary Franck, #3351
Grimm, Mary Franck, #3352
Grimm, Mary Franck, #3353
Grimm, Mary Franck, #3354
Grimm, Mary Franck, #3355
Grimm, Myra E., #3437
Grimm, Nellie, #3416
Grimm, Nellie, #3451
Grimm, Nettie, #3422
Grimm, Odo R., #3453
Grimm, Orpha M., #3440
Grimm, Paul H., #3439
Grimm, Robert W., #3430
Grimm, Sarah, #3358
Grimm, Sarah, #3359
Grimm, Sarah Susan, #3376
Grimm, Sarah Susan, #3377
Grimm, Sarah Susan, #3378
Grimm, Sarah Susan, #3399
Grimm, Sophia C., #3401
Grimm, Sophia Cecilia, #3368
Grimm, Sophia Cecilia, #3369
Grimm, Sophia Cecilia, #3370
Grimm, Susanna, #3355
Grimm, Thomas G., #3351
Grimm, Virgie, #3452
Grimm, Walter L., #3442
Grimm, Wilbur M., #3443
Grimm, William A., #3435
Grimm, William C., #3441
Grimm, William E., #3446
Grimm, William N.G., #3426
Grimm, William N.G., #3427
Grimm, William O., #3394
Grimm, Wm. W., #3401
Grosch, Amalia, #3284
Grosch, Anna Maria, #3280
Grosch, Anna Maria, #3282
Grosch, Anna Maria, #3296
Grosch, Anna Maria, #3297
Grosch, Benjamin Franklin, #3289
Grosch, Catharine, #3306
Grosch, Cathrine, #3285
Grosch, Conradt Clement, #3287
Grosch, Conradt Clement, #3300
Grosch, Elisabeth, #3294
Grosch, Elisabeth, #3305
Grosch, Frederick, #3279
Grosch, Frederick, #3307
Grosch, Frederick David, #3288
Grosch, Frederick David, #3301
Grosch, George Washington, #3292
Grosch, George Washington, #3304
Grosch, Henry, #3281
Grosch, John Frederick, #3293
Grosch, Juliana, #3303
Grosch, Julianna, #3291
Grosch, Lewis A., #3308

Grosch, Lewis Andrew, #3286
Grosch, Sara, #3283
Grosch, Sophia, #3290
Grosch, Sophia, #3302
Grosh, Ann E., #3335
Grosh, Ann E.L., #3324
Grosh, Ann E.L. Snyder, #3331
Grosh, Catharine, #3335
Grosh, Catharine E., #3328
Grosh, Catherine, #3331
Grosh, Frederick, #3277
Grosh, Frederick, #3278
Grosh, Geo., #3335
Grosh, George, #3331
Grosh, George W., #3329
Grosh, George W., #3334
Grosh, Henry I.F., #3325
Grosh, Henry I.F., #3337
Grosh, Henry Levin Fisher, #3332
Grosh, Otis S., #3326
Grosh, Otis S.[?], #3330
"Grosh, Sr.", Frederick, #3295
"Grosh, Sr.", Henry, #3327
Grove, Catharina, #3265
Grove, Catharina, #3266
Grove, Daniel, #3262
Grove, Daniel L., #3272
Grove, Daniel S.[or L.], #3249
Grove, Daniel S.[or L.], #3252
Grove, Elias, #3257
Grove, Elias S., #3273
Grove, Frances Louise, #1343
Grove, Harriet, #3261
Grove, Harriet B., #3267
Grove, Harry C., #1352
Grove, Harry Clyde, #1347
Grove, Harry Clyde, #1350
Grove, Harry Clyde (Dr.), #1346
Grove, Hope, #2767
Grove, Jacob, #3256
Grove, Jacob H., #3275
Grove, Jeannette Baker, #1344
Grove, Jeremiah, #3264
Grove, Joseph, #3260
Grove, Lovina, #3259
Grove, Mary, #3255
Grove, Philip, #3249
Grove, Philip, #3250
Grove, Philip, #3253
Grove, Philip, #3270
Grove, Richard Duckett, #1342
Grove, Samuel, #3258
Grove, Stephen P., #3276
Grove, Stephen Philip, #3263
Grove, Susan, #3268
Grove, Susan (Duckett), #1382
Grove, Susann, #6714
Grove, William T.[?], #6717
"Grove, Jr.", Harry Clyde (Dr.), #1347
"Grove, Sr.", Harry Clyde, #1382
Grubb, Joseph Lewis, #3507
Grubb, Joseph Lewis, #8174
Grymes, Mabel, #8274
Gulden, J.C., #7782
Gunnell, John J. H., #1914
Guy___nner[?], Catharine, #8372

H., A., #1980
H., A.C., #1985
H., B.[?]C., #1981
H., C., #1976
H., C.G., #1982
H., D., #1984
H., David, #1976
H., E., #1986
H., E., #1990
H., Elonore, #1977
H., F.I., #1988
H., G., #1979
H., J., #1978
H., Joh, #1976
H., Joh, #1989
H., John, #1992
H., S.M., #1983
H., W.O.N., #1987
H., W.W., #6378
Ha_____, Jacob, #2825
Hagan, Bernice Jane, #1574
Hagan, Betres, #1571
Hagan, Betres, #1572
Hagan, Beverly Syvle[?] Jean[?], #1540
Hagan, Charlette Joesephine, #1567
Hagan, Clayton Eugene, #1542
Hagan, Daisy May, #1566
Hagan, Freda Louise, #1576
Hagan, Gerald Frank, #1539
Hagan, Harlen Huffer, #1569
Hagan, Harold Lawrence, #1553
Hagan, Harold Lawrence, #1554
Hagan, Harry Lee, #1578
Hagan, Harry Lee, #1579
Hagan, Helen, #1538
Hagan, Howard L., #1563
Hagan, Howard Luther, #1556
Hagan, JoAnn Eusebia, #1584
Hagan, JoAnn Eusebia, #1590
Hagan, John Heflebower, #1543
Hagan, John Heflebower, #1564
Hagan, John Thomas, #1588
Hagan, John Vernon, #1557
Hagan, John Vernon, #1558
Hagan, Jophes Lee, #1573
Hagan, Joseph Clayton, #1589
Hagan, Joseph Lee, #1580
Hagan, Joseph Norris, #1551
Hagan, Joseph Norris, #1552
Hagan, Leon Viola, #1545
Hagan, Lillian Viola, #1561
Hagan, Mable Hellen Velettie[?], #1559
Hagan, Mable Hellen Velettie[?], #1560
Hagan, Mary Etta, #1575
Hagan, Mary Susan, #1548
Hagan, Mary Susie, #1562
Hagan, Patricia Ann Wheeler, #1581
Hagan, Ralph Austin, #1570
Hagan, Ralph Samuel, #1555
Hagan, Ralph Samuel, #1565
Hagan, Thomas Wayne, #1583
Hagan, Thomas Wayne, #1587
Hagan, Thomas Wayne, #1588
Hagan, Thomas Wayne, #1589
Hagan, Thos. Hefflebower, #1546
Hagan, Thos. Hefflebower, #1547

Hagan, Timothy Howard, #1586
Hagan, Timothy Lee, #1582
Hagan, Timothy Lee, #1585
Hagan, Timothy Lee, #1586
Hager, Andrew, #3248
Hager, Andrew H., #3228
Hager, Andrew H., #6866
Hager, Anna Bell, #7752
Hager, Annie, #7755
Hager, Carrie, #3238
Hager, Carrie L.[?], #6882
Hager, Daniel, #3226
Hager, David, #3231
Hager, David, #6864
Hager, David, #6869
Hager, Edward, #3233
Hager, Edward, #6871
Hager, Eleanor, #7750
Hager, Elizabeth, #8588
Hager, Emma Virginia, #7751
Hager, Jacob, #7748
Hager, Jacob, #7750
Hager, Jacob, #7751
Hager, Jacob, #7752
Hager, Jacob, #7755
Hager, Jacob C., #7753
Hager, James Thornton, #7742
Hager, John, #3229
Hager, John, #6867
Hager, Johnathan, #3239
Hager, Johnathan, #6883
Hager, Jonas H., #3227
Hager, Jonas H., #6865
Hager, Jonathan, #3219
Hager, Jonathan, #3230
Hager, Jonathan, #6857
Hager, Jonathan, #6859
Hager, Jonathan, #6868
Hager, Jonathan, #8587
Hager, Jonathan, #3221
Hager, "Jonathan ""The Miller", #7748
Hager, Kate K., #3234
Hager, Kate K.[?], #6872
Hager, L.E., #6861
Hager, L.E., #6862
Hager, S.E., #3223
Hager, S.E., #3224
Hager, Sallie A. (Mrs.), #3248
Hager, Susan, #7750
Hager, Susan, #7751
Hager, Susan, #7752
Hager, Susan, #7755
Hager, Susan E., #3232
Hager, Susan E., #6870
Hager, Willey Gra., #7754
Hager, William H., #3225
Hager, William H., #6863
Hagerman, Adie, #4640
Hagerman, Alice, #4639
Hagerman, Anna, #3706
Hagerman, Luther, #4641
Hagerman, Mary, #4638
Hagerman, Mary, #4639
Hagerman, Mary, #4640
Hagerman, Mary, #4641
Hagerman, Mary, #4642
Hagerman, Nanie, #4638
Hagerman, Willy, #4642
Haldeman, Harry Harvey, #7934
Hall, Elizabeth Bowie, #2704
Hall, Elizabeth Bowie, #2705

INDEX
Pages are not numbered; numbers refer to the entry number at the beginning of each record.

Hall, Elizabeth Bowie, #2706
Hall, Elizabeth Bowie, #2707
Hall, Elizabeth Bowie, #2708
Hall, Elizabeth Bowie, #3946
Hall, Elizabeth Bowie, #3947
Hall, Elizabeth Bowie, #3948
Hall, Elizabeth Bowie, #3949
Hall, Elizabeth Bowie, #3950
Hall, J.I., #4044
Hall, James, #2703
Hall, James, #2704
Hall, James, #3945
Hall, James, #3946
Hall, Mary DuBois, #7743
Ham, David, #1973
Ham, Sarah, #7313
Ham, Sarah, #7320
Ham[?], Elizabeth, #1974
Hamaker, Anna, #7965
Hamaker, Danl., #7972
Hamaker, Danl., #7973
Hamaker, Ephraim, #7966
Hamaker, Ephraim, #7967
Hamaker, John Hubrect, #7958
Hamaker, Maria, #7964
Hamaker, Peter, #7961
Hamaker, Peter, #7962
Hamaker, Peter, #7964
Hamaker, Peter, #7965
Hamaker, Peter, #7966
Hamaker, Peter, #7967
Hamaker, Peter, #7968
Hamaker, Peter, #7969
Hamaker, Peter, #7970
Hamaker, Peter, #7971
Hamaker, Peter, #7972
Hamaker, Peter, #7973
Hamaker, Samuel, #7959
Hamaker, Solomon, #7968
Hamaker, Solomon, #7969
Hamaker, Sophia, #7970
Hamaker, Sophia, #7971
"Hamaker, Jr.", Adam, #7959
"Hamaker, Sr.", Adam, #7956
"Hamaker, Sr.", Adam, #7957
Hamill, Ashman, #7981
Hamill, E.B. (Dr.), #7988
Hamill, E.B. (Dr.), #8006
Hamill, Eleanor, #7984
Hamill, Eleanor, #7985
Hamill, Eliz., #7983
Hamill, Geo. A., #7998
Hamill, George, #7987
Hamill, Irene Hughes, #7990
Hamill, Irene Hughes, #7992
Hamill, Irene Hughes, #8019
Hamill, Irene Hughes, #8023
Hamill, James, #7987
Hamill, Mary, #7976
Hamill, Mary, #7987
Hamill, Mary Eliz., #7989
Hamill, Mary Eliz., #7991
Hamill, Mary Eliz., #7993
Hamill, Mary Eliz., #7994
Hamill, Mary Eliz., #7995
Hamill, Rebecca, #7986
Hamill, Robert, #7977
Hamill, Robert, #7978
Hamill, S.B., #7975
Hamill, Wm., #7974

Hamill, Wm., #7979
Hamill, Wm., #7981
Hamill, Wm., #7982
Hamill, Wm., #7983
Hamill, Wm., #7984
Hamill, Wm., #7985
Hamill, Wm., #7986
Hamill, Wm., #7988
Hamill, Wm. Cromwell, #7982
"Hamill, DDS", Geo. Ashman (Dr.), #7999
Hamilton, Clara, #573
Hamilton, Lucile, #573
Hamilton, William, #573
Hamlin, Marceltells[?], #5609
Hammaker, Adam, #8039
Hammaker, Amanda, #8041
Hammaker, Amanda, #8042
Hammaker, Anna, #8008
Hammaker, Anna, #8009
Hammaker, Anna, #8010
Hammaker, Anna, #8011
Hammaker, Anna, #8012
Hammaker, Anna, #8013
Hammaker, Anna, #8014
Hammaker, Anna, #8015
Hammaker, Anna, #8016
Hammaker, Anna, #8017
Hammaker, Anna, #8018
Hammaker, Anna, #8020
Hammaker, Anna, #8033
Hammaker, Ephraim, #8038
Hammaker, Ephraim, #8039
Hammaker, Ephraim, #8040
Hammaker, Ephraim, #8041
Hammaker, Ephraim, #8042
Hammaker, Ephraim, #8043
Hammaker, Ephraim, #8044
Hammaker, Ephraim, #8045
Hammaker, Geo. Wm., #3073
Hammaker, Lizzie, #8045
Hammaker, Mary, #8034
Hammaker, Mary, #8046
Hammaker, Mary, #8047
Hammaker, Mary, #8048
Hammaker, Mary, #8049
Hammaker, Mary, #8050
Hammaker, Mary, #8051
Hammaker, Mary, #8052
Hammaker, Mary, #8053
Hammaker, Mary, #8054
Hammaker, Mary, #8055
Hammaker, Mary, #8056
Hammaker, Peter, #8008
Hammaker, Peter, #8040
Hammaker, Saml., #8043
Hammaker, Stewart, #8044
Hammett, Wm., #2109
Hammie, Jacob, #7550
Hammie, Jacob, #7551
Hammond, Cath., #1971
Hammond, Charles E., #2993
Hammond, Charles W., #3417
Hammond, Eleanor, #1970
Hammond, Eliza, #2055
Hammond, John, #1969
Hammond, Nora F. (Miss), #2993
Hammond, Rebecca, #2004
Hammond, Rebecca, #2022
Hammond, Rebecca, #8442

Hammond, Rebecca C., #2027
Hank, A.S., #6264
Hankey, Rev., #4378
Hanline, Elmer, #1102
Hanline, Mary Susan, #1152
Hanm[?], John, #1972
Hanner, Rev., #920
Happel, Sue rosalie, #1518
Harbaugh, J. Earl, #3068
Hardey, Ann P., #8438
Hardey, Ann Priscilla, #8478
Hardey, Editha, #8478
Hardey, George, #8478
Hardey, Priscilla, #8437
Hardwick, ____ Thomas, #6395
Hardwick, Alan, #6463
Hardwick, Alan, #6467
Hardwick, Alan Edward, #6452
Hardwick, Albert, #6297
Hardwick, Albert, #6298
Hardwick, Albert, #6299
Hardwick, Albert, #6300
Hardwick, Albert, #6427
Hardwick, Albert, #6428
Hardwick, Albert, #6429
Hardwick, Albert, #6459
Hardwick, Albert Birtwell, #6288
Hardwick, Albert Birtwell, #6289
Hardwick, Albert Birtwell, #6420
Hardwick, Albert Birtwell, #6455
Hardwick, Albert Birtwell, #6473
Hardwick, Alberta, #6299
Hardwick, Alberta, #6429
Hardwick, Alberta, #6460
Hardwick, Ambrose, #6465
Hardwick, Ambrose, #6471
Hardwick, Ambrose Ottey, #6457
Hardwick, Ambrose Smedley, #6291
Hardwick, Ambrose Smedley, #6422
Hardwick, Ambrose Smedley, #6433
Hardwick, Ambrose Smedley, #6434
Hardwick, Ambrose Smedley, #6435
Hardwick, Ambrose Smedley, #6474
Hardwick, Arlene Frances, #6440
Hardwick, Arthur James, #6263
Hardwick, Arthur James, #6276
Hardwick, Arthur James, #6277
Hardwick, Carol Vivien, #6437
Hardwick, Charles Jones, #6265
Hardwick, Charles Jones, #6286
Hardwick, Charles Jones, #6287
Hardwick, Charles Jones, #6419
Hardwick, Charles Jones, #6454
Hardwick, Charles Jones, #6469
Hardwick, Dennis, #6466
Hardwick, Dennis Roger, #6451
Hardwick, Donald Louis, #6450
Hardwick, Dorothy Marie, #6442
Hardwick, Dorothy Marie, #6445
Hardwick, Edith, #6396
Hardwick, Edith, #6397
Hardwick, Edith, #6398
Hardwick, Edith, #6399
Hardwick, Elizabeth, #6428
Hardwick, Elizabeth, #6461

Hardwick, Elizabeth, #6298
Hardwick, Elsie, #6290
Hardwick, Elsie, #6300
Hardwick, Elsie, #6301
Hardwick, Elsie, #6302
Hardwick, Elsie, #6303
Hardwick, Elsie, #6421
Hardwick, Elsie, #6430
Hardwick, Elsie, #6431
Hardwick, Elsie, #6432
Hardwick, Elsie, #6456
Hardwick, Elsie, #6462
Hardwick, Elsie, #6463
Hardwick, Elsie, #6464
Hardwick, Elsie, #6470
Hardwick, George W., #6439
Hardwick, George W., #6440
Hardwick, Gilbert Wm., #6446
Hardwick, Harold, #6434
Hardwick, Harry, #6285
Hardwick, Harry, #6286
Hardwick, Harry, #6287
Hardwick, Harry, #6288
Hardwick, Harry, #6289
Hardwick, Harry, #6290
Hardwick, Harry, #6291
Hardwick, Harry, #6292
Hardwick, Harry, #6293
Hardwick, Harry, #6294
Hardwick, Harry, #6295
Hardwick, Harry, #6354
Hardwick, Harry, #6355
Hardwick, Harry, #6356
Hardwick, Harry, #6357
Hardwick, Harry, #6374
Hardwick, Harry, #6375
Hardwick, Harry, #6376
Hardwick, Harry, #6377
Hardwick, Harry, #6396
Hardwick, Harry, #6397
Hardwick, Harry, #6398
Hardwick, Harry, #6399
Hardwick, Harry, #6418
Hardwick, Harry, #6419
Hardwick, Harry, #6420
Hardwick, Harry, #6421
Hardwick, Harry, #6422
Hardwick, Harry, #6423
Hardwick, Harry, #6424
Hardwick, Harry, #6425
Hardwick, Harry, #6426
Hardwick, Harry, #6460
Hardwick, Harry, #6461
Hardwick, Harry (Henry) William, #6282
Hardwick, Harry (Henry) William, #6283
Hardwick, Harry (Henry) William, #6284
Hardwick, Harry T.H., #6353
Hardwick, Harry Thomas, #6383
Hardwick, Harry Thomas , #6367
Hardwick, Harry William Byrne, #6285
Hardwick, Harry William Byrne, #6453
Hardwick, Harry William Rynn, #6264
Hardwick, Harry Wm. Byrne, #6418
Hardwick, Harry Wm. Byrne, #6468
Hardwick, Henry Th., #6259
Hardwick, Henry Thomas, #6276
Hardwick, Henry Thomas, #6277
Hardwick, Henry Thomas, #6278

INDEX
Pages are not numbered; numbers refer to the entry number at the beginning of each record.

Hardwick, Henry Thomas, #6279
Hardwick, Henry Thomas, #6280
Hardwick, Henry Thomas, #6281
Hardwick, Henry Thomas, #6282
Hardwick, Henry Thomas, #6283
Hardwick, Henry Thomas, #6284
Hardwick, Henry William, #6261
Hardwick, Ida Hazel, #6322
Hardwick, Ida Hazel, #6323
Hardwick, Ida Hazel, #6363
Hardwick, Ida Hazel, #6379
Hardwick, Ida Hazel, #6391
Hardwick, Jessie, #6292
Hardwick, Jessie, #6293
Hardwick, Jessie, #6423
Hardwick, Jessie, #6424
Hardwick, Jessie, #6458
Hardwick, Jessie, #6472
Hardwick, John Brent, #6464
Hardwick, Leonard Paul, #6357
Hardwick, Leonard Paul, #6377
Hardwick, Leonard Paul, #6399
Hardwick, Margorie, #6435
Hardwick, Mary, #6370
Hardwick, Mary, #6371
Hardwick, Mary, #6372
Hardwick, Mary, #6373
Hardwick, Mary (Mollie) May, #6348
Hardwick, Mary May, #6349
Hardwick, Mary May, #6350
Hardwick, Mary May, #6351
Hardwick, Mary May, #6352
Hardwick, Mary May, #6366
Hardwick, Mary May, #6382
Hardwick, Mildred, #6296
Hardwick, Mildred, #6426
Hardwick, Miriam Elizabeth, #6444
Hardwick, Mollie, #6250
Hardwick, Mollie, #6251
Hardwick, Mollie, #6252
Hardwick, Mollie, #6253
Hardwick, Mollie A., #6254
Hardwick, Mollie A., #6390
Hardwick, Molly May, #6394
Hardwick, Phebe, #6285
Hardwick, Phebe, #6286
Hardwick, Phebe, #6287
Hardwick, Phebe, #6288
Hardwick, Phebe, #6289
Hardwick, Phebe, #6290
Hardwick, Phebe, #6291
Hardwick, Phebe, #6292
Hardwick, Phebe, #6293
Hardwick, Phebe, #6294
Hardwick, Phebe, #6295
Hardwick, Richard Eugene, #6347
Hardwick, Richard Eugene, #6369

Hardwick, Richard Eugene, #6385
Hardwick, Richard Raymond, #6449
Hardwick, Robert Earle, #6447
Hardwick, Robert Earle, #6448
Hardwick, Robert Earle, #6449
Hardwick, Robert Earle, #6450
Hardwick, Robert Earle, #6451
Hardwick, Robert Earle, #6452
Hardwick, Robert Henry, #6266
Hardwick, Robert Henry, #6310
Hardwick, Robert Henry, #6311
Hardwick, Robert Sterling, #6355
Hardwick, Robert Sterling, #6375
Hardwick, Robert Sterling, #6397
Hardwick, Sadie Alma, #6250
Hardwick, Sadie Alma, #6251
Hardwick, Sadie Alma, #6256
Hardwick, Sadie Alma, #6312
Hardwick, Sadie Alma, #6313
Hardwick, Sadie Alma, #6317
Hardwick, Sadie Alma, #6318
Hardwick, Sadie Alma, #6319
Hardwick, Sadie Alma, #6320
Hardwick, Sadie Alma, #6321
Hardwick, Sarah, #6267
Hardwick, Sarah, #6384
Hardwick, Sarah, #6385
Hardwick, Sarah Elisabeth, #6260
Hardwick, Sarah Elizabeth, #6280
Hardwick, Sarah Elizabeth, #6281
Hardwick, Stanley Eugene, #6354
Hardwick, Stanley Eugene, #6374
Hardwick, Stanley Eugene, #6396
Hardwick, Thomas Dean, #6356
Hardwick, Thomas Dean, #6376
Hardwick, Thomas Dean, #6398
Hardwick, Thomas Howard, #6441
Hardwick, Thomas Howard, #6442
Hardwick, Thomas Howard, #6443
Hardwick, Thomas Howard, #6444
Hardwick, Webster, #6392
Hardwick, Webster Melbourne, #6324
Hardwick, Webster Melbourne, #6325
Hardwick, Webster Melbourne, #6364
Hardwick, Webster Melbourne, #6380
Hardwick, William, #6322
Hardwick, William, #6323
Hardwick, William, #6324
Hardwick, William, #6325
Hardwick, William, #6326
Hardwick, William, #6327
Hardwick, William, #6328

Hardwick, William, #6362
Hardwick, William Charles, #6250
Hardwick, William Charles, #6251
Hardwick, William Charles, #6252
Hardwick, William Charles, #6253
Hardwick, William Charles, #6255
Hardwick, William Charles, #6262
Hardwick, William Charles, #6278
Hardwick, William Charles, #6279
Hardwick, William Charles, #6307
Hardwick, William Charles, #6309
Hardwick, William Charles, #6310
Hardwick, William Charles, #6311
Hardwick, William Charles, #6312
Hardwick, William Charles, #6313
Hardwick, William Charles, #6314
Hardwick, William Charles, #6315
Hardwick, William Charles, #6316
Hardwick, William Charles, #6346
Hardwick, William Charles, #6347
Hardwick, William Charles, #6365
Hardwick, William Charles, #6393
Hardwick, William Murdock Webster, #6252
Hardwick, William Murdock Webster, #6253
Hardwick, William Murdock Webster, #6314
Hardwick, William Murdock Webster, #6315
Hardwick, William Murdock Webster, #6316
Hardwick, William Webster, #6390
Hardwick, William Webster, #6391
Hardwick, William Webster, #6392
Hardwick, William Webster, #6393
Hardwick, Wm. C., #6384
Hardwick, Wm. C., #6385
Hardwick, Wm. C., #6390
Hardwick, Wm. C., #6436
Hardwick, Wm. C., #6437
Hardwick, Wm. C., #6438
Hardwick, Wm. Charles, #6368
Hardwick, Wm. Charles, #6369
Hardwick, Wm. Charles, #6381
"Hardwick, III", Thomas Howard, #6443
"Hardwick, Jr.", Harry William, #6294
"Hardwick, Jr.", Harry William, #6295
"Hardwick, Jr.", Harry William, #6296
"Hardwick, Jr.", Harry William, #6297
"Hardwick, Jr.", Robert Earle, #6448
"Hardwick, Jr.", William Charles, #6346
"Hardwick, Jr.", Wm. C., #6384
"Hardwick, Jr.", Wm. C., #6438
"Hardwick, Jr.", Wm. Charles, #6368
Hardwicke, Elizabeth, #6268
Hardwicke, Elizabeth, #6269
Hardwicke, Henry Thomas, #6272
Hardwicke, Henry Thomas, #6273

Hardwicke, Henry Thomas, #6274
Hardwicke, Mary, #6270
Hargreaves, Amelia Ellen (Grayston), #4754
Hargreaves, Harold, #4740
Harkey, Rev., #3129
Harman, Alice (Miss), #575
Harp, Joshua, #5045
Harp, Mary Ellen, #3397
Harris, Annie K., #6740
Harris, C.W., #6743
Harris, Charles P., #6741
Harris, Helen J., #6742
Harris, John Presley, #7937
Harrison, Mary E., #2179
Harrison, Mary E., #2180
Harrison, T.L., #2177
Harrison, T.L., #2179
Harrison, T.L., #2180
Harry, [female], #2113
Harry, [female], #2114
Harry, [female], #2115
Harry, [female], #2116
Harry, George I., #2113
Harry, George I., #2114
Harry, George I., #2115
Harry, George I., #2116
Harry, George I.[?], #2110
Harry, George I.[?], #2111
Harry, George I.[?], #2112
Harry, Joseph, #2110
Harsh, Fanny, #6776
Harsh, John W., #4176
Harshour, T., #1591
Harsle, Jennie Newcomer, #4223
Hart, C.C., #2222
Hart, Elizabeth, #4665
Hart, John DeWit (Capt.), #4673
Hart, John Dewit[?], #4664
Hart, Kate, #4656
Hart, Kate, #4658
Hart, Rebecca P., #5993
Hartle, Asiaah Mearl, #859
Hartle, Charles Elles, #861
Hartle, Dorothy Irene, #860
Hartle, Edna L., #867
Hartle, Edna Lavene, #856
Hartle, Ellen Grace, #858
Hartle, Frank Albert, #862
Hartle, Isaac M., #871
Hartle, Lea Blanch, #854
Hartle, Leah B., #866
Hartle, Ralph H., #870
Hartle, Ralph Harland, #857
Hartle, Sarah Ann, #869
Hartle, W.B., #865
Hartle, W.B., #868
Hartle, William Berkley, #855
Hartman, Rebecca (Miss), #518
Hartsock, S.M., #281
Haskins, , #1010
Haskinson, Oliva , #2523
Hassett, Elizabeth Haines, #1662
Hassett, Elizabeth Haines, #1663
Hastings, Clarence Henry, #6635
Hastings, Clarence Henry, #6636
Hastings, Margaret Louise, #6644
Hastings, Margaret Louise, #6645
Hastings, Walter Henry, #6626
Hastings, Walter Henry, #6627
Hatch, Tryphena, #3741

INDEX
Pages are not numbered; numbers refer to the entry number at the beginning of each record.

Hatch, Tryphena, #3742
Hatch, Tryphena, #3743
Hatch, Tryphena, #3744
Hatch, Tryphena, #3745
Hatch, Tryphena, #3746
Hatch, Tryphena, #3747
Hatch, Tryphena, #3748
Hatch, Tryphena, #3749
Hatch, Tryphena, #3750
Hatch, Tryphena, #3751
Hatch, Tryphena, #3752
Hatch, Tryphena, #3753
Hatch, Tryphena, #3754
Hatch, Tryphena, #3755
Hatch, Tryphena, #3756
Hatch, Tryphena, #3757
Hatch, Tryphena, #3758
Hatch, Tryphina, #3785
Hawkins, Agnes L., #5217
Hawkins, Benjaman F.N., #5240
Hawkins, Charles Leo, #5244
Hawkins, Edward Mack Curtis, #6197
Hawkins, Emma V., #5246
Hawkins, Ethel L., #5219
Hawkins, Geneieve W., #5239
Hawkins, Kathleen Gertrude, #5220
Hawkins, Maggie M., #5218
Hawkins, Reuben W., #5245
Hawkins, Reuben Waeton[?], #5211
Hawkins, Rua A., #5216
Hawkins, Rueben W., #5215
Hawkins, Thomas Alexander, #2107
Hawkins, Thomas Alexander, #2108
Hawkins, Vera F., #5242
Hawkins, Virginia, #5221
Hawkins, William A., #5243
"Hawkins, Jr.", Reuben W., #5241
Hawthorn, Florence (Wilson), #6676
Hawthorn, Harry Edward, #6690
Hayman, E.T., #2607
Hayman, Edgar Thomas, #2569
Hayman, Edgar Thomas, #2570
Hayman, Edgar Thomas, #2583
Hayman, Edgar Thomas, #2600
Hayman, Elijah R., #2583
Hayman, Elijah Robert, #2600
Haynes, Sara Lavina, #2336
Haynes, Sara Lavina, #2337
Hays, Abner (Mrs.), #500
Hays, Ann B., #496
Hays, Loveney, #3269
Hays, Marian, #3337
Hays, Rebecca, #1150
Haywood, John, #2326
Haywood, John, #2326
Hazelhurst, Juliana Eleanor, #7558

Hazelhurst, Maria Eleanor, #7588
Hazlett, Henry, #3938
Hazlett, Henry, #3939
Hazlett, Mary Paul, #3939
Hazlett[?], Henry, #2696
Hazlett[?], Henry, #2697
Hazlett[?], Mary Pauls, #2697
Heard, Albert, #1517
Heard, Albert, #702
Heard, Albert, #703
Heard, Albert, #705
Heard, Albert, #706
Heard, Albert, #707
Heard, Alberta, #707
Heard, Alberta, #709
Heard, Hellen Firey, #705
Heard, Mary Catharine, #706
Heard, Mary Catharine, #708
Heard, Mollie E., #704
Heard, Mollie E., #705
Heard, Mollie E., #706
Heard, Mollie E., #707
Heard, Mollie E., #710
Heatin, Andrew J., #5757
Heaton, Andrew J., #5735
Hebb, Anna Myrtle, #55
Hebb, Clyde E., #38
Hebb, Clyde Edgar, #61
Hebb, Clyde Edgar, #62
Hebb, Clyde Edwin, #49
Hebb, Emma Kate, #5825
Hebb, Emma R., #36
Hebb, Emma Roberts, #46
Hebb, Florance Simmons, #48
Hebb, Glenn Edwin, #62
Hebb, Henry C., #40
Hebb, Henry C., #41
Hebb, Henry Clifford, #50
Hebb, Henry Clifford, #63
Hebb, Henry Clifford, #64
Hebb, Henry Clifford, #67
Hebb, Henry Clifford, #68
Hebb, John H., #35
Hebb, John Hanson, #42
Hebb, Johon H., #53
Hebb, Kate Elizabeth, #47
Hebb, Mary Alice, #54
Hebb, Mary Alice, #5828
Hebb, Mary C., #52
Hebb, Mary Catharine, #43
Hebb, Patricia Ann, #51
Hebb, Patricia Ann, #67
Hebb, William A., #37
Hebb, William Adam, #57
Hebb, William Adam, #58
Hebb, William Adam, #59
Hebb, William Adam, #63
Hebb, William Adam, #64
Hebb, William Adams, #45
Hebb, Wm. A., #56
Heck, Elizabeth (Mrs.), #1482
Heck, Elizabeth (Mrs.), #1483
Heck, George W., #1443
Heck, George Washington, #1469
Heck, Harriet J., #1442
Heck, Harriet J., #1447
Heck, Italene Commella, #1481
Heck, John, #1437
Heck, John, #1439

Heck, John, #1440
Heck, John, #1441
Heck, John, #1442
Heck, John, #1443
Heck, John, #1444
Heck, John, #1445
Heck, John, #1453
Heck, John, #1454
Heck, John, #1468
Heck, John N., #1440
Heck, Josephine D., #1439
Heck, Mary E., #1441
Heck, Mary E., #1446
Heck, William Gary, #1480
Heck, Willie W., #1444
Heck, Willie W., #1448
Hedrick, , #1018
Hedrick, , #4896
Hefastay, Dorothy Vivien, #6436
Hefastay, Dorothy Vivien, #6437
Hefastay, Dorothy Vivien, #6438
Hefastay, Vivien, #6343
Hefastay, Vivien, #6344
Hefastay, Vivien, #6345
Heieton, Jean, #6892
Heldabrand, Jacob, #4998
Heldabrand, Mary, #4998
Heldabrand, Maryan M., #4998
Helferstay, Carrie May, #6732
Helferstay, Harriet Elizabeth, #6756
Helferstay, Harry Kimble, #6735
Helferstay, Harry Kimble, #6753
Helferstay, James Oscar, #6730
Helferstay, James Oscar, #6750
Helferstay, Leroy, #6739
Helferstay, Leroy Cofron, #6738
Helferstay, Mildred V., #6739
Helferstay, Minnie, #6740
Helferstay, Minnie, #6741
Helferstay, Minnie, #6742
Helferstay, Minnie L., #6743
Helferstay, Minnie Lee, #6731
Helferstay, Nellie M., #6744
Helferstay, Nellie Mildred, #6733
Helferstay, Nettie L., #6745
Helferstay, Nettie Louise, #6736
Helferstay, Rena West, #6734
Helferstay, Rena West, #6751
Helferstay, William G., #6752
Helferstay, William Gattrell, #6737
Helferstay, William R., #6728
Helferstay, William R., #6754
Helferstay, Wm., #6727
Hellane, David Lee, #954
Hellane, Joseph Glen, #953
Hellane, Julia, #8509
Hellane, Louisa, #4842
"Hellane, Jr.", Joseph Glen, #934
Henderson, James, #6052
Henderson, James, #6141
Henderson, James, #6149
Henderson, James, #6568
Henderson, James, #6568
Henderson, James, #6572
Henderson, James, #6574
Henderson, James, #6575
Henderson, James, #6577
Henderson, James Sebastian Hamilton, #6574
Henderson, Jas., #6578

Henderson, S.H., #6578
Henderson, Sarah, #6052
Henderson, Sarah, #6141
Henderson, Sarah, #6149
Henderson, Sarah, #6568
Henderson, Sarah, #6569
Henderson, Sarah, #6570
Henderson, Sarah, #6571
Henderson, Sarah, #6572
Henderson, Sarah, #6574
Henderson, Sarah, #6577
Henderson, Sarah, #6578
Henderson, Sarah Anne, #6052
Henderson, Sarah Anne, #6140
Henderson, Sarah Anne, #6141
Henderson, Sarah Anne, #6572
Henderson, Sarah Anne, #6573
Henderson, Sarah Anne, #6576
Henderson, Sarah Anne, #6577
"Henderson, Jr.", James, #6569
"Henderson, Sr.", James, #6571
Hendry, James, #4698
Heneberger, A.E., #8277
Heneberger, Andrew E., #8272
Heneberger, Andrew E., #8287
Heneberger, Andrew E., #8304
Heneberger, Andrew E., #8323
Heneberger, Andrew Eli, #8313
Heneberger, Andrew Ellis, #8290
Heneberger, Barbara Maxine, #8276
Heneberger, Edgar, #8279
Heneberger, Edgar, #8297
Heneberger, Edwin, #8298
Heneberger, Edwin H., #8282
Heneberger, Edwin Randolph Grymes, #8275
Heneberger, Edwin Randolph Grymes, #8295
Heneberger, Elizabeth, #8319
Heneberger, Elizabeth (Bear), #8315
Heneberger, Elizabeth Catherine, #8316
Heneberger, Ellis Clark, #8314
Heneberger, Ellis Clark, #8318
Heneberger, Frances, #8312
Heneberger, Harry Bailey, #8285
Heneberger, Harry Bailey, #8300
Heneberger, John, #8283
Heneberger, John, #8302
Heneberger, Lucien, #8281
Heneberger, Lucien G., #8274
Heneberger, Lucien G., #8301
Heneberger, Lucien Randolph, #8291
Heneberger, Lucien Randolph, #8305
Heneberger, Mabel, #8301
Heneberger, Maggie, #8284
Heneberger, Maggie, #8299
Heneberger, Mary, #8307
Heneberger, Mary, #8320
Heneberger, Mary Ann, #8311
Heneberger, Mary Breese, #8278
Heneberger, Mary Breese, #8286
Heneberger, Mary E., #8303
Heneberger, Mary Ella, #8273
Heneberger, Mary Ella, #8280
Heneberger, Peter, #8306
Heneberger, Peter, #8308
Heneberger, Peter, #8309
Heneberger, Peter, #8310
Heneberger, Peter, #8321
Heneberger, Susan Jane, #8317
"Henenberger, Sr.", Alfred A., #8341

INDEX

Pages are not numbered; numbers refer to the entry number at the beginning of each record.

"Henenberger, Sr.", Alfred A., #8342
"Henenberger, Sr.", Alfred A., #8343
Hening, George Griffin, #8278
Hening, Lillian Bailey, #8292
"Hening, Jr.", George Griffin, #8293
Henneberger, Albertus, #8209
Henneberger, Albertus, #8220
Henneberger, Albertus, #8221
Henneberger, Alfred, #8204
Henneberger, Alfred, #8212
Henneberger, Alfred, #8232
Henneberger, Alfred, #8250
Henneberger, Alfred, #8263
Henneberger, Alfred, #8270
Henneberger, Alfred, #8358
Henneberger, Alfred, #8360
Henneberger, Alfred Augustus, #8209
Henneberger, Alfred Augustus, #8210
Henneberger, Alfred Augustus, #8230
Henneberger, Alfred Augustus, #8270
Henneberger, Alfred Garfield, #8205
Henneberger, Alfred Garfield, #8206
Henneberger, Ann Catherine, #8246
Henneberger, Augustus J., #8240
Henneberger, Augustus J., #8257
Henneberger, Cather. (Mrs.), #8271
Henneberger, Catherine, #8238
Henneberger, Catherine, #8239
Henneberger, Catherine, #8240
Henneberger, Catherine, #8241
Henneberger, Catherine, #8242
Henneberger, Catherine, #8243
Henneberger, Catherine, #8244
Henneberger, Catherine, #8245
Henneberger, Catherine, #8246
Henneberger, Catherine, #8247
Henneberger, Catherine, #8248
Henneberger, Catherine, #8249
Henneberger, Catherine, #8250
Henneberger, Catherine , #8243
Henneberger, Catherine (Mrs.), #8255
Henneberger, Clara, #8222

Henneberger, Clara, #8223
Henneberger, Clinton, #8249
Henneberger, Clinton, #8261
Henneberger, Douglas Wade, #8265
Henneberger, Douglas Wade, #8363
Henneberger, Eva, #8228
Henneberger, Eva, #8229
Henneberger, Evelyn, #8358
Henneberger, Evelyn Gertrude, #8366
Henneberger, Evelyn Gertrude, #8367
Henneberger, George W., #8245
Henneberger, George W., #8252
Henneberger, George Wampler, #8216
Henneberger, George Wampler, #8217
Henneberger, Harry Lincoln , #8218
Henneberger, Harry Lincoln , #8219
Henneberger, Hiram, #8248
Henneberger, Hiram, #8259
Henneberger, John, #8237
Henneberger, John, #8239
Henneberger, John, #8240
Henneberger, John, #8241
Henneberger, John, #8242
Henneberger, John, #8243
Henneberger, John, #8244
Henneberger, John, #8245
Henneberger, John, #8246
Henneberger, John, #8247
Henneberger, John, #8248
Henneberger, John, #8249
Henneberger, John, #8250
Henneberger, John, #8253
Henneberger, John, #8271
Henneberger, John J., #8242
Henneberger, John J., #8258
Henneberger, Karel, #8336
Henneberger, Karel, #8360
Henneberger, Lula May, #8207
Henneberger, Lula May, #8208
Henneberger, Margaret, #8247
Henneberger, Margaret, #8262
Henneberger, Mark Wendel, #8235
Henneberger, Mark Wendel, #8236
Henneberger, Mark Wendel, #8264
Henneberger, Mark Wendel, #8336
Henneberger, Mark Wendel, #8337
Henneberger, Mark Wendel, #8361
Henneberger, Mark Wendel, #8362
Henneberger, Mark Wendel, #8368
Henneberger, Mary Catherine, #8214
Henneberger, Mary Catherine, #8215
Henneberger, Mary E., #8231
Henneberger, Mary E., #8270

Henneberger, Mary Elizabeth, #8213
Henneberger, Nellie, #8224
Henneberger, Nellie, #8225
Henneberger, Nina, #8226
Henneberger, Nina, #8227
Henneberger, Sarah Ann, #8241
Henneberger, Sarah Ann, #8260
Henneberger, Susan, #8244
Henneberger, Susan, #8256
Henneberger, William, #8239
Henneberger, William, #8251
"Henneberger, III", Alfred A., #8360
"Henneberger, III", Alfred Augustus, #8233
"Henneberger, III", Alfred Augustus, #8234
"Henneberger, Jr.", Alfred, #8336
"Henneberger, Jr.", Alfred A., #8358
"Henneberger, Jr.", Alfred A., #8359
"Henneberger, Jr.", Alfred Augustus, #8210
"Henneberger, Jr.", Alfred Augustus, #8211
"Henneberger, Jr.", Alfred Augustus, #8233
"Henneberger, Jr.", Alfred Augustus, #8234
"Henneberger, Jr.", Alfred Augustus, #8235
"Henneberger, Jr.", Alfred Augustus, #8236
"Henneberger, Jr.", Alfred Augustus, #8265
"Henneberger, Jr.", Alfred Augustus, #8268
"Henneberger, Sr.", Alfred Augustus, #8266
"Henneberger, Sr.", Alfred Augustus, #8269
"Henneberger, Sr.", Alfred Augustus, #8364
"Henneberger, Sr.", Alfred Augustus, #8365
"Henneberger, Sr.", Evelyn Bitzberger, #8267
Henry[? Or Harry], Tarma Bell, #2069
Herb, D.S., #173
Herb, Daniel S., #171
Herb, Daniel S., #174
Herb, Daniel S., #175
Herb, Daniel S., #178
Herb, Daniel S. , #179
Herb, Henrietta, #173
Herb, Henrietta, #174
Herb, Henrietta, #178
Herb, J. Newton, #177
Herb, J. Newton, #2150
Herb, James Newton, #174
Herb, James Newton, #180
Herb, Lillian, #173
Herb, Lillian, #178
Herb, Susan O., #181
Herb, Susan O., #2132
Herney, Helen M., #811
Heron, Agnes[?], #5668
Heron, Elazabath, #5667

Heron, Elazabeth, #5671
Heron, Grefel, #5666
Heron, Helen, #5661
Heron, Helen, #5673
Heron, Helen, #5674
Heron, Jean, #5662
Heron, Jean, #5665
Heron, John, #5658
Heron, John, #5663
Heron, John, #5664
Heron, John, #5665
Heron, John, #5666
Heron, John, #5667
Heron, John, #5668
Heron, John, #5669
Heron, John, #5669
Heron, John, #5670
Heron, John, #5671
Heron, John, #5672
Heron, John, #5673
Heron, John, #5674
Heron, John, #5674
Heron, Margaret, #5660
Heron, Mary, #5670
Heron, Robert, #5656
Heron, Robert, #5657
Heron, Robert, #5659
Heron, Robert, #5664
Heron, William, #5673
Herr, [daughter], #3155
Herr, [daughter], #3156
Herr, [daughter], #3177
Herr, [daughter], #3178
Herr, [son], #3199
Herr, [son], #3200
Herr, Ann Williams, #3165
Herr, Ann Williams, #3166
Herr, Anna, #6960
Herr, Anna, #6961
Herr, Anna, #6962
Herr, Anna, #6963
Herr, Anna, #6964
Herr, Anna, #6965
Herr, Anna, #6966
Herr, Anna, #6967
Herr, Anna, #6968
Herr, Anna, #6969
Herr, Anna, #6970
Herr, Anna, #6971
Herr, Anna, #6972
Herr, Anna, #6973
Herr, Anna, #6974
Herr, Catharine, #3137
Herr, Catharine, #3139
Herr, Catharine, #3140
Herr, Catharine, #3141
Herr, Catharine, #3142
Herr, Catharine, #3143
Herr, Catharine, #3144
Herr, Catharine, #3145
Herr, Catharine, #3146
Herr, Catharine, #3147
Herr, Catharine, #3148
Herr, Catharine, #3149
Herr, Catharine, #3150
Herr, Catharine, #3151
Herr, Catharine, #3152
Herr, Catharine, #3153
Herr, Catharine, #3154
Herr, Catharine, #3155
Herr, Catharine, #3156

INDEX
Pages are not numbered; numbers refer to the entry number at the beginning of each record.

Herr, Catharine, #3179
Herr, Edward G.W., #3193
Herr, Edward Green Williams, #3163
Herr, Edward Green Williams, #3164
Herr, Eleanor, #3147
Herr, Eleanor, #3148
Herr, Eleanor, #3180
Herr, Eliza, #3130
Herr, Eliza, #3149
Herr, Eliza, #3150
Herr, Elizabeth, #3143
Herr, Elizabeth, #3144
Herr, Elizabeth, #3176
Herr, Elizabeth Beecher, #3173
Herr, Elizabeth Beecher, #3174
Herr, George Washington, #3153
Herr, George Washington, #3154
Herr, Henrietta, #3204
Herr, Henrietta Catharine, #3161
Herr, Henrietta Catharine, #3162
Herr, Henrietta Catharine Cyester, #3191
Herr, Henry, #3139
Herr, Henry, #3140
Herr, Henry C., #3132
Herr, Henry C., #3133
Herr, Henry Clay, #3159
Herr, Henry Clay, #3160
Herr, Irene Virginia, #3202
Herr, Isabella, #3135
Herr, Isabella, #3171
Herr, Isabella, #3172
Herr, John, #3126
Herr, John, #3127
Herr, John, #3136
Herr, John, #3137
Herr, John, #3138
Herr, John, #3141
Herr, John, #3142
Herr, John, #3143
Herr, John, #3144
Herr, John, #3145
Herr, John, #3146
Herr, John, #3147
Herr, John, #3148
Herr, John, #3149
Herr, John, #3150
Herr, John, #3151
Herr, John, #3152
Herr, John, #3153
Herr, John, #3154
Herr, John, #3155
Herr, John, #3156
Herr, John, #3157
Herr, John, #3158
Herr, John, #3159
Herr, John, #3160
Herr, John, #3161
Herr, John, #3162
Herr, John, #3179
Herr, John, #3187
Herr, John, #3203
Herr, John, #3211

Herr, John P., #3131
Herr, John P., #3185
Herr, John Peter, #3151
Herr, John Peter, #3152
Herr, Margaret R., #3139
Herr, Mary Ann, #3128
Herr, Mary Ann, #3141
Herr, Mary Ann, #3142
Herr, Samuel Horatio, #3167
Herr, Samuel Horatio, #3168
Herr, Samuel Horatio, #3188
Herr, Sarah, #3138
Herr, Sarah, #3157
Herr, Sarah, #3158
Herr, Sarah, #3159
Herr, Sarah, #3160
Herr, Sarah, #3161
Herr, Sarah, #3162
Herr, Sarah, #3189
Herr, Sarah, #3212
Herr, Sarah E., #3140
Herr, Sarah Elizabeth, #3201
Herr, Sarah Jane, #3169
Herr, Sarah Jane, #3170
Herr, Susanna, #3129
Herr, Susanna, #3145
Herr, Susanna, #3146
Herr, Susannah, #3183
Herr, William L., #3134
Herr, William L., #3192
Herr, William LaFayette, #3157
Herr, William LaFayette, #3158
Hershey, A.M., #6165
Hershey, A.M., #6167
Heskett, Alcinda L., #5210
Heskett, Alcinda L., #5214
Heskett, Clarissa Amanda, #5206
Heskett, Clarissa Amanda, #5207
Heskett, William, #5204
Heskett, William, #5205
Heskett, Wm., #5206
Heskett, Wm., #5207
Hess, Addie M., #8324
Hess, Addie M., #8328
Hess, Addie M., #8329
Hess, Addie M., #8330
Hess, Catharina, #3250
Hess, Catharina, #3254
Heymering, Henry, #4330
Heymering, Henry, #4331
Heymering, Henry Wood, #4331
Heymering, Henry Wood, #4341
Heymering, Henry Wood, #4353
Heymering, Marinus, #4338
Heymering, Marinus, #4339
Heymering, Marinus, #4351
"Heymering, Jr.", Marinus, #4330
"Heymering, Jr.", Marinus, #4340
"Heymering, Jr.", Marinus, #4352
Heyser, William, #8407
Hibarger, Alice, #3705
Hibbarel, N., #596
Hidd[?], Ednor[?] Mary, #2688

Highbarger, Catharine, #658
Hightower, Rev., #4534
Hilbish, Henrietta, #172
Hilbish, Henrietta, #176
Hill, Ida Frances, #5824
Hill, Reuben, #1516
Hill, Reuben, #665
Hill, Willard, #3115
Hill, Willard, #3124
Hilleary, George, #2609
Hilleary, Harriett, #2611
Hilleary, Henry, #2609
Hilleary, Henry, #2610
Hilleary, Henry, #2611
Hilleary, Laura Claggett, #8438
Hilleary, Laura Claggett, #8480
Hilleary, Laura Claggett, #8500
Hilleary, Thomas, #2610
Hilleary, Wm. H., #8480
Hilliary, Harriet, #2604
Hilliary, Harriet, #2605
Hindman, Anne, #1474
Hindman, Elizabeth, #1477
Hindman, Isabaella, #1470
Hindman, Isabaella, #1471
Hindman, Isabaella, #1472
Hindman, Isabaella, #1473
Hindman, Isabaella, #1474
Hindman, Isabaella, #1475
Hindman, Isabaella, #1476
Hindman, Isabaella, #1477
Hindman, Isabaella, #1478
Hindman, James, #1475
Hindman, Jane, #1472
Hindman, John, #1470
Hindman, John, #1470
Hindman, John, #1471
Hindman, John, #1472
Hindman, John, #1473
Hindman, John, #1474
Hindman, John, #1475
Hindman, John, #1476
Hindman, John, #1477
Hindman, John, #1478
Hindman, Margaret, #1478
Hindman, Mary, #1476
Hindman, Mary, #1479
Hindman, Sarah, #1463
Hindman, Sarah, #1473
Hindman, Sarah, #1491
Hindman, William, #1471
Hindman[?], John[?], #1451
Hiskett, Alcinda L., #5277
Hitt, John W., #4955
Hitt, John W., #4984
Hitt, John Wesley, #4982
Hitt, Nancy, #4984
Hobbs, Kenneth L., #5912
Hobbs, Kenneth L., #5920
Hobbs, Kenneth L., #5921
Hobbs, Kenneth L., #5926
Hobbs, Mary Lee, #5921
Hochrein, Margaret Ellen, #6340
Hochrein, Margaret Ellen, #6341
Hochrein, Margaret Ellen, #6416
Hochrein, Margaret Ellen, #6417
Hochrein, Margaret Ellen, #6439
Hochrein, Margaret Ellen, #6440
Hoff, Francis C., #2880
Hoff, Harison, #2880
Hoff, Martha, #2880

Hoffman, [blank], #7271
Hoffman, Albert, #2734
Hoffman, Annrebecca, #5811
Hoffman, Christena, #5468
Hoffman, Conrod, #5793
Hoffman, Conrod, #5807
Hoffman, David A., #2207
Hoffman, David A., #2215
Hoffman, David Allen (Dr.), #2200
Hoffman, David Allen (Dr.), #2201
Hoffman, David Allen (Dr.), #2202
Hoffman, David Allen (Dr.), #2203
Hoffman, David Allen (Dr.), #2204
Hoffman, Donald, #2153
Hoffman, Edgar Brown, #2201
Hoffman, Edgar Brown, #2205
Hoffman, Edgar Brown, #2206
Hoffman, Edgar Brown, #2207
Hoffman, Edgar Brown, #2208
Hoffman, Edgar Brown, #2209
Hoffman, Edgar Brown, #2210
Hoffman, Edith M., #3112
Hoffman, Edith M., #3122
Hoffman, Effie Louise, #2203
Hoffman, Effie Louise, #2218
Hoffman, Effie Louise, #2219
Hoffman, Effie R., #2206
Hoffman, Elias, #3114
Hoffman, Elias, #3116
Hoffman, Elias, #3125
Hoffman, Elis.th. [Elisabeth], #5463
Hoffman, Elisabeth, #5461
Hoffman, Elizabeth, #5808
Hoffman, George, #5796
Hoffman, George, #5797
Hoffman, George, #5803
Hoffman, George, #5804
Hoffman, Goege, #5795
Hoffman, Ida, #3111
Hoffman, Ida, #3121
Hoffman, Isabell, #3109
Hoffman, Isabell, #3119
Hoffman, John, #5810
Hoffman, John Adams, #2202
Hoffman, John Adams, #2211
Hoffman, John Adams, #2212
Hoffman, John Adams, #2213
Hoffman, John Adams, #2214
Hoffman, John Adams, #2215
Hoffman, John Adams, #2216
Hoffman, John Adams, #2216
Hoffman, John Adams, #2217
Hoffman, Jos.h. [Joseph], #5466
Hoffman, Jos.h. [Joseph], #5480
Hoffman, Lizzie Catharine, #3395
Hoffman, Martha Dandelia (Mrs.), #2759
Hoffman, Mary, #2151
Hoffman, Mary, #2213
Hoffman, Mary, #5796
Hoffman, Mary, #5804
Hoffman, Mary, #5809
Hoffman, Mary, #2217
Hoffman, Mary J., #3118
Hoffman, Nichol, #5466
Hoffman, Nichol, #5467
Hoffman, Nichol, #5468
Hoffman, Nicholas, #5464
Hoffman, Nicholas, #5479
Hoffman, Nicholas, #5480
Hoffman, Nicolas, #5476

INDEX
Pages are not numbered; numbers refer to the entry number at the beginning of each record.

Hoffman, Patricia Ann, #7271
Hoffman, Rachel, #5466
Hoffman, Rachel, #5467
Hoffman, Rachel, #5468
Hoffman, Rachel, #5479
Hoffman, Rachel, #5480
Hoffman, Randolph, #5794
Hoffman, Randolph, #5805
Hoffman, Ripley C., #2214
Hoffman, Ripley Christian (Dr.), #2204
Hoffman, Russell Embich, #2208
Hoffman, Sarah, #5806
Hoffman, Sarah D., #3113
Hoffman, Sarah D., #3117
Hoffman, Sarah Elizabeth, #3110
Hoffman, Sarah Elizabeth, #3120
Hoffman, Sue M., #4301
Hoffman, Susan, #5467
Hoffman, Verona, #2210
Hoffman, Victor, #2209
Hoffman, Wallace, #2212
"Hoffman, Jr.", John Adams, #2152
Hoffmaster, Sarah V.J., #787
Hoffmaster, Sarah V.J., #790
Hoffmaster, Sarah V.J., #791
Hoffmaster, Sarah V.J., #792
Hoffmaster, Sarah V.J., #793
Hoffmaster, Sarah V.J., #794
Hoffmaster, Sarah V.J., #795
Hofhour, Rev., #5052
Hogmire, Amalia, #3298
Hogmire, Catharine, #3220
Hogmire, Catharine, #3221
Hogmire, Catharine, #6858
Hogmire, Catharine, #6859
Hoke, Sarah Velma, #6346
Hoke, Sarah Velma, #6347
Holbird, Henry B., #918
Holbird, James, #919
Holbird, Mary Jane, #896
Holbird, Mary Jane, #917
Holbird, Sarah Ann, #897
"Holbird, Jr.[?]", James[?], #898
Holland, R.C., #3135
Hollingsworth, Isaac, #1204
Hollingsworth, Isaac, #1206
Hollingsworth, Rachel, #1205
Hollingsworth, Rachel, #1207
Hollis, C.W., #2905
Hollis, Edna, #7931
Hollis, Edna, #7932
Hollis, Edna, #7933
Hollis, Edna, #7934
Hollis, Edna, #7935
Hollis, Edna, #7936
Hollis, Edna, #7937
Hollis, Mary Louise, #2906
Hollis, Mary Louise, #2907
Hollis, Mary Louise, #2909
Hollis, Mary Louise, #2910
Hollis, Mary Louise, #2911
Hollis, Philip, #2905
Hollis, Philip Boyd, #2900
Hollis, Philip Boyd, #2901
Hollis, Philip Boyd, #2906

Hollis, Phyllis Bowling, #2901
Hollis, Phyllis Bowling, #2902
Hollis, Phyllis Bowling, #2904
Holmead, Rev., #5909
Holmes, John F.[?], #3780
Holmes, Minnie, #4285
Holmes, Nellie Armor, #4285
Holmes, Sarah Jane (Miss), #3802
Holmes, Thomas, #4275
Holmes, Thomas, #4285
Holmes, John F., #3766
Holsworth, Elizabeth, #812
Hont[?], , #1008
Hood, John Pope, #5700
Hood, John Westly, #5694
Hood, Luke, #5695
Hood, Luke Pearce, #5701
Hood, Michael, #3614
Hood, Pamela, #3612
Hood, Pete, #3622
Hood, Peter, #3641
Hood, William Aron, #5699
Hooper, Mary Cath., #7996
Hooper, Mary Cath., #7997
Hopkins, Angela Marie, #3051
Hopkins, J.A., #5043
Hopkins, John Thompson, #3050
Hopkins, Samuel Earl, #3052
Hopkins, Sara B., #3049
Hopkins, Sara B., #3050
Hopkins, Sara B., #3051
Hopkins, Sara B., #3052
Hopkins, William F., #3040
Hopkins, Wm. F., #3046
Hopkins, Wm. F., #3049
Hopkins, Wm. F., #3050
Hopkins, Wm. F., #3051
Hopkins, Wm. F., #3052
"Hopkins, Jr.", Wm. F., #3049
Horine, Elizabeth, #2913
Horn, Edith, #6374
Horn, Edith, #6375
Horn, Edith, #6376
Horn, Edith, #6377
Horn, Edith Maxine, #6353
Horn, Edith Maxine, #6354
Horn, Edith Maxine, #6355
Horn, Edith Maxine, #6356
Horn, Edith Maxine, #6357
Horn[?], Clara (Miss), #7253
Horne, Barbara, #1408
Horne, Barbara, #1409
Horne, Cindy Louise, #1409
Horne, Cindy Louise, #5295
Horne, Michael, #1408
Horne, Michael, #5294
Horne, Ned, #1408
Horne, Ned, #1409
Horne, Ned, #5294
Horne, Ned, #5295
Horne, Ned V., #1390
Horne, Ned V., #5301
Hoskins, , #4888
Hoskinson, Oliva[?], #2522
Hotchinson[?], Elenora C., #2527
Hott, J.W. (Bishop), #4289
Hott, J.W. (Bishop), #4290
Hott, James W., #3399

Houch, Jacob, #7162
Houch, Margre M., #7161
Houch, Margre M., #7162
Houck, Jacob, #7131
Houck, Margaret M., #7130
Houck, Margaret M., #7131
Houck, Maria, #7131
Houffman, Rev., #3144
Hout, H.R.W., #5509
Hout, Henry R.T.S., #5500
Hout, Henry R.T.S., #5506
Hout, Susie May S., #5502
Hout, Urillah V., #5510
Hout, , #4886
Howard, Agnes, #1072
Howard, Agnes, #1073
Howard, Agnes, #1074
Howard, Agnes, #1075
Howard, Agnes, #1076
Howard, Agnes, #1077
Howard, Anna, #1069
Howard, Christopher Leroy, #1033
Howard, Christopher Leroy, #1056
Howard, Daniel Cridle, #1063
Howard, Daniel Cridle, #1064
Howard, Eliza Bradley, #1074
Howard, Emma Wilson, #1050
Howard, Frances Loose, #6952
Howard, G.W., #1055
Howard, Geo. W., #1041
Howard, Geo. W., #1042
Howard, Geo. W., #1043
Howard, Geo. W., #1044
Howard, Geo. W., #1045
Howard, Geo. W., #1046
Howard, Geo. W., #1047
Howard, Geo. W., #1048
Howard, Geo. W., #1049
Howard, Geo. W., #1050
Howard, Geo. W., #1051
Howard, Geo. W., #1052
Howard, Geo. W., #1053
Howard, Geo. W., #1067
Howard, Geo. W., #1068
Howard, George, #1069
Howard, George N.[?], #1040
Howard, George W., #1030
Howard, George W., #1077
Howard, Harriet L., #1048
Howard, Harriet L., #1054
Howard, Harriet Louise, #638
Howard, Harriett L., #1052
Howard, Hinman, #1037
Howard, James Hatten, #1034
Howard, John M., #1044
Howard, John Preston, #5555
Howard, John Preston, #5564
Howard, Leonard C., #1058
Howard, Leonard Credle, #1035
Howard, Lois, #1033
Howard, Lois, #1056
Howard, Lois, #1058
Howard, Lois A., #1043
Howard, Lois A., #1051
Howard, Lois A., #1055
Howard, Lois A., #1057
Howard, Lois A., #1060
Howard, Lois A., #1061
Howard, Lois Ann, #1029
Howard, Lois Ann, #1034

Howard, Lois Ann, #1035
Howard, Lois Ann, #1036
Howard, Lois Ann, #1037
Howard, Luca A., #1045
Howard, Lucretia A., #1062
Howard, Lucy H., #1040
Howard, Lucy H., #1041
Howard, Lucy H., #1042
Howard, Lucy H., #1043
Howard, Lucy H., #1044
Howard, Lucy H., #1045
Howard, Lucy H., #1046
Howard, Lucy H., #1047
Howard, Lucy H., #1048
Howard, Lucy H., #1049
Howard, Lucy H., #1050
Howard, Lucy H., #1051
Howard, Lucy H., #1052
Howard, Lucy H., #1053
Howard, Margaret Ann, #1031
Howard, Mary Leah (Middlekauff), #5560
Howard, Mary M., #1041
Howard, Nancy, #1072
Howard, O.Z., #1053
Howard, O.Z.[?], #1049
Howard, Parliament [female], #1075
Howard, Precilla[?] Easter, #1065
Howard, Precilla[?] Easter, #1066
Howard, Thomas Pasteur, #1036
Howard, Thurza, #1073
Howard, W.[?] H., #1055
Howard, Walter H., #1061
Howard, Waltor H., #1047
Howard, Will H., #1062
Howard, Will. H., #1057
Howard, Will. H., #1059
Howard, Will. H., #1060
Howard, Will. H., #1061
Howard, William, #1067
Howard, William, #1069
Howard, William, #1071
Howard, William, #1072
Howard, William, #1073
Howard, William, #1074
Howard, William, #1075
Howard, William, #1076
Howard, William, #1077
Howard, William D., #1060
Howard, William Daniel, #1032
Howard, William H., #1028
Howard, William H., #1042
Howard, William H., #1076
Howard, William H., #6893
Howard, Wm., #1033
Howard, Wm., #1034
Howard, Wm., #1035
Howard, Wm., #1036
Howard, Wm., #1037
Howard , Wm., #1056
Howard , Will., #1058
Howe, Rev., #4531
Hoye, W.S., #5042
Hroh, Henry, #523
Huber, Annie L., #7632
Huber, Annie L., #7633
Huber, Annie L., #7634
Hubley, Anna Catharine Rauna, #7759
Hubley, Anna Catharine Rauna, #7760
Hubley, Anna Catherine Raum, #7771
Hubley, Anna Catherine Raum, #7772

INDEX
Pages are not numbered; numbers refer to the entry number at the beginning of each record.

Hubley, Anna Catherine Raum, #7773
Hubley, Anna Catherine Raum, #7774
Hubley, Anna Catherine Raum, #7775
Hubley, Anna Catherine Raum, #7776
Hubley, Anna Catherine Raum, #7777
Hubley, Anna Catherine Raum, #7778
Hubley, Anna Catherine Raum, #7779
Hubley, Anna Catherine Raum, #7780
Hubley, Anna Catherine Raum, #7781
Hubley, Anna Catherine Raum, #7782
Hubley, Anna Catherine Raum, #7783
Hubley, Anna Catherine Raum, #7784
Hubley, Anna Catherine Raum, #7785
Hubley, Mary, #7768
Hubley, Michael, #7760
Hubley, Michael, #7768
Hudson, Edward Carlyle, #6749
Huffer, Alfred, #3087
Huffer, Alfred, #3088
Huffer, Clarence E., #3074
Huffer, Clarence E., #3075
Huffer, Dorah M., #3069
Huffer, Dorah M., #3070
Huffer, Elizabeth, #3083
Huffer, Elizabeth, #3084
Huffer, Ivy Z.[?], #3063
Huffer, Ivy Z.[?], #3064
Huffer, Ivy Z.[?], #3065
Huffer, Ivy Z.[?], #3081
Huffer, Jacob, #3089
Huffer, John, #3053
Huffer, John, #3054
Huffer, John, #3055
Huffer, John, #3058
Huffer, John, #3059
Huffer, John, #3085
Huffer, John, #3086
Huffer, John, #3093
Huffer, John, #3094
Huffer, Jonas O.[or Q.], #3104
Huffer, Jonas O.[or Q.], #3105
Huffer, Jonas O.[or Q.], #3106
Huffer, Jonas Z.[?], #3058
Huffer, Jonas Z.[?], #3059
Huffer, Jonas Z.[?], #3062
Huffer, Jonas Z.[?], #3063
Huffer, Jonas Z.[?], #3064
Huffer, Jonas Z.[?], #3065
Huffer, Jonas Z.[?], #3066
Huffer, Jonas Z.[?], #3067
Huffer, Jonas Z.[?], #3068
Huffer, Jonas Z.[?], #3069
Huffer, Jonas Z.[?], #3070
Huffer, Jonas Z.[?], #3071
Huffer, Jonas Z.[?], #3072
Huffer, Jonas Z.[?], #3073
Huffer, Jonas Z.[?], #3074
Huffer, Jonas Z.[?], #3075
Huffer, Jonas Z.[?], #3078
Huffer, Jonas Z.[?], #3079
Huffer, Jonas Z.[?], #3080
Huffer, Jonas Z.[?], #3090
Huffer, Jonas Z.[?], #3091
Huffer, Mary, #3092
Huffer, Mary G., #3066
Huffer, Mary G., #3067
Huffer, Mary G., #3068
Huffer, Rhuannah, #3082
Huffer, Sarah, #3393
Huffer, Sarah A. Huffer, #3071
Huffer, Sarah A. Huffer, #3072
Huffer, Sarah A. Huffer, #3073
Huffer, , #4875
"Huffer, III", John, #3099
"Huffer, III", John, #3100
"Huffer, III", John, #3101
"Huffer, III", John, #3104
"Huffer, III", John, #3105
"Huffer, III", John, #3106
"Huffer, Jr.", John, #3094
"Huffer, Jr.", John, #3095
"Huffer, Jr.", John, #3096
"Huffer, Jr.", John, #3099
"Huffer, Jr.", John, #3100
"Huffer, Jr.", John, #3101
Huffman, Elizabeth, #3448
Huffman, Rev., #6808
Huffman, Rev., #6809
Huffman, Rev., #6831
Huffman, Rev., #6848
Huffman, Rev., #6850
Hughes, Irene, #7988
Hughes, Samuel, #3503
Hull, Hannah, #1383
Hummer, Andrew Leo, #4160
Hummer, Andrew Leo, #4163
Hummer, Hannah Ardinger, #4160
Hummer, Hannah Ardinger, #4161
Hummer, Hannah Ardinger, #4162
Hummer, Katherine, #1702
Hummer, Katherine, #1703
Hummer, Katherine, #1704
Hummer, Katherine, #1705
Hummer, Katherine, #1706
Hummer, Katherine, #1707
Hummer, Katherine Elizabeth, #4163
Hummer, Katherine Elizabeth, #4164
Hummer, Katherine Elizabeth, #4167
Hummer, Katherine Elizabeth, #4168
Hummer, Katherine Elizabeth, #4169
Hummer, Katherine Elizabeth, #4170
Hummer, Leo, #1699
Hummer, Leo, #1702
Hummer, Leo, #1703
Hummer, Leo, #4162
Hunt, Heather Susan, #6932
Hunt, Jonathan Ross, #6933
Hunt, William, #1335
Huntzberry, Etta May, #3403
Hurfmyer, Rev., #7784
Hurst, Juliet Frances, #1912
Hurst, Lucy, #1913
Hurst, Mary, #1912
Hurst, Mary, #1913
Hurst, William, #1912
Hurst, William, #1913
Hutchinson, Rachel A., #1928
Hutchinson, Sarah, #6144
Hutchinson, Sarah E., #6180
Hutchinson, Sarah E., #6181
Hutchinson, Sarah E., #6182
Hutchinson, Sarah E., #6183
Hutchinson, Sarah E., #6184
Hutchinson, Thomas Hunter, #1928
Hutchinson, Wm. E., #1928
Hutchison, Frank R., #2556
Hutchison, Nora (Sole), #2556
Hutzel, Alice, #4649
Hutzel, Calren[?], #4635
Hutzel, Charley, #4636
Hutzel, Clemmie, #4637
Hutzel, Corma[?], #4650
Hutzel, Elesis[?], #4652
Hutzel, Elizabeth, #4632
Hutzel, Ellsworth, #4648
Hutzel, Elmer, #4653
Hutzel, George, #4634
Hutzel, John, #4633
Hutzel, John, #4634
Hutzel, John, #4635
Hutzel, John, #4636
Hutzel, John, #4637
Hutzel, Jonas , #4645
Hutzel, Jonas , #4646
Hutzel, Luther, #4649
Hutzel, Luther, #4650
Hutzel, Luther, #4651
Hutzel, Luther, #4652
Hutzel, Luther, #4653
Hutzel, Maude, #4651
Hutzel, Russell, #4646
Hutzel, Samuel, #4647
Hutzel, Samuel, #4648
Hutzel, Septimus, #4633
Hutzel, Vernon, #4645
Hutzel, Webster, #4647
Huyett, Anna Virginia, #3039
Huyett, Anna Virginia, #3044
Huyett, Anna Virginia, #3045
Huyett, Daniel, #2578
Huyett, Daniel, #2579
Huyett, Margaretta Brinham, #2578
Huyett, Margaretta Brinham, #2579
Huyett, Margaretta O., #2578
Huyett, Margaretta O., #2579
Huyett, Margaretta O., #2606
Huyett, Margaretta Ozella, #2567
Idle, Willyi[?] A., #681
Ingram, Ada Viola, #1817
Ingram, Ada Viola, #1818
Ingram, Elva L., #8105
Ingram, Elva L., #8106
Ingram, J. Roy, #1815
Ingram, J. Roy, #1816
Ingram, J. Roy, #8105
Ingram, J. Roy, #8106
Ingram, J. Wilbur, #1815
Ingram, J. Wilbur, #8069
Ingram, J. Wilbur, #8105
Ingram, R. Leon, #1816
Ingram, R. Leon, #8070
Ingram, R. Leon, #8106
Irvin, Benjamin, #1929
Irvin, James Wm., #1929
Irvin, Mary Jane, #1929
Irvine, A.H., #2403
Jackson, ___bert Earle, #6334
Jackson, ___bert Earle, #6335
Jackson, ___bert Earle, #6336
Jackson, ___bert Earle, #6337
Jackson, ___bert Earle, #6338
Jackson, ___bert Earle, #6339
Jackson, _lbert William, #6342
Jackson, Agnes D., #1227
Jackson, Alan Edward, #6339
Jackson, Alan Edward, #6415
Jackson, Amelia P., #1216
Jackson, Amelia P., #1217
Jackson, Andrew, #1213
Jackson, Arabella E., #1219
Jackson, Arabella E., #1220
Jackson, Arlene Frances, #6341
Jackson, Arlene Frances, #6417
Jackson, Carol Vivien, #6344
Jackson, Dennis Roger, #6338
Jackson, Dennis Roger, #6414
Jackson, Donald Louis, #6337
Jackson, Donald Louis, #6413
Jackson, Dorothy M., #6409
Jackson, Dorothy Marie, #6330
Jackson, Dorothy Marie, #6331
Jackson, Dorothy Marie, #6406
Jackson, George Willard, #6319
Jackson, George Willard, #6340
Jackson, George Willard, #6402
Jackson, George Willard, #6416
Jackson, George Willard, #6417
Jackson, Geroge Willard, #6341
Jackson, Gilbert William, #6320
Jackson, Gilbert William, #6403
Jackson, Harry Thomas, #6328
Jackson, Howard, #6317
Jackson, Howard, #6318
Jackson, Howard, #6319
Jackson, Howard, #6320
Jackson, Howard, #6321
Jackson, Howard Thomas, #6313
Jackson, Jennie, #940
Jackson, John Tyler P., #1218
Jackson, Jos., #2108
Jackson, Lillie, #941
Jackson, Lucy A., #1224
Jackson, Lucy A., #1225
Jackson, Maggie, #935
Jackson, Maria Louisa, #1228
Jackson, Maria Louisa, #1229
Jackson, Maria Louisa, #1230
Jackson, Mary L., #1223
Jackson, Mary May, #6327
Jackson, Matiedan, #921
Jackson, Miriam Elizabeth, #6333
Jackson, Mirriam Elizabeth, #6408
Jackson, Penelope, #1231
Jackson, Penelope, #1232
Jackson, Rachel, #1214
Jackson, Rachel, #1215
Jackson, Richard Raymond, #6336
Jackson, Richard Raymond, #6412

INDEX
Pages are not numbered; numbers refer to the entry number at the beginning of each record.

Jackson, Robert Earle, #6318
Jackson, Robert Earle, #6401
Jackson, Robert Earle, #6410
Jackson, Robert Earle, #6411
Jackson, Robert Earle, #6412
Jackson, Robert Earle, #6413
Jackson, Robert Earle, #6414
Jackson, Robert Earle, #6415
Jackson, Sadie A., #6400
Jackson, Sadie A., #6401
Jackson, Sadie A., #6402
Jackson, Sadie A., #6403
Jackson, Sadie A., #6404
Jackson, Spencer, #1208
Jackson, Spencer, #1209
Jackson, Spencer, #1210
Jackson, Spencer, #1213
Jackson, Thomas Howard, #6329
Jackson, Thomas Howard, #6330
Jackson, Thomas Howard, #6331
Jackson, Thomas Howard, #6332
Jackson, Thomas Howard, #6333
Jackson, Thomas Howard, #6334
Jackson, Thomas Howard, #6400
Jackson, Thomas Howard, #6401
Jackson, Thomas Howard, #6402
Jackson, Thomas Howard, #6403
Jackson, Thomas Howard, #6404
Jackson, Thomas J., #1221
Jackson, Thomas J., #1222
Jackson, William, #938
Jackson, William Charles, #6321
Jackson, William Charles, #6326
Jackson, William Charles, #6343
Jackson, William Charles, #6344
Jackson, William Charles, #6345
Jackson, William Charles, #6404
"Jackson, III", Thomas Howard, #6332
"Jackson, III", Thomas Howard, #6407
"Jackson, Jr.", Robert Earle, #6335
"Jackson, Jr.", Robert Earle, #6411
"Jackson, Jr.", Spencer, #1226
"Jackson, Jr.", Thomas Howard, #6317
"Jackson, Jr.", Thomas Howard, #6400
"Jackson, Jr.", Thomas Howard, #6405
"Jackson, Jr.", Thomas Howard, #6406

"Jackson, Jr.", William Charles, #6345
Jacobs, Virginia, #2689
Jacobs, Virginia, #2690
Jacobs, Virginia, #3930
Jacobs, Virginia, #3931
Jacobs, William, #4929
Jacobs, William H., #3671
Jacques, Lancelot, #218
Jacques, Libie, #1595
Jacques, Mary, #218
Jacques, Mary, #218
Jamerson, Charles, #157
Jamerson, John, #156
Jamerson, Minny V., #160
Jamerson, Susan E., #159
Jamerson, Thomas W., #158
Jamison, Alf, #150
Jamison, Barbara A., #2771
Jamison, Birtha M., #164
Jamison, Blanche D., #167
Jamison, Clinton H., #166
Jamison, Dannie Lee, #170
Jamison, David W., #2766
Jamison, George W., #168
Jamison, Harvey, #4045
Jamison, Harvey L., #169
Jamison, Harvey L., #2768
Jamison, Harvey Lester, #151
Jamison, Harvey Lester, #152
Jamison, James, #148
Jamison, James, #161
Jamison, James, #163
Jamison, Lestser Martin, #149
Jamison, Martha May (Brill), #155
Jamison, Marvin L., #2772
Jamison, Mary E., #145
Jamison, Mary E., #162
Jamison, Mary E., #34
Jamison, Maude Ellen (Shoemaker), #146
Jamison, Maude Ellen (Shoemaker), #147
Jamison, Wayne B., #2773
Jamison, Worthington J., #165
Jautze, Margaretha, #5638
Jenkins, Harry, #7362
Jenkins, Henry, #7361
Jenkins, Henry, #7362
Jenkins, Henry, #7363
Jenkins, Rev., #8269
Jenkins, Robert, #7363
Jennings, Annie (Spielman), #968
Jennings, Catharine A., #3132
Jennings, Laura Elizabeth, #970
Jennings, Laura Elizabeth, #971
Jennings, Nellie S., #975
Jennings, Nellie S., #976
Jennings, William[?] S., #973
Jennings, William[?] S., #974
Jennings, , #4865
"Jennings, Jr.[?]", Samuel, #966
"Jennings, Jr.[?]", Samuel, #967
Jennings[?], Anna Estelle, #980
Johns, Dr., #7575
Johns, Emma Julia, #5873
Johns, Emma Julia, #5883
Johns, Emma Julia, #5888
Johns, Henry, #7577

Johns, James Saml., #5871
Johns, James Samuel, #5887
Johns, John, #5869
Johns, John, #5874
Johns, John, #5875
Johns, John, #5876
Johns, John, #5884
Johns, John, #5894
Johns, John Nelson, #5872
Johns, John Nelson, #5886
Johns, Julia, #5874
Johns, Julia, #5875
Johns, Julia, #5876
Johns, Julia M., #5868
Johns, Julia M., #5884
Johns, Julia M., #5895
Johns, Julia Marinda, #5875
Johns, Luther Richard, #5889
Johns, Luther Rinehard[?], #5876
Johns, Margaret Crabb, #2661
Johns, Margaret Crabb, #2662
Johns, Margaret Crabb, #2663
Johns, Margaret Crabb, #2664
Johns, Margaret Crabb, #2665
Johns, Margaret Crabb, #2666
Johns, Margaret Crabb, #2667
Johns, Margaret Crabb, #3900
Johns, Margaret Crabb, #3903
Johns, Margaret Crabb, #3904
Johns, Margaret Crabb, #3905
Johns, Margaret Crabb, #3906
Johns, Margaret Crabb, #3907
Johns, Margaret Crabb, #3908
Johns, Margaret Crabb, #3909
Johns, Margaret Crabb, #3910
Johns, Margret Louisia, #5870
Johns, Stella Malissa, #5874
Johns , Margaret Crabb, #2660
Johnson, Agnes Elizabeth, #394
Johnson, Agnes Elizabeth, #395
Johnson, Agnes Elizabeth, #396
Johnson, Arthur Bair, #410
Johnson, Arthur Bair, #411
Johnson, Benjamin F., #377
Johnson, Benjamin Franklin, #378
Johnson, Benjamin Franklin, #379
Johnson, Benjamin Franklin, #380
Johnson, Benjamin Samuel, #389
Johnson, Benjamin Samuel, #390
Johnson, Benjamin Samuel, #391
Johnson, Catherine, #8538
Johnson, Clarence Francis, #408
Johnson, Clarence Francis, #409
Johnson, Cora Elizabeth, #379
Johnson, Cora Elizabeth, #381
Johnson, Cora Elizabeth , #382
Johnson, Edwin Franklin, #401
Johnson, Edwin Franklin, #402
Johnson, Frederick Foltz, #397
Johnson, Frederick Foltz, #398
Johnson, Helen Francis, #406
Johnson, Helen Francis, #407
Johnson, Irvin Wertz, #399
Johnson, Irvin Wertz, #400
Johnson, Mary Grace, #383
Johnson, Maurice Needy, #403
Johnson, Maurice Needy, #404
Johnson, Maurice Needy, #405
Johnson, Olive Louise, #384
Johnson, Olive Louise, #385
Johnson, Paul William, #386

Johnson, Paul William, #387
Johnson, Paul William, #388
Johnson, Rhoda Myrtle, #392
Johnson, Rhoda Myrtle, #393
Johnson, Ritch, #8539
"Johnson, M.D.", James , #1367
Johson, William, #8550
Johson, William, #8551
Jones, Annie L., #726
Jones, Bertha, #6342
Jones, Bertha Catherine, #6446
Jones, Bertha E., #7678
Jones, Bertha Elizabeth, #7720
Jones, Bertha Elizabeth, #7721
Jones, Bertha Elizabeth, #7727
Jones, Bertha Elizabeth, #7728
Jones, Bertha Elizabeth, #7729
Jones, Bertha Elizabeth, #7730
Jones, Bertha Elizabeth, #7731
Jones, Bertha Elizabeth, #7732
Jones, Bertha Elizabeth, #7733
Jones, Bertha Elizabeth, #7734
Jones, Bertha Elizabeth, #7735
Jones, Bertha Elizabeth, #7736
Jones, Bertha Elizabeth, #7737
Jones, Bertha Elizabeth, #7738
Jones, Bertha Elizabeth, #7739
Jones, Bertha Elizabeth, #7740
Jones, Bertha Elizabeth, #7741
Jones, Catharine, #5694
Jones, Charles Edward, #5697
Jones, E.H., #7008
Jones, E.H., #7218
Jones, Frank C., #1126
Jones, Harrison Piper, #2585
Jones, Joseph C., #5693
Jones, Joseph Chiswell, #5698
Jones, Mary Elizabeth, #5695
Jones, Mary Wilson, #2572
Jones, MaryElizabeth, #5696
Jones, Maurice Hepborn, #2571
Jones, Maurice Hepborn, #2585
Jones, Maurice Hepborn, #2589
Jones, Minnie A., #2585
Jones, Nancy, #1178
Jones, , #6305
Kabele, Rev., #4532
Kaetge[?], Ira L., #976
Kaetgel, Miriam Ea____[?], #982
Kaetgel, Sterling[?] Dayne[?], #981
Kaetzel, Addie, #2994
Kaetzel, Addie M., #2965
Kaetzel, Addie M., #2966
Kaetzel, Addie M., #2967
Kaetzel, Addie M., #2968
Kaetzel, Adelaide M., #2992
Kaetzel, Annie Laura, #2973
Kaetzel, Bertie Rebbecca, #3005
Kaetzel, Bessie Corine, #2971
Kaetzel, Blanche L., #3015
Kaetzel, Catherain V., #3018
Kaetzel, Charles C., #3019
Kaetzel, Charles Claude, #3028
Kaetzel, Christian, #3011
Kaetzel, Christian Theobald, #2999
Kaetzel, Cora Elizabeth, #3001
Kaetzel, Dorothy G., #3020
Kaetzel, Dorothy Grace, #3029
Kaetzel, Edith Virginia, #3004
Kaetzel, Edna L., #3031
Kaetzel, Elizabeth, #3013

INDEX

Pages are not numbered; numbers refer to the entry number at the beginning of each record.

Kaetzel, Ethel Viola, #3006
Kaetzel, Garland Bovie[?], #3007
Kaetzel, Harry David, #2980
Kaetzel, James Henry, #3002
Kaetzel, John Franklin, #2975
Kaetzel, John Franklin, #2979
Kaetzel, June M., #3017
Kaetzel, June Marie, #3026
Kaetzel, Katie Mozell[?], #3008
Kaetzel, Laura M., #2970
Kaetzel, Laura M. (Mrs.), #2977
Kaetzel, Lewis, #2964
Kaetzel, Lewis, #2971
Kaetzel, Lewis, #2972
Kaetzel, Lewis, #2973
Kaetzel, Lewis, #2974
Kaetzel, Lewis, #2975
Kaetzel, Lewis, #2976
Kaetzel, Lewis, #2995
Kaetzel, Lewis P., #2978
Kaetzel, Lewis P., #2994
Kaetzel, Lewis P.[?], #2969
Kaetzel, Loretta Jean, #3032
Kaetzel, Louise, #3024
Kaetzel, Mary Alice A., #2976
Kaetzel, Mary Elizabeth, #3000
Kaetzel, Maud C., #2974
Kaetzel, Nettie Naomi, #3003
Kaetzel, Pearl Virginie, #2972
Kaetzel, Robert Lee, #3009
Kaetzel, Virginia, #3027
Kaetzel, Wanda LaRue, #3021
Kaetzel, William, #3025
Kaetzel, William L., #3016
Kaetzel, William Lewis, #3037
Kaetzel, William Lewis, #3038
Kagans[?], , #6114
Kamps[?], Margaret A., #7016
Kane, Albert G., #7342
Kane, Albert Graichen, #7366
Kane, Albert Graichen, #7367
Kane, Albert Graichen, #7368
Kane, Albert Graichen, #7369
Kane, Albert Graichen, #7370
Kane, Albert Graichen, #7371
Kane, Albert Graichen, #7372
Kane, Albert Graichen, #7373
Kane, Albert Graichen, #7374
Kane, Ann Rebecca, #7339
Kane, Ann Rebecca, #7352
Kane, Ann Rebecca, #7353
Kane, Ann Rebecca, #7354
Kane, Ann Rebecca, #7355
Kane, Ann Rebecca, #7356
Kane, Ann Rebecca, #7357
Kane, Ann Rebecca, #7358
Kane, Blanche Va., #7371
Kane, "Camillis Powell ""Mick", #7364
Kane, "Camillis Powell ""Mick", #7365
Kane, Capitolia, #7343
Kane, "Capitolia ""Sis", #7375

Kane, "Capitolia ""Sis", #7376
Kane, "Capitolia ""Sis", #7377
Kane, Charley Rouse, #7374
Kane, Cornillis P., #7341
Kane, Eva Bell, #7370
Kane, Frank W., #7346
Kane, Frank Ward, #7382
Kane, Frank Ward, #7383
Kane, Frank Ward, #7384
Kane, Hattie B., #7347
Kane, Hattie Belle, #7385
Kane, James Oscar[?], #7372
Kane, John N., #7335
Kane, John N., #7336
Kane, John N., #7348
Kane, John W., #7338
Kane, John W., #7350
Kane, John W., #7351
Kane, Laura V., #7340
Kane, Laura Virginia, #7359
Kane, Laura Virginia, #7360
Kane, Laura Virginia, #7361
Kane, Laura Virginia, #7362
Kane, Laura Virginia, #7363
Kane, Lillian May, #7373
Kane, Maggie, #7351
Kane, Margaret, #7384
Kane, Margaret Ann, #7349
Kane, Margret A., #7337
Kane, Mora Ethel, #7368
Kane, Rosa L., #7345
Kane, Rosa Lillian, #7380
Kane, Rosa Lillian, #7381
Kane, Rosa Lillian, #7391
Kane, Rosa Lillian, #7400
Kane, Rosa Lillian, #7401
Kane, Rosa Lillian, #7402
Kane, Rosa Lillian, #7403
Kane, Theodore Paul, #7369
Kane, Walter Joshua, #7378
Kane, Walter Joshua, #7379
Kane, Walter W., #7344
Karicoff, J.W., #2728
Karras, Elicia Poling, #700
Karras, Justin Poling, #701
Karras, Philip, #686
Karras, Philip, #700
Karras, Philip, #701
Kauffman, Frances, #6975
Kauffman, Lester, #2997
Kauffman, Mary Ann, #7426
Kauffman, MaryAnn, #7431
Kausler, Catarina, #2942
Kausler, Catarina, #2943
Kausler, Catarina, #2944
Kausler, Catarina, #2945
Kausler, Catarina, #2946
Kausler, Catarina, #2947
Kausler, Catarina, #2948
Kausler, Catarina, #2949
Kausler, Catarina, #2950
Kausler, Catarina, #2951
Kausler, Catarina, #2952
Kausler, Catarina, #2953
Kausler, Catarina, #2954
Kausler, Catarina, #2955
Kausler, Catarina, #2956
Kausler, Catarina, #2957
Kausler, Catarina, #2958
Kausler, Catarina, #2959
Kausler, Catarina, #2960

Kausler, Catarina, #2961
Kausler, Catarina, #2962
Kaylor, Isouria, #5033
Kaylor, John W., #5033
Kaylor, Mary (Miss), #5034
Kearns, Mary Jane, #3028
Keating, Edward Smith , #4414
Keating, Fannie Winter, #4392
Keating, Fannie Winter, #4393
Keating, Fannie Winter, #4394
Keating, George Winter, #4397
Keating, George Winter, #4398
Keating, Howard Thomas, #4415
Keating, John, #4390
Keating, John, #4412
Keating, John, #4413
Keating, John, #4414
Keating, John, #4415
Keating, John, #4416
Keating, John, #4417
Keating, John, #4418
Keating, John A., #4356
Keating, John M., #4423
Keating, John Marshall, #4399
Keating, John Marshall, #4400
Keating, Lillie Marshall, #4390
Keating, Lillie Marshall, #4391
Keating, Lottie Russell, #4395
Keating, Lottie Russell, #4396
Keating, Maggie Mason, #4412
Keating, Marion, #4416
Keating, Percy Varnell[?], #4413
Keating, Templie Eugenia, #4417
Keating, Templie Eugenia, #4418
Keblinger, W., #1225
Keedy, Laura Loose, #6953
"Keedy, Jr.", Henry H., #6889
Keefer, Catharine Margaretta, #4060
Keefer, Catharine Margaretta, #4061
Keefer, Catharine Margaretta, #4062
Keefer, Catharine Margaretta, #4063
Keefer, Catharine Margaretta, #4064
Keefer, Catharine Margaretta, #4065
Keefer, Catharine Margaretta, #4066
Keefer, Rev., #8219
Keefer, Rev., #8221
Keiffer, J. Spangler, #5020
Keller, Isaac, #3160
Keller, Isaac, #3170
Kelley, Margaret L., #3646
Kemp, Catharine Ann, #7386
Kemp, Catharine Ann, #7394
Kemp, Catharine Ann, #7395
Kemp, Catharine Ann, #7396
Kemp, Catharine Ann, #7397
Kemp, Granmother, #5861
Kemp, Susanna, #5851
Kemp, Susanna, #5852
Kendall, Alma Nelson, #2932
Kendall, Dorothy Winifred, #2935
Kendall, Findly J., #2922
Kendall, John McNaughton, #2936
Kendall, Katie Elizabeth, #2934
Kendall, Larry, #317

Kendall, Mabel Louise, #2924
Kendall, Mabel Louise, #2933
Kendall, Mabel Louise, #2939
Kendall, Robert McNaughton, #2928
Kendall, Robert McNaughton, #2929
Kendall, Robert McNaughton, #2937
Kendall, Roy McNaughton, #2923
Kendall, Roy McNaughton, #2931
Kendall, Winifred Belle, #2920
Kendall, Winifred Belle, #2929
Kenney, Susan Jean, #6899
Kentner, Cristena, #5853
Kentner, Cristena, #5854
Kentner, Elizabeth, #5854
Kentner, Jacob, #5854
Kerlin, A.K., #2832
Kershner, Benjamin F., #4570
Kershner, Bessie, #323
Kershner, Elizabeth, #4568
Kershner, Fannie G., #363
Kershner, Franklin H., #370
Kershner, Myrtle, #324
Keyes, Jean Woodhead, #6659
Kidd, Ednor Mary, #3929
Kieffer, J. Spangler, #429
Kieffer, J. Spangler, #6801
Kieffer, J.S., #1519
Kieffer, Rev., #6804
Kight, Casper E., #7432
Kight, Casper E., #7433
Kight, Casper E., #7433
Kight, Casper Ellsworth, #7429
Kight, Theodore J., #7432
Kilcher, Ann Candace , #277
Kilcher, James Conrad, #284
Kilcher, Katherine Starr , #276
Kimble, Mary Maxine, #8275
King, Alonzo (Rev.), #3789
King, Alonzo (Rev.), #3811
King, Ella, #429
King, Ella, #430
King, Ella, #431
King, Ella, #432
King, Ella, #433
King, Ella, #434
King, Ella, #435
King, Ella, #436
King, Ella, #437
King, Ella, #438
King, Ella, #439
King, Ella, #440
King, John, #7594
King, John, #7638
King, Tryphena C. (Mrs.), #3796
Kiracofe, Alic J., #5298
Kiracofe, Alice J., #1387
Kiracofe, C.V., #1431
Kiracofe, Catharine Virginia, #1432
Kiracofe, Hannah May, #1431
Kiracofe, J.W., #1384
Kiracofe, J.W., #1431
Kiracofe, J.W., #1432
Kiracofe, John Wesley (Rev.), #1434
Kiracofe, John Wesley (Rev.), #1435
Kiracofe, M. Josephine, #1430
Kiracofe, M. Josephine, #5308
Kiracofe, Mary Josephine, #1401
Kirby, Catharine, #5690
Kirby, Charles H., #5675
Kirby, Edward, #5685
Kirby, Edward S., #5676

INDEX
Pages are not numbered; numbers refer to the entry number at the beginning of each record.

Kirby, Eliza, #5681
Kirby, Eliza, #5682
Kirby, Elizabeth, #5691
Kirby, Hannah, #5686
Kirby, James, #5683
Kirby, John, #5684
Kirby, John A., #5680
Kirby, Joseph, #5692
Kirby, Lucy, #5688
Kirby, MaryE., #5679
Kirby, Sarah, #5687
Kirby, Sarah J., #5678
Kirby, Stephen, #5689
Kirby, Susan E., #5677
Kise, M., #1229
Kissell, Emanuel M. (Mrs.), #502
Kissell, Jacob (Mrs.), #503
Kitzmiller, [infant son], #2432
Kitzmiller, [infant son], #2433
Kitzmiller, Augustus, #2427
Kitzmiller, Augustus, #2428
Kitzmiller, Augustus, #2430
Kitzmiller, Augustus, #2431
Kitzmiller, Augustus, #2441
Kitzmiller, Augustus, #2442
Kitzmiller, Augustus, #2449
Kitzmiller, Augustus Ambrose, #2443
Kitzmiller, Augustus Ambrose, #2444
Kitzmiller, Augustus Ambrose, #2445
Kitzmiller, Bertie L., #2429
Kitzmiller, Bertie Lorena, #2434
Kitzmiller, Blanche, #1124
Kitzmiller, Clementine, #2449
Kitzmiller, Clementine (Wilson), #2441
Kitzmiller, Clementine (Wilson), #2442
Kitzmiller, Eve ___rene, #4514
Kitzmiller, Evelyn Irene, #4532
Kitzmiller, Laverne Earl, #4534
Kitzmiller, LeRoy Iller, #4522
Kitzmiller, Margaret M., #1125
Kitzmiller, Mary V., #2449
Kitzmiller, Mary Wilson, #2435
Kitzmiller, Melvin LeRoy, #4515
Kitzmiller, Melvin[?], #4533
Kitzmiller, Nathaniel, #1085
Kitzmiller, Nevin David, #4516
Kitzmiller, Raymond Eugene, #4517
Kitzmiller, Raymond Eugene, #4541
Kitzmiller, Susan, #2439
Kitzmiller, Susan, #2440
Kitzmiller, Susan, #2448
Kitzmiller, Washington, #2439
Kitzmiller, Washington, #2440

Kitzmiller, Washington, #2448
Kitzmiller, William, #2439
Kitzmiller, William, #2440
Kitzmiller, William, #2448
Kitzmiller Bertie L., , #2436
Kitzmiller Bertie L., , #2437
Kitzmiller Bertie L., , #2438
Kitzmiller[?], LeRoy Iller, #4501
Kline, Charlott, #4500
Kline, David, #4500
Kline, I., #1598
Kline, I., #1600
Kline, Richard, #1868
Kline, Richard, #1869
Kline, Rose E., #4499
Kline, Rose E., #4500
Klose, Ronald, #8264
Klose, Ronald, #8368
Knadle, E.B., #2436
Knadle, E.B., #2437
Knadle, E.B., #2438
Knadler, Bertie K., #2447
Knadler, Bertie Lorena, #2445
Knadler, Bertie Lorena, #2446
Knadler, Dorothy Margaret, #2438
Knadler, E.B., #2445
Knadler, E.B., #2446
Knadler, Edward B., #2429
Knadler, Edward B., #2447
Knadler, Frances Etelka, #2436
Knadler, Ruth Wilson, #2437
Knadler, Ruth Wilson, #2456
Knauss, Anna, #2122
Knauss, Anthony, #2129
Knauss, Antonis, #2122
Knauss, Sarah Louisa, #2128
Knauss, Sarah Louisa, #2129
Knauss, Sarah Lousia, #2122
Knauus, Anna, #2129
Kneale, Gladys Matilda (Grayston), #4752
Kneale, Harry, #4742
Knecht, Robert William, #2998
Knepper, Freddie[?], #7093
Knepper, George, #7091
Knepper, Lewis F., #7033
Knepper, Lewis F., #7034
Knepper, Myrtle V., #7094
Knepper, Nellie D., #7092
Knode, Alonzo, #2886
Knode, Amelia, #2111
Knode, Blackford Westenhaver, #2882
Knode, Blackford Westenhaver, #2883
Knode, Blackford Westenhaver, #2884
Knode, Blackford Westenhaver, #2885
Knode, Blackford Westenhaver, #2886
Knode, Charles Lane, #2912
Knode, Charles Lane, #2917
Knode, Edgar Lane, #2916
Knode, Ella, #2883
Knode, John Cadwallader, #2899
Knode, John Calvin, #2887
Knode, John Calvin, #2888

Knode, John Hubert, #2918
Knode, John Ott, #2897
Knode, John Ott, #2898
Knode, John Ott, #2899
Knode, John Ott[?], #2890
Knode, Louise Blackford, #2891
Knode, Louise Blackford, #2892
Knode, Louise Blackford, #2900
Knode, Louise Blackford, #2901
Knode, Louise Blackford, #2906
Knode, Lula, #2885
Knode, Mary C., #2912
Knode, Saml., #2912
Knode, Samuel, #2919
Knode, Samuel C., #2913
Knode, Samuel C., #2914
Knode, Samuel C., #2916
Knode, Willard Westenhaver, #2889
Knode, William, #2884
Knodle, Mary A., #6708
Knodle, Mary Ann, #6707
Knodle, William, #6701
Knodle, William, #6706
Knouff, Sarah (Miss), #508
Knox, [female], #7659
Knox, [female], #7670
Knox, Charles McLean, #7617
Knox, Charles McLean, #7618
Knox, Charles McLean, #7619
Knox, Charles McLean, #7645
Knox, Charles McLean, #7658
Knox, Charles McLean, #7677
Knox, Elizabeth, #7630
Knox, Elizabeth, #7631
Knox, Elizabeth Harriet, #7620
Knox, Elizabeth Harriet, #7621
Knox, Elizabeth Harriet, #7646
Knox, Elizabeth Harriet, #7660
Knox, Euphemia M., #7644
Knox, Euphemia Mason, #7614
Knox, Euphemia Mason, #7615
Knox, Euphemia Mason, #7616
Knox, Euphemia Mason, #7657
Knox, Helen M., #7642
Knox, Helen Margaret, #7608
Knox, Helen Margaret, #7609
Knox, Helen Margaret, #7610
Knox, Helen Margaret, #7655
Knox, John, #7601
Knox, John, #7605
Knox, John, #7606
Knox, John, #7607
Knox, John, #7635
Knox, John, #7639
Knox, John, #7641
Knox, John, #7654
Knox, Jos. H. Mason, #7619
Knox, Jos. H. Mason, #7645
Knox, Margaret, #7651
Knox, Margaret, #7652
Knox, Margaret, #7653
Knox, Margaret, #7654
Knox, Margaret, #7655
Knox, Margaret, #7656
Knox, Margaret, #7657
Knox, Margaret, #7658
Knox, Margaret, #7659
Knox, Margaret, #7660
Knox, Margaret, #7661
Knox, Margaret, #7669

Knox, Martha Virginia, #7622
Knox, Martha Virginia, #7623
Knox, Martha Virginia, #7661
Knox, Martha Virginia , #7647
Knox, Rachel Rebecca, #7599
Knox, Rachel Rebecca, #7600
Knox, Rachel Rebecca, #7601
Knox, Rachel Rebecca, #7639
Knox, Rachel Rebecca, #7652
Knox, Rebecca (Mrs.), #7667
Knox, Rebecca Hodge (Mrs.), #7626
Knox, Samuel, #7594
Knox, Samuel, #7597
Knox, Samuel, #7598
Knox, Samuel, #7599
Knox, Samuel, #7600
Knox, Samuel, #7601
Knox, Samuel, #7602
Knox, Samuel, #7602
Knox, Samuel, #7603
Knox, Samuel, #7603
Knox, Samuel, #7604
Knox, Samuel, #7604
Knox, Samuel, #7605
Knox, Samuel, #7606
Knox, Samuel, #7607
Knox, Samuel, #7608
Knox, Samuel, #7609
Knox, Samuel, #7610
Knox, Samuel, #7611
Knox, Samuel, #7612
Knox, Samuel, #7613
Knox, Samuel, #7614
Knox, Samuel, #7615
Knox, Samuel, #7616
Knox, Samuel, #7617
Knox, Samuel, #7618
Knox, Samuel, #7619
Knox, Samuel, #7620
Knox, Samuel, #7621
Knox, Samuel, #7622
Knox, Samuel, #7623
Knox, Samuel, #7635
Knox, Samuel, #7638
Knox, Samuel, #7639
Knox, Samuel, #7640
Knox, Samuel, #7640
Knox, Samuel, #7641
Knox, Samuel, #7642
Knox, Samuel, #7643
Knox, Samuel, #7644
Knox, Samuel, #7645
Knox, Samuel, #7646
Knox, Samuel, #7647
Knox, Samuel, #7650
Knox, Samuel, #7652
Knox, Samuel, #7653
Knox, Samuel, #7653
Knox, Samuel, #7654
Knox, Samuel, #7655
Knox, Samuel, #7656
Knox, Samuel, #7657
Knox, Samuel, #7658
Knox, Samuel, #7659
Knox, Samuel, #7660
Knox, Samuel, #7661
Knox, Samuel, #7668
Knox, Samuel, #7672
Knox, Sarah M., #7643
Knox, Sarah Mary, #7611
Knox, Sarah Mary, #7612

INDEX
Pages are not numbered; numbers refer to the entry number at the beginning of each record.

Knox, Sarah Mary, #7613
Knox, Sarah Mary, #7656
Kohr, Ethel B., #1835
Koons, Anna Bell, #851
Koons, Donald W., #849
Koons, G. Clinton, #846
Koons, Harry C., #847
Koons, Margaret V., #848
Koons, Melvin[?] F., #852
Koons, Nancy Lee, #853
Koons, Rayetta, #845
Koons, Ruth N., #850
Koontz, Agnes C., #2847
Koontz, Blanche, #2836
Koontz, Blanche M., #2846
Koontz, Edna E., #2849
Koontz, Elmer W., #2853
Koontz, Floyd L., #2843
Koontz, Floyd L., #2852
Koontz, Floyd Leslie, #2856
Koontz, Fred E., #2837
Koontz, Fred E., #2848
Koontz, Gladys F., #2851
Koontz, H.C., #2860
Koontz, Harry C., #2838
Koontz, Harry C., #2850
Koontz, Henry C., #2839
Koontz, Henry C., #2844
Koontz, Henry C., #2855
Koontz, Henry C., #2861
Koontz, Henry C., #4930
Koontz, Leona V., #2842
Koontz, Leona V., #2854
Koontz, Willie M., #2845
Koontz, Willie V., #2840
Koontz, Willmina Virginia (Mrs.), #2855
Koontz, , #2857
Kottcamp, A.Francis, #3452
Kratz, Anna E., #7236
Kratz, Elsie, #7008
Kratz, Elsie, #7009
Kratz, Elsie, #7010
Kratz, Elsie, #7011
Kratz, Elsie, #7012
Kratz, Elsie, #7013
Kratz, Elsie, #7014
Kratz, Elsie, #7015
Kratz, Elsie, #7218
Kratz, Elsie, #7223
Kratz, Elsie, #7240
Kraus, Mollie, #7364
Kretzer, Benj. F., #6586
Kretzer, Benjamin F., #6607
Kretzer, Henrietta, #6587
Kretzer, Henrietta, #6608
Kretzer, Hyatt, #39
Kroft, Abraham, #185
Kroft, Abraham, #187
Kroft, Catherine (Ross), #186
Kroft, Charlotte, #194
Kroft, David, #189
Kroft, Drusilla Katherine, #191
Kroft, Elizabeth, #190
Kroft, John, #188
Kroft, Katharine, #195
Kroft, Mary Jane, #192
Kroft, Sarah Ann, #193
Krouse, [father of Elizabeth], #8035

Krouse, [father of Elizabeth], #8036
Krouse, [father of Elizabeth], #8037
Krouse, Elizabeth, #7962
Krouse, Elizabeth, #7963
Krouse, Elizabeth, #7964
Krouse, Elizabeth, #7965
Krouse, Elizabeth, #7966
Krouse, Elizabeth, #7967
Krouse, Elizabeth, #7968
Krouse, Elizabeth, #7969
Krouse, Elizabeth, #7970
Krouse, Elizabeth, #7971
Krouse, Elizabeth, #7972
Krouse, Elizabeth, #7973
Krouse, Elizabeth, #8008
Krouse, Geo. E., #5041
Krouse, Mary, #7963
Krouse, Mazie K. (Mrs.), #5041
Krouse, Peter, #7963
Krug, Rebecca, #6095
Kugler, Phyllis, #6697
Kuhn, Ada, #1821
Kuhn, Ada, #1822
Kuhn, Ada Viola, #1800
Kuhn, Ada Viola, #1801
Kuhn, Ada Viola, #8065
Kuhn, Ada Viola, #8099
Kuhn, Ada Viola, #8100
Kuhn, Ada Violet, #1811
Kuhn, Anna Amelia, #1782
Kuhn, Anna Amelia, #1783
Kuhn, Anna Amelia, #1806
Kuhn, Anna Amelia, #8071
Kuhn, Anna Amelia, #8082
Kuhn, Anna Amelia, #8089
Kuhn, Anna Amelia, #8090
Kuhn, Edward A., #1776
Kuhn, Edward A., #1808
Kuhn, Edward Abraham, #1798
Kuhn, Edward Abraham, #1799
Kuhn, Edward Abraham, #8093
Kuhn, Edward Abraham, #8094
Kuhn, Elva, #1815
Kuhn, Elva, #1816
Kuhn, Elva Louise, #1814
Kuhn, Elva Louise, #8068
Kuhn, Elva Louise, #8104
Kuhn, Frank, #1787
Kuhn, Frank, #1788
Kuhn, Frank, #8074
Kuhn, Frank Brewer, #1812
Kuhn, Frank Brewer, #8066
Kuhn, Frank Brewer, #8101
Kuhn, Frank Brewer, #8102
Kuhn, Harry, #1805
Kuhn, Harry G., #1777
Kuhn, Harry G., #1778
Kuhn, Harry G., #1793
Kuhn, Harry G., #8079
Kuhn, Harry Gustavus, #8087
Kuhn, Harry Gustavus, #8088
Kuhn, Jacob, #1789
Kuhn, Jacob, #1790
Kuhn, Jacob, #8076
Kuhn, Jacob Frederic, #1810
Kuhn, Jacob Frederic, #8064
Kuhn, Jacob Frederic, #8097
Kuhn, Jacob Frederic, #8098
Kuhn, Jacob Frederick, #1794

Kuhn, Jacob Frederick, #1795
Kuhn, Jacob Frederick, #8081
Kuhn, Jacob Frederick, #8084
Kuhn, John, #1777
Kuhn, John, #1778
Kuhn, John, #1779
Kuhn, John, #1780
Kuhn, John, #1782
Kuhn, John, #1783
Kuhn, John, #1784
Kuhn, John, #1785
Kuhn, John, #1786
Kuhn, John, #1787
Kuhn, John, #1788
Kuhn, John, #1789
Kuhn, John, #1790
Kuhn, John, #1793
Kuhn, John, #1794
Kuhn, John, #1795
Kuhn, John, #1796
Kuhn, John, #1797
Kuhn, John, #1798
Kuhn, John, #1799
Kuhn, John, #1800
Kuhn, John, #1801
Kuhn, John, #1802
Kuhn, John, #1803
Kuhn, John, #8071
Kuhn, John, #8072
Kuhn, John, #8075
Kuhn, John, #8076
Kuhn, John, #8079
Kuhn, John, #8081
Kuhn, John, #8087
Kuhn, John, #8088
Kuhn, John, #8089
Kuhn, John, #8090
Kuhn, John, #8091
Kuhn, John, #8092
Kuhn, John, #8093
Kuhn, John, #8094
Kuhn, John, #8095
Kuhn, John, #8096
Kuhn, John, #8097
Kuhn, John, #8098
Kuhn, John, #8099
Kuhn, John, #8100
Kuhn, John, #8101
Kuhn, John, #8102
Kuhn, John, #8103
Kuhn, John, #8104
Kuhn, John Joseph, #1785
Kuhn, John Joseph, #1786
Kuhn, John Joseph, #1809
Kuhn, John Joseph, #8063
Kuhn, John Joseph, #8073
Kuhn, John Joseph, #8085
Kuhn, John Joseph, #8086
Kuhn, John Joseph, #8095
Kuhn, John Joseph, #8096
Kuhn, Libbie, #1813
Kuhn, Libbie, #8067
Kuhn, Libbie G., #1802
Kuhn, Libbie G., #8103
Kuhn, Mahala, #1777
Kuhn, Mahala, #1778
Kuhn, Mahala, #1780
Kuhn, Mahala, #8077
Kuhn, Mahala, #8078
Kuhn, Mahala, #8079
Kuhn, Mahala, #8081

Kuhn, Mahala, #8087
Kuhn, Mahala, #8088
Kuhn, Mahala, #8089
Kuhn, Mahala, #8090
Kuhn, Mahala, #8091
Kuhn, Mahala, #8092
Kuhn, Mahala, #8093
Kuhn, Mahala, #8094
Kuhn, Mahala, #8095
Kuhn, Mahala, #8096
Kuhn, Mahala, #8097
Kuhn, Mahala, #8098
Kuhn, Mahala, #8099
Kuhn, Mahala, #8100
Kuhn, Mahala, #8101
Kuhn, Mahala, #8102
Kuhn, Mahala, #8103
Kuhn, Mahala, #8104
Kuhn, Mahala (Brewer), #1791
Kuhn, Mahala (Brewer), #1792
Kuhn, Mahalah, #1804
Kuhn, Mahalah, #8071
Kuhn, Mahalah, #8072
Kuhn, Mary Amanda, #1796
Kuhn, Mary Amanda, #1797
Kuhn, Mary Amanda, #8083
Kuhn, Mary Amanda, #8091
Kuhn, Mary Amanda, #8092
Kuhn, Minnie Amanda, #1784
Kuhn, Minnie Amanda, #1807
Kuhn, Minnie Amanda, #8072
Kurtz, Benjamin, #3148
Kurtz, Benjamin, #3150
Kurtz, Benjamin, #3152
Kutern, Maria Elizabeth, #2154
Kutern, Maria Elizabeth, #2155
Kutern, Maria Elizabeth, #2156
Kyle, Marsha, #7351
Lachman, G.W., #7762
Lackman, G.W., #7798
Lackman, Margaret (Aughinbaugh), #7797
Lafferty, Anna, #1889
Lafferty, George, #1910
Lafferty, Van, #1870
Lafferty, Van, #1879
Lafferty, Van, #1898
Lafferty, Van, #1899
Lambert, Catherine, #3655
Lambert, Dale Kirkham[?], #3648
Lambert, David Orien, #3649
Lambert, Donald ____, #3647
Lambert, Kristie Anne, #3656
Lanahan, Rev., #7171
Lancy, Geneva, #7095
Lancy, Maggie M., #7096
Lancy, , #7036
Landis, Harriet Elizabeth, #84
Landis, Hattie E., #74
Landis, Joseph, #72
Landis, Joseph, #81
Landis, Joseph, #86
Landis, Lillian Mae, #70
Landis, Lillie May, #75
Landis, Rebecca, #82
Landis, Rebecca Ripple, #73
Lane, Catherine, #8394
Lane, John C., #2913
Lane, John C., #8370
Lane, Mary, #8373
Lane, Mary, #8381

INDEX
Pages are not numbered; numbers refer to the entry number at the beginning of each record.

Lane, Mary Catharine, #2913
Lane, Mary Catharine, #2915
Lane, Mary Catharine, #2916
Lane, Mary Catharine, #2919
Lane, Seth, #8393
Lane, Seth, #8394
Lane[?], William (Rev.), #2116
Langdon, Almira, #372
Langdon, Lilian E., #372
Langdon, Lilian E., #375
Langdon, William, #372
Lantz, Annie C., #5348
Lantz, Martha, #570
Lantz, Martha H.[?], #530
Lantz, Martha Hadessah, #522
Lantz, Martha U.[?] (Miss), #571
Lantz, Mary B., #558
Larew, Abraham, #1160
Larew, Jacob, #1161
Larew, Noah, #1158
Larew, Rachel, #1159
Larque, Jenie[?] A.[?], #3771
Larque, Jenie[?] A.[?], #3781
Latrobe, Agnes Catherine, #7561
Latrobe, Agnes Catherine, #7572
Latrobe, Agnes Catherine, #7573
Latrobe, B.H., #7586
Latrobe, B.H., #7591
Latrobe, Benjamin H., #7558
Latrobe, Benjamin Henry, #7574
Latrobe, Benjamin Henry, #7575
Latrobe, C.H., #7580
Latrobe, Charles H., #7560
Latrobe, Charles H., #7563
Latrobe, Charles H., #7578
Latrobe, Charles H., #7589
Latrobe, Charles H., #7590
Latrobe, Charles Hazelhurst, #7566
Latrobe, Charles Hazelhurst, #7567
Latrobe, Edward, #7568
Latrobe, Edward, #7569
Latrobe, Edward, #7586
Latrobe, Eleanor Breckenridge, #7579
Latrobe, Ellen Hazelhurst, #7591
Latrobe, Elsie Gamble, #7578
Latrobe, Gamble, #7580
Latrobe, J.E., #7586
Latrobe, L.B., #7580
Latrobe, Laura Riggs, #7585
Latrobe, Letitia B., #7578
Latrobe, Lettie G., #7589
Latrobe, Maria Eleanor, #7576
Latrobe, Maria Eleanor, #7577
Latrobe, Mary E., #7583
Latrobe, Mary Elizabeth, #7562
Latrobe, Mary Elizabeth, #7570
Latrobe, Mary Elizabeth, #7571

Latrobe, Rosa Wirt (Robinson), #7590
"Latrobe, Jr.", B.H., #7562
"Latrobe, Jr.", B.H., #7563
"Latrobe, Jr.", B.H. (Rev.), #7585
"Latrobe, Jr.", Benjamin H., #7565
Laurence, Annie C., #5350
Laurence, Annie C., #5351
Laurence, Annie C., #5352
Laurence, Emma V.[?], #5351
Laurence, Mary E., #5350
Laurence, William, #5346
Laurence, William, #5348
Laurence, William, #5350
Laurence, William, #5351
Laurence, William, #5352
Laurence, Willie K., #5352
Lawrence, Laura F.[?], #7765
Lawrence, Mary E., #5349
Layman, Diana Lynn, #5287
Layman, Wm., #1391
Laymon, Clifford R., #5291
Laymon, Clifford Roy, #1412
Laymon, Dawn Marie, #1413
Laymon, Dawn Marie, #5292
Laymon, Deana Lynn, #5289
Laymon, Diana, #1410
Laymon, Dilliom[?], #5289
Laymon, Dilliom[?], #5290
Laymon, Dilliom[?], #5291
Laymon, Dilliom[?], #5292
Laymon, Dilliom[?], #5293
Laymon, John C., #5293
Laymon, John Carroll, #1414
Laymon, Phyllis, #1410
Laymon, Phyllis, #1411
Laymon, Phyllis, #1412
Laymon, Phyllis, #1413
Laymon, Phyllis, #1414
Laymon, William, #1410
Laymon, William, #1411
Laymon, William, #1412
Laymon, William, #1413
Laymon, William, #1414
Laymon, William, #5302
Laymon, Wm. H., #5288
"Laymon, Jr.", William H., #1411
"Laymon, Jr.", Wm. H., #5290
Leary, Edward, #3825
Leary, Edward, #3826
Leary, Edward, #3829
Leary, Edward, #3840
Leary, Elizabeth, #3825
Leary, Elizabeth, #3826
Leary, Elizabeth, #3829
Leary, Elizabeth (Brown), #3839
Leary, George B., #3826
Leary, Hadassah, #3829
Leary, Hadassah, #3825
Leashman, R.C., #5931
Leasure, Anna Atelia[?], #8382
Leasure, Anna Atelia[?], #8383
Leasure, Catharine, #8392
Leasure, Christian, #8372
Leasure, Christian, #8405
Leasure, Elijah C., #8404
Leasure, Elijah C.[?], #8386

Leasure, John Henry, #8397
Leasure, John Henry, #8403
Leasure, Margaret Allis, #8385
Leasure, Margaret Allis[?], #8379
Leasure, Martin Luther, #8396
Leasure, Martin Luther, #8401
Leasure, Mary Elizabeth, #8400
Leasure, Sarah Jane, #8384
Leasure, Sarah Jane, #8398
Leasure, Susan Catharine, #8402
Leasure, William Henry, #8395
Leasure, William Henry, #8399
Leatherman, Elva (Young), #2834
Leatherman, Godfrey, #4494
Leatherman, Lloyd Young, #2835
Leatherman, William Brown, #2832
Leatherman, William Brown, #2833
Lechron[?], Danl. H., #8374
Lee, Auburn R., #5934
Lee, Charles B., #5943
Lee, Chas. Bery, #5930
Lee, Clarence C., #5952
Lee, Estelle, #5935
Lee, Farris C., #5946
Lee, Grace, #5937
Lee, Grace A., #5939
Lee, Grace Adelaide, #5950
Lee, Hannah, #2700
Lee, Hannah, #2701
Lee, Hannah, #2702
Lee, Hannah, #2703
Lee, Hannah, #3942
Lee, Hannah, #3943
Lee, Hannah, #3944
Lee, Hannah, #3945
Lee, Harold Mathew, #5940
Lee, Harold Matthew, #5951
Lee, Mace Alta, #5949
Lee, Martha A., #5933
Lee, Martha A., #5934
Lee, Martha A., #5935
Lee, Martha A., #5936
Lee, Martha A., #5937
Lee, Martha A., #5938
Lee, Martha A., #5942
Lee, Martha Adelaide, #5929
Lee, Martha E., #5947
Lee, Mary, #5936
Lee, Mary M., #5912
Lee, Mary M., #5948
Lee, Matthew R., #5911
Lee, Matthew R., #5932
Lee, Matthew R., #5934
Lee, Matthew R., #5935
Lee, Matthew R., #5936
Lee, Matthew R., #5937
Lee, Matthew R., #5941
Lee, Matthew R., #5942
Lee, Matthew Richard, #5928
Lee, Richard A., #5945
Lee, Richard Auburn, #5927
Lee, Ruth E., #5944
Lees[?], Elizabeth Ann (Cochran), #783
Lefevere, Ann W., #3196
Lefevere, Ann W., #3197
Lefevere, Samuel, #3196
Legget, Jno. E. (Dr.), #647
Lehman, Anna May, #239

Lehman, Annie M., #247
Lehman, Clegget M., #231
Lehman, Cleggett M., #246
Lehman, Cleggett Middlekauff, #237
Lehman, Elizabeth A., #244
Lehman, Elizabeth A., #246
Lehman, Elizabeth A., #247
Lehman, Elizabeth A., #248
Lehman, Elizabeth A., #249
Lehman, Emma Florence, #238
Lehman, J. William, #233
Lehman, John F., #245
Lehman, John F., #246
Lehman, John F., #247
Lehman, John F., #248
Lehman, John F., #248
Lehman, John F., #249
Lehman, John S., #230
Lehman, John S., #235
Lehman, John S., #237
Lehman, John S., #238
Lehman, John S., #239
Lehman, John S., #240
Lehman, John S., #241
Lehman, John S., #242
Lehman, John S., #243
Lehman, John William, #243
Lehman, Lizzie, #242
Lehman, Lizzie A., #236
Lehman, Lizzie A., #237
Lehman, Lizzie A., #238
Lehman, Lizzie A., #239
Lehman, Lizzie A., #240
Lehman, Lizzie A., #241
Lehman, Lizzie A., #242
Lehman, Lizzie A., #243
Lehman, Lizzie M., #232
Lehman, Maud, #234
Lehman, Maud, #241
Lehman, Minnie K., #249
Lehman, Minnie Kate, #240
Leisure, Christian, #8376
Leisure, Elijah, #8371
Leisure, Elijah, #8391
Leisure, Elizabeth, #8378
Leisure, Susannah, #8377
Leiter, Abraham, #6984
Leiter, Abraham, #6991
Leiter, Ann, #525
Leiter, Ann, #552
Leiter, Anna Mary, #531
Leiter, Anna Mary, #537
Leiter, Barbara Virginia, #533
Leiter, Barbara Virginia, #539
Leiter, Barbara Virginia, #549
Leiter, Barbara Virginia, #556
Leiter, David, #578
Leiter, David, #579
Leiter, Edna (Martin), #585
Leiter, Edward Benton, #6999
Leiter, Eliza Jane, #6997
Leiter, Elizabeth M., #565
Leiter, Emma Susan, #6986
Leiter, George A., #563
Leiter, George Abraham, #553
Leiter, George Thompson, #6996
Leiter, J. Carrington, #567
Leiter, J. Harry, #566
Leiter, J. Harry, #568
Leiter, James F., #529
Leiter, James F., #557

INDEX
Pages are not numbered; numbers refer to the entry number at the beginning of each record.

Leiter, James F., #571
Leiter, James Freeland, #522
Leiter, James Freeland, #555
Leiter, James M. (Mrs.), #498
Leiter, James W.[?], #554
Leiter, James William, #545
Leiter, James William, #546
Leiter, Jeremiah, #578
Leiter, John William, #6995
Leiter, Joseph, #523
Leiter, Joseph, #524
Leiter, Joseph, #551
Leiter, Joseph, #6993
Leiter, Joseph (Mrs.), #497
Leiter, Joseph G., #535
Leiter, Joseph G., #541
Leiter, Leevi Ziegler, #534
Leiter, Leevi Ziegler, #564
Leiter, Levi Zeigler, #540
Leiter, Levi Zeigler, #559
Leiter, Lizzie Carrie, #557
Leiter, Lizzie Carver, #536
Leiter, Lizzie Carver, #542
Leiter, Lizzie Carver, #550
Leiter, Louisa (Miller), #6985
Leiter, Louisa Miller, #7006
Leiter, Lydia Ann, #6987
Leiter, Marsha[?] H., #557
Leiter, Martha Alice, #547
Leiter, Martha Alice, #548
Leiter, Mary Beatty, #6994
Leiter, Mary Beatty, #7004
Leiter, Mary Catherine, #7000
Leiter, Mary Elizabeth, #569
Leiter, Mary Elizebth [sic], #526
Leiter, Sarah Drusilla, #6998
Leiter, Sarah Drusilla, #7005
Leiter, Theresa (Downing), #580
Leiter, Titus Benton, #532
Leiter, Titus Benton, #538
Leiter, Titus Benton, #560
Leiter, Vannie[?] Kate, #543
Leiter, Vannie[?] Kate, #544
Leiter, Virginia (Eckstine), #582
Leiter, , #583
"Leiter, Jr.", Abraham, #7003
"Leiter, Jr.", Samuel, #579
"Leiter, Jr.", Samuel, #581
"Leiter, Sr.", Abraham, #7002
"Leiter, Sr.", Samuel, #581
"Leiter, Sr.", Samuel, #583
Leonard, Anamay, #924
Leonard, Anamay, #929
Leonard, Cary, #927
Leonard, Cary, #937
Leonard, Lara Lee, #926
Leonard, Laura, #920
Leonard, Laura Lee, #930
Leonard, Maggie, #931
Leonard, Maggie C., #925
Leonard, Matilda, #923
Leonard, Matilda, #943
Leonard, Matilda, #960
Leonard, Walter, #921
Leonard, Walter, #922
Leonard, Walter, #939
Leonard, Walter, #958
Leonard, William Henry, #928

Leonard, William Henry, #936
Lerch, Anna Elizabeth, #2124
Lerch, Harvey Joseph, #2125
Lerch, Harvey Joseph, #2130
Lerch, Hiram Anthony, #2126
Lerch, Hiram Anthony, #2131
Lerch, Joseph, #2120
Lerch, Joseph, #2121
Lerch, Joseph, #2128
Lerch, Joseph, #2148
Lerch, Miranda Adaline, #2123
Lerch, Miranda Adaline, #2136
Lerch, Reuben, #2120
Lerch, Reuben, #2121
Lerch, Reuben, #2123
Lerch, Reuben, #2124
Lerch, Reuben, #2125
Lerch, Reuben, #2126
Lerch, Reuben, #2127
Lerch, Reuben, #2128
Lerch, Reuben, #2130
Lerch, Reuben, #2131
Lerch, Reuben O., #2148
Lerch, Reuben O., #2149
Lerch, Reubon O., #2133
Lerch, Sarah, #2123
Lerch, Sarah, #2124
Lerch, Sarah, #2125
Lerch, Sarah, #2126
Lerch, Sarah, #2127
Lerch, Sarah, #2130
Lerch, Sarah, #2131
Lerch, Sarah Louisa (Knauss), #2134
Lerch, Sarah Louise (Mrs.), #2143
Lerch, Susan, #2120
Lerch, Susan, #2121
Lerch, Susan, #2128
Lerch, Susan Ottila, #2127
Lerch, Susie O., #2150
Lerch, Susin O., #177
Lesher, John, #1593
Lesher, John, #1613
Lesher, Nancy Katherine, #1613
Leslie, James, #2863
Leslie, James, #2864
Leslie, James, #2865
Leslie, James, #2879
Leslie, James H., #2864
Leslie, James H.[?], #2879
Leslie, Jane, #2863
Leslie, Jane, #2864
Leslie, Jane, #2865
Leslie, Jane, #2879
Leslie, Mary Elisabeth, #2863
Leslie, Susan J.[?], #2865
Letch, Catharine, #7943
Letch, Catharine, #7944
Lewis, Almira, #5900
Lewis, Almira, #5902
Libby, Noah W., #6937
Lightle, Leora M., #1514
Line, Catharine, #2451
Line, Clara Virginia, #420
Line, Clara Virginia, #425
Line, Elizabeth, #3096
Line, Elizabeth, #3097
Line, Elizabeth, #3098
Line, Elizabeth, #3099
Line, Elizabeth, #3100

Line, Elizabeth, #3101
Line, F_____[?], #421
Line, Flora B., #426
Line, Florra Bell, #418
Line, Frank Howard, #427
Line, Ida Elizabeth, #419
Line, Ida Elizabeth, #424
Line, Malinda C., #428
Line, Malinda Catherine, #423
Line, Malinda Cathrine, #417
Line, Suana (Susan?), #2238
Line, Susan, #2184
Line, Thomas Franklin, #416
Line, Thomas Franklin, #422
Line, , #4869
Linebaugh, Benjamin F., #2733
Linebaugh , Mary E. (Mrs.), #2756
Linger, Margaret Ruth (Miss), #3414
"Linger, Sr.", John, #6097
"Linger, Sr.", John, #6098
Link, Adam, #335
Link, Bill, #337
Link, Dennis, #338
Link, John, #334
Link, Lester, #339
Link, Margaret M., #325
Link, Margaret M., #326
Link, Margaret M., #327
Link, Margaret M., #328
Link, Margaret M., #329
Link, Margaret M., #330
Link, Margaret M., #331
Link, Margaret M., #332
Link, Margaret M., #333
Link, Margaret May, #323
Link, Margaret May, #324
Link, Martha, #342
Link, Rebecca, #340
Link, Sally, #341
Link, Wesley, #336
Link, Wm., #333
Link, Wm., #334
Link, Wm., #335
Link, Wm., #336
Link, Wm., #337
Link, Wm., #338
Link, Wm., #339
Link, Wm., #340
Link, Wm., #341
Link, Wm., #342
Liskey, Argielle Buff, #78
Liskey, Catherine Marie, #2401
Liskey, Emma Theresa, #2392
Liskey, Franklin Clyde, #2402
Liskey, Ida Catherine (Brown), #2386
Liskey, Ida Catherine (Brown), #2387
Liskey, John Michael, #2390
Liskey, John Michael, #2391
Liskey, Leon Wilson, #2399
Liskey, Leon Wilson, #2400
Liskey, Lillian Mae (Landis), #83
Liskey, Lloyd Wayne, #77
Liskey, Luther Harring, #2388
Liskey, Luther Harring, #2389
Liskey, Roberft Clinton, #2384
Liskey, Roberft Clinton, #2385
Liskey, Robert Brown, #2397
Liskey, Robert Brown, #2398

Liskey, Robert Clinton, #2383
Liskey, Robert Clinton, #2388
Liskey, Robert Clinton, #2389
Liskey, Robert Clinton, #2390
Liskey, Robert Clinton, #2391
Liskey, Robert Clinton, #2392
Liskey, Robert Clinton, #2393
Liskey, Robert Clinton, #2394
Liskey, Robert Clinton, #2395
Liskey, Robert Clinton, #2396
Liskey, Robert Clinton, #2397
Liskey, Robert Clinton, #2398
Liskey, Robert Clinton, #2399
Liskey, Robert Clinton, #2400
Liskey, Robert Clinton, #2401
Liskey, Robert Clinton, #2402
Liskey, Stella Pearl, #2393
Liskey, Stella Pearl, #2394
Liskey, Winnie D., #2395
Liskey, Winnie D., #2396
"Liskey, Jr.", Robert Brown, #71
"Liskey, Jr.", Robert Brown, #76
"Liskey, Sr.", Robert Brown, #70
"Liskey, Sr.", Robert Brown, #80
"Liskey, Sr.", Robert Brown, #85
Litsinger, W.R., #2200
Litten, George M., #8510
Llewelyn, Cordelia Reese, #1920
Llewelyn, Elizabeth, #1920
Llewelyn, Thomas, #1920
Locher[?], Mary, #3274
Lockwood, Henrietta M., #4314
Lockwood, Marietta Maria, #4332
Loflin, Lola, #4334
Logan, Nellie Mildred, #6760
Logan, W., #6744
Long, Abram D., #2819
Long, Abram D., #2827
Long, Abram D., #2828
Long, Abram D., #2829
Long, Abram D., #2830
Long, Abram D., #7544
Long, Abram D., #7553
Long, Abram D., #7554
Long, Abram D., #7555
Long, Abram D., #7556
Long, Abram Devenport, #2817
Long, Abram Devenport, #7542
Long, Ann E., #2819
Long, Ann E., #2827
Long, Ann E., #2828
Long, Ann E., #7553
Long, Ann E., #7554
Long, Ann Elizabeth, #2816
Long, Ann Elizabeth, #2818
Long, Ann Elizabeth, #7543
Long, Ann Elizabeth, #7544
Long, Ann Elizabeth, #7551
Long, Anthony, #5856
Long, Catherine, #5856
Long, Earl Downey, #2778
Long, Elizabeth, #2820
Long, Elizabeth, #7545
Long, Elizabeth D., #2826
Long, Elizabeth D., #7552
Long, Elizabeth M., #2831
Long, Elizabeth M., #7557
Long, Elizabeth Mary, #2827
Long, Elizabeth Mary, #7553
Long, Georgia A. (Miss), #5043
Long, Guy, #2806

INDEX
Pages are not numbered; numbers refer to the entry number at the beginning of each record.

Long, Guy, #2807
Long, Guy, #2808
Long, Guy, #2809
Long, Guy, #2810
Long, Guy, #2811
Long, Guy, #2812
Long, Guy, #2813
Long, Guy, #2814
Long, Guy Mohler, #2777
Long, Hadassah, #4023
Long, Hadassah, #4024
Long, Hadassah (Brown), #3843
Long, Hadassah (Downey), #3708
Long, Helen, #2807
Long, Helen, #2808
Long, Helen Saxton, #4027
Long, Helen Saxton, #4028
Long, I. Peaerle, #2776
Long, I. Pearle, #2789
Long, I. Pearle, #2790
Long, I. Pearle, #2791
Long, I. Pearle, #2792
Long, I. Pearle, #2793
Long, I. Pearle, #2794
Long, I. Pearle, #2795
Long, I. Pearle, #2796
Long, I. Pearle, #2797
Long, Ida C., #2775
Long, Ida C., #2782
Long, Ida C., #2787
Long, Ida C., #2788
Long, Ida C., #2805
Long, Ina Pearle, #2762
Long, Ina Pearle, #4018
Long, Ina Pearle, #4019
Long, Isaac S., #4032
Long, James, #2821
Long, James, #2822
Long, James, #7546
Long, James, #7547
Long, John, #2823
Long, John, #2824
Long, John, #7548
Long, John, #7549
Long, John W., #5041
Long, Joshua, #2761
Long, Joshua, #2774
Long, Joshua, #2781
Long, Joshua, #2786
Long, "Joshua ""Papa", #2804
Long, Lena, #2811
Long, Lena, #2812
Long, Lena M., #4030
Long, Lola Blanche, #2780
Long, Lola Blanche, #2785
Long, Maria, #5855
Long, Maria, #5856
Long, Mary, #204
Long, Maxwell B., #4336
Long, Maxwell B., #4338
Long, Merle Chester, #2809
Long, Merle Chester, #2810
Long, Minnie (Burgan), #2806
Long, Minnie S., #4029
Long, Pearle, #4013
Long, Sally, #7554
Long, Saly, #2828
Long, Simon, #4031
Long, Simon Welty, #2784

Long, Simon Wlety, #2779
Loose, Anna, #6916
Loose, Anna, #6946
Loose, Carey, #6890
Loose, Carry, #6913
Loose, Grace Cannon[?], #6915
Loose, Henrietta A., #6912
Loose, Henrietta B., #6902
Loose, Henrietta B., #6945
Loose, Henrietta Baectell, #6951
Loose, Henry C., #6886
Loose, Henry C., #6903
Loose, Henry C., #6943
Loose, Henry Clay, #6949
Loose, J. Pearson, #6892
Loose, J. Pearson, #6949
Loose, "Jennie ""(Laura V. Pearson)", #6908
Loose, "Jennie ""(Laura Va.)", #6944
Loose, Jos. B., #6885
Loose, Jos. B., #6901
Loose, Joseph B., #6942
Loose, Joseph Edward, #6907
Loose, Joseph Edward, #6940
Loose, Joseph Pearson, #6909
Loose, Joseph Pearson, #6948
Loose, Laura Virginia, #6889
Loose, Laura Virginia, #6911
Loose, M. Frances, #6888
Loose, Margaret Francie, #6904
Loose, Margaret Francis, #6941
Loose, Mary Francie, #6910
Loose, Mary Lizzie, #6906
Loose, Mary Lizzie, #6939
Loose, Nelly, #6891
Loose, Nelly, #6914
Loose, Samuel Baechtel, #6887
Loose, Samuel Baechtel, #6905
Loose, Trace[?] Cannon, #6954
Lorcch[?], D.B., #971
Lorcch[?], D.B., #972
Lord, Eizabeth Heather E'Lea[?], #6773
Lord, Elizabeth Heather, #6749
Lord, Michelle Louise, #6772
Lorentz, , #6107
Lorrence, F.D., #7159
Loudenslager, Mary E., #2729
Loving, Ruth, #1222
Lowe, Benjamin Franklin, #470
Lowe, Cephias, #225
Lowe, Charles S., #471
Lowe, Charles S., #490
Lowe, Charles Swearingin, #226
Lowe, David Smith, #465
Lowe, Doro Elphrada, #489
Lowe, Doro. E., #472
Lowe, Dousilla, #229
Lowe, Elisa, #227
Lowe, Eliza, #478
Lowe, Elizabeth, #220
Lowe, Elizabeth, #221
Lowe, Elizabeth, #463
Lowe, Elizabeth, #474
Lowe, Elizabeth, #476
Lowe, Elizabeth[?] Etta[?], #483
Lowe, Eveline, #477

Lowe, Frederic, #485
Lowe, James Edmun, #482
Lowe, John, #469
Lowe, John B., #463
Lowe, John B., #474
Lowe, John B., #475
Lowe, John B., #492
Lowe, John Booth, #228
Lowe, Joseph, #224
Lowe, Joseph, #468
Lowe, Joseph, #487
Lowe, Joshua Smith, #467
Lowe, Linthy[?], #479
Lowe, Margret, #484
Lowe, Maria, #221
Lowe, Martin Luther, #473
Lowe, Mary, #222
Lowe, Mary Almeda, #480
Lowe, Rhodai, #491
Lowe, Robert, #219
Lowe, Robert, #221
Lowe, Robert, #463
Lowe, Robert, #474
Lowe, Robert Boothe[?], #488
Lowe, Robert Bothe[?], #466
Lowe, Sinthanna[?], #486
Lowe, Susan R., #493
Lowe, Susannah, #223
Lowe, William, #481
Lower, Wm. T., #3397
Lowery, Bettie B., #233
Lowery, Frank E., #4630
Lowery, William L. (Rev.), #4630
Lowman, Pearl Virginia (Kaetzel), #2982
Lowrie, Harriet, #6113
Lowrie, Harriet, #6114
Lowrie, Harriet, #6115
Lowrie, Harriet, #6116
Lowrie[?], Delia, #6113
Lowrie[?], Eliza, #6115
Lowrie[?], Jane, #6114
Lowrie[?], Martha, #6116
Lowry, Delia Maria, #6136
Lowry, Harriet, #6135
Lowry, Harriet, #6136
Lowry, Harriet, #6137
Lowry, Harriet, #6138
Lowry, Harriet, #6139
Lowry, Harriet Eliza, #6138
Lowry, Jane Sophia, #6137
Lowry, Juliet Rebecca, #6135
Lowry, Martha Ann, #6139
Lowry, , #6101
Luciman, Adelheid, #6008
Lucincna, Adelheid, #6017
Lum, Alta V., #2735
Lum, Alta Virginia, #2746
Lum, Birtha Viola, #2745
Lum, Birtha Viola, #2748
Lum, Catherine (Mrs.), #2754
Lum, Charles Ausker, #2741
Lum, Clara Elizabeth, #2747
Lum, Clara Elizabeth, #2744
Lum, Elizebeth C., #2751
Lum, Elizebeth Cathrine, #2737
Lum, John A., #2760
Lum, John Alvy, #2730
Lum, John Alvy, #2739
Lum, Martha Van Dela, #2743
Lum, Martha Van Della, #2734

Lum, Mary E.M., #2733
Lum, Mary Esty May, #2742
Lum, Minnie M. (Mrs.), #2758
Lum, Oscar A., #2732
Lum, Samuel Luther, #2738
Lum, Samuel Luther, #2750
Lum, Samuel S., #2729
Lum, William E., #2731
Lum, William E., #2749
Lum, William Emory, #2740
Lum, William S., #2728
Lum, William S., #2752
Lum, William Sihon, #2736
Lumm, W.E., #2757
Lumm, William E., #2753
Lumn, Henry, #2336
Lumn, Sara Alice, #2333
Lumn, Sara Alice, #2336
Lupton, Joseph, #1201
Lupton, Joseph, #1201
Lupton, Joseph, #1202
Lupton, Mary, #1201
Lupton, Rachel, #1203
Lutz, Nancy, #1789
Lutz, Nancy, #1790
Lutz, Nancy, #8076
Lyday, Anna, #1614
Lyday, Anna, #1615
Lyday, Anna, #1616
Lyday, Anna, #1617
Lyday, Anna, #1618
Lyday, Anna, #1619
Lyday, Anna, #1620
Lyday, Anna, #1621
Lyday, Anna, #1622
Lyday, Samuel (Mrs.), #501
Lynch, Martin Edward, #5556
Lynch, Martin Edward, #5570
Lynch, Mildred Catherine (Middlekauff) Toms, #5559
Lyons[?], Martha E., #5910
Maasty[?], Ellin B., #5399
Mabe, Ann, #696
Mabe, Ann, #697
Mabe, Marcella Ann, #684
Machs, Benj., #1661
Magaruder[?], Florence Stevinson, #2084
Magruder, Bradley, #3958
Magruder, Henry, #1941
Magruder[?], Bradley[?], #2714
Mahon, Louise J., #214
Main, Anna Mary, #5641
Main, Elisabeth, #5643
Main, George, #5640
Main, George, #5641
Main, George A., #5654
Main, George A., #5655
Main, George Adam, #5644
Main, Henry Luther, #5637
Main, John, #5637
Main, John, #5642
Main, John George, #5654
Main, John George, #5655
Main, Martha, #5637
Main, Marthe, #5636
Main, Mary Elizabeth, #5653
Malone, Hannah, #1680
Malone, Hannah, #4089
Malott, Francis, #588
Malott, Harriett, #580

INDEX
Pages are not numbered; numbers refer to the entry number at the beginning of each record.

Malott, Harriett, #588
Malotte, Frances, #40
Malotte, Frances, #64
Malotte, Frances, #65
Malotte, Frances, #66
Malotte, Frances, #67
Manning, Franklin, #3791
Marders, Elder, #5910
Margan, Rev., #746
Markley, R., #8234
Markwood, H., #3388
Markwood, H., #3389
Markwood, H., #3390
Marshall, Andrew, #7610
Marshall, Andrew, #7642
Marshall, Benjamin A., #7612
Marshall, Benjamin A., #7643
Marshall, Helen Margaret, #7676
Marshall, James H., #7639
Marshall, John H. (Hon.), #7601
Marshall, Rachel Rebecca Knox, #7636
Marshall[?], George H., #4956
Martin, A.C., #3186
Martin, Annah H., #5595
Martin, Annah H., #5612
Martin, Augustus C., #3130
Martin, Daniel, #5608
Martin, Daniel M., #5597
Martin, Edgar Thuston, #4711
Martin, Edna, #581
Martin, Eliza, #3186
Martin, Elizann H., #5598
Martin, Ella David, #6702
Martin, Ely M., #5603
Martin, Fanney M., #5602
Martin, Fannie E., #5611
Martin, H., #1746
Martin, H., #8119
Martin, Helene Jane, #4709
Martin, Jacob M., #5596
Martin, Jacob M., #5606
Martin, John M., #5601
Martin, Jonas M., #5605
Martin, Laura V., #4707
Martin, Laura V., #4709
Martin, Laura V., #4711
Martin, Leda M., #5604
Martin, Lydia, #5610
Martin, M., #1746
Martin, M., #8119
Martin, Maria, #1747
Martin, Maria, #1748
Martin, Maria, #1749
Martin, Maria, #1750
Martin, Maria, #1751
Martin, Maria, #1752
Martin, Maria, #1753
Martin, Maria, #1754
Martin, Maria, #1755
Martin, Maria, #1756
Martin, Maria, #1757
Martin, Maria Ellen, #1746
Martin, Maria Ellen, #8119
Martin, Martha M., #5600
Martin, Mattie, #5609
Martin, Robert Startzman, #4714
Martin, Solomon M., #5599

Martin, Solomon W., #5594
Martin, Solomon W., #5612
Martin, W. Edgar, #4697
Martin, W.E., #4709
Martin, W.E., #4711
"Martin, M.D.", Solomon M., #5607
Martindale, T.D., #2190
Mary, , #7628
Mason, Agnes, #1070
Mason, Agnes, 1071
Mason, Henry M., #7558
Mason, Joshua, #1070
Mason, Meta R. (Miss), #7645
Mason, Meta. R., #7619
Mason, Nancy, #1070
Masser, Rev., #4361
Mathers, Mary Jane, #1460
Mathews, Elder, #2787
Mathews, Merce, #1594
Mathews, Mercer, #1638
Mathews, Mercer, #1639
Mathews, Mercer, #1640
Mathews, Mercer, #1641
Mathews, Mercer, #1642
Mathias, Anne Louise, #6897
Mathias, Anne Louise, #6922
Mathias, Helen Loose Miller, #6957
Mathias, Jane Loose, #6898
Mathias, Jane Loose, #6921
Mathias, Philip Heagy, #6894
Maudy, Matilda, #3831
Maywell, George, #6266
McAllister, Geo. W., #914
McAllister, Geo. W., #915
McAllister, George W., #908
McBee, Mary Gertrude (Miss), #1469
McBride, Catharine, #2612
McBride, William F., #2983
McCaitey, Barbery, #5402
McCauley, Harriet, #5954
McCauley, Harriet, #5995
McCauley, Harriet, #5997
McCauley, James, #4952
McCauley, James, #4981
McCauley, James, #4985
McCauley, Lena R., #4985
McCauley, Lizzie, #4957
McCauley, Wm. Harvey, #36
McCausland, Glenn, #7834
McCausland, John Glen, #7809
McCausland, John Glen, #7810
McCausland, , #7834
McClearey, Eleanor, #1519
McCollister, Amby[?], #4602
McCollister, Lavina (Miss), #4603
McCollister, Margaret (Miss), #4604
McCollister, Mary Ellen, #4606
McCollister, Mathas[?] James, #4605
McCollister, Murten[?] William, #4607
McColloch, John (Major), #2280
McCoy, Amelia Catherine, #2855

McCoy, Amelia Catherine, #3674
McCoy, Clara Ardinger, #1742
McCoy, Clara Ardinger, #4139
McCoy, Ethel L.[?], #5483
McCoy, Theodore Elsworth, #5495
McCoy, Violetta, #5489
McCoy, Violetta, #5490
McCullough, Elizabeth, #7801
McCune, Walter A., #3416
McCurdy, James, #7627
McCurdy, James, #7628
McCurdy, James, #7629
McCurdy, Margaret, #7629
McDonald, Esther Ann, #1919
McDonald, Jackson, #1919
McDonald, John William, #1919
McDowell, Emily (Gabby), #1362
McDowell, Nathan, #1368
McElvain, George, #2119
McGill, Ellen, #8480
McGinley, Sarah, #7592
McGinley, Sarah, #7593
McGlaughlin, , #5783
McGraw, Fannie (Leiter), #561
McIlhenny, Mary (Miss), #4571
McIlvaine, Robert, #2118
McInturff[?], Frederick, #721
McInturff[?], Frederick, #723
McInturff[?], Maryann, #722
McKee, Ann Louisa Henrietta, #5624
McKee, Elisajane, #5616
McKee, Elisajane, #5625
McKee, Evaline, #5620
McKee, Evaline, #5626
McKee, Ferdinand, #5619
McKee, Ferdonand, #5630
McKee, Isabella, #5614
McKee, Isabella, #5627
McKee, James, #5615
McKee, James B., #5633
McKee, John, #5613
McKee, John, #5621
McKee, John, #5629
McKee, John, #5631
McKee, John, #5634
McKee, John, #5635
McKee, Laura, #5623
McKee, Leander, #5622
McKee, Leander, #5632
McKee, Mary Elizabeth (Mrs.), #2502
McKee, Robert, #5617
McKee, William, #5618
McKee, William B., #5628
McKilley[?], Margaret Ann, #1465
McLanahan, A.C.H., #1625
McLanahan, A.C.H., #1633
McLanahan, Amelia, #1626
McLanahan, Anna, #1632
McLanahan, Catherine A., #1591
McLanahan, Catherine A., #1624
McLean, Moses, #7624
McLean, Moses, #7625
McLean, Rachel, #7593
McLean, Rachel, #7594
McLean, Rachel, #7625
McMahon, John (Major), #2275
McMahon, John (Major), #2276
McMahon, Nancy, #2274
McMahon, Nancy, #2275

McMahon, Nancy, #2276
McMahon, Nancy, #2290
McMahon, Nancy, #2291
McMahon, Nancy, #2292
McMahon, Nancy, #2293
McMahon, Nancy, #2294
McMahon, Nancy, #2295
McMahon, Nancy, #2296
McMahon, Nancy, #2297
McMahon, Nancy, #2298
McMahon, Nancy, #2299
McMahon, Nancy, #2300
McMann, Rev., #4360
McNabb, Francis, #7354
McNabb, George, #7356
McNabb, Hallie, #7353
McNabb, James H., #7352
McNabb, James H., #7353
McNabb, James H., #7354
McNabb, James H., #7355
McNabb, James H., #7356
McNabb, James H., #7357
McNabb, James H., #7358
McNabb, Jim, #7358
McNabb, John , #7357
McNabb, Ruth, #7355
McNamee, Elizabeth K. (Miss), #7252
McNamee, Sallie V., #5608
McNeal, Marguerite, #886
McQuiller, Joseph M., #5216
McSherry, Margaret A., #7641
McVicker, Margaret Rae, #3637
McWhenny [McIlhenny], Margaret A., #7607
Mead, Samiel, #1895
Mealey, Edw. M., #7500
Mealey, Edward Merryman, #7540
Mealey, Edward Windsor, #7501
Mealey, Edward Windsor, #7502
Mealey, Edward Windsor, #7511
Mealey, Elizabeth Frances (Windsor), #7535
Mealey, Frederick Samson, #7514
Mealey, Frederick Samson, #7539
Mealey, Joseph Albert, #7512
Mealey, Joseph Albert, #7537
Mealey, Laura Gertrude (Parks), #7541
Mealey, Richard Clinton, #7513
Mealey, Richard Clinton, #7538
Mehn, Adam, #5648
Mehn, Adam, #5649
Mehn, Adam, #5650
Mehn, Adam, #5651
Mehn, Adam, #5652
Mehn, Elisabeth, #5649
Mehn, Georg Adam, #5638
Mehn, John Frederick, #5650
Mehn, John George, #5652
Mehn, Maria Magdalena, #5651
Menn, May Adam, #5639
Mentzer, Walter H., #2770
Merckle, Anna Emogene, #802
Merckle, Claude Owen, #804
Merckle, Claudia Frances, #811
Merckle, Edward E., #813
Merckle, Esby Franklin, #812
Merckle, Frances H., #807
Merckle, Frances Helene, #803
Merckle, Mathis, #812
Merckle, Robert C., #811
Merckle, Robert E., #810

INDEX
Pages are not numbered; numbers refer to the entry number at the beginning of each record.

Merckle, Robert E., #814
Merckle, Robert E. (Mrs.), #814
Merckle, Robert E.L., #801
Merckle, Robert L. (Sgt.), #814
Merckle, Robert Lee, #808
Merckle, Robert Lee, #809
Merriken, Alphonza Elizabeth (Miss), #1279
Merriman[?], Robert, #5220
Metcalf, Horace, #3788
Metz, Myrtle, #3441
Metzel, John, #745
Metzer, D., #6142
Michael, Anna Maria, #5586
Michael, Georg Willhelm, #5588
Michael, Georg Willhelm, #5589
Michael, Heinrich Christan, #5587
Michael, Jacob Jonathan, #5582
Michael, Jacob Jonathan, #5583
Michael, Johann Christoph, #5581
Michael, Johann Gottlieb, #5584
Michael, Johann Gottlieb, #5585
Michael, Johann Willhelm, #5590
Michael, Johann Willhelm, #5591
Michael, Jonathan, #5579
Michael, Matilda, #5592
Michael, Matilda, #5593
Mickey, Sallie, #3450
Middlekauff, An Susen, #8142
Middlekauff, Ann M., #5515
Middlekauff, Ann Maria, #5530
Middlekauff, Ann Maria, #5531
Middlekauff, Barbara, #5541
Middlekauff, Corneae Cunningham, #8141
Middlekauff, Cornelius, #4569
Middlekauff, Cornelius C., #8149
Middlekauff, Cornelius C., #8153
Middlekauff, Daniel, #5538
Middlekauff, Daniel, #5543
Middlekauff, Daniel , #5536
Middlekauff, Emma, #5548
Middlekauff, Emma C., #5518
Middlekauff, Emma C., #5532
Middlekauff, Emma C., #5533
Middlekauff, Emma Irene, #5569
Middlekauff, Emma Irene, #5578
Middlekauff, Emma K., #5512
Middlekauff, Emma Mariah, #5573
Middlekauff, Franklin Earl, #5565

Middlekauff, Franklin Earl, #5574
Middlekauff, Hilda Jean (Miss), #2996
Middlekauff, Jacob, #5546
Middlekauff, Jane, #5557
Middlekauff, Johannes, #8599
Middlekauff, John C., #2996
Middlekauff, John C. (Rev.), #2996
Middlekauff, Jonathan, #5511
Middlekauff, Jonathan, #5514
Middlekauff, Jonathan, #5534
Middlekauff, Jonathan, #5535
Middlekauff, Jonathan B., #5521
Middlekauff, Jonathan B., #5528
Middlekauff, Jonathan B., #5529
Middlekauff, Jonnaton, #5545
Middlekauff, Josebh [sic], #5547
Middlekauff, Joseph M., #5522
Middlekauff, Joseph M., #5523
Middlekauff, Joseph Melvin, #5516
Middlekauff, Julia A.P., #5519
Middlekauff, Julia A.P., #5526
Middlekauff, Julia A.P., #5527
Middlekauff, Leah Mary, #5564
Middlekauff, Leonard, #8139
Middlekauff, Leonard, #8147
Middlekauff, Leonard, #8152
Middlekauff, Lizzie, #230
Middlekauff, Marea, #5537
Middlekauff, Marea, #5538
Middlekauff, Marea, #5540
Middlekauff, Maria Elizabeth, #8598
Middlekauff, Mary A. Eliz.[?], #8145
Middlekauff, Mary Leah, #5575
Middlekauff, Mildred, #5568
Middlekauff, Mildred C., #5570
Middlekauff, Mildred Catherine, #5571
Middlekauff, Naomi Supinger, #5561
Middlekauff, Nellie F., #4696
Middlekauff, Peter, #5544
Middlekauff, Polly, #8140
Middlekauff, Ruth, #5567
Middlekauff, Ruth, #5577
Middlekauff, Saml. O., #5524
Middlekauff, Saml. O., #5525
Middlekauff, Samual, #5542
Middlekauff, Samuel Clenton, #8144
Middlekauff, Samuel Osker, #5517
Middlekauff, Susan, #5539
Middlekauff, Susan (Mrs.), #4569
Middlekauff, Walter Cornelius, #8146
Middlekauff, William C., #5520
Middlekauff, William Clyde, #5558
Middlekauff, William Clyde, #5566

Middlekauff, William Clyde, #5576
Middlekauff, William L., #5552
Middlekauff, William L., #5563
Middlekauff, William Lycurgus[?], #5572
Middlekauff, Wm. C., #5513
"Middlekauff, Jr.", Leonard, #8148
Middlekauff-McBride, Annie L. (Mrs.), #2981
Midlar[?], Jane, #4496
Midlar[?], Mary Jane, #4495
Midlar[?], Mary Jane, #4496
Midlar[?], Sebastian, #4496
Milburne, L.R., #6147
Miler, Sophia, #5858
Miller, Absam, #4942
Miller, Anna (Brown), #3838
Miller, Anna Elizabeth (Lerch), #2135
Miller, Annie Florence, #5820
Miller, Barbra, #5834
Miller, Bessie Lind, #5814
Miller, Bessie Lind, #5826
Miller, Brian Patrick, #6936
Miller, Carly Nicole, #6938
Miller, Catharina, #5469
Miller, Catharina, #5475
Miller, Catherine, #6958
Miller, Christine Amber, #6930
Miller, Daniel, #5837
Miller, David, #5492
Miller, David, #5493
Miller, David, #6713
Miller, David Scott, #6899
Miller, David Scott, #6923
Miller, DeWitt L., #2998
Miller, Elisabeth, #5469
Miller, Elisabeth, #5470
Miller, Elisabeth, #5471
Miller, Elisabeth, #5472
Miller, Elisabeth, #5473
Miller, Elisabeth, #5474
Miller, Elisabeth, #5475
Miller, Elizabeth, #5477
Miller, Elizabeth, #5833
Miller, Elizabeth, #5852
Miller, Emma Kate, #5818
Miller, Estella Rachel, #41
Miller, Estella Rachel, #69
Miller, Esther, #5836
Miller, Ezra[?] M., #5485
Miller, Father, #5508
Miller, Flora B., #5086
Miller, Frank Edson, #5819
Miller, Frank Edson, #5830
Miller, G. Arthur, #3208
Miller, Goldie V., #5504
Miller, Grace Yvonne, #4047
Miller, H., #3560
Miller, Hager, #3245
Miller, Hager, #3246
Miller, Hager, #6880
Miller, Hager, #6881
Miller, Hannah, #5472
Miller, Harold E., #2771
Miller, Helen Loose, #6894
Miller, Helen Loose, #6918
Miller, Henry, #5461
Miller, Henry, #5462
Miller, Henry, #5469
Miller, Henry, #5470

Miller, Henry, #5471
Miller, Henry, #5472
Miller, Henry, #5473
Miller, Henry, #5474
Miller, Henry, #5478
Miller, Henry, #5812
Miller, Henry, #5821
Miller, Henry, #5823
Miller, Henry, #5827
Miller, Henry Carlton, #5817
Miller, Henry Carlton, #5829
Miller, Henry Loose, #6895
Miller, Henry Loose, #6920
Miller, Ida Frances, #5816
Miller, J. Garvin, #3247
Miller, Jac.b. [Jacob] Henry, #5474
Miller, Jacob, #4060
Miller, Jacob Henry, #5459
Miller, Jacob Henry, #5460
Miller, James E., #5702
Miller, Jno., #6578
Miller, Johannes, #5471
Miller, John, #5831
Miller, John, #5832
Miller, John, #5833
Miller, John, #5834
Miller, John, #5835
Miller, John, #5836
Miller, John, #5837
Miller, John, #5838
Miller, John, #5839
Miller, John, #5851
Miller, John, #5852
Miller, John, #5857
Miller, John, #6711
Miller, Joseph, #3432
Miller, Kyle Gregory, #6935
Miller, Laura, #5096
Miller, Laura C., #5489
Miller, Laurra C., #5488
Miller, Louisa, #6984
Miller, Louisa, #6992
Miller, M. Alice, #37
Miller, Mae L., #3435
Miller, Magdalana Sager, #5493
Miller, Magdalana Sager, #5494
Miller, Margaret Ann, #4943
Miller, Marjorie, #698
Miller, Marjorie, #699
Miller, Marjorie Eileen, #685
Miller, Martin, #5482
Miller, Martin L., #5097
Miller, Martin Luther, #5494
Miller, Mary, #5838
Miller, Mary (Mrs.), #7001
Miller, Mary Alice, #57
Miller, Mary Alice, #5815
Miller, Mary Alice, #60
Miller, Mary Alice, #63
Miller, Mary Alice, #64
Miller, Mary Cecil (Mrs.), #4056
Miller, Mary Ellen, #7893
Miller, Minnie F., #5335
Miller, Mother, #5507
Miller, Myrtle Virginia, #4046
Miller, Nannie, #5496
Miller, Nannie, #5497
Miller, Nellie Loose, #6955
Miller, Rachel, #5473
Miller, Rev., #4173
Miller, Rev., #6727

INDEX
Pages are not numbered; numbers refer to the entry number at the beginning of each record.

Miller, Samuel, #5840
Miller, Sarie C. (Miss), #2498
Miller, Scott Richard, #6931
Miller, Sophia, #5839
Miller, Sue, #5499
Miller, Susan, #5813
Miller, Susan, #5822
Miller, Susan Winroth, #6900
Miller, Susan Winroth, #6924
Miller, Susann, #6709
Miller, Susann, #6710
Miller, Susanna, #5470
Miller, Susanna, #5832
Miller, Susanna, #5833
Miller, Susanna, #5834
Miller, Susanna, #5835
Miller, Susanna, #5835
Miller, Susanna, #5836
Miller, Susanna, #5837
Miller, Susanna, #5838
Miller, Susanna, #5839
Miller, Susannah, #5862
Miller, Susannah, #8371
Miller, Urilah V.[?], #5501
Miller, Urillah V., #5506
Miller, Victor Davis, #6896
Miller, Victor Davis, #6917
Miller, William, #6712
Miller, , #7960
"Miller, Jr.", Victor D., #6891
"Miller, Jr.", Victor D., #6956
"Miller, Jr.", Victor Davis, #6919
Milliken, Andrew, #214
Milliken, Elizabeth Bell, #216
Milliken, Jane Mary, #217
Milliken, Thomas Edgar, #215
Mills, Albert Franklin, #5388
Mills, Alice V., #5421
Mills, Alice Virginia, #5370
Mills, Allie Lizzey May, #5453
Mills, Alta May E., #5365
Mills, Alte[?] Lizze May, #5410
Mills, Amos A., #5431
Mills, Amos Calvin, #5376
Mills, Arlander, #5455
Mills, Asa Marion, #5394
Mills, Aslander, #5399
Mills, Aslander, #5402
Mills, Bruffe , #5455
Mills, Carry Mahala, #5441
Mills, Charles Amos Calvin, #5454
Mills, Charles E., #5443
Mills, Charles Edgar, #5415
Mills, Charles H., #5378
Mills, Charles Johnson, #5396
Mills, Charles P.[?], #5452
Mills, Charles William Edgare, #5416
Mills, Daisy R., #5383
Mills, Daisy Viola, #5367
Mills, Daisy Viola, #5418
Mills, David E., #5424
Mills, David Elmer, #5369
Mills, Denton W., #5414
Mills, Dewitt Clinton, #5393
Mills, Eda Louise Ellen, #5373

Mills, Elmer, #5411
Mills, Elmer Franklin, #5372
Mills, Eva/Iva Irene, #5386
Mills, Franklin Webster, #5440
Mills, George Anne, #5385
Mills, George F., #5401
Mills, George F., #5403
Mills, George Franklin Webster, #5409
Mills, George Walter, #5439
Mills, Groege Franklin Webster, #5407
Mills, Hare[?] Milton Arlander, #5456
Mills, Ida Camilla, #5368
Mills, Ida Camilla, #5419
Mills, Ida Comila, #5458
Mills, Izora Alverta, #5366
Mills, James J., #5391
Mills, James J., #5393
Mills, James J., #5394
Mills, James J., #5395
Mills, James J., #5396
Mills, James J., #5397
Mills, James J., #5430
Mills, James J., #5444
Mills, James J., #5445
Mills, John A., #5442
Mills, John Allen Wood, #5438
Mills, John Allenwood, #5406
Mills, John D., #5432
Mills, Joseph, #5381
Mills, Joseph F., #5389
Mills, Lizie, #5390
Mills, Lizzie J., #5375
Mills, Lulu May, #5384
Mills, Mahala, #5417
Mills, Mahala, #5457
Mills, Maria, #5422
Mills, Mary Catherine, #5371
Mills, Mary E., #5392
Mills, Mary E., #5393
Mills, Mary E., #5394
Mills, Mary E., #5395
Mills, Mary E., #5396
Mills, Mary E., #5397
Mills, Mary E., #5445
Mills, Mary E.W., #5377
Mills, Mary G.[?], #5435
Mills, Minnie May, #5395
Mills, Nancy Ann, #5436
Mills, Nancy Ann, #5451
Mills, Nelsan Arlander, #5448
Mills, Nelson anladey[?], #5408
Mills, Nickler Raman, #5449
Mills, Orlando B., #5397
Mills, Orlando B., #5445
Mills, Oscar, #5412
Mills, Oscar T.B., #5413
Mills, Pleasant Gertrude, #5380
Mills, Rober[?], #5398
Mills, Robert, #5428
Mills, Robert J.[?], #5434
Mills, Robert S., #5382
Mills, Robert S., #5420
Mills, Robert Sheridan, #5387
Mills, Robt. L., #5374
Mills, Samuel J.[?], #5429
Mills, Sarah Ann, #5433
Mills, Sarah Ann, #5450
Mills, Sarah Annie, #5400

Mills, Sarah Annie, #5423
Mills, Sarah Catharine, #5405
Mills, Sarah[?] Annie, #5425
Mills, Sary[?] Cathrine, #5437
Mills, William E. Bruffey, #5427
Mills, William E.B., #5404
Mills, William E.B., #5446
Mills, William Ellsworth, #5379
Mills, , #6118
Mills[?], Janet E., #3636
Milton, Mary Ellen, #1892
Miner, Jno., #6576
Mines, Jno., #6054
Mines, Jno., #6151
Mines, Jno., #6153
Mines, Jno., #6155
Mines, Jno., #6157
Mines, Lio, #6140
Mines, Rev., #6585
Minkland, Rev. Dr., #8274
Mitchell, Carrie B., #3123
Mitchell, Clarence F., #5219
Mitchell, Florence V., #1247
Mitchell, Florence V., #1248
Mitchell, John E., #1246
Mitchell, John E., #1247
Mitchell, John E., #1248
Mitchell, John E., #1249
Mitchell, John E., #1249
Mittag, Ann Catherine, #8254
Moeller, John F., #7759
Monroe, Thos., #1602
Monroe, Thos., #1604
Monroe, Thos., #1606
Moomau, Lydia, #1080
Moomau, Lydia, #1081
Moomau, Lydia, #1082
Moore, Beatrice C., #582
Moore, C., #680
Moore, Catharine, #666
Moore, Catharine, #691
Moore, Elisabeth, #668
Moore, Franklin J., #668
Moore, L.T. (Col.), #5046
Moore, Mary (Mrs.), #5046
Moreland, David W., #1151
"Morgart, RN", Julia Helen, #282
Morison, Esther, #3830
Morrow, Martha Ellen, #2798
Moser, Mary E. (Summers) (Mrs.), #4623
Moser[?], Josiah, #5484
Mother, ,
Mount, Ann Jane, #4738
Mowen, Kenneth F., #887
Mson, James, #7604
Mson, James, #7640
Muck, Abraham F., #5039
Muck, Elizabeth Ann (Mrs.), #5039
Muhlenberg, H., #6961
Mullen, Emma, #5563
Mullendore, Cecelia Elizabeth, #593
Mullendore, Daniel, #590
Mullendore, Martha A., #3394
Mullendore, Sophia, #591
Mullendore, Violetta Matilda, #592
Mullikin, Mary, #2628
Mullikin, Mary, #2630
Mullikin, Mary, #2631

Mullikin, Mary, #2632
Mullikin, Mary, #2633
Mullikin, Mary, #2634
Mullikin, Mary, #2635
Mullikin, Mary, #2636
Mullikin, Mary, #3869
Mullikin, Mary, #3871
Mullikin, Mary, #3872
Mullikin, Mary, #3873
Mullikin, Mary, #3874
Mullikin, Mary, #3875
Mullikin, Mary, #3876
Mullikin, Mary, #3877
Mummert, Mary, #2799
"Munday, Jr.", John Henry, #2467
Murdock, John, #743
Murdock, John, #746
Murdock, John, #749
Murphey, Catharine, #8561
Murphey, John Edmond, #8508
Murphy, Dennis (Dr.), #2113
Murphy, Ellen Carey (Coleman), #8499
Murphy, Mary Lois, #7940
Murphy, Matthew Hilt, #7930
Murphy, Matthew Hilt, #7938
Murphy, Matthew Hilt, #7939
Murphy, Matthew Hilt, #7940
Murphy, Matthew Hilt, #7941
Murphy, Matthew Samuel, #7941
Musser, [unreadable], #6060
Musser, [unreadable], #6061
Musser, Abraham, #6087
Musser, Abraham, #6088
Musser, Abraham, #6226
Musser, Abraham, #6227
Musser, Ada Cary, #6192
Musser, Adam, #6091
Musser, Ann Maria, #6067
Musser, Ann Maria, #6068
Musser, Ann Maria, #6245
Musser, Ann Maria, #6246
Musser, Anna Maria, #6045
Musser, Anna Maria, #6048
Musser, Anna Maria, #6212
Musser, Anne Catherine, #6181
Musser, Annie Laurie, #6190
Musser, Annie Laurie, #6199
Musser, Caroline Beall, #6147
Musser, Caroline Beall, #6162
Musser, Caroline Beall, #6163
Musser, Catharine, #6076
Musser, Catharine, #6077
Musser, Catharine, #6218
Musser, Christiana, #6025
Musser, Christiana, #6062
Musser, Christiana, #6092
Musser, Christiana, #6096
Musser, Christiana Catharine, #6030
Musser, Christiana Catharine, #6235
Musser, Christiana Catharine, #6236
Musser, Christianie C., #6174
Musser, Christianna Catharine, #6040
Musser, Christina Catherine, #6156
Musser, Christina Catherine, #6157
Musser, Elisabeth, #6201
Musser, Elisabeth, #6202
Musser, Elisabeth, #6203
Musser, Elizabeth, #6069
Musser, Elizabeth, #6213
Musser, Elizabeth Mary, #6182
Musser, Emma, #6044

INDEX
Pages are not numbered; numbers refer to the entry number at the beginning of each record.

Musser, Emma, #6244
Musser, Flavel A., #6177
Musser, Flavel Augustus, #6056
Musser, Flavel Augustus, #6154
Musser, Flavel Augustus, #6155
Musser, Frances E., #6194
Musser, Frances E., #6201
Musser, G., #6029
Musser, G., #6030
Musser, G., #6031
Musser, G., #6034
Musser, G., #6035
Musser, G., #6043
Musser, G., #6044
Musser, G., #6045
Musser, G., #6046
Musser, G., #6047
Musser, Geo., #6028
Musser, Geo., #6033
Musser, Geo., #6576
Musser, Geo., #6580
Musser, George, #6025
Musser, George, #6025
Musser, George, #6026
Musser, George, #6027
Musser, George, #6032
Musser, George, #6033
Musser, George, #6036
Musser, George, #6042
Musser, George, #6042
Musser, George, #6050
Musser, George, #6051
Musser, George, #6060
Musser, George, #6061
Musser, George, #6063
Musser, George, #6064
Musser, George, #6066
Musser, George, #6067
Musser, George, #6068
Musser, George, #6069
Musser, George, #6070
Musser, George, #6071
Musser, George, #6072
Musser, George, #6073
Musser, George, #6073
Musser, George, #6074
Musser, George, #6074
Musser, George, #6075
Musser, George, #6076
Musser, George, #6077
Musser, George, #6078
Musser, George, #6079
Musser, George, #6080
Musser, George, #6081
Musser, George, #6082
Musser, George, #6083
Musser, George, #6084
Musser, George, #6085
Musser, George, #6086
Musser, George, #6087
Musser, George, #6088
Musser, George, #6089
Musser, George, #6090
Musser, George, #6092
Musser, George, #6096
Musser, George, #6140
Musser, George, #6142
Musser, George, #6148

Musser, George, #6204
Musser, George, #6205
Musser, George, #6206
Musser, George, #6207
Musser, George, #6208
Musser, George, #6209
Musser, George, #6210
Musser, George, #6211
Musser, George, #6212
Musser, George, #6213
Musser, George, #6214
Musser, George, #6215
Musser, George, #6216
Musser, George, #6216
Musser, George, #6217
Musser, George, #6218
Musser, George, #6219
Musser, George, #6220
Musser, George, #6221
Musser, George, #6222
Musser, George, #6223
Musser, George, #6224
Musser, George, #6225
Musser, George, #6226
Musser, George, #6227
Musser, George, #6228
Musser, George, #6229
Musser, George, #6230
Musser, George, #6239
Musser, George, #6240
Musser, George J., #6172
Musser, George James, #6053
Musser, George James, #6054
Musser, George James, #6059
Musser, George James, #6144
Musser, George James, #6150
Musser, George James, #6151
Musser, George James, #6179
Musser, George James, #6180
Musser, George James, #6181
Musser, George James, #6182
Musser, George James, #6183
Musser, George James, #6184
Musser, H.Y. [Henry Young], #6049
Musser, Henrich, #6225
Musser, Henrieta, #6228
Musser, "Henrietta ""(Harriet)", #6089
Musser, "Henrietta ""(Harriet)", #6090
Musser, Henry, #6085
Musser, Henry, #6086
Musser, Henry M., #6146
Musser, Henry M., #6171
Musser, Henry M., #6201
Musser, Henry M., #6202
Musser, Henry M., #6203
Musser, Henry Marcellus, #6195
Musser, Henry Marcellus, #6202
Musser, Henry Martyn, #6166
Musser, Henry Martyn, #6167
Musser, Henry Young, #6046
Musser, Henry Young, #6247
Musser, Jacob, #6075
Musser, Jacob, #6217
Musser, Jacob, #6219
Musser, Jacob Graeff, #6034
Musser, Jacob Graff, #6241

Musser, Jaub[?], #6078
Musser, Johan Adam, #6222
Musser, Johan Adam, #6223
Musser, Johannes, #6210
Musser, Johannes, #6211
Musser, Johannes, #6215
Musser, John, #6066
Musser, John, #6072
Musser, John Adam, #6081
Musser, John Adam, #6082
Musser, M., #6029
Musser, M., #6030
Musser, M., #6031
Musser, Margaretta Schaum, #6047
Musser, Margaretta Schaum, #6050
Musser, Margaretta Schaum, #6248
Musser, Margaretta Schaum, #6249
Musser, Maria C., #6169
Musser, Mary, #6026
Musser, Mary, #6028
Musser, Mary, #6037
Musser, Mary, #6051
Musser, Mary, #6148
Musser, Mary, #6231
Musser, Mary Elleanor, #6031
Musser, Mary Ellen, #6164
Musser, Mary Ellen, #6165
Musser, Mary Ellen, #6237
Musser, Mary Ellen, #6238
Musser, Mary J., #6189
Musser, Mary J., #6190
Musser, Mary J., #6191
Musser, Mary J., #6192
Musser, Mary J., #6193
Musser, Mary Jett, #6193
Musser, Mary Jett, #6200
Musser, Mattheus, #6220
Musser, Mattheus, #6221
Musser, Matthias, #6079
Musser, Matthias, #6080
Musser, Minnie Palmer, #6189
Musser, Minnie Palmer, #6197
Musser, Paul, #6060
Musser, Paul, #6061
Musser, Rebecca, #6064
Musser, Rebecca, #6065
Musser, Rebecca, #6099
Musser, Rebecca, #6100
Musser, Rebecca, #6101
Musser, Rebecca, #6102
Musser, Rebecca, #6103
Musser, Rebecca, #6104
Musser, Rebecca, #6105
Musser, Rebecca, #6106
Musser, Rebecca, #6209
Musser, S., #6034
Musser, S., #6035
Musser, S., #6043
Musser, S., #6044
Musser, S., #6045
Musser, S., #6046
Musser, S., #6047
Musser, Salmi (Salome), #6214
Musser, Sarah, #6033
Musser, Sarah, #6041
Musser, Sarah, #6042
Musser, Sarah, #6050

Musser, Sarah, #6055
Musser, "Sarah ""(Salome)", #6070
Musser, "Sarah ""(Salome)", #6071
Musser, Sarah Anne, #6055
Musser, Sarah Anne, #6056
Musser, Sarah Anne, #6058
Musser, Sarah Anne, #6144
Musser, Sarah Anne, #6145
Musser, Sarah Anne, #6146
Musser, Sarah Anne, #6149
Musser, Sarah Anne, #6150
Musser, Sarah Anne, #6151
Musser, Sarah Anne, #6152
Musser, Sarah Anne, #6153
Musser, Sarah Anne, #6154
Musser, Sarah Anne, #6155
Musser, Sarah Anne, #6156
Musser, Sarah Anne, #6157
Musser, Sarah Anne, #6158
Musser, Sarah Anne, #6159
Musser, Sarah Anne, #6160
Musser, Sarah Anne, #6161
Musser, Sarah Anne, #6162
Musser, Sarah Anne, #6163
Musser, Sarah Anne, #6164
Musser, Sarah Anne, #6165
Musser, Sarah Anne, #6166
Musser, Sarah Anne, #6167
Musser, Sarah Anne, #6168
Musser, Sarah Elizabeth, #6035
Musser, Sarah Elizabeth, #6184
Musser, Sarah Elizabeth, #6185
Musser, Sarah Elizabeth, #6242
Musser, Sarah Fairfax, #6191
Musser, Sarah Fairfax, #6198
Musser, Sarah M., #6175
Musser, Sarah Marie, #6152
Musser, Sarah Marie, #6153
Musser, Sebastian Graff, #6029
Musser, Sebastian Graff, #6233
Musser, Sebastian Graff, #6234
Musser, Sebatian Graff, #6039
Musser, Susan J., #6176
Musser, Susan Jane, #6158
Musser, Susan Jane, #6159
Musser, Susanna, #6043
Musser, Susanna, #6243
Musser, Susie, #6196
Musser, Susie, #6203
Musser, Wilhelm, #6224
Musser, William, #6028
Musser, William, #6038
Musser, William, #6051
Musser, William, #6052
Musser, William, #6055
Musser, William, #6056
Musser, William, #6057
Musser, William, #6083
Musser, William, #6084
Musser, William, #6092
Musser, William, #6140
Musser, William, #6142
Musser, William, #6144
Musser, William, #6145
Musser, William, #6146
Musser, William, #6148
Musser, William, #6149
Musser, William, #6150
Musser, William, #6151
Musser, William, #6152
Musser, William, #6153

INDEX
Pages are not numbered; numbers refer to the entry number at the beginning of each record.

Musser, William, #6154
Musser, William, #6155
Musser, William, #6156
Musser, William, #6157
Musser, William, #6158
Musser, William, #6159
Musser, William, #6160
Musser, William, #6161
Musser, William, #6162
Musser, William, #6163
Musser, William, #6164
Musser, William, #6165
Musser, William, #6166
Musser, William, #6167
Musser, William, #6168
Musser, William, #6169
Musser, William, #6170
Musser, William, #6183
Musser, William, #6232
Musser, William, #6536
Musser, William, #6576
Musser, William, #6580
Musser, William H., #6173
Musser, William H., #6189
Musser, William H., #6190
Musser, William H., #6191
Musser, William H., #6192
Musser, William H., #6193
Musser, William H., #6197
Musser, William H., #6198
Musser, William H., #6199
Musser, William Henderson, #6145
Musser, William Henderson, #6160
Musser, William Henderson, #6161
Musser, William Henderson, #6186
Musser, William Henderson, #6188
Musser, Wm., #6573
Myers, Ann C., #5311
Myers, Ann C. [mother], #5326
Myers, Annie M., #5110
Myers, Annie Mary, #5120
Myers, Benjamin F., #5315
Myers, Benjamin F., #5325
Myers, Bertha V., #5322
Myers, Bertha V., #5337
Myers, Carrie M., #5317
Myers, Carrie May, #5328
Myers, Charles Learitt, #5340
Myers, Charles Leavitt, #5361
Myers, Charles M., #5110
Myers, Charles M., #5316
Myers, Chas. McC., #5334
Myers, Cora E., #5321
Myers, Edith, #38
Myers, Edith, #62
Myers, Elizabeth, #5112
Myers, Elizabeth, #5113
Myers, Evans M., #5111
Myers, Evans Miller, #5116
Myers, George Summer, #4336
Myers, Harry G., #5323
Myers, Harry Grafton, #5336
Myers, Henry Samuel, #5344
Myers, Henry Samuel, #5359

Myers, Ida Virginia, #5339
Myers, Ida Virginia, #5360
Myers, Jacob, #5310
Myers, Jacob, #5324
Myers, Jacob A., #5114
Myers, Jacob C. [father], #5327
Myers, Jno. [father], #5341
Myers, Jno. D., #5349
Myers, Jno. D., #5353
Myers, John, #5357
Myers, John D., #5342
Myers, John Daniel, #5362
Myers, John William, #5314
Myers, John William, #5330
Myers, Kathrian, #5356
Myers, Lemuel Edgar, #5345
Myers, Lemuel Edgar, #5364
Myers, Leroy, #3024
Myers, Lucy H., #1039
Myers, Mabel Kendall, #2921
Myers, Mabel Virginia, #2940
Myers, Mabel Virginia , #2925
Myers, Margaret E., #5338
Myers, Margaret Ellen, #5313
Myers, Marshall Howard, #5363
Myers, Mary Aileen, #7476
Myers, Mary cathern, #5312
Myers, Mary E., #5354
Myers, Mary Elizabeth, #5343
Myers, Mary Elizabeth, #5358
Myers, Mary Lantz, #5347
Myers, Mary Lantz, #5355
Myers, Melbrey Kate, #7477
Myers, Minnie F., #5320
Myers, N. Effie, #5101
Myers, Noah Etta, #5103
Myers, Noah W., #5319
Myers, Noah Washington, #5332
Myers, Patrick Eugene, #1590
Myers, Peter, #4443
Myers, Peter, #4444
Myers, Rebecca, #4443
Myers, Rosa Almy, #5115
Myers, Sue M., #7484
Myers, Ulysses S., #5318
Myers, Ulysses S., #5333
Myers, Will, #7475
Nalley, Hilda Irene, #2405
Nalley, Hilda Irene, #2410
Nalley, Leroy Edward, #2408
Nalley, Leroy Edward, #2415
Nalley, William H., #2403
Nalley, William H., #2404
Nalley, William H., #2406
Nalley, William Richard, #2411
Nally, Clara B., #2421
Nally, Clara Bell, #2426
Nally, Johon E., #2424
Nally, Joseph J., #2420
Nally, Joseph J., #2425
Neal, Adam, #1166
Neal, Ann Eliza, #1186
Neal, Captolia, #1168
Neal, Charles Benton, #1162
Neal, Charles Wesley, #1171
Neal, Charles Wesley, #1183
Neal, Eliza Adel, #1163
Neal, Eliza J., #1167
Neal, Eliza J., #1168
Neal, Eliza[?], #1166

Neal, Eliza[?] G., #1164
Neal, Elley, #1167
Neal, Emory Nelson, #1172
Neal, Emory Nelson, #1182
Neal, Emry, #1162
Neal, Enoch Jones, #1185
Neal, Frances Asbury, #1173
Neal, Francis Asbury, #1189
Neal, J.C.W., #1170
Neal, James, #1178
Neal, James, #1180
Neal, James, #1181
Neal, James, #1182
Neal, James, #1183
Neal, James, #1184
Neal, James, #1185
Neal, James, #1186
Neal, James, #1187
Neal, James, #1188
Neal, James, #1189
Neal, James (Mrs.), #1174
Neal, James E., #1177
Neal, James E.[?], #1165
Neal, James Emory, #1187
Neal, James Emry, #1175
Neal, John Curtis, #1181
Neal, L.[?] S.[?], #1179
Neal, Mary Elizabeth, #1184
Neal, Mary Malindia, #1164
Neal, Mary Malindia, #1176
Neal, Nancy, #1180
Neal, Nancy, #1181
Neal, Nancy, #1182
Neal, Nancy, #1183
Neal, Nancy, #1184
Neal, Nancy, #1185
Neal, Nancy, #1186
Neal, Nancy, #1187
Neal, Nancy, #1188
Neal, Nancy, #1189
Neal, S.[?] L., #1164
Neal, S.L., #1166
Neal, S.L., #1167
Neal, S.L., #1168
Neal, S.L., #1176
Neal, Sarah, #1162
Neal, Stansbary [?] L., #1169
Neal, Stansbury Lawrence, #1188
Neal, William, #1180
Necholls, Maryann, #1938
Needy, Alice J., #5307
Needy, Alice J. (Kiracofe), #1402
Needy, Alice J. (Kiracofe), #1429
Needy, Alice J.E., #5279
Needy, Cora E., #377
Needy, E.L., #1387
Needy, E.L., #1403
Needy, E.L., #1427
Needy, E.L., #5278
Needy, E.L., #5298
Needy, Earl Kiracofe, #1405
Needy, Earl Kiracofe, #5281
Needy, Earle Kiracofe, #1428
Needy, Earle Kiracofe, #5306
Needy, Edna M., #1388
Needy, Edna M., #5299
Needy, Edna Myrtle, #1404
Needy, Edna Myrtle, #5280
Needy, Edward L., #5305
Needy, Hazel Ruth, #1406
Needy, Hazel Ruth, #1425

Needy, Hazel Ruth, #5304
Needy, Katharine L., #1389
Needy, Katharine L., #1416
Needy, Katharine L., #5300
Needy, Katharine Louise, #1407
Needy, Katharine Louise, #5283
Needy, Ruth Hazel, #5282
Neel, Isabella, #6579
Neel, Joseph, #6579
Neel, Rosanna __ne, #6578
Neel, Rosanna __ne, #6579
Negley, Rose, #6887
Neibert, Alice, #320
Neibert, Betty Jeanene, #306
Neibert, Betty Jeanene, #309
Neibert, Betty Jeanene, #310
Neibert, Betty Jeanene, #314
Neibert, Betty Jeanene, #315
Neibert, Christian Phillip, #318
Neibert, Christian Phillip, #319
Neibert, Christian Phillip, #320
Neibert, Christian Phillip, #321
Neibert, Christian Phillip, #322
Neibert, Edgar, #318
Neibert, Ella, #322
Neibert, Faye Rene, #308
Neibert, Faye Rene, #312
Neibert, Faye Rene, #313
Neibert, Faye Rene, #316
Neibert, Lillian, #321
Neibert, Richard Duane, #307
Neibert, Richard Duane, #311
Neibert, Scott A., #319
Neibert, Scott Alvey, #302
Neibert, Scott Alvey, #303
Neibert, Scott Alvey, #304
Neibert, Scott Alvey, #306
Neibert, Scott Alvey, #307
Neibert, Scott Alvey, #308
Neibert, Scott Alvey, #309
Neibert, Scott Alvey, #310
Neibert, Scott Alvey, #311
Neibert, Scott Alvey, #312
Neibert, Scott Alvey, #313
Nelson, Elizabeth Johnston, #2931
Nelson, J.K., #4301
Netty, Ada Belle, #5748
Netty, Bertha Irene, #5747
Netty, Bertie Eugene, #5746
Netty, Clara M., #5734
Netty, Clara Maria, #5725
Netty, Clara Maria, #5743
Netty, Clara Maria, #5744
Netty, Clara Maria, #5745
Netty, Clara Maria, #5746
Netty, Clara Maria, #5747
Netty, Clara Maria, #5748
Netty, Lydia Ellen, #5744
Netty, William Henry, #5745
Nety, Clara M., #5756
Newcomer, Altha Massinne[?], #4204
Newcomer, Ann, #1973
Newcomer, Anna Sherrick, #7332
Newcomer, Besse (Spickler), #4227
Newcomer, Charles Jacob, #4191
Newcomer, Charles Jacob, #4218
Newcomer, Edmond Motter, #4197
Newcomer, Edmund M., #4220
Newcomer, Emma Margarette, #4205
Newcomer, Emma R., #4214
Newcomer, Frank Sherrick, #7324

INDEX
Pages are not numbered; numbers refer to the entry number at the beginning of each record.

Newcomer, George L., #4224
Newcomer, George Lester, #4200
Newcomer, Grason E., #4177
Newcomer, Grason Earle, #4199
Newcomer, Grason Earle, #4226
Newcomer, Guy Luttrell, #4206
Newcomer, Harry M., #4213
Newcomer, Henry, #7334
Newcomer, Henry M., #4174
Newcomer, Henry M., #4217
Newcomer, Henry Martin, #4195
Newcomer, John B., #4175
Newcomer, John Brewer, #4192
Newcomer, John Brewer, #4212
Newcomer, John Brewer[?], #4201
Newcomer, "Joseph G. ""Joe", #4208
Newcomer, Julia E., #4207
Newcomer, Keefer Brewer, #4203
Newcomer, Mary J., #4176
Newcomer, "Mary Jane ""Jen", #4193
Newcomer, Nellie Inez, #4190
Newcomer, Samuel C., #4221
Newcomer, Samuel Cadwell, #4196
Newcomer, Susan Emma, #4194
Newcomer, Susan Emma, #4219
Newcomer, Victor H., #7314
Newcomer, Victor H., #7322
Newcomer, Victor H., #7331
Newcomer, Virginia Sherrick, #7315
Newcomer, Virginia Sherrick, #7323
Newcomer, William D., #4222
Newcomer, William Rudolph, #4198
Newlin, Ida, #7350
Newlin, Ida, #7351
Newman, Maria B., #873
Newman, Maria B., #876
Nichles, John Ashton, #7437
Nichol, , #8054
Nicholas, Rev., #7746
Nichols, Elizabeth, #993
Nichols, Jacob, #1002
Nichols, Jacob, #985
Nichols, Jacob, #992
Nichols, Mr., #4884
Nichols, , #1006
Nichols, , #8051
Nicholson, Matilda, #4630
Nicholson, Nellie Faire, #6658
Nickels, Joseph, #5486
Nickels, Joseph, #5487
Nickolson, Rev., #230
Nicodemus, John L., #7315

Nicodemus, John Luther, #7316
Nicodemus, John Luther, #7317
Nicodemus, Virginia S., #7318
Nihiser, Rev., #1103
Nikirk, A. Russell, #7498
Nikirk, Albert Russell, #7492
Nikirk, Ellen Catherine, #7494
Nikirk, Ernest Boone, #7489
Nikirk, George Roy, #7495
Nikirk, Grace May, #7491
Nikirk, Harry Wilson, #7490
Nikirk, Joseph, #7485
Nikirk, Joseph, #7486
Nikirk, Joseph, #7488
Nikirk, Joseph, #7489
Nikirk, Joseph, #7490
Nikirk, Joseph, #7491
Nikirk, Joseph, #7492
Nikirk, Joseph, #7493
Nikirk, Joseph, #7494
Nikirk, Joseph, #7495
Nikirk, Joseph, #7497
Nikirk, Mollie E., #3060
Nikirk, Mollie E., #3061
Nikirk, Mollie E., #3062
Nikirk, Mollie E., #3063
Nikirk, Mollie E., #3064
Nikirk, Mollie E., #3065
Nikirk, Mollie E., #3066
Nikirk, Mollie E., #3067
Nikirk, Mollie E., #3068
Nikirk, Mollie E., #3069
Nikirk, Mollie E., #3070
Nikirk, Mollie E., #3071
Nikirk, Mollie E., #3072
Nikirk, Mollie E., #3073
Nikirk, Mollie E., #3074
Nikirk, Mollie E., #3075
Nikirk, Mollie E., #3078
Nikirk, Mollie E., #3079
Nikirk, Mollie E., #3080
Nikirk, Mollie E., #3106
Nikirk, Mollie E., #3107
Nikirk, Mollie E., #3108
Nikirk, Walter Edward, #7488
Nikirk, William Fagne, #7493
Nikirk, William Fagne, #7496
Nobel, Beverly Alice, #5907
Nobel, Norma May, #5908
Nobel, Norman, #5906
Nobel, Norman, #5907
Nobel, Norman, #5908
Noble, Fred B., #4305
Noble, Norman Geo., #5904
Noble, Thomas, #5903
Noble, Thomas William, #5900
Noland, Peter Chilton, #6928
Noland, Susan Mathias, #6929
Norris, Alcinda L., #5227
Norris, Alcinda L., #5228
Norris, Alcinda L., #5229
Norris, Alcinda L., #5238
Norris, Amanda, #5222
Norris, Amanda, #5232
Norris, Annie E., #5191
Norris, Annie Eliza, #5227
Norris, Annie Eliza, #5233
Norris, Annie[?] E., #5177
Norris, Arthur J., #5266
Norris, Carlton E., #5263
Norris, Carlton E., #5276

Norris, Catharine, #5231
Norris, Charles E., #5259
Norris, Charles E., #5275
Norris, Charles W., #5180
Norris, Charlotte Louisa, #5228
Norris, Charts[?] W., #5194
Norris, Claud M., #5261
Norris, Daissy V., #5182
Norris, Daissy V., #5183
Norris, Daisy May, #1544
Norris, Daisy V., #5196
Norris, Daniel E., #5181
Norris, Daniel E., #5195
Norris, Daniel W., #5178
Norris, Daniel W., #5192
Norris, Earl, #5272
Norris, Earl W., #5267
Norris, Elen, #5169
Norris, Elizbeth (Mrs.), #5161
Norris, Emma E., #5198
Norris, Emma V., #5215
Norris, Emma Virginia, #5229
Norris, Evente[?] Earl, #5149
Norris, Evente[?] Earl, #5150
Norris, Franklin W., #5264
Norris, Genie M., #5158
Norris, Genie M., #5159
Norris, Genie M., #5160
Norris, H. Pearl, #3208
Norris, H. Pearl, #3209
Norris, Henrietta Pearl, #3217
Norris, Henrietta Pearl, #3218
Norris, Henry, #5176
Norris, Henry, #5190
Norris, Ida, #5274
Norris, Ida R., #5260
Norris, Isabella, #3194
Norris, Jennie M., #5199
Norris, John, #5208
Norris, John, #5209
Norris, John, #5210
Norris, John, #5212
Norris, John, #5213
Norris, John, #5214
Norris, John, #5222
Norris, John, #5223
Norris, John, #5224
Norris, John, #5225
Norris, John, #5226
Norris, John, #5227
Norris, John, #5228
Norris, John, #5229
Norris, John, #5230
Norris, John, #5231
Norris, John, #5236
Norris, John, #5277
Norris, John A., #5170
Norris, John A., #5175
Norris, John F., #5141
Norris, John F., #5142
Norris, John F., #5146
Norris, John F., #5158
Norris, John F., #5159
Norris, John F., #5160
Norris, John F., #5163
Norris, John F., #5168
Norris, John F., #5170
Norris, John F., #5175
Norris, John Marion, #5157
Norris, John Scott, #5147
Norris, John Scott, #5148

Norris, John Scott, #5164
Norris, John W., #5235
Norris, John William, #5226
Norris, Joseph A., #5268
Norris, Ma__le Ellin, #5142
Norris, Maclen[?], #5185
Norris, Marguerite, #5153
Norris, Marvin Scott, #5156
Norris, Mary, #5262
Norris, Mary, #5271
Norris, Mary B., #3215
Norris, Mary C., #5179
Norris, Mary C., #5193
Norris, Mary Elizabeth, #5146
Norris, Mary Elizebeth, #5167
Norris, Mary Etta, #5143
Norris, Mary Etta, #5159
Norris, Mary J., #5197
Norris, Mary Jane, #5184
Norris, Mary Jane, #5224
Norris, Milton V.A., #3206
Norris, Minnie Ellen, #5158
Norris, Minnie Ellen, #5186
Norris, Minnie Ellin, #5172
Norris, Patrick, #5200
Norris, Patrick, #5201
Norris, Patrick, #5202
Norris, Patrick, #5203
Norris, Patrick, #5225
Norris, Patrick H., #5234
Norris, Paul, #5273
Norris, Paul L., #5269
Norris, Pearl Frances Regina, #5153
Norris, Preston B., #5270
Norris, Sarah, #5202
Norris, Sarah, #5203
Norris, Sarah A., #5222
Norris, Sarah A., #5223
Norris, Sarah A., #5224
Norris, Sarah A., #5226
Norris, Sarah A., #5230
Norris, Sarah Elizabeth, #5223
Norris, Scott, #5153
Norris, T.T., #3194
Norris, Thomas E., #5166
Norris, Thomas Envey, #5145
Norris, Thomas W., #3135
Norris, Upton, #3216
Norris, Upton O., #3207
Norris, Upton O., #3214
Norris, Virginia M., #5146
Norris, Virginia M., #5163
Norris, Virginia M., #5171
Norris, Willard Hodges, #5154
Norris, Willard Hodges, #5155
Norris, William Earl, #5151
Norris, William F.[?], #5265
Norris, William H., #5165
Norris, William Henry Fenton, #5144
Norris, William Henry Fenton, #5152
Norris, Wm. A., #5151
Norris, Wm. A., #5188
Norris[?], Eleanor Jane, #6489
Norton[?], Martha Elizabeth, #4446
Nouier[?], Catharine Elizabeth, #6488
Nussear, Agnes (Mrs.), #2417
Nussear, Henry Arthur, #2405
Nussear, Mary Norma, #2412
"Nussear, Jr.", Henry Arthur, #2413
Nutt, Aaron, #7135

INDEX
Pages are not numbered; numbers refer to the entry number at the beginning of each record.

Nutt, Addie, #7208
Nutt, Addie, #7209
Nutt, Addie (Miss), #7199
Nutt, Emma, #7203
Nutt, Emma, #7210
Nutt, Emma (Miss), #7201
Nutt, General, #7200
Nutt, General, #7212
Nutt, Jennie, #7214
Nutt, Jennie R., #7204
Nutt, Leonard, #7218
Nutt, Leonard P., #7222
Nutt, Luther Peterman, #7220
Nutt, Mary, #7207
Nutt, Mary, #7213
Nutt, Mary (Mrs.), #7216
Nutt, Mary (Snyder), #7137
Nutt, Nancy Jane, #7135
Nutt, Nellie, #7205
Nutt, Nellie, #7215
Nutt, Nellie (Miss), #7202
Nutt, Nelson, #7117
Nutt, Nelson, #7134
Nutt, Nelson, #7135
Nutt, Nelson, #7136
Nutt, Nelson, #7150
Nutt, Nelson, #7202
Nutt, Nelson, #7211
Nutt, Ralph Leonard, #7221
Nutt, Sibyl Lucile, #7219
Nutt, Viola, #7206
Nutt, Viola, #7217
Oberly, Susan, #2148
O'Brian, George A., #2721
O'Donnell, Frank, #5499
O'Donnell, Lester, #5499
Officer, Arthur H., #2195
Officer, Arthur H., #2198
Officer, Edgar T., #2192
Officer, Florence M., #2196
Officer, Gertrude H., #2194
Officer, Jennie C., #2193
Officer, Robert A., #2197
Officer, Samuel P., #2190
Officer, Samuel P., #2192
Officer, Samuel P., #2193
Officer, Samuel P., #2194
Officer, Samuel P., #2195
Officer, Samuel P., #2196
Officer, Samuel P., #2197
O'N., E., #1972
Onderdonk, Buy Latrobe, #7583
Onderdonk, Henry, #7562
Onderdonk, Henry, #7583
O'Neal, E.D.[?], #1965
O'Neal, Elias, #1963
O'Neal, Rober, #1964
O'Neal[?], Elia[?], #1962
Osbourn, Sarah Jane, #3195
Osbourn, Thomas F., #3205
Osbourn, William, #3195
Osbourne, Sarah Jane, #3198
Ostrander, Martha, #5893
Ostrander, Martha Atwell, #5892
Ostrander, Robert, #5893
Oswald, Allen Heck, #8024
Oswald, Geo. B., #1520
Oswald, Geo. B., #1529
Ott, J.D., #8369

Otto, Ruth E.V., #5505
Ottry, Phebe, #6418
Ottry, Phebe, #6419
Ottry, Phebe, #6420
Ottry, Phebe, #6421
Ottry, Phebe, #6422
Ottry, Phebe, #6423
Ottry, Phebe, #6424
Otty, Phebe, #6284
Overdear, Anna, #7959
Overdear, Polly, #7960
Owen, S.N., #2473
Owen, S.W., #1517
Owen, S.W., #1520
Owen, S.W., #2606
Owen, S.W., #2607
Owen, S.W., #702
Oyeman, Anna Catharina Margeretha, #6018
Oyeman, Evalena Dorothy, #6022
Oyeman, Geo. F.C., #6019
Oyeman, Henrietta Marie, #6020
Oyeman, Henrietta Marie, #6329
Oyeman, Henrietta Marie, #6405
Oyeman, Henrietta Marie, #6406
Oyeman, Henrietta Marie, #6441
Oyeman, Henrietta Marie, #6442
Oyeman, Henrietta Marie, #6443
Oyeman, Henrietta Marie, #6444
Oyeman, Johann Herman, #6006
Oyeman, Johann Herman, #6011
Oyeman, Johann Herman, #6016
Oyeman, John F.[?], #6002
Oyeman, John F.[?], #6003
Oyeman, Julienne[?], #6507
Oyeman, Marie, #6330
Oyeman, Marie, #6331
Oyeman, Marie, #6332
Oyeman, Marie, #6333
Oyeman, Marie, #6334
Oyeman, Robert T.[?], #6001
Oyeman, Robert T.[?], #6004
Oyeman, Robert T.[?], #6005
Oyeman, Robert Theodore, #6021
Oyeman, William Fricke, #6023
Oyeman, William Fricke, #6024
P_____, H.C., #2070
Page, C.R., #8019
Palmer, E.P., #8278
Paret, Bishop, #637
Parker, Ruthanna, #5749
Parker, Ruthanna, #5750
Parker, Ruthanna, #5760
Parks, Elisabeth, #5705
Parks, Elisabeth, #5706
Parks, Laura Gertrude, #7501
Parks, Lester A., #1127
Parnell, Daniel, #7850

Parnell, Frances Elizabeth, #7848
Parnell, Kathryn Ann, #7849
Parnell, Ural Clay, #7847
Parnell, Ural Clay, #7848
Parnell, Ural Clay, #7849
Parnell, Ural Clay, #7850
Patterson, Carl E., #6358
Patterson, Carl E., #6359
Patterson, Carl E., #6360
Patterson, Carl E., #6361
Patterson, Leon Allen, #6359
Patterson, Leon Allen, #6360
Patterson, Sharon Ann, #6361
Paul, Mary, #2694
Paul, Mary, #3938
Paul[?], Mary, #3935
Paull, Mary, #2621
Paull, Mary, #3867
Pauls, Mary, #2696
Payne, Margaret, #2583
Payne, Margaret, #2600
Pearson, Jennie[?], #6886
Peck, Rev., #6805
Pence, Eva, #588
Pence, Eva, #589
Penner, Calvin R., #6639
Penner, Calvin R., #6640
Penner, Charles R., #6642
Penner, Charles R., #6643
Penner, Daniel Albert, #6631
Penner, Daniel Albert, #6647
Penner, Edward L., #6637
Penner, Edward L., #6638
Penner, George W., #6633
Penner, George W., #6634
Penner, J.J., #6649
Penner, John J., #6632
Penner, Margaret E., #6641
Penner, Mary Louise, #6624
Penner, Mary Louise, #6625
Penner, Mary Louise, #6629
Penner, Samuel, #6625
Penner, Samuel, #6628
Penner, Samuel, #6650
Penner, William, #6648
Penner, William H., #6646
Penner, William Henry, #6630
Pennington, Sarah, #1467
Pennington, Sarah Rochester, #3652
Pensinger, Anna Lee, #884
Pensinger, Anna Lee, #888
Pensinger, Harry Richard, #882
Pensinger, Harry Richard, #895
Pensinger, Henry, #873
Pensinger, L. Roy, #895
Pensinger, Linford Roy N., #876
Pensinger, Linford Roy N., #885
Pensinger, Linford S., #886
Pensinger, Linford Snyder, #881
Pensinger, Lorraine Elizabeth, #880
Pensinger, Lorraine Elizabeth, #890
Pensinger, M. Evelyn, #893
Pensinger, M. Jane, #889
Pensinger, Maria B., #875
Pensinger, Maria B., #885
Pensinger, Maria B., #891
Pensinger, Maria Jane, #878
Pensinger, Mary, #895

Pensinger, Mary Evelyn, #879
Pensinger, Rebecca, #873
Pensinger, Virginia Raye, #883
Pensinger, Virginia Raye, #887
Pensinger, William J., #873
Pensinger, William J., #874
Pensinger, William J., #876
Pensinger, William J., #885
Pensinger, William J., #892
Penson[?], Ira (Rev.), #3796
Perkins, Wm. H. (Dr.), #7109
Perrott, Alexander R., #2470
Perrott, Alexander Rudolph, #2457
Perrott, Alexander Rudolph, #452
Perrott, Effie Elnora, #2463
Perrott, Effie Elnora, #458
Perrott, Effie Naomi, #2470
Perrott, Effie Naomi, #2471
Perrott, Elva V., #2468
Perrott, Elva Virginia, #2466
Perrott, Elva Virginia, #461
Perrott, Elva Virginia, #462
Perrott, Hazel Louise, #2458
Perrott, Hazel Louise, #453
Perrott, Jacob M., #2473
Perrott, Jacob Martin, #2469
Perrott, Jacob Martin, #2470
Perrott, John Rohyer, #2461
Perrott, John Rohyer, #456
Perrott, Laura Mildred Susan, #2462
Perrott, Laura Susan, #457
Perrott, Martin Reichard, #2459
Perrott, Martin Reichard, #454
Perrott, Maud Irene, #2465
Perrott, Maud Irene, #460
Perrott, Oliver, #5083
Perrott, Oliver, #5085
Perrott, Robert Lee, #2464
Perrott, Robert Lee, #459
Perrott, Wilbur V., #2472
Perrott, Wilbur Vincen, #2460
Perrott, Wilbur Vincent, #455
Perrpout, Rev., #6658
Perry, Clifton Edward, #2414
Perry, Thomas L., #3033
Perry[?], Clifton Edward, #2422
Philip, Joh Hann[?], #1974
Philips, Rev., #7335
Philips, Samuel, #8204
Philips, Samuel, #8215
Phillips, Amanda, #1953
Phillips, Carl, #890
Phillips, George W., #599
Phillips, Thomas, #1954
Phleegen[?], L.H., #4360
Phleeges[?], John Winter, #4440
Pickard, U.D., #5938
Pickard, U.D., #5939
Pickenpaugh, , #6119
Pierce, ___h Lewis, #7713
Piersel, Barbara, #4340
Pillsbury, W.H.H., #2205
Piper, Beula, #2364
Piper, Beula, #2365
Piper, Beula, #2366
Piper, Beula, #2367
Piper, Beula, #2368
Piper, Beula, #2369
Piper, Beula, #2370
Piper, Beula, #2371
Piper, Beula, #2372

INDEX
Pages are not numbered; numbers refer to the entry number at the beginning of each record.

Pittenger, D.S., #835
Pittenger, David L., #834
Pittenger, George B. McClellen, #844
Pittenger, H.F., #838
Pittenger, Harry Tecumseh Sherman, #842
Pittenger, Isabella S., #840
Pittenger, Lillie May, #841
Pittenger, Louisa J., #839
Pittenger, Marthe J., #7746
Pittenger, Thomas Alvey, #843
Pittenger, W.D., #837
Pittman, Sarah Ellen, #2930
Plummer, Alice E., #5129
Plummer, Alice E., #5137
Plummer, Alice Estella, #5133
Plummer, F. Berry, #6774
Plummer, Fannie Virginia, #5130
Plummer, Fannie Virginia, #5135
Plummer, Gertrude May, #5132
Plummer, Henry E., #5127
Plummer, Henry E., #5128
Plummer, Henry E., #5136
Plummer, Henry E., #5139
Plummer, Henry Edward, #5134
Plummer, Mary Ellen, #5131
Poe, Matilda (Miss), #517
Poe, Sophia (Miss), #516
Poffenberger, Agnes Stella, #7729
Poffenberger, Agnes Stella, #7730
Poffenberger, Alice Louise, #7739
Poffenberger, Christian M., #5117
Poffenberger, Clarence Glenwood, #7732
Poffenberger, Clarence Glenwood, #7733
Poffenberger, Deloris Mae, #7682
Poffenberger, Dolores Mae, #7686
Poffenberger, Elizabeth Ray, #5104
Poffenberger, Elizabeth Raye, #5124
Poffenberger, Ettie Pauline, #5109
Poffenberger, Harvey Cecil, #5108
Poffenberger, Harvey Cecil, #5125
Poffenberger, Harvey L., #5101
Poffenberger, Harvey Line, #5102
Poffenberger, Harvey Line, #5121
Poffenberger, Ira David, #7687
Poffenberger, Ira David, #7688

Poffenberger, Ira Grayson, #7678
Poffenberger, Ira Grayson, #7679
Poffenberger, Ira Grayson, #7684
Poffenberger, Ira Grayson, #7689
Poffenberger, Ira Grayson, #7727
Poffenberger, Ira Grayson, #7728
Poffenberger, Irene E. Reeder, #7683
Poffenberger, Irene Isabell, #7741
Poffenberger, Irma Elizabeth, #7734
Poffenberger, Irma Elizabeth, #7735
Poffenberger, Jack Ruddoff, #864
Poffenberger, Jack Rudolph, #872
Poffenberger, Jacob Evans, #5105
Poffenberger, Jacob Evans, #5123
Poffenberger, Janice Marie, #7681
Poffenberger, Janice Marie, #7685
Poffenberger, Jos., #7430
Poffenberger, Joseph, #7426
Poffenberger, Leonard Ellsworth, #7740
Poffenberger, Maggie (Miss), #1334
Poffenberger, Margie Leona, #7736
Poffenberger, Mary Ann Frances, #5126
Poffenberger, Mary Ann Francis, #5106
Poffenberger, Mary Ann R., #5118
Poffenberger, Noah Ettie, #5119
Poffenberger, Norman Myers, #5107
Poffenberger, Norman Myers, #5122
Poffenberger, Owen Edward, #7678
Poffenberger, Owen Edward, #7718
Poffenberger, Owen Edward, #7719
Poffenberger, Owen Edward, #7727
Poffenberger, Owen Edward, #7728
Poffenberger, Owen Edward, #7729
Poffenberger, Owen Edward, #7730
Poffenberger, Owen Edward, #7731
Poffenberger, Owen Edward, #7732
Poffenberger, Owen Edward, #7733

Poffenberger, Owen Edward, #7734
Poffenberger, Owen Edward, #7735
Poffenberger, Owen Edward, #7736
Poffenberger, Owen Edward, #7737
Poffenberger, Owen Edward, #7738
Poffenberger, Owen Edward, #7739
Poffenberger, Owen Edward, #7740
Poffenberger, Owen Edward, #7741
Poffenberger, Theodore Rosevelt, #7737
Poffenberger, Woodrow Wilson, #7738
Poffenberger, Woodward M., #4302
"Poffenberger, Jr.", Owen Edward, #7731
Poffenburger, Deloris M., #7715
Poffenburger, Ira Grayson, #7716
Poffenburger, Janice Marie, #7712
Poling, A.W., #680
Poling, Albert, #691
Poling, Albert W., #667
Poling, Albert W., #669
Poling, Albert W., #690
Poling, Baby, #673
Poling, C.H., #681
Poling, C.H., #688
Poling, Catharine, #668
Poling, Catharine, #669
Poling, Catharine, #687
Poling, Chandler Miller, #698
Poling, Christina Lynn, #694
Poling, Columbus Hall, #669
Poling, Columbus Hall, #691
Poling, David R., #666
Poling, Edward L., #698
Poling, Edward L., #699
Poling, Edward Lee, #678
Poling, Edward Lee, #685
Poling, Emerson, #696
Poling, Emerson, #697
Poling, Harry Emerson, #677
Poling, Harry Emerson, #684
Poling, James, #694
Poling, James, #695
Poling, James Nathan, #695
Poling, James Newton, #676
Poling, James Newton, #683
Poling, John Robert, #696
Poling, M.B., #680
Poling, Mark Edward, #697
Poling, Martin B., #667
Poling, Mary Alice, #671
Poling, Mary Alice, #689
Poling, Newton, #676
Poling, Newton, #677
Poling, Newton, #678
Poling, Newton, #679
Poling, Newton L., #682
Poling, Newton Lyon, #672
Poling, Newton Lyon, #693
Poling, R., #680
Poling, Rebecca, #700

Poling, Rebecca, #701
Poling, Rebecca Jeanne, #679
Poling, Rebecca Jeanne, #686
Poling, Ruth, #667
Poling, Ruth, #674
Poling, Ruth, #675
Poling, Travis Edward, #699
Poling, Virginia S., #676
Poling, Virginia S., #677
Poling, Virginia S., #678
Poling, Virginia S., #679
Poling, W.A., #688
Poling, Wendell Idleman, #670
Poling, Wendell J., #688
Poling, Willye Idelman, #692
Polling, Albert W., #666
Pollinger, Elizabeth, #3881
Pollinger, Elizabeth, #3882
Pomp, Thomas, #2146
Pomss, Thomas, #2121
Poppen, Alvin W., #2903
Poppen, Daniel Victor, #2902
Poppen, Daniel Victor, #2903
Poppen, Daniel Victor, #2904
Poppen, Grace, #2903
Poppen, Kimberly Hollis, #2904
Posey, Sarah, #5212
Posey, Sarah A., #5209
Potter, William D., #594
Pottinger, Elizabeth, #2641
Pottinger, Elizabeth, #2646
Pottinger, Elizabeth, #2647
Potts, Elisabeth, #1881
Potts, Ezekiel, #1881
Powell, Sarah, #6259
Powell, Sarah, #6274
Powell, Sarah, #6275
Powell, Sarah, #6276
Powell, Sarah, #6277
Powell, Sarah, #6278
Powell, Sarah, #6279
Powell, Sarah, #6280
Powell, Sarah, #6281
Powell, Sarah, #6282
Powell, Sarah, #6283
Powell, Sarah, #6284
Powell, William, #6271
Powles, Ruth, #6698
Prentice, Eliza P., #3786
Price, Alfred A., #4287
Price, Alfred Armor, #4272
Price, Amelia Wild, #4287
Price, Augustus, #4272
Price, Augustus, #4273
Price, Augustus Richard, #4273
Price, Augustus W., #4277
Price, Augustus W., #4282
Price, Emma, #4272
Price, Emma, #4273
Price, Emma Elizabeth (Armor), #4288
Prichard, Annie E., #595
Prichard, Annie E., #599
Prichard, Annie E., #602
Prichard, Elizabeth F., #607
Prichard, George, #597
Prichard, George, #600
Prichard, George, #608
Pritchard, M. Susan (Miss), #7748
Pritchard, Samuel, #7749
Pritchard, Susan, #7749
Prtichard, Mary, #7749

INDEX
Pages are not numbered; numbers refer to the entry number at the beginning of each record.

Pymont, , #6268
Quantrill, A.R., #8411
Quantrill, Catharine C., #8412
Quantrill, Eliza, #8374
Quantrill, Eliza, #8408
Quantrill, J.D.E., #8373
Quantrill, J.D.E., #8380
Quantrill, J.D.E., #8390
Quantrill, Jesse D.E., #8410
Quantrill, Judith Ann, #8387
Quantrill, Judith Ann, #8390
Quantrill, Mary, #8369
Quantrill, Mary, #8388
Quantrill, Mary Ann, #8406
Quantrill, Pretzman, #8389
Quantrill, Pretzman[?], #8388
Quantrill, Thomas, #8387
Quantrill, Thomas, #8390
Quantrill, Thos. H., #8409
Rabbais, Sebastian, #1518
Rabuck, Sarah Jane, #5755
Rabuck, Sarah Jane, #5761
Rahauser, Frederick, #187
Rahauser, Jonathan, #3126
Rahauser, Jonathan, #3142
Rahauser, Jonathan, #3146
Ramacciotti, Mary B., #8505
Ramsburg, Rev., #5483
Ramsey, Chester Sylvester, #5090
Ramsey, Flora B., #5088
Ramsey, Flora B., #5099
Ramsey, Jessie Beatrice, #5089
Ramsey, Laura Jane, #5092
Ramsey, Lena Gray, #5093
Ramsey, Margaret M., #5091
Ramsey, Sarah J., #5100
Ramsey, Sylvester, #5098
Ramsey, Vivian Belle, #5095
Ramsey, W.H., #5086
Ramsey, W.H., #5087
Ramsey, Wiliam L., #5094
Randal, Walter B., #6185
Raney, John T.[?], #7187
Raney, Susan Ann, #7186
Raney, Susan Ann, #7187
Raney, Susan Ann, #7188
Raney, Susan Ann, #7189
Raney, Susan Ann, #7190
Raney, Susan Ann, #7191
Raney, Susan Ann, #7192
Rankin, Elizabeth K., #7665
Rankin, Elizabeth K., #7666
Rankin, Elizabeth Watson, #7630
Rankin, Elizabeth Watson, #7665
Rankin, Harry Huber, #7632
Rankin, James, #7629
Rankin, Jere C., #7632
Rankin, Jere C., #7633
Rankin, Jere C., #7634
Rankin, Jerry, #7648
Rankin, Jerry, #7649
Rankin, Johnston, #7665
Rankin, Johnston, #7666
Rankin, Margaret Johnston, #7666
Rankin, Margaret Johston, #7631

Rankin, Maria Louise, #7634
Rankin, Maria Louise, #7649
Rankin, Mary Jane, #7633
Rankin, Mary Jane, #7648
Rankin, S. Johnston, #7621
Rankin, S. Johnston, #7646
Rankin, Samuel Johnston, #7630
Rankin, Samuel Johnston, #7631
Rankin, Samuel Johnston, #7674
Rathen, Don, #8276
Rawlings, Frederick, #1266
Rawlings, Frederick, #1280
Rawlings, Frederick, #1281
Rebaugh, John, #3455
Reed, Reuben Walter, #2564
Reed, Reuben Walter, #2565
Reeder, Bettie Marie, #7710
Reeder, Betty Cronise, #7701
Reeder, Betty Cronise, #7702
Reeder, Daniel, #7694
Reeder, Daniel, #7695
Reeder, Dennis Elwood, #7709
Reeder, Ernest Winfred, #7708
Reeder, Hiram, #7690
Reeder, Hiram, #7691
Reeder, Imogene Bernice Hardez, #7714
Reeder, Irene Elizabeth, #7679
Reeder, Irene Elizabeth, #7680
Reeder, Irene Elizabeth, #7706
Reeder, Irene Elizabeth, #7717
Reeder, John Luther, #7680
Reeder, John Luther, #7703
Reeder, John Luther, #7705
Reeder, John Luther, #7706
Reeder, John Luther, #7707
Reeder, John Luther, #7708
Reeder, John Luther, #7709
Reeder, John Luther, #7710
Reeder, John Luther, #7711
Reeder, John Luther, #7722
Reeder, John Luther, #7723
Reeder, John Luther, #7725
Reeder, Mae Gertrude, #7707
Reeder, Marcia Copeland, #7711
Reeder, Otho James, #7698
Reeder, Otho James, #7699
Reeder, Otho James, #7700
Reeder, Rose Ann (Longman), #7692
Reeder, Rose Ann (Longman), #7693
Reeder, Susan (Beachley), #7696
Reeder, Susan (Beachley), #7697
Reese, Lydia, #5040
Reetzell[?], Carry Pearson Loose, #6950
Reifsnider, Anna Mariah, #2506
Reifsnider, Anna Mariah, #2520
Reifsnider, Anna Mariah, #7855
Reifsnider, Anna Mariah, #7857
Reily, James R., #3154
Reily, Rev., #3158
Reinharat[?], Ann Catharine, #3271

Reinhart[?], Christian, #3271
Reityet, William R., #6890
Remsburg, Annie[?] E., #3643
Remsburg, Mary Catherine, #5329
Remsburg, Peter, #5331
Reynolds, James W., #3129
Reynolds, James W., #3181
Reynolds, James W., #3182
Reynolds, Ruth Estella, #5565
Reynolds, Susanna, #3181
Rhineman, John, #2895
Rhineman, Mary Jane, #2895
Rhineman, Minnie Edington, #2895
Rhineman, Minnie Edington, #2896
Rhodes, Elizabeth, #5606
Rhorback, Cornelius, #4843
Rice, Edrie J., #605
Rice, Edrie[?], #599
Rice, J.E.B., #6775
Rice, John, #598
Rice, John, #603
Rice, John, #606
Rice, Rhoda B., #609
rice, S.L., #4303
Richardson, Alice Morris, #1234
Richardson, Clarenc Rich., #8001
Richardson, Daniel Stewart, #8000
Richardson, Daniel Stewart, #8001
Richardson, Daniel Stewart, #8002
Richardson, Daniel Stewart, #8003
Richardson, Daniel Stewart, #8004
Richardson, Francis Samuel, #8000
Richardson, H.J., #7440
Richardson, Hariot Virginia, #1237
Richardson, Hariot Virginia, #1240
Richardson, Hariot Virginia, #1241
Richardson, Hariot Virginia, #1242
Richardson, Hariot Virginia, #1243
Richardson, Hariot Virginia, #1244
Richardson, Hariot Virginia, #1245
Richardson, Harry Earnest, #8004
Richardson, James William, #1235
Richardson, James William, #1236
Richardson, Maria Louisa, #1246
Richardson, Maria Louisa, #1247
Richardson, Maria Louisa, #1248
Richardson, Maria Louisa, #1249
Richardson, Martha Linton, #1239
Richardson, Mary Anette, #1210
Richardson, Mary Anette, #1211
Richardson, Mary Anette, #1212
Richardson, Mary Anette, #1213
Richardson, Mary Anette, #1238
Richardson, Richard Alexander, #1233
Richardson, Richard Alexander, #1234
Richardson, Richard Alexander, #1235
Richardson, Richard Alexander, #1236
Richardson, Richard Alexander, #1237
Richardson, Richard Alexander, #1238
Richardson, Richard Alexander, #1239
Richardson, Robert Howard, #8003
Richardson, Sallie, #8022

Richardson, Sallie J., #8000
Richardson, Sallie J., #8001
Richardson, Sallie J., #8002
Richardson, Sallie J., #8003
Richardson, Sallie J., #8004
Richardson, Sallie J., #8031
Richardson, William P., #1246
Richardson, Wm. Alfred, #8002
Ricketts, George, #5996
Ricketts, George, #5999
Ricketts, Jane, #5999
Ricketts, Louisa Jane, #5996
Ricketts, Thomas, #5999
Rickird, Kattie M., #5160
Ricktis[?], George, #5956
Ridd, Edna, #2620
Ridennour, Daniel Newton, #7417
Ridenor, Jacob, #7406
Ridenour, Alice, #5061
Ridenour, Alice, #5068
Ridenour, Catharine Elizabeth, #5032
Ridenour, Catharine M., #1878
Ridenour, Catharine M., #1907
Ridenour, Charles Augustus, #5057
Ridenour, Charles Edward, #7413
Ridenour, Christopher, #1878
Ridenour, Christopher, #1907
Ridenour, Courtney A., #5050
Ridenour, Courtney A., #5051
Ridenour, Daniel, #7425
Ridenour, Daniel Nuton, #7412
Ridenour, David, #5040
Ridenour, David A., #3500
Ridenour, David M., #5048
Ridenour, Doris Gertrude, #5033
Ridenour, Edna Jane, #5030
Ridenour, Effa Jane, #7419
Ridenour, Effa Jane, #7421
Ridenour, Eliz., #1907
Ridenour, Elizabeth, #1878
Ridenour, Elizabeth, #5072
Ridenour, Emma Arbelan, #7416
Ridenour, Emma Jane, #5058
Ridenour, Emma Jane, #5067
Ridenour, Etta, #7420
Ridenour, Frank Leslie, #5062
Ridenour, Frank Leslie, #5069
Ridenour, George Melanchthon, #7411
Ridenour, James William, #5059
Ridenour, Jane, #5051
Ridenour, Jennie G., #5025
Ridenour, Jennie Gertrude, #5029
Ridenour, John, #5051
Ridenour, John Edward, #5060
Ridenour, John Edward, #5070
Ridenour, John He, #7423
Ridenour, John Henry, #7409
Ridenour, John L., #5021
Ridenour, John L., #5024
Ridenour, John L., #5028
Ridenour, John L., #5049
Ridenour, Laura Virginia, #5055
Ridenour, Lewis Machelon, #7415
Ridenour, Lewis Machelon, #7418
Ridenour, Manday Catharine, #7410
Ridenour, Mary C., #1516
Ridenour, Mary C., #1537
Ridenour, Mary C. (Miss), #665
Ridenour, Mary Cornelia, #5053
Ridenour, Mary Ellen Rebecca, #7408
Ridenour, Mary Kate, #5063

INDEX
Pages are not numbered; numbers refer to the entry number at the beginning of each record.

Ridenour, Oliver Burkhart, #5056
Ridenour, Samuel, #5052
Ridenour, Samuel, #5053
Ridenour, Samuel, #5054
Ridenour, Samuel, #5055
Ridenour, Samuel, #5056
Ridenour, Samuel, #5057
Ridenour, Samuel, #5058
Ridenour, Samuel, #5059
Ridenour, Samuel, #5060
Ridenour, Samuel, #5061
Ridenour, Samuel, #5062
Ridenour, Samuel, #5063
Ridenour, Samuel, #5064
Ridenour, Samuel, #5073
Ridenour, Sarah Elizabeth, #7414
Ridenour, Sophia Ann, #5054
Ridenour, Sophia Ann, #5066
Ridenour, Susan, #3474
Ridenour, Susanna, #7407
Ridenour, Susannah, #7422
Ridenour, Welty Andrew, #5031
Ridenour, William, #7424
Rideout, Eliza, #8540
Rider, Rev., #6807
Ridgeley, Kate, #7158
Ridgeley, Mary, #7157
Ridgeley, Mary, #7159
Ridgeley, Richard, #7155
Ridgeley, Richard, #7157
Ridgeley, Richard, #7158
Ridgeley, Richard, #7170
Ridgeley, Richard, #7171
Ridgeley[?], Richard, #7112
Ridgely, Ruxton M., #3041
Rinehart, E.T., #7616
Rinehart, E.T., #7644
Rinehart, Euphemia Mason, #7671
Rinehart, Even. Thomas, #7673
Rinehart, Marmie, #7637
Rinehart, Mary Helen, #7662
Rinehart, Mary Helen, #7663
Rinehart, Mary Helen, #7664
Rinehart, Mary Magdalene (Summer), #4575
Rinehart, Samuel (M.D.), #7672
Ringer, Eberhard, #8584
Ringer, Jacob (Mrs.), #8586
Ringer, John (of R), #415
Ringer, Julean, #413
Ringer, Mary, #414
Ringer, Rhegattin Juliana, #8585
Ringer, Robert, #412
Ringleb, Mary Ida, #6309
Ringleb, Mary Ida, #6310
Ringleb, Mary Ida, #6311
Rittenhouse, Rev., #173
Ritter, Servis (Mrs.), #499
Rizer, Mary Martha, #7390
Rizer, Mary Martha, #7398
Rizer, Mary Martha, #7399
Robaugh, John, #250
Robbins, Donna Jeanne, #8264

Robbins, Donna Jeanne, #8337
Robbins, Donna Jeanne, #8368
Roberdeau, Heriot Triplett, #1233
Roberdeau, Heriot Triplett, #1234
Roberdeau, Heriot Triplett, #1235
Roberdeau, Heriot Triplett, #1236
Roberdeau, Heriot Triplett, #1237
Roberdeau, Heriot Triplett, #1238
Roberdeau, Heriot Triplett, #1239
Roberts, Rebecca H., #3133
Robertson, Lois (Middlekauff), #5554
Robinson, A.C. (Dr.), #7564
Robinson, Rosa W., #7563
Robinson, Rosa W., #7564
Rogers, Emily J., #2219
Rogers, John F., #2218
Rogers, John F., #2219
Rogers, John F., #2220
Rogerson, Maud, #3430
Rohrback, Ann S., #4844
Rohrback, Anna Mary, #1024
Rohrback, Anna Mary, #1025
Rohrback, Anna Mary, #4902
Rohrback, Anna Mary, #4903
Rohrback, Barbara, #1018
Rohrback, Barbara, #1019
Rohrback, Barbara, #4896
Rohrback, Barbara, #4897
Rohrback, Barbara, #986
Rohrback, Barbara (Barks), #996
Rohrback, Barbara (Barks), #997
Rohrback, Catharine, #1010
Rohrback, Catharine, #1011
Rohrback, Catherine, #4888
Rohrback, Catherine, #4889
Rohrback, Cornelious, #1000
Rohrback, Cornelious, #990
Rohrback, Cornelious, #1026
Rohrback, Cornelius, #1027
Rohrback, Cornelius, #4904
Rohrback, Cornelius, #4905
Rohrback, Daniel, #1016
Rohrback, Daniel, #1017
Rohrback, Daniel, #4894
Rohrback, Daniel, #4895
Rohrback, Elias, #1020
Rohrback, Elias, #1021
Rohrback, Elias, #4898
Rohrback, Elias, #4899
Rohrback, Elias, #989
Rohrback, Elias, #999
Rohrback, Elizabeth, #1006
Rohrback, Elizabeth, #1007
Rohrback, Elizabeth, #4884
Rohrback, Elizabeth, #4885
Rohrback, Franklin, #4844
Rohrback, Henry, #1005
Rohrback, Henry, #1006
Rohrback, Henry, #1007
Rohrback, Henry, #1008
Rohrback, Henry, #1009

Rohrback, Henry, #1010
Rohrback, Henry, #1011
Rohrback, Henry, #1012
Rohrback, Henry, #1013
Rohrback, Henry, #1014
Rohrback, Henry, #1015
Rohrback, Henry, #1016
Rohrback, Henry, #1017
Rohrback, Henry, #1018
Rohrback, Henry, #1019
Rohrback, Henry, #1020
Rohrback, Henry, #1021
Rohrback, Henry, #1022
Rohrback, Henry, #1023
Rohrback, Henry, #1024
Rohrback, Henry, #1025
Rohrback, Henry, #1026
Rohrback, Henry, #1027
Rohrback, Henry, #4878
Rohrback, Henry, #4879
Rohrback, Henry, #4880
Rohrback, Henry, #4881
Rohrback, Henry, #4882
Rohrback, Henry, #4883
Rohrback, Henry, #4884
Rohrback, Henry, #4885
Rohrback, Henry, #4886
Rohrback, Henry, #4887
Rohrback, Henry, #4888
Rohrback, Henry, #4889
Rohrback, Henry, #4890
Rohrback, Henry, #4891
Rohrback, Henry, #4892
Rohrback, Henry, #4893
Rohrback, Henry, #4894
Rohrback, Henry, #4895
Rohrback, Henry, #4896
Rohrback, Henry, #4897
Rohrback, Henry, #4898
Rohrback, Henry, #4899
Rohrback, Henry, #4900
Rohrback, Henry, #4901
Rohrback, Henry, #4902
Rohrback, Henry, #4903
Rohrback, Henry, #4904
Rohrback, Henry, #4905
Rohrback, Henry, #994
Rohrback, Henry, #995
Rohrback, Henry B., #4892
Rohrback, Henry B., #4893
Rohrback, Henry B., #988
Rohrback, Henry Barks, #1014
Rohrback, Henry Barks, #1015
Rohrback, Jacob, #987
Rohrback, Jacob, #998
Rohrback, Jacob (Col.), #4847
Rohrback, Jacob H., #1012
Rohrback, Jacob H., #1013
Rohrback, Jacob H., #4890
Rohrback, Jacob H., #4891
Rohrback, John H., #1004
Rohrback, John H., #1005
Rohrback, John H., #4882
Rohrback, John H., #4883
Rohrback, Joseph L., #4846
Rohrback, Mary, #1008
Rohrback, Mary, #1009
Rohrback, Mary, #4886
Rohrback, Mary, #4887
Rohrback, Mary (Mrs.), #4847
Rohrback, Noah, #1022

Rohrback, Noah, #1023
Rohrback, Noah, #4900
Rohrback, Noah, #4901
Rohrback, William, #4845
Rohrback, William Wagner, #4844
Rohrer, Albert Martin, #5007
Rohrer, Albert Martin, #5013
Rohrer, Anna[?] R., #5016
Rohrer, Becca[?], #4643
Rohrer, Becca[?], #4644
Rohrer, Carrie, #4643
Rohrer, Clarence H., #5016
Rohrer, Clarence H., #5017
Rohrer, Clarence Henry, #5006
Rohrer, Clarence Henry, #5011
Rohrer, Corah[?] Ellen, #5010
Rohrer, Daniel, #3410
Rohrer, Daniel A., #3404
Rohrer, David, #4988
Rohrer, David, #5000
Rohrer, Edgar F.[?], #5004
Rohrer, Edger Frank, #5014
Rohrer, Elizabeth, #3407
Rohrer, Elizabeth, #4997
Rohrer, Estella May, #5503
Rohrer, Flora M., #5003
Rohrer, Florie May, #5012
Rohrer, Harriet Matilda, #4999
Rohrer, Harriet Matilda, #5002
Rohrer, Helen H., #5019
Rohrer, Henry, #4986
Rohrer, Ivon Delmar, #5018
Rohrer, Jacob A., #4996
Rohrer, Jacob M., #5003
Rohrer, Jacob M., #5004
Rohrer, Jacob M., #5005
Rohrer, Jacob M., #5007
Rohrer, Jacob M., #5008
Rohrer, Jacob M., #5010
Rohrer, Jacob M., #5011
Rohrer, Jacob M., #5012
Rohrer, Jacob M., #5013
Rohrer, Jacob M., #5014
Rohrer, Jacob M., #5015
Rohrer, John, #4989
Rohrer, John M., #4997
Rohrer, Joseph, #4987
Rohrer, LaVerne Baker, #2800
Rohrer, Lillie M., #5003
Rohrer, Lillie M., #5004
Rohrer, Lillie M., #5005
Rohrer, Lillie M., #5007
Rohrer, Lillie M., #5010
Rohrer, Lillie M., #5011
Rohrer, Lillie M., #5012
Rohrer, Lillie M., #5013
Rohrer, Lillie M., #5014
Rohrer, Lillie M., #5015
Rohrer, Lillie M., #5009
Rohrer, Louise S., #5018
Rohrer, Magdaline, #3093
Rohrer, Magdaline, #3094
Rohrer, Margaret, #3409
Rohrer, Margaret Ellen, #4992
Rohrer, Marie C., #5017
Rohrer, Martha E., #4995
Rohrer, Mary, #4986
Rohrer, Mary, #4987
Rohrer, Mary, #4988
Rohrer, Mary, #4989
Rohrer, Mary, #4990

INDEX

Pages are not numbered; numbers refer to the entry number at the beginning of each record.

Rohrer, Mary, #4991
Rohrer, Mary, #4992
Rohrer, Mary, #4993
Rohrer, Mary, #4994
Rohrer, Mary, #4995
Rohrer, Mary, #4996
Rohrer, Mary, #4999
Rohrer, Mary, #5000
Rohrer, Mary, #5001
Rohrer, Mary, #5002
Rohrer, Maryan ____[?], #4994
Rohrer, Miriam Lee, #2802
Rohrer, Nelda Jean, #2801
Rohrer, Nelda Jean, #2803
Rohrer, Samuel J., #3404
Rohrer, Samuel J., #3405
Rohrer, Samuel J., #3406
Rohrer, Samuel J., #3407
Rohrer, Samuel J., #3408
Rohrer, Samuel J., #3409
Rohrer, Samuel J., #3410
Rohrer, Sophia Jane, #4993
Rohrer, W. Newton, #2798
Rohrer, William, #4990
Rohrer, William, #5001
Rohrer, William Arthur, #2798
Rohrer, Winfield S.[?], #4991
Rohrer, Winifred, #3426
Rohrer, Wm., #2800
Rohrer, Wm., #2801
Rohrer, Wm., #2802
Rohrer, Wm. A., #2763
"Rohrer, Jr.", Ivon Delmar, #5019
"Rohrer, Jr.", John M., #4986
"Rohrer, Jr.", John M., #4987
"Rohrer, Jr.", John M., #4988
"Rohrer, Jr.", John M., #4989
"Rohrer, Jr.", John M., #4990
"Rohrer, Jr.", John M., #4991
"Rohrer, Jr.", John M., #4992
"Rohrer, Jr.", John M., #4993
"Rohrer, Jr.", John M., #4994
"Rohrer, Jr.", John M., #4995
"Rohrer, Jr.", John M., #4996
"Rohrer, Jr.", John M., #4997
"Rohrer, Jr.", John M., #4999
"Rohrer, Jr.", John M., #5000
"Rohrer, Jr.", John M., #5001
"Rohrer, Jr.", John M., #5002
Rolfe, Rev., #1279
Rose, H. Adelaide, #5909
Rosenstal, Joanna M., #3455
Rosensteel[?], Joanna Margaret, #3458
Ross, Catharine, #196
Ross, Catharine, #197
Ross, Catherine, #187
Ross, Lidia, #1826
Ross, Lidia, #8058
Ross, Rev. Dr., #2919
Roth, Althea, #1700
Roth, Althea, #1701
Roth, Althea, #4165
Roth, Althea, #4166
Rothrauff, N., #8373
Roudabush, G.J., #725
Roulette, Annie Elizabeth, #4934

Roulette, Benjamin Franklin, #4939
Roulette, Carrie May, #4940
Roulette, Carrie May, #4946
Roulette, John Daniel, #4935
Roulette, Joseph Clinton, #4936
Roulette, Margaret Ann, #4933
Roulette, Margaret Ann, #4947
Roulette, Otho William, #4937
Roulette, Otho William, #4945
Roulette, Susan Rebecca, #4938
Roulette, Ulyssis Sheridan, #4941
Roulette, William, #4932
Roulette, William, #4933
Roulette, William, #4943
Roulette, William, #4944
Roulette, William, #4948
Roundthaler, Rev., #8206
Roundthaler, Rev., #8208
Roundthaler, Rev., #8229
Rowe, Minnie May, #2730
Rowland, Abraham, #2278
Rowland, Ann ____, #4950
Rowland, Ann Maria, #4963
Rowland, Ann Maria, #4978
Rowland, Benjamin, #4951
Rowland, Benjamin, #4983
Rowland, Benjamin H., #4973
Rowland, Benjamin Henry, #4962
Rowland, Catharine, #4953
Rowland, Catharine, #4964
Rowland, Eliza, #4983
Rowland, Henry, #4958
Rowland, Henry, #4971
Rowland, John E., #4957
Rowland, John Emmert, #4967
Rowland, John Emmert[?], #4977
Rowland, John S., #4949
Rowland, John Shively, #4960
Rowland, John Shively, #4975
Rowland, Joseph M., #4954
Rowland, Joseph Martin, #4969
Rowland, Lena, #4952
Rowland, Lena, #4965
Rowland, Mary (Shively), #4959
Rowland, Mary (Shively), #4972
Rowland, Mary E., #4956
Rowland, Mary Ellen, #4968
Rowland, Nancy, #4978
Rowland, Nancy Emmert, #4961
Rowland, Nancy Emmert, #4976
Rowland, Nancy H., #4955
Rowland, Nancy H., #4966
Rowland, Samuel David, #4970
Rowland, Samuel David, #4974
Royer, [female], #8053
Royer, [female], #8054
Royer, A., #7248
Royer, Dan., #8047
Royer, Ella, #8055
Royer, Ella, #8056
Royer, G.A., #7229
Royer, Jane, #7978
Royer, Jno., #8048

Royer, Lizzie, #8052
Royer, Mary, #8050
Royer, Mary, #8051
Royer, Rev., #7225
Royer, Rev., #7227
Royer, Rev., #7243
Royer, Saml., #8046
Royer, Saml., #8047
Royer, Saml., #8048
Royer, Saml., #8049
Royer, Saml., #8050
Royer, Saml., #8051
Royer, Saml., #8052
Royer, Saml., #8053
Royer, Saml., #8054
Royer, Saml., #8055
Royer, Saml., #8056
Royer, Saul, #8034
Royer, Thos., #8049
Ruch, Daniel, #5022
Ruch, Daniel, #5026
Ruch, Dan'l, #5023
Ruch, Kate, #5027
Ruch, Kate (Bishop), #5023
Ruck, Daniel, #5020
Ruck, Ralph R., #5082
Rucker, Genie M., #5141
Rucker, Virginia, #5175
Ruff, John K., #3380
Rupp, Ulysses S.G., #6703
Russell, George M., #1256
Ruth, Francis, #4372
Ryan, Malvina (Miss), #577
Sagle, Mabel, #2857
Saler, Catrin, #5549
Saler, Nancy Ann, #5550
Sanders, David Benjamin Franklin, #2608
Sandlass, [blank], #6465
Sandlass, Viola, #6303
Sandlass, Viola, #6304
Sandlass, Viola, #6305
Sandlass, Viola, #6433
Sandlass, Viola, #6434
Sandlass, Viola, #6435
Sands, Samuel A., #1823
Sanford, F.[?] P.[?], #5773
Sanford, F.[?] Ruthanna, #5759
Sanford, Frances Ruthanna, #5753
Sanford, Frances Ruthanna, #5763
Sanford, Frances Ruthanna, #5764
Sanford, Frances Ruthanna, #5765
Sanford, Frances Ruthanna, #5766
Sanford, Francis Parker, #5751
Sanford, Francis Parker, #5761
Sanford, George Pinkney, #5752
Sanford, George Pinkney, #5770
Sanford, Joseph Francis, #5749
Sanford, Joseph Francis, #5750
Sanford, Joseph Francis, #5760
Sanford, Joseph Francis, #5769
Sanford, Robert Parker, #5754
Sanford, Ruthann, #5737
Sanford, Ruthanna Parker, #5768
Sanford, Sarah Jane, #5771
Sanner, Alice, #7388
Sanner, R.R., #7387
Santee, J.W., #5349
Satterfield, Kathleen Marie, #5296
Satterfield, Thomas, #1392
Satterfield, Thomas, #5296

Satterfield, Thomas, #5297
Satterfield, Thomas, #5303
Satterfield, Tracy Lynn, #5297
Schaefer, David F., #4370
Schaeffer, Frederick, #4848
Schaeffer, Sophia C. (Mrs.), #4848
Schantz, Ida, #2139
Schantz, Ida, #2140
Scheafer, D.F., #4354
Scheafer, D.F., #4374
Schenkel, Hunt Hardinge, #6927
Schenkel, Philip Mathias, #6926
Schenkel, Robert Downs, #6925
Schenkel, Stuart Pearson, #6934
Schidleman, Emma T. (Mrs.), #1328
Schinkel, Robert Downs, #6897
Schlosser, Eliz., #8148
Schlosser, Elizabeth, #8143
Schlosser, John, #8143
Schlosser, John, #8150
Schlosser, John, #8151
Schlosser, Peter, #8150
Schlosser, Susannah, #8151
Schmid, Elgina Marie, #8268
Schmid, Karel, #8233
Schmid, Karel, #8234
Schmid, Karel, #8235
Schmid, Karel, #8236
Schmid, Karel Marie, #8265
Schmiding, Anna Maria, #5579
Schmiding, Anna Maria, #5580
Schmidt, Rev., #4046
Schneider, Anna Maria, #7141
Schneider, Caspar, #7141
Schneider, Jacob, #8590
Schneider, Peter, #7141
Schneider, Peter, #7142
Schneider, Peter, #8589
Schofield, Gertrude Annie, #4741
Schone, Eva[?] A. Fricke, #6515
Schriver, Susann, #5821
Scobey, Mary Ann, #4280
Scobey, Rachel, #4274
Scobey[?], Rachel, #4231
Scott, Ellen, #5162
Scott, Ellen, #5189
Scott, George Marshall, #7637
Scott, Helen, #7664
Scott, William, #7637
Scott, William Henry, #5173
Scott, William Henry, #5174
Scott, Wm., #7662
Scott, Wm., #7664
Seibert, Daniel S., #6805
Seibert, Louila E., #6839
Seidenstricker, , #4230
Seigleitz, Frank C., #8507
Seiss, Mary C., #35
Sellman, Matilda, #294
Sellman, Matilda, #4005
Sencenbach, Maude L. (Miss), #2142
Sensaman, Mariah, #8375
Severson, Doyles, #7854
Severson, Harlan, #7853
Severson, Harlan, #7854
Shafer, Charles F., #8372
Shafer, Ellen Newcomer, #3601
Shafer, Margaret C., #3251
Shafer, Margaret C., #3252
Shaffer, ____ M., #4438
Shaffer, Ann, #4438

INDEX
Pages are not numbered; numbers refer to the entry number at the beginning of each record.

Shaffer, Ann, #4439
Shaffer, Ann, #4440
Shaffer, Ann Matilda (Winter), #4421
Shaffer, C.M., #4438
Shaffer, C.M., #4439
Shaffer, C.M., #4440
Shaffer, Charles Hamil[?], #4439
Shaffer, Christian[?] M., #4357
Shaffer, Francis Winter, #4437
Shank, Abraham, #5606
Shank, Abraham, #6779
Shank, Abraham, #6801
Shank, Abraham, #6810
Shank, Abraham, #6812
Shank, Abraham, #6813
Shank, Abraham, #6814
Shank, Abraham, #6815
Shank, Abraham, #6816
Shank, Abraham, #6817
Shank, Abraham, #6818
Shank, Abraham, #6819
Shank, Abraham, #6820
Shank, Abraham, #6821
Shank, Abraham, #6822
Shank, Abraham, #6823
Shank, Abraham, #6824
Shank, Abraham, #6825
Shank, Abraham, #6826
Shank, Abraham, #6827
Shank, Abraham, #6828
Shank, Abraham, #6829
Shank, Abraham, #6836
Shank, Abraham, #6837
Shank, Barbara E., #4579
Shank, Charley Abraham, #6816
Shank, Charley Abraham, #6817
Shank, Charley Abraham, #6834
Shank, Christley Speaker, #6818
Shank, Christley Speaker, #6819
Shank, Esther (Miss), #521
Shank, Fanny Leah, #6812
Shank, Fanny Leah, #6813
Shank, Fanny Leah, #6832
Shank, Fredrick Arthur, #6826
Shank, Fredrick Arthur, #6827
Shank, Henry, #6800
Shank, Jacob Harman, #6814
Shank, Jacob Harman, #6815
Shank, Jacob Harman, #6833
Shank, John C., #6806
Shank, John Chester, #6828
Shank, John Chester, #6829
Shank, Loulia E., #6805
Shank, Loulia Elizabeth, #6824
Shank, Loulia Elizabeth, #6825
Shank, M. Bertha, #6803
Shank, Margaret Bertha, #6820
Shank, Margaret Bertha, #6821

Shank, Maria, #6800
Shank, Mary N., #6804
Shank, Mary Naomi, #6822
Shank, Mary Naomi, #6823
Shank, Noah, #3504
Shank, Noah , #3490
Shank, Rachel, #5465
Shank, Sarah, #6837
Shank, Shristley Speaker, #6835
Shank, Susan, #8038
Shank, Susan, #8039
Shank, Susan, #8040
Shank, Susan, #8041
Shank, Susan, #8042
Shank, Susan, #8043
Shank, Susan, #8044
Shank, Susan, #8045
Shank, Susan (Frey), #3499
Shank, Susan (Mrs.), #3504
Shelton, J.B., #2187
Shenk, William Gordon, #2409
Shenk, William Gordon, #2416
Sherick, Anna, #7312
Sherrick, Anna, #7321
Sherrick, Anna, #7334
Sherrick, Barbara, #7325
Sherrick, Jacob, #7327
Sherrick, Jacob, #7328
Sherrick, Joseph, #7312
Sherrick, Joseph, #7313
Sherrick, Joseph, #7319
Sherrick, Joseph, #7326
Sherrick, Joseph, #7329
Sherrick, Mary H., #7314
Sherrick, Sarah, #7330
Sherrick, Sarah, #7333
Shilling, Beatrice Pearl (Mrs.), #3030
Shillingburg, Amelia Frances (Sollars), #1131
Shillingburg, Ann Amelia, #1085
Shillingburg, Beall Davis, #1111
Shillingburg, Bertha Mildred, #1110
Shillingburg, Carrie, #1113
Shillingburg, Carrie, #1123
Shillingburg, Edward S., #1103
Shillingburg, Edward S., #1104
Shillingburg, Edward S., #1105
Shillingburg, Edward S., #1106
Shillingburg, Edward S., #1107
Shillingburg, Edward S., #1108
Shillingburg, Edward S., #1109
Shillingburg, Edward S., #1110
Shillingburg, Edward S., #1111
Shillingburg, Elizabeth Kitzmiller, #1089
Shillingburg, Elizabeth Kitzmiller, #1090
Shillingburg, Ella Rea, #1118
Shillingburg, Grover C., #1101
Shillingburg, Grover Cleveland, #1104
Shillingburg, Hannah, #1084
Shillingburg, Infant, #1106
Shillingburg, Infant, #1107
Shillingburg, Isabella, #1086
Shillingburg, James B., #1128

Shillingburg, James Bryan, #1117
Shillingburg, James G., #1112
Shillingburg, James G., #1113
Shillingburg, James G., #1114
Shillingburg, James G., #1115
Shillingburg, James G., #1116
Shillingburg, James G., #1117
Shillingburg, James G., #1118
Shillingburg, James G., #1119
Shillingburg, James G., #1120
Shillingburg, James G., #1121
Shillingburg, James G., #1132
Shillingburg, James Gibson, #1100
Shillingburg, John King, #1114
Shillingburg, John King, #1125
Shillingburg, Ledah, #1102
Shillingburg, Ledah Ann Frances, #1108
Shillingburg, Leona Mae, #1119
Shillingburg, Leona May, #1127
Shillingburg, Lewis D., #1078
Shillingburg, Lewis D., #1079
Shillingburg, Lewis D., #1080
Shillingburg, Lewis D., #1133
Shillingburg, Lydia, #1098
Shillingburg, Olin Lee, #1105
Shillingburg, Rebecca, #1091
Shillingburg, Russel Bryon, #1109
Shillingburg, Samuel Sollars, #1116
Shillingburg, Sarah F., #1083
Shillingburg, Sarah Francis, #1099
Shillingburg, Sarah I., #1129
Shillingburg, Sarah Isabella, #1120
Shillingburg, Tony W., #1130
Shillingburg, Tony Wilson, #1115
Shillingburg, Tony Wilson, #1124
Shillingburg, William, #1087
Shillingburg, William, #1088
Shimer, Orpha Kendall, #2928
Shimer, Orpha Kendall, #2941
Shimp, Rossie[?], #7366
Shimp, Rossie[?], #7368
Shimp, Rossie[?], #7369
Shimp, Rossie[?], #7370
Shimp, Rossie[?], #7371
Shimp, Rossie[?], #7372
Shimp, Rossie[?], #7373
Shimp, Rossie[?], #7374
Shindle, Ann M., #5511
Shipley, Rev., #4366
Shoaff, , #1609
Shoap, Hugh W., #2927
Shomaker, George, #6254
Shomaker, George, #6257
Shomaker, George, #6258
Shomaker, Mollie Amanda, #6306
Shomaker, Mollie Amanda, #6307
Shomaker, Mollie Amanda, #6308
Shomaker, Mollie Amanda, #6312
Shomaker, Mollie Amanda, #6313
Shomaker, Mollie Amanda, #6314
Shomaker, Mollie Amanda, #6315
Shomaker, Mollie Amanda, #6316
Shook, Jane, #4173
Shook, Jane, #4180
Shook, Jane, #4181
Shook, Jane, #4182
Shook, Jane, #4183
Shook, Jane, #4184
Shook, Jane, #4185

Shook, Jane, #4186
Shook, Jane, #4187
Shook, Jane, #4188
Shook, Jane, #4189
Shotts, Christena, #5867
Shotts, Cristena, #5865
Shotts, Daniel, #5847
Shotts, Daniel, #5848
Shotts, Elizabeth, #5842
Shotts, Elizabeth, #5843
Shotts, Elizabeth, #5844
Shotts, Elizabeth, #5853
Shotts, Elizabeth, #5855
Shotts, Elizabeth, #5866
Shotts, Henry, #5841
Shotts, Henry, #5842
Shotts, Henry, #5842
Shotts, Henry, #5843
Shotts, Henry, #5844
Shotts, Henry, #5852
Shotts, Henry, #5853
Shotts, Henry, #5855
Shotts, Katharine, #5841
Shotts, Maria, #5864
Shotts, Martha R., #5864
Shotts, Mary E., #5865
Shotts, Mary Elizabeth, #5846
Shotts, Michael, #5865
Shotts, Michael C., #5853
Shotts, Michael Christian, #5844
Shotts, Michael[?], #5846
Shotts, Peter P., #5860
Shotts, Peter Philip, #5843
Shotts, Philip, #5841
Shotts, Samuel H., #5855
Shotts, Samuel H., #5864
Shotts, Samuel Henry, #5845
Shotts, Samuel Henry, #5849
Shotts, Samuel Henry, #5850
Show, Amelia C., #3682
Show, Amelia Catherine McCoy, #4920
Show, Ann Francis[?], #3679
Show, Ann Mary, #3676
Show, Ann Mary, #3680
Show, Ann Mary, #4907
Show, Ann Mary, #4916
Show, Annie F., #3671
Show, Annie F., #4910
Show, Annie F., #4928
Show, Annie F., #4929
Show, Charles W., #3672
Show, Charles W., #4909
Show, Charles W., #4927
Show, Charles Wesley, #3678
Show, George Elmer, #3681
Show, George Elmer, #3690
Show, George Elmer, #4914
Show, George Elmer, #4919
Show, John A., #3670
Show, John Andrew, #3675
Show, John Andrew, #4906
Show, John Andrew, #4915
Show, John Andrew, #4925
Show, Maggie E., #3669
Show, Margaret Elizabeth, #3677
Show, Margaret Elizabeth, #4908
Show, Margaret Elizabeth, #4926
Show, Sarah Cathien, #4913
Show, Sarah Cathren, #3689
Show, William Henry, #3673
Show, William Henry, #3688

INDEX
Pages are not numbered; numbers refer to the entry number at the beginning of each record.

Show, Willmenia Massa Virginia, #3687
Show, Willmina M.V., #4911
Show, Willmina M.V., #4917
Show, Willmina M.V., #4930
Show, Winnie Frances, #3692
"Show, Jr.", William Henry, #4912
"Show, Jr.", William Henry, #4918
"Show, Jr.", William Henry, #4931
Showalter, Olive Stover[?], #4819
Showe, Wilimina, #2860
Showe, Willia M.[?], #2861
Showe, William Henry, #2855
Shrader, Marget E., #5401
Shrader, Marget E., #5403
Shrader, Susan I., #877
Shrigley, Caroline Susan Rebeca, #4450
Shrigley, Ellon Agusta Mas[?], #4455
Shrigley, Enoch M., #4449
Shrigley, Enoch Murry, #4446
Shrigley, Enoch Murry, #4447
Shrigley, Enoch Raylord[?], #4453
Shrigley, Ida Ann Florence, #4456
Shrigley, James Andrew Winfield Scott, #4454
Shrigley, James Vincent, #4458
Shrigley, John Henry Dill, #4452
Shrigley, Joseph Thomas Hanson, #4451
Shrigley, Lewelin Marshall, #4459
Shrigley, Martha, #4449
Shrigley, Mary Luesa Penelope, #4449
Shrigley, Thadeus Langley, #4457
Shryock, George French, #1193
Shryock, George French, #1194
Shryock, Henry R., #1197
Shryock, Henry R., #1198
Shryock, Lenol Martin, #1199
Shryock, Lenol Martin, #1200
Shryock, Lewis Justin, #1191
Shryock, Lewis Justin, #1192
Shryock, Lewis P., #1190
Shryock, Phebe, #1190
Shryock, Phebe, #1195
Shryock, Phebe, #1196
Shue, Alan (Rev.), #3451
Shupe, Adam, #1975
Shupe, Catha., #1975
Shupe, Catharine, #1969
Shupe, Dorothy, #1975
Shupp, Isaac Hamilton, #889
Sidney Mark, , #4058
Sifferd, , #2168
Sigafoose, Minnie Lee, #6758
Sigler, Jane[?], #2772
Sigler, Lillie V. (Miss), #4675

Sigler, Mary, #4797
Sigler, Mary, #4798
Simms, Rev., #5932
Simms, Rev., #5933
Simms, Rev., #5934
Simms, Rev., #5935
Simms, Rev., #5936
Simms, Rev., #5937
Simon, J.S., #8211
Simon, J.S., #8269
Simon, R., #3030
Simpson, [female], #1932
Simpson, Wm., #1931
Simpson, Wm., #1932
Singer, Frederick, #2137
Singer, Frederick, #2138
Singer, Raymond Frederick, #2137
Singer, Raymond Frederick, #2138
Sisler, Martha, #6851
Sisler, Martha, #6852
Sisler, Martha, #6853
Sisler, Martha, #6854
Sisler, Martha, #6855
Sisler, Martha, #6856
Sisler, Martha J., #6808
Siter[?], Annie L., #6989
Sites, William E., #6990
Slifer, L.B., #3414
Slifer, Luther, #3440
Slifer, Rodney LaTaine, #3414
Slifer, Virgie, #3409
Slifer, Virgie, #3410
Slifer, Virgie (Miss), #3408
Slingley, Martha Elizabeth, #4448
Slonacher, Charles E., #8324
Slonak, Nora B., #8347
Slonak, Nora B., #8348
Slonak, Nora B., #8349
Slonaker, Andrew, #8335
Slonaker, C., #8325
Slonaker, C., #8326
Slonaker, C., #8327
Slonaker, C.O., #8333
Slonaker, C.O., #8334
Slonaker, Chas. O., #8352
Slonaker, Chas. O., #8353
Slonaker, Chas. O., #8354
Slonaker, Nettie, #8338
Slonaker, Nettie G., #8344
Slonaker, Nettie G., #8345
Slonaker, Nettie G., #8346
Smalley, Elan, #597
Smallwood, Elizabeth, #8552
Smallwood, Kimberly Jane, #1585
Smallwood, Kimberly Jane, #1586
Smeltzer, J.P., #4384
Smice, Ada B., #5736
Smice, Ada Belle, #5730
Smice, Ada Belle, #5758
Smice, Amelia, #5714
Smice, Beit E., #5737
Smice, Bert E., #5759
Smice, Bert E., #5762
Smice, Bert E., #5764
Smice, Bert E., #5765
Smice, Bert E., #5766

Smice, Bert Raymond, #5766
Smice, Bertha Irene, #5767
Smice, Bertha Irine, #5729
Smice, Bertha Irine, #5739
Smice, Bertie Eugene, #5728
Smice, Bobert Eugene, #5732
Smice, Bobert Eugene, #5764
Smice, Clara Maria, #5741
Smice, Elisabeth, #5709
Smice, Elizabeth, #5719
Smice, Frances Ruthanna, #5733
Smice, Frances Ruthanna, #5765
Smice, Geo. W., #5734
Smice, Geo. W., #5742
Smice, Geo. W., #5744
Smice, Geo. W., #5745
Smice, Geo. W., #5746
Smice, Geo. W., #5747
Smice, Geo. W., #5748
Smice, Geo. W., #5756
Smice, Geo. W., #5772
Smice, George, #5713
Smice, George Washington, #5724
Smice, George Washington, #5740
Smice, John, #5712
Smice, Lydia C., #5735
Smice, Lydia E., #5757
Smice, Lydia Ellen, #5726
Smice, Margaret, #5707
Smice, Maria, #5710
Smice, Maria, #5711
Smice, Mary, #5717
Smice, Mary L., #5720
Smice, Mary L., #5721
Smice, Nage[?], #5718
Smice, Peter, #5704
Smice, Peter, #5706
Smice, Susannah, #5708
Smice, Thomas, #5715
Smice, Thomas, #5716
Smice, William, #5738
Smice, William Henry, #5727
Smilli, E.H., #1649
Smith, Albert H., #3399
Smith, Augustus Kenley, #2225
Smith, Benjamin F., #2241
Smith, Betsey, #2239
Smith, Carlyle Fillmore, #6599
Smith, Carlyle Fillmore, #6617
Smith, Catharine, #5213
Smith, Cecelia A., #6325
Smith, Claude McPhearson, #6594
Smith, Claude McPhearson, #6610
Smith, David, #6588
Smith, David, #6623
Smith, Doris, #2363
Smith, Doris Rose, #863
Smith, E., #2141
Smith, Earl H., #3418
Smith, Edward (Rev.), #4361
Smith, Elizabeth, #2237
Smith, Elizabeth B.G., #4944
Smith, Emily, #2200
Smith, Emily, #2201
Smith, Emily, #2202
Smith, Emily, #2203
Smith, Emily, #2204
Smith, Emily, #2232
Smith, Emily, #2247
Smith, Emily , #2199
Smith, F. Lester, #6615

Smith, Fannie C., #6592
Smith, Fannie C., #6605
Smith, Fannie Cecelia, #6600
Smith, Frances Loose, #6893
Smith, Franklin Lester, #6597
Smith, Franklin Lester, #6612
Smith, Frisby, #6623
Smith, George Howard, #1819
Smith, George Howard, #1820
Smith, George W., #2240
Smith, Gilbert, #2358
Smith, Gilbert, #2359
Smith, Gilbert, #2360
Smith, Gilbert, #2361
Smith, Gilbert, #2362
Smith, Gilbert, #2363
Smith, Helen Kuhn, #1822
Smith, Hiram J., #3398
Smith, Horace C., #2248
Smith, Horace Christopher, #2221
Smith, Horace Christopher, #2222
Smith, Horace Christopher, #2224
Smith, Horace Christopher, #2225
Smith, Horace Christopher, #2226
Smith, Horace Christopher, #2227
Smith, Horace Christopher, #2228
Smith, Howard, #1821
Smith, Howard, #1822
Smith, Howard Cage, #1821
Smith, Idelia Cordelia, #6596
Smith, Idella C., #6603
Smith, J.H., #1651
Smith, Jackie, #2359
Smith, Jean, #2230
Smith, John, #4109
Smith, John A., #2199
Smith, John A., #2242
Smith, John A., #2245
Smith, John Adams, #2172
Smith, John Adams, #2184
Smith, John Adams, #2185
Smith, John Adams, #2186
Smith, John Adams, #2187
Smith, John Adams, #2224
Smith, Joshua, #464
Smith, Julean, #2233
Smith, Mahlon H.[?], #3401
Smith, Margrete, #2235
Smith, Maria, #4108
Smith, Maria, #4109
Smith, Maria Ardinger, #1712
Smith, Mary, #2228
Smith, Mary, #464
Smith, Mary Ann, #6589
Smith, Mary Jane, #2186
Smith, Mary Jane, #2187
Smith, Mary Jane, #2190
Smith, Mary Jane, #2191
Smith, Mary Jane, #2192
Smith, Mary Jane, #2193
Smith, Mary Jane, #2194
Smith, Mary Jane, #2195
Smith, Mary Jane, #2196
Smith, Mary Jane, #2197
Smith, Mary Jane, #2246
Smith, Matilda, #2234
Smith, Mattie Leutishia, #632
Smith, Mattie V., #631
Smith, Mattie V., #632
Smith, Mattie Virginia (Braxton), #634
Smith, Millard Fillmore, #6609

INDEX
Pages are not numbered; numbers refer to the entry number at the beginning of each record.

Smith, Murta C., #6593
Smith, Myrta C., #6602
Smith, Norman Scott, #6598
Smith, Norman Scott, #6618
Smith, Patsy, #2360
Smith, Peggy, #2361
Smith, Rhody, #474
Smith, Rhody Lowe, #464
Smith, Robert, #2181
Smith, Robert, #2183
Smith, Robert, #2184
Smith, Robert, #2229
Smith, Robert, #2236
Smith, Robert, #2238
Smith, Robert, #2243
Smith, Robert McL., #6947
Smith, Robert McLanahan[?], #6888
Smith, Roberta, #2362
Smith, Sophia, #2227
Smith, Susan, #2244
Smith, Susan Line, #2182
Smith, Susan Line, #2183
Smith, Virginia D., #693
Smith, Virginia Dare, #682
Smith, Warren, #2226
Smith, Willard F., #6591
Smith, William, #2231
Smith, William , #631
Smith, William , #632
Smith, William Daniel, #631
"Smith, Jr.", Fannie C., #6606
Smiths, Mary D., #2335
Snaveley, Roy Webster, #6595
Snavely, Ada R., #39
Snavely, Ada Rebecca, #44
Snavely, Ida C., #6590
Snavely, Ida C., #6604
Snavely, , #8042
Sndier, Harriet (Miss), #509
Snider, John T., #7128
Snider, Leonard, #7121
Snider, Leonard, #7122
Snider, Louisa, #7125
Snider, Mary, #7124
Snider, Otho, #7123
Snider, Peter, #7126
Snider, Rebecca (Charlton), #7122
Snider, Sarah Ann, #7129
Snider, William B., #7127
Snyder, A.E., #3338
Snyder, A.E., #3339
Snyder, A.E., #3340
Snyder, A.E., #3341
Snyder, A.E., #3342
Snyder, A.E., #3343
Snyder, A.E., #3344
Snyder, A.E., #3345
Snyder, Ada May (Beck), #6692
Snyder, Adam, #1383
Snyder, Adam, #1393
Snyder, Adam, #1394
Snyder, Adam, #1426
Snyder, Adam, #1432
Snyder, Ann Eliza, #7044
Snyder, Anne Eliza, #7073
Snyder, Anne Eliza, #7074
Snyder, Anthony, #7179

Snyder, Anthony, #7180
Snyder, Anthony, #7184
Snyder, Anthony, #7185
Snyder, Bessie Cora, #7260
Snyder, Bruce, #7270
Snyder, C.W.[or V.], #1384
Snyder, Casper, #7143
Snyder, Casper, #7172
Snyder, Catharine M., #8419
Snyder, Catharine M., #8420
Snyder, Catharine V.[?], #1395
Snyder, Cathrine, #7270
Snyder, Cathrine, #7271
Snyder, Charles Bruce, #7266
Snyder, Charles Dickson, #7264
Snyder, Charles Dixon, #7253
Snyder, Charles Dixon, #7257
Snyder, Clara, #7265
Snyder, Clyde, #7267
Snyder, Clyde, #7268
Snyder, Cornelius K., #7021
Snyder, Cornelius K., #7238
Snyder, Cornelius K., #7251
Snyder, Cornelius Kratz, #7010
Snyder, Cornelius Kratz, #7224
Snyder, Cornelius Kratz, #7225
Snyder, Cornelius Kratz, #7241
Snyder, Daniel Clyde, #7254
Snyder, Daniel Clyde, #7259
Snyder, Daniel J., #7252
Snyder, Daniel J., #7255
Snyder, Daniel J., #7261
Snyder, David[?], #1424
Snyder, Dick, #7265
Snyder, Dixon, #7266
Snyder, Elisabeth E., #1399
Snyder, Elizabeth H. (Mrs.), #7262
Snyder, Elizabeth H.[?], #7256
Snyder, Elizabeth Louise, #7268
Snyder, Ella Dellinger, #3342
Snyder, Ella Dellinger, #3343
Snyder, Elsie (Kratz), #7239
Snyder, Francis Frederick, #7188
Snyder, Frederick, #7079
Snyder, George G., #7016
Snyder, George Grosh, #7013
Snyder, George Grosh, #7230
Snyder, George Grosh, #7231
Snyder, George Grosh, #7244
Snyder, George Grosh, #7245
Snyder, Hannah, #1394
Snyder, Hannah, #1432
Snyder, Hariet (Bryan), #7057
Snyder, Harriet, #7183
Snyder, Harriet Bryan, #7048
Snyder, Harriet Henrietta, #7086
Snyder, Harry G., #8423
Snyder, Harry G., #8424
Snyder, Helen Louise, #7014
Snyder, Helen Louise, #7232
Snyder, Helen Louise, #7233
Snyder, Hester, #1791
Snyder, Hester, #1792
Snyder, Hester, #8078
Snyder, Howard F.H., #8427
Snyder, Irene, #3081
Snyder, Ivy Z.[?], #3078
Snyder, Ivy Z.[?], #3079

Snyder, Ivy Z.[?], #3080
Snyder, J. Edmond, #3065
Snyder, J. Edmond, #3076
Snyder, J. Edmond, #3077
Snyder, J. Edmond, #3080
Snyder, J. Edmond, #3081
Snyder, Jacob C., #7049
Snyder, Jacob C., #7069
Snyder, Jacob C., #7070
Snyder, Jacob C., #7071
Snyder, Jacob C., #7072
Snyder, Jacob C., #7073
Snyder, Jacob C., #7074
Snyder, Jacob C., #7075
Snyder, Jacob C., #7076
Snyder, Jacob C., #7077
Snyder, Jacob C., #7078
Snyder, Jacob C., #7079
Snyder, Jacob C., #7080
Snyder, Jacob C., #7081
Snyder, Jacob C., #7082
Snyder, Jacob C., #7083
Snyder, Jacob C., #7084
Snyder, Jacob C., #7085
Snyder, Jacob C., #7086
Snyder, Jacob C., #7115
Snyder, Jacob Casper, #7048
Snyder, Jacob Casper, #7050
Snyder, Jacob Casper, #7053
Snyder, Jacob Casper, #7056
Snyder, Jacob Casper, #7174
Snyder, Jacob Casper, #7175
Snyder, James Thomas, #7190
Snyder, John Francis, #7191
Snyder, John Francis, #7197
Snyder, John L., #7166
Snyder, John L., #7167
Snyder, John Leiter, #6653
Snyder, John S.B., #7045
Snyder, John S.B., #7077
Snyder, John S.B., #7078
Snyder, John W., #1400
Snyder, John W., #1423
Snyder, John Y.[?], #7118
Snyder, Joseph, #7195
Snyder, Kate, #8021
Snyder, Larncia A., #1422
Snyder, Larncia[?] A., #1398
Snyder, Lela Lucinda, #8428
Snyder, Lela Lucinda, #8429
Snyder, Leonard, #3336
Snyder, Leonard, #7110
Snyder, Leonard, #7113
Snyder, Leonard, #7114
Snyder, Leonard, #7116
Snyder, Leonard, #7117
Snyder, Leonard, #7118
Snyder, Leonard, #7130
Snyder, Leonard, #7134
Snyder, Leonard, #7143
Snyder, Leonard, #7144
Snyder, Leonard, #7145
Snyder, Leonard, #7147
Snyder, Leonard, #7177
Snyder, Leonard, #7178
Snyder, Leonard, #7196
Snyder, Leonard, #7240
Snyder, Leonard P., #3344
Snyder, Leonard P., #3345
Snyder, Leonard P., #7007
Snyder, Leonard P., #7008
Snyder, Leonard P., #7010

Snyder, Leonard P., #7011
Snyder, Leonard P., #7012
Snyder, Leonard P., #7013
Snyder, Leonard P., #7014
Snyder, Leonard P., #7015
Snyder, Leonard P., #7020
Snyder, Leonard P., #7237
Snyder, Leonard P., #7250
Snyder, Leonard Williams, #7193
Snyder, Leonard Williams, #7198
Snyder, Lizzie E., #1386
Snyder, Louisa, #7112
Snyder, Louisa, #7155
Snyder, Louisa, #7156
Snyder, Louisa, #7157
Snyder, Louisa, #7158
Snyder, Louise, #7272
Snyder, Luth[?], #7249
Snyder, Luther Peterman, #7015
Snyder, Luther Peterman, #7018
Snyder, Luther Peterman, #7234
Snyder, Luther Peterman, #7235
Snyder, Mae Esther, #3439
Snyder, Maggie M. (Deahl), #7153
Snyder, Maggie M. (Houck), #7120
Snyder, Margaret M., #7132
Snyder, Margre M. (Houch), #7163
Snyder, Maria, #7050
Snyder, Maria Luisa, #7194
Snyder, Mariah, #7080
Snyder, Mariah, #7081
Snyder, Mary, #7106
Snyder, Mary, #7117
Snyder, Mary, #7134
Snyder, Mary, #7149
Snyder, Mary, #7150
Snyder, Mary, #7151
Snyder, Mary, #7202
Snyder, Mary Catherine, #7189
Snyder, Mary E., #885
Snyder, Mary Emma, #7258
Snyder, Mary Emma, #7263
Snyder, Mary Eva[?], #8434
Snyder, Mary J., #1397
Snyder, Mary J., #1421
Snyder, Mary Margaret, #7022
Snyder, Mary Margaret, #7023
Snyder, Mary Margaret, #7024
Snyder, Mary Margaret, #7025
Snyder, Mary Margaret, #7026
Snyder, Mary Margaret, #7027
Snyder, Mary Margaret, #7028
Snyder, Mary Margaret, #7029
Snyder, Mary Margaret, #7030
Snyder, Mary Margaret, #7031
Snyder, Mary Margaret, #7032
Snyder, Mary Margaret, #7033
Snyder, Mary Margaret, #7034
Snyder, Mary Margaret, #7035
Snyder, Mary Margaret, #7036
Snyder, Mary Margaret, #7037
Snyder, Mary Margaret, #7038
Snyder, Mary Margaret, #7039
Snyder, Mary Margaret, #7040
Snyder, Mary Margaret, #7041
Snyder, Mary Margaret, #7042
Snyder, Mary Margaret, #7043
Snyder, Mary Margaret, #7075
Snyder, Mary Margaret, #7076
Snyder, Mary Otis, #3333
Snyder, Mary Otis, #3338

INDEX
Pages are not numbered; numbers refer to the entry number at the beginning of each record.

Snyder, Mary Otis, #3339
Snyder, Maudy M., #8425
Snyder, Maudy M., #8426
Snyder, Nina[?] O., #8421
Snyder, Nina[?] O., #8422
Snyder, Otho, #7114
Snyder, Otho, #7197
Snyder, Otho, #7198
Snyder, Otho A., #7147
Snyder, Otho A., #7148
Snyder, Otho A., #7186
Snyder, Otho A., #7188
Snyder, Otho A., #7189
Snyder, Otho A., #7190
Snyder, Otho A., #7191
Snyder, Otho A., #7192
Snyder, Otho A., #7196
Snyder, Paul Elbert, #8432
Snyder, Paul Elbert, #8433
Snyder, Peter, #7160
Snyder, Peter, #7161
Snyder, Peter, #7172
Snyder, Peter, #7173
Snyder, Peter, #7176
Snyder, Peter L., #7119
Snyder, Peter Leonard, #7130
Snyder, Peter Leonard, #7133
Snyder, Ralph Leonard, #7012
Snyder, Ralph Leonard, #7019
Snyder, Ralph Leonard, #7228
Snyder, Ralph Leonard, #7229
Snyder, Ralph Leonard, #7240
Snyder, Ralph Leonard, #7242
Snyder, Ralph Leonard, #7243
Snyder, Rebecca, #3336
Snyder, Rebecca, #7113
Snyder, Rebecca, #7114
Snyder, Rebecca, #7116
Snyder, Rebecca, #7117
Snyder, Rebecca, #7118
Snyder, Rebecca, #7147
Snyder, Rebecca, #7196
Snyder, Rebecca (Charlton), #7145
Snyder, Rebecca (Charlton), #7146
Snyder, Rebecca Jane, #7192
Snyder, Richard Franklin, #7269
Snyder, Robert, #7272
Snyder, Roy Samuel, #8430
Snyder, Roy Samuel, #8431
Snyder, S.J., #1385
Snyder, Samuel J., #8416
Snyder, Samuel J., #8417
Snyder, Samuel J., #8418
Snyder, Sarah Ann, #7168
Snyder, Sarah Ann, #7169
Snyder, Sarah J., #1396
Snyder, Sarahan, #7111
Snyder, Sibyl Lucile, #7017
Snyder, Sibyl Lucile, #7226
Snyder, Sibyl Lucile, #7227
Snyder, Sibyl Lucile, #7246
Snyder, Sibyl Lucile, #7247
Snyder, Sibyl Lucile, #7248
Snyder, Susan, #7197
Snyder, Susan, #7198
Snyder, Susan (Mrs.), #7181
Snyder, Susan Ann, #7046
Snyder, Susan Ann, #7082

Snyder, Susan Ann, #7083
Snyder, Syble Lucile, #7011
Snyder, Tarleton[?], #7047
Snyder, Tarleton[?], #7084
Snyder, Tarleton[?], #7085
Snyder, Viola Willetta, #3340
Snyder, Viola Willetta, #3341
Snyder, William B., #7116
Snyder, William Clyde, #7267
Snyder, Wm. B., #3335
Snyder, Wm. B., #3336
Snyder, Wm. B., #3338
Snyder, Wm. B., #3339
Snyder, Wm. B., #3340
Snyder, Wm. B., #3341
Snyder, Wm. B., #3342
Snyder, Wm. B., #3343
Snyder, Wm. B., #3344
Snyder, Wm. B., #3345
Snyder, Wm. B., #7164
Snyder, Wm. B., #7165
Sole, A.B., #2524
Sole, A.B., #2531
Sole, Charels E., #2540
Sole, "Charles Ephriam ""Dutch", #2548
Sole, "Charles Ephriam ""Dutch", #2549
Sole, "Charles Ephriam ""Dutch", #2550
Sole, Elenora C., #2536
Sole, George M., #2533
Sole, Grover C., #2555
Sole, Grover C., #2559
Sole, Grover C., #2560
Sole, Grover C., #2561
Sole, Grover C., #2562
Sole, Groves C., #2541
Sole, H.E., #2525
Sole, Hattie V.[?], #2542
Sole, Hugh E., #2534
Sole, John E., #2526
Sole, John E., #2535
Sole, Jonas O., #2538
Sole, Joseph H., #2532
Sole, Joseph Henry, #2543
Sole, Joseph Henry, #2544
Sole, Josephus H., #2528
Sole, Josepus H., #2537
Sole, Nonnie (Goddard), #2553
Sole, Nonnie (Goddard), #2554
Sole, Nonnie (Goddard), #2555
Sole, Oliva, #2543
Sole, Olivia, #2530
Sole, W. D., #2523
Sole, W.C., #2545
Sole, W.C., #2546
Sole, W.C., #2557
Sole, W.C., #2558
Sole, W.D., #2529
Sole, W.D., #2547
Sole, William, #2543
Sole, William, #2549
Sole, William, #2560
Sole, William C., #2539
Sole, William C., #2551
Sole, William C., #2552
Sole, Willliam D., #2521
Soles, Hattie, #805
Soles, Josephus, #806
Sollars, Amelia Frances, #1112

Sollars, Amelia Frances, #1122
Sollars , Amelia Frances, #1113
Sollars , Amelia Frances, #1114
Sollars , Amelia Frances, #1115
Sollars , Amelia Frances, #1116
Sollars , Amelia Frances, #1117
Sollars , Amelia Frances, #1118
Sollars , Amelia Frances, #1119
Sollars , Amelia Frances, #1120
Sollers[?], Anna, #2086
Somerville, Florence Regenia, #31
Somerville, Gertrude Elaine, #32
Somerville, Harry Francis, #33
Somerville, Jane Henrietta (Curtis), #635
Souders, Birdie M.B., #5076
Souders, Daniel L., #5078
Souders, Elcie Elizabeth, #5080
Souders, Leon Summers, #5079
Souders, Lillie M., #5075
Souders, Lilly May (Mrs.), #5084
Souders, Lovease Barbria, #5081
Souders, Nathan J., #5077
Souders, Ronald Lewis, #2991
Souders, William A., #5074
South, Amelia, #7273
Sowers, Alice, #2373
Sowers, Becky, #2376
Sowers, Bonnie Lee, #949
Sowers, Charles, #2372
Sowers, Charles, #2373
Sowers, Charles, #2374
Sowers, Charles, #2375
Sowers, Charles, #2376
Sowers, Charles, #2377
Sowers, Howard Winter, #932
Sowers, Janice, #2377
Sowers, Karen, #2375
Sowers, Virginia E., #963
Sowers, Virginia Elizabeth Cock, #946
Sowers, Wilma, #2374
Spangle, Louise, #5635
Sparrow, Allen, #109
Sparrow, Allen _____[?], #115
Sparrow, Allen Kestor, #135
Sparrow, Anna Eliza Frances[?], #120
Sparrow, Charles Alferd, #117
Sparrow, Charles L., #142
Sparrow, Charley Leslie[?], #139
Sparrow, Effie Martin, #132
Sparrow, Effie Mary (Martin), #126
Sparrow, Eliza, #110
Sparrow, Elizabeth Aanna, #111
Sparrow, Ella May, #134
Sparrow, Emma J., #129
Sparrow, Emma Jane, #140
Sparrow, Emma Jane, #141
Sparrow, Emory Melvin, #118
Sparrow, Harry[?] Menard[?], #136
Sparrow, Harvey M., #133
Sparrow, Henry Clay, #119
Sparrow, Herbert C., #121
Sparrow, Herbert C., #127
Sparrow, Herbert Cory[?], #138
Sparrow, Howard E., #131
Sparrow, Howard Edwin, #113
Sparrow, Lelia (Shank), #128

Sparrow, Martha Ellen, #114
Sparrow, Martin H., #125
Sparrow, Mary E., #123
Sparrow, Mary Florance, #116
Sparrow, William H., #122
Sparrow, William H., #124
Sparrow, William Thomas, #112
Sparrow, Willie Edwin, #143
Sparrow, Willie[?] Edwin, #137
Speaker, Ama May, #6787
Speaker, Anna M., #6778
Speaker, Fannie neomi, #6796
Speaker, Fanny, #6782
Speaker, Fanny, #6794
Speaker, Fanny Neomi, #6786
Speaker, Harman, #6776
Speaker, Harman, #6781
Speaker, Henry, #6783
Speaker, Henry, #6792
Speaker, Hiram, #6777
Speaker, Hiram, #6793
Speaker, Mary V., #6780
Speaker, Mary Virginia, #6788
Speaker, Nacey Hellen, #6785
Speaker, Sarah E., #6779
Speaker, Sarah E., #6801
Speaker, Sarah E., #6802
Speaker, Sarah Elizabeth, #6784
Speaker, Sarah Elizabeth, #6811
Speaker, Sarah Elizabeth, #6812
Speaker, Sarah Elizabeth, #6813
Speaker, Sarah Elizabeth, #6814
Speaker, Sarah Elizabeth, #6815
Speaker, Sarah Elizabeth, #6816
Speaker, Sarah Elizabeth, #6817
Speaker, Sarah Elizabeth, #6818
Speaker, Sarah Elizabeth, #6819
Speaker, Sarah Elizabeth, #6820
Speaker, Sarah Elizabeth, #6821
Speaker, Sarah Elizabeth, #6822
Speaker, Sarah Elizabeth, #6823
Speaker, Sarah Elizabeth, #6824
Speaker, Sarah Elizabeth, #6825
Speaker, Sarah Elizabeth, #6826
Speaker, Sarah Elizabeth, #6827
Speaker, Sarah Elizabeth, #6828
Speaker, Sarah Elizabeth, #6829
Spealaman, Jason, #4815
Spealman, Ann M., #4824
Spealman, Ann M., #4826
Spealman, Anne Mary, #4829
Spealman, Barbara E., #4827
Spealman, Daniel , #4792
Spealman, David, #4791
Spealman, Effie May, #4818
Spealman, Emanuel, #4793
Spealman, Emanuel, #4803
Spealman, Emanuel, #4813
Spealman, Emanuel, #4817
Spealman, Evelyn, #4823
Spealman, Ezra, #4794
Spealman, Ezra, #4795
Spealman, Harvey, #4821
Spealman, Harvey Loomer[?], #4819
Spealman, Herbert, #4821
Spealman, Jacob, #4788
Spealman, Jacob, #4810
Spealman, Jacob, #4811
Spealman, Jacob, #4816
Spealman, John, #4785
Spealman, John, #4786

INDEX
Pages are not numbered; numbers refer to the entry number at the beginning of each record.

Spealman, John, #4787
Spealman, John, #4788
Spealman, John, #4789
Spealman, John, #4789
Spealman, John, #4790
Spealman, John, #4791
Spealman, John, #4792
Spealman, John, #4793
Spealman, John, #4794
Spealman, John, #4795
Spealman, John, #4796
Spealman, John, #4797
Spealman, John, #4798
Spealman, John, #4801
Spealman, John [father], #4799
Spealman, John [father], #4800
Spealman, Joseph, #4790
Spealman, Joseph, #4812
Spealman, Lawson, #4804
Spealman, Losson, #4796
Spealman, Martha Jane, #4831
Spealman, Martin Lewis[?], #4820
Spealman, Mary Alice, #4828
Spealman, Mary Ann, #4785
Spealman, Mary Ann, #4814
Spealman, Susan, #4786
Spealman, Violet, #4822
Spealman, William H., #4787
Spealman, William H., #4824
Spealman, William H., #4825
Spealman, William Henry, #4830
"Spealman, Sr.", John, #4802
"Spealman, Sr.", Mary, #4805
Spear, Martha, #1466
Spessard, Aldine Leon, #2989
Spessard, Charles Earl, #2985
Spessard, Charles W., #2992
Spessard, Darla Jean, #2991
Spessard, Elizabeth, #3075
Spessard, Harry David, #2987
Spessard, Leon Aldine, #2967
Spessard, Lewis Cleggett, #2968
Spessard, Lewis Cleggett, #2990
Spessard, Robert Dean, #2997
Spessard, Russell Leon, #2986
Spessard, Woodward E., #232
"Spessard, Jr.", Charles W., #2966
"Spessard, Jr.", Charles William, #2988
"Spessard, Sr.", Charles W., #2965
"Spessard, Sr.", Charles W., #2966
"Spessard, Sr.", Charles W., #2967
"Spessard, Sr.", Charles W., #2968
Spicer[?], Soppia, #4241
Spickler, Besse V., #4177
Spickler, Mary A., #836
Spickler, Mary Ann, #834
Spicknall, J. Turnbull, #284
Spicknall, J. Turnbull, #285
Spielman, Amthe[?], #7745

Spielman, Ann, #4809
Spielman, Ann M., #4838
Spielman, Anna M. (Mrs.), #4850
Spielman, Anna Mary, #4859
Spielman, Anna Mary, #4860
Spielman, Anna Mary, #4861
Spielman, Anna Mary, #4862
Spielman, Anna Mary, #4863
Spielman, Anna Mary, #4864
Spielman, Anna Mary, #4865
Spielman, Anna Mary, #4865
Spielman, Anna Mary, #4866
Spielman, Anna Mary, #4866
Spielman, Anna Mary, #4867
Spielman, Anna Mary, #4868
Spielman, Anna Mary, #4869
Spielman, Anna Mary, #4870
Spielman, Anna Mary, #4871
Spielman, Anna Mary, #4872
Spielman, Anna Mary, #4873
Spielman, Anna Mary, #4874
Spielman, Anna Mary, #4875
Spielman, Anna Mary, #4876
Spielman, Anna Mary, #4877
Spielman, Barbara Ellen, #4861
Spielman, Barbara Ellen, #4862
Spielman, Cora, #3429
Spielman, Elizabeth, #4834
Spielman, Elizabeth Catherine, #4875
Spielman, Ezra, #4806
Spielman, Ezra, #4807
Spielman, George Noah, #4832
Spielman, George Noah, #4871
Spielman, George Noah, #4872
Spielman, Harvey A., #4835
Spielman, Harvey Albert, #4876
Spielman, Jacob Everett, #4833
Spielman, Jacob Everett, #4837
Spielman, Jacob Everett, #4873
Spielman, Jacob Everett, #4874
Spielman, Martha Jane, #4869
Spielman, Martha Jane, #4870
Spielman, Mary Alice, #4863
Spielman, Mary Alice, #4864
Spielman, Mary Elizabeth, #4807
Spielman, Mary F., #7744
Spielman, Mary M. , #4840
Spielman, Mary M. , #4841
Spielman, Mary M. (Mrs.), #4849
Spielman, Otha Allen, #4877
Spielman, Otha Aten.[?], #4836
Spielman, William, #4850
Spielman, William H., #4839
Spielman, William Henry, #4867
Spielman, William Henry, #4868
Spielman, Wm., #4808
Spielman, Wm., #4809
Spielman, , #1024
Spielman, , #4902
"Spielman, Jr.", William H., #969
"Spielman, Sr.", William H., #4857
"Spielman, Sr.", William H., #4858

"Spielman, Sr.", William H., #4859
"Spielman, Sr.", William H., #4861
"Spielman, Sr.", William H., #4862
"Spielman, Sr.", William H., #4863
"Spielman, Sr.", William H., #4864
"Spielman, Sr.", William H., #4865
"Spielman, Sr.", William H., #4866
"Spielman, Sr.", William H., #4867
"Spielman, Sr.", William H., #4868
"Spielman, Sr.", William H., #4869
"Spielman, Sr.", William H., #4870
"Spielman, Sr.", William H., #4871
"Spielman, Sr.", William H., #4872
"Spielman, Sr.", William H., #4873
"Spielman, Sr.", William H., #4874
"Spielman, Sr.", William H., #4875
"Spielman, Sr.", William H., #4876
"Spielman, Sr.", William H., #4877
Spielman[?], Mary Magdalene, #4855
Spielman[?], Mary Magdalene, #4856
Spilman, A.H., #3134
Spindle, Addison Beebe, #5918
Spindle, Benj. T., #5910
Spindle, Benj. T., #5913
Spindle, Benjm., #5924
Spindle, Benjm. T., #5909
Spindle, Benjm. T., #5914
Spindle, Benjm. T., #5915
Spindle, Benjm. T., #5931
Spindle, Forris[?] Thomas, #5919
Spindle, Forris[?] Thomas, #5923
Spindle, H. Addelaide, #5914
Spindle, H. Adelaide, #5922
Spindle, Martha A., #5911
Spindle, Martha Adelaide, #5916
Spindle, Martha E., #5915
Spindle, Martha E., #5925
Spindle, Pansly[?] Purington, #5917
Spreacher, Bessie Bell, #576
Sprecher, Eliza A., #576
Sprecher, Mary M., #8593
Sprecher, Mary M., #8594
Sprecher, William H., #576
"Stackhouse, Jr.", Will, #1866
Stake, William Elmer, #2519
Staley, Carolyn Elizabeth, #2882
Staley, Carolyn Elizabeth, #2883
Staley, Carolyn Elizabeth, #2884
Staley, Carolyn Elizabeth, #2885
Staley, Carolyn Elizabeth, #2886
Stangle, L.A., #7703
Stansbury, Carroll ____, #1661
Stapleford, Edmund, #4777
Stapleford, Edmund, #4778
Stapleford, Edmund Russell Blake, #4780
Stapleford, Lillie, #4779
Stapleford, Lillie Dale, #4781
Startzman, C., #3130
Startzman, C., #4291
Startzman, Charles Christian, #4705
Startzman, Charles Christian, #4718
Startzman, Christian, #3174
Startzman, Clara E., #4698
Startzman, Clara Ellen, #4723
Startzman, Daniel R., #4695

Startzman, Daniel R., #4701
Startzman, Daniel R., #4715
Startzman, Esther Cornelia, #4710
Startzman, Laura V., #4697
Startzman, Laura Virginia, #4719
Startzman, Lillie, #4702
Startzman, Lily, #4695
Startzman, Lily, #4716
Startzman, Mary E.[or C.], #4708
Startzman, Mary Elizabeth, #4722
Startzman, Max W., #4699
Startzman, Max W., #4706
Startzman, Max William, #4721
Startzman, Nancy Helen (Speaker), #6797
Startzman, Nellie F., #4710
Startzman, Nellie F., #4712
Startzman, Nellie F., #4713
Startzman, Paul R., #4724
Startzman, Paul Raymond, #4700
Startzman, R. Newton, #4696
Startzman, R. Newton, #4712
Startzman, R. Newton, #4713
Startzman, Richard Newton, #4703
Startzman, Richard Newton, #4710
Startzman, Richard Newton, #4717
Startzman, Rosalie, #4713
Startzman, Susan, #4704
Startzman, Susan, #4720
Startzman, Vernon Newton, #4712
Stattan, Geo. W., #3394
Statton, A.B., #885
Statton, George W., #7485
Steam, C.T., #3398
Steck, Michael, #2185
Steck, Michael, #2245
Steele, Axel W., #3437
Steffey, Nellie J.[?], #4215
Stein, Evalyn Marguerite, #2141
Stein, Harvey E., #2141
Steinman, Sophia, #2224
Steinman, Sophia, #2225
Steinman, Sophia, #2226
Steinman, Sophia, #2227
Steinman, Sophia, #2228
Steinman, Sophia E., #2222
Steinman, Sophia E., #2223
Steinmetz, Hannah, #1710
Steinmetz, Hannah, #1711
Steinmetz, Hannah, #1715
Steinmetz, Hannah, #1716
Steinmetz, Hannah, #1717
Steinmetz, Hannah, #1718
Steinmetz, Hannah, #1719
Steinmetz, Hannah, #1720
Steinmetz, Hannah, #1721
Steinmetz, Hannah, #1722
Steinmetz, Hannah, #1723
Steinmetz, Hannah, #1724
Steinmetz, Hannah, #1725
Steinmetz, Henry, #1711
Stelling, G.F., #873
Stephens, Benjamin, #1916
Stephens, Nancy, #1916
Stephens, Thomas, #1916
Stephey, Daniel, #8026
Stevens, Neill Graham, #6199
Stewart, Elizabeth, #2871
Stewart, Elizabeth, #2872
Stewart, George William, #2872
Stewart, Jane, #2881

INDEX
Pages are not numbered; numbers refer to the entry number at the beginning of each record.

Stewart, John, #1251
Stewart, John, #1252
Stewart, John, #1253
Stewart, John, #1253
Stewart, John, #1254
Stewart, John, #1257
Stewart, John, #1258
Stewart, Margaret, #1254
Stewart, Margaret, #1256
Stewart, Martha, #2862
Stewart, Martha, #2881
Stewart, Martha Jane, #2871
Stewart, Mary Ellen, #1252
Stewart, Mary Ellen, #1255
Stewart, Maryann, #2862
Stewart, Thomas, #2862
Stewart, Thomas, #2871
Stewart, Thomas, #2872
Stewart, Thomas, #2881
Stickel, Mary Veda (Miss), #8596
Stickel, Mary Veda (Miss), #8597
Stine, Frank L., #7679
Stine, Mildred Phyllis, #5553
Stine, Victor F., #5562
Stine, Victor Francis, #5567
Stine[?], Samy[?], #4644
Stinemetz, Hannah, #4106
Stinemetz, Hannah, #4107
Stinemetz, Henry, #4107
Stoakes, Frank, #4737
Stock, Lizzie, #7764
Stocksdale, Geo., #5912
Stockslager, David S., #2993
Stone, Lucy Alvera, #4355
Stone, M. Bertha, #6841
Stone, Oscar J., #6803
Stone, Oscar James, #6840
Stone, W.H., #4304
Stoner, Emma J. (Summer), #4576
Stoner[?], Aron, #3854
Storm, Allice C., #4689
Storm, Frances E., #747
Storm, Frances M., #4693
Storm, Frank E., #4687
Storm, Frank E., #744
Storm, Harriet C., #4692
Storm, Hattie, #4688
Storm, Hattie, #4694
Storm, Hattie, #744
Storm, Hattie, #748
Storm, Hattie, #757
Storm, John F., #4691
Storm, Katie E., #744
Storm, Pauline S., #4690
Stouffer, Almira Virginia, #1867
Stouffer, Almira Virginia, #1868
Stouffer, D.[?] C., #4677
Stouffer, Edith G., #4686
Stouffer, Frances Louise, #1865
Stouffer, Frances Louise, #1866
Stouffer, Frank McKaig, #4682
Stouffer, Fred Hallle[?], #4683

Stouffer, James L., #4680
Stouffer, James Lee, #1863
Stouffer, James Lee, #1864
Stouffer, James Lee, #1865
Stouffer, James Lee, #1866
Stouffer, James Lee, #1867
Stouffer, James Lee, #1868
Stouffer, Joseph P., #4685
Stouffer, Lois Ann, #4681
Stouffer, M.V., #4676
Stouffer, Nancy, #3582
Stouffer, Ranskin[?] A., #4678
Stouffer, Richard Z.[?], #4684
Stouffer, William H., #4675
Stouffer, William V., #4679
Stover, Mae Elverta[?], #4820
Stratton, Edward, #3623
Stratton, Edward, #3638
Straub, Catharine (Hager), #3241
Straub, Catherine Hager, #6876
Straub, Harry H., #3242
Straub, Harry H., #6877
Straub, L.D., #6860
Straub, L.D., #6862
Straub, Norman B., #3243
Straub, Norman B., #3244
Straub, Norman B., #6878
Straub, Norman B., #6879
Straub, S.D., #3222
Straub, S.D., #3224
Strawn[?], Juanita, #4821
Streets, Charles Cunnungham, #1092
Streets, Charles Cunnungham, #1093
Streets, Hannah, #1092
Streets, John Green, #1094
Streets, Streit Lingham, #1095
Streets, Wm., #1092
Streets, Wm., #1084
Strobel, Carrie May, #6757
Strock, Henry F., #234
Struble, Peter A., #3125
Stull, Dorothy, #1772
Stull, Dortha, #8113
Summer, Alvey B., #4581
Summer, Alvey B., #4597
Summer, Ann M.E., #4601
Summer, Anna Maria, #4590
Summer, Barbara E., #4583
Summer, Benjamin R., #4577
Summer, Benjamin R., #4580
Summer, Bettie Barten[?], #4660
Summer, Charles C., #4584
Summer, Charles C., #4596
Summer, Edward C., #4593
Summer, Edward Clinton, #4587
Summer, Ellie May, #4659
Summer, Emma J., #4582
Summer, H.[or K.?], #4659
Summer, J. Wesley, #4657
Summer, J.W., #4656
Summer, John, #4574
Summer, John, #4598
Summer, John, #4600
Summer, John G., #4586
Summer, John G., #4595

Summer, Lillian Ka___[?], #4661
Summer, Madeline, #4700
Summer, Mary Magdalene, #4591
Summer, Mary[?], #4662
Summer, Sarah E., #4585
Summer, Sarah E., #4592
Summer, Thomas H., #4578
Summer, Thomas H., #4589
Summer, William J., #4588
Summer, William J., #4594
Summers, Bettie Baxter[?], #4667
Summers, Caroline M., #4616
Summers, Dolly M., #4618
Summers, Ellie Mary, #4666
Summers, Emma #4611
Summers, Emma (Mrs.), #4620
Summers, Emma (Mrs.), #4631
Summers, Emma A., #4615
Summers, Ezra D., #4617
Summers, Ezra Daniel, #4622
Summers, J. Wesley, #4670
Summers, J.W., #4673
Summers, James, #4627
Summers, James Eugene, #4621
Summers, James V., #4613
Summers, John W., #4663
Summers, Kate (Hart), #4672
Summers, Kate (Hart), #4673
Summers, Mary E., #4614
Summers, Mary Lizzie, #2732
Summers, Michael F., #4612
Summers, Michael Francis, #4626
Summers, Nathaniel, #4669
Summers, Rebecca, #4627
Summers, Sarah Ann, #4627
Summers, Sarah Waring[?], #4668
Summers, Simon, #4629
Summers, Simon G., #4631
Summers, Simon P., #4610
Summers, Simon P., #4619
Summers, Simon P., #4627
Summers, Wallie Waring, #4671
Supinger, Naomi, #5566
Sutton, Francis Eskridge, #93
Sutton, Francis Eskridge (Lieutenant), #102
Sutton, Harriett, #103
Sutton, Henry Carroll, #92
Sutton, Henry Carroll, #99
Sutton, Henry Carroll (Dr.), #105
Sutton, Mary Louise, #100
Sutton, Mary Louise, #94
Sutton, Richard Eskridge, #87
Sutton, Richard Eskridge, #89
Sutton, Richard Eskridge (Dr.), #104
Swain, Benjimine, #1327
Swain, Benjmine, #1334
Swain, Benny, #1319
Swain, Charles Luther, #1320
Swain, Charles Rubin, #1325
Swain, Emma Traphenia[?], #1316
Swain, James Fleven[?], #1322
Swain, John P., #1324
Swain, John P., #1332
Swain, Manzela Virginia, #1317
Swain, Samuel, #1323
Swain, Susan Elizabeth (Mrs.), #1329
Swain, William, #1326
Swain, William B., #1318

Swan, Jane Savanah[?], #4228
Sward[?], Sarah, #2103
Swayne, Benjamine, #1333
Swayne, Charles Reuben, #1315
Swayne, Charles Reuben, #1331
Swayne, Isabela, #1313
Swayne, Isabella, #1330
Swayne, Samuel Lewis, #1314
Swayne, Susan Elizabeth, #1321
Sweetsiy, Seth, #598
Swentzel, F., #4355
Swigert, Dessie, #7813
Swigert, Dessie, #7814
Swope, Louisa, #2334
Swope, Mary Ann, #2332
Swope, Mary Ann, #2334
Swope, May, #3445
Swope, Rev., #1635
Syester, A.K. (Hon.), #2115
Syrus, Frank, #3235
Syrus, Frank, #6873
Syrus, Harry, #3236
Syrus, Harry, #3240
Syrus, Harry, #6874
Syrus, Harry, #6884
Talbot[?], Ann Elizabeth, #6490
Talbott, John, #6491
Talbott, Joseph, #6492
Talley, Pearl, #3427
Tapman, Ambrose Smedley, #6303
Tapman, Ambrose Smedley, #6304
Tapman, Ambrose Smedley, #6305
Tapman, Edward Brent, #6302
Tapman, Harold, #6304
Tapman, John, #6300
Tapman, John, #6301
Tapman, John, #6302
Tapman, John, #6303
Tapman, John, #6462
Tapman, John, #6463
Tapman, John, #6464
Tapman, John Allen, #6301
Tapman, Marjorie, #6305
Tappan, D.S., #2211
Taxman, John, #6431
Taxman, John, #6432
Taxman[?], E. Brent, #6432
Taxman[?], John, #6430
Taxman[?], John Allen, #6431
Taylor, Alice, #281
Taylor, Edith M., #1101
Taylor, H.D., #2179
Taylor, John Milton, #292
Taylor, Mary J., #7804
Taylor, Mary Jane, #7761
Tery[?], Butbr[?], #3508
Thomas, Beatie E., #3400
Thomas, Julia Frances Foltz, #6762
Thomas, Milo E., #6746
Thomas, Milo Edwin, #6761
Thomas, Rachel (Heiller[?]), #5481
Thomas, William Kirley, #6331
Thomas, Wm. K., #6409
Thomas, Wm. K., #6445
Thompson, Chatharine L. (Miss), #1934
Thompson, Ella, #2550
Thompson, Rev., #8223
Thompson, Rev., #8225
Thompson, Rev., #8227
Thompson, Richard, #7841
Thompson, Richard, #7842

INDEX
Pages are not numbered; numbers refer to the entry number at the beginning of each record.

Thompson, Richard R., #7811
Thompson, Richard R., #7812
Thompson, Tommy, #3619
Thompson, Virginia, #3642
Thompson, Wm. K., #3620
Thompson, , #7841
Tigh, Margery, #4817
Timmins, Anna Maria (Mrs.), #2499
Timmins, Anna Mariah, #2518
Timmins, Daniel Bird, #2483
Timmins, Daniel Reifsnider, #2507
Timmins, David B., #2474
Timmins, David Bird, #2492
Timmins, David Byers, #2475
Timmins, David Byers, #2477
Timmins, David Byers, #2478
Timmins, David Byers, #2479
Timmins, David Byers, #2480
Timmins, David Byers, #2481
Timmins, David Byers, #2482
Timmins, David Byers, #2483
Timmins, David Byers, #2484
Timmins, David Byers, #2500
Timmins, David Byers, #2501
Timmins, David Byers, #2514
Timmins, Denton Hartzell, #2482
Timmins, Denton Hartzell, #2491
Timmins, Emlyetta, #2510
Timmins, Emma Almeda, #2479
Timmins, Emma Almeda, #2493
Timmins, Frank Elmer, #2481
Timmins, Frank Elmer, #2490
Timmins, Harry O., #2496
Timmins, Harry O., #2497
Timmins, Harry O., #2498
Timmins, Henry Clay, #2517
Timmins, Ida May, #2477
Timmins, Ida May, #2486
Timmins, Joseph, #2515
Timmins, Joseph Edward, #2480
Timmins, Joseph Edward, #2489
Timmins, Mary Ann, #2476
Timmins, Mary Ann, #2485
Timmins, Mary Elizabeth, #2516
Timmins, Matilda, #2513
Timmins, Philip Shoemaker, #2509
Timmins, Rebecca Jane, #2494
Timmins, Rebecca Jane, #2512
Timmins, Susann, #2511
Timmins, William, #2520
Timmins, William, #7855
Timmins, William Lane, #2478
Timmins, William Lane, #2487
Timmins, William W., #7874
Timmins, William Walls, #2495

Timmins, William Walls, #2508
Timmins, William Walls, #7856
Timmins, William Ward, #2505
Timmins, Wm. W., #2499
Timmons, Anna Mariah, #7872
Timmons, Anna Mariah (Mrs.), #7874
Timmons, Daniel Bird, #7891
Timmons, Daniel Bird, #7892
Timmons, Daniel Reifsnider, #2504
Timmons, Daniel Reifsnider, #7858
Timmons, David B., #7875
Timmons, David Byers, #7868
Timmons, David Byers, #7876
Timmons, David Byers, #7877
Timmons, Denton Hartzell, #7889
Timmons, Denton Hartzell, #7890
Timmons, Emiyetta[?], #7863
Timmons, Emma Almeda, #7884
Timmons, Emma Almeda, #7885
Timmons, Frank Elmer, #7888
Timmons, Henry Clay, #7871
Timmons, Howell, #2503
Timmons, Ida May, #7880
Timmons, Ida May, #7881
Timmons, Joseph, #7869
Timmons, Joseph Edward, #7886
Timmons, Joseph Edward, #7887
Timmons, Mary Ann, #7878
Timmons, Mary Ann, #7879
Timmons, Mary Elizabeth, #7870
Timmons, Matilda, #7867
Timmons, Philip Shoemaker, #7861
Timmons, Philip Shoemaker, #7862
Timmons, Rebecca Jane, #7865
Timmons, Rebecca Jane, #7866
Timmons, Susann, #7864
Timmons, W.E., #2503
Timmons, William Elmer Stake, #7873
Timmons, William Lane, #7882
Timmons, William Lane, #7883
Timmons, William Walls, #7859
Timmons, William Walls, #7860
Tittus, T.T., #5482
Titus, Rev., #4174
Todd, John, #214
Tombaugh, J., #2761
Tombaugh, J.M., #4013
Tomlinson, Drusilla, #2283
Tomlinson, Drusilla, #2284
Tomlinson, Drusilla, #2285
Tomlinson, Drusilla, #2305
Tomlinson, Drusilla, #2306
Tomlinson, Drusilla, #2307
Tomlinson, Drusilla, #2308
Tomlinson, Drusilla, #2309
Tomlinson, Drusilla, #2310

Tomlinson, Drusilla, #2311
Tomlinson, Drusilla, #2312
Tomlinson, Drusilla, #2313
Tomlinson, Drusilla, #2314
Tomlinson, Jemima, #2287
Tomlinson, Jemima, #2288
Tomlinson, Jemima, #2289
Tomlinson, Joseph (Colonel), #2284
Tomlinson, Joseph (Colonel), #2285
Tomlinson, Rudolf Adolfus, #2286
Toms, Oscar Ray, #5551
Toms, Oscar Ray, #5568
Toms, Viola, #2339
Toms, Viola, #2340
Toms, Viola, #2341
Toms, Viola, #2342
Tonhbaugh, "Elizabeth (""Aunt"")", #7758
Torbitt[?], Bessie, #5111
Townsend, David, #7806
Trapmill, Joseph, #4357
Trapnell, Jno., #4364
Trapnell, Joseph, #4356
Trapnell, Joseph, #4393
Trapnell, Joseph, #4396
Triplett, Alexander, #1244
Triplett, Edna Linton, #1243
Triplett, Hayward, #1237
Triplett, Hayward, #1240
Triplett, Hayward, #1241
Triplett, Hayward, #1242
Triplett, Hayward, #1242
Triplett, Hayward, #1243
Triplett, Hayward, #1244
Triplett, Hayward, #1245
Triplett, Pelham, #1245
Triplett, Roberdeau, #1240
Triplett, Roderick, #1241
Tritch, Avril May, #6847
Tritch, Avril May, #6848
Tritch, Eric, #6847
Tritch, Eric, #6848
Tritch, Eric, #6849
Tritch, Eric, #6850
Tritch, Eric E., #6809
Tritch, Eric Edgar, #6830
Tritch, Eric Edgar, #6831
Tritch, Irene Carey, #6847
Tritch, Irene Carey, #6848
Tritch, Irene Carey, #6849
Tritch, Irene Carey, #6850
Tritch, Margaret, #6830
Tritch, Margaret, #6831
Tritch, Roy, #6830
Tritch, Roy, #6831
Tritch, Roy Eric, #6849
Tritch, Roy Eric, #6850
Tritefoe, Sarah, #3511
Tritefoe, Sarah, #3512
Tritefoe, Sarah, #8178
Tritefoe, Sarah, #8179
Tritsch, Roy, #6807
Trott, Norman L., #3414
Trovenger, Joseph, #8155
Trovinger, Ann Malenda, #8164
Trovinger, Ann Malinda, #4552
Trovinger, Barbary, #4547
Trovinger, Barbary, #4561
Trovinger, Barbary, #8159

Trovinger, Benton, #4551
Trovinger, Benton, #8163
Trovinger, Catharine, #4556
Trovinger, Catharine, #8168
Trovinger, Daniel, #4549
Trovinger, Daniel, #4567
Trovinger, Daniel, #8161
Trovinger, Eliz., #8155
Trovinger, Eliz., #8160
Trovinger, Elizabeth, #4543
Trovinger, Elizabeth, #4548
Trovinger, Emily, #4554
Trovinger, Emily, #8166
Trovinger, Fanny, #4553
Trovinger, Fanny, #4562
Trovinger, Fanny, #8165
Trovinger, Franklen, #8167
Trovinger, Franklin, #4555
Trovinger, John, #4544
Trovinger, John, #4563
Trovinger, John, #4565
Trovinger, John, #8156
Trovinger, Joseph, #4542
Trovinger, Joseph, #4543
Trovinger, Joseph, #4545
Trovinger, Joseph, #4550
Trovinger, Joseph, #4559
Trovinger, Joseph, #4560
Trovinger, Joseph, #4569
Trovinger, Joseph, #8154
Trovinger, Joseph, #8157
Trovinger, Joseph, #8162
Trovinger, Joseph (Major), #4573
Trovinger, Marten Luther, #8170
Trovinger, Martin Luther, #4558
Trovinger, Nancy Amelia, #4557
Trovinger, Nancy Amelia, #8169
Trovinger, Samuel, #4546
Trovinger, Samuel, #4566
Trovinger, Samuel, #8158
Trovinger, Sarah E., #4563
Trovinger, Susan Kate (Miss), #8149
Trumpower, Alma Elizabeth, #904
Trumpower, Andrew N., #909
Trumpower, Beulah Mayble, #903
Trumpower, Calven, #910
Trumpower, Clyde Oscar, #900
Trumpower, Findley Frisby, #907
Trumpower, Harold Percy, #906
Trumpower, Iva Belle, #902
Trumpower, John William, #912
Trumpower, Joseph, #913
Trumpower, Joseph P., #911
Trumpower, Mary Jane, #908
Trumpower, Percy H., #913
Trumpower, Thomas, #896
Trumpower, Thomas, #916
Trumpower, Vernon Blaine, #901
Trumpower, Walter Lloyd, #905
Turlang, Annie L., #5447
Turner, Joan Eileen, #1549
Turner, Joan Eileen, #1550
Turner, John D., #4571
Turner, John D., #7746
Turner, John D., #7747
Turner, Margaret, #7747
Turner, Nancy Jean, #1541
Turner, Richard Lee, #1577
Tuttrell, Guy A., #4177
Tweedy, Elenor, #4759
Tweedy, Eliza Jane, #4757

INDEX
Pages are not numbered; numbers refer to the entry number at the beginning of each record.

Tweedy, Eliza Jane, #4773
Tweedy, James, #4765
Tweedy, James, #4769
Tweedy, James B., #4766
Tweedy, James[?] Bell[?], #4772
Tweedy, John, #4755
Tweedy, John, #4762
Tweedy, Johnston W., #4767
Tweedy, Maria, #4756
Tweedy, Martha, #4776
Tweedy, Martha Maria, #4763
Tweedy, Mary Ann, #4760
Tweedy, Mary Ann, #4774
Tweedy, Robert L., #4764
Tweedy, Samuel, #4758
Tweedy, Samuel, #4775
Tweedy, Sarah E., #4768
Tweedy, Sarah Edith[?], #4771
Tweedy, William, #4761
Tweedy, William, #4770
Twigg, Daniel Fenton, #4509
Twigg, Daniel Fenton, #4538
Twigg, David Finley, #4530
Twigg, David Finley[?], #4513
Twigg, Elizabeth, #4506
Twigg, Elizabeth, #4536
Twigg, Essie Anna, #4501
Twigg, Essie Anna, #4521
Twigg, Henry Martin, #4510
Twigg, Henry Martin, #4527
Twigg, John, #4519
Twigg, John, #4520
Twigg, John W., #4499
Twigg, John Wesley, #4507
Twigg, John Wesley, #4525
Twigg, Leucizer Marthar Matilda, #4512
Twigg, Leuezesa[?] Marthar Matilda, #4529
Twigg, Martha, #4504
Twigg, Martha, #4507
Twigg, Martha, #4508
Twigg, Martha, #4509
Twigg, Martha, #4510
Twigg, Martha, #4524
Twigg, Martha, #4525
Twigg, Martha, #4526
Twigg, Martha, #4527
Twigg, Martha, #4528
Twigg, Martha, #4529
Twigg, Martha, #4538
Twigg, Martha, #4539
Twigg, Martha, #4540
Twigg, Martha Ellen, #4519
Twigg, Martha Ellen, #4531
Twigg, Mary Jane, #4503
Twigg, Mary Jane, #4505
Twigg, Mary Jane, #4506
Twigg, Mary Jane, #4535
Twigg, Mary Jane, #4536
Twigg, Rose E., #4518
Twigg, Rose E., #4519
Twigg, Rose E., #4520
Twigg, Samuel Mirchant, #4511
Twigg, Samuel Mirchant, #4528

Twigg, Sarah Catharine, #4505
Twigg, Sarah Catharine, #4537
Twigg, William Edward, #4520
Twigg, Wm., #4495
Twigg, Wm., #4497
Twigg, Wm., #4502
Twigg, Wm., #4503
Twigg, Wm., #4504
Twigg, Wm., #4505
Twigg, Wm., #4506
Twigg, Wm., #4507
Twigg, Wm., #4508
Twigg, Wm., #4509
Twigg, Wm., #4510
Twigg, Wm., #4523
Twigg, Wm., #4524
Twigg, Wm., #4525
Twigg, Wm., #4526
Twigg, Wm., #4527
Twigg, Wm., #4528
Twigg, Wm., #4529
Twigg, Wm., #4535
Twigg, Wm., #4536
Twigg, Wm., #4538
Twigg, Wm., #4539
Twigg, Wm., #4540
Twigg, Wm. Albert, #4508
Twigg, Wm. Albert, #4526
Twigg, Wm. Albert, #4539
Unger, Ella David, #6719
Unger, Ella David, #6725
Unger, Harry B., #6704
Unger, Harry Benton, #6702
Unger, Henry Benton, #6718
Unger, Henry Benton, #6726
Unger, J. Elvin, #6703
Unger, John Elvin, #6721
Unger, Lillie May, #6720
Unger, William Frederick, #6722
Unger, William Frederick, #6724
Urian, Abbie A., #2715
Urian, Abbie A., #2721
Urian, Abbie A., #2722
Urian, Abbie A., #2723
Urian, Abbie A., #2724
Urian, Abbie A., #2726
Urian, Abbie A., #2727
Urian, Abbie A. , #2725
Urian, Adam S., #2726
Urian, John Frederick, #2727
Urian, Phoebe, #2721
Uter[?], Catherine M., #6525
Vars[?], Eleanor, #2685
Vars[?], Eleanor, #2686
Vars[?], Eleanor, #2687
Vars[?], Eleanor, #3925
Vars[?], Eleanor, #3926
Vars[?], Eleanor, #3927
Vars[?], Eleanor, #3928
Vars[?], Eleanor, #3929
Vars[?], Eleanor, #3930
Vass[?], Eleanor, #2619
Vickers, Jennie, #5975
Vickers[?], Jennie, #5959
Vincel, Earline Amanda, #8189
Vincel, Earling Amanda, #3522
Vincel, Larah Eizbeth, #8186
Vincel, Laura Jane, #3521
Vincel, Laura Jane, #8188

Vincel, Luisa Virginia, #3520
Vincel, Luisa Virginia, #8187
Vincel, Sarah Elizbeth, #3519
Vinson, Eva M., #4304
Vinton, R.L., #7295
Vinton, R.S., #1301
Wachter, M., #4380
Wagner, Beverly Diane, #7272
Wagner, Harry Martin, #6723
Wagner, Samuel, #1464
Wagoner, John, #1970
Walker, J.E., #6426
Walker, John E., #6296
Wallace, Anna, #2211
Wallace, Anna, #2212
Wallace, Anna, #2213
Wallace, Anna, #2214
Wallace, Anna, #2215
Wallace, Anna, #2216
Wallace, Anna, #2217
Walling, Eliza, #1302
Walling, Eliza, #7296
Walling, Eliza (Miss), #1294
Walling, Eliza (Miss), #7287
Walling, Elizabeth, #1297
Walling, Elizabeth, #7290
Walling, Elizabeth, #7291
Walling, Elizabeth, #7292
Walling, Elizabeth, #7294
Walling, Elizabeth, #7295
Walling, Herman Dorsey, #1298
Walling, Herman Dorsey, #1299
Walling, James, #1295
Walling, James, #7288
Walling, James (Capt.), #1305
Walling, James (Capt.), #7304
Walling, James (Col.), #1304
Walling, James (Col.), #7303
Walling, Mary, #1306
Walling, Mary, #7305
Walling, Mercy, #1296
Walling, Mercy, #7289
Walling, Mercy (Miss), #1293
Walling, Mercy (Miss), #7286
Walling, Nancy, #7293
Wallington, Rev., #4047
Walmsley, Anne Elizabeth, #5979
Walmsley, Anne Elizabeth, #5983
Walmsley, Anne Elizabeth, #5995
Walmsley, Charles Edward, #5964
Walmsley, Daniel McCullough, #5970
Walmsley, Harriet, #5994
Walmsley, Harriet M., #5988
Walmsley, Harriet McCauley, #5987
Walmsley, Harriet McClauley, #5969
Walmsley, Harriet Vickers, #5975
Walmsley, Harriet Vickers, #5976
Walmsley, Hugh Beard, #5966
Walmsley, Hugh Beard, #5992
Walmsley, James G., #5960
Walmsley, James Gooding, #5977
Walmsley, James Gooding, #5981
Walmsley, James Gooding, #5994
Walmsley, Jennie Vickers, #5989
Walmsley, John M., #5959
Walmsley, John M., #5989
Walmsley, John McCauley, #5980
Walmsley, John McCauley, #5984

Walmsley, John McCauley, #5988
Walmsley, Louisa J., #5956
Walmsley, Louisa Jane, #5962
Walmsley, Louisa Jane, #5999
Walmsley, Margaret B., #5986
Walmsley, Margaret Beard, #5968
Walmsley, Margaret Beard, #5985
Walmsley, Mary C., #5997
Walmsley, Mary Carroll, #5982
Walmsley, Mary Gooding, #5991
Walmsley, MaryCarroll, #5978
Walmsley, Peggy Eliza, #5971
Walmsley, Philip M., #5986
Walmsley, Philip McCauley, #5963
Walmsley, R.M., #5974
Walmsley, Robert, #5986
Walmsley, Robert H.[?], #5992
Walmsley, Robert M., #5955
Walmsley, Robert M., #5957
Walmsley, Robert M., #5958
Walmsley, Robert M., #5961
Walmsley, Robert M., #5972
Walmsley, Robert M., #5973
Walmsley, Robert M., #5988
Walmsley, Robert M., #5993
Walmsley, Robert M., #5995
Walmsley, Robert M., #5997
Walmsley, Robert M., #5998
Walmsley, Robert Miller, #5996
Walmsley, Robert Miller, #6000
Walmsley, Robt., #5994
Walmsley, Robt. M., #5953
Walmsley, Robt. M., #5954
Walmsley, Robt. M., #5965
Walmsley, Robt. M., #5990
Walmsley, William Gibbs, #5967
Walsmely, John, #5975
Waltz, John E.K., #5042
Wampler, Helen (Miss), #511
Wampler, Mary E., #8204
Wantz, Laura Virginia, #5071
Ward, Wm. McK., #8272
Warenfels, Adam, #4474
Warenfels, Catharine, #4481
Warenfels, Daniel, #4482
Warenfels, Daniel Theodore, #4478
Warenfels, Evean Catharine, #4477
Warenfels, Frederick, #4480
Warenfels, Jacob, #4472
Warenfels, John, #4471
Warenfels, John, #4479
Warenfels, Josiah, #4473
Warenfels, Magdalena, #4485
Warenfels, Margret, #4483
Warenfels, Sarah, #4484
Warenfeltz, Adam Nicholas, #4465
Warenfeltz, Charls Frederick Santee, #4467
Warenfeltz, George Marelous, #4460
Warenfeltz, Henry Mlow[?], #4470
Warenfeltz, Jacob Wiliam, #4464
Warenfeltz, Josiah Jefferson, #4461
Warenfeltz, Martha E., #4468
Warenfeltz, Martha E., #4469
Warenfeltz, Maryan Elizabeth, #4463
Warenfeltz, Philip Terrances, #4462
Warenfeltz, Sarah Jane Rebecca, #4466
Warenfelz, John Godfrey, #4476
Warner, J.R., #7610
Warner, J.R., #7612
Warner, J.R., #7616

INDEX
Pages are not numbered; numbers refer to the entry number at the beginning of each record.

Warner, J.R., #7623
Warner, J.R., #7642
Warner, J.R., #7643
Warner, J.R., #7644
Warner, J.R., #7647
Warrenfels, Catharina, #4486
Warrenfels, Daniel, #4487
Warrenfels, Jacob, #4492
Warrenfels, John, #4491
Warrenfels, Magdalene, #4490
Warrenfels, Rebecca, #4488
Warrenfels, Sarah, #4489
Warrenfeltz, Ethel Irene, #5490
Warrenfeltz, Ethel Irene, #5491
Warrenfeltz, Jacob M., #5483
Warrenfeltz, Stuart Martin, #5491
Warrenfeltz, Susan, #4475
Washington, Ida , #8547
Wassler, , #8056
Watkins, Margaret, #348
Watkins, Margaret A., #350
Watts, Elizabeth, #2056
Watts, Elizabeth, #2057
Watts, Sarah, #2057
Watts, Wm., #2057
Way, E.J., #5981
Way, E.J., #5982
Way, E.J., #5983
Way, E.J., #5984
Ways[?], Ernest, #6521
Ways[?], Gertrude May Fricke, #6513
Ways[?], Gertrude May Fricke, #6520
Ways[?], John Henry, #6522
Wbee[?], Henry, #4818
Weakley, Mary, #2323
Weaver, H., #3392
Webster, J.J.G., #6251
Webster, J.J.G., #6307
Weddle, Elizabeth (Mrs.), #3010
Weeks[?], Barbara Jean, #3639
Weeks[?], Simon, #3856
Weiderman, L.T., #6253
Weidman, Mary, #7378
Weil, "Abelohen" ""[Apollonia]", #5648
Weil, Apollonia, #5649
Weil, Apollonia, #5650
Weil, Apollonia, #5651
Weil, Apollonia, #5652
Weis, Alfred, #2957
Weis, Alfred, #2958
Weis, Amalia, #2947
Weis, Amalia, #2948
Weis, Anna Maria Elizabeth, #2953
Weis, Anna Maria Elizabeth, #2954
Weis, Catarina Christina, #2959
Weis, Catarina Christina, #2960
Weis, Georg Weigandt, #2961
Weis, Georg Weigandt, #2962

Weis, Heinrich, #2942
Weis, Heinrich, #2943
Weis, Heinrich, #2944
Weis, Heinrich, #2945
Weis, Heinrich, #2946
Weis, Heinrich, #2947
Weis, Heinrich, #2948
Weis, Heinrich, #2949
Weis, Heinrich, #2950
Weis, Heinrich, #2951
Weis, Heinrich, #2952
Weis, Heinrich, #2953
Weis, Heinrich, #2954
Weis, Heinrich, #2955
Weis, Heinrich, #2956
Weis, Heinrich, #2957
Weis, Heinrich, #2958
Weis, Heinrich, #2959
Weis, Heinrich, #2960
Weis, Heinrich, #2961
Weis, Heinrich, #2962
Weis, Heinrich Kausler, #2949
Weis, Heinrich Kausler, #2950
Weis, James Hendricks, #2955
Weis, James Hendricks, #2956
Weis, Johannes, #2943
Weis, Johannes, #2944
Weis, Samuel, #2945
Weis, Samuel, #2946
Weis, William Jacob, #2951
Weis, William Jacob, #2952
Weller, Anna Mary, #6846
Weller, Charles, #6804
Weller, Cormorea Lee, #6852
Weller, Dixie Dee, #6855
Weller, John Arthur , #6843
Weller, John Charles, #6853
Weller, Loulia Margaret, #6842
Weller, Margaret, #6807
Weller, Mary N., #6838
Weller, Richard Dudley, #6856
Weller, Roger Francis, #6845
Weller, Willa Jane, #6851
Weller, William C., #6808
Weller, William C., #6851
Weller, William C., #6852
Weller, William C., #6853
Weller, William C., #6854
Weller, William C., #6855
Weller, William C., #6856
Weller, William Charles, #6844
Weller, William Sisler, #6854
Wells, David Beachley, #279
"Wells, III", Samuel Robert , #278
"Wells, Jr.", Samuel R., #285
Welty, Amelia, #7281
Welty, Amelia, #7284
Welty, Daniel, #7274
Welty, Ida Cora, #2761
Welty, Jennie , #5021
Welty, Martin L., #7278
Welty, Martin Luther, #7283
Welty, Michael, #7273
Welty, Michael, #7280
Welty, Michael, #7282
Welty, Rackel Ann, #7276
Welty, Sarow Elen, #7277
Welty, Susan, #4025
Welty, Susan, #4026
Welty, William Alforde, #7279

Welty, William Alfred, #7285
Welty, William Geary, #7275
Werking, Nancy, #694
Werking, Nancy, #695
Werking, Nancy Luetta, #683
Werner, Anna, #7806
Werner, Elizabeth, #1504
Weston, Arthur Hazelhurst, #7584
Weston, Bnj. Latrobe, #7581
Weston, Corn., #7581
Weston, Corn., #7582
Weston, Corn., #7584
Weston, Cornelius, #7561
Weston, Henry Bancroft, #7582
Weston, Kate, #7581
Weston, Kate, #7582
Weston, Kate, #7584
Westrata, Katherine, #7405
Westrata, Wm., #7405
Whaley, Susie B., #7427
Whaley, Susie Belle, #7449
Whaley, Susie Belle, #7450
White, Rev. Dr., #8277
White, Samuel, #6197
Whittney, Caroline H., #3790
Whyte, Anne Harriet, #101
Whyte, Anne Harriet, #96
Whyte, Arthur Titherington, #100
Whyte, Arthur Titherington, #106
Whyte, Arthur Titherington, #91
Whyte, Mary Sutton, #107
Whyte, Mary Sutton, #108
Wigton, R. Benton, #7985
Wilcox, Thomas S., #6651
Wiles, Nellie, #3442
Wilkes, Olive, #1836
Willhide, Emma R., #725
Williams, Anamay, #942
Williams, Anamay, #959
Williams, Caroline Gratia[?], #5998
Williams, Catharine L., #2705
Williams, Catharine L., #3947
Williams, Covah[?], #3949
Williams, Covela[?], #2707
Williams, Elizabeth Ann, #6584
Williams, Elizabeth Ann, #6585
Williams, Elleonor, #6585
Williams, Laura, #2706
Williams, Laura, #3948
Williams, Maria, #2708
Williams, Maria, #2711
Williams, Maria, #2712
Williams, Maria, #2713
Williams, Maria, #2714
Williams, Maria, #3950
Williams, Maria, #3951
Williams, Marion, #929
Williams, Otho Holland (Gen.), #2704
Williams, Otho Holland (Gen.), #2705
Williams, Otho Holland (Gen.), #2706
Williams, Otho Holland (Gen.), #2707
Williams, Otho Holland (Gen.), #2708
Williams, Otho Holland (Gen.), #3946

Williams, Otho Holland (Gen.), #3947
Williams, Otho Holland (Gen.), #3948
Williams, Otho Holland (Gen.), #3949
Williams, Otho Holland (Gen.), #3950
Williams, Sarah Catharine, #25
Williams, Zachariah, #6585
Williamson, Bessie, #2085
Willson, , #1250
Wilson, A.A., #4359
Wilson, Alice, #6651
Wilson, Alice, #6700
Wilson, Anna, #6668
Wilson, Anna, #6679
Wilson, Anna Louisa, #1340
Wilson, Arthur G., #6658
Wilson, Arthur Granville, #6689
Wilson, Charles Norton, #6673
Wilson, Charles Walter, #1338
Wilson, Chas., #6689
Wilson, Chas. Granville, #6677
Wilson, Chas. Granville, #6678
Wilson, Chas. M, #6677
Wilson, Chas. M, #6678
Wilson, Chas. N., #6682
Wilson, Clementine, #2445
Wilson, Clementine A., #2427
Wilson, Clementine A., #2428
Wilson, Clementine A., #2431
Wilson, Clyde H., #2584
Wilson, Clyde Huyett, #2568
Wilson, Clyde Huyett, #2580
Wilson, Clyde Huyett, #2598
Wilson, Edith Louise, #6619
Wilson, Edith Louise, #6620
Wilson, Edward, #6680
Wilson, Edward, #6688
Wilson, edwin C., #4303
Wilson, Edwin C., #4308
Wilson, Elias Baker, #1339
Wilson, Elizabeth, #2574
Wilson, Elizabeth, #2593
Wilson, Elizabeth Brewer , #2595
Wilson, Florence Isabell, #6672
Wilson, Frances Kendall, #2938
Wilson, Grace Irene, #6657
Wilson, Grace Irene, #6674
Wilson, Granville, #6667
Wilson, Granville, #6675
Wilson, Harriet Hillery, #2594
Wilson, Harry Edward, #6671
Wilson, Isaac, #1335
Wilson, Isaac, #1336
Wilson, Isaac, #1338
Wilson, Isaac, #1339
Wilson, Isaac, #1340
Wilson, Isaac, #1341
Wilson, Isaac, #1348
Wilson, Isaac, #1349
Wilson, Jennie M., #6681
Wilson, John H., #2567
Wilson, John H., #2582
Wilson, John H., #2596
Wilson, John H., #2606
Wilson, John Hamilton, #2575
Wilson, John Hamilton, #2595
Wilson, Juliet A., #3737
Wilson, Law., #2611
Wilson, Margaretta H., #2607
Wilson, Margaretta Helen, #2569
Wilson, Margaretta Helen, #2582
Wilson, Margaretta O., #2582

INDEX
Pages are not numbered; numbers refer to the entry number at the beginning of each record.

Wilson, Margaretta O., #2596
Wilson, Mary (Adams), #2597
Wilson, Mary A., #2584
Wilson, Mary A., #2599
Wilson, Mary Adams, #2571
Wilson, Mary Adams, #2584
Wilson, Mary Elenora, #1341
Wilson, Mary Elizabeth, #2576
Wilson, Mary Elizabeth, #2591
Wilson, MaryElen Virginia, #6669
Wilson, Millard Calvin, #6621
Wilson, Millard Calvin, #6622
Wilson, Myrta Smith, #6611
Wilson, Noah McKendree, #6602
Wilson, Pearl N., #4313
Wilson, Rufus, #2602
Wilson, Rufus H., #2566
Wilson, Rufus Hillary, #2605
Wilson, Rufus Hillery, #2594
Wilson, Rufus Hillery, #2595
Wilson, Susan Alice, #6652
Wilson, Susan Alice, #6661
Wilson, Susan Alice, #6662
Wilson, Susan Alice, #6663
Wilson, Susan Alice, #6670
Wilson, Susan Rebecca (Baker), #1349
Wilson, William, #2452
Wilson, William C., #2926
"Wilson, Jr.", Lancelot #2594
"Wilson, Jr.", Lancelot [or Lawrence], #2604
"Wilson, Jr.", Lancelot [or Lawrence], #2605
"Wilson, Jr.", Rufus Hilery, #2592
"Wilson, Jr.", Rufus Hilliary, #2577
"Wilson, Sr.", Rufus H., #2573
Winder, John, #3128
Windle, James B.[?], #3933
Windle, James E., #2692
Windsor, Edward Mealey, #7536
Windsor, Elizabeth, #7500
Windsor, Elizabeth Frances, #7540
Windsor, Elizabeth H., #7507
Windsor, Emily C., #7510
Windsor, Fanny, #7499
Windsor, Fanny, #7504
Windsor, Fanny, #7531
Windsor, John H., #7509
Windsor, John H., #7532
Windsor, Joseph R., #7508
Windsor, Joseph R., #7534
Windsor, Newman, #7499
Windsor, Newman, #7503
Windsor, Newman, #7533
Windsor, Richard T., #7505
Windsor, Robert N., #7506
Wingert, Bessie (Emmert), #3668
Wingert, Lewis Emmert, #3651

Wingert, Lewis Emmert, #3652
Wingert, Lewis Peters, #3666
Wingert, Lewis Peters, #3667
Wingert, Lewis Peters, #3668
Wingert, Philip Carter, #3653
Wingert, Theresa, #3654
Wingert[?] Lewis P., , #3650
Winkleback, Orvis, #3423
Winroth[?], Esther Madelyn, #6895
Winston, A.O., #1220
Winter, Alvina E., #4360
Winter, Alvina Elizabeth, #4377
Winter, Alvina Elizabeth, #4378
Winter, Ann Matilda , #4369
Winter, Ann Matilda , #4370
Winter, Anne Matilda, #4357
Winter, Benjamin, #4401
Winter, Blanche, #4430
Winter, Catharine, #4401
Winter, Catharine, #4406
Winter, Charles Thomas, #4375
Winter, Charles Thomas, #4376
Winter, Charles Thomas, #4407
Winter, E., #4371
Winter, E., #4373
Winter, E., #4375
Winter, E., #4377
Winter, E., #4379
Winter, E., #4381
Winter, E.C., #4408
Winter, E.C.C., #4359
Winter, E.C.C., #4362
Winter, E.C.C., #4363
Winter, E.C.C., #4365
Winter, E.C.C., #4409
Winter, E.C.C., #4433
Winter, E.C.C. (Dr.), #4410
Winter, E.V., #4363
Winter, E.V., #4365
Winter, E.V., #4408
Winter, Elizabeth, #4369
Winter, Elizabeth A., #4428
Winter, Elizabeth Ann, #4425
Winter, Emma Temple, #4388
Winter, Emma Temple, #4432
Winter, Estelle Vannet, #4385
Winter, Eugene C.C. (Dr.), #4430
Winter, Eugene Charles Curtis, #4383
Winter, Eugene Charles Curtis, #4384
Winter, F.B., #4445
Winter, Francis, #4385
Winter, Francis, #4386
Winter, Francis, #4387
Winter, Francis, #4388
Winter, Francis, #4389
Winter, Francis B., #4355
Winter, Francis B., #4431
Winter, Francis Benjamin, #4373
Winter, Francis Benjamin, #4374
Winter, Francis Benjamin, #4419
Winter, Francis Benjamin, #4420
Winter, Francis Benjamin, #4426

Winter, Francis C., #4408
Winter, Francis E., #4363
Winter, Francis E., #4364
Winter, Frank Benjamin, #4386
Winter, Homer Gibson, #4427
Winter, Homer Gibson, #4436
Winter, J.[?]T.[?], #4434
Winter, J.[?]T.[?], #4435
Winter, J.[?]T.[?], #4436
Winter, Jno. Thomas Hirst[?], #4434
Winter, John, #3162
Winter, John, #3164
Winter, John, #3166
Winter, John, #3172
Winter, John (Rev.), #4404
Winter, John T.[?] (Dr.), #4358
Winter, John Thomas, #4381
Winter, John Thomas, #4382
Winter, John Thomas, #4422
Winter, Johon (Rev.), #4411
Winter, L., #4433
Winter, L.A., #4385
Winter, L.A., #4386
Winter, L.A., #4387
Winter, L.A., #4388
Winter, L.A., #4389
winter, Lillie V., #4409
Winter, Louisa Ellen, #4387
Winter, Louisa Ellen, #4431
Winter, Lucy Alvira, #4420
Winter, Lucy Alvira, #4431
Winter, Luly A., #4445
Winter, Luther G.[?], #4405
Winter, Mary E., #4361
Winter, Mary Ellen, #4371
Winter, Mary Ellen, #4372
Winter, Maud A., #4365
Winter, Maud A., #4366
Winter, Maud Alvira, #4409
Winter, Maud Alvira, #4433
Winter, Minsia[?] Sherman, #4435
Winter, Odilon Fortney, #4389
Winter, Sarah E., #4411
Winter, T., #4371
Winter, T., #4373
Winter, T., #4375
Winter, T., #4377
Winter, T., #4379
Winter, T., #4381
Winter, Tempie[?], #4412
Winter, Tempie[?], #4413
Winter, Tempie[?], #4414
Winter, Tempie[?], #4415
Winter, Tempie[?], #4416
Winter, Tempie[?], #4417
Winter, Tempie[?], #4418
Winter, Templeanna, #4390
Winter, Templeanna Mason, #4379
Winter, Templeanna Mason, #4380
Winter, Thomas, #4354
Winter, Thomas, #4367
Winter, Thomas, #4369
Winter, Thomas, #4424
Winter, Thomas, #4425
Winter, Thomas, #4429
Winter, Thos., #4428
Winter, Yempre[?], #4356
"Winter, Sr.", Benjamin, #4402
Winters, David B., #3502
Winters, John, #3168

Winters, John, #3502
Winters, Valentine, #7134
Wise, Amanda (Flory), #1631
Wise, Augustus Joseph, #2963
Wise, Charly _oise[?], #1610
Wise, Harry, #1608
Wise, Harry, #1609
Wise, Harry, #1630
Wise, John C., #1592
Wise, John C., #1608
Wise, John C., #1609
Wise, John C., #1610
Wise, John C., #1611
Wise, John C., #1612
Wise, John C., #1630
Wise, John Eeloise[?], #1612
Wise, Sarah Catherine, #1611
Wise, William E., #5043
Wishard, Donna Jean, #3022
Wishard, Lucinda Kay, #3023
Wishard, Woodrow, #3026
Wishard, Woodrow W., #3033
Wishard, Woodrow W., #3034
Witherow, Margaret, #7594
Witherow, Margaret, #7595
Witherow, Margaret, #7596
Witherow, Margaret, #7599
Witherow, Margaret, #7600
Witherow, Margaret, #7601
Witherow, Margaret, #7602
Witherow, Margaret, #7603
Witherow, Margaret, #7604
Witherow, Margaret, #7605
Witherow, Margaret, #7606
Witherow, Margaret, #7607
Witherow, Margaret, #7608
Witherow, Margaret, #7609
Witherow, Margaret, #7610
Witherow, Margaret, #7611
Witherow, Margaret, #7612
Witherow, Margaret, #7613
Witherow, Margaret, #7614
Witherow, Margaret, #7615
Witherow, Margaret, #7616
Witherow, Margaret, #7617
Witherow, Margaret, #7618
Witherow, Margaret, #7619
Witherow, Margaret, #7620
Witherow, Margaret, #7621
Witherow, Margaret, #7622
Witherow, Margaret, #7623
Witherow, Margaret, #7635
Witherow, Margaret, #7638
Witherow, Margaret, #7639
Witherow, Margaret, #7640
Witherow, Margaret, #7641
Witherow, Margaret, #7642
Witherow, Margaret, #7643
Witherow, Margaret, #7644
Witherow, Margaret, #7645
Witherow, Margaret, #7646
Witherow, Margaret, #7647
Witherow, Samuel, #7593
Witherow, Samuel, #7594
Witherow, William, #7592
Witherow, William, #7593
Witmer, A.S., #269
Witmer, Amos, #264
Witmer, Andrew S., #250
Witmer, Andrew S., #251
Witmer, Ann Elizabeth, #256

INDEX
Pages are not numbered; numbers refer to the entry number at the beginning of each record.

Witmer, Ben, #1971
Witmer, Clara, #280
Witmer, Elizabeth, #260
Witmer, Emily S., #253
Witmer, Emily S., #265
Witmer, Henry J., #258
Witmer, Jacob A., #254
Witmer, Joseph M., #255
Witmer, Leander S., #257
Witmer, Lydia, #262
Witmer, Martha, #261
Witmer, Milton, #3579
Witmer, Milton, #3580
Witmer, Milton, #8025
Witmer, Nancy, #268
Witmer, Sarah, #250
Witmer, Sarah, #252
Witmer, Sarah A., #3599
Witmer, Sarah Catherine, #259
Witmer, Sarah Catherine, #266
"Witmer, Sr.", Jacob, #263
"Witmer, Sr.", Jacob, #267
Witmor, Pharas B., #5610
Witte, E., #3377
Wodf[?], Daniel, #4950
Wolf, (Miss), #8036
Wolf, C.E., #1654
Wolf, Daniel, #2786
Wolf, Daniel, #2861
Wolf, Daniel, #4980
Wolf, Daniel Elmer, #207
Wolf, David, #204
Wolf, David, #205
Wolf, David, #207
Wolf, David, #208
Wolf, David, #209
Wolf, David, #210
Wolf, David, #211
Wolf, David, #212
Wolf, David, #213
Wolf, Joseph Albert, #208
Wolf, Joseph Albert, #212
Wolf, Lizzie Angela, #210
Wolf, Mary, #206
Wolf, Mary, #207
Wolf, Mary, #208
Wolf, Mary, #209
Wolf, Mary, #210
Wolf, Mary, #211
Wolf, Mary, #212
Wolf, Mary, #213
Wolf, Mary Elen, #209
Wolf, Mary Elen, #213
Wolf, Mary Margaret, #6703
Wolf, Victor Ellsworth, #211
Wolfe, Clarence E., #1659
Wolfe, Dollie (Summers), #4624
Wolfe, Melvin E., #4628
Wolfe, Sherman, #4628
Wolfe, William Leroy, #737
Wolfinger, Annie Mary (Leiter), #562
Wolfinger, Mary I.[?] (Miss), #505
Wolfkiel, Allice, #5800
Wolfkiel, Curtis, #5801
Wolfkiel, John, #5799
Wolfkiel, Lorrenzo, #5802

Wolfkiel, losson[?], #5798
Woltz, Charles William, #1286
Woltz, Charles William, #7300
Woltz, Eli, #1311
Woltz, Eli, #7310
Woltz, Elie, #1282
Woltz, Elie, #1294
Woltz, Elie, #1298
Woltz, Elie, #7287
Woltz, Elie, #7291
Woltz, Elie, #7292
Woltz, Elie, #7294
Woltz, Elie, #7295
Woltz, Eliee, #1300
Woltz, Eliza, #1283
Woltz, Eliza, #1312
Woltz, Eliza, #7311
Woltz, Elizabeth, #1298
Woltz, Elizabeth, #1300
Woltz, Frances Jane, #1300
Woltz, Frances Jane, #1301
Woltz, Frances Jane, #1308
Woltz, Frances Jane, #7294
Woltz, Frances Jane, #7295
Woltz, Frances Jane, #7307
Woltz, Francis Jane, #1290
Woltz, George Washington, #1285
Woltz, George Washington, #1307
Woltz, George Washington, #7299
Woltz, George Washington, #7306
Woltz, Herman Dorsey, #1291
Woltz, Herman Dorsey, #1310
Woltz, Herman Dorsey, #7309
Woltz, Herman G., #7291
Woltz, Herman G., #7292
Woltz, James Walling, #1284
Woltz, James Walling, #7298
Woltz, John Reynolds, #1288
Woltz, John Reynolds, #7302
Woltz, Martin S., #1309
Woltz, Martin S., #7308
Woltz, Martin Startzman, #1292
Woltz, Mary Eliza, #1289
Woltz, Mary Eliza, #1303
Woltz, Mary Eliza, #7297
Woltz, Samuel Armstrong, #1287
Woltz, Samuel Armstrong, #7301
Wood, Ann Rebecca, #1278
Wood, Carlton Emerson, #4321
Wood, Caroline, #1264
Wood, Caroline, #1265
Wood, Caroline, #1266
Wood, Caroline, #1267
Wood, Caroline, #1268
Wood, Caroline, #1280
Wood, Caroline, #1281
Wood, Charles, #1274
Wood, Dallas, #1704
Wood, Dallas, #4167
Wood, Edith (England), #4336
Wood, Edith E., #4349
Wood, Eliza Jane, #1272
Wood, Elizabeth, #1277
Wood, H.H., #1261
Wood, H.H., #1262

Wood, H.H., #1264
Wood, H.H., #1265
Wood, H.H., #1266
Wood, H.H., #1267
Wood, H.H., #1269
Wood, H.H., #1270
Wood, H.H., #1271
Wood, H.H., #1272
Wood, H.H., #1273
Wood, H.H., #1274
Wood, H.H., #1275
Wood, H.H., #1276
Wood, H.H., #1277
Wood, H.H., #1278
Wood, H.W., #1269
Wood, Hannah, #1705
Wood, Hannah, #4168
Wood, Henry Millard, #4320
Wood, Henry Millard, #4335
Wood, Henry Millard, #4348
Wood, Jean Millard, #4336
Wood, Lafayette, #1275
Wood, Mary Elizabeth, #4330
Wood, Mary Elizabeth, #4331
Wood, Mary Elizabeth, #4337
Wood, Mary Elizabeth, #4338
Wood, Mary Elizabeth, #4350
Wood, Mary Elizabeth, #4351
Wood, Mattie Ellen, #1706
Wood, Mattie Ellen, #4169
Wood, Oliver C., #1273
Wood, Oscar, #1270
Wood, Rebecca, #1263
Wood, Rebecca, #1264
Wood, Rebecca, #1265
Wood, Rebecca, #1266
Wood, Rebecca, #1267
Wood, Rebecca, #1269
Wood, Rebecca, #1270
Wood, Rebecca, #1271
Wood, Rebecca, #1272
Wood, Rebecca, #1273
Wood, Rebecca, #1274
Wood, Rebecca, #1275
Wood, Rebecca, #1276
Wood, Rebecca, #1277
Wood, Rebecca, #1278
Wood, Robert, #1703
Wood, Robert, #1704
Wood, Robert, #1705
Wood, Robert, #1706
Wood, Robert, #1707
Wood, Robert, #4164
Wood, Robert, #4167
Wood, Robert, #4168
Wood, Robert, #4169
Wood, Robert, #4170
Wood, Roberta Ann, #1707
Wood, Roberta Ann, #4170
Wood, Tumeson(?), #1276
Wood, William, #1259
Wood, William A., #1271
Wood, Wm. A., #1279
Wood, , #4328
Wood, , #4329
Wooddy, John W., #1927
Wooddy, John Wm., #1927
Wooddy, Mary A., #1927
Worenfels, Alice E., #5127
Wright, Flosie Bell, #5703
Wright, Lucille, #3431

Wyand, [male], #4294
Wyand, Caleb, #4291
Wyand, Caleb, #4292
Wyand, Caleb, #4309
Wyand, D.H., #2453
Wyand, D.H., #2454
Wyand, D.H., #2455
Wyand, Emery E., #4307
Wyand, Emory C., #4301
Wyand, Emory Elmer, #4295
Wyand, Eva L., #4305
Wyand, Eva Luaretta, #4300
Wyand, Eva M., #4312
Wyand, Kate E., #2453
Wyand, Kate E., #2454
Wyand, Kate E., #2455
Wyand, Lurilla Penelope, #4306
Wyand, Lurilla[?] Penelope, #4298
Wyand, Merta Catharine, #4297
Wyand, Mertie C., #4302
Wyand, Ora B., #4304
Wyand, Ora B., #4311
Wyand, Ora Blessing, #4296
Wyand, Pearl N., #4303
Wyand, Perlie Naomi, #4299
Wyand, Sarah (Blessing), #4310
Wyand, Sarah A.P. (Blessing), #4293
Wyand, Willie C., #2453
Wyand, Willie C., #2454
Wyand, Willie C., #2455
Yeager, Elisbeth Ann, #899
Yeakel, I.C., #1469
Yeakle[?], Sara Lousisa, #3501
Yeates, Jenny Estelle, #7565
Yellman, Anna Catharina Margaretha, #6012
Yellman, Anna Chatarina Margaretha, #6006
Yerty, Daniel, #1001
Yerty, Daniel, #983
Yerty, Daniel, #991
Yerty, Elizabeth, #984
Yerty, Mr., #4884
Yingling, Blanche H., #4362
Yingling, Elizabeth, #6301
Yingling, Elizabeth, #6431
Yong, Mary, #5795
Young, Christiana, #6063
Young, Christiana, #6064
Young, Christiana, #6066
Young, Christiana, #6067
Young, Christiana, #6068
Young, Christiana, #6069
Young, Christiana, #6070
Young, Christiana, #6071
Young, Christiana, #6072
Young, Christiana, #6073
Young, Christiana, #6074
Young, Christiana, #6075
Young, Christiana, #6076
Young, Christiana, #6077
Young, Christiana, #6078
Young, Christiana, #6079
Young, Christiana, #6080
Young, Christiana, #6081
Young, Christiana, #6082
Young, Christiana, #6083
Young, Christiana, #6084
Young, Christiana, #6085
Young, Christiana, #6086
Young, Christiana, #6087

INDEX
Pages are not numbered; numbers refer to the entry number at the beginning of each record.

Young, Christiana, #6088
Young, Christiana, #6089
Young, Christiana, #6090
Young, Christina, #6205
Young, Christina, #6207
Young, Christina, #6208
Young, Christina, #6209
Young, Christina, #6210
Young, Christina, #6211
Young, Christina, #6212
Young, Christina, #6213
Young, Christina, #6214
Young, Christina, #6215
Young, Christina, #6216
Young, Christina, #6217
Young, Christina, #6218
Young, Christina, #6219
Young, Christina, #6220
Young, Christina, #6221
Young, Christina, #6222
Young, Christina, #6223
Young, Christina, #6224
Young, Christina, #6225
Young, Christina, #6226
Young, Christina, #6227
Young, Christina, #6228
Young, Elva Viola, #2832
Young, Pauline, #3025
Young[?], John M.[?], #3532
Zeigler, George Fredk., #6774
Zeigler, Kate E., #495
Zeigler, Mary C. (Miss), #504
Zeigler, Robert Lee, #6775
Zeller, Amelia, #1831
Zeller, Ann Amelia, #1850
Zeller, Anna C., #1840
Zeller, Annsecelia, #1832
Zeller, Bruce, #1843
Zeller, Charles, #1851
Zeller, Charles G., #1835
Zeller, Charles G., #1844
Zeller, Charles Garfield, #1860
Zeller, Daniel, #1858
Zeller, Daniel E., #1833
Zeller, Daniel E., #1841
Zeller, Daniel E., #1842
Zeller, Daniel E., #1843
Zeller, Daniel E., #1844
Zeller, Daniel E., #1845
Zeller, Daniel E., #1846
Zeller, Daniel E., #1847
Zeller, Daniel Edward, #1861
Zeller, David H., #1856
Zeller, Dennis T., #1714
Zeller, Dennis T., #1836
Zeller, Dennis T., #1837
Zeller, Dennis T. (Mrs.), #1743
Zeller, Dennis Tobias, #1698
Zeller, Dennis Tobias, #4113
Zeller, Ellen (Ardinger), #1696
Zeller, Henry S., #1831
Zeller, Henry S., #1832
Zeller, Henry S., #1838
Zeller, Henry S., #1839
Zeller, Margaret Louise, #1855
Zeller, Mary E., #1848

Zeller, Mary Louise (Cunningham), #1859
Zeller, Mary Louise (Cunningham), #1861
Zeller, Rachel E., #1841
Zeller, Rachel E., #1842
Zeller, Rachel E., #1849
Zeller, Rachel Elizabeth, #1862
Zeller, Rachel Elizabeth, #1863
Zeller, Rachel Elizabeth, #1865
Zeller, Rachel Elizabeth, #1866
Zeller, Rachel Elizabeth, #1867
Zeller, Rachel Elizabeth, #1868
Zeller, Tobias D., #1846
Zeller, William W., #1853
Zeller, William W., #1854
Zeller, William Wagner, #1852
Zeller, William Wayne, #1845
Zerger, Geo. W., #1930
Ziegler, Ann, #523
Ziegler, Barbara, #527
Ziegler, Barbara, #528
Zittle, Emmaline, #4629
Zittle, Michael, #4608
Zittle, Michael, #4609
Zittle, Michael, #4654
Zittle, Michael, #4655
, Ann Maria, #3277
, Anna, #1909
, Bertha, #4333
, C., #1992
, Catharine, #1911
, Catharine M., #8418
, Charles, #2715
, E., #1989
, Elisabeth, #481
, Elisabeth, #484
, Elizabeth, #1001
, Elizabeth, #1002
, Elizabeth, #3278
, J., #1992
, Maria Ellen, #1744
, Mary May, #6386
, Mary May, #6387
, Mary May, #6388
, Mary May, #6389
, Nora, #2545
, P.[?], #1989
, P.[?], #1990
, Rebecca, #1262
, Sarah J., #4931
, Williams, #5958
[?], Ernest, #6511
[?], John, #4978
[?], Margaret E. Cross[?], #6482
[blank], "Father", #2419
[blank], "Mother", #2418
[blank], "Mother", #2423
[blank], [infant], #8331
[blank], [infant], #8332
[blank], Agnes, #5248
[blank], Agnes, #7518
[blank], Albert, #5253
[blank], Ann Maria, #8543
[blank], Anna, #2087
[blank], Benjamin Augustus, #1922
[blank], Caroline, #8541
[blank], Cecelia Agnes, #1687
[blank], Charles, #5251
[blank], Clyde H., #4000

[blank], Coliar, #8542
[blank], Daniel, #4493
[blank], Elizabeth, #2050
[blank], Ely, #7529
[blank], Emma Catharina, #6009
[blank], Emma Chatarina, #6015
[blank], Ephraim, #7527
[blank], Ethel, #5252
[blank], Ezekiel, #2050
[blank], Floyd W., #3998
[blank], Frances V., #4001
[blank], Frances V., #4002
[blank], Franklin, #5249
[blank], Frielin, #7520
[blank], Geneieve[?], #5256
[blank], George, #7526
[blank], Hannah, #1664
[blank], Hannah, #4072
[blank], Hannah, #7515
[blank], Harvey[?], #8544
[blank], Helen, #5672
[blank], Jane, #1357
[blank], Jane, #1358
[blank], Jerry, #7524
[blank], Jesse, #7516
[blank], Jiles, #7523
[blank], Jordan, #7517
[blank], Kathleen, #5255
[blank], Kathleen J., #3999
[blank], Kathleen Marie, #1419
[blank], Lally Earle, #1358
[blank], Lewis, #7528
[blank], Lewis[?], #5723
[blank], Lindy, #7522
[blank], Lisa, #7530
[blank], Lou, #7766
[blank], Maggie, #5250
[blank], Maria Ellen, #8117
[blank], Maria Susan, #1966
[blank], Marion, #3419
[blank], Mary, #7521
[blank], Mary Ellen, #5722
[blank], Negro Bill, #8548
[blank], Negro Sam, #8549
[blank], Patricia, #1419
[blank], Patricia, #1420
[blank], Ralph, #7519
[blank], Ritter, #7525
[blank], Robert Theodore, #6010
[blank], Rua, #5247
[blank], Sherley Mareget, #1568
[blank], Tom, #1419
[blank], Tom, #1420
[blank], Tommy, #1357
[blank], Tracy Lynn, #1420
[blank], Vera, #5258
[blank], Virginia, #5257
[blank], Walter, #5254
[blank], Susan Marie, #1991
[no maiden name given], Maryann, #723
[unreadable], Alice V., #5424
[unreadable], Henrietta, #6509
[unreadable], Nelson Charlton, #6898
[unreadable], Sarah, #3299
[unreadable], Warren, #2071
[unreadable], Warren, #2076